SPORTS LAW

Patrick K. Thornton, JD, LLM
Adjunct Professor
The University of Houston Law Center
Adjunct Professor
South Texas College of Law

JONES AND BARTLETT PUBLISHERS

Sudbury, Massachusetts

BOSTON   TORONTO   LONDON   SINGAPORE

World Headquarters

Jones and Bartlett Publishers	Jones and Bartlett Publishers	Jones and Bartlett Publishers
40 Tall Pine Drive	Canada	International
Sudbury, MA 01776	6339 Ormindale Way	Barb House, Barb Mews
978-443-5000	Mississauga, Ontario L5V 1J2	London W6 7PA
info@jbpub.com	Canada	United Kingdom
www.jbpub.com		

Jones and Bartlett's books and products are available through most bookstores and online booksellers. To contact Jones and Bartlett Publishers directly, call 800-832-0034, fax 978-443-8000, or visit our website, www.jbpub.com.

Substantial discounts on bulk quantities of Jones and Bartlett's publications are available to corporations, professional associations, and other qualified organizations. For details and specific discount information, contact the special sales department at Jones and Bartlett via the above contact information or send an email to specialsales@jbpub.com.

This publication is designed to provide accurate and authoritative information in regard to the Subject Matter covered. It is sold with the understanding that the publisher is not engaged in rendering legal, accounting, or other professional service. If legal advice or other expert assistance is required, the service of a competent professional person should be sought.

Production Credits
Acquisitions Editor: Shoshanna Goldberg
Senior Associate Editor: Amy L. Bloom
Senior Editorial Assistant: Kyle Hoover
Production Manager: Julie Champagne Bolduc
Associate Production Editor: Jessica Steele Newfell
Associate Marketing Manager: Jody Sullivan
V.P., Manufacturing and Inventory Control: Therese Connell
Composition: Glyph International
Cover Design: Scott Moden
Cover Images: (top) © Photogolfer/Dreamstime.com; (bottom) © Rob Byron/ShutterStock, Inc.
Printing and Binding: Malloy, Inc.
Cover Printing: Malloy, Inc.

Library of Congress Cataloging-in-Publication Data
Thornton, Patrick K.
  Sports law/Patrick K. Thornton.
      p. cm.
  Includes bibliographical references and index.
  ISBN-13: 978-0-7637-3650-7 (alk. paper)
  ISBN-10: 0-7637-3650-3
  1. Sports—Law and legislation—United States. I. Title.
  KF3989.T48 2010
  344.73'099—dc22

                                                    2009050588

6048

Printed in the United States of America
14   13   12   10   9   8   7   6   5   4   3   2

To my wife, Alison, and our sons, Samuel and George.

CONTENTS

PREFACE

When I accepted my award for the "most improved player" in Pop Warner football I thought at that time my prospects for a professional sports career were fading. I knew they were completely gone when I accepted the "most spirited player" award on my high school basketball team. At that point I began to think about a career in academics, which eventually led me to study sports law.

If a student inquired about a course in sports law at a university or law school 25 years ago, that student may have encountered a blank stare. Fortunately, that is not the case today. The business of sports has become a multimillion-dollar industry with sports law leading the way. The topics of sports law run the gamut of legal and societal issues, dealing with many categories of law, including contracts, torts, intellectual property, labor relations, and antitrust and agency law. The rise of interest in sports law mirrors the explosion of the interest in sports in society and the business of sports.

Sports Law takes a look at the major legal cases, statutes, and regulations that explore a variety of legal issues in sports law. Each chapter includes questions and notes to encourage further study in that specific area of law. This text assists both sports law students and sports practitioners as they progress in their desired careers in the sports industry.

Sports Law begins by examining sports law in terms of the impact it has had on race, politics, religion, and society in general. As readers peruse the first chapter, they will gain an appreciation for sports law and the effect of sports on society. Chapter 1 is written with a less "legal" viewpoint than the remaining chapters of the book. It contains anecdotes and examples of great moments and players in sports and discusses their impact on legal issues within the sports world. It also deals with issues of race relations in sports, sports ethics, and the ever-growing problem of violence in sports.

Many people think of player contracts when they think of sports law. They may think of David Beckham's or Eli Manning's multimillion-dollar contracts. Chapter 2 introduces sports contracts between players, teams, coaches, and sponsors. This chapter explores the Uniform Player Contract (UPC) in professional sports and issues relating to contract bonuses, contract guarantees, breaches of contract, and remedies for a breach of contract.

Chapter 3 explores the interrelationship between antitrust and sports law. Players, franchises, universities, and others historically have used antitrust law to attempt to strike down unreasonable restraints of trade in violation of the Sherman Antitrust Act. The chapter presents *Flood v. Kuhn* (a case that many consider to be the most significant case in U.S. sports law), which deals with Curt Flood's challenge against baseball's reserve clause. Antitrust law also is discussed in the context of competing leagues, franchise relocation, and amateur athletics.

Chapter 4 naturally moves from antitrust law to labor law and collective bargaining, as these are now favored over antitrust law in sports law. Collective bargaining, arbitration, unfair labor practices, strikes, and lockouts all are examined in this chapter. Chapter 5 discusses the many issues surrounding sports agents, such as an agent's duty of care, standard representation agreements, and the regulation of agents by universities, leagues, and other entities. *Jerry Maguire* put sports agents on the map with its overused phrase, "Show Me the Money"; there is no doubt sports agents have become a major force in sports law and business over the past 30 years. Agents perform many duties on behalf of their clients, including the negotiation of player and endorsement contracts.

Chapter 6 discusses the profound effect of tort law on sports law. The number of sports participants suing one another recently has increased. There are several cases and problems discussing "participant versus participant" liability. When NHL "enforcer" Todd Bertuzzi retaliated against opponent Steve Moore and broke his neck during an NHL game, Moore sued Bertuzzi for his actions on the ice, alleging he was assaulted. There are a variety of torts discussed in the context of sports, including defamation, right of privacy and publicity, negligence, and medical malpractice.

Race and discrimination law are always hot topics in sports and are the focus of Chapter 7. For example, the NFL's Rooney Rule—requiring club owners to interview minority candidates for vacant head coaching positions in the NFL—was initiated by super-lawyer Johnnie Cochran.

Chapter 8 focuses on intellectual property, a growing area of sports law. Teams are concerned with trademark and licensing issues and often take legal measures to protect their intellectual property rights. Copyright law, trade secrets, and patent law are discussed in this chapter.

Women's participation in both youth and professional sports has greatly increased over the last few years. Mackenzie Brown is a great example. She tossed a perfect game in little league (against a full team of boys!) retiring all 18 batters she faced, striking out 12. Title IX has greatly changed amateur athletics since its institution in 1972. Multiple cases in Chapter 9 explore Title IX as well as general cases discussing gender equity in sports.

The National College Athletic Association (NCAA) deserves its own chapter in any sports law textbook. It is the largest and most powerful governing body of amateur sports in the United States. Chapter 10 focuses on many aspects of the NCAA, ranging from scholarships and eligibility issues to antitrust law, specific NCAA rules, and rule enforcement. Eligibility is the key to amateur athletics and is the focus of Chapter 11. An athlete's right to participate is the most essential issue for an athlete and questions of due process and equal protection can come into play under certain circumstances.

Chapter 12 examines the always-debated topic of drug testing in sports. No issue in sports law seemed to garner more attention in recent years than drug testing and doping. The cases and materials in this chapter explore drug testing at both the professional and amateur levels.

There is little doubt that sports law has become international in nature. Many U.S. professional leagues are playing games outside the United States. Many sports stars are international athletes in today's global marketplace. Chapter 13 explores international sports law, the Olympics, and the Court of Sport Arbitration.

I hope you will enjoy your study of sports law. It is my desire that your reading and study of this text will provide you with further knowledge about sports and the law, and that it will increase your passion for both. Good luck in your studies.

ACKNOWLEDGMENTS

A good book needs input from a variety of people, and this book is no exception. There are many people to thank for their help with this project. To my father, Jack, with whom I have had more conversations about sports than anyone else. Even though his point of view on legal issues in sports sometimes differs from mine, his opinions are still well developed, helping over the years to create much of the foundation for this book. A large debt of gratitude goes to my mother, Jennie, for all of the support she provided throughout the years.

There are two people who deserve a special acknowledgment, whom I could have not written this book without: Michael Flint and Jackie Faccini. Both assisted in the typing and reviewing of the manuscript and have given great input and advice. I also was fortunate to receive contributions and advice from several outstanding legal scholars along the way. One is my good friend and colleague of many years, Dr. Larry Ruddell (Davidson). Thanks to him for his review of the manuscript and numerous insights. A special acknowledgment goes to my long-time friend Mark Schwartz (Texas A&M), with whom—next to my father—I have had more conversations about sports than anyone else. I want to thank my father-in-law, Gene Hewett (U.S. Air Force), for his keen insight and use of the English language. I also had outstanding contributions from many others (in no particular order): Steve Elkington (Houston, PGA Professional); Joe Branch (Northwestern); Mike Bourke (Boston College); Melissa Wiseman (Texas Tech); Seth Daniel; Nick Nichols (Rice); Ronnie Ren (Rice); G. Ray Thornton (Texas State); Tim Purpura (Loyola); Mike Janecek (Texas A&M); Matt Mitten (Marquette); Dr. Richard "Hutch" Divorak (Georgia Southern); Doug Gerhman (Arizona State); Mike Laramie (Michigan); Kenny Waldt (Texas); Joseph Promo (Michigan State); Waco Thornton (U.S. Navy); David Brickey (Michigan State); Cheryl Thornton; Ron Sutton (Michigan State); Paul Duguay (Michigan); Dr. John "Rusty" Brooks (Texas Tech); Dennis Chalupa (Pepperdine); Sam Webb (TCU); Dr. Yuri Yatsenki (Kiev University); Dr. Darlene Serrato (Houston); Oliver Luck (West Virginia); Greg Kondritz (Vanderbilt); librarian Dean Riley (Missouri); Jesse Marcos (SWT); Kevin Erwin (Houston); Bryan Teel (Texas); Jack Dolphin (Australian IP lawyer); Kathleen Stischer-Burnette (Texas); Massimo Cocchia (Rome, Michigan); Jon Maire (Michigan); William Little (Notre Dame); E. Brian McGeever (Rice); Mark Willis (Texas A&M); Kurt Kilman (Michigan State); Anne Bachle-Fifer (Michigan); John Bloomstrom, Terry Kastein, and Josh Lovelady (Houston, Detroit Lions); and Caroline Shantor (Columbia).

Thanks to the many deans and department heads that hired me to teach sports law, including John Nussbaumer, who gave me my first position teaching sports law at The Thomas M. Cooley Law School; Lylene Pilkenton (South Texas College of Law); Richard Alderman (University of Houston Law School); Marian Dent (Pericles, Moscow, Russia); my good mate Gordon Walker (Latrobe Law School, Melbourne, Australia); James (Jimmy) Disch and Dr. Clark Haptonstall (Rice); Itziar Murillo (ISDE, Madrid, Spain); Gabriela Sonato (IE Business School, Madrid, Spain); and Lynn Buzzard (Handong Law School, South Korea).

Much of the information in this book has been collected through research as well as through the experiences I have had in the sports industry and in the classroom teaching sports law. I have been fortunate to teach sports law to undergraduates, graduate students, law students, and LLMs in a variety of countries. Those experiences have assisted me immensely in writing this book. I am very proud of the many outstanding students I have taught sports law to over the past 15 years in the United States and across the globe, in places like South Korea, Australia, Russia, and Spain. They have all contributed to the book in some fashion. It has been a pleasure to teach all of them.

Of course, a great deal of thanks and credit goes to my mentor in sports law, Walter T. Champion, Jr., the George Foreman Chair of Sports Law at Texas Southern University Law School. Walt—in his unique style—has given great insight over the past 15 years in the sports law area.

Thank you also to the reviewers of *Sports Law*. Their voices, critiques, and suggestions truly made this a better text:

- Thomas H. Sawyer, EdD, Indiana State University
- John Miller, PhD, Texas Tech University
- Anthony G. Weaver, PhD, MA, Elon University
- Bruce A. Larson, EdD, University of Kentucky
- Lisa Dukes, Lecturer Kinesiology, Iowa State University
- Deborah Hanks, JD, Cardinal Stritch University
- Chad D. McEvoy, EdD, Illinois State University
- Kristi L. Schoepfer, JD, Winthrop University
- Leigh Ann Danzey-Bussell, PhD, Marian College
- Ellen M. Zavian, George Washington University
- Joseph P. Jacobs, Jr., PhD, McDaniel College

Finally, to the fantastic people at Jones and Bartlett Publishers. I cannot say enough about all of them: Kyle Hoover, Shoshanna Goldberg, Jacqueline Geraci, Julie Bolduc, and Jody Sullivan. Thanks also to Anupriya Tyagi at Glyph International and Cindy Kogut for their invaluable contributions to the production of this book. I appreciate their patience and input in making this a real "page turner."

CHAPTER 1

SPORTS IN SOCIETY

THE INFLUENCE OF SPORTS

Sports have had a strong hold on Americans for over a century. Boys, girls, men, and women alike have enjoyed participating in and watching a variety of professional and amateur sports for many years. Sports in many ways are a metaphor for life. Young people can learn teamwork, sportsmanship, and perseverance and develop many other admirable qualities when participating in sports. Boys and girls alike dream of hitting a home run in the bottom of the ninth and winning the championship while playing for their favorite ball club. In the fabulous musical comedy *Damn Yankees*,[1] a middle-aged Washington Senator's fan, Joe Boyd, a real estate salesman, sells his soul to the devil to become a 22-year-old slugging outfielder for the Senators named Joe Hardy. Hardy then leads the lowly Senators to the American League Pennant over the much-hated Yankees.

Maybe that displays a little too much commitment, but many fans take their baseball and sports very seriously. Eric James Torpy, for example, was always a big fan of Celtics great Larry Bird. After his lawyer reached a plea agreement for a 30-year prison term, Torpy decided he wanted to spend 33 years in prison instead of 30 to match Larry Bird's jersey number 33. Torpy was accused of robbery and shooting with intent to kill. According to Oklahoma County District Judge Ray Elliott, "He said if he was going to go down, he was going to go down in Larry Bird's jersey. We accommodated his request and he was just as happy as he could be."[2] Scott Wiese was a dedicated fan of the Chicago Bears—so dedicated that he signed a pledge at a Chicago bar in front of other fans two days before the 2007 Super Bowl promising to change his name to Peyton Manning if the Bears lost. The score was Colts 29, Bears 17. Wiese started the process of the name change the next week. His lawyer commented, "I never doubted him. He's a man of his word."[3]

Sporting greats have existed in every field. To appreciate sports is to appreciate the people who play sports. A plethora of athletes, both professional and amateur, have provided exciting moments for millions of fans over the last hundred years. There are too many athletes and great teams to list,

---

[1] Based on the book *The Year the Yankees Lost the Pennant*, by Douglass Wallop (Norton 1954).
[2] *Man Requests 33-Year Sentence to Match Bird's Number*, CBS SportsLine.com, Oct. 20, 2005.
[3] *Bears Fan Prepares to Become Peyton Manning*, FoxSports.com, Feb. 8, 2007.

but a few should be acknowledged to gain a greater appreciation of sports and the effect sports have had on American culture and society.

George Herman "Babe" Ruth[4] and Tyrus Raymond Cobb[5] dominated baseball from the 1900s to the 1930s, with Ruth becoming an American icon. Cobb was known for his aggressive style on the base paths as well as everywhere else. The Boston Red Sox's Ted Williams is considered by many to be baseball's greatest hitter. He was the last player to bat over .400 for an entire season, with a stunning .406 average for the 1941 season. Williams sat at .399 on the last day of the season, which would have given him a .400 season mathematically, but he felt he could not properly attain the .400 mark while sitting on the bench. On the final day he went 6 for 8 in a doubleheader, ending the season with a spectacular .406 average. In Williams's last at-bat in the Major Leagues, he did what every Major Leaguer dreams of doing, hitting a home run. After he rounded the bases and ducked into the dugout for the last time, the fans pleaded with him to take a bow, but he would not come out of the dugout. Fans chanted for a curtain call, but he refused. Noted writer John Updike, who was covering the game for *The New Yorker*, penned a now-famous line about Williams refusing to acknowledge fans, noting poignantly that "gods don't answer letters."

The sport of baseball had suffered a black eye after the "Black Sox" scandal in the 1919 World Series in which several White Sox players took bribes to throw games. (The events surrounding this World Series were made famous in the movie *Eight Men Out* [Orion Pictures 1988].) Babe Ruth proved to be the cure for baseball through the 1920s with his bat and his larger than life personality. Babe Ruth dominated baseball like no other figure, both as a batter and pitcher.[6]

There are numerous outstanding athletes in all sports. Red Grange (the Galloping Ghost) put professional football on the map with his outstanding play in the 1920s. Professional football was first played as an organized league in 1920, with the Akron Pros winning the first league title. Professional football has produced such star players as Bronko Nagurski, Sid Luckman, Y. A. Tittle, Otto Graham, Bobby Layne, Jim Brown, Johnny Unitas, Gale Sayers, Dick Butkus, Lance Alworth, Bart Starr, Earl Campbell, Barry Sanders, Joe Montana, Jerry Rice, Tom Brady, and Peyton Manning.

Jim Thorpe was thought to be the greatest athlete ever to have lived, especially in light of his performance at the 1912 Olympics. Sweden's King Gustav V told Thorpe during the 1912 games, "Sir, you are the greatest athlete in the world." Thorpe responded with "Thanks King."[7] Thorpe also played professional football and basketball, and once even won a ballroom dancing contest.

George Mikan of the Minneapolis Lakers was the first great star of professional basketball. Bill Russell could be considered the greatest winner in professional sports history, leading the Boston Celtics to eleven NBA Championships in 13 years. Wilt Chamberlain dominated the game like no other basketball player, once averaging 50.4 points a game for an entire season. Michael Jordan is given credit for restoring the popularity of the NBA, along with Magic Johnson and Larry Bird. John Wooden coached UCLA to seven consecutive NCAA basketball championships and ten all together.

---

[4] George Herman "Babe" Ruth was beloved by baseball fans. Much has been written about the Babe. It has been argued that his 1921 season with the New York Yankees was the greatest single season ever had in any sport.

[5] Cobb was a controversial figure, beloved by some, despised by others. He still holds the highest lifetime batting average of any baseball player in history at .367. In a rather amusing line from the movie *Field of Dreams* (Universal Studios 1989), Shoeless Joe Jackson (Ray Liotta) comments on Cobb's request to play: "No one could stand the S.O.B. when we were alive so we told him to stick it."

[6] Ruth at one time held the World Series record for consecutive scoreless innings and was 94–46 with a 2.28 career ERA as a pitcher. He clubbed 714 home runs. He is the all-time slugging leader in baseball at .690.

[7] Greg Botelho, *Roller-coaster Life of Indian Icon, Sports' First Star*, CNN.com, July 14, 2004.

Rod Laver, Bill Tilden, Arthur Ashe, and Don Budge helped put men's tennis on the map. Women tennis stars have included the likes of Alice Marble (four-time U.S. Champion), Althea Gibson (who won eleven major titles during the 1950s), Margaret Court, Chris Evert, Billy Jean King, and Martina Navratilova. Bob Mathias dominated track and field and was the youngest decathlon champion ever at 17. He also served as a U.S. Congressman from 1967 to 1974. Dick Fosbury revolutionized the high jump with the "Fosbury Flop." Carl Lewis dominated track and field in the last part of the 20th century, winning nine Olympic gold medals. Pelé proved to be an international sports star because of his soccer prowess and is regarded by many as the greatest footballer (soccer player) of all time. He was declared the athlete of the century by the International Olympic Committee and has been simply referred to as the "King of Football."

Gordie Howe was "Mr. Hockey" for over a 31-year career in the NHL and World Hockey Association (WHA). At age 46 he was named the Most Valuable Player (MVP) of the WHA. Wayne Gretzky, "the Great One," owns virtually all of hockey's scoring records. He also won eight consecutive NHL MVP Awards (nine in ten years) and led his team to four Stanley Cup Championships. His 215 points (162 assists) in a season is considered one of sports' most unbreakable records.

Boxing has seen such greats as "Gentleman Jim" Corbett (heavyweight champion in 1892), Jack Dempsey, Joe Louis, Sonny Liston, Muhammad Ali, Rocky Marciano, Sugar Ray Robinson, and Joe Frazier. Golf has legends such as Walter Hagen, Bobby Jones, Ben Hogan, Sam Snead, Jack Nicklaus, Arnold Palmer, and more recently Tiger Woods. And let's not forget Babe Didrikson, who was the founding lady of the LPGA. In recent years athletes such as Tiger Woods, David Beckham, Cal Ripken, Anna Sorenstam, Pete Sampras, Steve Yzerman, Alex Rodriquez, and Sidney Crosby have dominated the headlines. These athletes have achieved celebrity status by virtue of their athletic ability and are some of the most easily recognized people in the world.

ESPN's biography program, *SportsCentury*, listed the greatest 100 athletes of the 20th century in January 1999. The most represented sport was baseball, with 23 athletes in the top 100. Interestingly, Jim Thorpe was listed in the baseball, football, and track and field categories. The top 50 are shown in Table 1-1. Do you agree with *SportsCentury*'s list? Where is Tiger Woods? Should he be placed on the list now? Who else deserves consideration?

Certainly, sports have become more commercialized in the last 20 years. Players and coaches make more money. Tiger Woods made in excess of $100 million in endorsements alone in 2007. David Beckham signed a contract with the Los Angeles Galaxy of the MLS worth approximately $250 million. Television has increased the exposure of sports at all levels and created opportunities for all parties involved in sports. Sports have become an entertainment product in the United States.

Americans participate in and watch a variety of sports; however, baseball has always been considered the American pastime. The first professional game was thought to have been played in 1869. The first World Series was played in 1903. Why is baseball considered America's national game? Why not football, basketball, hockey, or even golf? What is the greatest sport?

Sports have created some exciting moments for millions of fans for over a hundred years. If you are a sports fan, then you can certainly recall a great sporting event you have attended or witnessed on television. There are some moments in sports history that have dominated the sports landscape, such as Johnny Vander Meer's back-to-back no-hitters for the Reds in 1938, and Britain's Roger Bannister becoming the first man to break the four-minute mile in 1954. Bobby Thomson's "shot heard around the world," a home run that gave the New York Giants the pennant over their dreaded rival, the Brooklyn Dodgers, in 1951 is considered by many to be the greatest moment in sports history.

TABLE 1-1

Top 50 Athletes of the 20th Century	
1. Michael Jordan	26. Kareem-Abdul Jabbar
2. Babe Ruth	27. Jerry Rice
3. Muhammad Ali	28. Red Grange
4. Jim Brown	29. Arnold Palmer
5. Wayne Gretzky	30. Larry Bird
6. Jesse Owens	31. Bobby Orr
7. Jim Thorpe	32. Johnny Unitas
8. Willie Mays	33. Mark Spitz
9. Jack Nicklaus	34. Lou Gehrig
10. Babe Didrikson	35. Secretariat
11. Joe Louis	36. Oscar Robertson
12. Carl Lewis	37. Mickey Mantle
13. Wilt Chamberlain	38. Ben Hogan
14. Hank Aaron	39. Walter Payton
15. Jackie Robinson	40. Lawrence Taylor
16. Ted Williams	41. Wilma Rudolph
17. Magic Johnson	42. Sandy Koufax
18. Bill Russell	43. Julius Erving
19. Martina Navratilova	44. Bobby Jones
20. Ty Cobb	45. Bill Tilden
21. Gordie Howe	46. Eric Heiden
22. Joe DiMaggio	47. Edwin Moses
23. Jackie Joyner-Kersee	48. Pete Sampras
24. Sugar Ray Robinson	49. O.J. Simpson
25. Joe Montana	50. Chris Evert

Source: Courtesy of Baseball Reference. www.baseball-reference.com/bullpen/SportsCentury.

In the 1954 World Series, Willie Mays's catch of a Vic Wertz fly ball at the Polo Grounds is considered to be the greatest baseball catch of all time.

Some great moments in sports have been achieved by everyday players. Only one perfect game has ever been tossed in the history of the World Series: Don Larsen, with an 81–91 lifetime record, achieved the feat in the 1956 World Series against the Brooklyn Dodgers. Wilt Chamberlain's 100-point game in 1962 in the NBA is considered one of the most untouchable records in professional basketball. In the 1968 Super Bowl, Joe Namath led the underdog Jets to a major upset of the Baltimore Colts led by Johnny Unitas. The win by the Jets was one of the factors that led to the eventual merger of the NFL and American Football League (AFL) in 1970.

The Miracle Mets of 1969 and Reggie Jackson's monstrous home run in the 1971 All-Star Game in Detroit were landmark moments in sports, as were the perfect season by the Miami Dolphins in the NFL in 1973, Hank Aaron passing Babe Ruth on the all-time home run list with 755 in 1974, and the 1982 buzzer-beater win in the NCAA Finals, with North Carolina State prevailing over the Cougars of Houston. The 1980 U.S. Olympic hockey team's victory over the heavily favored Russians created a feeling of national pride in the United States and is considered by many to be the one greatest moment in U.S. sports history.

A sports moment cannot be much more dramatic than Kirk Gibson's home run in the 1988 World Series against the Oakland Athletics. Gibson could barely walk to the plate. However, in a pinch hitting role, he drilled a pitch by Dennis Eckersley into the right-field stands, providing fans with one of the shining moments in baseball folklore. The University of Texas Longhorns, led by Vince Young, beat the University of Southern California in the 2005 Rose Bowl 42–39, winning college football's National Championship in what many consider to be one of the greatest college football games of all time. For many, their greatest moment in sports is more personal. It might be a son or daughter scoring a basket, hitting a home run, scoring the winning goal, or wining a race.

Although sports have produced some thrilling moments over the years for fans and players alike, they have also provided a few "goats" and unfortunate plays as well. Consider the unbelievable day that Roy Riegels had in the 1929 Rose Bowl. Riegels was the captain-elect of the University of California football team for the 1929 season. In the granddaddy of all errors, Riegels picked up a fumble by a Georgia Tech player and ran to the wrong end zone, resulting in a safety for Georgia Tech. Cal lost the Rose Bowl 8–7. The win gave Georgia Tech the National Championship. At halftime Riegels told his coach he could not come out for the second half because he was humiliated. He was encouraged to do so by his teammates and coach and played an outstanding second half, even blocking a Georgia Tech punt. Unfortunately, after the game he was dubbed "Wrong Way Riegels" and received offers of marriage and sponsorships alike: the proposed sponsorships were for upside-down cake, a backward marathon, and a necktie with Riegels running the wrong way.

Notwithstanding the play, Riegels was a great football player and was named to several All-American teams after the 1929 season. He was certainly a good sport about the whole thing. In September of 1971, some 42 years after the event, the 1928 Georgia Tech team was inducted into the Georgia Tech Hall of Fame. Riegels and Benny Lorn, Riegels' teammate who tried to tackle him before he went into the end zone, were both invited to the event and accepted. They were both presented with membership cards to the Georgia Tech Letterman's Club. After his induction, Riegels said, "Believe me, I feel I've earned this." Riegels recovered pretty well from the episode in the 1929 Rose Bowl, earning All-American honors, serving in World War II, coaching both high school and college football, and running his own oil company. He is in the Rose Bowl's Hall of Fame and Cal's Hall of Fame—not a bad lifetime achievement.

One last note on Riegels that shows his esteemed character: In 1957 Jan Bandringa intercepted a pass for Paramount High School and ran 55 yards to his own end zone, resulting in a safety, giving Centennial High a 9–7 victory. Bandringa received a letter from Riegels that said, "For many years I've had to go along and laugh whenever my wrong-way run was brought up, even though I've grown tired listening and reading about it. But it certainly wasn't the most serious thing in the world. I regretted doing it, even as you do, but you'll get over it." How do you think Riegels' blunder would have been treated in today's media circus with sports talk radio and sports television? Riegels must have been a good sport and a person with a solid character. In the professional ranks, Vikings defensive end Jim Marshall recovered a fumble and ran the wrong way, resulting in a safety for the 49'ers.

Riegels called Marshall to issue condolences. I guess you could say it was an elite club. Marshall holds the record for the most opponents' fumbles recovered in the NFL and started 270 consecutive NFL games. He also appeared in several Pro Bowls and was a member of the Vikings' famous "Purple People Eaters" defense.

Bill Buckner was an All-Star first baseman for the Boston Red Sox; however, mentioning his name to a Red Sox fan might incite a certain level of hostility. Buckner's now-infamous error allowed the New York Mets the opportunity to capture the 1986 World Series title. The Red Sox faithful would have to wait another 18 years before winning a World Series title and breaking the mysterious "Curse of the Bambino."[8]

Sports have created some of the greatest moments for some and the worst for others. Take the tragic case of Donnie Moore. Moore was a good pitcher for the California Angels. The Angels were one pitch away from going to the 1986 World Series when Dave Henderson of the Red Sox drilled a pitch from Moore into the left-field stands for a Red Sox victory. Moore's life after the pitch was filled with turmoil and eventually ended in an attempted murder of his wife and his suicide.

Occasionally sports are able to transcend their surroundings and the game itself. The following event involving baseball player Rick Monday was one of those times. Monday was an outstanding performer in the Major Leagues for 19 seasons while hitting .264 and slugging a respectable 241 home runs. He was an MLB All-Star in 1968 and 1976 and had led Arizona State to the 1965 College World Series Championship. He was the first overall pick in the 1968 MLB draft. He may, however, be best remembered for his flag-saving moment in a 1976 game between the Dodgers and Cubs. William Thomas and his 11-year-old son had run onto the field at Dodger Stadium with an American flag and some matches with the intent of burning the flag. Monday, a 6-year veteran of the Marine Corps, quickly swiped the flag away from the two protestors, much to the delight of the crowd, which broke out singing "God Bless America." Monday has been offered $1 million for the flag but has turned it down. Baseball's Hall of Fame voted Monday's action as one of the 100 classic moments in the history of baseball.[9] The moment was captured by photographer James Roark of the *Los Angeles Herald Examiner*, who was nominated for the Pulitzer Prize for snapping the photograph.

It is unquestioned that sports have a substantial influence on the American landscape. They have influenced our culture, politics, and moral outlook over the last 200 years. Sports are replete with examples of how athletes have influenced our culture. Jesse Owens put to rest the myth of Aryan supremacy in the 1936 Olympics before a cast of Nazi soldiers and Adolf Hitler himself by winning four Olympic gold medals. However, upon his return to the United States, he remarked, "When I came back home, I couldn't live where I wanted. I wasn't invited to shake hands with Hitler, but I wasn't invited to the White House to shake hands with the president, either."[10] The upset victory of Texas Western, with the first all–African American lineup in college basketball, over the perennial college basketball power Kentucky was a major landmark for race and sports. Jackie Robinson, an All-American football player at UCLA, was the first to break baseball's color barrier in 1947 and endured racial hatred while doing so.

---

[8] The "Curse of the Bambino" is the Boston Red Sox faithful's explanation for the Red Sox World Series drought. For further study, see Dan Shaughnessy, The Curse Of The Bambino (2004).

[9] USA TODAY, Apr. 25, 2006.

[10] Jim Platt & James Buckley, Sports Immortals: Stories of Inspiration and Achievement (Triumph Books 2002).

Sports and politics have always had a close relationship. Many U.S. presidents played sports. Gerald Ford was offered professional contracts by the Green Bay Packers and the Detroit Lions after playing linebacker and center on the 1933 and 1934 undefeated National Championship teams for the Michigan Wolverines. President Ford was an outstanding all-around athlete, even appearing in the college all-star game in Chicago against the Bears. Jack Kennedy (Harvard), Richard Nixon (Whittier College), Ronald Reagan (partial football scholarship, Eureka College), and Dwight D. Eisenhower (Army) all played college football. Eisenhower once tackled Jim Thorpe during an Army–Carlisle college clash. Ronald Reagan was affectionately known as "the Gipper" for his portrayal of Notre Dame halfback George Gipp in *Knute Rockne, All American* (Warner Bros. 1940). He uttered one of the most famous lines in Hollywood history in this movie: "Sometimes when the team is up against it and the breaks are beating the boys, tell them to go out there with all they've got and win just one for the Gipper." Reagan was also a lifeguard for many years as a youth, and the Ronald Reagan Library credits him with saving approximately 77 lives over a period of seven years. George H. W. Bush (the 41st president) played second base on the Yale baseball team. George W. Bush (the 43rd president) was a part owner of the Texas Rangers baseball team and was a cheerleader at Yale.

Many former athletes have also been involved in the political arena at levels other than the presidency. Byron White was a member of the U.S. Supreme Court, but he might be best known as "Whizzer White" to many from his football playing days at the University of Colorado. Jack Kemp led the Buffalo Bills to two AFL Championships before he was a U.S. Congressman from New York. He was also the vice presidential candidate in the 1996 presidential election. Tom Osborne was the University of Nebraska head football coach for many years and parlayed that position into a seat in the U.S. Congress. Jim Bunning was an outstanding pitcher for the Philadelphia Phillies, among other teams, compiling a lifetime record of 224–181. He pitched a perfect game against the New York Mets in 1964 and had a no-hitter for the Tigers in 1958. Bunning became a U.S. Senator from Kentucky in 1998. Bill Bradley, a Rhodes Scholar, was also a U.S. Congressman and was a critical part of two NBA Championships for the New York Knicks. Arnold Schwarzenegger was a five-time Mr. Universe and seven-time Mr. Olympia and became governor of California. Jim Ryun, an outstanding runner, served in Congress from Kansas. In 1966, the 19-year-old Ryun set a world mile record of 3:55:3. NFL Hall of Famer Steve Largent served in Congress, as did the aforementioned decathlon champion Bob Mathias.

Many famous athletes served their country in the armed forces, leaving lucrative and successful athletic careers in the process. Christy Mathewson served in World War I and unfortunately suffered mustard gas poisoning during a training exercise in Europe. Mathewson was one of the five original members of the Baseball Hall of Fame in 1939. (The other members were Babe Ruth, Ty Cobb, Honus Wagner, and Walter Johnson.) Ted Williams batted .344 and hammered 521 home runs for the Boston Red Sox. How many more home runs and RBIs could he have had if not for his two tours of duty as a pilot in World War II and Korea? President George H. W. Bush awarded Williams the Presidential Medal of Freedom for his 19 seasons with the Red Sox and the 5 seasons he missed due to war service. Eddie Collins, Yogi Berra, Stan Musial, Joe DiMaggio, Phil Rizzuto, Nellie Fox, and Willie Mays were all outstanding baseball players who also served in the military. More recently, NFL standout Pat Tillman left a lucrative career in the NFL with the Arizona Cardinals. Tragically, he lost his life in the service of his country in Afghanistan in 2005.

SPORTS ETHICS

Sports and sports law involve ethical decision making. Sports lawyers and managers are faced with ethical dilemmas in everyday practice. Sports ethics is a burgeoning field, and much has been written recently in this area.

Consider the following ethical dilemma, which arose from an incident that occurred during the 1908 baseball season. It was September 23, and the New York Giants were playing the Chicago Cubs in a crucial game for the National League pennant. Hall of Famer Christy Mathewson was pitching for the Giants, with the game tied at 1–1 in the bottom of the ninth. With two outs, the Giants had runners on first (Fred Merkle) and third (Harry McCormick). The batter, Birdwell, hit a single, driving home McCormick from third with the apparent winning run. Merkle, seeing McCormick cross the plate with the apparent winning run, stopped before running all the way to second and headed for the clubhouse in jubilation. Fans poured onto the diamond, wildly celebrating an apparent Giants victory. The Cubs' second baseman, Johnny Evers ("Evers to Tinkers to Chance"),[11] realizing Merkle never touched second, yelled for the Cubs center fielder to throw him the ball. He knew if they could get the ball and touch second he could create a force out[12] at second base, and the winning run would not count. Giants pitcher McGinnity saw what Tinkers was up to and stepped in, intercepted the Cubs' center fielder's throw to Tinkers, and immediately threw the ball into the stands. A fan caught the ball as a prized trophy. However, before he could start home with it, he was chased and knocked down by two Cubs fans, who took the ball and threw it to Joe Tinker, who then relayed it to Evers. Evers then stepped on second amid all the chaos. (There is some dispute about whether it was the actual ball hit by Birdwell, but it was a baseball.) Evers looked for an umpire, but none had seen the play. (It's a shame that instant replay did not exist in 1908.)

The Cubs appealed, and later that night Hank O'Day, home plate umpire, ruled that Merkle was out and the game had ended in a tie; it was too dark to resume play, however. As a result, the Cubs and Giants ended the season in a tie for first place. A playoff was necessary to determine which team would advance to the World Series. The Giants' players did not want to play the game, but the Giants' owner urged them to take the field. They eventually did play and lost, with the Cubs thus "earning" a trip to the Fall Classic.

A board of directors determined whether or not to have a playoff. (This was prior to the creation of the office of Baseball Commissioner.) Affidavits had been submitted by many players from both teams claiming ownership of the truth of the events that transpired that day. Christy Mathewson had been coaching first base at the time of the play. He submitted an affidavit that said that Merkle had not reached second base. George Dovey was on baseball's board of directors at the time and stated with regard to the affidavit submitted by Mathewson:

> You may not realize what that affidavit, offered to us voluntarily, meant to Mathewson. First of all, it meant a share in the World Series. Also, had the disputed game stood as it ended, without technicality, Mathewson would have led all National League pitchers for the season. Miner [Mordecai] Brown beat him out of the honor in the post-season game. We took all the other affidavits and threw them in the waste basket. Matty's word was good enough for us.[13]

---

[11] This was the most famous double-play combination in baseball history. Their prowess was lauded in the poem "Baseball's Sad Lexicon" (1910) by Franklin Pierce Adams.

[12] Force Out: The putout of an advancing baserunner who is forced to move to the next base. Paul Dickson, *The Baseball Dictionary, 3rd Edition*, W. W. Norton & Company, 2009.

[13] Philip Seib, The Player: Christy Mathewson, Baseball and the American Century 51 (2003).

Unfortunately for Merkle, his mishap forever became known as "Merkle's Boner."[14] The baseball public never let Merkle forget his play in the 1908 pennant deciding game as a 19-year-old. Merkle did have a very respectable Major League career, batting .273 with 61 home runs. Notwithstanding the outcome of the season, the Giants' owner had gold medals made for all the Giants' players that read "The Real Champions, 1908."[15]

How many people would do what PGA golfer Greg Chalmers did? He disqualified himself from play in the 2001 Kemper Insurance Open after he discovered he had committed a rules violation. In the opening round he had hit a poor shot and later, upset with himself over the shot, made a comment to a caddie who was working for another golfer about the club he had used. His remarks constituted a violation of U.S. Golf Association Rule 8.1, which prevented a golfer from giving advice to another golfer during tournament play. Chalmers was unaware of the rule until three days after the remark, when he learned about it in a conversation with a fellow golfer. Chalmers subsequently forfeited his potential winnings (in the amount of $94,500).[16] How much integrity does it take to report your own rules violation and leave $94,500 on the table?

Keeping track of what down it is in a football game would seem to be a simple task, especially in an Ivy League contest. However, in the 1940 contest between Cornell and Dartmouth, Cornell, by virtue of a mistake by the referee, received five downs and scored on the fifth, giving it an apparent 7–3 victory over its Ivy League rival. Cornell came into the game with an 18-game winning streak. The Big Red had a first and goal at the Dartmouth (Big Green) 5-yard line with one minute left in the game. Cornell called a time-out, but a delay of game penalty moved the ball back to the 6-yard line. On fourth down, a Cornell pass was knocked down by a Dartmouth defender, but the referee became confused at this point because the scoreboard was still showing third down. Cornell was allowed to run another play, scoring a touchdown. The day after the game, the referee issued a statement apologizing for the error. After reviewing the film the next day, Cornell coach Snavely realized his team made its winning touchdown on the fifth down. In an unprecedented act, Snavely and Cornell's Athletic Director Jim Lynalt sent a telegraph to Dartmouth and offered congratulations to the "gallant" Dartmouth team on their victory. Dartmouth gladly accepted. Dartmouth football history lists the game as a 3–0 victory.[17] Cornell also conceded a Dartmouth win.[18] ESPN's *College Football Encyclopedia* lists the score as a 3–0 Dartmouth victory as well. This fifth-down play is noted as one of the top ten moments in college football.[19]

Similar events occurred in a Colorado–Missouri game in 1991 in which Colorado was given five downs and scored a touchdown on the fifth, winning the game 33–31. Colorado won the National Championship in 1991 with an 11–1–1 record. No concessions were made after the game. Should there have been? What action should have been taken by the university? The coach? Alumni? What repercussions would have resulted from a Colorado concession? Colorado coach Bill McCartney later founded Promisekeepers, a Christian men's group, in 1990. He later admitted he was "truly remorseful" about the fifth-down play and the result. He retired as the Colorado coach in 1994.

---

[14] Geoffrey C. Ward, Baseball: An Illustrated History (1994).

[15] One wonders how much Merkle's gold medal might be worth in today's sports memorabilia market.

[16] Fred Bowen, *An Honest Mistake*, Wash. Post, June 8, 2001.

[17] DartmouthSports.com, http://www.dartmouthsports.com.

[18] Cornell University, http://www.cornellbigred.com.

[19] ESPN College Football Encyclopedia: The Complete History of the Game (Michael McCambridge ed., 2005).

Most would argue that cheating in sports is unethical and unsportsmanlike. How should sports treat cheating? Should participants be fined, suspended, or both? What are the appropriate penalties for a player who bends the rules a little? Does it matter whether a player intentionally cheats or just unknowingly breaks the rules of the game? Do some sports tolerate cheating more than other sports?

One of the more famous cheaters in sports history was Rosie Ruiz, who entered the 1980 Boston Marathon with the intent of winning, like all the other participants. She did win, but her victory was a Pyrrhic victory at best. The word *marathon* would seem to indicate "running" to most—not riding a subway. Rosie must have been confused, because she took some form of motorized vehicle to make up lost ground. She was, of course, disqualified from the race. She was able to achieve the third-fastest time ever recorded for a female runner until that time. (It boggles the mind how a marathon runner could take a subway train but only finish with the third-fastest time in history.) Ruiz had evidently previously cheated in the New York City Marathon as well when she ran there to qualify for the Boston Marathon. She is banned for life from the Boston Marathon.

Not to be outdone by Ruiz, Abbes Tehami started a marathon in Brussels on September 17, 1991—or at least that is what officials thought. Evidently, along the way Tehami was able to find the time to stop and shave. When he crossed the finish line, he had no mustache, whereas when the person identified as Abbe Tehami began the run, he was sporting a mustache. It was determined that his coach actually started the race and ran seven and a half miles, after which the two veered off course and switched the number 62 bib. The race organizer Milou Blavier, upon seeing Tehami in the race, stated, "Gee, this is some comeback." Tehami never claimed his $7,150 winnings. As he crossed the finish line, he and his coach disappeared, evidently realizing that they had been busted.

Danny Amante was an overpowering Little League pitcher. Well, who wouldn't be if you were 14 and pitching to 12-year-olds? He dominated the 2001 Little League World Series, tossing a perfect game in the process. His team's regional championship was taken away, as was the team's third-place finish in the 2001 Little League World Series.

In a 1995 game between the University of Virginia (UVA) and Virginia Tech, Antonio Banks, a cornerback for Virginia Tech, intercepted a pass and ran it back for a touchdown in a 36–29 victory for the Hokies. Television replays showed UVA head athletic trainer Joe Gieck moving onto the field and attempting to stick out his left leg to trip Banks as he ran past for the touchdown. He denied trying to trip the player, but Terry Holland, Director of Virginia Athletics, started an investigation, and Gieck was prohibited from representing the Cavaliers at athletic events until the investigation was completed.[20]

When the New York Knicks were pursuing NBA championships in the 1970s, they engaged in a subtle tactic to prevent teams from running the court against them. It was said that certain Knicks players carried needles in their uniforms while playing, and at the right moment would deflate the ball to make it "softer."[21]

Major League Baseball's all-time hit leader Pete Rose gambled on games he actually managed for the Cincinnati Reds. Ken Caminiti admitted to taking steroids during his 1999 MVP season with the San Diego Padres. Should MLB rescind the MVP award because of his admission? Ron McKelvey

---

[20] Frederick J. Day, Clubhouse Lawyer: Law in the World of Sports 375–376 (2002).
[21] *Id.* at 369.

had a great college football career—about eight years long, to be exact. By using fake Social Security numbers, he was able to play football at several schools, including the University of Texas. Once his fraud was revealed, he was immediately dismissed from the university. Tim Johnson was the manager of the Toronto Blue Jays in 1998 and led them to a third-place finish. He was fired because he lied about serving in Vietnam as a Marine. George O'Leary resigned as head coach at the University of Notre Dame after discrepancies were found in his academic background. How should these acts be viewed? What action should be taken?

A football coach was banned for life from coaching after he allegedly cheated during a high school football game. Videotape showed the coach moving a down marker to assist his team in gaining a first down on a fourth-down play against a rival school. The coach's team scored on the drive and eventually won the game 13–12. The Rules Committee of the California Interscholastic Federation banned the coach for life after reviewing the matter.[22]

The following should be placed in the "How low can you go?" category: During the 2000 Sydney Paralympics, the Spanish "intellectually disabled" basketball team won the gold medal. However, the Spanish Paralympic Committee later discovered that 10 of the 12 players possessed no mental deficiency whatsoever. The scandal led to an overhaul of the Paralympic movement.

A Little League team from Colchester, Vermont, was leading Portsmouth, New Hampshire, 9–8. It was the top of the sixth (and last) inning, and Colchester merely needed three outs to advance to the New England Regional Championships. However, when the Colchester team had completed its turn at bat in the bottom of the fifth, it was discovered that not all players had a turn at bat. League rules require all players to bat at least once; if not, then the game is to be forfeited. Colchester's coach realized in the top of the sixth that one of his players had not batted. The coach realized the only way he could win was for Portsmouth to score so his team could get another at bat to win and avoid the forfeit. This circumstance led to a carnival atmosphere, with Colchester attempting to allow Portsmouth to score and Portsmouth refusing to score. The coach for Colchester instructed his pitcher to walk the first batter and then "wild pitch" the runner around so he could score and tie the game 9–9. Mark McCauley, Portsmouth's coach, got wise to the plan and told his players not to score and to intentionally strike out. The umpires eventually ejected the Colchester coach and pitcher. Colchester won the game 9–8 on the scoreboard, but Portsmouth won by forfeit 6–0. Was that the correct decision? Did the coaches and players act ethically under the circumstances? What should each coach have done under the circumstances?

Paul McCoy was a star running back for Matewan High School in Matewan, Michigan. Matewan had a 35–0 halftime lead over Burch, and McCoy had achieved 300 yards rushing and five touchdowns at the half. McCoy's coach, realizing McCoy had a chance to break the U.S. high school rushing and touchdown record in a single game, started the third quarter with a no-huddle offense. Matewan players also stopped running back punts to give McCoy a shot at the record. McCoy rushed for 661 yards on 28 carries and scored ten touchdowns in a 64–0 victory. There was some dispute about the high school rushing record, but the National Federation of State High School Associations showed the national record as being 619 yards in 1995. The Matewan coach defended his actions: "Why should there be any guilty feelings? Our school's smaller than they are. Why should I punish my kids for having a pretty good team? We were going to score 60 points if Paul doesn't even get on the bus."

---

[22] Mitch Stephens, *Oceanside Holds off El Cajon Valley*, NFLHS.com.

Was the conduct of the Matewan coach ethical? Was it unsportsmanlike? What is the difference? Is it unethical to "run up" the score on an opponent? Should there be a difference in amateur or professional athletics? Should college football consider the scores of games in ranking teams? Could failing to score enough points in a college football game affect a university financially? Are schools encouraged to run up the score on opponents?

Do you consider the following a "win at all costs" scenario? On June 23, 2006, in Bountiful, Utah, the Yankees were playing the Red Sox for the championship. No, not *that* championship—the Mueller Park Mustang League 10 and Under Championship. Red Sox player Romney Oaks was at the plate in the last inning with two outs and a runner on third. Romney struck out, ending the game and giving the Yankees a 9–8 victory. The victory and how it was achieved became the subject of a national debate. Romney's growth had been stunted by a malignant cranial tumor at the age of four. In a strategic move, Yankees coach Bob Farley chose to walk Jordan Bleak, the Red Sox's best hitter, to get to Romney in the last inning. Bleak already had a triple and a home run in his previous at bats. Romney proceeded to strike out. The Yankees advanced to the Little League World Series as a result of the win.[23] How do you view this situation? Was Romney's weakness exploited by the Yankees to win? Do you take the position that any player who is on the field playing the game should be treated just like everyone else? The Yankees were playing by the rules, but did they win the right way?

What ethical dilemmas do the following scenarios in sports present?

- A pitcher doctors the ball during a game.[24]
- A player steals another team's signs during a baseball game.
- A pitcher throws a brush-back pitch to a batter to "send a message."
- A hockey goalie knows a puck has passed the red line for a goal but pulls it out of the net before a referee sees it.
- A football player trips a runner in the open field who is running for a touchdown.
- A hockey player starts a fight with an opposing player in an attempt to get him thrown out of the game.
- An athlete uses a legal drug to enhance his performance on the field even though the league has banned the drug.
- A defensive back knows that the opposing quarterback had off-season knee surgery and during the game attempts to tackle him in the area of the surgery to put him out of the game.
- A baseball player knows he missed first base and is called out by the umpire. He then attempts to convince the umpire he actually touched the base.
- An NFL team is 1–14 going into the last game of the season. The team knows they can improve the team by finishing last and getting the first draft pick of next year's draft. Several players on the team try to lose the game on purposefully.

---

[23] Greg Garber, *Youth Team Pays High Price in Win-At-All-Costs Game*, ESPN.com, Aug. 15, 2006.

[24] "Doctoring" a baseball refers to placing a foreign substance on the ball to gain an advantage over the batter. Don Sutton, like many successful pitchers, was accused of doctoring the ball. When Sutton was confronted about whether he had ever applied a foreign substance, he responded, "Not true at all. Vaseline is manufactured right here in the United States." Day, *supra* note 20.

- A high school football team is beating its opponent 70–3 with two minutes to go in the game. The team scores a touchdown and then decides to go for a two-point conversion to break the school's record of 77 points.
- A Major League baseball player "corks" his bat to improve his hitting.
- A professional athlete admits to the media that he does not give 100% every game.
- A college basketball coach recruits a player, knowing that the player cannot perform the academic work required to be successful at the university.
- A league passes a rule that states minority candidates should be given preference in the interviewing process for coaching and administrative positions.
- A professional sport league plays a full schedule of games two days after a national tragedy.
- A professional pitcher "grooves" a pitch to a retiring player in his last at bat, and the player hits a home run.

Problem 1-1

John Allen accepted the head coaching position at New Mexico State University and signed a five-year contract paying him $500,000 a year, with incentives that possibly would raise his pay to as much as $700,000 yearly. After completing one football season at New Mexico State and finishing with a record of 7–5, Allen was offered the head coaching position at Arizona State University (ASU). On the same day that he was contacted by ASU about the head coach position, he signed an extension of his contract with New Mexico State for an additional five years. His contract with New Mexico State allowed for a buyout of his contract for $1 million. Two days after he signed the extension with New Mexico State, he signed a new contract with ASU, which paid New Mexico State $1 million to buy out the coach's contract. ASU gave Allen an eight-year deal worth $1.2 million a year. Allen has complied with all his contractual obligations to New Mexico State. What ethical considerations does his decision to accept the job at ASU raise? If he did nothing illegal and has not breached his contract with New Mexico State, does that mean he has acted ethically? What other parties are affected by his decision?

SPORTS VIOLENCE

Unfortunately, violence has become a major issue in both amateur and professional sports, and violence both by fans and players has increased in the last few years. Professional leagues and owners have attempted to take steps to ensure that violence does not threaten fan safety. Owners do not want fans afraid to attend games for fear of violent acts.

There are too many incidents to name here, but a few are instructive. One of the more famous events that took place in the NBA was a fight between the Detroit Pistons and the Indiana Pacers. This brawl eventually spilled over into the stands, and fans and players began to fight each other.

The NBA levied heavy fines and suspensions to all players involved. Latrell Sprewell was suspended by the NBA and fined for his alleged choking of his coach, P. J. Carlesimo. The event garnered national attention.

Well-respected professor Kenneth Shropshire's article about Latrell Sprewell takes an interesting look at race and sports in society. Although Shropshire readily admits that Sprewell is not a "choir boy," he makes some interesting arguments in Sprewell's defense. He also discusses sports and their role in society as a whole:

> Let me be clear: Sprewell's record is not a good one. Prior to the choking incident, Sprewell had feuded with his previous coach, Don Nelson; his driver's license had been revoked or suspended six times; and he had been under house arrest for three months for a reckless driving incident. These events, coupled with past allegations of violence against fellow players, including an alleged two-by-four assault, made him no one's ideal client. But success in the league was Sprewell's dream. Would a White player's dream have been stomped on in the same manner in order to deliver a broader, get-back-in-your-place message?
>
> An examination of the game itself tells us much about our own society. In the past, I've written that sports is a microcosm of society. I have concluded recently that this is an overstatement. Among other differences, the absence of inter-gender relationships reduces the value of sports as the ideal model. Further, the basketball model is Black and White, quite different from the real America. Baseball, with its increasing Latino component, is potentially a better model, but it is not as entrenched in urban culture as is basketball. Taking a hard look at the racial realities in basketball, a business perceived to be a bastion of equal opportunity for African Americans, provides a view of where we are in broader American society. For greater progress in the legislatures, our courts, and other sectors of society, more of those who have not directly felt or seen racism and other forms of discrimination need to believe it still exists. Those who doubt that the effects of racism in sports continue also need to accept that the majority of those striving to participate in the American Dream through sports no longer look like Bob Feller, and may, in fact, look like Latrell Sprewell.[25]

Texas Rangers relief pitcher Francisco Cordero used his powers for bad when he threw a chair into the stands and injured a spectator. He was suspended by Major League Baseball for 16 games because of his actions. He was sued for damages by the injured party and her husband, and the case was settled by the parties prior to trial.

In an infamous incident in baseball in 1966, San Francisco Giants pitcher Juan Marichal hit Dodgers catcher John Roseboro in the head with a bat. Marichal was subsequently suspended. Roseboro sued Marichal but eventually dropped the lawsuit. Marichal was fined $1,750 and suspended for a week. Years later Marichal expressed remorse for the incident. In one of the darker days of boxing, Mike Tyson bit off part of the ear of boxer Evander Holyfield during a boxing match.

Tennis great Monica Seles was stabbed by a Steffi Graf fan, Gunter Parche, in Hamburg, Germany, while playing in a match in 1993. Before that she had won 30 single titles in just five years. Player and fan violence took a turn for the worse on May 16, 2000, when Dodgers catcher Chad Krueter was punched in the back of the head by a fan who took the cap off his head. Krueter and several

---

[25] Kenneth L. Shropshire, *Beyond Sprewell: The New American Dream*, 4 J. GENDER RACE & JUST. 1, 13 (2000).

teammates rushed into the crowd, and a major brawl broke out between fans and players. Several Dodgers players and coaches were suspended as a result. An injured spectator was arrested for disorderly conduct. Several lawsuits were filed against the players, the Dodgers, and the Cubs as a result.[26]

Hockey has always had a reputation for fighting. In fact, hockey is one of the few sports that employs the services of a penalty box, which suspends a player's participation privileges for a short period of time for breaking the rules of the game. Most other sports will merely toss a player out of the game for misconduct. How much violence should professional hockey tolerate?

Two hockey incidents garnered significant attention because of the excessive violence involved. In 2000, Donald Brasher was assaulted on the ice during a game by noted enforcer Marty McSorley. McSorley was convicted of assault with a deadly weapon. He received an 18-month conditional discharge sentence and no jail time. Brasher suffered injuries as the result of the attack. In 2004, Steve Moore was struck across the head with a stick in a vicious attack by Todd Bertuzzi of the Vancouver Canucks. Bertuzzi was suspended by the league and lost over $500,000 in pay as a result of the suspension. Moore sued Bertuzzi in a civil lawsuit seeking millions of dollars in damages. NHL commissioner Gary Bettman stated, "This is not a part of our game, it has no place in our game, and it will not be tolerated in our game." Bertuzzi was suspended and was eventually reinstated 17 months later. He pled guilty to criminal charges, received a year probated sentence, and was forced to do 80 hours of community service.

One of the more violent acts in the history of sports was committed by Kermit Washington of the Los Angeles Lakers against NBA All-Star and head coach Rudy Tomjanovich of the Houston Rockets. Washington violently attacked Tomjanovich, punching him in the face and destroying his face beyond recognition. Tomjanovich later sued the Lakers and won a large verdict, primarily due to his attorney's skilled representation. Attorney Nick Nichols handled the case for Tomjanovich and was able to persuade a jury to return a large verdict in his client's favor. The case was later settled before a hearing on the appeal.

Football is by its nature a violent sport. How much on-field violence should be tolerated by a professional football league? How should off-the-field violence be treated? What role should a players union have in ensuring a player receives fair discipline from the team, league, or commissioner for acts of violence? In 2006, Albert Haynesworth stepped on the head of Dallas Cowboys center Andre Gurode with his cleats while Gurode was helmetless. He later apologized to Gurode but was suspended by the NFL.

Violence in youth sports has also increased. What can be done to curb the violence in youth sports? Is there too much parental supervision in sports for children? Are sports taken too seriously by parents at the youth sports level? Are there too many organized sports for youth? What about instituting a parent-free zone at the youth sports events where only kids and referees are allowed to participate? Should there be sportsmanship rules for parents and coaches when they participate in youth sports? On July 5, 2000, in Boston, Massachusetts, a fight took place in a youth hockey game between a player's father and his coach. The coach died the day after the fight. The parent was convicted of involuntary manslaughter and sentenced to six to ten years in prison.[27]

---

[26] Walter Champion, *The Great Dodgers–Wrigley Field Melee: A Bar Exam Question in the Making?*, 2 TEX. REV. SPORTS & ENT. L. 43 (2001).

[27] Law News, http://www.cnn.com/lawcenter, Jan. 11, 2002.

RACE AND SPORTS

Sports and race have been the subject of much discussion for many years. In baseball the color barrier was broken in 1947 by Jackie Robinson of the Brooklyn Dodgers. The Dodgers' general manager, Branch Rickey, specifically chose Robinson because of his character as well as athletic skill because he knew Robinson would face harassment and discrimination when he came to the major leagues. Black players played in the Negro Leagues for many years before the color barrier was broken in baseball. Today Major League Baseball has players from many different countries and different races.

Early Lloyd was the first black player in the NBA in 1952, playing with the Boston Celtics. Bill Russell won 11 championships as a player with the Boston Celtics in 13 seasons and was also named player manager of the Celtics in 1966. Russell experienced racism early in his life and was outspoken on civil rights issues. Above all else, Bill Russell was a winner, and isn't that the essence of sports—to win?

Consider the following statements made by athletes and executives in sports. Are the statements racist? Are they inappropriate? Are they to be considered free speech? How should they be viewed? When an athlete, coach, or sports executive makes a comment that could be considered racist or disparaging, what discipline measures should be taken?

In 2004 Larry Bird said that he thought the NBA lacked enough white superstars. "You know, when I played, you had me and Kevin [McHale] and some others throughout the league. I think it's good for a fan base because, as we all know, the majority of the fans are white America. And if you just had a couple of white guys in there, you might get them a little excited."[28] What do you think of Bird's remarks? Would it have been different if Bird were an active player? Should his comments be treated the same as the remarks made by John Rocker as in Case 1-2, Arbitration Regarding John Rocker, later in the chapter? The NBA took no action against Bird for his remarks. Did "Larry the Legend" get a break because of his stature and contributions to the league?

Golfer Fuzzy Zoeller said of Tiger Woods after he won the Masters Golf Tournament, "That little boy is driving well and he's putting well. He's doing everything it takes to win. So, you know what you guys do when he gets in here? You pat him on the back and say congratulations and enjoy it and tell him not to serve fried chicken next year. Got it? . . . [O]r collard greens or whatever the hell they serve." Zoeller lost several endorsement contracts as a result of his remarks. Do you consider his remarks racist? Should the PGA have taken steps to discipline Zoeller? Is this a different situation because golf is an individual sport? How do you compare these remarks to those of Bird? To those of John Rocker? Should any of these remarks be considered free speech?

In 1981 Al Campanis was fired after his controversial remarks on Ted Koppel's ABC's *Nightline* program. On April 6, 1987 *Nightline* devoted its program to the 40th anniversary of Jackie Robinson's Major League debut. Campanis had worked with the Dodgers since 1943 and was actually Jackie Robinson's teammate on the minor league team, Montreal Royals in 1946, the year before Robinson broke baseball's the color barrier.

Consider some of the outrageous statements made by Marge Schott, former owner of the Cincinnati Reds, such as saying that "Hitler was good in the beginning, but he went too far."[29] Why she was discussing Adolf Hitler at all is still a mystery, but she must have felt compelled to comment on the most hated person in the history of the world for some reason. She was also said to have used racial remarks

---

[28] Phil Taylor, *Bird's Comments About White Players in NBA Unwise, But Not Untrue*, SI.com, June 14, 2004.
[29] N.Y. TIMES, Nov. 29, 1992.

in describing players. She was suspended from baseball on February 3, 1993, for one year and fined $25,000 for language the executive council stated was "racially and ethically offensive." Should she have been treated differently because she was the owner of a team instead of a player? What disciplinary power does a commissioner of a league have over an owner for conduct detrimental to the league?

Consider also the comments of the former manager of the Chicago Cubs, Dusty Baker:

> Personally, I like to play in the heat. You know, it's easier for me. I mean, it's easier for most Latin guys and most minority people because most of us come from heat. You know, you don't find too many brothers from New Hampshire and Maine and upper peninsula and Michigan, right? I mean, you know, we're brought over here for the heat. Right? I mean, ain't that—isn't that history? Weren't we brought over here because we could take the heat?

Do you agree with Dusty Baker's version of history? What actions, if any, should have been taken against him?

On ESPN's *Sunday NFL Countdown*, Rush Limbaugh commented on Philadelphia Eagles quarterback Donovan McNabb, stating:

> Sorry to say this, I don't think he's been that good from the get-go. I think what we've had here is a little social concern in the NFL. The media has been very desirous that a black quarterback do well. There is a little hope invested in McNabb, and he got a lot of credit for the performance of his team that he didn't deserve. The defense carried this team.[30]

Do you believe Limbaugh should have been fired for his comments? Do you consider them racist?

Ozzie Guillen, manager of the Chicago White Sox, was fined by Major League Baseball and ordered to attend sensitivity training for his use of a derogatory term ("fag") to describe Jay Mariotti, a *Chicago Sun-Times* writer. The commissioner of baseball addressed Guillen's remarks, stating: "Baseball is a social institution with responsibility to set appropriate tone and example. Conduct or language that reflects otherwise will not be tolerated. The use of slurs embarrasses the individual, the club and the game." In his defense Guillen stated: "I don't have anything against those people. In my country, you call someone something like that and it is not the same as in this country." He later apologized for the remarks and added that he had gay friends, attended WNBA games, went to a Madonna concert, and planned to go to the Gay Games in Chicago.

Coach Bill Parcells described his surprise football plays as follows: "[N]o disrespect for the Orientals, but what we call Jap plays. OK. Surprise things." He later apologized for his remarks.[31]

Hank Greenberg was a star baseball player with the Detroit Tigers in the 1930s and 1940s. Hank was Jewish, endured anti-Semitism, and was subject to harassment by other players. He was a hero and a source of inspiration in the Jewish community. An excellent documentary film on Greenberg, *The Life and Times of Hank Greenberg* (20th Century Fox 1999), explains this issue. He left baseball in 1941 to enroll in the U.S. Army, where he served four years. Amazingly, in his first game back for the Tigers he hit a home run. He is now in the baseball Hall of Fame.

---

[30] *Limbaugh's Comments Touch Off Controversy*, ESPN.com, Oct. 1, 2003.

[31] *Parcells Apologized for Making Ethnic Remark*, ESPN.com, June 9, 2004, http://sports.espn.go.com/nfl/news/story?id=1817592.

Should sports teams use Native American tribes as names for teams and as mascots? Does it matter if the team is a professional or amateur team? Should there be a distinction between college and high school? The National Collegiate Athletic Association (NCAA) has taken a position in this matter, banning the use of Native American mascots by sports teams during postseason play. This issue has been the subject of much debate; even interscholastic sports have addressed the issue.[32] Some universities have appealed the NCAA's ruling and received waivers for the use of their mascots. Catawba College (Catawba Indians), Central Michigan University (Chippewas), Florida State University (Seminoles), Mississippi College (Choctaws), and the University of Utah (Utes) won their appeals against the NCAA after each showed it had the approval of local tribes to use the nicknames.

The College of William & Mary is phasing out the use of two Indian feathers in its athletic logo after losing a battle with the NCAA. The following letter from the president of William & Mary discusses the NCAA rules on the mascot issue.

October 10, 2006

Dear Fellow Members of the William & Mary Community:

I write concerning the National Collegiate Athletic Association's dispute with the College over our nickname and logo.

During the past several months, the NCAA has reviewed William & Mary's athletic insignia to determine whether they constitute a violation of Association standards. On the more important front, the Committee concluded that the College's use of the term "Tribe" reflects our community's sense of shared commitment and common purpose. Accordingly, it will remain our nickname. The presence of two feathers on the logo, though, was ruled potentially "hostile and abusive." We appealed that determination. The decision was sustained and has become final. We must now decide whether to institute legal action against the NCAA or begin the process of altering our logo.

I am compelled to say, at the outset, how powerfully ironic it is for the College of William & Mary to face sanction for athletic transgression at the hands of the NCAA. The Association has applied its mascot standards in ways so patently inconsistent and arbitrary as to demean the entire undertaking. Beyond this, William & Mary is widely acknowledged to be a principal exemplar of the NCAA's purported, if unrealized, ideals.

Not only are our athletic programs intensely competitive, but according to the Association's own Academic Progress Reports, the College ranks

---

[32] Lauren Brock, *A New Approach to an Old Problem: Could California's Proposed Ban on "Redskins" Mascots in Public Schools Have Withstood a Constitutional Challenge?*, 12 SPORTS LAW. J. 71 (Spring 2005); John B. Rhode, *The Mascot Name Change Controversy: A Lesson in Hypersensitivity*, 5 MARQ. SPORTS L. J. 141 (Fall 1994).

fifth among all institutions of higher learning in scholastic excellence. Each year, we graduate approximately 95% of our senior student
athletes. During the past decade, two William & Mary athletes have
been named Rhodes Scholars and 42 elected to membership in Phi Beta
Kappa, the national honorary society founded at the College in 1776.
Meanwhile, across the country, in the face of massive academic under-
performance, embarrassing misbehaviors on and off the field, and
grotesque commercialization of intercollegiate athletics, the NCAA has
proven hapless, or worse. It is galling that a university with such a
consistent and compelling record of doing things the right way is
threatened with punishment by an organization whose house, simply put,
is not in order.

Still, in consultation with our Board of Visitors, I have determined
that I am unwilling to sue the NCAA to further press our claims. There
are three reasons for my decision. I'll explain them in order.

First, failing to adhere to the NCAA logo ruling would raise the substantial possibility that William & Mary athletes would be foreclosed
from competing at the level their attainments and preparations merit.
Two years ago, for example, we hosted a thrilling semifinal national
championship football game against James Madison University. At present,
we are barred from welcoming such a competition to Williamsburg—in
football or any other sport. I believe it is our obligation to open
doors of opportunity and challenge for our students, not to close
them. I will not make our athletes pay for our broader disagreements
with a governing association. We have also consulted with our coaches
and student athletic advisory council on the matter. They are of the
same mind.

Second, given the well-known challenges that this and other universities face—in assuring access to world-class education, in supporting
the research and teaching efforts of our faculties, and in financing
and constructing twenty-first-century laboratories and facilities—I am
loath to divert further energies and resources to an expensive and
perhaps multi-faceted lawsuit over an athletic logo. Governing
requires the setting of priorities. And our fiercest challenges reside
at the core of our mission. I know, of course, that more than one
member of our understandably disgruntled community would likely be
willing to help finance litigation against the NCAA. Those dollars are
better spent in scholarship programs.

Third, the College of William & Mary is one of the most remarkable
universities in the world. It was a national treasure even before
there was a nation to treasure it. I am unwilling to allow it to
become the symbol and lodestar for a prolonged struggle over Native
American imagery that will likely be miscast and misunderstood—to the

detriment of the institution. Our challenge is greatness. Our defining purpose is rooted in the highest ideals of human progress, achievement, service, and dignity. Those are the hallmarks of the College of William & Mary. They will remain so.

I know this decision will disappoint some among us. I am confident, however, that it is the correct course for the College. We are required to hold fast to our values whether the NCAA does so or not. In the weeks ahead, we will begin an inclusive process to consider options for an altered university logo. I invite you to participate. And I am immensely grateful for your efforts and energies on behalf of the College.

Go Tribe. Hark upon the gale.

Sincerely,

Gene R. Nichol

President

College of William & Mary

Source: Courtesy of The College of William & Mary, President's Office.

Many schools, both high schools and colleges, have changed their logos as a result of this debated issue. Professional sports have team names such as Braves, Indians, Chiefs, Warriors, and Blackhawks. Should professional sports take steps to curb the use of these names in the same fashion as amateur sports has attempted to do so? The Washington Bullets changed their name to the Wizards for obvious reasons. Should the Buffalo Sabres follow suit? The original name of the Houston Astros was the Colt .45s. The Houston Dynamo franchise was originally named the 1836, the year of Texas's independence from Mexico, but was changed to the Dynamo after protest by the Hispanic community.

What arguments can you make that Native American mascots are insulting and demeaning to Native Americans? The U.S. Commission on Civil Rights has weighed in on the mascot issue:

The U.S. Commission on Civil Rights calls for an end to the use of Native American images and team names by non-Native schools. The Commission deeply respects the rights of all Americans to freedom of expression under the First Amendment and in no way would attempt to prescribe how people can express themselves. However, the Commission believes that the use of Native American images and nicknames in school is insensitive and should be avoided. In addition, some Native American and civil rights advocates maintain that these mascots may violate anti-discrimination laws.

These references, whether mascots and their performances, logos, or names, are disrespectful and offensive to American Indians and others who are offended by such stereotyping. They are particularly inappropriate and insensitive in light of the long history of forced assimilation that American Indian people have endured in this country.

Since the civil rights movement of the 1960s many overtly derogatory symbols and images offensive to African-Americans have been eliminated. However, many secondary schools, post-secondary institutions, and a number of professional sports teams continue to use Native American nicknames and imagery.[33]

PROFESSIONAL SPORTS

Professional sports leagues dominate the landscape in the United States, where there are what most consider four major sports: baseball, football, basketball, and hockey. Millions of fans attend professional sports events in the United States every year. The Super Bowl is one of the most watched television events every year, and commercial advertisers pay millions of dollars to advertise to people watching the game. The World Series is a staple of American life in October. Professional sports players have seen huge increases in salary in the recent past, and players unions have led the charge in securing higher salaries and better benefits for players. Athletes have always been celebrities in the United States, but with the ever-increasing popularity of sports and the increase in television exposure, many professional athletes have become household names.

Leagues, unions, players, and commissioners are the major players in the governance of professional sports. There are many legal and business issues in professional sports, which are addressed in later chapters. For example, since the mid-1960s professional sports have seen a rapid increase in the number of teams in each of the four major sports leagues. Franchise movement has been a major issue in recent years. Teams have moved from one city to another at a steady pace. Numerous new stadiums have been built. Many teams have been lured away to a new city because of a promise to build a new stadium or arena. Professional sports can garner major television revenue as well. Networks continue to pay large amounts of money to telecast a variety of professional sports in the United States. The PGA Tour displays the talents of the top golfers in the world, including Tiger Woods. In addition to the four major sports, U.S sports leagues exist for lacrosse, soccer, bowling, tennis, stock car racing (NASCAR), and a few other sports. Minor league baseball is also extremely popular in America.

Case Analysis

The cases in this chapter are an introduction to the various areas of sports law. Many who watch sports argue that sports have become too commercialized and are now just about money. That was never more apparent than in Case 1-1, *Popov v. Hayashi*, 2002 WL 31833731 (Cal. Superior 2002), in which the dispute was over the historic 73rd home run ball hit by Barry Bonds. Legal concepts relating to the ownership of personal property are present.

---

[33] Commissioner Elsie Meeks. Adopted by the United States Commission on Civil Rights.

Case 1-2 is an arbitration decision dealing with former Atlanta Braves pitcher John Rocker. The arbitrator details his decision concerning the alleged free speech rights of Rocker and the commissioner's attempts to discipline him for his statements. In Case 1-3, *Bellecourt v. Cleveland*, 104 Ohio St.3d 439 (Ohio 2004), some fans took matters into their own hands by setting a likeness of the Cleveland Indians mascot on fire in protest of its use. Case 1-4, *Cox v. National Football League*, 889 F.Supp. 118 (S.D. N.Y. 1995), deals with fan "interaction" with NFL player Bryan Cox and his lawsuit against the NFL for discrimination. The final case in the professional sports introduction, Case 1-5, *Castillo v. Tyson*, 701 N.Y.S.2d 423 (N.Y. App. Div. 2000), deals with one of the most unusual sports events to ever take place. In the Evander Holyfield–Mike Tyson heavyweight match-up, Tyson bit off a part of his opponent's ear. The remaining chapters focus on specific areas of law in sports law.

Is baseball a business? Of course it is. Sports memorabilia has become a big business (see *Fitl v. Strek* in Chapter 2, dealing with a dispute over a Mickey Mantle baseball card). Who owns balls that are hit into the grandstand? Many balls that make their way into the stands have become extremely valuable. That was the issue in this case dealing with the record 73rd home run ball hit by Barry Bonds.

📖 CASE 1-1 *Popov v. Hayashi*

2002 WL 31833731 (Cal. Superior 2002)

MCCARTHY, J.

Facts

In 1927, Babe Ruth hit sixty home runs. That record stood for thirty four years until Roger Maris broke it in 1961 with sixty one home runs. Mark McGwire hit seventy in 1998. On October 7, 2001, at PacBell Park in San Francisco, Barry Bonds hit number seventy three.

The event was widely anticipated and received a great deal of attention.

The ball that found itself at the receiving end of Mr. Bond's bat garnered some of that attention. Baseball fans in general, and especially people at the game, understood the importance of the ball. It was worth a great deal of money and whoever caught it would bask, for a brief period of time, in the reflected fame of Mr. Bonds.

With that in mind, many people who attended the game came prepared for the possibility that a record setting ball would be hit in their direction. Among this group were plaintiff Alex Popov and defendant Patrick Hayashi. . . . Both men brought baseball gloves, which they anticipated using if the ball came within their reach.

They, along with a number of others, positioned themselves in the arcade section of the ballpark. This is a standing room only area

located near right field. It is in this general area that Barry Bonds
hits the greatest number of home runs. The area was crowded with
people on October 7, 2001 and access was restricted to those who held
tickets for that section.

Barry Bonds came to bat in the first inning. With nobody on base and a
full count, Bonds swung at a slow knuckleball. He connected. The ball
sailed over the right-field fence and into the arcade.

Josh Keppel, a cameraman who was positioned in the arcade, captured
the event on videotape. . . .

In addition to the Keppel tape, seventeen percipient witnesses testified as to what they saw after the ball came into the stands. The testimony of these witnesses varied on many important points. Some of the
witnesses had a good vantage point and some did not. . . .

The factual findings in this case are the result of an analysis of the
testimony of all the witnesses as well as a detailed review of the
Keppel tape. Those findings are as follows:

When the seventy-third home run ball went into the arcade, it landed
in the upper portion of the webbing of a softball glove worn by Alex
Popov. While the glove stopped the trajectory of the ball, it is not
at all clear that the ball was secure. Popov had to reach for the ball
and in doing so, may have lost his balance.

Even as the ball was going into his glove, a crowd of people began to
engulf Mr. Popov. He was tackled and thrown to the ground while still
in the process of attempting to complete the catch. Some people intentionally descended on him for the purpose of taking the ball away,
while others were involuntarily forced to the ground by the momentum
of the crowd.

Eventually, Mr. Popov was buried face down on the ground under several
layers of people. At one point he had trouble breathing. Mr. Popov was
grabbed, hit and kicked. People reached underneath him in the area of
his glove. Neither the tape nor the testimony is sufficient to establish which individual members of the crowd were responsible for the
assaults on Mr. Popov.

The videotape clearly establishes that this was an out of control mob,
engaged in violent, illegal behavior. Although some witnesses testified in a manner inconsistent with this finding, their testimony is
specifically rejected as being false on a material point.

Mr. Popov intended at all times to establish and maintain possession
of the ball. At some point the ball left his glove and ended up on the
ground. It is impossible to establish the exact point in time that
this occurred or what caused it to occur.

Mr. Hayashi was standing near Mr. Popov when the ball came into the stands. He, like Mr. Popov, was involuntarily forced to the ground. He committed no wrongful act. While on the ground he saw the loose ball. He picked it up, rose to his feet and put it in his pocket.

Although the crowd was still on top of Mr. Popov, security guards had begun the process of physically pulling people off. Some people resisted those efforts. . . .

Mr. Hayashi kept the ball hidden. He asked Mr. Keppel to point the camera at him. At first, Mr. Keppel did not comply and Mr. Hayashi continued to hide the ball. Finally after someone else in the crowd asked Mr. Keppel to point the camera at Mr. Hayashi, Mr. Keppel complied. It was only at that point that Mr. Hayashi held the ball in the air for others to see. Someone made a motion for the ball and Mr. Hayashi put it back in his glove. It is clear that Mr. Hayashi was concerned that someone would take the ball away from him and that he was unwilling to show it until he was on videotape. Although he testified to the contrary, that portion of his testimony is unconvincing.

Mr. Popov eventually got up from the ground. He made several statements while he was on the ground and shortly after he got up which are consistent with his claim that he had achieved some level of control over the ball and that he intended to keep it. . . . When he saw that Mr. Hayashi had the ball he expressed relief and grabbed for it. Mr. Hayashi pulled the ball away.

It is important to point out what the evidence did not and could not show. Neither the camera nor the percipient witnesses were able to establish whether Mr. Popov retained control of the ball as he descended into the crowd. Mr. Popov's testimony on this question is inconsistent on several important points, ambiguous on others and, on the whole, unconvincing. We do not know when or how Mr. Popov lost the ball.

Perhaps the most critical factual finding of all is one that cannot be made. We will never know if Mr. Popov would have been able to retain control of the ball had the crowd not interfered with his efforts to do so. Resolution of that question is the work of a psychic, not a judge.

Legal Analysis

. . . An award of the ball to Mr. Popov would be unfair to Mr. Hayashi. It would be premised on the assumption that Mr. Popov would have caught the ball. That assumption is not supported by the facts. An award of the ball to Mr. Hayashi would unfairly penalize Mr. Popov. It would be based on the assumption that Mr. Popov would have dropped the ball. That conclusion is also unsupported by the facts.

Both men have a superior claim to the ball as against all the world. Each man has a claim of equal dignity as to the other. We are, therefore, left with something of a dilemma.

Thankfully, there is a middle ground.

. . . There is no reason, however, that the same remedy cannot be applied in a case such as this, where issues of property, tort and equity intersect.

The concept of equitable division has its roots in ancient Roman law. As Helmholz points out, it is useful in that it "provides an equitable way to resolve competing claims which are equally strong." Moreover, "[i]t comports with what one instinctively feels to be fair".

. . . The principle at work here is that where more than one party has a valid claim to a single piece of property, the court will recognize an undivided interest in the property in proportion to the strength of the claim.

Application of the principle of equitable division is illustrated in the case of *Keron v. Cashman* (1896) 33 A. 1055. In that case, five boys were walking home along a railroad track in the city of Elizabeth New Jersey. The youngest of the boys came upon an old sock that was tied shut and contained something heavy. He picked it up and swung it. The oldest boy took it away from him and beat the others with it. The sock passes from boy to boy. Each controlled it for a short time. At some point in the course of play, the sock broke open and out spilled $775 as well as some rags, cloths and ribbons.

The court noted that possession requires both physical control and the intent to reduce the property to one's possession. Control and intent must be concurrent. None of the boys intended to take possession until it became apparent that the sock contained money. Each boy had physical control of the sock at some point before that discovery was made.

Because none could present a superior claim of concurrent control and intent, the court held that each boy was entitled to an equal share of the money. Their legal claims to the property were of equal quality, therefore their entitlement to the property was also equal.

Here, the issue is not intent, or concurrence. Both men intended to possess the ball at the time they were in physical contact with it. The issue, instead, is the legal quality of the claim. With respect to that, neither can present a superior argument as against the other.

Mr. Hayashi's claim is compromised by Mr. Popov's pre-possessory interest. Mr. Popov cannot demonstrate full control. Albeit for different reasons, they stand before the court in exactly the same legal position as did the five boys. Their legal claims are of equal quality and they are equally entitled to the ball.

The court therefore declares that both plaintiff and defendant have an equal and undivided interest in the ball. Plaintiff's cause of action for conversion is sustained only as to his equal and undivided interest. In order to effectuate this ruling, the ball must be sold and the proceeds divided equally between the parties.

The parties are ordered to meet and confer forthwith before Judge Richard Kramer to come to an agreement as to how to implement this decision. If no decision is made by December 30, 2002, the parties are directed to appear before this court on that date at 9:00 am.

The court retains jurisdiction to issue orders consistent with this decision. The ball is to remain in the custody of the court until further order.

Source: Courtesy of Westlaw; reprinted with permission.

For further study see Paul Finkelman, *Fugitive Baseballs and Abandoned Property: Who Owns the Home Run Ball?* 23 CARDOZO LAW REVIEW 1609–1633 (2002).

John Rocker had an ongoing and somewhat friendly rivalry with Mets' fans as a member of the Atlanta Braves. He would incite Mets' fans when he would dart out of the visiting team's bullpen and sprint to the pitcher's mound in relief. This arbitration decision concerns off-season statements by Rocker in an interview with a reporter from *Sports Illustrated* magazine.

CASE 1-2   *Arbitration Regarding John Rocker*

THE MAJOR LEAGUE BASEBALL ARBITRATION PANEL

In the Matter of Arbitration

THE MAJOR LEAGUE BASEBALL PLAYERS ASSOCIATION

Panel Decision No. 104, Grievance No. 2000-3

Player: John Rocker

Introduction

On January 31, 2000, Allan H. "Bud" Selig, the Commissioner of Baseball, imposed discipline on John Rocker, a pitcher for the Atlanta Braves, for having engaged in conduct not in the best interests of baseball. Selig specifically referred to "certain profoundly insensitive and arguably racist statements" made by Rocker that were reported in the December 27,

1999 issue of Sports Illustrated. Selig charged that: "Your comments in Sports Illustrated have harmed your reputation, have damaged the image and goodwill of Major League Baseball and the Atlanta Braves and have caused various other harms to the Club and the game."

John Rocker, who now is 25 years old, began his minor league career in the Braves' organization in 1994. During the 1998 season he was called up to the Braves' Major League team as a relief pitcher. In 1999 he became the Braves' closer. His pitching performance during the 1999 regular season and the post-season was outstanding.

During the 1999 season, a mutual and growing antagonism developed between Rocker and the fans at Shea Stadium, the home of the New York Mets, Atlanta's principal rival in the National League East. Mets' fans used abusive and profane language and gestures to taunt Rocker, and he responded in kind. Some, according to Rocker, also threw various objects at him. The ongoing feud received widespread coverage in the media. The situation was exacerbated by critical comments in the press about Rocker and comments he made to the press attacking Mets' fans.

The relationship between Rocker and the Mets' fans intensified after the Braves swept the Mets in a late September series at Shea. The two teams met again in the National League Championship Series. In the third game—the first in that series to be played at Shea—the Braves won 1-0, and Rocker saved the game. Following the game, when Rocker approached the Braves' dugout after doing some interviews, a large group of hostile Mets' fans threatened to surge down onto the field from behind the Braves' dugout. The fans verbally attacked Rocker and he responded in kind. MLB Director of Security Kevin Hallinan was present, and at the hearing he described the situation as being as bad as any he had seen in his fourteen years in baseball. In his view, only quick and effective action by the New York Police Department prevented the fans from physically assaulting Rocker.

Before the start of the fourth game of the NLCS, Hallinan arranged a meeting with Rocker, Braves' Manager Bobby Cox and Braves' General Manager John Schuerholz in which Hallinan expressed his security concerns and asked Rocker to show restraint. Rocker expressed his willingness to do so, and he testified that he did "tone it down" after that meeting. Nonetheless, when Rocker went out onto the field, Hallinan subsequently reported:

> His appearance on the field triggered an immediate reaction by the Mets fans who loudly booed, and greeted him with obscenities and verbal abuse. Rocker responded by sticking out his tongue and yelling obscenities at the fans. He departed for the bullpen

where he continued to engage in a verbal exchange of hostilities with New York Mets fans.

There were no further meetings or discussions with Rocker regarding his interaction with New York fans, either during the remainder of the NLCS with the Mets or during the World Series, which the Braves lost to the Yankees in four straight games. Rocker testified that he was hit with a battery at Yankee Stadium during the third game of the World Series, but there were no other major incidents with New York fans.

On December 12, 1999, Rocker was interviewed by a reporter for Sports Illustrated. Rocker had agreed to the interview ahead of time, to obtain publicity, and it was conducted in Atlanta where he resides. The reporter spent the better part of the day driving around with Rocker in his vehicle, as he went about his business. He recorded Rocker's comments. Rocker testified that he asked the reporter to keep certain remarks off the record and, with one exception, the reporter complied with his requests.

On December 22, 1999, the Sports Illustrated article first appeared on the magazine's website, and it later appeared in print. It landed like a bombshell, creating a huge nationwide furor, which had not abated by the time of the arbitration hearing in early February 2000. The statements which triggered the Commissioner's decision to discipline Rocker are contained in the following excerpts from the article, and Rocker does not dispute they accurately reflect what he said:

> . . . "So many dumb asses don't know how to drive in this town," he says . . . "They turn from the wrong lane. They go 20 miles per hour. It makes me want—Look! Look at this idiot! I guarantee you she's a Japanese woman." A Beige Toyota is jerking from lane to lane. The woman at the wheel is white. "How bad are Asian women at driving?"
>
> JOHN ROCKER has opinions, and there's no way to sugarcoat them. They are politically incorrect, to say the least, and he likes to express them.
>
> - On ever playing for a New York team: "I would retire first. It's the most hectic, nerve-racking city. Imagine having to take the [Number] 7 train to the ballpark, looking like you're [riding through] Beirut next to some kid with purple hair next to some queer with AIDS right next to some dude who just got out of jail for the fourth time right next to some 20-year-old mom with four kids. It's depressing."
> - On New York City itself: "The biggest thing I don't like about New York are the foreigners. I'm not a very big fan of foreigners. You can walk

an entire block in Times Square and not hear anybody speaking English. Asians and Koreans and Vietnamese and Indians and Russians and Spanish people and everything up there. How the hell did they get in this country?"

. . . In passing, he calls an overweight black teammate "a fat monkey." Asked if he feels any bond with New York Knicks guard Latrell Sprewell, notorious for choking coach P.J. Carlesimo two years ago, Rocker lets out a snarl of disgust. "That guy should've been arrested, and instead he's playing basketball," he says. "Why do you think that is? Do you think if he was Keith Van Horn—if he was white—they'd let him back? No way." Rocker is rarely tongue-tied when it comes to bashing those of a race or sexual orientation different from his. "I'm not a racist or prejudiced person," he says with apparent conviction. "But certain people bother me."

Immediately after publication of the article, the Braves issued a statement disassociating the Club from the viewpoints attributed to Rocker. In consultation with his agents, Rocker issued a public apology, in which he stated:

While I have evidenced strong competitive feelings about New York fans in the past, and take responsibility for things I have said publicly, including the Sports Illustrated article, I recognize that I have gone way too far in my competitive zeal. I want everybody to understand that my emotions fuel my competitive desire. They are a source of energy for me, however I have let my emotions get the best of my judgment and have said things which, when read with cold, hard logic, are unacceptable to me and to my country. Even though it might appear otherwise from what I've said, I am not a racist. I should not have said what I did because it is not what I believe in my heart.

I was angry and basically firing back at the people of New York. It is time to stop this process.

I fully intend to learn from this experience. Everyone makes mistakes and I hope everyone can put this aside and begin with a fresh start in the 2000 season.

I am contrite.

Commissioner Selig testified that when he read the article he was "stunned" and "shocked". After deliberating with other MLB officials and conferring with the Braves' management, he made the decision to impose the discipline challenged in this grievance. He testified that he based his decision on several factors, including his belief that "all of us in Major League Baseball have a social responsibility". As he stated in his news release announcing the discipline:

> Major League Baseball takes seriously its role as an American institution and the important social responsibility that goes with it, said Selig. We will not dodge our responsibility. Mr. Rocker should understand that his remarks offended practically every element of society and brought dishonor to himself, the Atlanta Braves and Major League Baseball.
>
> The terrible example set by Mr. Rocker is not what our great game is about and, in fact, is a profound breach of the social compact we hold in such high regard.

The Commissioner also took into account security concerns and reports from the Atlanta Club that the controversy spawned by Rocker's remarks was affecting its business and the community. On January 5, 2000 the Atlanta City Council unanimously adopted a resolution condemning Rocker's remarks. A coalition of community organizations, many representing groups that were maligned by Rocker's remarks, as well as other individuals (including Jesse Jackson) and groups, demanded swift and decisive action by the Braves and the Commissioner. The Commissioner received literally thousands of communications condemning and, in some instances, defending Rocker's remarks. Many of these communications, while disapproving of Rocker's words, opposed disciplining him on free speech grounds. The Commissioner stressed that the controversy engendered by Rocker's remarks was all that "people want to talk about" with him, and was detracting from his efforts to "move baseball forward".

Source: Courtesy of Westlaw; reprinted with permission.

In the following case, the plaintiffs sued, stating their free speech rights had been violated after they were arrested for burning in effigy a likeness of "Chief Wahoo," the Cleveland Indians mascot, near the Indians' ballpark, Jacobs Field.

 CASE 1-3 *Bellecourt v. Cleveland*

104 Ohio St.3d 439 (Ohio 2004)

O'CONNOR, J.

April 10, 1998, opening day for the Cleveland Indians baseball team, was a blustery day in downtown Cleveland. Among the onlookers near Jacobs Field, the Indians' ballpark, were throngs of cheering fans as well as groups of spirited protestors. The protestors, including appellees Vernon Bellecourt, Juan Reyna, James Watson, Charlene Teters, and Zizwe Tchiquka, perceived the team's moniker and Chief Wahoo logo as disparaging to Native American culture.

Following animated yet peaceful speeches and marches, the protestors entered a cordoned area near Jacobs Field. In the presence of several safety personnel, the protestors doused a newspaper-stuffed effigy of Chief Wahoo with lighter fluid and set it afire. As the fire struggled to spread, Bellecourt sprayed additional lighter fluid on the effigy. The fire then quickly accelerated, and within seconds the effigy disintegrated, sending burning remnants to the sidewalk. Cleveland police extinguished what remained of the fire and arrested Bellecourt, Tchiquka, and Reyna. Shortly thereafter, Watson and Teters ignited an accelerant-soaked effigy of Little Black Sambo—apparently as an emblematic condemnation of the use of racially offensive symbols. Police then arrested Watson and Teters. Though appellant, the city of Cleveland, booked appellees on charges of aggravated arson and detained appellees overnight, the city did not prosecute appellees for violating any law.

. . . . [A]ppellees sued the city, the arresting officers and their commander, David Regetz, and Chief of Police Rocco Pollutro for civil-rights violations stemming from their allegedly baseless arrest and detention. . . .

Our ultimate inquiry is whether Cleveland is liable to appellees pursuant to Section 1983, Title 42, U.S. Code, for violating their constitutional right to free speech. Such liability will attach to a municipality only if the municipality itself has inflicted a constitutionally significant injury by executing a policy or custom. Because a violation of a constitutional right is prerequisite to a Section 1983 violation, our threshold inquiry is whether Cleveland violated appellees' constitutional right to free speech. If so, we would then proceed to resolve whether a Cleveland policy or custom was the "'moving force [behind] the constitutional violation.'"

Without question, the effigy burnings were constitutionally protected speech. Moreover, appellees concede, and we agree, that extinguishment of the waning flames after the effigies had disintegrated does not raise an issue of constitutional significance because by that time, the protected speech had concluded. Appellees urge, however, that the right to free speech is hollow if it is exercised at the expense of arrest. Though we generally agree with this proposition, we find it inapplicable here because any suppression of speech was incidental to Cleveland's important interest in preventing harm caused by fire.

When speech and nonspeech elements are part of the same course of conduct, "a sufficiently important governmental interest in regulating the nonspeech element can justify incidental limitations on First Amendment freedoms." A regulation is sufficiently justified "if it is within the constitutional power of the Government; if it furthers an important or substantial governmental interest; if the governmental interest is unrelated to the suppression of free expression; and if the incidental restriction on alleged First Amendment freedoms is no greater than is essential to the furtherance of that interest."

The threshold issue to *O'Brien*'s test is whether a governmental interest asserted by Cleveland is implicated on the facts before us. If the city has not asserted a pertinent interest, then we cannot apply *O'Brien*'s test, and the city will have failed to justify its infringement upon appellees' right to free speech.

In *Johnson,* Texas claimed, in part, that its interest in preventing breaches of the peace justified arresting Johnson for burning an American flag. The Supreme Court held that this interest was insufficient because "no disturbance of the peace actually occurred or threatened to occur because of Johnson's burning of the flag." Moreover, there was no indication that Johnson's provocative speech was intended to incite or likely to incite lawless conduct. In sum, Johnson was arrested for exercising a constitutional right, not for conduct that threatened the state's interest in maintaining order.

As in *Johnson,* the conduct in question here involved expression via the burning of a symbol. Unlike in *Johnson,* however, the facts here indicate that Cleveland's asserted interest in preserving public safety was implicated. In the judgment of Cleveland's police officers, the windy conditions coupled with the spraying of additional accelerant on the already burning effigies created a hazard that was their responsibility to remedy. Though appellees emphasize that they set the fire in a cordoned area devoid of flammable property, the police were obligated to protect the public, including the protestors themselves. A video of the effigy burnings and arrests is part of our record. It shows a protestor spraying accelerant on a burning effigy and then retreating from the rapidly growing fire before burning pieces of the disintegrating effigy began floating in the wind and landing in the proximity of the protestors. These facts implicate Cleveland's asserted interest in public safety.

Having determined that a governmental interest was implicated on the facts before us, we now apply *O'Brien*'s test to determine whether that interest justified an infringement upon appellees' freedom of speech. The parties do not dispute, nor do we question, that safety regulations are within Cleveland's constitutional powers or that such regulation furthers an important or substantial government interest that is generally unrelated to the suppression of free expression. Therefore, the first three prongs of *O'Brien*'s test are satisfied.

Appellees assert, however, that their arrests were not essential to further Cleveland's safety interest. In support of their position, appellees argue that prior to arrest, police should have warned them of dangers inherent to burning effigies or that the burnings would result in their arrests. In effect, appellees argue that the city erred by forgoing the lesser restriction of warnings in favor of the greater restriction of arrests.

The success of appellees' argument depends on the applicability of strict scrutiny, the highest level of constitutional analysis. Here, however, our analysis is based on *O'Brien*'s relatively lenient standard that "is little, if any, different from the standard applied to time, place, or manner restrictions." . . . Thus, appellees' "less restrictive means" argument is without merit.

Further, appellees' argument presumes that warnings would have obviated a fire hazard or that they were arrested merely for burning effigies. To be sure, the police knew that protestors intended to burn effigies. There is no indication, however, that the police had prior knowledge of the dangerous manner in which the effigies were to be burned, and it would be utterly impractical to require police to be so prescient as to issue appropriate warnings. Moreover, the record demonstrates that Cleveland arrested appellees not because they burned effigies, but because of a perceived public safety threat in the manner in which they burned the effigies. Under the facts before us, we determine that the arrests were narrowly tailored to Cleveland's asserted interest in preserving public safety. Therefore, the fourth prong of *O'Brien*'s test is satisfied, and any incidental limitation on appellees' First Amendment freedoms was justified. Accordingly, Cleveland is not liable to appellees. . . .

Source: Courtesy of Westlaw; reprinted with permission.

In this case, NFL player Bryan Cox sued the NFL under Title VII, requesting that the court find the NFL responsible for the racial abuse of fans directed toward African American players.

📖 CASE 1-4 *Cox v. National Football League*

889 F.Supp. 118 (S.D. N.Y. 1995)

BAER, District Judge.

Plaintiff filed this suit pursuant to Title VII of the Civil Rights Act of 1964, 42 U.S.C. § 2000e, seeking that defendant National Football League ("N.F.L.") "take some affirmative action to stop fans from

subjecting black football players to racial abuse." The parties stipulated to dismiss the action without prejudice, agreeing that the Court
would retain jurisdiction over the matter to determine whether plaintiff is entitled to attorneys' fees as a "prevailing party" in a Title
VII case. . . .

Background

Plaintiff Bryan Cox, a member of the National Football League's Miami
Dolphins during the 1993 season, claims that when he entered Rich Stadium, the Buffalo Bills' home field, on September 23, 1993 immediately
before the start of a game, several fans subjected him to

> an intense barrage of verbal abuse, much of which was based on
> race. Shouts of "nigger," "monkey," "we will kill you," and a
> string of racially-based obscenities were heard by several
> witnesses. One fan had rigged up a black dummy with Bryan's
> number and the words "Wanted Dead" on it, and then hung the dummy
> on a noose.

It was in this context, Cox relates, that he later made an "obscene
gesture" to the crowd, for which the N.F.L. fined him $10,000.

Defendants, meanwhile, note that prior to the game at issue, Cox had
been quoted as stating, "'I don't like the Buffalo Bills as a team
. . . I don't like the city, I don't like the people in the city . . .
I wouldn't care if any of those people fell off the face of the
[E]arth . . . Don't ask me to name the guys I hate. You can name them
all.'" Defendants apparently find it relevant that Cox appealed not
only this fine on January 25, 1994, but two others that the N.F.L. had
assessed during the 1993 season ("one for kicking a player in the head
[and] one for profane and abusive conduct towards game officials"), as
they mention same in their limited, four-page letter brief.

Defendants assert that the January 25 appeal, which was heard in
accordance with the applicable collective bargaining agreement, constituted the first time Cox had ever "advised the [N.F.L.] that he
had been the target of any racial abuse," as Cox cited the alleged
abuse in arguing that it warranted his obscene gesture. While await-
ing the ruling, Cox filed a charge of discrimination with the Equal
Employment Opportunity Commission ("EEOC") on March 23, 1994. On
April 15, 1994, the N.F.L. reduced Cox's fine to $3,000, stating that
"'some of the fan conduct in question was racially offensive and
unacceptable, but Bryan's response was inappropriate.'" Cox obtained
a "right-to-sue" letter from the EEOC on April 28, 1994 and filed the

instant suit against the N.F.L. on July 27, 1994. The next day, the N.F.L. distributed revised guidelines requiring, among other things, that teams remove from the stadiums fans who take part in "racial taunts."

Discussion

In order to be deemed a "prevailing party" in a Title VII action and thereby obtain attorneys' fees, a plaintiff need not obtain a final judicial adjudication; rather, it is sufficient if the case is settled with plaintiff obtaining a significant part of the relief he or she sought. In addition, the plaintiff must show that his or her actions in pursuing the claim constituted the "catalyst" that caused defendant to provide that relief. *Smith v. University of N. Carolina*, 632 F.2d 316, 347 (4th Cir.1980). Here, the N.F.L. argues that Cox's "vague request" in his complaint that the N.F.L. be required to take some "affirmative action" to eradicate the racially hostile atmosphere does not "entitle [him] to claim credit for the specific revisions made by the League to its security guidelines." Defs.' Letter Br. at 4. Moreover, the N.F.L. claims, it began the process of revising its guidelines soon after it learned of the racial taunts at the January 25 hearing, which demonstrates that the revised guidelines cannot be attributed to Cox's adversarial efforts; instead, it was the mere knowledge of the incident that spurred the N.F.L. to act.

The Second Circuit has explained that a "plaintiff may be considered a prevailing party even though the relief ultimately obtained is not identical to the relief demanded in the complaint, provided the relief obtained is of the same general type." *Koster v. Perales*, 903 F.2d 131, 134-35 (2d Cir.1990) (citation omitted). While I do not agree with plaintiff's assertion that the revised guidelines were "precisely the relief sought in [Cox]'s lawsuit," I do find that removing fans who engage in racial taunting does provide Cox with—at the very least—"the same general type" of relief that he sought.

Whether or not Cox's pursuit of his claim was responsible for bringing about the changed N.F.L. security guidelines presents a closer question. In support of his position, plaintiff quotes from a statement the N.F.L. made after this suit was filed: "'We have implemented new security measures for the 1994 season to address Bryan's concerns and to supplement previous procedures. . . . The steps were taken in part because of the incident last season involving Bryan Cox which highlighted the issue of racial harassment of players and coaches by fans.'" Although this statement was issued immediately after Cox filed his suit, the statement is not necessarily inconsistent with the N.F.L.'s claim that it took action as soon as it learned of the incident at the January 25 hearing. According to the N.F.L., moreover, an N.F.L. executive began working on the guideline revisions "shortly after" the January 25 hearing and presented the proposals to the teams at the annual spring meeting in May 1994 and to the players at their training camps at an unspecified point in July 1994.

Indeed, the N.F.L. might argue that, at most, it was responding to the appeal Cox made pursuant to the collective bargaining agreement, and not to the EEOC charge, which was not filed until late March, nor this lawsuit, which was not initiated before July. Relevant authority, however, renders this argument unpersuasive. . . . I find it sufficient that the appeal, the EEOC charge, and this lawsuit all were undertaken as a result of the same incident. Plaintiff will not effectively be penalized for having chosen to pursue the financial relief he sought solely in the collective bargaining setting.

There remains one issue of fact that, if resolved, could be determinative of the instant motion. If plaintiff can establish that the N.F.L. knew, or should have known, of the September 23, 1993 racial taunting incident prior to the January 25 hearing, the N.F.L.'s failure to initiate security guideline revision until after the hearing could support a finding that Cox's appeal motivated the N.F.L.'s ensuing action. If, however, this cannot be shown, the Court will address the difficult question of whether Cox's appeal caused the N.F.L. to take action, as opposed, or in addition, to the N.F.L.'s mere learning of the incident. . . .

Conclusion

Plaintiff will provide his supporting papers addressing the remaining issues of fact discussed above and detailing the amount of fees to which he feels he is entitled to the defendants and the Court by July 5, 1995. Defendants will provide any additional information bearing on their position to the plaintiff and the Court by the same date. . . .

SO ORDERED.

Source: Courtesy of Westlaw; reprinted with permission.

What steps should professional leagues take to curb violence? Should fans be banned from further attendance of sporting events or even fined? Did the NFL act appropriately in reacting to the allegations made by Cox?

In a 1997 heavyweight fight between Evander Holyfield and Mike Tyson, Tyson bit off part of Holyfield's ear in the third round of the fight. It is one of the most odd and controversial moments in the history of professional sports. The fight was stopped and Tyson disqualified. This decision upset the plaintiffs in the following case, who brought a class action lawsuit against Mike Tyson, fight promoters, and telecasters seeking a refund of the money paid by the viewers to watch the fight.

📖 CASE 1-5 *Castillo v. Tyson*

701 N.Y.S.2d 423 (N.Y. App. Div. 2000)

ROSENBERGER, J.P., WILLIAMS, RUBIN, ANDRIAS and BUCKLEY, JJ.

MEMORANDUM DECISION.

Judgment, Supreme Court, New York County, entered November 6, 1998, dismissing the complaint, and bringing up for review an order which, in a class action by fight fans against a boxer, fight promoters and fight telecasters seeking a refund of the money plaintiffs paid to view a fight in which the boxer was disqualified for biting his opponent's ear, granted defendants' motion to dismiss the complaint for failure to state a cause of action. . . .

Plaintiffs claim that they were entitled to view a "legitimate heavyweight title fight" fought "in accordance with the applicable rules and regulations" of the governing boxing commission, i.e., a fight that was to end either in an actual or technical knockout or by decision of the judges after 12 rounds, and that they are entitled to their money back because the fight ended in a disqualification. Many legal theories are invoked in support this claim—breach of contract, breach of implied covenant of good faith and fair dealing, unjust enrichment, breach of express and implied warranties, tortious interference with contractual relations, "wantonness", fraud, negligent representation—none of which have merit. Plaintiffs are not in contractual privity with any of the defendants, and their claim that they are third-party beneficiaries of one or more of the contracts that defendants entered into among themselves was aptly rejected by the motion court as "contrived". Nothing in these contracts can be understood as promising a fight that did not end in a disqualification. The rules of the governing commission provide for disqualification, and it is a possibility that a fight fan can reasonably expect. Plaintiffs could not reasonably rule out such a possibility by the boxer's and promoters' public statements predicting a "sensational victory" and "the biggest fight of all time" . . . and assuming other representations were made promising or implying a "legitimate fight", there can be no breach of warranty claim absent privity of contract between plaintiffs and defendants, and also because defendants provided only a service. Nor is a claim of fraud supported by plaintiffs' allegations that the boxer's former trainer predicted that the

```
boxer would get himself disqualified if he failed to achieve an early knockout
and that the boxer came out without his mouthpiece in the beginning of the
round that he was disqualified. Plaintiffs' claim for unjust enrichment was
properly dismissed by the motion court on the ground that plaintiffs received
what they paid for, namely, "the right to view whatever event transpired". We
have considered plaintiffs' other arguments, including that the action should
not be dismissed before plaintiffs have had an opportunity to conduct disclo-
sure, and find them unpersuasive.
```

Source: Courtesy of Westlaw; reprinted with permission.

AMATEUR SPORTS

Amateur sports exist at many levels in the United States. Millions of people participate in individual and team sports. Adults and children play a variety of sports in recreational, YMCA, or adult sports leagues. Millions of others participate just for the enjoyment of playing individual or team sports. This section functions as a short introduction to the issues involved in amateur sports. Chapters 10 and 11 deal specifically with the NCAA and eligibility in amateur sports. The concept of amateurism is discussed fully in those chapters.

High school and college sports are very popular, with millions of fans attending games at both levels, and both are highly regulated in the United States. Each has bodies that address a variety of legal issues relating to eligibility, drug testing, and amateur status. Millions of students play college sports, ranging from the junior college level to big-time college athletics. An NCAA final or Bowl Championship Series (BCS) game will be watched by millions, with large payouts to the winning schools. The following quote from a 1961 decision discusses the positives and negatives of amateur sports:

> Indeed, corruption of an amateur athlete is peculiarly distasteful. The athlete generally performs before the child in him wholly turns to man and thus is still unformed in character. Since at least as long ago as the founding of the republic, we have thought that participation in amateur sports is a valuable training for our youth, for their responsibilities in the armed services, in their civilian occupations and generally as citizens. Indeed few quotations are better known and more approved than the remark attributed to the Duke of Wellington that the Battle of Waterloo was won on the playing fields of Eton. We have believed that participation in athletics is not only healthful exercise but that it also inculcates and nourishes such desirable qualities as steadfastness, spirit, loyalty and team play. Violation of 382(1) can only tend to subvert the basic principles of amateur sport. Virtue there is in striving with one's whole spirit, but only evil can come from lack of effort that is bought.[34]

College sports in America are extremely popular and can also be very lucrative. Student-athletes participate at a variety of collegiate levels in a myriad of difficult sports ranging from football to rodeo. Bowl games for college football teams can provide a large payday to the university, especially if the game is designated as a BCS game. Table 1-2 provides an example of how lucrative it can be to have one's school appear in a bowl game. How do bowl payouts for universities affect the salary and bonuses of coaches? How do they affect the university as a whole? How do they affect a university's football schedule or the conference in which the university plays?

---

[34] Sollazzo v. P. A. Esperdy, 285 F.2d 341, 343 (2nd Cir. 1961).

TABLE 1-2

BOWL SCHEDULE AND PAYOUTS: 2008–2009				
Date	*Bowl*	*Location*	*TV Network*	*Payouts*
Dec. 20	EagleBank Bowl Wake Forest 29, Navy 19	Washington, DC	ESPN	$1 million
Dec. 20	New Mexico Bowl Colorado State 40, Fresno State 35	Albuquerque, NM	ESPN	$750,000
Dec. 20	St. Petersburg Bowl South Florida 41, Memphis 14	St. Petersburg, FL	ESPN2	$1 million
Dec. 20	Las Vegas Bowl Arizona 31, BYU 21	Las Vegas, NV	ESPN	$1 million
Dec. 21	New Orleans Bowl Southern Miss 30, Troy 27 (OT)	New Orleans, LA	ESPN	$325,000
Dec. 23	Poinsettia Bowl TCU 17, Boise State 16	San Diego, CA	ESPN	$750,000
Dec. 24	Hawaii Bowl Notre Dame 49, Hawaii 21	Honolulu, HI	ESPN	$750,000
Dec. 26	Motor City Bowl Florida Atlantic 24, Central Michigan 21	Detroit, MI	ESPN	$750,000
Dec. 27	Meineke Car Care Bowl West Virginia 31, North Carolina 30	Charlotte, NC	ESPN	$1 million
Dec. 27	Champs Sports Bowl Florida State 42, Wisconsin 13	Orlando, FL	ESPN	$2.13 million
Dec. 27	Emerald Bowl California 24, Miami (Fla.) 17	San Francisco, CA	ESPN	$750,000
Dec. 28	Independence Bowl Louisiana Tech 17, Northern Illinois 10	Shreveport, LA	ESPN	$1.1 million
Dec. 29	PapaJohns.com Bowl Rutgers 29, N.C. State 23	Birmingham, AL	ESPN	$300,000
Dec. 29	Alamo Bowl Missouri 30, Northwestern 23	San Antonio, TX	ESPN	$2.25 million

(Continued)

TABLE 1-2 (Continued)

BOWL SCHEDULE AND PAYOUTS: 2008–2009				
Date	*Bowl*	*Location*	*TV Network*	*Payouts*
Dec. 30	Humanitarian Bowl Maryland 42, Nevada 35	Boise, ID	ESPN	$750,000
Dec. 30	Holiday Bowl Oregon 42, Oklahoma State 31	San Diego, CA	ESPN	$2.2million
Dec. 30	Texas Bowl Rice 38, Western Michigan 14	Houston, TX	NFL	$750,000
Dec. 31	Armed Forces Bowl Houston 34, Air Force 28	Fort Worth, TX	ESPN	$750,000
Dec. 31	Sun Bowl Oregon State 3, Pittsburgh 0	El Paso, TX	CBS	$1.9 million
Dec. 31	Music City Bowl Vanderbilt 16, Boston College 14	Nashville, TN	ESPN	$1.6 million
Dec. 31	Insight Bowl Kansas 42, Minnesota 21	Tempe, AZ	NFL	$1.2 million
Dec. 31	Chick-fil-A Bowl SU 38, Georgia Tech 3	Atlanta, GA	ESPN	$2.92 million
Jan. 1	Outback Bowl Iowa 31, South Carolina 10	Tampa, FL	ESPN	$3.2 million
Jan. 1	Capital One Bowl Georgia 24, Michigan State 12	Orlando, FL	ABC	$4.25 million
Jan. 1	Gator Bowl Nebraska 26, Clemson 21	Jacksonville, FL	CBS	$2.25 million
Jan. 1	Rose Bowl USC 38, Penn State 24	Pasadena, CA	ABC	$17 million
Jan. 1	Orange Bowl Virginia Tech 20, Cincinnati 7	Miami, FL	FOX	$17 million
Jan. 2	Cotton Bowl Ole Miss 47, Texas Tech 34	Dallas, TX	FOX	$3 million

TABLE 1-2 (CONTINUED)

BOWL SCHEDULE AND PAYOUTS: 2008–2009				
Date	*Bowl*	*Location*	*TV Network*	*Payouts*
Jan. 2	Liberty Bowl Kentucky 25, East Carolina 19	Memphis, TN	ESPN	$1.8 million
Jan. 2	Sugar Bowl Utah 31, Alabama 17	New Orleans, LA	FOX	$17 million
Jan. 3	International Bowl Connecticut 38, Buffalo 20	Toronto, Canada	ESPN2	$750,000
Jan. 5	Fiesta Bowl Texas 24, Ohio State 21	Glendale, AZ	FOX	$17 million
Jan. 6	GMAC Bowl Tulsa 45, Ball State 13	Mobile, AL	ESPN	$750,000
Jan. 8	BCS Title Game Florida 24, Oklahoma 14	Miami, FL	FOX	$17 million

Case Analysis

The cases in this section address legal issues that are prevalent in amateur sports. In Case 1-6, *Dambrot v. Central Michigan University*, 55 F.3d 1177 (6th Cir. 1995), a basketball coach was fired after his use of the N-word during a halftime basketball speech. He sued, arguing that his actions constituted free speech. Case 1-7, *Hale v. Antoniou*, 2004 WL 1925551 (Me. 2004), deals with violence in amateur sports. When an out-of-control parent took his frustrations out on a youth hockey participant, the young boy and his parents sued the "over-the-top" father for damages. In Case 1-8, *Cronk v. Suffren Sr. High School*, 809 N.Y.S.2d 480 (N.Y. Sup. 2005), a high school football coach was sued by a player who alleged the coach had assaulted him. These cases present unique issues in the amateur sports arena.

How do you motivate a losing squad? Do you give them the "win one for the Gipper" speech or one of Knute Rockne's famous halftime speeches? In this case a coach at Central Michigan University took a different angle in an attempt to motivate his players. He was terminated for his actions and subsequently sued, arguing that he was engaging in free speech at the time.

📖 CASE 1-6   *Dambrot v. Central Michigan University*

55 F.3d 1177 (6th Cir. 1995)

KEITH, Circuit Judge.

Statement of the Case

On May 12, 1991, Dambrot became the head coach of the Central Michigan University men's basketball team. His responsibilities as head coach included, among other things, offering and renewing player scholarships, deciding which players could remain on the team, determining the amount of playing time for each player and selecting assistant coaches. This lawsuit arises from events which occurred during the 1992–93 men's basketball season.

The 1992 CMU men's basketball team was made up of eleven African Americans and three Caucasians. The team's full-time coaching staff included two assistant coaches, Derrick McDowell (an African American) and Barry Markwart (a Caucasian). The part-time coaching staff included one voluntary graduate assistant, Chip Wilde (a Caucasian), three managers (all Caucasian), and a professional trainer (a Caucasian).

In January of 1993, Dambrot used the word "nigger" during a locker room session with his players and coaching staff either during the halftime or at the end of a basketball game in which the team lost to Miami University of Ohio. According to Dambrot's testimony, Dambrot told the players they hadn't been playing very hard and then said "Do you mind if I use the N word?" After one or some of the players apparently indicated it was okay, Dambrot said "you know we need to have more niggers on our team. . . . Coach McDowell is a nigger, . . . Sand[er] Scott who's an academic All-American, a Caucasian, I said Sand[er] Scott is a nigger. He's hard nose, [sic] he's tough, et cetera." He testified he intended to use the term in a "positive and reinforcing" manner. The players often referred to each other using the N-word during games and around campus and in the locker room. Dambrot stated he used the word in the same manner in which the players used the term amongst themselves, "to connote a person who is fearless, mentally strong and tough."

Prior to the January incident, the record shows Dambrot had used the N-word on at least one other occasion. In November, Dambrot apparently addressed the team after a practice and said he wanted the players to 'play like niggers on the court' and wished he had more niggers on the basketball court. He then said he did not want the team to act like niggers in the classroom. When asked why he made these statements Dambrot stated:

> Well, that's really a very easy question for me to answer, because we had had an incident early in the year where we had five or six basketball players, some of our bigger kids on our team, in a math class. And our kids were aggressive, tough, you know, a little bit loud, abrasive. And the lady was intimidated, because it was the first year that she ever had taught. And they almost got kicked out of the math class. A matter of fact, Dave Keilitz, myself, Pat Podoll, Doug Nance, who is the faculty rep, and then the head of the department—I don't remember his name—the math department, met and discussed the situation. And it was my feeling that you can't be aggressive, tough, hard-nosed, abrasive in class, or you're going to get thrown out of classes, especially at a school like Central Michigan where the faculty members don't understand a lot about black people or have many black people in class. And I think our players understood what I meant by, 'Don't be niggers in the classroom.'

The news Dambrot had used the N-word in the locker room incident became known to persons outside the basketball team. In February 1993, Keilitz interviewed members of the men's basketball team at Dambrot's request. Keilitz reported all the African American players he interviewed said they were not offended by the coach's use of the term. At some point after those interviews, a former member of the men's basketball team, Shannon Norris, complained to the university's affirmative action officer, Angela Haddad, regarding Dambrot's use of the N-word during the November incident. The affirmative action officer confronted Dambrot who admitted using the word but stated he used it in a positive manner. The officer viewed Dambrot's use of the word as a violation of the university's discriminatory harassment policy and recommended Dambrot be disciplined. Dambrot accepted the proposed disciplinary action in lieu of a more formal investigation and was suspended without pay for five days.

News of the locker room incident spread through the campus after Dambrot was suspended. An article in the student newspaper was printed in which Dambrot told his side of the story. The statement was characterized by the district court as "considerably more explanatory and defensive than apologetic in tone." Students staged a demonstration and local, regional and national news media reported accounts of the incident at CMU.

On April 12, 1993, Keilitz, the athletic director, informed Dambrot he would not be retained as head coach for the 1993-94 season. The university stated that it believed Dambrot was no longer capable of effectively leading the men's basketball program.

Dambrot instituted a lawsuit on April 19, 1993, alleging, *inter alia,* he was fired because he used the term "nigger," and the termination violated his First Amendment rights to free speech and academic freedom. Several members of the basketball team joined the lawsuit alleging the university's discriminatory harassment policy was overbroad and vague and violated their First Amendment rights.

Dambrot's use of the N-word is even further away from the marketplace of ideas and the concept of academic freedom because his position as coach is somewhat different from that of the average classroom teacher. Unlike the classroom teacher whose primary role is to guide students through the discussion and debate of various viewpoints in a particular discipline, Dambrot's role as a coach is to train his student athletes how to win on the court. The plays and strategies are seldom up for debate. Execution of the coach's will is paramount. Moreover, the coach controls who plays and for how long, placing a disincentive on any debate with the coach's ideas which might have taken place.

While Dambrot argues and we accept as true that he intended to use the term in a positive and reinforcing manner, Dambrot's total message to the players is disturbing. Corey Henderson, one of the players on the 1992-93 team touched on the concern in his deposition testimony.

Q: What did that phrasing that he had wanted you to play like niggers on the basketball floor but not be niggers in the class-room mean to you as a students? [sic]

A: I really am not sure. Because in the context he was trying to use it in, I mean, nigger I guess as a—he wanted us—I guess he wanted us to play harder, I suppose, and I didn't understand why if it was good enough on the court then why it wasn't good enough in the classroom.

I mean, I was kind of shocked that he used that word being a coach and all because he—I didn't think that was appropriate for him to use that word, him or any coach, talking to a group of mostly young adult black males. I didn't think it was right for him to use that word.

But then I was kind of disgusted when he said not being one in the classroom. I didn't understand why it was good enough on the court but not good enough in the classroom.

The First Amendment protects the right of any person to espouse the view that a "nigger" is someone who is aggressive in nature, tough, loud, abrasive, hard-nosed and intimidating; someone at home on the court but out of place in a classroom setting where discipline, focus, intelligence and interest are required. This same view has been and is held about African Americans by many who view the success of Black athletes as a result of natural athletic ability and the success of Black executives as the result of affirmative action.

What the First Amendment does not do, however, is require the government as employer or the university as educator to accept this view as a valid means of motivating players. An instructor's choice of teaching methods does not rise to the level of protected expression. Assuming but not deciding, Dambrot is subject to the same standards as any teacher in a classroom (as opposed to a locker room setting), Dambrot's speech served to advance no academic message and is solely a method by which he attempted to motivate—or humiliate—his players. In the instant case, the University has a right to terminate Dambrot for recklessly telling these young men to be athletically ardent but academically apathetic in his attempt to boost athletic performance. The University has a right to terminate Dambrot for telling his players that success on the basketball court is not premised on the same principles of discipline, focus and drive that bring success in the classroom. The University has a right to disapprove of the use of the word "nigger" as a motivational tool just as the college in *Martin* was not forced to tolerate profanity. Finally, the University has a right to hold Coach Dambrot to a higher standard of conduct than that of his players. Dambrot's resort to the First Amendment for protection is not well taken.

For the foregoing reasons, Dambrot's speech cannot be fairly characterized as touching a matter of public concern.

Source: Courtesy of Westlaw; reprinted with permission.

In the following case the parents of a 15-year-old boy sued a parent of another player after the father of the opposing player went to the locker room after the game and allegedly assaulted the 15-year-old. The lawsuit alleged a civil assault under Maine law as well as intentional infliction of emotional distress. The plaintiff asked the court to award punitive damages as well. Should the plaintiff recover on these theories and be entitled to punitive damages?

📖 CASE 1-7 *Hale v. Antoniou*

2004 WL 1925551 (Me. 2004)

Background

The plaintiff Jordan Hale is fifteen years old and currently attends Falmouth High School. He was thirteen at the time of the incident that is the subject of this lawsuit.

When Jordan was in the seventh grade, he signed up to play in the Casco Bay hockey league. On December 10, 2001, Jordan's team played another team on which Michael Antoniou was a player. Jordan knew Michael and they were friends. Jordan also knew Michael's father, the defendant Demetri Antoniou.

Towards the end of the hockey game, Jordan and Michael collided. Jordan had lowered his shoulder and checked Michael. Michael went down onto the ice. Michael took a while to get up, and Jordan could tell Michael had been jarred by the hit. Michael returned to his team bench, and the game ended about ten seconds later. No penalty was called against Jordan.

From the defendant's perspective, it appeared as if Jordan drove his hockey stick onto Michael's "right jaw and right neck." The defendant testified that he thought his son might have suffered a concussion. In fact, Michael was injured as a result of the hit.

After the game, the teams went to their respective locker rooms. Jordan was in the locker room for about five minutes and had already started getting out of his hockey equipment when he saw the defendant at the doorway of his team's locker room. According to Jordan,

> I was talking to one of my teammates. And out of the corner of my eye I saw him—saw him and Mr. Scala kind of, like—Mr. Scala was leaning against the door; and he was kind of walking—stepped in front of him. And I didn't really pay any attention to it. I thought he was congratulating the team. And then I heard what he was saying. And then I saw Mr. Scala push him out. . . . I don't know what he said the first [sic]. But I heard him say, No. 7, stay away from my fucking kid. I'll get you next time.

Jordan does not recall the defendant saying anything else.

Jordan testified that the defendant had Michael's hockey stick in his left hand, which the defendant was pointing at him as he spoke. He also testified that it all happened very quickly, in a matter of seconds. In addition, Jordan stated that it looked as if the defendant would continue his advance toward him had Scala not stepped in between them.

According to the defendant, after the game, he was looking for his son's locker room. The defendant testified that he stepped into the locker room of Jordan's team and told Scala that "No. 7 was a fucking asshole." He also testified that at the time that he made this comment, he could not see "No. 7," nor did he know that No. 7 was Jordan Hale.

Scala testified that the defendant asked him where Jordan was, came into the locker room with a "hockey stick under—a bag on his shoulder, a hockey stick under his arm," and said, "Jordan Hale is an asshole," not "number seven is an asshole." Scala also testified that the defendant's statement caused him to "kind of stop[ ] in [his] tracks" and that after making the statement, "[the defendant] kept walking into the locker room." Scala went on to testify that "[the defendant] raised his stick and started pointing at Jordan and said I will get you get you next time. At which case I stepped in front of him. . . ." Scala asked the defendant to leave the locker room and the defendant left immediately. Scala did not notice how Jordan seemed in the locker room after the defendant left.

The parties dispute whether the defendant carried a hockey stick into the locker room. The parties also dispute whether the defendant's remarks were made to Scala or to both Scala and Jordan. In addition, they dispute whether the defendant made eye contact with Jordan and whether at the time of the incident, the defendant was "more angry with the coach for condoning aggressive behavior [than with Jordan]."

The parties also dispute whether Jordan was shaken up by the incident. At his deposition, the plaintiff testified that after the incident, he finished undressing and talked with his teammates and that when he left the locker room five minutes after the incident, he did not tell his father what had happened, although he told him "vaguely that night." He also testified that when his father asked him what the defendant said, he answered that he "didn't hear [the defendant]" because he "didn't want this to turn into anything that big" and because he "didn't want to make a big deal out of it." Jordan testified that he did not want to make a big deal about the incident because he "didn't think it was that important."

However, in his affidavit, Jordan testified that after the incident, when he tried to stand up, his knees buckled and he had to sit back down. In addition, both Jordan and his mother have offered testimony that Jordan is very private about his feelings generally and tries to downplay emotions and emotional situations.

Although Jordan has done fine in athletics since the incident, and has performed at a high level, including making the varsity high school soccer team as a freshman, there was a period of several games and weeks after the incident when he was not his usual self and when his play changed dramatically. The change was so pronounced that Scala noticed it. In addition, Jordan saw a counselor for three sessions.

Discussion

A. Civil Assault

"An actor is subject to liability to another for assault if (a) he acts intending to cause a harmful or offensive contact with the person of the other or a third person, or an imminent apprehension of such a contact, and (b) the other is thereby put in such imminent apprehension." *Restatement (Second) Torts,* § 21 (1965). Where the actor does not act intentionally, he will not be liable to the other for an apprehension caused by his actions.

In the present action, Jordan testified that the defendant was pointing a hockey stick at him as he said, "No. 7 stay away from my fucking kid." In addition, Scala testified that the defendant asked where Jordan was, came into the locker room with a "hockey stick under—a bag on his shoulder, a hockey stick under his arm," and said, "Jordan Hale is an asshole." Scala also testified that after he made that statement, "[the defendant] kept walking into the locker room." Collectively, this testimony creates a dispute regarding whether the defendant acted intending to cause Jordan imminent harm or imminent apprehension of harm.

There is also a dispute about whether Jordan was put in imminent apprehension by the defendant's acts. Jordan stated in his deposition that he saw Scala push the defendant out. In his affidavit, he followed up on his deposition testimony and stated that from his perspective, that it looked as if the defendant would continue his advance towards him had Scala not pushed the defendant out. In addition, Jordan also stated that after the incident, his knees buckled and he had to sit back down. Viewing these facts collectively in a light most favorable to Jordan, who was thirteen years old at the time of the incident it is possible that Jordan was put in imminent apprehension by the defendant's acts.

Accordingly, the defendant's motion for summary judgment on the plaintiffs' claim for civil assault is denied.

B. Intentional Infliction of Emotional Distress

To establish a defendant's liability for intentional infliction of emotional distress, a plaintiff must prove that (1) the defendant engaged in intentional or reckless conduct that inflicted serious emotional distress or would be substantially certain to result in serious emotional distress; (2) the defendant's conduct was so extreme and outrageous as to exceed all possible bounds of decency and must be regarded as atrocious and utterly intolerable; and (3) the plaintiff suffered serious emotional distress as a result of the defendant's conduct. "Serious emotional distress means emotional distress, created by the circumstances of the event, that is so severe that no reasonable person could be expected to endure it."

Here, there are the admissible material facts before the court that create a dispute as to whether the defendant acted intentionally or recklessly to cause Jordan emotion[al] harm. The same facts that create a dispute about the intent element of the civil assault claim also create a dispute about the intent element of Jordan's claim for intentional infliction of emotional distress.

In addition, the parties dispute whether the defendant's alleged behavior of swearing at, pointing a hockey stick at, and threatening a thirteen-year-old was so extreme and outrageous to exceed all possible bounds of decency. "Where reasonable men may differ, it is for the jury, subject to the control of the Court, to determine whether, in a particular case, the conduct has been sufficiently extreme and outrageous to result in liability."

Finally, there are facts before the court that create a dispute as to whether Jordan suffered serious emotional distress as a result of the defendant's conduct. Jordan claims he was shaken up by the incident. Although he stated that he didn't think the incident was important and that he didn't want to make a big deal about it, Jordan and his mother claim that Jordan is very private about his feelings generally and tries to downplay emotions and emotional situations. In addition, Jordan saw a counselor regarding the incident. Finally, Jordan's hockey coach testified that there was a period following the incident in which Jordan was not his usual self and Jordan's play changed dramatically.

Accordingly, the defendant's motion for summary judgment on Jordan's claim for intentional infliction of emotional distress is denied.

Decision

. . . Defendant's Motion for Summary Judgment is DENIED.

Source: Courtesy of Westlaw; reprinted with permission.

After a trial in this matter, a jury found no assault but did find that the defendant's actions constituted the tort of intentional infliction of emotional distress. Why did the jury fail to find assault under these facts? The defendant was never criminally charged. Should he have been? What punishment or discipline should the father have received for his actions? Should he have been suspended from any further participation in this youth sports league or was this just the case of a parent blowing off a little steam?

The Little League code of conduct for parents and its pledges for players and parents follow.

Sport Parent Code of Conduct

Preamble

The essential elements of character building and ethics in sports are embodied in the concept of sportsmanship and six core principles: trustworthiness, respect, responsibility, fairness, caring, and good citizenship. The highest potential of sports is achieved when competition reflects these "six pillars of character."

I therefore agree:

1. I will not force my child to participate in sports.
2. I will remember that children participate to have fun and that the game is for youth, not adults.
3. I will inform the coach of any physical disability or ailment that may affect the safety of my child or the safety of others.
4. I will learn the rules of the game and the policies of the league.
5. I (and my guests) will be a positive role model for my child and encourage sportsmanship by showing respect and courtesy, and by demonstrating positive support for all players, coaches, officials and spectators at every game, practice or sporting event.
6. I (and my guests) will not engage in any kind of unsportsmanlike conduct with any official, coach, player, or parent such as booing and taunting, refusing to shake hands, or using profane language or gestures.
7. I will not encourage any behaviors or practices that would endanger the health and well-being of the athletes.
8. I will teach my child to play by the rules and to resolve conflicts without resorting to hostility or violence.
9. I will demand that my child treat other players, coaches, officials and spectators with respect regardless of race, creed, color, sex or ability.
10. I will teach my child that doing one's best is more important than winning, so that my child will never feel defeated by the outcome of a game or his/her performance.
11. I will praise my child for competing fairly and trying hard, and make my child feel like a winner every time.

12. I will never ridicule or yell at my child or other participants for making a mistake or losing a competition.
13. I will emphasize skill development and practices and how they benefit my child over winning. I will also de-emphasize games and competition in the lower age groups.
14. I will promote the emotional and physical well-being of the athletes ahead of any personal desire I may have for my child to win.
15. I will respect the officials and their authority during games and will never question, discuss, or confront coaches at the game field, and will take time to speak with coaches at an agreed upon time and place.
16. I will demand a sports environment for my child that is free from drugs, tobacco, and alcohol, and I will refrain from their use at all sports events.
17. I will refrain from coaching my child or other players during games and practices, unless I am one of the official coaches of the team.

Source: Courtesy of Little League Baseball, Inc.

The Little League Pledge

I trust in God

I love my country

And will respect its laws

I will play fair

And strive to win

But win or lose

I will always do my best

Source: Courtesy of Little League Baseball, Inc.

The Little League Parent/Volunteer Pledge

I will teach all children to play fair and do their best.

I will positively support all managers, coaches and players.

I will respect the decisions of the umpires.

I will praise a good effort despite the outcome of the game.

Source: Courtesy of Little League Baseball, Inc.

In this case, a coach was sued for battery, among other causes of action, after he threw a high school player to the ground.

📖 **CASE 1-8** *Cronk v. Suffern Sr. High School*

809 N.Y.S.2d 480 (N.Y. Sup. 2005)

MARY H. SMITH, J.

This is an action to recover money damages for defendants' alleged "tortious conduct" in "denying plaintiff Dustin Cronk the opportunity to participate as a player on the School's varsity baseball team during his third year. . ." Plaintiffs specifically allege that these actions included "improper retaliation, conspiracy and deliberate indifference and neglect with respect to the customs and policies of the Defendants." Plaintiffs denominate two separate causes of action; first, for intentional infliction of emotional distress and second, "improper termination from baseball program.". . .

According to plaintiffs' . . . testimony, on October 22, 2002, plaintiff Dustin Cronk ("Dustin") was a member of the Suffern High School varsity football team, weighing approximately 200 pounds. Dustin, along with his teammates and the coaching staff, was on the field, but he was sidelined from actual participation due to a separated shoulder injury sustained several days earlier. Dustin testified that he was standing in front of Coach McNally, "joking around, just blocking his view," "purposely," whereupon Coach McNally suddenly grabbed him and threw him to the ground. Dustin got up and told Coach McNally, "Don't ever f'in touch me again." According to Dustin, Coach McNally "had it out for [him] that week," having days before kicked him out of gym class for insubordination, Dustin claiming that he merely had been laughing during the showing of a movie, and having him participate in gym activities when he was not supposed to be engaging in physical activity because of his shoulder injury. Dustin had related the incident to his parents and his mother telephoned Coach Faherty that night; Dustin's father then spoke with the principal the following day.

According to Dustin, the following day, Coach McNally and Coach Delaney, the head coach, isolated Dustin before practice and told Dustin that he should have worked out the problem after the incident instead of leaving and that he should not have gotten his parents involved because he was "going to have to grow up—not grow up, but learn to deal with problems on my own, and not get your parents involved so much." Thereafter, Dustin went to football practice. Several days later, Dustin had spoken with the principal about the incident. Following this discussion, Dustin testified that after a football practice the following week, all four coaches kept him after, saying, "we thought we worked everything out, why is this still going on" and, they referred to an earlier incident involving physical contact between a different coach and another student, leaving Dustin with the impression that they believed "it was okay" what Coach McNally did.

Dustin testified that he played the remaining three games left in the football season. Nothing further was said or done about this incident.

Dustin then tried out for the varsity baseball team in the spring and, having played past years, he was "stunned" when he did not make the team; he believed that he was a better player who possessed superior skills to a number of other students who made the team. Coach McNally was not involved with baseball, but Dustin testified that, because the "coaches are all friends," he did not make the team because of the incident with Coach McNally.

Dustin and his parents then filed, on or about March 19, 2003, a report with the Ramapo Police Department relating to the October 22, 2002 incident involving Coach McNally.

It appears from Mrs. Cronk's . . . testimony that the police, following their investigation, ultimately had concluded that there was a "lack of evidence to support the Cronk complaint, this case should be closed." According to Mrs. Cronk, students who had been interviewed by the police relating to this incident were later shown copies of the final prepared reports and they said that the preparing officers had "lied" about what the students had told the officers. Mrs. Cronk had testified that the initial police investigation was "compromised" by the investigating officer's familiarity with Coach McNally.

Dustin and Mrs. Cronk both testified that Dustin has not undergone any psychological counseling as a result of this incident. Also, Dustin testified that he played varsity football his senior year after this incident, following his having been cut from the varsity baseball team.

. . . . [D]efendant now is moving for summary judgment dismissing the complaint, arguing that "Plaintiffs cannot prove that the District was negligent in the hiring, training and supervision of the Suffern High School employees, and plaintiffs cannot prove negligence, intentional infliction of emotional distress or battery." Further, defendant contends that plaintiffs' Second Cause of Action for retaliation and wrongful exclusion from the baseball team is not a recognized cause of action and that same is akin to "educational malpractice" which is not cognizable in New York.

Plaintiffs oppose the motion, arguing that, contrary to defendant's interpretation of the complaint, plaintiffs have not pleaded a cause of action for negligent hiring, training and supervision of the Suffern

High School employees. Further, plaintiffs argue that the claim of battery "is but one aspect of the course of conduct asserted" in plaintiffs' First cause of action and that it was the battery "that touched off the series of events that resulted in the emotional distress to be suffered by plaintiff. . . . After the battery came the confrontation with the coaching staff, the failure of the school administration to properly react, and his being kept off the baseball team. . ." Plaintiffs deny that this is an action akin to educational malpractice because plaintiffs do not assert that the judgment of the School was based upon any statutory standard, and they state that "this is simply a case in which a nonsensical decision was made, for which the only explanation is that defendants were being vindictive."

. . . After this Court's careful reading of the record at bar and the parties' respective arguments, and upon application of the foregoing legal standard, defendant's motion for summary is granted in its entirety based upon the analysis *infra*. While this Court would have been inclined to sever from the First cause of action plaintiffs' stated claim for assault, finding that a triable issue of fact exists with respect thereto, patently, said claim is time-barred pursuant to the one-year statute of limitations. . . . Accordingly, this action is hereby dismissed.

"In order to prevail on a claim for intentional infliction of emotional distress, a plaintiff must plead and prove that a defendant engaged in extreme and outrageous conduct and that such conduct intentionally or recklessly caused severe emotional distress' (citations omitted). Said conduct must transcend the bounds of decency and be regarded as atrocious and utterly intolerable in a civilized community." (Citations omitted) . . . Further, a plaintiff is required to establish that severe emotional distress was suffered, which is "supported by medical evidence, not the mere recitation of speculative claims." While contemporaneous medical treatment is not required, there must be an evidentiary showing that the alleged conduct caused mental or physical symptoms that indicate the presence of emotional distress.

Based upon the foregoing, the Court necessarily finds that the claim for intentional infliction of emotional distress must be dismissed. Firstly, plaintiffs do not allege nor demonstrate through evidentiary submissions that Dustin has suffered mental or physical symptoms that indicate the presence of emotional distress related to the alleged actions. This failure alone is sufficient to dismiss said claim.

Additionally, however, the Court cannot find based upon the unrefuted circumstances presented that Coach McNally's action of grabbing and throwing Dustin to the ground, even when combined with the further claimed ensuing confrontations between Dustin and the football coaches and the allegedly inadequate response of the school, while all wholly inappropriate and unacceptable, whether individually or collectively, meets the rigorous standard of stating a viable claim for intentional infliction of emotional distress. The claim therefore is subject to dismissal on this basis, as well.

As to the Second cause of action, this Court is unaware of any viable claim for a student's exclusion from a sports team, allegedly motivated solely by retaliation, as here is alleged. Although the Court agrees with plaintiffs that, contrary to defendant's argument, this is not akin to a claim for educational malpractice, nevertheless, plaintiffs have failed to cite any authority or case law supporting the existence of such a claim. It also is to be noted that plainly the alleged damages caused by this alleged tortious action, i.e., that Dustin was hindered in gaining further recognition and/or prospective college scholarship offers, is highly speculative, likely incapable of being proven and, in any event, completely unsupported by the record at bar.

Source: Courtesy of Westlaw; reprinted with permission.

Do you agree with the court's ruling in this case? Should the coach have been suspended for his actions? Should the coach have been criminally charged? How should schools and school districts treat coaches who physically assault players? What level of discipline should coaches be allowed to administer to players during the coaching process? Is this the kind of discipline that should end up in the court system? How else could this have been resolved? Did the coaches act ethically under the circumstances? What about the player and his parents?

NOTES AND DISCUSSION QUESTIONS

The Influence of Sports

1. How have sports changed society? How have sports changed over the past 50 years? How have sports changed America over the last 100 years? How have sports influenced politics? Religion?
2. Americans participate in a variety of sports and attend both professional and amateur sports activities at increasing rates. NASCAR and professional wrestling are both popular among Americans and are also "big business."
3. There are very few professional athletes in the United States when compared with the population. The chances of a person becoming a professional athlete are very slim. There has been much debate about whether athletes should be role models for children. Are they? Should they be?

Sports Ethics

4. Define sports ethics. What other ethical considerations do sports present? How should ethical decisions be applied in professional sports? Amateur sports?

Sports Violence

5. What can be done to stem the tide of violence in sports? How should violence against spectators be dealt with on the professional level? Should fans be banned from further events? How would a league or team enforce such a ruling?

6. What steps should professional leagues take to curb violence? What should they do to ensure that fans do not entice players to violent acts? Should each stadium have a fan code of conduct?

7. What rules and procedures should be in place to prevent violent acts from occurring in amateur sports? What can be done to curtail the "win at all costs" attitude in youth sports? How can a balance be achieved between being competitive and allowing the kids to have fun?

Race and Sports

8. Should professional teams take action against the use of Native American mascots such as that taken by the NCAA? How would the league or commissioner enforce such a ban?

9. For an interesting case exploring the relationship between sports law, religion, free speech, and race, see *Williams v. Eaton*, 333 F. Supp. 107 (D. Wyo. 1971). Fourteen football players sued after they were suspended from the team for a protest. They wore black arm bands in protest of the university's and conference's use of student monies and facilities to play host to Brigham Young University, alleging racist policies on the part of the Mormon Church.

10. Do you believe the commissioner was correct in the discipline he levied against John Rocker? How are players' free speech rights limited? What if a player participated in an anti-war rally or anti-abortion march in the offseason? Would the commissioner have the right to suspend him based on his actions?

Professional Sports

11. Would Popov have to catch the ball in the same manner that is equivalent to an out in baseball to claim possession of it under the law? What is the difference between having possession of and exercising dominion over the ball? Should he have to make a "baseball" move with the ball before he is entitled to claim dominion over the ball? Do you agree with the court's notion of "equitable division"? How long does a spectator have to possess a ball thrown or hit into the stands before he or she can claim ownership? The court found that Popov had actually possessed the ball meaning to claim ownership. If he did, wouldn't the ball be considered lost after he gained possession and then be required to be returned to its rightful owner? The ball eventually sold for $450,000, which was less than Popov's legal fees. He refused to pay his lawyer and was sued.

12. Popov sued Hayashi for conversion, trespass to chattel, assault, and battery. If you were the judge, how would you rule on these claims? (See www.courttv.com, *Popov v. Hayashi*: Complaint.) Popov's petition stated in part:

> 6) On or about October 7, 2001, POPOV and DEFENDANT HAYASHI were in attendance of the San Francisco Giants Baseball at Pacific Bell Park. POPOV and

DEFENDANT HAYASHI were located in the Arcade area, in the standing room only seats, behind right field directly in line with the plaque commemorating Barry Bonds 500th career home run. POPOV was to the right of DEFENDANT HAYASHI by approximately twelve feet.

7) During the first inning, Barry Bonds hit his 73rd home run of the year setting a new single season home run record. The single season home run record is one of the most hallowed records in all of baseball and indeed, all sporting endeavors. The home run was hit to right field directly to POPOV. POPOV successfully caught the BASEBALL in his baseball mitt and brought the mitt containing the BASEBALL to his torso.

8) Based upon the express and implied promises of the San Francisco Giants and Major League Baseball that baseball fans are entitled to keep any balls which are caught as a souvenir, POPOV successfully obtained possession of THE BASEBALL.

9) Within seconds after catching the ball, POPOV was attacked, assaulted and battered by no less than six and as many as fifteen, individuals, including DEFENDANT HAYASHI and individual DOE Defendants. POPOV had the baseball firmly and securely in his grasp before being assaulted and battered by the Defendants. Many of these individuals knocked POPOV to the cement ground and piled on top of him. POPOV landed on his left cheek and left side of his torso. Upon landing on the ground, POPOV felt THE BASEBALL in his mitt pressing against his rib cage. POPOV began to immediately scream "GET OFF" and "HELP."

13. The ball hit by Mark McGwire to break Roger Maris's long-standing single-season home run record of 61 sold for $3.2 million. How does the reputation of the player who hit the ball affect its selling price? Eddie Murray's 500th home run ball was auctioned for $500,000.[35] At Wrigley Field, fans have the habit of throwing an opposing player's ball back after a home run. Would a fan have enough gumption to throw back a valuable ball?

The odd case of *Boston Red Sox Baseball Club v. Mientkiewicz* presented new issues in the ownership of balls. Doug Mientkiewicz fielded the final out for the 2004 Red Sox World Championship team. He jokingly referred to the ball as his "retirement," although he initially agreed to loan the ball to the Red Sox for display along with the World Series trophy. Mientkiewicz was traded to the New York Mets three months after the Red Sox won the World Series. The Red Sox argued that they were entitled to possession of the ball and sued their first baseman. The Red Sox argued that Mientkiewicz, as their former employee, came into possession of the ball through his course of employment with the Sox organization; therefore, the Red Sox were the rightful owners of the ball. The commissioner's office also filed a grievance against Mientkiewicz, claiming that he had no ownership rights to the ball. The Red Sox and Mientkiewicz eventually agreed to settle the matter. Red Sox Club president Larry Lucchino stated, "An amicable agreement

---

[35] See Carrie Muskat, *Where Have All the 500 Balls Gone?*, MLB.com, Apr. 18, 2001.

was reached several weeks ago when it was suggested that the Baseball Hall of Fame and Museum become the custodian of the ball."

14. Should Mike Tyson be held personally responsible to those viewers who paid to see the fight? What if Tyson had refused to box at all? Could the plaintiffs have recovered damages under those circumstances?

Amateur Sports

15. In *Dambrot*, the plaintiff asserted he was protected by free speech concerns. Do you agree with the court's decision? What if an African American coach at an historically black college had engaged in the same activity? Would the result be the same? Should the result be the same? Why was Dambrot's halftime speech not a matter of public concern?

16. The recruiting practices of high school basketball are examined in the movie *Hoop Dreams*. The film can be viewed as a documentary and a comment on winning at all costs at the high school level. After viewing the film, consider what affects recruiting practices have on student-athletes. What ethical considerations are present for coaches in such situations? One of the high school basketball players who was depicted in the movie aptly stated: "People always say to me, 'When you get to the NBA, don't forget about me.' Well, I should've said back, 'If I don't make it to the NBA, don't forget about me.'"[36]

SUGGESTED READINGS AND RESOURCES

Angell, Roger. *The Summer Game*. New York: Viking Press, 1972.

Bouton, Jim. *Ball Four*, 2d ed. New York: Collier Books, 1990.

Boxill, Jan. *Sports Ethics: An Anthology*. Malden, MA: Blackwell, 2003.

Cahan, Richard, & Jacob, Mark. *The Game That Was: The George Brace Baseball Photo Collection*. Chicago: Contemporary Books, 1996.

Chadwick, Alex. *Illustrated History of Baseball*. New York: Portland House, 1988.

Feinstein, John. *The Majors*. Boston: Little, Brown, 1999.

Gent, Peter. *North Dallas Forty*. New York: William Morrow, 1973.

Harwell, Ernie. *Tuned to Baseball*. South Bend, IN: Diamond Communications, 1985.

Haskins, D., with Wetzel, D. *Glory Road: My Story of the 1966 NCAA Basketball Championship and How One Team Triumphed Against the Odds*. New York: Hyperion, 2005.

Jones, Donald G., & Daley, Elaine L. *Sports Ethics in America*. New York: Greenwood Press, 1992.

MacCambridge, Michael (ed.). *ESPN Sports Century*. New York: Hyperion, 1999.

---

[36] William Gates, in *Hoop Dreams* (Fine Line Features 1994).

McMillen, Tom. *Out of Bounds: How the American Sports Establishment Is Being Driven by Greed and Hypocrisy—and What Needs to Be Done About It*. New York: Simon & Schuster, 1992.

Ritter, Lawrence S (comp.). *The Glory of Their Times: The Story of the Early Days of Baseball Told by the Men Who Played It*. New York: Perennial, 2002.

Sowell, Mike. *The Pitch That Killed*. Chicago: Ivan R. Dee, 2004.

Stoddard, Brian. *Saturday Afternoon Fever: Sport in the Australian Culture*. North Ryde, NSW, Australia: Angus & Robertson, 1999.

Sullivan, George. *The Gamemakers: Pro Football's Great Quarterbacks—From Baugh to Namath*. New York: Putnam, 1971.

Thorn, John, & Palmer, Pete. *The Hidden Game of Baseball: A Revolutionary Approach to Baseball and Its Statistics*. Garden City, NY: Doubleday, 1984.

Whittingham, Richard. *Rites of Autumn: The Story of College Football*. New York: Free Press, 2001.

Wolf, David. *Foul! The Connie Hawkins Story*. New York: Holt, Rinehart and Winston, 1972.

REFERENCE MATERIALS

Alexander, Charles C. *Ty Cobb*. New York: Oxford University Press, 1984.

Arvaniti, Nellie. *Ethics in Sport: The Greek Educational Perspective on Anti-Doping*. 9 SPORT IN SOCIETY 354 (2006).

Apparelyzed. *The 2012 London Paralympic Games—Disabled Olympic Games*. http://www.apparelyzed.com/london-paralympic-games/index.html.

Berlow, Lawrence H. *Sports Ethics: A Reference Handbook*. Santa Barbara, CA: ABC-CLIO, 1994.

Bissinger, H. G. *Friday Night Lights: A Town, a Team and a Dream*. Reading, MA: Addison-Wesley, 1990.

Bowman, John S (ed.). *Ivy League Football*. New York: Crescent Books, 1988.

Brown, Gerry, & Morrison, Michael (eds.). *ESPN Sports Almanac 2003*. New York: Hyperion, 2002.

Catawba Wins Appeal on Mascot Issue. INDIAN COUNTRY TODAY, June 12, 2006, http://www.indiancountrytoday.com/archive/28209949.html.

Champion, Walter T. *Sports Law in a Nutshell*. St. Paul, MN: Thomson/West, 2005.

Cheater, Cheater . . . The Worst Cases of Sports Cheating. CBC Sports Online, http://www.cbc.ca/sports/columns/top10/chets.html.

Cheating Coach Gets One-Year Suspension. NORTH COUNTY TIMES, Nov. 30, 2005.

Cosell, Howard, & Whitfield, Shelby. *What's Wrong with Sports*. New York: Simon & Schuster, 1991.

Davis, Chase. *Sox Drop Suit Over Series Ball, Agree to Arbitration with Mientkiewicz*. BOSTON GLOBE, Dec. 17, 2005.

DesJardins, Joseph R. *Business, Ethics, and the Environment*. Upper Saddle River, NJ: Pearson/Prentice Hall, 2007.

The Document of Appeal Sent by the College to the NCAA Regarding Use of the Tribe Athletic Logo. W&M News, June 15, 2006, http://web.wm.edu/news/.

Drehs, Wayne. *Notre Dame Players Wonder What's Next.* ESPN.com, Dec. 2001.

Feinstein, John. *The Punch, One Night, Two Lives, and the Fight That Changed Basketball Forever.* Boston: Little, Brown, 2002.

French, Peter A. *Ethics and College Sports.* Lanham, MD: Rowman & Littlefield, 2004.

Garber, Greg. *Youth Team Pays High Price in Win-At-All-Costs Game.* ESPN.com, Aug. 14, 2006.

Grimsley, Will, & The Associated Press Sports Staff. *A Century of Sports.* Maplewood, NJ: Hammond, 1971.

Guillen Apologizes for Use of Homosexual Slur. ESPN.com, June 21, 2006.

Howe, Gordie, with Condron, Frank. *Gordie Howe: My Hockey Memories.* Buffalo, NY: Firefly Books, 1999.

Johnson, William Oscar. *The Olympics.* New York: Time-Life, 1996.

Koenig, Kelly B. *Mahmoud Abdul-Rauf's Suspension for Refusing to Stand for the National Anthem: A "Free Throw" for the NBA and Denver Nuggets, or a "Slam Dunk" Violation of Abdul-Rauf's Title VII Rights?* 76 WASHINGTON UNIVERSITY LAW QUARTERLY 377 (1998).

Leavy, Jane. *Sandy Koufax: A Lefty's Legacy.* New York: HarperCollins, 2002.

Lefteroff, Lindsay M. Korey. *Excessive Heckling and Violent Behavior at Sporting Events: A Legal Solution?* 14 UNIVERSITY OF MIAMI BUSINESS LAW REVIEW 119 (Fall/Winter 2005).

Lipsyte, Robert, & Levine, Peter. *Idols of the Game: A Sporting History of the American Century.* Atlanta, GA: Turner, 1995.

Lowitt, Bruce. *'Wrong Way' Riegels Takes Off into History.* ST. PETERSBURG TIMES, Sept. 26, 1999.

Marathon Imposter Foiled by a Mustache. N.Y. TIMES, Sept. 17, 1991.

Maravich, Pete, & Campbell, Darrel. *Pistol Pete: Heir to a Dream.* Nashville, TN: Thomas Nelson, 1987.

McCambridge, Michael (ed.). *ESPN College Football Encyclopedia: The Complete History of the Game.* New York: Hyperion Books, 2005.

McCartney 'Remorseful' About Fifth-Down Play. SI.com, June 20, 1998.

Menke, Frank G. *The Encyclopedia of Sports.* New York: A. S. Barnes, 1955.

Merron, Jeff. *Presidential Superlatives.* ESPN.com, July 27, 2004.

Miss Ruiz Loses Her Title. N.Y. TIMES, April 30, 1980, B8.

Morgan, William J (ed.). *Ethics in Sport.* Champaign, IL: Human Kinetics, 2007.

Most Memorable Moment of the Century. CBS SportsLine.com, http://ps1.sportsline.com/u/football/college/1999/century/momentofcentury.htm.

NCAA Puts Bradley on Watch List. ESPN.com, April 28, 2006.

Nelson, Murray R. *Bill Russell: A Biography.* New York: Greenwood Press, 2005.

Perlman, Seth. *NCAA Bans Indian Mascot During Postseason.* USAToday.com, http://www.usatoday.com/sports/college/2005-08-05-indian-mascots-ruling_x.htm.

Play Ball! Quotes on America's Favorite Pastime. Kansas City, MO: Andrews McMeel, 1995.

Povich, Shirley. *Best Player—Not Best Man.* WASHINGTON POST, Jan. 1, 1995.

Reilly, Rick. *Paralympic Paradox.* SI.com, Dec. 5, 2000.

Shatzkin, Mike (ed.). *The Ballplayers: Baseball's Ultimate Biographical Reference.* New York: Arbor House/William Morrow, 1990.

Sowell, Mike. *One Pitch Away: The Players' Stories of the 1986 League Championships and World Series*. New York: Macmillan USA, 1995.

Sports Illustrated's Not-So-Great Moments in Sports. Warner Home Video, 1989.

Toomey, Bill, & King, Barry. *The Olympic Challenge*. Reston, VA: Reston Publishing , 1984.

Wallop, Douglass. *The Year the Yankees Lost the Pennant*. New York: W. W. Norton, 2004.

Ward, Geoffrey C. *Baseball: An Illustrated History*. New York: Alfred A. Knopf, 1994.

Whitley, David. *Teddy Ballgame Made Fenway Memories*. ESPN.com, http://espn.go.com/sportscentury/features/00016638.html.

Wieberg, Steve. *NCAA Allowing Florida State to Use Its Seminole Mascot*. USA TODAY, Aug. 23, 2005.

William & Mary to Change Athletic Logo. Indian Country Today, Oct. 20, 2006.

Yesterday in Sport. New York: Time-Life Books, 1968.

CHAPTER 2

CONTRACTS

Contracts are formed in every area of the sports industry. There are contracts for broadcasting deals, sponsorships, ticket sales, facility leases, merchandising and licensing, and players and coaches. The law of contracts emanates from several sources, such as the common law, the Uniform Commercial Code (UCC), and federal and state statutes. The common law principles of contract law apply to sports contracts. The UCC has been enacted in every state and governs commercial transactions between merchants. It is applicable to many contracts in sports as well.

Lawyers, agents, and executives within the sports industry are called on to examine, draft, and interpret contracts frequently as part of their job. A player's agent must be familiar with the terms of the standard player contract as well as other supporting documents to properly represent his or her client. A management executive must understand how salary caps and a luxury tax operate and how they interact with the standard player contract and the collective bargaining process as a whole to properly represent management interests. Facility managers must understand the concept of risk and contract provisions dealing with risk and insurance. Those involved in the marketing and sponsorship areas must grasp the specific provisions dealing with issues such as the right of publicity of athletes, moral clauses, specific uses of the product, territorial rights, and termination. Those working with a college or university may be called on to interpret the National Letter of Intent, sponsorship contracts, or facility leases in the course of their employment.

This chapter addresses the uniqueness of sports contracts and how they are used and interpreted within the sports industry. It provides a short overview of contract law and how contract principles are applied to contracts in sports generally. Standard player contracts, bonus clauses and addenda to contracts, the concept of guaranteed contracts, the negotiation of sports contracts, endorsement agreements, and contracts for coaches are also reviewed.

Sports merchandising and the sale of sport memorabilia are a multimillion-dollar industry in the United States. One just needs to browse the Internet to gain a sense of how athletes, teams, and other sports personalities, both professional and amateur, market themselves and their memorabilia. Case 2-1, *Fitl v. Strek,* 690 N.W.2d 605 (Neb. 2005), illustrates how contract principles apply to the world of sports merchandising. It involves a dispute over a 1952 Topps Mickey Mantle baseball card (a very valuable card in the business of sports card trading) and its relationship to the Nebraska UCC.

📖 CASE 2-1 *Fitl v. Strek*

690 N.W.2d 605 (Neb. 2005)

Wright, J.

Facts

In September 1995, Fitl attended a sports card show in San Francisco, California, where Strek was an exhibitor. Fitl subsequently purchased from Strek a 1952 Mickey Mantle Topps baseball card for $17,750. According to Fitl, Strek represented that the card was in near mint condition. After Strek delivered the card to Fitl in Omaha, Nebraska, Fitl placed it in a safe-deposit box.

In May 1997, Fitl sent the baseball card to Professional Sports Authenticators (PSA), a grading service for sports cards that is located in Newport Beach, California. PSA reported to Fitl that the baseball card was ungradable because it had been discolored and doctored.

On May 29, 1997, Fitl wrote to Strek and indicated that he planned to pursue "legal methods" to resolve the matter. Strek replied that Fitl should have initiated a return of the baseball card in a timely fashion so that Strek could have confronted his source and remedied the situation. Strek asserted that a typical grace period for the unconditional return of a card was from 7 days to 1 month.

In August 1997, Fitl sent the baseball card to ASA Accugrade, Inc. (ASA), in Longwood, Florida, for a second opinion. ASA also concluded that the baseball card had been refinished and trimmed.

On September 8, 1997, Fitl sued Strek, alleging that Strek knew the baseball card had been recolored or otherwise altered and had concealed this fact from him. Fitl claimed he had reasonably relied upon Strek's status as a reputable sports card dealer. Strek's answer generally denied Fitl's allegations.

In a trial to the court, Fitl appeared with counsel and offered evidence. Strek was represented by counsel but did not appear or offer any evidence. Fitl testified that he was in San Francisco over the Labor Day weekend of 1995, where he met Strek at a sports card show. Fitl subsequently purchased from Strek a 1952 Mickey Mantle Topps baseball card and placed it in a safe-deposit box. In 1997, Fitl retrieved the baseball card and sent it to PSA, a sports card grading service.

Steve Orand testified that he had been a sports card collector for 27 years and that he bought, sold, and traded cards. He testified that

PSA originated in 1996 or 1997 and was a leader in the sports card grading industry. He stated that PSA would not grade an altered card because alteration would totally devalue the card. He opined that any touchup or trimming of a card would render the card valueless and that an altered card is worth no more than the paper on which it is printed.

Orand examined the baseball card in question the week before trial and said that the edges of the card had been trimmed and reglued. One spot on the front of the baseball card and a larger spot on the back had been repainted, which left the card with no value. He testified that the standard for sports memorabilia was a lifetime guarantee and that a reputable collector would stand behind what he sold and refund the money if an item were fake or had been altered.

The district court entered judgment for Fitl in the amount of $17,750 and costs. The court found that Fitl had notified Strek as soon as he realized the baseball card was altered and worthless and that Fitl had notified Strek of the defect within a reasonable time after its discovery. The court rejected Strek's theory that Fitl should have determined the authenticity of the baseball card immediately after it had been purchased.

Assignment of Error

Strek claims that the district court erred in determining that notification of the defective condition of the baseball card 2 years after the date of purchase was timely pursuant to Neb. U.C.C. § 2-607(3)(a).

Analysis

. . . The district court found that Fitl had notified Strek within a reasonable time after discovery of the breach. Therefore, our review is whether the district court's finding as to the reasonableness of the notice was clearly erroneous.

Section 2-607(3)(a) states: "Where a tender has been accepted . . . the buyer must within a reasonable time after he discovers or should have discovered any breach notify the seller of breach or be barred from any remedy [.]" "What is a reasonable time for taking any action depends on the nature, purpose and circumstances of such action." Neb. U.C.C. § 1-204(2).

The notice requirement set forth in § 2-607(3)(a) serves three purposes. It provides the seller with an opportunity to correct any defect, to prepare for negotiation and litigation, and to protect itself against stale claims asserted after it is too late for the seller to investigate them. "Whether the notice given is satisfactory and whether it is given within a reasonable time are generally questions of fact to be measured by all the circumstances of the case."

. . . The most important one is to enable the seller "to make efforts to cure the breach by making adjustments or replacements in order to minimize the buyer's damages and the seller's liability." A second policy is to provide the seller "a reasonable opportunity to learn the facts so that he may adequately prepare for negotiation and defend himself in a suit." A third policy, designated the "least compelling" by the court, is the same as the policy behind statutes of limitation: "to provide a seller with a terminal point in time for liability."

Fitl purchased the baseball card in 1995 and immediately placed it in a safe-deposit box. Two years later, he retrieved the baseball card, had it appraised, and learned that it was of no value. Fitl testified that he had relied on Strek's position as a dealer of sports cards and on his representations that the baseball card was authentic. In *Cao v. Nguyen*, 258 Neb. 1027, 607 N.W.2d 528 (2000), we stated that a party is justified in relying upon a representation made to the party as a positive statement of fact when an investigation would be required to ascertain its falsity. In order for Fitl to have determined that the baseball card had been altered, he would have been required to conduct an investigation. We find that he was not required to do so. Once Fitl learned that the baseball card had been altered, he gave notice to Strek.

. . . [O]ne of the most important policies behind the notice requirement of North Carolina's equivalent to § 2-607(3)(a) is to allow the seller to cure the breach by making adjustments or replacements to minimize the buyer's damages and the seller's liability. However, even if Fitl had learned immediately upon taking possession of the baseball card that it was not authentic and had notified Strek at that time, there is no evidence that Strek could have made any adjustment or taken any action that would have minimized his liability. In its altered condition, the baseball card was worthless.

Strek claimed via his correspondence to Fitl that if Strek had received notice earlier, he could have contacted the person who sold him the baseball card to determine the source of the alteration, but there is no evidence to support this allegation. In fact, Strek offered no evidence at trial. His letter is merely an assertion that is unsupported. Earlier notification would not have helped Strek prepare for negotiation or defend himself in a suit because the damage to Fitl could not be repaired. Thus, the policies behind the notice requirement, to allow the seller to correct a defect, to prepare for negotiation and litigation, and to protect against stale claims at a time beyond which an investigation can be completed, were not unfairly prejudiced by the lack of an earlier notice to Strek. Any problem Strek may have had with the party from whom he obtained the baseball card was a separate matter from his transaction with Fitl, and an investigation into the source of the altered card would not have minimized Fitl's damages.

Strek represented himself as a sports card dealer at a card show in San Francisco. After Fitl expressed interest in a specific baseball card, Strek contacted Fitl to sell him just such a card. Orand stated that a reputable dealer will stand behind what he sells and refund the money if an item is fake or has been altered. In the context of whether a rejection of goods was made in a reasonable amount of time, we have stated that "when there is no precise rule of law which governs, the question of what, under the circumstances of a particular case, is a reasonable amount of time is usually a question for the jury."

The district court found that it was reasonable to give Strek notice of a defect 2 years after the purchase. This finding was not clearly erroneous. . . . [T]he burden is on the buyer to show a breach with respect to the goods accepted. Fitl presented evidence that the baseball card was not authentic, as he had been led to believe by Strek's representations. Strek did not refute Fitl's evidence.

Conclusion

The judgment of the district court is affirmed.

Source: Courtesy of Westlaw; reprinted with permission.

CONTRACT LAW

Contracts dominate daily business dealings in America. Parties enter into contracts to gain a better understanding of the rights and responsibilities of each party to the agreement. Contracts should clearly state the obligations of each party to the contract and also state the repercussions if a party fails to fulfill those obligations. Parties exchange goods and services in the stream of commerce on an everyday basis through written or oral contracts. Some contracts are more detailed than others, but it is wise for all parties to an agreement to fully understand the terms of a contract before reaching an agreement. Sports contracts are governed by the basics of contract law but possess some unique features as well. It is essential to have a basic understanding of contract law to determine how sports contracts function and how they can be interpreted. This chapter is not meant to be a treatise on contracts but merely to provide the reader with a rudimentary overview of the subject of contracts so the reader may have the necessary background to understand contract law in the context of sports law and business.

Contracts Defined

Contract law deals with the concept of the formation and enforcement of agreements between parties. Contracts provide stability to the marketplace so that businesspersons are able to rely on the good faith of others when planning and engaging in business. Not all promises are enforceable contracts. A contract has been defined as "[a]n agreement between two or more parties which creates an obligation to do or not to do a particular thing."[1] The *Restatement (Second) of Contracts* defines a contract as "a promise or set of promises for the breach of which the law gives a remedy, or the performance of which the law in some way recognizes as a duty."

Elements of a Binding Contract

To form a contract, the following elements must be met:

1. The parties to the contract must be competent to enter into a contract.
2. The contract must contain proper subject matter for a contract. In other words, the contract cannot be for an illegal purpose.
3. Consideration must be exchanged between the parties.
4. There must be mutuality of agreement between the parties.
5. Mutuality of obligations must exist between the parties.[2]

The first requirement for contract formation is capacity. All parties to the contract should be competent to enter into the contract.[3] A contract is not valid unless all parties to the contract are competent and are able to bind themselves to the contract.[4] A party might lack the necessary capacity if he or she is a minor, under the care of a guardian, or intoxicated at the time the party enters into the contract. Disputes have arisen over the issue of minors signing sports contracts. In *Central Army Sports Club v. Arena Ass'n.*, 952 F. Supp. 181 (S.D.N.Y. 1997), for example, the court found a Russian hockey player's signature on a standard player contract voidable because he signed it before he was eighteen years of age. The court summarized the issue as follows:

> The Court credits the submissions of Michael Solton, the defendants' expert on Russian law, for the proposition that Russia's Civil Code governs the Player's Contract. That code states that contracts in which a person under eighteen years old is a signing party are voidable at the option of the minor unless the minor obtained the express written consent of his parents or guardian. Parenthetically, the same rule obtains under New York and Michigan law. Accordingly, since Samsonov signed the Player's Contract when he was 17 years old without the appropriate parental consent, the agreement is a voidable contract.[5]

The National Letter of Intent (NLI) is a binding agreement between a prospective student-athlete and institution. It provides the following with regard to required signatures: "My parent or legal guardian

---

[1] Black's Law Dictionary, 322 (6th ed. 1990).

[2] Thomas v. Leja, 468 N.W.2d 58 (Mich. Ct. App. 1991); Haden v. David J. Sacks, P.C., 2007 WL 686898 (Tex. App.-Houston [I Division] 2007).

[3] *In re* Meredith's Estate, 266 N.W. 351 (Mich. 1936).

[4] Universal C.I.T. Credit Corp. v. Daniel, 243 S.W.2d 154, 159 (Tex. 1951).

[5] *Central Army Sports Club*, 952 F. Supp. at 190 n.9.

is required to sign this NLI if I am less than 21 years of age at the time of my signing, regardless of my marital status. If I do not have a living parent or a legal guardian, the person who is acting in the capacity of a guardian may seek permission from the NLI Steering Committee to sign this NLI."

A contract must also be for a legal purpose to be enforceable. A court will not enforce an illegal contract.[6] Likewise, a court will not enforce a contract that violates a statute or is against public policy.[7] For example, a contract between an agent and student-athlete that violates NCAA rules is considered against public policy and is not enforceable.[8] A contract to do something that is prohibited by statute is illegal and therefore unenforceable. Contracts for gambling where that it is prohibited are thus illegal.

A contract must also have consideration to be valid. *Consideration* is the value given in return for a promise. It is a legal detriment that has been bargained for in exchange for a promise.[9] "[N]o contract is enforceable . . . without the flow of consideration—both sides must get something out of the exchange."[10] In *Philadelphia v. Lajoie*, discussed later in this chapter, a player argued that he was allowed to abandon his contract because it lacked consideration, but the court disagreed. Courts will not question the adequacy of consideration exchanged between the parties, only that consideration has in fact been exchanged. A party can incur a legal detriment by promising to give something of legal value or by refraining from doing something.[11] For example, if John's Sporting Goods store offers Jared $50,000 to stop using a trademark similar to John's store, a valid agreement has been formed between the parties. The consideration between the parties is the money John is giving to Jared and Jared's forbearance to not use the trademark. Mutuality of agreement and obligation must also exist for there to be a valid contract.[12]

A valid contract exists after the parties have agreed to all material facts of the contract and a meeting of the minds has occurred.[13] "It is well established that a contract comes into being once the parties have reached a meeting of the minds, on the essential terms and have manifested the intent to be bound by those terms."[14]

Courts will examine the concepts of offer and acceptance to determine whether a meeting of the minds has in fact occurred. There must be an offer and an acceptance to constitute a contract.[15] An *offer* has been defined as "the manifestation of willingness to enter into a bargain, so made as to justify another person in understanding that his assent to that bargain is invited and will conclude it."[16] The following are generally not considered to constitute offers under contract law:

- Expressions of opinion
- Statements of intention

---

[6] Manning v. Noa, 76 N.W.2d 75 (Mich. 1955).

[7] Lansing Ass'n of Sch. Adm'rs v. Lansing Sch. Dist. Bd. of Educ., 549 N.W.2d 15 (Mich. Ct. App. 1996).

[8] Walters v. Fullwood, 675 F. Supp. 155 (S.D.N.Y. 1987).

[9] Higgins v. Monroe Evening News, 272 N.W.2d 537 (Mich. 1978).

[10] Schulz v. U.S. Boxing Ass'n, 105 F.3d 127 (3d Cir. 1997) (citing Continental Bank of Pennsylvania v. Barclay Riding Academy, Inc., 459 A.2d 1163, 1171 (N.J. 1983)).

[11] Hamer v. Sidway, 27 N.E. 256 (N.Y. 1891).

[12] Thomas v. Leja, 468 N.W.2d 58 (Mich. Ct. App. 1991); Bacon v. Karr, 139 So.2d 166 (Fla. App. 1962).

[13] Groulx v. Carlson, 440 N.W.2d 644 (Mich. Ct. App. 1989); Bullock v. Harwick, 30 So.2d 539 (1947).

[14] Forte Sports, Inc. v. Toy Airline Gliders of America, Inc., 371 F. Supp. 648 (2004) (citing Schulz v. U.S. Boxing Ass'n, 105 F.3d 12, 136 (3d Cir. 1997)).

[15] Mathieu v. Wubbe, 47 N.W.2d 670 (Mich. 1951).

[16] RESTATEMENT (SECOND) OF CONTRACTS § 24 (1979).

- Preliminary negotiations
- Agreement to agree
- Advertisements

Acceptance has been defined as a willingness to be bound by the terms of the offer. There are no magic words required to constitute acceptance.[17] "Acceptance must contain an assent—or meeting of the minds—to the essential terms contained in the offer."[18] The essential terms of the contract must be definite enough to provide a basis for enforcement of the agreement.[19]

Many sports contracts are entered into through the process of an offer by one party and a counteroffer by the opposing party. Negotiations may continue until the parties reach an agreement and have a meeting of the minds, thereby creating a binding and enforceable contract. Many contract negotiations are started by a team making an offer with an "offer sheet" that must be responded to by the player within a certain amount of time set forth by the collective bargaining agreement (CBA).

Problems in Formation

If a contract has been entered into by parties who have the requisite capacity, valid consideration has been exchanged, and an enforceable contract exists for all other elements, the contract may still be unenforceable if genuineness of assent between the parties has not occurred. A party may assert that misrepresentation, mistake, duress, or undue influence occurred during the formation of a contract and thus, no true meeting of the minds of the parties occurred; therefore, no enforceable contract exists.[20] When a party has been induced to enter into a contract by fraud or misrepresentation, the contract can usually be voided based on the fact that the parties failed to voluntarily consent to the terms of the contract.[21] The innocent party can rescind the contract and be returned to the original position the party was in before the contract. In *Vokes v. Arthur Murray, Inc.*, 212 So.2d 906 (Fla. 1968), the issue was whether statements by the instructor at the famous dance studio could be interpreted as statements of fact or opinion. Vokes sued, stating that the instructor at the school misrepresented to her that she was in fact a good dancer.

Mistakes in contracts can create problems of formation as well. There are two types of mistakes: unilateral and mutual. A *unilateral mistake* occurs when one of the parties to the contract makes a mistake as to some material fact contained in the contract.[22] A unilateral mistake does not usually allow a party to rescind the contract unless the opposing party knows or should have known about the mistake or when a unilateral mistake was due to a mathematical error in the contract.[23] A *mutual mistake* occurs when "both parties, at the time of contracting, share a misconception about a basic

---

[17] Gillespie v. Budkin, 902 So.2d 849 (Fla. 2005).

[18] *Id.* at 850 (citing to Nichols v. Hartford Ins. Co. of the Midwest, 834 So.2d 217, 219 (Fla. 1st DCA 2002)).

[19] Biddle v. Johnsonbaugh, 664 A.2d 159, 163 (Pa. Super. Ct. 1995).

[20] Brewer v. Royal Ins. Co. of America, 283 Ga. App. 312, 314; 641 S.F.2d 291 (Ga. App. 2007); Pursely v. Pursely, 144 S.W.2d 820, 826 (Ky. 2004).

[21] Industrial Commercial Elec. Inc. v. McLees, 101 P.3d 593 (Alaska 2004).

[22] BRJM, LLC v. Outsport Systems, Inc., 100 Conn. App. 143, 917 A.2d 605 (Conn. App. 2007).

[23] Crenshaw County Hospital Board v. St. Paul Fire & Marine Ins. Co., 411 F.2d 213 (5th Cir. 1969).

assumption of vital fact upon which they base their bargain."[24] A mutual mistake in a contract might lead to a rescission of that contract.[25]

Undue influence or duress can also allow a party to rescind a contract. A contract induced by undue influence is voidable at the option of the duped party. Duress has been defined as follows:

(a) any wrongful act of one person that compels a manifestation of apparent assent by another to a transaction without his volition, or

(b) any wrongful threat of one person by words or other conduct that induces another to enter into a transaction under the influence of such fear as precludes him from exercising free will and judgment, if the threat was intended or should reasonably have been expected to operate as an inducement.[26]

If proven, duress can allow a party to rescind a contract. In today's sports business, most players are represented by agents, but duress still can be asserted as a defense in a contract action.

Unconscionability can also create problems in the formation of contracts. A case dealing with this concept in the sports context was *Connecticut Professional Sports Corp. v. Heyman*, 276 F. Supp. 618 (S.D.N.Y. 1967), in which a player contract was deemed unconscionable and therefore unenforceable. To determine unconscionability, "[t]he basic test is whether, in the light of the general commercial background and the commercial needs of the particular trade or case, the clauses involved are so one-sided as to be unconscionable under the circumstances existing at the time of the making of the contract. . . . The principle is one of the prevention of oppression and unfair surprise . . . and not of disturbance of allocation of risks because of superior bargaining power."[27]

Interpretation

Issues relating to the interpretation of a contract can be essential to a contract dispute. The parties may believe they are entering into a contract and that they have reached a meeting of the minds on all essential terms of the contract, but they may be operating under different assumptions as a result of the parties' differing interpretation of a word or phrase found in the contract. Courts could be asked to determine the parties' intent in interpreting the following phrases, among others, in a sports contract:

- Right of first refusal
- Guarantee
- No-cut
- All-Star
- All Pro
- Champion
- Dangerous activity

---

[24] Alea London, Ltd. v. Bono-Soltysiak Enterprises, 186 S.W.3d 403, 415 (Mo. App. E.D. 2006).
[25] Industrial Com'n of North Dakota v. Noacck, 721 N.W.2d 698 (N.D. 2006).
[26] RESTATEMENT (SECOND) OF CONTRACTS, § 492 (1979).
[27] U.C.C. § 2-302 cmt. 1 (1977).

The following rules relating to contract interpretation provide guidance in the context of sports contracts. When interpreting a contract, the court gives effect to the intent of the parties involved in the contract.[28] "When the words of a contract are clear and explicit and lead to no absurd consequences, no further interpretation may be made in search of the parties intent."[29] Any ambiguity in a contract will be construed against the drafter of the contract.[30]

Remedies for a Breach of Contract

Several remedies are available to the nonbreaching party in a contract. Parties are entitled to damages for breach of contract and can also seek equitable remedies when a contract has been breached. A party may seek the following remedies:

- Damages
  - Compensatory
  - Consequential
  - Punitive
- Equitable remedies
  - Specific performance
  - Rescission
  - Restitution

The purpose of awarding damages to the nonbreaching party is to make that party whole under the contract.[31] A nonbreaching party can receive "benefit of the bargain" damages, which place the injured party in the same position they would have been had the contract not been breached.[32] *Compensatory damages* are damages available to the nonbreaching party to recover direct losses and costs.[33] *Consequential damages* are losses caused indirectly by a breach of contract. These damages, which are also referred to as "special" damages, attempt to compensate the nonbreaching party for any additional losses they may have incurred as a result of the defendant's breach of contract.[34] *Punitive damages*, also referred to as "exemplary" damages, are designed to punish a defendant for improper conduct.

Specific performance of a contract is an equitable remedy available to the nonbreaching party that calls upon the opposing party to perform the contract. It will not usually be granted unless monetary damages are inadequate.[35] Specific performance is a remedy reserved for when the subject matter of the contract is unique. Paintings, sculptures, land, and rare coins can be considered unique, such that monetary damages would be inadequate to compensate the plaintiff. For example, if A proposed to sell B a 1952

---

[28] Terry Barr Sales Agency v. All-Lock Co., 96 F.3d 174 (6th Cir. 1996).

[29] Sports Tech, Inc. v. SFI Manufacturing, Inc., 838 So.2d 807 (2003); Dillion v. DeNooyer Chevrolet Geo, 217 Mich. App. 163, 550 N.W.2d 846, 848–849 (Mich. Ct. App. 1996) (finding a plaintiff disqualified from a contest after breaking the rules of the contract by smoking in the vehicle).

[30] Quade v. Anderson, 829 F. Supp. 220 (W.D. Mich. 1993).

[31] Corl v. Huron Castings, Inc., 544 N.W.2d 278 (Mich. Ct. App. 1996).

[32] Tim-Bob, Inc. v. Mehling, 443 N.W.2d 451 (Mich. Ct. App. 1989); Taylor v. Colo. State Bank, 165 Colo. 576, 580, 440 P.2d 772, 774 (Colo. 1968).

[33] 24 WILLISTON ON CONTRACTS § 64.12 (4th ed. 1990).

[34] Schonfeld v. Hillard, 218 F.3d 164 (2d Cir. 2000).

[35] RESTATEMENT (SECOND) OF CONTRACTS, § 359.

Topps Mickey Mantle baseball card and then refused to perform, thus breaching the contract, the appropriate remedy for A would be specific performance because the card is unique. Specific performance of a contract is an order by a court to require a breaching party to perform obligations under the contract. Although a professional athlete's skills are considered to be unique, courts will not usually enforce a specific performance remedy for personal service contracts under most circumstances (see "Enforcement of Sports Contracts and Contract Defenses," later in this chapter).

Parties may agree to the damages that will be caused in the case of a breach of the contract in the form of a liquidated damages clause. Based on the freedom of contract, this clause will be upheld as long as the amount is not unconscionable, does not operate as a penalty, and does not offend public policy.[36] When a breach of contract occurs, the nonbreaching party must take reasonable steps to lessen or mitigate opposing party's damages.[37] With these basic contract principles in mind, let us turn to an analysis of how they relate to sports contracts.

APPLICATION OF CONTRACT LAW TO SPORTS

Contract Formation

Offer and Acceptance   When does a valid offer and acceptance occur? Is the league commissioner's approval necessary to form a valid contract?[38] That was one of the issues discussed in Case 2-2, *Los Angeles Rams Football Club v. Cannon*, 185 F. Supp. 717 (D.C. Cal. 1960). Billy Cannon was an All-American halfback at Louisiana State University (LSU) in 1958 and 1959 and the winner of the coveted Heisman Trophy. When Cannon left LSU, a fierce competition was going on between the established National Football League (NFL) and the upstart American Football League (AFL). The Los Angeles Rams had successfully signed Cannon to a $50,000 contract, but within a few weeks he also signed a contract with the Houston Oilers of the AFL for $100,000. It is against this backdrop that the following case is discussed.

📖 CASE 2-2   *Los Angeles Rams Football Club v. Cannon*

185 F. Supp. 717 (D.C. Cal. 1960)

```
LINDBERG, District Judge.

. . . [P]laintiff prays for an injunction to restrain defendant from
playing football or engaging in related activities for anyone other
than plaintiff without the plaintiff's consent during the term of a
```

---

[36] *In re* Trans World Airlines, Inc., 145 F.3d 124 (Del. 1990).
[37] National Football League Players' Ass'n v. National Football League Management Council, 188 Cal.App.3d 192 (Cal. App. 1986); *also see* 24 WILLISTON ON CONTRACTS § 64.27 (4th ed. 1990).
[38] *See* Detroit Football Co. v Robinson, 186 F. Supp. 993 (E.D. LA 1960).

contract or contracts allegedly entered into by the parties on November 30, 1959. . . .

Defendant denies he ever entered into a contract or contracts as alleged and further claims, as defenses to plaintiff's claims, fourteen affirmative defenses. The first six, in substance, deny that the defendant ever entered a binding contract or contracts but that defendant merely made an offer which was not accepted prior to revocation. The others, in brief, consist of fraud and deceit on the part of plaintiff, acting through Pete Rozelle, then the General Manager of the Rams. . . .

The defendant, Billy Cannon, is a remarkable football player who has just finished his collegiate career with Louisiana State University. The last intercollegiate game he participated in was the Sugar Bowl game on January 1, 1960. Prior to that time, however, on November 28, 1959, or early in the morning of the 29th, he was contacted by telephone by Pete Rozelle, now Commissioner of the National Football League, but who was then and at all times material to the dispute here involved General Manager for the Los Angeles Rams. . . .

There is no question about the call being made but there is serious dispute as to the conversation had. However, we can safely assume that it had to do with football. . . .

The telephone call . . . occurred less than thirty-six hours before the annual selection meeting [draft] of the National Football League which was held in Philadelphia, Pennsylvania.

The Rams, after sifting an astonishing amount of information through a complex scouting system, concluded that Billy Cannon was the player of the current graduating crop they would most like to see on their team. The Rams, by virtue of ten losses and only two wins last season were tied for last place in the League, but as every cloud has its silver lining this fact also tied them for first draft choice at the above-mentioned selection meeting. The tie was to be broken by the flip of a coin. . . .

It has been the Rams' contention throughout that this position on the draft is so valuable that careful steps are undertaken to assure the team having the choice that it is not wasted on a player not willing to play for that team. . . .

Following the press interview Cannon and Rozelle went to Rozelle's hotel room where Cannon signed three sets of National Football Player Contract forms covering the years 1960, 1961 and 1962, and took possession of two checks, one for $10,000 and the other for $500.

Mr. Rozelle, on or about December 1st, left one set of said forms as filled out—that set embracing the 1960 season—with the then acting Commissioner, Mr. Gunsel.

Some two weeks later Billy Cannon was contacted on behalf of a Mr. K. S. Adams, Jr., who is the owner or part owner of the Houston Oilers, a football club in the recently-formed American Football League. On or about December 22nd Cannon met with Mr. Adams and others in Baton Rouge and negotiations were had with respect to a so-called personal service contract including the playing of football.

On December 30, 1959 Billy Cannon sent to the Rams a letter wherein he announced that he no longer desired to play for the Rams, purportedly revoked any offer he may have made to play for the Rams, and returned therewith the two checks above mentioned uncashed and unendorsed.

Prior thereto, however, it is contended that Mr. Gunsel approved the contract for the 1960 season . . . [P]laintiff tak[es] the position that [the Commissioner's signature] is an unimportant ministerial act concerning only the League and the Club, while the defendant takes the position that it is an act absolutely essential to the formation of a contract. . . .

It is the opinion of this court that on this issue the defendant must prevail. Approval by the Commissioner is essential to the formation of a contract here and this is so because the terms of the document make it so. Keeping in mind that these forms were furnished by the Rams and not Billy Cannon, the court calls particular attention to the words regarding approval: 'This agreement shall become valid and binding upon each party hereto only when, as and if it shall be approved by the Commissioner.' . . .

This clause is too definite to be ignored. It jumps out at you. The words employed are too strong to permit of ambiguity. Their selection was obviously made with great care so that there would be no dispute about their meaning, and this court attaches to them the only meaning it can—that is, that the agreement shall only become valid and binding if, as and when approved by the Commissioner. . . .

Judgment will be for defendant, with costs. . . .

Source: Courtesy of Westlaw; reprinted with permission.

Consideration   Philadelphia 76'ers guard Alen Iverson refers to himself as "The Answer." Reebok marketed Iverson's shoes as "The Answer 1." In 2002, a DVD was released entitled *Alen Iverson: The Answer.* Case 2-3, *Blackmon v. Iverson,* 324 F. Supp.2d 602 (D.C. Pa. 2003), revolves around the origin of that nickname. The plaintiff (Blackmon) sued Iverson on several legal theories, stating that he suggested Iverson use "The Answer" as his nickname. The opinion in Case 2-3 focuses on the court's decision relating to Blackmon's breach of contract claims.

CASE 2-3   *Blackmon v. Iverson*

324 F. Supp.2d 602 (D.C. Pa. 2003)

MCLAUGHLIN, District Judge.

Analysis

The essence of all three of the plaintiff's claims is that the defendant took and used the plaintiff's ideas without compensating the plaintiff. . . .

. . . Courts have also been willing to give protection to ideas under various other legal theories: idea misappropriation; contract; quasi-contract or unjust enrichment; implied contracts; property theories; and confidential relationship theories. The plaintiff's claims fall into this latter category of protection.

. . . .

Breach of Contract

The plaintiff claims that he entered into an express contract with the defendant pursuant to which he was to receive twenty-five percent of the proceeds that the defendant received from marketing products with "The Answer" on them. The defendant argues that there was not a valid contract because the claim was not timely filed under the Pennsylvania statute of limitations, the terms of the contract were not sufficiently definite, and there was no consideration alleged.

Under Pennsylvania law, a plaintiff must present clear and precise evidence of an agreement in which both parties manifested an intent to be bound, for which both parties gave consideration, and which contains sufficiently definite terms.

Consideration confers a benefit upon the promisor or causes a detriment to the promisee and must be an act, forbearance, or return promise bargained for and given in exchange for the original promise. Under Pennsylvania and Virginia law, past consideration is insufficient to support a subsequent promise.

It is difficult to analyze the alleged contract because the complaint describes various promises that were made by the defendant at various times. This problem with the plaintiff's alleged contract became even clearer at the hearing on the motion. Counsel for the plaintiff gave various dates for the formation of the alleged contract[] (the "agreement and the discussions took place in early 1994;" "the last part of the contract didn't really take place until 1997;" "there was a meeting of the minds that took place in 1994, albeit the last . . . part of that contract didn't really take place until after Mr. Iverson had gotten into the pros;" "there was an initial understanding in 1994 that is then modified for a more specific situation in 1996;" "in Philadelphia in 1997 there is a modification of the original understanding;" "the original contract could have been rescinded, it could have been modified by the parties;" and the contract "most importantly came into being in 1996"). On this basis alone, the complaint fails adequately to set forth the elements required for a contract claim.

The Court, nevertheless, will consider whether there was consideration at the various times the plaintiff alleges the formation of a contract.

The plaintiff has argued that, in exchange for the defendant's promise to pay the twenty-five percent, the plaintiff gave three things as consideration: (1) the plaintiff's idea to use "The Answer" as a nickname to sell athletic apparel; (2) the plaintiff's assistance to and relationship with the defendant and his family; and (3) the plaintiff's move to Philadelphia.

According to the facts alleged by the plaintiff, he made the suggestion that the defendant use "The Answer" as a nickname and for product merchandising one evening in 1994. This was before the defendant first promised to pay; according to the plaintiff, the promise to pay was made later that evening. The disclosure of the idea also occurred before the defendant told the plaintiff that he was going to use the idea in connection with the Reebok contract in 1996, and before the sales of goods bearing "The Answer" actually began in 1997.

Regardless of whether the contract was formed in 1994, 1996, or 1997, the disclosure of "The Answer" idea had already occurred and was, therefore, past consideration insufficient to create a binding contract.

The plaintiff also argued that the plaintiff's relationship with and assistance to the defendant and his family and the defendant's move to Philadelphia during the 1997–1998 season constituted consideration for the defendant's promise to pay. There is no allegation in the complaint that these actions by the plaintiff were in exchange for the defendant's promise to pay.

According to the complaint, the plaintiff's relationship and support for the defendant, his "surrogate father" role, began in 1987, seven

years before the first alleged promise to pay was made. There is no
allegation that the plaintiff began engaging in this conduct because
of any promise by the defendant, or that the plaintiff continued his
gratuitous conduct in 1994, 1996, or 1997 in exchange for the promise
to pay. These actions are not valid consideration.

Even when the complaint is construed broadly, there is no allegation
that the move was required in exchange for any promise by the defendant to pay. In the absence of valid consideration, the plaintiff has
no claim for breach of an express contract.

Source: Courtesy of Westlaw; reprinted with permission.

Definiteness   What terms are required to be included in a contract so formation of a binding
contract can occur? If the terms of the agreement are not reasonably certain, the contract will fail.[39]
For a valid contract to exist, the contract must identify the parties; the subject matter of the contract,
including the work to be performed; the consideration to be paid; and the time of payment, delivery,
or performance. What if the contract is missing any of these elements? A court may still enforce the
contract if the terms can be made definite in the light of the surrounding circumstances.

Interpretation of Sports Contracts

After a contract is entered into between parties, questions regarding the interpretation of that contract may occur. Courts are called on to decide the parties' intent when they entered into the contract.
Parties may attach different meanings to a particular paragraph or word in the contract, thereby
changing the obligations of the parties. When do you know if you are really the champion or just the
"interim" champion? That would seem to be a relatively simple proposition, but not so in the convoluted
world of boxing, as demonstrated in Case 2-4, *Rocchigiani v. World Boxing Council, Inc.*, 131 F.
Supp. 2d 527 (S.D. N.Y. 2001).

📖 CASE 2-4 *Rocchigiani v. World Boxing Council, Inc.*

131 F. Supp. 2d 527 (S.D. N.Y. 2001)

OWEN, District Judge.

Although the old adage is that one should roll with the punches, the
wholly arbitrary and unfair conduct of the defendant in this case
would leave anyone down for the proverbial count. The defendant World
Boxing Council is a major prizefighting ranking organization that certifies and recognizes championship boxers in various weight divisions

---

[39] R.K. Chevrolet, Inc. v. Hayden, 480 S.E.2d 477 (Va. 1997).

throughout the world. The WBC promulgates rules and regulations which govern its sanctioned bouts, including the percentage of the "purse" that individual boxers receive from WBC fights. Plaintiff Graciano Rocchigiani is a professional light heavyweight boxer (175 lbs.) and a German citizen.

Prior to November 1997, Roy Jones, Jr. was the WBC's undisputed Light Heavyweight Champion. WBC rules required Jones to defend his title against the next highest ranked challenger, Michael Nunn, by November 1997. Jones, for whatever reason, informed the WBC that he would not participate in the fight against Nunn. As a result, the WBC deemed its Light Heavyweight Title vacant and scheduled a fight between Nunn and Rocchigiani. On March 21, 1998, Rocchigiani defeated Nunn in the WBC Light Heavyweight Championship in Berlin. Promotional material printed in conjunction with the bout, such as tickets and posters, indicated that the fight was for the WBC Light Heavyweight Championship. At the end of the match, a WBC official presented Rocchigiani with the Title belt and, moreover, announced him to the viewing public as the world champion. From April through June 1998, WBC listed Rocchigiani as "champion" in its official rankings. The WBC's President also wrote several letters congratulating Rocchigiani on his victory and referred to Rocchigiani as the world champion therein.

The written agreement setting up the event stated that the fight was for the "WBC World Championship." The parties executed the agreement in Berlin on March 20, 1998, the day before the Rocchigiani-Nunn bout. The contract contained several pages of specific rules regarding fight mechanics, such as the three knock-down rule, number of trainers in each fighter's corner, scoring system, mouthpiece requirement, permissible weight of the boxing gloves, procedures in case a fighter is cut, a list of common fouls such as hitting below the belt, and even a space to be filled in regarding the color of the trunks worn by each fighter. The agreement, drafted on standard form by the WBC, also provided that the fight would be governed by the WBC Rules relating to world championship bouts. The WBC promulgates these rules and incorporates them by reference into its sanctioned bouts. Additionally, provision WC-39 of the contract addressed disputes related to a subject not specifically covered by the written agreement and purported to vest final decision on any such problem with the WBC.

Rocchigiani, as the new champion, had the right to defend his Title against Jones, the former champion. As the champion, Rocchigiani would be entitled to a high or higher percentage of the Title purse under WBC rules. A few months after Rocchigiani's victory over Nunn, in June 1998, however, the WBC suddenly declared Rocchigiani the "Interim" Light Heavyweight Champion and changed the rankings by designating

Jones, previously the undisputed Title-holder, as the "Champion in Recess." The WBC, as stated by President Jose Sulaimán in his deposition of June 2, 2000, called the designation of Rocchigiani as champion in its rankings a "typographical error."

The WBC then set new terms for a championship bout between Jones and Rocchigiani, which included a purse split substantially less favorable than Rocchigiani believed he, as champion, was entitled to under WBC rules. When Rocchigiani protested, the WBC replied that its Board of Governors voted at the 1997 WBC Annual Convention that Rocchigiani and Nunn would fight for the interim title. The minutes show that the Board voted unanimously to sanction the Rocchigiani-Nunn bout for the interim title. The minutes of the 1997 Convention, however, were not finalized until October 1998—*eleven months after the Convention, seven months after [the] Rocchigiani-Nunn bout and one month after Rocchigiani filed this action*. WBC contends that the Board of Governors decided the bout was only for the interim championship and that German promoters referred to the event as a fight for the "WBC (Interim) Lightheavyweight" title. WBC also takes the position that its own rules, incorporated by reference in the fight agreement, allow the Board of Governors to exercise its discretion and, at any time, make such a modification.

Not long after Rocchigiani's victory over Nunn, Premier Network, a German cable television network, offered to broadcast the Rocchigiani-Jones bout and to pay Rocchigiani for his participation. The deal was never consummated, however, because in late June 1998, the WBC revoked Rocchigiani's championship creating confusion as to who was the real champion. Rocchigiani petitioned for reconsideration of this decision through an attorney, but was repeatedly denied reinstatement.

Rocchigiani initiated this diversity action on September 28, 1998 claiming breach of contract, breach of the duty of good faith and fair dealing, and seeking relief in equity. He claims damages in the amount of $1,225,000 and now moves for summary judgment. WBC also moves for summary judgment on the grounds that it had discretion to sanction the bout as the *interim* championship fight, Rocchigiani did not exhaust administrative remedies and that equitable relief is not warranted because Rocchigiani has an adequate remedy at law. . . .

Rocchigiani is entitled to summary judgment on his breach of contract claim embodied by the first cause of action in the supplemental and amended complaint. Under New York law, "[T]he initial interpretation of a contract is a matter of law for the court to decide." "Included in this initial interpretation is the threshold question of whether the terms of the contract are ambiguous." A contract is unambiguous if it "has a definite and precise meaning, unattended by danger of mis-conception in the purport of the [agreement] itself, and concerning which there is no reasonable basis for a difference of opinion." If a contract is unambiguous, I am "required to give effect to the contract as written and may not consider extrinsic evidence to alter or inter-pret its meaning." Contractual language whose meaning is otherwise plain is not ambiguous merely because the parties urge different interpretations in the litigation.

The language in the written agreement admits of only one possible interpretation: the Rocchigiani-Nunn bout was for the WBC Light Heavy-weight Championship. The word "interim" is nowhere to be found within the four corners of the document. The WBC drafted the agreement, uti-lizing its standard form, and is and was fully capable of explicitly designating the bout as for the "interim" Title. However, it did not do so. The contract is clear and unambiguous because there can be no mistake regarding what was meant by the words "WBC World Championship bout of Lightheavyweight 175 pounds . . . [.]" These words cannot rea-sonably be mistaken for WBC *Interim* World Championship bout of Lightheavyweight 175 pounds.

WBC argues that the Light Heavyweight Championship language appears only in the "recital" clause of the contract and is therefore unen-forceable. This argument truly causes a raised eyebrow. First, the only place in the WBC's standard form contract designating the nature of the bout is the preamble or recital clause; there is a blank and the weight class is to be filled in by hand. Second, nothing in the remainder of the contract states the Rocchigiani-Nunn bout was for a title other than the Light Heavyweight title.

WBC also relies on its own rules, incorporated by reference into the fight agreement, granting it general discretion to classify bouts, establish purse splits and championships. These clauses, however, cannot be read as vesting the organization with the power to act *nunc pro tunc* and agree that a bout is for one particular title and, subse-quently, unilaterally reclassify the substance of that bout by making it something else. WBC claims to have the authority to undo that which has already been done. The provisions granting WBC general discretion to make final determinations cannot be given the wholly unreasonable meaning defendant proposes. It would swallow the purpose and sanctity of the contract because WBC could, apparently at any time, rescind that which was properly bargained-for and obtained through a party's performance. Indeed, WBC's arguments undermine the basic principles of contract which, *inter alia,* are to protect the expectations of the parties and provide certainty where the future would otherwise be uncertain.

```
Having determined that the terms of the contract are that the
Rocchigiani-Nunn bout was for the championship, I need not examine the
intent of the parties, although disputed, because their intent is not
relevant to the summary judgment inquiry. The dispute with regard to
the 1997 WBC Convention and other assertions that all parties "knew"
the Rocchigiani-Nunn bout was for the interim championship and not for
the championship are immaterial in light of the plain language of the
fight agreement. . . .
```

Source: Courtesy of Westlaw; reprinted with permission.

Problem 2-1

Review the following provision dealing with the possible renegotiation of an endorsement contract. Assume the parties have entered into a three-year contract. How do you interpret the player's renegotiation opportunities? How would you draft this provision?

> RENEGOTIATION OF CONTRACT. ATHLETE agrees that if during the second Contract Year, ATHLETE is voted on the original ballot to play in the NFL Pro Bowl Game <u>and</u> is among the top five (5) wide-receivers in the NFL, then COMPANY shall meet with ATHLETE to renegotiate in good faith mutually acceptable terms for the ATHLETE Endorsement and related services in connection with the development, promotion, and sale of COMPANY'S products. If after engaging in good faith discussions, the parties have failed to reach a mutually satisfactory agreement, then this Contract shall be deemed to be terminated effective as of the conclusion of the second Contract Year and no Base Compensation for the third Contract Year shall be due to ATHLETE. The termination provisions set forth in this paragraph are subject to the COMPANY'S right of first refusal. If this Contract is terminated after the second Contract Year based on the condition precedents set forth in this paragraph, the COMPANY shall be able to bind ATHELTE to a third Contract Year by matching any offers ATHLETE receives from any other parties as long as COMPANY matches the same terms of other offers and does so within ten (10) days after ATHLETE receives the offer.

Enforcement of Sports Contracts and Contract Defenses

Specific performance is not the favored remedy for breach of a personal services contract. Enforcement problems would arise if specific performance were required. If a company hires an entertainer to sing at a concert and the entertainer fails to appear, the appropriate remedy would be to award damages to the plaintiff. That proposition has been tested in sports contracts many times.[40] The team "snubbed" by the player is usually limited to a *negative injunction*, which is an order precluding a player from playing for another team. Most contracts will provide for a *negative covenant*,

---

[40] *See* James T. Brennan, *Injunction Against Professional Athletes Breaching Their Contracts,* 34 BROOKLYN LAW REVIEW 61 (1967).

which binds the player to a team in the event a player attempts to breach a contract and move to another team. Many modern cases would now be sent through the arbitration process to be resolved.[41]

For a professional sports team to obtain an injunction to prevent a player from playing for another team, the team who originally contracted with the player must show (1) that damages are an inadequate remedy because of the player's unique skill; and (2) that if the injunction is not granted, the team will suffer irreparable harm.[42] When a team cannot be adequately compensated in monetary damages, it will seek a negative injunction to prevent the player from playing for another team. After the *Lajoie* case, outlined in Case 2-5, *Philadelphia Ball Club v. Lajoie*, 51 A. 973 (Pa. 1902), more emphasis was placed on the issue of the player's unique skills and whether the team seeking the injunction had suffered irreparable harm.[43] Now most standard player contracts provide that the player posseses unique skills. For example, the NHL's standard player contract states:

> The Player represents and agrees that he has exceptional and unique knowledge, skill and ability as a hockey player, the loss of which cannot be estimated with certainty and cannot be fairly or adequately compensated by damages. The Player therefore agrees that the Club shall have the right, in addition to any other rights which the Club may possess, to enjoin him by appropriate injunctive proceedings without first exhausting any other remedy which may be available to the Club, from playing hockey for any other team and/or for any breach of any of the other provisions of this contract.[44]

This clause binds the player to the club and allows the team the right to seek an injunction in the case of a breach of contract by the player.

Case 2-5, *Philadelphia Ball Club v. Lajoie*, 51 A. 973 (Pa. 1902), is a landmark case involving former batting champion and Hall of Famer Napoleon Lajoie and deals with the concept of the negative injunction.

📖 CASE 2-5 *Philadelphia Ball Club v. Lajoie*

51 A. 973 (Pa. 1902)

POTTER, J.

The defendant in this case contracted to serve the plaintiff as a baseball player for a stipulated time. During that period he was not to play for any other club. He violated his agreement, however, during the term of his engagement, and, in disregard of his contract, arranged to play for another and a rival organization. The plaintiff, by means of this bill, sought to restrain him during the period covered by the contract. The court below refused an injunction, holding that to warrant the interference prayed for 'the defendant's services

---

[41] Boston Celtics Ltd. Partnership v. Shaw, 908 F.2d 1041 (1st Cir. 1990).

[42] Professional Sports, Ltd. v. Virginia Squires Basketball Club, Ltd. Partnership, 373 F. Supp. 946 (W.D. Tex. 1974); Cincinnati Bengals, Inc. v. Bergey, 453 F. Supp. 129 (S.D. Ohio 1974).

[43] *See* Central New York Basketball, Inc. v. Barrett, 181 N.E.2d 506 (1961).

[44] Courtesy of the NHLPA.

must be unique, extraordinary, and of such a character as to render it impossible to replace him; so that his breach of contract would result in irreparable loss to the plaintiff.' In the view of the court, the defendant's qualifications did not measure up to this high standard. The trial court was also of opinion that the contract was lacking in mutuality, for the reason that it gave plaintiff an option to discharge defendant on 10 days' notice, without a reciprocal right on the part of defendant.

. . . We think, however, that in refusing relief unless the defendant's services were shown to be of such a character as to render it impossible to replace him he has taken extreme ground. It seems to us that a more just and equitable rule is . . . 'Where one person agrees to render personal services to another, which require and presuppose a special knowledge, skill, and ability in the employée, so that in case of a default the same service could not easily be obtained from others, although the affirmative specific performance of the contract is beyond the power of the court, its performance will be negatively enforced by enjoining its breach. . . . The damages for breach of such contract cannot be estimated with any certainty, and the employer cannot, by means of any damages, purchase the same service in the labor market.' We have not found any case going to the length of requiring, as a condition of relief, proof of the impossibility of obtaining equivalent service. It is true that the injury must be irreparable; but . . . 'The argument that there is no 'irreparable damage' would not be so often used by wrongdoers if they would take the trouble to discover that the word 'irreparable' is a very unhappily chosen one, used in expressing the rule that an injunction may issue to prevent wrongs of a repeated and continuing character, or which occasion damages which are estimated only by conjecture, and not by any accurate standard.' We are therefore within the term whenever it is shown that no certain pecuniary standard exists for the measurement of the damages. . . .

The court below finds from the testimony that 'the defendant is an expert baseball player in any position; that he has a great reputation as a second baseman; that his place would be hard to fill with as good a player; that his withdrawal from the team would weaken it, as would the withdrawal of any good player, and would probably make a difference in the size of the audiences attending the game.' We think that, in thus stating it, he puts it very mildly, and that the evidence would warrant a stronger finding as to the ability of the defendant as an expert ball player. He has been for several years in the service of the plaintiff club, and has been re-engaged from season to season at a constantly increasing salary. He has become thoroughly familiar with the action and methods of the other players in the club, and his own work is peculiarly meritorious as an integral part of the team work which is so essential. In addition to these features which render his services of peculiar and special value to the plaintiff, and not easily replaced, Lajoie is well known, and has great reputation among the patrons of the sport, for ability in the position which he filled, and was thus a most attractive drawing card for the public. He may not be the sun in the baseball firmament, but he is certainly a bright particular star. We feel, therefore, that the evidence in this case justifies the conclusion that the services of the defendant are of such a unique character, and display such a special knowledge, skill, and ability, as renders them of peculiar value to the plaintiff, and so difficult of substitution that their loss will produce 'irreparable injury,' in the legal significance of that term, to the plaintiff. . . .

But the court below was also of the opinion that the contract was lacking in mutuality of remedy, and considered that as a controlling reason for the refusal of an injunction. The opinion quotes the nineteenth paragraph of the contract, which gives to the plaintiff a right of renewal for the period of six months, beginning April 15, 1901, and for a similar period in two successive years thereafter. The seventeenth paragraph also provides for the termination of the contract upon 10 days' notice by the plaintiff. But the eighteenth paragraph is also of importance, and should not be overlooked. It provides as follows: '(18) In consideration of the faithful performance of the conditions, covenants, undertakings, and promises herein by the said party of the second part, inclusive of the concession of the options of release and renewal prescribed in the seventeenth and nineteenth paragraphs, the said party of the first part, for itself and its assigns, hereby agrees to pay to him for his services for said term the sum of twenty-four hundred dollars, payable as follows,' etc. And, turning to the fifth paragraph, we find that it provides expressly for proceedings, either in law or equity, 'to enforce the specific performance by the said party of the second part, or to enjoin said party of the second part from performing services for any other person or organization during the period of service herein contracted for; and nothing herein contained shall be construed to prevent such remedy in the courts, in case of any breach of this agreement by said party of the second part, as said party of the first part, or its assigns, may elect to invoke.'

We have, then, at the outset, the fact that the paragraphs now criticised and relied upon in defense were deliberately accepted by the defendant, and that such acceptance was made part of the inducement for the plaintiff to enter into the contract. We have the further fact that the contract has been partially executed by services rendered, and payment made therefore, so that the situation is not now the same as when the contract was wholly executory. The relation between the parties has been so far changed as to give to the plaintiff an equity, arising out of the part performance, to insist upon the completion of the agreement according to its terms by the defendant. This equity may be distinguished from the original right under the contract itself, and it might well be questioned whether the court would not be justified in giving effect to it by injunction, without regard to the mutuality or nonmutuality in the original contract. The plaintiff has so far performed its part of the contract in entire good faith, in every detail, and it would therefore be inequitable to permit the defendant to withdraw from the agreement at this late day. . . .

. . . In the contract now before us the defendant agreed to furnish his skilled professional services to the plaintiff for a period which might be extended over three years by proper notice given before the close of each current year. Upon the other hand, the plaintiff retained the right to terminate the contract upon 10 days' notice and the payment of salary for that time and the expenses of defendant in getting to his home. But the fact of this concession to the plaintiff is distinctly pointed out as part of the consideration for the large salary paid to the defendant, and is emphasized as such; and owing to the peculiar nature of the services demanded by the business, and the high degree of efficiency which must be maintained, the stipulation is not unreasonable. Particularly is this true when it is remembered that the plaintiff has played for years under substantially the same regulations.

We are not persuaded that the terms of this contract manifest any lack of mutuality in remedy. Each party has the possibility of enforcing all the rights stipulated for in the agreement. It is true that the terms make it possible for the plaintiff to put an end to the contract in a space of time much less than the period during which the defendant has agreed to supply his personal services; but mere difference in the rights stipulated for does not destroy mutuality of remedy. Freedom of contract covers a wide range of obligation and duty as between the parties, and it may not be impaired, so long as the bounds of reasonableness and fairness are not transgressed. . . .

. . . The defendant sold to the plaintiff, for a valuable consideration, the exclusive right to his professional services for a stipulated period, unless sooner surrendered by the plaintiff, which could only be after due and reasonable notice and payment of salary and expenses until the expiration. Why should not a court of equity protect such an agreement until it is terminated? The court cannot compel the defendant to play for the plaintiff, but it can restrain him from playing for another club in violation of his agreement. No reason is given why this should not be done, except that presented by the argument, that the right given to the plaintiff to terminate the contract upon 10 days' notice destroys the mutuality of the remedy. But to this it may be answered that, as already stated, the defendant has the possibility of enforcing all the rights for which he stipulated in the agreement, which is all that he can reasonably ask. Furthermore, owing to the peculiar nature and circumstances of the business, the reservation upon the part of the plaintiff to terminate upon short notice does not make the whole contract inequitable.

In this connection another observation may be made, which is that the plaintiff, by the act of bringing this suit, has disavowed any intention of exercising the right to terminate the contract on its own part. This is a necessary inference from its action in asking the court to exercise its equity power to enforce the agreement made by the defendant not to give his services to any other club. Besides, the remedy by injunction is elastic and adaptable, and is wholly within the control of the court. If granted now, it can be easily dissolved whenever a change in the circumstances or in the attitude of the plaintiff should seem to require it. The granting or refusal of an injunction or its continuance is never a matter of strict right, but is always a question of discretion, to be determined by the court in view of the particular circumstances.

Upon a careful consideration of the whole case, we are of opinion that the provisions of the contract are reasonable, and that the consideration is fully adequate. The evidence shows no indications of any attempt at overreaching or unfairness. Substantial justice between the parties requires that the court should restrain the defendant from playing for any other club during the term of his contract with the plaintiff. . . .

Source: Courtesy of Westlaw; reprinted with permission.

Mitigation of Damages   The breaching party to the contract can always assert that the plaintiff failed to mitigate or lessen the plaintiff's damages. The nonbreaching party has a duty to mitigate its own damages. The concept of mitigation of damages can be described as follows:

(1) Except as stated in Subsection (2), damages are not recoverable for loss that the injured party could have avoided without undue risk, burden, or humiliation.
(2) The injured party is not precluded from recovery by the rule stated in Subsection (1) to the extent that he has made reasonable but unsuccessful efforts to avoid loss.[45]

---

[45] RESTATEMENT (SECOND) OF CONTRACTS § 350.

THE STANDARD PLAYER CONTRACT

All major sports leagues use standard player contracts. Standard contracts are used in the Women's National Basketball Association (WNBA), and in the international sports world. Star players are sometimes able to modify the standard player contract through the negotiation process by adding incentives and bonus clauses; however, the majority of professional athletes will sign a standard player contract without modification.

The standard player contract is a product of the collective bargaining process. Management and labor have negotiated what they have deemed to be a contract suitable for both parties, each arguing for provisions that support the best interests of either labor or management. Legal and business issues arise when teams attempt to modify the standard player contract. Instead of proceeding through the court system to litigate contractual issues, players and management have determined that those matters will be decided by binding arbitration. This chapter discusses labor arbitration only in the context of contract disputes and interpretation of those disputes. This section addresses some of the cases that have interpreted the standard player contract.

Case Interpreting Provisions of the Standard Player Contract

All standard player contracts in sports have a skills clause that allows the team to cut a player from a team if the player fails to possess the requisite skill to continue to be on the team. The Uniform Player Contract for Minor League Baseball, for example, has a skills clause that reads as follows:

XIX. Termination

. . . .

B. Club may terminate this Minor League Uniform Player Contract upon the
    delivery of written or telegraphic notice to Player if Player at any
    time shall:
    . . . .
    4. Fail in the judgment of Club to exhibit sufficient skill or compet-
       itive ability to qualify or to continue as a professional baseball
       player as a member of Club's team . . .

Paragraph 11 of the NFL's standard player contract allows a team to terminate a player's contract if the team determines there are better players on the squad. The NFL's standard player contract includes the following provision:

11. SKILL, PERFORMANCE AND CONDUCT. Player understands that he is competing with other players for a position on Club's roster within the applicable player limits. If at any time, in the sole judgment of Club, Player's skill or performance has been unsatisfactory as compared with that of other players competing for positions on Club's roster, or if Player has engaged in personal

conduct reasonably judged by Club to adversely affect or reflect on Club, then Club may terminate this contract. In addition, during the period any salary cap is legally in effect, this contract may be terminated if, in Club's opinion, Player is anticipated to make less of a contribution to Club's ability to compete on the playing field than another player or players whom Club intends to sign or attempts to sign, or another player or players who is or are already on Club's roster, and for whom Club needs room.[46]

A standard player contract will typically include obligations on the part of the player to keep himself or herself in good physical condition to be able to perform services on behalf of the team. The standard player contract for the NHL states the following with regard to physical condition of the player:

2. The Player agrees to give his services and to play hockey in all League Championship, All Star, International, Exhibition, Play-Off and Stanley Cup games to the best of his ability under the direction and control of the Club in accordance with the provisions hereof.

The Player further agrees,

a. to report to the Club training camp at the time and place fixed by the Club, in good physical condition,

b. to keep himself in good physical condition at all times during the season . . .

Source: Courtesy of the NHLPA.

In Case 2-6, *Tillman v. New Orleans Saints Football Club,* 265 So.2d 284 (La. Ct. App. 1972), a dispute arose about whether the player could physically perform under the NFL's standard player contract.

📖 CASE 2-6 *Tillman v. New Orleans Saints Football Club*

265 So.2d 284 (La. Ct. App. 1972)

GULOTTA, Judge.

This appeal is from a judgment dismissing plaintiff's claim for $7,499.99 allegedly due on a written contract entered into between plaintiff and defendant on June 14, 1967. This was a National Football League Standard Player's Contract. Under its terms, the defendant was

---

[46] Courtesy of Westlaw.

to pay plaintiff, a football player, $12,000 for the 1967 football season, subject, however, to right of prior termination by the Saints as specified therein upon the giving of written notice to plaintiff.

During practice drill, before the commencement of the regular season, Tillman suffered a torn ligament of the knee.

Plaintiff was waived by the Saints on November 1, 1967, was paid $4,500.01, and his salary was terminated. On April 23, 1969, he filed this action for unpaid wages alleging that under the contract the Saints had no right to waive him, because he was injured at the time.

The questions before us are . . . (2) whether plaintiff was physically able to perform his services under the contract at the time it was terminated on November 1, 1967.

. . . Turning now to the question of whether plaintiff was physically able to play at the time his contract was terminated, the record reflects the team physician, Dr. Kenneth Saer, performed an operation on July 10, 1967, to repair the injury. Plaintiff's leg was placed in and remained in a cast until August 3, 1967.

Tillman was instructed to return to the Saints' training camp to begin regaining muscle strength through exercise by weightlifting and bicycle riding. The doctor testified that at this time plaintiff 'was doing quite well, his wound was well-healed'. It was on October 24, 1967, that Dr. Saer felt plaintiff was able to return to full play. His testimony was:

'I would say on October 24th if this were a person playing football, if this was one of the players playing he had a position to play they would play. The average football player would play before that time.'

In response to the question whether plaintiff was physically capable of playing professional football insofar as his right knee (the injured knee) was concerned, the doctor responded:

'I thought he was. Again, I thought he was on October 24th.'

Dr. Saer submitted a report dated April 13, 1971, in which he stated that plaintiff did have some 'residual disability and early degenerative arthritic changes in the knee joint.' However, we note that he further stated:

'Such changes are very commonly seen in the professional football player as a result of injuries in college or professional leagues. A large majority of professional football players with similar injuries and similar relatively mild disability would continue to play with this residual disability. The only other

physician who saw plaintiff was Dr. Harold G. Hutson, an ortho-
pedic surgeon in Little Rock, Arkansas. Two reports of Dr. Hutson
dated November 22, 1967, and April 3, 1968, were stipulated in
evidence. In the latter report, Dr. Hutson stated in regard to
his examination of plaintiff on November 21, 1967.

'It was my impression at that time that this patient was not
ready to return to full duty as a professional football player.'

However, Dr. Hutson erroneously concluded in his report that plaintiff
'had a repair of the medial collateral ligament and the anterior cruciate ligament.' Dr. Saer indicated, to the contrary, there was no
damage to the cruciate ligament but only to the medial collateral ligament and that tears to both ligaments, which was the mistaken impression of Dr. Hutson, would have been considerably worse. With this in
mind, we cannot give much weight to Dr. Hutson's conclusion that
plaintiff was unable to play football.

The trial judge accepted the opinion of the club physician and concluded
plaintiff was physically able to play professional football at the time
the contract was terminated. We find no error in this conclusion.

Plaintiff seeks to invoke the provisions of Paragraph 15 of the agreement, which provides:

Player may, within seventy-two hours after his examination by the
Club Physician, submit at his own expense to an examination by a
physician of his choice. If the opinion of such physician with
respect to Player's physical ability to render the services required
of him by this contract is contrary to that of the Club Physician,
the dispute shall be submitted to a disinterested physician to be
selected by the Club Physician and Player's Physician or, if they
are unable to agree, by the Commissioner of the National Football
League, and the opinion of such disinterested physician shall be
conclusive and binding upon the Player and the Club.

However, because we have concluded that the opinion of Dr. Hutson was
based upon a mistaken impression as to the extent of the injury and
have accorded little weight to his evaluation, we find no basis for
the application of this provision requiring the dispute to be submitted to a third, disinterested physician. The medical testimony of Dr.
Hutson does not satisfy us that there is indeed a dispute. Furthermore, plaintiff failed to comply with the provisions of Paragraph 15
of the agreement which require that an examination is to be had by the
player within 72 hours from that by the club physician.

Finally, we find no merit to plaintiff's contention that because
defendant failed to notify him in writing of his termination as

required by the contract, there was in effect no notice given, and, therefore, the contract was not terminated. It is uncontroverted that Tillman had actual knowledge on November 1, 1967, that he was waived. Counsel for plaintiff stipulated as of that date, the Saints had communicated this fact; furthermore, Tillman alleged in his original petition that he was notified by defendant of the termination of his contract. When Tillman left the Saints' camp in November, 1967, his actions indicated he had knowledge of his release. Moreover, the record is clear that by plaintiff's admissions and acquiescence to the notice, he waived his contractual right to a letter of termination.

Written notice would have been superfluous in this instance and mere ceremony. The law will not require a vain and useless thing.

Accordingly, the judgment of the trial court is affirmed.

Affirmed.

Source: Courtesy of Westlaw; reprinted with permission.

Teams have a major stake in ensuring that players are kept in good physical condition, especially if they have signed the player to a guaranteed contract. They do not want to assume the risk that a player will get injured participating in another sport. Therefore, a player's extracurricular activities are also addressed in the standard player contract.

Many players have been subjected to scrutiny for their off-season activities. For example, the Atlanta Hawks attempted to suspend Michael Sojourner without pay based on Paragraph 17 of the Uniform Player Contract because of an off-season injury he sustained. Sojourner broke his kneecap when executing a slam dunk while he was practicing at the University of Utah. The arbitrator found in favor of Sojourner, stating that slam dunking was not a "dangerous activity" and that the injury did not occur while he was playing for another team or exhibition game.[47]

It was reported that the Cleveland Browns attempted to recoup a portion of the bonus paid to Kellen Winslow after he tore his anterior cruciate ligament in an off-season motorcycle accident. Some off-field accidents are tolerated, however. The Milwaukee Brewers always seemed to look the other way when Hall of Famer Robin Yount engaged in numerous off-season dangerous activities.

Problem 2-2

James Kason is an outfielder with the Oakland Athletics. His contract prohibits him from engaging in dangerous off-season activities. While on vacation with his family, he attended a minor league baseball game in which his college roommate was the starting pitcher. The manager of the minor league team asked him to throw out the first pitch. He did not warm up, and during the throw to the plate he suffered a dislocated shoulder. He subsequently

---

[47] *In re* Arbitration Between National Basketball Ass'n and National Players Ass'n (Michael Sojourner) June 14, 1978, as referred to in Martin J. Greenberg & James T. Gray, 1 Sports Law Practice (2d ed. 1998).

missed the first 35 games of the season with the A's. His contract specifically provided the following: "Player shall not play baseball for any other team during the off-season nor shall the player engage in any of the following activities during the off-season, including but not limited to football, or any impromptu or competitive game of football, baseball or softball, lacrosse, hai-alai, lawn bowling, bowling, horseback riding, car racing, parachuting, basketball, ice or field hockey, track and field activities, table tennis, tennis, polo, karate, cricket, badminton or any other form of martial arts." Does the team have the legal right to terminate the player's contract? What defenses can the player assert? How would an arbitrator rule in this matter?

BONUS AND ADDENDUM CLAUSES TO CONTRACTS

Many players are able to negotiate bonus clauses to the standard player contract. Bonus clauses can include performance bonuses based on statistics compiled by the player or team or bonuses based on awards given by the team or league. NFL players, for example, can receive a variety of bonuses, including roster bonuses, signing bonuses, workout bonuses, and award bonuses, along with a variety of statistical bonuses.

Players have been able to negotiate some interesting and unusual bonus clauses in their contracts. Outfielder Carlos Beltran negotiated a private suite while traveling on the road for the New York Mets. Padres outfielder Phil Nevin signed a four-year, $34 million contract in November 2001. The contract indicated that he could become a free agent if the construction of the Padres new ballpark ever stopped and did not resume within one year. Nevin's agent wanted the clause in the contract because he believed the team could not be a contender without a new stadium. The San Francisco Giants had difficulty trading Livan Hernandez because his 2004 option of $6 million became guaranteed if he pitched a paltry 217 innings in 2004.

Bonus clauses are not a new invention. In 1919, Chicago White Sox pitcher Eddie Cicotte had a $10,000 bonus in his contract payable to him if he won 30 games. According to the book *Eight Men Out* by Eliot Asinof (1963), Cicotte was benched late in the season so that Charles Comisky would not have to pay the bonus. He finished with a win–loss record of 28 and 12. In 1959, slugger Rocky Colavito was apparently going to receive a bonus for not hitting 40 home runs, because the Indians wanted him to strike out less. He didn't try hard enough, however, and finished the 1959 season with 42 home runs and 86 strikeouts.[48] In 1972, Oakland Athletics owner Charlie Finley inserted a clause in each player's contract offering $300 if he grew a mustache. Many players on the team took him up on the offer.

Manny Ramirez was able to procure a clause in his contract stating that if any other Red Sox player receives a no-trade clause he will get one as well. Houston Astros owner Drayton McLane, Jr. made good on his promise to award All-Star pitcher Roy Oswalt a tractor as a bonus if he won Game 6 of the National League Championship Series against the St. Louis Cardinals in 2005. The owner of the Astros stated, "Each year, with our players, I ask them what their goals are. . . ." "I said,

---

[48] Jonathan Fraser Light, the Cultural Encyclopedia of Baseball (2d ed. 2005).

'Roy, what is one of your goals?' He said, 'To own a bulldozer.' That kind of took me back a little bit. I had never heard that before." As a rookie Oswalt told the owner, "You know, I'd really pick up my performance if I had a bulldozer. I know I would. No longer would I have to spend my mornings sculpting my own personal golf course with a silly lawn tractor. I could sleep more and come to the park refreshed." Motivated by the opportunity to cash in on the bonus, Oswalt won Game 6 of the 2005 NLCS as well as the NLCS MVP leading the Astros to their first World Series appearance. After receiving the Caterpillar DGN XL tractor worth approximately $200,000 Oswalt stated: "There are going to be a lot of jealous people around where I live [Weir, Miss.]. I'm going to try to hire [it] out and make a little money in the off season." Baseball contracts can contain a wide variety of bonus clauses; however, some clauses in baseball are prohibited. Major League Baseball rules state: "No contract shall be approved for playing, pitching or batting skill; or which provides for the payment of a bonus contingent on the standing of the club at the end of the championship season." Therefore, no bonuses can be based on the batting average of a player, runs batted in, runs scored, stolen bases, or pitcher wins. Bonuses have been negotiated based on the number of plate appearances, total number of games played, or innings pitched.

Some players have been able to negotiate attendance clauses in their contracts. Hall of Fame pitcher Bob Feller had an attendance clause in his contract with the Cleveland Indians in the 1940s. Roger Clemens's contract contained a clause that paid him a bonus if the Astros drew 2.8 million fans in 2005 and also provided that for each 100,000 fans that attended, he could earn up to an additional $3.4 million. Michael Jordan was not able to obtain an attendance clause during the negotiation of his first contract with the Chicago Bulls. The Bulls were averaging approximately 6,000 fans a game before Jordan arrived, but he was told by ownership that because he was drafted in the first three spots in the NBA draft, he was required to bring in spectators.

The following provisions are examples of what might be included as award bonuses in an addendum to a standard player contract for a Major League pitcher:

Award Bonuses

```
In addition to the salary set forth above, Player shall be entitled
to the following award bonuses for each year of the term of the
Contract:

1. If Player wins the Cy Young Award, the sum of $150,000 (One Hundred
   Fifty Thousand Dollars).
2. If Player places second in the voting for the Cy Young Award, $50,000
   (Fifty Thousand Dollars).
3. If Player places third in the voting for the Cy Young Award, $25,000
   (Twenty Five Thousand Dollars).
4. If Player is selected to the All-Star team, $75,000 (Seventy Five Thou-
   sand Dollars).
5. If Player is Division Series MVP, $50,000 (Fifty Thousand Dollars).
6. If Player is League Championship Series MVP, $50,000 (Fifty Thousand
   Dollars).
```

7. If Player is World Series MVP, $150,000 (One Hundred Fifty Thousand Dollars).

8. If Player is Gold Glove winner, $50,000 (Fifty Thousand Dollars).

In the Canadian Football League, bonuses have been negotiated for various players if they met specified conditions such as the following:

- Division All Star
- CFL All Star
- CFL Rookie of the Year
- CFL Most Outstanding Player in any category
- Player participates in 51% of offensive plays from the line of scrimmage
- Player starts and plays 51% of all offensive plays (excluding special teams)
- Player accumulates passing yards greater than or equal to 4,000 yards
- Player receives a bonus for maintaining weight
- Player receives a bonus for maintaining roster spot
- Division Most Outstanding Canadian
- CFL Most Outstanding Canadian
- Division Rookie of the Year
- Bonus for starting on the offensive side of the ball
- Player to receive bonus for making the active roster first game of the season and participating in a minimum of one play
- Player to receive a bonus for reporting to training camp and passing physical
- Player to receive a bonus for participating in 51% of all long snaps
- Player to receive a bonus as team nominee for Most Outstanding Player in any category
- Player to receive a bonus as CFL leader in kickoff return yardage or average yards per kickoff

Bonuses in the CFL could range from $500 to $70,000 (Canadian dollars) based on the bonus provision. Some players have even negotiated that the bonus be paid in U.S. dollars.

The collective bargaining agreement of the Arena Football League set forth the various performance bonuses that were allowed to be given by teams:

Allowable Performance Bonuses

A. Team Performance Bonuses
(per season or league leader basis only)
   1. Total points scored by team
   2. Total points allowed by team
   3. Total offense (net yards)
   4. Total defense (net yards)
   5. Net difference takeaways/giveaways
   6. Sacks allowed
   7. Team undefeated for regular season

    8. Quality for playoffs

    8a. Quality for home playoff games

   9. Division Champion

  10. Arena Bowl Participant

  11. Arena Bowl Champion

B. Individual Performance Bonuses

(per occurrence, per game, per season, team leader or league leader basis only)

  12. Starts

  13. 20-man roster

  14. Points scored

  15. TDs scored

  16. Rushing TDs

  17. Receiving TDs

  18. Receptions

  19. Number of rushes

  20. Rushing yards

  21. Receiving yards

  22. Rushing and receiving yards

  23. Average yards gained per rush

  24. Average yards gained per reception

  25. Average yards gained per rush or reception

  26. QB rating

  27. QB passing TDs

  28. QB touchdowns (running or passing)

  29. QB passing yards

  30. QB passes completed

  31. QB completion percentage

  32. QB interception percentage

  33. QB average yards per completed pass

  34. All-purpose yards

  35. Sacks allowed

  36. Interceptions

  37. Interception return yards

  38. Interceptions returned for TD

  39. Passes broken up

  40. Hurries

  41. Sacks

  42. Tackles

  43. Tackles for loss

  44. Forced fumbles

  45. Fumble recoveries

  46. Fumble return yards

  47. Fumble return TD

  48. Total return yards

49. Kicks returned for TD

50. Kick return yards

51. Field goals

52. Field goal percentage

53. Field goals in ranges: 0-30; 30-44; 45-50; 50+

54. Game winning field goals (must be last points scored in game)

55. Kicking PATs

C. Honors

(per occurrence only)

56. Any official league single game record broken

57. Any official league season record broken

58. Any official league career record broken

59. Club MVP (year end)

60. Club Ironman (year end)

61. All-Arena League First Team

62. ArenaBowl MVP

63. ArenaBowl Ironman

64. AFL Offensive Player of Year

65. AFL Defensive Player of Year

66. AFL Lineman of Year

67. AFL Kicker of Year

68. AFL Rookie of Year

69. AFL Ironman of Year

70. Offensive Player of Week

71. Defensive Player of Week

72. MVP of Game

73. Ironman of Week

74. Ironman of Game

Source: Courtesy of Westlaw; reprinted with permission.

Problem 2-3

You represent one of the best relief pitchers in Major League Baseball. You are in the process of negotiating his contract with the Philadelphia Phillies. Assume you were able to select only three of the following bonus clauses. Which ones would you select? What would be your negotiating strategy? What other bonus clauses might you suggest? What bonuses is he more likely to achieve?

1. A bonus clause for innings pitched, $75,000

2. A bonus clause for league MVP, $250,000

3. A bonus clause for most saves, $50,000

4. A bonus clause for World Series MVP, $250,000

5. A bonus clause for most appearances by a pitcher in the league, $100,000

6. A bonus clause for most wins in the league, $200,000

7. A bonus clause for winning the Cy Young Award, $150,000

Signing Bonus

Many players will receive a one-time bonus for merely signing the contract. Joe Namath received the largest bonuses of his era when the New York Jets of the AFL gave him a record $427,000 and a new Lincoln Continental in 1967. Signing bonuses have continued to increase over the years, as Table 2-1 shows for professional baseball for the years 1965 to 2004.

It has become common practice in the NFL to pay the signing bonus over an extended period of time to make more room under the salary cap for players. Because of all the ramifications of the signing bonus, the actual wording of the bonus has become critical.

Rider to USFL Signing Contract Between Houston USFL Joint Venture and Jim Kelly

Dated June 9, 1983.

As additional consideration for the execution of USFL Player Contracts for the years 1984, 1985, 1986, 1987, and 1988 and for the *Player's* adherence to all provisions of said contracts, *Club* agrees to pay *Player* the sum of ONE MILLION DOLLARS ($1,000,000) as follows: $200,000 shall be paid upon *Player* passing physical examination at time of signing Contract for 1984 year: and an additional $160,000 shall be paid on June 1 of each of 1984, 1985, 1986, 1987, and 1988.

It is expressly understood that no part of the bonus herein is part of any salary in the contracts specified above.

In the event *Player,* in any of the years 1984, 1985, 1986, or 1987 fails or refuses to report to *Club,* or leaves *Club* without its consent, or if for the year 1988 *Player* fails or refuses to report to club, then *Player* shall receive no bonus installment applicable for that year or any future year under this Signing Bonus Rider, unless such a breach is cured by *Player* within the time required under paragraph 12(a) of the Contract, which paragraph 12(a) appears in the Addendum to Contract.

Source: Courtesy of Westlaw; reprinted with permission.

TABLE 2-1

| | | | | | Signing |
| ALL-TIME NUMBER ONE OVERALL MAJOR LEAGUE BASEBALL DRAFT PICKS, 1965–2005 | | | | | |

Year	Player	Pos	Team	School	Signing Bonus
1965	Rick Monday	OF	Athletics	Arizona State University	$104,000
1966	Steve Chilcott	C	Mets	Lancaster, CA	$75,000
1967	Ron Blomberg	1B	Yankees	Atlanta, GA	$65,000
1968	Tim Foli	SS	Mets	Canoga Park, CA	$74,000
1969	Jeff Burroughs	OF	Senators	Long Beach, CA	$88,000
1970	Mike Ivie	C	Padres	Decatur, GA	$75,000
1971	Danny Goodwin	C	White Sox	Peoria, IL	(Didn't sign)
1972	Dave Roberts	3B	Padres	University of Oregon	$70,000
1973	David Clyde	LHP	Rangers	Houston, TX	$125,000
1974	Bill Almon	SS	Padres	Brown University	$90,000
1975	Danny Goodwin	C	Angels	Southern University	$125,000
1976	Floyd Bannister	LHP	Astros	Arizona State University	$100,000
1977	Harold Baines	OF	White Sox	St. Michaels, MD	$32,000
1978	Bob Horner	3B	White Sox	Arizona State University	$175,000
1979	Al Chambers	OF	Mariners	Harrisburg, PA	$60,000
1980	Darryl Strawberry	OF	Mets	Los Angeles, CA	$152,500
1981	Mike Moore	RHP	Mariners	Oral Roberts University	$100,000
1982	Shawon Dunston	SS	Cubs	Brooklyn, NY	$135,000
1983	Tim Belcher	RHP	Twins	Mt. Vernon Nazarene College	(Didn't sign)
1984	Shawn Abner	OF	Mets	Mechanicsburg, PA	$150,000
1985	B.J. Surhoff	C	Brewers	University of North Carolina	$150,000
1986	Jeff King	3B	Pirates	University of Arkansas	$160,000
1987	Ken Griffey, Jr.	OF	Mariners	Cincinnati, OH	$169,000
1988	Andy Benes	RHP	Padres	University of Evansville	$235,000
1989	Ben McDonald	RHP	Orioles	Louisiana State University	$350,000
1990	Chipper Jones	SS	Braves	Pierson, FL	$275,000
1991	Brien Taylor	LHP	Yankees	Beaufort, NC	$1,550,000
1992	Phil Nevin	3B	Astros	Cal State Fullerton	$750,000
1993	Alex Rodriguez	SS	Mariners	Miami, FL	$1,000,000
1994	Paul Wilson	RHP	Mets	Florida State University	$1,550,000
1995	Darin Erstad	OF	Angels	University of Nebraska	$1,575,000
1996	Kris Benson	RHP	Pirates	Clemson University	$2,000,000
1997	Matt Anderson	RHP	Tigers	Rice University	$2,500,000

(Continued)

TABLE 2-1 (CONTINUED)

ALL-TIME NUMBER ONE OVERALL MAJOR LEAGUE BASEBALL DRAFT PICKS, 1965–2005					
Year	*Player*	*Pos*	*Team*	*School*	*Signing Bonus*
1998	Pat Burrell	1B	Phillies	University of Miami	$3,015,000
1999	Josh Hamilton	OF	Devil Rays	Raleigh, NC	$3,960,000
2000	Adrian Gonzalez	1B	Marlins	Chula Vista, CA	$3,000,000
2001	Joe Mauer	C	Twins	St. Cretin-Derham Hall High School	$5,150,000
2002	Bryan Bullington	RHP	Pirates	Ball State University	$4,000,000
2003	Delmon Young	OF	Devil Rays	Camarillo High School, CA	$3,700,000
2004	Matt Bush	SS	Padres	Mission Bay High School, El Cajon, CA	$3,150,000
2005	Justin Upton	SS	Diamondbacks	Great Bridge High School, Chesapeake, VA	$6,100,000

Source: Courtesy of Baseballchronology.com.

In Case 2-7, *Alabama Football, Inc. v. Wright*, 452 F. Supp. 182 (N.D. Tex. 1977), a defunct football franchise in a defunct league (the World Football League) sought return of a signing bonus, arguing that no consideration existed between the parties, thereby making the contract unenforceable.

📖 CASE 2-7 *Alabama Football, Inc. v. Wright*

452 F. Supp. 182 (N.D. Tex. 1977)

ROBERT M. HILL, District Judge.

ORIGINAL COMPLAINT

The initial controversy centers itself around the definition of the word "bonus." In April of 1974 the parties entered into a contract whereby Wright agreed to play professional football for Alabama for the years 1977, 1978 and 1979. As per the terms of such contract Alabama, a member of the World Football League, paid Wright a $75,000 bonus at the time of the execution of the agreement. Subsequent to the execution of this agreement Alabama and the World Football League ceased to exist, thus making the whole of the contract incapable of being performed.

Alabama now seeks the return of the $75,000 claiming a total failure of consideration for the contract and contending that unjust enrichment will result if Wright is allowed to keep such bonus amount. Alabama specifically argues that the term "bonus" in the context of the relevant contract means compensation paid for services which were to be performed in the future by Wright for the benefit of Alabama. Therefore, since the unavoidable demise of Alabama and consequently Wright's inability to perform the contemplated future services, the advanced bonus should be returned for failure of mutual exchange of consideration.

Wright denies this claim. He argues that the word "bonus" in the context of the relevant contract and in the world of professional football means simply the payment of money in consideration for signing the contract. It is argued that the act of signing itself is full consideration for the bonus paid. Wright also argues that in addition to signing the contract he gave other valuable consideration for the bonus payment made by Alabama. Such other consideration is described as forbearance in negotiating with the Dallas Cowboys, Wright's existing employer, and with all other professional football teams for the 1975–1977 football seasons and allowing Alabama to publicize his name in promotions for Alabama's team. Accordingly, Wright asserts there has been due consideration given Alabama for its payment of the bonus.

In the court's opinion Wright's argument is most compelling. The contract between the two parties is unambiguous. Therefore, this court's responsibility is to construe the intent of the parties and the terms of the contract from the language of the document itself and the surrounding circumstances at its execution. In considering the word "bonus" in the context of the contract and the usage made of such word in professional football, the court finds that the parties intended Wright to be paid a $75,000 bonus upon his execution of a player's contract with Alabama and that no further services were contemplated by the parties as a condition to such payment or the retention of such payment by Wright. The bonus was not paid merely in anticipation of Wright's future services as a football player, but in exchange for a fully performed act, Wright's signing of the contract. The court finds such contractual provision to be reasonable and fair.

Additionally, the court finds that Alabama benefited from the execution of Wright's player contract. Such benefit consisted of obtaining Wright's playing services by at the latest the 1977 football season and for subsequent playing seasons and obtaining an exclusive agreement prohibiting Wright from negotiating or executing any other contract with any other professional football club in any football league. Even assuming the contract required more than the execution of the contract, these benefits accruing to Alabama upon execution of the contract would provide ample consideration to support the bonus payment. . . .

```
Wherefore, Alabama's motion for summary judgment is overruled;
Wright's motion for summary judgment on the Original Complaint is sus-
tained. . . .
```

Source: Courtesy of Westlaw; reprinted with permission.

NFL teams have attempted to retrieve all or part of signing bonuses paid to players for various reasons. The Miami Dolphins prevailed at arbitration against Ricky Williams for the return of his signing bonus. Arbitrator Richard Bloch awarded the Dolphins $8,616,373 from Williams, who announced in July 2004 that he was retiring. The $8.6 million award included $5.3 million in contract incentives as well as a $3.3 million portion of a signing bonus paid to Williams by the New Orleans Saints in 1999. The Dolphins asserted that because Williams had retired and failed three drug tests, they were entitled to recoup bonuses paid to him.[49] The New England Patriots withheld $8.75 million of Terry Glenn's $11.5 million bonus, stating he violated the morals clause in his contract when he tested positive under the NFL Substance Abuse Policy. The Seattle Seahawks took the position that because of Jeremy Stevens's drunk driving conviction, they could withhold a portion of his signing bonus.

Problem 2-4

Curtis Antoine is an outstanding leadoff hitter for the Detroit Tigers. He has everything desired of an outstanding leadoff hitter. He gets on base regularly, makes contact with the ball, can steal a base when needed to keep his team out of the dreaded "twin killing," and can hit with power. He is able to negotiate into his contract a bonus clause that gives him a $50,000 bonus if he makes 700 plate appearances for the Tigers during the season. By game 160 of the season, he has 696 plate appearances. Before the start of game 161, the manager tells Antoine he will only be used in a pinch hitting role for the last two games of the season because the Tigers would like to see how the rookies can perform for next season. He fails to get any more plate appearances for the remainder of the season and subsequently fails to qualify for the bonus in his contract. The Tigers finish the season with a win–loss record of 70–92, 14 games back of their division leader. Antoine believes the team purposely sat him down the last two games of the season to avoid paying the bonus. Does he have any remedy against the team for the failure to pay the bonus? What defense will the team assert? How would you advise him if you were his agent?

Interpretation of Bonus Clauses

Disputes can arise over bonus provisions in contracts if they are not drafted carefully. Former Minnesota Vikings Hall of Famer Alan Page had a dispute with the Vikings over a provision in his contract that stated "said player shall receive a bonus in the amount of $2,500 if he is selected 'All Pro' by any of the following: AP, UPI, PFW, or the *Sporting News.*" He was chosen as one of the defensive tackles on the "All-NFL" team selected by UPI and the *Sporting News* as well as being named to

---

[49] J. Cole, SAN DIEGO UNION-TRIBUNE, Sept. 25, 2004.

the AP's second-team "All-NFL" squad. He subsequently requested payment of the bonus from the Vikings. The issue was how to define "All-Pro." Jim Finks of the Vikings testified that to him, "All-Pro" meant that the player was selected as the top player at the position in the entire league. Finks had drafted the clauses in question on behalf of the Vikings. NFL Commissioner Pete Rozelle ruled in favor of Page, finding he was entitled to the $2,500 bonus. The team had specifically stated that the UPI and the *Sporting News* would serve to determine if Page were entitled to the bonus. The problem was that neither of those entities used the term "All-Pro" but instead chose two All-Conference Teams, AFC and NFC. Page had been named to the "All-NFC" team, which was the highest designation he *could* receive because there was no "All-Pro" team chosen. Page's legal skill became better known when he became Justice Page and served on the Minnesota Supreme Court for many years.

Option Clauses

An *option* contract is an offer that is considered irrevocable for a specific period of time.[50] Option contracts are sometimes used in player contracts as well as endorsement agreements. A player and team may agree to a particular length of a contract, but they can also give each party an option to extend the contract. Player contracts have contained option clauses in which the team retains the right to a player at a certain salary. In today's sporting world, option contracts are usually negotiated as an addendum to the standard player contract.

Teams or players can agree to option clauses, and they can appear in all forms. Former Houston Texans quarterback David Carr signed a seven-year, $46.75 million contract as a rookie. The final three years of the contract were voidable if he reached certain performance incentives. Therefore, his contract would have expired on March 3, 2006. However, the Texans had the option to "buy back" the voidable years. The first option was that the team could pay Carr a bonus of $5.5 million to buy back two seasons, with base salaries of $5 million for 2006 and $5.25 million for 2007. The second option was for the Texans to pay an $8 million bonus to buy back three seasons, with base salaries of $5.25 million in 2006 and 2007 and a salary of $6 million in 2008. The Texans exercised the second option, retaining Carr for three more seasons.

Many contract clauses allow the team to acquire the player's rights for the next season. Charles Hennigan had an option clause in his contract with the Houston Oilers when he was traded to the San Diego Chargers. The option clause was in dispute after the Chargers cut Hennigan from the squad. This is shown in Case 2-8, *Hennigan v. Chargers Football Co.*, 431 F.2d 308 (5th Cir. 1970).

📖 CASE 2-8 *Hennigan v. Chargers Football Co.*

431 F.2d 308 (5th Cir. 1970)

AINSWORTH, Circuit Judge:

. . . [W]e must determine whether a former professional football player is entitled to compensation from his Club for the 1967 season of the American Football League (AFL). The player was sent home when

---

[50] George v. Schuman, 168 N.W. 486 (Mich. 1918).

he reported for the team's 1967 training camp too injured to play. Terminated without pay, he seeks redress under the terms of the contract establishing the various rights and obligations of the player and his Club during the so-called option year to which every AFL player commits himself when he signs a standard contract to play football in the League. . . . The issues with which we deal are (1) whether the team's 'renewal' of the player's 1964-1966 contract obligated the Club to pay the player salary in 1967 under the injury clause of the contract and (2) whether this 'renewal' required the Club to pay the player under the 'no-cut' clause of the 1964-1966 contract.

I.

. . . On March 19, 1964, Charles T. Hennigan, appellee, signed an AFL Standard Players Contract (AFL Contract) for three years with the Houston Oilers, Inc., a member club of the AFL. A 'no-cut' clause was made a part of that contract. . . . Both the Standard Players Contract form and the 'no-cut' clause form used by the parties are among the standard forms the League requires its member clubs to use. . . .

Hennigan claims that the Chargers broke the promises made in paragraph 3 (compensation provision) and paragraph 10 (option provision) with respect to the 1967 football season. He makes this claim under the following circumstances, which the parties do not dispute: Hennigan engaged in professional football as a player for the Houston Oilers through the 1966 football season. While in the performance of his services, as a professional football player for the Oilers, Hennigan sustained injuries to his right knee during both the 1965 and 1966 football seasons. In March 1967 the Oilers exercised the Club's right under paragraph 9 of the contract with Hennigan and assigned the contract to the San Diego Chargers. In April 1967 the Chargers, as the assignee of Hennigan's AFL Contract, exercised the 'renewal' option under paragraph 10 of the Contract by means of a letter. . . . In July 1967 Hennigan reported as directed to the Chargers for the beginning of the training season. Upon reporting, he was examined by the Chargers' physician as required by paragraph 6 of the AFL Contract. The physician determined that Hennigan's right knee, which had been operated upon in February 1967, would not at this time 'stand up to the stress and strain of professional football.' Accordingly, the physician recommended that Hennigan be rejected for service as a player. . . . On the basis of the physician's report, the Chargers claimed the right under paragraph 6 to terminate its contractual relations with Hennigan because of Hennigan's physical incapacity to perform services as a professional football player, and a wire was mailed to the AFL

President. . . . Hennigan returned home and performed no services for the Chargers during the 1967 football season.

This suit was subsequently commenced by Hennigan against the Chargers to recover the salary that would have otherwise been payable to him for the 1967 football season had the Chargers not acted to terminate the player's contract. Hennigan . . . contended that because he had sustained the disabling injury to his right knee while performing services under the AFL Contract the Oilers had assigned to the Chargers, paragraph 15 of that contract (the injury clause) obligated the Chargers, by virtue of the latter's exercise of the 'renewal' option, to pay him his salary for the 1967 season. Secondly, and in any event, he contended that the 'no-cut' clause added to paragraph 6 was applicable and operative during the 1967 season and expressly precluded the Chargers from terminating the 'renewed' contract because of Hennigan's lack of capacity to play professional football. . . .

II.

In paragraph 15 (the injury clause) of the AFL Contract, the words 'In the event that Player is injured in the performance of his services under this contract' set forth a condition precedent, the occurrence of which must take place before the Club's duty to perform the promises it makes in that paragraph arises. It is undisputed that Hennigan was injured while performing services for the Houston Oilers. . . . By accepting the assignment, the Chargers assumed the Oilers' obligations to Hennigan under paragraph 15 and the 'no-cut' clause added to paragraph 6 of the 1964 contract. Hennigan contends that the Chargers, by exercising the 'renewal' option in paragraph 10, became obligated to pay him his salary for the 1967 football season, notwithstanding that he was sent home after failing the Club's physical examination, because the contract under which he was injured in 1965 and 1966 and the 'renewed' contract under which he reported to the Chargers in 1967 were one and the same. Therefore, he claims the Chargers Club was not relieved of the obligation to pay him for the 1967 season (the 'further term' of the 'renewed' contract) because he was physically incapable of passing the Club's physical examination at the beginning of the 1967 training season. The Club does not dispute the fact of Hennigan's injuries or when they occurred. . . . [The Chargers] contend instead that its exercise of the 'renewal' option had the effect of creating a new contract with Hennigan. Because Hennigan's disabling injuries occurred in 1965 and 1966, before the 1967 contract was made, the Club contends that the condition precedent to its duty to pay Hennigan for the 1967 season never took place, that is, Hennigan was not injured while in the performance of any services required of him by the option-year contract. . . .

This case, ultimately, turns upon the meaning that should be ascribed to the term 'renewal' . . . in the AFL Contract . . . with the Houston Oilers in 1964. . . . The option to 'renew' for a 'further term' may mean, as the Chargers and the AFL contend, that the Club has the right to hold the player to a new, one-year contract, as distinguished from the then existing, possibly multiyear contract. On the other hand, the option to 'renew' may mean, as Hennigan contends and the District Court concluded, that the Club has the right to keep the then existing, possibly multiyear contract in force for one more year, with the respective rights and obligations of the Club and the player in the last year as specified in paragraph 10. . . .

Our analysis of the AFL Contract leads us to the conclusion that, when the Chargers exercise the 'renewal' option, in essence a new contract was established. . . .

Our reading of the AFL Contract finds support in the clear purpose and effect of paragraph 10. The paragraph grants the Club an option on the player's services as a professional football player. . . . Unless the player signs a new AFL Contract, itself with a fixed term and an option provision, the Club is entitled in the option year to fix the player's salary, certainly an important consideration to the professional athlete, at an amount 10 percent less than the player was receiving previously. Moreover, the player is not entitled to whatever bonus or other payments he may have been receiving previously unless such payments are specifically agreed upon by the Club and the player. . . .

If a player under contract with an AFL Club is injured while performing services required of him by that contract, and the player is thereafter unable to perform services because of that injury, the Club is obligated under paragraph 15 to pay him his salary for the balance of the contract term, notwithstanding that the player is no longer able to fulfill the warranty he makes in paragraph 6.

[W]e do not find that the option to 'renew,' when reasonably interpreted, was meant to have the effect upon its exercise of carrying forward injuries suffered during the previous term as occurrences giving rise to the Club's duty to compensate the player in the option year under paragraph 15. If this were the effect, then a retired player attempting to return to professional football as a player could require the Club holding the option on his services to decide at its peril whether to exercise that option. Should the option be exercised, the Club would assume the risk that it might have to pay salary to a

```
person unable to perform any services because of injuries sustained
prior to his retirement. . . .
```

```
From our conclusion that the exercise of its option on Hennigan's ser-
vices by the Chargers had the effect of making a new contract with the
player for a term of one year, it follows that Hennigan was not enti-
tled to compensation for the 1967 football season from the Chargers.
. . . He was terminated for his inability to pass the physical exami-
nation. . . . [T]he 'no-cut' clause, by its terms, expired on May 1,
1967. Therefore, summary judgment should have been granted in favor of
the Chargers on the issue of their liability to Hennigan.
```

```
Reversed.
```

```
Source: Courtesy of Westlaw; reprinted with permission.
```

Other Significant Clauses in Player Contracts

A variety of other specialty clauses can be inserted into players' contracts. They are too numerous to name here, but a few deserve special attention. Some players are able to negotiate no-trade clauses in their contracts. Some clauses provide that the player cannot be traded without the player's consent. Other clauses may allow a player to list teams to which the player cannot be traded or specify a specific division or conference to which the player can or cannot be traded. Most standard player contracts include an "assignment clause" that allows the team to trade a player without the player's consent. The assignment clause listed in the NFL's standard player contract is as follows:

> Unless this contract specifically provides otherwise, Club may assign this contract and Player's services under this contract to any successor to Club's franchise or to any other Club in the League. Player will report to the assignee Club promptly upon being informed of the assignment of his contract and will faithfully perform his services under this contract. The assignee club will pay Player's necessary traveling expenses in reporting to it and will faithfully perform this contract.[51]

Negotiating a "no-cut" clause for a player is rare in most sports leagues, but especially in the NFL. Under a no-cut clause, a team can actually cut the player but may still be responsible for the player's salary for the remainder of the season.[52] What about a clause in a contract that states a player must be "loyal" to a team or forfeit his signing bonus? A "loyalty clause" found its way into the majority of the players' contracts of the Cincinnati Bengals for the 2002 season, sometimes referred to as the "Carl Pickens Clause." Pickens was a former wide receiver with the Bengals who routinely engaged in tirades against the team and management. The matter went to arbitration on December 14, 2000. This is shown in Case 2-9, National Football League Players Ass'n (on Behalf of the Cincinnati Bengals Players) v. National Football League Management Council (on Behalf of the Cincinnati Bengals), December 14, 2000.

---

[51] Courtesy of Westlaw; reprinted with permission.

[52] G. Roberts, *The First Annual Sports Dollars & Sense Conference: A Symposium on Sports Industry Contracts and Negotiations,* 3 Marq. Sports L. J. 29 (1992).

📖 CASE 2-9 *National Football League Players Ass'n (on Behalf of the Cincinnati Bengals Players) v. National Football League Management Council (on Behalf of the Cincinnati Bengals)*

December 14, 2000

The grievance in this case, filed July 27, 2000, protests the Club's inclusion of a provision in players' contracts that makes their signing bonus contingent on their refraining from making derogatory comments. The so-called "loyalty clause" requires the forfeiture of part or all of the bonus if:

> . . . in Club's sole judgment [sic] Player at any time makes any public comment to the media, including but not limited to the newspaper, magazines, television, radio or Internet or that is derogatory of or criticizing teammates, club coaches, Club management or the Club's operation or policies ("voluntary breach or failure to perform"). . . .

The Association says this provision violates Article VIII of the CBA, which establishes a maximum discipline schedule, including penalties applicable to "conduct detrimental to Club". Because players and teams cannot bargain individual contract terms that are inconsistent with the CBA, says the Association, the appended prohibition must be considered void.

Issue

Does the inclusion of the contested language in individual contracts violate the terms of the collective bargaining agreement?

Source: Courtesy of Westlaw; reprinted with permission.

How would you decide this arbitration? What legal issues are present?

Problem 2-5

Consider the Bengals' "loyalty clause" arbitration decision. Would a player be subject to losing a signing bonus for any of the following actions?

1. Giving an interview after the game criticizing the team's offensive scheme.
2. Posting, on the player's personal website, a statement that says, "We need to improve our special team play and I think coaching is a large part of that."

3. Telling a teammate that the owner is greedy.

4. Stating on a radio program, "If we are ever going to make it to the playoffs on a consistent basis, ownership is going to have to consider making some changes to the organization."

GUARANTEED CONTRACTS

Some players have the ability to negotiate a guaranteed contract. The term *guaranteed* is subject to interpretation as well. Many clauses in player contracts state that the player's salary will be paid regardless of whether he is on the team. There are very few guaranteed contracts for NFL players because of the high amount of risk involved. In 2002, only 3% of players on NFL rosters were paid regardless of whether they made an NFL club.[53] In 1970, John Vallely signed a uniform player contract with the Atlanta Hawks that contained an addendum that stated that the contract was "on a no-cut guaranteed basis." Vallely was subsequently traded to the Houston Rockets, who assumed his contract. In September 1972 Vallely was released by the Rockets. The Rockets continued to pay him even though he was not listed on the roster. However, because he was not on the club's roster, he failed to qualify for the league's pension plan. Vallely filed a grievance, arguing that his contract was guaranteed and therefore he was entitled to pension benefits. The issue in arbitration was whether the denial of pension benefits was a violation of the collective bargaining agreement. The arbitrator found in favor of Vallely, ruling that his guaranteed salary also entitled him to other benefits the contract provided.[54]

What actually constitutes a guaranteed contract? What language is necessary in a contract to make it guaranteed? The following provisions could be found in a player's contract dealing with a guarantee clause.

II. Guarantee

The Club and the Player agree that the multi-year Contract, of which this Addendum is a part, is "guaranteed" in the manner and under the terms and conditions set forth below. It is the intent of the Parties that this "guarantee" and the specific and important exceptions to it are central and fundamental to their agreement and the Parties acknowledge the importance and material quality of these provisions to their respective interests.

A. *Agreement to Pay if the Contract Is Not Terminated*

The Club guarantees, in the event that this Contract is not terminated, to pay the Player in full all payments stipulated in Paragraph

---

[53] *NFL Peace Guaranteed, Salaries Aren't,* Street & Smith's SportsBusiness Journal, Aug. 12–18, 2002.

[54] In the Matter of Arbitration Between National Basketball Association (Houston Rockets) and National Basketball Players Association (John S. Vallely), Peter Seitz, Arbitrator, Oct. 2, 1974.

2 of the Contract and in Paragraph 1 of this Addendum; provided, however, that the Club shall be relieved of its obligation to pay Player's salary during any period that the Player does not render his services under the Contract due to:

1. Voluntary retirement as an active Player or any unauthorized failure or refusal to render his services hereunder;

2. A labor dispute (including without limitation a strike, a lockout, or a sympathy strike);

3. Placement on any of the lists set out in Major League Rule 15 or any similar rule which may hereafter be adopted.

4. Suspension by the Club or by action of the League President or the Commissioner of Baseball (unless overturned through the appropriate appeal process, if any);

5. Intentional self-injury, suicide or attempted suicide;

6. The use of any type of illegal drug (unless the Player demonstrates that such use was accidental), the misuse of prescription or over-the-counter drugs or alcohol abuse or dependency;

7. Unless expressly authorized in writing by the Club, participation, or physical, mental or emotional injury or incapacity resulting from participation, in the following activities or sports: any competitive organized game of touch football, basketball, softball, volleyball, handball, paddleball, racquetball or squash; any competitive organized or impromptu game of tackle football, soccer, field hockey, ice hockey, roller hockey, polo, lacrosse or rugby; fencing, sky diving, bungee jumping, hunting, gliding or hang gliding, horse racing, boxing, wrestling, karate, judo, jujitsu or any martial art, in-line or other roller skating, ice skating, water or snow skiing, snowmobiling, bobsledding, spelunking, jai-alai, bicycle racing, motorboat or auto racing, motorcycling, white water canoeing, woodchopping, rodeo surfing with a surfboard, piloting, learning to operate or serving as a crew member of an aircraft, parachuting, participation in the "Superteams" or "Superstars" activities or other television or motion picture athletic competitions or any other sport involving a substantial risk of personal injury.

8. Incapacity due to an allegation and/or adjudication that player engaged in a criminal or felonious act (including without limitation civil or criminal incarceration or probation as a form of incapacity, but excluding traffic violations).

9. Incapacity caused by the HIV virus, AIDS and/or any related conditions; provided, however, that his exclusion shall be null and void in the event that (i) Player successfully completes an insurance examination (including an HIV test if required) within 120 days of the execution of this Agreement, such that the Club will be able to obtain general disability insurance coverage, including coverage for HIV and/or AIDS

related disabilities, or (ii) Club fails to have such insurance examination administered within such 120-day period.

B. *Agreement to Pay Salary if the Contract Is Terminated*

10. The Club guarantees that if the Contract is terminated because the Player fails, in the opinion of the Club's management, to exhibit sufficient skill or competitive ability to qualify or continue as a member of the Club's team (Paragraph 7(b)(2) of the Contract), the Player shall nevertheless continue to receive the unpaid balance of the salary stipulated in Paragraph 2 of the Contract for the term of the Contract, including previously earned award and incentive bonuses. Subject to the immediately following sentence, the foregoing agreement to continue to pay the Player's salary beyond the date of termination applies whether or not such failure to exhibit sufficient skills or competitive ability is due to Player's inability to display sufficient professional skills or competitive ability, or is due to physical or mental incapacity or death which is incurred on or off the baseball field or which is incurred before, during or after the Championship season. Notwithstanding anything to the contrary herein, the Club shall have the right to terminate this Contract and cease to make further salary payments to Player, and the agreement to continue the Player's salary shall not apply beyond the date of termination, in any case of Player's physical or mental disability or incapacity or death due all or in <u>substantial</u> part to or attributable all or in <u>substantial</u> part to any of those causes specified in Paragraph A5, 6, 7, 8 or 9 of this Addendum, but in the case of A8, only if the Player is found guilty (including pursuant to a plea of <u>nolo contendere</u> or a similar plea) of such act by a recognized court of law.

11. If the Club terminates the Contract pursuant to Paragraph 7(b)(1) or 7(b)(3) of the Contract, which the Club can only do for conduct on the part of the Player that is substantial and material in nature, all obligations of both Parties hereunder, including the obligation to pay the Player in full the salary stipulated in Paragraph 2 of the Contract, shall cease on the date of termination except the obligation to pay the Player compensation and award and incentive bonuses earned to said date.

12. In the event the Contract is terminated and during its prescribed term the Player signs a Uniform Player's Contract with another Major League Club or Clubs, notwithstanding anything to the contrary in this Paragraph, the Club's total obligations to the Player in any year shall be reduced by the amounts which the Player earns during that year from any Club or Clubs, including amounts deferred to later years, if any, and bonuses. In the event the Player refuses to accept a Uniform Player's Contract offered by a Major League Club other than the Club

which released him, the Player shall forfeit that portion of the salary which would not have been payable had he accepted such other Contract.

C. Conversion to a Non-Guaranteed Contract

The Player and the Club mutually acknowledge and agree that the Club is entering into this salary guarantee provision based upon the Player's representation he is in first class physical condition, and that, in an effort to maintain his first class physical condition, the Player will adhere to any reasonable training rules and/or conditioning programs established by the Club. In the event that the Club determines that the Player is no longer in first class physical condition due to the use of any type of illegal drug (unless Player demonstrates that such use was accidental), the misuse of prescription or over-the-counter drugs or alcohol abuse of dependency, or due to the Player's failure to adhere to such training rules or conditioning programs, the Club may, at its discretion, convert this guaranteed Contract into a non-guaranteed Contract by providing written notice of such conversion to the Player. Such determination by the club shall be based on competent medical evidence and is subject to verification by an independent physician mutually agreeable to the Club and the Player. The Player and the Club agree that the Club's rights under this Paragraph are in addition to and distinct from the rights set forth in Paragraph 7(b) of the Contract and elsewhere in this Addendum and that the Club's exercise of its rights under this Paragraph shall not affect the enforceability of any of the other rights and/or obligations created by this Contract and its Addenda.

*Source: Loaiza V Loaiza,*130 S.W.3d 894 (Tex. Ct. App> 2004). Courtesy of Westlaw.

NEGOTIATION OF SPORTS CONTRACTS

An agent, lawyer, or businessperson who negotiates a contract on behalf of a player must properly arm himself or herself with sufficient information to represent the client. This information might include the following:

- The collective bargaining agreement.
- The standard player contract.
- The league bylaws and constitution.
- Relevant court cases or administrative proceedings dealing with issues relating to the negotiation.
- Contracts of similar players.
- Information relating to player salaries and benefits.

Players do not always employ an agent to negotiate their contract. Former Major League Baseball MVP Willie Hernandez represented himself during negotiations with the Detroit Tigers and proved to be a formidable opponent. He threatened to demand a trade unless he was given a contract similar to other relievers in baseball.

An agent must understand terms such as *free agency*, *salary cap*, and *rights of first refusal* and possess a general understanding of how the economics of sports leagues operate to get his or her client the best contract available. Professional unions can be very helpful to agents in the negotiation of contracts. They can provide information on contracts signed by players so the agent can compare a proposed contract to signed contracts already entered into. Information relating to player salaries, bonuses, and contractual terms is readily available to agents today. Salaries of players are printed in newspapers and posted on the Internet. This information was not always available to agents in the past, making it difficult to be able to negotiate a good contract on behalf of a client. "In 1980 none of the NBA players' salaries or contract terms were available to agents or players, and thus as in football in 1974, the only people who had information on players' contracts were the few player agents who had actually negotiated those contracts."[55]

Salary negotiations for many players can be relatively simple. Players drafted in the later rounds of the NFL draft will most likely earn the league minimum salary with a small bonus and will sign the standard player contract. The only negotiating left to the agent would be the amount of the bonus. Collective bargaining has set the minimum salaries of most professional leagues, thereby reducing some negotiations to a relatively simple process for later-round draft picks and undrafted free agents. However, star players' contracts will require a knowledgeable and skilled negotiator. An agent who is familiar with the economic structure of the league as well as the relevant contract provisions that might be included in such a contract will have an advantage during negotiations. If an agent has negotiated previous contracts with an owner or a general manager of a particular team, the agent might have gained valuable knowledge for the next negotiation. Knowing the ropes gives the agent and player a negotiating advantage.

A player's representative must consider the following during negotiation of a player contract:

- Potential contract guarantees
- Incentives or bonus provisions
- No-trade clauses
- No-cut clauses
- Signing bonuses
- Injury protection provision
- Disability insurance
- Renewal contract provisions

Having a database of salary information is essential to negotiation. Agents must be familiar with players who are similarly situated in relation to the agent's client. Understanding performance statistics is also essential for the negotiation of a good contract. If a team offers an offensive lineman a $1 million bonus for being named NFL MVP, the agent would be wise to spend negotiation capital elsewhere. Negotiating a bonus for an American player in the Canadian Football League for Most

---

Outstanding Canadian would obviously be fruitless. Knowing what bonuses are attainable for a player is essential for the negotiation of a good contract. Understanding how each club in a league operates is also valuable. If an agent represented an undrafted free agent in the NFL, the agent would want to perform due diligence to determine whether the team has a history of signing a large number of undrafted free agents or whether it is a team that signs a large number of veteran free agents. Other considerations might be a factor during negotiations as well. For instance, some states have a state income tax. That issue may be a deciding factor between two offers made to a player. A player's personal preference regarding a particular team or location may also dominate the negotiations.

Negotiating strategies will change for different player contracts in different situations. A sports agent must understand the particularities of the sport his or her client plays to get a good deal on the player's behalf. If an agent is representing a player labeled as a "franchise player" by the Denver Broncos under the NFL's CBA, negotiations would surely differ from those of an agent representing a punter drafted in the seventh round by the Detroit Lions.

Negotiating a contract for a player selected in the fifth round of the Major League Baseball amateur draft would require specific knowledge of that sport, including the following:

- Professional Baseball Rules' College Scholarship Plan.
- Standard incentive bonus plan.
- Salary bonus paid in previous years to players in the first five rounds.
- Bonuses previously paid to players at the same position as the drafted player.

If an agent were called upon to negotiate a player's contract with the Canadian Football League (CFL), the agent's negotiations would be limited to a certain extent. Information would be available to the representative about players at certain positions and the salary range for those players. For instance, if an agent were representing an offensive tackle in the negotiation of a CFL contract, the salary range might be from $40,000 to $300,000 (U.S. dollars), depending on the player's experience with the team and the age of the player. Quarterbacks could demand more money when negotiating a CFL contract, but it would be fruitful for the agent to clearly understand the length of that contract just in case the player has a desire to play in the NFL.

It takes a great deal of skill, knowledge, and experience to negotiate a multimillion-dollar sports contract. Many top negotiators in the field of sports law, such as Scott Boras, Arm Tellum, Seth Daniel, and Tom Condon, use successful negotiation techniques to persuade opposing parties to their point of view. Each player representative brings to the table a set of negotiating skills and tactics. Negotiating a sports contract takes excellent negotiating skills combined with a special knowledge of the sporting world.

Agents and players have employed a variety of negotiation strategies over the years in the attempt to secure a better contract. Holding out for a better contract is a ploy that has been used by many players. Joey Galloway was not the first. Babe Ruth held out on a regular basis. This led sports writer Milton Richman to conclude, "Every time I'd see the annual headline 'Ruth Holds Out,' I'd automatically know winter was over and spring was here."[56] Holdouts do occur in today's sports world, but renegotiation of contracts has led to many players signing contracts in their last season of their current contract. Renegotiation of a contract by a player is also a tool that has been used many times for leverage to a better contract.

---

[56] Milton Richman, *Today's Sports Paradise,* UPI, Feb. 27, 1984.

Renegotiation is a strategy that has worked for some star athletes. Some players and agents will attempt to renegotiate a contract to which they had previously agreed, citing a change in circumstances since the original deal was structured. Boston lawyer and original sports agent Bob Wolf considered renegotiation of a contract improper, stating, "I've never blackmailed a club into negotiating. That's what it is, what else could it be called?"[57]

Another way for an athlete to gain an advantage during negotiation is to receive competitive offers from other teams. This was more common when major sports leagues had competition that could match the salary offers of the major teams. For example, in the 1980s the United States Football League (USFL) was a start-up league that went head to head with the NFL in signing players. Many NFL stars actually signed large contracts with the USFL and later played in the NFL, including Jim Kelly, Steve Young, and Herschel Walker. Heisman Trophy winner Walker signed a three-year, $3.9 million contract with the New Jersey Generals of the USFL. The Generals sold 36,000 season tickets, almost half of them purchased between Walker's signing and the opening game. One of the owners of the Generals was Donald Trump.[58] Rival leagues can assist a player during negotiations if the league can compete with an established sports league. The Canadian Football League cannot match the offers of the NFL; therefore, players do not have the leverage to negotiate using offers from the CFL as a valid tool when negotiating with an NFL team. In today's sports market, there are no realistic rivals to the four major sports leagues in the United States that could provide negotiation leverage for a player.

Free agency has clearly had an effect on a player's ability to negotiate a better contract. Since the institution of free agency in sports, player salaries have risen dramatically. In baseball, the arbitration process is a negotiating tool that has been used both by teams and players. Some athletes can use college as a negotiating tool to increase offers from teams. Outstanding high school baseball players can either attend college and play baseball or accept an offer from a professional team to play baseball. Players and their agents have used the "threat" of playing baseball in college as a negotiating tactic to receive a better offer from a team.

Negotiations with different teams can clearly lead to different results. A baseball agent knows what Major League teams are willing to offer a contract to a free agent player. The Yankees and Red Sox are traditionally active in the free agent market in baseball, whereas the Tampa Bay Rays and Kansas City Royals are not. An agent would do well to understand the economic structure of baseball and its impact on free agency to gain an advantage for his or her client during negotiations.

An agent representing a star player in the NFL would certainly be required to know the salary cap situation of the team with which he or she was negotiating. Other factors can determine a particular negotiation for a player. Some athletes prefer to play in a certain location for their own reasons. Gordie Howe chose to play with the Houston Aeros in the now-defunct World Hockey Association so that he could play alongside his two sons. A left-handed power hitter would certainly take into consideration the park of the club he was negotiating with to ensure his success as a power hitter. Free agent pitchers have taken into consideration whether they could be successful in pitching in the thin air of Coors Field for the Colorado Rockies, although it has not stopped some from signing lucrative contracts with the Colorado club.

---

[57] Howard Slusher, *Love Him or Hate Him,* Sport, Feb. 1983, at 18.
[58] *See* http://www.thisistheusfl.com.

ENDORSEMENT CONTRACTS

Sponsorship and endorsement contracts have become standard fare for many athletes. Professional athletes can makes millions of dollars if they acquire corporate sponsorship or endorsement deals. The negotiation of such deals can be crucial to the player's livelihood and future. Endorsers desire athletes who present a clean, wholesome image for their products. Corporations thus require athletes to sign a contract that contains a morals clause, whereby the company can terminate the agreement if the player places the company in a bad light or brings harm to the company's reputation.

Corporations who retain athletes to represent the company take the risk that the athletes might tarnish the reputation of the product by involvement in off-the-field conduct that is inappropriate. Because so much is at stake, corporations are now taking more precautions to ensure that they have the ability to terminate a contract if an athlete places the corporation in a bad light. A survey conducted in 1997 indicated that fewer than one-half of all endorsement contracts included a morals clause. That number had risen to a minimum of 75% by 2003.[59]

NBA player Latrell Sprewell was fined by Converse after his physical altercation with coach P. J. Carlesimo. PGA golfer John Daly's contract with Wilson was terminated following various drinking binges, including an episode at the Player's Championship in which Daly trashed his hotel room and subsequently withdrew from the tournament.[60] Kmart terminated the services of Fuzzy Zoeller after statements he made about Tiger Woods; Zoeller lost the remaining two years on his contract. NBA star Kobe Bryant was charged with one count of sexual assault in Eagle County, Colorado. None of his endorsers invoked a morals clause against Bryant. McDonald's, however, did not renew his endorsement contract after 2003.

Case 2-10, *Milicic v. Basketball Marketing Co.*, Inc., 857 A.2d 689 (Pa. Super. Ct. 2004), deals with an endorsement agreement in the context of the tort of intentional interference with contractual relations.

📖 CASE 2-10 *Milicic v. Basketball Marketing Co., Inc.*

857 A.2d 689 (Pa. Super. Ct. 2004)

McCAFFERY, J.

Appellant, The Basketball Marketing Company Inc. d/b/a AND 1, asks us to determine whether the trial court erred by issuing a preliminary injunction against it. Specifically, Appellant argues it did no more than send letters to its competitors informing them that it had a valid contract with Appellee, Darko Milicic, and that this did not rise to the level of wrongful conduct. For the reasons stated herein, we hold that the trial court properly granted Appellee's Petition for a Preliminary Injunction. Consequently, we affirm.

---

[59] Eric Fisher, *Sosa Flap to Change Endorsement Deals,* WASH. TIMES, June 8, 2003, at CO3.
[60] Ron Sirak, *Nice Birthday Gift: Wilson Drops Daly,* CHATTANOOGA FREE PRESS, Apr. 29, 1997, at D3.

The trial court summarized the pertinent facts and relevant procedural history as follows:

Appellant is a Delaware Corporation with its principal place of business in Paoli, Pennsylvania. Appellant is in the business of the marketing, distribution and sale of basketball apparel and related products. Appellee, Darko Milicic, is an 18 year-old basketball player from Serbia, and was the 2003 second overall draft pick by the National Basketball Association's Detroit Pistons.

The parties entered into an endorsement agreement ("the agreement") on June 15, 2002, when [Appellee] was just 16 years-old, whereby [A]ppellant would pay [Appellee] certain monies and provide him with products in exchange for [Appellee's] endorsement. The agreement was twice amended, revising the amount of compensation and to whom the payments would be sent, however all other provisions remained the same, including the choice of law clause mandating the agreement to be governed by the laws of Pennsylvania.

Although [Appellee] was virtually unknown in the United States at the time the agreement was executed, by April of this year his status had significantly changed and it was widely known he was likely to be a top five N.B.A. draft pick. As one would expect, [Appellee] was then in a position to sign a more lucrative endorsement deal and in June 2003, he proposed a buy out of the agreement. The parties agreed that [Appellee] would speak with other companies to determine the potential value of another agreement for negotiation purposes relating to the buy-out.

On June 20, 2003, four days after his 18th birthday, [Appellee] made a buy-out offer to [A]ppellant, which was refused. About six days later, [Appellee] sent [A]ppellant a letter disaffirming the agreement. He began returning all monies and products (or their equivalent value) he had received pursuant to the agreement.

Appellant refused to accept [Appellee's] letter as a negation of the agreement. On July 11, 2003, [A]ppellant wrote letters to Adidas America ("Adidas") and Reebok International Ltd. ("Reebok"), both of whom, according to the letters, were believed to have offered endorsement contracts to [Appellee]. In the letters, [A]ppellant informed the recipients that it was "involved in a contractual dispute" with [Appellee] and that the "agreement is valid and enforceable and will remain in force for several more years." Appellant also requested copies of all communication between [Appellee] and the respective companies.

Based upon [A]ppellant's letter, Adidas ceased negotiations and a nearly finalized endorsement agreement was not executed. [Appellee] filed the underlying Complaint seeking a Temporary Restraining Order, a Preliminary Injunction and Declaratory Relief. The Court granted the TRO and after a hearing, and consideration of briefs filed by both parties, granted the Preliminary Injunction. This timely appeal followed.

(Trial Court Opinion, October 23, 2003, at 1-3) (footnotes and citations omitted).

Appellant raises the following issues for our review:

1. WHETHER THERE WERE REASONABLE GROUNDS FOR THE COURT BELOW TO FIND THAT APPELLEE/PLAINTIFF MET HIS BURDEN TO ESTABLISH THAT THE APPELLANT/DEFENDANT HAD ENGAGED IN ACTIONABLE (*I.E.*, WRONGFUL) CONDUCT REGARDING APPELLANT/DEFENDANT'S COMMUNICATION WITH CERTAIN OF ITS COMPETITORS?

. . . .

In this case, Appellee alleges that Appellant breached a duty imposed by common law because Appellant's conduct constituted intentional interference with prospective contractual relations.[61] As stated above, we agree with the reasoning employed by the trial court in its determination that Appellee is likely to succeed on his underlying effort to invalidate the endorsement contract between the instant parties. Accordingly, Appellant's action of sending letters indicating that a valid contract *did* exist to entities already negotiating with Appellee, with the express purpose of halting such negotiations, would certainly support a valid claim for intentional interference with prospective contractual relations.

Indeed, a prospective contractual relationship between Appellee and Adidas was actively being pursued, which appears to be exactly why Appellant sent Adidas the letter. Appellant, without privilege or justification, engaged in conduct which deliberately attempted to harm the negotiations and which, in fact, did stop Adidas from entering into a contract with Appellee. Therefore, the trial court certainly had "apparently reasonable grounds" upon which to issue a preliminary injunction. . . .

Based upon the foregoing reasons, we hold that Appellant's conduct in sending out the letters to its competitors did support a valid potential claim for intentional interference with prospective contractual

---

[61] The requisite elements for a claim of intentional interference with prospective contractual relations are as follows:
   (1) the existence of a contractual or prospective contractual relation between the complainant and a third party;
   (2) purposeful action on the part of the defendant specifically intended to harm the existing relation or to prevent a prospective relation from occurring; (3) the absence of privilege or justification on the part of the defendant; and
   (4) the occasioning of actual legal damage as a result of the defendant's conduct.

```
relations, and that Appellee proved the essential prerequisites neces-
sary for injunctive relief. . . .

Order affirmed.
```

Source: Courtesy of Westlaw; reprinted with permission.

Problem 2-6

Your client had recently signed an endorsement agreement with Adidas Corporation. The contract states the following: "Company may revoke this agreement if player commits any act of moral turpitude which reflects poorly on the Company's reputation or diminishes the Company's good will in the marketplace." Your client was arrested for allegedly assaulting a fellow patron in a bar fight. He was shown on television in handcuffs, wearing a hat bearing the company's logo. This picture was displayed on television many times for the next several weeks. The player claimed he was innocent. The company invoked the clause and sent the player a notice that it was terminating the contract. Six months after the player received the termination notice, the local prosecutor dismissed all charges against the player. The player now wants to sue the company for breach of contract. Was the company's position legally sound when it terminated the contract? How could the morals clause be drafted better?

COACHES' CONTRACTS

In the last ten years coaches as well as players have seen substantial increases in their salary and bonuses. Many coaches have achieved the same notable status as famous players. At the professional and collegiate levels, coaches are being given large contracts over a longer period of time. Some coaches are paid based on potential and are hired by a professional team or a university because they have been successful at other places. Coaches are given less time to win than they have in the past; the days of building a winning program over a long period of time are over. Coaches at the professional level will receive pressure from owners and fans to win and get their team to the playoffs or else. Major college football and basketball coaches feel the heat from alumni, fans, students, and the university to produce a winner and to advance to a Bowl Championship Series game for football or the NCAA tournament in basketball. No major college coach can survive a losing season or, heaven forbid, consecutive losing seasons without the local radio sports talk show calling for his or her head.

Coach Larry Brown has won more games in the NBA than anyone. He has coached 11 teams and in 2005 coached the NBA champion Detroit Pistons. After winning the NBA Championship, he left Detroit to coach the New York Knicks in an attempt to turn around the Knicks and put them on the winning track once again. His contract with the Knicks was for five years and between $50 and $60 million. Tom Penders is another well-known coach, who is noted for turning around college basketball programs. He coached at the University of Texas, Rhode Island, and Fordham, where he was successful. In 2004 he landed at the University of Houston, where he brought back a winning tradition that earned him a five-year contract. Mike Krzyzewski, Duke's basketball coach, could write his own ticket to coach anywhere he wants. After Bobby Knight was fired by Indiana University, Texas Tech was quick to hire him in an effort to improve its basketball program.

After the Texas Longhorns won the 2005 Rose Bowl, the university promptly awarded their coach, Mack Brown, a ten-year contract extension worth $25 million. Why are college football coaches paid so well? If they are able to get the school to a Bowl Championship Series game, the university will receive a $14 to $17 million payday. Coaches usually receive a larger bonus for getting their team to a bowl game than they do for improving the graduation rates of student-athletes.

Universities have dismissed coaches for what they considered improper behavior that embarrassed the university. Mike Price procured the job of a lifetime at the University of Alabama but never coached a game there. He was dismissed by the university after it was discovered he had engaged in some extracurricular activity. Coach Price sued Time, Inc. and Don Yaeger over an article Yaeger wrote containing allegations of improper behavior and sexual misconduct.[62]

Larry Eustachy, an Iowa State basketball coach, was dismissed from his post after he was photographed at a student party holding a beer can and kissing young women on the cheek. The photograph appeared in the *Des Moines Register*. Eustachy later admitted he had made poor decisions.[63]

Rick Neuheisel's contract was terminated by the University of Washington because the university said he had gambled in violation of his contract and NCAA rules. He sued the University of Washington and the NCAA and received a $4.5 million judgment. The university had argued that Neuheisel's contract allowed him to be fined for acts of dishonesty, and that he had been fined for gambling on NCAA basketball as well as for lying when first questioned by the NCAA.[64] Neuheisel had participated in an NCAA basketball pool and won $25,000.

A college coach is called on to function in many capacities in today's competitive coaching market. He or she has to fill the duties of a coach, recruiter, counselor, radio talk show host, public relations expert, and sometimes an athletic director as well. The following are clauses which might appear in a college coach's contract:

- *Position.* The University agrees to employ Employee as Head Baseball Coach, under the terms and conditions set forth in this Agreement.
- *Employee responsibilities.* Employee agrees to accept employment under the duties of Head Baseball Coach in the Department of Intercollegiate Athletics;
  a. Employee shall devote full effort in faithfully and diligently carrying out the duties of Head Baseball Coach in the Department of Intercollegiate Athletics;
  b. Employee shall actively comply with and support all University rules and regulations;
  c. Employee shall adhere to all applicable rules and regulations of the NCAA, and the established bodies that govern intercollegiate athletics and the University. In the event Employee becomes aware, or has reasonable cause to believe, that violations of these organizations' constitutions, by-laws, interpretations, rules or regulations may have taken place, Employee shall report same promptly to the Director of Intercollegiate Athletics (the "Director");
  d. Employee shall carry out all other Department duties as assigned by the Director; and
  e. Employee shall comply with all applicable laws of the United States and the State of _____ .

---

[62] *Bad Behavior: How He Met His Destiny at a Strip Club,* SPORTS ILLUSTRATED, May 8, 2003. *Also see* Price v. Time, Inc. et al., 2003 WL 23273874 (N.D. Ala. 2003).

[63] Tom Witosky, *Eustachy's Party Behavior Called 'Poor Judgment,'* DES MOINES REGISTER, Apr. 28, 2003.

[64] *Neuheisel Said He Feels Vindicated by Settlement,* ESPN.com, March 8, 2005.

Coaches are usually given incentives to ensure that student-athletes meet certain academic standards. An example follows.

- *Academic expectations.* In the performance of his duties, Employee shall be directly responsible to and under the supervision of the Director. Without limitation of the foregoing, Employee in the performance of his duties shall conduct himself at all times in a manner consistent with his position as an instructor of students. The parties agree that, although this employment contract is sports-related, the primary purposes of the University and this Agreement are educative. Thus, the parties recognize and agree that satisfactory academic performance and normal and ordinary progress toward obtaining a baccalaureate degree by student-athletes participating in the University's intercollegiate athletic programs are of paramount importance. Employee will make every effort to ensure that student-athletes participating in the baseball program graduate. Employee will receive the following performance incentives related to the graduation rate of student-athletes participating in the baseball program or entering the program thereafter who have exhausted their athletic eligibility. If the graduation rate is 75%, Employee shall receive $80,000 in additional compensation. If the graduation rate is 70–74%, Employee shall receive $60,000. If the graduation rate is 65–69%, Employee shall receive $40,000. The University shall pay to Employee any additional compensation earned to adhere to and follow the academic standards and requirements of the University in regard to the recruitment and eligibility of prospective and current student-athletes for the sports program. All academic standards, requirements, and policies of the University shall be observed by the Employee at all times and shall not be compromised or violated at any time.

The following is a standard clause in a coach's contract dealing with termination for cause.

- *Termination by university with cause.* University shall have the right to terminate this Agreement for just cause prior to its normal expiration. The term "just cause" shall include, in addition to and as examples of its normally understood meaning in employment contracts, any of the following:
  - a. Violation by Employee of any of the material provisions of this Agreement not corrected by Employee within twenty (20) days following receipt of notification of such violation from the University.
  - b. Refusal or unwillingness by Employee to perform his duties hereunder in good faith to the best of Employee's abilities.
  - c. Any serious act of misconduct by Employee, including but not limited to an act of dishonesty, theft or misappropriation of University property, moral turpitude, insubordination, or act injuring, abusing, or endangering others.
  - d. A serious or intentional violation of any law, rule, regulation, constitutional provision, by-law, or interpretation of the University, the state of _____, conference, or the NCAA, which violation may, in the sole discretion of the University, reflect adversely upon the University or its athletic program in a material way.
  - e. Any other conduct of Employee seriously and materially prejudicial to the best interests of the University or its athletic program.

All coaches must comply with NCAA regulations. The following provisions deal with a coach's responsibilities for compliance with NCAA regulations.

- *NCAA violations.* Without limitation upon any right or remedy of the institution in the event Employee breaches this Agreement, it is specifically agreed that if the Employee is found to be in violation of NCAA rules and regulations, the Employee shall be subject to disciplinary or corrective action as set forth in the NCAA enforcement procedure. If the Employee is found to have been involved in material or intentional violations of NCAA or Conference rules and regulations, the University may take one or more of the following actions that it deems appropriate: (a) termination of employment for cause; or (b) in accordance with University policies and procedures, suspension for such period of time as the institution shall determine, or other corrective action.

The following is a standard clause giving a coach permission to interview at other universities.

- *University approval prior to negotiation with other schools.* The parties agree that, should another coaching opportunity be present to Employee, or should Employee be interested in another coaching position during the term of this Agreement, Employee must notify the University's Director of Intercollegiate Athletics of such opportunity or interest and permission must be given to Employee by the Director before any discussions can be held by the Employee with the anticipated coaching position principals, which permission shall not be unreasonably withheld.

The major provisions that might be included in a college coach's contract are as follows:

- Position
- Employee responsibilities
- Duration or term of contract
- Renewal provisions
- Compensation and benefits
  - Base salary
  - Postseason compensation
  - Media compensation
  - Shoe, apparel, and equipment contracts
  - Benefits
  - Payments toward enhanced retirement income
  - Housing allowance
  - Courtesy car
  - Spousal travel expenses and family travel budget
  - Country club membership
  - Academic incentives
- Academic expectations for student-athletes
- Collateral opportunities
  - Provisions stating university obligations are primary
  - Provisions stating that NCAA rules, state law, and university policy shall be followed
- Use of university facilities
- Termination by university with cause
- Termination for disability
- Termination by university without cause

- Breach by employee of the contract
- University approval prior to negotiation with other schools

In Case 2-11, *O'Connor v. St. Louis American League Baseball Co.*, a baseball manager was fired for allegedly allowing an opposing player, Napoleon Lajoie, to hit safely so Lajoie would win the 1910 batting race against Ty Cobb. A jury trial found in favor of the manager. The manager had claimed the club breached its contract when they terminated it one year early. O'Connor objected and filed a lawsuit against his former club which he won! The team appealed, and O'Connor won on appeal as well.

CASE 2-11 *O'Connor v. St. Louis American League Baseball Co.*

181 S.W. 1167 (Mo. Ct. App. 1916)

Plaintiff . . . avers that on the _____ day of October, 1909, he and defendant entered into a contract wherein and whereby defendant agreed to employ plaintiff as manager of the St. Louis American League Baseball Club for a period of two years, namely, the years 1910 and 1911, at a salary of $5000 a year. . . . [D]efendant discharged plaintiff and refused to allow him to continue as manager of the Baseball Club. . . . failed and refused to allow plaintiff to continue as manager of the club and, although often requested, has failed and refused and neglected to pay plaintiff the balance of $5000 due him under the terms of the contract[.] [P]laintiff demands judgment for that amount, interest and costs.

. . . [T]hat in the season ending on or about October 15th, 1910, there was keen rivalry in the American League for highest honors in batting average between one Cobb, a player in the League, playing with the team representing the city of Detroit, and one Lajoie, playing with the team representing the city of Cleveland in the League; that the final series between the teams representing the city of Cleveland and defendant was played at Sportsman's Park in the city of St. Louis in October, 1910; that the last two games of the series were played on or about October 9th, 1910, and were played on the same afternoon; that during the playing of these two games and during the season beginning on or about April 15th, 1910, and ending on or about October 15th, 1910, plaintiff was acting as the manager of the players representing the defendant club (the Browns); that plaintiff was desirous of favoring Lajoie, who played the position of second baseman on the Cleveland team, in his contest for batting honors with Cobb of the Detroit team, and to the end that Lajoie might be successful in making the highest average for batting honors in the League and in making a higher percentage than Cobb, unmindful and in disregard and in violation of his duties, plaintiff instructed one Corriden, who played the position of third baseman of the defendant club, to play so far back of his regular and ordinary position as third baseman as to allow Lajoie to make what are known as "base hits," which Lajoie could not and would not have made had it not been for the instructions by plaintiff to Corriden; that as a result of the instructions so given, and as a result of Corriden not playing his ordinary and regular position as third baseman, Lajoie succeeded in the two games so played in making 6 base hits; that the balls so struck by Lajoie were what is known as "bunted" balls and all of the balls so hit by Lajoie could have been properly fielded and Lajoie would not have made the base hits had it not been for the position in which Corriden was so playing under the instructions of plaintiff; that by giving these instructions to Corriden plaintiff violated his contract with defendant and brought the game of professional baseball into disrepute in the city of St. Louis and throughout the country, and because of his unfaithful act under his contract, plaintiff was given his unconditional release from the employment of defendant, and that if plaintiff had a contract with defendant for the playing season of 1911, which defendant denies, the conduct and behavior of plaintiff, as above set out, forfeited his further right to employment by defendant and entitled defendant to dispense with the further services of plaintiff.

. . . . On cross-examination plaintiff was asked as to what took place at the concluding games in which the St. Louis Club played, then playing against the Clevelands. . . . It may be said that plaintiff testified that he knew Lajoie and Cobb, and knew that these two men are supposed to be the best ball players in the country; that in the League, in the season of 1910, Cobb led in the batting and Lajoie was second, the difference between them, however, being a mere fraction. He further testified that he had not given Corriden, who played at third base, any special instructions that day as to where he was to play but that he had given all the members of his club instructions "to play back for Lajoie"; had given these instructions to his whole infield and outfield; had not given Corriden any special instructions, but gave him and the other members of the team these instructions, because of his knowledge of the hard hitting of Lajoie. In brief, plaintiff denied specifically all the charges set out in the answer, declaring that he had played that game of ball the same as any other game of baseball he had ever played in his life; that it was as square a game as he had ever played and he had not given any player any instructions that he ought not to have given to have them play an honest game of baseball; had given them the same instructions as in any other games of baseball that he was ever in; had not had any talk or understanding whatever with Lajoie that day or for that game. In this last he was uncontradicted.

The line of defense on cross-examination of plaintiff was to the end of showing that he had endeavored to favor Lajoie by purposely playing Corriden so far back of the third base that balls from Lajoie could not be fielded, all of which plaintiff denied.

. . . Mr. Byron Bancroft Johnson, president of the American League, testified that he wrote a letter to plaintiff October 11th, 1910, to the effect that his attention had been called by newspaper reports to the Cleveland-St. Louis game played on the preceding Sunday (the 9th); that the papers "boldly assert that the manner in which Lajoie secured his hits made it appear that the players on your team were trying to 'boost' his batting average," and he wanted O'Connor and other named players to submit a statement of the facts and report to him (Johnson) at once. O'Connor and others appeared before Johnson with the result that Johnson recommended to Hedges that he dismiss O'Connor.

Other witnesses for defendant testified to the fact of plaintiff causing Corriden to play some distance back of third base and that Lajoie had "bunted" the balls sent to him so that they fell short of third base and short of where Corriden was playing. The witnesses, however, admitted that they could not tell from the way Lajoie held his bat whether he intended to "bunt" or make a hard hit in any given play.

. . . [T]he burden was upon defendant to prove and establish to the satisfaction of the jury by the preponderance or greater weight of the evidence that plaintiff was desirous of favoring Lajoie to the end that Lajoie might be successful in making the highest average for batting honors and in making a higher average than one Cobb, and that plaintiff instructed one Corriden, who played the position of third baseman for defendant, to play so far back of his regular and ordinary position as third baseman as to allow Lajoie to make base hits, and that Lajoie could not and would not have made these hits had not Corriden played so far back of his ordinary and regular position as third baseman.

. . .The jury returned a verdict in favor of plaintiff for the sum of $5000, judgment following.

. . . [W]e find that the verdict, in so far as it finds there was no legal ground for the discharge of plaintiff, is fully warranted. There is no substantial evidence that plaintiff was desirous of favoring Lajoie in his contest for batting honors over Cobb, or that he, in disregard and in violation of his duties, and to favor Lajoie, instructed Corriden to play so far back of his regular position as to allow Lajoie to make successful hits, and which he could not otherwise

have made. To have sustained these charges, the jury would have had to
act on the vaguest suspicion. It is true that Lajoie "bunted" and that
Corriden, being far back from third base, was not able to handle the
balls so "bunted." But the jury must have found that there was no substantial evidence that plaintiff or anyone else could have anticipated, from his manner of holding his bat, that Lajoie intended to
"bunt" all of them. Even the fact that he did "bunt" the first,
according to the evidence, evidently did not convince the jury that
plaintiff should have anticipated his bunting any others. Failing to
satisfy the jury on this very material point, as we must assume from
the verdict was the case, defendant was bound to fail in its effort to
prove good cause for the discharge of plaintiff.

Source: Courtesy of Westlaw; reprinted with permission.

NOTES AND DISCUSSION QUESTIONS

Contract Law

1. Sports contract disputes can involve many different legal issues. In *Yarde Metals, Inc. v. New England Patriots Ltd. Partnership*, 834 N.E.2d 1233 (Mass. Apt. Ct. 2005), the plaintiff was suing the New England Patriots because its season tickets had been revoked. In its defense, the Patriots asserted that "on October 13, 2002, an individual named Mikel LaCroix," using a ticket from Yarde's account, was "ejected from Gillette Stadium for throwing bottles in the seating section." Mikel LaCroix was a business associate of Yarde and was using the ticket for the game in question. In his defense it was asserted: "LaCroix, along with others, used available women's restrooms to answer the call of nature. These patrons were unimpeded by security guards, but for some unexplained reason, as he left the women's restroom, LaCroix was arrested, removed from the stadium, and charged with the crime of disorderly conduct."

   The court, in finding for the Patriots, stated, "The purchase of a ticket to a sports or enter-tainment event typically creates nothing more than a revocable license."[65] The court further stated, "Although the Patriots labored under an initial misunderstanding as to why Yarde's guest had been ejected, Yarde later informed the Patriots of the restroom incident. The Pa-triots confirmed their decision to revoke the tickets and offered Yarde a refund for the re-maining tickets for the season. While we agree with the two motion judges who have heard motions in this case that the Patriots' response seems harsh, it did not have the effect of di-verting to itself the profits or benefits of the value of the season tickets. We assume that any resale of the tickets would only make the Patriots whole for the revenue it lost from Yarde." If a sports ticket is a revocable license, under what circumstance can a ticket be revoked? Was the Patriots' decision too harsh under the circumstances?

2. In *Fitl v. Strek*, the court found in favor of the plaintiff, awarding him $17,750. The Nebraska Uniform Commercial Code requires the buyer to notify the seller "within a reasonable time after he discovers or should have discovered any breach. . . ." Fitl bought the card on

---

[65] *Yarde Metals*, 834 N.E.2d at 658.

September 20, 1995, but did not give notice to the seller until May 20, 1997. Is that a reasonable period of time? The 1952 Topps Mickey Mantle rookie card has sold at prices as high as $250,000.[66]

Application of Contract Law to Sports

3. Parties can assert many defenses to a breach of contract action. They can assert lack of consideration, that no "meeting of the minds" occurred, or that no valid offer or acceptance existed. "Unclean hands" was asserted successfully in many cases starting in the 1960s.[67] In 2006 an Orange County jury found that Angel Baseball L.P. did not breach its contract with the City of Anaheim when it changed its name to "The Los Angeles Angels of Anaheim." The Angels have a 33-year lease to play their home games in the city-owned stadium in Anaheim, California. The City of Anaheim argued that Angels Baseball, L.P. breached the lease agreement, which intended to identify Anaheim as the city where the Angels played. After the Angels changed their name to include Los Angeles, they were sued by the city of Anaheim over the stadium lease. The Angels franchise history is as follows:

Los Angeles Angels, 1961–1964
California Angels, 1965–1996
Anaheim Angels, 1997–2004
Los Angeles Angels of Anaheim, 2005–present

Anaheim had spent $20 million to renovate the stadium for the Angels. A jury determined that the Angels could keep the geographically confusing name after four hours of deliberation. By a nine to three vote, the jury found that the Angels did not violate the stadium lease that required them to "include the name Anaheim therein." The city had demanded $373 million in damages that it claimed it would lose in media and tourism revenue. During spring training 2005, in a game between the Dodgers and the Angels, the Angels were announced as "the Los Angeles Angels of Anaheim" and the Dodgers as "the Los Angeles Dodgers of Los Angeles." How would you have drafted the lease differently? What ethical concerns does this legal problem present? What obligation should the owner have to the city where the team plays?

4. Do you believe that the plaintiff in *Blackmon v. Iverson* could be successful under the doctrine of promissory estoppel? *Promissory estoppel* is defined as follows: "A promise which the promisor should reasonably expect to induce action or forbearance on the part of the promisee or a third person and which does induce such an action or forbearance is binding if injustice can be avoided only by enforcement of the promise."[68] What other theories of recovery could the plaintiff in *Blackmon v. Iverson* have alleged in an attempt to recover from Iverson? Did Iverson actually make an enforceable promise?

---

[66] *See* http://www.themick.com.
[67] *See* New York Football Giants, Inc. v. Los Angeles Chargers Football Club, Inc., 291 F.2d 471 (5th Cir. 1961).
[68] RESTATEMENT (SECOND) OF CONTRACTS § 90(1).

5. In *Campione v. Adamar of New Jersey, Inc.*, 643 A.2d 42 (N.J. 1993), a casino patron sued the casino on various theories. Campione was a noted "card counter," that is, a player of a certain level of skill "who utilizes information concerning the cards remaining in the shoe to their advantage" in both methods of play and for betting.[69] He alleged, among many things, that the defendant casino violated contract law when it failed to pay him his winning bet of $350. "He further claims this is a breach of an implied contractual duty of the defendant to supply a fair game of chance giving fair odds."[70] The court, in finding that a valid offer and acceptance occurred, stated:

> When Campione placed a bet of $350 on the table after the casino employee had lowered the maximum bet to $100, he presented an offer to the casino. The casino then had the option to reject the offer by informing Campione that he had bet above the limit established for the table, and requesting that he lower his bet to a maximum of $100. No casino employee did so. As a result, when the casino allowed Campione to pursue the hand with his $350 bet, this constituted an acceptance of Campione's offer. Therefore, a binding contract was formed between Campione and the casino, and the casino was obliged to pay Campione the full amount of his winning bet.[71]

6. Pete Rozelle, general manager of the Rams during the negotiations with Billy Cannon, later became the NFL commissioner. Why did Rozelle have Cannon sign contracts prior to his eligibility expiring? Cannon played four seasons with the Houston Oilers, where he led the AFL in rushing in 1961 and played on three AFL Championship teams.

7. For an interesting contract interpretation problem, see *Twin City Fire Insurance Company v. Delaware Racing Association*, 840 A.2d 624 (Del. 2003). Three riders were injured while "breezing" their horses. The insurance company denied coverage on the ground that they were "practicing or participating in horseracing," which was excluded by the insurance policy. The trial court ruled that "breezing" a racehorse does not constitute practicing or participating in horseracing. The insurance company appealed. The policy provided in part:

> Description of Designated "Athletic Activity":

> HORSERACING.

> The policy does not apply to "bodily injury" to any person while practicing or participating in any "Athletic Activity" shown in the above Schedule. For purposes of this endorsement, "Athletic Activity" means physical fitness activity including gym classes or similar activities; or a sports or athletic contest or exhibition that you [the insured] sponsor.[72]

> The issue presented "was the activity in which the breeze riders were engaged in 'horseracing' within the meaning of the above quoted policy exclusion."[73] The Court of Appeals determined that the "breeze activity" was not "participating in horseracing."

---

[69] Campione v. Adamar of New Jersey, Inc., 643 A.2d 42 (N.J. 1993) (quoting Phillip Abram & Joel S. Greenberg, *The Effects of Eliminating the Surrender Rule at the Atlantic City Casinos,* Apr. 28, 1981).

[70] *Campione,* 643 A.2d at 44.

[71] *Id.* at 77.

[72] *Id.* at 626.

[73] *Id.* at 628.

8. In *Machen v. Johnson*, 174 F. Supp. 522 (S.D.N.Y. 1959), the court enjoined the defendant from boxing an opponent until a rematch against the plaintiff was held.

9. All professional sports leagues now require the commissioner to approve player contracts.

10. In many cases dealing with negative injunctions, the issue arises as to whether the player possesses "special, exceptional and unique skill" as a professional athlete. A golfer on the PGA Tour is exceptional because of his golfing talents, but he may not be exceptional or unique when compared with other golfers on the tour. How is it determined whether a player possesses unique athletic qualities? The contract at issue in *Dallas Cowboys Football Club, Inc. v. Harris*, 348 S.W. 2d 37 (Tex. Civ. App. 1961), stated the following:

> 8. The Player hereby represents that he has special, exceptional and unique knowledge, skill and ability as a football player, the loss of which cannot be estimated with any certainty and cannot be fairly or adequately compensated by damages and therefore agrees that the Club shall have the right, in addition to any other rights which the Club may possess, to enjoin him by appropriate injunction proceedings against playing football or engaging in activities related to football for any person, firm, corporation or institution and against any other breach of this contract.

The court stated the rule as follows:

> It is well established in this State and other jurisdictions that injunctive relief will be granted to restrain violation by an employee of negative covenants in a personal service contract if the employee is a person of exceptional and unique knowledge, skill and ability in performing the service called for in the contract.[74]

If anyone would know whether a football player had exceptional skill, it would be coach Tom Landry. He testified as follows:

> Q. Paragraph 8 of the Plaintiff's contract says: 'Player hereby represents he has special, exceptional and unique knowledge and skill and ability as a football player'? A. Well, I think the boy probably represents himself as being unique in that respect. Now, maybe he is not the best judge of his ability. Q. Well, whether or not a man is unique is a matter of opinion, isn't it? A. I think that is probably true as far as forming a conclusion; yes.[75]

The player testified as follows:

> Q. Now, have you looked up to definition of 'unique' in the dictionary? A. No, sir; I haven't. Q. Well, I am reading from the New Century Dictionary here, and it says: 'Of which there is but one, or sole, or only'; Do you think you are the only defensive halfback? A. Not by any means of the imagination. Q. It says, 'Unparalleled, or unequal'—you think you are unparalleled or unequal? A. I wish I were, now. Q. Do you think you are? A. No, sir; I am not. I know my own ability. Q. It says, 'something of which there is only one'; are you the only defensive halfback? A. No. I am not. Q. 'Something without parallel or equal of its kind'; are you that kind of defensive halfback? A. No. I wish I was.[76]

The court found in the club's favor, stating that Harris did have special and exceptional skill.

---

[74] Ibid at p. 42
[75] Ibid at p. 43
[76] Ibid at p. 43

11. Napoleon Lajoie was one of baseball's first superstars. He was inducted to the Hall of Fame in 1937. On May 23, 1901, he became the first player in baseball to be walked with the bases loaded.

> Second baseman Napoleon "Larry" Lajoie combined grace in the field with power at the bat. Renowned for hitting the ball hard, Lajoie topped .300 in 16 of his 21 big league seasons, ten times batting over .350 for a lifetime average of .339. In 1901, making the jump from the Phillies to the Athletics of the new American League, Lajoie dominated the junior circuit. He captured the Triple Crown, led league second basemen in fielding average and batted .422—an American League mark that has yet to be topped.[77]

> For an excellent in-depth discussion of the Lajoie litigation, see Roger I. Abrams, *Legal Bases: Baseball and the Law* (Temple University Press 1998).

The Standard Player Contract

12. What is the purpose of having a standard player contract for all players? What antitrust concerns could this raise? Should star players be able to modify the standard player contract?

13. Many players engage in off-season activities which may in some respects be in breach of their contract. Chicago Bulls point guard Jay Williams was injured in a motorcycle accident in the off-season; the Bulls honored one year of his contract and entered into a settlement agreement for the remaining two years of the contract.

14. All major sports leagues have standard player contracts. They can be located in the Collective Bargaining Agreement of each league.

Bonus and Addendum Clauses to Contracts

15. What is the consideration exchanged between the parties under contract law for a signing bonus? Under what circumstances can a team reclaim a signing bonus from a player? What happens if a player receives a signing bonus but retires the next day?

16. For another case dealing with a request for repayment of a signing bonus, see *Alabama Football, Inc. v. Stabler*, 319 So.2d 678 (Ala. 1975). In that case, the court found in favor of Ken "the Snake" Stabler.

17. For an interesting look at a professional athlete's division of property under a divorce decree, read the court's full opinion in *Loaiza v. Loaiza*, 130 S.W.3d 894 (Tex. Crim. App. 2004). A baseball player's former wife had appealed a lower court's decision dividing the marital assets. She complained he breached his fiduciary duty to her and committed "fraud on the community estate" by doing away with and hiding assets just prior to the divorce. She presented evidence at trial that her former husband had made the following expenditures from the marital estate without her knowledge:

---

[77] National Baseball Hall of Fame and Museum, *Nap Lajoie*, http://www.baseballhalloffame.org.

- $64,732.32 on a Lexus for his girlfriend Ashley.
- Approximately $30,000 in down payments on cars for his girlfriend's sister, mother, and brother.
- $145,809.33 to pay Ashley's medical bills.
- $78,436.56 to Ashley's mother, primarily for child care for his and Ashley's child, but also including $6,548.68 in payments made before the child's birth.
- $75,000 for the option to buy a house he had leased for Ashley and himself.
- $82,550 in payments to his girlfriend's mother.
- $118,745.38 [$70,000 + $48,745.38] in gifts or loans to other members of his girlfriend's family.
- Approximately $145,000 on hotels and airfare for trips that he did not go on, including trips involving Ashley and her family.
- $38,800 on Rolex watches later sold to teammates.
- Approximately $105,500 in checks and cash advances to himself that he could not account for.

It has been aptly stated: "It is well settled in the law that courts look with disfavor upon gifts by the husband to 'strangers' to the marriage, particularly of the female variety."[78]

Guaranteed Contracts

18. Former New England Patriots kicker Adam Vinatieri's 2002 $5.375 million contract was almost completely guaranteed. That is exceptional for a placekicker in the NFL. Do you believe that players maintain a higher level of competition if they do not have a guaranteed contract? Former Yankee Aaron Boone was waived by the team in 2004 after he was injured in a pick-up basketball game. Playing basketball was one of the prohibited activities in his contract that turned his contract into a nonguaranteed contract. The injury cost him approximately $900,000 of his one-year, $5.75 million contract.

19. In *Loaiza v. Loaiza* (Tex. Ct. App. 2004), a divorce case, it was disputed whether a baseball player's contract was guaranteed.

> The contract at issue is comprised of a Uniform Player's Contract (UPC) and an addendum between the Toronto Blue Jays and appellee. The addendum begins by stating that it "shall be deemed to amend and modify any provisions of, or rules or regulations governing, the UPC inconsistent herewith." The UPC contract provides that "[f]or performance of the Player's services and promises hereunder the Club will pay Player the sum of [$]4,000,000.00 (Four Million dollars) for 2001, and $5,800,000.00 (Five Million Eight Hundred Thousand Dollars) for 2002."
>
> Section D of the addendum is entitled "GUARANTEE." Under section D, the "Club and Player agree that Player's base salary for the 2001, and 2002 Major League Championship Seasons is 'guaranteed' in the manner and under the terms and conditions set forth below." The contract goes on to list the circumstances under which the club is relieved of its guarantee to pay appellee's base salary: (a) voluntary retirement;

---

[78] Osuna v. Quintana, 993 S.W.2d 201, 209 (Tex. Civ. App.-Corpus Christi 1999).

(b) labor dispute; (c) placement on any of the lists set out in Major League Rule 15; (d) suspension by the club; (e) intentional self-injury or suicide; (f) use of illegal drugs, misuse of prescription drugs, or alcohol dependency; (g) engaging in any inherently dangerous act or sport (e.g.: skydiving); (h) incapacity due to an allegation that player engaged in a criminal act; (i) HIV or AIDS; and (j) *refusal to render services.* Under section D, the payment is still guaranteed, however, if the "[c]ontract is terminated because Player fails . . . to exhibit sufficient skill or competitive ability to qualify or continue as a member of [the] Club," even in the case of death or physical or mental incapacity incurred on or off the baseball field, before, during, or after the season.

Regardless of the above, the contract provides that the obligation to continue payments beyond the date of termination will cease if the player's death or physical or mental incapacity is due to: (1) intentional self injury; (2) use of illegal drugs, misuse of prescription drugs, or alcohol dependency; (3) engaging in an inherently dangerous act, activity, or sport; (4) the player's own criminal act; or (5) incapacity due to the HIV virus or AIDS. The club also has the right under the addendum to convert the guaranteed contract into a non-guaranteed contract in the event that the club discovers that the player is not in first class physical condition due to the use of illegal drugs, misuse of prescription drugs, or alcohol dependency. Additionally, the player is required to complete physical examinations, by a doctor so the club can obtain insurance on the player. If the player refuses to cooperate with the examinations the guarantee is null and void.[79]

The court in that the contract was non-guaranteed because the player could always refuse to perform under the contract.

Negotiation of Sports Contracts

20. Some players have a good negotiating stance prior to signing a contract. For example, when John Elway was going from Stanford to the NFL, he made it well known that he would not play for the Baltimore Colts. He was drafted by the Colts as the No. 1 pick in the 1983 NFL draft. He announced he would play baseball for the Yankees, so the Colts traded him to the Denver Broncos, where he won two Super Bowls. Steve Francis refused to play for the expansion Vancouver Grizzlies even though he was taken in the first round with the second overall pick of the NBA draft. He was then traded to the Houston Rockets.[80] Eli Manning also used star power to force the San Diego Chargers to trade him to the New York Giants immediately after he was drafted.

Endorsement Contracts

21. For a case involving the interpretation of an endorsement agreement, see *Nike v. Champion*, 25 Fed. Appx. 605 (2002). In that case, Gary Payton, "the Glove," had entered into an exclusive contract with Nike, and the court examined those contractual provisions in conjunction with the National Basketball Player Association's group licensing agreement.

---

[79] Loaiza, supra at p 899.

[80] For further study, see Alex Nyberg Stuart, *This Is Not a Game: Top Sports Agents Share Their Negotiating Secrets,* CFO MAGAZINE, Jan. 1, 2006.

Coaches' Contracts

22. Many contracts provide for a set amount of damages to be awarded to the parties if a breach occurs. Liquidated damages were an issue in *JKC Holding Company, LLC v. Washington Sports Ventures, Inc.*, 264 F.3d 459 (4th Cir. 2001), a case dealing with the purchase of the Washington Redskins. "Liquidated damages provisions are based on the principle of just compensation and may not be used to reap a windfall or to secure performance by the compulsion of disproportion."[81] In *Vanderbilt University v. DiNardo*, 174 F.3d 751 (6th Cir. 1999), Coach DiNardo argued on appeal that the district court erred when it found that a liquidated damage clause did not operate as an unlawful penalty under Tennessee law. The court of appeals found the liquidated damages provision enforceable, but reversed the district court's conclusion that the contract addendum was enforceable as a matter of law.

23. The winner of the 1910 batting race, Case 2-11, *O'Connor v. St. Louis American League Baseball Co.*, was to have received a new automobile, a Chalmers "30," to be donated by Hugh Chalmers, owner of the Chalmers motor car company. Cobb sat out the last two games of the season, stating he had a recurring eye problem that had begun to flare up. (Compare with Ted Williams, who went six for eight in a doubleheader on the last day of the season to finish at .406 in 1941.) He had previously missed a series with Cleveland, Lajoie's team, due to the eye condition. Lajoie needed to have an outstanding finish to the season to beat Cobb for the batting title. On the last day of the season Lajoie played a doubleheader against St. Louis and manager Jack O'Connor. Lajoie went eight for nine in the final two games of the season. How he actually got the hits, which were almost all bunt singles became a disputed point in the O'Connor lawsuit. A well-known sportswriter of the day wrote the following commentary:

> As the world knows now, Tyrus Raymond Cobb is less popular than Napoleon Lajoie. Perhaps Cobb is the least popular player who ever lived. And why? Whether you like or dislike this young fellow, you must concede him one virtue: what he has won, he has taken by might of his own play. He asks no quarter and gives none. Pistareen ball players whom he has "shown up" dislike him. Third basemen with bum arms, second basemen with tender shins, catchers who cannot throw out a talented slider—all despise Cobb. And their attitude has infected the stands. Why do they so resent Cobb when he plays the game at every point on the field, giving his best at every moment, and makes life miserable for those less willing?
>
> Ahhh—one wonders. Here is the best man in all the world at his game, without the shade of doubt; the best of any time. Is it because he is swell-headed? But Cobb is not—he is, indeed, not spoiled at all. He is a gentle, well-mannered youth off the field, full of boyish life and spirits. On the field, he is full of the ebullience of his 24 years and of power and success. Hated why? What player gives the fans so much value for their money?[82]

---

[81] *In re* Coastline Steel Prod., Inc., 93 Misc.2d 255, 402 N.Y.S.2d 947, 950 (Sup.Ct. 1978).
[82] Ty Cobb, My Life in Baseball 98 (University of Nebraska Press 1993).

When the official stats were released, Cobb finished at .384944 and Lajoie at .384084. Research by *Total Baseball, The Ultimate Baseball Encyclopedia* showed that Lajoie actually was the winner at .384 to .383, but Cobb is still listed as the batting champion. In the end, both players were given new cars.

Batting Average[83]

1. Cobb (Detroit)   .383
2. Lajoie (Cleveland)   .384
3. Speaker (Boston)   .340
4. Collins (Philadelphia)   .324
5. Knight (New York)   .312

24. In *Strader v. Collins*, 280 A.D. 582, 586 (N.Y. 1952), the plaintiff was the head football coach of the New York Yankees. He sued the team after he was discharged. The defendant asserted that the coach could no longer perform his duties as head coach due to his physical condition. In finding in favor of the team, the court stated the following:

> In every contract of employment there is an implied condition that the employee will be physically capable of performing his duties at the time appointed. See, Fahey v. Kennedy, 230 App.Div. 156, 243 N.Y.S. 396.
>
> We think that under these circumstances the ultimate issue in the case was the actual physical condition of the plaintiff and his ability in the future to do the work required of him by the contract of employment. As this issue involves proof of a condition precedent implied in the contract, the burden of establishing fulfillment rests with the plaintiff.[84]

25. After reading Case 2-11, *O'Connor v. St. Louis American League Baseball Co.*, 181 S.W. 1167 (Mo. Ct. App. 1916), consider the following scenario: Suppose a manager instructs his pitcher to "groove" a pitch to an opposing player who is retiring at the end of this season. The manager's team is ahead 8–2 in the eighth inning of the game. The opposing player hits a home run, which ignites a rally, and the opposing team wins 9–8. Could the owner of the team terminate the manager's contract under this scenario?

SUGGESTED READINGS AND RESOURCES

Abrams, Roger I. *Legal Bases: Baseball and the Law*. Philadelphia: Temple University Press, 1998.

Cox, R., with Skidmore-Hess, D. *Free Agency and Competitive Balance in Baseball*. Jefferson, NC: McFarland, 2005.

Day, F. *Clubhouse Lawyer: Law in the World of Sports*. New York: iUniverse Star, 2004.

Gorman, J., & Calhoun, K. *The Name of the Game: The Business of Sports*. New York: John Wiley & Sons, 1994.

---

[83] G. Gillette & P. Palmer, The ESPN Baseball Encyclopedia 203 (4th ed. 2007).

[84] *Strader*, 280 A. D. at 586.

Howard, D., & Crompton, J. *Financing Sports*, 2d ed. Morgantown, WV: Fitness Information Technology, 2003.

Kelley, B. *Baseball's Biggest Blunder: The Bonus Rule of 1953–1957*. Lanham, MD: Rowman & Littlefield, 1996.

Quirk, J., & Fort, R. *Pay Dirt: The Business of Professional Team Sports*. Princeton, NJ: Princeton University Press, 1997.

Rosen, F., & Burton, B. *Contract Warriors*. New York: Penguin Group, 2005.

Schaaf, Phil. *Sports, Inc.: 100 Years of Sports Business*. Amherst, NY: Prometheus Books, 2004.

Westerbeek, H., & Smith, A. *Sports Business in the Global Marketplace*. New York: Palgrave Macmillan, 2003.

REFERENCE MATERIALS

Avery, D., & Rosen, J. *Complexity at the Expense of Common Sense? Emerging Trends in Celebrity Endorsement Deals*. 23 ENTERTAINMENT & SPORTS LAW 13 (Summer 2005).

Ballpark Digest, http://www.ballparkwatch.com.

Brazener, Robert A. *Employer's Termination of Professional Athlete's Services as Constituting Breach of Employment Contract*. 57 AMERICAN LAW REPORTS 3d 257 (2006).

Champion, W. T. *Fundamentals of Sports Law*. St. Paul, MN: Thomson/West, 2004.

Del Barba, Brad. *Addendum's for the Minor League Uniform Player Contract*. At The Yard, Jan. 29, 2003.

Devine, James R. *The Legacy of Albert Spalding, the Holdouts of Ty Cobb, Joe DiMaggio, and Sandy Koufax/Don Drysdale, and the 1994–95 Strike: Baseball's Labor Disputes Are as Linear as the Game*. 31 AKRON LAW REVIEW 1 (1997).

Epstein, Adam. *Sports Law*. Clifton Park, NY: Thomson/Delmar Learning, 2003.

Faber, Daniel M. *The Evolution of Techniques for Negotiation of Sports Employment Contracts in the Era of the Agent*. 10 UNIVERSITY OF MIAMI ENTERTAINMENT AND SPORTS LAW REVIEW 165 (Spring 1993).

Givony, Jonathan. *NBA CBA Principal Deal Points, Rookie and Minimum Salaries*. DraftExpress, Aug. 2, 2005, http://www.draftexpress.com.

Greenberg, Martin J. *Drafting of Player Contracts and Clauses*. 4 MARQUETTE SPORTS LAW JOURNAL 51 (Fall 1993).

Greenberg, Martin J. *Representation of College Coaches in Contract Negotiations*. 3 MARQUETTE SPORTS LAW JOURNAL 101 (Fall 2002).

Hansen, Danielle D. *Sports Attorneys and Contracts*. Lawcrossing, 2006, http://www.lawcrossing.com.

Heubeck, T., & Scheuer, J. *Incentive Contracts in Team Sports: Theory and Practice*. University of Hamburg, Germany, Sept. 7, 2002.

Inside the Minds: The Business of Sports—Executives from Major Sports Franchises on How a Team Operates Behind the Scenes. Boston: Aspatore Books, 2004.

Light, Jonathan F. *The Cultural Encyclopedia of Baseball*, 2d ed. Jefferson, NC: McFarland, 2005.

Marshall, Jason R. *Fired in the NBA! Terminating Vin Baker's Contract: A Case-Study in Collective Bargaining, Guaranteed Contracts, Arbitration, and Disability Claims in the NBA*. 12 SPORTS LAWYERS JOURNAL 1 (Spring 2005).

Mitten, M., Davis, T., Smith, R., & Berry, R., *Sports Law and Regulation: Cases, Materials, and Problems*. New York: Aspen, 2005.

Robert, Hillman A. *Principles of Contract Law*. St. Paul, MN: Thomson West, 2004.

Roberts, Gary R. *Interpreting the NFL Player Contract*. 3 MARQUETTE SPORTS LAW JOURNAL 29 (Fall 1992).

Sipusic, David J. *Instant Replay: Upon Further Review, the National Football League's Misguided Approach to the Signing Bonus Should be Overturned*. 8 SPORTS LAWYERS JOURNAL 207 (2001).

Street & Smith's SportsBusiness Journal.

Weiler, Joseph M. *Legal Analysis of the NHL Player's Contract*. 3 MARQUETTE SPORTS LAW JOURNAL 59 (Fall 1992).

C H A P T E R   3

ANTITRUST LAW

The Sherman Antitrust Act has shaped the structure of professional and amateur sports for the last 40 years. It has been used by a variety of entities to effect change in the sports world. Players, colleges and universities, owners, alumni, business owners, and even cheerleaders have attempted to use the antitrust laws to strike down what they perceived to be anticompetitive rules and regulations. Professional sports leagues institute regulations so they can operate smoothly and efficiently. Some of the regulations have been challenged as anticompetitive under the Sherman Antitrust Act. Individual sports have also seen their share of antitrust challenges.

In the 1970s professional athletes began using antitrust laws to challenge restraints such as player drafts, restrictions on player movement, standard player contracts, player corporations, and salary caps. Leagues began to assert the nonstatutory labor exemption as a defense to antitrust lawsuits, arguing that any antitrust lawsuits brought on behalf of players should be dismissed based on labor law. The nonstatutory labor exemption has become an extremely effective tool in the defense of antitrust claims and is discussed fully later in this chapter.

The Sherman Act was passed by Congress in 1890 with the overall goal of protecting fair competition in the marketplace and preventing monopolies. The act exists to promote customer welfare, protect individuals against the corruptive practices of big business, and offer individuals protection from monopolistic and anticompetitive behavior. Starting in the early 1900s, employers in a variety of industries sued under the Sherman Act to prevent unions from organizing.[1] In response, the Clayton Act was passed by Congress in 1914. In 1934, the Norris–LaGuardia Act, 29 U.S.C. §§ 101–105, was enacted because courts had been narrowly construing the scope of union activity that was immune from antitrust liability. The two statutes created a statutory exemption, providing labor unions with immunity from antitrust liability for their efforts to further their members' economic interests.

Because of the unique nature of sports, courts have sought to apply federal antitrust laws in a consistent fashion while addressing individual rules from a variety of leagues. In *St. Louis*

---

[1] Loene v. Lalor, 208 U.S. 274 (1908).

Convention & Visitors Commission v. National Football League, 154 F.3d 851 (8th Cir. 1998), the court discussed antitrust laws in the context of a sports league:

> Section 1 of the Sherman Antitrust act makes it unlawful to form a conspiracy in restraint of trade. 15 U.S.C. § 1. Restraints which have 'pernicious virtue' are illegal per se under Section 1 without inquiry into the reasonableness of the restraint of trade. . . . Analysis of whether a restriction's harm to competition outweighs any procompetitive effects is necessary if the anticompetitive impact of a restraint is less clear or the restraint is necessary for a product to exist at all. . . . Some trade restrictions by sports leagues have been held to fall into this category. . . .[2]

Professional sports teams and organizations are unique under antitrust laws. The court in the seminal case of *Flood v. Kuhn* noted that "[t]he importance of the antitrust laws to every citizen must not be minimalized. They are as important to baseball players as they are to football players, lawyers, doctors, or members of any other class of workers. Baseball players cannot be denied the benefits of competition merely because club owners view other economic interests as being more important. . . ."[3] As in any other business, teams desire to ensure a maximum profit. However, unlike other entities that sell the same product and compete for the same customer base, clubs in professional sports leagues have no desire to drive other member clubs out of the marketplace. All clubs have an interest in ensuring that all teams in the league are competitive ongoing ventures so as to maintain the league's success. Each club depends on the other for success while at the same time competing for an individual customer base. The Detroit Lions of the National Football League clearly have an interest in selling more team merchandise than their division rival, the Chicago Bears, but they have no interest in seeing the Chicago Bears franchise fold. The Lions' success as a franchise is dependent on their competitor's success as well. In describing this unique relationship in the NFL, one federal district court stated:

> [T]he NFL clubs which have 'combined' to implement the draft are not *competitors* in any economic sense. The clubs operate basically as a joint venture in producing an entertainment product—football games and telecasts. No NFL club can produce this product without agreements and joint action with every other team. To this end, the League not only determines franchise locations, playing schedules, and broadcast terms, but also ensures that the clubs receive equal shares of telecast and ticket revenues. These economic joint venturers 'compete' on the playing field, to be sure, but here as well cooperation is essential if the entertainment product is to attain a high quality: only if the teams are 'competitively balanced' will spectator interest be maintained at a high pitch. No NFL team, in short, is interested in driving another team out of business, whether in the counting-house or on the football field, for if the League fails, no one team can survive.[4]

A defendant's business activities or anticompetitive conduct must be connected to interstate commerce to be subject to scrutiny under federal antitrust laws.[5] Under Section 1 antitrust cases, courts are generally looking for an agreement between parties that results in a restraint of trade, whereas Section 2 antitrust cases are concerned with the operations of a monopoly. If Section 1 of the Sherman Act were

---

[2] *St. Louis Convention,* 154 F.3d 851 at 861.
[3] Flood v. Kuhn, 407 U.S. 258, 292 (1972).
[4] Smith v. Pro Football, Inc., 593 F.2d 1173 (D.C. Cir. 1979).
[5] Summit Health, Ltd. v. Pinhas, 500 U.S. 322 (1991).

read literally, it would strike down every contract as illegal.[6] Section 1 of the Sherman Act prohibits agreements and collective action that unreasonably restrain trade:

> Every contract, combination in the form of trust or otherwise, or conspiracy, in restraint of trade or commerce among the several States, or with foreign nations, is declared to be illegal. Every person who shall make any contract or engage in any combination or conspiracy hereby declared to be illegal shall be deemed guilty of a felony, and, on conviction thereof, shall be punished by fine not exceeding $10,000,000 if a corporation or, if any other person, $350,000, or by imprisonment not exceeding three years, or by both said punishments, in the discretion of the court.[7]

A plaintiff must prove three elements for an activity to be deemed in violation of Section 1 of the Sherman Act. It must be proven that "(1) there was an agreement among the league and member teams in restraint of trade; (2) it was injured as a direct and proximate result; and (3) its damages are capable of ascertainment and not speculative."[8]

A plaintiff must show that two or more persons acted in concert to restrain trade.[9] The first requirement of a Section 1 antitrust claim is to prove "concerted activity." Section 1 of the Sherman Act "does not prohibit independent business decisions but only prohibit[s] concerted action."[10] There does not have to be direct evidence of concerted action; it can be inferred from the words and conduct of the parties.[11] The alleged conspiracy must have a unity of purpose or common design and understanding.[12]

Section 2 of the Sherman Act guards against attempted monopolization.[13] Whereas Section 1 requires two or more persons to engage in the illegal activity, Section 2 applies to one or more persons. Section 2 reads as follows:

> Every person who shall monopolize, or attempt to monopolize, or combine or conspire with any other person or persons, to monopolize any part of the trade or commerce among the several States, or with foreign nations, shall be deemed guilty of a felony [and shall be punished].

Every contract can be viewed as a restraint; therefore, the Supreme Court has held that only restraints that are deemed "unreasonable" will be actionable under the Sherman Antitrust Act.[14] In *Chicago Board of Trade v. United States*, 246 U.S. 231 (1918), Justice Louis Brandeis stated the following with regard to antitrust laws:

> Every agreement concerning trade, every regulation of trade, restrains. To bind, to restrain is of their very essence. The true test of legality is whether the restraint imposed is such as merely regulates

---

[6] National Bancard Corporation (NaBanco) v. Visa U.S.A., 779 F.2d 592, 597 (11th Cir. 1986) (citing NCAA v. Board of Regents of University of Louisiana, 468 U.S. 85 (1984)).

[7] 15 U.S.C. § 1.

[8] St. Louis Convention & Visitors Comm'n v. NFL, 154 F.3d 861 (8th Cir. 1998) (citing Admiral Theatre Corp. v. Douglas Theatre, 585 F.2d 877, 883–84 (8th Cir. 1978)).

[9] Brenner v. World Boxing Council, 675 F.2d 445 (1982).

[10] JES Properties, Inc. v. USA Equestrian, Inc., 2005 WL 112665 (M.D. Fla.).

[11] *Id.*

[12] *Id.* (citing Michelman v. Clark–Schwabel Fiber Glass Corp., 534 F.2d 1036, 1043 (2nd Cir.) *cert. denied* 429 U.S. 885 (1976)).

[13] 15 U.S.C. § 2.

[14] NHLPA v. Plymouth Whalers Hockey Club, 419 F.3d 462, 469 (6th Cir. 2005) (citing NCAA v. Bd. of Regents of Univ. of Okla., 468 U.S. 85, 98 (1984)).

and perhaps thereby promotes competition or whether it is such as may suppress or even destroy competition.

Courts have used three standards to evaluate an antitrust problem: rule of reason, per se, and a "quick look" approach. Most sports antitrust problems today are evaluated by the rule of reason standard.[15] Under a rule of reason analysis, the plaintiff must show "significant anticompetitive effects within a relevant market."[16] If the plaintiff is able to meet this burden, then the defendant must present evidence of any procompetitive effect of the restraint justifying the anticompetitive injuries.[17] If the defendant succeeds, the burden then shifts back to the plaintiff to show that any legitimate objectives can be achieved in a substantially less restrictive manner.[18] This test has been described as follows:

> Under the rule of reason, a restraint must be evaluated to determine whether it is significantly anticompetitive in purpose or effect. . . . If, on analysis, the restraint is found to have legitimate business purposes whose realization serves to promote competition, the 'anticompetitive evils' of the challenged practice must be carefully balanced against its 'procompetitive virtues' to ascertain whether the former outweigh the latter. A restraint is unreasonable if it has the 'net effect' of substantially impeding competition.[19]

If an activity is anticompetitive on its face, then it will be deemed a per se violation under the Sherman Act. The per se test is reserved for restraints that have a very clear antitrust effect. It is applied when the challenged restraint is "entirely void of redeeming competitive rationale."[20] Under a per se analysis, the court will not examine the practice's impact on the market or the procompetitive justifications for the restraint.[21] This standard is applied only in clear-cut cases.[22]

In *Eureka Urethane, Inc. v. PBA, Inc.*, 746 F. Supp. 915, 931 (E.D. Mo. 1990), the court summarized the per se rule as follows:

> There are certain business combinations and practices which are so pernicious and devoid of redeeming attributes that they are considered to be unreasonable restraints on interstate or foreign commerce per se. If a party is injured as a result of a per se violation of §1 of the Sherman Act, he need not allege or prove any particular effect or impact of the violation on interstate or foreign commerce; the existence of such an effect or impact is conclusively presumed.

The "quick look" test is applied when the practice has obvious anticompetitive effects, such as price fixing. Under the quick look, it is unnecessary to examine whether the defendant possessed market power.

---

[15] Bryant v. United States Polo Ass'n, 631 F. Supp. 71 (1986).

[16] *Plymouth Whalers*, 419 F.3d at 469.

[17] *Id.*

[18] Worldwide Basketball and Sports Tours, Inc. v. Nat'l Collegiate Athletic Ass'n, 388 F.3d 955, 959 (6th Cir. 2004).

[19] *Smith*, 593 F.2d at 1183.

[20] NHLPA v. Plymouth Whalers Hockey Club, 325 F.3d 712, 718 (6th Cir. 2003).

[21] *Id.*

[22] Continental T.V., Inc. v. GTE Sylvania Inc., 433 U.S. 36, 49–50, (1977).

Case 3-1, *Major League Baseball Properties, Inc. v. Salvino, Inc.,* 2005 WL 3097883 (S.D.N.Y. 2005), is an example of how antitrust laws apply to the business aspects of sports. It deals with antitrust law in the context of the licensing of intellectual property by Major League Baseball. The court determined that the rule of reason was the appropriate standard and found that Major League Baseball did not violate antitrust law when enforcing its intellectual property rights.

CASE 3-1 *Major League Baseball Properties, Inc. v. Salvino, Inc.*

2005 WL 3097883 (S.D.N.Y. 2005)

CASEY, J.

I. Background

. . . MLBP has been the worldwide agent for licensing the use of intellectual property rights owned or controlled by MLB Clubs, the Baseball Office of the Commissioner ("BOC"), and MLBP on retail products. A series of agreements known as the Agency Agreement govern MLBP's operations and relationships with the Clubs. The Agency Agreement distinguishes between products sold at retail and those that Clubs give away as part of a promotion at a game. Retail items—even if they are sold at a concession stand inside a MLB stadium—must be licensed through MLBP. "Giveaways," however, do not require a license from MLBP as long as they do not include the marks of another Club, MLBP, or the BOC. Similarly, Clubs may sell products not licensed by MLBP at stadium concession stands provided the products do not use any marks owned by MLBP or the BOC.

Prior to MLBP's assumption of all licensing responsibility and authority, potential licensees had to approach each Club separately to obtain a license for MLB intellectual property. For example, in 1965, the Houston Astros refused to permit Topps Chewing Gum to make or sell a baseball card with an Astros team photo. Similarly, Coca-Cola did not include MLB Clubs in an "under the cap" promotion it ran in the 1960s because it was "too cumbersome" to obtain licensing rights from each Club individually. MLBP contends that its current organization provides efficient protection, quality control, and design of MLB's intellectual property, as well as efficiencies in promotions, advertising, sales, administration, and licensing operations. Salvino claims there are less restrictive ways to achieve efficient licensing operations.

Between 1989 and 2001, Salvino obtained licenses from MLBP to use MLB intellectual property on baseball figurines. Under the MLBP license agreement signed by Salvino, Salvino promised it would not use the Logos in any manner other than as licensed. . . . In 1998, Salvino began selling plush bean-filled bears known as Bammers. MLBP contends

that Salvino did not request a license to use MLBP intellectual property on the Bammers, but did obtain a license from the MLB Players
Association to use MLB player names on them. Salvino claims it tried
to obtain a license from MLBP to use MLB logos and other intellectual
property on its Bammers. Salvino sold its Bammers to retailers,
including MLB Clubs and stadium concession stands.

Colin Hagen of MLBP assumed responsibility for the Salvino account in
late 1998. He met with Wayne Salvino, Salvino's vice president, to
discuss the possibility of a license for Club trademarks on Bammers in
the spring of 1999. MLBP claims it never received a license application from Salvino. Salvino claims that Wayne Salvino personally delivered a completed license application to Hagen, although it has not
produced a copy of the completed form. Regardless, MLBP did not issue
Salvino a license to use MLB intellectual property on Bammers.

In March 1999, MLBP granted a non-exclusive license to Team Beans to
use certain MLB intellectual property on bean-filled bears. Team Beans
also obtained an exclusive license for the use of Club marks on plush
bears with sewn-on authentic uniforms and a non-exclusive license for
other categories of bears, including bean-filled bears similar to Bammers. MLBP claims Salvino tried to make its Bammers match Club uniforms as much as possible, including, for example, by using color
matches provided in the MLBP Style Guide that Salvino received in conjunction with its previously obtained MLBP licenses. In 2000, Salvino
placed the city or state name across the chest of certain of its Bammers. The parties dispute whether Salvino told Clubs and retailers
that it had an MLBP license for its Bammers.

In October 1999, MLBP learned that Salvino was making and selling Bammers with the Arizona Diamondbacks logo to the Diamondbacks Club store
without a MLBP license. Salvino claims the Diamondbacks ordered these
Bammers. Regardless, MLBP sent a cease-and-desist letter to Salvino
and Salvino responded by filing a lawsuit against MLBP. . . .

II. Discussion

. . . .

B. MLBP's Motion for Summary Judgment on Salvino's Antitrust Claims

Section 1 of the Sherman Act prohibits "[e]very contract, combination
in the form of trust or otherwise, or conspiracy, in restraint of trade
or commerce among the several States." 15 U.S.C. § 1. The Supreme Court
has limited § 1 of the Sherman Act "to prohibit only unreasonable
restraints of trade." Independent conduct falls outside the purview of
this provision. To prove a § 1 violation, a plaintiff must demonstrate:
(1) a combination or some form of concerted action between at least two

legally distinct economic entities that (2) unreasonably restrains trade under a *per se* or rule or reason analysis.

The parties disagree over how the Court should analyze Salvino's Sherman Act claim. MLBP argues that a rule of reason analysis is required. Salvino contends that the per se rule should be applied, but that even a quick look would demonstrate that MLBP's organization places unreasonable restraints on competition. [T]he categories of analysis of anticompetitive effect are less fixed than terms like 'per se,' 'quick look,' and 'rule of reason' tend to make them appear. . . . The essential inquiry remains the same—whether or not the challenged restraint enhances competition.

For conduct to be illegal *per se*, it must fall within the narrow range of behavior that is considered so plainly anti-competitive and so lacking in redeeming pro-competitive value that it is presumed illegal without further examination. . . .

This Court cannot say that the organization of MLBP and its licensing authority is a *per se* violation of § 1 of the Sherman Act. . . . Similarly, this Court finds that MLBP's role in licensing MLB intellectual property is not a naked restraint on trade . . . courts have declined to apply the *per se* rule to sports leagues where cooperation among competitors can under some circumstances have legitimate purposes as well as anticompetitive effects.

Under a rule of reason analysis, which is applied where the economic impact of certain practices is not immediately obvious . . . conduct will be deemed illegal only if it unreasonably restrains competition. . . . The plaintiff bears the burden of demonstrating that the challenged behavior had an actual adverse effect on competition as a whole in the relevant market. Evidence that the plaintiff has been harmed as an individual competitor will not suffice. If the plaintiff meets its burden, the burden shifts to the defendant to offer evidence of the pro-competitive effects of its agreement. The burden then shifts back to the plaintiff to prove that any legitimate competitive benefits offered by the defendant could have been achieved through less restrictive means. Ultimately, the factfinder must engage in a careful weighing of the competitive effects of the agreement—both pro and con—to determine if the effects of the challenged restraint tend to promote or destroy competition.

Under a quick look analysis, the plaintiff is relieved of its initial burden of showing that the challenged restraints have an adverse effect on competition because the anticompetitive effects are obvious. Under an abbreviated or 'quick-look' analysis . . . an observer with even a rudimentary understanding of economics could conclude that the arrangements in question would have an anticompetitive effect on customers and markets. . . . The Court finds, therefore, that the rule of reason is the appropriate review for Salvino's claim.

Accordingly, Salvino bears the initial burden of showing that the challenged action has had an *actual* adverse effect on competition as a whole in the relevant market. The mere fact that Salvino did not receive an MLBP license for its Bammers is not sufficient. Salvino has not offered any evidence of an adverse effect on competition resulting from MLBP's licensing authority. Indeed, Salvino did not respond to MLBP's arguments regarding the rule of reason analysis and instead urged the Court to analyze its claims under the *per se* rule or quick look doctrine, neither of which would require Salvino to make a showing of adverse effect on the market. Further, Salvino does not dispute MLBP's stated increase in MLBP-licensed products since MLBP took over licensing authority for MLB intellectual property. Salvino only takes issue with MLBP's proffered reasons for the increase, i.e., it claims the increase is a product of the "licensing boom" and not a result of MLBP's centralized process.

Where the plaintiff is unable to demonstrate such actual effects . . . it must at least establish that defendants possess the requisite market power and thus the capacity to inhibit competition market-wide. Salvino argues that a showing of market power is unnecessary, and dismisses as immaterial MLBP's attempts to define the relevant market. Salvino cannot escape its burden of demonstrating MLBP's market power in light of its inability to demonstrate an actual adverse effect on competition. The Court finds that Salvino has failed to offer any evidence of MLBP's actual adverse effect on the market or its sufficient market power. Accordingly, Salvino cannot demonstrate under the rule of reason that MLBP places unreasonable restraints on trade. MLBP's motion for summary judgment on Salvino's § 1 Sherman Act claim is granted. . . .

Source: Courtesy of Westlaw; reprinted with permission.

PROFESSIONAL SPORTS

Player Restraints

Starting in the 1970s, professional athletes began using the antitrust laws to challenge restraints instituted by leagues through league rules. Federal antitrust laws have been used to defeat rules instituted by leagues dealing with a player's ability to play for the club of his or her own choosing as well as rules limiting the amount of money a player can earn. All professional sports leagues' collective bargaining agreements (CBAs) contain player movement systems dictating the requirements a player must attain to achieve free agency. Antitrust laws have been used to challenge player restraints; however, not all restraints are illegal—only those that are deemed unreasonable.[23]

---

[23] Standard Oil v. United States, 221 U.S. 1, 31 S.Ct. 502, 55 L.Ed. 619 (1911).

Restraints could be in the form of a specific player movement system dealing with a player's right to market his or her services on the open market to several teams, or a particular rule that may limit a player's salary, such as a salary cap or luxury tax. Restraints can also come in the form of standard player contracts or a draft system of players.[24] Although all players in major sports leagues are required to sign the standard player contract, that contract can be modified to a certain extent. Therefore, the standard player contract cannot be considered a true restraint because if a player has enough negotiating power he can force the team to add addenda to the standard player contract to obtain a more favorable contract. All these restraints and a few others have been challenged by professional players using antitrust laws.

Leagues, players, and clubs have actually agreed to a variety of restraints through the collective bargaining process, including annual player drafts, restrictive player movement systems, salary caps, standard player contracts, and different salaries for players on developmental squads. Even though these are restraints, both parties have agreed to them, after determining they are necessary for the functioning of the league.

Professional leagues and member clubs have asserted that the nonstatutory labor exemption prevents antitrust lawsuits by the players. NFL players challenged the draft and free agency rules on antitrust grounds in the 1970s.[25] Players in the NBA were successful in challenging player restraints on antitrust grounds.[26] Baseball players were unsuccessful in their antitrust challenge against the reserve clause. The United States Supreme Court relied upon the doctrine of stare decisis in upholding baseball's antitrust exemption to antitrust laws.[27]

In one of the first cases involving player restraints, Joe Kapp, a former Most Valuable Player (MVP) in the Canadian Football League, alleged that certain NFL rules violated the antitrust laws and caused his expulsion from the National Football League.[28] Kapp alleged that league tampering rules, the standard player contract, and the NFL's Rozelle Rule were all unreasonable restraints of trade. In defense, the league argued as follows:

> [D]efendants argue that professional league sport activities, such as football, must be distinguished from other kinds of business activities which have been held to be per se antitrust violations; that league sports activities are so unique that the per se rule is inapplicable; that, although club teams compete on the playing field, the clubs are not, and indeed cannot be, competitors with one another in a business way because the very purpose of a professional sports league is to provide reasonably matched teams for field competition to attract and sustain the interest and patronage of the fans; that the success of the league as a joint venture of its clubs depends upon the ability of each club to do this; that, if each member club were allowed by the league to engage in free-for-all competition for the best or better players, then the most strongly financed or otherwise better advantaged clubs would be able to sign up and monopolize the best or better players, leaving only average or mediocre players for the other clubs with the effect of destroying the evenly matched field competition that brings fans to the games.[29]

A jury found in favor of Kapp. On appeal, the Ninth Circuit found in favor of the league.

---

[24] *Smith*, 593 F.2d at 1188 (striking down the NFL draft as an illegal restraint of trade under the Sherman Act).

[25] *Smith*, 593 F.2d; Kapp v. National Football League, 586 F.2d 644 (9th Cir. 1978).

[26] Robertson v. Nat'l Basketball Ass'n, 389 F. Supp. 867 (S.D.N.Y. 1975).

[27] *Flood*, 407 U.S. at 258.

[28] *Kapp*, 586 F.2d 644.

[29] Kapp v. NFL, 390 F. Supp. 79 (N.D. Cal. 1974).

In *Mackey v. NFL*, 543 F.2d 606 (8th Cir. 1976), the NFL's "Rozelle Rule" was challenged by NFL players and determined to be an antitrust violation. The rule stated that when a player's contract ended and he switched teams, the new team was required to compensate the former team by way of draft choices, current players, or cash. If the structure of the transaction could not be worked out between the teams, then the commissioner would make the decision or the award. This system restricted player movement and was challenged in *Mackey* as an antitrust violation. Players have also challenged salary caps as antitrust violations.[30] Salary caps have been instituted by most professional leagues. The National Hockey League instituted a salary cap after the 2004 NHL season was canceled. The National Football League and the National Basketball Association both have salary caps. The NBA's cap has been referred to as a "soft cap."

After *Mackey v. NFL*, players began challenging terms that were in existing CBAs. In *McCourt v. California Sports, Inc.*, 600 F.2d 1193 (6th Cir. 1979), the plaintiff, Dale McCourt, was the Red Wings' leading scorer as a rookie. McCourt was awarded to the Los Angeles Kings as compensation for the Red Wings signing the Kings' goaltender, Rogatien Vachon. The 1976 collective bargaining agreement of the NHL required that an "equalization payment" be made by the signing team to the team losing the player under NHL Bylaw 9A. McCourt refused to play for the Kings and instead filed a lawsuit challenging the restraint as an unreasonable restraint under the Sherman Act. The Sixth Circuit Court for the Federal Court of Appeals found in favor of the NHL, stating:

> [I]t is apparent that the inclusion of the reserve system in the collective bargaining agreement was the product of good faith, arm's-length bargaining, and that what the trial court saw as a failure to negotiate was in fact simply the failure to succeed, after the most intensive negotiations, in keeping an unwanted provision out of the contract. This failure was a part of and not apart from the collective bargaining process, a process which achieved its ultimate objective of an agreement accepted by the parties. . . .
>
> Assuming without deciding that the reserve system incorporated in the collective bargaining agreement was otherwise subject to the antitrust laws, whether the good faith, arm's-length requirement necessary to entitle it to the non-statutory labor exemption from the antitrust laws applies is to be governed by the developed standards of law applicable elsewhere in the field of labor law and as set forth in Mackey, supra. So viewed, the evidence here, as credited by the trial court, compels the conclusion that the reserve system was incorporated in the agreement as a result of good faith, arm's-length bargaining between the parties. As such it is entitled to the exemption. . . .[31]

In another case dealing with player restraint, Case 3-2, *Smith v. Pro Football, Inc.*, 593 F.2d 1173 (D.C. Cir. 1979), the court held that the NFL's draft of college players was in violation of antitrust laws.

James "Yazoo" Smith was an All-American defensive back at the University of Oregon and was drafted by the Washington Redskins in the first round of the 1968 NFL draft. He signed a one-year contract for $50,000, which included a $20,000 signing bonus. In the last game of the 1968 season, he suffered a career-ending neck injury. Washington paid him an additional $19,800, which was the amount he would have received had he played out his option year. Two years later Smith filed a lawsuit alleging that the NFL rookie draft was in violation of antitrust laws. He argued that if not for the draft, he would have received a more lucrative contract from the Redskins. The court in *Smith* found the draft in violation of antitrust laws:

---

[30] Wood v. National Basketball Association, 602 F. Supp. 525 (S.D.N.Y. 1984).
[31] *McCourt*, 600 F.2d at 1203.

📖 CASE 3-2 *Smith v. Pro Football, Inc.*

593 F.2d 1173 (D.C. Cir. 1979)

. . . Confining our inquiry, as we must, to the draft's impact on competitive conditions, we conclude that the draft as it existed in 1968 was an unreasonable restraint of trade. The draft was concededly anticompetitive in purpose. It was severely anticompetitive in effect. It was not shown to have any significant offsetting procompetitive impact in the economic sense. Balancing the draft's anticompetitive evils against its procompetitive virtues, the outcome is plain. The NFL's defense, premised on the assertion that competition for players' services would harm both the football industry and society, are unveiling; there is nothing of procompetitive virtue to balance, because the Rule of Reason does not support a defense based on the assumption that competition itself is unreasonable.

. . . .

. . . Without intimating any view as to the legality of the following procedures, we note there exist significantly less anticompetitive alternatives to the draft system which has been challenged here. The trial judge found that the evidence supported the viability of a player selection system that would permit "more than one team to draft each player, while restricting the number of players any one team might sign." A less anticompetitive draft might permit a college player to negotiate with the team of his choice if the team [that] drafted him failed to make him an acceptable offer. The NFL could also conduct a second draft each year for players who were unable to reach agreement with the team [that] selected them the first time. Most obviously, perhaps, the District Court found that the evidence supported the feasibility of a draft that would run for fewer rounds, applying only to the most talented players and enabling their "average" brethren to negotiate in a "free market." The least restrictive alternative of all, of course, would be for the NFL to eliminate the draft entirely and employ revenue-sharing to equalize the teams' financial resources, a method of preserving "competitive balance" nicely in harmony with the league's self-proclaimed "joint-venture" status.

. . . .

[A] player draft can survive scrutiny under the rule of reason only if it is demonstrated to have positive, economically procompetitive benefits that offset its anticompetitive effects, or, at least, if it is demonstrated to accomplish legitimate business purposes and to have a net anticompetitive effect that is insubstantial. Because the NFL draft as it existed in 1968 had severe anticompetitive effects and no demonstrated procompetitive virtues, we hold that it unreasonably restrained trade in violation of § 1 of The Sherman Act. . . .[32]

Source: Courtesy of Westlaw; reprinted with permission.

In a dissenting opinion in *Smith*, however, Judge MacKinnon argued that the draft was necessary, stating:

In my view, there are compelling reasons why the draft has continued so long without serious challenge. In effect a player draft is *natural* for league sports. Competitive equality among the component teams is an inherent requirement for meaningful sports competition and the survival of a conference or league high school, college, or professional and all of its members. Close rivalries are the backbone of any successful sport. When the NFL established the draft, its objective was to give each team the same fair *opportunity* to be competitive; it sought to achieve a competitive balance among all the League's teams, that is, to "try to equalize the teams." The intended result was to create a situation where each League game would become a closer contest, where spectator interest in the game and the players themselves would be increase[d], where the interesting individual contests would create an interesting League championship race, and where ultimately the teams and their players would benefit from the greater income resulting from the increased fan interest.

. . . .

All major sports, in recognition of the need for competitive balance, have drafts. Hockey and basketball have drafts, and baseball instituted a draft when it became clear from the long domination of the New York Yankees that the farm system was not producing competitive balance. . . .[33]

. . . .

The Rule of Reason and the College Player Draft.

. . . [T]he important consideration is the Effect of the draft. The majority concludes that the draft strips the players of "any real bargaining power," lowers their salaries, and suppresses if not destroys competition for their services. I disagree. The majority opinion and

---

[32] *Smith*, 593 F.2d at 1188–89.
[33] *Id.* at 1197–98.

the trial court only looked at the draft from the players' side and only at a portion of that. As for bargaining power, the operation of the draft also restrains the team from dealing with other players (even though there are exceptions, discussed below). This is particularly true when a team drafts for a position, as the Redskins did in drafting Smith as their first round choice in 1968. The Redskins drafted Smith in the first round to fill a need at the "free safety position." In using their first round draft choice to select a player for that particular position, they practically put all of their eggs in one basket for that year. In selecting Smith, they passed over[,] or did not reach, all other players of nearly equal ability for that position. After the Redskins had exercised their first draft selection, these other players would be chosen by other teams with later picks, and would thus not be available in later rounds. Even if another player was later available, it would be a waste of a valuable draft choice for the Redskins to use any subsequent choice to draft for that same position, since the position needed only one player and the team had other needs to fill as well. That is the way the 1968 player draft went for the Redskins. After they had drafted Smith first to fill that position, the team practically had to sign him if they wanted to fill what they considered was a vital team vacancy. These circumstances gave Smith very substantial bargaining leverage, as his professional negotiating agent frequently reminded the Redskins. Also, a first round draft choice commands considerable publicity in the locality, and the team is under very considerable pressure from its fans to sign the player and thereby put the first-round pick in a uniform. Smith was the beneficiary, as a first round choice, of such public pressure. . . .[34]

Source: Courtesy of Westlaw; reprinted with permission.

Many of the player restraints that once existed are now in effect and found in collective bargaining agreements in a revised form, agreeable to both management and labor. These restraints have now been agreed to by players and management through the collective bargaining process and can no longer be challenged as antitrust violations. Once the parties have agreed to a "restraint" through the collective bargaining process, and the negotiations have in fact taken place in good faith and occurred at arm's length, then the nonstatutory labor exemption prevents a successful antitrust challenge.

The current NFL draft is composed of 7 rounds with 32 teams selecting players, with supplemental draft picks awarded each year to NFL clubs. Prior to 1993 the NFL draft could consist of more than 7 rounds with numerous teams selecting. The reduction of draft rounds creates more free agents. However, statistically, the chances are less than 15% that an undrafted rookie will earn a roster spot on an NFL club. Is it more advantageous for the players' union that the draft be 7 rounds or more than 7 rounds?

---

[34] *Id.* at 1211–12.

In *Wood v. National Basketball Ass'n,* 809 F.2d 954 (2nd Cir. 1987), Leon Wood sued, alleging he had been a victim of the NBA's salary cap because he was offered only the league minimum salary when he entered the NBA draft. A salary cap operates to limit a team's payroll within a league. The salary cap could, under certain circumstances, restrain the amount a particular player could earn in a year. For instance, if a player were a free agent and wanted to play for a certain team, a scenario could exist whereby the team could not afford to sign that player if the team did not have enough money under the salary cap of the league to pay the free agent. Wood asserted that the college draft and the salary cap were in violation of antitrust laws and that the NBA was not shielded by the non-statutory labor exemption. The salary cap had been negotiated by management and labor and became a part of the NBA's collective bargaining agreement, therefore Wood's case was dismissed.

In *Mackey v. National Football League,* 16 NFL players took on the NFL's Rozelle Rule, which had been named after the NFL commissioner, Pete Rozelle. The Mackey case was decided a few years after the first collective bargaining agreement had been entered into in professional sports. It was a significant case in that it analyzed the relationship between antitrust law and labor law in the context of a collective bargaining agreement. The NFL's Rozelle Rule stated:

> Any player, whose contract with a League club has expired, shall thereupon become a free agent and shall no longer be considered a member of the team of that club following the expiration date of such contract. Whenever a player, becoming a free agent in such manner, thereafter signed a contract with a different club in the League, then, unless mutually satisfactory arrangements have been to the former club one or more players, from the Active, Reserve, or Selection List (including future selection choices) of the acquiring club as the Commissioner shall be final and conclusive.[35]

Numerous NFL players challenged the NFL's Rozelle Rule on the basis that the rule kept players' salaries low and prevented players from marketing their services to the highest bidder. Players who were free agents were having difficulty finding teams to sign them to a new contract. It was against that background that *Mackey* was decided. See Case 3-3, *Mackey v. National Football League,* 543 F.2d 606 (8th Cir. 1976) below.

📖 CASE 3-3 *Mackey v. National Football League*

543 F.2d 606 (8th Cir. 1976)

```
LAY, Circuit Judge.

This is an appeal by the National Football League (NFL) . . . from a
district court judgment holding the "Rozelle Rule" to be violative of
the Sherman Act, and enjoining its enforcement.

This action was initiated by a group of present and former NFL play-
ers. . . . Their complaint alleged that the defendants' enforcement of
the Rozelle Rule constituted an illegal combination and conspiracy in
restraint of trade denying professional football players the right to
```

---

[35] NFL Constitution § 12.1(H).

freely contract for their services. Plaintiffs sought injunctive
relief and treble damages.

The district court held that the defendants' enforcement of the Rozelle
Rule constituted a concerted refusal to deal and a group boycott, and
was therefore a per se violation of the Sherman Act. Alternatively, finding
that the evidence offered in support of the clubs' contention that the
Rozelle Rule is necessary to the successful operation of the NFL insufficient to justify the restrictive effects of the Rule, the court concluded that the Rozelle Rule was invalid under the Rule of Reason
standard. Finally, the court rejected the clubs' argument that the
Rozelle Rule was immune from attack under the Sherman Act because it had
been the subject of a collective bargaining agreement between the club
owners and the National Football League Players Association (NFLPA).

The defendants raise two basic issues on this appeal: (1) whether the
so-called labor exemption to the antitrust laws immunizes the NFL's
enforcement of the Rozelle Rule from antitrust liability; and (2) if
not, whether the Rozelle Rule and the manner in which it has been
enforced violate the antitrust laws.

History

The NFL, which began operating in 1920, is an unincorporated association comprised of member clubs which own and operate professional
football teams. It presently enjoys a monopoly over major league professional football in the United States.

. . . The NLRB recognized the NFLPA as a labor organization, and as
the exclusive bargaining representative of all NFL players. Since that
time, the NFLPA and the clubs have engaged in collective bargaining
over various terms and conditions of employment.

Antitrust Issues

We turn, then, to the question of whether the Rozelle Rule, as implemented, violates § 1 of the Sherman Act, which declares illegal "every
contract, combination . . . or conspiracy, in restraint of trade or
commerce among the several States." The district court found the
Rozelle Rule to be a per se violation of the Act. Alternatively, the
court held the Rule to be violative of the Rule of Reason standard.

Per Se Violation

We review next the district court's holding that the Rozelle Rule is
per se violative of the Sherman Act [because it significantly deters
clubs from negotiating with and signing free agents and thus operates
as a group boycott or concerted refusal to deal.]

. . . There is substantial evidence in the record to support the district court's findings as to the effects of the Rozelle Rule. We think, however, that this case presents unusual circumstances rendering it inappropriate to declare the Rozelle Rule illegal per se without undertaking an inquiry into the purported justifications for the Rule.

Rule of Reason

The focus of an inquiry under the Rule of Reason is whether the restraint imposed is justified by legitimate business purposes, and is no more restrictive than necessary.

In defining the restraint on competition for players' services, the district court found that the Rozelle Rule significantly deters clubs from negotiating with and signing free agents; that it acts as a substantial deterrent to players playing out their options and becoming free agents; that it significantly decreases players' bargaining power in contract negotiations; that players are thus denied the right to sell their services in a free and open market; that as a result, the salaries paid by each club are lower than if competitive bidding were allowed to prevail; and that absent the Rozelle Rule, there would be increased movement in interstate commerce of players from one club to another.

We find substantial evidence in the record to support these findings. Witnesses for both sides testified that there would be increased player movement absent the Rozelle Rule. . . .

In support of their contention that the restraints effected by the Rozelle Rule are not unreasonable, the defendants asserted a number of justifications. First, they argued that without the Rozelle Rule, star players would flock to cities having natural advantages such as larger economic bases, winning teams, warmer climates, and greater media opportunities; that competitive balance throughout the League would thus be destroyed; and that the destruction of competitive balance would ultimately lead to diminished spectator interest, franchise failures, and perhaps the demise of the NFL, at least as it operates today. Second, the defendants contended that the Rozelle Rule is necessary to protect the clubs' investment in scouting expenses and player developments costs. Third, they asserted that players must work together for a substantial period of time in order to function effectively as a team; that elimination of the Rozelle Rule would lead to increased player movement and a concomitant reduction in player continuity; and that the quality of play in the NFL would thus suffer, leading to reduced spectator interest, and financial detriment both to the clubs and the players. Conflicting evidence was adduced at trial by both sides with respect to the validity of these asserted justifications.

The district court held the defendants' asserted justifications unavailing. As to the clubs' investment in player development costs, Judge Larson found that these expenses are similar to those incurred by other businesses, and that there is no right to compensation for this type of investment. With respect to player continuity, the court found that elimination of the Rozelle Rule would affect all teams equally in that regard; that it would not lead to a reduction in the quality of play; and that even assuming that it would, that fact would not justify the Rozelle Rule's anticompetitive effects. As to competitive balance and the consequences which would flow from abolition of the Rozelle Rule, Judge Larson found that the existence of the Rozelle Rule has had no material effect on competitive balance in the NFL. Even assuming that the Rule did foster competitive balance, the court found that there were other legal means available to achieve that end e.g., the competition committee, multiple year contracts, and special incentives. The court further concluded that elimination of the Rozelle Rule would have no significant disruptive effects, either immediate or long term, on professional football. In conclusion the court held that the Rozelle Rule was unreasonable in that it was overly broad, unlimited in duration, unaccompanied by procedural safeguards, and employed in conjunction with other anticompetitive practices such as the draft, Standard Player Contract, option clause, and the no-tampering rules.

We agree that the asserted need to recoup player development costs cannot justify the restraints of the Rozelle Rule. That expense is an ordinary cost of doing business and is not peculiar to professional football. Moreover, because of its unlimited duration, the Rozelle Rule is far more restrictive than necessary to fulfill that need.

We agree, in view of the evidence adduced at trial with respect to existing players['] turnover by way of trades, retirements and new players entering the League, that the club owners' arguments respecting player continuity cannot justify the Rozelle Rule. We concur in the district court's conclusion that the possibility of resulting decline in the quality of play would not justify the Rozelle Rule. We do recognize, as did the district court, that the NFL has a strong and unique interest in maintaining competitive balance among its teams. The key issue is thus whether the Rozelle Rule is essential to the maintenance of competitive balance, and is no more restrictive than necessary. The district court answered both of these questions in the negative.

We need not decide whether a system of inter-team compensation for free agents moving to other teams is essential to the maintenance of competitive balance in the NFL. Even if it is, we agree with the district court's conclusion that the Rozelle Rule is significantly

more restrictive than necessary to serve any legitimate purposes it
might have in this regard. First, little concern was manifested at
trial over the free movement of average or below average players.
Only the movement of the better players was urged as being detrimental to football. Yet the Rozelle Rule applies to every NFL player
regardless of his status or ability. Second, the Rozelle Rule is
unlimited in duration. It operates as a perpetual restriction on a
player's ability to sell his services in an open market throughout
his career. Third, the enforcement of the Rozelle Rule is unaccompanied by procedural safeguards. A player has no input into the
process by which fair compensation is determined. Moreover, the
player may be unaware of the precise compensation demanded by his
former team, and that other teams might be interested in him but for
the degree of compensation sought. . . .

In sum, we hold that the Rozelle Rule, as enforced, unreasonably
restrains trade in violation of § 1 of the Sherman Act. . . .

Appeal Dismissed.

Source: Courtesy of Westlaw; reprinted with permission.

Players have also challenged eligibility restrictions dealing with regulations on when they
could become a professional. Former American Basketball Association (ABA) and NBA star
Spencer Haywood challenged the NBA's draft eligibility rule in a case that made it to the U.S.
Supreme Court.[36] The NBA draft rule stated that a player could not enter the NBA draft until four
years after the date of his high school graduation. Haywood had won All-American honors in college and also won an Olympic medal in the 1968 Summer Games. After one year at the University
of Detroit, he signed a contract with the Denver Rockets of the ABA and received Rookie of the
Year honors. Haywood eventually left the Rockets in a contract dispute. He then agreed to a six-year
contract with the Seattle SuperSonics of the NBA. The NBA commissioner disapproved the contract
based on Haywood's ineligibility. Haywood sued, and the Federal District Court found in his favor,
holding the four-year rule as per se illegal as a "group boycott" under the Sherman Antitrust Act.
The ruling in Haywood stated the following:

Section 2.05 of the bylaws of the NBA provides as follows:
　'High School Graduate, etc. A person who has not completed high school or who has completed
high school but has not entered college, shall not be eligible to be drafted or to be a Player until four
years after he has been graduated or four years after his original high school class has been graduated, as
the case may be, nor may the future services of any such person be negotiated or contracted for, or otherwise reserved. Similarly, a person who has entered college but is no longer enrolled, shall not be eligible
to be drafted or to be a Player until the time when he would have first become eligible had he remained

---

[36] Haywood v. National Basketball Ass'n, 401 U.S. 1204 (1971).

enrolled in college. Any negotiations or agreements with any such person during such period shall be null and void and shall confer no rights whatsoever; nor shall a Member violating the provisions of this paragraph be permitted to acquire the rights to the services of such person at any time thereafter.'

Section 6.03, while included in the bylaws as a part of the draft provisions, further defines eligibility for the NBA and reinforces the rule that a player cannot sign with an NBA team prior to four years after the graduation of his high school class. Section 6.03 provides as follows:

'Persons Eligible for Draft. The following classes of persons shall be eligible for the annual draft:

'(a) Students in four-year colleges whose classes are to be graduated during the June following the holding of the draft;

'(b) Students in four-year colleges whose original classes have already been graduated, and who do not choose to exercise remaining collegiate basketball eligibility;

'(c) Students in four-year colleges whose original classes have already been graduated if such students have no remaining collegiate basketball eligibility;

'(d) Persons who become eligible pursuant to the provisions of Section 2.05 of these bylaws.'[37]

The NBA asserted its reasons for the rule:

. . . Three reasons have been suggested for having the four-year college rule. First, the NBA has suggested that it is financially necessary to professional basketball as a business enterprise. It seems clear . . . that this does not provide a basis for exemption from the antitrust laws with regard to group boycotts, unless it qualifies under the [exception]. As discussed earlier, Silver does not exempt the present rules from illegality.

A second reason given by the NBA is that this type of regulation is necessary to guarantee that each prospective professional basketball player will be given the opportunity to complete four years of college prior to beginning his professional basketball career. However commendable this desire may be, this court is not in a position to say that this consideration should override the objective of fostering economic competition which is embodied in the antitrust laws. If such a determination is to be made, it must be made by Congress and not the courts.

Finally, Haywood has suggested that at least one of the reasons for the four-year college rule is that collegiate athletics provides a more efficient and less expensive way of training young professional basketball players than the so-called 'farm team' system, which is the primary alternative. Even if this were true, it would not, of course, provide a basis for antitrust exemption. . . .[38]

The court found in favor of Haywood, stating that the rule constituted a group boycott under the antitrust laws. Do the reasons set forth by the NBA in *Haywood* still exist today? Compare those to the rationale by the league set forth in *Clarett v. National Football League*, Case 3-4 (later in this section).

The current eligibility rule found in the 2005 NBA's CBA states:

---

[37] Denver Rockets v. All–Pro Management, Inc., 325 F. Supp. 1049 (D.C. Cal. 1971).
[38] *Id.* at 1066.

Article X: Player Eligibility and NBA DRAFT

Section 1. Player Eligibility. . . .

(b) A player shall be eligible for selection in the first NBA Draft with respect to which he has satisfied all applicable requirements of Section 1(b)(i) below. . .:

    (i) The player (A) is or will be at least 19 years of age during the calendar year in which the Draft is held, and (B) with respect to a player who is not an international player (defined below), at least one (1) NBA Season has elapsed since the player's graduation from high school (or, if the player did not graduate from high school, since the graduation of the class with which the player would have graduated had he graduated from high school); and

    (ii) (A) The player has graduated from a four-year college or university in the United States (or is to graduate in the calendar year in which the Draft is held) and has no remaining intercollegiate basketball eligibility; or

        (B) The player is attending or previously attended a four-year college or university in the United States, his original class in such college or university has graduated (or is to graduate in the calendar year in which the Draft is held), and he has no remaining intercollegiate basketball eligibility; or

        (C) The player has graduated from high school in the United States, did not enroll in a four-year college or university in the United States, and four calendar years have elapsed since such player's high school graduation; or

        (D) The player did not graduate from high school in the United States, and four calendar years have elapsed since the graduation of the class with which the player would have graduated had he graduated from high school; or

        (E) The player has signed a player contract with a "professional basketball team not in the NBA" (defined below) that is located anywhere in the world, and has rendered services under such contract prior to the Draft; or

        (F) The player has expressed his desire to be selected in the Draft in a writing received by the NBA at least sixty (60) days prior to such Draft (an "Early Entry" player); or

        (G) If the player is an "international player" (defined below), and notwithstanding anything contained in subsections (A) through (F) above:

            (1) The player is or will be twenty-two (22) years of age during the calendar year of the Draft; or

            (2) The player has signed a player contract with a "professional basketball team not in the NBA" (defined below)

that is located in the United States, and has rendered
services under such contract prior to the Draft; or

(3) The player has expressed his desire to be selected in
the Draft in a writing received by the NBA at least
sixty (60) days prior to such Draft (an "Early Entry"
player).

Source: National Basketball Association 2005 Collective Bargaining
Agreement.

Maurice Clarett, a former Ohio State student-athlete, challenged the NFL's eligibility rules on antitrust grounds, claiming they constituted an unreasonable restraint upon his ability to market his services in the NFL. NFL bylaws prohibited member clubs from selecting any college football player through the draft who had not first exhausted all college football eligibility, graduated from college, or been out of high school for three football seasons. In 1990 the NFL had changed the league policy relating to entering the NFL draft by allowing any player who was more than three years out of high school to apply for "special eligibility" to enter its amateur draft. Many college players took advantage of this year and applied for the NFL draft; however, the league would strictly enforce its policy regarding being three years out of high school. Prior to the implementation of that rule, the NFL would typically deny eligibility to anyone who applied who had not completed four years of college.

Maurice Clarett believed he was ready to make the transition to the NFL from Ohio State, but NFL draft eligibility rules prevented him from playing in the NFL. As a freshman he played on the Ohio State National Championship team that went 14–0, culminating in a double-overtime victory over the University of Miami in the Fiesta Bowl. He was awarded for his outstanding play as a freshman when he was voted the best running back in college football by the *Sporting News*. He was also named Big Ten Freshman of the Year. Clarett was six feet tall and 230 pounds, and many teams and scouts indicated they believed he could play in the NFL after his freshman season. Clarett was eventually drafted in the 2005 NFL as the 101st pick in the third round of the NFL draft by the Denver Broncos. He was later released by the Denver Broncos during training camp.

In August of 2003, Clarett requested the NFL grant him a hardship exemption for the 2004 draft under the "special eligibility" application. The NFL denied his application. Clarett eventually filed a federal lawsuit, and the federal district court granted Clarett's motion for summary judgment, which prevented the NFL from refusing his entry into the 2004 NFL draft.[39] The NFL appealed, and the Second Circuit found in favor of the NFL, stating that the nonstatutory labor agreement protected the NFL's eligibility rules.[40] Even though the collective bargaining agreement between the NFL and the Players Association failed to include any specific reference outlining the three-year eligibility rule, the executive director of the NFLPA had given his approval for the draft rules, and that was enough for the court to allow the rule to be shielded by the nonstatutory labor exemption. The Second Circuit did not address the application of the draft rule to the antitrust laws, even though the federal district court did analyze the draft rules pursuant to the antitrust laws.

---

[39] Clarett v. National Football League, Inc., 2003 WL 22469936 (2003).
[40] Clarett v. NFL, 369 F.3d 124 (2nd Cir. 2004).

The following is the complaint filed by Maurice Clarett against the NFL in federal district court in New York. What legal issues can you spot in it? Examine paragraph 31. Do you agree with those particular allegations made by Clarett?

CASE 3-4 *Clarett v. National Football League*

369 F.3d 124 (2nd Cir. 2004)

Civil Action No.: 03-CV-7441, September 23, 2003, 2003 WL 22469936

Jury Trial Demanded

Parties and Jurisdiction

1. Plaintiff Maurice Clarett ("Clarett") is an individual with a primary residence in Youngstown, Ohio.
2. Defendant National Football League, Inc. ("defendant" or "NFL") is an entity doing business and registered to do business in New York, with an office located at 280 Park Avenue, New York, New York 10017.
3. Jurisdiction is founded upon 28 U.S.C. § 1331. Specifically, the federal question arises under the Sherman Act, 15 U.S.C. § 1-3, and the Clayton Act, 15 U.S.C. § 15. . . . .

Trade and Commerce

6. The activities of the defendant, as described in this Complaint, occurred within interstate commerce; had, and continue to have, a substantial effect on interstate trade and commerce; and have unreasonably restrained, and continue to restrain, interstate trade and commerce.

Facts

7. The defendant, a professional football league, engages in various forms of interstate commerce and is subject to federal antitrust laws. The NFL enjoys a monopoly over professional football in the United States.
8. The NFL is a distinct market for professional football for which there are no reasonable substitutes in the United States.
9. The NFL began operating in 1920 as the American Professional Football Association, an unincorporated association comprised of member clubs which owned and operated professional football teams.
10. At present, the NFL is composed of thirty-two (32) separately incorporated clubs in cities throughout the United States. Representatives of each of the clubs form the NFL Management Committee, which performs various administrative functions such as organizing and scheduling games, and promulgating rules.

11. Until 1968, the NFL's operations were unilaterally controlled by the club owners.

12. In 1968, the NLRB recognized the National Football League Players Association ("NFLPA") as a labor organization within the meaning of 29 U.S.C. Section 152(5).

13. In 1993, the NFL Management Committee and the NFLPA negotiated a Collective Bargaining Agreement ("CBA"), which has been extended three times and will not expire until the 2007 season.

14. The NFL bylaws include a rule prohibiting any player who has not completed three college seasons, or is not three years removed from high school graduation, from joining the NFL ("the Rule").

15. The CBA, which comprises 292 pages, 61 articles, appendices from A through N, and 357 sections, does not contain the Rule.

16. The Rule is not the product of bona fide arm's length negotiation between the NFL and the NFLPA.

17. The purpose of the Rule is to perpetuate a system whereby college football serves as an efficient and free farm system for the NFL by preventing potential players from selling their services to the NFL until they have completed three college seasons.

18. Clarett was born on XX/XX/1983 and graduated high school in December 2001.

19. While in high school, Clarett was a member of his school's football team. Among the honors he received was selection as the USA Today Offensive Player of the Year after his senior season, as well as being chosen as "Mr. Football" by the Associated Press. During his high school career, Clarett ran for 4,675 yards and 65 touchdowns.

20. After he graduated from high school, Clarett enrolled in Ohio State University ("OSU").

21. During the 2002–2003 football season, Clarett was a first-year member of the OSU Football Team ("Team").

22. The Team and Clarett enjoyed complete success during the 2002–2003 football season, winning all fourteen of their games, the Fiesta Bowl, and the undisputed national championship.

23. Clarett rushed for over 1,200 yards and scored 18 touchdowns. Among his honors, Clarett was named to several 2003 preseason All-America teams, voted the No. 1 running back in college football by the Sporting News, named a first-team All-Big Ten pick, and was named Big Ten Freshman of the Year.

24. Clarett was interested in entering the 2003 National Football League Draft ("2003 Draft") but was prevented from doing so by the Rule.

25. Representatives of the NFL, including Commissioner Paul Tagliabue, stated publicly that the NFL would not let Clarett enter the 2003 Draft or any draft prior to his senior year at OSU.

26. The NFL is the only major professional sport, unlike baseball, basketball or hockey, which prohibits the drafting of players who have not completed three college seasons or who are not three years removed from high school graduation.

27. As a result of the NFL's position on this issue, Clarett did not de-
    clare himself eligible for the 2003 Draft and re-enrolled at OSU.
28. Clarett is currently enrolled in his second year at Ohio State.
29. Playing football professionally is the only means by which Clarett can
    profit from his athletic ability.
30. There is no other league of professional football that is comparable
    to the NFL.
31. Had Clarett been eligible for the 2003 Draft, it is almost certain
    he would have been selected in the beginning of the First Round and
    would have agreed to a contract and signing bonus worth millions of
    dollars.

Count One

32. Plaintiff hereby incorporates Paragraphs One through Thirty-One as if
    each were set forth in full.
33. The Sherman Act declares illegal, among other things, "every contract,
    combination . . . or conspiracy, in restraint of trade or commerce
    among the several states."
34. The Rule is a per se violation of the Sherman Act.
35. The Rule is a group boycott and a concerted refusal to deal with in-
    dividuals such as Clarett.
36. The Rule substantially burdens competition without advancing any im-
    portant interest of active football players as employees.
37. The restraint the Rule imposes is justified by no legitimate business
    purpose.
38. The Rule is harmful to competition as it provides for a total exclu-
    sion of players who have not completed three college seasons or are not
    three years removed from high school graduation, notwithstanding their
    ability to perform in the market and compete for available positions
    in the league.
39. The Rule is not expressly part of the existing CBA, is not the prod-
    uct of bona fide arms-length negotiation, and is, thus, not subject to
    the nonstatutory labor exemption to the antitrust laws.
40. Moreover, the Rule does not concern wages, hours or other terms and
    conditions of employment and is not a mandatory subject of collective
    bargaining within the meaning of the National Labor Relations Act (29
    U.S.C. § § 151-169).
41. In addition, the direct effect of the Rule is a restraint of amateur
    athletes who were strangers to the collective bargaining process be-
    tween the NFL and NFLPA without advancing any important union goal.
    Thus, the Rule is unlawful.
42. Defendant's actions constitute concerted conduct and an unreasonable
    restraint of trade, in violation of the Sherman Act, 15 U.S.C. § 1 et
    seq. and the Clayton Act, 15 U.S.C. § 15.

43. As a direct result of defendant's unlawful conduct, Clarett has suffered substantial loss and damage.

WHEREFORE plaintiff Maurice Clarett seeks an Order declaring the Rule
unlawful and him eligible for a Supplemental Draft to be held within
10 days from the date of the Order, or eligible for the next year's
draft if a Supplemental Draft is impractical, damages, including lost
income as a result of being declared ineligible for the 2003 Draft,
treble damages and attorney's fees as permissible under the Sherman
and Clayton Acts, together with interest and costs of suit.

Source: Courtesy of Westlaw; reprinted with permission.

The federal district court analyzed the draft rule using antitrust analysis. The NFL argued that Clarett had
failed to carry his burden of proof, and in support of its position argued "the NFL has offered substantial evidence demonstrating that the rule is reasonable and serves legitimate, procompetitive interests. The NFL's evidence confirms, for example, that the eligibility rule is intended in part to reduce the increased likelihood of
injury, and the resulting harm that would be imposed on the NFL clubs and others, due to the fact that until they
reach their early twenties, most players are not sufficiently mature physically and psychologically to endure the
rigors of the high-impact, high visibility world of NFL football. The NFL has supplemented this evidence with
expert testimony confirming that, from a medical standpoint, these concerns are well grounded and that the eligibility rule is quite reasonable."[41]

Clarett argued that the rule did indeed have noncompetitive effects:

D. The Effects of the Rule

The NFL is the only major sport organization that prohibits players
from entering its draft until a prescribed period after high school
graduation. The National Basketball Association, Major League Baseball
and the National Hockey League have no such restrictions. By virtue of
the Rule, the NFL member teams have agreed with one another not to
hire players until three NFL seasons have elapsed since the players
graduated from high school. Because of the NFL teams' concerted
refusal to deal with this segment of the talent pool, these players
are absolutely and unreasonably restricted from competing for positions in the League and are unlawfully delayed or prevented from earning a livelihood in their chosen profession.

By forcing prospective players to wait until three NFL seasons have
elapsed before becoming eligible for its draft, the NFL is able to

---

[41] Memorandum of the National Football League in Opposition to Plaintiff's Motion for Summary Judgment and in
Support of the NFL's Cross–Motion for Summary Judgment Non–Statutory Labor Exemption, Clarett v. National
Football League, Inc., 2003 WL 23220600 (S.D.N.Y. 2003).

maintain a free and efficient "farm" system for developing players. College football acts in effect as a minor league, for which the NFL incurs no expenses. While Major League Baseball teams each spend an average of nine million dollars annually for the minor league system, the NFL teams spend virtually nothing on a player development system; instead, the only such costs incurred by NFL teams are for their scouts, to whom the NCAA grants easy and ready access. Under the current system, NFL teams take no financial risks of investing in players while they are in college. Indeed, if a player suffers an injury while in the NCAA, or does not develop as expected, which reduces his value or renders him unable to play professionally, the NFL teams lose nothing. College football is a willing partner in this cozy arrangement as it generates millions of dollars for the colleges without their having to incur the expense of player salaries. Players who are otherwise able to compete with the best in their profession must bide their time on the farm working for nothing.

For extremely talented players like Maurice Clarett, who are otherwise able to compete for a position at the professional level, there are no comparable options. Not only are members of this segment of the talent pool arbitrarily foreclosed from plying their trade for three seasons, they are also prevented during that time from enjoying the opportunity to reap other financial rewards attendant upon becoming a professional athlete, such as endorsement and appearance income. As one respected sports economist has estimated, valuing the cost of tuition and board and dividing it by the estimated number of hours dedicated to the sport, the median hourly wage for a college football athlete is just $7.69. Moreover, if these players suffer career-ending injury while playing at the college level, their opportunity for financial rewards in football will be forever lost.[42]

Source: Courtesy of Westlaw; reprinted with permission.

The plaintiff also presented to the court a comparison of Maurice Clarett to other NFL players in support of his position:

E. Maurice Clarett Compared to Other NFL Players

Clarett, who is 6 feet tall and weighs 230 pounds, will be about eight weeks shy of his 21st birthday at the start of the 2004 NFL season. In the last few years, there have been several players in the NFL who were as young or younger than Clarett will be at the start of the 2004 NFL season. When the 2000 NFL season began, five players

---

[42] Memorandum of Law in Support of Plaintiff's Motion for Summary Judgment, Clarett v. National Football League, Inc., 2003 WL 23220596 (S.D.N.Y. 2003).

were 21 years old. During the 2001 NFL season, seven NFL players were 21 years old. At the start of the 2002 NFL season, eight NFL players were 20 years old. Clinton Portis, the great running back with the Denver Broncos, turned 21 at the start of the 2002 NFL season. Clarett is as tall or taller and weighs as much or more than NFL running back legends Walter Payton, Barry Sanders, and Gale Sayers when they played football. Of the top 20 rushing leaders after the 5th week of the 2003 NFL season, Clarett weighed as much as or more than 17 of them and was as tall or taller than 15 of them.FN23. In addition, Emmitt Smith, who has rushed for more yards than any player in the history of the NFL, was 20 years old when drafted in 1990, and weighs less and is shorter than Clarett.[43]

Source: Courtesy of Westlaw; reprinted with permission.

FN23. The top 20 rushing leaders after the 5th week of the 2003 NFL season, with their height and weight are: (1) Jamal Lewis, 5'11", 240 lbs.; (2) Stephen Davis, 6'0", 230 lbs.; (3) Ahman Green, 6'0", 217 lbs.; (4) Priest Holmes, 5'9", 213 lbs.; (5) LaDainian Tomlinson, 5'10", 221 lbs.; (6) Clinton Portis, 5'11", 205 lbs.; (7) Deuce McAllister, 6'1", 221 lbs.; (8) Fred Taylor, 6'1", 234; (9) Moe Williams, 6'1", 205 lbs.; (10) Ricky Williams, 5'10", 226 lbs.; (11) Tiki Barber, 5'10", 200 lbs.; (12) William Green, 6'0", 215 lbs.; (13) Shaun Alexander, 5'11", 225 lbs.; (14) Anthony Thomas, 6'2", 228 lbs.; (15) Troy Hambrick, 6'1", 233 lbs.; (16) Garrison Hearst, 5'11", 215 lbs.; (17) Trung Canidate, 5'11", 215 lbs.; (18) Edgerrin James, 6'0", 214 lbs.; (19) Amos Zereoue, 5'8", 212 lbs.; (20) Michael Pittman, 6'0", 218 lbs.

Source: Memorandum of Law in Support of Plaintiff's Motion for Summary Judgment, Clarett v. National Football League, Inc., 2003 WL 23220596 (S.D.N.Y. 2003).

After the federal district court found in favor of Clarett, several college football students declared for the 2005 NFL draft. The most notable was Mike Williams, an All-American wide receiver from the University of Southern California. He would most likely have been picked in the first round of the 2004 NFL draft, but when the NFL prevailed on appeal, Williams was ruled ineligible for the 2004 draft. When he had declared his eligibility for the 2004 NFL draft, he had also retained an agent and received financial benefits based on his athletic ability. The NCAA subsequently declared him ineligible to play at USC. Williams terminated the relationship with his agent and repaid the financial benefits he had received, but the NCAA still declared him ineligible. He was forced to sit out the entire 2004 college football season but was selected as the tenth overall pick in the 2005 NFL draft by the Detroit Lions.

---

[43] *Id.*

Antitrust Exemptions

The law has carved out multiple exemptions to antitrust law. Many regulations and policies of sports would seem to violate antitrust law but are not deemed in violation of the Sherman Act because they fall under certain exemptions. Baseball, for example, has had a longtime historical exemption to antitrust laws. The NFL has several exemptions which in some respects excludes it from antitrust scrutiny. Finally, the nonstatutory labor exemption protects union–management agreements that have been entered into after good-faith bargaining by the parties from any antitrust violations.

Baseball   Baseball is unique in its exemption from antitrust laws. It has been described as a "narrow application of *stare decisis*."[44] Football, basketball, hockey, boxing, professional bowling, golf, tennis, and even wrestling are all subject to antitrust scrutiny. Baseball's exemption, although largely historical, has been kept mostly intact since *Federal Baseball v. National League of Professional Baseball Clubs*, 259 U.S. 200 (1922). In *Federal Baseball*, the U.S. Supreme Court first considered the applicability of the federal antitrust laws to baseball. In that case, Justice Holmes declared that professional baseball was not a business that was involved in interstate commerce.[45] Subsequently, in *Toolson v. New York Yankees*, 346 U.S. 356 (1953), the Supreme Court upheld *Federal Baseball,* stating that any decision that allowed the application of the antitrust laws to baseball should be addressed by the legislature. Conversely, in other cases the Supreme Court has determined that particular sports are subject to antitrust laws, such as basketball in *Robertson v. National Basketball Ass'n.*, 622 F.2d 34 (2nd Cir. 1980), football in *Radivich v. National Football League*, 352 U.S. 445 (1957), and boxing in *United States v. International Boxing Club, Inc.*, 348 U.S. 236 (1955). These sports are all subject to antitrust laws because of business activity occurring in "interstate commerce."

Baseball's exemption from antitrust laws was once again challenged in *Flood v. Kuhn*, 402 US 528 (1972). Prior to the free agency era in sports, all baseball players were bound by a clause in their contract known as the *reserve clause*. The reserve clause essentially stated that teams had the right to unilaterally renew a player's contract following each season. In essence, the reserve clause allowed teams to retain all rights to a player and thereby prevented a player from seeking contract offers from other teams for his services. The club could buy, sell, or trade a player without the player's input into the decision. It was against this background that Curt Flood brought his case to the U.S. Supreme Court in 1972.

Flood was the co-captain of the 1967 World Series champion St. Louis Cardinals and was one of the best center fielders in baseball. He won seven Gold Glove Awards for his outstanding play in center field. In 1968, the cover of *Sports Illustrated* touted Flood as "the best centerfielder in baseball," quite an honor considering Hall of Famer Willie Mays was the center fielder at the time for the San Francisco Giants.

At the beginning of the season, with the reserve clause still in place, Flood had sought a raise from the Cardinals. The Cardinals' owner, August "Cussie" Bush, was well known for quashing attempts at labor organizing at his breweries and had very little sympathy for ballplayers. He did not give Flood the raise he requested. The next season Flood once again asked for a raise and was turned down. In October of 1969, Flood was informed he was being traded to the Philadelphia Phillies as part of a seven-player deal. Even though he was not allowed to refuse the trade, on Christmas Eve 1969 he sent the following letter to Commissioner of Baseball Bowie Kuhn:

---

[44] Flood v. Kuhn, Supra.
[45] *Federal Baseball*, 259 U.S. at 209 (1922).

Dear Mr. Kuhn:

After 12 years in the Major Leagues, I do not feel that I am a piece
of property to be bought and sold irrespective of my wishes. I believe
that any system which produces that result violates my basic rights as
a citizen and is inconsistent to laws of the United States and of the
several states. It is my desire to play baseball in 1970, and I am
capable of playing. I received a contract from the Philadelphia club,
but I believe I have the right to consider offers from other clubs
before making any decision. I therefore request that you make known to
all Major League clubs my feelings in this matter and advise them of
my availability for the 1970 season.

                                        Sincerely,

                                        Curt Flood

Source: Courtesy of www.bizofbaseball.com.

After reading the letter, Kuhn refused Flood's request. Flood refused to play for the Philadelphia ball club, gave up a $90,000-per-year salary, and retired from baseball. Later, Flood did play 13 games for the Washington Senators in 1971 but retired immediately thereafter. On July 16, 1970, Flood filed an antitrust lawsuit challenging the century-old reserve clause. In his case, Case 3-5, *Flood v. Kuhn*, 407 U.S. 258 (1972), before the Supreme Court, Flood argued that *Federal Baseball* and *Toolson* should be overturned and that the reserve clause was in violation of the Sherman Antitrust Act. The court ruled against Flood, upholding baseball's reserve clause.

📖 CASE 3-5 *Flood v. Kuhn*

407 U.S. 258 (1972)

Mr. Justice BLACKMUN delivered the opinion of the Court.

For the third time in 50 years the Court is asked specifically to rule
that professional baseball's reserve system is within the reach of the
federal antitrust laws. . . .

II. The Petitioner

The petitioner, Curtis Charles Flood, born in 1938, began his major
league career in 1956 when he signed a contract with the Cincinnati
Reds for a salary of $4,000 for the season. He had no attorney or
agent to advise him on that occasion. He was traded to the St. Louis
Cardinals before the 1958 season. Flood rose to fame as a center
fielder with the Cardinals during the years 1958–1969. In those 12
seasons he compiled a batting average of .293. His best offensive

season was 1967 when he achieved .335. He was .301 or better in six of the 12 St. Louis years. He participated in the 1964, 1967, and 1968 World Series. He played errorless ball in the field in 1966, and once enjoyed 223 consecutive errorless games. Flood has received seven Golden Glove Awards. He was co-captain of his team from 1965-1969. He ranks among the 10 major league outfielders possessing the highest lifetime fielding averages.

But at the age of 31, in October 1969, Flood was traded to the Philadelphia Phillies of the National League in a multi-player transaction. He was not consulted about the trade. He was informed by telephone and received formal notice only after the deal had been consummated. In December he complained to the Commissioner of Baseball and asked that he be made a free agent and be placed at liberty to strike his own bargain with any other major league team. His request was denied.

Flood then instituted this antitrust suit in January 1970 in federal court for the Southern District of New York. The defendants (although not all were named in each cause of action) were the Commissioner of Baseball, the presidents of the two major leagues, and the 24 major league clubs. In general, the complaint charged violations of the federal antitrust laws and civil rights statutes, violation of state statutes and the common law, and the imposition of a form of peonage and involuntary servitude contrary to the Thirteenth Amendment. . . . Petitioner sought declaratory and injunctive relief and treble damages.

Flood declined to play for Philadelphia in 1970, despite a $100,000 salary offer, and he sat out the year. After the season was concluded, Philadelphia sold its rights to Flood to the Washington Senators. Washington and the petitioner were able to come to terms for 1971 at a salary of $110,000. Flood started the season but, apparently because he was dissatisfied with his performance, he left the Washington club on April 27, early in the campaign. He has not played baseball since then. . . .

IV. The Legal Background

A.

Federal Baseball Club v. National League, 259 U.S. 200 (1922), was a suit for treble damages instituted by a member of the Federal League (Baltimore) against the National and American Leagues and others. The plaintiff obtained a verdict in the trial court, but the Court of Appeals reversed. The main brief filed by the plaintiff with this Court discloses that it was strenuously argued, among other things, that the business in which the defendants were engaged was interstate commerce; that the interstate relationship among the several clubs, located as they were in different States, was predominant; that organized baseball represented an investment of colossal wealth; that it was an engagement in moneymaking; that gate receipts were divided by agreement between the home club and the visiting club; and that the business of baseball was to be distinguished from the mere playing of the game as a sport for physical exercise and diversion. See also 259 U.S., at 201-206. . . .

In the years that followed, baseball continued to be subject to intermittent antitrust attack. The courts, however, rejected these challenges on the authority of *Federal Baseball*. In some cases stress was laid, although unsuccessfully, on new factors such as the development of radio and television with their substantial additional revenues to baseball. For the most part, however, the Holmes opinion was generally and necessarily accepted as controlling authority. . . .

C.

The Court granted certiorari, 345 U.S. 963 (1953), in the *Toolson*, *Kowalski*, and *Corbett* cases, cited in rm 12 and 13 and, by a short per curiam (Warren, C.J., and Black, Frankfurter, Douglas, Jackson, Clark, and Minton, JJ.), affirmed the judgments of the respective courts of appeals in those three cases. *Toolson v. New York Yankees, Inc.*, 346 U.S. 356 (1953). *Federal Baseball* was cited as holding 'that the business of providing public baseball games for profit between clubs of professional baseball players was not within the scope of the federal antitrust laws,' 346 U.S., at 357. . . .

[There are] four reasons for the Court's affirmance of *Toolson* and its companion cases: (a) Congressional awareness for three decades of the Court's ruling in Federal Baseball, coupled with congressional inaction. (b) The fact that baseball was left alone to develop for that period upon the understanding that the reserve system was not subject to existing federal antitrust laws. (c) A reluctance to overrule *Federal Baseball* with consequent retroactive effect. (d) A professed desire that any needed remedy be provided by legislation rather than by court decree. The emphasis in Toolson was on the determination, attributed even to Federal Baseball, that Congress had no intention to include baseball within the reach of the federal antitrust laws. Two Justices (Burton and Reed, JJ.) dissented, stressing the factual aspects, revenue sources, and the absence of an express exemption of organized baseball from the Sherman Act. 346 U.S., at 357. . . .

V.

. . . In view of all this, it seems appropriate now to say that:

1. Professional baseball is a business and it is engaged in interstate commerce.

2. With its reserve system enjoying exemption from the federal antitrust laws, baseball is, in a very distinct sense, an exception and an anomaly. *Federal Baseball* and *Toolson* have become an aberration confined to baseball.

3. Even though others might regard this as 'unrealistic, inconsistent, or illogical,' the aberration is an established one, and one that has been recognized not only in *Federal Baseball* and *Toolson*, but in *Shubert, International Boxing, and Radovich*, as well, a total of five consecutive cases in this Court. It is an aberration that has been with us now for half a century, one heretofore deemed fully entitled to the benefit of stare decisis, and one that has survived the Court's expanding concept of interstate commerce. It rests on a recognition and an acceptance of baseball's unique characteristics and needs.

4. Other professional sports operating interstate—football, boxing, basketball, and, presumably, hockey and golf—are not so exempt.

5. The advent of radio and television, with their consequent increased coverage and additional revenues, has not occasioned an overruling of *Federal Baseball* and *Toolson*.

6. The Court has emphasized that since 1922 baseball, with full and continuing congressional awareness, has been allowed to develop and to expand unhindered by federal legislative action. Remedial legislation has been introduced repeatedly in Congress but none has ever been enacted. The Court, accordingly, has concluded that Congress as yet has had no intention to subject baseball's reserve system to the reach of the antitrust statutes. This, obviously, has been deemed to be something other than mere congressional silence and passivity. . . .

Accordingly, we adhere once again to *Federal Baseball* and *Toolson* and to their application to professional baseball. We adhere also to *International Boxing* and *Radovich* and to their respective applications to professional boxing and professional football. If there is any inconsistency or illogic in all this, it is an inconsistency and illogic of long standing that is to be remedied by the Congress and not by this Court. If we were to act otherwise, we would be withdrawing from the conclusion as to congressional intent made in *Toolson* and from the concerns as to retrospectivity therein expressed. Under these circumstances, there is merit in consistency even though some might claim that beneath that consistency is a layer of inconsistency. . . .

The conclusion we have reached makes it unnecessary for us to consider the respondents' additional argument that the reserve system is a mandatory subject of collective bargaining and that federal labor policy therefore exempts the reserve system from the operation of federal antitrust laws. . . .

And what the Court said in Federal Baseball in 1922 and what it said in Toolson in 1953, we say again here in 1972; the remedy, if any is indicated, is for congressional, and not judicial, action.

The judgment of the Court of Appeals is affirmed.

Judgment affirmed. . . .

This Court's decision in *Federal Baseball Club v. National League*, 259 U.S. 200 (1922), is a derelict in the stream of the law that we, its creator, should remove. Only a romantic view of a rather dismal business account over the last 50 years would keep that derelict in midstream.

Mr. Justice MARSHALL, with whom Mr. Justice BRENNAN joins, dissenting. . . .

Source: Courtesy of Westlaw; reprinted with permission.

Baseball's antitrust exemption has been narrowed by later decisions. In *Piazza v. Major League Baseball*, 831 F. Supp. 420 (E.D. Penn. 1993), the court held that the proposed sale and relocation of a baseball team was not protected by baseball's exemption. The court stated:

Applying these principles of *stare decisis* here, it becomes clear that, before *Flood*, lower courts were bound by both the *rule* of *Federal Baseball* and *Toolson* (that the business of baseball is not interstate commerce and thus not within the Sherman Act) and the *result* of those decisions (that baseball's reserve system is exempt from the antitrust laws). The Court's decision in *Flood*, however, effectively created the circumstance referred to by the Third Circuit as "result stare decisis," from the English system. In *Flood*, the Supreme Court exercised its discretion to invalidate the *rule* of *Federal Baseball* and *Toolson*. Thus no rule from those cases binds the lower courts as a matter of *stare decisis*. The only aspect of *Federal Baseball* and *Toolson* that remains to be followed is the result or disposition based upon the facts there involved, which the Court in *Flood* determined to be the exemption of the reserve system from the antitrust laws. . . .

For these reasons, I conclude that the antitrust exemption created by *Federal Baseball* is limited to baseball's reserve system, and because the parties agree that the reserve system is not at issue in this case, I reject Baseball's argument that it is exempt from antitrust liability in this case.[46]

In examining the prior decisions involving baseball and the antitrust laws, the court found that when the U.S. Supreme Court directly addressed baseball's antitrust exemption, it was only in the context of the reserve clause.

---

[46] *Id.* at 438.

In *Minnesota Twins Partnership v. State*, 592 N.W. 847 (Minn. 1999), a court was called on once again to deal with baseball's antitrust exemption when the league attempted to disband the Minnesota Twins. The court found that the sale and relocation of the Twins was exempted from antitrust scrutiny because it was an integral part of the business of baseball. The court found that the number of teams allowed to compete in the league was a decision that was integral to the game of baseball. The court stated:

> The *Piazza* opinion is a skillful attempt to make sense of the Supreme Court's refusal to overrule *Federal Baseball*, an opinion generally regarded as "not one of Mr. Justice Holmes' happiest days." But *Piazza* ignores what is clear about *Flood*—that the Supreme Court had no intention of overruling *Federal Baseball* or *Toolson* despite acknowledging that professional baseball involves interstate commerce. Although the facts of *Flood* deal only with baseball's reserve system, the Court's conclusion in *Flood* is unequivocal. . . .
>
> As intellectually attractive as the *Piazza* alternative is, we are compelled to accept the paradox the Supreme Court acknowledged in *Flood* when it declined to overrule *Federal Baseball*. . . .
>
> We choose to follow the lead of those courts that conclude the business of professional baseball is exempt from federal antitrust laws. Further, we conclude that the sale and relocation of a baseball franchise, like the reserve clause discussed in Flood, is an integral part of the business of professional baseball and falls within the exemption.[47]

The Curt Flood Act of 1998 was the end result of many bills that had been placed before Congress in an attempt to dismantle with or block baseball's historical antitrust exemption. The act modified the Sherman Antitrust Act to allow Major League Baseball players the same rights and remedies as some other professional athletes. The act allows antitrust challenges only to conduct or agreements by those persons "in the business of organized professional Major League Baseball directly relating to or affecting employment of Major League Baseball players to play baseball at the Major League level."[48] It specifically denies any remedy to a player for terms and conditions of his employment arising out of the collective bargaining process. Furthermore, the act does not affect the application of the nonstatutory labor exemption.[49]

```
Curt Flood Act of 1998 (15 U.S.C. § 27)
```

Section 1. Short Title.

```
This Act may be cited as the "Curt Flood Act of 1998."
```

Section 2. Purpose.

```
It is the purpose of this legislation to state that major league base-
ball players are covered under the antitrust laws (i.e., that major
```

---

[47] *Id*. at 856.
[48] 15 U.S.C. § 526b(a).
[49] 15 U.S.C. § 26b(d)(4).

league baseball players will have the same rights under the antitrust laws as do other professional athletes, e.g., football and basketball players), along with a provision that makes it clear that the passage of this Act does not change the application of the antitrust laws in any other context or with respect to any other person or entity.

Section 3. Application of the Antitrust Laws to Professional Major League Baseball

The Clayton Act (15 U.S.C. §§12 *et seq.*) is amended by adding at the end the following new section:

Sec. 27 (a) Subject to subsections (b) through (d), the conduct, acts, practices, or agreements of persons in the business of organized professional major league baseball directly relating to or affecting employment of major league baseball players to play baseball at the major league level are subject to the antitrust laws if engaged in by the person in any other professional sports business affecting interstate commerce.

(b) No court shall rely on the enactment of this section as a basis for changing the application of the antitrust laws to any conduct, acts, practices, or agreements other than those set forth in subsection (a). This section does not create, permit, or imply a cause of action by which to challenge under the antitrust laws, or otherwise apply the antitrust laws to, any conduct, acts, practices, or agreements that do not directly relate to or affect employment of major league baseball players to play baseball players to play baseball at the major league level.

Source: Courtesy of Westlaw; reprinted with permission.

Nonstatutory Labor Exemption   The U.S. Supreme Court established the nonstatutory labor exemption in *Allen Bradley Co. v. Local Union No. 3, International Brotherhood of Electrical Workers*, 325 U.S. 797, 65 S.Ct. 1533 (1945). The nonstatutory labor exemption flows from the statutory labor exemption and protects from antitrust scrutiny union–management agreements that result from good-faith negotiations. It is based on the premise that the law favors collective bargaining over antitrust laws. One of the more difficult questions that has arisen in this area is the extent management can claim the protection of the nonstatutory labor exemption. What happens if the parties cannot agree during the collective bargaining process as to the terms and conditions of employment? How far does the nonstatutory labor exemption go to protect management from antitrust lawsuits?

The labor exemption will protect management from antitrust challenges even after a CBA has expired. Labor law requires parties to the CBA to maintain the status quo and make efforts to enter into a new agreement until they reach an impasse. Only when there is a total breakdown of negotiations between union and management will an impasse be declared. Strikes or lockouts might follow an impasse. The duty to maintain the status quo expires once an impasse is reached and the employer has bargained in good faith. The employer may then unilaterally impose changes to mandatory subjects of collective bargaining without fear of antitrust scrutiny.

The terms of collective bargaining continue after expiration because labor law requires all parties to maintain the status quo and engage in continued bargaining in an attempt to reach a new agreement until they reach an impasse.[50] This creates an environment that furthers the policy of collective bargaining and hopefully leads to stable labor relations. Sometimes an impasse can be temporary; therefore, the process of collective bargaining is not over until the first impasse occurs.

In *Powell v. National Football League*, 930 F.2d 1293 (8th Cir. 1989) *cert. denied*, 498 U.S. 1040 (1991), the court considered whether the terms of an expired collective bargaining agreement lose their antitrust immunity if the parties reached an impasse in their efforts to negotiate a new agreement. *Powell v. NFL* held that the exemption continues even after the parties have reached an impasse. The federal district court in *Powell* found as follows:

Our reading of the authorities leads us to conclude that the League and the Players have not yet reached the point in negotiations where it would be appropriate to permit an action under the Sherman Act. The district court's impasse standard treats a lawful stage of the collective bargaining process as misconduct by defendants, and in this way conflicts with federal labor laws that establish the collective bargaining process, under the supervision of the National Labor Relations Board, as the method for resolution of labor disputes.

In particular, the federal labor laws provide the opposing parties to a labor dispute with offsetting tools, both economic and legal, through which they may seek resolution of their dispute. A union may choose to strike the employer . . . and the employer may in turn opt to lock out its employees. . . . Further, either side may petition the National Labor Relations Board and seek, for example, a cease-and-desist order prohibiting conduct constituting an unfair labor practice. . . . To now allow the Players to pursue an action for treble damages under the Sherman Act would, we conclude, improperly upset the careful balance established by Congress through the labor law.

. . . After a collective bargaining agreement has expired, an employer is under an obligation to bargain with the union before it may permissibly make any unilateral change in terms and conditions of employment which constitute mandatory subjects of collective bargaining. After impasse, an employer may make unilateral changes that are reasonably comprehended within its pre-impasse proposals.

. . . .

---

[50] National Labor Relations Act § 8(9)(5), (d), 29 U.S.C. § 158 (a)(5), (d) (1982).

. . . Following the expiration of the 1982 Agreement, the challenged
restraints were imposed by the League only after they had been for-
warded in negotiations and subsequently rejected by the Players. The
Players do not contend that these proposals were put forward by the
League in bad faith. We therefore hold that the present lawsuit cannot
be maintained under the Sherman Act. Importantly, this does not entail
that once a union and management enter into collective bargaining,
management is forever exempt from the antitrust laws, and we do not
hold that restraints on player services can never offend the Sherman
Act. We believe, however, that the nonstatutory labor exemption protects agreements conceived in an ongoing collective bargaining relationship from challenges under the antitrust laws. "[N]ational labor
policy should sometimes override antitrust policy," and we believe
that this case presents just such an occasion. . . .

. . . In sum, we hold that the antitrust laws are inapplicable under
the circumstances of this case as the nonstatutory labor exemption
extends beyond impasse. We reverse the order of the district court.
. . .[51]

Source: Courtesy of Westlaw; reprinted with permission.

The only U.S. Supreme Court decision in a sports labor antitrust case is *Brown v. Pro Football Inc.*, 518 U.S. 231 (1996). The *Brown* case dealt with the issue of developmental squad players in the NFL. The developmental squad would consist of first- and second-year NFL players who failed to make the roster but whom teams needed for practice purposes and as possible replacements for injured players. The NFLPA wanted developmental squad contracts to be negotiated in the same manner as NFL player contracts. The NFL had unilaterally created these squads, and instead of engaging in negotiations with the NFLPA about salaries for developmental squad players, the league unilaterally implemented its own salary, starting at $1,000 a week for each player. This salary was well below the minimum salary for roster players. The NFLPA filed an antitrust lawsuit against the NFL over the issue of the developmental players' salaries.

The federal district court found that the labor exemption expired when the collective bargaining agreement expired. The case went to trial in the fall of 1992, and a jury awarded $10 million to 235 developmental squad players. The case was reversed on appeal, holding that the nonstatutory labor exemption protected the league from all antitrust lawsuits brought by players or their representatives relating to conduct that occurred during the collective bargaining process. The players appealed to the U.S. Supreme Court, Case 3-6, *Brown v. Pro Football, Inc.*, 518 U.S. 231 (1996). The United States Supreme Court held that when the league unilaterally imposed a fixed salary for developmental squad players, it was protected from antitrust scrutiny under the nonstatutory labor exemption.

---

[51] *Powell*, 930 F.2d at 1301–04.

CASE 3-6 *Brown v. Pro Football, Inc.*

518 U.S. 231 (1996)

Justice BREYER delivered the opinion of the Court.

The question in this case arises at the intersection of the Nation's labor and antitrust laws. A group of professional football players brought this antitrust suit against football club owners. The club owners had bargained with the players' union over a wage issue until they reached impasse. The owners then had agreed among themselves (but not with the union) to implement the terms of their own last best bargaining offer. The question before us is whether federal labor laws shield such an agreement from antitrust attack. We believe that they do. This Court has previously found in the labor laws an implicit antitrust exemption that applies where needed to make the collective-bargaining process work. Like the Court of Appeals, we conclude that this need makes the exemption applicable in this case.

I.

We can state the relevant facts briefly. In 1987, a collective-bargaining agreement between the National Football League (NFL or League), a group of football clubs, and the NFL Players Association, a labor union, expired. The NFL and the Players Association began to negotiate a new contract. In March 1989, during the negotiations, the NFL adopted Resolution G-2, a plan that would permit each club to establish a "developmental squad" of up to six rookie or "first-year" players who, as free agents, had failed to secure a position on a regular player roster. Squad members would play in practice games and sometimes in regular games as substitutes for injured players. Resolution G-2 provided that the club owners would pay all squad members the same weekly salary.

The next month, April, the NFL presented the developmental squad plan to the Players Association. The NFL proposed a squad player salary of $1,000 per week. The Players Association disagreed. It insisted that the club owners give developmental squad players benefits and protections similar to those provided regular players, and that they leave individual squad members free to negotiate their own salaries.

Two months later, in June, negotiations on the issue of developmental squad salaries reached an impasse. The NFL then unilaterally implemented the developmental squad program by distributing to the clubs a uniform contract that embodied the terms of Resolution G-2 and the $1,000 proposed weekly salary. The League advised club owners that paying

developmental squad players more or less than $1,000 per week would
result in disciplinary action, including the loss of draft choices.

In May 1990, 235 developmental squad players brought this antitrust
suit against the League and its member clubs. The players claimed that
their employers' agreement to pay them a $1,000 weekly salary violated
the Sherman Act. See 15 U.S.C. § 1 (forbidding agreements in restraint
of trade). The Federal District Court denied the employers' claim of
exemption from the antitrust laws; it permitted the case to reach the
jury; and it subsequently entered judgment on a jury treble-damages
award that exceeded $30 million. The NFL and its member clubs appealed.

The Court of Appeals (by a split 2-to-1 vote) reversed. The majority
interpreted the labor laws as "waiv[ing] antitrust liability for
restraints on competition imposed through the collective-bargaining
process, so long as such restraints operate primarily in a labor
market characterized by collective bargaining." 50 F.3d 1041, 1056
(C.A.D.C.1995). The court held, consequently, that the club owners
were immune from antitrust liability. We granted certiorari to review
that determination. Although we do not interpret the exemption as
broadly as did the Appeals Court, we nonetheless find the exemption
applicable, and we affirm that court's immunity conclusion.

II.

The immunity before us rests upon what this Court has called the
"nonstatutory" labor exemption from the antitrust laws. The Court
has implied this exemption from federal labor statutes, which set
forth a national labor policy favoring free and private collective
bargaining, which require good-faith bargaining over wages, hours,
and working conditions, and which delegate related rulemaking and
interpretive authority to the National Labor Relations Board
(Board). . . .

B.

The Government argues that the exemption should terminate at the point
of impasse. After impasse, it says, "employers no longer have a duty
under the labor laws to maintain the status quo," and "are free as a
matter of labor law to negotiate individual arrangements on an interim
basis with the union."

Employers, however, are not completely free at impasse to act independently. The multiemployer bargaining unit ordinarily remains
intact; individual employers cannot withdraw. The duty to bargain
survives; employers must stand ready to resume collective bargaining.
And individual employers can negotiate individual interim agreements

with the union only insofar as those agreements are consistent with "the duty to abide by the results of group bargaining." Regardless, the absence of a legal "duty" to act jointly is not determinative. This Court has implied antitrust immunities that extend beyond statutorily *required* joint action to joint action that a statute "expressly or impliedly allows or assumes must also be immune."

More importantly, the simple "impasse" line would not solve the basic problem we have described above. Labor law permits employers, after impasse, to engage in considerable joint behavior, including joint lockouts and replacement hiring. Indeed, as a general matter, labor law often limits employers to four options at impasse: (1) maintain the status quo, (2) implement their last offer, (3) lock out their workers (and either shut down or hire temporary replacements), or (4) negotiate separate interim agreements with the union. What is to happen if the parties cannot reach an interim agreement? The other alternatives are limited. Uniform employer conduct is likely. Uniformity—at least when accompanied by discussion of the matter—invites antitrust attack. And such attack would ask antitrust courts to decide the lawfulness of activities intimately related to the bargaining process.

The problem is aggravated by the fact that "impasse" is often temporary, it may differ from bargaining only in degree, it may be manipulated by the parties for bargaining purposes, and it may occur several times during the course of a single labor dispute, since the bargaining process is not over when the first impasse is reached. How are employers to discuss future bargaining positions during a temporary impasse? Consider, too, the adverse consequences that flow from failing to guess how an *antitrust* court would later draw the impasse line. Employers who erroneously concluded that impasse had *not* been reached would risk antitrust liability were they collectively to maintain the status quo, while employers who erroneously concluded that impasse *had* occurred would risk unfair labor practice charges for prematurely suspending multiemployer negotiations. . . .

For these reasons, we hold that the implicit ("nonstatutory") antitrust exemption applies to the employer conduct at issue here. That conduct took place during and immediately after a collective-bargaining negotiation. It grew out of, and was directly related to, the lawful operation of the bargaining process. It involved a matter that the parties were required to negotiate collectively. And it concerned only the parties to the collective-bargaining relationship. . . .

The judgment of the Court of Appeals is affirmed. . . .

It is so ordered. . . .

Source: Courtesy of Westlaw; reprinted with permission.

The nonstatutory labor exemption was expanded onto the basketball context in *Caldwell v. American Basketball Ass'n Inc.*, 1991 WL 270473 (S.D.N.Y. 1991). In that case a former basketball player who had been suspended from the league brought an antitrust lawsuit. The issue before the court was whether the suspension flowed from the collective bargaining agreement and was then subject to the nonstatutory labor exemption. The court found that the suspension arose from the CBA and not the particular terms of Caldwell's player contract. On appeal, Caldwell lost at the Second Circuit Court of Appeals, which held that his antitrust claims were barred by the nonstatutory labor exemption.

Sports Broadcasting Exemption   Congress has created various antitrust exemptions for professional football. For instance the NFL and TV networks are allowed to sell a unitary television package. Secondly, "blackouts" for home games in the home territory are also exempted from antitrust scrutiny. Finally, the combined merger of the AFL and NFL draft systems are also exempt as well. The exemption for sports broadcasting reads as follows:

§ 1291. Exemption from antitrust laws of agreements covering the telecasting of sports contests and the combining of professional football leagues

```
The antitrust laws . . . shall not apply to any joint agreement by or
among persons engaging in or conducting the organized professional
team sports of football, baseball, basketball, or hockey, by which any
league of clubs participating in professional football, baseball, bas-
ketball, or hockey contests sells or otherwise transfers all or any
part of the rights of such league's member clubs in the sponsored
telecasting of the games of football, baseball, basketball, or hockey,
as the case may be, engaged in or conducted by such clubs. In addi-
tion, such laws shall not apply to a joint agreement by which the
member clubs of two or more professional football leagues, which are
exempt from income tax under section 501(c)(6) of the Internal Revenue
Code of 1986 [26 U.S.C.A. 501(c)(6)], combine their operations in
expanded single league so exempt from income tax, if such agreement
increases rather than decreases the number of professional football
clubs so operating, and the provisions of which are directly relevant
thereto.[52]
```

League Versus League

There has been much litigation in the antitrust area dealing with disputes between rival leagues. Start-up leagues have sued established leagues, arguing that the practice of the established league constitutes a monopoly and that it is in violation of antitrust laws. The NFL has seen

---

[52] 15 U.S.C. § 1291.

its share of rival leagues appear on the horizon. The World Football League (WFL), the American Football League (AFL), the United States Football League (USFL) and the XFL have all attempted to compete against the NFL. Some had more success than others.

In *American Football League v. National Football League*, 323 F.2d 124 (4th Cir. 1962), the burgeoning American Football League and its franchise owners brought an antitrust action against the owners of the NFL franchises. The court ruled in favor of the NFL finding it was not a monopoly as alleged by the AFL. In 1960 the AFL started with 8 teams. The AFL and the NFL began playing one another in the 1966 Super Bowl. The NFL was thought to be the dominant league; however, the first two Super Bowls were split between the two leagues. The New York Jets, under the leadership of Joe Namath, knocked off the heavily favored Baltimore Colts and their Hall of Fame quarterback, Johnny Unitas, 16–7. The 1967 Super Bowl victory for the Jets was also a victory for the AFL and a major breakthrough for the league. The AFL signed and produced great stars such as George Blanda, Lance Alworth, Daryle "Mad Bomber" Lamonica, Mike Garrett (USC Heisman Trophy winner), Billy Cannon (Heisman Trophy winner), Bubba Smith, George Webster, Len Dawson, Charlie Hennigan, Jan Stenerud, Jim Nance, Babe Parilli, Otis Taylor, Jim Ringo, and Matt Snell, to name a few.

Franchise Relocation

Antitrust laws have also been at issue when franchises relocate. Numerous franchises have been added to professional sports leagues in the last 40 years, while others have relocated. Owners may have different reasons to move a professional sports franchise to a new city. Many cities attempt to lure a professional franchise with the promise of a new facility. Franchises must provide fans with a first-class facility in which to watch the sport. A facility must also provide all the comforts that go along with watching a sport. Gone are the days when a hot dog and a beer were the only choices at the national pastime. Owners must provide fans with a myriad of food and entertainment choices while at the park.

In the NFL, there has been significant franchise movement since 1984:

- Cleveland Browns to the Baltimore Ravens
- Houston Oilers to the Tennessee Titans
- Los Angeles Rams to the St. Louis Rams
- Los Angeles Raiders to the Oakland Raiders
- Baltimore Colts to the Indianapolis Colts
- St. Louis Cardinals to Phoenix Cardinals

The following franchises were added to the NFL since 1995:

- Cleveland Browns (1999)
- Houston Texans (2002)
- Jacksonville Jaguars (1995)
- Carolina Panthers (1995)

In *Los Angeles Memorial Coliseum Commission v. National Football League*, 726 F.2d 1381 (1984), the issue facing the court was whether the Oakland Raiders could move to Los Angeles. After the Raiders' lease expired with the Oakland Coliseum in 1978, the club's managing partner, Al Davis, signed an agreement with Los Angeles Coliseum officials outlining the terms of the Raiders' proposed move to Los Angeles. The Raiders had to overcome Rule 4.3 of Article IV of the NFL Constitution, which stated:

> The League shall have exclusive control of the exhibition of football games by member clubs within the home territory of each member. No member club shall have the right to transfer its franchise or playing site to a different city, either within or outside its home territory, without prior approval by the affirmative vote of three-fourths of the existing member clubs of the League.

Other NFL teams voted 22–0 against the move by the Raiders, with five teams abstaining. The Raiders subsequently filed an antitrust action against the NFL and its member clubs. A jury returned a verdict for the Raiders for $11.55 million in damages, which was trebled because the team was the prevailing party in an antitrust lawsuit. The Ninth Circuit Court of Appeals affirmed the jury's verdict. The court found that the NFL's three-fourths rule was a violation of antitrust law partly based on the fact that the regulation was an unreasonable restraint of trade.

AMATEUR ATHLETICS AND ANTITRUST LAW

Antitrust law has had a major impact on amateur sports as well. Alleged illegal restraints have been challenged at the amateur level as well as at the professional level. (Antitrust law in regard to the NCAA is discussed in Chapter 10.) The same legal analysis is applied for antitrust cases at both levels. The majority of courts have given deference to amateur sports associations to preserve the integrity and character of amateur athletics.

In Case 3-7, *Hairston v. Pacific 10 Conference*, 101 F.3d 1315 (1996), several collegiate athletes sued their conference, alleging antitrust violations after the conference suspended them for recruiting violations.

📖 CASE 3-7 *Hairston v. Pacific 10 Conference*

101 F.3d 1315 (1996)

```
Before: WRIGHT, HALL and TROTT, Circuit Judges.
```

I.

```
Appellants are former and current University of Washington ("UW")
football players. Appellee, the Pacific-10 Conference ("Pac-10"), is
an unincorporated association of ten universities situated in Califor-
nia, Arizona, Oregon and Washington, formed for the purpose of "estab-
lishing an athletic program to be participated in by the members."

On November 5, 1992, the Seattle Times reported that UW's star quar-
terback, Billy Joe Hobert, had received three loans totalling $50,000
from an Idaho businessman. After investigating the allegations, UW
```

officials suspended Hobert and declared him permanently ineligible to play amateur football. One month later, the *Los Angeles Times* published a series of articles alleging that UW's football program had violated several NCAA rules. At this time, UW, in conjunction with Pac-10 officials, began investigating these alleged irregularities.

After conducting an eight-month investigation into the allegations of recruiting improprieties, the Pac-10 placed the UW football team on probation for recruiting violations. The levied sanctions included: (1) a two-year bowl ban covering the 1993 and 1994 seasons; (2) a one-year television revenue ban; (3) a limit of 15 football scholarships each for the 1994-95 and the 1995-96 academic years; (4) a reduction in the number of permissible football recruiting visits from 70 to 35 in 1993-94 and to 40 in 1994-95; and (5) a two-year probationary period.

The imposition of penalties on the UW Huskies devastated both the players and their fans. In an effort to have the sanctions rescinded, appellants filed a complaint against the Pac-10. In their complaint, appellants alleged antitrust violations under Section One of the Sherman Act, 15 U.S.C. § 1, and breach of contract. They argued that the penalties were "grossly disproportionate to the University's violations" and evidence of a conspiracy engineered by UW's Pac-10 competitors to sideline UW's football program and thereby improve their own records and odds of winning a post-season bowl game berth. Besides injunctive relief appellants also sought damages, which would include the cost of air fare, lodging, meals and expenses related to a trip to play in a post-season bowl game.

IV.

Section 1 of the Sherman Act prohibits "[e]very contract, combination . . . or conspiracy, in restraint of trade or commerce among the several States[.] . . ."15 U.S.C. § 1. In order to establish a claim under Section 1, the players must demonstrate: "(1) that there was a contract, combination, or conspiracy; (2) that the agreement unreasonably restrained trade under either a per se rule of illegality or a rule of reason analysis; and (3) that the restraint affected interstate commerce."

The first and third elements of this test are not at issue. The Pac-10 members' agreement to sanction UW fulfills the "contract, combination, or conspiracy" prong.

Under the rule of reason, the fact-finder examines the restraint at issue and determines whether the restraint's harm to competition outweighs the restraint's procompetitive effects. The plaintiff bears the initial burden of showing that the restraint produces significant anticompetitive effects within the relevant product and geographic markets. If the plaintiff meets this burden, the defendant must come forward with evidence of the restraint's procompetitive effects. The plaintiff must then show that "any legitimate objectives can be achieved in a substantially less restrictive manner."

Here, the plaintiffs met their initial burden by showing that the Pac-10 members banned UW from participating in bowl games for two years. The Pac-10 replied with evidence showing that there are significant procompetitive effects of punishing football programs that violate the Pac-10's amateurism rules. The burden then returned to the athletes to show that the Pac-10's procompetitive objectives could be achieved in a substantially less restrictive manner. The players' burden of proof at the summary judgment stage of the proceedings was not high; all they had to do was present more than a "mere scintilla of evidence to support [their] case."

The athletes claim that the Pac-10's penalties were grossly disproportionate to UW's violations. However, they do not offer even the thinnest reed of support for this proposition. They point to the testimony of Robert Aronson, a law professor at the University of Washington, who analyzed the sanctions imposed against the UW compared to sanctions imposed against similar institutions. Aronson, however, testified that the penalties were within the range of appropriate penalties. The players also claim that the NCAA's report on the Pac-10's sanctions concludes that the penalties were disproportionate. It does not. The report actually states that the Pac-10's penalties were too lenient, not that they were too harsh. In short, the athletes have presented no evidence that would allow a jury to find in their favor. Hence summary judgment was proper.

VI.

Appellants have failed to show that the penalties the Pac-10 imposed constituted an unreasonable restraint of trade.

Source: Courtesy of Westlaw; reprinted with permission.

MISCELLANEOUS ANTITRUST ISSUES

Antitrust laws have been applied to many sports. In *Elliott v. United Center*, 126 F.3d 1003 (7th Cir. 1997), a regulation that prohibited fans from entering an area with food that was purchased outside the arena was challenged. Independent peanut vendors sued, claiming the center monopolized the market for food sales at and around the arena in violation of the Sherman Act. The court disagreed, ruling that the United Center's rule did not violate antitrust law. In *Fieldturf Inc. v. Southwest*

Recreational Industries, Inc., 235 F. Supp. 2d 708 (E.D. Ky. 2002), a company that manufactured Astroturf sued its competitors on antitrust grounds, but the court found that the plaintiff failed to establish the existence of a monopoly. One of the significant issues in addressing an antitrust problem is defining the relevant geographic and product market. The broader a market is defined, the smaller the market share will be for the entity alleged to be monopolizing.

There have been many antitrust lawsuits dealing with equipment use. In *In re Baseball Bat Antitrust Litigation*, 75 F. Supp. 2d 1189 (D. Kan. 1999), a manufacturer of wooden baseball bats sued a manufacturer of aluminum bats. The court held that no antitrust injury was present. In *Eureka Urethane, Inc. v. PBA, Inc.*, 746 F. Supp. 915 (E.D. Mo. 1990), a manufacturer of bowling balls brought an antitrust action against a bowling association when the association refused to sanction one of its balls for tournament play. The defendant, the Professional Bowlers Association (PBA), refused to allow the plaintiff to manufacture the "Bud Ball." The plaintiff had obtained a license from Anheuser Busch for the use of the Budweiser bow tie logo. The bow tie was placed on a bowling ball colored in Budweiser red. PBA rules stated the following:

Rule VII, Section A [before any bowler can use any new equipment in PBA competition it must have PBA clearance].

Rule VII, Section E [prohibits logos on bowling balls other than the original under which they were manufactured].

Rule XI, Section I and J [before any bowler can avail himself of an incentive offer, the offer must have PBA approval].

Rule XVIII, Section D [proscribes speech by PBA bowlers during interviews of the name of a commercial organization or product unless it relates to the tournament's title sponsor].

Rule XX, Section A [logos competitive with a title sponsor are precluded from appearing on a player's shirt].

Source: Courtesy of Westlaw.

The court granted summary judgment in favor of the defendant, finding that the association did not engage in anticompetitive behavior when it prohibited the use of the ball.

Case 3-8, *Gunter Harz Sports, Inc. v. U.S. Tennis Ass'n, Inc.*, 665 F.2d 222 (8th Cir. 1981), deals with the use of certain tennis rackets in tournament play.

📖 CASE 3-8 *Gunter Harz Sports, Inc. v. U.S. Tennis Ass'n, Inc.*

665 F.2d 222 (8th Cir. 1981)

PER CURIAM.

This matter involves a rule of the United States Tennis Association (USTA) which effectively prohibits the use of a certain tennis racket in sanctioned tournaments. The manufacturer of the racket, Harz Sports, brought an antitrust action against the USTA. The district court ruled that the USTA is subject to the Sherman Act but, following a trial on the merits, found no antitrust violation, 511 F.Supp. 1103. We affirm.

The district court applied a thorough rule of reason analysis. Briefly, the court found that the USTA legitimately functions as a private, nonprofit regulating body to ensure that competitive tennis is conducted in an orderly fashion and to preserve the essential character of the game as played in organized competition. USTA regulation of racket characteristics is rationally related to these goals. Moreover, the court found that the particular rule at issue here does not extend beyond what is necessary to further such goals and provides adequate procedural safeguards to protect against arbitrary enforcement of the rule. These findings have substantial support in the record and we find no merit in the contrary assertions by Harz Sports.

The USTA does not dispute the district court's findings, but contends that it should not be subject to the antitrust laws in the first instance. The International Tennis Federation, as amicus curiae, similarly argues against judicial involvement absent evidence of "extraordinary anticompetitive animus." We cannot agree. Antitrust regulation is proper when, as here, an association wields enormous economic clout by virtue of its exclusive control over the conduct of a major sport. See Mackey v. National Football League, 543 F.2d 606 (8th Cir. 1976), cert. denied, 434 U.S. 801, 98 S.Ct. 28, 54 L.Ed.2d 59 (1977). Nonprofit amateur sports associations also have been subject to antitrust regulation. When an athletic association's action serves to protect fair competition in the game and does not involve improper collusion with commercial interests or "an agreement with business competitors in the traditional sense," courts have followed a rule of reason approach. Id. . . .

Source: Courtesy of Westlaw; reprinted with permission.

NOTES AND DISCUSSION QUESTIONS

Professional Sports

1. In *Salvino v. MLBPA, supra,* Case 3-1, why did the court select the rule of reason standard instead of the per se standard argued by the plaintiffs? What procompetitive effects did the MLBPA's expert note? Do you agree with the expert's opinions?
2. How does the application of antitrust law differ within the context of the sports world? How does it differ with regard to professional versus amateur sports?
3. In *CHA-CAR, Inc. v. Calder Race Course, Inc.,* 752 F.2d 609 (1985), the court was trying to determine whether to apply the rule of reason analysis or a per se standard. A race track

owner allowed a limited number of stalls to horses that the owner determined to be the best horses. The plaintiffs were thoroughbred racehorse trainers who were competing for spaces at the defendant's track. The trainers sued, alleging the defendant's practice of assigning stall space to favored competitors of the plaintiffs was a violation of Section 1 of the Sherman Act. The court found in favor of the defendant owners, stating, "the conduct in the instant case might well be [a] legitimate business decision."[53] They found that some horses would be denied a stall and some trainers would suffer economic harm no matter how the allocation was made.[54]

4. In *John v. American Contract Bridge League*, 2004 WL 392930, the plaintiff sued the defendant on a variety of legal theories, including the claim that the defendant engaged in a group boycott under Section 1 of the Sherman Act. The plaintiff was a professional bridge player who was suspended from sanctioned bridge play for 4 months by the defendant's ethical oversight committee. After an investigation, the committee found that the plaintiff had violated bridge rules. The plaintiff appealed his suspension through an administrative process, and his punishment was increased to 18 months. The court found that the defendant was entitled to summary judgment on plaintiff's claims under the Sherman Act. The plaintiff had argued that the court should apply the per se rule, citing *Blalock v. Ladies Professional Colt Ass'n*, 359 F. Supp. 1260, 1265-66 (N.D. GA 1973). The court, in finding in favor of the defendant, stated:

> Since *Blalock* was decided, the Supreme Court and the circuits have analyzed such cases involving restrictions in sports and other competitive leagues under the rule of reason. When the trade allegedly being restrained concerns a competitive sport, the Court has recognized, the *per se* rule creates problems because the competition would be impossible without collective agreements among competitors about the rules of the competition and enforcement of those rules.[55]

Compare with *Bridge Corp. of America v. American Contract Bridge League*, 428 F.2d 1365 (9th Cir. 1970), which applies the rule of reason to a plaintiff's claim that the defendant refused to sanction a tournament using a new scoring computer.

5. Would you consider a professional draft an unreasonable restraint of trade? If so, why does every professional league have a draft? Do you believe the drafts fulfill the purpose as set forth in *Smith v. Pro Football*? Is it true that if no draft existed, all draftees would want to play for the New York Yankees, Los Angeles Lakers, or the Detroit Red Wings?

6. What is the rationale behind baseball's exemption from antitrust law? How has baseball's exemption been narrowed since *Flood v. Kuhn*? What was the historical basis for the exemption?

7. Each NFL team has a "practice squad" consisting of eight players. A player can only be on a practice squad for two years and then must make an NFL roster to keep playing in the league.

8. The AFL argued that the NFL's expansion into Minneapolis and Dallas was part of an illegal effort on the part of NFL owners to obtain a monopoly over professional football.

---

[53] *CHA–CAR*, 752 F.2d at 614.
[54] *Id.*
[55] *Id.* at 7.

The Fourth Circuit found that the AFL had not proven its case. It found that the AFL failed to show that the NFL did not possess the power to monopolize the relevant market and that if the NFL did have any form of a monopoly, it was a natural monopoly. The AFL Dallas franchise moved to Kansas City in 1963. The Dallas Texans won the 1963 AFL Championship game in overtime against the Houston Oilers, 20–17. The Kansas City Chiefs were the first AFL team in the Super Bowl, losing to the Green Bay Packers, 35–14.

9. The former United States Football League also sued the NFL on antitrust grounds. Although the USFL did win a jury verdict in the amount of $1 (which was tripled to $3 under antitrust law), the court found that the NFL's success over the USFL was due to the poor management of the USFL and was not totally the result of antitrust violations on the part of the NFL.

10. *Zimmerman v. National Football League*, 632 F. Supp. 398 (D.D.C. 1986) involved a supplemental draft of the NFL. Zimmerman alleged that the supplemental draft violated Section 1 of the Sherman Act because it forced him to negotiate with only one NFL team. Zimmerman was selected in the first round of the June 5 NFL supplemental draft by the New York Giants. The NFL's supplemental draft was a "response to the USFL's rapid emergence as a viable competitor to the NFL for the services of college football players preparing to enter the professional ranks."[56] Zimmerman had signed a contract with a USFL team. The court, in reliance upon *Mackey v. NFL*, found in favor of the NFL:

> We come then to the final prong of the *Mackey* test and what both parties have recognized as the crucial issue of this case: Whether the agreement was the product of *bona fide,* arm's length bargaining between the parties. This analysis denies the labor exemption to anticompetitive agreements imposed unilaterally by one party, usually management, without regard to the interests of the other. Protecting such agreements would not further the congressional policy favoring collective bargaining. Plaintiff seeks to show that the supplemental draft was unilaterally imposed by the NFL on a weak union and that the characterization of the conversations between Upshaw and Donlan as "bargaining" involving other disputed issues such as roster size was simply a charade, designed by counsel after the fact to immunize the supplemental draft from antitrust challenge.[57]

> In sum, the Court finds that the agreement to allow a supplemental draft in 1984 satisfies all prongs of the *Mackey* test. The defendants cannot be liable under the antitrust laws for the effects of that agreement.[58]

11. Golf has been relatively free of antitrust challenges. The PGA Tour was formed in 1968 as a nonprofit organization. There is no union for professional golfers; therefore, golf has been able to stay away from labor strikes, lockouts, and intense labor negotiations. For further study, see Charles R. Daniel II, *The PGA Tour: Successful Self-Regulation or Unreasonably Restraining Trade?* 4 SPORTS LAWYERS JOURNAL (Spring 1997).

---

[56] *Zimmerman*, 632 F. Supp. at 401.
[57] *Id.* at 406.
[58] *Id.* at 408.

Harry Toscano, a senior professional golfer, brought an action against the Professional Golfers Association (PGA) and other defendants alleging that the PGA used its media rights and events rules to prevent a competing senior golf tour from being formed.[59] The question presented was whether the plaintiff had standing to sue on antitrust grounds. The Senior PGA Tour sponsors golf tournaments for players older than 50 years. The Senior PGA Tour rules prevented tour members from participating in nontour events that were scheduled on the same day as a Senior PGA event unless they obtained a written release from the tour commissioner. The court found that the plaintiff's alleged injuries were not sufficient to allow standing to bring a claim against the PGA on the basis that its rules were anticompetitive.

12. Is the restriction on 18-year-olds in the NBA an antitrust violation? If so, how? What defenses can be asserted in its defense? Noted American basketball broadcaster, Dick Vitale, questioned the purpose of the 19-year age limit in the NBA:

> I find it mind-boggling that the people in charge of the NBA and NCAA can't come up with a logical system that benefits everyone. There should be a way for a phenom like LeBron James (and potentially a Greg Oden) to get a chance to play at the NBA level when he's ready. . . .
>
> We need some sanity. College helps you mature as a person. Staying in school allows you to be a kid and not deal with the day-to-day pressure of pro basketball until you become better-prepared.
>
> With the addition of the NBA's 19-year-old age minimum, I don't see a major change from the current state of the game. Big deal—it will look good that the NBA isn't taking kids straight out of the high school ranks. Now, though, more high schoolers might enroll in prep schools for a postgraduate year before joining the pros.
>
> The NBA is all about ego, ego, ego. Some kids who stayed in the draft don't get it. They aren't ready, and it's really sad. Just look at the product we see on the court today; it isn't what it used to be.

Could a plaintiff contest the age requirements for the NBA on antitrust grounds? The league now requires a potential player to be at least 19 years old before he can enter the NBA draft. Are the arguments for the age requirement different from other sports? For a scholarly examination of this issue, see Nicholas E. Wurth, *The Legality of an Age-Requirement in the National Basketball League After the Second Circuit's Decision in* Clarrett v. NFL, 3 DePaul J. Sports Law & Contemporary Problems 103 (Summer 2005).

13. Even though Flood lost his antitrust challenge at the Supreme Court, baseball players were able to achieve free agency status through labor arbitration. It could be argued that Curt Flood is one of the reasons baseball players enjoy the large salaries they do today. He took a chance in challenging the reserve clause, and it essentially ended his baseball playing days. Flood, a native Houstonian, passed away in 1997.

14. Some leagues have attempted to gain immunity under Section 1 of the Sherman Act by structuring the league as a single entity with owners investing in the league and not the team. The single-entity defense for sports leagues has been rejected in several cases.[60]

---

[59] New York Cent. R. Co. v. U.S., 201 F. Supp. 1106 (D.C.N.Y. 1962).
[60] Sullivan v. NFL, 34 F.3d 1091 (1st Cir. 1994); *Smith*, 593 F.2d 1173.

In Los Angeles Memorial Coliseum Com'n v. NFL, Spencer Williams, district judge, concurring in part and dissenting in part, stated:

> . . . I conclude that the N.F.L. is, as a matter of law, a single entity insofar as this aspect of its operations is concerned, and not subject to the strictures of Sherman Act § 1. . . .

> . . .The N.F.L. cannot truly be separated from its member clubs, which are simultaneously franchisees and franchisors. The Raiders did not, and do not now, seek to compete with the other clubs in any sense other than in their win/loss standings; they do not challenge the plethora of other ancillary regulations attendant to the league structure, including the draft, regulation and scheduling of meetings between teams, and the system of pooled and shared revenues among the clubs because they wish to remain within its beneficial ambit. . . .

The profound interdependency of the N.F.L. and member clubs in the daily operation and strategic marketing of professional football belies the district court's conclusion that each member club is an individual and economically meaningful competitor. The dispositive factor in determining whether the member clubs are capable of conspiring to restrain competition—the *sine qua non* of the Sherman Act § 1—by reason of Rule 4.3, is the extent, if any, of their competition in an economic sense. Virtually every court to consider this question has concluded that N.F.L. member clubs do *not* compete with each other in the economic sense.

By riveting its attention upon the "single entity" issue, as a sort of talismanic affirmative defense to the appellees' charges here, the district court overlooked the dispositive inquiry of whether Rule 4.3, as an instrument of the N.F.L. member clubs, violated the Sherman Act § 1, by restricting any economically independent entities from supplying goods or services related to professional football to the individual clubs. I use "upstream flow" as shorthand for products and services like players and coaches, television services, potential investors and the myriad of other integrated industries; member clubs do have independent and economically significant identities apart from the collective N.F.L. for the limited purposes of their extra-league dealings with those upstream suppliers. See Weistart & Lowell, *Law of Sports*, § 5.11 (1978), 687, 692 esp. n. 86. Thus, § 1 can and should protect the competitive aspects of player drafts, disallow cross-ownership bans and exclusive television and equipment contracts, by insuring that any one club's interaction outside the confines of intra-league regulation of production of the sport is unfettered by the working of any intraleague rule. . . .

The paradox to which I return, as the root of why the N.F.L., as well as other sports leagues, must be regarded as a "single entity" is that the keener the on-field competition becomes, the more successful their off-the-field, and ultimately legally relevant, collaboration. The formal entities, including the member clubs—including the Raiders—which the district court ruled to be competitors cannot compete, because the only product or service which is in their separate interests to produce can only result as a fruit of their joint efforts. This systemic cooperation trickles down to all members of the league, regardless of their on-the-field record, at least to the extent of the shared revenues. . . .

A ruling that the N.F.L. cannot enforce Rule 4.3 is effectively ruling that it may not enforce any collective decision of its member clubs over the dissent of a club member, although this is precisely what each owner has contractually bargained for in joining the enterprise. . . .

There was no evidence before the district court establishing that a member club of the N.F.L. could, or would seek to, defect to the U.S.F.L., thereby transferring its assets in quest of greater exploitation. Only such a showing, or an alternative theory, supported by evidence in the record could illustrate that any particular member club had an intrinsic value shorn of its affiliation with the N.F.L., and thus could support the district court's result. We find no such evidence in the record. *C.f. Associated Press, supra* (newspapers which sought to affiliate did not share revenues, and each produced separate and distinct products with intrinsic value). There is no evidence that any of the member clubs' investors would have committed time or capital investment without the existing league structure. Without the league, professional football becomes a pursuit no more substantial than a group of finely-tuned athletes traveling haphazardly about, in search of playing competition. . . .

No "antitrust exemption" for the N.F.L. would be created by holding that it is a single economic entity for purposes of regulating franchise location. Section 2 of the Sherman Act, prohibiting monopolies and attempts to monopolize, remains fully applicable to all N.F.L. intra-league rules and activities. . . .

The purposes for which the N.F.L. should be viewed as a single entity, impervious to § 1 attack, must be functionally defined as those instances in which member clubs must coordinate intra-league policy and practice if the joint product is to result. . . .[61]

15. Why do the MLB and NHL allow players to come into the league directly out of high school, but the NFL does not? Do you agree with the argument that football players coming right out of high school are not physically ready to play in the NFL? What other reasons could the NFL argue in support of the regulation?

16. What antitrust challenges are left for professional players after *Clarett v. NFL*? The nonstatutory labor exemption seems to be expanding. This will make it difficult for any professional player to bring a successful antitrust lawsuit arising from a labor dispute with a team. The nonstatutory labor exemption would most likely not apply to individual sports such as golf, track and field, boxing, or tennis. Usually, these athletes are not organized and do not engage in a collective bargaining process.

17. In *Neeld v. National Hockey League*, 594 F.2d 1297 (9th Cir. 1979), a one-eyed hockey player sued the NHL on antitrust grounds. NHL Bylaw 12.6 stated:

A player with only one eye, or one whose eyes has a vision of only three-sixtieths (3-60ths) or under, shall not be eligible to play for a Member Club.

The district court granted summary judgment for the NHL, holding that Bylaw 12.6 was not in violation of the Sherman Act. The Ninth Circuit affirmed the lower court's ruling:

---

[61] Los Angeles Memorial Coliseum Commission v. NFL ("Raiders"), 726 F.2d 1381 (9th Cir.), *cert. denied,* 469 U.S. 990 (1984).

The bylaw is not motivated by anticompetitiveness and Neeld does not actually contend that it is. Further, any anticompetitive effect is at most De minimis, and incidental to the primary purpose of promoting safety, both for Neeld, who lost his eye in a hockey game, and for all players who play with or against him. We take judicial notice that ice hockey is a very rough and physical contact sport, and that there is bound to be danger to players who happen to be on Neeld's blind side, no matter how well his mask may protect his one good eye. Also of some importance and legitimate concern to the League and its members is the possibility of being sued for personal injuries to Neeld himself or to others, if Neeld is permitted to play.[62]

In finding for the NHL, the court of appeals stated that the purpose behind the antitrust laws is "to maintain and promote competition."[63] Only unreasonable restraints are illegal.[64] The court determined that the evidence supported the reasonableness of the bylaw and that safety was the primary concern for the NHL. Suppose Neeld's case had been brought under the Americans with Disabilities Act of 1990. Would the result have been different? What reasonable accommodation could be made by the NHL?

Amateur Athletics and Antitrust

18. Antitrust law was applied in the gentlemanly game of polo when a player verbally abused a referee during a match and was subsequently suspended. In *Brant v. United States Polo Ass'n*, 631 F. Supp. 71 (S.D. Fla. 1986), the plaintiff sued on antitrust and defamation grounds. The plaintiff alleged that his suspension was in violation of Section 1 of the Sherman Act. The suspension was based on the plaintiff's confrontation with an umpire during a match. Plaintiff insulted the referee, and his insults were deemed to be "foul." Plaintiff used several derogatory phrases toward the umpire, including referring to him as the "fucking umpire."[65] The court dismissed the plaintiff's lawsuit, stating that the plaintiff failed to show that his 44-day suspension would have an anticompetitive effect on his team, his polo club, or the formation of a rival league.

SUGGESTED READINGS AND RESOURCES

Allison, John R. *Professional Sports and the Antitrust Laws: Status of the Reserve System.* 25 Baylor Law Review 1 (1973).

Delaney, K., & Eckstein, R. *Public Dollars, Private Stadiums: The Battle over Building Sports Stadiums.* New Brunswick, NJ: Rutgers University Press, 2003.

Euchner, Charles C. *Playing the Field: Why Sports Teams Move and Cities Fight to Keep Them.* Baltimore, MD: John Hopkins University Press, 1994.

Goldstein, Seth M. *Out of Bounds Under the Sherman Act? Player Restraints in Professional Team Sports.* 4 Pepperdine Law Review 285 (1977).

---

[62] *Neeld*, 594 F.2d at 1300.

[63] *Id.* at 1297.

[64] *Id.* (citing Chicago Board of Trade v. United States, 246 U.S. 231, 238 38 S.Ct. 242, 62 L.Ed. 683 (1918)).

[65] *Brant*, 631 F. Supp. at 73.

Leahy, P. J. *Application of Federal Antitrust Laws to Baseball: Hearing Before the Committee on the Judiciary, U.S. Senate.* Darby, PA: Diane Publishing, 2003.

Meritore, Barton J. *Baseball's Antitrust Exemption: The Limits of Stare Decisis.* 12 Boston College Industrial and Commercial Law Review 1 (1971).

United States Congress, Senate Committee on the Judiciary Staff. *BCS or Bust: Competitive and Economic Effects of the Bowl Championship Series on and off the Field: Hearing Before the Committee on the Judiciary, United States Senate, One Hundred Eighth Congress, First Session, October 29, 2003.* Washington, DC: U.S. Government Printing Office, 2004.

Zimbalist, A. S. *May the Best Team Win: Baseball Economics and Public Policy.* Washington, DC: Brookings Institution Press, 2003.

REFERENCE MATERIALS

Allison, J. R. *Professional Sports and the Antitrust Laws: Status of the Reserve System.* 25 Baylor Law Review 1 (1973).

Altman, P. *Stay Out for Three Years After High School or Play in Canada—and for Good Reason.* 70 Brooklyn Law Review 569 (2004–2005).

Calabrese, J. *Antitrust and Baseball.* 36 Harvard Journal on Legislation 531 (1999).

Champion, W. T. *Fundamentals of Sports Law.* St. Paul, MN: Thomson/West, 2004.

Daniel, C. R., II. *The PGA Tour: Successful Self-Regulation or Unreasonably Restraining Trade?* 4 Sports Lawyers Journal 41 (1997).

Eppel, J. P. *Professional Sports (Antitrust Exemptions: A Symposium).* 33 American Bar Association Antitrust Law Journal 69 (1967).

Gerba, J. *Instant Replay: A Review of the Case of Maurice Clarett, the Application of the Non-Statutory Labor Exemption, and Its Protection of the NFL Draft Eligibility Rule.* 73 Fordham Law Review 2383 (2005).

Goldstein, S. M. *Out of Bounds Under the Sherman Act? Player Restraints in Professional Team Sports.* 4 Pepperdine Law Review 285 (1977).

Grewe, R. *Antitrust Law and the Less Restrictive Alternatives Doctrine: A Case Study of its Application in the Sports Context.* 9 Sports Lawyers Journal 227 (2002).

Itri, S. Maurice Clarett v. National Football League, Inc.: *An Analysis of Clarett's Challenge to the Legality of the NFL's Draft Eligibility Rule Under Antitrust Law.* 11 Villanova Sports and Entertainment Law Journal 303 (2004).

Jacobs, M., & Winter, R. K. *Antitrust Principles and Collective Bargaining by Athletes: Of Superstars in Peonage.* 81 Yale Law Journal 1 (1971).

Kaplan, M. *Application of Federal Antitrust Laws to Professional Sports.* 18 American Law Reports 489 (2005).

Leavell, J. F., & Millard, H. L. *Trade Regulation and Professional Sports.* 26 Mercer Law Review 603 (1975).

Leshanski, J. *What Every Baseball Fan Should Know: The Curt Flood Case Part 1 (of 4).* At Home Plate. http://www.athomeplate.com/flood.shtml.

Martin, P. L. *The Labor Controversy in Professional Baseball: The Flood Case.* 23 Labor Law Journal 567 (1972).

Meritore, B. J. *Baseball's Antitrust Exemption: The Limits of Stare Decisis.* 12 Boston College Industrial and Commercial Law Review 1 (1971).

Messeloff, D. *The NBA's Deal with the Devil: The Antitrust Implications of the 1999 NBA–NBPA Collective Bargaining Agreement.* 10 FORDHAM INTELLECTUAL PROPERTY, MEDIA AND ENTERTAINMENT LAW JOURNAL 521 (2000).

Mitten, M., Davis, T., Smith, R., & Berry, R. *Sports Law and Regulation: Cases, Materials, and Problems.* New York: Aspen, 2005.

Monopsony in Manpower: Organized Baseball Meets the Antitrust Laws. 62 YALE LAW JOURNAL 576 (1953).

Nottingham, D. *Keeping the Home Team at Home: Antitrust and Trademark Law as Weapons in the Fight Against Professional Sports Franchise Relocation.* 75 UNIVERSITY OF COLORADO LAW REVIEW 1065 (2004).

Professional Football Telecasts and the Blackout Privilege. 57 CORNELL LAW REVIEW 297 (1972).

Rosenthal, L. *From Regulating Organization to Multi-Billion Dollar Business: The NCAA Is Commercializing the Amateur Competition It Has Taken Almost a Century to Create.* 13 SETON HALL JOURNAL OF SPORT LAW 321 (2003).

Ross, S. *Antitrust Options to Redress Anticompetitve Restraints and Monopolistic Practices by Professional Sports Leagues.* 52 CASE WESTERN LAW REVIEW 133 (2001).

Struck, T. *Facility Issues in Major League Soccer: What Do Soccer Stadiums Have to Do with Antitrust Liability?* 14 MARQUETTE SPORTS LAW REVIEW 551 (2004).

The Super Bowl and the Sherman Act: Professional Team Sports and the Antitrust Laws. 81 HARVARD LAW REVIEW 418 (1967).

Tygart, T. *Antitrust's Impact on the National Football League and Team Relocation.* 7 SPORTS LAWYERS JOURNAL 29 (2000).

Vallee, J. *Antitrust.* 32 TEXAS TECH LAW REVIEW 599 (2001).

Wurth, N. *The Legality of an Age-Requirement in the National Basketball League After the Second Circuit's Decision in* Clarett v. NFL. 3 DEPAUL JOURNAL OF SPORTS LAW AND CONTEMPORARY PROBLEMS 103 (2005).

Yu, D. *The Reconciliation of Antitrust Laws and Labour Laws in Professional Sports.* 6 SPORTS LAWYERS JOURNAL 159 (1999).

CHAPTER 4

LABOR RELATIONS IN SPORTS

Labor law has become a mainstay in the sports industry and has now taken precedence over antitrust law in resolving disputes between management and labor. Collective bargaining is the staple of labor relations, and collective bargaining agreements (CBAs), which govern the complicated relationship among players, teams, and leagues, can be the result of protracted negotiations between management and labor. Players and management have attempted to form a partnership that is agreeable to all parties, dividing the revenues of their sport. Professional sports unions were not formed until the 1950s and collective bargaining agreements followed thereafter. Professional sports has seen its share of labor strife, with lockouts and strikes occurring numerous times as each party attempted to force its will on the other during protracted labor negotiations. The parties eventually agree to a new CBA with the hope that labor peace will continue.

Players have attempted to unionize for many years. John Montgomery Ward (a Columbia Law School graduate) was both an outstanding ballplayer (he was selected to baseball's Hall of Fame in 1964) and a labor organizer. Ward organized the Brotherhood of National League Players in the late 1880s and continued to represent professional baseball players against management after he left baseball as a player.[1]

Marvin Miller was named executive director of the Major League Baseball Players Association (MLBPA) in 1966 and was instrumental in the players' making great strides toward bigger salaries and more benefits for players. Miller once stated that "[t]he essential dignity of equals sitting down together just can't be overemphasized." Miller was a noted labor organizer and assisted players in eventually gaining free agency and striking down baseball's reserve clause, which had prevented players from declaring free agency and gaining economic freedom.

After Curt Flood's challenge to baseball's reserve clause was defeated at the U.S. Supreme Court in *Flood v. Kuhn* (see Chapter 3), free agency for baseball players was eventually achieved through the Messersmith/McNally labor arbitration decision and its subsequent appeals through the courts. *Kansas City Royals v. Major League Baseball Players' Ass'n*, 532 F.2d 615 (8th Cir. 1976). The labor arbitration

---

[1] Bryan Di Salvatore, *A Clever Base-Ballist: The Life and Times of John Montgomery Ward*, The Johns Hopkins University Press, 2001.

decision forced management to the bargaining table and resulted in an increase in player's rights under a new Basic Agreement. Since 1968 there have been several work stoppages, either by way of strike or lock-out, in Major League Baseball. Lockouts occurred in 1973, 1976, and 1990, and strikes occurred in 1972, 1981, 1985, and 1994 to 1995. The 1994–1995 strike was the longest in baseball history, resulting in the cancellation of the 1994 World Series. Many baseball fans said they would never return to the sport because of the work stoppage and the subsequent cancellation of the World Series, but attendance figures since then have shown otherwise. Fans continue to flock to the ballpark in record numbers.

The National Football League Players Association (NFLPA) was formed in 1956. Since that time there have been several strikes or lockouts, with the most recent strike occurring in 1987. The NBPA was formed in 1954 behind the leadership of Boston Celtic great Bob Cousy. The NBA has had two lockouts, the first in 1995 and another in 1998. The National Hockey League Players Association (NHLPA) was formed in 1958 and has had two work stoppages. The NHL lost the entire 2004 hockey season as a result of a players' strike. Strikes and lockouts have been common since the institution of player unions as both players and management have used the tools available to them in attempts to force their will on the other party during labor negotiations.

This chapter explores labor relations between players and management, examining the rights and responsibilities of each party under federal law as well as significant provisions of the collective bargaining agreements of professional leagues. The duty of unions to fairly represent members is also reviewed, as well as issues relating to the arbitration process between management and labor.

NATIONAL LABOR RELATIONS ACT

Professional sports are governed by the National Labor Relations Act (NLRA).[2] Baseball received the protection of the NLRA in 1969.[3] The National Labor Relations Board (NLRB) asserted jurisdiction over football in *National Football League Management Council*, 203 N.L.R.B. 165 (1973). Once professional sports came under the jurisdiction of the NLRA, labor and management became subject to the act and all parties were given all the rights set forth in the act. At one time, sports were not viewed as a business and therefore were not subject to the protection of the NLRA. However, it is now well settled that the NLRA and its corresponding protections apply to professional sports. The NLRB may decline jurisdiction over an industry if its impact on interstate commerce is not substantial enough. For example, the NLRB refused to exercise jurisdiction over the thorough-bred horse racing industry, finding it to be only a local activity.[4] It is the policy of the NLRB to encourage parties to engage in collective bargaining.

The following are significant excerpts from the National Labor Relations Act outlining the policies of the NLRA, relevant definitions, and rights of employees to organize.

§ 151. Findings and Declaration of Policy

The denial by some employers of the right of employees to organize and the refusal by some employers to accept the procedure of collective bargaining lead to strikes and other forms of industrial strife or

---

[2] 29 U.S.C. §§ 151–166.
[3] American League of Professional Baseball Clubs, 180 N.L.R.B. 190 (1969).
[4] Walter A. Kelly, 139 N.L.R.B. 744 (1962).

unrest, which have the intent or the necessary effect of burdening or obstructing commerce. . . .

The inequality of bargaining power between employees who do not possess full freedom of association or actual liberty of contract, and employers who are organized in the corporate or other forms of ownership association substantially burdens and affects the flow of commerce, and tends to aggravate recurrent business depressions, by depressing wage rate and the purchasing power of wage earners in industry and by preventing the stabilization of competitive wage rates and working conditions within and between industries.

Experience has proved that protection by law of the right of employees to organize and bargain collectively safeguards commerce from injury, impairment, or interruption, and promotes the flow of commerce by removing certain recognized sources of industrial strife and unrest, by encouraging practices fundamental to the friendly adjustment of industrial disputes arising out of difference as to wages, hours, or other working conditions, and by restoring equality of bargaining power between employers and employees. . . .

It is hereby declared to be the policy of the United States to eliminate the causes of certain substantial obstructions to the free flow of commerce and to mitigate and eliminate these obstructions when they have occurred by encouraging the practice and procedure of collective bargaining and by protecting the exercise by workers of full freedom of association, self-organization, and designation of representatives of their own choosing, for the purpose of negotiating the terms and conditions of their employment or other mutual aid or protection.

§ 152. Definitions

. . . .

(2) The term "employer" includes any person acting as an agent of an employer, directly or indirectly, but shall not include the United States or any wholly owned Government corporation, or any Federal Reserve Bank, or any State or political subdivision thereof, or any person subject to the Railway Labor Act, 45 U.S.C.A. §151, as amended from time to time, or any labor organization (other than when acting as an employer), or anyone acting in the capacity of officer or agent of such labor organization.

(3) The term "employee" shall include any employee, and shall not be limited to the employees of a particular employer, unless this subchapter explicitly states otherwise, and shall include any individual whose work has ceased as a consequence of, or in connection

with, any current labor dispute or because of any unfair labor
practice, and who has not obtained any other regular and substantially equivalent employment, but shall not include any individual
employed as an agricultural laborer, or in the domestic service of
any family or person at his home, or any individual employed by his
parent or spouse, or any individual having the status of an independent contractor, or any individual employed as a supervisor, or
any individual employed by an employer subject to the Railway Labor
Act, 45 U.S.C.A. §151, as amended from time to time, or by any
other person who is not an employer as herein defined.

. . . .

(8) The term "unfair labor practice" means any unfair labor practice
    listed in section 158 of this title.

(9) The term "labor dispute" includes any controversy concerning
    terms, tenure or conditions of employment, or concerning the asso-
    ciation or representation of persons in negotiating, fixing, main-
    taining, changing, or seeking to arrange terms or conditions of
    employment, regardless of whether the disputants stand in the
    proximate relation of employer and employee.

. . . .

§ 157. Right of Employees as to Organization, Collective Bargaining, etc.

Employees shall have the right to self-organization, to form, join, or
assist labor organizations, to bargain collectively through representatives of their own choosing, and to engage in other concerted activities for the purpose of collective bargaining or other mutual aid or
protection, and shall also have the right to refrain from any or all of
such activities except to the extent that such right may be affected by
an agreement requiring membership in a labor organization as a condition of employment as authorized in section 158(a)(3) of this title.[5]

One of the first duties of the NLRB was to determine the appropriate bargaining unit for a sport. The bargaining unit is usually the sport as a whole instead of individual teams or certain positions (such as a union for quarterbacks only). Once recognized, the designated union becomes the sole bargaining representative for all members. For example, the CBA of the Women's National Basketball Association (WNBA) acknowledges the Women's National Basketball Players Association (WNBPA) as the appropriate bargaining unit for labor in the WNBA.

In Case 4-1, *Morio v. North American Soccer League*, 501 F. Supp. 633 (D.C.N.Y. 1980), the court examined the issue of whether an unfair labor practice had been committed by failing to bargain exclusively with the players union.

---

[5] 29 U.S.C.A. §§ 151–157.

CASE 4-1 *Morio v. North American Soccer League*

501 F. Supp. 633 (D.C.N.Y. 1980)

MOTLEY, District Judge.

This is an action brought by Petitioner, . . . National Labor Relations Board, for and on behalf of the National Labor Relations Board
(the Board) in which she seeks a temporary injunction pursuant to
Section 10(j) of the National Labor Relations Act. . . . Respondents in
this action are the North American Soccer League and its 21 constituent
member clubs in the United States. The action is now before the court
upon the issuance of an order to show cause why the temporary injunctive relief prayed for by Petitioner should not be granted. . . .
The North American Soccer League Players Association (the Union) was
permitted to intervene in the action and to participate in the hearing. . . . Upon the entire record, the court finds and concludes that
Petitioner has reasonable cause to believe and there is reasonable
cause to believe that Respondents have engaged in unfair labor practices and that Petitioner is entitled to the temporary injunctive
relief sought in this action. . . .

The unilateral changes which Respondents admit have occurred since
September 1, 1978, in the terms and conditions of employment, may violate the employer's obligations to bargain with the exclusive bargaining representative of the players. The duty to bargain carries with it
the obligation on the part of the employer not to undercut the Union
by entering into individual contracts with the employees. In NLRB v.
Katz, 369 U.S. 736 (1962), the Supreme Court noted: "A refusal to
negotiate in fact as to any subject which is within s 8(d) and about
which the Union seeks to negotiate violates s 8(a)(5)."

. . . Respondents' most vigorous opposition comes in response to Petitioner's application for an order requiring Respondents to render
voidable, at the option of the Union, all individual player contracts,
whether entered into before or after the Union's certification on
September 1, 1978. Respondents claim that such power in the hands of the
Union, a non-party to this action, would result in chaos in the industry and subject Respondents to severe economic loss and hardship since
these individual contracts are the only real property of Respondents.

It should be noted, at the outset, that the relief requested by Petitioner is not a request to have all individual contracts declared null
and void. It should be emphasized that Petitioner is not requesting
that the "exclusive rights" provision of the individual contracts,
which bind the players to their respective teams for a certain time,

be rendered voidable. Moreover, the Board seeks an order requiring Respondents to maintain the present terms and conditions in effect until Respondents negotiate with the Union—except, of course, for the unilateral changes—unless and until an agreement or a good faith impasse is reached through bargaining with the Union. Petitioner does not, however, seek to rescind that unilateral provision which provided for the present summer schedule. The Board has consciously limited its request for relief to prevent any unnecessary disruption of Respondents' business. The Board is seeking to render voidable only those unilateral acts taken by the Respondents, enumerated above, which Respondents admit have in fact occurred.

These unilateral changes appear to modify all existing individual contracts entered into before September 1, 1978, in derogation of the Union's right to act as the exclusive bargaining agent of all employees in the unit.

The court finds that Petitioner is entitled to the temporary injunctive relief which it seeks with respect to all of the individual contracts. The individual contracts entered into since September 1, 1978, are apparently in violation of the duty of the Respondents to bargain with the exclusive bargaining representative of the players. The Act requires Respondents to bargain collectively with the Union. The obligation is exclusive. This duty to bargain with the exclusive representative carries with it the negative duty not to bargain with individual employees. Medo Photo Supply Corp. v. NLRB, 321 U.S. 678, (1944). . . .

In National Licorice Co. v. NLRB, 309 U.S. 350 (1940), the Supreme Court held that the Board has the authority, even in the absence of the employees as parties to the proceeding, to order an employer not to enforce individual contracts with its employees which were found to have been in violation of the NLRA. Petitioner is seeking temporary relief to this effect as to those individual contracts entered into before September 1, 1978, as well as relief with respect to those contracts entered into prior to September 1, 1978. The evidence discloses that Petitioner has reasonable cause to believe that Respondents have used, and will continue to use, the individual contracts entered into prior to September 1, 1978, to forestall collective bargaining. . . .

Injunction granted.

Source: Courtesy of Westlaw; reprinted with permission.

Case 4-2, *North American Soccer League v. N.L.R.B.*, 613 F.2d 1379 (5th Cir. 1980), examined the question of what the "appropriate unit" is for collective bargaining purposes. In the majority of sports, the sport as a whole is determined to be the bargaining unit, as opposed to a particular position on a team or the team itself. The union desires the largest unit possible, whereas management wants a "divide and conquer" strategy to be able to put itself in a better bargaining position. In *North American Soccer League v. NLRB*, the court held the league and its member clubs to be "joint employers." The North American Soccer League (NASL) disputed the NLRB's certification of "all NASL players of clubs based in the United States" as the appropriate bargaining unit.

📖 CASE 4-2 *North American Soccer League v. N.L.R.B.*

613 F.2d 1379 (5th Cir. 1980)

RONEY, Circuit Judge:

The correct collective bargaining unit for the players in the North American Soccer League is at issue in this case. Contrary to our first impression, which was fostered by the knowledge that teams in the League compete against each other on the playing fields and for the hire of the best players, our review of the record reveals sufficient evidence to support the National Labor Relations Board's determination that the League and its member clubs are joint employers, and that a collective bargaining unit comprised of all NASL players on clubs based in the United States is appropriate. Finding petitioners' due process challenge to be without merit, we deny the petition for review and enforce the collective bargaining order on the cross-application of the Board.

The North American Soccer League is a non-profit association comprised of twenty-four member clubs. The North American Soccer League Players Association, a labor organization, petitioned the NRLB for a representation election among all NASL players. The Board found the League and its clubs to be joint employers and directed an election within a unit comprised of all the soccer players of United States clubs in the League. Excluded from the unit were players for the clubs based in Canada, because the Board concluded its jurisdiction did not extend to those clubs as employers.

Players in the unit voted in favor of representation by the Association. After the League and its clubs refused to bargain, the Board found them in violation of Sections 8(a)(1) and (5) of the National Labor Relations Act, 29 U.S.C.A. ss 158(a)(1) and (5), and ordered collective bargaining. The League and its member clubs petitioned this Court for review. The Board's cross-application seeks enforcement of that order.

The settled law is not challenged on this petition for review. Where an employer has assumed sufficient control over the working conditions of the employees of its franchisees or member-employers, the Board may require the employers to bargain jointly. The Board is also empowered to decide in each case whether the employee unit requested is an appropriate unit for bargaining. The Board's decision will not be set aside unless the unit is clearly inappropriate. Thus the issues in this case are whether there is a joint employer relationship among the League and its member clubs, and if so, whether the designated bargaining unit of players is appropriate.

Joint Employers

Whether there is a joint employer relationship is "essentially a factual issue," and the Board's finding must be affirmed if supported by substantial evidence on the record as a whole.

The existence of a joint employer relationship depends on the control which one employer exercises, or potentially exercises, over the labor relations policy of the other. In this case, the record supports the Board's finding that the League exercises a significant degree of control over essential aspects of the clubs' labor relations, including but not limited to the selection, retention, and termination of the players, the terms of individual player contracts, dispute resolution and player discipline. Furthermore, each club granted the NASL authority over not only its own labor relations but also, on its behalf, authority over the labor relations of the other member clubs. The evidence is set forth in detail in the Board's decision and need be only briefly recounted here. North American Soccer League, 236 N.L.R.B. (No. 181).

The League's purpose is to promote the game of soccer through its supervision of competition among member clubs. Club activities are governed by the League constitution, and the regulations promulgated thereunder by a majority vote of the clubs. The commissioner, selected and compensated by the clubs, is the League's chief executive officer. A board of directors composed of one representative of each club assists him in managing the League.

The League's control over the clubs' labor relations begins with restrictions on the means by which players are acquired. An annual college draft is conducted by the commissioner pursuant to the regulations, and each club obtains exclusive negotiating rights to the players it selects. On the other hand, as the Board recognized, the League exercises less control over the acquisition of "free agent" players and players "on loan" from soccer clubs abroad.

The regulations govern interclub player trades and empower the commissioner to void trades not deemed to be in the best interest of the League. Termination of player contracts is conducted through a waiver system in accordance with procedures specified in the regulations.

The League also exercises considerable control over the contractual relationships between the clubs and their players. Before being permitted to participate in a North American Soccer League game, each player must sign a standard player contract adopted by the League. The contract governs the player's relationship with his club, requiring his compliance with club rules and the League constitution and regulations. Compensation is negotiated between the player and his club, and special provisions may be added to the contract. Significantly, however, the club must seek the permission of the commissioner before signing a contract which alters any terms of the standard contract.

Every player contract must be submitted to the commissioner, who is empowered to disapprove a contract deemed not in the best interest of the League. The commissioner's disapproval invalidates the contract. Disputes between a club and a player must be submitted to the commissioner for final and binding arbitration.

Control over player discipline is divided between the League and the clubs. The clubs enforce compliance with club rules relating to practices and also determine when a player will participate in a game. The League, through the commissioner, has broad power to discipline players for misconduct either on or off the playing field. Sanctions range from fines to suspension to termination of the player's contract.

Although we recognize that minor differences in the underlying facts might justify different findings on the joint employer issue, the record in this case supports the Board's factual finding of a joint employer relationship among the League and its constituent clubs.

Having argued against inclusion of the Canadian clubs in the NLRB proceeding, petitioners contend on appeal that their exclusion renders the Board's joint employer finding, encompassing 21 clubs, inconsistent with the existence of a 24-club League. The jurisdictional determination is not before us on appeal, however, and the Board's decision not to exercise jurisdiction over the Canadian clubs does not undermine the evidentiary base of its joint employer finding.

Even assuming the League and the clubs are joint employers, they contend that Greenhoot, Inc., 205 N.L.R.B. 250 (1973), requires a finding of a separate joint employer relationship between the League and each of its clubs, and does not permit all the clubs to be lumped together with the League as joint employers. In Greenhoot, a building management company was found to be a joint employer separately with each building owner as to maintenance employees in the buildings covered by its contracts. The present case is clearly distinguishable, because here each soccer club exercises through its proportionate role in League management some control over the labor relations of other clubs. In Greenhoot, building owners did not exercise any control through the management company over the activities of other owners.

Appropriate Unit

The joint employer relationship among the League and its member clubs having been established, the next issue is whether the leaguewide unit of players designated by the Board is appropriate. Here the Board's responsibility and the standard of review in this Court are important.

The Board is not required to choose the most appropriate bargaining unit, only to select a unit appropriate under the circumstances. The determination will not be set aside "unless the Board's discretion has been exercised 'in an arbitrary or capricious manner.'"

Notwithstanding the substantial financial autonomy of the clubs, the Board found they form, through the League, an integrated group with common labor problems and a high degree of centralized control over labor relations. In these circumstances the Board's designation of a leaguewide bargaining unit as appropriate is reasonable, not arbitrary or capricious.

In making its decision, the Board expressly incorporated the reasons underlying its finding of a joint employer relationship. The Board emphasized in particular both the individual clubs' decision to form a League for the purpose of jointly controlling many of their activities, and the commissioner's power to disapprove contracts and exercise control over disciplinary matters. Under our "exceedingly narrow" standard of review, no arguments presented by petitioners require denial of enforcement of the bargaining order.

Thus the facts successfully refute any notion that because the teams compete on the field and in hiring, only team units are appropriate for collective bargaining purposes. Once a player is hired, his working conditions are significantly controlled by the League. Collective bargaining at that source of control would be the only way to effectively change by agreement many critical conditions of employment.

Source: Courtesy of Westlaw; reprinted with permission.

THE UNION'S DUTY OF FAIR REPRESENTATION

A players' union is called on to represent a diverse group of individuals who have individual interests but essentially the same goal—to maximize their revenues and improve working conditions for all players. The union has an obligation to its members to represent and serve their interests. It must represent equally both the superstar and the proverbial clipboard-holding quarterback. A union must listen to all its members, evaluate all essential data, and attempt to obtain the most favorable CBA it can for its members. Although it is true that some members may not be satisfied with any deal that is negotiated, it is difficult to prevail in a lawsuit against a union for a breach of its duty of fair representation. The NLRA grants exclusive authority to the union to handle all negotiations on behalf of the bargaining unit. Many times a union must sacrifice certain individual rights to achieve the common goal. They must take into consideration the bargaining unit as a whole rather than a few individual superstars when trying to gain the upper hand on management.

The phrase "duty of fair representation" is incapable of a precise definition.[6] There is no code that explicitly prescribes the standards that govern unions in representing their members in processing grievances. Furthermore, whether a union has breached its duty of fair representation depends on the facts of each case.[7] The NLRA requires a union to fairly represent all members of the bargaining unit.[8] It has been determined that any breach of a union's duty of fair representation is considered an unfair labor practice.[9] However, mere negligence on the part of a union does not establish a breach of the duty of fair representation.[10] It is essential that unions be given discretion to act on what they believe to be the best interests of their members.[11] If a union proceeds on some reasoned basis, then it will not breach its duty of fair representation.[12] Unions are therefore given much leeway to make decisions regarding what they believe to be in the best interests of union members.

In Case 4-3, *Peterson v. Kennedy*, 771 F.2d 1244 (9th Cir. 1985), the plaintiff alleged that the NFLPA breached its duty of fair representation when it failed to properly process a grievance claim. Was this mere negligence on the part of the union or more egregious conduct?

📖 CASE 4-3　*Peterson v. Kennedy*

771 F.2d 1244 (9th Cir. 1985)

REINHARDT, Circuit Judge:

The district court concluded that the evidence presented was legally insufficient to sustain the jury's verdict that the union breached its duty of fair representation. We agree. After reviewing all of the evidence in the light most favorable to Peterson, we conclude that the union did not breach its duty of fair representation; the record is devoid of evidence that the union acted in an arbitrary, discriminatory, or bad faith manner.

---

[6] St. Clair v. Local 515, Int'l Bhd. of Teamsters, etc., 422 F.2d 128, 130 (6th Cir. 1969).

[7] *See* Thompson v. Brotherhood of Sleeping Car Porters, 316 F.2d 191 (4th Cir. 1963); Trotter v. Amalgamated Ass'n of Street Railway Employees, 309 F.2d 584 (6th Cir. 1962), *cert. denied*, 372 U.S. 943 (1963); Griffin v. International Union, United Automobile, Aerospace, and Agricultural Implement Workers of America, UAW, 469 F.2d 181, 182 (4th Cir. 1972).

[8] Steele v. Louisville & N.R. Co., 323 U.S. 192 (1944).

[9] National Labor Relations Board v. Miranda Fuel Company, 140 N.L.R.B. 181 (1962).

[10] Peters v. Burlington Northern R. Co., 931 F.2d 534 C.A. 9 (Mont. 1990).

[11] Herring v. Delta Airlines. Inc., 894 F.2d 1020, 1023 (9th Cir. 1990).

[12] Eichelberger v. NLRB, 765 F.2d 851, 856 (9th Cir. 1985).

The duty of fair representation is a judicially established rule imposed on labor organizations because of their status as the exclusive bargaining representative for all of the employees in a given bargaining unit. The Supreme Court recently explained the basis and scope of the duty:

> The duty of fair representation exists because it is the policy of the National Labor Relations Act to allow a single labor organization to represent collectively the interests of all employees within a unit, thereby depriving individuals in the unit of the ability to bargain individually or to select a minority union as their representative. In such a system, if individual employees are not to be deprived of all effective means of protecting their own interests, it must be the duty of the representative organization to "serve the interests of all members without hostility or discrimination toward any, to exercise its discretion with complete good faith and honesty, and to avoid arbitrary conduct." 462 U.S. at 164 n. 14.

A union breaches its duty of fair representation only when its conduct toward a member of the collective bargaining unit is "arbitrary, discriminatory, or in bad faith." The duty is designed to ensure that unions represent fairly the interests of all of their members without exercising hostility or bad faith toward any. It stands "as a bulwark to prevent arbitrary union conduct against individuals stripped of traditional forms of redress by the provisions of federal labor law."

The Supreme Court has long recognized that unions must retain wide discretion to act in what they perceive to be their members' best interests. To that end, we have "stressed the importance of preserving union discretion by narrowly construing the unfair representation doctrine." We have emphasized that, because a union balances many collective and individual interests in deciding whether and to what extent it will pursue a particular grievance, courts should "accord substantial deference" to a union's decisions regarding such matters.

A union's representation of its members "need not be error free." We have concluded repeatedly that mere negligent conduct on the part of a union does not constitute a breach of the union's duty of fair representation. . . .

Whether in a particular case a union's conduct is "negligent," and therefore non-actionable, or so egregious as to be "arbitrary," and hence sufficient to give rise to a breach of duty claim, is a question that is not always easily answered. A union acts "arbitrarily" when it simply ignores a meritorious grievance or handles it in a perfunctory manner, for example, by failing to conduct a "minimal investigation" of a grievance that is brought to its attention. We have said that a union's conduct is "arbitrary" if it is "without rational basis," or is "egregious, unfair and unrelated to legitimate union interests." In *Robesky v. Qantas Empire Airways Ltd.*, 573 F.2d 1082, 1089-90 (9th Cir.1978), we held that a union's unintentional mistake is "arbitrary" if it reflects a "reckless disregard" for the rights of the individual employee, but not if it represents only "simple negligence violating the tort standard of due care. . . ."

There are some significant general principles that emerge from our previous decisions. In all cases in which we found a breach of the duty of fair representation based on a union's arbitrary conduct, it is clear that the union failed to perform a procedural or minister- ial act, that the act in question did not require the exercise of judgment and that there was no rational and proper basis for the union's conduct. . . .

We have never held that a union has acted in an arbitrary manner where the challenged conduct involved the union's judgment as to how best to handle a grievance. To the contrary, we have held consistently that unions are not liable for good faith, non-discriminatory errors of judgment made in the processing of grievances. We have said that a union's conduct may not be deemed arbitrary simply because of an error in evaluating the merits of a grievance, in interpreting particular provisions of a collective bargaining agreement, or in presenting the grievance at an arbitration hearing. In short, we do not attempt to second-guess a union's judgment when a good faith, non-discriminatory judgment has in fact been made. It is for the union, not the courts, to decide whether and in what manner a particular grievance should be pursued. We reaffirm that principle here.

Sound policy reasons militate against imposing liability on unions for errors of judgment made while representing their members in the col- lective bargaining process. In *Dutrisac*, we recognized that holding unions liable for such errors would serve ultimately to "defeat the employees' collective bargaining interest in having a strong and effective union." If unions were subject to liability for "judgment calls," it would necessarily undermine their discretion to act on behalf of their members and ultimately weaken their effectiveness. In the long run, the cost of recognizing such liability would be borne not by the unions but by their memberships. Not only would the direct costs of adverse judgments be passed on to the members in the form of increased dues, but, more importantly, unions would become increasingly reluctant to provide guidance to their members in collective bargaining disputes. Such a result would be inconsistent with our oft-repeated commitment to construe narrowly the scope of the duty of fair representation in order to preserve the unions' discretion to decide how best to balance the collective and individual interests that they represent. . . .

Whether liability for a loss occasioned by ordinary negligence of the union might be spread more equitably among the membership as a whole, rather than be borne by the individual member who is harmed, is no longer an open question.

In applying the foregoing principles to the case at hand, we conclude, as a matter of law, that Peterson failed to establish that the NFLPA breached its duty of fair representation. As mentioned, Peterson does not contend that the union acted in a discriminatory or bad faith manner toward either him or his grievance. He relies exclusively on his claim that the union's error was so egregious as to be "arbitrary." We disagree. The alleged error was one of judgment. Viewing the evidence in the light most favorable to Peterson, the most that can be said is that the union provided him with incorrect advice and did not alter its judgment until it was too late to rectify the error. In this case, deciding whether to file an injury or a non-injury grievance was not a purely mechanical function; the union attorneys were required to construe the scope and meaning of the injury and non-injury grievance provisions of the collective bargaining agreement and to determine which of the two grievance procedures was more appropriate. As we have indicated earlier, the answer was not as simple as a literal reading of the two contract sections might indicate. . . .

Although the union's representatives may have erred in initially advising Peterson to file an injury grievance and in failing to recognize its mistake in time to file a non-injury grievance in its stead, we are unwilling to subject unions to liability for such errors in judgment. Accordingly, we affirm the district court's conclusion that the evidence presented was insufficient, as a matter of law, to support the jury's verdict against the union. . . .

Appeal denied.

Source: Courtesy of Westlaw; reprinted with permission.

The *Peterson* case shows how difficult it is to prevail on a claim for breach of duty of good faith. What else does the plaintiff have to show to win? In Case 4-4, *Sharpe v. National Football League Players Ass'n*, 941 F. Supp. 8 (D.D.C. 1996), former NFL player Shannon Sharpe sued the NFLPA, alleging that the union had breached its duty of fair representation to him. Why did the court dismiss his claim?

📖 CASE 4-4   *Sharpe v. National Football League Players Ass'n*

941 F. Supp. 8 (D.D.C. 1996)

JUNE L. GREEN, District Judge.

I. Introduction

This matter is before the Court on the Defendant National Football League Players Association's ("Defendant") Motion to Dismiss. The Court holds that before it may consider the Plaintiff's complaint, the Plaintiff must receive, at least, an adverse decision from an arbitrator on his contract claim against his former employer. Since the arbitrator has not decided that claim, the Plaintiff's Complaint must be dismissed.

II. Facts

The Plaintiff was a professional football player for the Green Bay Packers ("Packers") of the National Football League ("NFL"). The Plaintiff was also a member of the collective bargaining unit represented by the Defendant with the right to be represented by the Defendant in individual grievance matters against the Packers. The Defendant is the exclusive collective bargaining representative for present and future professional football players in the NFL, representing such players in injury grievance claims against the players' employer-clubs.

In May 1993, the Defendant and the NFL Management Council signed a new collective bargaining agreement that controlled employment disputes between players and teams. In particular, the agreement provides for the filing of injury grievances by players against their employer-teams.

In 1991, the Plaintiff signed a contract that obligated him to play for the Packers through the year 2000. The Plaintiff was scheduled to be paid an installment on his 1995 salary by March 15, 1995. In the final week of the 1994 NFL season, the Plaintiff participated in a game and did not receive any injury. The Plaintiff alleges that, in February 1995, the Packers coerced him into having surgery and led him to believe that the team would pay his 1995 salary. After the surgery, the Plaintiff became physically unable to perform under the contract he signed with the Packers. The Packers subsequently terminated the Plaintiff.

On March 8, 1995, the Plaintiff submitted to arbitration an injury grievance against the Packers seeking the remainder of his 1995 salary.

He alleged that the Packers wrongfully terminated him when he was physically unable to perform under his contract.

The Plaintiff alleges that the Defendant urged him to withdraw his grievance and then, without Plaintiff's knowledge, secretly agreed with the NFL Management Council that the Defendant would expedite Plaintiff's claim and not treat it as an injury grievance. In addition, the Plaintiff alleges that the Defendant has left the arbitrator and the Management Council with the "impression" that the Defendant did not believe in the legitimacy of Plaintiff's claim. The Plaintiff argues that the secret agreement would deprive the Plaintiff of the following: (1) the ability "to fully pursue the injury grievance claim[;]" (2) due process rights and important guidelines and procedures; (3) the necessary time to prepare his case; (4) the right to supplement the hearing record. The Plaintiff, therefore, believes that the Defendant did not represent him in good faith.

The Plaintiff then filed this action alleging that the Defendant breached its duty of fair representation of the Plaintiff.

III. Discussion

Under the contract that the Plaintiff signed with the Packers, he agreed that any contractual dispute between the Packers and him would "be submitted to final and binding arbitration in accordance with the procedure called for in any collective bargaining agreement in existence at the time the event giving rise to any such dispute occurs." The extant collective bargaining agreement contains two grievance procedures, each of which results in binding arbitration: (1) an injury grievance procedure; and (2) a non-injury grievance procedure, through which all other disputes "pertaining to terms and conditions of employment of NFL players will be resolved exclusively. . . ."

The Plaintiff has chosen to arbitrate his dispute with the Packers while suing the Defendant before this Court. Yet, a suit against an employer alleging a breach of the collective bargaining agreement and a suit against the union for breach of the union's duty of fair representation are "inextricably interdependent." To prevail on either claim, an employee-union member must prove a violation of the employment contract and demonstrate the union's breach of duty. "The employee may, if he chooses, sue one defendant and not the other; but the case he must prove is the same whether he sues one, the other, or both."

The Plaintiff is obligated to arbitrate his contract claim against the Packers by virtue of his employment contract, the collective bargaining agreement and federal labor policy. Indeed, the Plaintiff has submitted his claim against the Packers to arbitration and it is pending.

The focus, therefore, "is no longer on the reasons for the union's failure to act but on whether, contrary to [an] arbitrator's decision, the employer breached the contract and whether there is substantial reason to believe that a union breach of duty contributed to [an] erroneous outcome of the contractual proceedings." Consequently, before the Court can entertain the Plaintiff's claim against the Defendant for breach of its duty of fair representation, the Plaintiff must receive, at least, an adverse decision from an arbitrator on his claim against the Packers. Since no such decision has yet been rendered, the Plaintiff's complaint is premature and must be dismissed.

The Court shall, therefore, grant the Defendant's Motion to Dismiss.

IV. Conclusion

In order to consider the Plaintiff's claim that the Defendant breached its duty of fair representation, the Plaintiff must submit his contract claim against the Packers to arbitration and, at least, receive an adverse decision. Since the arbitrator has not resolved this dispute, the Plaintiff's complaint must be dismissed.

Source: Courtesy of Westlaw; reprinted with permission.

COLLECTIVE BARGAINING

Collective bargaining is the process by which a group of workers negotiates as a collective unit with management to establish the working conditions, salaries, and benefits for all employees. Both parties must negotiate in good faith or the proceedings can be considered an unfair labor practice.[13] Management cannot unilaterally impose its will upon the union for new terms that relate to subjects of mandatory collective bargaining until the parties have reached an impasse in negotiations. It would be an unfair labor practice to do so before impasse. The parties' labor negotiations will, it is hoped, produce a collective bargaining agreement that outlines the compromise agreement. The CBA takes precedent over league rules, bylaws, and individual agreements between players and teams.

A CBA can be a lengthy, comprehensive document. It is developed by labor law experts and covers almost every conceivable issue that might arise between the parties. Courts recognize the CBA as an enforceable contract; any material breach will give a cause of action to a party to the CBA. The CBA establishes the individual rights of the parties and also implements federal labor policy. Courts use the traditional rules of contract interpretation to determine whether the CBA has been breached. Section 301 of the Labor Management Relations Act provides parties with the power to file a federal lawsuit for violations of the CBA.[14]

---

[13] 29 U.S.C. § 158(b).
[14] 29 U.S.C.A. § 185.

In the sports context, individual players still have the authority to negotiate certain aspects of their employment contract even though the union is considered the sole representative for union members during the collective bargaining process. Players and their agents are able to negotiate their own salaries in excess of the league minimum, as well as bonus clauses, without the assistance of the union as long as they are not in violation of the CBA.

A typical collective bargaining agreement in sports addresses the following topics:

- *Free agency and player mobility systems.* How can players move within the league? How many years do they have to be in the league before they can declare free agency?
- *Salary caps and luxury taxes.* What is the amount of the cap and how long does it last? How is the cap or luxury tax number determined? Is there a minimum amount teams must spend on payroll?
- *Standard player contracts.* What terms make up the standard player contract? To what extent can this standard contract be revised through collective bargaining?
- *Revenue sharing.* What constitutes "revenue" for the league? How are the revenues to be divided?
- *Grievance and arbitration procedures.* When can a player go to arbitration? How does the arbitration process work? Can a party still pursue a remedy through the court system if arbitration is agreed to in the CBA?
- *Player agents.* Who can be a player agent? Is an examination required? What qualifications must an agent have to be approved as an agent? To what extent can an agent be disciplined by the union for poor representation?
- *Off-season workouts, medical examinations, and physical conditions of players.* Who determines whether a player is physically fit to play? Can a player have a second medical opinion if he or she suffers an injury?
- *Player drafts.* How are players drafted into a league? How does the draft function? How many draft rounds are there?
- *Drug testing programs.* Who can be tested and how frequently? What drugs are included in the testing program? What happens if a player tests positive? How does the drug program treat multiple offenders?
- *Player salaries and benefits.* What are the minimum salaries for players? Are veterans and rookies treated differently? Who is entitled to a pension and benefits?
- *Licensing and marketing of players.* Who owns the publicity rights of players? Can players opt out of such a program? How are licensing revenues determined and divided?
- *Player conduct and discipline.* What player conduct can be regulated? What about off-field or off-season misconduct? What fines can be levied? Can a player be fined by both a team and the league?

This list is not exhaustive but rather presents a general overview of the issues that can be negotiated between management and labor.

Each party has duties and responsibilities that arise from the collective bargaining agreement. All major sports leagues now have CBAs that govern the relationship between the parties. Through the collective bargaining process, management and labor have attempted to arrive at an agreement that satisfies both parties. They must form a partnership that will govern their relationship for an extended period of time and maximize benefits and revenues for both management and labor. Each party wants to negotiate the best terms it can and wants to avoid any possible labor strife. Given the huge increase in the popularity of sports in the last 30 years, owners and players arrive at the negotiating table with their own interests in mind along with the added incentive of dividing up the pie of revenues generated by the particular sport. Players are concerned with items such as salaries, injury protection, job security, free agency, pension benefits, and the vast realm of licensing and marketing opportunities for professional players. Owners have some of the same concerns but from a different perspective. Their concerns can include stadium issues, team payroll, guaranteed contracts for players, and revenue streams, with the primary purpose of attracting fans to the stadium.

Conflict between players and management has led to strikes and lockouts in professional sports. The players run the risk of fans becoming disengaged or apathetic after they see multi million-dollar ballplayers complaining about their salaries and working conditions. Owners run the risk of a shutdown of the sport and of being perceived as greedy by fans, which could turn into a public relations nightmare. The players and owners know all too well the repercussions of a "work stoppage," whether that occurs by way of strike or lockout. It has been estimated that the 1994 players' strike in baseball cost both parties approximately $1,000,000,000. The players lost approximately $243,000,000 in wages, and the owners lost approximately $376,000,000 in attendance and television revenues in 1994 and $326,000,000 in revenue for lost attendance in 1995. Certainly, damage is done to the reputation of the sport, which must be remedied by the goodwill of the players and management after a work stoppage. After the 2004 players' strike in the National Hockey League, fans returned to hockey with a slight increase in attendance.

Collective bargaining requires a lot of give and take from both sides. Historically, the parties have been willing to sacrifice the game itself to push their point. Each side presents different arguments. The players argue that their services are unique and that without them the sport could not exist. That is certainly a valid point in light of the owners' attempt in 1987 to play NFL games with replacement players. The players also argue that their careers are short and thus they need to achieve their earning power in a very short period of time. Players argue that they are the ones taking the risks of career-ending injuries and that they are the reason the fans attend games. They are the "entertainers" of the sports world.

Alternatively, the owners assert that they have taken the risk of investing in the team and therefore they should be able to control the destiny of the franchise. They also assert that a larger payroll does not always guarantee success on the court, field, or ice. Owners have historically stated that they are losing money and that the sport will not be able to survive if players' salaries continue to rise.

Both sides have valid points, and both have fought hard through the collective bargaining process to make headway in creating a collective bargaining agreement that all parties can live with.

Player Salaries and Team Payrolls

One of the results of the increased power of the MLBPA has been the huge increase in player salaries. Salaries have risen extravagantly since the institution of free agency and collective bargaining. Baseball's salary arbitration process has also been a factor in increasing players' salaries. Conversely, salary caps and luxury taxes can decrease players' salaries. The average salary for a

Major League Baseball player in 2009 was $2,996,106.[15] The ten teams with the highest salaries of 2009 were as follows:

1. New York Yankees, $201 M.
2. New York Mets, $135 M.
3. Chicago Cubs, $135 M.
4. Boston Red Sox, $122 M.
5. Detroit Tigers, $115 M.
6. Los Angeles Angels, $113 M.
7. Philadelphia Phillies, $113 M.
8. Houston Astros, $103 M.
9. Los Angeles Dodgers, $100 M.
10. Seattle Mariners, $98 M.

The two teams in the 2006 World Series, the Detroit Tigers and the St. Louis Cardinals, ranked 14th and 11th, respectively, in salary for the 2006 season. In the 2008 World Series, the Philadelphia Phillies defeated the Tampa Rays. The Phillies' payroll was approximately $98 million, whereas the Rays' payroll was approximately $43 million. The Rays' payroll was next to last in the major leagues.

There is a wide discrepancy among the payrolls of the Major League teams, with the New York Yankees having a larger payroll than other teams. It is clear that the owner of the Yankees wants to win the World Series every year. It is understandable that ballplayers with the Yankees may thus feel a little more pressure to perform than players in some other franchises do. However, if baseball is interested in achieving competitive balance, how can that goal be achieved given the wide discrepancy in team payrolls? Does the gap in payroll affect the overall competition of the league?

A Major League Baseball team plays 162 games a year. Before the season begins, it is almost a given that the worst team in the league will win at least one-third of its games and the best team will lose one-third of its games. There are always exceptions, of course. Consider the 1962 New York Mets (40–120), and the 2003 Detroit Tigers (43–119). The remaining one-third of the games are played to determine the eventual champion.

The minimum salary in Major League Baseball for the 2010 season is $400,000, the NFL's minimum salary for 2010 is $325,000 and the NHL's minimum salary for the 2009–2010 season was $500.000. The number of professional athletes is very small considering the number of people who participate in amateur sports.

Salary Caps and Luxury Taxes

Because of the continuing increase in player salaries, owners have argued that some limit on player salaries should be introduced to allow professional sports to function competitively. The increase in baseball salaries has been a perennial concern for baseball. Albert Goodwill Spalding expressed apprehension about the issue in 1881, stating, "Professional baseball is on the wane. Salaries must come down or the interest of the public must be increased in some way. If one or the other does not happen, bankruptcy stares every team in the face." One of the ways owners have

---

[15] www.bizofbaseball.com

attempted to decrease or hold down salaries of players is through the implementation of salary caps or luxury taxes.

Unions and management in all major sports, have battled over limiting player salaries through these methods over the last 20 years. In the early 1980s, NBA management and the players union agreed to a salary cap. In 1981, 16 of the 23 NBA teams showed losses, and the league had rumors of rampant drug usage. Television ratings were low and so was game attendance. By the end of the 1980s, the NBA was a successful and growing league. Many factors contributed to the rise of the NBA, including marquee players such as Michael Jordan, Larry Bird, and Magic Johnson. In 1993, the NFL instituted its salary cap.

The operation of a salary cap is an extremely complicated calculation and will only be addressed in summary here. Baseball does not have a salary cap but rather a luxury tax. The WNBA also has a salary cap.

The NHL salary cap was set at $56 million per team for the 2009–2010 season. NHL teams were required to spend at least $40 million on player salaries for 2009–2010. The cap figure includes salary and bonuses. All leagues have certain limits on player salaries.

The NBA's salary cap is often referred to as a "soft cap," whereas the NFL's has been referred to as a "hard cap." NBA teams can exceed the cap on a regular basis because of the "Larry Bird exception." The NBA allows teams to exceed the salary cap by resigning their own free agents at an amount up to the maximum salary.

The most common way NFL teams attempt to circumvent the salary cap is by extrapolating guaranteed signing bonuses over the life of the contract. The NFL salary cap has grown from approximately $34 million in 1993 to $128 million for the 2009 season. Internationally, Australian Rules Football has had a salary cap since the 1980s.

Does a salary cap create competitive balance or mediocrity? Do you believe that fans would rather see one dominating team in a sport or different teams competing for the title every year? If all teams in the NFL have the same amount of money to spend on payroll, then all teams should be able to compete for the NFL title every year. In Major League Baseball, the Yankees outdistanced the second-biggest spender in 2009 by a large margin. In baseball, the teams with the largest payroll generally make it to the playoffs. Do owners generally get what they pay for with regard to sports salaries?

Player Mobility and Free Agency

For many years players had no ability to change teams because of the reserve clause or other contractual restrictions, and as a result players' salaries basically stayed relatively dormant. One of the results of collective bargaining has been the increase of players moving from team to team, increasing the amount of salary offers players receive. Major league baseball achieved free agency through the labor arbitration process, whereas other sports used the antitrust laws to strike down what they perceived to be as unreasonable restraints on player movement.

Since the implementation of the NFL's Rozelle Rule and its subsequent demise, players have fought for free agency, that is, the ability to market themselves in the open market to receive their fair market value. *Free agent* (FA) has become a well-known term in team sports. Leagues have established different categories of free agency. Each major sports league has different rules on how a player achieves free agency status. If a player is able to achieve full free agency status, then that player may be able to command substantial offers from several clubs, thereby driving up the player's negotiation price.

Unrestricted free agency (UFA) is the most valued type of free agency in any player movement system. It is usually given to a player who has achieved a certain level of service within the league and whose contract has expired with his or her present team. These players are then able to enter the market with an opportunity to receive offers from several teams in an attempt to receive fair market value for their services. *Restricted free agency* (RFA) means a player can market his or her services to other clubs but that the player's current team holds a right of first refusal or some other mechanism to restrict a player's movement. A restricted free agent can receive offers from competing clubs, but the player's current team might have the opportunity to match that offer. The restricted free agent may be able to garner an increase in salary but may not be able to move to another team.

The NFL provides for "franchise players" and "transition players" in its CBA. After an NFL player reaches the pinnacle of unrestricted free agency, an NFL club may still retain his rights through the designation of that player as the team's "franchise player" under the CBA. In Major League Baseball, players can achieve free agency status after six years of Major League service.

Problem 4-1

Which of the following might be considered a mandatory subject of collective bargaining?

a. The structuring of a player movement system for a professional league.
b. The designated hitter rule in baseball.
c. The type of shoes a baseball player can wear.
d. The number of games scheduled in a championship season.
e. The playoff structure of a league.
f. Implementation of a time clock for a batter to step into the batter's box in MLB.
g. Increasing the number of games in the World Series.
h. Increasing or decreasing roster size.
i. The type of ball used in the sport.

ARBITRATION

Through collective bargaining, management and labor have agreed to avoid the litigation process by resolving their disputes through binding arbitration, with certain exceptions. Arbitration cases in professional sports can involve salary disputes, discipline of players, injury grievances, and contractual disputes, among other matters. If an arbitration clause is present in the CBA, arbitration will usually be the sole remedy for a player to pursue a grievance. Courts give great deference to an arbitrator's ruling and are therefore hesitant to overrule an arbitrator's decision.

The first legal issue to be addressed in an arbitration case is whether the claim is arbitrable under the CBA. Is it one of the matters that was contemplated by the parties to be subject to the arbitration process when they entered into the CBA? Arbitration is usually less expensive and quicker than litigation, and can also be confidential under certain circumstances. Lawsuits can be costly and very time-consuming. Arbitration is an alternative dispute resolution method that all parties can agree to and hope to abide by in resolving a dispute. Most standard player contracts in professional sport leagues contain a very broad arbitration clause describing all matters that are subject to arbitration. Parties can also agree who will arbitrate the matter as well.

Salary

After the 1976 basic agreement was signed, the Major League Baseball Players Association wanted free agency but not for all players every year. The MLBPA believed that if players were able to declare themselves free agents every year of their career, the free agent market would become saturated and result in a decrease of players' salaries. Because of that belief, the players association entered into a deal that allowed players to achieve free agency after six years of service in the Major Leagues. The MLB salary arbitration system was implemented in the 1976 basic agreement.

The salary arbitration system was seen as a compromise between the reserve clause and unrestricted free agency. Salary arbitration is available to those players in MLB who have three or more years but less than six years of service at the Major League level. If a player has between two and three years of service, he can qualify for salary arbitration if he has 86 days of service at the Major League level for the previous season and also ranks in the top 17 of all Major League players who are eligible for arbitration for the same reasons. These players are commonly known as "super two" players.

Baseball's arbitration process began in 1976 and presents a unique dispute resolution system. Each party presents a confidential offer to the arbitrator, and the arbitrator is required to select from the proposed offers presented by the parties. This is commonly referred to as "final offer" arbitration. Each party presents arguments in support of its position to a single arbitrator. It is fundamental to say that arbitration in baseball has increased salaries. Alfonso Soriano "lost" his arbitration case with the Washington Nationals and had to settle for the losing figure of $10 million per season. He had requested $12 million at arbitration. To date it was the highest salary ever awarded in arbitration. In 2006 Alfonso Soriano had a batting average of .277 while hitting 46 home runs, knocking in 95 RBIs, and stealing 41 bases. Despite his contributions, the Washington Nationals finished the season with a 71–91 record, in last place in the National League Eastern Division.

Many players settle their case prior to arbitration so they can avoid the adversarial arbitration process. At the arbitration hearing, clubs will argue that the player is not worth as much as he is claiming with the player arguing he is worth the claimed amount. Arbitrations are statistically driven, with experts testifying on both sides about the player's performance in different situations. The arbitration hearing will go far beyond the wins and losses for pitchers and batting averages for hitters. The arbitration will explore in detail how the player performs and contributes to the club's success.

Baseball's collective bargaining agreement outlines the criteria and procedure of baseball's arbitration process. The MLB Basic Agreement sets forth the following arbitration provisions:

F. Salary Arbitration

. . . .

(12) *Criteria*

(a) The criteria will be the quality of the Player's contribution to his Club during the past season (including but not limited to his overall performance, special qualities of leadership and public appeal), the length and consistency of his career contribution, the record of the Player's past compensation, comparative baseball salaries (see paragraph (13) below for confidential salary data), the existence of any physical or mental defects on the part of the Player, and the recent performance record of the Club including but not limited to its League standing and attendance as an indication of public acceptance (subject to the exclusion stated in (12) subparagraph (b)(i) below). Any evidence may be submitted which is relevant to the above criteria, and the arbitration panel shall assign such weight to the evidence as shall appear appropriate under the circumstances. The arbitration panel shall, except for a Player with five or more years of Major League service, give particular attention, for comparative salary purposes, to the contracts of Players with Major League service not exceeding one annual service group above the Player's annual service group. This shall not limit the ability of a Player or his representative, because of special accomplishment, to argue the equal relevance of salaries of Players without regard to service, and the arbitration panel shall give whatever weight to such argument as is deemed appropriate.

(b) Evidence of the following shall not be admissible:

    (i) The financial position of the Player and the Club;

    (ii) Press comments, testimonials or similar material bearing on the performance of either the Player or the Club, except that recognized annual Player awards for playing excellence shall not be excluded;

    (iii) Offers made by either Player or Club prior to arbitration;

    (iv) The cost to the parties of their representatives, attorneys, etc.;

    (v) Salaries in other sports or occupations.[16]

Source: MLB Basic Agreement, 2007–2011.

Tal Smith has been involved in professional baseball for over 50 years and is a noted expert on baseball arbitration. The following are insightful excerpts from an interview he gave relating to the baseball arbitration process.

BizBall: I want to shift over to something that is a large part of this—a large part of your history and what you do now. The arbitration process is something that is, to most baseball fans, a mystical process. When the process was first put in place, the vast majority of cases were won by players or, rather, player agents.

    When John McMullen let you go, you first assisted the A's with arbitration cases with Mike Morris and Tony Armas.

    Do you recall these first cases, and how you approached it?

Smith: Gene Michael—I forget the others on there—we did four cases. I've done some cases since—in Houston in '80; I helped Sandy Alderson in 1981 with their two cases.

    I started getting calls when I lost my consulting practice. It was even before that. I guess I announced that in April. I had only done the Oakland stuff. I was getting calls from

---

[16] *See* J. Gordon Hylton, *The Historical Origins of Professional Baseball Grievance Arbitration*, 11 MARQ. SPORTS L. REV. 175 (2001).

people who wanted to ask questions or get a little help on this and that. Dick Wagner was one. Obviously, Oakland, Roy Eisenhart, had called and that's what got me to go out there to help them with their two cases.

That's when I lost the consulting practice and I started getting calls. I think Jim Campbell, the GM in Detroit at the time, was the first one. He asked if I'd handle their arbitration. Well, obviously, I knew the GMs and they knew me and, as I said, maybe we had done some innovative things during our Astros days in the '70s with contracts, the options and the performance clauses and so on and so forth. So Campbell called and asked if I'd do it. One thing led to another. He talked to some other people and I started getting some inquiries. We ended up representing six clubs in 1982.

I put together a team. Gerry Hunsicker was part of it; Steve Mann, who had worked for Bill Wright and was brought in as an analyst in the late '70s for a year or so for the Astros. I put together a team of people that I knew and we lost the first case in '82 to Willie Mays Aikens and won the next seven, including three against Dick Moss and three for the Yankees. That sort of set us off on that.

As far as how we did it, I just have a sense of what's important in establishing a player's value and tried to present in a well organized, orderly fashion to an arbitrator and make the distinction between players that are arbitration eligible and those that are free agents. To me, they were two different markets at that time. I think over a period of time a lot of clubs lost sight of that and lost that advantage. That's a long drawn out thing that I'd be happy to talk to you about at some other time. It's a theory that worked very well until the clubs, by their own practice, killed it.

BizBall: In the early days of arbitration you seemed to adapt where others did not on management's side of the table. You seemed to grasp that statistical analysis played a key role in presenting your case to the arbiter. Did you try and pass on what was working for you to others to try and get owners and GMs to understand how the arbitration process worked?

Smith: At one time, we were representing 13 clubs. In one year, as you know, 1986, we handled 96 filings and actually presented 25 cases. I really suspect—at that time I think—that the union was trying to test us and see if they could break us perhaps from the standpoint of volume.

I have certain theories, beliefs, and philosophies as to how to approach this and how the salary structure should be determined. Some people embraced it and others didn't understand it, I don't think. I think they really clouded the distinction between someone that's got additional service—that has six years—and has earned the right to be a free agent is different from somebody—a third-year player—eligible for salary arbitration. The Basic Agreement, to me, clearly distinguishes on service and affords and grants players various rights depending upon that service. Those rights should have different value. As I said, all that's been clouded and, as time went on, we had to adjust because there were too many examples of clubs ignoring that or doing things that just didn't make a whole lot of sense. You know, frankly, a lot of the problem is that Clubs are responsible for the actions of others, whether deemed appropriate or not.

BizBall: In your opinion, how often does the arbiter already know which figure he will choose— just by viewing each side's written submission? In other words, how often does oral argument sway the arbiter?

Smith: As you probably know, there isn't any brief submitted in advance. While, presumably, the arbitrator comes up with this as it stands—ideally not even knowing who the player is going to be. It is basically an oral presentation backed up by your written exhibits. I'm not sure that's generally understood. There are some arbitrators that are obviously well-informed fans that have their own opinions. That's why I think it's important for them not to know in advance. I don't want them going to a scouting notebook or something of that nature and form their conclusions based on what somebody else has written. I think they should come in as much as possible with an open mind and listen to the evidence that is presented.

I'm sure we're all human and, if it's a prominent player, it's tough to win cases with prominent players. I still maintain, along with everyone in the room, that we won the case with Don Mattingly with the Yankees. I can recall leaving the hearing and walking down the street with union reps and agents and everything else and everybody more or less conceded that the club had prevailed, not because Mattingly wasn't a great player—he was a great player—it's a question of what's the appropriate value. Yet, when we got the decision, it was in favor of the player. It was a case heard in New York with a New York arbitrator. Those things happen.

I think the decisions in those days prior to the institution of a panel, I think if you were to poll both sides—the union reps or the agents, and the club practitioners—I'm not sure (before the decision) that they would get half of them right. We all have a sense you go in as an advocate, you present your case and you've got a pretty good idea as to whether you won or not. But, sometimes the arbitrator didn't see it the same way and you get surprises on both sides. We got some wins—some calls for us—that really surprised us.

BizBall: Sabermetrics, especially among the baseball community, is fairly well known, but you started to collect data and present that with computer analysis. In the process, I think that some people believe that there's just this overwhelming flow of statistical analysis that is done. Is it a case where actually 'less is more' in some cases? You're dealing with arbitrators who may not fully understand baseball.

Smith: As a standpoint? I think that very clearly you run the risk of overkill. You've got to keep this pretty basic. In the first place, you've only got an hour. It is not an exercise that is really designed for some of the more sophisticated or advanced sabermetricians. It's got to be more fundamental and basic than that; otherwise you'll confuse the issue. You still get back to comparing one player to another, as to what the salary should be and so on. I think you've got to be very, very careful. I've got an appreciation for sophisticated statistics, but I don't think that's the exercise that's involved when you get into arbitration.

BizBall: There seems to be—and maybe this is just a cycle—there seems to be a decline in cases that are going to hearing. I can only think of three this season. Why do you think there has been a decline or do you just think it's just the way this off-season cycle went?

Smith: Well, it may be somewhat of a cycle. It had seemed that one group this year didn't settle, that went down to the wire; as a matter of fact, the actual cases were relief pitchers and all the late settlements seemed to be relief pitchers and not the frontline closers. To some degree that goes in cycles, because there have been settlements among a certain group—whether it's the MLS 3 relief pitchers which was basically the group that was late in getting issues resolved. It sort of impacts everybody in that class. It's a time-consuming process.

You'd have to talk to agents. Some agents enjoy the process, but I think there's risk for agents. If they lose a case, then they risk losing the client. If they win the case, it's probably because the player feels that he's a very good player. From a club standpoint, there's some tendency to feel that they don't want to subject the player to it. I don't think it's all that negative. We've done almost 150 cases, I think, and I can only recall two or three where I thought there was any animosity and so on. I think the tone is really established. To me it's nothing more than an ongoing discussion or debate, the same as you would have in negotiations, except for the fact that it's being presented to a third party. It's not one where you have to be derisive or castigate the player or anything else. I mean the numbers are the numbers. When you're negotiating, if a guy hit .220 or .235 you bring that out in your negotiations. If he's got an ERA of 5.00, you're telling the agent that; you're telling the player that. So now you're simply telling that to a third party. I don't think it has to be denigrating.

There are some people that think that it's just not in the club's best interests to subject the player to that. I don't necessarily subscribe to that. I don't think there's all that much harm done. I still see many players that we've arbitrated against. Of course, everybody likes to win. I like to win; the player likes to win. But I don't think it's affected our relationships or dealings. They still go out of their way in most cases to speak. Barry Bonds speaks to me. We beat Bonds twice and Barry and I still kid—you may call it agitate—about it. I don't think it has any lasting consequences. Most of them will say, "I still came out ahead anyway." Bobby Bonilla—I worked with Bobby twice and I won both of those cases—now works with the Union. When I see him during arbitration season, he'll sort of joke about it and say, "I still came out way ahead because the money's so great to begin with."

BizBall: What's the most memorable case that you were involved in?

Smith: Oh boy, that's hard to say. I mean it was interesting doing the Bonds and Bonilla cases. The Bonds case is one of those players. Mattingly is one of the toughest losses, because I have great respect for Don as a player, I clearly thought we won that case. I don't know if I can single out one over the other. We've done so many over the years. We've been upset about some of the calls, some of the decisions and what not, but it sort of evens out because you win some cases you didn't think you were going to win.

Source: Tal Smith, interview by Maury Brown, The Biz of Baseball, Oct. 9, 2005, www.bizofbaseball.com. Courtesy of The Biz of Baseball.

Grievances

A variety of grievance arbitrations have been asserted, ranging from discipline of players to uniform issues, disputes over ownership of balls, off-field activities, and contract disputes.[17] Grievance arbitration functions to handle a variety of disputes and provides an expedient manner to resolve them. For example, Latrell Sprewell became involved in a scuffle with his coach, P. J. Carlesimo, in 1997. While the team was practicing, Carlesimo and Sprewell began yelling profanities at each other, and then Sprewell grabbed Carlesimo around the neck and began choking him. Sprewell was suspended 68 games for his conduct, with a loss of pay of $6.4 million. He appealed the decision of the arbitrator and lost.

---

[17] Sprewell v. Golden State Warriors, 266 F.3d 979 (9th Cir. 2001).

In Case 4-5, *White v. National Football League*, 149 F. Supp.2d 858 (D. Minn. 2001), the arbitrator was deciding whether a "bye week" in the NFL counted as a regular season game under the CBA for free agency purposes. Is this the type of matter that should be arbitrated? What do players do during the bye week in the NFL? Do they practice? Even though there is no game, are they still performing the obligations of their contract? When interpreting whether a bye week means a game, does it matter when the bye week was actually instituted in the NFL? Why might that be important?

CASE 4-5 *White v. National Football League*

149 F. Supp.2d 858 (D. Minn. 2001)

Order

DOTY, District Judge.

This matter is before the court on the objections of class counsel and the National Football League Players' Association ("NFLPA") to the decision of Special Master Jack H. Friedenthal dated March 15, 2001. . . . [T]he court affirms the special master's decision.

Background

This case arises out of a proceeding commenced by class counsel and the NFLPA regarding the status of Kyle Richardson ("Richardson"), a punter for the Baltimore Ravens last season. Under the Collective Bargaining Agreement and the Stipulation and Settlement Agreement (hereafter collectively referred to as the "CBA"), a NFL player is entitled to become an Unrestricted Free Agent if he has four or more Accrued Seasons. The CBA further specifies that a player is credited with an Accrued Season if he was on full pay status for six or more regular season games. *See* CBA Art. XVIII, § 1(a). Richardson has three Accrued Seasons in the NFL apart from his service in 1997.

In the 1997 season, Richardson was on full pay status with two different clubs during five weeks when those clubs engaged in regular season games. Additionally, he was on full pay status during a sixth week when the club that was paying him had a bye. The special master determined that Richardson was prevented from receiving a fourth Accrued Season, thereby denying him unrestricted free agency, since his team had a bye week during one of his qualifying weeks of full pay status for the six or more regular season games.

The sole question that the special master addressed, now before this court, is whether the bye week, during which Richardson was on full pay status, counts as a "game" for purposes of defining an Accrued Season under the provisions of the CBA. Special Master Friedenthal concluded that the clear language of the CBA provides that a player will only be credited with an Accrued Season if he is on full pay status for a total of six or more regular season games in a given year and that games played by other NFL teams during a week in which a player's team has a bye cannot count toward the calculation of an Accrued Season. For the reasons stated, the court concurs with the special master and affirms his decision.

. . . .

Discussion

The parties do not dispute the relevant language of the CBA but rather its interpretation. . . . [T]he court must give effect and meaning to every term of the contract, making every reasonable effort to harmonize all of its terms. The contract must also be interpreted so as to effectuate, not nullify, its primary purpose.

Class counsel argues that a player should be credited with a "game" under the definition of an Accrued Season when his team is on a bye week so long as he is on full pay status and there are other regular season games being played during that week. In other words, they believe that CBA Art. XXVIII, § 1(a) should be interpreted to read as "six or more *weeks* during the regular season." To support this position, class counsel points out that a player on a team with a bye week is still required to practice and is still entitled to receive 1/17th of his regular season salary. Class counsel also argues that there are other instances in the NFL's Constitution and Bylaws where a "week" is treated as a "game."

The court, however, is unpersuaded by this argument. The court acknowledges that there is no explicit guidance as to whether the regular season games referred to in this provision are limited to games played by the player's team or whether this provision should be interpreted to encompass the period of time in which the player is on full pay status and regular season games are being played regardless of whether the player's team has a bye week. However, the court agrees with the special master's conclusion that the language here, in specifying "six or more regular season *games*," contemplates a certain level of participation or readiness to participate. (Emphasis added.) That is, the choice of the word "games" must be construed to denote its plain and obvious meaning. If the parties intended that only the number of *payments* or the number of *weeks* that games were played in the league were to be used to calculate an Accrued Season, it would have been more logical for the parties to simply draft the provision to require "six or more payments" or "full pay status for six or more weeks."

This provision does not state "weeks" or "payments," but "games." The court may not rewrite the parties' agreement to substitute the term "weeks" for the term "games" since this would defeat the intent of the parties as indicated by the plain language of the contract.

Class counsel also asserts that this provision is ambiguous and that any interpretation should avoid arbitrary or discriminatory results. The court cannot conclude that the provision here is ambiguous. Considered in the context of the CBA as a whole, and based upon the previous discussion, the court does not believe that reasonable minds could differ as to what this provision means. *See id.* Article XVIII § 1(a) clearly and unambiguously specifies "six or more regular season games," not "weeks" or "payments."

Moreover, contrary to class counsel's assertions, the court is not convinced that affirming the special master's interpretation of this provision leads to an arbitrary or discriminatory result. The distinction between games and weeks was drawn by the parties in the CBA, not by the special master or this court. The requirement that a player be on full pay status for six or more regular season games is no more arbitrary or discriminatory than any other bright line rule, such as the agreement to require full pay status for six as opposed to five or seven games. The fact that players may be required to perform other services or receive an allotment of compensation during bye weeks does not suggest anything arbitrary or irrational, but instead reflects one of the many compromises reached by the parties during the course of negotiations.

Class counsel also stresses that the court must reach a fair and reasonable result in interpreting this provision that is consistent with the purposes sought to be attained by the parties. The language of the CBA demonstratively reflects that when the parties intend to refer to "weeks," as opposed to "games," they do so clearly and unequivocally. Similarly, when the parties intend a "bye week" to count as a "game," it is explicitly and clearly stated in the language of the CBA.

The court thus believes that its interpretation of Article XVIII § 1(a), i.e., construing the definition of an Accrued Season to count only games actually played by a team that is paying a player and not bye weeks in which other NFL teams are playing games, reflects a fair and reasonable interpretation of the CBA since it is consistent with other provisions in the CBA and is in conformance with the purposes of the parties as reflected in the record. Had the parties intended the word "games" to simply means "weeks," they would have explicitly provided, as they did elsewhere, that a bye week counts as a game. *See, e.g.,* CBA Art. XXXIV § 4(b).

The court therefore concludes that under settled principles of contract interpretation, the term "weeks," cannot be substituted for the term "games." This court has applied this principle of contract interpretation since the beginning of the CBA. As this court noted in the *Grabach-Hobart* proceeding:

"By employing different language in different sections of the SSA, it is clear that the parties recognized and understood the difference between "sole control" and "likely to be earned." Had the parties intended "likely to be earned" to be the test for the portion of signing bonuses over voidable contract years, they could have so agreed." *See White v. NFL*, 972 F.Supp. 1230, 1239 (D.Minn.1997).

Thus, this court will not read into the CBA under the guise of contract construction a condition that the parties did not insert or intend to add.

. . . . [T]he court affirms Special Master Friedenthal's conclusion that the intent of the parties is reflected in the unambiguous language providing that "a player shall receive one Accrued Season for each season during which he was on . . . full pay status for a total of six or more regular season games." CBA Art. XVIII § 1(a). And under this provision, a player cannot count toward an Accrued Season a game played by other NFL teams during a week in which the team that pays him has a bye. Since Kyle Richardson was on full pay status for only five regular season games during the 1997 season, he cannot receive credit for an Accrued Season for that season.

Accordingly, IT IS HEREBY ORDERED that the objections of class counsel are overruled and the decision of the special master is affirmed.

Source: Courtesy of Westlaw; reprinted with permission.

UNFAIR LABOR PRACTICES

The National Labor Relations Board enforces the NLRA regarding unfair labor practices. Section 8(d) of the NLRA requires management and labor to "meet at reasonable times and confer in good faith with respect to wages, hours, and other terms and conditions of employment." If either side fails to do so, it can be considered an unfair labor practice. The National Labor Relations Board cannot coerce or force either the union or employer to agree to a specific proposal or to make any concessions.[18] The NLRA describes unfair labor practices as follows.

---

[18] United Steelworkers of America, AFL-CIO v. N.L.R.B., C.A.D.C. (1970); 441 F.2d 1005, 142 U.S. App. D.C. 315, *cert. denied*, 93 S. Ct. 50, 409 U.S. 846, 34 L. Ed. 2d. 87.

§ 158. Unfair Labor Practices

(a) Unfair labor practices by employer

It shall be an unfair labor practice for an employer—

(1) to interfere with, restrain, or coerce employees in the exercise of the rights guaranteed in section 157 of this title;

(2) to dominate or interfere with the formation or administration of any labor organization or contribute financial or other support to it. . . .

(3) by discrimination in regard to hire or tenure of employment or any term or condition of employment to encourage or discourage membership in any labor organization. . . .

(4) to discharge or otherwise discriminate against an employee because he has filed charges or given testimony under this subchapter;

(5) to refuse to bargain collectively with the representatives of his employees. . . .

An unfair labor practice can arise in a variety of situations. For instance, it is considered an unfair labor practice for an employer to promote decertification of a union.[19] The NLRA promotes the freedom of employees to select a bargaining representative, and it would be considered an unfair labor practice for an employer to encourage or discourage employees from joining a bona fide union.[20] An employer cannot attempt to influence employees to join one union over another.[21] If an employer uses threats and coercion to interfere with an employee's right of organization under the act, it is considered an unfair labor practice.[22] In the context of sports, labor relations issues have arisen regarding leagues interfering with the players' right to unionize, leagues refusing to recognize players' unions as the exclusive bargaining representatives, and employers retaliating against players for engaging in union activity.

If a team releases a player because of union activity, that can constitute an unfair labor practice. In *N.L.R.B v. Nordstrom d/b/a Seattle Seahawks*, 292 NLRB 899 (1985), wide receiver Sam McCullum alleged that the Seahawks cut him because of his union activity. McCullum had been selected as the team's union representative. He implemented a "solidarity handshake" that he engaged in with his teammates and opposing players prior to the first preseason games of the 1982 season. This did not win favor with the coaching staff of the Seahawks. McCullum started every preseason game for the Seahawks but was cut from the team after the Seahawks acquired another wide receiver. The NFLPA and McCullum alleged that his union activities had cost him his job. The Seahawks defended, stating that McCullum was cut based on lack of skill. The Seattle Seahawks sought a review of the NLRB's ruling that McCullum had been released by the team for engaging in union-related activities. Eleven years after his release, McCullum was vindicated when a federal court affirmed the NLRB's proceeding and affirmed an award of $301,000 in back pay to the wide receiver.

Generally speaking, unions desire to bargain over a wide range of issues, whereas management attempts to carefully narrow the specific issues to be addressed. As mentioned previously, unions and management have a duty to bargain in good faith over wages, hours, and other terms and conditions.

---

[19] N.L.R.B. v. Birmingham Publishing Company, C.A. 5, 262 F.2d 2 (1958).
[20] N.L.R.B. v. Stowe Spinning Co., 165 F.2d 609 (1947), *rev'd on other grounds*, 336 U.S. 226 (1949).
[21] N.L.R.B. v. Fotochrome, Inc., 343 F.2d 631 (1965), *cert. denied*, 382 U.S. 833.
[22] N.L.R.B. v. Coast Delivery Service, Inc., 437 F.2d 264 (Cal. 1971).

Problem 4-2 explores the issue of what is a subject of mandatory bargaining. What obligations do the parties have to disclose information to the opposing party?

Problem 4-2

You are the agent for Mike Jones, a recent graduate of the University of Northern Iowa who was drafted as a deep snapper in the seventh round of the NFL draft by the Green Bay Packers. Jones's father was a member of a union his entire working life, and Mike feels very dedicated to union activity because of his father. He wants to be the union representative for the Packers. He also plans to wear a headband while on the sidelines during the first preseason game in honor of his father, who recently passed away. The headband states "Unions Forever." As his agent, how would you advise him? What could be the repercussions of his actions? What actions can be taken by the league or team against Jones? What are his rights as a union member?

After the signing of the 1985 basic agreement, baseball owners began to conspire with one another on how to hold down salaries in baseball. The owners entered into an unspoken gentlemen's agreement to attempt to drive down the market price for star players by failing to offer free agents a significant contract. The owners as a collective group refused to sign star free agents. Kirk Gibson was the 1984 World Series Most Valuable Player (MVP) for the Detroit Tigers, who beat the San Diego Padres. Gibson was unable to attract any offers whatsoever from other clubs after his great season and showing in the World Series. The National League MVP for the 1984 season was Andre Dawson, "the Hawk." He was forced to sign a blank contract with the Cubs that paid him less than he had earned the previous season. The Players Association filed a grievance in 1985 and filed a second grievance in 1986 after more free agents were not able to receive their full market value. After the 1987 season, the owners began using an information bank when they traded offers about players. The Players Association filed a third grievance, asserting that this practice was collusion among owners. The average salary for a Major League Baseball player declined from 1986 to 1987. The players' challenge to the owners' collusion was upheld through the arbitration process, and the three cases were eventually settled for $280,000,000, with funds being distributed to individual players through the MLBPA.

Players have the right to strike under the NLRA. If they do strike, management has the right to hire replacement workers, which it did for the 1987 NFL season. That particular strike lasted three weeks. When players returned from the strike, clubs retaliated against them. Case 4-6, *National Labor Relations Board v. National Football League Management Council*, 309 NLRB 78 (1992), examines the NFL players' right to strike and the retaliation that occurred.

📖 CASE 4-6 *National Labor Relations Board v. National Football League Management Council*

309 NLRB 78 (1992)

BY CHAIRMAN STEPHENS AND MEMBERS DEVANEY AND OVIATT

The parties began negotiations for a successor to the 1982–1987 agreement early in 1987. These negotiations were unsuccessful and, on

September 21, 1987, after the second week of regular season play, the players went out on strike. The Respondents immediately began hiring temporary replacements for the striking players. Because certain Clubs were unable to assemble complete teams in time for the games scheduled for September 27-28, 1987, the Respondents canceled those games.

The Respondents also substantially modified the NFL's complex personnel rules governing the hiring of players and their eligibility to play in a game. . . .

Only players on a Club's Active list were eligible to play in a game. The Respondents' rules usually provide that, for games played on a Saturday or Sunday, each Club must establish its Active list for the game by 2 p.m. New York time the day prior to that game. For Monday night games, the deadline is 2 p.m. New York time the day of the game.

In response to the strike, the Respondents substantially modified these rules. On September 29, 1987, the NFL Management Council Executive Committee (CEC) eliminated roster limits until 4 p.m. New York time on October 3, 1987. Clubs were permitted an unlimited number of players on their Inactive lists with a 45-player Active list limit for participating in the games on October 4-5. The deadline for establishing the Active lists was set at 4 p.m. New York time on October 3, and a deadline of 12 p.m. noon local time on Friday (October 2) was established for signing nonroster players. The CEC also established a deadline of 12 p.m. noon local time on October 2 for strikers to report in order to be eligible to play in the Sunday or Monday games.

On October 1, the above rules were modified to establish a 3 p.m. Friday New York time deadline for strikers to report in order to be eligible for that weekend's games or for Clubs to sign nonroster players.

On October 5, the CEC further modified its eligibility rules for returning strikers. The deadline for signing nonroster players was moved back to 4 p.m. New York time Saturday for teams playing on Sunday, and to 4 p.m. New York time on Monday for teams playing that night. For strikers, however, the reporting deadline was set at 1 p.m. New York time on Wednesdays. Strikers reporting after that time were not eligible to play in the following weekend's game, could not be paid for that game, and were exempt from counting against the Club's Active or Inactive list until 4 p.m. New York time on the day following that game. This rule was in effect on Thursday October 15, when the Union advised the Respondents that the strike was over; on the basis of this rule all strikers who had not reported prior to the deadline were declared ineligible to play in the games scheduled for October 18-19 and were not paid for that game. . . .

The judge found, and we agree, that the Union unconditionally offered to return to work on Thursday October 15. For the reasons that follow, we find that the Respondents unlawfully discriminated against the strikers by maintaining and enforcing the Wednesday eligibility deadline to preclude their participation in or payment for the games played on October 18-19.

The Supreme Court has recognized that "there are some practices which are inherently so prejudicial to union interests and so devoid of significant economic justification . . . that the employer's conduct carries with it an inference of unlawful intent so compelling that it is justifiable to disbelieve the employer's protestations of innocent purpose." American Ship Building Co. v. NLRB, 380 U.S. 300 (1965). If an employer's conduct falls within this category, "the Board can find an unfair labor practice even if the employer introduces evidence that the conduct was motivated by business considerations." NLRB v. Great Dane Trailers, 388 U.S. 26, 34 (1967).

On the other hand, if the impact on employee rights of the discriminatory conduct is comparatively slight, an antiunion motivation must be proved to sustain the charge if the employer has come forward with evidence of legitimate and substantial business justifications for the conduct. Thus, in either situation, once it has been proved that the employer engaged in discriminatory conduct which could have adversely affected employee rights to some extent, the burden is upon the employer to establish that it was motivated by legitimate objectives since proof of motivation is most accessible to him.

Applying these principles to this case, we find as an initial matter that the Wednesday deadline rule clearly constitutes discriminatory conduct which adversely affects employee rights. On its face, the rule discriminates against strikers by applying different, and more stringent, standards for eligibility to participate in NFL games (and to be paid for such participation). Moreover, the rule also adversely affects one of the most significant rights protected by the Act—the right to strike. The Board and the courts, applying the principles of Great Dane, have long recognized that the right to strike includes the right to full and complete reinstatement upon unconditional application to return. . . .

As in Laidlaw, the Respondents—in reliance on their Wednesday reporting deadline—offered the striking employees who reported for work on October 15 "less than the rights accorded by full reinstatement" (i.e., the right to participate in the games scheduled for October 18-19 and to be paid for those games). Laidlaw, supra, 171 NLRB at 1368. Thus, the Wednesday deadline adversely affected the striking

employees in the exercise of their right to strike or to cease participating in the strike, by prohibiting the full and complete reinstatement, for the October 18-19 games, of those employees who chose to
return to work after the Respondents' deadline had passed.

We need not decide whether, as the General Counsel contends, the
Respondents' conduct was inherently destructive of employee rights.
Even assuming that the impact on employee rights of the Wednesday
deadline rule for strikers was "comparatively slight," the burden
still rests with the Respondents to establish "legitimate and substantial business justifications" for the rule. For the reasons that
follow, we find that the Respondents have not made the required
showing.

The Respondents assert that the Wednesday deadline was justified by
the Clubs' need for sufficient time to prepare returning players for
game conditions. In this regard, the Respondents presented evidence
that the strikers' physical condition would be expected to deteriorate
as the strike progressed. In addition, NFL Management Council official
Eddie LeBaron testified that players could not maintain their "football
condition" without participating in practices involving physical
contact. The Respondents also assert that they particularly did not
wish to risk injuries to so-called franchise players.

The Respondents also assert that the rule is justified by their goal
of ensuring that each Club operates from the same competitive position. Thus, the Wednesday deadline would give each Club the same
amount of preparation time with returning players, prevent situations
in which a replacement squad was "mismatched" against a squad composed
of veterans who had reported late in the week, and ensure that Clubs
could prepare for specific players during the Wednesday and Thursday
practices when game plans were typically practiced.

Finally, the Respondents assert that the Wednesday deadline was justified in light of substantial administrative difficulties allegedly
posed if strikers returned at a late date in the week. These alleged
difficulties included the question of how to merge replacement squads
and strikers, as well as the logistics of practicing and evaluating
two squads of players at the same time and arranging transportation to
away games for late-reporting players.

In evaluating the Respondents' justifications, we initially note the
unprecedented nature of the Wednesday deadline and the absence of any
evidence that the Respondents have imposed a deadline of this type on
employees outside of a strike setting. In particular, the record shows
that players who withheld their services in pursuit of individual
goals (i.e., players holding out for a more lucrative contract) are

not subject to comparable restraints on their status on their return. Rather, such players are eligible to play immediately so long as they are included in the Club's active roster. . . .

It is undisputed that the Wednesday deadline was only applicable to striking players. The Respondents could and did sign nonstrikers to contracts subsequent to the date the strikers were declared ineligible. . . .

Under these circumstances, we find that the Respondents have not established legitimate and substantial justifications for the deadline rule. While it may be true that some striking employees' physical conditioning declined during the strike, the same considerations were present in the case of holdouts and of replacement players. . . .

We also find that the Respondents' asserted competitiveness concerns are unpersuasive. Although the Respondents were entitled to ensure that all clubs operated under the same rules, adopting a deadline which discriminated against strikers was unnecessary to the achievement of this goal. The Respondents' argument that Clubs needed the practice time provided by the Wednesday deadline to prepare the strikers to play (and, for the purpose of those practices, needed to know who would be playing for its opponent) is contradicted by their willingness to allow nonstrikers with substantially less preparation time to play in those games. . . .

The Respondents also provide no explanation for the fact that the initial deadline for returning strikers, 12 noon on Friday (later modified to 3 p.m. New York time), would have provided the Clubs with less time to accomplish the reinstatement of returning strikers than they actually had when the strikers reported on October 15. . . .

In sum, the Respondents' Wednesday deadline prohibited employees who returned from the strike on October 15 from playing in the following weekend's games and prohibited their Club from paying them for that game on the basis of their absence from the Club during the strike. The only players subject to such restrictions were those who chose to participate in the strike, a concerted activity protected by the Act. Players absent from their Club for other reasons were not subject to any similar restriction on their eligibility to participate in games; players ineligible to play for other reasons were nevertheless still entitled to be paid. Accordingly, for the reasons stated above, we find that the Respondents' maintenance and enforcement of its Wednesday deadline rule violated Section 8(a)(1) and (3) of the Act. . . .

To remedy the unfair labor practices which we have found, we shall order the Respondents to cease and desist, and to take certain

```
affirmative action necessary to effectuate the purposes of the Act.
Specifically, we shall order the Respondents to make whole all
employees who were denied wages and declared ineligible for the
games played on October 18 and 19, 1987, on the basis of the Respon-
dents' Wednesday eligibility rule for strikers, with interest com-
puted in the manner set forth in the judge's decision. The
Respondents shall also make whole those injured players denied com-
pensation on account of their participation in the strike in the
manner set forth in the judge's decision. . . .
```

Source: Courtesy of Westlaw; reprinted with permission.

NOTES AND DISCUSSION QUESTIONS

Collective Bargaining

1. What is required of management and labor during the collective bargaining process? Under what circumstances could management or labor be considered to be acting in "bad faith" during labor negotiations?

2. Do you agree with the operation of baseball's luxury tax system? Should owners be required to spend a minimum amount for payroll to keep their team competitive? The NBA's luxury tax has a "floor" requiring owners to keep a minimum payroll. If a team owner wants to spend as much money as he or she can to produce a winner, why shouldn't the owner be allowed to do so?

3. Do you believe professional athletes make too much money? Examine the pay scale for "The Celebrity 100" list published by *Forbes* magazine for details of the salaries of famous people. Consider the fact that actor Jim Carrey earned $20 million[23] for his role in *The Cable Guy*. Are professional athletes also entertainers? The average career for an NFL players is less than four years.

4. After cancellation of the 1994 World Series, many fans swore they would never again attend a baseball game. In 2009, Major League Baseball drew 73.4 million spectators through the turnstiles. A person could argue based on these figures that no one person can ruin the game of baseball. It is, in essence, the national pastime.

5. In October 2006, MLB and the players union extended their CBA for five more years, through 2011. The majority of the key points of the former CBA were kept intact, including revenue sharing and the luxury tax. The deal was the longest in baseball history (five years). If a strike or lockout does not occur during the term of the basic agreement, baseball would experience 16 consecutive years without a concerted action by union or management. Management wanted to get a deal done so the luxury tax would remain in place for the 2007 season. The threshold for the luxury tax was set at $136.5 million, rising

---

[23] www.imbd.com (See biography for Jim Carrey)

continuously until 2011, when it is set to be $178 million. The minimum salary increased from $327,000 to $380,000. It will be $390,000 for 2008, $400,000 in 2009, and adjusted for the cost of living in 2011.[24]

6. In terms of baseball economics, when a star free agent becomes available, only a few teams in Major League Baseball are able to make offers to the free agent. In recent years the majority of MLB teams were unable to compete for superstar free agents. How can a professional sports league operate competitively if a majority of the teams cannot compete in the open market for the best players? How can owners draw fans to the stadium if the team does not have a realistic chance of winning before the season starts?

7. Not only have player salaries risen because of collective bargaining, but also average ticket prices have risen in all four major sports. Major League Baseball's average ticket price rose from $9.14 in 1991 to $25.40 in 2008. Average ticket prices in the NFL and NBA have gone up over $20 during that same time frame. More specifically, the NFL average ticket price was $25.21 in 1991, and in 2009 the average ticket cost $75.00, and the average ticket in the NBA has gone from $22.52 in 1991 to $48.83 in 2008. The NHL's average ticket price has seen a less dramatic increase over the years, going from $33.49 in 1994 to $51.41 in 2009–2010.[25]

8. Professional leagues have taken action against teams that have exceeded the salary cap. The NFL fined 49'ers executives Carmen Policy and Dwight Clark $400,000 and $200,000, respectively, for salary cap violations. The 49'ers were required to pay a $300,000 team fine and also gave up a fifth round draft choice in 2001 and a third round draft choice in 2002. What should the penalty be if a team exceeds salary cap restrictions? Fines? Draft picks? Forfeits? A combination of these? Was the penalty meted out to Policy and Clark too harsh?

Arbitration

9. Do you approve of baseball's arbitration process? Would it operate more fairly for the owners if the arbitrator could negotiate a settlement between the two numbers instead of being required to choose between two numbers? How do you view the adversarial process of arbitration? Is it harmful to the relationship between the parties that the team is required to demean the player's accomplishments during the hearing?

10. Grievances come in all shapes and forms. In 2006 the NBPA filed a grievance over the length of shorts worn by players. League rules provided that players' shorts could not be below 0.1 inch above the knee. Over $10,000 in fines were given to several players, and NBA teams were fined $50,000 for each violation. The NBA deputy commissioner stated, "These are rules, just as there are rules with other parts of the game." The union argued during the grievance that players were being unfairly penalized for wearing uniforms made by Reebok. Billy Hunter, head of the NBPA, stated, "I understand the need to appeal to a

---

[24] *MLB, MLBPA Reportedly Reach Tentative Deal on Five-Year CBA*, Street & Smith's SportsBusiness Daily, Oct. 23, 2006.
[25] Fox Sports.com.

fan base who buy tickets, but sometimes I think it's like throwing the baby out with the bath water." He further stated, "Too much scrutiny is going on, and what it's doing is interfering with the play."[26] Do you believe this is the type of issue that should be subject to labor arbitration?

11. In 2006, an arbitrator ruled that the Tennessee Titans could not prevent quarterback Steve McNair from using their training facility while he was under contract with the team. The Titans were attempting to renegotiate McNair's contract to reduce the salary cap impact before training camp so they could pursue other free agents. During a contract dispute with the Titans, McNair was asked to conduct his training away from the team's complex. The Titans were concerned that if McNair were injured while working out with the team, the team might be responsible for the "cap figure" if he were unable to play. The NFLPA argued that as long as McNair was under contract he had a right to be on the premises. The NFLPA prevailed through the arbitration process.

12. Barry Bonds was fined $5,000 by Major League Baseball for wearing wristbands that violated baseball uniform rules. His wristbands were larger than allowed and also contained a logo design not allowed by Major League Baseball rules.[27]

13. In *Major League Baseball Players Association v. Garvey*, 532 U.S. 1015 (2001), former MLB star Steve Garvey argued at the Supreme Court that an arbitration decision regarding his claim for damages arising from collusion should be vacated. The Court was called upon to determine the scope of an arbitration decision. Garvey had alleged that his contract with the San Diego Padres had not been extended because of collusion and made a claim for $3 million. The arbitrator denied his claim, expressing doubt as to the veracity of a letter from Ballard Smith, the Padres' president and CEO from 1979 to 1987, in support of Garvey's claims. The U.S. Supreme Court affirmed the arbitration decision, denying Garvey's claims for damages due to collusion.

14. Arbitration in sports can cover a variety of topics. In *Allen v. McCall*, 521 So.2d 182 (1988), a dispute arose concerning the amount an agent was entitled to for negotiating a contract. The agent invoked the arbitration provisions under the NFLPA regulations that governed contract advisors. The court of appeals reversed the arbitration decision based on the fact that the arbitrator had failed to consider whether the agent had received notice of the arbitration hearing.

15. On November 19, 2004, the NBA experienced a blight on the good name of the sport. With less than a minute left in a game between the Detroit Pistons and the Indiana Pacers, a fight broke out between players after Ron Artest committed a flagrant foul against Detroit Pistons player Ben Wallace. Players began to fight with one another, and the fight eventually moved into the stands as Artest began to fight Detroit Piston fans. NBA Commissioner David Stern subsequently levied fines against nine players and suspended them for a total of 140 games. Ron Artest was suspended by the NBA for the rest of the season. Two other Pacers players, Stephen Jackson and Jermaine O'Neal, were also suspended,

---

[26] Marc Stein, *Union Files Grievance over Fines for Long Shorts*, ESPN.com.

[27] Barry M. Bloom, *Bonds Fined for Apparel Violation; Slugger Will Appeal Decision Regarding His Wristbands*, MLB.com.

Jackson for 30 games and O'Neal for 25. The NBA immediately took action and appealed the commissioner's ruling to a grievance arbitration, stating that the CBA did not allow such punishment by the commissioner. The league argued that any appeal must be made directly to the commissioner, not a grievance arbitrator. The opinion in *National Basketball Association v. National Basketball Players Association, Ron Artest, Stephen Jackson, Anthony Johnson, and Jermaine O'Neal*, 2005 WL 22869 (S.D.N.Y. 2005) was the result of the NBA filing a declaratory judgment action asserting that the arbitrator did not have jurisdiction to hear the appeal. Under what circumstances does the commissioner have the sole authority to render discipline for player misconduct and hear appeals of any decision that is rendered? When is a decision by the commissioner of a sports league arbitratable?

Unfair Labor Practices

16. Immediately after the NFL's first CBA was agreed to, NFL owners unilaterally instituted a rule that imposed a $200 fine on any player who left the bench during a fight. The NFLPA argued that the unilateral implementation of this rule was a "refusal to bargain" in violation of federal labor law. The owners argued that the commissioner had established the rule under his authority. The NLRB determined that the rule originated from the owners and that because the rule was a mandatory subject of bargaining, it was an unfair labor practice to unilaterally implement the rule.[28]

17. In 2000 the owners of the Arena Football League threatened to cancel the entire 2000 season after a player's antitrust lawsuit had been filed. Several players formed the Arena Football League Players Association (AFLPA) but did not unionize so that they could avoid the nonstatutory labor exemption, which would have most likely barred their claim. Shortly thereafter the owners recognized the Arena Football League Players Organizing Committee (AFLPOC) as the players' sole bargaining representative. In September 2000, the NLRB filed an unfair labor challenge against the AFL, stating that club owners and league officials had threatened players and illegally promised them benefits to coerce them to accept the AFLPOC as their union. After the complaint was filed, the AFL reached a settlement that paid AFL players $5 million in damages.[29]

    Consider the case of Korey Stringer, the former Minnesota Vikings player who died after collapsing on the playing field. Stringer, an All-Pro lineman, died in a team practice that was being held in conditions of high heat and humidity. Stringer weighed 335 pounds and was in full pads at the time of his death. Stringer's death was the first recorded death from heatstroke in the NFL. Stringer's estate subsequently filed a wrongful death lawsuit against the Minnesota Vikings for $100 million. Kelci Stringer v. NFL, et al., Case No. 2:03-cv-665 (S.D. Ohio).

---

[28] NFLPA v. NLRB, 503 F.2d 12 (8th Cir. 1974).
[29] *Arena Football League Players Sign Six-Year CBA*, SportsBusiness.com, Sept. 28, 2001.

SUGGESTED READINGS AND RESOURCES

Dowbiggin, Bruce. *Money Players: How Hockey's Greatest Stars Beat the NHL at Its Own Game*. Toronto: McClelland & Stewart, 2003.

Korr, Charles P. *The End of Baseball as We Knew It: The Players Union, 1960–81*. Urbana: University of Illinois Press, 2002.

Lewis, Michael. *Moneyball: The Art of Winning an Unfair Game*. New York: W. W. Norton, 2004.

Smart, Barry. *Sport Star: Modern Sport and the Cultural Economy of Sporting Celebrity*. London: Sage Publications, 2005.

Staudohar, Paul D. *Playing for Dollars: Labor Relations and the Sports Business*. Ithaca, NY: ILR Press, 1996.

Wetzel, Dan, & Yaeger, Don. *Sole Influence: Basketball, Corporate Greed, and the Corruption of America's Youth*. New York: Warner Books, 1999.

Zimbalist, Andrew S. *Unpaid Professionals: Commercialism and Conflict in Big-Time College Sports*. Princeton, NJ: Princeton University Press, 2001.

REFERENCE MATERIALS

Backman, Scott. *NFL Players Fight for Their Freedom: The History of Free Agency in the NFL*. 9 SPORTS LAWYERS JOURNAL 1 (2002).

Baker, Thomas A., & Connaughton, Dan. *The Role of Arbitrability in Disciplinary Decisions in Professional Sports*. 16 MARQUETTE SPORTS LAW REVIEW 123 (2005).

Champion, Walter T. *Collective Bargaining*. In *Fundamentals of Sports Law*. St. Paul, MN: Thomson/West, 2004.

Cochran, James. *Data Management, Exploratory Data Analysis, and Regression Analysis with 1969–2000 Major League Baseball Attendance*. 10 JOURNAL OF STATISTICS EDUCATION (2002), http://www.amstat.org/publications/jse/v10n2/datasets.cochran.html.

Cohen, George. *Major Sports League Collective Bargaining Agreements Relating to Grievance Arbitration and Salary Arbitration*. In *Entertainment, Arts, and Sports Law: ALI-ABA Course of Study*. American Law Institute–American Bar Association, SK035 ALI-ABA 341, 2005.

Conti, Jonathan. *The Effect of Salary Arbitration on Major League Baseball*. 5 SPORTS LAWYERS JOURNAL 221 (1998).

Donegan, Frederick. *Examining the Role of Arbitration in Professional Baseball*. 1 SPORTS LAWYERS JOURNAL 183 (1994).

Edel, Martin. *Panel III: Restructuring Professional Sports Leagues*. 12 FORDHAM INTELLECTUAL PROPERTY, MEDIA AND ENTERTAINMENT LAW JOURNAL 413 (2002).

Farmer, Amy, Pecorino, Paul, & Stango, Victor. *The Causes of Bargaining Failure: Evidence from Major League Baseball*. 47 JOURNAL OF LAW AND ECONOMICS 543 (2004).

Findlay, Hilary. *Rules of a Sport-Specific Arbitration Process as an Instrument of Policy Making*. 16 MARQUETTE SPORTS LAW REVIEW 73 (2005).

Fisher, Franklin M., Maxwell, Christopher, & Schouten, Evan S. *The Economics of Sports Leagues—The Chicago Bulls Case*. 10 MARQUETTE SPORTS LAW JOURNAL 1 (1999).

Fleming, Joseph Z. *The Use of the Infield Fly Rule and Evaluation of Comments by Yogi Berra as Precedent for Resolving Disputes Under Labor, Employment Discrimination and Humanitarian Relief Laws Affecting Sports, Arts, and Entertainment Industries.* In *Entertainment, Arts, and Sports Law: ALI-ABA Course of Study.* American Law Institute–American Bar Association, SK035 ALI-ABA 263, 2005.

Gould, William B., IV. *Labor Issues in Professional Sports: Reflections on Baseball, Labor and Antitrust Law.* 15 STANFORD LAW AND POLICY REVIEW 61 (2004).

Heller, Adam. *Creating a Win-Win Situation Through Collective Bargaining: The NFL Salary Cap.* 7 SPORTS LAWYERS JOURNAL 375 (2000).

Kaplan, Richard. *The NBA Luxury Tax Model: A Misguided Regulatory Regime.* 104 COLUMBIA LAW REVIEW 1615 (2004).

Lipinski, Tracy. Major League Baseball Players Ass'n v. Garvey *Narrows the Judicial Strike Zone of Arbitration Awards.* 36 AKRON LAW REVIEW 325 (2003).

Lord, Richard. *Arbitration and Professional Sports.* 20 WILLISTON ON CONTRACTS §56:10 (2004).

Masteralexis, Lisa. *Antitrust and Labor Law: Professional Sport Applications.* In *Law for Recreation and Sports Managers*, 3d ed., 663 (D. Cotton & T. J. Wilde eds.). Dubuque, IA: Kendall/Hunt, 2003.

McCormick, Robert. *Labor Loopholes: Has Collective Bargaining Become Professional Sports' Final Attraction?* 4 VILLANOVA SPORTS AND ENTERTAINMENT LAW JOURNAL 39 (1997).

Meyer, Jeffrey. *The NFLPA's Arbitration Procedure: A Forum for Professional Football Players and Their Agents to Resolve Disputes.* 6 OHIO STATE JOURNAL ON DISPUTE RESOLUTION 107 (1990).

Nissim, Ari. *The Trading Game: NFL Free Agency, the Salary Cap, and a Proposal for Greater Trading Flexibility.* 11 SPORTS LAWYERS JOURNAL 257 (2004).

Pollack, Jason. *Take My Arbitrator, Please: Commissioner "Best Interests" Disciplinary Authority in Professional Sports.* 67 FORDHAM LAW REVIEW 1645 (1999).

Pulver, Ian. *A Face Off Between the National Hockey League and the National Hockey League Players' Association: The Goal a More Competitively Balanced League.* 2 MARQUETTE SPORTS LAW JOURNAL 39 (1991).

Riemer, Stuart. *Albert Pujols: Major League Baseball Salary Arbitration from a Unique Perspective.* 22 CARDOZO ARTS AND ENTERTAINMENT LAW JOURNAL 219 (2004).

Rosenbaum, Dan. *The Brave New World of the NBA Luxury Tax.* University of North Carolina at Greensboro, March 2004.

Rosentraub, Mark. *Governing Sports in the Global Era: A Political Economy of Major League Baseball and Its Stakeholders.* 8 INDIANA JOURNAL OF GLOBAL LEGAL STUDIES 121 (2000).

Wiseman, Frederick, & Chatterjee, Sangit. *Team Payroll and Team Performance in Major League Baseball: 1985–2002.* 1 ECONOMICS BULLETIN 1–10 (2003).

Zimbalist, Andrew. *Competitive Balance in Sports Leagues.* 3 JOURNAL OF SPORTS ECONOMICS 111 (2002).

CHAPTER 5

AGENTS

Sports agents generally did not exist prior to the era of free agency in sports. Now almost every professional athlete has an agent representing his or her interests. From National Football League superstars to players in the WNBA, professional athletes have selected agents to handle issues such as contract negotiations, endorsements, business matters, legal issues, and financial planning.

Sports agents were popularized by Hollywood in the movie *Jerry Maguire,* starring Tom Cruise. Cruise, a sports agent, has an overnight epiphany of what he considers the "greedy" side of the sports business. He subsequently writes a memorandum discussing the ethics of the sports business and distributes it to the firm at which he works. He is at first highly praised for his efforts and then immediately fired. The movie's most well-known line, "Show me the money," has become the mantra of professional sports over the past few decades. Another sports agent was featured in Home Box Office's popular series *Arliss*. Arliss Michaels claimed to be the "working man's friend" as he wheeled and dealed his way through the sports world performing a myriad of duties for multimillion-dollar professional athletes.

How easy is it to become a sports agent? The process was once described as follows:

> Anyone can be an agent; every frustrated jock, every accountant who is bored, every lawyer who is doing pig iron contracts feels that athletic representation could be a lot more exciting, and it offers some vicarious thrills. The Hillside Strangler could be an agent.[1]

The idea of sports agents can be traced as far back as the career of Harold "Red" Grange, better known as the "Galloping Ghost." Grange was the original star of professional football and is thought by some to have been the greatest professional football player ever and one of the main reasons the professional game gained such popularity. Upon his arrival in professional football, the Chicago Bears put together a barnstorming tour in which they displayed his talents, playing 19 games in 62 days. In the 1920s his agent, Charles "Cash and Carry" Pyle, represented Grange in a

---

[1] RUXIN, AN ATHLETE'S GUIDE TO AGENTS 22 (1989).

variety of deals, including his playing contract, endorsement deals, and movie rights. The day after Grange played his last game at the University of Illinois in 1925, Pyle negotiated a contract with George Halas of the Chicago Bears on behalf of his client for a purported $3,000 per game and a percentage of gate receipts.

Hollywood movie producer and sports agent J. Williams Hayes represented All-Star pitchers Sandy Koufax and Don Drysdale in contract negotiations with the Los Angeles Dodgers in the mid-1960s. The era of free agency had not yet arrived in professional sports, so the use of an agent was unusual at that time. In the mid-1960s, Major League Baseball players were still shackled by the dreaded reserve clause, which gave a player only two options: he could either retire or be traded to another team. Koufax and Drysdale threatened to hold out and not play for the 1965 season unless the Dodgers agreed to increase their salaries. In 1964 Koufax had earned $85,000 as one of the best pitchers in baseball, and Drysdale had earned $80,000. Their agent suggested they engage in a joint holdout and then promptly demanded $1 million over three years to be divided equally between the two or, alternatively, argued that each should receive $167,000 annually. The Dodgers rejected the offer but eventually increased their salaries to $125,000 for Koufax and $115,000 for Drysdale for the next season. Superstars such as Grange, Koufax, and Drysdale thus used the services of an agent, but they were certainly the exception during their era. The overwhelming majority of athletes went unrepresented.

The former Detroit Tigers great Earl Wilson was one of the first players to use the services of an agent when he called upon attorney Bob Woolf to negotiate his playing contract with the Boston Red Sox in 1964. During contract negotiations, however, Wilson was prevented from bringing not only his agent to the negotiations but also any family members. If Wilson needed counsel regarding his contract during the negotiation process, he was required to leave the meeting and telephone Woolf from a pay phone. This is quite a different environment from the high-powered negotiations that can occur today between a player and management. Woolf would later represent such notable athletes as Joe Montana, Larry Bird, and Carl Yastrzemski.

One of the more legendary stories about the attitude toward sports agents involved a "discussion" between All-Pro center Jim Ringo and Hall of Fame Coach Vince Lombardi. When Ringo arrived at the Green Bay Packers' training camp, he informed Lombardi that he had retained an agent to represent him in contract negotiations with the Packers. Lombardi responded by informing Ringo that he was negotiating with the wrong team and that the negotiations should be taking place with the Philadelphia Eagles because that was where Ringo had just been traded.

The use of agents has increased substantially in the past 25 years. This increase can be attributed to many factors, including the increase in popularity of sports, the broadcasting of sports on television, the rising salaries for professional players, the extensive and complex nature of collective bargaining agreements in professional sports, the rise of labor unions, and the increased ability of a player to generate income in addition to his or her playing contract. Many sports agents and sports lawyer groups have now been formed, including the Black Sports Agents Association, the Sports Lawyers Association, and the Association of Professional Sports Agents located in England, Scotland, and Wales.

Today, many large sports representation firms exist, such as the International Management Group (IMG), Assante Sports Management Group, and SFX Sports. They represent a myriad of different athletes for a variety of different matters. IMG was the first large sports management firm. It was founded by Mark McCormack, who met Arnold Palmer while playing golf for William & Mary College. After McCormack graduated from law school, Palmer asked him to review an endorsement contract.

That was the start of a sports management firm that now has 70 offices in 30 countries and represents such notable athletes as Tiger Woods and Peyton Manning.

The sports agent business has seen a large growth of big firms in the past few years with a trend of consolidating smaller ones into larger firms. Agencies that have been purchased include F.A.M.E., owned by David Falk, best known for representing Michael Jordan; Tellem and Associates, owned by Arn Tellem, a well-known NBA agent; Hendricks Sports Management, elite baseball agents; and Speakers of Sports. These firms combine sports representation with the entertainment interests of the athlete. Large firms not only represent the athletes in contract negotiations but also perform many other functions as well. Sports firms have become a "one-stop shop" for professional athletes, handling both the athletes' business and personal needs.

Sports agents can be lawyers, certified public accountants, financial planners, or business executives. An agent must possess a good working knowledge of the sport in which he or she practices, must understand the economic issues of the sport, and must also have a working knowledge of labor relations, contracts, and business. These are all essential to any agent who represents professional athletes. For instance, an agent negotiating an NFL contract for a top draft pick must understand the ramifications of the salary cap, know the categories of free agency under the collective bargaining agreement, be able to negotiate a contract with an NFL team executive, and be able to interpret and analyze specialized legal clauses pertinent to his or her client's contract. Finally, the agent must have knowledge about the financial and tax ramifications of any deal that is entered into on behalf of the player.

It is imperative that the agent build a relationship of trust with his or her client. The agent is acting as a fiduciary on the part of a player, so it is essential that open communication and trust exist between the two parties so the agent may achieve the best results for the player. A network of contacts is important to an agent as well. The more individuals an agent knows, the better he or she is able to perform the duties of an agent. It is an advantage for agents and their client if the agent is able to establish professional working relationships with general managers, owners, and other executives of professional teams. If a player's agent is "connected" with the sports world, the agent will have a definite advantage over those agents who are not and may be able to achieve a better result for his or her client. This fact is one of the major reasons it is so difficult for new agents to break into the agent business: players tend to flock to the agents who are experienced and who already have clients and connections within the sports world.

As will be explored later in this chapter, many steps have been taken to regulate the conduct of agents and to ensure they are qualified to represent professional athletes. The idea of becoming a sports agent has now been popularized to the point at which there are companies on the Internet that offer courses in athlete management, covering topics such as NCAA compliance, contract negotiations, preparing for professional drafts, recruitment of clients, and dealing with legal and financial issues.

The popularity and intrigue of representing professional athletes have caused a glut of agents in the market. In actuality, the majority of registered sports agents with the four major professional leagues have no clients. There are approximately 3,500 professional athletes in the four major sports leagues, the NFL, NBA, NHL, and MLB. In reality, a very small number of agents represent a large number of players, leaving the majority of agents with no clients.

For a potential first-round draft pick in the National Football League, an agent in today's competitive market must arrange for a line of credit for the player from the time the player plays his last college game to the time he receives a signing bonus from his new NFL team. The agent will also be required to pay for training with a highly regarded training facility that will properly prepare the player for the NFL Combine, an event that occurs in February during which NFL teams evaluate collegiate players entering the NFL draft the following April. The agent could also be called on to arrange for financing for a new car or home during this span for the player and even the player's family members. Agents must take precautions in ensuring that the potential NFL player makes a smooth transition from his last day as a collegian to the first day he signs a professional contract. The agent must be able to provide these types of services immediately to the client upon the player's last collegiate game or the agent will not be able to compete for the top collegiate players entering the NFL draft. This makes it difficult for new agents to the most elite players.

Coaches have agents as well, but their numbers are even smaller. The majority of coaches needing agents are at the NCAA Division I college level in football and basketball. This scarcity has created fierce competition for clients among agents for players and coaches alike.

DUTIES AND RESPONSIBILITIES OF AGENTS

A sports agent may be called on to perform many functions for the client. These tasks can include tax preparation and advice, marketing of the athlete, legal advice, estate and financial planning, career counseling for the athlete's postcareer plans, and advice on media relations. Negotiating a contract for an athlete is just one of the many responsibilities an agent may have in the representation process.

The law has defined agency as "the fiduciary relation [that] results from the manifestation of consent by one person to another that the other shall act in his behalf and subject to his control, and consent by the other to so act."[2] The law imposes a fiduciary duty upon an agent. This duty involves a relationship of trust and confidence between the agent and the principal. In any agency relationship, one party agrees to act on behalf of the other and in the latter's best interest. One of the primary functions of the agent is to carry out the desires and wishes of the principal. The agent must be loyal to the principal and furthermore it is incumbent upon the agent to act solely and exclusively in the best interest of the principal and not in the interest of the agent or other parties.

The agency relationship involves a principal, who retains an agent to represent the principal's interests to a third party. In the sports context, the principal is the athlete, and the agent is the party the athlete retains to represent him or her. Both agency and contract law govern this relationship. An agent has certain duties under the law that must be discharged to the principal. These include the following:

- A duty to act in the best interest of the principal.
- A duty to keep the principal informed of all significant matters concerning the agency relationship.
- A duty to obey instructions given to the agent by the principal concerning the agency relationship.
- A duty to account to the principal for all funds handled on the principal's behalf.
- A duty to exercise reasonable care in the performance of the agent's duties.

---

[2] RESTATEMENT (SECOND) OF AGENCY § 1(1).

Problem 5-1

Art Shamsky is just starting out in the agent business. He has negotiated one contract for a player in the Canadian Football League but has not negotiated any NFL contracts. He is contacted by a cousin whose roommate is a potential high-round draft pick in the NFL. Shamsky is able to sign the player to a standard representation agreement. Shamsky begins to call various scouts of NFL teams to tell them about the player. All the scouts agree that the player will go no lower than the third round of the upcoming NFL draft. Based on this information and other research Shamsky has performed, he assures the player that he will be taken in the first three rounds of the NFL draft. Shamsky also tells the player he will be able to get him at least a $300,000 signing bonus based on the information he has received from the NFL scouts and general managers. The player is actually drafted in the sixth round of the NFL draft and only receives a signing bonus of $85,000. The player fires Shamsky and plans to file a civil lawsuit against him based on breach of contract and breach of fiduciary duty. Will the player win his lawsuit? Does the agent have any defenses to the lawsuit?

Case 5-1, *Bias v. Advantage International, Inc.*, 905 F.2d 1558 (D.C. Cir. 1990), involves the former number-one draft pick of the Boston Celtics, Len Bias, whose estate sued his former agent. Bias died of a cocaine overdose two days after he was selected as the second overall pick in the 1986 NBA draft. The lawsuit alleged that the agent failed to properly perform his duties as an agent because he failed to finalize an endorsement contract before the death of Bias and also failed to procure life insurance on Bias's behalf before he died.

📖 CASE 5-1 *Bias v. Advantage International, Inc.*

905 F.2d 1558 (D.C. Cir. 1990)

SENTELLE, Circuit Judge:

I. Background

On April 7, 1986, after the close of his college basketball career, Bias entered into a representation agreement with Advantage whereby Advantage agreed to advise and represent Bias in his affairs. Fentress was the particular Advantage representative servicing the Bias account. On June 17 of that year Bias was picked by the Boston Celtics in the first round of the National Basketball Association draft. On the morning of June 19, 1986, Bias died of cocaine intoxication. The Estate sued Advantage and Fentress for two separate injuries allegedly arising out of the representation arrangement between Bias and the defendants.

First, the Estate alleges that, prior to Bias's death, Bias and his parents directed Fentress to obtain a one-million dollar life insurance policy on Bias's life, that Fentress represented to Bias and Bias's parents that he had secured such a policy, and that in reliance on Fentress's assurances, Bias's parents did not independently seek to buy an insurance policy on Bias's life. Although the defendants did obtain increased disability coverage for Bias, in a one-million dollar disability insurance policy with an accidental death rider, they did not secure any life insurance coverage for Bias prior to his death.

Second, on June 18, 1986, the day after he was drafted by the Boston Celtics, Bias, through and with Fentress, entered into negotiations with Reebok International, Ltd. ("Reebok") concerning a potential endorsement contract. The Estate alleges that after several hours of negotiations Fentress requested that Bias and his father leave so that Fentress could continue negotiating with Reebok representatives in private. The Estate alleges that Fentress then began negotiating a proposed package deal with Reebok on behalf of not just Bias, but also other players represented by Advantage. The Estate contends that Fentress breached a duty to Bias by negotiating on behalf of other players, and that because Fentress opened up these broader negotiations he was unable to complete the negotiations for Bias on June 18. The Estate claims that as a result of Fentress's actions, on June 19, when Bias died, Bias had no contract with Reebok. The Estate alleges that the contract that Bias would have obtained would have provided for an unconditional lump sum payment which Bias would have received up front.

The District Court awarded the defendants summary judgment on both of these claims. With respect to the first claim, the District Court held, in effect, that the Estate did not suffer any damage from the defendants' alleged failure to obtain life insurance for Bias because, even if the defendants had tried to obtain a one-million dollar policy on Bias's life, they would not have been able to do so. The District Court based this conclusion on the facts, about which it found no genuine issue, that Bias was a cocaine user and that no insurer in 1986 would have issued a one-million dollar life insurance policy, or "jumbo" policy, to a cocaine user unless the applicant made a misrepresentation regarding the applicant's use of drugs, thereby rendering the insurance policy void.

With respect to the Estate's second claim, the District Court concluded that the defendants could not be held liable for failing to produce a finished endorsement contract with Reebok before Bias's death because the defendants had no independent reason to expedite the signing of the endorsement contract to the extent argued by the Estate, and because the defendants could not have obtained a signed contract before Bias's death even if they had tried to do so.

A. Bias's Prior Drug Use

The defendants in this case offered the eyewitness testimony of two former teammates of Bias, Terry Long and David Gregg, in order to show that Bias was a cocaine user during the period prior to his death. Long and Gregg both described numerous occasions when they saw Bias ingest cocaine, and Long testified that he was introduced to cocaine by Bias and that Bias sometimes supplied others with cocaine.

. . . The Estate offered affidavits from each of Bias's parents stating that Bias was not a drug user; the deposition testimony of Bias's basketball coach, Charles "Lefty" Driesell, who testified that he knew Bias well for four years and never knew Bias to be a user of drugs at any time prior to his death; and the results of several drug tests administered to Bias during the four years prior to his death which may have shown that, on the occasions when the tests were administered, there were no traces in Bias's system of the drugs for which he was tested.

Because the Estate's generalized evidence that Bias was not a drug user did not contradict the more specific testimony of teammates who knew Bias well and had seen him use cocaine on particular occasions, the District Court determined that there was no genuine issue as to the fact that Bias was a drug user. We agree.

Bias's parents and coach did not have personal knowledge of Bias's activities at the sorts of parties and gatherings about which Long and Gregg testified. The drug test results offered by the Estate may show that Bias had no cocaine in his system on the dates when the tests were administered, but, as the District Court correctly noted, these tests speak only to Bias's abstention during the periods preceding the tests. . . .

The Estate is not entitled to reach the jury merely on the supposition that the jury might not believe the defendants' witnesses. We thus agree with the District Court that there was no genuine issue of fact concerning Bias's status as a cocaine user.

B. The Availability of a Jumbo Policy in Light of Bias's Prior Drug Use

The defendants submitted affidavits from several experts who testified that in their expert opinions no insurer in 1986 would have issued a jumbo policy without inquiring, at some point in the application process, about the applicant's prior drug use. Dr. Achampong testified that insurers inquire about prior drug use at some stage of the application process, generally either in the initial application, during the medical examination, during the follow-up character investigation, or at some other stage. Dr. Achampong further concluded that an affirmative answer to this question renders an applicant uninsurable. . . . Bernard R. Wolfe, a licensed insurance agent experienced in evaluating the insurance needs of professional athletes, offered essentially the same opinion that insurance companies do not issue substantial term life insurance policies without first investigating an applicant's prior drug use and that insurance companies do not issue substantial term life insurance policies to applicants who use cocaine.

The District Court thus concluded that the Estate had failed to rebut the defendants' showing that as a cocaine user Bias would have been unable to obtain a jumbo policy. The District Court recognized that Bias might have been able to obtain a policy by lying about his prior drug use, but rightly concluded that such a knowing and material misrepresentation in response to a direct question would have rendered void any policy which Bias thereby obtained.

We agree with the District Court. The defendants offered evidence that *every* insurance company inquires about the prior drug use of an applicant for a jumbo policy at *some point* in the application process. . . . The Estate failed to name a single particular company or provide other evidence that a single company existed which would have issued a jumbo policy in 1986 without inquiring about the applicant's drug use. Because the Estate has failed to do more than show that there is "some metaphysical doubt as to the material facts," the District Court properly concluded that there was no genuine issue of material fact as to the insurability of a drug user. . . .

IV. The Reebok Contract

We find no merit in the Estate's claim based on the Reebok contract negotiations. Neither the language of the representation agreement between Bias and Advantage nor any other evidence could support a finding that the defendants breached any duty to Bias by failing to push to obtain a signed contract on June 18, 1986.

Even if the defendants were under some duty to try to sign a contract for Bias as quickly as possible, the Estate has offered no evidence to rebut the defendants' showing that the contract could not possibly have been signed prior to Bias's death, irrespective of the defendants' actions. The defendants offered testimony from Reebok officials that the language of any agreement between Reebok and Bias would have had to be reviewed by the Reebok legal department before Reebok would have signed the agreement. The Estate did not counter the defendants' evidence that an endorsement contract cannot be negotiated, drafted, and signed in a single day. In fact, the Estate's own expert testified that a contract between Bias and Reebok could not feasibly have been signed on June 18, 1986. The Estate must do more than merely argue that the feasibility of obtaining a signed endorsement contract in a single day is a question for the jury; it must offer some basis for its claim that a jury could reasonably conclude that the contract could have been drafted and signed on June 18. Because the Estate failed to do this, we affirm the District Court's award of summary judgment to the defendants on this claim.

Source: Courtesy of Westlaw; reprinted with permission.

REPRESENTATION AGREEMENTS

What terms and conditions should govern the player/agent relationship outside the scope of the common law duties imposed on the parties? Prior to the union influence in sports, agents and players would negotiate individual contracts for representation. This resulted in many different versions of representation agreements, with different fee structures and different legal obligations placed on the parties. With the rise of the influence of unions in sports, major sports leagues began to require agents to use a "standard representation agreement" when signing a potential client to a contract. This has created uniformity of representation agreements and allows the parties to have a better understanding of their obligations.

The National Football League Players Association (NFLPA) and the National Basketball Players Association (NBPA) have standard representation agreements that dictate the terms and conditions between an agent and a player. All agents desiring to represent players in the NFL and NBA must use the standard representation agreement or they cannot represent a player. MLBPA still allows agents to develop their own representation agreements with players.

The standard agreement contains clauses dealing with the fiduciary responsibility of the agent, arbitration provisions governing disputes between players and agents, and fee structures. The influence of the NFLPA has led to a concise agreement that the parties sign that allows the player to terminate the relationship between the parties upon five days' written notice. The following are significant excerpts from the NFLPA standard representation agreement.

This AGREEMENT made this _____ day of _____, 201_____, by and between _____ hereinafter (Player), _____ and thereinafter (Contract Advisor)

WITNESSETH:

In consideration of the mutual promises hereinafter made by each to the other. Player and Contract Advisor agree as follows . . .

2. Representations

Contract Advisor represents that in advance of executing this Agreement, he/she has been duly certified as a Contract Advisor by the NFLPA. Player acknowledges that the NFLPA certification of the Contract Advisor is neither a recommendation of the Contract Advisor, nor a warranty by NFLPA of the Contract Advisor's competence, honesty, skills or qualifications.

Contract Advisor hereby discloses that he/she (check one): [ ] represents or has represented; [ ] does not represent and has not represented NFL management personnel in matters pertaining to their employment by or association with any NFL club. (If Contract Advisor responds in the affirmative. Contract Advisor must attach a written addendum to this Agreement listing names and positions of those NFL Personnel represented.)

3. Contract Services

Player hereby retains Contract Advisor to represent, advise, counsel, and assist Player in the negotiation, execution, and enforcement of his playing contract(s) in the National Football League.

In performing these services, Contract Advisor acknowledges that he/she is acting in a fiduciary capacity on behalf of Player and agrees to act in such manner as to protect the best interests of Player and assure effective representation of Player in individual contract negotiations with NFL Clubs. Contract Advisor shall be the exclusive representative for the purpose of negotiating player contracts for Player. However, Contract Advisor shall not have the authority to bind or commit Player to enter into any contract without actual execution thereof by Player. Once Player agrees to and executes his player contract, Contract Advisor agrees to also sign the player contract and send a copy (by facsimile or overnight mail) to the NFLPA and the NFL Club within 48 hours of execution by Player. If Player and Contract Advisor have entered into any other agreements or contracts relating to services other than the individual negotiating services described in this Section, describe the nature of the other services covered by the separate agreements:

4. Compensation for Services

If Contract Advisor succeeds in negotiating an NFL Player Contract acceptable to Player and signed by Player during the term hereof, Contract Advisor shall receive a fee of three percent (3%) of the compensation received by Player for each such playing season, unless a lesser percent (%) or amount has been agreed to by the parties and is noted in the space below. The parties hereto have agreed to the following lesser fee:

In computing the allowable fee pursuant to this Section 4 the term "compensation" shall include only base salaries, signing bonuses, reporting bonuses, roster bonuses and any performance incentives actually received by Player. The term "compensation" shall not include any "honor" incentive bonuses (i.e. ALL PRO, PRO BOWL, Rookie of the Year), or any collectively bargained benefits.

5. Payment of Contract Advisor's Fee

Contract Advisor shall not be entitled to receive any fee for the performance of his/her services pursuant to this Agreement until Player receives the compensation upon which the fee is based. However, Player may enter into an agreement with Contract Advisor to pay any fee attributable to deferred compensation due and payable to Player in advance of when the deferred compensation is paid to Player, provided that Player has performed the services necessary under his contract to entitle him to the deferred compensation. Such fee shall be reduced to its present value as specified in the NFLPA Regulations (see Section 4(b)). Such an agreement must also be in writing, with a copy sent to the NFLPA. In no case shall Contract Advisor accept, directly or indirectly, payment of any fees hereunder from Player's club. Further, Contract Advisor is prohibited from discussing any aspect of his/her fee arrangement hereunder with any club.

6. Expenses

Player shall reimburse Contract Advisor for all reasonable and necessary communication expenses (i.e., telephone and postage) actually incurred by Contract Advisor in connection with the negotiation of Player's NFL contract. Player also shall reimburse Contract Advisor for all reasonable and necessary travel expenses actually incurred by Contract Advisor during the term hereof in the negotiation of Player's NFL contract, but only if such expenses and approximate amounts thereof are approved in advance by Player. Player shall promptly pay all such expenses upon receipt of an itemized, written statement from Contract Advisor. . . .

7. Disclaimer of Liability

Player and Contract Advisor agree that they are not subject to the control or direction of any other person with respect to the timing, place, manner or fashion in which individual negotiations are to be conducted pursuant to this Agreement (except to the extent that Contract Advisor shall comply with NFLPA Regulations) and that they will save and hold harmless the NFLPA, its officers, employees and representatives from any liability whatsoever with respect to their conduct or activities relating to or in connection with this Agreement or such individual negotiations.

8. Disputes

Any and all disputes between Player and Contract Advisor involving the meaning, interpretation, application, or enforcement of this Agreement or the obligations of the parties under this Agreement shall be resolved exclusively through the arbitration procedures set forth in Section 5 of the NFLPA Regulations Governing Contract Advisors. . . .

11. Filing

This contract is signed in quadruplicate. Contract Advisor agrees to deliver two (2) copies to the NFLPA within five (5) days of its execution, one (1) copy to the Player, and retain one (1) copy for his/her files. Contract Advisor further agrees to submit any other executed agreements between Player and Contract Advisor to NFLPA.

12. Term

The term of this Agreement shall begin on the date hereof and shall continue for the term of any player contract executed pursuant to this Agreement; provided, however, that either party may terminate this Agreement effective five (5) days after written notice of termination is given to the other party. Notice shall be effective for purposes of this paragraph if sent by certified mail, postage prepaid, return receipt requested to the appropriate address contained in this Agreement.

If termination pursuant to the above provision occurs prior to the completion of negotiations for an NFL player contract(s) acceptable to Player and signed by Player, Contract Advisor shall be entitled to compensation for the reasonable value of the services performed in the attempted negotiation of such contract(s) provided such services and time spent thereon are adequately documented by Contract Advisor. If termination pursuant to the above provision occurs after Player has signed an NFL player contract negotiated by Contract Advisor, Contract Advisor shall be entitled to the fee prescribed in Section 4 above for negotiation of such contract(s).

In the event that Player is able to renegotiate any contract(s) previously negotiated by Contract Advisor prior to expiration thereof, Contract Advisor shall still be entitled to the fee he/she would have been paid pursuant to Section 4 above as if such original contract(s) had not been renegotiated. If Contract Advisor represents Player in renegotiation of the original contract(s), the fee for such renegotiation shall be based solely upon the amount by which the compensation in the renegotiated contract(s) exceeds the compensation in the original

contract(s), whether or not Contract Advisor negotiated the
original contract(s).

If the Contract Advisor's certification is suspended or revoked by the
NFLPA or the Contract Advisor is otherwise prohibited by the NFLPA
from performing the services he/she has agreed to perform herein, this
Agreement shall automatically terminate, effective as of the date of
such suspension or termination.

Source: Courtesy of Westlaw; reprinted with permission.

AGENT FEES

Some professional sports leagues have set limits on the fees agents can charge for negotiating a
player's contract. The Major League Baseball Players Association (MLBPA) allows the market to
govern the fees of player agents and has not set any limitations on agent fees. The agent fee is negotiated between the player and his agent. However, an MLB agent cannot charge a fee to a player
unless the player's salary, after deducting the agent's fee, exceeds the minimum salary guaranteed by
baseball's Basic Agreement.

The standard representation agreement of the NBPA states the following with regard to fees:

The Player shall pay fees to the Agent for services performed pursuant
to this Agreement in accordance with the following provisions:

(A) If the Player receives only the minimum compensation under the NBA-NBPA
collective bargaining agreement (CBA) applicable for the playing season or seasons covered by the individual contract, the Agent shall receive a fee of two percent (2%) of the compensation received by the
player for each such season, unless a lesser percent (%) or amount has
been agreed to by the parties and is noted in the space below. . . .

(B) If the Player receives compensation in excess of the minimum compensation applicable under the CBA for one or more playing seasons, the Agent
shall receive a fee of four percent (4%) of the compensation received
by the Player for each such playing season, unless a lesser percent (%)
or amount has been agreed to by the parties and is noted in the space
below. . . .

(C) If the Player is a rookie drafted in the first round of the NBA Draft
who receives compensation in accordance with the "Rookie Scale" set
forth in Article VIII of the CBA, the Agent shall receive a fee that
is the higher of: (i) 4% of the compensation in excess of the 80% amount
that is guaranteed under the Rookie Scale; or (ii) the amount payable
under subparagraph (A) above by a rookie who receives only the minimum
compensation under Article II, Section 6(b) of the CBA, unless a lesser
percent (%) or amount has been agreed to by the parties and is noted
in the space below. . . .

In computing the allowable fee pursuant to paragraph 3(A),(B) or
(C) above, the term "compensation" shall include base salary, signing
bonus and any performance bonus actually received by the player; no
other benefits provided in the player contract shall be taken into
account in the computing of the fee—including, but not limited to,
the fact that the contract guarantees compensation to the player for
one or more seasons, the value of a personal loan, an insurance policy,
an automobile, or a residence, etc.

Source: Courtesy of Westlaw; reprinted with permission.

Prior to the 1987 CBA, the limit on fees for agents in the NFL was 5%. Since that time the fees for agents have slowly been reduced. The current maximum fee allowed by the NFLPA for an agent negotiating a player contract is 3%. However, the NFLPA is exploring the option of reducing the agent fee once again to a maximum of 2%. Competition has been so great for clients in the NFL that some agents have even reduced their fee to 1% for certain players, and some agents will waive fees altogether for the player's first contract just to sign a player. If a player is drafted in the seventh round of the NFL draft and receives a signing bonus and signs a standard player contract for the league's minimum salary, the agent can collect 3% on both the minimum salary amount and the signing bonus.

Even if an agent is successful in negotiating a player contract, there is no guarantee the agent will receive a fee. A player could be drafted in the NFL draft or sign a rookie free agent contract and subsequently be cut from the team; in this case, the agent would receive no fee. The agent could negotiate an NFL player contract in April but the player could be cut from the team the week before the first game in September. The agent would receive no fee even though he or she had negotiated the player's contract and may have expended sums on recruiting, training, and other expenses on behalf of the player.

The fee limitations set by the leagues only apply to player contracts and not endorsement contracts or other work performed by the agent. Agents can charge a higher fee for endorsement contracts or other legal or business-related work performed on behalf of the client. Large sports management firms charge as much as 20% for the negotiation of an endorsement contract on behalf of a client. Most leagues require the agent to provide an itemized list of expenses incurred by the agent and to seek approval by the player before incurring any expenses. If a dispute arises between a player and an agent over fees, the matter is required to be settled through binding arbitration.

Some players have chosen to pay agents an hourly fee to negotiate a contract or perform business services.[3] Some believe this results in a lower fee for the agent, depending on the amount of the contract being negotiated. Former Baltimore Orioles general counsel Lon Babby later became a well-known sports agent. He represented Rickie Weeks, the number-two pick in the 2003 Major League Baseball draft. Weeks signed a contract with the Milwaukee Brewers with a signing bonus of $3.6 million.[4] Most agents might collect as much as 5% of any signing bonus as their fee. Instead of charging 5%, Babby billed Weeks for the work he performed at an hourly rate. Babby did the same for many of his NBA clients. His practice of billing hourly attracted NBA star Grant Hill to sign with Babby. Tim Duncan and many other NBA players followed Hill and retained Babby as their agent. Babby says his fees are capped at a certain level corresponding with the amount of time he spends

[3] Berger, Brian, *Making a Case for Doing Away with Full-Time Agents,* Sports Business Radio, November 19, 2007.
[4] Haudricourt, Tom, *Brewers Sign Rickie Weeks,* Baseball America, August 5, 2003.

on the matter. He says players end up with a better deal if they are charged an hourly fee. Some agents believe this practice tarnishes the profession of the sports agent.

In Case 5-2, *Brown v. Woolf*, 554 F. Supp. 1206 (D.C. Ind. 1983), the agent was sued for fraudulent misrepresentation and breach of fiduciary duty. The aforementioned Woolf was one of the first successful sports agents in the sports world. His former client sued him, and Woolf sought to have the case dismissed on summary judgment. The court found that a question of fact existed as to whether or not Woolf engaged in fraudulent misrepresentation during his representation of the plaintiff, so his motion for summary judgment was denied.

📖 CASE 5-2 *Brown v. Woolf*

554 F. Supp. 1206 (D.C. Ind. 1983)

STECKLER, District Judge.

This matter comes before the Court on the motions of defendant, Robert G. Woolf, for partial summary judgment and for summary judgment. Fed.R.Civ.P. 56.

The complaint in this diversity action seeks compensatory and punitive damages and the imposition of a trust on a fee defendant allegedly received, all stemming from defendant's alleged constructive fraud and breach of fiduciary duty in the negotiation of a contract for the 1974–75 hockey season for plaintiff who was a professional hockey player. Plaintiff alleges that prior to the 1973–74 season he had engaged the services of defendant, a well known sports attorney and agent, who represents many professional athletes, has authored a book, and has appeared in the media in connection with such representation, to negotiate a contract for him with the Pittsburgh Penguins of the National Hockey League. Plaintiff had a professionally successful season that year under the contract defendant negotiated for him and accordingly again engaged defendant's services prior to the 1974–75 season. During the negotiations in July 1974, the Penguins offered plaintiff a two-year contract at $80,000.00 per year but plaintiff rejected the offer allegedly because defendant asserted that he could obtain a better, long-term, no-cut contract with a deferred compensation feature with the Indianapolis Racers, which at the time was a new team in a new league. On July 31, 1974, plaintiff signed a five-year contract with the Racers. Thereafter, it is alleged the Racers began having financial difficulties. Plaintiff avers that Woolf continued to represent plaintiff and negotiated two reductions in plaintiff's compensation including the loss of a retirement fund at the same time defendant was attempting to get his own fee payment from the Racers. Ultimately the Racers' assets were seized and the organizers defaulted on their obligations to plaintiff. He avers that he received only $185,000.00 of the total $800,000.00 compensation under the Racer contract but that defendant received his full $40,000.00 fee (5% of the contract) from the Racers.

Plaintiff alleges that defendant made numerous material misrepresentations upon which he relied both during the negotiation of the Racer contract and at the time of the subsequent modifications. Plaintiff further avers that defendant breached his fiduciary duty to plaintiff by failing to conduct any investigation into the financial stability of the Racers, failing to investigate possible consequences of the deferred compensation package in the Racers' contract, failing to obtain guarantees or collateral, and by negotiating reductions in plaintiff's compensation from the Racers while insisting on receiving all of his own. Plaintiff theorizes that such conduct amounts to a prima facie case of constructive fraud for which he should receive compensatory and punitive damages and have a trust impressed on the $40,000.00 fee defendant received from the Racers.

. . . By his motion for summary judgment, defendant attacks several aspects of plaintiff's claims against him. He argues (1) that plaintiff cannot recover on a breach of contract theory because Robert G. Woolf, the individual, was acting merely as the agent and employee of Robert Woolf Associates, Inc. (RWA), (2) that defendant's conduct could not amount to constructive fraud because (a) plaintiff alleges only negligent acts, (b) there is no evidence defendant deceived plaintiff or violated a position of trust, (c) there is no showing of harm to the public interest, and (d) there is no evidence that defendant obtained an unconscionable advantage at plaintiff's expense.

. . . Indiana cases contain several formulizations of the tort of constructive fraud. Generally it is characterized as acts or a course of conduct from which an unconscionable advantage is or may be derived . . . or a breach of confidence coupled with an unjust enrichment which shocks the conscience . . . or a breach of duty, including mistake, duress or undue influence, which the law declares fraudulent because of a tendency to deceive, injure the public interest or violate the public or private confidence. . . . Another formulization found in the cases involves the making of a false statement, by the dominant party in a confidential or fiduciary relationship or by one who holds himself out as an expert, upon which the plaintiff reasonably relies to his detriment. The defendant need not know the statement is false nor make the false statement with fraudulent intent. . . .

The Court believes that both formulizations are rife with questions of fact, *inter alia,* the existence or nonexistence of a confidential or fiduciary relationship and the question of reliance on false representations as well as questions of credibility.

Defendant argues that despite the customary existence of such fact questions in a constructive fraud case, judgment is appropriate in this instance because plaintiff has produced nothing to demonstrate the existence of fact questions.

. . . In this case, defendant has offered affidavits, excerpts of depositions, and photocopies of various documents to support his motions. He contends that such materials demonstrate that reasonable minds could not conclude that defendant did the acts with which the complaint charges him. In response, plaintiff rather belatedly offered portions of plaintiff's depositions as well as arguing that issues such as those raised by a complaint based on constructive fraud are inherently unsuited to resolution on a motion for summary judgment.

Having carefully considered the motions and briefs and having examined the evidentiary materials submitted, the Court concludes that summary judgment would not be appropriate in this action. The Court is not persuaded that there are no fact questions remaining unresolved in this controversy such that defendant is entitled to judgment as a matter of law. As movant for summary judgment, defendant bears the "heavy burden" of clearly demonstrating the absence of any genuine issue of a material fact.

By reason of the foregoing, defendant's motions for partial summary judgment and for summary judgment are hereby DENIED.

Source: Courtesy of Westlaw; reprinted with permission.

The following excerpts from the NFLPA regulations relating to agent fees set forth the maximum fees that NFL agents can receive. They also set forth the timing of the payment of those fees. (The NFLPA refers to its agents as "contract advisors.")

Section 4: Agreements Between Contract Advisors and Players; Maximum Fees

B. Contract Advisor's Compensation

1. The maximum fee which may be charged or collected by a Contract Advisor shall be three percent (3%) of the "compensation" (as defined within this Section) received by the player in each playing season covered by the contract negotiated by the Contract Advisor.
2. The Contract Advisor and player may agree to any fee which is less than the maximum fee set forth in (1) above.
3. As used in this Section 4(B), the term "compensation" shall be deemed to include only salaries, signing bonuses, reporting bonuses, roster bonuses, and any performance incentives earned by the player during the term of the contract (including any option year) negotiated by the Contract Advisor. For example, and without limitation, the term compensation

shall not include any "honor" incentive bonuses (e.g. ALL PRO, PRO BOWL, Rookie of the Year), or any collectively bargained benefits or other payments provided for in the player's individual contract.

4. A Contract Advisor is prohibited from receiving any fee for his/her services until and unless the player receives the compensation upon which the fee is based. However, these Regulations recognize that in certain circumstances a player may decide that it is in his best interest to pay his Contract Advisor's fee in advance of the receipt of any deferred compensation from his NFL club. Accordingly, a player may enter into an agreement with a Contract Advisor to pay the Contract Advisor a fee advance on deferred compensation due and payable to the player. Such fee advance may only be collected by the Contract Advisor after the player has performed the services necessary under his contract to entitle him to the deferred compensation. Further, such an agreement between a Contract Advisor and a player must be in writing, with a copy sent by the Contract Advisor to the NFLPA.

For purposes of determining the fee advance, the compensation shall be determined to be an amount equal to the present value of the deferred player compensation. . . .

5. A Contract Advisor who is found to have violated Section 3(B)(2) or (3) of these Regulations shall not be entitled to a fee for services provided to a player who was the subject of an improper inducement under Section 3(B)(2) or (3). In the event that the Contract Advisor collects any fees from the player before a finding of such violation, he/she shall be required to reimburse the player for such fees. If the improper inducement was a loan of money or property which was to be repaid or returned to the Contract Advisor, the money or property need not be repaid or returned by the player who was the subject of the improper inducement under Section 3(B)(2) or (3). . . . .

Source: Courtesy of Westlaw; reprinted with permission.

CONFLICTS OF INTEREST

One of the primary functions of an agent is to avoid all actual or potential conflicts of interest. It is incumbent upon the agent to avoid a conflict of interest so that the agent can dedicate his or her efforts fully to the principal's concerns. Conflicts of interest raise concerns about an agent's fiduciary duty required under the law. For example, it would be a conflict of interest and a breach of an agent's duty of loyalty to the principal to represent two principals in the same transaction unless both principals were fully aware of the situation and consented to the representation. If an agent makes full disclosure of any conflict of interest and the athlete is fully aware of the existing conflict, the agent will not have breached any fiduciary duty owed to the athlete. The duty of confidentiality also requires the agent to keep all information received by the principal in confidence during the relationship. The agent's duty of confidentiality continues even after the agent–athlete relationship has been terminated.

Possible conflict situations could exist for an agent by representing players on the same team at the same position. They could also exist if an agent represented a coach and player on the same team. The standard representation agreement for NFL contract advisors specifically requests that the agent disclose whether he or she also represents anyone in a management capacity for an NFL club.

Case 5-3, *Detroit Lions, Inc. v. Argovitz*, 580 F. Supp. 542 (6th Cir. 1984), is an example of a situation in which an agent, who was also functioning as an owner, failed to properly disclose all potential and real conflicts of interests so that a player could make a fully informed decision regarding his future team. Billy Sims was a professional football player who was represented by Jerry Argovitz. Sims was unaware that Argovitz was also the owner of a team called the Houston Gamblers. Argovitz wanted to sign Sims to a contract with the Houston Gamblers. The Gamblers were a professional team in the United States Football League (USFL). The USFL was formed in 1982 and attempted, with some success, to lure away top players from the NFL to play in its newly formed league. The league was successful in signing quarterbacks Steve Young and Jim Kelly as well as running back Herschel Walker to long-term contracts. The USFL disbanded in 1986 still owing millions of dollars to players on signed contracts. It is against this backdrop that this case is presented.

CASE 5-3 *Detroit Lions, Inc. v. Argovitz*

580 F. Supp. 542 (6th Cir. 1984)

Memorandum Opinion

DeMASCIO, District Judge.

The plot for this Saturday afternoon serial began when Billy Sims, having signed a contract with the Houston Gamblers on July 1, 1983, signed a second contract with the Detroit Lions on December 16, 1983. On December 18, 1983, the Detroit Lions, Inc. (Lions) and Billy R. Sims filed a complaint in the Oakland County Circuit Court seeking a judicial determination that the July 1, 1983, contract between Sims and the Houston Gamblers, Inc. (Gamblers) is invalid because the defendant Jerry Argovitz (Argovitz) breached his fiduciary duty when negotiating the Gamblers' contract and because the contract was other-wise tainted by fraud and misrepresentation. . . .

For the reasons that follow, we have concluded that Argovitz's breach of his fiduciary duty during negotiations for the Gamblers' contract was so pronounced, so egregious, that to deny recision would be unconscionable.

Sometime in February or March 1983, Argovitz told Sims that he had applied for a Houston franchise in the newly formed United States Football League (USFL). In May 1983, Sims attended a press conference in Houston at which Argovitz announced that his application for a franchise had been approved. The evidence persuades us that Sims did not know the extent of Argovitz's interest in the Gamblers. He did not know the amount of Argovitz's original investment, or that Argovitz was obligated for 29 percent of a $1.5 million letter of credit, or that Argovitz was the president of the Gamblers' Corporation at an annual salary of $275,000 and 5 percent the yearly cash flow. The defendants could not justifiably expect Sims to comprehend the ramifications of Argovitz's interest in the Gamblers or the manner in which that interest would create an untenable conflict of interest, a conflict that would inevitably breach Argovitz's fiduciary duty to Sims. Argovitz knew, or should have known, that he could not act as Sims' agent under any circumstances when dealing with the Gamblers. Even the USFL Constitution itself prohibits a holder of any interest in a member club from acting "as the contracting agent or representative for any player."

Conclusions of Law

. . . .

3. The relationship between a principal and agent is fiduciary in nature, and as such imposes a duty of loyalty, good faith, and fair and honest dealing on the agent.

4. A fiduciary relationship arises not only from a formal principal-agent relationship, but also from informal relationships of trust and confidence.

5. In light of the express agency agreement, and the relationship between Sims and Argovitz, Argovitz clearly owed Sims the fiduciary duties of an agent at all times relevant to this lawsuit.

6. An agent's duty of loyalty requires that he not have a personal stake that conflicts with the principal's interest in a transaction in which he represents his principal. As stated in *Burleson v. Earnest*, 153 S.W.2d 869 (Tex.Civ.App. 1941):

> (T)he principal is entitled to the best efforts and unbiased judgment of his agent. . . . (T)he law denies the right of an agent to assume any relationship that is antagonistic to his duty to his principal, and it has many times been held that the agent cannot be both buyer and seller at the same time nor connect his own interests with property involved in his dealings as an agent for another.

7. A fiduciary violates the prohibition against self-dealing not only by dealing with himself on his principal's behalf, but also by dealing on his principal's behalf with a third party in which he has an interest, such as a partnership in which he is a member. . . .

8. Where an agent has an interest adverse to that of his principal in a transaction in which he purports to act on behalf of his principal, the transaction is voidable by the principal unless the agent disclosed all material facts within the agent's knowledge that might affect the principal's judgment.

9. The mere fact that the contract is fair to the principal does not deny the principal the right to rescind the contract when it was negotiated by an agent in violation of the prohibition against self-dealing. . . .

The question, therefore, does not relate to the *mala fides* of the agent nor to whether or not a greater sum might have been procured for the property, nor even to whether or not the vendor received full value therefore. The self-interest of the agent is considered a vice which renders the transaction voidable at the election of the principal without looking into the matter further than to ascertain that the interest of the agent exists.

10. Once it has been shown that an agent had an interest in a transaction involving his principal antagonistic to the principal's interest, fraud on the part of the agent is presumed. The burden of proof then rests upon the agent to show that his principal had full knowledge, not only of the fact that the agent was interested, but also of every material fact known to the agent which might affect the principal and that having such knowledge, the principal freely consented to the transaction.

11. It is not sufficient for the agent merely to inform the principal that he has an interest that conflicts with the principal's interest. Rather, he must inform the principal "of all facts that come to his knowledge that are or may be material or which might affect his principal's rights or interests or influence the action he takes."

12. Argovitz clearly had a personal interest in signing Sims with the Gamblers that was adverse to Sims' interest—he had an ownership interest in the Gamblers and thus would profit if the Gamblers were profitable, and would incur substantial personal liabilities should the Gamblers not be financially successful. Since this showing has been made, fraud on Argovitz's part is presumed, and the Gamblers' contract must be rescinded unless Argovitz has shown by a preponderance of the evidence that he informed Sims of every material fact that might have influenced Sims' decision whether or not to sign the Gamblers' contract.

13. We conclude that Argovitz has failed to show by a preponderance of the evidence either: (1) that he informed Sims of the following facts, or (2) that these facts would not have influenced Sims' decision whether to sign the Gamblers' contract:

    a. The relative values of the Gamblers' contract and the Lions' offer that Argovitz knew could be obtained.

    b. That there was significant financial differences between the USFL and the NFL not only in terms of the relative financial stability of the Leagues, but also in terms of the fringe benefits available to Sims.

   c. Argovitz's 29 percent ownership in the Gamblers; Argovitz's $275,000 annual salary with the Gamblers; Argovitz's five percent interest in the cash flow of the Gamblers.

   d. That both Argovitz and Burrough failed to even attempt to obtain for Sims valuable contract clauses which they had given to Kelly on behalf of the Gamblers.

   e. That Sims had great leverage, and Argovitz was not encouraging a bidding war that could have advantageous results for Sims.

14. Under Texas law, a nonbinding prior act cannot be ratified, and the right to seek recision cannot be waived, unless the party against whom these defenses are asserted had full knowledge of all material facts at the time the acts of ratification or waiver are alleged to have occurred. . . .

17. As a court sitting in equity, we conclude that recision is the appropriate remedy. We are dismayed by Argovitz's egregious conduct. The careless fashion in which Argovitz went about ascertaining the highest price for Sims' service convinces us of the wisdom of the maxim: no man can faithfully serve two masters whose interests are in conflict. Judgment will be entered for the plaintiffs rescinding the Gamblers' contract with Sims. IT IS SO ORDERED.

Source: Courtesy of Westlaw; reprinted with permission.

Problem 5-2

Jim Pastel is a well-known sports agent in the world of professional football. He worked as an agent for 17 years representing NFL players for contract negotiations with all NFL teams. During his career as a sports agent, he worked closely with representatives from the NFLPA in drafting regulations for agents and arguing arbitration cases on behalf of players against the league for disputes between teams and players. During these 17 years he became familiar with negotiation strategies of the union as well as developing a comprehensive knowledge of contracts and salary structure. He also became well acquainted with all team owners in the leagues. During the selection process for the NFL commissioner, his name is put forth as a possible candidate. The NFL calls him for an interview. Pastel is interested in the position and decides he will go through the interview process. What legal or ethical considerations are present in this scenario? How would his interview for the commissioner's job affect his current NFL clients? If he is offered the position, should he accept? Why or why not?

Problem 5-3

Jeremy Rollins is a star player for a new NHL franchise, the Houston Ice Breakers. After three years and three losing seasons, the team files for bankruptcy. Its biggest creditor is Rollins. The team owes him $36 million based on the contract Rollins signed that brought him to Houston from Detroit. Rollins's lawyer advises him that if he files a claim with the bankruptcy court as a creditor he will recover only a very small amount of the money that is owed to him. Instead, his lawyer advises him to buy the team and become its principal owner since he is the team's biggest creditor. He follows his lawyer's advice and becomes the owner of the Ice Breakers as well as its star player. Does his dual capacity as owner-player present any problems for Rollins in his capacity as an owner or player? What action, if any, should the league or union take under the circumstances? What ethical considerations are present for Rollins?[5]

COMPETITION AMONG AGENTS

The competition for top draft picks in professional sports is extreme and fierce and sometimes can lead to questionable behavior among agents vying for top athletes. There are many reasons for increased competition for clients, including the increase in the number of agents and the amount of money involved in the transactions. It is sometimes difficult to prove that another agent improperly solicited or stole a client. Very often, the testimony that is needed to establish such proof must be extracted from the player who has just recently retained the very agent who is accused of the impropriety. The player is often not willing to testify against his or her new agent, which makes it difficult for the agent who is alleging the wrongdoing to prove misconduct.

Common law remedies are available to agents who believe that other agents have improperly solicited or taken clients from them. An agent will sometimes assert that the competing agent engaged in acts that constitute the tort of wrongful interference with contractual relations. To be successful in a case under this tort, a plaintiff must prove the following elements:

- A valid, enforceable contract must exist between two parties.
- A third party must know that this contract exists.
- This third party must intentionally cause one of the two parties to the contract to breach the contract.
- The interference must be for the purpose of advancing the economic interest of the third party.[6]

The NFLPA has taken significant steps to attempt to curb unethical and illegal behavior by agents. It requires all registered contract advisors to list their "runners," that is, individuals who perform recruiting on their behalf. The NFLPA and other player associations have also taken an aggressive stance in disciplining agents who violate union regulations while recruiting clients.

---

[5] *PLUS: HOCKEY—PITTSBURGH; Lemieux Cleared to Buy Penguins,* The New York Times, August 26, 1999.
[6] Kallok v. Medtronic, Inc., 573 N.W.2d 356 (Minn. 1998).

Litigation between superagent Leigh Steinberg and David Dunn highlights the problem of competition for clients in the sports business. Dunn left the employment of Steinberg to begin his own sports agency and took with him several significant clients of the firm. Steinberg sued Dunn, alleging that Dunn breached a covenant not to compete that he had signed with the firm whereby Dunn was to not solicit clients or take clients with him when he left the firm. The case went to trial in Los Angeles, and a jury returned a verdict in favor of Steinberg in the amount of $44.66 million in 2002. The jury determined that Dunn had breached the covenant not to compete and also engaged in unfair competition when he took clients from the firm. Dunn eventually filed for bankruptcy protection after the judgment was entered. The verdict did not scare away clients for Dunn, however. Dunn now owns his own agency, Athletes First, a sports agency representing NFL players.

Unions have also passed regulations that penalize and discipline agents who steal clients. The NFLPA regulations for agents specifically address this issue:

B. Prohibited Conduct

```
Contract Advisors are prohibited from:

.  .  .  .

21. (a) Initiating any communication, directly or indirectly, with a player
        who has entered into a Standard Representation Agreement with an-
        other Contract Advisor and such Standard Representation Agreement
        is on file with the NFLPA if the communication concerns a matter
        relating to the:
            (i) Player's current Contract Advisor;
           (ii) Player's current Standard Representation Agreement;
          (iii) Player's contract status with any NFL Club(s); or
           (iv) Services to be provided by prospective Contract Advisor
                either through a Standard Representation Agreement or
                otherwise.
    (b) If a player, already a party to a Standard Representation Agree-
        ment, initiates communication with a Contract Advisor relating to
        any of the subject matters listed in Section 3(B)(21)(a) the Con-
        tract Advisor may continue communications with the Player regard-
        ing any of those matters.
    (c) Section 3(B)(21) shall not apply to any player who has less than
        sixty (60) days remaining before his NFL Player Contract expires,
        and he has not yet signed a new Standard Representation Agreement
        with a Contract Advisor within the sixty (60) day period.
    (d) Section 3(B)(21) shall not prohibit a Contract Advisor from send-
        ing a player written materials which may be reasonably interpreted
        as advertising directed at players in general and not targeted at
        a specific player.
```

Source: Courtesy of Westlaw; reprinted with permission.

Another dispute dealing with sports agents vying for top stars was *Speakers of Sports, Inc. v. ProServ, Inc.*, Case 5-4, 178 F.3d 862 (7th Cir. 1999). In this case the plaintiff alleged that ProServ made false promises to a player that caused him to change agents. When ProServ was unable to produce the results it had promised, the player left ProServ and signed with another firm to represent him. The court was left to decide the question of whether the statements made by ProServ constituted a tort or whether the firm's conduct was merely part of the competitive process that takes place in the lucrative sports agent business.

CASE 5-4 *Speakers of Sport, Inc. v. ProServ, Inc.*

178 F.3d 862 (7th Cir. 1999)

POSNER, Chief Judge.

Ivan Rodriguez, a highly successful catcher with the Texas Rangers baseball team, in 1991 signed the first of several one-year contracts making Speakers his agent. ProServ wanted to expand its representation of baseball players and to this end invited Rodriguez to its office in Washington and there promised that it would get him between $2 and $4 million in endorsements if he signed with ProServ—which he did, terminating his contract (which was terminable at will) with Speakers. This was in 1995. ProServ failed to obtain significant endorsement for Rodriguez and after just one year he switched to another agent who the following year landed him a five-year $42 million contract with the Rangers. Speakers brought this suit a few months later, charging that the promise of endorsements that ProServ had made to Rodriguez was fraudulent and had induced him to terminate his contract with Speakers.

. . . Speakers could not sue Rodriguez for breach of contract, because he had not broken their contract, which was, as we said, terminable at will. Nor, therefore, could it accuse ProServ of inducing a breach of contract. . . . But Speakers did have a contract with Rodriguez, and inducing the termination of a contract, even when the termination is not a breach because the contract is terminable at will, can still be actionable under the tort law of Illinois, either as an interference with prospective economic advantage, or as an interference with the contract at will itself. . . .

There is in general nothing wrong with one sports agent trying to take a client from another if this can be done without precipitating a breach of contract. That is the process known as competition, which though painful, fierce, frequently ruthless, sometimes Darwinian in its pitilessness, is the cornerstone of our highly successful economic system. Competition is not a tort but on the contrary provides a defense (the "competitor's privilege") to the tort of improper interference. . . . It does not privilege inducing a breach of contract,

Soderlund Bros., Inc. v. Carrier Corp., supra, 215 Ill.Dec. 251, 663 N.E.2d at 8—conduct usefully regarded as a separate tort from interfering with a business relationship without precipitating an actual breach of contract—but it does privilege inducing the lawful termination of a contract that is terminable at will.

There would be few more effective inhibitors of the competitive process than making it a tort for an agent to promise the client of another agent to do better by him which is pretty much what this case comes down to. It is true that Speakers argues only that the competitor may not make a promise that he knows he cannot fulfill, may not, that is, compete by fraud. Because the competitor's privilege does not include a right to get business from a competitor by means of fraud, it is hard to quarrel with this position in the abstract, but the practicalities are different. If the argument were accepted and the new agent made a promise that was not fulfilled, the old agent would have a shot at convincing a jury that the new agent had known from the start that he couldn't deliver on the promise. Once a case gets to the jury, all bets are off. The practical consequence of Speakers' approach, therefore, would be that a sports agent who lured away the client of another agent with a promise to do better by him would be running a grave legal risk.

This threat to the competitive process is blocked by the principle of Illinois law that promissory fraud is not actionable unless it is part of a scheme to defraud, that is, unless it is one element of a pattern of fraudulent acts. By requiring that the plaintiff show a pattern, by thus not letting him rest on proving a single promise, the law reduces the likelihood of a spurious suit; for a series of unfulfilled promises is better (though of course not conclusive) evidence of fraud than a single unfulfilled promise.

. . . The promise of endorsements was puffing not in the most common sense of a cascade of extravagant adjectives but in the equally valid sense of a sales pitch that is intended, and that a reasonable person in the position of the "promisee" would understand, to be aspirational rather than enforceable—an expression of hope rather than a commitment. It is not as if ProServ proposed to employ Rodriguez and pay him $2 million a year. That would be the kind of promise that could found an enforceable obligation. ProServ proposed merely to get him endorsements of at least that amount. They would of course be paid by the companies whose products Rodriguez endorsed, rather than by ProServ. ProServ could not force them to pay Rodriguez, and it is not contended that he understood ProServ to be warranting a minimum level of endorsements in the sense that if they were not forthcoming ProServ would be legally obligated to make up the difference to him.

It is possible to make a binding promise of something over which one has no control; such a promise is called a warranty. But it is not plausible that this is what ProServ was doing—that it was guaranteeing Rodriguez a minimum of $2 million a year in outside earnings if he signed with it. The only reasonable meaning to attach to ProServ's so-called promise is that ProServ would try to get as many endorsements as possible for Rodriguez and that it was optimistic that it could get him at least $2 million worth of them. So understood, the "promise" was not a promise at all. But even if it was a promise (or a warranty), it cannot be the basis for a finding of fraud because it was not part of a scheme to defraud evidenced by more than the allegedly fraudulent promise itself.

It can be argued, however, that competition can be tortious even if it does not involve an actionable fraud . . . or other independently tortious act, such as defamation, or trademark or patent infringement, or a theft of a trade secret; that competitors should not be allowed to use "unfair" tactics; and that a promise known by the promisor when made to be unfulfillable is such a tactic, especially when used on a relatively unsophisticated, albeit very well to do, baseball player. Considerable support for this view can be found in the case law. But the Illinois courts have not as yet embraced the doctrine, and we are not alone in thinking it pernicious. The doctrine's conception of wrongful competition is vague—"wrongful by reason of . . . an established standard of a trade or profession,". . . . Worse, the established standards of a trade or profession in regard to competition, and its ideas of unethical competitive conduct, are likely to reflect a desire to limit competition for reasons related to the self-interest of the trade or profession rather than to the welfare of its customers or clients. We agree with Professor Perlman that the tort of interference with business relationships should be confined to cases in which the defendant employed unlawful means to stiff a competitor . . . and we are reassured by the conclusion of his careful analysis that the case law is generally consistent with this position as a matter of outcomes as distinct from articulation.

Invoking the concept of "wrongful by reason of . . . an established standard of a trade or profession," Speakers points to a rule of major league baseball forbidding players' agents to compete by means of misrepresentations. The rule is designed to protect the players, rather than their agents, so that even if it established a norm enforceable by law Speakers would not be entitled to invoke it; it is not a rule designed for Speakers' protection. In any event its violation would not be the kind of "wrongful" conduct that should trigger the tort of intentional interference; it would not be a violation of law.

The seller can be hurt even if the customer is not; but to allow the seller to obtain damages from a competitor when no consumer has been hurt is unlikely to advance the consumer interest. Allowing Speakers to prevail would hurt consumers by reducing the vigor of competition between sports agents. The Rodriguezes of this world would be disserved, as Rodriguez himself, a most reluctant witness, appears to believe. Anyway, we don't think that the kind of puffing in which ProServ engaged amounts to an unfair method of competition or an unfair act or practice. . . .

We add that even if Speakers could establish liability under either the common law of torts or the deceptive practices act, its suit would fail because it cannot possibly establish, as it seeks to do, a damages entitlement (the only relief it seeks) to the agent's fee on Rodriguez's $42 million contract. That contract was negotiated years after he left Speakers, and by another agent. Since Rodriguez had only a year-to-year contract with Speakers—terminable at will, moreover—and since obviously he was dissatisfied with Speakers at least to the extent of switching to ProServ and then when he became disillusioned with ProServ of *not* returning to Speakers' fold, the likelihood that Speakers would have retained him had ProServ not lured him away is too slight to ground an award of such damages. Such an award would be the best example yet of puffing in the pie-in-the-sky sense. AFFIRMED.

Source: Courtesy of Westlaw; reprinted with permission.

Problem 5-4

Josh James works as a sports agent for IJK Sports. He is assigned the task of representing several minor league baseball players, some of whom have the potential to make it to the major league level. After two years at the agency, one of the IJK clients assigned to Josh, Jimmy Slayton, breaks into the big leagues as a pitcher with the Cleveland Indians. Slayton telephones Josh and tells him he wants to leave IJK and wants Josh to represent him. He also tells Josh he has told two of his friends who play for the Chicago Cubs about him and that they are interested in Josh representing them as well. The Cubs players are currently represented by a well-known baseball agent. Josh wants to capitalize on this opportunity. What is the best way he should proceed? What are his legal and ethical duties to his employer and to the other agent? Will he be able to represent these players? If he leaves IJK with Jimmy Slayton as his client, does IJK have a cause of action against Josh? If so, on what basis?

THE REGULATION OF SPORTS AGENTS

Necessity for Regulation

Many different entities have attempted to regulate sports agents. Federal and state laws have been passed outlining the duties, responsibilities, and prohibited conduct of sports agents. Professional sports unions, universities, states, and the National Collegiate Athletic Association (NCAA) have all implemented rules and regulations in an attempt to monitor the conduct of sports agents. Players' unions have a major stake in ensuring that all individuals who are certified by the union as agents are qualified to represent union members. All these entities have a vested interest in protecting players from the unethical and illegal conduct of sports agents. Each has attempted, through its own respective processes, to ensure that the individuals representing a player are qualified and are engaging in ethical and legal conduct while performing the duties of a sports agent.

One of the motivating factors for the regulation of agents has been the extreme competition for clients in the professional sports industry. The popularity of sports as well as the amount of money involved has led to an increase in the number of individuals who desire to call themselves sports agents. Many individuals seek to become agents because of the large amount of money at stake, but they may not possess the necessary background or qualifications to perform the job. The sports agent profession can be very lucrative. For example, if an NFL agent is able to sign a first-round draft pick, that agent could receive as much as $300,000. Agent David Dunn's negotiation of first-round draft pick Carson Palmer's contract netted him in excess of $420,000. Compare that with the 1983 contract signed by John Elway of Stanford, which paid his agent, Marv Demoff, $40,000. Clearly, this has created a competitive market for the representation of NFL players.

Although most agents provide competent, well-intended advice and counsel, there are always a few agents who fail to take the player's best interest into consideration. The sports agent business is replete with stories of athletes being exploited by agents. In 2002, William H. "Tank" Blank, one of the most infamous sports agents, was found guilty of defrauding numerous NFL clients. He was sentenced to 60 months in prison and ordered to pay restitution in the amount of $12 million for defrauding clients over a three-year period by inducing players to invest in fraudulent investment schemes.

Howard Jay Colub represented such stars as Cedric Maxwell, Art Howe, Lance Parrish, and George Foster. He was found guilty of fraud and theft while performing his duties as a sports agent. Colub recommended to several clients that they should invest in a national trucking organization. The clients gave Colub funds to purchase trucks, but he promptly placed the funds in his personal account. He also persuaded clients to invest in several other potential businesses, took the money, and deposited those funds in his personal account as well. He subsequently was sentenced to 12 years in prison for his crimes.

An episode involving former Heisman Trophy winner Andre Ware tested the Texas Athlete Agent Act. Team America, a sports agent firm, employed Johnny Rodgers, a former Heisman Trophy winner himself, to recruit Ware to the firm as a client. Rodgers then engaged in a series of unethical and illegal acts in his failed attempts to sign Ware to a representation contract. Rodgers contacted Ware's mother and told her that her son should sign a contract with the agency notwithstanding the fact that Ware had one year of eligibility remaining. Rodgers later met Joyce Ware, Andre's mother, at LaGuardia Airport and claimed to be a representative from the Downtown Athletic Club, the sponsor of the Heisman Trophy. He took Mrs. Ware shopping in New York and, during this shopping spree, purchased a fur coat for her. When she arrived home Mrs. Ware found that cash had been placed in her purse. She informed her son of these incidents and he, acting ethically, promptly contacted the University of Houston's athletic director and informed the university of the circumstances. The university reported the actions of Johnny Rodgers to the Texas secretary of state; Rodgers was fined $10,000 for his improper conduct and for violating the Texas Athlete Agent Act. The following are the findings of the state of Texas relating to the team and Johnny Rodgers:

```
Based on the above facts it is the conclusion of THE SECRETARY OF
STATE that prior to December 20, 1989, TEAM AMERICA and/or JOHNNY
RODGERS were not registered with the secretary of state as athlete
agents pursuant to art. 8871, sec. 2(a);
```

That TEAM AMERICA and/or JOHNNY RODGERS are athlete agents as defined by art. 8871, sec. 1(a);

That ANDRE WARE is an athlete as defined in art. 8871 sec. 1(a)(5)(A);

That TEAM AMERICA and/or JOHNNY RODGERS, acting in concert or separately and in violation of art. 8871 secs. 2(a) and (7) contacted ANDRE WARE through his mother;

That during the time the contacts were made ANDRE WARE was located within the State of Texas;

That TEAM AMERICA and/or JOHNNY RODGERS acting in concert or separately gave $300.00 cash, purchased gifts and provided free hotel lodging, things of value, for and on behalf of MRS. WARE, the mother of ANDRE WARE, with the intent to induce ANDRE WARE to enter into an agreement by which the parties will represent the athlete in violation of sec. 6(b)(4) of art. 8871;

That the financial package entitled CASH FLOW AND TAX PROJECTIONS PREPARED FOR ANDRE WARE was prepared in Houston, Texas in concert with and/or on behalf of TEAM AMERICA and/or JOHNNY RODGERS with the intent to induce ANDRE WARE to sign an agent contract and/or a financial services contract with TEAM AMERICA and/or JOHNNY RODGERS; and

That all of said parties acting in concert or separately violated art. 8871, sec. 1(a), *et seq.*

Civil Penalty

THE SECRETARY OF STATE, concluding that violations of art. 8871 have occurred and considering the violations to be serious in nature imposes the following civil penalties in accordance with sec. 9(b) of art. 8871:

TOTAL ECONOMIC ATHLETIC MANAGEMENT OF AMERICA INCORPORATED, a Nebraska Corporation, d/b/a TEAM AMERICA, should be and is hereby assessed a civil penalty of TEN THOUSAND DOLLARS ($10,000.00); and

JOHNNY RODGERS should be and is hereby a civil penalty of TEN THOUSAND DOLLARS ($10,000.00).

Source: Courtesy of Westlaw; reprinted with permission.

Union Regulations

Unions clearly have an obligation to ensure that agents are qualified to represent union members. As of 2009, there were approximately 750 NFL contract advisors certified by the NFLPA, and a large portion of those contract advisors had no NFL clients. A very small number of agents represent the bulk of NFL players. In comparison, for the 2007 season, there were approximately 300 agents certified by the Major League Baseball Players Association for 700 players. Eight tandems of agents represented 41% of the $2.5 billion in salaries paid out by major league teams in the 2007 season.[7]

To further regulate agents, the NFLPA has taken measures that have resulted in a reduction of the number of agents. An agent must negotiate one NFL standard player contract every three years or be required to apply for recertification by the union. The annual dues for the 2009 season for an NFLPA contract advisor were $1,200 if the contract advisor represented less than 10 active players and were $1,700 if the contract advisor represented 10 or more active players. In 1985 the application fee to become an NFLPA contract advisor was a mere $35. The applicant must also pass a written examination. The exam covers issues dealing with collective bargaining, player benefits, and other matters relating to the representation of NFLPA players. The applicant is also required to attend a seminar approved by the NFLPA to remain certified with the league. Applicants are prohibited from recruiting or signing players until they have passed the exam and received certification from the league.

NFLPA regulations require that all new applicants not only have a four-year college degree from an accredited university but also possess a postgraduate degree from an accredited college or university. The NFLPA will waive this requirement under exceptional circumstances. This amendment was not retroactive and did not apply to those contract advisors who have already received certification from the NFLPA. This was clearly an attempt by the NFLPA to increase the quality of its contract advisors but should also have the effect of reducing the number of contract advisors.

The NFLPA expressed concerns about whether contract advisors had insurance coverage available to them for any potential liability that might result from their negligent actions as contract advisors. The NFLPA Executive Committee subsequently required that all contract advisors obtain malpractice insurance to cover any potential liability they may face when performing their duties as a contract advisor.

All professional leagues require prospective agents to complete an application to become an agent. The application typically inquires into the applicant's qualifications to represent a player, including the following:

- Education
- Business experience
- Financial management experience
- Discipline measures taken against the applicant by any professional associations
- Other athletes represented by the applicant
- Employment history
- Financial background of the applicant

The following document is the application required by the NFLPA for its prospective agents. Do you think the application is extensive enough? Is the union asking the necessary questions of its potential agents? What other information would you like to know before the agent's application is approved by the NFLPA? Are there privacy issues the union should concern itself with?

---

[7] Schwartz, Peter J., *Baseball's Best Agents,* Forbes, September 22, 2007.

Application for Certification as an NFLPA Contract Advisor

I, _____ . . . hereby apply for certification as an NFLPA Contract Advisor pursuant to the NFLPA Regulations Governing Contract Advisors. . . .

In advance of completing and signing this Application, I have read the NFLPA Regulations Governing Contract Advisors, which were provided to me along with this Application.

In submitting this Application, I agree to comply with and be bound by these Regulations (including but not limited to the maximum fee schedule), which are incorporated herein by reference and any subsequent amendments thereto.

I understand that making any false or misleading statement of a material nature in answering any question on this Application can result in denial or revocation of Certification. Further, I understand and agree that during the period of time between my filing of this Application for Certification and my Certification by the NFLPA, I am prohibited from directly or indirectly soliciting any players for representation as a Contract Advisor. . . .

I agree that if granted Certification I will save and hold harmless the NFLPA, its officers, employees, and representatives from any liability whatsoever resulting from my acts of commission or omission in providing services to any player in connection with his individual contract negotiations with an NFL Club or in connection with any subsequent enforcement of such individual contract or any other contracts involving any player I represent.

I agree that if I am denied Certification or if subsequent to obtaining Certification it is revoked or suspended pursuant to the Regulations, the exclusive method for challenging any such action is through the arbitration procedure set forth in the Regulations.

. . . .

2. Education

a. Law or other graduate school attended:

_____

b. Colleges or Universities attended:

_____

c. High School attended:

_____

d. If you have not received a degree from an accredited four year college/university, list below the negotiating experience you wish the NFLPA to consider in lieu of a college degree.

---

3. Current Occupation/Employment

. . . .

b. Please list below the names of employers, addresses, telephone numbers, positions held, and dates of all your employment for the past ten (10) years. . . .

---

4. Lawyers and Law Graduates

a. Have you been admitted to the Bar in any jurisdiction?

. . . .

c. Have you ever been disbarred, suspended, reprimanded, censured, or otherwise disciplined or disqualified as an attorney, as a member of any other profession, or as a holder of any public office?

---

d. Are any charges or complaints currently pending against you regarding your conduct as an attorney, as a member of any profession, or as a holder of public office?

---

e. Has your right to practice before any governmental office, bureau, agency, commission, etc., ever been restricted, suspended, withdrawn, denied, or terminated?

---

5. All Applicants

a. Are you a member of any business or professional organization which directly relates to your occupation or profession?

---

b. Please list any occupational or professional licenses or other similar credentials (i.e., Certified Public Account, Chartered Life Underwriter, Registered Investment Advisor, etc.) you have obtained other than college or graduate school degrees. . . .

---

c. Are you registered or have you applied to be registered pursuant to any state statutes regulating athlete agents?

---

d. Have you ever been denied an occupational or professional license, franchise or other similar credentials for which you applied?

_____

. . . .

f. Have you ever been suspended, reprimanded, censured, or otherwise disciplined or disqualified as a member of any profession, or as a holder of any public office?

_____

g. Are any charges or complaints currently pending against you regarding your conduct as a member of any profession, or as a holder of public office?

_____

h. Has your right to engage in any profession or occupation ever been restricted, suspended, withdrawn, or terminated?

_____

6. All Applicants

a. Have you ever been charged with, indicted for, convicted of, or pled guilty or pled no contest to a criminal charge, other than minor traffic violations ($100 fine or less)?

_____

b. Have you ever been a defendant in any civil proceedings in which allegations of fraud, misrepresentation, embezzlement, misappropriation of funds, conversion, breach of fiduciary duty, forgery, professional negligence, or legal malpractice were made against you?

_____

c. Have you ever had legal proceedings brought against you by any player, players association, professional sports club or league (NFL or otherwise) for any reason?

_____

d. Have you ever been adjudicated insane or legally incompetent by any court?

_____

e. Were you ever suspended or expelled from any college, university, graduate school, or law school?

_____

f. Has any surety or any bond on which you were covered been required to pay any money on your behalf?

_____

g. Are there any unsatisfied judgments of continuing effect against you (other than alimony or child support)?

_____

h. Have you ever been declared bankrupt or been an owner or part owner of a business which has declared bankruptcy?

_____

8. Professional Sports Experience

a. Please list below (or attach a list which includes) the names of every NFL player, including rookies, you are now representing or have represented in the past in individual contract negotiations with NFL Clubs, including the dates of such representation and the NFL Club(s) involved:

_____

b. Apart from professional football, list any other professional sports in which you currently represent or have previously represented any professional athletes, state whether you have been approved or certified as agent in such sport (and the date of approval) and for each such sport specify the number of athletes you currently represent.

_____

c. (Optional—applicant may refrain from answering if he/she desires.) Please list below the names of any other professional athletes, entertainers, or celebrities you are now representing or have represented in the past, indicating the type of representation, the dates of representation, and the employers involved:

_____

9. NFL Management Personnel

List the names of any coaches, general managers or other management officials of any NFL Club you presently represent or have represented in the past regarding employment with their respective Clubs:

_____

10. Related Businesses and Personnel

a. List the name, address and phone number for each firm or organization with which you are currently affiliated where the business of representing professional athletes is customarily conducted.

_____

. . . .

11. Business Services

```
a. What services do you or your firm provide to Players?
   (Please check each service provided.)
   [ ] Contract Negotiation    [ ] Estate Planning
   [ ] Tax Planning            [ ] Financial Planning
   [ ] Investment Counseling   [ ] Appearances/Endorsements
Other Services (Explain) _____ .
b. Do you manage, invest or in any other manner handle funds for NFL players?
   _____

If yes, are you currently registered under the Investment Advisor's
Act? If no, explain why:
   _____
```

One of the more powerful tools available to a union is the power to discipline an agent for improper conduct. Every professional sports union sets forth in its regulations the type of conduct that is prohibited by agents. When agents engage in prohibited conduct, the union can fine the agent or revoke the license granted to the agent. Punishment by the union can range from a reprimand to decertification. Agents are provided with an appeal process for any discipline they may receive.

In December 2003, arbitrator Roger Kaplan found that former NFL player and agent Sean Jones had violated NFLPA regulations in his financial dealings with former NFL player Chris Dishman but reduced the union's discipline from decertification to a two-year suspension. Dishman sued Jones in a civil lawsuit and received a judgment in the amount of $396,000.[8]

In 2004, the NFLPA disciplinary committee filed a complaint against contract advisor Hadley Engelhard stating that he gave his NFLPA website password to a reporter and also changed his agent fee for a player without properly informing the player. The disciplinary committee of the NFLPA voted to issue a letter of reprimand and levied a fine of $10,000 for each offense.

NFL agent Jerome Stanley was suspended by the NFLPA's disciplinary committee for missing a deadline to file for free agency on behalf of his client, Dennis Northcutt of the Cleveland Browns. Northcutt had signed a seven-year contract with the Browns that required him to notify the team by November 19 if he was going to void the final three years of the contract. Northcutt indicated he was eager to test the free agent market and was anticipating receiving in the neighborhood of a five-year contract with a $5 million signing bonus. He was unable to void the contract because of the missed deadline by his agent.

Every major sports player's union has regulations dealing with agent misconduct. The following are provisions for dealing with agent misconduct found in the MLB regulations.

Section 3: Standard of Conduct for Player Agents; General Requirements; Prohibited Conduct; Miscellaneous

Introduction

```
The primary objectives of the MLBPA in issuing these Regulations are
to enable each Player to make an informed selection of his Player Agent
after receiving full disclosure of the pertinent facts concerning those
```

---

[8] SportsBusiness Daily, Dec. 8, 2003, http://www.sportsbusiness.daily.com/.

persons who serve or are eligible to serve as Player Agents, including the fees they charge for the various services they render; to ensure that Player Agents shall provide the individual Players whom they represent with effective representation free from any actual or potential conflict of interest; and to provide both Players and Player Agents with an effective and expeditious procedure for resolving any disputes concerning their contractual obligations.

. . . .

B. The following conduct by a Player Agent may result in the revocation or suspension of the Player Agent's certification, or in other disciplinary action:

. . . .

(2) Providing or causing to be provided money or any other thing of value to any Player (including a minor league player or amateur athlete), the purpose of which is to induce or encourage such Player to utilize the Player Agent's services;

(3) Providing or causing to be provided money or any other thing of value to (a) a member of a Player's (including a minor league player's or amateur athlete's) family, or (b) any other person (other than a person in the regular and principal employ of the Player Agent), the purpose of which is to induce or encourage such Player or any other Player (including a minor league player or amateur athlete) to utilize the Player Agent's services;

(4) Providing or causing to be provided materially false or misleading information to any Player (including a minor league player or amateur athlete) either in the context of seeking to be selected as a Player Agent for such Player or any other Player (including a minor league player or amateur athlete), or in the course of representing a Player as his agent;

(5) Holding or seeking to hold, either directly or indirectly, a financial interest in any Major League Baseball Club or in any other business venture that would create an actual or potential conflict of interest between the Player Agent and any Player-client(s);

(6) Being employed by, serving as an officer of, or representing, either directly or indirectly, Major League Baseball, the American or National Leagues, any Club or affiliated entity, or representing, either directly or indirectly, any management or supervisory level employee or official of them, without the prior written authorization of the MLBPA;

(7) Soliciting or accepting money or anything of value from any Major League Baseball Club, a League, the Commissioner's Office, or any officer, employee or agent of them, in circumstances where to do so would create an actual or potential conflict of interest between the Player Agent and any Player-clients;

(8) Engaging in any other activity which, in the Association's judgment, creates an actual or potential conflict of interest with the effective representation of Players, provided that the representation of two or more Players on any one Club shall not per se violate this provision;

(9) Negotiating and/or agreeing to any provision in a Player contract which eliminates or reduces any Player benefit contained in any collectively bargained agreement between the Major League Baseball Clubs and the MLBPA;

(10) Concealing from a Player, or from the MLBPA, any material facts relating to the functions described in Section 1(A), above;

(11) Failing to advise the Player and to report to the MLBPA any known or reasonably suspected violations of a Uniform Player's Contract, or of the Basic Agreement, by a Club or Clubs, the League, the Commissioner's Office or any officer, employee or agent of them;

(12) Engaging in unlawful conduct and/or conduct involving dishonesty, fraud, deceit, misrepresentation, or other conduct which reflects adversely on his fitness as a Player Agent;

(13) Failing to utilize the impartial arbitration proceedings contained herein as the exclusive method for resolving claims or disputes, or otherwise violating any of the other requirements set forth in these Regulations. . . .

Source: Courtesy of Westlaw; reprinted with permission.

Problem 5-5

Carlos Williams represents some of the most elite players in the NBA. He has negotiated over $400 million in contracts with 27 different NBA teams during his career. General managers in the NBA speak very highly of him and call him the NBA's most ethical and toughest negotiator. Unbeknownst to the league or union, Williams began to fall behind in tax payments to the IRS. He negotiated a payment schedule with the IRS whereby he agreed to pay $1.5 million over a period of five years to repay all the back taxes that he owed. The union found out about his agreement with the IRS and is contemplating taking disciplinary action against Williams. Does it have a basis to take such action? What basis does Williams have to challenge any disciplinary measures taken by the league?

In the arbitration decision, Case 5-5, *In the Matter of the Agent Certification Application of Stephen M. Woods,* a former NBA agent challenged the league's decision to suspend his license based on prohibited conduct under the NBPA regulations.

CASE 5-5 *In the Matter of the Agent Certification Application of Stephen M. Woods*

Opinion and Award

On January 5, 1999, the agent certification of Stephen M. Woods was revoked by the NBPA Committee on Agent Regulation.

. . . .

Section 2: Requirements for Certification

A. Applying for Certification

To be eligible for certification, the applicant must have received a degree from an accredited four year college/university. The Committee shall have the authority to determine whether relevant negotiating experience can substitute for any year(s) of education.

On June 20, 2000, Woods appealed the Committee's action. At essentially the same time, he filed information requests asking for the educational background of all NBPA-certified agents and the means to contact those agents. Shortly thereafter, at my direction, the Committee provided Woods with the educational background and negotiating experience of the 12 agents who did not have four-year degrees together with the telephone numbers of the 300 plus agents certified by the Union.

Woods further argued that his negotiating experience and the fact that he had served as an Adjunct Professor at the University of South Carolina fully compensated for his non-attendance at a four-year college and that the Committee's action in finding otherwise, and denying his application, at least in part, on the educational ground, was arbitrary and personally insulting.

The real question here . . . is . . . whether its denial of his reapplication was reasonable given all the circumstances. In the Committee's view, it was.

The Regulations require a degree from a four-year college or university or, in the Committee's reasonable discretion, a showing of relevant negotiating experience sufficient to off-set the lack of a college education. As the Committee now knows, since his present application, unlike his prior application, makes this clear, Woods never attended college. In contrast, the overwhelming majority of the some 300 agents certified by the NBPA graduated from an accredited college or university and possess four-year degrees. Of the 12 who do not, 11 attended colleges or universities in the United States or other countries for varying periods of time. (Only one of the 11 had less than two years of college.) Nine of those 11 demonstrated negotiating experience in the representation of professional athletes sufficient, in the judgment of the Committee, to overcome their lack of a degree; the other two demonstrated negotiating experience in other capacities. Only one of the certified agents, other than Woods, did not attend any college. Before becoming an agent, however, he owned and operated a business generating annual sales of $20 million. The Committee contends that a comparison of the education and experience of these individuals with that of Woods, particularly since he failed to detail his previous negotiating experience despite repeated requests that he do so, justify its conclusion that he has failed to demonstrate sufficient relevant experience to overcome his lack of college training.

Thus, there can be no question that the Union can authorize the use of agents, if it so wishes, and, once it does so, can also pass upon the qualifications of those who apply. In other words, the Union has no obligation to certify or re-certify Woods or anyone else as an agent. Its sole duty in this regard is to be reasonable in its determinations. . . .

Award

The decision of the NBPA Committee on Agent Regulations not to approve the application of Stephen M. Woods as a certified agent at this time was reasonable in the circumstances of the case under review. It is therefore affirmed.

George Nicolau, Impartial Arbitrator

Source: Courtesy of Westlaw; reprinted with permission.

Case 5-6, *Rosenhaus v. Star Sports, Inc.*, 929 So.2d 40 (Fla. App. 3 Dist. 2006), involved a dispute between two agents and the method by which the dispute should be handled. The interpretation of Section 5 of the NFLPA's standard representation agreement, "Arbitration Procedures," was at issue.

📖   CASE 5-6   *Rosenhaus v. Star Sports, Inc.*

929 So.2d 40 (Fla. App. 3 Dist. 2006)

Before GERSTEN, FLETCHER, and SUAREZ, JJ.

SUAREZ, J.

Drew and Jason Rosenhaus and Rosenhaus Sports Representation, Inc., appeal from the denial of a motion to dismiss and to compel arbitration. We reverse.

Star Sports, Inc. ("Star"), filed a multi-count complaint in the Circuit Court of Miami-Dade County against Drew Rosenhaus, Jason Rosenhaus, and

Rosenhaus Sports Representation, Inc., a Florida corporation, alleging intentional interference with an advantageous business relationship and tortious interference with a contractual right. The complaint alleges that Star is in the business of providing marketing and related services to professional football players in the National Football League ("NFL"), and that Drew and Jason Rosenhaus are both certified Contract Advisors with the National Football League Players Association ("NFLPA"). The complaint alleges that Star entered into a written contract referred to as a "Marketing Agreement" with Anquan Boldin, a professional football player in the NFL, wherein Star was to be Boldin's exclusive agent for marketing and related services. The complaint also alleges that Drew and Jason Rosenhaus intentionally and unjustifiably interfered with this Marketing Agreement by directly soliciting Boldin to have Jason and Drew Rosenhaus and/or Rosenhaus Sports Representation, Inc., represent him in his marketing endeavors and to exclude Star from representing him. Drew and Jason Rosenhaus and Rosenhaus Sports Representation, Inc., filed a motion to dismiss the complaint and to compel arbitration, claiming the exclusive remedy for a dispute between two Contract Advisors relating to a Marketing Agreement is through arbitration pursuant to Section 5, the Arbitration Procedures provision, contained in the Agent Regulations of the NFLPA. The trial court denied the motion and this appeal from the non-final order was timely filed.

There are three elements to consider in ruling on a motion to compel arbitration: (1) whether the parties have entered into a valid arbitration agreement; (2) whether an arbitrable issue exists; and (3) whether the right to arbitration has been waived. Two of the three elements are not presented on appeal. The issue of whether the parties entered into a valid arbitration agreement is not in dispute. All parties are members of the NFLPA and are "Contract Advisors," as defined by that organization. All parties agree that, as Contract Advisors, they are bound by the Agent Regulations promulgated by the NFLPA which detail the obligations, rights, and liabilities of Contract Advisors. All parties agree that the Agent Regulations contain a provision requiring certain disputes between Contract Advisors to be resolved through arbitration. The issue of whether the right to arbitration has been waived has not been raised on appeal. The only issue before us is whether the claims of intentional interference with an advantageous business relationship and intentional interference with the Marketing Agreement, are arbitrable claims pursuant to Section 5, Arbitration Procedures, of the Agent Regulations.

Whether a particular issue is subject to arbitration is a matter of contract interpretation. . . . Arbitration is required only as to those disputes to which the parties have expressly agreed. The arbitration clause must refer to the subject matter which is in dispute.

To determine whether the parties in this case agreed to arbitrate an issue relating to the Marketing Agreement, we must look at the scope of the language of the Agent Regulations.

The Arbitration Procedures provision of the NFLPA Agent Regulations states as follows:

Section 5 - Arbitration Procedures

A. Disputes

This arbitration procedure shall be the exclusive method for resolving any and all disputes that may arise from the following:

. . . .

5. A dispute between two or more Contract Advisors with respect to whether or not a Contract Advisor interfered with a contractual relationship of a Contract Advisor and player in violation of Section 3(B)(21). . . .

A dispute between two Contract Advisors is required to be resolved through arbitration if the violation alleged is the interference by one Contract Advisor with the contract of another Contract Advisor and an NFL player in violation of Section 3(B)(21) of the Agent Regulations.

Section 3(B)(21), entitled Prohibitive Conduct, states in pertinent part:

B. Prohibited Conduct

Contract Advisors are Prohibited from:

21.(a) Initiating any communication, directly or indirectly, with a player who has entered into a Standard Representation Agreement with another Contract Advisor and such Standard Representation Agreement is on file with the NFLPA if the communication concerns a matter relating to the:

. . . .

(iv) Services to be provided by prospective Contract Advisor *either* through a Standard Representation Agreement *or otherwise*. (emphasis added)

Therefore, prohibited conduct occurs when one Contract Advisor communicates with a player who has entered into a Standard Representation Agreement with another Contract Advisor and the communication concerns a matter relating to the services provided by the Contract Advisor to the player either through a Standard Representation Agreement or otherwise. The document in question is the Marketing Agreement entered into by Star and Boldin. The issue is whether the Marketing Agreement is a service "otherwise" provided by Star to Boldin, within the meaning of Section

3(B)(21)(iv). If the Marketing Agreement is such a service, the question of whether the Rosenhauses intentionally interfered with Star's business relationship and contractual rights with Boldin is an issue which the Agent Regulations require to be resolved through arbitration. If it is not, the issue is one which may be resolved in the circuit court.

The word "otherwise" is not defined in the Agent Regulations. As such, we may look to the dictionary to determine the plain and ordinary meaning of the word. Black's Law Dictionary and Webster's New Collegiate Dictionary define the word "otherwise" as "in a different manner; in another way; or in other ways." *Black's Law Dictionary* 992 (5th ed.1979); *Webster's New Collegiate Dictionary* 806 (1980). Therefore, the Agent Regulations prohibit communication by one Contract Advisor with an NFL player if the communication relates to services to be provided to that player by another Contract Advisor either through the Standard Representation Agreement or "in a different manner; in another way; or in other ways."

We conclude that, since the Marketing Agreement is an agreement whereby Star was to provide services to Boldin by marketing his name and obtaining endorsements and promotions for him, the Marketing Agreement is a service provided in a different manner; in another way, or in other ways (a service provided "otherwise"). The issue of whether the Rosenhauses initiated communication with Boldin and intentionally interfered with Star's Marketing Agreement with Boldin is an issue which the Arbitration Procedures of the NFLPA Agent Regulations require to be resolved through arbitration. As Contract Advisors with and members of the NFLPA, Star and the Rosenhauses are bound by the Agent Regulations and are required to resolve the claims of intentional interference with an advantageous business relationship and tortious interference with a contractual right through arbitration.

We therefore reverse the trial court's denial of the appellants' motion to dismiss and to compel arbitration and remand for further proceedings consistent herewith.

Source: Courtesy of Westlaw; reprinted with permission.

Federal Regulation

In 2007 Congress passed the Sports Agent Responsibility and Trust Act (SPARTA), the first-ever federal law aimed at regulating sports agents.[9] The law was coauthored by former University of Nebraska football coach Tom Osborne. The act does not preempt any state laws relating to agents but instead was meant to supplement the already existing Uniform Athletes Agent Act.

---

[9] 15 USCA §§ 7801–7807 (2004).

The goal of SPARTA is to keep college athletes eligible and to protect them from unscrupulous agents. It sets forth guidelines for agents regarding the recruiting of student-athletes and delineates penalties for those agents who violate the act. The act also gives a state attorney general the right to bring a civil lawsuit against any agent who violates the act. Universities have also been given the right to bring a civil lawsuit against any agent who causes damage to the university for improper conduct under the law.

State Regulation

An agent will sometimes have clients in different states and will be faced with the dilemma of how to comply with each state's law regarding athlete agents. A California agent may be recruiting a student-athlete at Louisiana State University who is from Florida. Where would the agent register to be in compliance with state law? What law or regulations would apply to his or her actions?

In 2000, the National Conference of Commissioners on Uniform State Laws completed the draft of the Uniform Athletes Agent Act (UAAA). They then sent it for adoption by the individual states. As of July, 2007, the UAAA had been adopted by 36 states and two territories. One of the purposes of the passage of the UAAA was, obviously, to create uniformity among the many states that had passed laws dealing with athlete agents.

The UAAA is a uniform act regulating athlete agents who deal with students. State regulation is still required under the law. An agent must register where his or her principal place of business is located. The uniform law would allow for reciprocity for the registration of agents in any state that has enacted the UAAA. The UAAA also addresses the contents of a representation agreement, sets forth a list of prohibited acts for agents, and provides a remedy for schools that are harmed by an agent's actions or conduct.

Regulation by the NCAA

The National Collegiate Athletic Association is the governing body for collegiate athletics in the United States. Its membership consists of over 1,250 private and public colleges and universities. One of the primary missions of the NCAA is to maintain the concept of amateurism. The NCAA also has the difficult tasks of maintaining the integrity of athletics at the collegiate level and of monitoring the activities of student-athletes, agents, coaches, boosters, and others involved in athletic programs. The NCAA has the power to discipline agents, student-athletes, and universities if they are found to be in violation of NCAA rules or regulations.

The NCAA has promulgated numerous rules and regulations involving the conduct of agents. For instance, student-athletes may lose their eligibility to play if they agree to be represented by an agent for the purpose of marketing their athletic ability or agree to be represented before they complete their eligibility.

The NCAA desires each student-athlete make an intelligent, well-informed decision when selecting an agent. It has created the following list of questions that a student-athlete should pose to any prospective agent.

```
Note: When you use this questionnaire to interview agents other than
at agent day functions, the first question you should ask is "Where
are you registered?"

1. Where and when did you graduate from law school?

2. If you are not a lawyer, what are your educational credentials?
```

3. Have you ever been disbarred, suspended, reprimanded, censured or otherwise disciplined or disqualified as an attorney or as a member of any other profession?

4. Are there currently any complaints or charges pending against you regarding your conduct as an attorney or as a member of any other profession?

5. Have you ever been implicated or investigated for any violations of NCAA or professional league rules?

6. Are you an NFLPA certified contract advisor?

7. Did you take the NFLPA Collective Bargaining Agreement Test? What was your score? If you did not take the test, why not?

8. Do you have ownership interests in your company? (Are you a firm or agency partner or strictly an employee?)

9. Can you supply me with a list of current and former clients?

10. What services do you offer to your clients other than contract negotiations (financial planning, tax advice, etc.)? Do you mind if I use my own accountant or financial planner?

11. Who will be negotiating my contract?

12. How many clients have you lost, and what was the reason for their departure? Can you provide me with a list of their phone numbers?

13. Who do you consider to be your top clients?

14. What have you done to advance the careers of your clients on and off the field?

15. Do you provide an annual statement to your clients? May I see an example?

16. How do you keep your clients informed of charges?

17. What is your fee structure? Are your fees negotiable?

18. How and when are you to be paid?

19. What is the duration of the agreement?

20. What are the procedures for terminating the agreement?

21. What happens to our agreement if I fail to make the team; if I am waived; or if I get injured?

22. If I am likely to be a free agent, how can you help maximize my chances of making a team?

23. Do you have any connections with NFL Europe, the CFL, or the Arena Football League?

24. Have you ever had a dispute with a client and if so, how was it resolved?

Source: © National Collegiate Athletic Association, 2006–2008. All rights reserved. Reprinted with permission.

Norby Walters and Lloyd Bloom show the extremes to which some agents will go to attempt to sign star college athletes to contracts. They offered lavish gifts to student-athletes, and even used strong-arm tactics and threatened student-athletes with physical harm in their recruiting and signing process. They were highly successful in signing top draft picks; however, their tactics eventually led to their downfall. In 1988 they were both indicted by a grand jury on seven counts of mail fraud and conspiracy under the Racketeer Influenced and Corrupt Organizations Act (RICO) and were found guilty on all seven counts.

In the court's opinion in Case 5-7, *Walters v. Fullwood,* 675 F. Supp. 155 (S.D.N.Y. 1987), the court was deciding whether agreements entered into between Walters and Bloom as agents and their clients, were in violation of NCAA regulations. Walters and his partner Bloom signed over 50 student-athletes to contracts while they were still eligible to participate in collegiate athletics.

📖 CASE 5-7   *Walters v. Fullwood*

675 F. Supp. 155 (S.D.N.Y. 1987)

BRIEANT, Chief Judge.

. . . Defendant Brent Fullwood, a Florida resident, was an outstanding running back with the University of Auburn football team in Alabama. . . . At an unspecified time during his senior year at Auburn, Fullwood entered into an agreement with W.S. & E., . . . ("the W.S. & E. agreement"). The agreement was dated January 2, 1987, the day after the last game of Fullwood's college football career, and the first day he could sign such a contract without forfeiting his amateur status under sec. 3-1-(c) of the N.C.A.A. Constitution. . . . The contract . . . granted W.S. & E. the exclusive right to represent Fullwood as agent to negotiate with professional football teams after the spring draft of the National Football League ("N.F.L."). Walters and Bloom were the corporate officers and sole shareholders of W.S. & E. As a provisionally certified N.F.L. Players' Association ("N.F.L.P.A.") contract advisor, Bloom was subject to the regulations of that body governing agents ("N.F.L.P.A. Agents' Regulations"), which require the arbitration of most disputes between players and contract advisors.

On August 20, 1986, W.S. & E. paid $4,000 to Fullwood, who then executed a promissory note in plaintiffs' favor for that amount. . . . At various times throughout the 1986 season, plaintiffs sent to Fullwood or his family further payments that totaled $4,038.

. . . While neither plaintiffs nor defendants have specifically admitted that the W.S. & E. agency agreement was post dated, they have conspicuously avoided identifying the actual date it was signed. There is a powerful inference that the agreement was actually signed before or during the college football season, perhaps contemporaneously with the August 20 promissory note, and unethically postdated as in other cases involving these plaintiffs.

At some point prior to the N.F.L. spring 1987 draft, Fullwood repudiated his agreement with W.S. & E., and chose to be represented by defendant George Kickliter, an attorney in Auburn, Alabama.

As anticipated, Fullwood was taken early in the N.F.L. draft. The Green Bay Packers selected him as the fourth player in the first round; he signed a contract with them. . . .

In March, 1987, Walters and Bloom brought suit . . . alleging (1) that Fullwood breached the W.S. & E. agency agreement, (2) that Fullwood owed them $8,038 as repayment for the funds he received during the autumn of 1986, which are now characterized as loans. . . .

"We are living in a time when college athletics are honeycombed with falsehood, and when the professions of amateurism are usually hypocrisy. No college team ever meets another today with actual faith in the other's eligibility." —President William Faunce of Brown University, in a speech before the National Education Association, 1904. *Quoted in* J. Betts, *America's Sporting Heritage 1850–1950,* 216 (1974).

The N.C.A.A. was organized in 1906 largely to combat such evils. Its constitution provides in relevant part that:

"Any individual who contracts or who has ever contracted orally or in writing to be represented by an agent in the marketing of the individual's athletic ability or reputation in a sport no longer shall be eligible for intercollegiate athletics in that sport."

N.C.A.A. Constitution, sec. 3-1-(c). Section 3-1-(a) prohibits any player from accepting pay in any form for participation in his college sport, with an exception for a player seeking, directly without the assistance of a third party, a loan from an accredited commercial lending institution against future earnings potential solely in order to purchase insurance against disabling injury.

This Court concludes that the August 1986 loan security agreement and the W.S. & E. agency agreement between Fullwood and the plaintiffs violated sections 3-1-(a) and 3-1-(c) of the N.C.A.A. Constitution, the observance of which is in the public interest of the citizens of New York State, and that the parties to those agreements knowingly betrayed an important, if perhaps naive, public trust. . . . [W]e decline to serve as "paymaster of the wages of crime, or referee between thieves". We consider both defendant Fullwood's arbitration rights under the N.F.L.P.A. Agents' Regulations, and plaintiffs' rights on their contract and promissory note with Fullwood, unenforceable as contrary to the public policy of New York. "The law 'will not extend its aid to either of the parties' or 'listen to their complaints against each other, but will leave them where their own acts have placed them.'"

. . . An agreement may be unenforceable in New York as contrary to public policy even in the absence of a direct violation of a criminal statute, if the sovereign has expressed a concern for the values underlying the policy implicated. . . .

Even in the context of a non-criminal contract, "a prime and long-settled public policy closes the doors of our courts to those who sue to collect the rewards of corruption."

. . . New York case law prevents judicial enforcement of contracts the performance of which would provoke conduct established as wrongful by independent commitments undertaken by either party. . . .

All parties to this action should recognize that they are the beneficiaries of a system built on the trust of millions of people who, with stubborn innocence, adhere to the Olympic ideal, viewing amateur sports as a commitment to competition for its own sake. Historically, amateur athletes have been perceived as pursuing excellence and perfection of their sport as a form of self-realization, indeed, originally, as a form of religious worship, with the ancient games presented as offerings to the gods. . . .

There also is a modern, secular purpose served by secs. 3-1-(a) and 3-1-(c) of the N.C.A.A. Constitution. Since the advent of intercollegiate sports in the late 19th century, American colleges have struggled, with varying degrees of vigor, to protect the integrity of higher education from sports-related evils such as gambling, recruitment violations, and the employment of mercenaries whose presence in college athletic programs will tend to preclude the participation of legitimate scholar-athletes.

Sections 3-1-(a) and 3-1-(c) of the N.C.A.A. Constitution were instituted to prevent college athletes from signing professional contracts while they are still playing for their schools. The provisions are rationally related to the commendable objective of protecting the academic integrity of N.C.A.A. member institutions. A college student already receiving payments from his agent, or with a large professional contract signed and ready to take effect upon his graduation, might well be less inclined to observe his academic obligations than a student, athlete or not, with uncertainties about his future career. Indeed, he might not play at his college sport with the same vigor and devotion.

The agreement reached by the parties here, whether or not unusual, represented not only a betrayal of the high ideals that sustain amateur athletic competition as a part of our national educational commitment; it also constituted a calculated fraud on the entire spectator public. Every honest amateur player who took the field with or against Fullwood during the 1986 college football season was cheated by being thrown in with a player who had lost his amateur standing.

In August 1986, Brent Fullwood was one of that select group of college athletes virtually assured of a lucrative professional sports contract

immediately upon graduation, absent serious injury during his senior
year. The fruits of the system by which amateur players become highly
paid professionals, whatever its flaws, were soon to be his. That is
precisely why plaintiffs sought him out. Both sides of the transaction
knew exactly what they were doing, and they knew it was fraudulent and
wrong. This Court and the public need not suffer such willful conduct
to taint a college amateur sports program.

Source: Courtesy of Westlaw; reprinted with permission.

Problem 5-6

Paul Thomas is an attorney who is trying to break into the sports agent business. A friend
of his knows a possible first-round NFL draft pick who is attending the University of Oklahoma.
The friend introduces Thomas to Jamison, who is in his junior year at the university. Jamison
tells Thomas he is "taking offers" from potential agents and that he needs about $2,500 a month
for the rest of his college career to maintain his "lifestyle." Thomas agrees to pay Jamison and
continues to pay him $2,500 through the player's senior year. After Jamison's senior year, Okla-
homa is invited to play in the Alamo Bowl against Northwestern, with a payout to each university of $1.2 million. Three days before the bowl game, Jamison is declared ineligible and
Oklahoma is banned from playing in the bowl game by the NCAA because of violations of
NCAA rules. An investigation by the NCAA, based on a tip, revealed the payments by the
agent to the player. The University of Oklahoma now seeks to recover $1.2 million because of
the lost bowl game opportunity. It seeks damages to the reputation of the university as well. It
names Thomas and Jamison as defendants in a civil lawsuit. Will the university prevail? What
is the relevant law in this case? What damages has the University of Oklahoma sustained?

Regulation by Universities and Colleges

Colleges and universities have taken steps to ensure that student-athletes are protected from
unscrupulous agents. Many athletic departments and professional sports counseling panels of universities have "agent days" on campus to allow agents to be interviewed by student-athletes. Universities believe they can better control the conduct of agents on campus by hosting such events. The
University of Alabama and Ohio State University are two major universities that have held very
successful agent days. At Alabama, agents who have at least five current clients are able to make a
20-minute presentation to rising senior football student-athletes and their parents. The university
stresses this is the only chance that agents will have to meet with student-athletes prior to the end of
the season. Agents are able to present materials to prospective clients as well as to make a short oral
presentation. The purpose of agent day is to regulate contact between the university's student-athletes
and agents and to give student-athletes a wide variety of agents from which to choose. As part of their
ongoing attempts at the regulation of agents, universities are also performing criminal background
checks on potential agents who want to interview student-athletes.[10]

---

[10] Interview with Chris King, Associate Athletic Director for Compliance, University of Alabama.

Problem 5-7

You have recently secured the job of your dreams as associate athletic director at your alma mater, Michigan State University. The head of the compliance department has requested that you draft a detailed program for agent regulation on campus and submit the proposal to the professional sports counseling panel of the university for its approval. What elements would you include in such a proposal? What would be your major concerns in drafting such a program?

NOTES AND DISCUSSION QUESTIONS

Duties and Responsibilities of Agents

1. What are the basic qualifications a sports agent should possess? Should agents be required to have a graduate degree or to have substantial business experience before they are certified as a sports agent?

2. What are the primary duties of a sports agent?

3. Under what circumstances could a player win a case against an agent for breach of fiduciary duty?

4. In Case 5-1, *Bias v. Advantage*, do you believe the agent breached his fiduciary duty? Do you believe that the agent breached the fiduciary duty owned to Len Bias by negotiating endorsement contracts for several players at the same time? What is a reasonable time period for an agent to complete the negotiation of an endorsement contract on behalf of a player?

Representation Agreements

5. Is the standard representation agreement a good idea? What are the advantages and disadvantages of such an agreement? Why do some leagues require standard agreements and some do not?

Agent Fees

6. Should unions be able to set limits on fees for agents or should the market control agent fees? Should all unions have a set fee for agents?

7. Was it unethical for the agent in Case 5-2, *Brown v. Woolf*, to take the entire fee he was owed under the contract even though the player received a reduced amount of what he was owed under the contract? Is an agent ever required to reduce his or her fees during negotiations? At what point during the negotiations is an agent allowed to take his or her fee?

Conflicts of Interest

8. Which of the following pose a conflict of interest for a sports agent?
   a. Representing two players on the same team at the same position.
   b. Representing a player and coach on the same team.
   c. Representing NFL management personnel and a player simultaneously.

    d. A sports management firm that continues to represent a player who retires and later becomes the general manager of a Major League team.

9. What are the potential problems that exist for an agent who represents a player for both contract negotiations and financial matters?

10. Assume that an agent represents two NFL players who do play the same position and are both unrestricted free agents. During negotiations with an NFL club, the agent is told by the general manager that salary cap considerations only allow the signing of one star player. Does the agent have an irreconcilable conflict of interest in this scenario? What are the agent's duties in this case? Suppose an agent is told by a team that his client, player A, needs to take a salary cut to make room on the squad for player B, who is also represented by the agent. What conflict of interest issues arise under the circumstances? Can the agent continue to represent both players?

Competition Between Agents

11. Do you agree with the court's decision in Case 5-4, *Speakers of Sports v. ProServ*? Suppose an agent told a player that his new marketing company would make the player the "most well-known golfer on the PGA Tour." Would the golfer have a cause of action against the agent if the agent failed to keep this promise?

The Regulation of Sports Agents

12. Who should have the primary responsibility for regulation of sports agents: the state, universities, leagues, unions, or the NCAA?

13. At what point should a players' union step in and regulate a dispute between agents over the signing of a player? Do you think this type of activity is unusual in the sports agent business?

14. In *Collins v. National Basketball Players' Ass'n*, 976 F.2d 740 (10th Cir. 1992), an agent challenged the authority of the union to regulate agents and lost. This case stands for the proposition that unions have the authority to regulate agents.

15. Should unions require that all agents carry liability insurance in case the agent commits malpractice during the negotiation of a contract? If the league failed to require agents to carry negligence insurance, how would someone such as Dennis Northcutt recover any damages he incurred as a result of his agent's negligence?

16. Was it proper for the NFLPA to attempt to decertify agent David Dunn for his filing of personal bankruptcy? When should a players' union be able to discipline an agent for business dealings that are not related to the representation of a sports client?

17. What further steps should a league or university take to prevent agents from stealing clients from one another?

18. Should leagues be able to limit the number of agents who are certified? Would this create antitrust issues?

19. Should leagues require each potential agent pass a test before he or she is certified? What material should the applicants be tested on? What should be the required passing score? How many chances should applicants have to pass the exam?

20. Should agents be required to attend continuing education courses that include an ethical component to continue to be certified by the league?

21. In *Barry Rona and Major League Baseball Players' Association* (Arbitration 1993), the Major League players union rejected Barry Rona's application under section 2(c) of its regulations, which allowed the union to refuse certification to anyone whose conduct "may adversely affect his credibility [or] integrity . . . to serve in a representative and/or fiduciary capacity on behalf of players." The union stated that Rona was an integral part of the collusion of baseball owners in the 1980s to keep player salaries down. The decision, however, stated:

> [T]he Arbitrator finds that the Players Association acted arbitrarily and capriciously in rejecting Rona's application.

> The Players Association's conclusion that Rona was part of the collusion in the 1985 and 1986 free agent markets because he was a leading figure in the PRC [Player Relations Committee] is fundamentally at odds with the Code's very clear position that lawyers do not act unethically merely because they represent individuals or institutions that are found to have engaged in wrongful activities. And there is no evidence, nor any finding by Chairman Roberts or Chairman Nicholau that it was or should have been obvious to Rona that his clients were acting "merely for the purpose of harassing or maliciously injuring any person". . . . On the contrary, he expressed his "concerns" to his clients, asked them directly whether they were involved in collusion to destroy the free agent markets in 1985 and 1986 and, when they replied negatively, allowed them to so testify under oath before the Roberts and Nicholau Panels. Rona acted entirely properly . . . in allowing his clients to have their day in court to attempt under oath to refute the circumstantial evidence that they were engaged in collusion can hardly be termed taking a "frivolous legal position". . . . This Arbitrator believes that these are not even close questions. For the foregoing reasons the Arbitrator concludes that the Players Association's rejection of Rona's application because of his alleged involvement in the 1985 and 1986 collusion was arbitrary and capricious.

Do you believe the arbitrator was right in this situation? Could a former general manager of a team become an agent? What about an agent who goes to the management side? What ethical and legal ramifications does this pose?

22. Should leagues be able to regulate the financial advisors of players in the same manner that they regulate agents? How could this be done? *See,* Shropshire, Kenneth L. and Davis, Timothy, *The Business of Sports Agents,* University of Pennsylvania Press, 2008, pp. 140–143.

23. Should colleges and universities be able to require that potential agents for student-athletes at their university already have clients in order to be able to come to campus and interview student-athletes?

24. Should all agents be required to be attorneys? *See generally,* Carfagna, Peter A., *Representing the Professional Athlete,* Thomson Reuters, 2009.

25. Should there be a Uniform Code of Ethics for sports agents? If so, what should be contained in the code?

26. For an interesting dispute between well-known agents, see *Smith v. IMG Worldwide, Inc.,* 437 F. Supp. 2d 297 (E.D. Penn. 2006) (an African-American agent sued a white agent alleging defamation and interference with contractual relations). *For a general discussion of*

the case see, Shropshire, Kenneth L. and Davis, Timothy, *The Business of Sports Agents,* Supra, p. 64.

27. Do you believe enough has been done to regulate the conduct of sports agents? If not, what else could be done?

SUGGESTED READINGS AND RESOURCES

Crasnick, Jerry. *License to Deal: A Season on the Run with a Maverick Baseball Agent.* Emmaus, PA: Rodale, 2005.

Dunn, David L. *Regulation of Sports Agents: Since at First It Hasn't Succeeded, Try Federal Legislation.* 39 HASTINGS LAW JOURNAL 1031 (1988).

Ehrhardt, Charles W., & Rogers, J. Mark. *Tightening the Defense Against Offensive Sports Agents.* 16 FLORIDA STATE UNIVERSITY LAW REVIEW 633 (1988).

Fox, Dana. *Regulating the Professional Sports Agents: Is California in the Right Ballpark?* 15 PACIFIC LAW JOURNAL 1230 (1984).

Lefferts, L. J. *The NFL Players Association's Agent Certification Plan: Is It Exempt from Antitrust Review?* 26 ARIZONA LAW REVIEW 699 (1984).

Lewis, Michael. *Moneyball: The Art of Winning an Unfair Game.* New York: W. W. Norton, 2003.

The Offer Sheet: An Attempt to Circumvent NCAA Prohibition of Professional Contracts, 14 LOYOLA OF LOS ANGELES LAW REVIEW 141 (1988).

Roberts, Marc, with Digeronimo, Theresa Foy. *Roberts Rules! Success Secrets from America's Most Trusted Sports Agent.* Franklin Lakes, NJ: Career Press, 1998.

Rosenhaus, Drew, with Yaeger, Don, & Rosenhaus, Jason. *A Shark Never Sleeps: Wheeling and Dealing with the NFL's Most Ruthless Agent.* New York: Pocket Books, 1997.

Ruxin, Robert H. *Unsportsmanlike Conduct: The Student Athlete, the NCAA, and Agents.* 8 JOURNAL OF COLLEGE AND UNIVERSITY LAW 347 (1981–1982).

Shropshire, Kenneth L. *Agents of Opportunity: Sports Agents and Corruption in Collegiate Sports.* Philadelphia: University of Pennsylvania Press, 1990.

Shropshire, Kenneth L., & Davis, Timothy. *The Business of Sports Agents.* Philadelphia: University of Pennsylvania Press, 2003.

Simon, Ron. *The Game Behind the Game: Negotiating in the Big Leagues.* Stillwater, MN: Voyageur, 1993.

Wood, Richard P., & Mills, Michael R. *Tortious Interference with an Athletic Scholarship: A University's Remedy for the Unscrupulous Sports Agent.* 40 ALABAMA LAW REVIEW 141 (1988).

REFERENCE MATERIALS

Barner, Tamara L. *Show Me the . . . Ethics? The Implications of the Model Rules of Ethics on Attorneys in the Sports Industry.* 16 GEORGETOWN JOURNAL OF LEGAL ETHICS 519–33 (2005).

Bogad, Melissa Steedle. *Maybe Jerry Maguire Should Have Stuck with Law School: How the Sports Agent Responsibility and Trust Act Implements Lawyer-Like Rules for Sports Agents.* 27 CARDOZO LAW REVIEW 1889 (2006).

Caswell, M. *Merriman Declares 'Lights Out' on Minicamp.* The Mighty 1090 AM, 2005.

Champion, Walter T. *Sports Law: Cases, Documents, and Materials.* New York: Aspen, 2005.

Champion, Walter T. *Sports Law in a Nutshell*, 2d ed. St. Paul, MN: West Group, 2000.

Couch, Bryan. *How Agent Competition and Corruption Affects Sports and the Athlete-Agent Relationship and What Can Be Done to Control It.* 10 SETON HALL JOURNAL OF SPORT LAW 111–36 (2000).

Doman, M. *Attorneys as Athlete-Agents: Reconciling the ABA Rules of Professional Conduct with the Practice of Athlete Representation.* 5 TEXAS REVIEW OF ENTERTAINMENT AND SPORTS LAW 37–77 (2003).

Firm Accused of Legal Malpractice. ESPN.com, Jan. 13, 2005.

Genzale, J. *There's Real Muck Behind Sleazy Image.* Street and Smith's SportsBusiness Journal, http://www.sportsbusinessjournal.com.

Greenberg, Martin J., & Gray, James T. *Sports Law Practice*, 2d ed. Charlottesville, VA: Lexis Law Publishing, 1998.

Hyman, M. *Agents Who Play as Rough as Linebackers.* BusinessWeek Online, Sept. 27, 2004.

Kaesebier, C. *Membership Programs Tap Unique Resources for Educational Efforts.* NCAA NEWS, May 27, 2002.

Kertscher, T. *'Len Bias Law' Use Called County's 1st.* MILWAUKEE JOURNAL SENTINEL, May 9, 2005.

King, B. *Babby Brings Billable Hours to Baseball.* Street & Smith's SportsBusiness Journal, 2003, http://www.sportsbusinessjournal.com.

Masteralexis, Lisa Pike, Barr, Carol A., & Hums, Mary A. *Principles and Practice of Sport Management*, 2d ed. Sudbury, MA: Jones and Bartlett, 2005.

Mitten, Matthew J., Davis, Timothy, Smith, Rodney, & Berry, Robert. *Sports Law and Regulation.* New York: Aspen, 2005.

Mullen, Liz. *Arbitrator Upholds NFLPA Discipline for Agent over Employee's Actions.* Street and Smith's SportsBusiness Journal, April 15, 2002, http://www.sportsbusinessjournal.com.

Mullen, Liz. *Ekuban: Deals with My Ex-Agent Ruined Credit.* Street and Smith's SportsBusiness Journal, Feb. 17, 2003, http://www.sportsbusinessjournal.com.

Mullen, Liz. *NFL Agent to Appeal Union Decertification Vote.* Street and Smith's SportsBusiness Journal, Oct. 27, 2003, http://www.sportsbusinessjournal.com.

Mullen, Liz. *NFLPA Decertifies Hodari, Issues Complaints Against 2.* Street and Smith's SportsBusiness Journal, Nov. 17, 2003, http://www.sportsbusinessjournal.com.

Mullen, Liz. *Sleaze Factor Off the Charts, Agents Allege.* Street and Smith's SportsBusiness Journal, June 24, 2002, http://www.sportsbusinessjournal.com.

Roberts, Marc, with Digeronimo, Theresa Foy. *Roberts Rules! Success Secrets from America's Most Trusted Sports Agent.* Franklin Lakes, NJ: Career Press, 1998.

Robinson, A. *Cubs' Wilson Clarifies Agent Situation.* MERCURY NEWS, May 18, 2005.

Sammataro, James G. *Business and Brotherhood, Can They Coincide? A Search into Why Black Athletes Do Not Hire Black Agents.* 42 HOWARD LAW JOURNAL 535–68 (1999).

Shropshire, Kenneth L., & Davis, Timothy. *The Business of Sports Agents.* Philadelphia: University of Pennsylvania Press, 2003.

Simon, Ron. *The Game Behind the Game: Negotiating in the Big Leagues.* Stillwater, MN: Voyageur, 1993.

CHAPTER 6

TORTS AND RISK MANAGEMENT

GENERAL CONCEPTS

Risk management issues have become very important for sports management personnel, leagues, stadium owners, and teams. Understanding liability issues is essential for all involved in sports to avoid possible litigation and legal difficulties. A *tort* is defined as a civil wrong not arising from a breach of contract. The word *tort* is French for "wrong." Tort law has been described as a vehicle to compensate those who have suffered injuries from wrongful conduct. It covers a wide variety of wrongful conduct and injuries and provides a remedy for acts that may have caused physical injury or that have interfered with physical safety or freedom of movement. Most businesses today are well aware of tort liability and risk management issues and take them into consideration in business planning.

A tort action is typically a civil action brought by a plaintiff to seek compensation for damages incurred by the plaintiff or to seek some other remedy allowed by law. One of the purposes of tort law is to deter or prevent similar conduct by the same party or others in the future. One who commits a tort is referred to as a *tortfeasor,* and an action or conduct that constitutes a tort is referred to as *tortious behavior*. Torts can either be classified as intentional torts or negligence. An *intentional tort* requires intent on the part of the tortfeasor. *Intent* has been defined as "the desire to bring about certain results." Intentional torts can include assault and battery, intentional infliction of emotional distress, defamation, invasion of the right of privacy, misrepresentation, and intentional interference with contractual or business relations. *Negligence* is "conduct which involves an unreasonably great risk of causing damage,". . . "which falls below the standard established by law for the protection of others against unreasonable risk of harm."[1]

Some torts can also be classified as crimes. For example, assault and battery is a crime and can also form the basis of a civil action by a plaintiff. If A hits B with a hockey stick without provocation, A could be subject to prosecution by the state and could also be sued by B in a civil action for damages sustained, by A's wrongful conduct, subject to any defense that A might assert against B.

---

[1] Dan B. Dobbs, Robert E. Keeton and David G. Owen, *Prosser and Keeton on Torts, Fifth Edition*, West Publishing, 1988, citing to Second Restatement of Torts, § 282.

A wave of tort reform legislation has been passed in the United States. Legislation has been introduced at the state and federal levels to limit the amount of damages a plaintiff may receive for pain and suffering in a tort lawsuit. One of the major purposes of the passage of this type of legislation is to prevent the filing of frivolous lawsuits and to prevent juries from awarding verdicts inconsistent with the evidence. This chapter does not attempt to discuss every tort in the law but only those torts and tort defenses pertinent to the discussion of sports law.

NEGLIGENCE

Negligence is by far the most popular theory of recovery for spectators and for those who are injured while participating in sporting activities. Negligence claims have been brought against coaches, participants, stadium owners, concessionaires, leagues, and referees, alleging that their conduct failed to meet the "reasonable person" standard required in negligence law.

Negligence is an unintentional tort to a person, property, or reputation. The alleged wrongdoer does not intend the consequences of his or her actions. The conduct of the actor creates a risk, and that risk must be foreseeable. If no risk has been created by the actor's conduct, then there is no negligence. However, the risk must be such that a reasonable person engaging in the same kind of conduct would anticipate the risk involved and take steps to guard against it.

To be successful in a negligence action against a defendant, the plaintiff must prove four elements:

1. A duty of care was owed to the plaintiff.
2. The defendant breached that duty.
3. The breach of the duty was a proximate cause or legal cause of the plaintiff's injuries.
4. The plaintiff suffered damages.[2]

If the plaintiff fails to prove all four elements, then the negligence case fails.

Accidents occur every day; however, a plaintiff will not have a cause of action based on negligence arising from an accident unless the plaintiff can first establish that a duty of care was owed by the defendant to the plaintiff. A question arises regarding how to distinguish an accident from unreasonable behavior that causes injury. Judge Learned Hand once stated that negligence is determined by "the likelihood that his conduct will injure others, taken with the seriousness of the injury if it happens, and balanced against the interest which he must sacrifice to avoid the risk."[3]

In deciding whether a duty of care has been breached, a jury will determine how a reasonable person would have acted under the same or similar circumstances. Under negligence law, if an individual is found to owe a duty of care to others, then that individual must conduct himself or herself in a manner so as to avoid injury to another party. Whether a person's conduct constitutes a breach of duty is determined on a case-by-case basis. Whether a duty exists is usually a question of law that depends on the relationship between the parties and the risks involved.[4] There is no tort liability unless the defendant is found to owe a duty to the plaintiff.[5]

---

[2] Sanders v. Kuna Joint School District, 876 P.2d 154 (Idaho Ct. App. 1994); *Also see, Prosser and Keeton on Torts*, Supra pp. 164–165.

[3] Conway v. O'Brien, 111 F.2d 611, 612 (C.A.2 1940).

[4] Thomas v. Wheat, 143 P.3d 767 (Okla. Civ. App. 2006).

[5] Henderson v. Volpe-Vito, Inc., 2006 WL 1751832 (Mich. Ct. App. 2006).

Duty of Care

In Case 6-1, *Vaillancourt v. Latifi*, 840 A.2d 1209 (Conn. App. Ct. 2004), the plaintiff sued the organizer of a recreational league, alleging that the league owed him a duty of care when he sustained an injury in a softball game. The court was called upon to determine whether a duty of care existed under the circumstances.

CASE 6-1   *Vaillancourt v. Latifi*

840 A.2d 1209 (Conn. App. Ct. 2004)

DRANGINIS, J.

The issue in this personal injury action is whether the organizer of a recreational athletic league is liable for the injuries a competitor sustains during the heat of the game. Under the facts alleged in the complaint, the organizer of the league is not responsible for the plaintiff's injuries, as nothing it did or did not do was the legal cause of those injuries. We therefore affirm the judgment of the trial court.

In July, 2000, the plaintiff commenced an action for injuries he allegedly sustained while he was playing softball in a league organized by the YMCA. The plaintiff alleged that in March, 1998, the YMCA solicited teams for its industrial softball league (league). Teams were required to register and to pay a fee to participate in the league. During a league game on July 15, 1998, the plaintiff, the catcher for his team, was attempting to tag the defendant Vaheem Latifi, who was running to home plate from third base. Latifi ran into the plaintiff and caused him to fall to the ground. The plaintiff alleged that Latifi acted with intent and malice. As a result of the collision, the plaintiff suffered injuries, primarily a broken arm. The fifth count also alleged that in exchange for the fee paid by each team, the YMCA was obligated to provide competitors with facilities, organization and instruction "to run a safe league."

. . . [T]he YMCA denied, among other things, that it was obligated to provide a safe league and that it had been negligent. The YMCA thereafter filed a motion claiming that it was entitled to summary judgment as a matter of law because the umpire on the date of the game was an independent contractor, it did not owe the plaintiff a duty of care and nothing that it did or did not do was the legal cause of the plaintiff's injuries. In granting the motion for summary judgment, the court concluded that there was no evidence before it regarding the scope of the duty, either direct or vicarious, that the YMCA owed the plaintiff or that it had breached its duty. We affirm the judgment of the trial court, albeit on different grounds, as we conclude that nothing the YMCA did or did not do was the legal cause of the plaintiff's injuries.

On appeal, the plaintiff claims that it was improper for the court to conclude that the YMCA did not owe him an independent or vicarious duty of care and that there were no genuine issues of material fact in that regard. As a matter of law, the YMCA did not owe the plaintiff a duty of care, as nothing alleged in the complaint was the legal cause of his injuries.

The plaintiff's cause of action "invokes the well established proposition that a tortfeasor is liable for all damages proximately caused by its negligence." The elements of a negligence cause of action are duty, breach, proximate cause and injury.

"To prevail on a negligence claim, a plaintiff must establish that the defendant's conduct legally caused the injuries. . . . [L]egal cause is a hybrid construct, the result of balancing philosophic, pragmatic and moral approaches to causation. The first component of legal cause is causation in fact. Causation in fact is the purest legal application of . . . legal cause. The test for cause in fact is, simply, would the injury have occurred were it not for the actor's conduct."

"Because actual causation, in theory, is virtually limitless, the legal construct of proximate cause serves to establish how far down the causal continuum tortfeasors will be held liable for the consequences of their actions. . . . The fundamental inquiry of proximate cause is whether the harm that occurred was within the scope of foreseeable risk created by the defendant's negligent conduct. . . . In negligence cases such as the present one, in which a tortfeasor's conduct is not the direct cause of the harm, the question of legal causation is practically indistinguishable from an analysis of the extent of the tortfeasor's duty to the plaintiff."

"Duty is a legal conclusion about relationships between individuals, made after the fact, and imperative to a negligence cause of action. The nature of the duty, and the specific persons to whom it is owed, are determined by the circumstances surrounding the conduct of the individual. . . . Although it has been said that no universal test for [duty] ever has been formulated . . . our threshold inquiry has always been whether the specific harm alleged by the plaintiff was foreseeable to the defendant. The ultimate test of the existence of the duty to use care is found in the foreseeability that harm may result if it is not exercised."

"A simple conclusion that the harm to the plaintiff was foreseeable, however, cannot by itself mandate a determination that a legal duty exists. Many harms are quite literally foreseeable, yet for pragmatic reasons, no recovery is allowed. . . . A further inquiry must be made, for we recognize that duty is not sacrosanct in itself, but is only an expression of the sum total of those considerations of policy which lead the law to say that the plaintiff is entitled to protection. . . . While it may seem that there should be a remedy for every wrong, this is an ideal limited perforce by the realities of this world."

Our Supreme Court has recognized that the very nature of athletic competition makes it reasonably foreseeable that competitors may be injured during the contest. "In athletic competitions, the object obviously is to win. In games, particularly those played by teams and involving some degree of physical contact, it is reasonable to assume that the competitive spirit of the participants will result in some rules violations and injuries. . . . Some injuries may result from such violations, but such violations are nonetheless an accepted part of any competition."

. . . Our Supreme Court appreciated the tension between promoting vigorous athletic competition and protecting competitors. As a matter of policy, it concluded that a balance between the two objectives can be achieved "by allowing a participant in an athletic contest to maintain an action against a coparticipant only for reckless or intentional conduct and not for merely negligent conduct."

. . . As a matter of public policy, we acknowledge the tension between promoting competition via athletic leagues and protecting competitors from injury. Here, we need not decide the type of action an injured athlete must allege to prevail against the organizer of an athletic league. Instead, we conclude that the plaintiff failed to allege material facts with respect to the mechanism of his injury that gave rise to a duty owed him by the YMCA. The negligent acts the plaintiff alleged were not the proximate cause of his injury.

The plaintiff alleged that in exchange for a fee, the YMCA owed competitors a duty to operate the league safely. According to the plaintiff, the YMCA breached that duty by failing to select, employ and train its umpires to protect and to prevent vicious attacks on competitors. The essence of the plaintiff's claim is that the umpire failed to prevent Latifi's running into the plaintiff. That claim is predicated on the assumption that Latifi demonstrated unsportsmanlike behavior prior to the collision. The plaintiff concedes, however, that Latifi did nothing prior to the collision to alert anyone that he intended to cause the plaintiff harm or to otherwise require Latifi's removal from the game. Individuals who serve as officials at athletic competitions are not clairvoyant and we do not presume that they can foresee a malicious and intentional act of bad sportsmanship such as that alleged by the plaintiff. As a matter of law, the umpire's failure to eject Latifi from the game prior to the time he ran into the plaintiff was not the proximate cause of the plaintiff's injuries.

In his brief and at oral argument, the plaintiff argued that the YMCA was responsible for his injuries because it did not ensure that the umpire informed the competitors of the rules of the league, particularly the rule that a runner coming to home plate must slide rather than knock down the catcher. Although the plaintiff did not allege that the YMCA was negligent in that manner, he made the argument at the hearing on the motion for summary judgment.

The plaintiff contends that had the umpire ensured that everyone who participated in the game on July 15, 1998, knew of the slide rule, the plaintiff would not have been injured. We are not persuaded. Highly competitive members of athletic teams often take chances and risks that cause them to forget or to ignore the rules of the game. Their intent is to win, however, not to hurt other competitors. For that reason, an injured competitor must allege and prove recklessness against the competitor who causes an injury.

Furthermore, both this court and our Supreme Court have concluded that even when an actor has been warned or is aware of behavior that creates a risk of injury to others, the actor may fail to take heed. We cannot speculate here about what might have happened if the umpire had informed Latifi of the slide rule.

We conclude that the court properly granted the YMCA's motion for summary judgment because the complaint failed to allege any acts or omissions of the YMCA that were the legal cause of the plaintiff's injuries. As a matter of law, therefore, the YMCA did not owe the plaintiff a duty of care.

The judgment is affirmed.

Source: Courtesy of Westlaw; reprinted with permission.

Breach of Duty

A breach of duty occurs if a judge or jury determines that a reasonable person in the position of the defendant acted negligently. The question is not necessarily how a particular person would act but rather how society would judge that an ordinarily prudent person (i.e., a "reasonable person") would act under the same or similar circumstances. In Case 6-2, *Lindaman ex rel. Lindaman v. Vestal Cent. School Dist.*, 785 N.Y.S.2d 549 (N.Y. App. Div. 2004), the parents of a seven-year-old sued a school district, alleging that the district was negligent when it allowed a group of second graders to play a multiple-ball version of dodge ball. The court was asked to determine whether the defendant's conduct was negligent.

CASE 6-2   *Lindaman ex rel. Lindaman v. Vestal Cent. School Dist.*

785 N.Y.S.2d 549 (N.Y. App. Div. 2004)

Rose, J.

Plaintiffs commenced this action to recover for injuries sustained by the seven-year-old infant plaintiff (hereinafter plaintiff) when she became entangled with another student, fell on a hardwood floor and fractured her left arm during a multiple-ball version of the game of dodge ball in her second-grade gym class on defendant's premises. Defendant moved for summary judgment dismissing the complaint, asserting that the game was appropriate, safe and adequately supervised by a teacher, and the accident was unforeseeable. In opposition, plaintiffs asserted that, because of its known dangers, the game was inappropriate for seven-year-old children, making it foreseeable that plaintiff would be injured. Supreme Court found questions of fact as to whether the activity was appropriate for children of plaintiff's age and a proximate cause of her injuries, and denied the motion. Defendant now appeals.

We affirm. While schools are not insurers of the safety of their students, they are under a duty to exercise the same degree of care as would a reasonably prudent parent placed in comparable circumstances. This duty includes the obligation to assign students to supervised athletic activities that are within their abilities. Whether a school's conduct met this duty and was a proximate cause of a particular injury are generally questions of fact.

When defendant met its initial burden to show that the dodge ball game was safe and appropriate through the testimony of its athletic director, plaintiffs offered in response the deposition testimony of Robert Moyer, the teacher who was supervising the activity when plaintiff was hurt, and an affidavit of Steve Bernheim, an expert in sports, recreational and educational safety. Moyer admitted that he had no documentation concerning the appropriateness of using dodge ball with second-grade students, he had never observed any of defendant's other teachers use the activity with second graders and no one ever advised him that it was appropriate at that grade level. Bernheim asserted that, while there are no established standards of age-appropriateness for dodge ball, it is recognized as a potentially dangerous activity and has been banned by several school districts in New York and elsewhere. He also opined that traditional dodge ball is not appropriate for students below the fourth-grade level and the chaotic, multiple ball version being played here, without a neutral or safety zone in the center of the game area as prescribed in defendant's own guidelines, was particularly dangerous for younger children.

Inasmuch as this action turns upon whether defendant's use of a particular form of dodge ball with children in the second grade was safe and appropriate, and this is to be gauged by the standard of what a reasonably prudent parent would do if he or she were in possession of the available information, we agree with Supreme Court that Bernheim's affidavit has probative force under these circumstances, despite his failure to cite any formally recognized standard of age-appropriateness for dodge ball.

Source: Courtesy of Westlaw; reprinted with permission.

Proximate Cause

Also essential to any successful tort case is that the plaintiff prove that the defendant's wrongful activity caused the harm or injury to the plaintiff. Proximate cause can also be described as legal cause. Questions of proximate cause are tied directly to the concept of foreseeability. For liability to be imposed on a defendant, the defendant's conduct must have created a foreseeable risk of injury. If an individual breaches a duty of care and another individual suffers damages, the wrongful conduct of the defendant must also have caused the damages for a negligence case to be sustained.

To determine whether the causation element has been met, two questions are posed: Is there causation in fact? Were the defendant's actions a proximate cause of the injury?[6] If an injury would not have occurred without the defendant's conduct, then the causation in fact requirement is met. Causation in fact is also referred to as the "but for" test. But for the wrongful acts of the defendant, the injury would not have occurred. However, causation in fact is easily met in virtually every scenario. A plaintiff could argue, for example, that if the defendant had not been born then the wrongful conduct would not have occurred. Its application is virtually limitless. Because of this, courts have established proximate cause or legal cause as the benchmark for meeting the third element of a negligence case. Proximate cause or legal cause is present when the nexus between the wrongful conduct of the defendant and the plaintiff's injuries is strong enough to require imposing liability on the tortfeasor. Both causation in fact and proximate cause must be present for the plaintiff to succeed in a negligence action. If a defendant's conduct meets the test of causation in fact but a court determines that the defendant's wrongful conduct is not the proximate cause or legal cause of the injury, then the plaintiff's negligence case will fail. A plaintiff is not required to eliminate all of the other potential causes in proving proximate cause. They only need to prove a sufficient evidentiary basis from which causation can be reasonably inferred and furthermore, the causation is only required to be a "substantial factor" in causing the injury.

---

[6] *See generally, Prosser and Keeton on Torts,* Supra, §42, p. 272.

Damages

For a plaintiff to prove a negligence case, the party must also have suffered damages. If an alleged wrongdoer breached a duty of care and causation was present, the plaintiff must still have suffered an injury to have a viable negligence claim. The most common remedy for a tort victim is money damages. However, plaintiffs can also seek injunctive relief under tort law if money damages are deemed inadequate.

Damages can be categorized as nominal, compensatory, or punitive. *Nominal damages* are obviously a very small award. These damages are awarded when the law recognizes a technical invasion of the plaintiff's rights, but no economic harm has been done to the plaintiff. In *United States Football League v. National Football League*, 842 F.2d 1335 (2nd Cir. 1988), a jury awarded nominal damages of $1 to the USFL in an antitrust lawsuit against the NFL. The amount awarded was then trebled to $3 as required under antitrust law.

Compensatory damages are available to make the plaintiff "whole." In a personal injury lawsuit, the plaintiff can seek damages for wage loss, pain and suffering, disfigurement, and medical expenses. The purpose behind *punitive damages* is to punish the wrongdoer and to prevent the wrongdoer and others from engaging in similar conduct in the future; however, punitive damages are not available to a plaintiff in every state.

DEFAMATION

Sports have become an intrinsic part of the American landscape. Individuals think nothing of calling their local sports radio station and berating the local sports heroes, coaches, referees, broadcasters, or owners. Sports is a topic of conversation for millions of people in the United States every day through a variety of media and electronic outlets. Television and radio sports shows abound, with talking heads, callers, and hosts spouting the latest information concerning the minutiae of each player's performance and sordid details about superstars' personal lives. Could any of these "discussions" ever constitute the tort of defamation? Could a player or coach ever sue a radio talk show host, television anchorperson, journalist, or fan for public remarks made about the athlete?

The free speech protections of the First Amendment are not absolute. Defamation is not protected speech under the First Amendment. There are two types of defamation: libel and slander. Orally damaging a person's reputation constitutes *slander*, whereas using the written word involves the tort of *libel*.

Black's Law Dictionary, 8th ed., defines defamation as follows: "The act of harming the reputation of another by making a false statement [written or oral] to a third person. If the alleged defamation involves a matter of public concern, the plaintiff is constitutionally required to prove both the statement's falsity and the defendant's fault." One of the key questions in any defamation case is whether the defendant's statement is one of fact or opinion. If the statement constitutes only opinion, then there is not an actionable tort. However, a difficult question can arise when the statement constitutes a hybrid statement consisting of both fact and opinion. A statement based on false or undisclosed facts can also constitute defamation.

To be held actionable, a defamatory statement must also be "published." If A tells B that he is a fraud and a thief and it is a false statement but is not communicated to a third party, then the publication requirement has not been met and no defamation has occurred. The defamatory state-ment must be communicated to a third party to meet the publication requirement.

At common law, the courts recognized that certain types of statements are defamation per se and therefore need no proof of injury. They are as follows:

- Those which impute to a person the commission of some criminal offense involving moral turpitude, for which the party, if the charge is true, may be indicted and punished.
- Those which impute that a person is infected with some contagious disease, where if the charge is true, it would exclude the party from society.
- Those which impute to a person unfitness to perform the duties of an office or employment of profit, or want of integrity in the discharge of the duties of such an office or employment.
- Those which prejudice such person in his or her profession or trade.[7]

Truth is an absolute defense against any defamation claim. A defendant may also assert privilege against a plaintiff's defamation claim under certain circumstances. If false and defamatory statements are made about a public figure, then absent a showing of actual malice, there is no defamation. What constitutes a public figure as defined under defamation law? Public figures are usually individuals who have been placed in the public limelight. The category can include entertainers, politicians, and anybody else who becomes known to the public because of their position or activities in the community.

In *Cobb v. Time, Inc.*, 278 F.3d 629 (6th Cir. 2002), a former professional boxer brought a libel action against *Time* alleging defamation. In reversing a jury verdict of $8.5 million in compen-satory damages and $2.2 million in punitive damages, the court found that Cobb was a public figure under the *New York Times* standard and that he had failed to prove "actual malice" on the part of the defendant.

A college track coach who had sued a school magazine for libel on the basis of an article claim-ing that he had dropped several black athletes from the team for participating in a boycott of a dis-criminating organization was also held to be a public figure.[8] A high school football coach was held to be a public figure for purposes of defamation for actions related to the coach's arrest for bookmak-ing and alleged grade changes for football players.[9] However, the head basketball coach of a small junior college in New Orleans with a largely local student body was declared not to be a public figure under defamation law.[10]

For a statement to be made with actual malice it must be made with either knowledge of falsity or a reckless disregard of the truth. Public figures have a greater burden of proof in defamation cases than private individuals because they must meet the actual malice standard set forth in *New York Times v. Sullivan*, 376 U.S. 254, 84 S. Ct. 710, 11 L. Ed. 2d 686 (1964).

In Case 6-3, *Cohen v. Marx*, 211 P.2d 320 (Cal. Dist. Ct. App. 1949), involving the famous comedian Groucho Marx, a boxer fighting under the nickname of "Canvasback Cohen" sued the entertainer and the American Broadcast Company (ABC) for statements made by Marx about the boxer. The court discussed the notion that the plaintiff had waived his right to privacy by placing himself in the public light as a professional athlete. The decision gives an early indication that a court will view an athlete as a public figure.

---

[7] Tronfeld v. Nationwide Mutual Insurance Company, 636 S.E.2d 447, 449–50 (Va. 2006).
[8] Vandenburg v. Newsweek, Inc., 507 F.2d 1024 (5th Cir. 1975).
[9] Brewer v. Roger*s*, 439 S.E.2d 77 (Ga. Ct. App. 1993).
[10] Flose v Delgado Community College, 776 F. Supp. 1133 (E.D. LA 1996).

CASE 6-3 *Cohen v. Marx*

211 P.2d 320 (Cal. Dist. Ct. App. 1949)

McCOMB, J.

The essential allegations of plaintiff's complaint as amended were that:

In 1933, he had entered the prize ring as a professional boxer under the name of "Canvasback Cohen"; that he continued this ring career, losing decisions, until about 1939, when he abandoned the prize ring as a career; that on January 12, 1949, defendant Groucho Marx broadcast over a program of the defendant American Broadcast Company on its program "You Bet Your Life," "I once managed a prize-fighter, Canvasback Cohen. I brought him out here, he got knocked out, and I made him walk back to Cleveland."

The sole question presented for our determination is:

Did plaintiff, by entering the prize ring, seeking publicity, and becoming widely known as a prize fighter under the name of "Canvasback Cohen" waive his right to privacy?

This question must be answered in the affirmative. A person who by his accomplishments, fame, or mode of life, or by adopting a profession or calling which gives the public a legitimate interest in his doings, affairs, or character, is said to become a public personage, and thereby relinquishes a part of his right of privacy.

Applying the foregoing rule to the facts in the present case it is evident that when plaintiff sought publicity and the adulation of the public, he relinquished his right to privacy on matters pertaining to his professional activity, and he could not at his will and whim draw himself like a snail into his shell and hold others liable for commenting upon the acts which had taken place when he had voluntarily exposed himself to the public eye. As to such acts he had waived his right of privacy and he could not at some subsequent period rescind his waiver. . . .

Source: Courtesy of Westlaw; reprinted with permission.

Problem 6-1

Jerry Billings is a well-known sports radio host. Many famous sports celebrities appear on his radio show. He is famous for examination and critique of the social side of sports as well as his intricate knowledge of the sports business. On his show he continually berates players, coaches, and owners for their lack of business knowledge and social awareness in today's sporting scene. One day on his show, Billings states that the owner of the professional football team the

San Antonio Dragons is a "loser," a "deadbeat," and "unscrupulous." He ends his rampage by stating that the owner was able to buy the team with the money he made from his "nefarious business activities." The owner did not hear the broadcast but is told of the remarks by a friend and later obtains a transcript of the show. After reading the transcript, he contacts his lawyer about filing a civil lawsuit against the radio station and Billings. Does he have a viable claim against Billings or the station? If so, under what theory? How would a court rule on this case? Would the owner of the Dragons be a public figure under defamation law? Would the talk show host be protected by the First Amendment? See *Stepien v. Franklin*, 528 N.E.2d 1324 (Ohio Ct. App. 1988).

In Case 6-4, *Smith v. McMullen*, 589 F. Supp. 642 (D.C. Tex. 1984), a former general manager of a major league baseball team sued an owner over statements the owner made to a newspaper referring to him as a "despicable human being." The court addressed the issue of whether the statement was pure opinion, fact, or a hybrid statement.

📖 CASE 6-4 *Smith v. McMullen*

589 F. Supp. 642 (D.C. Tex. 1984)

McDONALD, District Judge.

Facts

The case upon which the present motion is based involves an action for slander brought by plaintiff Tal Smith, former general manager of the Houston Astros, against defendant John J. McMullen, Chairman of the Board of the Houston Sports Association and current owner of the Astros. Plaintiff alleges that the defendant made certain defamatory statements to a reporter for the *Houston Chronicle* on April 23, 1983. These comments, which were published in the *Chronicle* on April 24, were essentially as follows:

> Houston Astros Chairman of the Board John McMullen, reacting angrily to recent criticism of his team, said Saturday night that Houston's baseball franchise "was the worst in baseball when I bought it in 1979.

> "And I can prove it by the price I paid for the franchise (never fully detailed to the public).

> "The 25 men on the field today are better than the Astros' 25-man team when I bought the club."

> . . . .

> McMullen said he is tired of reading suggestions that Smith was the architect of the Astros' success.

"How can you keep writing that?" McMullen asked. "You'd better start writing the truth. Tal Smith is a despicable human being. It's unfair and wrong for people to keep giving him credit."

Defendant made these statements about plaintiff despite the fact that during plaintiff's tenure as general manager of the Astros, the team improved from last place in their division in 1975 to first place in 1980. In 1983, when defendant made the comments which are the basis of this action, the Astros were ranked in last place in the Western division.

Plaintiff contends that the statements which were published in the *Houston Chronicle* were defamatory and have injured him in his profession or business and impute unfitness for his employment in professional baseball. Defendant, on the other hand, denies that the comments were slanderous and maintains that his remarks were at most only words of vituperation or rhetoric hyperbole and that, in addition, they were statements of opinion protected by the First Amendment.

. . . Defendant filed the present Motion for Judgment on the Pleadings, alleging that from the face of the pleadings, it appears that defendant is entitled to judgment dismissing the complaint as a matter of law.

The cause of action upon which the present motion is based involves alleged slanderous statements. In order to constitute actionable slander under Texas law, there must be a defamatory statement orally communicated or published to a third party without legal excuse. The defamatory statement must be either actionable per se, i.e., defamatory in itself, or actionable per quod, i.e., not actionable on its face, but actionable only in view of the actual damages resulting from the slanderous words. In general, oral words are not actionable without pleading and proof of special damages. However, when a statement unambiguously and falsely imputes criminal conduct to another, it is actionable per se, and it is error to allow a jury to determine whether such statements are defamatory. Likewise, an oral defamation which "affects a person injuriously in his office, profession, or occupation" is also actionable per se without the pleading and proof of special damages. Alternatively, if a defamatory meaning may exist, but does not necessarily exist, then the statement is ambiguous and the court must allow a jury to determine whether the communication would be understood by the ordinary reader in a defamatory sense.

1. Rhetoric Hyperbole

Defendant's first contention is that the alleged comments . . . were, at most, only words of vituperation or rhetoric hyperbole and thus not actionable under Texas defamation law. The Court disagrees.

. . . Mere words of vituperation and abuse are not of themselves actionable and libelous. However, when evaluating a statement to determine whether the words are capable of a defamatory meaning, the words cannot be examined in isolation, but instead must be viewed in the context of the statement as a whole. In the case at bar, defendant has engaged in far more than mere name-calling; the totality of his statements, when viewed as a whole, are reasonably capable of a defamatory intent. Thus, defendant's remarks cannot be protected as mere hyperbole.

2. Opinion

Defendant's second contention is that the alleged comments attributed to him were statements of opinion that are protected by the First Amendment.

Pure opinion, which includes derogatory remarks and metaphorical language, clearly seems to fall within the protection of the First Amendment. Hybrid statements, by contrast, fall somewhere in between pure opinion and fact, and are defined as those statements which reflect the author's deductions or evaluations, but at the same time are laden with factual content. A hybrid statement is generally entitled to an absolute privilege as opinion only when it is accompanied by a full and accurate narration of the material background facts. If the author fails to provide the background facts upon which his statements are based, then the hybrid statement is not entitled to an absolute privilege.

In the case at bar, the Court concludes that defendant's remarks pertaining to plaintiff were hybrid in nature and were not pure opinion. The Court further finds that defendant failed to set forth any facts in support of his assertion that plaintiff had nothing to do with the apparent success of the Astros during his tenure as general manager. Thus, inasmuch as defendant's statements were no more than conclusory statements of unsupported fact, they are not privileged as opinion.

Conclusion

The question of whether the comments were in fact slanderous appropriately should be left to a determination by a jury. Defendant has failed to show that he is entitled to dismissal as a matter of law.

The Court notes at this point that the defendant has alleged that plaintiff is a public figure. If that allegation is correct, then plaintiff will be subject to the "actual malice" proof requirements enunciated in *New York Times v. Sullivan*, 376 U.S. 254.

Source: Courtesy of Westlaw; reprinted with permission.

In Case 6-5, *Montefusco v. ESPN Inc.,* 30 Media L. Rep. 2311 (3rd Cir. 2002), John Montefusco Jr. sued ESPN, alleging that the television sports giant was liable for the tort of defamation and also had invaded his privacy when ESPN analogized plaintiff's conviction of assault and criminal trespass to that of O.J. Simpson, "another ex-athlete accused of domestic violence." Montefusco took umbrage with this comparison and asserted that ESPN was liable for "defamation by implication." The court disagreed, finding in favor of ESPN.

📖 CASE 6-5 *Montefusco v. ESPN Inc.*

30 Media L. Rep. 2311 (3rd Cir. 2002)

NYGAARD, Circuit Judge.

Plaintiff John Montefusco, Jr., appeals from the dismissal of his defamation claim against ESPN, Inc. Montefusco, formerly a major league baseball pitcher for the San Francisco Giants, the Atlanta Braves and the New York Yankees, and once the National League's "Rookie of the Year," was the subject of a telecast by the ESPN sports news show, "SportsCenter."

In the SportsCenter telecast, ESPN described criminal proceedings in New Jersey concerning charges against Montefusco by his ex-wife, Doris Montefusco, of sexual and physical violence. Doris Montefusco charged Montefusco with rape, threatened murder, and three attempts to seriously injure her with extreme indifference to human life. The ESPN broadcast noted that a jury found Montefusco not guilty of eighteen felony counts, but convicted him of assault and criminal trespass. Several times throughout the telecast, Montefusco's case was analogized to that of O.J. Simpson, "another ex-athlete accused of domestic violence."

Montefusco sued ESPN for defamation and made a claim for false light invasion of privacy. Both the defamation claim and the false light claim were based on identical grounds. Montefusco argues that the comparison with Simpson implies that Montefusco is guilty of the crimes of which he was acquitted.

The District Court dismissed Montefusco's claim from the bench, finding that the telecast was not defamatory and that the sports news program was privileged to report such a comparison.

We agree. The jury decides whether a statement is defamatory only when the trial court determines that "the statement is reasonably susceptible to both a defamatory and a non-defamatory meaning."

In the instant case, none of the statements made in the sports news broadcast were defamatory: all of the statements related to the criminal charges were factually accurate, as was the comparison of Montefusco's case to Simpson's. We are satisfied as a matter of law that the telecast was truthful, and did not defame the Appellant. The District Court therefore did not err in dismissing Appellant's claims.

Appellant's theory of defamation-by-implication fails because the reported comparison does not imply that Montefusco is guilty of the crimes of which he was acquitted. Moreover, New Jersey has specifically held that there can be no libel by innuendo of a public figure where the facts in the challenged communication are true.

In addition, we find that the publication of the statements was privileged. Pursuant to New Jersey's "fair report privilege," ESPN's presentation was "accurate and complete," and did not mislead viewers as to the Simpson case or Montefusco's circumstances.

The judgment of the District Court will be affirmed.

Source: Courtesy of Westlaw; reprinted with permission.

RIGHT TO PRIVACY AND PUBLICITY RIGHTS

Professor William Prosser divided the right of privacy into four categories:

1. The use of a person's name, picture, or other likeness for commercial purposes without permission
2. Intrusion on an individual's affairs or seclusion
3. Publication of information that places a person in a false light
4. Public disclosure of private facts about an individual that an ordinary person would find objectionable[11]

The majority of states now recognize "the use of a person's name, picture, or other likeness for commercial purposes without permission" as a viable cause of action for infringement of the "right of publicity." Many states have statutes dealing with the right of publicity.[12] The right of publicity grants a person the exclusive right to control the commercial value and exploitation of his or her name, likeness, or personality.[13] The right of publicity protects the commercial interests of athletes and entertainers in their identities.[14] The tort is derived from the appropriation branch of the right of privacy. Other privacy torts protect primarily personal interests, whereas the right of publicity primarily protects the property interest in the publicity of one's name.[15]

One of the first cases to recognize an athlete's right to his own image was *O'Brien v. Pabst Sales Co.*, 124 F.2d 167 (5th Cir. 1941), *cert. denied* 315 U.S. 823 (1942). Davey O'Brien sued

---

[11] PROSSER AND KEETON ON THE LAW OF TORTS (5th ed. 1984); RESTATEMENT (SECOND) OF TORTS 3652A (1971).

[12] *See* 21 OKLA. STAT. ANN. § 839.1.

[13] Sinker v. Goldsmith, 623 F. Supp. 727 (D. Ariz. 1985).

[14] *See* Carson v. Here's Johnny Portable Toilets, Inc., 698 F.2d 831 (6th Cir. 1983), *appeal after remand,* 810 F.2d 104 (6th Cir. 1983); *also see* White v. Samsung Electronics America, Inc., 971 F.2d 1395 (9th Cir. 1992).

[15] Hirsch v. S.C. Johnson & Son, Inc., 280 N.W.2d 129 (Wis. 1979).

a beer producer that had used his picture as a football player without his permission. O'Brien had been actively involved in organizations that spoke out against the use of alcohol. He sued Pabst for invasion of privacy. He lost, but Justice Holmes in his now-famous dissent, stated that although there was no controlling authority on the issue, O'Brien still clearly had a property right in his endorsement.

HOLMES, Circuit Judge (dissenting).

There is no Texas statute or decision directly in point, but I think, under the Texas common law, the appellant is entitled to recover the reasonable value of the use in trade and commerce of his picture for advertisement purposes, to the extent that such use was appropriated by appellee.

The right of privacy is distinct from the right to use one's name or picture for purposes of commercial advertisement. The latter is a property right that belongs to every one; it may have much or little, or only a nominal, value; but it is a personal right, which may not be violated with impunity.

The great property rights created by the demands of modern methods of advertising are of comparatively recent origin, and may not have been in existence in January, 1840, but the common law of Texas is subject to growth and adaptation in the land of its adoption, as well as it was in the country of its origin. The capacity of the common law of Texas 'to draw inspiration from every fountain of justice' has not been diminished by time, though a century has passed since its adoption by the legislature of that state.

No one can doubt that commercial advertisers customarily pay for the right to use the name and likeness of a person who has become famous. The evidence in this case shows that appellant refused an offer by a New York beer company of $400 for an endorsement of its beer, and the appellee apparently recognized that it was necessary to obtain the consent of the various football players, because it required that releases be obtained from them. This admittedly was not done. The fact that appellant made this stipulation with the publishers of the calendars may save it from the infliction of punitive damages, but cannot relieve it from the payment of actual damages measured by the value of the unauthorized use of appellant's picture.

Texas statutes or decisions (if there were any) might make easier the task before us, but the absence thereof does not relieve us of the duty of finding and declaring the governing law of Texas and the forty other states of the Union in which a tort is alleged to have been committed by appellee in the use of appellant's picture for the purpose of advertising beer. If in any of those forty-one states a tort was

committed as alleged, the amount of damages proximately resulting
therefrom should have been submitted to the jury.

The decision of the majority leaves the appellant without remedy for
any non-libellous use made of his picture by advertisers of beer,
wine, whiskey, patent medicines, or other non-contraband goods, wares,
and merchandise. It also places every other famous stage, screen, and
athletic star in the same situation. If one is popular and permits
publicity to be given to one's talent and accomplishment in any art or
sport, commercial advertisers may seize upon such popularity to
increase their sales of any lawful article without compensation of any
kind for such commercial use of one's name and fame. This is contrary
to usage and custom among advertisers in the marts of trade. They are
undoubtedly in the habit of buying the right to use one's name or picture to create demand and good will for their merchandise. It is the
peculiar excellence of the common law that, by general usage, it is
shaped and molded into new and useful forms. [16]

Source: Courtesy of Westlaw; reprinted with permission.

Haelen Laboratories v. Topps Chewing Gum, Inc., 202 F.2d 866 (2d Cir. 1953), *cert. denied*, 346 U.S. 816 (1953), dealt with the right to use baseball players' images on bubble gum trading cards. In that case the court held that New York law recognized a common law right of publicity, which was a property right that could be transferred.

Today's athlete is also a celebrity who has a commercial value in his or her name, likeness, nickname, image, and identity worldwide. An athlete's right of publicity has become a valuable asset to the athlete as well as to his or her team and league. Sports teams and athletes generate millions of dollars each year promoting their products, services, images, and intellectual property rights. An endorsement by an athlete can be extremely valuable to a company, translating into large commercial gains worldwide. Many companies vie for the right to sign famous athletes to endorsement contracts to promote their products. Over the last few years athletes have endorsed many different types of products, including cars, financial services, food products, and even sexual aids. Tiger Woods is one of the most sought-after athletes in the world. In 2008 his endorsements were valued in excess of $117,000,000.

Athletes have become entertainers as well. Many professional sports players have become "actors," thereby increasing their exposure and possible marketability. Chuck Conners of *Rifleman* fame was one of the first athletes to have his own television series. Conners played first base for the Los Angeles Dodgers and also played for the Boston Celtics. Other athletes followed in making appearances on television and in the movies, including Jim Brown (*The Dirty Dozen*), Merlin Olsen (*Little House on the Prairie*), Alex Karras (*Against All Odds*), Bob Uecker (*Mr. Belvedere*), Dan Marino (*Ace Ventura, Pet Detective*), and Shaquille "Shaq" O'Neal (*Blue Chips*).

Many areas of the law come into play when the commercial value of an athlete's name or likeness is at stake. This include the common law right of privacy, the statutory right of publicity, federal

---

[16] O'Brien v. Pabst at 170–72.

and state trademark laws, unfair competition laws, and defamation law. Courts have been willing to extend the right of publicity to names, nicknames, caricatures, and even voices.[17]

In *Muhammad Ali v. Playgirl*, 447 F. Supp. 723 (S.D.N.Y. 1978), Ali sued the women's magazine, alleging that it was using his likeness when it published a drawing of an African American boxer sitting in a corner of a boxing ring who had Ali's facial features. The court found in favor of Ali, indicating that the right of publicity is not limited to an actual photograph but could be based merely on the use of the physical characteristics of the individual.

In a case involving football great Elroy "Crazylegs" Hirsch, Hirsch sued a manufacturer of shaving lotion, alleging that the company's use of his nickname "Crazylegs" to describe its shaving lotion was in violation of his right of publicity. He alleged that because he had used that nickname for many years as both a collegiate and amateur football player, his right of publicity has been infringed. The court remanded the case to the trial court, stating that the disputed identification issue would not prevent his claim.[18]

In another case dealing with the right of privacy, Kareem Abdul-Jabbar sued General Motors Corporation (GMC) for its use of his former name, Lewis Alcindor.[19] A television commercial played during the 1993 NCAA men's basketball tournament stated, "How about some trivia?" Immediately thereafter the words "You're talking to the champ" appeared on the screen. Then a voice asked, "Who holds the record for being voted the most outstanding player of this tournament?" The following words appeared on the screen: "Lewis Alcindor, UCLA, '67, '68, '69." A voice then asked, "Has any car made the *Consumer Digest*'s Best Buy List more than once? The Oldsmobile Eight-Eight has." The commercial then showed the car for several seconds, stated that the '88 had made the list three years in a row, and gave the price. The commercial ended by showing the on-screen message "A Definite First Round Pick," with a voice adding "It's your money" and a final printed message, "Demand Better, '88 by Oldsmobile."

GMC had never obtained consent from Abdul-Jabbar to use his name. After Abdul-Jabbar complained to GMC, the ad was withdrawn. Abdul-Jabbar sued, saying the use of his name was likely to confuse consumers as to his endorsement of the automobile. GMC asserted that Abdul-Jabbar had lost the rights to his birth name because he had "abandoned" his former name through nonuse. The court found in favor of Abdul-Jabbar, stating:

> While the Lanham Act has been applied to cases alleging appropriation of a celebrity's identity, the abandonment defense has never to our knowledge been applied to a person's name or identity. We decline to stretch the federal law of trademark to encompass such a defense. One's birth name is an integral part of one's identity; it is not bestowed for commercial purposes, nor is it "kept alive" through commercial use. A proper name thus cannot be deemed "abandoned" throughout its possessor's life, despite his failure to use it, or continue to use it, commercially.
>
> In other words, an individual's given name, unlike a trademark, has a life and a significance quite apart from the commercial realm. Use or nonuse of the name for commercial purposes does not dispel that significance. An individual's decision to use a name other than the birth name—whether the decision rests on religious, marital, or other personal considerations—does not therefore imply intent to set aside the birth name, or the identity associated with that name.

---

[17] Midler v. Ford Motor Co., 849 F.2d 460 (9th Cir. 1988), (Finding in favor of The Divine Miss M.)
[18] *Hirsch*, 90 Wis.2d 379 280 N.W.2d 129 (1979).
[19] Abdul-Jabbar v. General Motors, 85 F.3d 407 (9th Cir. 1996).

While the issue of whether GMC's use of the name Lew Alcindor constituted an endorsement of its product is far from clear, we hold that GMC cannot rely on abandonment as a defense to Abdul-Jabbar's Lanham Act claim.[20]

California and New York have both seen a great increase in the right of publicity lawsuits. Both states have right of publicity statutes outlining the relevant law. The California Right of Publicity Statute contains the following provisions:

(a) Any person who knowingly uses another's name, voice, signature, photo-graph, or likeness, in any manner, on or in products, merchandise, or goods, or for purposes of advertising or selling, or soliciting pur-chases of, products, merchandise, goods or services, without such per-son's prior consent, or, in the case of a minor, the prior consent of his parent or legal guardian, shall be liable for any damages sustained by the person or persons injured as a result thereof. In addition, in any action brought under this section, the person who violated the sec-tion shall be liable to the injured party or parties in an amount equal to the greater of seven hundred fifty dollars ($750) or the actual dam-ages suffered by him or her as a result of the unauthorized use, and any profits from the unauthorized use that are attributable to the use and are not taken into account in computing the actual damages. In es-tablishing such profits, the injured party or parties are required to present proof only of the gross revenue attributable to such use, and the person who violated this section is required to prove his or her deductible expenses. Punitive damages may also be awarded to the in-jured party or parties. The prevailing party in any action under this section shall also be entitled to attorney's fees and costs.

(b) As used in this section, "photograph" means any photograph or photographic reproduction, still or moving, or any videotape or live television trans-mission, of any person, such that the person is readily identifiable.

(1) A person shall be deemed to be readily identifiable from a photo-graph when one who views the photograph with the naked eye can rea-sonably determine that the person depicted in the photograph is the same person who is complaining of its unauthorized use.

(2) If the photograph includes more than one person so identifiable, then the person or persons complaining of the use shall be repre-sented as individuals rather than solely as members of a definable group represented in the photograph. A definable group includes, but is not limited to, the following examples: a crowd at any sporting event, a crowd in any street or public building, the audience at any theatrical or stage production, a glee club, or a baseball team.

---

[20] *Id.* at 412.

(3) A person or persons shall be considered to be represented as members of a definable group if they are represented in the photograph solely as a result of being present at the time the photograph was taken and have not been singled out as individuals in any manner.

(c) Where a photograph or likeness of an employee of the person using the photograph or likeness appearing in the advertisement or other publication prepared by or in behalf of the user is only incidental, and not essential, to the purpose of the publication in which it appears, there shall arise a rebuttable presumption affecting the burden of producing evidence that the failure to obtain the consent of the employee was not a knowing use of the employee's photograph or likeness.

(d) For purposes of this section, a use of a name, voice, signature, photograph, or likeness in connection with any news, public affairs, or sports broadcast or account, or any political campaign, shall not constitute a use for which consent is required under subdivision (a).

(e) The use of a name, voice, signature, photograph, or likeness in a commercial medium shall not constitute a use for which consent is required under subdivision (a) solely because the material containing such use is commercially sponsored or contains paid advertising. Rather it shall be a question of fact whether or not the use of the person's name, voice, signature, photograph, or likeness was so directly connected with the commercial sponsorship or with the paid advertising as to constitute a use for which consent is required under subdivision (a).

(f) Nothing in this section shall apply to the owners or employees of any medium used for advertising, including, but not limited to, newspapers, magazines, radio and television networks and stations, cable television systems, billboards, and transit ads, by whom any advertisement or solicitation in violation of this section is published or disseminated, unless it is established that such owners or employees had knowledge of the unauthorized use of the person's name, voice, signature, photograph, or likeness as prohibited by this section.

(g) The remedies provided for in this section are cumulative and shall be in addition to any others provided for by law.[21]

Source: Courtesy of Westlaw; reprinted with permission.

Case 6-6, *Doe v. TCI Cablevision*, 110 S.W.3d 363 (Mo. 2003), involves a professional hockey player, Tony Twist, and a marketer of comic books. Twist was a well-known "enforcer" in the NHL.

---

[21] Cal. Civ. Code § 3344.

He was called upon many times in his career to "even" issues on the ice on behalf of his teammates. He sued TCI Cablevision, arguing that a character in a comic book was based on him and that Twist was entitled to damages for the use of this likeliness.

📖 CASE 6-6   *Doe v. TCI Cablevision*

110 S.W.3d 363 (Mo. 2003)

LIMBAUGH, Judge.

I.

Tony Twist began his NHL career in 1988 playing for the St. Louis Blues, later to be transferred to the Quebec Nordiques, only to return to St. Louis where he finished his career in 1999, due to injuries suffered in a motorcycle accident. During his hockey career, Twist became the League's preeminent "enforcer," a player whose chief responsibility was to protect goal scorers from physical assaults by opponents. In that role, Twist was notorious for his violent tactics on the ice. Describing Twist, a *Sports Illustrated* writer said: "It takes a special talent to stand on skates and beat someone senseless, and no one does it better than the St. Louis Blues left winger." Austin Murphy, *Fighting For A Living: St. Louis Blues Enforcer Tony Twist, Whose Pugilistic Talents Appear To Run In The Family, Doesn't Pull Any Punches On The Job,* Sports Illustrated, Mar. 16, 1998, at 42. The article goes on to quote Twist as saying, "I want to hurt them. I want to end the fight as soon as possible and I want the guy to remember it."

Despite his well-deserved reputation as a tough-guy "enforcer," or perhaps because of that reputation, Twist was immensely popular with the hometown fans. He endorsed products, appeared on radio and television, hosted the "Tony Twist" television talk show for two years, and became actively involved with several children's charities. It is undisputed that Twist engaged in these activities to foster a positive image of himself in the community and to prepare for a career after hockey as a sports commentator and product endorser.

Respondent Todd McFarlane, an avowed hockey fan and president of Todd McFarlane Productions, Inc. (TMP), created *Spawn* in 1992. . . .

Spawn is "a dark and surreal fantasy" centered on a character named Al Simmons, a CIA assassin who was killed by the Mafia and descended to hell upon death. Simmons, having made a deal with the devil, was transformed into the creature Spawn and returned to earth to commit various violent and sexual acts on the devil's behalf. In 1993, a fictional character named "Anthony 'Tony Twist' Twistelli" was added to the *Spawn* storyline. The fictional "Tony Twist" is a Mafia don whose list of evil deeds includes multiple murders, abduction of children and sex with prostitutes. The fictional and real Tony Twist bear no physical resemblance to each other and, aside from the common nickname, are similar only in that each can be characterized as having an "enforcer" or tough-guy persona.

Each issue of the *Spawn* comic book contains a section entitled "Spawning Ground" in which fan letters are published and McFarlane responds to fan questions. In the September 1994 issue, McFarlane admitted that some of the *Spawn* characters were named after professional hockey players, including the "Tony Twist" character: "Antonio Twistelli, a/k/a Tony Twist, is actually the name of a hockey player of the Quebec Nordiques." And, again, in the November 1994 issue, McFarlane stated that the name of the fictional character was based on Twist, a real hockey player, and further promised the readers that they "will continue to see current and past hockey players' names in my books."

In April 1996, *Wizard,* a trade magazine for the comic book industry, interviewed McFarlane. In the published article, "Spawning Ground: A Look at the Real Life People Spawn Characters Are Based Upon," McFarlane is quoted as saying that he uses the names of real-life people to create the identities of the characters. Brief biographies and drawings of the *Spawn* characters follow the McFarlane interview. The paragraph devoted to the "Tony Twist" character contained a drawing of the character accompanied by the following description:

> First Appearance: Spawn # 6
>
> Real-Life Persona: Tony Twist.
>
> Relation: NHL St. Louis Blues right winger.
>
> The Mafia don that has made life exceedingly rough for Al Simmons and his loved ones, in addition to putting out an ill-advised contract on the Violator, is named for former Quebec Nordiques hockey player Tony Twist, now a renowned enforcer (i.e. "Goon") for the St. Louis Blues of the National Hockey League.

Below the character description was a photo of a Tony Twist hockey trading card, in which Twist was pictured in his St. Louis Blues hockey jersey.

In 1997, Twist became aware of the existence of *Spawn* and of the comic book's use of his name for that of the villainous character. On one occasion, several young hockey fans approached Twist's mother with Spawn trading cards depicting the Mafia character "Tony Twist." Subsequently, at an autograph session Twist was asked to sign a copy of the

Wizard article in which McFarlane was interviewed and Twist's hockey trading card was pictured. . . .

In this case, Twist seeks to recover the amount of the fair market value that respondents should have paid to use his name in connection with Spawn products and for damage done to the commercial value—in effect the endorsement value—of his name. Therefore, Twist's case, though brought as a misappropriation of name action, is more precisely labeled a right of publicity action. . . .

The court held "On the record here, the use and identity of Twist's name has become predominantly a ploy to sell comic books and related products rather than an artistic or literary expression, and under these circumstances, free speech must give way to the right of publicity."

Source: Courtesy of Westlaw; reprinted with permission.

Did Tony Twist have a viable lawsuit? What factors should the court examine to determine whether his right of publicity was infringed? The Missouri Court of Appeals affirmed a $15 million jury verdict in favor of Twist.[22]

In Case 6-7, *Newcombe v. Adolf Coors Co.*, 157 F.3d 686 (9th Cir. 1998), Don Newcombe, the 1956 National League's Most Valuable Player (MVP), sued Coors over its use of a drawing of a baseball player who was shown in a picturesque baseball stadium in a windup position. Newcombe argued that the figure in the ad was him, was used without his consent and was in violation of his right of publicity. Unbeknownst to the artist, the photograph he had used for his model was actually a photo of Newcombe pitching in the 1949 World Series at Ebbets Field in Brooklyn, New York. The situation was further complicated because of Newcombe's position as the spokesperson for the National Institute for Drug and Alcohol Abuse, combined with the fact that Newcombe himself was a recovering alcoholic.

📖 CASE 6-7 *Newcombe v. Adolf Coors Co.*

157 F.3d 686 (9th Cir. 1998)

HUG, Chief Judge.

. . . Newcombe contends that his likeness and identity were used without his permission in an advertisement for Killian's Irish Red Beer, and that this violated California's statutory and common law protections against commercial misappropriation. Newcombe also contends that the advertisement was negligently created, that the defendants intentionally inflicted emotional distress upon him and that because he is a known recovering alcoholic, using his likeness in a beer advertisement was defamatory.

---

[22] *Appeals Court Upholds $15M Verdict for Twist*, St. Louis Business Journal, June 20, 2006.

Facts and Procedural Background

Newcombe is a former major league baseball all-star who pitched for the Brooklyn Dodgers and other teams from 1949 until 1960. He had previously starred in the so-called Negro leagues and was one of the first African-American players to play in the major leagues after Jackie Robinson broke the color barrier in 1947. Newcombe is the only player in major league history to have won the Most Valuable Player Award, the Cy Young Award, and the Rookie of the Year Award. He was a four-time member of the National League All Star Team, he batted over .300 in four different seasons, and had the most wins of any pitcher in the National League in 1950, 1951, 1955, and 1956.

Newcombe's baseball career was cut short due to his service in the Army and a personal battle with alcohol. He is a recovering alcoholic and he has devoted a substantial amount of time using his fame to advocate the dangers of alcohol, including serving as a spokesperson for the National Institute on Drug and Alcohol Abuse pursuant to presidential appointments by Richard Nixon, Gerald Ford and Ronald Reagan. He is currently the Director of Community Relations with the Los Angeles Dodgers, where he continues an active role in fighting alcohol abuse.

Killian's Irish Red Beer, owned by Coors Brewing Co., published an advertisement in the February 1994 *Sports Illustrated* "swimsuit edition" that featured a drawing of an old-time baseball game. The drawing was on the left half of the full-page advertisement while the right half was filled with text and a picture of a glass of beer. The baseball scene focused on a pitcher in the windup position and the background included a single infielder and an old-fashioned outfield fence. The players' uniforms did not depict an actual team, and the background did not depict an actual stadium. However, Newcombe, along with family, friends and former teammates, immediately recognized the pitcher featured in the advertisement as Newcombe in his playing days.

Newcombe filed suit in California state court on March 10, 1994, alleging that his identity had been misappropriated in violation of California statutory and common law, that the advertisement was defamatory because it portrayed him—a recovering alcoholic—as endorsing beer, that the advertisement was negligently created, and that the defendants intentionally inflicted emotional distress upon him. He sought to enjoin the advertisement from future publication, and he asked for $100,000,000 in damages. In his complaint, Newcombe named Coors, Foote Cone & Belding Advertising ("Belding") (the creator of the ad) and Time Inc. (the publisher of *Sports Illustrated*) as defendants ("the defendants"). . . .

While denying that the pitcher in the advertisement was a "likeness" of Newcombe, Coors admitted that the drawing in the color advertisement was based on a newspaper photograph of Newcombe pitching in the 1949 World Series. The drawing and the newspaper photograph are virtually identical, as though the black and white newspaper photo had been traced and colored in. The only major differences between the newspaper photograph of Newcombe and the drawing of him are that the pitcher's uniform number has been changed from "36" to "39," and the bill of the hat in the drawing is a different color from the rest of the hat. Otherwise, the drawing in the advertisement appears to be an exact replica of the newspaper photograph of Newcombe.

Discussion

Newcombe contends that the defendants violated his right of privacy and used his likeness and identity to their commercial advantage in violation of his statutory rights under Cal. Civ.Code § 3344 and common law right of privacy. . . .

To sustain a common law cause of action for commercial misappropriation, a plaintiff must prove: "(1) the defendant's use of the plaintiff's identity; (2) the appropriation of plaintiff's name or likeness to defendant's advantage, commercially or otherwise; (3) lack of consent; and (4) resulting injury."

In assessing whether summary judgment against Newcombe was appropriate with respect to both his common law and statutory claims, we must first decide whether Newcombe's likeness was actually used. Necessarily, we must address how identifiable an image must be to constitute a likeness. . .

A person is deemed to be readily identifiable from a photograph "when one who views the photograph with the naked eye can reasonably determine that the person depicted in the photograph is the same person who is complaining of its unauthorized use."

Having viewed the advertisement, we hold that a triable issue of fact has been raised as to whether Newcombe is readily identifiable as the pitcher in the advertisement. Initially, we note that the drawing in the advertisement and the newspaper photograph of Newcombe upon which the drawing was based are virtually identical. The pitcher's stance, proportions and shape are identical to the newspaper photograph of Newcombe; even the styling of the uniform is identical, right down to the wrinkles in the pants. The defendants maintain that stance alone cannot suffice to render a person readily identifiable, and that even if it could, the drawing of the pitcher in the advertisement was essentially generic and could have been any one of thousands of people who have taken to the pitcher's mound to throw a baseball. We disagree.

It may be the case that Newcombe's stance is essentially generic, but based on the record before us, Newcombe is the only one who has such a stance. The record contains pictures of other pitchers in the windup position but none of these pitchers has a stance similar to Newcombe's, thus giving us no basis to reach the conclusion proposed by the defendants that the pitcher in the advertisement is "generic." Furthermore, Matthew Reinhard, the Art Director at Belding, declared that a prior work of Cassidy's, which depicted former San Francisco Giant pitcher Juan Marichal in his unorthodox high-leg-kick windup, would not have been suitable for the advertisement at issue because Marichal's windup was too distinctive. Reinhard's admission that a pitcher's windup could be so distinctive so as to make that player readily identifiable, regardless of the visibility of his face or the markings on the uniform, bolsters our determination that there is a genuine issue of material fact as to whether Newcombe's stance was so distinctive that the defendants used his likeness by using a picture of Newcombe's stance.

In addition to the identifiability of the pitcher in the advertisement as Newcombe based on the pitcher's stance, the pitcher's skin is moderately dark, which is quite similar to Newcombe's skin color. A jury could rationally find from this that Newcombe was readily identifiable, even though his facial features were not entirely visible. Furthermore, while the drawing in the advertisement was slightly altered from the newspaper photograph, that does not alter our conclusion that there is a genuine issue of material fact as to whether the advertisement made use of Newcombe's likeness. For example, the uniform number in the advertisement ("39") is only slightly different than Newcombe's number ("36")—the first number is the same and the second number is simply inverted and the advertisement utilized the same block style numbers that were used on Newcombe's jersey—and it is arguable that the similarity in numbers could either consciously or subconsciously conjure up images of Newcombe. Also, we do not find persuasive the fact that the coloring of the bill of the hat in the advertisement is different, in light of the fact that the rest of the uniform is identical to the uniform in the newspaper photograph of Newcombe.

Source: Courtesy of Westlaw; reprinted with permission.

Problem 6-2

Jack Bates is a professional football player with the Cincinnati Bengals. His agent has told him that he needs to be more of a "showman" on the field in order to become more well known to the fans. Bates, a wide receiver, determines that the next time he scores a touchdown he will perform his new creation, "the Bates Shuffle." During the next game, he scores a touchdown and performs the shuffle on the sideline. The fans love it. He continues to do his "Bates Shuffle" over the next two seasons every time he scores a touchdown. Fans have become well acquainted with the shuffle and cheer loudly every time he does it. One day while watching television in the off-season, Bates sees a twelve-year-old boy with a football performing what he recognizes as "the Bates Shuffle" in an advertisement for a local sporting goods store. Bates's friends recognize it as well. Bates contacts the store and asks them to remove the image of the "Bates Shuffle" from the commercial. The store refuses to remove the advertisement. Does Bates have a cause of action against the store for infringement upon his right of publicity? What defenses could the store assert?

PREMISES LIABILITY

Premises liability law stems from the law of negligence and delineates the guidelines by which the owner or occupier of land can be held liable for injuries sustained by individuals on the premises. Premises liability law requires a possessor of land to exercise reasonable care to protect individuals who come onto the property from harm.[23] The premises owner is not insurer of the safety of individuals who enter upon the premises and the land owner's duty is only to exercise reasonable care for their protection.[24] The owner's duty of care depends on the status of the person on the land.[25] An individual entering upon land is usually classified as either an invitee, licensee, or trespasser. A business visitor or invitee is a person who is invited to enter or remain on the land for a purpose directly or indirectly connected with business dealings connected with the possession of the land.[26] When a business owner invites patrons to enter the establishment, the owner is required to exercise ordinary care in keeping the premises safe for them.[27]

With regard to a business invitee, the landowner must (1) exercise reasonable care, (2) disclose to the invitee all dangerous conditions that are not likely to be discovered by the invitee, and (3) ensure that the premises are safe for the reception of the invitee or give warning to the invitee about dangers existing upon the land.[28] An owner of land violates its duty owed to invitees when it negligently allows conditions to exist on the property that imperil the safety of persons on the premises.[29] Landowners who invite individuals onto their premises are required to exercise reasonable care to protect them against foreseeable risks about which the owner knew or should have known.

A *licensee* has been defined as "a person who is privileged to enter or remain on land only by virtue of the possessor's consent."[30] A licensee comes upon the property for their own purposes

---

[23] Bucki v. Hawkins, 914 A.2d 491, 495 (R.I. 2007); Kirchner v. Shooters on the Water, Inc., 856 N.E.2d 1026, 1031–32 (Ohio Ct. App. 2006).

[24] Backer v. Pizza inn, Inc., 162 Ga.App. 682, 292 S.E.2d 562, 1982.

[25] Hiar v. Strong, 2006 WL 664242 at *1 (Mich. Ct. App. 2006).

[26] Stephens v. Bashas' Inc., 924 P.2d 117 (Ct. App. Div. 1 1996).

[27] Roberts v. Outback Steakhouse of Florida, 641 S.E.2d 253, 269 (Ga. Ct. App. 2007).

[28] Harris v. Niehans, 857 S.W.2d 222 (Mo. 1993).

[29] Keeran v. Spurgeon Mercantile Co., 191 N.W. 99 (Iowa 1922).

[30] Restatement (Second) of Torts § 330.

rather than for any purpose or interest of the landowner.[31] The basic duty owed to a licensee is to warn of known danger.[32] The landowner owes no duty of inspection to licensees. A *trespasser* is "a person who enters or remains upon land in possession of another without privilege to do so created by the possessor's consent or otherwise."[33] The trespasser is the least-protected class of plaintiffs; the landowner has no duty to make the premises safe for a trespasser. The landowner must only refrain from doing intentional harm to the trespasser. A person sneaking into a game without paying or going onto the playing surface without consent, before, during or after a game would be classified as a trespasser and therefore would be owed no duty of care by the owner of the premises.

A stadium owner has a relationship with a spectator that is similar to that of a landowner–invitee.[34] Fans who pay for tickets are business invitees because the cost of a ticket confers a benefit to the owner of the premises.[35] The spectator would be an invitee who is owed the highest duty of care by the premises owner.[36] Other examples of invitees include store customers, restaurant patrons, and amusement park entrants. Based on this relationship, a stadium owner owes a duty of care to ensure a spectator's safety and to exercise reasonable care toward the spectator. This requires a stadium owner to inspect the premises and make sure they are safe for all patrons. The stadium owner also has to provide adequate warnings to invitees/spectators of any possible dangers that exist on the premises. Those duties have included taking reasonable steps to protect spectators from the foreseeable acts of third parties, including other violent spectators. However, owners are not required to anticipate unforeseeable acts of third parties.

There have been lawsuits dealing with "field rushing" activities by students. When Wisconsin upset Michigan on October 30, 1993, thousands of fans ran onto the field in celebration. Seventy-three people were severely injured as a result. At a Ball State University football game, Andrew Bourne was paralyzed when a goalpost fell on him.[37] Several witnesses recounted that the following message had appeared on the scoreboard: "Do you think the goalposts are coming down? They look lonely." Fans who rush onto a field after a game are most likely trespassers; however, considering the scoreboard message at Ball State, could a university be deemed to have invited fans onto the field, thereby removing them from trespasser status under the law and making them invitees?

What obligations does a stadium owner have to provide adequate security for fans? In Case 6-8, *Iacono v. MSG Holding, L.P.*, 801 N.Y.S.2d 778 (N.Y. 2005), the plaintiffs asserted that Madison Square Garden was negligent when it failed to provide adequate security to prevent a riot that caused the plaintiff's injuries. One of the plaintiffs was a photographer for *Sports Illustrated* who was assigned to cover the boxing match being held at the Garden. Is the duty to a photographer different from that owed to spectators?

---

[31] McCurry v. Young Men's Christian Association, 210 Neb. 278, 313 N.W.2d 689, 691 (1981).

[32] *Hiar*, 2006 WL 664242.

[33] Restatement (Second) of Torts § 330.

[34] Dan B. Dobbs, The Law of Torts § 323 (2000).

[35] *Id.*

[36] Scott v. University of Michigan Athletic Association, 152 Mich. 684 (1908), (football); Crane v. Kansas City Baseball & Exhibition Co., 168 Mo.App. 301; 153 S.W. 1076 (1918), (baseball).

[37] Andrew Bourne, et al. v. Marty Gilman, Incorporated, 452 F.3d 632 (2006). Bourne sued Ball State and the manufacturer of the goal posts. He settled his case with Ball State for $300,000.

📖 CASE 6-8 *Iacono v. MSG Holdings, L.P.*

801 N.Y.S.2d 778 (N.Y. 2005)

This lawsuit is the product of a riot that took place at the conclusion of the July 11, 1996 heavyweight boxing match between Riddick Bowe and Andrew Golota. The riot was captured on film as part of the HBO telecast of the match. Golota appeared to be winning the bout and well on his way to a major upset, but somehow he did not stop hitting Bowe below the belt. Golota was disqualified in the seventh round because of the repeated low-blows. Soon after, the riot began. Members of both fighters' camps and entourages engaged one another in the ring, and the riot subsequently spread all over Madison Square Garden; individual fights broke out in the lobby and outside the building.

Plaintiff John Iacono is a photographer for Sports Illustrated who was assigned to work the Bowe-Golota fight. During the fight he was situated directly next to the ring with his elbows on the edge of the ring. When the fight was stopped, Mr. Iacono moved onto the apron of the ring (the edge of the ring outside of the ropes) to take victory photographs. While he attempted to take these pictures, the riot began. Mr. Iacono continued to photograph what he described as the "chaotic" scene at the ring for approximately twenty minutes, until he was punched in the face by an unknown person standing inside the ring.

The court found: "A jury here could reasonably find that the risk of a riot or stampede could have been averted, or its consequences contained, by adequate crowd-control measures which would have inhibited or prevented the eruption of precipitating incidents such as individual or group altercations, arguments or other provocative causes that defendant city failed to exercise reasonable care necessary under the circumstances to avoid the foreseeable risk.

Further, in determining whether MSG was negligent in controlling the riot, the applicable standard is that the landowner is only required to take reasonable measures to secure the premises. The plaintiffs introduce evidence that the measures taken were not reasonable in responding to and in diffusing the riot. In his affidavit, Mr. Blanche asserts that MSG security engaged the rioters. But, he concludes that MSG's response techniques were unreasonable, stating, for example, that the "taking on of the rioters on a one to one basis was a losing proposition for Madison Square Garden security personnel who had then lost control of the crowd." Therefore, plaintiffs' have set forth a question of fact on their second claim based on MSG's alleged negligence in controlling the riot."

Source: Courtesy of Westlaw; reprinted with permission.

How far does the concept of duty extend for a stadium owner? In Case 6-9, *Hayden v. University of Notre Dame*, 716 N.E.2d 603 (Ind. Ct. App. 1999), the court examined the duty a stadium owner has to protect fans from the violent or negligent acts of others.

CASE 6-9 *Hayden v. University of Notre Dame*

716 N.E.2d 603 (Ind. Ct. App. 1999)

KIRSCH, Judge.

Facts and Procedural History

On September 16, 1995, William and Letitia Hayden attended a football game on the Notre Dame campus. They were season ticket holders and sat in their assigned seats, which were in the south endzone behind the goalpost. During the second quarter of the game, one of the teams kicked the football toward the goal. The net behind the goalposts did not catch the ball, and it landed in the stands close to Letitia Hayden's seat. Several people from the crowd lunged for the ball in an effort to retrieve it for a souvenir. One of them struck Letitia Hayden from behind, knocking her down and causing an injury to her shoulder.

The Haydens brought suit against Notre Dame for failing to exercise care to protect Letitia Hayden. Notre Dame moved for summary judgment, arguing that it did not have a legal duty to protect Letitia Hayden from the intentional criminal acts of an unknown third person. The trial court granted Notre Dame's motion. The Haydens now appeal.

The Haydens claim that Notre Dame was negligent in failing to protect Letitia Hayden. In order to prevail on a claim of negligence, a plaintiff must prove: (1) a duty owed to the plaintiff by the defendant; (2) a breach of that duty by the defendant; and (3) injury to the plaintiff proximately caused by that breach. The only element at issue here is whether Notre Dame owed Letitia Hayden a duty under the circumstances. Whether a duty exists is generally a question of law for the court to determine.

The Haydens argue that this case is governed by premises liability principles and that the relevant standard of care is determined by

Letitia Hayden's status as an invitee. The parties do not dispute that Letitia Hayden was a business invitee of Notre Dame. Nonetheless, Notre Dame argues that it owed no duty to protect Letitia Hayden from a third party's criminal act. It contends that the third party's action was unforeseeable, and that it therefore owed no duty to anticipate it and protect Letitia Hayden, a business invitee.

Our supreme court recently decided several cases which articulated the test for determining when a landowner's duty to its invitees extends to protecting them against the criminal actions of third parties that occur on its land. In *Delta Tau Delta v. Johnson*, 712 N.E.2d 968 (Ind.1999), the court adopted a "totality of the circumstances" test for determining when such a duty arises. This test "requires landowners to take reasonable precautions to prevent foreseeable criminal actions against invitees." The court explained that, "[u]nder the totality of the circumstances test, a court considers all of the circumstances surrounding an event, including the nature, condition, and location of the land, as well as prior similar incidents, to determine whether a criminal act was foreseeable." "A substantial factor in the determination is the number, nature, and location of prior similar incidents, but the lack of prior similar incidents will not preclude a claim where the landowner knew or should have known that the criminal act was foreseeable."

Applying the totality of the circumstances test in the case before it, the court held that the defendant-fraternity owed a duty to the plaintiff, a young woman who attended a party at the fraternity house, to take reasonable precautions to protect her from sexual assault by third parties on its premises. The court looked at prior incidents of assault and forced alcohol consumption, as well as the fraternity's awareness of the prevalence of date rape (especially involving fraternity members) and of legal action taken against other fraternities for sexual assault, and concluded that under these circumstances such a duty existed.

Applying this test to the case before us, we find that the totality of the circumstances establishes that Notre Dame should have foreseen that injury would likely result from the actions of a third party in lunging for the football after it landed in the seating area. As a result, it owed a duty to Letitia Hayden to protect her from such injury. The Haydens were seated in Notre Dame's stadium to watch a football game. Notre Dame well understands and benefits from the enthusiasm of the fans of its football team. It is just such enthusiasm that drives some spectators to attempt to retrieve a football to keep as a souvenir. There was evidence that there were many prior incidents of people being jostled or injured by efforts of fans to retrieve the ball. Letitia Hayden testified that she and her husband had attended Notre Dame football games for many years, and that she witnessed footballs land in the seating area around her many times. On numerous occasions, she saw people jump to get the ball. She testified that she witnessed another woman injured a number of years earlier when people in the crowd attempted to retrieve a football, and that she was knocked off her seat earlier in the game by crowd members attempting to retrieve the ball prior to the incident in which she was injured.

William Hayden testified that the net behind the goalpost caught the ball only about fifty percent of the time that it was kicked. The other half of the time, the ball would fall in the seating area around his seat, and people would try desperately to retrieve the ball. He stated that a few years prior to this incident, he had been knocked off his feet and thrown into the next row by fans eager to retrieve a football, and that he had been jostled a number of times. He stated that Notre Dame ushers witnessed fans being jostled in scrambles for the ball, but did not make aggressive attempts to recover the balls. He testified that in prior years, student managers, who were Notre Dame employees, would aggressively attempt to retrieve balls from fans and were usually successful in returning the balls to the playing field. The managers, however, no longer tried to retrieve the balls and stayed on the playing field.

Based on the totality of the circumstances, we hold that Notre Dame owed Letitia Hayden a duty to take reasonable steps to protect her from injury due to the actions of other fans in attempting to retrieve footballs which land in the seating area. The trial court erred in finding that no duty existed and entering summary judgment in favor of Notre Dame.

Source: Courtesy of Westlaw; reprinted with permission.

Problem 6-3

Delta Tech has not won a home game in five years. On homecoming day it beat its arch-rival, Riverview A&M, 18–17 on the last play of the game with a field goal. After the game ended, students poured onto the field. Several students climbed on top of the goalpost and brought it to the ground. The goalpost landed on a 19-year-old freshman, injuring her severely. She seeks to file a civil lawsuit against Delta Tech for its failure to keep students from rushing the field after the game. No security was present at the game, and the rushing students had easy access to the field. There were signs posted along the field stating "No students are allowed on the playing surface during the game." How would a court decide this case? What defenses can the university assert on its behalf? Did the university do enough under the circumstances to prevent the student's injury?

Problem 6-4

James Jenkins celebrated his birthday by attending an NBA game between the Hawks and Celtics in Boston. James was a big Celtics fan, and the more they fell behind in the score, the more he drank. At the end of the third quarter, Jenkins went to the nearest concession area and purchased a gin and a tonic. His friends knew he was drunk at the time he purchased the gin and tonic. He was passed out for most of the fourth quarter and eventually woke up with two minutes to go in the game. He left the game and, while driving home, struck and killed a pedestrian. The estate of the pedestrian sued the NBA and the Boston Celtics organization, seeking damages. Does the estate have a viable lawsuit against the league or the Celtics or both? If so, under what theory? What defenses are available to the team and the league?

SPECTATOR INJURIES

Every year millions of fans pass through the gates of sports arenas to watch their favorite sports teams and players. Most fans want to see their heroes up close and personal. In today's sporting world a fan not only gets to see a game but also extracurricular activities during the sporting event, such as extravagant halftime shows, fireworks, concerts, mascots' antics, and cannons being fired, and sometimes can even participate in these activities. Stadium owners, teams, and leagues have realized that sporting events have become entertainment vehicles and that they need to keep the fans entertained and interested throughout the event with a myriad of other activities in addition to the sporting event itself. Throughout all this activity and distraction, potential liability situations exist. Stadium owners, leagues, and teams have become fully aware of risk management issues arising out of this activity.

Injuries can occur from activities that arise from the playing of the game itself, such as batted balls, a flying puck, or a thrown bat. During a baseball game, a ball can fly into the stands at a high rate of speed. Players can lose their grip on bats and can launch a two-pound missile into the crowd. A tragic event occurred at an NHL game between the Columbus Blue Jackets and Calgary Flames in Columbus, Ohio, when a 13-year-old girl was killed when a hockey puck struck her in the head. The NHL and the arena settled the case for $1.2 million.[38] Football, unlike baseball and hockey, has no real objects of danger flying into the crowd, but the NFL does fine its players for throwing balls into the stands or jumping into the stands.

Injuries can also occur as the result of mascot antics, vendors who spill food or drinks on fans, fans injuring other fans, and negligence issues concerning the design and maintenance of the stadium itself. Facility owners and operators owe a duty of care to spectators under negligence law to provide a safe environment to the fans so they can enjoy the game free of injury. Some states have passed statutes dealing with spectator liability, specifically dealing with baseball spectators.

Spectator violence has also increased in recent years. In a well-known incident that occurred in 2000 at Wrigley Field, several players for the Los Angeles Dodgers entered the stands and began to fight with Cubs fans behind the Cubs' dugout. The melee started when a Cubs fan

---

[38] Associated Press, *Coroner's Report: Puck Snapped Girl's Head Back, Damaging Artery,* Sports Illustrated, March 20, 2002.

removed the cap of a Dodger player. In another incident, Bill Spiers, a former Houston Astros player, was attacked by a fan in a game against the Milwaukee Brewers in 1998. His teammates left the bench and the bullpen to aid Spiers. He suffered a welt under his left eye and a bloody nose but chose to remain in the game. His assailant was charged with two counts of assault. Another incident of fan violence occurred in 2002 at Comiskey Park when a shirtless father-son team attacked Kansas City Royals' first-base coach Tom Gamboa. The father and son contended that the coach "got what he deserved" for making an obscene gesture. Gamboa maintained that he never acknowledges fans in the crowd. The father faced a felony aggravated battery charge, and the son was charged with two counts of aggravated battery. Gamboa suffered only a few cuts and bruises from the incident, even though a knife was found on the scene, apparently falling out of the pocket of one of the assailants.

Fan violence has not been limited to baseball. In 2001, Toronto Maple Leafs' Ty Domi fought with a fan in the penalty box during a game against the Philadelphia Flyers. Domi twice sprayed water over taunting fans in the front row before his attacker lunged against the glass to throw a punch at Domi that failed to connect. The glass separating the two collapsed, and Domi pulled his attacker into the penalty box. The fight ended when another player who was already in the penalty box broke up the fight. In another bizarre incident, tennis great Monica Seles was stabbed by a psychotic fan in 1993 when the fan charged onto the tennis court. Hollywood has addressed fan violence in the movie *The Fan,* starring Robert DeNiro and Wesley Snipes, in which a crazed fan played by DeNiro stalks and attempts to harm Snipes, who plays an outfielder with the San Francisco Giants. The plot outline was described as "an All-Star baseball player becomes the unhealthy focus of a down on his luck salesman."

It should be noted that interactions between fans and players are nothing new. In a 1928 case, *Atlanta Baseball Company v. Lawrence,* 144 S.E. 351 (Ga. Ct. App. 1928), a baseball player entered the stands after a fan "ragged" him. The court described the antics of the fans as follows:

> The plaintiff, accompanied by his little grandson and certain friends, was in attendance upon the game on the occasion named, on paid admission. "Plaintiff and said party were seated in said grandstand while said game was progressing, and the game began to go against the team of defendant. A number of spectators at said game, under the impression that the pitching of said McLaughlin was responsible for a large part of the poor showing made by the team of defendant, began to 'rag' said McLaughlin, as it is called; that is to say, began to make audible remarks that were not particularly complimentary to the pitching ability of said McLaughlin as displayed on said occasion. Said custom or 'ragging,' particularly if it is good-natured, consisting of criticisms upon the manner in which the game is being played, is a common custom at practically all the games played by defendant. Plaintiff joined in said 'ragging' only to the extent of saying, good naturedly, 'Give us another pitcher.' In so doing, plaintiff was really following the common custom indulged in by the patrons of defendant at the baseball games played by defendant's employees on said grounds. In making said remark plaintiff had no expectation and no ground for expectation that any offensive action would be indulged in by defendant or any of its employees on account thereof. So free was plaintiff from an anticipation of any consequences flowing from his good-natured 'ragging' that he was engaged in showing and explaining to his visiting friends a score card of said game which he had bought from defendant, and was sitting down in his seat when, to his astonishment, on looking up he saw standing over him in a threatening attitude said McLaughlin, who had just come in from his position as pitcher on the baseball diamond. Said McLaughlin was accompanied by several other employees of defendant, members of defendant's hired baseball team, and

the attitude of said McLaughlin was insulting and threatening. Without any provocation on the part of plaintiff, said McLaughlin proceeded to attack, beat, bruise, and wound plaintiff, inflicting several blows upon plaintiff, and battering and bruising plaintiff's face and person."[39]

The plaintiff sued the team, alleging that the team was responsible for the acts of its employee. However, the court found that the pitcher, by leaving the playing field and going into the stands, was not acting within the scope of his employment with the team.[40]

Because of the well-established rule that a spectator at a sporting event generally assumes all risks incidental to the game, teams have prevailed in the majority of lawsuits dealing with spectator injuries. However, some courts have found in favor of spectators when injuries occurred as a result of occurrences not "incidental to the game." In a lawsuit involving spectator injuries, the spectators will typically argue that the facility had inadequate safety barriers or that the defendant failed to warn them of the risks involved.

A ball going into the stands at a baseball game is a common occurrence. Case 6-10, *Teixiera v. New Britain Baseball Club, Inc.*, 41 Conn. L. Rptr. 777 (Sup. Ct. Conn. 2006), discusses baseball's unique limited duty rule.

📖 CASE 6-10   *Teixiera v. New Britain Baseball Club, Inc.*

41 Conn. L. Rptr. 777 (Sup. Ct. Conn. 2006)

SHABAN, J.

I. Facts and Procedural Background

On February 28, 2005 the plaintiff, Michael Teixiera, commenced a personal injury action . . . against the defendant, New Britain Baseball Club, Inc. (NBBC). . . . NBBC operates a baseball field known as New Britain Stadium (the stadium) in New Britain . . . [P]laintiff went there with his minor son to attend a Rock Cats game. While in line to enter the stadium, the plaintiff purchased two tickets for an all-you-can-eat barbeque that was held before the game in the Pepsi Picnic Patio (Patio). The plaintiff was escorted from the line to the Patio which was down the right field line adjacent to the permanent stands. Prior to the start of the game and just before the plaintiff and his son finished eating, two baseball players with the Rock Cats began throwing to one another in the right field area. Thereafter, while in the Patio, the plaintiff was struck in the testicles by an errantly thrown baseball.

The plaintiff claims in his complaint that NBBC caused the plaintiff's injuries and losses in that: it failed to have a fence of sufficient

---

[39] *Atlanta Baseball Co.*, 144 S.E. at 351.
[40] *Id.* at 352.

height separating the picnic area from the playing field; one or more baseball players on the field were allowed to throw baseballs perpendicular to the Patio; one or more baseball players on the field threw a baseball in the direction of the Patio despite the presence of the plaintiff and, no warning was given to the plaintiff of the thrown baseball.

. . . In support of its motion, the defendant argues that the plaintiff's negligence action against the defendant must fail because: . . . (2) plaintiff contractually assumed the risk of being struck by a thrown baseball; . . . and (5) under the "limited duty" rule, the defendant fulfilled its duty to the plaintiff.

"A possessor of land has a duty to an invitee to reasonably inspect and maintain the premises in order to render them reasonably safe . . . In addition, the possessor of land must warn an invitee of dangers that the invitee could not reasonably be expected to discover." However, "a possessor of land has no duty to warn an invitee of a dangerous condition when the invitee has actual knowledge of the condition . . . Warning an invitee against dangers which are either known to him or are so obvious to him that he may be expected to discover them is unnecessary." *Kurti v. Becker,* 54 Conn.App. 335, 344-45, 733 A.2d 916, cert. denied, 251 Conn. 909, 739 A.2d 1248 (1999).

. . .

III. Discussion

The plaintiff and the defendant both agree that the plaintiff was a business invitee and the court finds there is no question that he was such. . . Although Connecticut courts have not decided an issue relating to what type of duty a baseball stadium owner owes a spectator, the issue has been addressed in other jurisdictions. Collectively, those jurisdictions are split on the issue. While some jurisdictions believe that an owner of stadium should be held to the standard of reasonable care in maintaining a stadium relative to its invitees, it appears an approximately equal number of jurisdictions have adopted the reasoning of a "limited duty" rule. That rule holds that the owner is only responsible for screening the most dangerous section of the field (the area behind home plate). See *Akins v. Glen Falls City School District,* 53 N.Y.2d 325, 441 N.Y.S.2d 644, 424 N.E.2d 531, 533 (1981). The purpose and reasoning of such a rule is thoroughly set forth in *Benejam v. Detroit Tigers, Inc.,* 246 Mich.App. 645, 635 N.W.2d 219, 223 (Mich.App.2001) wherein the Court of Appeals of Michigan stated:

> [T]he limited duty rule does not ignore or abrogate usual premises liability principles. Instead, it identifies the duty of

baseball stadium proprietors with greater specificity than the usual "ordinary care/reasonably safe" standard provides. The limited duty precedents do not eliminate the stadium owner's duty to exercise reasonable care under the circumstances to protect patrons against injury . . . Rather, these precedents define that duty so that once the stadium owner has provided adequately screened seats for all those desiring them, the stadium owner has fulfilled his duty of care as a matter of law. The limited duty doctrine establishes the outer limits of liability and thereby prevents a jury from requiring a stadium owner to take precautions that are clearly unreasonable . . . By providing greater specificity with regard to the duty imposed on stadium owners, the rule prevents burgeoning litigation that might signal the demise or substantial alteration of the game of baseball as a spectator sport.

. . . [T]his court adopts the reasoning of the limited duty rule finding it to be applicable to owners and operators of baseball stadiums such as NBBC. In this case, NBBC had placed screen netting behind home plate which was approximately 30 feet in height and approximately 155 feet in length. The screened area behind home plate is available to those spectators who may desire seating safe from any thrown or batted balls which might otherwise enter the stands. It is also common knowledge that this is the area of the baseball field which has the highest frequency of a ball being in play whether it be thrown or batted. This is true not only during the game but also during pre-game activities where the frequency of activity and number of balls being used at one time is higher (e.g., batting practice, infield practice, players warming up, often all take place at the same time). The corollary to this is that the area down the outfield foul lines, furthest away from the home plate area, are the least likely to have a ball in play. Given the lessened level of risk of being struck by a thrown or batted ball in these areas, it is unnecessary to have the same extensive netting or other protections in place for the benefit of the spectators.

Although the plaintiff suffered his injury before the game started, the extent of the duty of an owner is not dependent upon the time at which a spectator is in the stadium. It would be highly impractical to require an owner to put into place levels of netting or screening before or after a game different than those required during the course of a game. Stadium owners are not guarantors of a spectator's safety. Other than the plaintiff's simple allegations that the fence along the Patio was insufficient, the plaintiff has offered no material evidence regarding the adequacy of that fencing (or of that behind home plate) relative to its location in the park under the circumstances that existed then and there.

Even if one were to assume (though this court does not rule on the issue) that there was a duty to warn the plaintiff, the evidence presented by the defendant overwhelmingly establishes that sufficient warnings regarding thrown or batted balls were provided to the plaintiff by the defendant.

8. That on July 3, 2004, the fence leading into the Pepsi Picnic Patio at New Britain Stadium had a sign posted on it that read: *Welcome to the Pepsi Picnic Patio* The New Britain Rock Cats ask that you *be alert at all times* to baseballs that may enter the picnic area from the field of play. You assume the risk and legal responsibility for any injury to your person or property arising out of your use of and presence in the picnic area."

. . . [T]he back of the ticket held by the plaintiff to enter the stadium had the following language: "The holder of this ticket assumes all the risks and danger incidental to the game of baseball including specifically (but not limited to) the danger of being injured by thrown bats and thrown or batted balls, and agrees that the participating clubs, their agents and players are not liable for injuries from such causes."

There is no question that although the conditions were open and obvious to the plaintiff, sufficient warnings were posted by the defendant for the benefit of its invitees to apprise them of conditions that were likely to exist while in the park. There was adequate notice to enable the plaintiff to take whatever precautionary measures he felt were appropriate under the circumstances to secure his safety.

Source: Courtesy of Westlaw; reprinted with permission.

In Case 6-11, *Nemarnik v. Los Angeles Kings Hockey Club, L.P.*, 127 Cal. Rptr. 2d 10 (Cal. Ct. App. 2002), the plaintiff alleged that the defendant was negligent because of failure to control a crowd in front of the plaintiff's fourth-row season-ticket seats. The area where the plaintiff was sitting was not protected by glass or screening. She alleged that the defendant had a duty to remove spectators from her line of sight and sued when she suffered injury after she was struck in the mouth by a hockey puck.

📖 CASE 6-11 *Nemarnik v. Los Angeles Kings Hockey Club, L.P.*

127 Cal. Rptr. 2d 10 (Cal. Ct. App. 2002)

ORTEGA, J.

Plaintiff Holly Ann Nemarnik was injured when, during pregame warm-ups at a Los Angeles Kings ice hockey game, a puck flew off the ice and struck her in the mouth. Plaintiff sued the Kings (The Los Angeles Kings Hockey Club, L.P.), the National Hockey League, and the owners and operators of the ice hockey venue.

Plaintiff's Factual Allegations

On April 18, 1999, plaintiff attended a Kings hockey game at the Forum. During the pregame warm-ups, several pucks were in play on the ice. Plaintiff had a fourth row, season ticket seat but could not see the ice because "there were more people congregating around her area than she had ever seen before. No ushers asked the crowd to go to their proper seats as required." Plaintiff "tried folding up her seat and sitting on the edge to obtain a clear view, but still could not see over the crowd the venue had allowed to form around and in front of her. [Plaintiff] was perplexed and distracted by the fact that she had never seen such a crowd form around her at any previous hockey game she had attended. She was unsure what to do about the situation. Ultimately, a puck did fly off the ice. [Plaintiff] was unable to see the puck come off the ice, heading directly toward her; she was unable to take evasive action. The hockey puck struck [plaintiff] in the mouth and face, causing severe injuries."

Plaintiff's theory of liability is that defendants were negligent in failing to prevent the spectators from milling around the ice during pregame warm-ups: "The suit was based on the fact that defendants, by allowing a crowd to form and to remain in an area where they were not supposed to be congregating, increased the normal risk inherent in attending a hockey game; i.e., while a puck leaving the ice might be a normal risk of attending a game, that risk was significantly increased by allowing the spectators' views to be blocked so that they could not see the puck coming, and take evasive action."

Due to the risk of hockey pucks leaving the ice during play, the Forum requires the usher staff to prevent latecomers from blocking the view of seated guests. The Forum's handbook for ushers and ticket takers states in part: "During game action you MUST stop latecomers from blocking the view of seated guests. Politely request all ticket holders to stand along the back wall (LOGE) or the base of the stairway (COLLONADE) until there is a stoppage of play. Following a whistle, instruct guests to quickly take their seats. All portals are to be kept clear." The handbook also states: "Approach people congregating around your section. Ask them if you can provide assistance in helping them find their seats. Politely remind them that no one may stand or congregate in or at the top of the aisles." The handbook further provides: "One of the primary functions of the guest services department is protecting the personal safety of all our guests. . . . The safety of our guests and staff MUST be a constant concern of all of our employees. Be aware of all physical conditions in your work area at all times. Report any problems immediately to your supervisor or building staff."

Obstructions of view caused by the unpredictable movements of other fans are an inherent and unavoidable part of attending a sporting event. Views are blocked whenever fans spontaneously leap to their feet or move to and from their seats.

. . . In this case, plaintiff contends an unusually large number of people were milling around in front of the ice, blocking her view. She emphasizes that she is not complaining about a single hot dog vendor walking by, or a lone fan standing up to cheer. Instead, she states, "a huge crowd of fans was crammed into the aisles down near the front of the ice rink, where her assigned seat was located. . . . Thus, there is a strong inference that the people blocking [plaintiff's] view of the ice were not actually assigned to the seating area where they were congregating [i.e., if the seats were all *occupied*, those seats could not have belonged to the people congregating near the rink around [plaintiff].]" She claims "there was nowhere around her for this mass of fans to sit down; the seats were full; people were all standing in the aisle; they were blocking her view in all directions. There were even people standing in her own ticketed seats, and she had to shoo them away."

As far as we are aware, however, no court has imposed a legal duty upon an athletic team, sports league, or sports arena to prevent large crowds of spectators, during pregame warm-ups, from congregating in the aisles near the front of the arena, or from blocking the views of seated spectators. We know of no published decision in which tort liability was upheld based upon the injured spectator's alleged inability to evade a flying bat, ball, or puck during pregame warm-ups due to the defendants' breach of its duty to prevent other fans from obstructing the plaintiff's view.

In this case, however, no one in defendants' employ had distracted or caused plaintiff to turn away from the ice. Just as baseball can be played without the antics of a costumed mascot, plaintiff claims ice hockey can be played without allowing large crowds of spectators to stand in front of the ice. Plaintiff claims that while the risk of being hit by a puck is an assumed risk, the risk of having one's view blocked by other spectators is not. Just as stadium owners owe no duty to eliminate the risk of injury from foul balls, we similarly conclude defendants owe no duty to eliminate the inherent risk of injury from flying pucks.

Source: Courtesy of Westlaw; reprinted with permission.

What about those injuries that occur during halftime, before or after the game, between innings, or even when a spectator participates in an event during a game?[41] In Case 6-12, *Dalton v. Jones*, 581 S.E.2d 360 (Ga. Ct. App. 2003), a spectator was struck by a baseball thrown by a player into the stands when she was on her way to the concession stands between innings. She sued the player and the team, alleging negligence, and stated that they were responsible for the injuries she had suffered.

📖 CASE 6-12 *Dalton v. Jones*

581 S.E.2d 360 (Ga. Ct. App. 2003)

ADAMS, Judge.

Plaintiff Jacqueline Dalton filed a negligence action against Andruw Jones, a major league baseball player, and the Atlanta National League Baseball Club, Inc. (Atlanta Braves) seeking to recover for injuries she allegedly sustained when she was struck by an errant baseball. Finding that Dalton assumed the risk of injury, the trial court granted summary judgment to both defendants. On appeal, Dalton contends that the trial court misapplied the doctrine of assumption of risk in the context of sports events and failed to properly apply the concept of gross negligence. We find no error and affirm.

On June 6, 2000, Dalton attended an Atlanta Braves baseball game held at Turner Field. According to Dalton, as she "was beginning to proceed towards the concession stand," she was suddenly hit in the face by a baseball. She alleged that Atlanta Braves' outfielder Jones "was negligent in throwing a baseball in the stands in between innings of the game." Claiming she sustained a permanent eye injury, she attributed that injury and "permanent disfigurement to her face" to the gross negligence of Jones. She also asserted that the Atlanta Braves were "negligent in not providing the Plaintiff with sufficient protection by failing to properly educate and train it[s] players as to the potential danger of such acts, and for failing to provide equipment in the stands to protect the spectators." Dalton's lawsuit relied exclusively on theories of negligence and gross negligence and did not allege any intentional conduct.

Jones and the Braves asserted the affirmative defense of assumption of risk and also claimed that Dalton failed to exercise ordinary care for her own safety. The trial court found the defense of assumption of risk precluded Dalton's recovery.

---

[41] *See* Taylor v. Baseball Club of Seattle, L.P., 130 P.3d 835 (Wash. Ct. App. 2006) (granting summary judgment for the Club based on spectators' claims for injuries that occurred during pregame warm-ups); *Also see* Loughran v. The Phillies, 888 A.2d 872 (Pa. Super. Ct. 2005).

1. Dalton contends that the trial court erred by misapplying the defense of assumption of risk. She claims that she did not assume the risk of this type of injury.

. . . Even assuming that Dalton can prove that Jones threw or tossed a baseball that went into the stands and further assuming that this baseball hit Dalton in the face, Dalton failed to show that the trial court erred in deciding the case adversely to her. We find, as did the trial court, that this case is controlled by Hunt v. Thomasville Baseball Co., 80 Ga.App. 572, 56 S.E.2d 828 (1949). Pursuant to the longstanding rule set forth in *Hunt:*

> [O]ne who buys a ticket for the purpose of witnessing a baseball game and who chooses or accepts a seat in a portion of the grandstand which his own observation will readily inform him is unprotected, voluntarily assumes the risks inherent in such a position, since he must be presumed to know that there is a likelihood of wild balls being thrown and landing in the grandstand or other unprotected areas.

It is undisputed that Dalton had a seat in an unprotected area of the stadium. By her own admission, Dalton did not see the ball coming toward her, and apparently was not keeping a close lookout on the field. Although Dalton asserts that Jones should have warned her and other spectators, no Georgia case has ever held that a warning is required before a baseball player throws a ball. In golf, unlike in baseball, when a golfer strikes an errant shot, he is expected to yell "fore" to warn his fellow golfers and spectators of the imminent danger. Even so, despite this duty to warn, "people who are on a golf course must assume the risk of being injured from a defected or hooked or sliced ball." We decline to impose a duty to warn on the game of baseball.

2. Dalton contends that the trial court misapplied the concept of gross negligence. She asserts that a jury should decide whether Jones displayed grossly negligent conduct and exhibited a total disregard for her safety by throwing a baseball into the stands.

Dalton's evidence, however, cannot sustain these assertions. . . . Dalton stated that "Jones and another Braves player . . . were pitching [the] ball back and forth to each other [after] coming back onto [the] field when it was time for [an]other player on the other team to hit the ball. Mr. Jones threw the ball into the stands around this time as I was just standing up to go and get a soda." But, in an apparent effort to avert summary judgment, Dalton offered an affidavit from her companion, Thomas Franklin, Sr., who testified that he saw Jones "without warning to the spectators, throw the ball into the

stands," between innings, when "the game was not in play at the time."
But Dalton offered no evidence to show that Jones intentionally, as
opposed to negligently, threw the baseball into the stands. And the
trial court in its order granting summary judgment noted that in fact,
at the motion hearing, Dalton's counsel conceded that Jones' actions
were not intentional. Therefore, even when the evidence is considered
in Dalton's favor, at most it shows that during an Atlanta Braves
game, while a spectator in an unprotected area of the stadium, Dalton
was accidentally hit by an errant baseball. Whether the ball was
thrown or tossed during an inning of play or between innings lacks
legal significance because, as the trial court noted, "this throw
occurred during a time which was necessary to the playing of the game,
during which time the Plaintiff has assumed the risk of injury from
bats, balls, and other missiles."

Judgment affirmed.

Source: Courtesy of Westlaw; reprinted with permission.

Does a sports photographer assume the risk of being injured during a sporting event? Even
though he or she is not classified as a spectator, what duty of care is owed to him or her? That was
the issue in Case 6-13, *Bereswill v. National Basketball Ass'n, Inc.*, 719 N.Y.S.2d 231 (N.Y. App.
Div. 2001), in which a photographer was injured during an NBA playoff game. A player dove for a
ball and fell onto the plaintiff, injuring him. The photographer sued, arguing that the defendants knew
of the potential risk, or increased the risk, that the plaintiff could sustain injuries.

📖 CASE 6-13 *Bereswill v. National Basketball Ass'n, Inc.*

719 N.Y.S.2d 231 (N.Y. App. Div. 2001)

Plaintiff, an award-winning photographer who has worked for *Newsday*
for more than 25 years, was taking photos from his usual spot near one
of the corners of the basketball court at Madison Square Garden during
a 1994 final round playoff game between the New York Knickerbockers
and the Houston Rockets when he was hit and injured by then New York
Knick Charles Oakley as Oakley dove out of bounds in pursuit of a
loose ball.

. . . Plaintiff argued that defendants' assumption of risk defense was
without merit since he was neither a participant in nor a spectator of
the game and was subject to an "inherent compulsion" to work despite
his misgivings about overcrowding along the baselines, where photographers had been assigned spots on the floor, within 2 to 3 feet of the
playing area. Plaintiff further argued that the National Basketball
Association (NBA), Madison Square Garden, and the Knicks created new
or enhanced risks that were not inherent to the sport by allowing

conditions to become so crowded, as a result of the additional media personnel present for the championship series, that he was unable to get out of Oakley's way.

The IAS Court properly granted summary judgment. Even as a non-participant, plaintiff is subject to a defense based on the doctrine of assumed risk. With respect to his claim of "inherent compulsion," plaintiff failed to present "evidence in admissible form that he had no choice in the matter but to obey a superior's direction to continue notwithstanding the danger."

Defendants did not enhance existing risks or create risks not inherent to the sport of professional basketball or to the taking of pictures at the games. Defendants' duty was "to make the conditions as safe as they appear to be. If the risks of the activity are fully comprehended or perfectly obvious, plaintiff has consented to them and defendant has performed its duty." Plaintiff testified he had taken photos at 400 to 500 basketball games at the Garden prior to the game during which he was hurt, had seen at least 40 to 50 instances of players leaving the court and landing in photographers' areas, and had been personally involved in 4 or 5 such incidents. Although plaintiff spoke to both NBA and Knick officials during the game and told them there were too many people in his general area, he remained in his assigned spot, notwithstanding the availability of alternative media sections. It is clear, in light of plaintiff's experience and conduct, that any increased risks were obvious to him, and that he fully comprehended the circumstances and willingly assumed the risk of continuing to working from the courtside spot in which the complained of collision eventually took place.

Source: Courtesy of Westlaw; reprinted with permission.

PARTICIPANT VERSUS PARTICIPANT LIABILITY

In recent years there has been an increase in litigation relating to injuries sustained by participants during sporting events. Generally, participants in sporting events assume all risks of unintentional injuries but not those that are inflicted intentionally or in willful disregard for the safety of others. The assumption of risk doctrine will usually thwart any attempt at recovery by an injured participant.

Professional Sports

The doctrine of assumption of risk makes it difficult to recover tort damages from another participant during a professional sporting event. Most would agree that professional football, baseball, basketball, and hockey players as well as boxers assume the risk of injuries they may sustain from the conduct of an opponent during a game. In hockey, every player understands he can be sent to the penalty box for a myriad of penalties, including fighting, high-sticking, boarding, cross-checking, and instigating. However, some violent acts in sports exceed the scope of the game. One of the more notable incidents was San Francisco Giants pitcher Juan Marichal striking Los Angeles Dodgers catcher John Roseboro in the head with a bat during a game in 1965. Roseboro sued Marichal in tort and settled for $7,500.

Tomjanovich v. California Sports, Inc., No. H-78-243 (S.D. Tex. 1979), is the most famous tort sports case involving participant liability. Kermit Washington punched Rudy Tomjanovich during an NBA game, causing severe injuries to Tomjanovich, who sustained a skull fracture, concussion, and facial injuries that diminished his career as a professional player. Tomjanovich was actually trying to break up a fight at the time of the incident. He sued the Los Angeles Lakers, arguing they encouraged players to start fights with other teams and asserting they were vicariously liable for the acts of Washington. Noted Houston sports attorney Nick Nichols was able to persuade a California jury that Tomjanovich was entitled to damages in excess of $1 million. This case was one of the early cases awarding damages in a participant liability case. Rudy Tomjanovich was later the coach of both the Lakers and the Rockets and won two World Championships with the Rockets in 1994 and 1995.

Bill Romanowski of the National Football League Oakland Raiders was sued by Marcus Williams for injuries Williams suffered when Romanowski hit him in the face during a practice drill in 2003. The punch ended Williams's career, causing some brain damage when his eye socket was crushed by Romanowski. The Raiders asserted they were not responsible for the conduct of Romanowski and fined him $60,000. Romanowski had been fined over $100,000 by the league in his career for head butting, headkicking, and spearing, all illegal activities in the NFL. The case went to trial in March 2005, and a jury awarded Williams $340,000. Williams was not satisfied with the verdict and was seeking a new trial when he and Romanowski agreed to settle the case for $415,000. Professional football is a violent game that would not usually lend itself to lawsuits between participants; however, because of the violent nature of the act committed by Romanowski, the matter was considered outside the scope of risk assumed even by a professional football player.

One of the most notorious incidents of violence in sports led to a civil lawsuit against Todd Bertuzzi of the Vancouver Canucks.[42] Steve Moore, former Colorado Avalanche forward and Moore's parents, filed a civil lawsuit against Bertuzzi, his teammate Brad May, Canucks head coach Mark Crawford, and Canucks general manager Brian Burke. The lawsuit arose out of an incident that occurred on February 16, 2004, in an NHL game between Colorado and Vancouver. The lawsuit alleged that Bertuzzi carried out an assault on the plaintiff at the request of the administration of the Vancouver hockey club. Todd Bertuzzi pled guilty to the charge of assault in a British Columbia court and was suspended from the league for the assault on Moore. Bertuzzi also received a $500,000 fine for his violent outburst against Moore, one of the largest fines ever issued in professional sports history.

In *McKichan v. St. Louis Hockey Club, L.P.*, 967 S.W.2d 209 (Mo. Ct. App. 1998), a professional hockey goaltender sued the opposing player and the owner of an opposing team for injuries the goaltender received when the opposing player charged into him. The defendant player filed a counterclaim against the goaltender for injuries the former had suffered. The players dismissed their claims against one another prior to trial and the case proceeded to trial solely against the owner on a theory of vicarious liability, asserting that the owner was responsible for the acts of his players. A jury returned an award of $175,000, but on appeal the trial court judgment was reversed. The court of appeals, finding in favor of the defendant, stated:

---

[42] Associated Press, *Moore Seeking $15M in Lost Wages, More in Damages*, ESPN.com, Feb. 15, 2006.

In practice, the concepts of duty, assumption of risk, and consent must be analyzed on a case-by-case basis. Whether one player's conduct causing injury to another is actionable hinges upon the facts of an individual case. *Ross,* 637 S.W.2d at 14. Relevant factors include the specific game involved, the ages and physical attributes of the participants, their respective skills at the game and their knowledge of its rules and customs, their status as amateurs or professionals, the type of risks which inhere to the game and those which are outside the realm of reasonable anticipation, the presence or absence of protective uniforms or equipment, the degree of zest with which the game is being played, and other factors.

We apply these concepts and factors to the case before us. The specific game was a professional hockey game, not an amateur game. It was not a pickup, school, or college game. Rough play is commonplace in professional hockey. Anyone who has attended a professional hockey game or seen one on television recognizes the violent nature of the sport. In order to gain possession of the puck or to slow down the progress of opponents, players frequently hit each other with body checks. They trip opposing players, slash at them with their hockey sticks, and fight on a regular basis, often long after the referee blows the whistle. Players regularly commit contact beyond that which is permitted by the rules, and, we are confident, do it intentionally. They wear pads, helmets and other protective equipment because of the rough nature of the sport.

Professional hockey is played at a high skill level with well conditioned athletes, who are financially compensated for their participation. They are professional players with knowledge of its rules and customs, including the violence of the sport. In part, the game is played with great intensity because its players can reap substantial financial rewards. We also recognize that the professional leagues have internal mechanisms for penalizing players and teams for violating league rules and for compensating persons who are injured.

In summary, we find that the specific conduct at issue in this case, a severe body check, is a part of professional hockey. This body check, even several seconds after the whistle and in violation of several rules of the game, was not outside the realm of reasonable anticipation. For better or for worse, it is "part of the game" of professional hockey. As such, we hold as a matter of law that the specific conduct which occurred here is not actionable.[43]

In Case 6-14, *Hackbart v. Cincinnati Bengals, Inc.,* 601 F.2d 516 (10th Cir. 1979), involving two NFL players, the court applied a "recklessness" standard in determining whether liability existed on the part of the defendant for the actions he took against another player during an NFL game.

📖 CASE 6-14   *Hackbart v. Cincinnati Bengals, Inc.*

601 F.2d 516 (10th Cir. 1979)

```
WILLIAM E. DOYLE, Circuit Judge.

The question in this case is whether in a regular season professional
football game an injury which is inflicted by one professional foot-
ball player on an opposing player can give rise to liability in tort
where the injury was inflicted by the intentional striking of a blow
during the game.
```

---

[43] *McKichan,* 967 S.W.2d.

The injury occurred in the course of a game between the Denver Broncos and the Cincinnati Bengals, which game was being played in Denver in 1973. The Broncos' defensive back, Dale Hackbart, was the recipient of the injury and the Bengals' offensive back, Charles "Booby" Clark, inflicted the blow which produced it . . .

Clark was an offensive back and just before the injury he had run a pass pattern to the right side of the Denver Broncos' end zone. The injury flowed indirectly from this play. The pass was intercepted by Billy Thompson, a Denver free safety, who returned it to mid-field. The subject injury occurred as an aftermath of the pass play.

As a consequence of the interception, the roles of Hackbart and Clark suddenly changed. Hackbart, who had been defending, instantaneously became an offensive player. Clark, on the other hand, became a defensive player. Acting as an offensive player, Hackbart attempted to block Clark by throwing his body in front of him. He thereafter remained on the ground. He turned, and with one knee on the ground, watched the play following the interception.

The trial court's finding was that Charles Clark, "acting out of anger and frustration, but without a specific intent to injure . . . stepped forward and struck a blow with his right forearm to the back of the kneeling plaintiff's head and neck with sufficient force to cause both players to fall forward to the ground." Both players, without complaining to the officials or to one another, returned to their respective sidelines since the ball had changed hands and the offensive and defensive teams of each had been substituted. Clark testified at trial that his frustration was brought about by the fact that his team was losing the game.

Due to the failure of the officials to view the incident, a foul was not called. However, the game film showed very clearly what had occurred. Plaintiff did not at the time report the happening to his coaches or to anyone else during the game. However, because of the pain which he experienced he was unable to play golf the next day. He did not seek medical attention, but the continued pain caused him to report this fact and the incident to the Bronco trainer who gave him treatment. Apparently he played on the specialty teams for two successive Sundays, but after that the Broncos released him on waivers. (He was in his thirteenth year as a player.) He sought medical help and it was then that it was discovered by the physician that he had a serious neck fracture injury. . . .

I. The Issues and Contentions

1. Whether the trial court erred in ruling that as a matter of policy the principles of law governing the infliction of injuries should be

entirely refused where the injury took place in the course of the game. . . .

5. The final issue is whether the evidence justifies consideration by the court of the issue of reckless conduct as it is defined in A.L.I. Restatement of the Law of Torts Second, s 500, because (admittedly) the assault and battery theory is not available because that tort is governed by a one-year statute of limitations.

II. Whether the Evidence Supported the Judgment

The evidence at the trial uniformly supported the proposition that the intentional striking of a player in the head from the rear is not an accepted part of either the playing rules or the general customs of the game of professional football. . . .

Thus the district court's assumption was that Clark had inflicted an intentional blow which would ordinarily generate civil liability and which might bring about a criminal sanction as well, but that since it had occurred in the course of a football game, it should not be subject to the restraints of the law; that if it were it would place unreasonable impediments and restraints on the activity. The judge also pointed out that courts are ill-suited to decide the different social questions and to administer conflicts on what is much like a battlefield where the restraints of civilization have been left on the sidelines.

We are forced to conclude that the result reached is not supported by evidence.

III. Whether Intentional Injury Is Allowed by Either Written Rule or Custom

Plaintiff, of course, maintains that tort law applicable to the injury in this case applies on the football field as well as in other places. . . .

The general customs of football do not approve the intentional punching or striking of others.

. . . .

V. Is The Standard of Reckless Disregard of the Rights of Others Applicable to the Present Situation?

The Restatement of Torts Second, s 500, distinguishes between reckless and negligent misconduct. Reckless misconduct differs from negligence, according to the authors, in that negligence consists of mere inadvertence, lack of skillfulness or failure to take precautions; reckless misconduct, on the other hand, involves a choice or adoption of a course of action either with knowledge of the danger or with knowledge of facts which would disclose this danger to a reasonable man. . . .

Therefore, recklessness exists where a person knows that the act is harmful but fails to realize that it will produce the extreme harm which it did produce. It is in this respect that recklessness and intentional conduct differ in degree.

In the case at bar the defendant Clark admittedly acted impulsively and in the heat of anger, and even though it could be said from the admitted facts that he intended the act, it could also be said that he did not intend to inflict serious injury which resulted from the blow which he struck. . . .

In sum, having concluded that the trial court did not limit the case to a trial of the evidence bearing on defendant's liability but rather determined that as a matter of social policy the game was so violent and unlawful that valid lines could not be drawn, we take the view that this was not a proper issue for determination and that plaintiff was entitled to have the case tried on an assessment of his rights and whether they had been violated.

The trial court has heard the evidence and has made findings. The findings of fact based on the evidence presented are not an issue on this appeal. Thus, it would not seem that the court would have to repeat the areas of evidence that have already been fully considered. The need is for a reconsideration of that evidence in the light of that which is taken up by this court in its opinion. We are not to be understood as limiting the trial court's consideration of supplemental evidence if it deems it necessary.

The cause is reversed and remanded for a new trial in accordance with the foregoing views.

Source: Courtesy of Westlaw; reprinted with permission.

Problem 6-5

Martin Londestar is a noted "enforcer" for the Detroit hockey club. He has incurred the most penalty minutes in the league for the last three seasons. Whenever an opposing player roughs up a star player on the Detroit team, Martin, at the encouragement of the Detroit organization, goes into action. In one particular game, Detroit's superstar, Joe Fasell, was unintentionally struck in the head with a stick by Miller, a player from the Los Angeles team. Miller was given a ten-minute misconduct penalty by the referee. Once he served the penalty, he was back in the game. Londestar, at the request of the coach, skated behind Miller and intentionally tripped him, causing him to fall into the boards headfirst. Miller was taken to a local hospital, where he was diagnosed with a neck fracture and his physician determined that his career in professional hockey was over. Miller wants to sue Londestar and the Detroit hockey club for damages in a civil action. What legal theories will he assert in seeking damages? What defenses are available to Londestar and the Detroit organization? Do you believe a jury would award damages to Miller in this case?

Problem 6-6

Carlos Mauricio is an offensive lineman for the Carolina Panthers. He is told by his line coach that Joe Cantu, the defensive lineman for the Green Bay Packers, suffered a severe ankle injury two weeks ago and that his ankle would be weak for the upcoming game against the Panthers. The coach tells Carlos that it would be to his advantage and to the team's advantage to have Cantu out of the game early and that if the opportunity presented itself, Mauricio should "target" Cantu's injured ankle. During the second quarter of the game between the Panthers and the Packers, Mauricio falls on Cantu's ankle while blocking him, crushing his ankle and putting Cantu on the injured reserved list for the rest of the season. Mauricio weighs 355 pounds and could have avoided falling on Cantu's ankle but chose not to. In the press conference following the game, when asked about the incident, Mauricio stated, "Cantu got what he deserved; he is the NFL's dirtiest player and I hope his career is over, he's gives the NFL a bad name." Cantu wants to sue Mauricio for his actions on the field. Will he win? What theory will Cantu use to prevail? Does Mauricio have any defenses to a tort action? What other defendants could be included in the lawsuit?

Amateur and Recreational Sports

The possibility of a participant suffering an injury exists in all contact sports. A negligence case arising from a sports injury can be based on failing to employ a competent coach, failing to provide adequate training or supervision, failing to provide safe equipment or facilities, requiring individuals to play, or even allowing mismatched players to compete against one another.

Courts have held that participants have assumed the risk of injury in skating, golfing, automobile racing, swimming and diving, touch football, softball, and several other sports.[44] When one participant brings a lawsuit against another participant, most courts have held that the defendant's conduct must be deemed reckless or intentional before a participant can recover, whereas a few have held that ordinary negligence is enough for a participant to recover.[45] Many cases have addressed participant liability, but the general agreement is that there is no recovery for participants' injuries unless the conduct of the defendant was wanton or reckless.[46]

---

[44] Reyes v. City of New York, 2007 WL 738906 (N.Y. App. Div. 2007) (holding that the defendant was entitled to judgment as a matter of law on plaintiff's claim for damages when he was struck by a ball in the dugout).

[45] Barakat v. Pordash, 842 N.E.2d 120, 122–23 (Ohio Ct. App. 2005) (applying a reckless or intentional standard). Lestina v. West Bend Mut. Ins. Co., 501 N.W.2d 28 (Wis. 1993) (applying the negligence standard).

[46] Hoke v. Cullinan, 914 S.W.2d 335 (Ky. 1995) (applying a reckless standard for injuries occurring in a tennis match).

In *Leonard ex rel. Meyer v. Behrens*, 601 N.W.2d 76 (Iowa 1999), the court found that an unsupervised paintball game was a contact sport and therefore dismissed the plaintiff's claims, applying a reckless standard. In *Kavanagh v. Trustees of Boston University*, 795 N.E.2d 1170 (Mass. 2003), a basketball player sued a university and an opposing player for injuries he sustained when he was punched by the opposing player. The court found in favor of the defendants on all counts. In discussing the standard to be used in deciding a participant liability case, the court stated:

> We must first address what standard is to be applied to claims that coaches are liable for causing their players to injure other players. Recognizing that, by their nature, competitive sports involve physical contact between opposing players, and that some degree of aggressiveness in play is essential to athletic competition, we have held that mere negligence on the part of a player does not suffice to impose liability for injuries inflicted by that player during competition. See *Gauvin v. Clark,* 404 Mass. 450, 454, 537 N.E.2d 94 (1989). Rather, an injured player must show that the other player's conduct amounted to recklessness before the law will impose liability. See *id*. Utilizing a standard of recklessness, as opposed to mere negligence, "furthers the policy that '[v]igorous and active participation in sporting events should not be chilled by the threat of litigation.'" *Id*. Just as players are entitled to play aggressively without fear of liability, a coach properly may encourage players to play aggressively. Indeed, a coach's ability to inspire players to compete aggressively is one of a coach's important attributes. The mere possibility that some players might overreact to such inspiration or encouragement should not, by itself, suffice to impose liability on a coach. As we do with the players themselves, we must impose liability only where a coach's behavior amounts to at least recklessness.[47]

In a case involving Super Bowlers "gone wild," a partygoer was injured in an informal game of touch football using a "peewee" football at halftime of the 1987 Super Bowl.[48] The plaintiff warned the defendant "not to play so rough or I was going to have to stop playing."[49] The defendant, in an attempt to intercept a pass, knocked the plaintiff down, stepped on her hand, and injured her finger. She had to have her finger amputated after three failed operations. The court found against the plaintiff, upholding the lower court's granting of a motion for summary judgment, stating that the defendant could only be held responsible if he intentionally injured someone or engaged in conduct that was so reckless as to be totally outside the range of the ordinary activity of the sport.

Nabozny v. Barnhill, 334 N.E.2d 258 (Ill. Ct. App. 1975), involved a soccer match between two amateur teams. The plaintiff was the goalkeeper, and the defendant was a forward on the opposing team. During the match, the defendant kicked the plaintiff in the head, causing injury, when the plaintiff was down on one knee holding the ball to his chest. Organizational rules stated that players were prohibited from making contact with the goalkeeper when he was in the penalty area and had possession of the ball. The court found in favor of the plaintiff, stating:

> . . . Individual sports are advanced and competition enhanced by a comprehensive set of rules. Some rules secure the better playing of the game as a test of skill. Other rules are primarily designed to protect participants from serious injury.

---

[47] *Kavanagh*, 795 N.E.2d at 1179.
[48] Knight v. Jewett, 834 P.2d 696 (Cal. 1992).
[49] *Id*. at 697.

For these reasons, this court believes that when athletes are engaged in an athletic competition; all teams involved are trained and coached by knowledgeable personnel; a recognized set of rules governs the conduct of the competition; and a safety rule is contained therein which is primarily designed to protect players from serious injury, a player is then charged with a legal duty to every other player on the field to refrain from conduct proscribed by a safety rule. A reckless disregard for the safety of other players cannot be excused. To engage in such conduct is to create an intolerable and unreasonable risk of serious injury to other participants. . . . Under the facts presented in the case at bar, we find such a duty clearly arose. Plaintiff was entitled to legal protection at the hands of the defendant. The defendant contends he is immune from tort action for any injury to another player that happens during the course of a game, to which theory we do not subscribe.[50]

Does a student athlete who is a discus thrower assume the risk of getting hit by a discus thrown by a teammate? That was the issue in Case 6-15, *Muller v. Spencerport Central School District*, 865 N.Y.S.2d 255 (2008).

📖 CASE 6-15   *Muller v. Spencerport Central School District*

865 N.Y.S.2d 255 (2008)

MARTOCHE, J.P., LUNN, FAHEY, AND PINE, JJ.

MEMORANDUM:

Plaintiffs commenced this action individually and as the parents of their daughter, a ninth-grade student who is a member of the junior varsity outdoor track and field team at Spencerport High School. At track practice, their daughter was struck in the head by a discus thrown by her teammate . . . while plaintiffs' daughter was waiting for her turn to throw the discus. . . .We agree with defendant that it met its initial burden by establishing that the risk of being struck by a discus is a "'perfectly obvious'" inherent risk in the sport and that plaintiffs' daughter "'assumed the [inherent] risks associated [with] this voluntary extracurricular sport.'" We conclude, however, that plaintiffs raised a triable issue of fact whether defendant's coaching staff "failed to provide proper supervision of the [discus throwing] activities, thereby exposing [plaintiffs' daughter] to unreasonably increased risks of injury."

. . . [I]t is well established that voluntary participants in sporting or recreational activities are not "deemed to have assumed the risks of reckless or intentional conduct.". . . [H]ere there is no evidence in the record before us that [her teammate's] conduct was anything other than an unfortunate accident.

Source: Courtesy of Westlaw; reprinted with permission.

---

[50] *Nabozny*, 334 N.E.2d at 260–61.

In Case 6-16, *Connell v. Payne*, 814 S.W.2d 486 (Tex. Crim. App. 1991), the plaintiff was a polo player who was injured when another player hit him in the eye with a mallet during a polo match. The court had to decide the question of the extent of the duty owed by one participant to another.

📖 CASE 6-16 *Connell v. Payne*

814 S.W.2d 486 (Tex. Crim. App. 1991)

BAKER, Justice.

This is a case of first impression in Texas. Alan B. Connell, Jr. suffered injuries when Robert B. Payne, Jr. swung a polo mallet and struck him in the eye during a match at Willow Bend Polo and Hunt Club. The jury's verdict was favorable to Payne and Willow Bend. The trial court entered a take-nothing judgment against Connell. Connell contends the trial court erred because it refused to submit jury questions on ordinary negligence and gross negligence. . . . We affirm the trial court's judgment.

The Game

All parties agree polo is a dangerous game. The risk of injury is high. It is common for injuries to occur even while players diligently follow the rules. To promote the safety of horse and rider, the game of polo stipulates certain "right-of-way" rules. One rule gives the right-of-way to the player closest to the parallel "line of the ball." A player who tries to take the ball away from an opponent having the line of the ball may not approach the opponent's horse at any angle greater than forty-five degrees. If two players are along the line of the ball, one player may "ride the opponent off the line." That is, the player may ride toward the opponent. The opponent must move away from the line of the ball to avoid a collision. The opponent loses the right of possession. Connell and Payne were on opposite teams in the match. During a play, both Connell and Payne rode to intercept the ball. Each tried to make a shot to benefit his team. Almost simultaneously, each swung his mallet at the ball. Connell's mallet struck the ball. Payne's mallet struck Connell in the eye. Connell lost the sight in that eye.

Procedural History

Connell sued Payne and Willow Bend for his injuries. He alleged Payne intentionally or recklessly caused his injury. He also alleged Payne was negligent and his conduct was gross negligence. He asserted Payne had a reputation for reckless play. He alleged Willow Bend knew of Payne's reputation and was negligent in allowing Payne to play. He also alleged Payne's and Willow Bend's negligence proximately caused his damages.

The parties tried the case to a jury. The trial court submitted a jury question that asked whether Payne intentionally or recklessly caused Connell's injury. The court also submitted jury questions that asked whether Willow Bend or Connell was negligent. The jury answered each of these questions "no." Based on these answers, the trial court entered a take-nothing judgment against Connell.

Connell asserts three points of error. In points one and two, he contends the trial court erred in failing to submit jury questions on whether Payne was negligent and whether Payne's conduct was gross negligence. Connell argues the trial court erred by applying an intentional or reckless standard.

The Legal Duty

No Texas court has decided the issue of the legal duty owed by one participant to another participant in a competitive contact sport. Connell argues the proper standard is negligence. He contends a recklessness standard holds him to an unreasonably high burden of proof. Connell contends if a participant in a competitive contact sport violates a safety rule, the injured party should have to prove only ordinary negligence. We disagree.

By participating in a dangerous contact sport such as polo, a person assumes a risk of injury. The risk involved in competing in contact sports is the basis for the historical reluctance of courts to allow players to recover damages for injuries received while participating in a competitive contact sport unless one participant deliberately injures another.

The Ohio Supreme Court recently considered a similar issue. That court reasoned a mere showing of negligence is not enough to allow recovery in sport or recreational activity. We agree. . . . A participant in a competitive contact sport expressly consents to and assumes the risk of the dangerous activity by voluntarily participating in the sport. We hold that for a plaintiff to prevail in a cause of action for injuries sustained while participating in a competitive contact sport, the plaintiff must prove the defendant acted "recklessly" or "intentionally." . . .

We affirm the trial court's judgment.

Source: Courtesy of Westlaw; reprinted with permission.

MEDICAL MALPRACTICE

Professional athletes are required to be in top physical condition to perform at their very best for their teams. A professional athlete's body is an asset to the team and the athlete. The team has an interest in ensuring that a player can perform at a top level to fulfill his or her contractual obligations to the team. The standard player contract in all major sports requires the player to maintain good physical condition. All professional and collegiate athletes are given extensive physical examinations to ensure they are ready to engage in athletic competition. Professional sports teams retain the services of a physician who will provide medical care and advice to their players. The team physician's main function is to provide medical care for team members. In the course of that duty, the physician will typically provide both medical advice and treatment. This creates a patient/physician relationship between the team physician and the player. Many team physicians actually pay for the privilege of being the team physician. Colleges and high schools also hire physicians and medical care personnel to perform physical examinations and to provide emergency medical care to participants in athletic events.

Team doctors can be pressured by many sources, including owners, coaches, or even players themselves, to find that a player is in condition to play, when in fact circumstances exist that might prove otherwise. Plaintiffs have sued a variety of medical providers, such as team physicians, athletic trainers, and universities, for failing to render proper medical care or advice. If a medical provider such as a doctor, hospital, or nurse fails to render proper care or treatment, the plaintiff may have a medical malpractice claim. A medical expert must testify on behalf of the plaintiff to establish the appropriate standard of care for the medical provider and state whether the standard of care has been breached. *Medical malpractice* is conduct that deviates from a reasonable standard of care:

> A plaintiff in a medical malpractice action is required to establish the following elements: (1) a duty owed by the health care provider to act according to the applicable standard(s) of care; (2) a breach of that duty; (3) an injury; and (4) a causal connection between the breach of the standard and the injury. With respect to the causation element, the plaintiff must show evidence that to a reasonable degree of medical probability, the injury claimed was proximately caused by the negligence of the defendant. (citations omitted).[51]

LIABILITY OF COACHES

Coaches play an integral part in the development of both professional and amateur athletes. They are for the most part given much discretion in the performance of their job when directing a team and making decisions affecting players. Some coaches are noted for harsh tactics and for a tough coaching style, whereas others, including some of the most successful coaches, have been very mild-mannered individuals. No one would argue that the coaching styles of Bobby Knight and John Wooden were the same, but both were successful in winning basketball games.

Coaches have been sued on a variety of theories, including failing to inspect equipment, improper or inadequate instruction, or failure to properly supervise an event or other participants. A coach has a duty to protect players from all foreseeable risks; moreover, a coach must use reasonable care to ensure the safety of all those under his or her supervision.

---

[51] Brumfield v. Ruyle, 2007 WL 1018475 (Tex. Ct. App.-Ft. Worth 2007).

In *Lamorie v. Warner Pac. College*, 850 P.2d 401 (Or. Ct. App. 1993), a 75-pound football player tried to tackle a 182-pound player and failed. The boy and his parents sued the coach for negligent supervision. The coach had promised the father that the boy would never play against anyone over 90 pounds. The injured player had signed a waiver assuming risk. The court found although the player had signed the waiver assuming the risk inherent to the sport of football, he did not assume the risk of a coach's negligent supervision. In *Baker v. Briarcliff Sch. Dist.*, 613 N.Y.S.2d 660 (N.Y. App. Div. 1994), a coach was held liable for injuries suffered in a game of field hockey for allowing a player to play without proper equipment and for failing to warn students about the risks of not wearing mouth guards.

In Case 6-17, *Prejean v. East Baton Rouge Parish School Bd.*, 729 So.2d 686 (La. Ct. App. 1999), a coach was sued for negligence when a young boy was injured during a basketball game in which the coach also participated.

📖 CASE 6-17 *Prejean v. East Baton Rouge Parish School Bd.*

729 So.2d 686 (La. Ct. App. 1999)

KUHN, J.

Facts and Procedural Background

Harvey was injured during a basketball practice on February 21, 1994, while his team practiced on an outdoor concrete court. The basketball team consisted of mainly fourth and fifth grade students and some third graders. Combs explained that the basketball team was organized through the Big Buddy Program, which he described as an organization which assists the schools by having volunteers work with the children in various extracurricular activities. Combs testified he had coached the team for approximately three to four years prior to Harvey's accident. . . . Neither of the coaches had received any instruction regarding the coaching of children from the school board.

Combs normally conducted warm-up and lay-up drills at the beginning of his practices and then would have the boys participate in a scrimmage. He testified that he generally played in the scrimmages with the boys if he did not have enough student players to form a team or if he wanted to demonstrate a particular technique. Combs explained that he engaged in a lot of "hands-on" work with the children so that he could teach various plays and defensive techniques.

On the day of the accident, Combs recalled that ten players participated in a scrimmage, nine students and himself, with five players on each team . . .

According to Combs' testimony, immediately prior to the accident in question, he and another student, Truman Ratcliff, were working on a "trapping and pressing" technique. Harvey was dribbling the ball down the court while facing Truman and Combs. At some point, Harvey lost the ball and Truman, Harvey and Combs all attempted to recover it. Combs stated that Harvey was in front of him and about four to five feet to his right. Truman was to Comb's left side when the ball became loose near mid-court. The ball went to Harvey's left when he lost control of it. In an attempt to recover the ball, Truman accelerated his speed and moved between Combs and Harvey. Truman was leaning down as he attempted to recover the ball. Combs explained, "I bumped Truman as he was going for the ball and he fell into Harvey." Combs specifically denied having pushed Truman and also denied having intentionally bumped Truman. According to Combs' testimony, he was running at a "slow jog" when he bumped into Truman and the lower part of his body bumped into the upper part of Truman's body. Truman fell on Harvey's legs which got tangled up causing Harvey to fall onto the hard surface of the basketball court. Combs called for emergency assistance when he saw that Harvey's left leg was injured. Harvey remained lying on the court until the paramedics arrived and transported him to a hospital emergency room.

Harvey recalled that when the accident happened, Combs had been demonstrating plays to the students and he (Harvey) was playing the position of guard. As he was dribbling the ball, it hit his foot and went to his left. Truman was moving from Harvey's right to recover the ball and was leaning down to get the ball which was rolling on the ground. Combs also attempted to recover the ball. Harvey explained that Truman's shoulder first hit Harvey's left knee, causing him to fall to the ground. Truman then fell on Harvey's leg. Harvey testified his leg broke when Truman fell on it. Harvey stated he did not know whether Combs had bumped into or pushed Truman. Harvey also testified that Combs did not usually participate in the scrimmages as a team player.

Harvey's younger brother, John Prejean, who was nine years old at the time of the accident, testified that he witnessed the accident. He explained that he had been watching the basketball practice and decided to walk back towards the school to get some water from the water fountain. When he was about halfway towards the water fountain, he looked back towards the court. Although he did not see the ball, he stated that when he turned around, he saw Combs push Truman to the side with his hands. He did not recall whether Combs used one or two hands when he pushed Truman. John said he did not see Harvey dribbling the ball, but saw Harvey running down the court playing defense. He described Combs as being to Harvey's right side and Truman as being between Harvey and Combs. He explained that Truman was leaning towards Harvey and running down the court when Combs pushed him.

Combs was approximately twenty-seven years old when the accident occurred, measured five foot six inches tall and weighed approximately one hundred eighty-two pounds. Harvey was eleven years old at the time of the accident and weighed about ninety pounds. Combs estimated that Harvey was about three to four inches shorter than himself and Truman was about six to seven inches shorter than himself.

Based on these findings, the court awarded plaintiff $35,000.00 in general damages and $15,682.00 in medical expenses. In accordance with this ruling, the court signed a judgment in favor of Mrs. Prejean and against the School Board and Combs, jointly, severally, and in solido, for the sum of $50,682.00.

The School Board and Combs have appealed contending that: (1) Combs' actions were not a cause-in-fact of Harvey's injuries; and (2) the School Board did not breach a legally imposed duty of care in favor of Harvey.

Analysis

Each negligence case must be analyzed based on the particular facts of the case. A defendant's duty in any given circumstance presents a legal question; i.e., what is the specific standard of care to be applied? The inquiry of whether a defendant's conduct breached that standard presents a factual question. . . .

A coach has the duty to exercise his or her specific responsibilities in such a manner as to protect those under his or her charge from foreseeable harm. The scope of such a broadly stated duty is necessarily fact-specific, to be determined on a case-by-case basis in light of the respective relationships and circumstances of the parties. Furthermore, a coach does not insure the safety of those in the coach's charge in all circumstances.

In the present case, the coach had a duty to act reasonably while supervising the basketball practice and to exercise his coaching duties in such a manner as to protect the student players from foreseeable harm.

The trial court found that the injury which occurred in this case was foreseeable when the coach chose to interject himself into the scrimmage with young children. The trial court reasoned that the risk of injury was great, and Combs breached a duty to protect Harvey from harm when Combs "attempted to retrieve a ball that two students were also attempting to retrieve. . . ." During the oral arguments before this court, plaintiff acknowledged that Combs' action of interjecting himself into the scrimmage was not the questionable conduct. We agree that a coach's physical participation in a game is not substandard conduct; physical demonstration of techniques by a coach is essential to learning in athletics. Rather, plaintiff asserted that Combs' substandard conduct was the manner in which he attempted to recover the loose ball.

We disagree with the trial court's conclusion that Combs breached a duty to the students by participating in the scrimmage and attempting to retrieve the ball. The record fails to establish that Combs' conduct in attempting to recover the loose ball presented any greater risk of injury to Harvey or the other players than the risk of injury generally involved in playing basketball. Virtually all team sports involve the risk of physical contact and, thus, the risk of injury.

The trial court found that Combs "bumped" Truman who then fell onto Harvey. The record establishes that as Truman attempted to recover the ball, he accelerated his speed and moved between Harvey and Combs. During this maneuver, Combs bumped into Truman. We find the trial court was manifestly erroneous in concluding that Harvey's injury was foreseeable as a result of Combs' action of participating in the scrimmage and attempting to recover the loose ball. A review of the record indicates this was an unfortunate accident, and given the fact Coach Combs merely "bumped" Truman who fell into Harvey, it was not foreseeable such a serious injury would result. We do not agree that Combs placed Harvey at risk of harm by participating in the scrimmage and attempting to recover the ball. Combs' actions did not constitute a breach of his duty to supervise his players in a reasonable manner *and* to protect the players from foreseeable harm. Because we conclude Combs did not breach the duty owed to the student players, we find no liability arising from Combs' conduct.

Source: Courtesy of Westlaw; reprinted with permission.

LIABILITY OF OFFICIALS AND REFEREES

Officials in sporting events have been sued for failure to inspect playing fields, failure to cancel an athletic contest because of bad weather, failure to control use of equipment, failure to enforce rules, failure to control the conduct of players, and failure to render first aid. There has been a long-standing reluctance to hold sports officials negligent.[52] Referees do have to enforce the rules of the game, but there is no independent tort for referee malpractice.[53] No court has recognized a viable cause of action for misapplication of a game rule or error in judgment.[54] There has been legislation introduced at the state level that grants immunity to officials or limits their liability in some fashion. The Mississippi State Legislature, for example, has enacted the following statute with regard to the immunity of officials:

---

[52] *See* Pape v. State, 90 A.D.2d 904; 456 N.Y.S.2d 863, 8 Ed. Law Rep. 158 (N.Y. App. Div. 1982) (holding referees do not have a duty to protect one basketball player from the aggressive actions of another player).

[53] Bain v. Gillispie, 357 N.W.2d 47 (Iowa Ct. App. 1984).

[54] Georgia High School Ass'n v. Waddell, 285 S.E.2d 7 (Ga. 1981).

```
Miss. Code Ann. § 95-9-3
```

(1) Sports officials who officiate athletic contests at any level of
    competition in this state shall not be liable to any person or
    entity in any civil action for injuries or damages claimed to have
    arisen by virtue of actions or inactions related in any manner to
    officiating duties within the confines of the athletic facility at
    which the athletic contest is played.

(2) For purposes of this section, sports officials are defined as
    those individuals who serve as referees, umpires, linesmen and
    those who serve in similar capacities but may be known by other
    titles and are duly registered or members of a local, state,
    regional or national organization which is engaged in part in
    providing education and training to sports officials.

(3) Nothing in this section shall be deemed to grant the protection
    set forth to sports officials who cause injury or damage to a
    person or entity by actions or inactions which are intentional,
    willful, wanton, reckless, malicious or grossly negligent. . . .

Source: Courtesy of Westlaw; reprinted with permission

TORT DEFENSES

Assumption of the Risk

If a plaintiff voluntarily enters a risky activity and knows about and understands that risk, he or she will be barred from recovery in tort.[55] The basic rule states that a plaintiff who voluntarily enters into a risky situation, knowing the risk involved, will be prevented from recovering in tort for damages. This is commonly referred to as the *assumption of the risk doctrine.*[56] This defense has been used very successfully in tort cases on behalf of stadium owners, participants, coaches, and school districts that have been sued. However, a party cannot assume a risk different from or greater than that normally associated with the activity. Assumption of the risk can be express or implied; that is, it can be assumed by express agreement between the parties or implied by the plaintiff's knowledge of the risk involved.

In Case 6-18, *Hawley v. Binghamton Mets Baseball Club Inc.*, 691 N.Y.S.2d 626 (N.Y. 1999), a spectator became a participant in a promotional activity between innings at a minor league baseball game. The court had to determine whether the minor league team was negligent in failing to advise the plaintiff of the risks inherent to the activity and also in failing to provide him with proper equipment.

---

[55] Grishman v. Porter, 2006 WL 1381654 (Cal. Ct. App. 2006).
[56] *Prosser and Keeton on Torts,* Supra, §68, Assumption of Risk.

📖 **CASE 6-18** *Hawley v. Binghamton Mets Baseball Club Inc.*

691 N.Y.S.2d 626 (N.Y. 1999)

Mercure, J.

Plaintiff Scott Hawley sustained the injuries forming the basis for this negligence action during the course of a "B-Mets Pop-Up Promotion." Plaintiff was selected in a drawing to participate in the promotion, which took place at Binghamton Mets Stadium in the City of Binghamton, Broome County, following a June 25, 1997 evening game, and entailed having plaintiff take the field and attempt to catch three fly balls that were projected into the air by a pitching machine. The complaint alleges that plaintiff successfully caught the first two balls but was struck in the face by the third, causing serious injuries to his eye. The claim of liability is predicated upon defendants' alleged failure to exercise reasonable care in the circumstances, to advise plaintiff of the risks and dangers attendant to the activity and to provide plaintiff with protective equipment. Concluding that plaintiff had assumed the risk of injury inherent in the activity and that defendants had not acted in a manner as to conceal or unreasonably increase those risks, Supreme Court granted the motions. Plaintiff appeals and we affirm.

. . . "[I]t is well-settled law that voluntary participants in sporting events assume the risk of injuries normally associated with the sport" unless "the conditions caused by the defendants' negligence are 'unique and created a dangerous condition over and above the usual dangers that are inherent in the sport.'" In making that determination, "the background of the skill and experience of the particular plaintiff" must be assessed.

Here, it is claimed that plaintiff, although an experienced amateur baseball and softball player, was unaware of, and thus did not assume, certain unique risks that were present on the night of the event and which were a proximate cause of his injury. Specifically, plaintiffs contend that "[t]he lights, the crowd, the myriad of insects and the excitement all combined to create a unique experience," precluding plaintiff's knowledge of the inherent risks. We disagree. As a frequent attendee at Binghamton Mets games, plaintiff was familiar with the conditions, including the lights and the insects. More important, by the time plaintiff fielded the first two fly balls he was well aware of the prevailing conditions and "[h]is continued participation in the [activity] in light of that awareness constituted assumption of risk as a matter of law."

We also reject the contention that the operator of the pitching machine enhanced plaintiff's risk by adjusting the machine so as to cause the balls to be projected progressively higher into the air. Other than plaintiff's uncertain deposition testimony that the second ball "seemed like it was higher" than the first and that the third ball "seemed to be a little higher" than the second, there is no evidence in the record to support plaintiff's theory. In any event, plaintiff should have reasonably expected to catch balls with varying trajectories while participating in a pop-fly contest.

Finally, although it may well be that plaintiff could have prevented or substantially diminished the injury to his eye by wearing protective eyewear, because the risk of fielding fly balls without wearing protective eyewear is so obvious, we reject the contention that defendants had a duty to provide such eyewear or warn plaintiff of the danger of wearing regular glasses.

Source: Courtesy of Westlaw; reprinted with permission.

What risks does a badminton participant assume? That was the question posed in Case 6-19, *Rosenbaum v. Bayis Ne'emon, Inc.*, 32 A.D.3d 534 (N.Y.A.D. 2006).

📖 CASE 6-19 *Rosenbaum v. Bayis Ne'emon, Inc.*

32 A.D.3d 534 (N.Y.A.D. 2006)

ROBERT W. SCHMIDT, J.P., DAVID S. RITTER, FRED T. SANTUCCI, and ROBERT J. LUNN, JJ.

In an action to recover damages for personal injuries, etc., the defendant Bayis Ne'Emon, Inc., d/b/a Camp Esther appeals from an order of the Supreme Court, Kings County (Schneier, J.), dated June 17, 2005, which denied its motion for summary judgment dismissing the complaint insofar as asserted against it.

ORDERED that the order is affirmed, with costs.

The plaintiff Moshe Rosenbaum (hereinafter the plaintiff) was injured when his foot slipped into a hole while playing a game of badminton on premises owned by the defendant Bayis Ne'Emon, Inc., d/b/a Camp Esther (hereinafter the appellant). The Supreme Court denied the appellant's motion for summary judgment dismissing the complaint insofar as asserted against it based on the doctrine of assumption of risk. We affirm.

"Participants in sporting events may be held to have consented to injury-causing events which are the known, apparent, or reasonably foreseeable risks of their participation.". . . However, the doctrine of assumption of risk will not serve as a bar to liability if the risk is "unassumed, concealed, or unreasonably increased[.]"

Here, the appellant failed to make a prima facie showing of entitlement to judgment as a matter of law. . . .

. . . The record indicates that at least a portion of the subject hole was concealed by an object which has been described by witnesses as being either a cesspool cover or a manhole cover and, as such, was not readily observable. Accordingly, it cannot be concluded as a matter of law that the plaintiff assumed the risk of the injury-causing event. . . .

Source: Courtesy of Westlaw; reprinted with permission.

Every baseball player understands the concept of a brushback pitch, or "high heat." Is that a risk a batter implicitly assumes? Case 6-20, *Avila v. Citrus Community College District,* 131 P.3d 383 (Cal. 2006), discusses this issue.

📖 CASE 6-20 *Avila v. Citrus Community College District*

131 P.3d 383 (Cal. 2006)

WERDEGAR, J.

During an intercollegiate baseball game at a community college, one of the home team's batters is hit by a pitch. In the next half-inning, the home team's pitcher allegedly retaliates with an inside pitch and hits a visiting batter in the head. The visiting batter is injured, he sues, and the courts must umpire the dispute. . . .

Jose Luis Avila, a Rio Hondo Community College (Rio Hondo) student, played baseball for the Rio Hondo Roadrunners. On January 5, 2001, Rio Hondo was playing a preseason road game against the Citrus Community College Owls (Citrus College). During the game, a Roadrunners pitcher hit a Citrus College batter with a pitch; when Avila came to bat in the top of the next inning, the Citrus College pitcher hit him in the head with a pitch, cracking his batting helmet. Avila alleges the pitch was an intentional "beanball" thrown in retaliation for the previous hit batter or, at a minimum, was thrown negligently. . . .

. . . Avila's complaint in essence alleges four ways in which the District breached a duty to Avila: by (1) conducting the game at all; (2) failing to control the Citrus College pitcher; (3) failing to provide umpires to supervise and control the game; and (4) failing to provide medical care. . . .

The second alleged breach, the failure to supervise and control the Citrus College pitcher, is barred by primary assumption of the risk. Being hit by a pitch is an inherent risk of baseball. The dangers of being hit by a pitch, often thrown at speeds approaching 100 miles per hour, are apparent and well known: being hit can result in serious injury or, on rare tragic occasions, death. FN9.

> FN9. Most famously, in August 1920, Cleveland Indians shortstop Roy Chapman was hit by a pitch from the New York Yankees' Carl Mays. He died the next day. (Sowell, The Pitch that Killed (1989) pp. 165-190; James, The Bill James Baseball Abstract (1985) pp. 131, 137.) At least seven other batters in organized baseball have been killed by pitches. (James, at pp. 131, 137.)

Being *intentionally* hit is likewise an inherent risk of the sport, so accepted by custom that a pitch intentionally thrown at a batter has its own terminology: "brushback," "beanball," "chin music." In turn, those pitchers notorious for throwing at hitters are "headhunters." Pitchers intentionally throw at batters to disrupt a batter's timing or back him away from home plate, to retaliate after a teammate has been hit, or to punish a batter for having hit a home run. Some of the most respected baseball managers and pitchers have openly discussed the fundamental place throwing at batters has in their sport. In George Will's study of the game, Men at Work, one-time Oakland Athletics and current St. Louis Cardinals manager Tony La Russa details the strategic importance of ordering selective intentional throwing at opposing batters, principally to retaliate for one's own players being hit. (Will, Men at Work (1990) pp. 61-64.) As Los Angeles Dodgers Hall of Fame pitcher Don Drysdale and New York Giants All Star pitcher Sal "The Barber" Maglie have explained, intentionally throwing at batters can also be an integral part of pitching tactics, a tool to help get batters out by upsetting their frame of mind. Drysdale and Maglie are not alone; past and future Hall of Famers, from Early Wynn and Bob Gibson to Pedro Martinez and Roger Clemens, have relied on the actual or threatened willingness to throw at batters to aid their pitching. (See, e.g., Kahn, The Head Game, at pp. 223-224; *Yankees Aced by Red Sox,* L.A. Times (May 31, 2001) p. D7 [relating Martinez's assertion that he would even throw at Babe Ruth].)

While these examples relate principally to professional baseball, "[t]here is nothing legally significant . . . about the level of play" in this case. The laws of physics that make a thrown baseball danger-ous and the strategic benefits that arise from disrupting a batter's timing are only minimally dependent on the skill level of the partici-pants, and we see no reason to distinguish between collegiate and pro-fessional baseball in applying primary assumption of the risk.

It is true that intentionally throwing at a batter is forbidden by the rules of baseball. (See, e.g., Off. Rules of Major League Baseball, rule 8.02(d); National Collegiate Athletic Assn., 2006 NCAA Baseball Rules (Dec. 2005) rule 5, § 16(d), p. 62.) But "even when a participant's conduct violates a rule of the game and may subject the violator to internal sanctions prescribed by the sport itself, imposition of *legal liability* for such conduct might well alter fundamentally the nature of the sport by deterring participants from vigorously engaging in activity that falls close to, but on the permissible side of, a prescribed rule." It is one thing for an umpire to punish a pitcher who hits a batter by ejecting him from the game, or for a league to suspend the pitcher; it is quite another for tort law to chill any pitcher from throwing inside, i.e., close to the batter's body—a permissible and essential part of the sport—for fear of a suit over an errant pitch. For better or worse, being intentionally thrown at is a fundamental part and inherent risk of the sport of baseball. FN11 It is not the function of tort law to police such conduct.

> FN11. The conclusion that being intentionally hit by a pitch is an inherent risk of baseball extends only to situations such as that alleged here, where the hit batter is at the plate. Allegations that a pitcher intentionally hit a batter who was still in the on-deck circle, or elsewhere, would present an entirely different scenario. (See Note, *Dollar Signs on the Muscle . . . and the Ligament, Tendon, and Ulnar Nerve: Institutional Liability Arising from Injuries to Student-Athletes* (2001) 3 Va. J. Sports & L. 80, 80, 111-112 [recounting the notorious 1999 incident in which Wichita State University pitcher Ben Christensen hit University of Evansville second baseman Anthony Molina with a pitch while Molina was still in the on-deck circle].)

In *Knight, supra,* 3 Cal.4th at page 320, 11 Cal.Rptr.2d 2, 834 P.2d 696, we acknowledged that an athlete does not assume the risk of a coparticipant's intentional or reckless conduct "totally outside the range of the ordinary activity involved in the sport." Here, even if the Citrus College pitcher intentionally threw at Avila, his conduct did not fall outside the range of ordinary activity involved in the sport. The District owed no duty to Avila to prevent the Citrus College pitcher from hitting batters, even intentionally. Consequently, the doctrine of primary assumption of the risk bars any claim predicated on the allegation that the Citrus College pitcher negligently or intentionally threw at Avila. . . .

Source: Courtesy of Westlaw; reprinted with permission.

Waivers and Releases

Many participants in sporting events are required to sign a waiver or release before they are allowed to participate. The release usually requires the participant to waive all rights that he or she has for any claims for damages arising from the activity. A waiver or release is an attempt by one party to escape liability from another party. Waivers and releases are generally not favored by the law, and some courts have found them unconscionable and contracts of adhesion and therefore unenforceable. Some have been held to be unenforceable based on public policy grounds.[57] Courts generally favor warnings over waivers. Releases can be enforceable under certain circumstances if it is clear that the parties intended that the defendant be "held harmless." For further study, see *School Districts' Negligence Release Forms: Are They Worth the Paper They're Printed On?*, 177 WEST'S EDUCATION LAW REPORTER 755 (2003).

The following is an example of a waiver clause found on the back of a ticket for the Boston Red Sox baseball club:

> "The holder assumes all risk and danger incidental to the game of baseball including specifically (but not exclusively) the danger of being injured by thrown bats and thrown or batted balls and agrees that the participant clubs, their agents and players are not liable for injuries resulting from such causes."[58]

In Case 6-21, *Cousins Club Corp. v. Silva,* 869 So.2d 719 (Fla. Dist. Ct. App. 2004), the parents of a boxer sued when their son suffered brain injuries during a boxing match. The boxer had signed a document entitled "Release, Assumption of Risk and Indemnification Agreement" prior to the boxing match. The question of the enforceability of this release was at issue.

📖 CASE 6-21 *Cousins Club Corp. v. Silva*

869 So.2d 719 (Fla. Dist. Ct. App. 2004)

TAYLOR, J.

The parents of Carlos E. Silva sued Club Boca individually and as legal guardians of their son to recover damages for severe brain injuries sustained by Carlos in a promotional boxing match held at the nightclub. The jury awarded Carlos $12,045,000 and his father and mother $50,000 and $250,000 respectively for loss of filial consortium. We affirm the final judgment for Carlos Silva, but reverse the derivative award to his parents. . . .

On November 3, 1997, Carlos Silva, then a nineteen-year-old college student, went to Club Boca to box in the club's Monday Night Boxing

---

[57] Wagenblast v. Odessa School District No. 105-157-166J, 758 P.2d 968 (Wash. 1988).
[58] Jane Costa v. The Boston Red Sox Baseball Club, 61 Mass. App. Ct. 299, (2004).

promotional event. Before the fight, Carlos signed a "Release, Assumption of the Risk and Indemnification Agreement." Carlos was to fight Charlie Mejia, a friend and former wrestling teammate. Mejia had boxed once before at the club, but Carlos had never been in a boxing match prior to this event.

Although the testimony at trial was not clear, some witnesses thought that within seconds into the first round Carlos got hit and fell through the ropes, hitting his head on a wooden stage located next to the ring. During the second round, Carlos received several blows to his head. The referee allowed the fight to continue. Club Boca did not have a ringside physician available for the boxing match.

At the end of the third round, Carlos just sat in his corner with his head down. The referee asked one of his friends to remove him so they could start the next fight. Finally, the referee had to help remove Carlos. Carlos sat in a chair and kept leaning his head forward. Within a few minutes, he was unresponsive although conscious. Then his head was completely down; he was unconscious, making snoring noises. His friends began requesting help. One friend ran to a bouncer and requested a paramedic. The bouncer finally came over and "yoked" Carlos up under the arms, dragging him outside. The bouncer thought that Carlos was drunk, even though one friend was screaming that Carlos was not drunk and should not be handled that way. Eventually someone called for medical assistance. Approximately forty-five minutes passed from the time that Carlos left the ring until he received emergency medical assistance.

According to the plaintiffs' expert medical testimony, Carlos sustained a subdural hematoma due to blows in the fight and/or hitting his head on the wooden stage and severe brain edema due to lack of oxygen. The experts testified that, although the subdural hematoma was significant, the severe brain edema was a result of the forty to forty-five minute delay in summoning medical attention. The lack of medical attention allowed the hematoma to get much larger and caused extremely high pressure to build up within Carlos' cranial cavity. Carlos' brain was so swollen that the neurosurgeon was forced to remove a part of the brain that controlled speech and motor functions on his right side. As a result, Carlos cannot speak or walk and remains in a partial vegetative state.

In their negligence count, the plaintiffs alleged that Club Boca was negligent in: (a) constructing the boxing ring adjacent to the fixed wooden stage in such a configuration as to be unreasonably dangerous to participants; (b) failing to provide a licensed physician and/or medical personnel to monitor the fight and the welfare of the participants; (c) continuing the fight following Carlos' acceleration from the ring; (d) failing to monitor the health and welfare of Carlos prior to, during, and following the fight; (e) failing to place some form of mat or protection upon the adjacent fixed wooden stage; (f) failing to timely summon an ambulance; (g) negligently handling the impaired Carlos following the fight; (h) failing to have the referee monitor the health and welfare of Carlos; (i) permitting the announcer, promoter and/or referee to incite the participants to continue fighting; (j) failing to warn the boxers of the lack of medical attention; (k) failing to make certain that the participants could not come in contact with the adjacent stage; (l) failing to warn the boxers that the adjacent stage was within such close proximity and was dangerous; and (m) failing to appropriately regulate the level and skill of the boxers they paired to fight. Club Boca asserted as affirmative defenses that the release and waiver signed by Carlos barred the action, that Carlos assumed the risks inherent in the boxing match, and that Carlos was comparatively negligent.

Release and Waiver

The document entitled "Release, Assumption of Risk and Indemnification Agreement" stated in pertinent part:

> In consideration of my participation in the above entitled event, and with the understanding that my participation in Monday Night Boxing is only on the condition that I enter into this agreement for myself, my heirs and assigns, I hereby assume the inherent and extraordinary risks involved in Monday Night Boxing and any risks inherent in any other activities connected with this event in which I may voluntarily participate.

We conclude that the trial court properly denied Club Boca's motion for summary judgment. The court determined that the release did not bar the plaintiff's lawsuit, because under the agreement the plaintiff assumed only the risks inherent in the boxing match, and thus, released liability only for injuries resulting from his voluntary participation in the boxing match. Further, the court ruled that the release did not clearly and unequivocally release Club Boca from liability for injuries to the plaintiff as a result of its own negligence.

We agree that, based on the language of the release, any negligence on the part of Club Boca fell outside the scope of the release. Thus, while Carlos may have been precluded from recovering for injuries resulting from any dangers inherent in boxing, he was not barred from recovering for injuries resulting from Club Boca's negligence.

In determining that Carlos' damages were mostly caused by Club Boca's negligence, rather than by any inherent risks in boxing, the jury specifically found that Club Boca was negligent in: (1) failing to provide or obtain medical treatment for Carlos; (2) failing to maintain its premises in a reasonably safe condition; and (3) failing to properly supervise the Monday Night Boxing event. The jury attributed 85% negligence to Club Boca and 15% to Carlos. It awarded $912,000.00 for past medical expenses; $8,500,000 for future medical expenses; $1,633,000 for future loss of earning ability; $100,000 for past pain and suffering and loss of enjoyment of life; and $900,000 for future pain and suffering and loss of enjoyment of life. The total award for Carlos Silva was $12,045,000. Carlos' mother was awarded $250,000 and his father $50,000 for loss of filial consortium. The trial court entered a final judgment on the verdict, reducing it to account for Carlos' 15% comparative negligence.

AFFIRMED in part; REVERSED in part and REMANDED.

Source: Courtesy of Westlaw; reprinted with permission.

Comparative Negligence

Comparative negligence is another defense to a tort action. In a negligence action, a jury can reduce any damages it finds the plaintiff is entitled to by the percentage of fault of the plaintiff. The doctrine of comparative negligence compares the negligence of the plaintiff with that of the defendant and can sometimes work to reduce the recovery of damages for the plaintiff. In some states that have adopted the comparative negligence doctrine, a plaintiff is allowed to recover damages even if the plaintiff's negligence is greater than that of the defendant. For instance, if a jury found a stadium owner negligent and returned a verdict for the plaintiff-spectator in the amount of $100,000, but also found that the plaintiff-spectator was 60% negligent, a judgment would be entered for $40,000 for the plaintiff-spectator. Some state laws provide for a "fifty percent rule," which prevents a plaintiff who is found to be more than 50% negligent from any recovery whatsoever.[59]

Immunity

Another defense to tort liability is sovereign immunity. Under the doctrine of sovereign immunity, a state or its agents cannot be held liable in tort absent their consent.[60] The doctrine was originally

---

[59] Alexander v. Kappa Alpha Psi Fraternity, Inc., 464 F. Supp.2d 751 (M.D. Tenn. 2006).
[60] Spera v. Waterford Bd. of Educ., 2007 WL 866262 (Conn. Super. Ct. 2007).

based on the ancient maxim "the king can do no wrong." The immunity defense differs in every state, and many states have exceptions to this defense.

In Case 6-22, *Bridges v. City of Carrasco, 982 So.2d 306, 2007-1593 (La.App.3 Cir.4/30/08),* a participant in a softball game brought a lawsuit after he was injured as a participant. The legal issue presented to the court was whether the sports association and its officials who ran the tournament were immune from tort liability under Louisiana law.

📖 CASE 6-22 *Bridges v. City of Carrasco*

982 So.2d 306, 2007-1593 (La.App.3 Cir.4/30/08)

PICKETT, J.

The plaintiffs, Charles and Cynthia Bridges, appeal a judgment of the trial court granting a motion for summary judgment filed by the defendant, United States Specialty Sports Association (USSSA) dismissing USSSA from the plaintiffs' suit for damages resulting from injuries Mr. Bridges sustained during a softball game. We affirm the judgment of the trial court.

Facts

The plaintiff, Charles Bridges, was injured on June 5, 2004, while participating in a softball tournament at Pelican Park in Carencro. The tournament was sponsored by the defendant, USSSA. The team of which Bridges was a member played a game Saturday morning, a second game on Saturday afternoon, and its third game at approximately 9:00 p.m. Saturday evening. Between the afternoon and night games it started to rain. Bridges stated that when he arrived at the field for the night game he noticed the infield, which was carpeted with an "Astroturf" type material, was in poor condition because of several hours of rain; however, he decided to play anyway. Bridges played shortstop. The softball game consisted of seven innings. In the fifth or sixth inning, Bridges was covering second base in an attempt to tag out a runner coming from first base. The areas around each base had no turf covering, but rather, had the dirt infield exposed. In attempting to take second base, the runner either slipped or slid in the dirt around second base causing a collision between the runner and the plaintiff. As a result of the collision, the plaintiff sustained a broken lower leg. This suit followed.

The plaintiff filed a petition for damages against both USSSA and the City of Carencro, alleging that the condition of the field around second base was the cause of his injuries and that because of the defective condition, the game should have been postponed. The only defendant before us is USSSA. The plaintiffs argue that it was the responsibility of the USSSA Tournament Manager, Marie Duplechin, to postpone the game due to the poor field conditions, and that her failure to do so resulted in the plaintiffs' injuries.

The action at issue in this case, is a motion for summary judgment filed by USSSA, who claims immunity under the provisions of La.R.S. 9:2798, which provides in part:

Limitation of liability of a volunteer athletic coach, manager, team volunteer health care provider, or official; definitions

A. Except as provided in Subsection B of this Section, no person shall have a cause of action against any volunteer athletic coach, manager, athletic trainer, team volunteer health care provider, or sports team official for any loss or damage caused by any act or omission to act directly related to his responsibilities as a coach, manager, athletic trainer, team volunteer health care provider, or official, while actively conducting, directing, or participating in the sporting activities or in the practice thereof, unless the loss or damage was caused by the gross negligence of the coach, manager, athletic trainer, team volunteer health care provider, or official . . .

USSSA submitted evidence proving that the umpire to whom Mr. Perry first pointed out the alleged defect in the pitcher's mound was a volunteer for USSSA. USSSA did admit that its umpires are paid a stipend of fifteen dollars per game, and submitted evidence of this stipend. The tournament directors also receive a stipend of ten dollars for each team entered in the tournament. USSSA asserted, and Mr. Perry agreed, that these payments are not enough to support a person and therefore could not be considered a salary. These payments meet the definition of "incidental compensation" under La.R.S. 9:2798(C). Therefore, La.R.S. 9:2798 applies, and USSSA's umpire and director are not liable for any injury Mr. Perry sustained.

The burden then shifts back to Mr. Perry to show that he could produce evidence proving that the umpire and director were not immune from liability. Mr. Perry produced no evidence, nor did he even argue that any such evidence might be produced at trial, to show that the umpire and director did not meet the elements required to take advantage of the immunity offered by La.R.S. 9:2798.

Since USSSA met its burden of proving that its umpire and director were immune from liability as per La.R.S. 9:2798, and because Mr. Perry could not meet his burden to produce factual support to the contrary, the trial court correctly granted USSSA's motion for summary judgment based also on immunity from liability under La.R.S. 9:2798.

In the case at bar, Ms. Duplechin, the tournament director, submitted an affidavit establishing that she was a volunteer (under the terms of

La.R.S. 9:2798). The plaintiffs argue that since "tournament director" is not one of the positions specifically listed in La.R.S. 9:2798, that she does not qualify for immunity under the statute. We agree that "tournament director" is not specifically listed, *however*, the statute does include "*official[s]*," *i.e.*,

A. Except as provided in Subsection B of this Section, no person shall have a cause of action against any volunteer athletic coach, manager, team volunteer health care provider, or sports team *official*. . . unless the loss or damage was caused by the gross negligence of the coach, manager, athletic trainer, team volunteer health care provider, or *official*." (Emphasis ours).

Just as we found umpires were covered by the statute in the *Perry* case, we find tournament directors to be covered in this case.

Finally, the plaintiffs argue that their allegation of "gross negligence" should preclude the granting of a summary judgment. The record establishes that after the rain, remedial steps were taken to improve the playing surface. In its answers to interrogatories the City of Carencro and Pelican Park, Inc. stated that the later "games were delayed approximately 30 to 60 minutes to give maintenance workers time to prepare the field for playing." The answers specifically state: "[t]he water was swept off and then turface/quick dry was spread over the dirt area and raked." The plaintiffs brought forth no deposition or affidavit which counter the defendants' claims of remedial action nor raise an issue of material fact regarding alleged gross negligence on the part of the defendants.

Accordingly, for the reasons stated above, the judgment of the trial court is affirmed. All costs of this appeal are assessed against the plaintiffs, Charles and Cynthia Bridges.

Source: Courtesy of Westlaw; reprinted with permission.

WORKERS' COMPENSATION

Workers' compensation laws established an administrative process for compensating injured workers who were injured in the job. The laws are often deemed "strict liability" because the payment of benefits is not based on any fault of the employer, but rather on the existence of an employment relationship. For the employer to be liable, the injury of the employee must be accidental and must have occurred in the course of employment without regard to the question of negligence.[61] The original purpose of the workers' compensation law was to provide for the injured

---

[61] Stringer v. Minnesota Vikings Football Club, Inc., 705 N.W.2d 746 (Minn. 2005).

worker and to curb lawsuits against the employer for every injury that occurred on the job. The law operates as an exclusive remedy for all injuries sustained by an employee during the scope of employment. Absent an intentional act or gross negligence on the part of the employer, the worker's only remedy against an employer for an injury on the job is the workers' compensation benefits.[62] Workers' compensation is usually required by the state for every employee, although some state laws have exceptions for certain numbers of workers, small business owners, and other categories. The theory behind workers' compensation law is that the employer has to bear the burden of the cost of the injury.

As mentioned previously, professional athletes usually assume all risks, including injury, inherent to the sport. The collective bargaining agreements of the major sports leagues provide for payment of benefits and some wages to an athlete if he or she sustains a sports-related injury during a sporting event. Professional athletes may also be eligible to receive state workers' compensation benefits for injuries they have sustained from playing a particular sport. In *Palmer v. Kansas City Chiefs*, 621 S.W.2d 350 (Mo. Ct. App. 1981), the workers' compensation claimant was denied benefits for injuries he sustained during a professional football game while executing a block. However, absent a specific exclusion under state law, professional athletes who are injured during the course of their employment might be able to recover workers' compensation benefits. Defenses that are normally available in tort actions, such as assumption of risk, and comparative or contributory negligence, are not available to the employer in a workers' compensation matter. For further discussion of professional athletes and workers' compensation benefits, see *Grabbing Them by the Ball: Legislature, Courts, and Team Owners Bar Non-Elite Professional Athletes from Workers' Compensation*, 8 AMERICAN UNIVERSITY JOURNAL OF GENDER, SOCIAL POLICY & THE LAW 623 (2000).

Amateur Athletes

In college athletics, the question is whether the student-athlete should be treated as an employee under workers' compensation law. What happens to a college athlete who is injured while on scholarship at the university? Some states, such as Florida and California, have specifically provided for college athletes to receive workers' compensation benefits if they are injured during a sports event at the university. The National Collegiate Athletic Association (NCAA) has a catastrophic insurance plan in place for NCAA member institutions. The policy covers players, coaches, managers, and cheerleaders who are injured during their activities.

In *Waldrep v. Texas Employers Ins. Ass'n*, 21 S.W.3d 692 (Tex. Ct. App. 2000), the court addressed the issue of whether a student-athlete, Kent Waldrep, was entitled to workers' compensation under Texas law after he was paralyzed in 1974 as a result of an injury he received during a college football game. Finally, in 1993, the Texas Workers Compensation Commission ruled that he was an employee of Texas Christian University (TCU) at the time of his injury; however, TCU's insurance provider appealed, and in 1997 a jury reversed that decision. The court, in finding that TCU did not have the right to direct all of Waldrep's activities during his stay at the school, affirmed the lower court's ruling that Waldrep was not entitled to workers' compensation.

---

[62] Quick v. Meyers Welding Fabricating, Inc., 649 So.2d 999 (La. Ct. App. 1994).

Professional Athletes

If fighting is penalized by game rules but is encouraged by the coach, can it be deemed part of a player's employment if he is instructed to start a fight? One of the requirements to receive workers' compensation benefits is "that the injury arise out of and in the course and scope of employment." In Case 6-23, *Norfork Admirals v. Jones*, 2005 WL 2847392 (Va. App. 2005), the Virginia Court of Appeals was called on to decide whether a hockey player who was injured after he initiated a fight during a game with an opponent was entitled to workers' compensation benefits.

CASE 6-23 *Norfolk Admirals v. Jones*

2005 WL 2847392 (Va. App. 2005)

ELDER, Judge.

. . . The record shows that on March 29, 2002, claimant, a right-hand-dominant, twenty-two-year-old male, was employed by the Norfolk Admirals as a hockey player, playing as a right-wing power forward. On that date, claimant took the ice and, following his coach's instructions, instigated a fight with an aggressive opposing player. As a result of the fight, claimant was sent to the penalty box, at which time he noticed that his right shoulder was sore and he could not lift his arm. At the end of the game, claimant went immediately to the team doctor to report the injury.

Following the injury, claimant took several days off with the agreement of employer's head athletic trainer, Kevin "Stu" Bender. Claimant's agent recommended that he not participate in the playoffs because he had been injured and did not yet have a contract for the 2002/2003 hockey season . . .

On May 16, 2002, Dr. Campbell performed surgery on the claimant's right shoulder, which included the insertion of six screws.

II. Analysis

A. *Injury by Accident Arising Out of and in the Course of Employment*

"In order to establish entitlement to compensation benefits, the claimant must prove, by a preponderance of the evidence, [(1)] an injury by accident which arose [(2)] out of and [(3)] in the course of his employment." Employer argues that because claimant was the aggressor in voluntary combat, the injury did not arise out of his employment. Claimant argues that he suffered an accidental injury as a result of a fight he engaged in at the instruction of his coach. He claims that fighting is a part of the history and game of hockey and that it constitutes a hazard to which he was exposed to a degree beyond that of the public at large.

1. Injury by Accident

Employer argues that intentional actions by any design are not accidental and, thus, are not compensable. The Workers' Compensation Act does not define "injury by accident." That phrase, however, has been defined by judicial interpretation. In *Southern Express v. Green*, 257 Va. 181, 509 S.E.2d 836 (1999), the Supreme Court stated that, "to establish an "injury by accident" a claimant must prove (1) that the injury appeared suddenly at a particular time and place and upon a particular occasion, (2) that it was caused by an identifiable incident or sudden participating event, and (3) that it resulted in an obvious mechanical or structural change in the human body." *Id.* at 187, 509 S.E.2d at 839. Here, the commission found evidence to support these factors, and we agree.

The particular time, place, and occasion of claimant's injuries was at the conclusion of a fight during the hockey game in which claimant played on March 29, 2002. The identifiable or precipitating event was the fight, which claimant instigated with a player on the opposing team on the instructions of his coach. Finally, claimant's doctor stated that the fight "materially aggravated" claimant's right shoulder injury, causing lesions of the anterior, inferior, and posterior labrum of the right shoulder, which indicates a mechanical or structural change that resulted in his injury. Thus, credible evidence supports the commission's finding that claimant sustained an injury by accident within the meaning of the Act rather than an impairment resulting from cumulative trauma.

2. Arising out of Employment

. . . in the case at bar, the evidence established that, at the time claimant was injured, he was performing a task that he was employed to perform. The commission found that fighting is an integral part of the game of hockey and that claimant's job on employer's hockey team was to be an "enforcer." This conclusion was supported by the deposition testimony of Lawrence J. Landon, Executive Director of the Professional Hockey Players' Association, who stated fighting is a part of hockey and is not prohibited by the league. He testified that the league rule on fighting is just a "policing mechanism or control mechanism because [fighting] is allowed." He said, "All fighting is part of the game." He also testified that, in fighting, claimant was doing what he was paid to do; that injury due to fighting is a foreseeable risk for any player in any game; and that games without fighting are the exception rather than the rule. The evidence also included claimant's testimony that his coach told him to "go get" a particular player on the opposing side, which claimant understood to mean, "go fight him." Although employer argues that claimant's fighting constituted willful misconduct, employer failed to rebut the evidence that fighting was a part of claimant's employment.

Employer argues that the commission engaged in overreaching and improperly took judicial notice in finding that fighting is a part of the game of hockey. We disagree. No judicial notice was taken. The commission considered the ample evidence before it on the issue of fighting in hockey. The evidence supports the commission's decision that claimant's injury can fairly be traced to his employment as a contributing proximate cause. "[W]hether an employee is guilty of willful misconduct and whether such misconduct is a proximate cause of the employee's accident are issues of fact." Although claimant conceded that fighting is voluntary and that he instigated the fight, the fight was not a personal undertaking but instead was directed against the other player as part of claimant's employment relationship and in furtherance of employer's business.

3. In the Course of Employment

The phrase, "in the course of employment," means that the injury took place "'within the period of employment, at a place where the employee may reasonably be, and while he is reasonably fulfilling duties of his employment or engaged in doing something incidental thereto.'" Claimant's injury occurred while he was employed as a hockey player, during a hockey game, and while he followed his coach's orders. Thus, ample evidence supported the commission's finding that claimant was injured in the course of his employment. . . .

III.

Because credible evidence supports the commission's decision that claimant sustained a compensable injury by accident arising out of and in the course of employment . . . we affirm the commission's award.

Affirmed.

Source: Courtesy of Westlaw; reprinted with permission.

NOTES AND DISCUSSION QUESTIONS

Negligence

1. In Case 6-2, *Lindaman ex rel. Lindaman v. Vestal Cent. School Dist.*, the court denied the defendant's motion for summary judgment, finding a question of fact existed as to whether the defendant was negligent. In your opinion, is this type of game appropriate for children of this age group? If not, what age is appropriate?

2. For an interesting case involving the concept of duty under negligence law, see *Kleinknecht v. Gettysburg College*, 989 F.3d 1360 (3d Cir. 1993), which addressed the issue of the duty owed to an intercollegiate athlete if he or she is injured while participating in sports on campus. What duty of care does a university owe an intramural participant in providing for his or her safety?

Defamation

3. Discuss whether the following individuals would be considered public figures for the purpose of defamation law.

   a. The winner of college football's Heisman Trophy
   b. A bronze medal winner in a swimming event at the Olympics
   c. The head high school football coach for the state champions
   d. The sports reporter for a local television station

4. In *Nussbaumer v. Time, Inc.*, 13 Media L. Rep. 1753 (Ohio Ct. App. 1986), the plaintiff sued the publisher of an article that appeared in *Sports Illustrated* alleging that the plaintiff, as vice president and player personnel director of an NFL team, was operating as a spy for management. The court discussed whether Nussbaumer was a "public figure" for the purposes of defamation and whether or not the article referring to the plaintiff as a "spy" for management constituted defamation under the law. The court found as follows:

   > The managing of a professional club attracts acute coverage. Decisions controlling what player will be on the field, coaching, and general management philosophy are publicized. News conferences are frequently held to announce changes that affect this area.
   >
   > When Nussbaumer accepted a front office job with the Browns, he stepped into the public eye. He was in charge of player selection. He helped arrange player trades with other clubs, select possible choices in the college player draft, and helped negotiate contracts with players on the team roster. All of these chores directly affect who will be playing for the team; hence, they attract a continuing media coverage.
   >
   > The relationship between the individuals charged with managing the team is also predictably in the limelight. Disagreements over players, coaching philosophy, or just personality clashes are predictably given great attention by the media. Each season the media covers dozens of stories stemming from office gossip or office politics. Stories of the firing of a coach because of a disagreement with the management are common. An individual involved in the management of professional sports teams has voluntarily stepped into the public eye. The organization he works for attracts and courts such attention that he is a public figure at least for the limited purpose of stories related to his job.
   >
   > The article dealt solely with the management of the Browns. It stated that Nussbaumer was spying on the head coach for the front office. Nussbaumer should be required to demonstrate actual malice on the part of the defendants.[63]

---

[63] *Nussbaumer,* 13 Media L. Rep. 1753.

Right to Privacy and Publicity Rights

5. For further study of this issue, see *Montana v. San Jose Mercury News*, 40 Cal. Rptr. 2d 639 (Cal. Ct. App 1995). In that case, the former NFL great Joe Montana sued a newspaper over its reproduction of an artist's rendition of Montana in the Super Bowl. Montana alleged that the newspaper misappropriated his name and likeness for commercial purposes by reproducing in poster form newspaper pages containing his photograph, thereby violating his right of privacy. The court found in favor of the newspaper, based on First Amendment grounds, stating:

> In the instant case, there can be no question that the full page newspaper accounts of Super Bowls XXIII and XXIC, and the 49'ers' four championships in a single decade, constituted publication of matters in the public interest entitled to First Amendment protection. Montana, indeed, concedes as much. The question he raises in this appeal is whether the relatively contemporaneous reproduction of these pages, in poster form, for resale, is similarly entitled to First Amendment protection. We conclude that it is. This is because Montana's name and likeness appeared in the posters for *precisely* the same reason they appeared on the original newspaper front pages: because Montana was a major player in the contemporaneous, newsworthy sports events. Under these circumstances, Montana's claim that SJMN used his face and name solely to extract commercial value from them fails.[64]

6. In 2004 Tiger Woods sued the manufacturer of a yacht when it used his name and likeness for commercial purposes. Attorneys for Woods sued in federal court, claiming that his contract with Christensen Shipyards, Ltd., barred the boat manufacturer from using the famous golfer's identity to promote the company. The lawsuit stated that the shipyard started a "widespread national campaign" using Woods's name and photos of the 155-foot yacht *Privacy*. It also says the company used the golfer's name and the pictures in a display at the Fort Lauderdale Boat Show. The lawsuit claimed damages for Woods because his privacy was violated. It was reported that Christensen Shipyards agreed to pay $1.6 million to settle the lawsuit. Associated Press, *'Privacy' for Tiger: Woods Settles Yacht Suit, NBC Sports,* May 8, 2006.

7. In *Facenda v. NFL Films, Inc., et al.*, 2007 WL 1314632 (E.D. Pa. 2007), the estate of the legendary sportscaster John Facenda (known as "the voice of God") sued over the use of Facenda's voice in the video game *Madden NFL '06*. The estate asserted claims for invasion of privacy, as well as unauthorized use of name or likeness under the Pennsylvania Right of Publicity Statute and under the Lanham Act. The court dismissed the right of privacy claim, but found that the estate was entitled to recover under the Lanham Act as well as the state right of publicity statute. The court found that although Facenda's voice was only used briefly, it did add commercial value to the video game.

8. Does every athlete have commercial value in his or her name? Does it matter whether the athlete is an amateur or professional? Suppose an individual owned the domain name Heismantrophywinner.com and placed on the website information relating to the statistics and success of each Heisman Trophy winner. Would a winner of that prestigious award have a

---

[64] *Montana,* 40 Cal. Rptr. 2d at 640–41.

cause of action against the domain owner for invasion of privacy or infringement of the right of publicity? Would athlete Deon Sanders have a cause of action under a right of privacy theory against the domain owner of www.deonsanderssucks.com? Could the domain name owner defend a lawsuit based on freedom of speech under the First Amendment? Could an athlete have a nickname protected as a domain name in the same fashion that Muhammad Ali had protection of the phrase "the Greatest" in *Ali v. Playgirl*? Consider the domain name www.thehockeypuck.com, which sends the viewer to a website that states:

> Hello, Dummies! Welcome to The Hockey Puck—the Ultimate Don Rickles Web Experience. We are the most complete source of Ricklesania on the web or anywhere. Whatever you're looking for, you'll find it here—articles, movie and television listings, pictures—even upcoming appearances by the man himself. You should be so lucky to have Mr. Warmth hurl an insult your way. We hope you'll come back often to learn more about one of the truly great comic geniuses of all time. Let's get crackin,' gang!

Who might have a cause of action against Rickles for the use of this domain name?

9. Could an athlete have a protected right of privacy in a particular move or style of play? For instance, does Tiger Woods have rights to the well-known fist-pumping move he uses after he makes a great shot? Does NBA Hall-of-Famer Kareem Abdul-Jabbar have privacy protection in his well-known basketball shoot named the "sky hook." Walker, Don, *Abdul-Jabbar's Manager: Kareem Owns "Sky Hook"*, The Business of Sports, June 2, 2009. *For further study see*, Eugene Volokh, *Freedom of Speech and the Right of Publicity*, Houston Law Review Vol. 40, 2003.

10. In *Pooley v. National Hole-In-One Ass'n*, 89 F. Supp. 2d 1108 (D. Ariz. 2000), the defendant used plaintiff Don Pooley's picture for only six seconds in its advertisement. Does that violate an individual's right of publicity? According to the court, it did, "It capitalized on Plaintiff's name, reputation, and prestige in the context of an advertisement. The promotional videotape went one step further and implied a false connection between the Plaintiff and its business. The Court finds that the use of Plaintiff's identity was strictly commercial and not protected by the First Amendment. . . ."[65] Would the result in this case have been the same if the defendant had not identified Pooley by name but only used a picture of him teeing off? What damages was Pooley being entitled to? How do you calculate damages in a right of publicity case?

Premises Liability

11. What duty of care does a stadium owner owe to a minor who attends a game? Does a minor understand the risk involved as spectator or a participant in a sporting event? What about a spectator who is wholly unfamiliar with the sport being played or who has never attended the sport?[66] In *City of Atlanta v. Merritt*, 323 S.E.2d 680 (Ga. Ct. App. 1984), an eight-year-old was struck in the face by a foul ball at a baseball game. The plaintiff alleged that the design of the stadium was defective and that the picnic area near the right-field line

---

[65] *Pooley*, 89 F. Supp. 2d at 1114.
[66] Gunther v. Charlotte Baseball, Inc., 854 F. Supp. 424 (D.S.C. 1994) (holding spectators assumed the risk of being hit by a foul ball even though they never had attended a game).

was not screened. In most cases, courts will find that minors know or should have known of the inherent risks of the game. However, in *Merritt*, the court held that a question of fact existed as to whether the eight-year-old understood and appreciated the risks involved from a foul ball.

12. In which of the following circumstances would a stadium owner be held liable?

    a. A drunk fan attacks another fan and injures him or her.

    b. A spectator slips and falls on a slick floor near the concession stands.

    c. A hot dog vendor spills hot water on a spectator.

    d. A player from the opposing team goes into the stands and assaults a fan after the fan has been "ragging" the player.

13. Does a written warning on the back of a ticket always provide a defense to a stadium owner? When should verbal warnings be given during a baseball game concerning objects going into the stands?

Spectator Injuries

14. In *Teixiera v. New Britain Baseball Club*, the spectator was injured before the game started. Should a stadium owner's liability be different for events that occur before and after the game? Were the warnings to spectators adequate in *Teixiera*?

15. In *Benejam v. Detroit Tigers*, 635 N.W.2d 219 (Mich. Ct. App. 2001), the court explored the limited duty rule, which imposes upon the stadium owner a limited duty to screen the area behind home plate and to further offer a sufficient amount of seating to those spectators who reasonably may be anticipated to request protected seating in the course of the game. The limited duty rule is essentially a unique baseball rule dealing with liability of stadium owners. Some courts have argued against a special rule for baseball, stating that ordinary principles of negligence law should apply.

    In *Benejam*, a young girl was sitting behind the net when a bat shattered and a fragment of it curved around the net and struck her. There was no hole in the net. A jury awarded the plaintiff $917,000. The verdict was overturned on appeal. The court found that there was a screen behind home plate and there was "no proof whatsoever that persons wanting seats protected by the screen could not be accommodated."

16. There are many cases dealing with golf law. If A tees off and hooks his drive to the tee box being used by B and injures B, can B prevail in his lawsuit against A for damages? Under what circumstances can a golfer be held liable for errant shots? Does the golfer have a duty to yell "fore" if he or she hits an errant shot? In *Outlaw v. Bituminous Ins. Co.*, So.2d 1350 (La. Ct. App. 1978), the court held that an adult owed a duty to a child golfer not to drive a ball in the child's direction while playing through. For a complete discussion of this issue, see Michael A. Shadiak, *Does a Golf Course Owner and/or Operator Owe a Duty of Care to Their Patrons to Protect Them from Lightning Strikes?*, 8 Seton Hall Journal of Sport Law 301–26 (1992).

    In *Thomas v. Wheat*, 143 P.3d 767 (Okla. Ct. App. 2006), a painter who was painting a house that bordered a golf course was struck by a golf ball. The painter sued the golfer, and the lower court granted the golfer's motion for summary judgment. On appeal, the court said that there was a material issue of fact as to whether the painter was within the zone of risk and whether the golfer's "fore" warning was effective.

17. What instruction would you give to a team mascot about getting fans involved in extracurricular activity? What liability concerns do mascots present? Although it is the general rule that stadium owners and teams are not liable for spectators, they do have a legal duty not to increase the risks of injury to spectators who are attending the event. In *Lowe v. California League of Professional Baseball*, 65 Cal. Rptr. 2d 105 (Cal. Ct. App. 1997), the antics of the club's mascot led the court to consider the question of a stadium owner's liability to a spectator. A spectator was attending a minor league baseball game and claimed that the defendant's mascot, "Tremor," a large dinosaur with a protruding tail, interfered with his view of the game and prevented him from seeing a foul ball that struck the plaintiff and caused injuries. The court of appeals reversed the lower court's granting of summary judgment, noting that the "antics of the mascot are not an essential or integral part of the playing of a baseball game" and that a question of fact existed as to whether the mascot's antics increased the inherent risk to the plaintiff.

18. The National Hockey League has a policy that prevents the seating of patrons while the puck is in play. What is the purpose of this rule? Should other sports adopt a similar rule?

19. What steps should a university take to prevent "field rushing activity" from taking place? Should universities be required to purchase goal posts that collapse for their stadiums?

Participant Versus Participant Liability

20. Consider the heated exchange that took place between Roger Clemens and Mike Piazza in the 2000 World Series. Piazza has had much success against Clemens in his career. During an at bat, Piazza's shattered bat flew in the direction of Clemens, who quickly scooped up the bat and discarded it in general direction of Piazza. If the bat had hit and injured Piazza, would Piazza have had grounds for a civil lawsuit against Clemens for damages? On what basis could a jury find Clemens liable?

21. Can a violation of a safety rule form the basis of a lawsuit? Consider an NFL player who commits a flagrant foul and receives an unsportsmanlike conduct penalty for hitting a player while he is out of bounds. If the latter player is injured as a result, would the violation of a rule of the game—in this case, unsportsmanlike conduct—form the basis of a civil lawsuit?[67] What if a baseball player "corked" his bat and then during an at bat lined a foul ball off the third-base coach's head, injuring him? (Corking a bat is a violation of league rules and allegedly assists the player in hitting the ball harder and farther.) Could the third-base coach prevail in a lawsuit against the player on the basis that the player had violated a rule of the game?

Medical Malpractice

22. Does a team physician have a duty to the team or to the player? Could a player sue a team doctor for failure to diagnose an injury? Consider the case of Jeff Novak, a former Southwest Texas State standout who sued the Jacksonville Jaguars' team physician, Stephen Lucke. Novak was awarded $4.35 million by a Jacksonville jury in July 1999. The verdict

---

[67] *See Nabozny*, 334 N.E.2d 258.

was overturned less than a week later by Judge Frederick Tygart, who indicated that he saw no evidence of negligence by Dr. Lucke. Novak best described the position of the team physician: "I think it's probably the toughest environment a doctor can have in the whole world. You've got coaches that want them on the field. You've got physicians who are tied up in wanting that team to win as well, and wanting to make the coach happy so he can be there again next year as the team doctor of the Jacksonville Jaguars." Novak had filed a medical malpractice lawsuit against the Jaguars's team physicians for medically clearing him to practice with a hematoma on his right leg. Coach Tom Coughlin testified in his deposition in the lawsuit that he "can and will exert as much pressure on the player and the doctors to get the player on the field." The case eventually settled for $2.2 million. Selena Robberts, *Sports of the Times; Coughlin's Biggest Risk is Rejection,* The New York Times, May 13, 2004.

Liability of Coaches

23. In which of the following scenarios could a coach be held liable for injuries to a student-athlete?

    a. Making a student run extra laps for being late to practice, as result of which the student suffers injuries.

    b. Requiring players to perform one-on-one tackling drills with a weight difference of 70 pounds between the two players.

    c. Requiring a player to continue playing notwithstanding that the player has suffered an injury.

Liability of Officials or Referees

24. Under what circumstances can a referee be held liable for negligence? What about a referee who accidentally gives a football team an extra down that allows the opposite team to score a touchdown and win the championship? What about a referee who miscalculates the time left in the game and allows one team extra time to kick a winning field goal?

Tort Defenses

25. Do releases at sporting events always provide a defense to the defendant? Consider a situation in which a participant fails to sign a release for a particular occurrence of an event but has participated in the event many times before. That was the case in *Beaver v. Grand Prix Karting Association, Inc.* 246 F.3d 905 (7th Cir. 2001). The plaintiff had been kart racing since 1985 and had signed a release many times in the past when participating in races. In 1994 she was injured while racing, and it was discovered that she had not signed a release for that race. The court, finding in favor of the defendant, stated:

> The death last month of race car legend Dale Earnhardt at the Daytona 500 was tragic, but not unpredictable. Indeed, the sport of automobile racing is a hazardous activity, and drivers on the NASCAR circuit know very well that they risk life and limb every time they get into a race. The same can be said, though to a lesser degree, to be sure, of go-kart racers. As karts have become faster and more maneuverable, the sport has

matured from little more than child's play to a rather dangerous activity. Although the risks of negotiating a race course at high speeds in a vehicle that offers little protection seem obvious, organizers of go-kart races have adopted the practice of requiring participants to sign a release flagging those risks and waiving claims arising from injuries sustained during a race. In this case we confront the question of whether such a release can be enforced against a racer who likely was aware of the requirement that she execute it, but somehow participated in the race without doing so.

. . . .

The question of whether assent to an exculpatory clause can be gleaned from a party's actions is generally a question of fact. . . . Based on the evidence presented, the jury reasonably concluded that it is the custom and practice of the go-kart industry, as well as the Elkhart Grand Prix, to require race participants to execute releases. The jury further reasonably concluded that Beaver was well-aware of this requirement and chose to participate in the 1994 race anyway. Under Indiana law, these facts sufficiently establish Beaver's assent to the release.[68]

In *Tuttle v. TRC Enterprises*, 2007 WL 610638; 830 N.Y.S.2d 854 (N.Y.A.D. 2007), a motorcycle rider sued a cycle park for injuries he sustained when he collided with a utility vehicle being driven by one of the park's employees on a scheduled "fun day" by the park. The court held that the release signed by the rider was void against public policy and not enforceable.

26. In *Tilson v. Russo*, 818 N.Y.S. 2d 311, 2006 N.Y. Slip Op. 05070, the plaintiff was an experienced horse rider who suffered injuries to her left shoulder when a horse named "Lady" bit her. The court of appeals affirmed the lower court's order granting the defendant's motion for summary judgment. The appeals court found that the risk of being bitten was inherent in sporting events involving horses and that the rider was aware of the risks involved in sporting events involving horses.

Workers' Compensation

27. Is a student-athlete an employee for purpose of workers' compensation law? What about a professional athlete? Suppose a student who is on an academic scholarship is injured on the way to a seminar to present research for the school. Would he or she be entitled to workers' compensation benefits as well?

SUGGESTED READINGS AND RESOURCES

Champion, Walter. *The Evolution of a Standard of Care for Injured Athletes: A Review of* Kleinknecht *and Progeny.* 1 Virginia Journal of Sports and Entertainment Law 290 (1999).

Davis, J. H. *"Fixing" The Standard of Care: Motivated Athletes and Medical Malpractice.* 12 American Journal of Trial Advocacy 715 (1988).

---

[68] *Beaver*, 246 F. 3d at 907.

Feinstein, John. *Next Man Up: A Year Behind the Lines in Today's NFL*. Boston: Little, Brown, 2005.

Feinstein, John. *The Punch: One Night, Two Lives, and the Fight That Changed Basketball Forever*. Boston: Little, Brown, 2002.

Fotiades, John M. *You're the Judge! How to Understand Sports, Torts and Courts*. Worcester, MA: Edgeworth & North Books, 1989.

Hanson, Laurel R. *Informed Consent and the Scope of a Physician's Duty of Disclosure*. 77 NORTH DAKOTA LAW REVIEW 71 (2001).

Hecht, Alexander N. *Legal and Ethical Aspects of Sports-Related Concussions: The Merrill Hoge Story*. 12 SETON HALL JOURNAL OF SPORT LAW 1 (2002).

Hollingsworth, Kerry L., Kleinknecht v. Gettysburg College: *What Duty Does a University Owe Its Recruited Athletes?* 19 THURGOOD MARSHALL LAW REVIEW 711 (1994).

Kionka, Edward J. *Torts in a Nutshell*, 3d ed. St. Paul, MN: West Publishing Company, 1999.

Lazaroff, Daniel E. *Torts and Sports: Participant Liability to Co-Participants for Injuries Sustained During Competition*. 7 UNIVERSITY OF MIAMI ENTERTAINMENT AND SPORTS LAW REVIEW 191 (1990).

Mitten, M. J. *Medical Malpractice Liability of Sports Medicine Care Providers for Injury to, or Death of, Athlete*. 33 AMERICAN LAW REPORTS 5TH 619, 1995.

Niles, Stewart E., & West, Roderick K. *In Whose Interest? The Return of the Injured Athlete to Competition*. 25 BRIEF 8 (1996).

Yasser, Ray. *In the Heat of Competition: Tort Liability of One Participant; Why Can't Participants Be Required to be Reasonable?* 5 SETON HALL JOURNAL OF SPORT LAW 253, 1995.

Yasser, Ray. *Torts and Sports: Legal Liability in Professional and Amateur Athletics*. Westport, CT: Quorum Books, 1985.

REFERENCE MATERIALS

Baseball Player's Right to Recover for Baseball-Related Personal Injuries from Nonplayer. 55 AMERICAN LAW REPORTS 4TH 664 (1987).

Caldarone, Justin P. *Professional Team Doctors: Money, Prestige, and Ethical Dilemmas*. 9 SPORTS LAWYERS JOURNAL 131 (2002).

Causes of Action Second Series Database. *Cause of Action for Injury to Sports Spectator*. 20 CAUSES OF ACTION 2D 361 (2004).

Champion, Walter T. *Sports Law: Cases, Documents, and Materials*. New York: Aspen, 2005.

Champion, Walter T. *Sports Law in a Nutshell*, 2d ed. St. Paul, MN: West Group, 2000.

Coleman, P., & Jarvis, R. M. *Hi-Jinks at the Ballpark: Costumed Mascots in the Major Leagues*. 23 CARDOZO LAW REVIEW 1635 (2002).

Colwell, W. B., & Schwartz, B. *Coaches' Liability for Injuries to Student Athletes*. 194 WEST'S EDUCATION LAW REPORT 765 (2005).

Cotton, Doyice J., Wolohan, John T., & Wilde, T. Jesse. *Law for Recreation and Sport Managers*, 2d ed. Dubuque, IA: Kendall/Hunt, 2001.

Cozzillio, Michael J., & Levinstein, Mark S. *Sports Law: Cases and Materials*. Durham, NC: Carolina Academic Press, 1997.

Fitzgerald, Timothy B. *The "Inherent Risk" Doctrine, Amateur Coaching Negligence, and the Goal of Loss Avoidance*. 99 NORTHWESTERN UNIVERSITY LAW REVIEW 889 (2005).

Foley, Allison M. *We, the Parents and Participant, Promise Not to Sue . . . Until There is an Accident. The Ability of High School Students and Their Parents to Waive Liability for Participation in School-Sponsored Athletics.* 37 SUFFOLK UNIVERSITY LAW REVIEW 439 (2004).

Goplerud, C. P., & Terry, N. P. *Allocation of Risk Between Hockey Fans and Facilities: Tort Liability After the Puck Drops.* 38 TULSA LAW REVIEW 445 (2003).

Greenberg, Martin J., & Gray, James T. *Sports Law Practice*, 2d ed. Charlottesville, VA: Lexis Law Publishing, 1998.

Halpin, Ty. *Player Given More Protection Under Baseball's New Slide Rule.* NCAA NEWS, Aug. 16, 2006.

Hiller, Aaron. *Rule 11 and Tort Reform: Myth, Reality, and Legislation.* 18 GEORGETOWN JOURNAL OF LEGAL ETHICS 809 (2005).

Horton, David. *Rethinking Assumption of Risk and Sports Spectators.* 51 UCLA LAW REVIEW 339 (2003).

Hurst, T., & Knight, J. *Coaches' Liability for Athletes' Injuries and Deaths.* 13 SETON HALL JOURNAL OF SPORT LAW 27 (2003).

Jarvis, Robert M. & Coleman, Phyllis. *Batter Up! From the Baseball Field to the Courthouse: Contemporary Issues Facing Baseball Practitioners.* 23 CARDOZO LAW REVIEW 1635 (2002).

Jarvis, Robert M., & Coleman, Phyllis. *Sports Law: Cases and Materials.* St. Paul, MN: West Group, 2005.

Jones, J. C. H., & Stewart, K.G. *Hit Somebody: Hockey Violence, Economics, the Law, and the* Twist *and* McSorley *Decisions.* 12 SETON HALL JOURNAL OF SPORT LAW 165 (2002).

Judge Rules in Tiger Woods' Favour in Yacht Case. Golf Today, http://www.golftoday.co.uk/news/yeartodate/news05/woods43.html.

Kilgannon, Corey. *Tiger Woods's Boat, Privacy, Attracts Plenty of Onlookers.* NEW YORK TIMES, June 18, 2006.

Kimpflen, John. *Injuries to Participants in Games of Amusement or Sports Activities.* 27A AMERICAN JURISPRUDENCE 2D *Entertainment and Sports Law* § 97 (2004).

Kionka, Edward J. *Torts in a Nutshell*, 3d ed. St. Paul, MN: West Publishing, 1999.

Langerman, Samuel. *Contact Sports Injury Cases.* 7 AMERICAN JURISPRUDENCE *Trials* 213 (2003).

McMurray, Erin E. *"I Expected Common Sense to Prevail":* Vowles v. Evans, *Amateur Rugby, and Referee Negligence in the U.K.* 29 BROOKLYN JOURNAL OF INTERNATIONAL LAW 1307 (2004).

Meshbesher, R. I., & Grant, C. M. *Sports Injury—Intentional Acts.* 18 AMERICAN JURISPRUDENCE 2D *Proof of Facts* § 217 (2005).

Miller, Thomas F. *Torts and Sports: Has Michigan Joined the Wrong Team with Ritchie-Gamester?* 48 WAYNE LAW REVIEW 113 (2002).

Mirne, Michael D. *The Brawl at Wrigley: An Analysis of Tort Liability.* 9 SPORTS LAWYERS JOURNAL 95 (2002).

Misinec, M. *When the Game Ends, the Pandemonium Begins: University Liability for Field-Rushing Injuries.* 12 SPORTS LAWYERS JOURNAL 181 (2005).

Mitten, Matthew J. *Medical Malpractice Liability of Sports Medicine Care Providers for Injury to, or Death of, Athlete.* 33 AMERICAN LAW REPORTS 5TH 619 (2005).

Mitten, Matthew J., Davis, Timothy, Smith, Rodney, & Berry, Robert. *Sports Law and Regulation: Cases, Materials, and Problems.* New York: Aspen, 2005.

Nichols, Nick C. *Sports Injury Revolution: Revisiting* Rudy Tomjanovich vs. Cal Sports Inc. dba Los Angeles Lakers. 1985.

Phillips, Jerry, Terry, N., Maraist, F., & McClellan, F. *Tort Law: Cases, Materials, Problems,* 2d ed. Charlottesville, VA: Michie, 1997.

Rigelhaupt, James L. *Liability to Spectator at Baseball Game Who Is Hit by Ball or Injured as Result of Other Hazards of Game.* 91 AMERICAN LAW REPORTS 3D 24 (2005).

Shepard, Jim. *Tiger Woods Publicity Rights Lawsuit Settled.* May 17, 2006, http://powerboat. about.com.

Sims, Andrew. *Panel I: Defamation in Sports.* 15 FORDHAM INTELLECTUAL PROPERTY, MEDIA & ENTERTAINMENT LAW JOURNAL 335 (2005).

Stone, B., Levin, M., & Gillman, R. *Tickets.* In 30 *West's Legal Forms,* 3d ed., § 34.2. St. Paul, MN: Thomson/West, 2004.

Sushner, Marc. *Are Amateur Sports Officials Employees?* 12 SPORTS LAWYERS JOURNAL 123 (2005).

Taxin, Michael F. *The Challenging Evolution of Sports: Why Performance Enhancing Drug Use Should Be Considered in Determining Tort Liability of Professional Athletes.* 14 FORDHAM INTELLECTUAL PROPERTY, MEDIA & ENTERTAINMENT LAW JOURNAL 817 (2004).

Weiler, Paul C., & Roberts, Gary R. *Sports and the Law: Text, Cases, Problems,* 3d ed. St. Paul, MN: Thomson/West, 2004.

Woodlief, Jennifer Lynn. *The Trouble with Charlie.* 9 ENTERTAINMENT AND SPORTS LAW 3 (1991).

Yasser, Raymond L., McCurdy, James R, Goplerud, C. Peter, & Weston, M. *Sports Law: Cases and Materials,* 4th ed. Cincinnati, OH: Anderson, 2000.

CHAPTER 7

DISCRIMINATION

Issues of race, equality, and discrimination are at the forefront of the sports world today, as they have been for the last century. Throughout the history of sports, equality has been a topic of much discussion and debate. For example, the 1936 Olympics in Berlin were supposed to showcase the National Socialist government in Germany and exhibit Aryan supremacy. However, U.S. Olympian Jesse Owens astounded the world as he won four gold medals in one day. Adolf Hitler refused to shake hands with any black athletes at the 1936 Olympics.

Dodger great Jackie Robinson broke Major League Baseball's (MLB) color barrier in 1949.[1] His number, 42, is the only retired number that hangs in every ballpark in the major leagues. Robinson was also a standout football player at UCLA. Prior to Robinson's breaking into the MLB, African American players were allowed to showcase their talents only in the Negro Leagues.[2] The National Football League was integrated from 1920 to 1934. However, in 1934, NFL owners entered into a gentlemen's agreement banning all black players. The NFL was once again integrated when Kenny Washington, also from UCLA, played with the Los Angeles Rams. Washington had once been a roommate of Jackie Robinson's at UCLA. Chuck Cooper was the first African American to be selected in the NBA draft when he was chosen by the Boston Celtics in 1950. Bill Russell was the first African American coach in major professional sports when he became the head coach of the Boston Celtics in 1966. However, despite winning multiple championships with the Celtics and playing on the U.S. Olympic basketball team in 1955, Russell spoke of how he was discriminated against when he wanted to move his family into an all-white neighborhood in Boston.

The unequal treatment of women, minorities, and disabled persons in the sports world has been addressed by the court system and legislation in recent years. Equality in sports presents a paradoxical picture today. Michelle Wie, a 16-year-old Korean girl, is playing golf on the PGA Tour, whereas in 2003 Martha Burk challenged the Augusta National Golf Club over its policy of excluding women

---

[1] J. Gordon Hylton, *American Civil Rights Law and the Legacy of Jackie Robinson*, 8 MARQ. SPORTS L.J. 387 (1998).

[2] Alfred D. Matthewson, *Major League Baseball's Monopoly Power and Negro Leagues*, 35 AM. BUS. L.J. 291 (1998).

as members.[3] Millions of white fans cheer African American student-athletes every year, but major college football programs continue to hire minority head coach candidates at a very slow pace. Sylvester Croom became the first African American coach in the history of the Southeastern Conference (SEC) when he was named head coach at Mississippi State University in 2003. Entering the 2009 college football season in the Football Bowl Subdivision (FBS), there were only seven African American coaches for 200 schools.[4] By comparison, 6 of the 32 NFL franchises had African American coaches. In 2002 Vonetta Flowers became the first African American athlete to win a gold medal at the Winter Olympics, participating in the two-person bobsled. Major strides have been made for disabled individuals participating in sports with the passage of the Americans with Disabilities Act of 1990 and the *PGA Tour v. Martin* decision discussed later in this chapter. Marv Levy, a Harvard graduate and former coach of the Buffalo Bills, was hired as the Bills' general manager and vice president in 2006 at the stellar age of 80. The Age Discrimination Act of 1967 prohibits discrimination against workers over 40 years old.

The topics of discrimination and equality in sports comprise a plethora of issues. This chapter focuses on the laws prohibiting discrimination and those who have challenged or used the laws in an attempt to combat discrimination based on sex, race, disability, religion, age, and national origin. Race is also discussed in Chapter 1, viewed in light of how it has played a role in the development of sports. Equal opportunity for women in sports is discussed more fully in Chapter 9, "Gender Equity and Women in Sports."

RACIAL DISCRIMINATION

A combination of statutes, judicial decisions, and interpretive regulations governs racial discrimination in the employment process. The difficulties involving race in society have produced much legislation and numerous court decisions. Plaintiffs can seek to remedy racial discrimination using a myriad of different legal theories, such as the following:

- The Fourteenth Amendment of the U.S. Constitution
- Title VII of the Civil Rights Act of 1964 as amended by the Civil Rights Act of 1991 (42 U.S.C § 2000e)
- The Civil Rights Act of 1866 (42 U.S.C § 1981)
- The Civil Rights Act of 1871 (42 U.S.C. § 1983)
- State statutes and constitutions and local legislation

Title VII of the Civil Rights Act of 1964 prohibits job discrimination against employees and applicants on the basis of race, color, natural origin, religion, and sex:

---

[3] Teri Thompson and Michael O'Keeffe, *Five Years After Martha Burk's Protest, Augusta Hasn't Changed*, New York Daily News, April 12, 2008.

[4] Ronnie Turner, *College Football: Minorities Trying to Break into Top Jobs*, The Salt Lake Tribune, June 22, 2009; *BCA Seeks More Minority Head Coaches in College Football*, Sports Business Daily, November 13, 2008; *also see* Neil Forrester, *The Elephant in the Locker Room: Does the National Football League Discriminate in the Hiring of Head Coaches?*, 34 McGeorge L. Rev. 877 (2003).

It shall be an unlawful employment practice for an employer—

(1) to fail or refuse to hire or to discharge any individual, or otherwise to discriminate against any individual with respect to his compensation, terms, conditions, or privileges of employment, because of such individual's race, color, religion, sex, or national origin; or

(2) to limit, segregate, or classify his employees or applicants for employment in any way which would deprive or tend to deprive any individual of employment opportunities or otherwise adversely affect his status as an employee, because of such individual's race, color, religion, sex, or national origin.[5]

Title VII applies to employers who have 15 or more employees, labor unions that operate hiring halls, employment agencies, and state and local governments. It has been referred to as "the single most important piece of legislation that has helped to shape and define employment rights in this country."[6] The Civil Rights Act of 1991 amended Title VII in many respects, including giving plaintiffs the right to seek compensatory and punitive damages in intentional discrimination cases.

The Equal Employment Opportunity Commission (EEOC) is the federal agency that enforces the federal laws prohibiting discrimination and it also provides oversight of all federal and equal employment opportunity regulations, practices, and policies. An individual alleging discrimination under Title VII must file a claim with the EEOC before he or she can bring a lawsuit against his or her employer. The EEOC can investigate the allegations and make an attempt to settle the case between the parties. If no settlement is reached, the EEOC has the authority to file a lawsuit against the employer on the employee's behalf. If the EEOC decides not to bring a lawsuit or decides not to investigate the case, the individual asserting discrimination may file a lawsuit on his or her own initiative against the employer.

Title VII covers both intentional and unintentional discrimination. Intentional discrimination by an employer is commonly referred to as *disparate treatment discrimination*.[7] Disparate treatment is the most common form of discrimination claim and can be difficult to prove. A typical disparate treatment case could involve an individual's claim that an employer treated him or her less favorably based on an impermissible factor such as race, age, or sex. For an unsuccessful applicant to prove a prima facie case of disparate treatment discrimination, the plaintiff must show the following: (1) he or she is a member of a protected class, (2) he or she applied and was qualified for the position, (3) he or she was rejected, and (4) the position remained open and the employer continued to seek applicants.[8] A protected class has been defined as "a class of persons with identifiable characteristics who historically have been victimized by discriminatory treatment for certain purposes. Depending on the context, these characteristics include age, color, gender, national origin, race, and religion."[9] Once the plaintiff has established a prima facie case, he or she has met the initial burden of proof. The burden of going forward then shifts to the employer, who must provide a legitimate, nondiscriminatory reason for the employment decision.[10] If the employer meets this burden, then the plaintiff must prove that this stated reason was merely pretextual.

---

[5] 42 U.S.C.A §2000e-2(a)1.

[6] Dawn D. Bennett-Alexander & Laura B. Pincus, Employment Law For Business (1995).

[7] Jackson v. University of New Haven, 228 F. Supp. 2d 156 (D.Conn. 2002).

[8] McDonnell Douglas Corp. v. Green, 411 U.S. 792, 802 (1973).

[9] Frank B. Cross and Roger LeRoy Miller, *The Legal Environment of Business: Text and Cases, Ethical, Regulatory, Global and E-Commerce Issues*, South-Western College/West; 7th Edition, 2008, p. 710.

[10] *Id.*, 802–04.

Discrimination can also take the form of *disparate impact discrimination*, which occurs when an employer adopts a practice or policy that seems neutral on its face but is shown to have an adverse impact on a protected class. In these types of cases a plaintiff alleges that an employment practice by the defendant "in fact falls more harshly on one group than another and cannot be justified by business necessity."[11] If a person can prove disparate impact discrimination, then it is not necessary to prove intent.[12] Examples of practices that may be subject to a disparate impact challenge include written tests, height and weight requirements, and subjective procedures, such as interviews. Many disparate impact cases are brought as class actions. Most often, proving this form of discrimination involves statistical proof about the employer's practices. The EEOC has promulgated quantitative guidelines to determine if employee selection and promotion rules have a disproportionate impact. These guidelines state that if the observed promotion or selection rate for any group is less than four-fifths of the rate for the group with the highest rate, then disproportionate impact will be assumed.

> A selection rate for any race, sex, or ethnic group which is less than four-fifths (or eighty percent) of the rate for the group with the highest rate will generally be regarded by the Federal enforcement agencies as evidence of adverse impact, while a greater than four-fifths rate will generally not be regarded by the Federal enforcement agencies as evidence of adverse impact.[13]

An employer can assert several defenses to an employment discrimination action. The first defense for the employer is to assert that discrimination did not take place or that the plaintiff has failed to meet the burden of proof. The employer can also attempt to justify discrimination on the basis of business necessity, a bona fide occupational qualification (BFOQ), a seniority system, or even employee misconduct. The business necessity defense can be a viable defense to disparate impact discrimination if the employer can show a connection between the business decision and job preference.

No decisions concerning employment on the basis of race, religion, age, sex, or national origin will be considered discrimination if they are based on a bona fide occupational qualification (BFOQ).[14] The BFOQ clause has been narrowly construed by courts, and the burden rests on the employer in asserting such a defense.[15] A BFOQ has been defined as follows: "a qualification that is reasonably necessary to the normal operation or essence of an employer's businesses."[16] For example, it may be permissible to set an age level for employees of fire and police departments to ensure safety.

An employer may also defend a discrimination case on the basis of a fair seniority system. Differences in employment conditions that result from such a system are permissible as long as there is no intent to discriminate. The "after-acquired evidence" doctrine can in some cases, operate as a defense to an employment discrimination lawsuit. If, during the process of a discrimination lawsuit, the employer finds evidence of an employee's misconduct that would have caused the employer to fire the employee, this fact can under certain circumstances, provide a defense to an employment discrimination action.

---

[11] International Brotherhood of Teamsters v. U.S., 431 U.S. 324, 336 n.15; 97 S. Ct. 1843; 52 L. Ed. 2d 396 (1977).
[12] Griggs v. Duke Power, 401 U.S. 424 (1971).
[13] 29 C.F.R. § 1607.4(d).
[14] 42 U.S.C.A. § 2000e-2(e).
[15] Grant v. General Motors, 908 F.2d 1303 (6th Cir. 1990).
[16] Frank v. United Airlines, Inc., 216 F.3d 845, 853 (9th Cir. 2000).

There have been many discrimination cases dealing with athletes from all sports. Many African American ballplayers played in the Negro Leagues before the color barrier in baseball was broken by Jackie Robinson. In 1993, MLB created a plan that provided medical coverage to former Negro League players. In 1997, it adopted a supplemental income plan that provided an annual payment of $10,000 to eligible players ("Negro League Supplemental Income Plan"). Individuals who had played in the Negro Leagues prior to 1948, were eligible for such payments. These two plans are referred to collectively as the "Negro League Plans." Subsequently, a group of Caucasian and Latino ballplayers sued MLB, claiming violation of Title VII by excluding them from medical and supplemental income plans devised for former Negro League players and also sued for battery claiming they were subjected to dangerous drugs without informed consent.[17]

As mentioned previously, there has been much debate about the hiring of minorities at both the professional and college levels of coaching. Super lawyer Johnnie Cochran brought this issue to light in a letter he sent to NFL Commissioner Paul Tagliabue about the state of minority hiring for coaching and front office positions. Shortly after the letter was received by the NFL, the league issued guidelines regarding its policy of interviewing and hiring NFL coaches.

In 2003, the Detroit Lions were looking for a head coach and hired former San Francisco 49'ers head coach Steve Mariucci. During the hiring process, the Lions failed to follow the league policy put in place after Johnnie Cochran's letter to the commissioner. Mariucci was the only candidate interviewed for the job, and no minority candidates were interviewed. (The Lions stated that five minority candidates had turned down interviews.) The league subsequently fined the Detroit Lions' president, Matt Millen, $200,000 for failing to follow league policy during the hiring process.[18] Gene Upshaw, executive director of the NFL Players Association (NFLPA), stated: "The Detroit Lions gave mere lip service to the agreed-upon minority hiring process, treating it almost as if a nuisance to their hiring of Steve Mariucci. The minority candidates were never given a fair chance to interview. In this case the Lions' position is indefensible." Do you agree with this policy? Should the NFL be able to require teams to interview minority candidates for all head coaching positions? For further study of the issue, see Patrick K. Thornton, *The Legacy of Johnnie Cochran, Jr.: The National Football League's Rooney Rule*, 33 THURGOOD MARSHALL LAW REVIEW 77 (2007).

SEX DISCRIMINATION

Title VII also prohibits discrimination based on sex. To establish a prima facie case of sex discrimination under Title VII, a plaintiff must prove that (1) she was a member of a protected class; (2) she was qualified for the position; (3) she was discharged or otherwise subjected to an adverse employment action; and (4) others, similarly situated but not of the protected class, were treated more favorably.[19] There can also be cases of reverse sex discrimination as well. For instance, in *Medcalf v. Trustees of University of Pennsylvania*, 71 Fed. Appx. 924 (3rd Cir. 2003), a crew coach alleged he had been the subject of reverse discrimination when the defendant failed to hire him as the women's crew coach. A jury returned a verdict in his favor, and the University of Pennsylvania appealed.

---

[17] Moran v. Selig, 447 F. 3d 748 (9th Cir. 2006).

[18] *PRO-FOOTBALL; Lions Fined Over Minority Hiring*, The New York Times, July 25, 2003.

[19] Peirick v. Indiana University-Purdue University Indianapolis Athletics Department, 2005 WL 1518663 at *8 (S.D. Ind. 2005).

Bernice Gera wanted to be a major league umpire. Only one thing stood in her way: she was a woman. In Case 7-1, *New York State Division of Human Rights v. New York-Pennsylvania Professional Baseball League*, 36 A.D.2d 364 (N.Y. App. Div. 1971), the issue was whether being a male was a bona fide occupational qualification for the position umpire.

CASE 7-1   *New York State Division of Human Rights v. New York-Pennsylvania Professional Baseball League*

---

36 A.D.2d 364 (N.Y. App. Div. 1971)

MARSH, Justice.

OPINION

Petitioners, New York-Pennsylvania Professional Baseball League and Vincent McNamara, its President, and the National Association of Professional Baseball Leagues and Phillip Piton, its President, in a proceeding pursuant to section 298 Executive Law, seek review and reversal of the decisions and orders entered by the Commissioner of the State Division of Human Rights and the Human Rights Appeal Board on the complaint of Bernice Gera. The orders of the Commissioner, affirmed with slight modification by the Appeal Board, determined, after a hearing, that petitioners had barred complainant from employment as an umpire because of her sex in violation of Sec. 296, Executive Law and directed petitioners to cease and desist such unlawful discriminatory practice and to take certain affirmative action with respect to New York teams and leagues, including the establishment of new physical standards which shall have a reasonable relation to the requirements of the duties of umpires and which do not discriminate against women as a group and other groups having smaller average stature than American men. The further direction was made that petitioners reconsider complainant's application for employment as an umpire with reference to such new physical standards.

The record on which the decision and orders under review were based reveals that the complainant, a female, was born June 14, 1931, is 5' 2" in height and weighs 129 pounds. She had played on her high school softball team, coached Little League teams and umpired games sponsored by the American Legion, Catholic Youth Organization, YMCA and the New York Police Department as well as at the Bridgeton, N.J. Semi-Professional Tournament and the National Baseball Congress, a league composed of Semi-Professional teams in Wichita, Kansas. Early in 1967, using the first name 'Bernie' and concealing her sex, she made an application for admission to the Al Somers School for umpires setting forth her age as 35, weight as 144 pounds and height as 5' 3". The Al Somers School was approved, supervised and subsidized by the Baseball

Umpire Development Program, which was organized under major league sponsorship in December 1964, five months after the enactment of the Federal Civil Rights Act, to establish standards for minor league umpires. Umpires hired by the various minor league presidents, subject to the approval of the President of the National Association, were required to be approved by the Baseball Umpire Development Program in order to secure payment of major league subsidies. The Baseball Umpire Development Program established as qualifications for umpires an age limit of 35, minimum height of 5' 10", minimum weight of 170 pounds, graduation from high school and from an approved umpire school.

Despite her obvious lack of physical qualifications required by the Umpire Development Program, the Somers School upon receiving complainant's application advised her by letter that she would be welcome to join the next class the following year. Upon telephoning the school to advise them of her sex she was told by Somers that since she had raised an important policy matter it would have to be discussed with the Administrator of the Baseball Umpire Development Program and she would be further advised. No additional acknowledgment was received concerning her application to the Somers School.

In the summer of 1968 complainant wrote the petitioner, McNamara, President of the New York-Pennsylvania League, requesting an application for an umpiring position without setting forth her qualifications. In response McNamara outlined various objections to hiring a female umpire and concluded: 'It is our professional opinion that it would be unwise to expose you or any other lady to situations such as those stated previously above.'

Subsequently complainant instituted a proceeding against the New York-Pennsylvania League and McNamara. While the proceeding was pending McNamara mailed an umpire questionnaire to complainant which she returned properly listing her age, height and weight. McNamara thereupon mailed a contract to her which she signed and returned and which he transmitted with his signature to petitioner Piton as President of the National Association for his approval, stating however to Piton, that he tendered the contract even though he did not consider complainant qualified, because of his having been importuned by the complainant and the Human Rights Commission. He said further that he felt that he had to execute the contract despite her lack of qualifications knowing that Piton would have to make the final decision. Piton disapproved the contract advising complainant that the National Association was guided by the standards established by the Umpire Development Program having to do with height, weight and age and that based upon her failure 'to meet the physical requirements for admission to the Umpire Development Program and for employment by the National Association

Leagues I have no alternative but to disapprove and invalidate your proposed contract.'

While as President of the National Association, Piton was required to approve all player and umpire contracts in the minor leagues, he testified that he wasn't sure he knew of the required standards as to height, weight and age prior to the summer of 1967 when complainant first made known her interest in umpiring in professional baseball.

Sec. 296, Executive Law provides:

'1. It shall be an unlawful discriminatory practice:

(a) For an employer, because of the age, race, creed, color, national origin or sex of any individual, to refuse to hire or employ or to bar or to discharge from employment such individual or to discriminate against such individual in compensation or in terms, conditions or privileges of employment. . . .

6. It shall be an unlawful discriminatory practice for any person to aid, abet, incite, compel or coerce the doing of any of the acts forbidden under this article or to attempt to do so.'

Whatever policy organized baseball may conceive to be in its best interests must yield to a public policy established in the interests of the whole of society as evidence[d] by the statutory law of the State.

Petitioners contend that the 'bona fide occupational qualification' exception to the law (Executive Law s 296, subd. 1(d) and Civil Rights Act of 1964, s 703, subd. (e); tit. 42 U.S.C. s 2000e-2(e)) is applicable herein and permits restricting the hiring of umpires to those of the male sex. This contention is unsound. Recent court decisions have required that this exception be affirmatively proved by the party claiming it. The courts have given this provision a narrow construction. In Weeks v. Southern Bell Telephone & Telegraph Co., the Court of Appeals for the Fifth Circuit stated at page 235 of 408 F.2d:

'(W)e hold that in order to rely on the bona fide occupational qualification exception an employer has the burden of proving that he had reasonable cause to believe, that is, a factual basis for believing, that all or substantially all women would be unable to perform safely and efficiently the duties of the job involved.'

Petitioners have not introduced evidence to support a factual basis for belief that women are not qualified for the job of a professional baseball umpire. Essentially the only evidence on this point is that the job would require some physical strain, travel and loss of weight, with a possibility of some physical injury. In the Weeks case, supra, the court stated that characterizing a job as 'strenuous' does not meet the burden required to show a bona fide occupational qualification and few jobs of a strenuous character do not involve some risk of physical injury.

Further support for the proposition that the bona fide occupational qualification exception does not apply to the position in question is found in the guidelines set down by the Equal Employment Opportunity Commission construing this provision. (See 16 C.F.R. Sec. 1604.1(a)). The courts have held that such guidelines are entitled to 'great deference.' Those guidelines have construed the bona fide occupational qualification exception very narrowly. They reject the proposition that an employer can refuse 'to hire an individual based on stereotyped characterizations of the sexes.' (29 C.F.R. Sec. 1604.1(a)(ii)). According to the Commission the exception is primarily to apply 'where it is necessary for the purpose of authenticity or genuineness . . . i.e., an actor or actress.' (29 C.F.R. Sec. 1604.1(a)(iv)(2)).

Significantly, and quite in opposition to the position now asserted by petitioners that being of the male sex is a bona fide occupational qualification for the hiring of umpires and that as a practical business policy baseball should not be required to hire female umpires, Bernard Deary, Administrator of the Umpire Development Program testified that a female applicant meeting the age, height and weight requirements of the Umpire Development Program and a graduate of an approved course would be recommended to the leagues for hiring as an umpire. Petitioner Piton as President of the National Association also testified that sex was no factor in his decision to disapprove complainant's contract.

In the light of the foregoing it would appear that it has not been established that being of the male sex is a bona fide occupational qualification for an umpire or that, as a matter of policy, hiring of umpires should be restricted to males.

It is uncontroverted that complainant failed to meet the height and weight standards required by petitioners and that such standards bar all but less than one percent of women for consideration of employment as professional baseball umpires. Our concern therefore is with whether the record supports the Commissioner's findings that petitioners have not established that these standards bear a reasonable relation to the requirements of the job.

Various witnesses for petitioners testified that the physical qualifications for a professional baseball umpire require that he be 5' 10" tall and 170 pounds in weight. Testimony was given that these standards were 'born of the judgment of men with long experience in professional baseball', that an umpire 'must be a person who commands respect of big fellows, big men', also to the increased size of professional baseball catchers, the possibility of confrontation with big athletes, physical strain, travel conditions, and length of games. While these factors are entitled to be taken into consideration in the hiring of an umpire, none of them, either individually or collectively, justify an inflexible standard of 5' 10" and 170 pounds. Despite testimony that very little deviation was permitted from these standards, considerable evidence appears to the contrary. This is not to say that these standards were created with the intent to prevent complainant or other women from receiving consideration for employment. Rather, it is meant that the failure to meet these standards should not be considered a Per se cause to bar such employment in the light of the uncontroverted evidence that such standards are inherently discriminatory. While undoubtedly height and weight are important in judging a person's ability to stand physical strain, it has not been demonstrated that persons 5' 10" and over are the only people capable of withstanding such strain. The evidence indicates that in the past, professional baseball umpires in both the major and minor leagues, including the petitioner McNamara, the present Administrator of the Baseball Umpire Development Program Bernard Deary, and the legendary Bill Klem of major league fame, failed to meet the standard height of 5' 10" or weight of 170 pounds with no indication of any deficiency in the quality of their performance. It would appear therefore, that the findings of the Commissioner were proper, and that the standards applied by the petitioners, inherently discriminatory against women, have not been justified in the record. The finding of discrimination based upon sex was a logical conclusion and is supported by the record as a whole.

Two other requirements were allegedly applied by petitioners to bar complainant's employment: age and graduation from an approved umpire training school. In view of the conflicting evidence produced as to the consistency of the application of these standards, the Commissioner's findings of discrimination are supported by the record. Moreover, there is no evidence that complainant would not have the knowledge, ability and skill to qualify for an umpire position. In fact the evidence demonstrated considerable previous experience in semi-professional, American Legion and youth organization baseball as well as graduation from an umpiring school from which organized baseball had taken umpires.

The finding that petitioner McNamara discriminated against complainant because she was a woman and by not affording her equal treatment with that accorded to male applicants is clearly established by the evidence. The finding that he failed to send complainant an application for an umpiring position is not inconsistent with the finding in the proceeding against the National Association and Piton which states that such an application was sent. The sending of this application by McNamara while this proceeding was pending, under all the circumstances presented was an equivocal act from which the Commissioner could draw various conclusions especially in light of the testimony of Piton that McNamara's 'decision to hire' the complainant was merely an attempt to throw it in the lap of his superiors. This type of action appears to be one of those 'subtleties of conduct' that are important factors in cases of alleged discrimination and therefore a court should not attempt to substitute its judgment for that of the Commissioner. . . .

Source: Courtesy of Westlaw; reprinted with permission.

Problem 7-1

Mary Johnson has loved hockey all of her life. She has been a hockey referee in many semi-professional leagues for the past seven years. She has received outstanding performance reviews for her work as a referee in the leagues she has worked. She now desires to be a referee in the Instructional Hockey League (IHL). She has filed an application for employment but the league has a rule that it does not allow women referees due to safety concerns for players and referees alike. Ms. Johnson is 5' 2" and weighs 105 pounds. Johnson filed a lawsuit against the IHL based on discrimination seeking employment with the league. What defenses does the league have against the lawsuit? How would a court rule in this case?

RELIGIOUS DISCRIMINATION

Sports and religion have always intermingled. For example, Billy Sunday was a well-known preacher in baseball circles in the 1890s.[20] A former Major League player, Sunday played eight seasons for Chicago, Philadelphia, and Pittsburgh and batted .248 while playing in 499 games. In 1891 he quit baseball to devote his time and energy to the Young Men's Christian Association (YMCA). He was an ordained preacher in the Presbyterian Church.[21]

Many athletes have exhibited sincere religious faith. The great Sandy Koufax refused to pitch in the first game of the 1965 World Series because it fell on the Jewish holiday Yom Kippur.[22]

---

[20] James v. Chalmers, *ISAIAH'S MANTLE.; Billy Sunday and the Fierce Prophets of Olden Times*, The New York Times, April 16, 1915.

[21] *For further study see*, Roger A. Bruns, *Preacher: Billy Sunday and Big-Time American Evangelism*, University of Illinois Press, 2002.

[22] William C. Rhodren, *Sports of the Times; Presence of Koufax Puts the Cap on a Great Day*, The New York Times, October 11, 2004.

Muhammad Ali refused to be drafted for the Vietnam War because of his religious beliefs and was subsequently stripped of his heavyweight title. NBA player Shawn Bradley followed his faith's calling on a two-year mission, thereby delaying the potential earnings of a career in the NBA. The great British track athlete Eric Liddell refused to run on Sunday during the 1924 Olympics because of his religious beliefs.[23] His story was turned into an Academy Award–winning movie, *Chariots of Fire*. Hank Greenberg was a great ballplayer for the Detroit Tigers and suffered much religious persecution during World War II because of anti-Semitism.[24]

In 1996, Mahmoud Abdul-Rauf of the Denver Nuggets was suspended by the NBA for his refusal to stand for the national anthem. He stated he could not participate in the anthem because the Koran forbade any participation in "nationalistic ritualism." He also said, "The American flag represents freedom, liberty and justice for the majority of us. The foundation of our country was built with bricks of racism, discrimination, segregation, deception, oppression—and our flag represents not only the foundation, but the first, second, third . . ., 19th and 20th floors of current freedom, liberty, racism and discrimination."[25] For most of the 1995–1996 season the Nuggets allowed him to stay in the locker room during the anthem. In March, fans began to call local radio stations and expressed their outrage regarding his failure to stand. The Nuggets then reversed their decision and required Mahmoud Abdul-Rauf to be present at the national anthem and to stand. The NBA eventually suspended him without pay on March 11, 1996, which would cost him about $30,000 a game. After a one-game suspension, Abdul-Rauf agreed to stand and pray silently as the anthem was played.[26]

Conflicts between religion and sports have also arisen at the high school and collegiate levels. These have included issues such as the scheduling of practices and games, the conducting of prayer sessions before games, the wearing of religious headwear during competition, and grooming policies.[27] The National Collegiate Athletic Association (NCAA) clashed with the concept of religious freedom regarding NCAA Rule 9.2. The rule was an attempt to do away with religious displays by players such as kneeling, removing their helmets, and crossing themselves in the end zone following a score. Liberty University, its football coach, and four of its players filed a lawsuit against the NCAA.[28] The lawsuit asked the court to determine whether the NCAA rule restricted the free exercise of religion. The plaintiff dismissed the lawsuit after the NCAA stated that praying was still permitted under the rules.[29] The First Amendment to the U.S. Constitution protects student-athletes from a state-endorsed religion. The Establishment Clause to the First Amendment "protects every individual's right to freedom of belief while the Free Exercise Clause protects the individual's freedom to practice his [or her] religion."[30]

---

[23] Barbara, Basler, *Chinese Grave's Secret: A Famed Runner Rests Here*, The New York Times, December 2, 1990.

[24] *For further study see*, Hank Greenberg and Ira Berkow, *Hank Greenberg: The Story of My Life*, Benchmark Press, 2001.

[25] *Pledging Allegiance to Flag*, Ariz. Republic, Apr. 28, 1996, at C14.

[26] Jason Diamos, *BASKETBALL; Abdul-Rauf's Plan: Stand, Pray and Play*, The New York Times, March 15, 1996.

[27] For a general discussion of the subject, see Scott C. Idleman, *Religious Freedom and the Interscholastic Athlete*, 12 Marq. Sports L. Rev. 295 (2001). *Also see* Gil Fired & Lisa Bradley, *Applying the First Amendment to Prayer in a Public University Locker Room: An Athlete's and Coach's Perspective*, 4 Marq. Sports L.J. 301 (1994).

[28] *SPORTS PEOPLE: COLLEGE FOOTBALL; School Sues Over Game Player*, The New York Times, September 1, 1995.

[29] Rajiv Chandrasekaran, *A Reverse in the End Zone: After Liberty's Challenge, NCAA Clarifies Rule, Allows Praying After Touchdowns*, Wash. Post, Sept. 2; 1995. *Also see, Does the NCAA's Football Rule 9.2 Impede the Free Exercise of Religion on the Playing Field?*, 16 Loyola L. & Ent. L. J. 445 (1995).

[30] Malnak v. Yogi, 440 F. Supp. 1284, 1316, n. 20 (D.C. N.J. 1977).

In *Keller v. Gardener Community Consolidated Grade School District*, 552 F. Supp. 512 (D.C. Ill., 1982), an elementary school student and his father challenged a rule that required attendance at practice in order to "suit up" in the game. Eleven-year-old Joseph Keller missed practice because he attended religion classes scheduled by the Catholic church at the same time basketball practice was held. The coach failed to make an exception for Joseph, and a lawsuit followed. In finding in favor of the defendant school district, the court stated:

> The only question remaining is whether the coach's rule violates the plaintiff's right to freedom of religion. It has long been established that the First Amendment rights are not absolute, and this includes particularly the right to the free exercise of religion. . . .
>
> Following this balancing approach, we first must consider the sincerity of the religious claim being advanced by Keller and the degree to which the challenged regulation interferes with religious belief or a vital religious practice based upon a belief. It is common knowledge that a catechism class such as that the plaintiff attends is a program of religious instruction, the purpose of which is to teach Catholic children the fundamental principles of their religion. Although an integral part of a Catholic's practices may be to learn the laws and rituals of the Catholic faith, and during certain stages of a practitioner's life the church may require a particular degree of knowledge of the religion, it is not mandatory that a fifth-grade child attend a formal catechism class. It would be sufficient for the student to learn the tenets of the Catholic faith directly from a priest or from some other member of the church community. Further, the actual teaching of the religious doctrine, while subject to variance among different diocese[s], is substantially the same.
>
> Keller admits that catechism classes are conducted by another Catholic church in the vicinity of the Gardner School District, which do not differ materially from the catechism classes offered in Dwight, and which do not pose scheduling conflicts with the school's basketball program. His conduct in attending catechism classes only in Dwight is a matter of personal preference stemming from his familiarity with a particular catechism class and its teachers. It cannot be said that the plaintiff has been denied the opportunity to participate in scheduled games because of conduct mandated by religious belief or necessity. Keller has not established an interference with his free exercise of religion, but only with his selection of a church in which it may be pursued. At the most, he has established only an excusable and de minimus burden upon his religious practice. . . .
>
> We must also pause to consider, as part of this balancing process, the impact on the basketball program of an alternative to the current school policy. An alternative scheduling arrangement would not be appropriate because the school could not successfully pre-arrange a practice schedule that would accommodate the religious education class of each of the many participants in the athletic program. And it would be unfair to allow a special exemption to the attendance rule for the benefit of those students who opt to observe their special religious classes, while disallowing similar exemptions for attending other activities to students who may not be adherents to a particular religious organization. Either alternative would be unworkable and ultimately would defeat the athletic program. Clearly the burden imposed on the school if it were forced to change its rule to accommodate Keller is considerable. . . .
>
> The plaintiff has failed to establish the uniqueness of the catechism program in Dwight, Illinois, and as a result he is unable to show that the burden on his free exercise of religion, if there is an interference at all, outweighs the burden that would be imposed upon the school were it to change its policy regarding unexcused absences. Balancing the interests involved, it appears unreasonable for the school to have to accommodate its basketball program to the petitioner's personal schedule or preference. . . .[31]

---

[31] *Id.* at 514–16.

In Case 7-2, *Johnson v. National Football League*, 1999 WL 892938 (S.D.N.Y. 1999), an NFL player asserted that he had experienced religious and racial discrimination under Title VII of the Civil Rights Act of 1964.

CASE 7-2 *Johnson v. National Football League*

1999 WL 892938 (S.D.N.Y. 1999)

CHIN, D.J.

In this *pro se* employment discrimination case, plaintiff J. Edwards Johnson V, a/k/a Yacub Abdul-Matin, contends that he was discriminated against because of his race and religion by the National Football League (the "NFL") and the other defendants in this case. In particular, Johnson—who played offensive tackle at the University of Miami for five years—contends that defendants violated his rights under Title VII of the Civil Rights Act of 1964, . . . and the Civil Rights Act of 1866, . . . by refusing to "employ" him as a football player in the NFL purportedly because of his race and religion and certain statements he had made concerning the subjects of race and religion.

Defendants NFL, Paul Tagliabue (Commissioner of the NFL), the Atlanta Falcons, Taylor Smith (President of the Atlanta Falcons), the NFL Europe League, and the President of the NFL Europe League (the "NFL Defendants") move . . . to . . . dismiss the complaint for failure to state a claim upon which relief may be granted or, alternatively, for summary judgment dismissing the complaint. Also named as defendants in this action are the Exclusive Sports Network, ESPN/ESPN 2, and the President of ESPN/ESPN 2 (the "ESPN Defendants"). The ESPN Defendants have not appeared in the action.

The NFL Defendants contend that the complaint should be dismissed because (1) plaintiff failed to file suit within ninety days after receipt of a right-to-sue letter from the Equal Employment Opportunity Commission (the "EEOC") and (2) the complaint fails to allege a viable claim of discrimination against the NFL Defendants under Title VII or § 1981. Alternatively, the NFL Defendants seek dismissal of the claims against the individual NFL Defendants on the grounds that individual liability is not available under Title VII and plaintiff has failed to allege the personal involvement required for individual liability under § 1981. Finally, the NFL defendants contend, in the alternative, that they are entitled to summary judgment.

For the reasons that follow, the motion to dismiss is granted in part and denied in part. The alternative motion for summary judgment is denied. In addition, the claims against the ESPN Defendants are dismissed *sua sponte*.

Summary of the Case

The facts alleged in the complaint are assumed to be true for purposes of this motion.

Johnson, who is African-American, played football for the University of Miami in Miami, Florida for five years. He started as an offensive tackle and also played defensive lineman. He had some difficulties, including suffering a broken arm and being suspended for missing classes, but he also had some success.

While at the University of Miami, Johnson converted to Islam as a religion and became a Muslim. A public controversy arose because of his involvement in the Islamic religion, and Johnson wrote two articles about race and religion that were published in the university newspaper. These articles, according to Johnson, were not well received by his coaches.

Before the start of the 1997–1998 college football season, Johnson was listed among potential draft selections for offensive linemen for the NFL. Johnson was interested in being drafted and he made that interest known to all the NFL teams. The Miami Dolphins invited Johnson for a "try-out" about a week before the draft, which was to be held on April 18 and 19, 1998. Other teams expressed some interest in Johnson as well.

On April 19, 1998, on a telecast of ESPN 2, a "ticker," or "scroll," at the bottom of the screen reported that Johnson had been drafted by the Atlanta Falcons in the fourth round. The ticker continued to report this information for half an hour. It was then reported, however, that the Atlanta Falcons had not drafted Johnson, but that they had selected a different player. The NFL Defendants contend that the ESPN 2 ticker was simply wrong and that the error was inadvertent. Johnson contends that he was in fact drafted and that the Atlanta Falcons then changed their minds.

Johnson was not signed by the Atlanta Falcons or any other NFL team. Johnson contends that immediately after the draft, his agent was contacted by the New York Giants, who initially expressed some interest in him but then changed their minds. At one point the Washington Redskins tentatively agreed to interview Johnson, but then "back[ed] out," because of "what had happened in Miami."

Johnson eventually filed a charge of discrimination with the EEOC. The EEOC did not address the charge on the merits, but issued Johnson a right-to-sue letter on March 26, 1999.

Johnson commenced this action by submitting his *pro se* complaint to the Court's *Pro Se* Office on June 23, 1999. The complaint was formally docketed by the Clerk of the Court on August 3, 1999.

This motion followed.

Discussion

A. The Timeliness of the Action

The NFL Defendants argue that the complaint must be dismissed because plaintiff failed to file his action within ninety days after receipt of a right-to-sue letter from the EEOC. The argument is rejected, as a factual matter.

It is true, as the NFL Defendants point out, that Johnson's complaint was not docketed until August 3, 1999, more than ninety days after Johnson received the March 26, 1999 right-to-sue letter. But the NFL Defendants overlook the fact that Johnson's complaint was received by the Court's *Pro Se* Office on June 23, 1999—within the ninety day period. Indeed, Johnson's original complaint is stamped "received" in the *Pro Se* Office on June 23, 1999. Hence, Johnson submitted the complaint to the Court within ninety days after receiving his right-to-sue letter. The complaint must be deemed "filed" for these purposes on June 23, 1999 and the action is timely. . . . Accordingly, this prong of the NFL Defendants' motion to dismiss is denied.

B. The Sufficiency of the Claims

The NFL Defendants contend that Johnson's complaint fails to state a claim upon which relief may be granted because it "does not allege any circumstances giving rise to an inference of discrimination by the NFL Defendants." Specifically, the NFL Defendants argue that the complaint complains of discriminatory treatment by the coaching staff at the University of Miami without alleging that the NFL Defendants were involved in, or responsible for, those actions.

The NFL Defendants read the *pro se* complaint too narrowly. Liberally construed, as it must be at this juncture, the *pro se* complaint sufficiently alleges a claim of discrimination against at least some of the NFL Defendants. Johnson alleges not just that the University of Miami coaching staff reacted negatively to issues of religion, but that "what happened in Miami" resulted in his being "[b]lackballed" in the NFL. He cites two examples of teams that were interested in signing him but then changed their minds because of "what happened in Miami." The complaint specifically charges that Johnson was denied an "equal opportunity" for employment in the NFL and its affiliate, NFL Europe, "based on his race, religion, and [expression of] rights as they relate to both race and religion." The complaint contends that Johnson was "'profiled' as a troublemaker because of his position at the University of Miami . . . for Racial Pride and Color." The complaint further alleges that the "profiling" resulted in his being denied "work-outs" and "tryouts," that the "profiling" resulted in his name being withdrawn by the Atlanta Falcons after they drafted him, and that the "profiling" and "blackballing" caused other teams also to withdraw their interest in him.

It is true that the complaint raises certain issues that may not be covered by Title VII or § 1981, but the complaint does allege that Johnson was denied employment opportunities because of a combination of race and religion. Accordingly, this aspect of the motion is denied.

C. The Individual Defendants

The claims against Tagliabue, Smith, and the unidentified President of the NFL Europe must be dismissed. First, individual officers or supervisors are not "employers" for purposes of Title VII and therefore may not be held individually liable under Title VII. Second, with respect to the claims under § 1981, the complaint contains no allegation of any individual involvement by any of the individual defendants. Hence, the NFL Defendants' motion to dismiss is granted to the extent the claims against the individual defendants are dismissed.

D. The Alternative Request for Summary Judgment

The NFL Defendants also move, in the alternative, for summary judgment. At this early stage of the litigation, however, Johnson has not had the opportunity to conduct discovery. Accordingly, the motion for summary judgment is denied, without prejudice to renewal after the parties have had an opportunity to conduct discovery.

E. The ESPN Defendants

The ESPN Defendants have not appeared in this action, but clearly there is no basis for holding them liable under Title VII or § 1981. Johnson did not apply to ESPN for employment, nor was Johnson in, or seeking to be in, any type of contractual relationship with any of the ESPN Defendants. Accordingly, the claims against the ESPN Defendants are dismissed *sua sponte*.

Conclusion

The NFL Defendants' motion to dismiss is granted only as to the claims against the individual defendants and it is otherwise denied. The NFL Defendants' alternative motion for summary judgment is denied, without prejudice to renewal after the completion of discovery. The claims against the ESPN Defendants are dismissed *sua sponte*.

Source: Courtesy of Westlaw; reprinted with permission.

Many interscholastic athletes have tested their rights under the Free Exercise Clause of the First Amendment. In Case 7-3, *Menora v. Illinois High School Ass'n*, 683 F.2d 1030 (7th Cir. 1982), a student sought to wear a yarmulke during a high school basketball game and was refused.

CASE 7-3　*Menora v. Illinois High School Ass'n*

683 F.2d 1030 (7th Cir. 1982)

POSNER, Circuit Judge.

Interscholastic high school sports in Illinois, including basketball, are conducted under the aegis of the Illinois High School Association, a private association of virtually all of the state's public and private (including parochial) high schools. A rule of the Association forbids basketball players to wear hats or other headwear, with the sole exception of a headband no wider than two inches, while playing. The principal concern behind this prohibition is that the headwear might fall off in the heat of play and one of the players might trip or slip on it, fall, and injure himself.

This rule is challenged in the present case as an infringement of the religious freedom of orthodox Jews. . . . [O]rthodox Jewish males are required by their religion "to cover their heads at all times except when they are (a) unconscious, (b) immersed in water or (c) in imminent danger of loss of life." There is no exception for playing basketball. Orthodox Jews who play basketball comply, or at least try to comply, with this requirement by wearing yarmulkes (small skull caps that cover the crown of the head) fastened to the hair with bobby pins. Ordinarily a yarmulke just perches on the head; the bobby pins are an acknowledgment of the yarmulke's instability on a bobbing head. But bobby pins are not a secure method of fastening; yarmulkes fastened by them fall off in the heat of play with some frequency. The Association has interpreted its rule to forbid the wearing of yarmulkes during play; and the plaintiffs in this lawsuit—two orthodox Jewish high schools in Chicago, the members of their interscholastic basketball teams, and the members' parents—contend that this interpretation forces them to choose between their religious observance and participating in interscholastic basketball, which as it happens is the only interscholastic sport in which the two schools participate.

As the plaintiffs had the burden of proving that their First Amendment rights were infringed by the Association's no-headwear rule, we are constrained on this record to conclude that they failed to make out a case and that the judgment in their favor must be vacated. As we have explained, they have no constitutional right to wear yarmulkes insecurely fastened by bobby pins and therefore they cannot complain if the Association refuses to let them do so because of safety concerns which, while not great, are not wholly trivial either. But it does not follow that the complaint should be dismissed. The district court should retain jurisdiction so that the plaintiffs can have an opportunity to propose to the Association a form of secure head covering that complies with Jewish law yet meets the Association's safety concerns. If the Association refuses to interpret or amend its rule to allow such a head covering to be worn by orthodox Jews, the district court should then proceed to determine, consistently with the analysis in this opinion, the plaintiffs' right to have the rule enjoined as a violation of their religious freedom.

We put the burden of proposing an alternative, more secure method of covering the head on the plaintiffs rather than on the defendants because the plaintiffs know so much more about Jewish law. The stipulation is singularly unilluminating about the content of that law, and because of the importance of avoiding false conflicts in constitutional adjudication we deprecate it as a basis for the decision of this case. Read literally, the stipulation would prevent orthodox Jews from getting haircuts, would require them to wear a hat or yarmulke to bed (though it could be removed after they fell asleep), and might even forbid them to play basketball while wearing yarmulkes fastened only by bobby pins, given the high probability that the yarmulke will fall off at some point during the game (or during the season) and cause—it would seem—a violation of religious law. To the extent that such questions of religious interpretation prove actually relevant to this case they should be addressed, in the first instance at least, by the plaintiffs when they propose to the Association in the further proceedings that we envisage on remand a more secure method of head covering. And if, despite counsel's representation at oral argument, we are incorrect in believing that Jewish religious law permits a more secure head covering than a yarmulke fastened only by bobby pins, this also can be raised on remand.

Source: Courtesy of Westlaw; reprinted with permission.

Problem 7-2

Kathy Mitchell is a devout Christian. She attends church regularly and is active in her youth group at church. She is an honor student and an All-District basketball player at Lamar High School. As part of her way to show her faith, she wears a cross around her neck on a chain. She wears the cross during games as well. During a game with their archrival, the opposing coach requests that the referee require Mitchell to remove her cross, citing a rule of the local High School Athletic Association that states: "During practice or competitive events student-athletes are prohibited from wearing any form of jewelry." Mitchell refuses to take off the cross, and the referee forfeits the match against Lamar High School. Mitchell files a lawsuit against the Association alleging religious discrimination. Will she win? What defenses are available?

AGE DISCRIMINATION

Athletes today are performing at higher levels and have longer careers than their predecessors, with some exceptions. Some of these past exceptions include Satchel Paige, a former Negro League great, who played Major League Baseball at the age of 59 with the Kansas City Athletics.[32] Gordie Howe played professional hockey in six decades. Howe played 22 seasons with the Detroit Red Wings and retired at age 43; however, he came back to the sport to play with his two sons for the Houston Aeros of the World Hockey League, scoring 508 points in 419 games. He "unretired" once more at the age of 51, scoring 51 points for the Hartford Whalers of the NHL while playing in 80 games. Hall of Famer Warren Moon played quarterback in the NFL well into his 40s, and George Foreman boxed in his 50s. In today's sports world many athletes are having viable athletic careers into their 40s and beyond.

The Age Discrimination in Employment Act of 1967 (ADEA) was passed by Congress to protect older workers in the employment process. The statute states in part:

```
(a) The Congress hereby finds and declares that—

    (1) in the face of rising productivity and affluence, older workers
        find themselves disadvantaged in their efforts to retain
        employment, and especially to regain employment when displaced
        from jobs;

    (2) the setting of arbitrary age limits regardless of potential for
        job performance has become a common practice, and certain other-
        wise desirable practices may work to the disadvantage of older
        persons;
```

---

[32] *See* Leroy Satchel Paige et al., Maybe I'll Pitch Forever: A Great Baseball Player Tells the Hilarious Story Behind the Legend (Doubleday 2000).

    (3) the incidence of unemployment, especially long-term unemployment
        with resultant deterioration of skill, morale, and employer
        acceptability is, relative to the younger ages, high among older
        workers; their numbers are great and growing; and their employment
        problems grave;
    (4) the existence in industries affecting commerce, of arbitrary
        discrimination in employment because of age, burdens commerce
        and the free flow of goods in commerce.
(b) It is therefore the purpose of this chapter to promote employment of
    older persons based on their ability rather than age; to prohibit
    arbitrary age discrimination in employment; to help employers and
    workers find ways of meeting problems arising from the impact of age
    on employment.[33]

    . . . .

(a) Employer practices
It shall be unlawful for an employer—

(1) to fail or refuse to hire or to discharge any individual or otherwise
    discriminate against any individual with respect to his compensa-
    tion, terms, conditions, or privileges of employment, because of
    such individual's age;
(2) to limit, segregate, or classify his employees in any way which
    would deprive or tend to deprive any individual of employment oppor-
    tunities or otherwise adversely affect his status as an employee,
    because of such individual's age; or
(3) to reduce the wage rate of any employee in order to comply with this
    chapter.[34]

The Age Discrimination in Employment Act of 1967 (ADEA) protects individuals who are 40 years of age or older from employment discrimination based on age. The ADEA's protections apply to both employees and job applicants. Under the ADEA, it is unlawful to discriminate against a person because of his or her age with respect to any term, condition, or privilege of employment, including hiring, firing, promotion, layoff, compensation, benefits, job assignments, and training. The courts have interpreted the ADEA to permit employers to favor older workers based on age even when doing so adversely affects a younger worker who is 40 or older. The ADEA applies to employers with 20 or more employees, including state and local governments, employment agencies, labor organizations, as well as the federal government. In order to establish a prima facie discharge

---

[33] 29 U.S.C.A. § 621.
[34] 29 U.S.C.A § 623.

case of age discrimination, a plaintiff must prove the following four elements: (1) he or she was discharged;[35] (2) he or she was at least 40 years old at that time; (3) he or she was performing his or her job duties at a level that met the employer's legitimate expectations at the time of the plaintiff's discharge; and (4) he or she was treated more harshly than other similarly situated younger employees.[36] Employers may assert as a defense to the lawsuit that age was not a determining factor in any adverse employment decision made by the employer.

In Case 7-4, *Moore v. University of Notre Dame*, 22 F. Supp. 2d 896 (N.D. Ind. 1998), the court was called on to determine the damages that should be awarded to the plaintiff under the ADEA after a jury found in favor of the plaintiff on his claim for age discrimination.

📖 CASE 7-4 *Moore v. University of Notre Dame*

22 F. Supp. 2d 896 (N.D. Ind. 1998)

SHARP, District Judge.

Plaintiff, Joseph R. Moore (Moore), filed a claim in this Court against The University of Notre Dame (Notre Dame) alleging age discrimination, retaliation, and defamation. . . . The case went to trial in Lafayette on July 9, 1998. On July 15, 1998, after four and one-half hours of deliberation, the Jury found that Notre Dame had violated the Age Discrimination in Employment Act (ADEA) and awarded Moore back pay in the amount of $42,935.28. Additionally, because the jury determined that Notre Dame's violation of ADEA was wilful, Plaintiff also was awarded liquidated damages in the additional amount of $42,935.28. Judgment must and now does enter in favor of the plaintiff, Joseph E. Moore and against the defendant, Notre Dame in the amount of $85,870.56. . . .

I. Relief Under the ADEA

The remedial scheme for a discriminatory discharge is designed to make a plaintiff who has been the victim of discrimination whole through the use of equitable remedies.

Moore now asks the Court to reinstate him in his former coaching position, or to award five year's front pay in lieu of reinstatement.

---

[35] Discharge can also include "An employee's reasonable decision to resign because of unendurable working conditions." *Pennsylvania State Police v. Suders*, 542 U.S. 129, 141 (2004).

[36] Alba v. Merrill Lynch & Co., 198 Fed. Appx. 294 (Va. Ct. App. 2006); Citing to *McDonnell Douglas Corp. v. Green*, 411 U.S. 792, 93 S. Ct. 1817, 36 L. Ed. 2d 668 (1973).

Notre Dame contends that Moore has received all relief to which he was entitled and therefore asks this Court to deny Moore's Motion for Reinstatement/Front Pay.

A. Reinstatement

Although reinstatement is the preferred remedy in a discrimination case, it is not always appropriate. The factors which should be considered when determining its propriety include, hostility in the past employment relationship and the absence of an available position for the plaintiff. Additionally, under ADEA, when a period for reinstatement is relatively short, such that plaintiff is close to retirement, the strong preference in favor of reinstatement is neutralized by the increased certainty of potential loss of pay permitting consideration of a front pay award.

1. Hostility

The decision to reinstate a discriminatorily terminated employee is consigned to the sound discretion of the district court which should not grant reinstatement "where the result would be undue friction and controversy." Evidence that hostility developed between the employer and employee during litigation may also be considered, but is not dispositive.

In the present case, Moore's reinstatement would cause significant friction as well as disruption of the current football program. Moore and Davie, his direct supervisor, are no longer on speaking terms. During trial, sufficient evidence was presented to infer that Moore and Davie would be unable to engage in a workable relationship. Reinstatement in this instance is impracticable. Moreover, even if hostility and undue friction were not a problem, reinstatement is not appropriate in this case.

2. Available Position

The Seventh Circuit has also held that reinstatement can reasonably be denied when "someone else currently occupies the employee's former position." The law is clear. Even if this Court determined that reinstatement is warranted, it is not an appropriate remedy in this case as there is no available position to which Moore could return. Therefore, the Court turns to the more difficult issue of whether front-pay is warranted.

B. Front Pay

Plaintiff is incorrect in stating that "if the Court rejects Moore's request for reinstatement, it *must* award him front pay." Front pay is an available remedy under ADEA, however, such an award remains discretionary with court. The Seventh Circuit has defined front pay as "a lump sum . . . representing the discounted present value of the difference between the earnings (an employee) would have received in his old employment and the earnings he can be expected to receive in his present and future, and by hypothesis, inferior, employment." . . . The court determines the amount of front pay to award depending on whether:

1. the plaintiff has a reasonable prospect of obtaining comparable employment;
2. the time period for the award is relatively short;
3. the plaintiff intends to work or is physically capable of working; and
4. liquidated damages have been awarded.

. . . Moreover, an award must be grounded in available facts, acceptable to a reasonable person and not highly speculative. It cannot be based simply on a plaintiff's own stated intentions with regard to how long he or she would have worked.

Notre Dame contends that Moore is not entitled to front pay because (1) evidence acquired by Notre Dame after Moore's discharge would have led to his discharge based on legitimate, nondiscriminatory reasons . . .

In the present case, Notre Dame argues that Moore's jury award of $42,935.28 and liquidated damages award of $42,935.28 makes him whole and that further compensation would "be a total award greater than the statute contemplates." The Court disagrees. Moore's 1996–97 annual salary was $79,552.08. Assuming an annual increase of 4%, his 1997-98 salary would have been $82,734.16 and his 1998-99 salary $86,043.53. In addition to loss of salary, Moore also lost several benefits. It is unlikely he will be able to duplicate the benefits and prestige the Notre Dame position provided him. Moreover, as Moore is at or near retirement age, it is unlikely he will find comparable employment at the salary level he enjoyed while at Notre Dame. The evidence showed that Moore had coached at Notre Dame for nine years and intended to continue in that position until retirement. Moore has been unable to replace his Notre Dame position with a comparable one. He is currently earning $46,600 and working three jobs. In this Court's opinion, the jury award has not "made him whole" and front pay may be appropriate.

4. Summary

The purpose of front pay under the Age Discrimination in Employment Act is to ensure that a person who has been discriminated against on the basis of age is made whole, not to guarantee every claimant who cannot mitigate damages by finding comparable work an annuity to age 70. Furthermore, the risk of non-continuity of future employment in a "volatile" field must be considered in determining an award of front pay, and the Court has considered this fact.

Defendant's argument that front pay is too speculative when the plaintiff's profession has a high turnover rate does not preclude a front-pay award. In this case, such an award is not "highly speculative." The Court has solid evidence concerning Moore's annual salary and the number of years he hoped to continue his employment. While Moore asserts that five years front pay is warranted, this Court disagrees. The evidence presented at trial establishes that Moore expressed a desire to work two more years and then retire. There was no guarantee that Davie would remain at Notre Dame longer than his current contract or that Moore would indefinitely remain in Davie's employ. The evidence also suggests that Moore and Davie had philosophical differences which may have led to a parting of the ways. With all evidence considered, the Court finds an award of two years front pay sufficient. The front pay is calculated as follows:

Had Moore remained at Notre Dame his total 1998 salary would have been $84,388.84. Subtracted from this amount is Moore's annual salary from his present employment. Moore testified that he currently earns $1,600 for his services as assistant football coach at Cathedral Preparatory School, $15,000 for his work with the Baltimore Ravens, and $30,000 from his work with Tollgrade Communications. His total current yearly earning amount is therefore $46,600. The difference between Moore's Notre Dame salary and his current salary is $37,788.84 per year. This amount is multiplied by a period of two years and yields a total of $75,577.68. Because the Court is not including an additional amount for lost benefits and is not factoring in any increase for the second year, no discounting of the front pay award is warranted. Thus, the total front pay award equals $75,577.68 plus post judgment interest.

Source: Courtesy of Westlaw; reprinted with permission.

Problem 7-3

Wilson Miller was an eight-time Pro-Bowl quarterback. At age 43 he still is able to play quarterback in the NFL. He is signed by the Denver Broncos to a contract and participates in the training camp. He is competing for the third-team quarterback position with Rusty Johnson, a 22-year-old rookie. Miller is cut from the team at the end of the camp in favor of Johnson. Miller was told by the head coach that although he had more experience reading defenses the owner wanted to go with the "new kid." He was also told by the head coach that Johnson had less propensity to get injured than Miller because of Miller's age. The assistant coach told

Miller that the owner told the head coach to keep the rookie over Miller because the Broncos have a very young fan base and the head coach wanted to "make his roster as young as possible," in order to attract more fans to the game. Miller files an age discrimination case against the Broncos. The Broncos admit that both quarterbacks are of the same level of skill and both fill the team's offensive scheme. The Broncos argue that keeping Johnson over Miller was a business necessity because more fans will buy season tickets as a result of Johnson's presence on the team. Johnson's hometown is Denver, Colorado, and he played his college football for the University of Colorado. Can Miller prevail in his age discrimination lawsuit? Is the business necessity defense a valid defense to an age discrimination case?

DISCRIMINATION AGAINST PEOPLE WITH DISABILITIES

Many notable athletes have participated in sporting events with disabilities or severe limitations. Pete Gray lost his right arm in a boyhood accident but still became a Major League Baseball player. While in the minor leagues he was named the Southern Association's Most Valuable Player in 1943, stealing 68 bases and batting .333. He played professionally for the St. Louis Browns in 1945, playing in 77 games and batting .245. Gray taught himself to throw and bat from the opposite side of the plate because of the loss of his arm.[37]

Monte Stratton returned to the pitching mound for the Chicago White Sox after his leg was amputated below the knee as a result of a hunting accident. His life was portrayed by Jimmy Stewart in the 1944 film *The Monte Stratton Story*.[38] Tom Dempsey was an outstanding placekicker with the New Orleans Saints and is the co-holder of the record for the longest field goal in NFL history, 63 yards. Dempsey was born without fingers on his right hand or toes on his right foot. Magic Johnson returned to play in the NBA notwithstanding his positive HIV status. In 2003, Marsha Wetzel became the first deaf female referee in NCAA Division I basketball.[39]

The Americans with Disabilities Act of 1990

The Americans with Disabilities Act of 1990 (ADA) was passed into law to prohibit discrimination in the employment process because of disability. According to the ADA, "individuals with disabilities continually encounter various forms of discrimination, including outright intentional exclusion, the discriminatory effects of architectural, transportation, and communication barriers, overprotective rules and policies, failure to make modifications to existing facilities and practices, exclusionary qualification standards and criteria, segregation, and relegation to lesser services, programs, activities, benefits, jobs, or other opportunities."[40] The act is designed to remedy that situation.

---

[37] *See*, William C. Kashatus, *One-Armed Wonder: Pete Gray, Wartime Baseball, and the American Dream*, McFarland & Company, 2001.

[38] Michael Lewis, *The Kick is Up and It's . . . A Career Killer*, The New York Times, October 28, 2007.

[39] Kelley King, *Who Is . . . Marsha Wetzel*, SI Vault, February 17, 2003.

[40] 42 U.S.C § 12101(a)(5).

The ADA is divided into four major sections:

Title I–Employment
Title II–Public Services
Title III–Public Accommodations and Services by Private Entities
Title IV–Telecommunications and Common Carriers

The precursor to the ADA was the Rehabilitation Act of 1973, which prohibited discrimination because of disability by federal government contractors and by those who receive federal financial assistance. Many disabled athletes asserted Section 504 of the Rehabilitation Act to establish their right to participate in collegiate athletics. The ADA is more extensive than the Rehabilitation Act. It covers employers with 15 or more employees and applies to both private and public employers. The ADA prohibits employers from discriminating in any aspect of the employment process against an otherwise qualified individual who possesses a disability as defined under the act.

The ADA defines a "qualified individual with a disability" as an individual with a disability who, with or without reasonable accommodations, can perform the essential functions of the employment that such individual holds or desires.[41] An employer is not required to hire a disabled person who is not capable of performing the duties of the job; however, the ADA does require the employer to make a "reasonable accommodation" for the disabled individual. An employer is not required to make an accommodation for an individual if that accommodation would impose undue hardship on the operation of the employer's business.

The ADA's definition of disability reads, in part, "disability means, with respect to an individual . . . (a) a physical or mental impairment that substantially limits one or more of the major life activities of such individual; (b) a record of such an impairment; or (c) being regarded as having such an impairment." Disabilities have been defined under the ADA to include blindness, alcoholism, morbid obesity, muscular dystrophy, and being HIV positive.

On September 25, 2008, the ADA was amended to clarify who is covered by the law's protections. The "ADA Amendments Act of 2008" revises the definition of "disability" to more broadly encompass impairments that substantially limit a major life activity. The amended language also states that mitigating measures, including assistive devices, auxiliary aids, accommodations, medical therapies and supplies (other than eyeglasses and contact lenses) have no bearing in determining whether a disability qualifies under the law. Changes also clarify coverage of impairments that are episodic or in remission that substantially limit a major life activity when active, such as epilepsy or post traumatic stress disorder. The amendments took effect January 1, 2009.

The owners and operators of public places of accommodation must allow disabled individuals to participate equally in the goods, services, and accommodations provided by the establishment. Owners and operators must make reasonable modifications in their policies to enable this goal to be achieved.

In Case 7-5, *PGA Tour, Inc. v. Martin*, 532 U.S. 661 (2001), the Supreme Court of the United States weighed in on the issue of whether the game of golf would be fundamentally changed by allowing a PGA golfer to use a golf cart while playing on the PGA Tour.

---

[41] 42 U.S.C.A. § 12131(2).

📖 CASE 7-5 *PGA Tour, Inc. v. Martin*

532 U.S. 661 (2001)

Justice STEVENS delivered the opinion of the Court.

This case raises two questions concerning the application of the Americans with Disabilities Act of 1990 to a gifted athlete: first, whether the Act protects access to professional golf tournaments by a qualified entrant with a disability; and second, whether a disabled contestant may be denied the use of a golf cart because it would "fundamentally alter the nature" of the tournaments to allow him to ride when all other contestants must walk.

I.

Petitioner PGA TOUR, Inc., a nonprofit entity formed in 1968, sponsors and cosponsors professional golf tournaments conducted on three annual tours. About 200 golfers participate in the PGA TOUR; about 170 in the NIKE TOUR; and about 100 in the SENIOR PGA TOUR. PGA TOUR and NIKE TOUR tournaments typically are 4-day events, played on courses leased and operated by petitioner. The entire field usually competes in two 18-hole rounds played on Thursday and Friday; those who survive the "cut" play on Saturday and Sunday and receive prize money in amounts determined by their aggregate scores for all four rounds. The revenues generated by television, admissions, concessions, and contributions from cosponsors amount to about $300 million a year, much of which is distributed in prize money.

There are various ways of gaining entry into particular tours. For example, a player who wins three NIKE TOUR events in the same year, or is among the top-15 money winners on that tour, earns the right to play in the PGA TOUR. Additionally, a golfer may obtain a spot in an official tournament through successfully competing in "open" qualifying rounds, which are conducted the week before each tournament. Most participants, however, earn playing privileges in the PGA TOUR or NIKE TOUR by way of a three-stage qualifying tournament known as the "Q-School."

Any member of the public may enter the Q-School by paying a $3,000 entry fee and submitting two letters of reference from, among others, PGA TOUR or NIKE TOUR members. The $3,000 entry fee covers the players' greens fees and the cost of golf carts, which are permitted during the first two stages, but which have been prohibited during the third stage since 1997. Each year, over a thousand contestants compete in the first stage, which consists of four 18-hole rounds at different locations.

Approximately half of them make it to the second stage, which also includes 72 holes. Around 168 players survive the second stage and advance to the final one, where they compete over 108 holes. Of those finalists, about a fourth qualify for membership in the PGA TOUR, and the rest gain membership in the NIKE TOUR. The significance of making it into either tour is illuminated by the fact that there are about 25 million golfers in the country.

Three sets of rules govern competition in tour events. First, the "Rules of Golf," jointly written by the United States Golf Association (USGA) and the Royal and Ancient Golf Club of Scotland, apply to the game as it is played. . . . Those rules do not prohibit the use of golf carts at any time.

Second, the "Conditions of Competition and Local Rules," often described as the "hard card," apply specifically to petitioner's professional tours. The hard cards for the PGA TOUR and NIKE TOUR require players to walk the golf course during tournaments, but not during open qualifying rounds. . . .

Third, "Notices to Competitors" are issued for particular tournaments and cover conditions for that specific event. . . .

II.

Casey Martin is a talented golfer. As an amateur, he won 17 Oregon Golf Association junior events before he was 15, and won the state championship as a high school senior. He played on the Stanford University golf team that won the 1994 National Collegiate Athletic Association (NCAA) championship. As a professional, Martin qualified for the NIKE TOUR in 1998 and 1999, and based on his 1999 performance, qualified for the PGA TOUR in 2000. In the 1999 season, he entered 24 events, made the cut 13 times, and had 6 top-10 finishes, coming in second twice and third once.

Martin is also an individual with a disability as defined in the Americans with Disabilities Act of 1990 (ADA or Act). Since birth he has been afflicted with Klippel-Trenaunay-Weber Syndrome, a degenerative circulatory disorder that obstructs the flow of blood from his right leg back to his heart. The disease is progressive; it causes severe pain and has atrophied his right leg. During the latter part of his college career, because of the progress of the disease, Martin could no longer walk an 18-hole golf course. Walking not only caused him pain, fatigue, and anxiety, but also created a significant risk of hemorrhaging, developing blood clots, and fracturing his tibia so badly that an amputation might be required. For these reasons, Stanford made written requests to the Pacific 10 Conference and the NCAA to waive for Martin their rules requiring players to walk and carry their own clubs. The requests were granted.

When Martin turned pro and entered petitioner's Q-School, the hard card permitted him to use a cart during his successful progress through the first two stages. He made a request, supported by detailed medical records, for permission to use a golf cart during the third stage. Petitioner refused to review those records or to waive its walking rule for the third stage. Martin therefore filed this action. A preliminary injunction entered by the District Court made it possible for him to use a cart in the final stage of the Q-School and as a competitor in the NIKE TOUR and PGA TOUR. Although not bound by the injunction, and despite its support for petitioner's position in this litigation, the USGA voluntarily granted Martin a similar waiver in events that it sponsors, including the U.S. Open.

III.

. . . [P]etitioner asserted that the condition of walking is a substantive rule of competition, and that waiving it as to any individual for any reason would fundamentally alter the nature of the competition. . . . Their testimony makes it clear that, in their view, permission to use a cart might well give some players a competitive advantage over other players who must walk. . . .

On the merits, because there was no serious dispute about the fact that permitting Martin to use a golf cart was both a reasonable and a necessary solution to the problem of providing him access to the tournaments, the Court of Appeals regarded the central dispute as whether such permission would "fundamentally alter" the nature of the PGA TOUR or NIKE TOUR. Like the District Court, the Court of Appeals viewed the issue not as "whether use of carts generally would fundamentally alter the competition, but whether the use of a cart by Martin would do so." That issue turned on "an intensively fact-based inquiry," and, the court concluded, had been correctly resolved by the trial judge. In its words, "[a]ll that the cart does is permit Martin access to a type of competition in which he otherwise could not engage because of his disability."

IV.

Congress enacted the ADA in 1990 to remedy widespread discrimination against disabled individuals. In studying the need for such legislation, Congress found that "historically, society has tended to isolate and segregate individuals with disabilities, and, despite some improvements, such forms of discrimination against individuals with disabilities continue to be a serious and pervasive social problem.". . .

In the ADA, Congress provided that broad mandate. To effectuate its sweeping purpose, the ADA forbids discrimination against disabled individuals in major areas of public life, among them employment (Title I of the Act), public services (Title II), and public accommodations (Title III). At issue now, as a threshold matter, is the applicability of Title III to petitioner's golf tours and qualifying rounds, in particular to petitioner's treatment of a qualified disabled golfer wishing to compete in those events.

. . . .

It seems apparent, from both the general rule and the comprehensive definition of "public accommodation," that petitioner's golf tours and their qualifying rounds fit comfortably within the coverage of Title III, and Martin within its protection. The events occur on "golf course[s]," a type of place specifically identified by the Act as a public accommodation. It would therefore appear that Title III of the ADA, by its plain terms, prohibits petitioner from denying Martin equal access to its tours on the basis of his disability. . . .

We need not decide whether petitioner's construction of the statute is correct, because petitioner's argument falters even on its own terms. . . .

In this case, however, the narrow dispute is whether allowing Martin to use a golf cart, despite the walking requirement that applies to the PGA TOUR, the NIKE TOUR, and the third stage of the Q-School, is a modification that would "fundamentally alter the nature" of those events.

. . . .

As an initial matter, we observe that the use of carts is not itself inconsistent with the fundamental character of the game of golf. From early on, the essence of the game has been shotmaking—using clubs to cause a ball to progress from the teeing ground to a hole some distance away with as few strokes as possible. . . . The walking rule that is contained in petitioner's hard cards, based on an optional condition buried in an appendix to the Rules of Golf, is not an essential attribute of the game itself.

Indeed, the walking rule is not an indispensable feature of tournament golf either. . . .

Petitioner, however, distinguishes the game of golf as it is generally played from the game that it sponsors in the PGA TOUR, NIKE TOUR, and (at least recently) the last stage of the Q-School—golf at the "highest level.". . . The walking rule is one such rule, petitioner submits, because its purpose is "to inject the element of fatigue into the skill of shot-making," and thus its effect may be the critical loss of a stroke. As a consequence, the reasonable modification Martin seeks would fundamentally alter the nature of petitioner's highest level tournaments even if he were the only person in the world who has both the talent to compete in those elite events and a disability sufficiently serious that he cannot do so without using a cart.

The force of petitioner's argument is, first of all, mitigated by the fact that golf is a game in which it is impossible to guarantee that all competitors will play under exactly the same conditions or that an individual's ability will be the sole determinant of the outcome. . . .

Further, the factual basis of petitioner's argument is undermined by the District Court's finding that the fatigue from walking during one of petitioner's 4-day tournaments cannot be deemed significant. . . .

Moreover, when given the option of using a cart, the majority of golfers in petitioner's tournaments have chosen to walk, often to relieve stress or for other strategic reasons. . . .

Under the ADA's basic requirement that the need of a disabled person be evaluated on an individual basis, we have no doubt that allowing Martin to use a golf cart would not fundamentally alter the nature of petitioner's tournaments. . . . [T]he purpose of the walking rule is to subject players to fatigue, which in turn may influence the outcome of tournaments. Even if the rule does serve that purpose, it is an uncontested finding of the District Court that Martin "easily endures greater fatigue even with a cart than his able-bodied competitors do by walking.". . . The purpose of the walking rule is therefore not compromised in the slightest by allowing Martin to use a cart. A modification that provides an exception to a peripheral tournament rule without impairing its purpose cannot be said to "fundamentally alter" the tournament. What it can be said to do, on the other hand, is to allow Martin the chance to qualify for, and compete in, the athletic events petitioner offers to those members of the public who have the skill and desire to enter. That is exactly what the ADA requires. As a result, Martin's request for a waiver of the walking rule should have been granted.

. . . .

The judgment of the Court of Appeals is affirmed.

It is so ordered.

Source: Courtesy of Westlaw; reprinted with permission.

In Case 7-6, *Montalvo v. Radcliffe*, 167 F.3d 873 (4th Cir. 1999), the parents of an HIV-positive 12-year-old boy sought protection under Title III of the ADA. Should HIV-positive athletes be allowed to participate in sports? Should a distinction be made between professional and amateur athletes in this regard? Should a distinction be made between contact and non-contact sports?

CASE 7-6   *Montalvo v. Radcliffe*

167 F.3d 873 (4th Cir. 1999)

NIEMEYER, Circuit Judge:

Michael Montalvo, a 12-year old boy with AIDS, was denied admission to a traditional Japanese style martial arts school because of his HIV-positive status.

In this case, U.S.A. Bushidokan concedes that its karate school is a place of public accommodation subject to the requirements of Title III and that Michael Montalvo is disabled for purposes of the ADA by virtue of being HIV-positive or having AIDS. . . . U.S.A. Bushidokan also concedes that it denied Michael participation in group karate classes on the basis of his HIV-positive status, the condition that concededly constitutes his disability. But U.S.A. Bushidokan contends that its exclusion of Michael was legally justified because Michael posed a "direct threat" to other members of the karate class. This contention presents two issues: (1) whether Michael's condition posed a significant risk to the health or safety of others and (2) whether reasonable modifications of policies, practices, or procedures were available to eliminate the risk as a significant one.

First, both the Montalvos' and U.S.A. Bushidokan's medical experts testified that blood-to-blood contact is a means of HIV transmission, and both experts agreed that AIDS is inevitably fatal. In addition, U.S.A. Bushidokan's expert testified without challenge that it was possible to become infected with the virus from blood splashing into the eyes or onto seemingly intact skin.

Second, the type of activity offered at U.S.A. Bushidokan emphasized sparring, attack drills, and continuous body interaction with the result that the participants frequently sustained bloody injuries, such as nose bleeds, cuts inside the mouth, and external abrasions. Radcliffe testified that blood from those injuries is "extremely likely" to come in contact with other students' skin. Even though U.S.A. Bushidokan had a policy of constantly monitoring for bloody injuries and removing for treatment participants with those injuries, the fast-paced, continuous combat exercises hampered U.S.A. Bushidokan's efforts to eliminate contact when such injury occurred.

From these facts and other similar evidence, the district court found that there is "a high frequency of minor but bloody abrasions among the students" and that the blood from such injuries is "extremely likely" to spill onto the hands, uniforms, and mouths of other students. The court also found that because of this likelihood and because of the ineffectiveness of the "universal precautions" for handling blood in the context of this hard-style karate, the risk of a student's transmitting HIV to another student was "significant." We agree.

The nature, duration, and severity of the risk and probability of transmission . . . indicate that a significant risk to the health and safety of others would exist if Michael were allowed to participate in the group karate classes. . . . The nature of the risk . . . is blood-to-blood or blood-to-eye contact, according to the testimony of both sides' experts. The duration of the risk . . . is for the length of Michael's life. The severity of the risk is extreme because there is no known cure for AIDS, and, as the Montalvos concede, AIDS is inevitably fatal. And although the exact mathematical probability of transmission is unknown, the mode of transmission is one which is likely to occur in U.S.A. Bushidokan's combat-oriented group karate classes because of the frequency of bloody injuries and body contact. Thus, the nature of the risk, combined with its severity, creates a significant risk to the health and safety of hard-style karate class members.

The experts in this case agreed that HIV can be transmitted through blood-to-blood contact, and the evidence showed that this type of contact occurred frequently in the karate classes at U.S.A. Bushidokan. Thus, the district court's finding that Michael Montalvo posed a significant risk to the health or safety of others is amply supported by the evidence.

B.

Even though Michael Montalvo's condition posed a significant risk to the health or safety of others, U.S.A. Bushidokan would still be required to admit him to group karate classes if a reasonable modification could have eliminated the risk as a significant one. The only modification which was both effective in reducing risk to an insignificant level and in maintaining the fundamental essence of

U.S.A. Bushidokan's program was its offer of private karate classes to Michael.

. . . To require U.S.A. Bushidokan to make its program a less combat-oriented, interactive, contact intensive version of karate would constitute a fundamental alteration of the nature of its program. The ADA does not require U.S.A. Bushidokan to abandon its essential mission and to offer a fundamentally different program of instruction.

Accordingly, we conclude that U.S.A. Bushidokan, in excluding Michael Montalvo from participating in its combat-oriented group karate classes, did not violate Title III of the ADA because Michael posed a significant risk to the health and safety of others that could not be eliminated by a reasonable modification. The judgment of the district court is AFFIRMED.

Source: Courtesy of Westlaw; reprinted with permission.

In Case 7-7, *Anderson v. Little League Baseball, Inc.*, 794 F. Supp. 342 (D. Ariz. 1992), a wheelchair-bound Little League coach wanted to continue as a base coach. The court discussed the issue of whether the coach was a "direct threat" to the safety of others under the ADA.

📖 CASE 7-7   *Anderson v. Little League Baseball, Inc.*

794 F. Supp. 342 (D. Ariz. 1992)

EARL H. CARROLL, District Judge.

Background

On July 24, 1991, Defendants Little League Baseball, Inc. and its President and Chief Executive Officer Dr. Creighton J. Hale adopted the following policy regarding base coaching:

. . . (coach in wheel chair) may coach from the dugout, but cannot be in the coachers box. Little League must consider the safety of the youth playing the game, and they should not have the added concern of avoiding a collision with a wheel chair during their participation in the game.

Plaintiff, who is confined to a wheelchair due to a spinal cord injury, has coached Little League Baseball for the past three years as an on-field base coach. Plaintiff alleges that defendants adopted this policy to prevent him from participating on the baseball field during the 1991 season-end tournament.

According to plaintiff, the local Little League refused to enforce defendants' policy. Plaintiff's team was eliminated early from the 1991 tournament. Defendants did not actively pursue the policy at that time.

Thereafter, the State District Administrators of Little League voted to oppose the policy and seek its reversal, and District Administrator Mike Kayes urged defendants to reconsider the policy. Other persons associated with Little League also encouraged defendants to reconsider the policy. . . .

Throughout the course of the 1991-1992 regular season, the local Little League refused to enforce the policy banning wheelchairs from the coachers box and allowed plaintiff to continue serving as an on-field base coach. Recently, plaintiff complains, defendants have attempted to require local Little League officials to exclude plaintiff from the field by threatening revocation of charters and tournament privileges. . . . Defendants' recent actions have led plaintiff to believe that defendants will not allow him to coach on the field during the 1992 season-end tournament which begins on July 8, 1992. Plaintiff was selected to coach the All-Star team in the tournament. Moreover, plaintiff is concerned that defendants will attempt to prevent him from coaching on the field next year.

. . . [P]laintiff asked this Court to enjoin defendants from preventing plaintiff from participating fully, coaching on the field, or otherwise being involved to the full extent of his responsibilities as coach. In addition, plaintiff requested that this Court enjoin defendants from intimidating or threatening players, parents of players, coaches, officials, umpires, or other persons involved in Little League Baseball and from attempting to induce them to boycott games because of plaintiff's participation.

Discussion

The "Americans with Disabilities Act" was enacted on July 26, 1990. In passing the Act, Congress recognized that one or more physical or mental disabilities affect more than 43,000,000 Americans whom society has tended to isolate and segregate because of their disabilities. Such discrimination exists in the areas of employment, housing, public accommodations, education, transportation, communication, recreation, institutionalization, health services, voting, and access to public services. Disabled individuals experience not only outright intentional exclusion, but also the discriminatory effects of architectural, transportation, and communication barriers, overprotective rules and policies, failure to make modification to existing facilities and practices, and relegation to lesser services, programs, activities, benefits, jobs, or other opportunities.

The Act's Subchapter III—Public Accommodations and Services Operated by Private Entities provides as follows:

> No individual shall be discriminated against on the basis of disability in the full and equal enjoyment of the goods, services, facilities, privileges, advantages, or accommodations of any place of public accommodation by any person who owns, leases (or leases to), or operates a place of public accommodation.

Many disabled people lead isolated lives and do not frequent places of public accommodation. "The extent of non-participation of individuals with disabilities in social and recreational activities is alarming.". . . The United States Attorney General has stated that we must bring Americans with disabilities into the mainstream of society "in other words, full participation in and access to all aspects of society."

The term "public accommodation" includes any gymnasium, health spa, bowling alley, golf course, or other place of exercise or recreation which affects interstate commerce. Plaintiff alleges that "public accommodation" includes Little League Baseball and its games. Further, plaintiff alleges that defendants are subject to the provisions of the Americans with Disabilities Act because they "own, lease (or lease to), or operate a place of public accommodation" within the meaning of the Act. . . .

Despite its prohibition against discrimination in public accommodations, Subchapter III provides:

> Nothing in this subchapter shall require an entity to permit an individual to participate in or benefit from the goods, services, facilities, privileges, advantages and accommodations of such entity where such individual poses a direct threat to the health or safety of others. The term "direct threat" means a significant risk to the health or safety of others that cannot be eliminated by a modification of policies, practices, or procedures or by the provision of auxiliary aids or services.

In determining whether an individual, such as plaintiff, poses a direct threat to the health or safety of others, a public accommodation must make an individualized assessment, based on reasonable judgment that relies on current medical knowledge or on the best available objective evidence, to ascertain: (1) the nature, duration, and severity of the risk; (2) the probability that the potential injury will actually occur; and (3) whether reasonable modifications of policies, practices, or procedures will mitigate the risk.

The Act's definition of "direct threat" codifies the standard first articulated by the United States Supreme Court . . . that a person suffering from the contagious disease of tuberculosis can be a handicapped person with the meaning of Section 504 of the Rehabilitation Act of 1973. . . . The Court recognized that there is a need to balance the interests of people with disabilities against legitimate concerns for public safety. "The determination that a person poses a direct threat to the health or safety of others may not be based on generalizations or stereotypes about the effects of a particular disability; it must be based on an individual assessment that conforms to the requirements of [28 C.F.R. § 36.208(c)]." An individualized inquiry is essential if the law is to achieve its goal of protecting disabled individuals from discrimination based on prejudice, stereotypes, or unfounded fear.

There is no indication . . . that defendants conducted an individualized assessment and determined that plaintiff poses a direct threat to the health and safety of others. In fact, there is no indication that defendants undertook any type of inquiry to ascertain "the nature, duration, and severity of the risk" posed by plaintiff; "the probability that the potential injury will actually occur;" or "whether reasonable modifications of policies, practices, or procedures will mitigate the risk" allegedly posed by plaintiff. Defendants' policy amounts to a absolute ban on coaches in wheelchairs in the coachers box, regardless of the coach's disability or the field or game conditions involved. Regrettably, such a policy—implemented without public discourse—falls markedly short of the requirements enunciated in the Americans with Disabilities Act and its implementing regulations.

The Court gives great weight to the fact that plaintiff has served as a Little League coach at either first base or third base for three years without incident. Moreover, plaintiff's significant contributions of time, energy, enthusiasm, and personal example benefit the numerous children who participate in Little League activities as well as the community at large. Plaintiff's work with young people teaches them the importance of focusing on the strengths of others and helping them rise to overcome their personal challenges.

The Court has no doubt that both plaintiff and the children with whom he works will suffer irreparable harm if defendants are permitted to arguably discriminate against plaintiff based upon his disability. Such discrimination is clearly contrary to public policy and the interests of society as a whole. In particular, such discrimination is contrary to the interests of plaintiff and everyone who is interested or participates in Little League activities, including the defendant organization and its officers.

The Court anticipates that the parties will respect these interests and cooperate so that the tournament will begin on schedule and the games will be played as they were during the regular season.

Accordingly,

IT IS ORDERED that . . . [d]efendants are enjoined from preventing or attempting to prevent plaintiff from participating fully, coaching on the field, or otherwise being involved to the full extent of his responsibilities as coach, under the auspices of Little League Baseball, Inc. Furthermore, defendants are enjoined from intimidating or threatening players, parents of players, coaches, officials, umpires, or other persons involved in Little League Baseball and from attempting to induce them to boycott games because of plaintiff's participation.

Source: Courtesy of Westlaw; reprinted with permission.

Problem 7-4

Cynthia Jones is an outstanding basketball player for the Women's Maryland Wheelchair Scholastic League. She believes she could also play and compete in a nonwheelchair league with footed players. She makes a request of her local city league that she be allowed to participate in a footed league. The league turns her down, citing safety concerns. She has told the league she will only compete outside the three-point line on the court and never go inside of that line. Does the league have a right to refuse her request? What reasonable accommodations could be made for her? *See Kuketz v. MDC Fitness Corp.*, 13 Mass. L. Rptr. 511 (Mass. Super. Ct. 2001).

SEXUAL HARASSMENT

Title VII protects employees against sexual harassment in the workplace. There have been many sexual harassment lawsuits involving athletes, coaches, school administrators, and others who are involved in sports. There is little doubt that sexual harassment in sports deters females from participating and developing as athletes. The development of sexual harassment policies by organizations will help to deter future sexual harassment. Sexual harassment consists of unwelcomed sexual advances, requests for sexual favors, and other physical and verbal conduct of a sexual nature when the conduct affects an individual's employment, unreasonably interferes with an individual's work performance, or creates an intimidating, hostile, or offensive work environment. The types of sexual harassment have been described as follows:

[C]ourts have consistently recognized two distinct categories of sexual harassment claims: *quid pro quo* harassment, and hostile work environment sexual harassment. Where the plaintiff can show 'that a tangible employment action resulted from a refusal to submit to a supervisor's sexual demands,' she establishes an explicit change in her terms or conditions of employment, resulting in a *quid pro quo* case of sexual harassment. Where, however, her claim targets a supervisor's 'severe and pervasive' sexually demeaning behavior rather than a fulfilled threat, the claim is properly characterized as a 'hostile work environment' claim.[42]

For a plaintiff to establish a claim for quid pro quo sexual harassment, he or she must prove that (1) the employee belongs to a protected group, (2) the employee was subject to unwelcome sexual harassment, (3) the harassment complained of was based on sex, (4) the employee's reaction to the harassment complained of affected a tangible employment action, and (5) the harasser was the employee's supervisor.[43]

To establish a claim for hostile work environment sexual harassment, the plaintiff must prove that (1) the employee was a member of a protected group, (2) the employee was subject to unwelcome harassment that was sufficiently severe or pervasive to create a hostile work environment, (3) the harassment complained of was based on the employee's sex, (4) the harassment resulted in a tangible employment action, and (5) the harasser was the employee's supervisor, although a hostile environment can arise from someone other than the employee's supervisor.[44] Although the phrase "hostile work environment" is not specifically mentioned in Title VII, a viable cause of action still exists under the statute.[45] The plaintiff must come forward and show "that a rational jury could find that the workplace is permeated with discrimination, intimidation, ridicule and insult."[46]

In *Fall v. Indiana University Board of Trustees*, 12 F. Supp. 2d 870 (N.D. Ind. 1998), the plaintiff was suing a university and its former chancellor for sexual harassment. In discussing hostile work environment sexual harassment, the court stated:

> To be sure, exactly what act or combination of actions may "objectively" constitute a hostile work environment is a rather gray area. The Supreme Court has cautioned that the standard for judging hostility must be "sufficiently demanding to ensure that Title VII does not become a 'general civility

---

[42] Alwine v. Buzas, 89 Fed. Appx. 196 (10th Cir. 2004).

[43] Burlington Industries, Inc. v. Ellerth, 524 U.S. 742 (1998); Faragher v. City of Boca Raton, 524 U.S. 775 (1998).

[44] Jew v. University of Iowa, 749 F. Supp. 946, 958 (S.D. Iowa 1990); Pavon v. Swift Trans Co. Inc., 192 F.3d 902, 908 (9th Cir. 1999).

[45] Clarke v. Bank of Commerce, 2007 WL 1072212 (N.D. Okla. 2007) (slip opinion).

[46] Davis v. U.S. Postal Serv., 142 F.3d 1334, 1341 (10th Cir. 1998); Montero v. AGCO Cor., 192 F.3d 856, 960 (9th Cir. 1999); However, after the Supreme Court's decision in *Burlington Industries v. Ellerth*, it is more difficult to try to distinguish prima facie cases. In that case the U.S. Supreme Court held, "We do not suggest the terms quid pro quo and hostile work environment are irrelevant to Title VII litigation. To the extent they illustrate the distinction between cases involving a threat which is carried out and offensive conduct in general, the terms are relevant when there is a threshold question whether a plaintiff can prove discrimination in violation of Title VII. When a plaintiff proves that a tangible employment action resulted from a refusal to submit to a supervisor's sexual demands, he or she establishes that the employment decision itself constitutes a change in the terms and conditions of employment that is actionable under Title VII. For any sexual harassment preceding the employment decision to be actionable, however, the conduct must be severe or pervasive. Because Ellerth's claim involves only unfulfilled threats, it should be categorized as a hostile work environment claim which requires a showing of severe or pervasive conduct."

code,'. . . . Moreover, the Supreme Court has repeatedly emphasized that "the objective severity of harassment should be judged from the perspective of a reasonable person in the plaintiff's position, considering 'all the circumstances.'"[47]

. . . .

In the words of Justice Scalia:

The inquiry requires careful consideration of the social context in which particular behavior occurs and is experienced by its target. A professional football player's working environment is not severely or pervasively abusive, for example, if the coach smacks him on the buttocks as he heads onto the field—even if the same behavior would reasonably be experienced as abusive by the coach's secretary (male or female) back at the office. . . . Common sense, and an appropriate sensitivity to social context, will enable courts and juries to distinguish between simple teasing or roughhousing . . . and conduct which a reasonable person in the plaintiff's position would find severely hostile or abusive.[48] (citations omitted)

In Case 7-8, *Kesner v. Little Caesar's Enterprises, Inc.*, 2002 WL 1480800 (E.D. Mich. 2002), the plaintiff was a flight attendant on a private plane used by the Detroit Tigers Baseball Club. She sued several entities, stating she had been the victim of sexual harassment by players on the team. After reading this case, do you believe the players' conduct constituted sexual harassment? If you do, what amount of damages should she receive from the sexual harassment that occurred?

 CASE 7-8 *Kesner v. Little Caesar's Enterprises, Inc.*

2002 WL 1480800 (E.D. Mich. 2002)

ZATKOFF, Chief J.

Plaintiff alleges that she was harassed by members of the Detroit Tigers. Plaintiff alleges that the harassment started on her first flight with the Tigers in April 2000, when a group of players were looking at pornographic material on one of the player's laptop computers. She alleges that the computer was positioned in a way that allowed Plaintiff, as well as at least one other flight attendant, Jenifer Campbell, to witness it. Plaintiff alleges that the harassment was thereafter continued. For instance, she alleges that some of the players repeatedly called her pejorative and profane names, such as "bitch," "cunt," and "hide." She alleges that some players would make comments with sexual innuendos. For example, Plaintiff alleges that when she would ask players if they wanted a dessert, players would occasionally reply by asking whether she had any "cooter pie" or "hair pie." Or else, she alleges that two players, Doug Brocail and Gregg

---

[47] *Fall*, 12 F. Supp. 2d at 877.
[48] *Id.*

Jefferies, asked her whether she would give her husband a "blowjob in a van?" Plaintiff also alleges that some of the players would touch or rub against her breasts and buttocks in a manner that she thought was inappropriate, and that made her uncomfortable.

Plaintiff alleges that the harassment from the players culminated in July 2000. Before the airplane took off, Plaintiff alleges that she noticed a player, Jeff Weaver, walk out of the lavatory. She saw a smoke cloud and smelled burnt marijuana following him out of the lavatory, and saw ashes inside the lavatory. Plaintiff alleges that she approached Weaver and Matt Anderson, who were sitting next to each other, and told them that smoking marijuana was not permitted on the flight. She alleges that Anderson responded by barking profanities at her, and calling her a "stupid bitch." Later that flight, she alleges that another player, Bobby Higginson, confronted and chastised her for reporting the marijuana smoking. A third player, Brad Ausmus, also confronted Plaintiff, and allegedly called her a "dumb bitch" for reporting the marijuana smoking incident. Plaintiff alleges that she was treated this way by the players because of her gender, and that she had never seen the players treat her male counterparts on the flight crew in the same manner.

Plaintiff's complaints extend beyond the treatment she received from the players; she alleges that she was mistreated by other members of the flight crew as well. Plaintiff alleges that two pilots, Al Long and Pat White, repeatedly touched her in a manner that she thought was "inappropriate," including repeatedly touching her breasts with their hands, and that a third pilot, Rob Mintari, touched her buttocks with his hands on three separate occasions.

Plaintiff had many difficulties with Mintari, who was the chief pilot. Plaintiff alleges that Mintari personally disliked Plaintiff, and stated that he would fire her if he had the chance. . . .

1. Sexual Harassment (Count I)

Plaintiff's first claim is for sexual harassment. . . .

Upon examining this statutory language, the Michigan Supreme Court has determined that there are five elements in a claim for sexual harassment based upon an intimidating, hostile, or offensive work environment:

(1) the employee belonged to a protected group;
(2) the employee was subjected to communication or conduct on the basis of sex;
(3) the employee was subjected to unwelcome sexual conduct or communication;

(4) the unwelcome sexual conduct or communication was intended to or in fact did substantially interfere with the employee's employment or created an intimidating, hostile, or offensive work environment; and

(5) respondeat superior.

Whether a work environment is intimidating, hostile, or offensive is determined by whether a reasonable person, in the totality of the circumstances, would perceive the conduct at issue as creating an intimidating, hostile, or offensive work environment. This is a question for the jury to decide. The Court finds that the alleged behavior—such as being called pejorative names such as "bitch," "cunt," and "hide," being asked about her sexual practices with her husband, and being touched on her breasts and buttocks without her consent—is sufficiently severe that, if it is found to be true, it could allow a reasonable person to find that it created an intimidating, hostile, or offensive work environment. . . .

Plaintiff states that she repeatedly told Gease, the director of flight operations, Mintari, the chief pilot, and Brown, the lead flight attendant, about her problems with the players. For instance, she complained to both Brown and Mintari about being asked by Doug Brocail and Gregg Jefferies whether she would give her husband a "blowjob in a van[.]" According to Plaintiff, Mintari replied that she had to go along with it because it was the baseball players' airplane. She also states in her deposition that she complained to the same group of superiors about being called a "bitch" repeatedly by the baseball players. She states that Gease witnessed Al Long put his hands on Plaintiff's breasts on at least two occasions and that she complained to Gease about Mintari placing his hands on her buttocks. Gease simply replied, however, that she "was to make Robby happy so that [she] could probably maintain [her] job."

Whether or not Plaintiff received the employee handbook that required her to report claims of sexual harassment to Oumedian, it is true that Gease was the head of Olympia Aviation, which is a named Defendant, and, if Plaintiff's allegations are true, then Gease, as well as Plaintiff's other superiors at Olympia Aviation, failed to respond to her complaints. Otherwise, the Court does not find that any of the other named Defendants, which are all corporate entities, can be held liable. Plaintiff fails to provide the Court with any evidence that Defendants Little Caesars Enterprises, Inc., Olympia Entertainment, Inc., or the Detroit Tigers, Inc., had any knowledge of Plaintiff's complaints. As for Ilitch Holdings, while Plaintiff did complain to Oumedian about Mintari, thus giving Ilitch Holdings some knowledge of the harassment, Ilitch Holdings took action, and terminated the person—Mintari—that Plaintiff complained of. Thus, these corporate

Defendants cannot be held liable for the harassing behavior of the baseball players and the other members of the flight crew. Therefore, Plaintiff's claim for sexual harassment may go forward with respect to Olympia Aviation, however, it may not with respect to any other named Defendant. . . .

The Court finds that Plaintiff produces probative evidence sufficient to raise a genuine issue of material fact regarding Plaintiff's claim of sexual harassment . . .

Source: Courtesy of Westlaw; reprinted with permission.

Problem 7-5

You have just been named the new athletic director at your alma mater. You are concerned about some statements that have been made to women trainers for the football team. It has been brought to your attention that student-athletes have made sexually explicit remarks to women trainers at practice and during games. You have scheduled a meeting with the university's general counsel about your concerns. What policies or procedures would you put into place to prevent sexual harassment from occurring in the future? Would you provide sexual harassment training to all student-athletes and staff? If so, what would the training consist of? Could the university be held liable for sexual harassment of a university employee by student-athletes?

NOTES AND DISCUSSION QUESTIONS

Racial Discrimination

1. In *Richardson v. Sugg*, 325 F. Supp. 2d 919 (E.D. Ark. 2004), former Arkansas coach Nolan Richardson alleged he had been fired as head coach based on his race. Richardson was a well-known basketball coach at the collegiate level. The case is insightful with regard to athletic administration and coaching at the collegiate level.

   Coach Richardson had called an Arkansas fan a "redneck SOB." Frank Boyles, Arkansas' athletic director, approached a writer for the *Hawgs Illustrated* magazine and asked him if he would do a column equating Richardson's statement with that of a Caucasian calling Richardson the N-word. After Richardson was fired, he sued, stating that Broyles's use of the N-word was evidence that he was fired because of his race. The court addressed this issue, stating:

   > It should ring out loudly and clearly—an African American calling a Caucasian person a redneck is nowise the same as a Caucasian person calling an African American a "N-word[ed]." Although some may argue that there is no real difference, they are wrong, and I suspect they know it. I think the following analysis makes this point well:

   > What about words like "honky," "redneck," and "cracker"? While those words can be harmful epithets in certain contexts, some have argued that such words are not comparably damaging to whites as are epithets hurled against people of color and other so-called minorities. In the view of two commentators:

The word "honky" is more a badge of respect than a put down. "Cracker," although disrespectful, still implies power, as does "redneck." The fact is that terms like "N-word[ed]," "spick," "faggot," and "kike" evoke and reinforce entire cultural histories of oppression and subordination. They remind the target that his or her group has always been and remains unequal in status to the majority group. Even the most highly educated, professional class African American or Latino knows that he or she is vulnerable to the slur, the muttered expression, the fishy glance on boarding the bus, knows that his degree, his accomplishments, his well-tailored suit are no armor against mistreatment at the hands of the least educated white.[49]

Do you think that Frank Broyles's use of the "N-word" was enough to show discriminatory intent on the part of the coach? Richardson's lawsuit was dismissed by the court, which stated that Richardson was not fired because of his race.

2. What are your impressions of the National Football League's Rooney Rule? Should a professional league require its owners to interview minority candidates when they hire head coaches? What about general managers, assistant managers, and other positions within the corporation? What role should the commissioner take in the hiring processes of professional sports teams? Should certain minorities have preference over others? For further study, see Bram A. Maravent, *Is the Rooney Rule Affirmative Action? Analyzing the NFL's Mandate to Its Clubs Regarding Coaching and Front Office Hires*, 13 SPORTS LAWYERS JOURNAL 233 (2006). Why are there so few minority coaches in Division I football? Should the NCAA require members to interview minority candidates for football and basketball coaching positions as well? There has been some discussion about implementing "The Eddie Robinson Rule," which would require that minority candidates be interviewed for head football coach openings at the collegiate level. *See*, Patrick K. Thornton, *The Increased Opportunity for Minorities in the National Football League Coaching Ranks: The Initial Success of the NFL's Rooney Rule,* Willamette Sports Law Journal, Spring 2009.

3. How do you view the debate over the use of Native American mascots? What school mascots might people find offensive? The Bombers? The Crusaders? The Chiefs? Some universities have changed their team names or mascots in response to pressure exerted by the NCAA. Stanford University renamed its team from the Indians to the Cardinals, and Marquette University changed from the Warriors to the Golden Eagles. The Washington Wizards in the NBA were originally the Bullets. The Houston Astros were called the Colt .45's from 1962 to 1965. In August 2005, the NCAA stated that any school using a Native American mascot would be prevented from hosting future postseason events. Major college football is not affected because there is no official NCAA tournament. The NCAA later announced that approval from American Indian tribes would be a primary factor in giving approval for schools that wanted to use Native American nicknames and mascots in postseason play. Florida State University sought approval from two Seminole groups to use their name for university sports teams. The NCAA subsequently removed these names from the list of banned mascots and team names. For a full discussion of the issue, see Chapter 1, "Sports in Society."

---

[49] *Richardson*, 325 F. Supp. 2d at 929.

4. In *Pro-Football, Inc. v. Harjo*, 415 F.3d 44 (D.C. Cir. 2005), several Native Americans petitioned the Trademark Trial and Appeal Board seeking cancellation of the registration of six trademarks used by the Washington Redskins. Section 1064(3) of the U.S. Trademark Act (Title 15) allows a party to file a petition to seek cancellation of a mark if they believe they will be damaged by the registration. The Washington Redskins revised fight song states: "Hail to the Redskins! / Hail to victory! / Braves on the Warpath, fight for old D.C.! / Run or pass and score, / We want a lot more! / Beat 'em, swamp 'em, touchdown, / Let the points soar! / Fight on, Fight on, / 'Till you have won, / Sons of Washington!"[50]

   Do you find this offensive? Would you consider any of the following professional team names or their mascots potentially offensive: the Atlanta Braves, the Cleveland Indians, the Cincinnati Reds, the Chicago Blackhawks, the Kansas City Chiefs, the New Orleans Saints, the Anaheim Angels, the New Jersey Devils, the Milwaukee Brewers?

5. The Houston MLS franchise was originally called "1836," signifying the year the city of Houston was founded. Several Hispanic groups stated that the name disparaged Mexican-Americans because the year also corresponded to the year Texas gained its independence from Mexico. See, *Spirit of 1836: Houston's New MLS Team Reveals Name*, Sports Business Daily, January 26, 2006.

6. Consider Allen Iverson's song "40 Bars." The song lyrics included the following lines: "Get murdered in a second in the first degree; / Come to me with faggot tendencies; /You'll be sleeping where the maggots be . . .; / Die reaching for heat, leave you leaking in the street; / Niggers screaming he was a good boy ever since he was born; / But fuck it he gone; / Life must go on; / Niggers don't live that long . . . " After the song's release, many civil rights groups and gay and lesbian groups, as well as NBA Commissioner David Stern, voiced displeasure with Iverson and his lyrics. The commissioner encouraged Iverson to revise the lyrics to a less offensive tone. Eventually Iverson canceled the release of the album. What actions, if any, should have been taken against Iverson for his controversial lyrics?

7. What racial issues do you believe are facing sports today? Do you believe progress has been made in resolving discrimination in sports?

Sex Discrimination

8. Under what circumstances can reverse discrimination exist as set forth in the *Medcalf* case?

9. *New York State Division of Human Rights v. New York-Pennsylvania Professional Baseball League* was decided in 1971. Do you think that the same argument would be made today to prevent women from becoming referees or umpires?

10. In *Graves v. Women's Professional Rodeo Association, Inc.*, 907 F.2d 71 (1990), a male barrel racer sued the Women's Professional Rodeo Association (WPRA) alleging that it denied him membership on the basis of his gender in violation of Title VII of the Civil Rights Act of 1964. The court found against Graves and discussed the following in dicta relating to the concept of BFOQ:

   > Although WPRA raised no defense beyond its failure to qualify as an "employer" under Title VII, we note that under the bona fide occupational qualification (BFOQ) exception

---

[50] In November 2009, the U.S. Supreme Court refused to hear the case. *NPR staff and wire reports, High Court Won't Hear Washington Redskins Case,* National Public Radio, Nov. 14, 2009. The original Redskins fight song included references to scalping and contained the phrase "Fight for old Dixie."

the organization probably would not have to admit males even if it had the requisite fifteen employees. The legislative history offers as an example of legitimate discrimination under the BFOQ exception to the proscriptions of Title VII "a professional baseball team for male players." 110 Cong.Rec. 7213 (1964). Presumably, being female would similarly constitute a BFOQ for competing in women's professional rodeo, in the same way that being female would constitute a BFOQ for competing in women's professional tennis or for membership in the Ladies' Professional Golf Association. In short, we do not believe that Title VII mandates the admission of men as competitors in women's professional sports.[51]

11. In *Smith v. City of Salem, Ohio*, 369 F.3d 912 (6th Cir. 2004), the Sixth Circuit Court of Appeals held that discrimination against a transsexual employee constitutes gender discrimination under Title VII. Smith was a lieutenant in the city's fire department and had been diagnosed with gender identity disorder. His coworkers made comments when he began dressing more femininely. The court, in finding in his favor, stated:

> Relying on *Price Waterhouse*—which held that Title VII's prohibition of discrimination "because of . . . sex" bars gender discrimination, including discrimination based on sex stereotypes—Smith contends on appeal that he was a victim of discrimination "because of . . . sex" both because of his gender non-conforming conduct and, more generally, because of his identification as a transsexual. We find both bases of discrimination actionable pursuant to Title VII.[52]
>
> . . . [D]iscrimination against a plaintiff who is a transsexual—and therefore fails to act like and/or identify with the gender norms associated with his or her sex—is no different from the discrimination directed against Ann Hopkins in *Price Waterhouse*, who, in sex-stereotypical terms, did not act like a woman. Sex stereotyping based on a person's gender non-conforming behavior is impermissible discrimination, irrespective of the cause of that behavior; a label, such as "transsexual," is not fatal to a sex discrimination claim where the victim has suffered discrimination because of his or her gender non-conformity. Accordingly, we hold that Smith has stated a claim for relief pursuant to Title VII's prohibition of sex discrimination.[53]

Religious Discrimination

12. Should student-athletes be able to recite prayers before games? What legal arguments have been made against such action?

13. How much religious expression should professional athletes be allowed to have during a game?

Age Discrimination

14. Did you believe the damages were sufficient in *Moore v. University of Notre Dame*? Should the plaintiff have been entitled to front pay? Under what circumstances would reinstatement not be the appropriate remedy?

---

[51] *Graves*, 907 F.2d at 73, n.3.
[52] *Smith*, 369 F.3d at 918.
[53] *Id.* at 921.

15. Do you agree with the law in setting 40 as the age at which discrimination can occur under the ADEA?

Discrimination Against People with Disabilities

16. In *PGA v. Martin*, the court found that walking is not an essential part of the game of golf. Do you agree? How far do PGA golfers walk during a PGA event?

17. What reasonable accommodations could be made for Jim Abbott, former California Angels pitcher? Abbott was born without a right hand but overcame his disability by becoming the collegiate player of the year at the University of Michigan and even tossed a no-hitter with the Yankees in 1993. Abbott pitched ten years in the major leagues. Could he argue he was entitled to a "special fielder" as a reasonable accommodation due to his disability?

18. For further study of HIV in sports, see Karen Ahearn, *HIV-Positive Athletes*, 7 Sports Lawyers Journal 279 (2000).

19. *Olinger v. United States Golf Assn.*, 205 F.3d 1001 (7th Cir. 2000), was a case decided the same day as *PGA v. Martin*. In the former case, a disabled golfer sued the U.S. Golf Association (USGA) under the ADA, requesting that he be able to use a cart. The USGA defended the case under Title III:

> In a nutshell, the USGA argues that the courses where the U.S. Open is played are "mixed use" facilities subject to Title III regulations "outside the ropes" where the general public has unfettered access to the course but not "inside the ropes," where the actual championship competition is conducted and access is tightly restricted. The USGA concedes that a golf course is listed as one of the examples of a place of public accommodation under the ADA. But the USGA says it is only properly classified as such when it is used for "exercise or recreation," and the U.S. Open is not conducted for those purposes: It is held to identify America's national golf champion.[54]

The court stated in response:

> Following this thinking, places like Green Bay's Lambeau Field and Chicago's Wrigley Field would be "mixed use" facilities. Although they would be subject to the ADA in general, their actual fields of strife—where Packers battle Bears and Cubs play Cardinals—would not be places of public accommodation under the ADA.

> While there may be some logic to this contention, we hesitate to embrace it for we can resolve this appeal, as did the district court, on a more narrow ground. Even assuming that the competitive part of the golf course on which the U.S. Open is played is a place of public accommodation covered by the ADA, Mr. Olinger cannot prevail because we believe his use of a cart during the tournament would fundamentally alter the nature of the competition.[55]

Ken Venturi was a witness for the defendant and stated that physical and mental fatigue is part of golf. He cited the specific situation of Ben Hogan, a famous golfer:

> Finally, Venturi recalled the amazing story of Ben Hogan. Hogan was severely injured in 1949 when his car collided with a Greyhound bus. He was told he would never walk

---

[54] *Olinger*, 205 F.3d at 1004–05.
[55] *Id.* at 1005.

again, let alone play golf. Yet the next year, he walked and won the U.S. Open. During the trial, Venturi was asked if there was any accommodation made to Hogan as a result of his accident. Venturi replied, 'They never thought about it. They never thought about carts. And knowing Ben Hogan as well as I have, he wouldn't take one.'[56]

20. In *Zona v. Clark University*, 436 F. Supp. 2d 287 (D. Mass. 2006), a university student-athlete brought an action against his coach, the university, and other defendants alleging he was entitled to recover under Title III of the ADA when the coach disclosed to the team that the student had bipolar disorder. The court noted that Title III does provide for a private cause of action, but that the plaintiff would only be entitled to injunctive relief and not monetary damages.

Sexual Harassment

21. Case 7-8, *Kesner v. Little Caesar's*, was tried before a jury in Detroit, Michigan, which returned a verdict of $200,000 on February 14, 2003. Do you believe the award was adequate for the harassment suffered? See, *Flight Attendant Wins Suit vs. Tigers*, Sporting News, February 14, 2003.

22. What actions should the owner of a team take against the players for the sexual harassment that occurred in *Kesner*? Could the commissioner take action against the Tigers' players under the best interest of baseball clause, as he did against John Rocker for his outburst? (See Chapter 1.) Can you make any distinction between the two?

23. Could a stadium owner be held liable for the sexual harassment of an usher by spectators? A business owner can be held liable for sexual harassment of customers if they fail to take appropriate acts to stop the harassment. *See* 27 C.F.R. § 1604.11(e). *Also see*, David Picker, *At Jets Game, a Halftime Ritual of Harassment*, The New York Times, November 20, 2007.

24. Same-sex sexual harassment is recognized by courts as a viable cause of action. See *Oncale v. Sundowner Offshore Services, Inc.*, 523 U.S. 75 (1998).

25. In *Bass v. World Wrestling Federation Entertainment, Inc.*, 129 F. Supp. 2d. 491 (D.C. Tex. 2001), the court, in finding for the plaintiff on her sexual harassment claim, stated:

> Plaintiff has produced sufficient allegations to sustain her cause of action on a hostile work environment theory. She claims that she and other female members of the WWF were subjected to "repeated and unwelcome sexual advances and intrusions" by male members of the WWF. Specifically, she alleges that certain male WWF members accosted Plaintiff and other female members while they were dressing, undressing, or showering. She recites an incident in which she was called "Mister" by a male member of the WWF who then simulated a sexual act with his microphone directed at her buttocks. Finally, she states that Lombardi sexually assaulted her by groping her breasts while pushing her up against a wall and pushing his body into hers. She claims these intrusions were subjectively unwelcome, humiliating, and offensive, and that they altered the terms or conditions of her employment. These allegations suffice to show a workplace permeated with discriminatory intimidation which was sufficiently severe or pervasive to alter the conditions of Plaintiff's employment and create both an objectively and subjectively hostile or abusive work environment.[57]

---

[56] *Id.* at 1007.
[57] *Bass*, 129 F. Supp. 2d. at 501.

SUGGESTED READINGS AND RESOURCES

Abdel-Shehid, Gamal. *Who Da Man? Black Masculinities and Sporting Cultures*. Toronto: Canadian Scholars' Press, 2005.

Beck, Melissa M. *Fairness on the Field: Amending Title VII to Foster Greater Female Participation in Professional Sports*. 12 Cardozo Arts and Entertainment Law Journal 241 (1994).

Blumenthal, Karen. *Let Me Play: The Story of Title IX—The Law That Changed the Future of Girls in America*. New York: Simon & Schuster Children's Publishing, 2005.

Brackenridge, Celia, & Fasting, Kari (eds.). *Sexual Harassment and Abuse in Sport: International Research and Policy Perspectives*. London: Whiting & Birch, 2002.

Bryant, Howard. *Shut Out: A Story of Race and Baseball in Boston*. Boston: Beacon Press, 2003.

Giampetro-Meyer, Andrea. *Recognizing and Remedying Individual and Institutional Gender-Based Wage Discrimination in Sport*. 37 American Business Law Journal 343 (2000).

Gohl, Sarah. *A Lesson in English and Gender: Title IX and the Male Student-Athlete*. 50 Duke Law Journal 1123 (2001).

Griffin, Pat. *Lesbians and Bisexual Women in Sport*. 70 JOPERD—The Journal of Physical Education, Recreation & Dance (1999).

Huber, Joseph H. *Strategies to Combat Age Discrimination in Interscholastic Sports*. Palaestra, Sept. 22, 1997.

Messner, Michael A. *Taking the Field: Women, Men and Sports*. Minneapolis: University of Minnesota Press, 2002.

Miller, Patrick B., & Wiggins, David K. (eds.). *Sport and the Color Line: Black Athletes and Race Relations in Twentieth Century America*. New York: Routledge, 2004.

Porto, Brian. *A New Season: Using Title IX to Reform College Sports*. Westport, CT: Praeger, 2003.

Reaves, Rhonda. *There's No Crying in Baseball: Sports and the Legal and Social Construction of Gender*. 4 Journal of Gender, Race and Justice 283 (2001).

Segrave, Kerry. *Age Discrimination by Employers*. Jefferson, NC: McFarland, 2001.

Sullivan, Kathleen A., Lantz, Patricia J., & Zirkel, Perry A. *Leveling the Playing Field or Leveling the Players? Section 504, the Americans with Disabilities Act, and Interscholastic Sports*. 33 Journal of Special Education 258 (2000).

Tokarz, Karen. *Women, Sports, and the Law: A Comprehensive Research Guide to Sex Discrimination in Sports*. Buffalo, NY: William S. Hein, 1986.

REFERENCE MATERIALS

Age Discrimination in Employment Act of 1967, Pub. L. No. 90-202, 81 Stat. 602 (1967).

Bowden, Terry. *Uneven Playing Field*. Rivals.com, June 30, 2005, http://rivals.yahoo.com/ncaa/football/news?slug=tb-minoritycoaches062905.

Champion, Walter T. *Sports Law: Cases, Documents, and Materials*. New York: Aspen, 2005.

Cozzillio, Michael J., & Levinstein, Mark S. *Sports Law: Cases and Materials*. Durham, NC: Carolina Academic Press, 1997.

Dennie, Chris. *Native American Mascots and Team Names: Throw Away the Key; The Lanham Act Is Locked for Future Trademark Challenges*. 15 Seton Hall Journal of Sports and Entertainment Law 197 (2005).

District Court Hears Arguments on Football Discrimination Suit. Duke University Office of News & Communications, Oct. 6, 2000, http://www.dukenews.duke.edu/2000/10/heathersueo06.html.

Epstein, Adam. *Sports Law.* Clifton Park, NY: Thomson/Delmar Learning, 2003.

Fried, Gil, & Bradley, Lisa. *Applying the First Amendment to Prayer in a Public University Locker Room: An Athlete's and Coach's Perspective.* 4 MARQUETTE SPORTS LAW JOURNAL 301 (1994).

Idleman, Scott C. *Religious Freedom and the Interscholastic Athlete.* 12 MARQUETTE SPORTS LAW REVIEW 295 (2001).

Koening, Kelly B. *Mahmoud Adbul-Rauf's Suspension for Refusing to Stand for the National Anthem: A "Free Throw" for the NBA and Denver Nuggets, or a "Slam Dunk" Violation of Abdul-Rauf's Title VII Rights?* 76 WASHINGTON UNIVERSITY LAW QUARTERLY 377 (1998).

Lapchick, Richard. *The 2005–2008 Racial and Gender Report Cards.* Orlando, FL: Institute for Diversity and Ethics in Sports, College of Business Administration, University of Central Florida, 2005.

Lapter, Alain. Bloom v. NCAA: *A Procedural Due Process Analysis and the Need for Reform.* 12 SPORTS LAWYERS JOURNAL 255 (2005).

Liu, Goodwin. *Race, Class, Diversity, Complexity.* 80 NOTRE DAME LAW REVIEW 289 (2004).

Lumpkin, Angela, Stoll, Sharon Kay, & Beller, Jennifer M. *Sport Ethics: Applications for Fair Play,* 3d ed. Boston: McGraw-Hill, 2003.

MacCambridge, Michael (ed.). *ESPN SportsCentury.* New York: Hyperion Books, 1999.

McKinny, Christopher J. *Professional Sports Leagues and the First Amendment: A Closed Market-place.* 13 MARQUETTE SPORTS LAW REVIEW 223 (2003).

Miller, Lori K. *Sport Business Management.* Gaithersburg, MD: Aspen, 1997.

Miller, Roger LeRoy, Jentz, Gaylord A., & Cross, Frank B. *West's Business Law: Extended Case Approach,* 2d ed. Mason, OH: Thomson/West, 2006.

Mitten, Matthew J, Davis, Timothy, Smith, Rodney, & Berry, Robert. *Sports Law and Regulations: Cases, Materials and Problems.* New York: Aspen, 2005.

Morgan, M. *Activists Push for More Black Coaches in College Football.* USA TODAY, 2002.

Nobile, Robert. *Liability for Sexual Harassment.* In *Essential Facts: Employment* §7:10. Mason, OH: Thomson/West, 2005.

Otos, Sally. Cohen v. Brown University: *Sports in the Legal Arena.* 3 SPORTS LAWYERS JOURNAL (1996).

Platt, Jim, & Buckley, James. *Sports Immortals: Stories of Inspiration and Achievement.* Chicago: Triumph Books, 2002.

Rank, Jessica E. *Is Ladies' Night Really Sex Discrimination? Public Accommodation Laws, De Minimis Exceptions, and Stigmatic Injury.* 36 SETON HALL LAW REVIEW 223 (2005).

Richey, Charles. *Manual on Employment Discrimination and Civil Rights Actions in the Federal Courts.* Eagan, MN: Thomson/West, 2005.

Rossein, Merrick T. *Disparate Impact.* In *Employment Discrimination: Law and Litigation.* Eagan, MN: Thomson/West, 2005.

Ruzicho, Andrew J., Sr., & Jacobs, Louis A. *Management Policies and Procedures.* In *Employment Practices Manual.* Eagan, MN: Thomson/West, 2005.

Stein, M. *Pacers' Jackson Calls Ban on Chains 'Racist Statement.'* ESPN.com, 2005.

Title VI of the Civil Rights Act of 1964, Pub. L. 88-352, tit. 6, § 601, 78 STAT. 252 (1964).

True, Jeffrey C. *The NCAA Celebration Rule: A First Amendment Analysis.* 7 SETON HALL JOURNAL OF SPORT LAW 129 (1997).

Twomey, David P. *Labor and Employment Law: Text and Cases,* 12th ed. Mason, OH: Thomson/South-Western/West, 2004.

Weiss, Michelle R. *Pay Equity for Intercollegiate Coaches: Exploring the EEOC Enforcement Guidelines.* 13 MARQUETTE SPORTS LAW REVIEW 149 (2002).

Yasser, Raymond L., McCurdy, James R., Goplerud, C. Peter, & Weston, M. *Sports Law: Cases and Materials,* 4th ed. Cincinnati, OH: Anderson, 2000.

CHAPTER 8

INTELLECTUAL PROPERTY

The purpose of intellectual property law is to promote creativity and provide a greater variety of products and services in the marketplace for the consumer. Intellectual property law gives businesses, inventors, writers, artists, and others protection in intangible property creations, allowing ownership rights in property that are balanced with public access to that property. The U.S. Constitution addresses intellectual property rights in Article 1, Section 8, Clause 8, which authorizes Congress "to promote the progress of science and useful arts, by securing for limited times to authors and inventors the exclusive rights to their respective writings and discoveries." Each form of intellectual property is the result of the investment of creative labor and intellectual capacity by the creator. In some situations intellectual property rights encompass several forms of intellectual property. For instance, an inventor could have patent protection as well as copyright protection in the same invention, such as a computer program. A trademark owner can also have copyright protection on their mark.

Intellectual property law has traditionally encompassed four areas: trademarks, copyrights, trade secrets, and patents. It can also involve many other areas of the law, including misappropriation, the tort of "passing off," false advertising, and the licensing of intellectual property. The umbrella of "unfair competition" covers a wide spectrum of intellectual property rights. This chapter explores all elements of intellectual property law in the context of the sports world. Licensing and sponsorship dominate the sports business landscape and are discussed as well.

TRADEMARKS

The purpose of trademark law is to prevent customer confusion. Consumers want to be able to rely on trademarks to assist them in purchasing goods in the marketplace and to have confidence in the goods they purchase. Consumers can benefit greatly when they are able to identify the origin of goods. Trademark law also assists business owners because it helps them create and protect the "goodwill" of their business. The average person in the United States cannot go through the day without coming into contact with numerous trademarks and service marks in the marketplace. Trademarks serve as labels "that identif[y] and distinguish a particular product,"[1] thus assisting to create certainty in the marketplace.

---

[1] Sport Supply Group, Inc. v. Columbia Casualty Company, 335 F.3d 453, 461 (5th Cir. 2003).

The Lanham Act, 15 U.S.C. § 1051 et seq., is the federal statute dealing with trademarks in the United States, and the U.S. Patent and Trademark Office (PTO) is the agency governing trademarks. The PTO is an agency in the United States Department of Commerce that issues patents to inventors and businesses for their inventions, and also provides trademark registration for business owners. Once a trademark has been registered with the PTO, all parties are on notice that the registrant of that mark owns the exclusive rights to that mark. The registrant is allowed to use the symbol ® to give notice to others that the mark is a registered mark with the PTO. The symbol ™ can be used with any common law usage of a mark. The United States has a dual system of trademark registration. An entity can obtain registration of a trademark at either the federal or state level.

The more distinctive a mark is, the more likely it is to receive trademark protection under the law. The law does not recognize every possible symbol for trademark protection. To avoid consumer confusion, the law states that only certain marks are allowed trademark protection. The first trademarks were merely names or identifying symbols that were attached to goods. Many companies now use slogans or phrases that also qualify as trademarks, such as Nike's "Just Do It," American Express's "Don't leave home without it," and the Processor Education Program and Dairy Management's "Got Milk?"[2] These slogans have become so well known that they are now common vernacular in the American marketplace.

The Lanham Act defines a trademark as follows:

> The term "trademark" includes any word, name, symbol, or device, or any combination thereof—
> (1) used by a person, or
> (2) which a person has a bona fide intention to use in commerce and applies to register on the principal register established by this Act, to identify and distinguish his or her goods, including a unique product, from those manufactured or sold by others and to indicate the source of the goods, even if that source is unknown.[3]

Colors, fragrances, and even sounds can constitute trademarks.[4] A service mark performs the same function as a trademark but is used to identify services rather than goods.

Whether a mark is entitled to protection depends essentially upon the classification or strength of the trademark. The initial issue in any action for trademark protection is whether the word, name, symbol, or device is protected by trademark law. Courts have generally divided trademarks into four categories:

1. Arbitrary or fanciful
2. Suggestive
3. Descriptive
4. Generic[5]

---

[2] *See* Nike, Inc. v. Circle Group Internet, Inc., 318 F. Supp. 2d 688 (N.D. Ill. 2004) (finding defendant was a cyber-squatter under federal law for using "justdoit.net").

[3] 15 U.S.C.A. § 1127.

[4] Qualitex Co. v. Jacobson Products Co., Inc., 115 S. Ct. 1300, 34 U.S.P.O. 2d 1161 (1995) (finding that a color could constitute a trademark).

[5] Half Price Books v. Barnesandnoble.com, 2003 WL 23175436 (N.D. Tex. 2003) at 3.

In *Major League Baseball Properties, Inc. v. Opening Day Productions, Inc.*, 385 F. Supp. 2d 256, 272 (S.D.N.Y. 2005), the court described the relevant categories as follows:

> . . . Whether a mark qualifies for § 43(a) protection depends on its classification within the system established by Judge Friendly in *Abercrombie & Fitch Co. v. Hunting World, Inc.*, 537 F.2d 4, 9 (2d Cir. 1976). That system incorporates four classes of marks, in ascending order of strength: (1) generic, (2) descriptive, (3) suggestive, and (4) arbitrary or fanciful. Suggestive and arbitrary marks are considered "inherently distinctive and entitled to protection" due to the fact that "their intrinsic nature serves to identify a particular source of a product." *Two Pesos, Inc. v. Taco Cabana, Inc.*, 505 U.S. 763, 768, 112 S. Ct. 2753, 120 L. Ed. 2d 615 (1992). Therefore, they are "automatically protected" without a showing of secondary meaning. A generic mark can never be protected, but a descriptive mark is eligible for protection if it has acquired secondary meaning. Therefore, a descriptive mark must have become distinctive of the particular producer's goods in commerce. Secondary meaning attaches to a mark when "a significant number of prospective purchasers understand the term when used in connection with the particular kinds of goods involved . . . as indicative of an association with a specific entity." *Bernard v. Commerce Drug Co.*, 964 F.2d 1338, 1343 (2d Cir. 1992).

A *fanciful* mark is a newly coined word that is created for the sole purpose of functioning as a trademark. Fanciful terms can include invented words such as "Xerox."[6] "Kodak" has been classified as a fanciful term for photographic supplies.[7] "Exxon" is also considered a fanciful trademark. An *arbitrary* mark has a common meaning, but that meaning is unrelated to the product itself. An arbitrary mark in no way describes the product or service it is meant to identify. "Ivory" has been held to be an arbitrary term referring to soap, but it is generic when referring to elephant tusks.[8] "Apple" is an arbitrary term when referring to computers.[9] "Bicycle" could be considered arbitrary when referring to playing cards. Both arbitrary and fanciful marks are completely unrelated to the goods with which they are associated.

Suggestive marks allude to the nature of the product but take some effort and imagination on the part of the public to make the connection between the product and its source. These types of marks indirectly describe the service or product they identify. "Coppertone" for tanning products, "Greyhound" for bus services, and "Mustang" for automobiles are all examples of suggestive marks. "Roach Motel" may be a suggestive mark as well.[10]

Descriptive marks usually describe some element of the product, such as size, the provider of the goods, or some particular characteristic of the goods. "Tender Vittles" as applied to cat food is descriptive.[11] Other examples of descriptive marks include "Healthy Choice" for nutritious food products,[12] "Thirst Aid" for drinks,[13] and "Soaker" for water gun.[14] The term "half price books" is

---

[6] Douglas Laboratories, Inc. v. Copper Tan Inc., 210 F. 2d 453 (2d. Cir. 1954).

[7] Kodak Co. v. Weil, 243 N.Y.S. 319 (1930).

[8] *Abercrombie & Fitch*, 537 F.2d at 9 n.6.

[9] *Half Price Books*, 2003 WL 23175436 at 3.

[10] Duluth News-Tribune v. Mesabi Pub. Co., 84 F.3d 1093, 1096 (8th Cir. 1996).

[11] Big O Tire Dealers, Inc. v. The Goodyear Tire & Rubber Company, 408 F. Supp. 1219 (D. Col. 1976), *aff'd*, 561 F.2d 1365 (10th Cir. 1977).

[12] ConAgra, Inc. v. George A. Hormel, & Co., 990 F.2d 368, 370 (8th Cir. 1993). The Lanham Act states that five years of continuous and substantial use serves as prima facie evidence that the mark has acquired secondary meaning under the act.

[13] Sands, Taylor & Wood Co. v. Quaker Oats Co., 978 F.2d 947, 952 (7th Cir. 1992), *cert. denied* 507 U.S. 1042 (1993).

[14] Talk To Me Products, Inc. v. Larami Corp., 804 F. Supp. 555, 562 (S.D.N.Y. 1992), *aff'd* 992 F.2d 469 (2d Cir. 1993).

categorized as either generic or descriptive.[15] Generic marks constitute the names of the goods or services themselves and are therefore not protectable under U.S. trademark law. Examples of generic marks include "Chocolate Fudge" for soda, "Crab House" for a seafood restaurant, "You Have Mail" (AOL), and "Hog" for large motorcycles. Owners can lose protection in a trademark if the mark becomes the common name of a product or service. Examples of marks that were once protectable but have now become generic include, "Zipper" for slide fasteners, "Thermos" for vacuum bottles, and "Yo-Yo" for returning tops.

The Lanham Act indicates that certain marks can never acquire trademark protection. Some of these are as follows:

- Generic marks
- Scandalous or immoral marks
- Marks that are deceptive
- Marks that are primarily a surname
- Marks in prior use

Trademark Infringement: "Likelihood of Confusion"

A trademark owner must always protect and "police" his or her trademark. An infringement of a trademark can cause the owner loss of profits as well as infringing upon the goodwill of the owner's mark and the owner's future business. A trademark owner must take the necessary legal steps to ensure no other parties infringed upon their mark. For a trademark owner to prevail in a trademark infringement lawsuit, the owner of the mark must show (1) ownership of a protectable mark and (2) likelihood of consumer confusion.[16]

Problem 8-1

Plaintiff Dallas Cowboys Football Club, Ltd. ("Dallas Cowboys" or "Cowboys") is the National Football League ("NFL") franchise in the Dallas, Texas, metropolitan area. Plaintiff NFL Properties, LLC, ("NFLP") is the marketing arm of the thirty-two NFL member clubs.

Defendant America's Team Properties, Inc. ("ATP"), is a Minnesota corporation with its principal place of business in Burnsville, Minnesota. Defendant was incorporated in 1998 to take assignment of U.S. Trademark Reg. No. 1,899,914 (for "clothing; namely, shirts") and exploit the mark commercially.

The '914 trademark registration was originally applied for by Terrence Nash ("Nash"), president and owner of MEOB, Inc. ("MEOB"), in June 1990, and was sold to ATP in 1998. In his intent-to-use application with the United States Patent and Trademark Office, Nash submitted a sworn declaration stating that he was unaware of any other person or firm that had the right to use the mark in commerce. Nash has stated he intended to sell one million t-shirts at $1 profit each to pay for his children's education. The '914 trademark was granted to MEOB in 1995.

Nash states that he sold or gave away t-shirts printed with "America's Team" at various sporting events and while traveling as a salesman. He received a license from the University of

---

[15] *Half Price Books*, 2003 WL 23175436 at 4.
[16] Fuddruckers, Inc. v. Doc's B.R. Others, Inc., 826 F.2d 837, 841 (9th Cir. 1987).

Washington and sold co-branded t-shirts outside Husky Stadium in 1990. He also licensed use of "America's Team" to a recreational league softball team in Texas. Nash claims he was completely unaware that the Dallas Cowboys, or any other entity, was referred to as "America's Team" at this time.

Nash claims a few sales between 1990 and 1994. In 1994, he sold t-shirts to four businesses. As a result of the registration and these sales, Defendant asserts it has a nationwide priority date of June 6, 1990, and the mark has been continually used in commerce since 1995. Thereafter, Nash spoke with many entities about potential licensing deals, including Nike, Reebok, and L.A. Gear, but none came to fruition.

Defendant ATP purchased the trademark from MEOB, Inc., in 1998 for $100. As part of the deal, MEOB's president and owner Brian Reichel ("Reichel") agreed to give Nash 49 percent of the proceeds from any subsequent sale of the registration. On May 14 and May 17, 1999, Defendant ran advertisements in the *USA Today* newspaper to auction the "America's Team" registration to the highest bidder with a minimum bid of $500,000. America's Team Properties also called the Dallas Cowboys to notify the team that the registration was up for sale. Defendant also contacted the team in October, November, and December 2003 to offer to sell the registration for $400,000. The Cowboys refused to pay.

Since purchasing the registration, ATP has sold clothing and assorted goods through its website, www.americasteamusa.com. Its "primary focus" has been to create a website and social networking site to promote the "America's Team Award" to "provide a four-year, full-ride scholarship to one high school team every year."

The Dallas Cowboys and NFLP filed this suit alleging Defendant ATP's actions infringe their common law rights in the trademark and their state trademark registration. The Cowboys assert that "America's Team" is a protectable mark and that the team has priority over America's Team Properties, Inc. Plaintiffs assert that "Defendant is a bad-faith infringer whose increasingly aggressive and harassing activities pose a significant threat to the business concerns of the Dallas Cowboys."

Defendant ATP filed a counterclaim against the Dallas Cowboys and NFLP, seeking a declaratory judgment that its registration is valid and that the Cowboys have no use priority, and further seeks cancellation of the Cowboys' state trademark registration in Texas.

The Cowboys assert the team has used "America's Team" as a service mark and trademark since 1979. The term was first used in commerce that year as the title of the Dallas Cowboys' 1978 season highlight film. The term was coined by Bob Ryan, an executive at NFL Films, working with Doug Todd, the Cowboys' public relations director. The name stuck, and the Cowboys actively encouraged its use to promote the team. The Cowboys allow sponsors, promoters, and charities to use the term in promotions.

Other examples abound of use in connection with the Dallas Cowboys. A 1979–1980 calendar sold by the Cowboys to the public used the term. In the 1980s, NFL Films sold a videocasette titled "America's Team: The Dallas Cowboys 1975–1979." Between 1986 and 1990, a NFLP licensee sold silver coins with the term engraved on them. The team used the term in various publications throughout the 1980s and 1990s. And since at least 1989, the Cowboys have used the term in presentations and sales pitches to potential sponsors and business partners.

By at least 1991, the Cowboys sold t-shirts emblazoned with the term. The team notes that the first use in commerce by MEOB and Nash was January 1995. The team argues that by this time, the term had been long associated with the Dallas Cowboys and had been used in commerce on sweatshirts, trading cards, belt buckles, and other items for years.

On October 30, 1992, the Dallas Cowboys obtained Texas trademark registration No. 5223517 for "Dallas Cowboys America's Team" for use on clothing. Since 1995, the Cowboys have made millions of dollars selling "America's Team" items including apparel, glassware, flags, blankets, towels, pins, footballs, toys, and holiday ornaments. The team has sold the items through various retail outlets, including thirty-three Official Dallas Cowboys Pro Shops in malls and airports, at Texas Stadium, a merchandise trailer, through catalogs, and on the Internet. The Cowboys also sell "America's Team" items through wholesalers and license its use to various manufacturers.

Since December 2003, Defendant has filed fifty-eight trademark applications with the USPTO for various uses of "America's Team" and related indicia. The Cowboys and NFLP have opposed many of the applications before the USPTO Trademark Trial and Appeal Board ("TTAB"), and the TTAB proceedings are suspended pending the outcome of this action.

Plaintiffs seek summary judgment on seven claims: declaration of noninfringement and nondilution, federal unfair competition, federal dilution, injury to business reputation or trademark under Texas law, common law trademark infringement, common law unfair competition, and further seek cancellation of Defendant's trademark registration. 2009 WL 819394 (N.D. Tex. 2009).

Source: Courtesy of Westlaw; reprinted with permission.

In Case 8-1, *Baseball America, Inc. v. Powerplay Sports, Ltd.,* 71 U.S.P.Q.2d 1844 (2004), the "opposer" objected to the trademark application of Powerplay Sports on several grounds, claiming that the proposed mark would cause "consumer confusion."

📖 CASE 8-1 *Baseball America, Inc. v. Powerplay Sports, Ltd.*

71 U.S.P.Q.2d 1844 (2004)

Opinion by Bottorff

Administrative Trademark Judge:

. . . [A]pplicant seeks registration on the Principal Register of the mark BASEBALL AMERICANA (in typed form; BASEBALL disclaimed) for goods identified in the application as "posters" . . . applicant seeks registration on the Principal Register of the mark BASEBALL AMERICANA (in typed form; BASEBALL disclaimed) for services recited in the application as "educational services, namely, conducting courses, seminars, conferences and workshops in the field of baseball history and trivia, and photography; organizing baseball exhibitions for stadiums, museums, theme parks, libraries and other public venues; providing facilities for educational, entertainment, sporting and cultural activities in the form of a baseball hall of fame and museum." . . . [B]oth applications include applicant's claim of acquired distinctiveness under Trademark Act Section 2(f), 15 U.S.C. §1052(f).

Opposer has opposed registration of the marks depicted in both of applicant's applications. As grounds for opposition in both cases, opposer has alleged that it is the prior user of the mark BASEBALL AMERICA on or in connection with various baseball-related goods and services; that it is the owner of Principal Register Registration . . . which is of the mark depicted . . . for goods identified in the registration as "publications, namely newspapers, books, and calendars relating to baseball, principally items concerning minor league and college baseball," and that applicant's mark, as applied to the goods and services identified in applicant's applications, so resembles opposer's previously-used and registered mark BASEBALL AMERICA as to be likely to cause confusion, to cause mistake, or to deceive. . . .

Opposer has established that it is the owner of a valid and subsisting registration of the mark BASEBALL AMERICA. . . .

. . . [W]e turn next to the question of whether opposer has established the "likelihood of confusion" element of its . . . opposition. . . .

We turn first to the issue of whether applicant's mark and the opposer's mark, when compared in their entireties in terms of appearance, sound and connotation, are similar or dissimilar in their overall commercial impressions. The test is not whether the marks can be distinguished when subjected to a side-by-side comparison, but rather whether the marks are sufficiently similar in terms of their overall commercial impression that confusion as to the source of the goods or services offered under the respective marks is likely to result. The focus is on the recollection of the average purchaser, who normally retains a general rather than a specific impression of trademarks. Moreover, where, as in the present case, the marks would appear on virtually identical goods and services, the degree of similarity between the marks which is necessary to support a finding of likely confusion declines.

Applying these legal principles in the present case, we find that opposer's mark BASEBALL AMERICA and applicant's mark BASEBALL AMERICANA are more similar than dissimilar when viewed in their entireties in terms of appearance, sound, connotation and overall commercial impression. Visually and aurally, the marks differ only as to the final two letters of applicant's mark. Although the marks are not identical in connotation, they are similar, in that Americana, by definition, pertains to America. Both marks generally connote "baseball in America" or "American baseball." Viewed in their entireties, we find that the marks create similar overall commercial impressions. When we factor in the legally identical nature of the parties' goods and services and the renown of opposer's mark, both of which decrease the degree of similarity between the marks which is necessary to find a likelihood of confusion, we find that the marks are sufficiently similar that confusion is likely to result from the parties' use of these marks on or in connection with their goods and services.

Next, we find that applicant's goods and services, as identified in the applications, are legally identical to goods and services as to which opposer has proven it is the prior user of its mark, i.e., posters and educational seminars in the field of baseball. We also find that applicant's goods and services are sufficiently related to the goods identified in opposer's pleaded registration that confusion is likely to result from the parties' use of these confusingly similar marks. Opposer's publications, like applicant's goods and services, all pertain to the sport of baseball. Moreover, opposer has published books which pertain, like applicant's goods and services, to the historical aspects of baseball.

We also find that the parties' respective goods and services are or could be marketed in the same trade channels to the same classes of purchasers, i.e., to baseball fans. Applicant has admitted as much. These are general consumers who would not be expected to exercise more than ordinary care in purchasing the goods and services. Likewise, applicant's and opposer's publications and services are inexpensive consumer items which can be purchased without a great degree of care.

Next, the evidence of record establishes that opposer's BASEBALL AMERICA magazine is considered in the trade to be a "publication of record" for statistics and other information pertaining to baseball and baseball players. Opposer's statistics, rankings and player evaluations are regarded by those in the trade, and by other media outlets, as definitive reference materials. For example, USA Today publishes opposer's rankings of college baseball teams, and identifies such rankings as the "Baseball America Top 25." Opposer's editors have appeared on ESPN as on-air commentators in connection with coverage of college baseball, the annual college and amateur baseball drafts, and the major league expansion draft. Readership of opposer's magazine is approximately 125,000 to 150,000 per issue, and opposer had 500,000 visitors to its baseballamerica.com website in the typical month of June 2003. Opposer selects the rosters and publishes the official game program for the All-Star Futures Game and the Legends and Celebrity Softball Game, which are played as part of the festivities surrounding the Major League All-Star Game each summer. Based on this evidence, we find that opposer's BASEBALL AMERICA mark is a well-known and indeed famous mark in the baseball field, a fact which weighs heavily in favor of a finding of likelihood of confusion.

After considering all of the evidence of record as it pertains to the relevant . . . evidentiary factors, . . . we conclude that applicant's mark, when used on and in connection with applicant's goods and services, so resembles opposer's mark, previously used and/or registered for identical or similar goods and services, that confusion as to source, sponsorship or affiliation is likely to result. . . .

Decision: Each of these consolidated oppositions is sustained.

Source: Courtesy of Westlaw; reprinted with permission.

When you hear the words "Baby Bombers," what do you think of? Do the New York Yankees come to mind? Does it make you think of the "Bronx Bombers"? In Case 8-2, *Hart v. New York Yankees Partnership*, 184 Fed. Appx. 972 (C.A. Fed. 2006), the New York Yankees filed an opposition with the Trademark Trial and Appeal Board objecting to the plaintiff's intent-to-use application for registering the mark BABY BOMBERS. The Yankees prevailed (as they most often do).

📖 CASE 8-2 *Hart v. New York Yankees Partnership*

184 Fed. Appx. 972 (C.A. Fed. 2006)

Before MICHEL, Chief Judge, PLAGER, Senior Circuit Judge, and BRYSON, Circuit Judge.

PER CURIAM.

Leon P. Hart filed an intent-to-use application with the United States Patent and Trademark Office to register the mark BABY BOMBERS for clothing and athletic wear. The New York Yankees Partnership and Staten Island Minor League Holdings, L.L.C. (collectively, the "New York Yankees" or "Yankees") filed an opposition, which the Trademark Trial and Appeal Board ("Board") sustained. We *affirm*.

The New York Yankees oppose Hart's mark on the basis of their use of the common law mark BABY BOMBERS in association with the New York Yankees major league baseball club and with the Yankees' minor league affiliate, the Staten Island Yankees baseball club. In order to establish their ground of opposition under section 2(d) of the Lanham Act, 15 U.S.C. § 1052(d), the Yankees must show that they have priority of use in the mark and that Hart's mark, when used on the goods set forth in the application, would create a likelihood of confusion with the Yankees' mark. Because the Yankees' BABY BOMBERS mark is unregistered, the Yankees must also show their mark is distinctive in order to establish priority.

. . . Hart's priority date is July 23, 2001, the date he filed his intent-to-use application. The Board found that the New York Yankees had used the term BABY BOMBERS in promotional materials to refer to their Staten Island minor league affiliate since its inception in 1999. The Board also found that the term had been used by the press to refer to both the minor league and major league Yankees teams for several years before Hart's priority date. Contrary to Hart's argument on appeal, the Board's finding that the Yankees have priority in the mark did not rely on uses of the term subsequent to July 23, 2001. There is ample evidence in the record that the term was used in connection with the Staten Island Yankees prior to 2001. Based on our examination of the record, we conclude that the Board's finding that the Yankees have priority in the BABY BOMBERS mark is supported by substantial evidence.

The Board also found that the Yankees' BABY BOMBERS mark was distinctive rather than merely descriptive of the qualities or characteristics of goods or services. Hart has alleged no specific error in the Board's analysis. Having reviewed the record, we are satisfied that the Board's finding of distinctiveness is supported by substantial evidence.

Finally, the Board determined that the mark BABY BOMBERS for clothing and athletic wear would be confusingly similar to the Yankees' identical mark when used in association with entertainment services involving baseball games. The Board considered the factors set forth in *In re E.I. DuPont DeNemours & Co.*, 476 F.2d 1357, 1361 (1973), especially the questions of similarity of the marks and whether Hart's goods and the Yankees' services are related. With regard to similarity of the marks, the Board noted that the marks clearly are identical in appearance and sound. The Board also found that the meaning and commercial impression of BABY BOMBERS would be identical to the extent that the mark, when used in connection with a minor league baseball team and on athletic clothing, suggests an association with the New York Yankees, who have been referred to as the Bronx Bombers for over seventy years. With regard to similarity of the parties' goods and services, the Board found that Hart's athletic clothing goods were sufficiently related to the Yankees' baseball exhibition services that consumers would likely believe Hart's products were approved or licensed by the Yankees. Hart's arguments have not convinced us that the Board's findings are unsupported by substantial evidence or that the Board erred in concluding that a likelihood of confusion exists between the marks. Because the New York Yankees have also established that they have priority in the BABY BOMBERS mark and that their mark is distinctive, we *affirm* the decision of the Board. . . .

Source: Courtesy of Westlaw; reprinted with permission.

Trademark Dilution

What happens if one party uses another party's trademark in an unwholesome or derogatory fashion? The legal concept of dilution encompasses a use of a trademark that tarnishes or dilutes the original mark because the viewing public will associate the original manufacturer's product with an unsavory product. Infringement under a dilution theory is a recent development in trademark law. The Federal Trademark Dilution Act (FTDA) was passed in 1995, giving owners of famous trademarks protection against those parties diluting or tarnishing their trademark. Many states have also passed dilution laws protecting "distinctive" or "famous" trademarks from unauthorized use. In effect, dilution laws protect the goodwill associated with a famous mark.

The FTDA (15 USCA § 1125) provides in pertinent part:

```
(c) Dilution by blurring; dilution by tarnishment

    (1) The owner of a famous mark shall be entitled . . . to an
        injunction against another person's commercial use in commerce
        of a mark or trade name, if such use begins after the mark has
        become famous and causes dilution of the distinctive quality
        of the mark. . . . In determining whether a mark is distinctive
        and famous, a court may consider factors such as, but not
        limited to—

        (A) the degree of inherent or acquired distinctiveness of the
            mark;
        (B) the duration and extent of use of the mark in connection
            with the goods or services with which the mark is used;
        (C) the duration and extent of advertising and publicity of the
            mark;
        (D) the geographical extent of the trading area in which the
            mark is used;
        (E) the channels of trade for the goods or services with which
            the mark is used;
        (F) the degree of recognition of the mark in the trading areas
            and channels of trade used by the marks' owner and the
            person against whom the injunction is sought;
        (G) the nature and extent of use of the same or similar marks
            by third parties; and
        (H) whether the mark was registered . . . or on the principal
            register. . . .
```

Dilution is only available to the holder of a "famous" mark.[17] Under dilution analysis, the mark holder is not required to prove that "likelihood of confusion" exists. Infringement by way of dilution can occur in two ways: tarnishment or blurring.[18] Tarnishment involves harm to the goodwill of the plaintiff's trademark caused by the defendant's conduct creating a link in the consumer's minds between the

[17] Washington Speakers Bureau, Inc. v. Leading Authorities, Inc., 33 F. Supp. 2d 488, 504 (E.D. Va. 1999).
[18] People for the Ethical Treatment of Animals v. Doughney, 2000 WL 943353 (E.D. Va. 2000).

plaintiff's mark and the poor quality of the defendant's goods. Under a "blurring" theory, the plaintiff's trademark loses some distinctiveness because of its association with the defendant's mark.[19] The law can also under some circumstances protect the owner of a trademark when a party uses that mark in an attempt at parody but still has the effect of tarnishing the mark.[20]

In Case 8-3, *NBA Properties v. Untertainment Records LLC*, 1999 WL 335147 (S.D.N.Y. 1999), NBA Properties sought an injunction against Untertainment Records for its use of an altered NBA logo. Instead of NBA Hall of Famer Jerry West bouncing a ball, a silhouetted player was shown holding a gun alongside a message containing the word "Drugs." The NBA alleged that the defendant was diluting its famous mark and infringing upon its goodwill.

📖 CASE 8-3 *NBA Properties v. Untertainment Records LLC*

1999 WL 335147 (S.D.N.Y. 1999)

BAER, District J.

Plaintiff NBA Properties, Inc. ("NBAP") brings this action against defendants Untertainment Records LLC, alleging trademark infringement, trademark dilution, unfair competition and state law violations of trademark dilution.

Here, the plaintiff moves for a temporary restraining order and preliminary injunction enjoining Vibe from future use of an advertisement and requiring defendant Vibe to use its best efforts to remedy the damage it has caused to NBAP by having published and disseminated the advertisement in the June/July issue of *Blaze* magazine. The composition of the advertisement contains the NBA logo and shows a silhouetted basketball player dribbling a basketball (the "NBA Logo") altered to put a handgun in one hand alongside the words "SDE SPORTS, DRUGS, & ENTERTAINMENT" (the "Advertisement" or "Ad"). Specifically, NBAP seeks an order that would recall page 11 (the page on which the Ad appears) in all copies of the magazine that have been disseminated. . . .

The defendant is ordered to cease use of the Advertisement in all future issues of *Blaze* magazine and any other Vibe publications, and the defendant is ordered to publish a corrective advertisement. . . .

II. Background

The NBA Logo in various forms is registered with the United States Patent and Trademark Office. NBAP is the proprietor of each of these marks and the registrations. The NBA Logo is heavily used, advertised and promoted in connection with telecasts of NBA games and other NBA

---

[19] Deere & Company v. MTD Products, Inc., 41 F.3d 39 (2nd Cir. 1994).
[20] Girl Scouts of USA v. Personality Posters Manufacturing Co., 304 F. Supp. 1228, 1233 (S.D.N.Y. 1969).

activities. It is commonly recognized as representing the NBA, its member teams and players, and its commercial ventures. The NBAP is the marketing and licensing arm of the NBA and has the exclusive right to exploit trademarks owned by the teams that comprise the NBA.

Untertainment is a producer of albums by artists including rapper Cameron Giles, known as "Cam'Ron." Untertainment is about to release an album by Cam'ron entitled "SDE Sports, Drugs, & Entertainment." In connection with the sale and promotion of that album, Untertainment had constructed itself or had constructed a 30' by 50' banner bearing the NBA trademark with the same alterations as the Ad, and placed it at the southwest corner of Lenox Avenue and 125th street in New York City. Untertainment submitted the Advertisement for publication in the June/July issue of *Blaze* magazine. Vibe is the publisher of *Blaze* magazine. *Blaze* is a start-up magazine and the June/July issue was its sixth issue. That same issue contains an advertisement for NBA Apparel.

The NBAP commenced this lawsuit, shortly after it learned of the banner and received numerous calls from distressed residents and representatives of school, community and church groups who expressed outrage at what they thought was the NBAP's sponsorship of the banner.

B. Clear Likelihood of Success on the Merits

1. Trademark Dilution Claims

The plaintiff alleges that Vibe's altered use of the NBA mark dilutes its distinctive quality in violation of section 43(c) of the Lanham Act. The Federal Trademark Dilution Act of 1995 (the "Dilution Act"), 15 U.S.C. § 1125(c), establishes a federal cause of action to ensure that famous trademarks are protected from unauthorized users who seek to trade on the fame and goodwill of the famous mark and dilute its image. The legislative history of the Act indicates that its purpose is "to protect famous trademarks from subsequent uses that blur the distinctiveness of the mark or tarnish or disparage it, even in the absence of a likelihood of confusion."

To prevail on its claim of trademark dilution in violation of section 43(c) of the Lanham Act, the plaintiff must establish that the mark is famous within the meaning of the statute, and there is a likelihood of dilution. Section 43(c) states that "the owner of a famous mark shall be entitled . . . to an injunction against another person's commercial use in commerce of a mark or trade name, if such use begins after the mark has become famous and causes dilution of the distinctive quality of the mark . . . ." 15 U.S.C. § 1125(c)(1).

The Dilution Act sets forth eight nonexclusive factors that courts may consider when determining whether the mark is famous: (A) the degree of inherent or acquired distinctiveness of the mark; (B) the duration and extent of use of the mark in connection with the goods or services with which the mark is used; (C) the duration and extent of advertising and publicity of the mark; (D) the geographical extent of the trading area in which the mark is used; (E) the channels of trade for the goods or services with which the mark is used; (F) the degree of recognition of the mark in the trading areas and channels of trade used by the marks' owner and the person against whom the injunction is sought; (G) the nature and extent of use of the same or similar marks by third parties. . . . In addition, the question of whether a mark is distinctive or famous under the Dilution Act is analogized to the strength of mark analysis conducted in conjunction with trademark infringement claims.

Based on a consideration of these factors, it appears indisputable that the NBA Logo is a famous mark. The NBA Logo is registered on the Principal Trademark Register of the United States in a variety of forms. It is a recognized symbol of the NBA and NBAP among consumers located both in the United States and around the world. Accordingly, the NBA Logo is a famous mark entitled to protection under the Dilution Act.

Dilution is defined as "the lessening of the capacity of a famous mark to identify and distinguish goods or services, regardless of the presence or absence of (1) competition between the owner of the famous mark and other parties, or (2) likelihood of confusion, mistake, or deception." Dilution under federal law can occur in two forms, either by blurring or tarnishment, and "mirrors the traditional New York dilution analysis, under which dilution can be founded upon." Blurring occurs when a party uses or modifies the plaintiff's mark and creates the possibility that the mark will lose the ability to serve a unique identifier. "Dilution through tarnishment occurs where the defendant uses the plaintiff's mark in association with unwholesome or shoddy goods or services."

Further, the Second Circuit affirmed a preliminary injunction based on dilution by tarnishment and stated in part:

> 'Tarnishment' generally arises when the plaintiff's trademark . . . is portrayed in an unwholesome or unsavory context likely to evoke unflattering thoughts about the owner's product. In such situations, the trademark's reputation and commercial value might be diminished because . . . the defendant's use reduces the trademark's reputation and standing in the eyes of consumers as a wholesome identifier of the owner's products or services.

```
The NBAP claims that linking the NBA Logo with violence and drugs will
adversely color the public's impressions of the NBA. I agree. The NBA
is bound to suffer negative associations from the juxtaposition of the
distorted NBA Logo containing the basketball player with a gun in his
right hand and the words "SPORTS, DRUGS, & ENTERTAINMENT." Indeed, the
outrage generated in response to the banner indicates that the Adver-
tisement placed the NBA Logo in an unwholesome and unsavory context in
the eyes of the public. Any suggestion that the NBAP or the NBA endorses
violence, gunplay or drug use, or that they have chosen to associate
themselves with those who do, will likely tarnish their reputation
with their corporate customers and partners, as well as the public
at large.

The plaintiff has made a clear showing that the defendant's publica-
tion will create negative associations with the NBA Logo and that
there is a likelihood of confusion under the tarnishment theory of
dilution. Thus, the plaintiff is entitled to injunctive relief based
on its claims of trademark dilution.

Source: Courtesy of Westlaw; reprinted with permission.
```

Problem 8-2

You are the marketing director for a new line of sporting wear. Your boss has asked you to come up with a slogan to market a new product to young teens. Your creativity is lacking, and after hours of toiling over the problem, you arrive at the slogan "Just did it." Your boss agrees with your choice, and the company begins to market its new product using that slogan. Nike, Inc., sends a cease and desist letter to your company's legal department stating that your company is infringing on Nike's trademark. How will a court decide this case? What other information do you need to know to properly decide this case? See *Nike, Inc. v. "Just Did It" Enterprises*, 6 F.3d 1225 (7th Cir. 1993).

Trademark Parody

The American cowboy humorist Will Rogers once stated, "Now everything is funny as long as it is happening to somebody else, but when it happens to you, why it seems to lose some of its humor, and if it keeps on happening, why the entire laughter kind of fades out of it."[21] Parody in trademark law mirrors that statement. Noted professor J. Thomas McCarthy writes, "[N]o one likes to be the butt of a joke, not even a trademark. But the requirement of trademark law is that a likely confusion of source, sponsorship, or affiliation must be proven, which is not the same thing as a 'right' not to be made fun of."[22]

---

[21] W. ROGERS, THE WRITINGS OF WILL ROGERS (1974).
[22] 2 J. MCCARTHY, TRADEMARKS AND UNFAIR COMPETITION § 31:38 at 670 (2d ed. 1984).

Many parties have asserted that their use of a mark was actually a parody of the mark and therefore not an infringement and defended the use of the mark on First Amendment grounds. The purpose of a parody is "to create a comic or satiric contrast to a serious work." A parody does not intend to confuse the public but makes its humorous point by association with the original work. Its actual point is to amuse the public, not to confuse. Courts have found a viable parody "only when there was a discernable direct comment on the original."[23] A parody or satire can also be provided First Amendment protection. In *Cardtoons, L.C. v. Major League Baseball Players' Ass'n*, 182 F.3d 1132 (10th Cir. 1999), the court found in favor of a plaintiff who was manufacturing baseball cards featuring caricatures of players, on the basis of the First Amendment.

There have been many sports-related lawsuits dealing with the use of parody under trademark law. For a serious look at the lovable Barney, see *Lyons Partnership v. Giannoulas*, 179 F.3d 384 (5th Cir. 1999). In that case, the best-known mascot in sports history, the San Diego Chicken, used a Barney look-alike in his act and proceeded to pummel Barney into oblivion. When the Chicken's owner was sued for trademark infringement, the "Chicken" was granted summary judgment on his defense that his use of a Barney look-alike was a parody under trademark law. The court summarized the defense as follows:

> Giannoulas offers a slightly different perspective on what happened. True, he argues, Barney, depicted with his large, rounded body, never changing grin, giddy chuckles, and exclamations like "Super-dee-Dooper!," may represent a simplistic ideal of goodness. Giannoulas, however, also considers Barney to be a symbol of what is wrong with our society—homage, if you will, to all the inane, banal platitudes that we readily accept and thrust unthinkingly upon our children. Apparently, he is not alone in criticizing society's acceptance of a children's icon with such insipid and corny qualities. Quoting from an article in The New Yorker, he argues that at least some perceive Barney as a "potbellied," "sloppily fat" dinosaur who "giggle[s] compulsively in a tone of unequaled feeblemindedness" and "jiggles his lumpish body like an overripe eggplant." The Internet also contains numerous web sites devoted to delivering an anti-Barney message. Giannoulas further notes that he is not the only satirist to take shots at Barney. Saturday Night Live, Jay Leno, and a movie starring Tom Arnold have all engaged in parodies at the ungainly dinosaur's expense. One Internet search service provides a list of links to anti-Barney websites, many of which contain warnings like the following: "If you're offended by material that suggests the killing of Barney, or like him in any way, please don't come here."
>
> Perhaps the most insightful criticism regarding Barney is that his shows do not assist children in learning to deal with negative feelings and emotions. As one commentator puts it, the real danger from Barney is "denial: the refusal to recognize the existence of unpleasant realities. For along with his steady diet of giggles and unconditional love, Barney offers our children a one-dimensional world where everyone must be happy and everything must be resolved right away." Giannoulas claims that, through careful use of parody, he sought to highlight the differences between Barney and the Chicken. Giannoulas was not merely profiting from the spectacle of a Barney look-alike making an appearance in his show. Instead, he was engaged in a sophisticated critique of society's acceptance of this ubiquitous and insipid creature. Furthermore, Giannoulas argues that he performed the sketch only at evening sporting events. The sketch would begin with the Chicken disco dancing. The Barney character would join the Chicken on the field and dance too, but in an ungainly manner that mimicked the real Barney's dance.

---

[23] Dr. Seuss Enterprises v. Penguin Books, Inc., 924 F. Supp. 1559, 1569 (S.D. Cal. 1996) *aff'd* 109 F. 3d 1394 (9th Cir. 1997).

The Chicken would then indicate that Barney should try to follow the Chicken's dance steps (albeit, by slapping the bewildered dinosaur across the face). At this point, Barney would break character and out-dance the Chicken, to the crowd's surprise. The Chicken would then resort to violence, tackling Barney and generally assaulting Barney. Barney would ultimately submit to the Chicken and they would walk off the field apparently friends, only for the Chicken to play one last gag on the back-in-character naive and trusting Barney. The Chicken would flip Barney over a nearby obstacle, such as a railing."[24]

After going to their respective litigating corners, each party came out fighting. Spokeswoman Kelly Lane issued a statement on behalf of Lyons Partnerships, the owner of Barney: "Lyons is obviously very disappointed by this ruling. Lyons continues to believe that the Chicken's use of a Barney look-alike confuses and upsets young children who see their friend Barney being beaten up. The partnership is weighing an appeal."[25] Giannoulas stated in response to the court's decision: "To paraphrase my purple adversary, I think the judge's decision is Super-Dee-Dooper."[26] Giannoulas noted that his parody was the only one subject to litigation. He further stated: "Hopefully, Barney will go back to being a peaceful playmate, rather than a litigious bully."[27]

In a case involving both trademark and copyright infringement, *Dallas Cowboys Cheerleaders, Inc. v. Pussycat Cinema, Ltd.*, 467 F. Supp. 366 (D.C.N.Y. 1979), the famous cheerleaders sued when the defendant made a 90-minute film entitled *Debbie Does Dallas*. The defendant asserted that the film was a parody or satire and therefore entitled to protection under trademark law. The court found that a preliminary injunction should be issued against the defendant on various legal grounds. The court stated:

> A parody is a work in which the language or style or another work is closely imitated or mimicked for comic effect or ridicule. A satire is a work which holds up the vices or shortcomings of an individual or institution to ridicule or derision, usually with an intent to stimulate change; the use of wit, irony or sarcasm for the purpose of exposing and discrediting vice or folly.
>
> In the present case, there is no content, by way of story line or otherwise, which could conceivably place the movie *Debbie Does Dallas* within any definition of parody or satire. The purpose of the movie has nothing to do with humor; it has nothing to do with a commentary, either by ridicule or otherwise, upon the Dallas Cowboys Cheerleaders. There is basically nothing to the movie *Debbie Does Dallas,* except a series of depictions of sex acts. The other phases of the movie the dialogue and the "narrative" are simply momentary and artificial settings for the depiction of the sex acts. The associations with the Dallas Cowboys Cheerleaders obviously play an important role in the film and in the advertising; but this is a role that has nothing to do with parody or satire. The purpose is simply to use the attracting power and fame of the Dallas Cowboys Cheerleaders to draw customers for the sexual "performances" in the film. The obvious intent of defendant Zaffarano and the others responsible for this film is to cash in upon the favorable public image of the Dallas Cheerleaders, including the image of a particular quality of feminine beauty and character.

---

[24] *Lyons Partnership*, 179 F.3d 384 at 386–87.
[25] Ken Ellingwood, *Winged Victory-Federal Judge Allows San Diego Chicken's Free-Range Comedy—He Can Continue Performing Skit That Mocks Barney Character*, Los Angeles Times, July 1, 1998.
[26] Ibid.
[27] Ibid.

Defendant argues that there is, at most, only a minor association with the Dallas Cheerleaders in the movie, since the scene with Debbie performing sex acts partly clothed in the Dallas Cheerleaders uniform is only a small part of the film. This is unrealistic. Debbie's "performance" is the culmination of the film. It is Debbie and her selection to be a cheerleader in Dallas (obviously a Dallas Cowboys Cheerleader) which give rise to the title, and the opportunity to display the uniform prominently in the advertising as well as to use the various slogans associating the film with the Dallas Cheerleaders.

In this connection, it is apparent that the movie and the advertising are intended to be closely connected, and are in fact closely connected. If injunctive relief is merited, it is not appropriate to limit such relief solely to the advertising, as defendant Zaffarano suggests. The use of the associations with the Dallas Cheerleaders both in the film and in the advertising, all have the single purpose of exploiting the Dallas Cheerleaders' popularity in order to attract customers to view the sex acts in the movie. . . .[28]

Trademarks and Domain Names

What happens when a famous trademark is also being used as a domain name by another party? Does the trademark owner have a legal right to prevent the owner of the domain name from the continuing use of the domain name? Congress passed legislation in an attempt to determine how to best resolve disputes between those who own domain names and trademarks. The most important tool for fighting cybersquatters has become the Anticybersquatting Consumer Protection Act of 1999 (ACPA).

When the domain name system first became available, many people were able to acquire otherwise protected trademarks of companies through the domain name registration process, an activity labeled *cybersquatting*. Cybersquatting was defined by the Second Circuit Court of Appeals in *Sporty's Farm v. Sportsman's Mkt., Inc.*, 202 F.3d 489, 493 (2nd Cir. 2000), as "involv[ing] the registration as domain names of well-known trademarks by non-trademark holders who then try to sell the names back to the trademark holder." Courts have described cybersquatting in many different ways, including "the internet version of a land grab."[29] There are many different types of cybersquatting. For example, many cybersquatters rely on the fact that people often make spelling or typing mistakes; these cybersquatters are known as "typosquatters."[30]

The evolution of cybersquatting has included such legal concepts as trademark infringement, unfair competition, First Amendment issues, and property ownership rights. In *People for Ethical Treatment of Animals v. Doughney*, 263 F.3d 359 (4th Cir. 2001), the plaintiffs brought claims of trademark infringement and unfair competition under the Lanham Act, whereas the defendant asserted that he was entitled to keep the domain name "peta.org" because his website was a constitutionally protected parody. The court found that the unauthorized use of the PETA trademark in a domain name was infringement.

Athletes have had conflicts with individuals who have taken the athlete's name in the form of a domain name. Courts have had to decide whether such an action is a violation of the athlete's right of publicity, violation of trademark law, or both. Does an athlete have trademark protection in his or her name? Some athletes and celebrities have argued that their famous name is equal to a common law trademark. Individuals may attempt to register an athlete's name as a domain name and use it as

---

[28] *Dallas Cowboys Cheerleaders*, 467 F. Supp. at 376.
[29] *Also see,* Virtual Works v. Volkswagen of America, Inc., 238 F.3d 264, 267 (4th Cir. 2001).
[30] *Abercrombie & Fitch Stores v. Zuccarini*, Case No. D2000-1004 (WIPO Nov. 1, 2001).

a fan website. Many cybersquatters have purchased the domain names of athletes and entertainers in hopes of making a profit by selling the name back to them. Some cybersquatters have successfully defended their use of such a domain name on First Amendment grounds.

Barry Zito, a star pitcher for the San Francisco Giants, had his name registered as a domain name by another party. He sought return of his domain name through the dispute resolution process of the Internet Corporation for Assigned Names and Numbers (ICANN).[31] Zito was able to wrestle away his domain name, barryzito.com, from the registrant. In an arbitration decision, *Barry v. Zito*, Claim Number: FA0207000114773 (2002), the panel found that Zito had built up "commercial value" in his name and was entitled to the return of the domain name. Many famous athletes have had their name, a portion of their name or their nickname taken and used by others as their domain name. These have included Tiger Woods,[32] Yao Ming,[33] and Terrell Owens.[34]

Unless you were an avid Philadelphia Phillies fan you might have never heard of Tyler Green. In Case 8-4, *Green v. Fornario*, 486 F. 3d 100, the dispute was over the domain name www.tylergreensports.com.

CASE 8-4 *Green v. Fornario*

486 F. 3d 100

I. Facts and Procedural History

A. Tyler Green

Tyler Green is a former pitcher for the Philadelphia Phillies. . . . Plagued by injuries from the get-go, Green was able to play only three full seasons in the Major Leagues. The apex of his career was a 1995 trip to the All Star Game.

Following his retirement from professional baseball in 2000, Green has stayed in the Philadelphia area . . . he regularly appears on regional television and radio baseball programs, and he participates in a variety of Phillies-related charitable events. From this evidence, Green no doubt retains some name recognition in the greater Philadelphia community.

B. Greg Fornario and Tyler Green Sports

Greg Fornario ran a business called Tyler Green Sports. A former bartender at a Philadelphia-area sports bar, Fornario decided in the late 1990s

---

[31] Effective December 1, 1999, ICANN initiated the Uniform Domain Name Resolution Policy.

[32] *Eldrick "Tiger" Woods v. Whitsan Bay Golf Shop,* FA0608000772886, National Arbitration Forum. (Dispute was over www.tigerwoodscoursedesign.com).

[33] Yao lost his dispute over yaoming.com. See, *Yao Ming c/o BDA Sports Management v. Evergreen Sports, Inc.,* FA 0304000154140, National Arbitration Forum.

[34] Terrell Eldorado Owens v. Aran Smith d/b/a/ Sportsphenoms.com and/or Sportsphenoms, D2003-0463.

to start a sports handicapping business. Handicappers are the stock analysts of the sports gambling world: they provide information to sports bettors. According to Fornario, he saw this as an easy way to make money, and so he acquired an 800 number, took out an ad in the paper, and waited for the calls to come in. There was a mix-up, however, with his 800 number, and so he discontinued the business after running the advertisement for only one day.

Fornario did, however, market this short-lived venture as Tyler Green Sports. He testified that the business was never affiliated with anyone named Tyler or Green. Rather, he purportedly came up with "Green" because handicapping businesses, he said, typically have some reference to money in their names. Green is, of course, the color of money, so it fit. Fornario then tried to come up with something "catchy" to put with Green. He settled on Tyler, he claimed, because he is an Aerosmith fan, and Stephen Tyler is the group's lead singer. Thus, Tyler Green Sports. He testified that at the time he had never heard of Tyler Green the baseball player. He admitted, however, to being a fan of all sports except hockey. The Philadelphia teams have no allure for him, as he is a New York native. He described himself as a "diehard" Yankees fan. While all of this is more than a mite shaky, it is Fornario's story, and he is sticking to it.

In 2000, Fornario, his handicapping business long defunct, resumed using the name Tyler Green Sports in trade. This time, he used it as the name of an entertainment promotion company. Specifically, the company made money by coming up with event ideas, putting them together, and selling them to venues. For example, it promoted a number of Philadelphia Eagles' pep rallies by lining up player appearances, taking care of decorations and advertising, and selling the pre-packaged events to sports bars. It also did traditional party planning. The company used the website http://www.tylergreensports.com to advertise its services. Fornario incorporated the company in Pennsylvania, and registered to it the name Tyler Green Sports. Before registering the name, he testified that he engaged an attorney to do a trademark search. According to Fornario, this search revealed that the name Tyler Green Sports was not registered to any business or person. Tyler Green Sports never achieved significant commercial success.

At the time that he began using the trade name Tyler Green Sports, Fornario had lived in the Philadelphia area for at least five years and had spent considerable time around sports as a fan, a bartender in a sports bar, and a nascent handicapper. From this, he seems the sort of person who would know of a pitcher on the Phillies' team. Still, finding that he knew of Green is not compelled by this record. Doing so here would require discrediting Fornario's testimony and deciding that Green was famous enough that Fornario could not but know of him.

While Tyler Green was known regionally in his short career and his post-retirement work continues to garner some attention, we cannot conclude that the record evidence of his recognition means that Fornario must have known of him.

We turn now to Green's § 1125(d) cybersquatting claim. That section—a relatively new addition to the Lanham Act—prohibits registering a domain name that is confusingly similar to a distinctive mark or dilutive of a famous mark with "a bad faith intent to profit" from it. 15 U.S.C. § 1125(d)(1)(A). For example, registering the site http://www.dupont.com with the hope of selling it to E.I. du Pont de Nemours and Company for an exorbitant price would be a quintessential act of cybersquatting.

To determine bad faith in this context, Congress has given us nine factors to consider:

(I)   the trademark or other intellectual property rights of the person, if any, in the domain name;

(II)   the extent to which the domain name consists of the legal name of the person or a name that is otherwise commonly used to identify that person;

(III)   the person's prior use, if any, of the domain name in connection with the bona fide offering of any goods or services;

(IV)   the person's bona fide noncommercial or fair use of the mark in a site accessible under the domain name;

(V)   the person's intent to divert consumers from the mark owner's online location to a site accessible under the domain name that could harm the goodwill represented by the mark, either for commercial gain or with the intent to tarnish or disparage the mark, by creating a likelihood of confusion as to the source, sponsorship, affiliation, or endorsement of the site;

(VI)   the person's offer to transfer, sell, or otherwise assign the domain name to the mark owner or any third party for financial gain without having used, or having an intent to use, the domain name in the bona fide offering of any goods or services, or the person's prior conduct indicating a pattern of such conduct;

(VII)   the person's provision of material and misleading false contact information when applying for the registration of the domain name, the person's intentional failure to maintain accurate contact information, or the person's prior conduct indicating a pattern of such conduct;

(VIII) the person's registration or acquisition of multiple domain names which the person knows are identical or confusingly similar to marks of others that are distinctive at the time of registration of such domain names, or dilutive of famous marks of others that are famous at the time of registration of such domain names, without regard to the goods or services of the parties; and

(IX)   the extent to which the mark incorporated in the person's domain name
       registration is or is not distinctive and famous. . . .

15 U.S.C. § 1125(d)(1)(B)(i).

Here, at least five of the nine factors appear to cut in Fornario's
favor. It is undisputed that he used the name Tyler Green in connection with a *bona fide* offering of services (factors III and VI). In
addition, there is no evidence that he provided misleading contact
information (factor VII), that he registered multiple confusing domain
names (factor VIII), or that he intended to divert internet users from
Tyler Green's own website (factor V). While applying the factors is a
holistic, not mechanical, exercise, we have little difficulty concluding that Fornario met the low threshold of having a colorable defense
to Green's cybersquatting claim.

It appears that Green's strongest claim was his § 1125(a) claim for
confusing misdescription. That section prohibits using in commerce any
name that is likely to cause confusion as to sponsorship of or affiliation with one's goods. 15 U.S.C. § 1125(a)(1)(A). Here, Green's claim
was that Fornario's use of his name created the false impression that
he was affiliated with, or otherwise approved of or sponsored,
Fornario's business. Given the evidence of Green's name recognition,
we believe that he would have had a good chance of succeeding on this
claim, as it is sensible to think that using the name of a regionally
known sports player in connection with a company that hosts events at
sports bars in that region would deceive people.

At the same time, likelihood of confusion is a factual issue, and we
will not presume to know what evidence Fornario could have produced
had he found it prudent to continue litigating the case. His business
activities appear to have little to do with baseball. Moreover, it is
unclear just how well-recognized, even regionally, Green was when
Fornario acted. So the evidence produced at discovery would be key.
While possible, we are not convinced that it is even probable that a
retired player, with a career neither long nor notable, would be well-
known enough to render use of his name in connection with a party and
event-planning business confusing to the typical consumer. Indeed, it
is plausible that Fornario's use of Tyler Green's name confused few
consumers. Thus, once again we cannot conclude that Fornario lacked a
colorable defense.

We do not know precisely why Fornario agreed to stop using the name
Tyler Green Sports so quickly. Likelihood of success almost certainly
went into the thought process, but, as the District Court noted,
Fornario probably also considered the financial position of his
business (precarious) and the value of the trade name (minimal).

Deciding to forgo costly litigation struck the District Court as a reasonable strategic decision, and we agree. In any event, given that Fornario met the low bar of a colorable claim to use the name Tyler Green Sports, it was reasonable for the District Court not to infer bad faith from his refusal to stop at Green's request. If anything, by settling quickly Fornario saved Green (who, we note, does not press a claim for damages) a great deal of trouble, and we are loathe to discourage such decisions by using them to support an inference of culpable conduct. Thus, we cannot conclude that the District Court clearly erred in declining to find that Fornario refused to heed Green's cease and desist letters in bad faith.

. . . .

Green argues that Fornario knowingly sought to profit from Tyler Green's name recognition. But the District Court found that Fornario did not know of Green when he began using the trade name Tyler Green Sports, and that finding (no matter our doubts) is not clearly erroneous. In addition, Green argues in effect that upon receiving the first cease and desist letter, Fornario immediately should have set off for Canossa. We cannot agree. If Fornario maintained a good-faith belief that he was rightfully using the trade name Tyler Green Sports, he was entitled to decline pre-litigation requests and defend his position as he saw fit. The District Court found that the evidence did not support a finding of bad faith, and that determination also is not clearly erroneous. Thus, we affirm the Court's conclusion that this case is not "exceptional" enough to merit an award of attorneys' fees to Green.

Source: Courtesy of Westlaw; reprinted with permission.

Problem 8-3

DeWayne Scott is a huge sports fan. He loves college football and follows the recruiting practices of all the major football programs. He has the idea of registering as domain names the names of the top 100 high school football players in the United States from a list he obtains from the Internet. He purchases the domain names for $29 each. Three years after he makes his purchases he strikes gold. The ninth player on the list, Jerome Wilkins, is a Heisman trophy candidate from the University of Maryland. Maryland wants to promote Wilkins as a candidate for the award and seeks the domain name from Scott. Is Scott required to transfer the name to the university? Would he have to transfer the name to Wilkins? What if he turns the website (www.JeromeWilkins.com) into a fan website touting him for the Heisman trophy?

COPYRIGHTS

Section 102 of the 1976 Copyright Act states that a copyright can exist "[i]n original works of authorship fixed in any tangible medium of expression."[35] A work of authorship must be original for the work to be protected under copyright law. The work must also possess a modicum of originality to qualify as a copyrighted work. The good news is that it is fairly easy to meet the creativity standard set forth under copyright law.[36] The work becomes a copyrighted work once it is "fixed" in a tangible medium of expression.

The works of authorship that are available for copyright protection under the act include the following:

- Literary works
- Musical works, including any accompanying words
- Dramatic works, including any accompanying music
- Pantomimes and choreographic music
- Pictorial, graphic, and sculptural works
- Motion pictures and other audiovisual works
- Sound recordings
- Architectural works[37]

Copyright law provides the owner of a copyright with a "bundle of rights." The owner of a copyright is given the sole authority to authorize or do the following:

- Reproduce the copyrighted work
- Prepare derivative works based on the copyrighted work (this is commonly referred to as the right to adapt the copyrighted work)
- Distribute copies or phonorecords of the copyrighted work
- Publicly perform the work (this right does not apply to pictorial, graphic, and sculptural works, architectural works, or sound recordings)
- Publicly display the work
- In the case of sound recordings, to perform the copyrighted work publicly by means of a digital audio transmission[38]

Registration is not required for a work to be able to receive copyright protection. However, U.S. authors must register any work prior to filing an infringement lawsuit. The ownership of a valid copyright protects the holder of that copyright from the unauthorized copying, display, and public performance of the work. The bundle of rights under copyright law also provides the owner with the right to prepare derivative works of the original work as well as the right of control the sale and distribution of the copyrighted work. Copyright ownership is limited to a certain extent under the act. Other parties may use a copyrighted work under the "fair use" doctrine, which is

---

[35] 15 U.S.C.A. § 102.
[36] Sebastian International, Inc. v. Consumer Contacts (PTY) Ltd., 664 F. Supp. 909 (D.N.J. 1987), *rev'd on other gds.*, 847 F.2d 1093 (3rd Cir. 1988).
[37] 15 U.S.C.A. § 102.
[38] 15 U.S.C.A. § 106.

discussed later in this chapter. The Copyright Act also provides for compulsory licensing of cable television broadcasts and musical compositions.

Copyright Infringement

If a party violates any of the exclusive rights of the copyright holder found in Section 106 of the Copyright Act, then infringement has occurred, absent a viable defense. A party can infringe a copyright directly or indirectly. To prove a copyright infringement case, a plaintiff must show "(1) ownership of a valid copyright; and (2) copying of a constituent element of the work that is original."[39] Defendants may also avail themselves of the fair use defense under copyright law to avoid an infringement claim.

An independent creation of copyrighted work is not a violation under the act. How can you prove that someone has copied your work? It is the unusual case in which a party has direct proof of a violation under the act. Therefore, the plaintiff must prove that copying occurred by showing that the defendant had "access" to the plaintiff's copyrighted work and that the defendant's work is "substantially similar" to the copyrighted elements of the plaintiff's protected work.

If a party infringes a copyright, the plaintiff can sue for damages or seek an injunction, or both. Damages can be actual profits lost as the result of the infringement. Case 8-5, *Hoch v. MasterCard International Incorporated and McCann-Erickson*, 284 F. Supp. 2d 1217, deals with legal issues surrounding possible copyright infringement in a commercial involving Major League Baseball.

 CASE 8-5 *Hoch v. MasterCard International Incorporated and McCann-Erickson*

284 F. Supp. 2d 1217

I. Background

Plaintiffs are two life-long friends in their forties who share a love of baseball and, in particular, the Minnesota Twins Major League Baseball team (Minnesota Twins). In 1998, they formed an organization, Citizens United for Baseball in Minnesota (CUBM) with the goal of keeping Major League Baseball (MLB) in Minnesota. Their efforts included a campaign to build a new baseball stadium to keep the Minnesota Twins in Minnesota. In support of this goal, Plaintiffs made a thirty-minute documentary in 1998 entitled *Twins—Now and Forever* (*Twins*). Plaintiffs created *Twins* by filming a ten-day road trip that included visits to baseball stadiums in Cleveland, Baltimore, and Denver, all of which had built stadiums in urban settings. In each city, Plaintiffs interviewed stadium represen-tatives, civic leaders, residents, and fans. The interviews emphasized that a MLB team and stadium can be an important community asset. Plaintiffs copyrighted *Twins* in 2001.

---

[39] Feist Publications, Inc. v. Rural Tel. Serv. Co., 499 U.S. 340, 361, 11 S. Ct. 1282, 1296, 113 L. Ed. 2d 358 (1991).

McCann-Erickson is an advertising agency that created a series of ads known as the "Priceless" campaign for MasterCard, a credit-card service company. As part of that series, McCann-Erickson created six ads, called the *Trip* ads, highlighting MasterCard's sponsorship of MLB. The *Trip* ads feature two twenty-something male friends on a road trip to visit all thirty MLB stadiums in one summer, purchasing necessities along the way with their MasterCard credit card. McCann-Erickson developed the idea in February 2001, and, after receiving approval from MasterCard and MLB, filmed the *Trip* ads shortly thereafter. MLB ballparks in five cities are depicted in the *Trip* ads: Cincinnati, Boston, Baltimore, San Francisco, and Seattle. Plaintiffs allege that the *Trip* ads infringe on their copyright for *Twins*.

The elements of a claim for copyright infringement are: (1) ownership of the copyright by the plaintiffs; and (2) copying by the defendants. The parties do not dispute that Plaintiffs own a valid copyright in *Twins,* so the Court's inquiry is limited to the second element. When, as is the case at hand, there is not direct evidence of copying, a plaintiff may use circumstantial evidence to prove copying. To establish copying through circumstantial evidence, Plaintiffs must show that Defendants had access to the work and that there is substantial similarity between the works. *See id.*

A. Access

Access is established by showing that a defendant had an "opportunity to view or to copy" plaintiff's work. *Id.* at 942. Establishing a "bare possibility of access is not enough; rather, [plaintiff] must prove that defendant[ ] had a reasonable possibility of viewing his work." *Id.* Access may not be inferred based on conjecture and speculation. Here, Plaintiffs assert two theories of access: widespread dissemination and corporate receipt.

1. Widespread Dissemination

A reasonable possibility of access may be established by evidence that prior to the creation of the infringing work, the copyrighted work was widely disseminated to the public. Plaintiffs made approximately 500 copies of *Twins*. They argue *Twins* achieved widespread dissemination based on the following: (1) *Twins* was shown once per day for one week at the Baseball Hall of Fame in Cooperstown, New York; (2) it was shown continuously in Minnesota at a CUBM booth for two days at "Twins Fest," a meet-the-players event for fans of the Minnesota Twins; (3) several hundred copies were handed to public officials in Minnesota; (4) Minnesota public television showed at least a portion of *Twins;*

(5) Plaintiffs were interviewed on local radio shows and in local papers; and (6) clips of *Twins* were available on CUBM website.

The Court's review of the case law reveals several reoccurring considerations in determinations of widespread dissemination: number of copies distributed, commercial success or notoriety, and national performances or distribution.

The evidence in this case reveals that *Twins'* distribution was limited in number and geography, was regionally broadcast, and met with virtually no commercial success. Most of the 500 copies were distributed in the Twin Cities and with the exception of the performances at the Baseball Hall of Fame, all the showings were in Minnesota. It is undisputed that no one associated with the creation of the *Trip* ads was in Cooperstown, New York, or in Minnesota during any of the showings of *Twins*. As to the airings on Minnesota public television, the record reveals that the broadcast took place after the onset of this litigation. Plaintiffs' regional notoriety gained from their appearances on radio and in print does not by itself create an opportunity for Defendants to view *Twins*. Turning to the CUBM website, notwithstanding Plaintiffs ability to track the number of site visits, the record contains no such information for months of February and March 2001 when Defendants created the ads. Without regard to the number of site visits, the clips of *Twins* available on the website contain less than 10% of the film. Indeed, Plaintiffs' letter to Allen Selig, Chief Executive Officer and Commissioner of Baseball, dated January 28, 2000, discloses Plaintiffs' difficulties in distributing *Twins* and in getting people to watch it. Viewing the evidence in the light most favorable to Plaintiffs, the Court concludes that *Twins* failed to obtain a level of widespread dissemination.

2. Corporate Receipt Doctrine

Plaintiffs assert that a reasonable possibility of access is established through the corporate receipt doctrine. *Nimmer on Copyright* describes the doctrine as follows:

> [E]vidence that a third party with whom both the plaintiff and defendant were dealing had possession of plaintiff's work is sufficient to establish access by defendant. But the proof must show that both plaintiff's and defendant's dealings took place concurrently, in order to give rise to an imputation of access. If the defendant is a corporation, the fact that one employee of the corporation has possession of plaintiff's work should warrant a finding that another employee (who composed defendant's work) had access to plaintiff's work, whereby reason of the physical

propinquity between the employees the latter has the opportunity to view the work in the possession of the former. 3 Melville B. Nimmer, *Nimmer on Copyright* § 13.02(A) (1992).

At its most basic level, the corporate receipt doctrine allows an inference of access to be drawn when there is a relationship—either based on a common employer or other dealings—between an intermediary who knows of plaintiff's work and the alleged copier. However, this relationship cannot be too attenuated so that access is established only "through a 'tort[u]ous chain of hypothetical transmittals.'"

Here, Plaintiffs offer two avenues under which the corporate receipt doctrine might applies: first through Selig, and second via David Mona, Chairman of the Minneapolis office of Weber Shandwick, a public relations firm. Plaintiffs contend Selig's admitted receipt of *Twins* acts as a corporate receipt because MLB has approval rights over MasterCard's MLB ads. It is undisputed that Selig is not, and has never been, involved with MasterCard's sponsorship deal. Selig's only role in relation to sponsorships is receipt of a report upon conclusion of a new sponsorship. The record further reflects MLB's first contact with McCann-Erickson regarding approval of the *Trip* ads took place after McCann-Erickson conceptualized the *Trip* ads into storyboards. Plaintiffs fail to offer any facts that could give rise to an inference of access through Selig.

With regard to Mona, it is undisputed that he received a copy of *Twins* from Plaintiffs. Plaintiffs assert the corporate receipt doctrine is satisfied insofar as: (1) the Interpublic Group is the parent company to both Mona's employer and McCann-Erickson, and (2) at some point in the early 1990s, Mona's company had a MasterCard account. First, it is undisputed that Mona has no relationships—business or personal—with anyone involved in the *Trip* ads. Additionally, Mona is located in Minnesota and has no physical proximity to the New York based Defendants. Second, although Mona's firm dealt with a MasterCard campaign in the early 1990s, the record reflects that Mona had no part in it. Plaintiffs have failed to produce evidence of a relationship that could tie Mona to McCann-Erickson or to MasterCard. Viewed in the light most favorable to the Plaintiffs, the evidence shows only the barest possibility based on hypothetical speculation and conjecture that Defendants had access to *Twins*.

B. Substantial Similarity

Even if Plaintiffs had shown a reasonable possibility of access, their claim would still fail as matter of law because the two works are not substantially similar. The Eighth Circuit follows a two-step analysis for substantial similarity. The first step, an objective extrinsic test, analyzes the similarity of ideas. If there is a substantial similarity of ideas, the second step, a subjective intrinsic test, evaluates the similarity of expression based on the response of a reasonable, ordinary person. Summary judgment is appropriate where "reasonable minds could not differ as to the absence of substantial similarity in expression."

1. Extrinsic Test

The extrinsic test focuses on alleged similarities in the objective details of the works. It requires a comparison of plot, theme, dialogue, mood, pace, setting, and sequence. A court applying the extrinsic test must "filter out and disregard the non-protectible elements in making its substantial similarity determination." The Court decides the extrinsic test as a matter of law and may rely on expert testimony to conduct the analysis.

Plot, Theme and Dialogue   Copyright law only protects the expression of ideas, not the ideas themselves. Accordingly, general plots or stock themes are not protected. The distinction between an idea and its expression is often difficult to ascertain.

In the case at hand, the two works share the similar idea of two male friends traveling on a road trip to visit baseball stadiums. Plaintiffs assert that the two works are substantially similar in that both feature "adventure-seeking friends who embark on a road trip that has at its heart the love of baseball, as shown through tradition, history and legends associated with the national pastime." Defendants produced expert testimony detailing numerous examples of road trips in film and literature, and travel books devoted entirely to baseball stadium road trips. Indeed, Plaintiffs' characterization applies with equal force to the film *Field of Dreams*. Plaintiffs' expert did not conduct analysis relevant to the extrinsic test, and he admits his lack of expertise in the areas of visual arts and baseball. The Court thus concludes that the idea of a baseball stadium road trip by automobile is an example of general, unprotected stock theme.

Similarly, *scenes a faire,* sequences of events that flow necessarily from the choice of a setting or situation, are not protected by copyrights. In the case at hand, this includes the visuals that flow from the basic idea of a road trip—highway signs, service stops, landmarks for geographic identification, and transportation by automobile. Plaintiffs argue that these "obvious similarities" preclude summary judgment. The Court disagrees and concludes the similarities are nothing more than *scenes a faire.*

Disregarding the unprotected stock themes and *scenes a faire,* a review of the plot, theme and dialogue reveals significant dissimilarity between the two works. Plaintiffs' thirty-minute film is a methodical journey that investigates the economic benefits to a community that builds a downtown baseball stadium. Plaintiffs spend a considerable portion of the film developing this plot by interviewing people involved with the stadiums, fans on the street, and local merchants. The narrative in *Twins* contains an explicit message as to the community benefits of urban baseball stadiums. On the other hand, the two friends in the *Trip* ads have a rather minimalist plot of visiting all thirty MLB ballparks in one summer. Their intent is to create "priceless" memories and to have fun. The characters in the *Trip* ads have little or no dialogue and the story telling depends significantly on the end-titles (*e.g.,* "26 stadiums down, 4 to go: priceless").

Mood and Pace   The mood of *Twins* earnestly reflects its purpose. Although Plaintiffs occasionally joke around with each other, their trip maintains a practical, orderly attitude commensurate with the goals of CUBM. In contrast, the three-and-one-half minutes of *Trip* ads moves at a lightning pace. The *Trip* ads evoke an entirely happy-go-lucky feel, comporting with freedoms associated with summertime youth.

Setting and Sequence   Plaintiffs assert that the geographic sequence is substantially similar between the works. A review of the paths taken in the works reveals no such similarity. *Twins* starts in Minnesota, goes through Chicago (exterior shot of Wrigley Field), to Cleveland, to Baltimore, to Denver and back to Minnesota. The *Trip* ads carve a path that starts in Cincinnati, goes to Boston, to Baltimore, to San Francisco, and then to Seattle. Plaintiffs also contend substantial similarities exist because both the *Trip* ads and *Twins* use similarly colored Volkswagen mini-buses decorated with stickers to effectuate their road trips. The Court agrees that there is clear similarity between the automobiles used. However, this lone common element does not justify a finding of substantial similarity under the extrinsic test.

2. Intrinsic Test

The intrinsic test is subjective and asks whether an ordinary, reasonable person would find the "total concept and feel of the works" to be substantially similar. In the instant case, the concept and feel of the two works are completely different. Whereas the *Trip* ads are snapshots

of carefree youths pursuing a summertime goal, *Twins* explores the economic benefits of urban baseball fields with the intent to raise money
and support for Plaintiffs' organization, CUBM. No reasonable person
could find these two works to be substantially similar.

In short, Plaintiffs have not submitted any evidence to create an
issue of fact as to whether Defendants had access to *Twins* and whether
Twins and the *Trip* ads are substantially similar. Viewing the record
in the light most favorable to Plaintiffs, no reasonable trier of fact
could find that Defendants copied *Twins*. The Court therefore grants
Defendants' motion.

Source: Courtesy of Westlaw; reprinted with permission.

Fair Use Defense

The fair use defense to copyright law allows use of a copyrighted work under certain circumstances notwithstanding the copyright owner's "bundle of rights" found in Section 106 of the Copyright Act. The Copyright Act of 1976 gave statutory recognition to the fair use doctrine, which is
sometimes used to resolve the potential conflicts between copyright ownership and free speech. This
defense under copyright law can be asserted by a defendant once the plaintiff has set forth a prima
facie case for infringement. Essentially, the court allows a defendant to escape liability based on a
"fair use" of the work, finding that infringement occurred, but excusing the use. The doctrine is
founded on principles of common sense and fairness and prevents the strict application of the copyright laws when that application would be deemed unfair or too rigorous.

The federal copyright statute provides the following with regard to fair use:

§107 Limitations on exclusive rights: Fair use

Notwithstanding the provisions of sections 106 and 106A, the fair use
of a copyrighted work, including such use by reproduction in copies or
phonorecords or by any other means specified by that section, for purposes such as criticism, comment, news reporting, teaching (including
multiple copies for classroom use), scholarship, or research, is not
an infringement of copyright. In determining whether the use made of a
work in any particular case is a fair use the factors to be considered
shall include—

(1) the purpose and character of the use, including whether such
    use is of a commercial nature or is for nonprofit educational
    purposes;
(2) the nature of the copyrighted work;
(3) the amount and substantiality of the portion used in relation to
    the copyrighted work as a whole; and
(4) the effect of the use upon the potential market for or value of
    the copyrighted work.

The fact that a work is unpublished shall not itself bar a finding of
fair use if such finding is made upon consideration of all the above
factors.[40]

There are many cases illustrating the fair use defense under copyright law. *Penguin Books, USA, Inc. v. Dr. Seuss Enterprises*, 924 F. Supp. 1559 (S.D. Cal. 1996), involved two parties that most individuals would never consider in the same context—O.J. Simpson and Dr. Seuss. In this case, Dr. Seuss Enterprises brought a lawsuit against a publisher that used copyrighted material in a book about the O.J. Simpson murder trial entitled *"The Cat Not in the Hat! A Parody by Dr. Juice."* The work purported to take a "fresh look" at the O.J. Simpson double-murder trial and used the distinctive writing style created by Theodore S. Geisel, better known to the world as Dr. Seuss. The court examined the issue of whether the book was an infringement of the works of Geisel or was fair use of a copyrighted work allowed under copyright law. The plaintiff sued for both copyright and trademark infringement. The court examined the fair use factors and arrived at the conclusion that the attempted parody was an infringing work notwithstanding the fact that the book actually referred to itself as a parody on the cover. One of the lines in the book read "one knife? / two knife? / red knife / dead wife." The court determined this to be an infringement of the Dr. Seuss book *One Fish Two Fish Red Fish Blue Fish*. The court also compared illustrations found in the Penguin book to those by Dr. Seuss, finding them infringing.[41]

TRADE SECRETS

The basic purpose of trade secret law is to protect against the theft of information by commercially unreasonable means. Trade secret law is actually more aligned in some respects with contract and tort law than intellectual property law. It is rudimentary that information must be kept secret for it to have trade secret protection. Absolute secrecy is not required, however; parties must simply take reasonable measures to maintain secrecy. There is no requirement to register a trade secret to have protection. Once a trade secret is disclosed, its protection is lost. A trade secret is defined by Section 4 of the Uniform Trade Secrets Act (UTSA) as "information, including a formula pattern, compilation, program, device, method, technique, or process, that: (i) derives independent economic value, actual or potential, from not being generally known to, and not being readily ascertainable by proper means by, other persons who can obtain economic value from its disclosure or use, and (ii) is the subject of efforts that are reasonable under the circumstances to maintain its secrecy."

Trade secrets can constitute customer habits, marketing techniques, research and development, customer lists, and pricing information. If a business cannot protect its information through trademarks, patents, or copyrights then it may be able to protect that information from competitors by deeming it a trade secret.

---

[40] 17 U.S.C.A. § 107.

[41] *For further study on fair use see*, Patrick K. Thornton, *The Limits of the Fair Use Doctrine: The Family Guy Ko's Carol Burnett in a Battle of Cultural Icons*, University of Baltimore Intellectual Property Law Journal, Volume 17, Number 1, Fall 2008.

Misappropriation of Trade Secrets

The theft of confidential business information can constitute the misappropriation of trade secrets. Violation of trade secret law can entitle the owner of the trade secret to damages or an injunction against further disclosure of the information. Section 757 of the *Restatement of Torts* states: "One who discloses or uses another's trade secret, without a privilege to do so, is liable to the other if (1) he discovered the secret by improper means; or (2) his disclosure or use constitutes a breach of confidence reposed in him by the other in disclosing the secret to him."

One of the problems facing businesses is what to do with employees who possess trade secrets and then leave to work for a competitor. Many employees are required to sign contracts containing covenants not to compete and confidentiality agreements relating to trade secrets in the event they leave to work for a competitor. When an employee takes confidential protected information to a competitor, the issue of trade secret protection can become the subject of extensive litigation.[42]

In Case 8-6, *Harvey Barnett v. Shidler*, 338 F.3d 1125 (10 Cir. 2003), the court reviewed trade secrets law in the context of methods of swimming instruction.

📖 CASE 8-6 *Harvey Barnett v. Shidler*

338 F.3d 1125 (10 Cir. 2003)

Before SEYMOUR, McKAY, and LUCERO, Circuit Judges.

LUCERO, Circuit Judge.

I.

In 1966, Dr. Harvey Barnett, the founder and president of ISR, began to develop the Infant Swimming Research program ("ISR program"), which plaintiffs describe as a "*scientific,* behavioral approach to pediatric drowning prevention." ISR's program utilizes a method known as "swim, float, swim," and contains nearly two-thousand "prompts and procedures" for teaching infants as young as six-months old how to survive in the water. In addition, the ISR program maintains safety protocols to keep children safe during instruction and provides a "BUDS" Record Sheet allowing parents to monitor children's bodily functions, diet, and sleep in order to evaluate physical responses to the ISR program.

In a five-week course, ISR trains and certifies instructors. ISR-certified instructors teach survival skills to infants in private lessons, ten minutes a day, five days a week for three to four weeks. Instructors receive a videotape entitled "Prompts and Procedures," which illustrates how to use behavioral conditioning in teaching infants and covers other water-safety issues. ISR's program also includes the ISR Master Instructor System, in which individuals become certified as Master Instructors to train other potential ISR instructors.

---

[42] See Callaway Golf Co. v. Dunlop Slazenger Group Americas, Inc., 318 F. Supp. 2d 205 (D. Del. 2004).

Dr. Barnett has written various books detailing some of the techniques and methods used in ISR's aquatic-survival program, including *Precision Strokes for Little Folks,* published in 1974. More than ten years later, he wrote, but never published, a manual entitled *The Science of Infant Swimming,* which is used to help instructors understand "the psychology of infants and young children, their anatomy, and the physics involved as their small bodies move through the water." In 1989, ISR began publishing the "Parent Resource Book," now in its ninth edition, an educational book distributed to parents regarding the dangers of infant drowning and the theory and processes used by ISR.

Judy Heumann, Ann Shidler, and Alison Geerdes, defendants in the instant case, are former ISR instructors who left the company in early 2000. ISR trained Heumann as an instructor and Master Instructor in 1984 and 1987, respectively. Shidler was trained as an instructor in 1990, and as a Master Instructor in 1993, and Geerdes was trained as an ISR instructor and worked for less than a year before leaving ISR. She is not a Master Instructor. Defendants paid fees ranging from $5,000 to $10,000 for the instruction.

While employed by ISR, Heumann, Shidler, and Geerdes each signed a "Non-disclosure and Confidentiality Agreement" and a license agreement containing a further "Confidentiality of Information" provision as well as a "Covenant Not to Compete." Notwithstanding these agreements, on leaving ISR in 2000, the three former employees started Infant Aquatic Survival ("IAS"), a new company devoted to teaching infant and child swimming in Colorado. It is this conduct that is the subject of this litigation. Defendants' program is allegedly similar to the ISR program in that it utilizes the same "swim, float, swim" method, implements some of the same safety protocols, uses a Daily Health Data Sheet similar to the BUDS sheet, uses a comparable registration form, and distributes a comparable parent resource book to parents of children enrolled in the IAS program. It is uncontested that defendant Shidler's husband sought to reserve the names Harvey Barnett, Inc. and Infant Swimming Research, Inc. with the Colorado Secretary of State. On more than one occasion, defendants falsely advertised that their program, IAS, had been in business since 1990.

ISR filed in district court a complaint against the defendants, alleging state-law claims of misappropriation of trade secrets, breach of contract, and unjust enrichment. . . .

A.

In evaluating the district court's decision regarding ISR's trade-secrets claim, we look to Colorado law. Colorado has adopted the

Uniform Trade Secrets Act, which defines a trade secret as "any scientific or technical information, design, process, procedure, formula,
[or] improvement . . . which is secret and of value." Colo.Rev.Stat.
§ 7-74-102. In order "[t]o be a 'trade secret' the owner thereof must
have taken measures to prevent the secret from becoming available to
persons other than those selected by the owner to have access thereto for
limited purposes." Trade-secret status is a question of fact. (holding
that in this context "doubts as to existence of triable issue of
fact . . . must be resolved in favor of the existence of triable issues").

Factors considered in determining whether a trade secret exists include:

(1) the extent to which the information is known outside the business;
(2) the extent to which it is known to those inside the business, i.e.,
by the employees; (3) the precautions taken by the holder of the trade
secret to guard the secrecy of the information; (4) the savings effected
and the value to the holder in having the information as against competitors; (5) the amount of effort or money expended in obtaining and
developing the information; and (6) the amount of time and expense it
would take for others to acquire and duplicate the information.

In arriving at its conclusion that the ISR program is not a trade
secret as a matter of law, the district court determined that
(1) "[v]ariations of the swim, float, swim method are known both
inside and outside the children's aquatic business," (2) ISR did not
take precautions to guard the secrecy of its information "until at least
1996, after hundreds of instructors had been trained and thousands of
students taught," (3) "[p]arents and bystanders were allowed to watch
and videotape lessons," and (4) "a variation on ISR's methods could be
created through a perusal of commercially available child psychology,
child health, and swimming instruction books." Ultimately, the court
found that "ISR allowed its program to become part of the public
domain before seeking protection . . . [and] the Prompts and Procedures, based on principles of behavioral conditioning, was already in
use to teach children swim, float, swim throughout the nation" and
thus "as a matter of law . . . ISR has no protectable trade secret."[43]

Source: Courtesy of Westlaw; reprinted with permission.

Problem 8-4

You are the head football coach at Harvard and have just discovered that your beloved
offensive coordinator has taken the head coaching job with your archrival, the Yale Bulldogs.
Your former employee has held a press conference asserting that he knows all the offensive

---

[43] The Court of Appeals reversed the district court's decision granting summary judgment in favor of defendants on
ISR's claim of misappropriation of trade of secrets.

schemes run by Harvard because he has a copy of the Harvard playbook and also has all of his former coaches' notes regarding football strategy, which he took with him when he went to Yale. He promises not to lose to Harvard as long as he is at Yale. You are furious because the employee had been an offensive coordinator on your staff for 15 years, dating back to your years at the Naval Academy. You want to seek legal action against your former employee. Is there any legal action that you could assert against the former employee or Yale?

In *Steinberg, Moorad & Dunn, Inc. v. David L. Dunn and Athletes First LLC*, 136 Fed. Appx. 6 (9th Cir. 2005), noted sports agent Leigh Steinberg sued David Dunn when he left the firm to establish his own sports agency firm and took some of Steinberg's clients with him. Steinberg sued Dunn and his corporation on a variety of legal theories, including breach of contract and trade secret misappropriation. The appeals court stated the following in finding against the plaintiffs for their claims for trade secret misappropriation:[44]

> . . . First, the district court correctly concluded that the client list information was available to all agents. Thus, this information was not a protectable trade secret in this case.
>
> Moreover, SMD's claim that "player[s] desires and preferences" is a trade secret is not supported by this record. It may be that California's "trade route" cases could be analogous here, but the evidence to which SMD points does not support the claim. The only evidence to which SMD points are two player depositions. The first suggests that Dunn, while at SMD and after resigning, talked with one athlete about securing marketing and endorsement deals. An inference could be made from this evidence, though the evidence is extremely vague, that this was a career goal of that athlete, known to Dunn as a result of his employment at SMD. There is, however, no suggestion that this information was confidential to the athlete or not generally known.
>
> Similarly, a second athlete's deposition shows that, as a result of Dunn's employment at SMD, Dunn knew of the athlete's hopes to become involved in entertainment. After Dunn's departure from SMD, Dunn directly used that information in an unsuccessful effort to secure that athlete as an Athletes First client. But again, there is no suggestion in the record that *this* particular information was confidential. SMD cites to *other* information about the athlete's objectives that *was* confidential—his unhappiness with his current team and his hopes to sign with a different one. However, the record does not support the contention that the athlete's hopes for entertainment opportunities, the alleged trade secret information here, was not generally known.
>
> Finally, SMD's claim that its "internal data about costs, budgets, profit margins and projections" qualifies for trade secret protection fails. SMD correctly points out that costs and pricing information can be shown to derive independent economic value and thus can be trade secrets. But this is only the case if the methods for setting such prices are not commonly-used industry formulas. This is because pricing policies could be valuable to competitors seeking to set lower prices. No pricing information that could be used to compete was taken.[45]

---

[44] A jury returned the jury in favor of Steinberg on his other claims for $44.6 million.
[45] *Steinberg*, 136 Fed. Appx. at 4–5.

PATENTS

Section 101 of Title 35 of the *United States Code* defines the categories of patentable inventions broadly: "whoever invents or discovers any new and useful process, machine, manufacture, or composition of matter, or any new and useful improvement thereof, may obtain a patent therefore, subject to the conditions and requirements of this title." A patent may only be obtained by filing an application with the U.S. Patent and Trademark Office. A patent is essentially a grant from the U.S. government that provides the owner of the patent with exclusive rights to that particular invention for a certain period of time.

For the PTO to grant a patent, three requirements must be met. The proposed patent must be novel, useful, and not obvious to a practitioner in the field. Novelty is shown by applying a set of technical rules to determine whether the applicant was the first to make the claimed patent. The second requirement, utility, has become a minor obstacle to receiving a patent. A patent application will not usually be rejected for lack of usefulness even if the claimed invention is deemed "experimental" and has no current use. The third requirement, "non-obviousness," is the most important requirement in patent law. It has been referred to as the "ultimate condition of patentability." The requirement examines whether the proposed invention is a technical advancement over the "prior art." If a proposed patent represents only a small step forward in the art, it will not merit patent protection, even if it is both new and useful. Furthermore, according to 35 U.S.C.A. Section 112, the patentee must provide a sufficiently good description of the invention so that a person of "ordinary skill in the art" could make and use the invention.

Once a patent is granted, the owner of the patent has the right to exclude all others from the use of that patent for a certain period of time. The owner can sue anyone who is infringing on the patent by using, selling, or making the patented invention without the authority of the patent owner. If a party infringes a patent, the aggrieved party may seek money damages or an injunction, or both, as a remedy for the infringement.

Many inventors have begun to obtain patent protection in the sports area. Patents in the sports area are sought to gain exclusive control to novel sports techniques and products in an attempt to exclude others from the market. Inventors have been granted patents in the sports arena for such things as a method for training baseball pitchers, a method for fitness training, and a method for putting a golf ball.[46]

In Case 8-7, *Application of Neely*, 361 F.2d 255 (1966), a patent applicant was appealing a rejection of his patent application dealing with the lighting of athletic fields.

📖 CASE 8-7 *Application of Neely*

United States Court of Customs and Patent Appeals

Patent Appeal No. 7583

361 F.2d 255 (1966)

KIRKPATRICK, Judge.

This is an appeal from a decision of the Board of Appeals affirming the examiner's rejection of claims 2, 3 and 10 of the appellant's

---

[46] Derek Bambauer, *Legal Responses to the Challenges of Sports Patents*, Harvard Journal of Law & Technology, Volume 18, Number 2, Spring 2005. See U.S. Patent No. 5,639,243 (issued June 17, 1997).

application serial No. 141,753 entitled 'Floodlighting of Athletic Fields,' as 'unpatentable over Cahill' 1,235,527. We consider this a section 103 rejection.

Claim 2 is as follows:

2. A method of floodlighting a hockey rink consisting in the steps of erecting two poles at diagonally opposite corners respectively of the rink with a plurality of floodlamps atop each pole, and directing the lamps toward respective spots on the playing surface of the rink in a pattern of substantially uniform light intensity throughout the playing surface with the axes of certain of the lamps directed toward the center zone of the rink from one pole crossing those from the other pole, thereby to illuminate the space above the playing surface.

Claim 3 provides that the lamps be directed towards spots on the playing surface of the rink 'in a pattern in which concentration of spots increases with an increase in distance of the spots from the poles.'

Claim 10 is not limited to a hockey rink and merely claims the location of poles, pointing out that it leaves both sides and both ends of the field 'free of view-obstructing poles' and, by adjusting the individual lights, illuminates the entire field to a desired minimum intensity.

The main reference considered by the board and by the examiner is the Cahill patent referred to above. That patent is for 'Illuminating Systems for Base-Ball and Other Games.' None of the sixteen claims refer to illuminating anything other than a baseball field and, although the specification refers to the illumination of large areas so that baseball and other games may be played at night, hockey rinks are nowhere mentioned.

There is no doubt that, as the appellant argues, Cahill's nine-pole illuminating system is designed to meet problems of lighting quite different from those presented by hockey rinks and that many considerations go to the 'crux' of Cahill's system for illuminating a baseball field and are not applicable to lighting a hockey ring where substantially all players, save the two goal keepers, are constantly and rapidly changing both position and direction of movement over the rink. However, that does not mean that a person with a knowledge of the lighting requirements of a hockey rink could not learn from Cahill the method of doing it. As the board, referring to light, said, 'the need for distribution and intensity, generally, would be as well known as for a baseball field.'

We fail to see anything in arranging floodlights and directing their beams so that a given area is lighted to the greatest advantage which would be beyond the capacity of a person ordinarily skilled in the art.

The essence of the method claimed is simply placing two poles at diagonally opposite corners and providing them with enough floodlights to adequately light a hockey rink. Certainly, it is obvious, when uniform illumination of an area is desired, to aim the floodlights at the spots which will produce uniform illumination and, if all lamps are of the same intensity, to increase the number of lamps aimed at a particular spot as the distance from the pole increases.

The appellant's application states that it is conventional to use four poles on each side of a hockey rink, and Cahill discloses the use of multiple poles with lamps selectively aimed. It can hardly be said that it is an unexpected result if the removal of most of the poles improves the spectators' view of the rink or that a two-pole system will be less expensive than a four-pole.

The decision of the board is affirmed.

Affirmed.

Source: Courtesy of Westlaw; reprinted with permission.

The Arena Football League received patent protection for its rules and method of play. U.S. Patent Number 4911443 (Issued March 27, 1990) states the summary of the invention as follows:

It is the primary object of the invention to provide a variation of traditional American football that demands virtually all of the athletic skills of traditional football, but which is faster paced and may be played inside existing sports facilities.

It is another object of the invention to provide a game that can be safely played with spectators seated in close proximity to the playing field.

It is still another object of the invention to provide sufficient precautions to protect the players from indoor hazards resulting from a relatively small playing field, yet not mitigate the hard-contact and fast-paced action of traditional American football.

In accordance with the present invention, a new game involving the advancement of a ball across a playing field and over an opponent's goal line has substantially the same rules as American football (e.g., NFL or NCAA) except that kicks or passes into the end zone may be deflected back onto the playing field as a "live" ball by a rebounding assembly that is proximate to the goal line, but elevated above the playing field. Preferably, the rebounding assembly extends in a plane normal to the playing field and parallel to the goal line and includes a centrally located opening defining a scoring area. Upon an attempted field goal—executed by either placement of the ball as in American football or a dropkick—an errant kick will cause the ball to hit the rebounding assembly instead of passing through the scoring area. Off the rebound and before the ball hits the playing field, the players of the team defending the goal associated with the rebounding assembly have a right to receive the ball. Once the ball has hit the playing field, it is free to be picked up and advanced by a player from either team. Forward passes that hit the rebounding assembly are live until the ball hits the ground.

In order to better assure that a ball kicked into the rebounding assembly is typically returned to the playing field, the assembly is comprised of resilient material that after absorbing the kinetic energy of ball, returns a significant portion of it to reflecting the ball off the rebounding assembly. Although the material comprising the rebounding assembly returns much of the kinetic energy to the ball, it also is sufficiently elastic so that the ball usually has a return trajectory that may be anticipated. More specifically, the preferred shape of the ball is that of the commonly known American football which is an oblong spheroid, and such a shape is conducive to erratic returns off the rebounding assembly. The elastic character of the rebounding assembly tends to negate the unpredictable effects of the oblong shape of the ball.

There has even been discussion about applying patent protection to "sports moves."[47] Could a player receive patent protection for a particular style of slam dunk or golf swing? PGA golfer Steve Elkington is considered by most golf experts to have the best golf swing on the PGA Tour, which has assisted him in winning ten PGA events and two majors. Could he receive patent protection in his "perfect" golf swing? Consider the famous high jumper Dick Fosbury, who revolutionized the sport when he began jumping over the bar backward, thereby creating the "Fosbury Flop," a move that earned him a gold medal in the 1968 Olympics. Many thought his move unorthodox at the time, but now all high jumpers use his "flop" method. Could he have received patent protection on this particular move? Hall of Fame pitcher Nolan Ryan received a patent entitled "Training Apparatus, Method for Training an Athlete, and Method for Producing a Training Device" in 1997. Portions of the "Summary of the Invention" in the patent application describe the invention as follows:

To use the system, the athlete stands on the starting pad and grips a suitable striking implement, such as a towel. The athlete executes a sequence of one or more movements in the manner required by the sport, beginning with the athlete stepping off the starting pad and ending with the athlete stepping with at least one foot onto the landing pad. During the movement sequence, the athlete swings the implement in the manner used in the sport and attempts to strike the target with the implement. For example, a baseball pitcher begins a delivery with a leg lift on the starting pad and strides to the landing pad while swinging the implement as though it were a baseball in an attempt to strike the target. In embodiments in which the target is rotatable, the target rotates or spins in response to being struck with the implement. The spinning target provides immediate and satisfying visual, aural and tactile feedback to the athlete. The extent to which the target spins is proportional to the force it experiences. In most sports, it is desirable to maximize the transfer of force from the athlete's arm to the implement.

The invention may further comprise a posture guide. The posture guide may have any suitable shape and may be made of any suitable material, such as mesh screening. It may be disposed in any suitable orientation between the starting and landing pads to constrain the athlete's movement. For example, as a baseball pitcher comes out of a leg lift and into a stride, the pitcher's upper body begins to tilt or hunch over with respect to vertical. Although the optimal tilt angle is dependent upon the individual pitcher's biomechanical profile, the pitcher should not vary the angle during training once the individual's biomechanically correct angle has been determined. To constrain the pitcher to this angle, a posture guide having a generally planar shape may be placed in an orientation parallel to the beam at an acute angle with respect to a plane connecting the starting and landing pads. Nevertheless, the shape and orientation of the posture guide may be adapted to suit the needs of athletes training for other sports.[48]

---

[47] J. Smith, *It's Your Move—No It's Not! The Application of Patent Law to Sports Moves*, 70 U. Colo. L. Rev. 1051 (1999).

[48] U.S. Patent No. 5,639,243.

In Case 8-8, *Baseball Display Co. v. Star Ballplayer Co.*, 35 F.2d 1 (3rd Cir. 1929), the court had to decide what amount of profits were available to a plaintiff whose patent relating to a manually operated scoreboard had been infringed.

📖 CASE 8-8 *Baseball Display Co. v. Star Ballplayer Co.*

35 F.2d 1 (3rd Cir. 1929)

WOOLLEY, Circuit Judge.

The District Court, having found the plaintiff's patent No. 1,321,940 valid and infringed (D.C.) 8 F.(2d) 46, referred the case to a master for accounting. After a sharp contest the master awarded the plaintiff $12,500 for profits, damages and interest. . . . [B]oth parties have appealed; the plaintiff because the award is inadequate, the defendants because it is excessive. . . .

The invention of the patent relates to means for portraying baseball games play by play to a crowd in the street. The device—of less value since the broadcasting of national series games by radio—represents a baseball field arranged on a vertical plane upon which, when placed on a building above the crowd and operated from the rear by men in touch with the telegraph, every play including pitched and batted balls, thrown balls and base running can be shown quite realistically. Oscanyan, the patentee, was not the first to conceive this general idea but he was first to conceive the mechanism which showed a player running step by step to base and thereafter showed him holding the base, playing off and sliding back, and running to the next base. This is done by a series of open slots separated by closed spaces in the base-to-base pathway and a white object representing the runner passing under the open slots. To see and follow the movement of a runner heightens the interest of spectators and is a thing of value in the structure. The defendant, Baseball Display Company, deliberately infringed this device by combining it with the other and old features of a baseball board. In this amusement art the plaintiff and the defendant did not sell their boards, but 'leased' them for terms of years at agreed 'rentals' to newspaper companies and then to only one company in a city, thereby tendering it an advertising advantage over its news competitors.

Continuing to use the words 'lease' and 'rentals' as they were used at the trial, the defendant made 30 separate leases of its boards embodying the feature of the patented invention, each for a period of five years at a named annual rental, with the privilege of renewal for a period of ten years at a named figure. After granting these leases and

letting its boards (with the plaintiff's base-running device) to newspapers, the defendant, at the end of the first year, abandoned the
plaintiff's base-running device and installed in the leased boards one
of its own for the remainder of the terms. The plaintiff sued for damages and also for profits on all leases for the whole of their terms
of five years and for their renewal terms (although it is doubtful
that there were any renewals) and for punitive damages as well. The
defendant . . . admitted liability for damages or profits for one year
of the terms of the leases, in the case of profits only such as were
earned after extensive overhead expenses had been deducted, which left
practically nothing, or in the case of damages only such, of course,
as were proved, but in no case both profits and damages.

The factors that entered into the master's accounting are reflected in
his tabulated recapitulation which is as follows:

Profits

$11,726.39 @50 per cent. $5,863 19

Subsequent royalty—50 per cent

@50 per cent.   1,350 00

                                                       $7,213 19

Damages

No. 5-Burkam-Herrick Publishing

Company, Dayton. 5 years,

@$200 a year. $1,000 00

No. 7-Times Publishing Company,

Erie, Pa. 5 years,

@$175.   875 00

No. 12-Lancaster Intelligencer,

Lancaster, Pa. 5 years,

@$100.   500 00

No. 16-Milwaukee (Goldenberg),

Milwaukee, Wis. 5 years,

@$350.   1,720 00

                                                 4,095 00

                                                       $11,308 19

To the total of damages and profits—the latter including interest compounded annually—the master added $1,191.80 somewhat in the nature of a penalty and recommended a decree for $12,500 which the court entered with interest. . . .

The main difficulty in the accounting lay in profits. The master properly eliminated rentals on renewals of leases. He refused, however, to limit profits on rentals to the one year of actual physical infringement to which, ordinarily, a plaintiff having suffered from infringement would only be entitled and allowed profits for the terms the leases actually ran, the most of them having run their full five year terms. For such an allowance neither the plaintiff nor the master produced precedents. Manifestly, the allowance was quite out of the ordinary; so, also, were the infringements. If the infringements can be separated from the leases, clearly the full time allowance of profits should not stand. But the long term leases were in part procured by the aid of the infringements, and while the actual infringements stopped at the end of one year the profits resulting from them continued for four years longer and during those years the leases shut out the plaintiff from that part of the field and held it for the defendant. Without the infringements there would have been no leases of the precise type here obtained. As the patented device figured directly and effectively in procuring them with their annually recurring profits we think the master was right in holding that the infringing torts were not limited to the first year of actual use and that in consequence the penalty for the torts should be co-extensive with the torts themselves.

What were the profits? The master could not find them from the defendant's evidence, so he employed an accountant of his own who, on the evidence of rentals and under the master's instruction as to their computation, found annual profits on the 30 leases in the amount of $9,541.47 which, after adding interest, compounded annually, made the total of $11,726.39 shown in the master's summary reproduced above. The master's figure of computed profits must, in the conflict of evidence, be accepted as right particularly in view of the uncertainty of the defendant's evidence of costs and profits. But in compounding interest as a penalty the master and the court fell into error. While the defendant should without doubt suffer a penalty for its wrongdoing, we find no authority or theory for inflicting it by compounding interest on profits and then charging interest on the interest thus compounded to the date of the decree and thereafter interest on the decree with this accumulated interest.

What share of the profits thus determined should be awarded the plaintiff? As the plaintiff's patented device was but a part of the leased baseball boards, this involves a question of apportionment. . . . The plaintiff contended that its device produced 70 per cent. to 90 per cent. of the profits; the defendant only 25 per cent. The master found that it produced 50 per cent. Evidence of what part one of several elements in an inventive combination precisely plays is from the nature of the thing seldom available. It is however certain that the plaintiff's element produced less than 90 per cent. of the profits yet more than 25 per cent. The profits were received from the leases and the leases were more easily procured because of the plaintiff's new base-running element added to old elements. Indeed it is doubtful if the defendant could have procured any of the contracts without it as it was the novel feature of an old board. At any rate the defendant pirated it and stressed it in getting business. The evidence sustains the master's finding of 50 per cent apportionment.

Was the plaintiff entitled to general damages? The master rightly found its evidence too weak to sustain a broad award, but, after allowing profits on all 30 leases, he allowed in addition damages on four of them in the sum of $4,095. The defendant assails this finding on the law that in an infringing accounting damages may not be added to profits on the same infringement and that when profits are in excess of damages a complainant is not entitled to recover damages in addition to profits.

Regarding a given infringement as one tort, as it may be and frequently is, these principles of law apply and are not open to question. Their application, however, to the case in hand depends upon the character of the infringements. Here they occurred by granting 30 leases embodying the invention of the plaintiff's patent. A grant of this number of leases to newspapers throughout the country did not constitute one inseparable act of infringement such as one act of infringement in a continuous use of a patented process. . . . On the contrary the infringements growing out of the 30 leases of the offending device may properly be regarded as 30 separate, distinct and wholly unrelated acts of infringement, to each of which the penalty for infringement, whether recovery of profits or damages, may be applied within the rule stated. Therefore there should be deducted from the total rentals which the master found as profits from the thirty leases the rentals on leases 5, 7, 12 and 16, and treating these four (because of the aggravated nature of the infringements and their damaging consequences to the plaintiff) as subject to the rule of damages, there should be allowed damages on them, proven to be in excess of profits and, because of the deliberate and willful infringement, also punitive damages in 50 per cent. of the actual. The matter of interest as to both profits and damages is controlled by the rules found in the authorities cited in Walker on Patents, Secs. 571, 736.

We direct that the decree be modified conformably with the following summary:

Profits from 30 leases of varying terms. . . .	$9,541 47	
Less profits from leases:		
No. 5.	$431 26	
No. 7.	556 26	
No. 12.	393 75	
No. 16.	515 00	1,896 27
Net profit from 26 leases.		$7,645 20
Defendant's share of net profits on 50.		
Per cent. apportionment.		3,822 60
Plaintiff's share—same.		$3,822 60
Damages (without profits) on leases Nos. 5, 7, 12 and 16.	$4,095 00	
Punitive damages 50 per cent. of actual.	2,047 50	6,143 50
		$9,965 10

Interest at 6 per cent. on profits from the date of the submission of the master's report to the date of modification of the decree.

. . . . . .

Interest at 6 per cent. on the new amount of the final decree, including damages, profits and interest on profits, from the date of modification to date of payment.

. . . . . .

Total.

```
All costs in the trial court shall be taxed against the defendants-
appellants and the costs on these appeals shall be taxed one-third
against the plaintiff-appellant and two-thirds against the defendants-
appellants.
```

```
The plaintiff's motion to dismiss the defendants' appeal is denied.
```

```
The decree when modified will be affirmed.
```

Source: Courtesy of Westlaw; reprinted with permission.

LICENSING AND SPONSORSHIPS

Sports marketing permeates our culture. The Super Bowl is the most-watched television program every year. Professional sports teams market their products on a worldwide scale to give their teams more visibility. The licensing of sports brands has become a multibillion-dollar venture worldwide. Corporations view sports events as a way to expand the reach of their products globally as well. Corporate America and the sports industry have become business partners on a worldwide basis, with both enhancing their revenues and bringing more athletes to their products. Teams, leagues, and players possess logos, names, memorabilia, designs, characters, and other forms of intellectual property that they must protect.

The sports industry has seen an increase in involvement with the law of intellectual property. Professional leagues and teams receive substantial revenues every year from the sale of various products containing team logos and slogans. Sporting events have become a launching pad for sponsors to market products to millions of individuals within a short period of time. The National Football League, Major League Baseball, the National Basketball Association, NASCAR, and the Olympics are all involved in intricate sponsorship agreements with a variety of different sponsors.

Naming rights for stadiums are a perfect example of sponsorships in professional and amateur sports. Having a sports stadium named after a large corporation is now standard fare in the sporting world for both professional and collegiate athletics. The Colorado Rockies play in Coors Field, and the Houston Astros in Minute Maid Park. The San Francisco Giants no longer play in Candlestick Park, but rather in AT&T Park. At the collegiate level sponsors line up to associate themselves with major college bowl games. Examples include the FedEx Orange Bowl, the Tostitos Fiesta Bowl, the AutoZone Liberty Bowl, The Chick-Fil-A Peach Bowl, the Meineke Car Care Bowl, and the Bell Helicopter Armed Services Bowl.

The License Agreement

A license to use another person's intellectual property is essentially a contract or agreement permitting the use of the designated intellectual property for a specific purpose. The license allows the owner of the intellectual property to retain ownership while still allowing its use within certain boundaries. The granting of a license creates a contractual relationship between the licensor and licensee. Licensing agreements can take many forms.

The following is a standard provision dealing with the granting of the license that might be found in a licensing agreement for trademarks.

A. LICENSEE acknowledges LICENSOR's exclusive rights in the Trademarks and, further, acknowledges that the Trademarks are unique and original to LICENSOR and that LICENSOR is the owner thereof. LICENSEE shall not, at any time during or after the effective Term of the Agreement, dispute or contest, directly or indirectly, LICENSOR's exclusive right and title to the Trademarks or the validity thereof.

LICENSOR, however, makes no representation or warranty with respect to the validity of any patent, trademark, or copyright that may issue or be granted therefrom.

B. LICENSEE acknowledges that the Trademarks have acquired secondary meaning.

C. LICENSEE agrees that its use of the Trademarks inures to the benefit of LICENSOR and that the LICENSEE shall not acquire any rights in the Trademarks as a result of this license.

The licensing agreement will also have a section dealing with the rights and obligations of the licensee and licensor:

A. LICENSOR hereby grants to LICENSEE, for the Term of this Agreement as recited in Schedule A attached hereto, the non-exclusive right and license to use the Property in connection with the Licensed Products as well as on packaging, promotional and advertising material associated herewith.

B. LICENSOR hereby grants to LICENSEE, for the Term of this Agreement as recited in Schedule A attached hereto, the non-exclusive right and license to manufacture, have manufactured, sell, distribute and advertise Licensed Products incorporating the Property in the Territory. The license includes, but is not limited to, a license under any and all patents and copyrights and any applications therefore which have been filed or may be filed in the future with respect to the Property. It is understood and agreed that this license shall pertain only to the Licensed Products and does not extend to any other product or service.

C. LICENSEE agrees that the Property of LICENSOR shall be used subject to the limitations on form identified in Schedule A, attached hereto.

D. LICENSEE may not grant any sublicenses to any third party without the prior express written consent of the LICENSOR, which may be withheld for any reason.

E. LICENSEE shall not make or authorize any use, direct or indirect, of the Property or the Licensed Products, like or similar, outside the Territory and will not knowingly sell the Licensed Products to persons who intend or are likely to resell them outside the Territory.

Professional Sports

Leagues and player unions also have become involved in marketing and licensing products on behalf of players and the league. The following is the provision dealing with group licensing in the WNBA's standard player contract:

(a) The Player hereby grants to WNBA Enterprises the right to use her Player Attributes in the manner set forth in the Agreement between WNBA Enterprises and the Women's National Basketball Players Association, made as of April 30, 1999 (the "Group License Agreement"), a copy of which will, upon her request be furnished to the player. The player agrees to adhere to all of the terms of the Group License Agreement, including, without limitation, the provisions prohibiting her from licensing her Player Attributes for use during any Season to any entity that competes with a WNBA Sponsor or WN7BA Licensee or a Designated Local Sponsor (as those terms are defined in the Group License Agreement), and the provisions requiring her to make certain appearances.

(b) Notwithstanding anything to the contrary contained in the Group License Agreement or this Contract, WNBA Enterprises may use the Player's name, nickname, and/or the Player's Player Attributes as such Player Attributes may be captured in game action footage or photographs, in any advertising, marketing or collateral materials or public service or marketing programs conducted by the WNBA, WN7BA Enterprises or any Team that, without regard to whether such use includes sponsor identification, is intended to (i) promote (x) a Team, the WNBA, players and/or the sport of basketball, (y) any game or competition in which a Team or a group of players participates or (z) any telecast or broadcast of such game or competition and/or (ii) further the development, popularity or growth of the WNBA and/or the sport of basketball (eg., in connection with basketball clinics, "grass roots" programs and similar non-commercial activities). WN7BA Enterprises shall be entitled to use the Player's Player Attributes individually pursuant to the preceding sentence and shall not be required to use the Player's Player Attributes in a group or as one of multiple players; provided, however, that no such use made by WNBA Enterprises shall constitute an endorsement or testimonial by the Player of any product or service.

(c) The Player agrees that the WNBA shall have the right to take and use her Pictures in accordance with the provisions of Article XX, Section 3 of the CBA.

Problem 8-5

James Thompson is a starting forward for the Utah Jazz. He is a rising star in the NBA. His neighbor invited him over to play the newest version of the video game *Destroyer Basketball*. Thompson discovers during the playing of the game that a figure on the team called the "Dragons" is extremely similar to his likeness. The player statistics list the player as being 6′ 6″, the same height as Thompson. The player is left-handed, as is Thompson. The character wears number 11; Thompson wears number 22. The player is listed in the game as having a value of "8," meaning he averages between 18 and 22 points per game. Thompson averaged 17.4 points a game in his last NBA season. Furthermore, Thompson has a unique "fall-away jumper" that is his "trademark" shot. The character in the video game performs a very similar fall-away jump shot. Does Thompson have any legal recourse against the manufacturer of the video game? If so, on what basis? What intellectual property rights are at issue in this situation?

NOTES AND DISCUSSION QUESTIONS

Trademarks

1. In *Major League Baseball Properties v. Opening Day Productions, Inc.*, 385 F. Supp. 2d 256 (S.D.N.Y. 2005), Major League Baseball brought a declaratory judgment action asking the court to find that the league was not an infringer of the term "Opening Day." The defendant, Opening Day Productions, argued that the term "opening day" was "arbitrary" and not a descriptive mark. If the mark were descriptive, the defendant would have to show "secondary meaning" under trademark law to garner trademark protection. The court in its ruling stated in part:

   . . . The parties are in dispute as to how to characterize the mark "opening day." Plaintiffs argue that the mark is descriptive while defendant argues that the mark is arbitrary. . . .

   In assessing a mark, a "[court] must be mindful that '[t]he focus in categorizing a mark is on how the words are used in context rather than their meaning in the abstract.'" . . . "[T]he word 'apple' would be arbitrary when used on personal computers, suggestive when used in 'Apple-A-Day' on vitamin tablets, descriptive when used in 'Tomapple' for combination tomato-apple juice and generic when used for apples." I J.T. McCarthy, "Trademarks and Unfair Competition," § 11:22, at 498-99 (2d ed.1984).

   The term "opening day" is proposed by defendant to be used on merchandise in connection with the opening day of the baseball season. As it was used, it is a descriptive mark, rather than one that could be classified as arbitrary. . . . [T]here is nothing rare or inventive about using the term "opening day" in the context of the opening day of the baseball season. The term does not leave much to the imagination. It does not require much thought be used in identifying its source or utility.

Since "Opening day" is a descriptive mark, defendant must show that it has acquired secondary meaning in order for it to be entitled to Lanham Act protection. Defendant must therefore show that "Opening day" has become distinctive of it's [sic] particular goods in commerce. . . .

Defendant cannot make this showing. Defendant has not offered any evidence that its goods have acquired secondary meaning in the marketplace. Consumers have not come to identify "opening day" products with defendant. In fact, both of the owners of defendant company stated in deposition that they do not believe that the public identifies the mark "opening day" with defendant's clothing line.[49]

How much of a realistic chance do you think Opening Day Productions had against Major League Baseball? Consider the term "Super Bowl." How should that be classified? What about a trademark for using "Super Bowl" in greeting cards?[50]

2. In *Lemon v. Harlem Globetrotters International, Inc.*, 437 F. Supp. 2d 1089 (D. Ariz. 2006), the plaintiffs alleged in part that their names "when combined with their nicknames and player numbers are 'fanciful' marks and are therefore inherently strong" and that no secondary meaning was needed to establish protection under the Lanham Act.[51] Plaintiffs asserted that a number combined with letters or words can be a fanciful mark, citing Professor McCarthy's treatise *Trademarks and Unfair Competition*, which gives "Chanel No. 5" and "V-8" as examples.[52] The court disagreed, stating:

A celebrity's persona is neither descriptive of a good or service nor "fanciful" within the meaning of trademark law. For example, the persona of Meadowlark Lemon—his image, name and jersey number—does not describe a good or service sold in commerce. Nor is it a merely fanciful phrase like V-8 vegetable juice. Rather, Plaintiff's Lemon's persona is a uniquely distinguishing characteristic that calls to mind a specific person and his publicly known sports personality.[53]

3. How would you categorize the word "playmakers"? Is it descriptive, generic, or suggestive? How could a television show entitled *Playmakers* tarnish the Playmakers Sports Agency? What damages would the agency be entitled to if it were able to prevail? In *March Madness Athletic Association, L.L.C. v. Netfire, Inc.*, 161 F. Supp. 2d 560 (N.D. Tex. 2001), the defendant owned the domain name marchmadness.com and argued that plaintiff's mark "March Madness" was generic, stating it referred to postseason basketball tournaments in general and not just to the NCAA tournament. The court stated, "March Madness is more akin to a descriptive mark than it is to an arbitrary or a suggestive mark. The term March Madness describes something mad, crazy, etc., that occurs in the month of March."[54]

---

[49] *Major League Baseball Properties*, 385 F. Supp. 2d at 253.

[50] *See* National Football League v. Jasper Alliance Corporation, 1990 WL 354523 (Trademark Tr. & App. Bd. 1990).

[51] *Lemon*, 437 F. Supp. 2d at 1094.

[52] 2 J. THOMAS MCCARTHY, MCCARTHY ON TRADEMARKS AND UNFAIR COMPETITION, § 7:15 (4th ed. 2005).

[53] *Lemon*, 437 F. Supp. 2d at 1095–96.

[54] *March Madness Athletic Ass'n*, 161 F. Supp. 2d at 571.

4. Do you believe that consumer confusion existed in Case 8-1, *Baseball America, Inc. v. Power-play Sports, Ltd.*? Was it problematic that Powerplay Sports was doing business in the same market channels as Baseball America?

5. Which of the following slogans do you believe trademark or copyright law would protect?

  a. Michael Buffer's "Let's get ready to rumble." See letsrumble.com

  b. Harry Caray's "Cubs Win"

  c. Al Michaels's "Do you believe in miracles?" (referring to the 1980 U.S. Olympic hockey team's victory over the Soviet Union)

  d. Yogi Berra's "It ain't over till it's over"

6. In *Foxworthy v. Custom Tees, Inc.*, 879 F. Supp. 1200 (N.D. Ga. 1995), the well-known comedian sued a t-shirt manufacturer for allegedly infringing upon the phrase "You might be a redneck." The court found that Foxworthy was entitled to trademark protection in the phrase because the public so closely associated him with it.[55] The court also found that Foxworthy was entitled to copyright protection in the phrase as well.

7. In *Kournikova v. General Media Communications, Inc.*, 278 F. Supp. 2d 1111 (C.D. Cal. 2003), the tennis star sued General Media Communications, claiming that photos of her appearing in *Penthouse* magazine constituted false advertising and false endorsement under the Lanham Act. The court granted summary judgment for the defendant, partially on the basis of the First Amendment.

8. An interesting domain name and trademark dispute occurred over SamBucks Coffee House. The owner of SamBucks Coffee House was Samantha Buck Lundberg. Starbucks Corporation sued her, alleging trademark infringement. She won at the lower court level, but on appeal the coffee giant prevailed. The owner asserted she was entitled to a fair use defense because she had the right to use her own name as the name of her business. The court found that "Sam Buck" was not Mrs. Lundberg's name and had not been her name for more than a decade. The court further found that "[e]ven if Lundberg had not abandoned the surname 'Buck' more than a decade ago, the alleged similarity between her mark and her name is not a defense to trademark infringement. The Ninth Circuit has held that there is no right to use an individual's own name in business where the use confuses the public."[56]

In *Starbucks v. Wolfe's Borough Coffee, Inc.*, 2005 WL 3527126 (S.D.N.Y.), 79 U.S.P.Q. 2d 1138 (2005), the coffee behemoth sought an injunction against the defendant for its use of the name Charbucks. After a two-day bench trial, the court found as follows:

> Plaintiff has failed to demonstrate that Defendant's use of the term "Charbucks" as part of the name of one of its lines of coffee has tarnished Starbucks' reputation, or is likely to lead the public to associate a lack of quality or prestige of Defendant's product with Plaintiff's goods.[57]

On appeal the lower court's judgment was vacated and remanded because the FTDA was amended, effective October 6, 2006, to entitle an owner of a famous mark to an injunction if the mark was likely to cause dilution rather than requiring the defendant to prove actual confusion.[58]

---

[55] *Foxworthy.*, 879 F. Supp. at 1211.

[56] Starbucks Corp. v. Lundberg, 2005 WL 3183858 (D. Or. 2005).

[57] *Wolfe's Borough Coffee*, 2005 WL 3527126 at 10.

[58] *Wolfe's Borough Coffee*, 477 F.3d 765, 766 (2007).

Under what circumstances could an individual use his or her name if it is also the name of a famous sports player?

   9. In *Sportvision, Inc. v. Sportsmedia Technology Corporation*, 2005 WL 1869350 (N.D. Cal. 2005), a dispute arose as to the ownership of the virtual yellow first-down marker used in televised football games. The plaintiff applied for a trademark in 2000 based on the following description:

> The mark consists of the color yellow used on a virtual line that appears as an image on a football field during a television or video broadcast of a football game. The portion of the drawing in dotted lines depicts a portion of an image of a football field including line markers, and serves to show positioning of the mark. The drawing is lined for the color yellow.[59]

When the plaintiff learned that the defendant was using a similar line, it requested the defendant to stop using the mark, asserting that the company was an infringer. After the plaintiff learned that the defendant had used the virtual yellow line indicator on *Monday Night Football*, the company sued. The court granted the defendant's motion for partial summary judgment, finding that the plaintiff's mark was merely "functional" and that no likelihood of confusion existed between the virtual first-down markers.

   10. Who owns the right to player statistics? More than any sport, baseball is clearly a game of numbers. Many baseball fans know the meaning of the following numbers:

   a. .406
   b. 755
   c. 56
   d. 2130

Can you identify them?[60] Does Bob Gibson have any property rights in his 1968 record-breaking 1.12 ERA in baseball? Does Nolan Ryan have a property right in the number 5,714, which represents his lifetime strikeout record in baseball?

   In 1996 several former Major Leaguers sued over MLB's use of their names and statistics in video games and game programs. Major League Baseball prevailed, asserting it had the right to use the information based on the freedom of the press.[61] In *NBA v. Motorola, Inc.*, 105 F.3d 841 (2d Cir. 1997), the NBA sued Motorola for copyright infringement when Motorola's pagers began to provide statistics and final scores to fans. The court found in favor of the defendant because the pagers only provided factual information from the broadcast, and thus there was no copyright infringement.

   In *CBC Distribution and Marketing, Inc. v. Major League Baseball Advanced Media*, 443 F. Supp. 2d 1077 (E.D. Mo. 2006), a fantasy game owner sued MLB Advanced Media seeking a declaratory judgment that it possessed the right to use statistics and data concerning Major League Baseball players in its games. The MLB Players Association also intervened in the lawsuit. The federal district court found that the plaintiff had not infringed upon the players'

---

[59] *Sportvision*, 2005 WL 1869350 at 1.
[60] *Answers:* (a) .406 is the batting average of Ted Williams, the last player to bat over .400 for a full season. (b) 755 is the number of home runs hit by Hank Aaron. (c) 56 represents the famous hitting streak of Joe DiMaggio in 1941. (d) 2,130 is the number of consecutive games played by Cal Ripken.
[61] Gionfriddo v. Major League Baseball, 114 Cal. Rptr. 2d 307 (Cal. Ct. App. 2001).

right of publicity because it had no "intent to obtain a commercial activity."[62] The court also found that the plaintiff's use of MLB player names and statistics was protected speech under the First Amendment.[63] *For further study see*, Patrick K. Thornton and Christopher James, *Down Two Strikes, Is Major League Baseball Already Out?: How the 8th Circuit Balked to Protect the Right of Publicity in C.B.C. v. MLB, Advanced Media*, South Texas Law Review, Volume 50, Number 2, Winter 2008.

11. Many celebrities and athletes have fought for their control of their domain names and won. Courts and arbitration panels have found that a person may acquire common law trademark rights in his or her name.[64] However, trademark rights must be established by secondary meaning. In *Yao Ming v. Evergreen Sports, Inc.*, FA 030400015140 (2003), the well-known NBA center was seeking return of the domain name yaoming.com. The panel refused to transfer the domain name to Yao, finding as follows:

> . . . In this case, Complainant merely states that the Complaint is based on "the name Yao Ming, which is the name of 7' 5" tall NBA star athlete Yao Ming . . . used in athletic entertainment and endorsement." Complainant failed to submit any evidence of how the name is used in athletic entertainment and/or endorsement or facts to support consumer knowledge. Bald assertions of consumer knowledge are not an adequate form of evidence to establish secondary meaning in a name.
>
> This decision, however, should not be construed as finding that Complainant could never establish that it has common law rights in the YAO MING mark or that Respondent is using the domain name in bad faith. If Complainant were to file a complete Complaint, alleging facts, providing actual evidence, and citing specific examples, a future Panel might have sufficient evidence upon which to base a decision.

The panel seems to be encouraging Yao to present evidence of his rights to the common law trademark use of his name. Why was Barry Zito entitled to the return of his domain name when Yao Ming was denied? Did you find it odd that the panel awarded Zito the domain name even though, at the time the original owner had obtained it, Zito had not made a name for himself as a professional ball player? Under what circumstances could a person be entitled to retain the domain name of a professional athlete?

Bruce Springsteen was not able to persuade a World Intellectual Property Organization (WIPO) panel that he was entitled to brucespringsteen.com, notwithstanding the fact that he is "the Boss" (WIPO No. D2000-15). Gordon Sumner, better known as Sting, is a world-famous musician who has been recording songs for more than 20 years. He alleged he was entitled to sting.com because of his use of the nickname. Although the WIPO panel ordered that the name be transferred to Sumner or be canceled, it did not find he had a common law right to the nickname:

> . . . Although it is accepted that the Complainant is world famous under the name STING, it does not follow that he has rights in STING *as a trademark or service mark*. . . .
> [T]he personal name in this case is also a common word in the English language,

---

[62] *CBC Distribution and Marketing*, 443 F. Supp. 2d at 1089; The case was affirmed on appeal, 505 F.3d 818 (8th Cir. 2007).

[63] *Id.* at 1098.

[64] Estate of Tupac Shakur v. Shakur Info Page, AF–0346 (eResolution Sept. 28, 2000).

with a number of different meanings. The following are the entries for "sting" from *Merriam-Webster's Collegiate Dictionary*:

> "sting 1: to prick painfully: as to pierce or wound with a poisonous or irritating process b: to affect with sharp quick pain or smart "hail stung their faces" 2: to cause to suffer acutely "stung with remorse" 3: overcharge, cheat: to wound one with or as if with a sting 4: an elaborate confidence game; specific: such a game worked by undercover police in order to trap criminals."

In light of the fact that the word "sting" is in common usage in the English language, with a number of meanings, this case can be distinguished from the other cases cited above in which the Complainants' personal name was found also to be an unregistered trademark or service mark to which the Uniform Policy applies. This Administrative Panel is inclined to the view, therefore, that the Complainant's name STING is not a trademark or service mark. . . .

Could Jerome Bettis argue he was entitled to thebus.com? Could the Great One, Wayne Gretzky, be entitled to www.thegreatone.com? What other sports or entertainment figures can you think of who might assert claims to domain names because of their nicknames, numbers, or playing style?

12. A party has a duty to protect and police its trademark to ensure no one else is using the mark. In 2006, Texas A&M University filed a lawsuit over the Seattle Seahawks' use of what the university believed to be an infringement of its noted "12th Man" trademark. What likelihood-of-confusion factors would be considered in this trademark litigation? Does it make a difference that the Seahawks are a professional team and the Aggies are collegiate? Is the "12th Man" mark suggestive, arbitrary, fanciful, descriptive, or generic? (The matter was eventually settled between the parties.)

13. In Case 8-2, *Hart v. New York Yankees Partnership*, the court noted, "The Board also found that the term BRONX BOMBERS had been used by the press to refer to both minor and major league Yankee teams for several years before Hart's priority date."[65] Is there a likelihood of confusion between "Baby Bombers" and "Bronx Bombers"?

14. Colleges and universities have gone to battle over the use of their trademarks.[66]

Copyrights

15. What damages is the plaintiff entitled to as a result of the proven infringement? Much litigation ensued dealing with the issue of damages in *Bouchat*.[67]

16. Under what circumstances could a party prove copyright infringement by direct evidence?

Patents

17. Could Michael Jordan receive patent protection for his famous slam dunk? What about sports players who possess a unique move? Are they entitled to patent protection?

---

[65] *Hart,* 184 Fed. Appx. at 973.

[66] Texas Tech University v. Speigelberg, 461 F. Supp. 2d 510 (N.D. Tex. 2006) (disputes over "Red Raider" marks); Board of Trustees University of Arkansas v. Professional Therapy Services, Inc., 873 F. Supp. 1280 (W.D. Ark. 1995) (The district court held as a matter of law that the University's Razorback trademarks were strong and distinctive).

[67] For further study, see Bouchat v. Champion Products, Inc. et al., 327 F. Supp. 2d 537 (D. Md. 2003); Bouchat v. Baltimore Ravens Football Club, Inc., and NFL Properties, 346 F.3d 514 (4th Cir. 2003).

18. Did you agree with the court's assessment of damages in Case 8-8, *Baseball Display Co. v. Star Ballplayer Co.*? What damages would you have assessed?
19. How do patent law and trade secrets overlap?
20. Why did the court find that Mr. Neely's invention for the lighting of athletic fields was properly rejected by the Patent Board of Appeals? How could he have changed the invention to prevent rejection?

Licensing and Sponsorships

21. What are the most important considerations in a licensing agreement? What types of intellectual property can be licensed?
22. Players, Inc., is the licensing arm of the NFLPA; its stated mission is to "take the helmet off" players and market them as personalities. NFL players grant the NFLPA their group licensing rights to use their name, number, likeness, and image. Players, Inc., currently has more than 80 licensing programs in effect for apparel, collectibles, trading cards, video games, and fantasy football games, to name a few examples.
23. How does the licensing of a particular player coordinate with his or her right of publicity?

Amateur Licensing

24. Many colleges and universities license their products. Major college football programs have entered into licensing agreements with Nike or Reebok for the use of logos appearing on players' uniforms during games.

SUGGESTED READINGS AND RESOURCES

Burleson, Tina Y., & Champion, Walter T. *Trade Dress as the Only Club in the Bag to Protect Golf Club Manufacturers from "Knock-Offs" of Their Prized Boutique Clubs.* 3 TEXAS REVIEW OF ENTERTAINMENT & SPORTS LAW 43 (2002).

Deutsch, Askan. *Sports Broadcasting and Virtual Advertising: Defining the Limits of Copyright Law and the Law of Unfair Competition.* 11 MARQUETTE SPORTS LAW REVIEW 41 (2000).

Handa, Sunny. *Retransmission of Television Broadcasts on the Internet.* 8 SOUTHWESTERN JOURNAL OF LAW AND TRADE IN THE AMERICAS 39 (2001–2002).

McEvilly, Theresa A. *Virtual Advertising in Sports Venues and the Federal Lanham Act §43(A): Revolutionary Technology Creates Controversial Advertising Medium.* 8 SETON HALL JOURNAL OF SPORT LAW 603 (1998).

Nothing but Internet. 110 HARVARD LAW REVIEW 1143 (1997).

Sableman, Mark. *Trademark Laws Underlie Sports Fortunes.* ST. LOUIS JOURNALISM REVIEW, Oct. 1, 1998.

Stabbe, Mitchell. *Fair or Fowl? Using Sports Teams' Trademarks Can Cost the Media Money.* AMERICAN JOURNALISM REVIEW, Aug. 1, 2005.

REFERENCE MATERIALS

Abromson, Henry M. *The Copyrightability of Sports Celebration Moves: Dance Fever or Just Plain Sick?* 14 MARQUETTE SPORTS LAW REVIEW 571 (2004).

Badgley, Robert A. *Domain Name Disputes*. New York: Aspen Law & Business, 2003.

Baharlias, Andrew D. *Yes, I Think the Yankees Might Sue if We Named Our Popcorn 'Yankees Toffee Crunch.' A Comprehensive Look at Trademark Infringement Defenses in the Context of the Professional and Collegiate Sports Industry*. 8 SETON HALL JOURNAL OF SPORT LAW 99 (1998).

Bambauer, Derek. *Legal Responses to the Challenges of Sports Patents*. 18 HARVARD JOURNAL OF LAW & TECHNOLOGY 401 (2005).

Bitman, Ronnie. *Rocking Wrigley: The Chicago Cubs' Off-Field Struggle to Compete for Ticket Sales with Rooftop Neighbors*. 56 FEDERAL COMMUNICATIONS LAW JOURNAL 377 (2004).

Chisum, Donald S., & Jacobs, Michael A. *Understanding Intellectual Property Law*. New York: M. Bender, 1996.

Cohen, Jay T. *I'll Trade You Scott Posednik for Alex Rodriguez: Fantasy Trademark and Copyright Protection*. 13 SPORTS LAWYERS JOURNAL 133 (2006).

Das, Proloy K. *Offensive Protection: The Potential Application of Intellectual Property Law to Scripted Sports Plays*. 75 INDIANA LAW JOURNAL 1073 (2000).

DiCarlo, Lisa. *With Tiger Woods, It's Nike, Nike Everywhere*. MSNBC.com, Apr. 15, 2004.

Ezer, Deborah J. *Celebrity Names as Web Site Addresses: Extending the Domain of Publicity Rights to the Internet*. 67 UNIVERSITY OF CHICAGO LAW REVIEW 1291 (2000).

Ferrelle, J. Rice. *Combating the Lure of Impropriety in Professional Sports Industries: The Desirability of Treating a Playbook as a Legally Enforceable Trade Secret*. 11 JOURNAL OF INTELLECTUAL PROPERTY LAW 149 (2003).

Fremlin, Robert. *Entertainment Law*. Rochester, NY: Lawyers Cooperative Publishing, 1990.

Greenberg, Martin J., & Gray, James T. *Sports Law Practice*, 2d ed. Charlottesville, VA: Lexis Law Publishing, 1998.

Hass, Bill. *Stadium Naming Good for Business*. NEWS & RECORD (Greensboro, NC), Dec. 15, 2004, C1.

Helms, Marisa. *TCF Wins U Stadium Naming Rights*. Minnesota Public Radio, March 24, 2005.

Hetzel, Dannean J. *Professional Athletes and Sports Teams: The Nexus of Their Identity Protection*. 11 SPORTS LAWYERS JOURNAL 141 (2004).

Kahn, Mark A. *May the Best Merchandise Win: The Law of Non-Trademark Uses of Sports Logos*. 14 MARQUETTE SPORTS LAW REVIEW 283 (2004).

Kane, Siegrun D. *Trademark Infringement Litigation 2004: "Lost in Translation."* 783 PLI/Pat 373 (2004).

Lindey, Alexander, & Landau, Michael. *Lindey on Entertainment, Publishing and the Arts: Agreements and the Law*, 3d ed. St. Paul, MN: Thomson/West, 2004.

Merges, Robert P., Menell, Peter S., & Lemley, Mark A. *Intellectual Property in the New Technological Age*, 2d ed. Gaithersburg, MD: Aspen Law & Business, 2000.

Nottingham, Don. *Keeping the Home Team at Home: Antitrust and Trademark Law as Weapons in the Fight Against Professional Sports Franchise Relocation*. 75 UNIVERSITY OF COLORADO LAW REVIEW 1065 (2004).

Oliveau, Maidie E. *What's in a Name? (Or, Why Pay Millions to Name a Building?)* 23 SPG ENTERTAINMENT & SPORTS LAWYER 1 (2005).

Pattishall, Beverly W., Hilliard, David C., & Welch, Joseph N. *Trademarks and Unfair Competition*, 4th ed. Newark, NJ: Lexis Publishing, 2000.

Phelps, William G. *Parody as Trademark or Tradename Dilution or Infringement*. 179 AMERICAN LAW REPORTS FEDERAL 181 (2005).

Rosenthal, Edward H. *Rights of Publicity and Entertainment Licensing.* 845 PLI/PAT 283 (2005).

Schechter, Roger E., and Thomas, John R. *Intellectual Property: The Law of Copyrights, Patents and Trademarks.* St. Paul, MN: Thomson/West, 2003.

Schwarz, A. *Claiming It Owns the Rights to Players' Names, Baseball Tells Fantasy Leagues to Pay Up. The Leagues Tell Baseball to Dream On.* 2005-DEC LEGAL AFFAIRS 22 (2005).

Simensky, Melvin, Selz, Thomas D., Burnett, Barbara, Lind, Robert C., & Palmer, Charles A. *Entertainment Law,* 2d ed. New York: M. Bender, 1998.

Smith, Jeffrey A. *It's Your Move—No It's Not! The Application of Patent Law to Sports Moves.* 70 UNIVERSITY OF COLORADO LAW REVIEW 1051 (1999).

Troutt, David Dante. *A Portrait of the Trademark as a Black Man: Intellectual Property, Commodification, and Redescription.* 38 UNIVERSITY OF CALIFORNIA AT DAVIS LAW REVIEW 1141 (2005).

Verna, Anthony. *www.WhatsInA.Name.* 14 SETON HALL JOURNAL OF SPORTS & ENTERTAINMENT LAW 153 (2004).

Voigt, Christian Maximilian. *"What's Really in the Package of a Naming Rights Deal?" Service Mark Rights and the Naming Rights of Professional Sports Stadiums.* 11 JOURNAL OF INTELLECTUAL PROPERTY LAW 327 (2004).

Williams, Jack F. *Symposium: Batter Up! From the Baseball Field to the Courthouse: Contemporary Issues Facing Baseball Practitioners: Who Owns the Back of a Baseball Card? A Baseball Player's Right in his Performance Statistics.* 23 CARDOZO LAW REVIEW 1705 (2002).

Withers, C. Knox. *Sine Qua Non: Trademark Infringement, Likelihood of Confusion, and the Business of Collegiate Licensing.* 11 JOURNAL OF INTELLECTUAL PROPERTY LAW 421 (2004).

CHAPTER 9

GENDER EQUITY AND WOMEN IN SPORTS

OVERVIEW

Historically, women have been discriminated against in sports and have not been provided with the same opportunities for participation as men. A vast disparity has existed between men's and women's sports in the provision of training facilities, adequate equipment, coaching staff, trainers, playing fields, recruitment for the sport, and adequate funding. Opportunities for girls at the interscholastic level had also been curtailed because of an overall attitude that girls could not play or had no desire to participate in sports at the same competitive level as boys. Many women around the world still do not have the equal opportunities for sports participation that U.S. women do.

Female amateur athletes have experienced much discrimination and harassment, which has limited their opportunities in athletics over a long period of time. Fortunately, this has begun to change. Girls and women are now participating in sports at the interscholastic and intercollegiate levels in record numbers, which are still increasing. More women are coaching at the collegiate level, and some strides are being made by women in athletic administration as well. Many of the archaic notions about women participating in sports have been discarded as women achieve greatness and notoriety in both amateur and professional sports.

Interest in women's sports has greatly increased as a result of the participation of girls in sports at an early age as well as the existence of laws that have given women the opportunity to participate fully. Parents of daughters have also taken an interest in involving girls in sports at a young age. More females are now participating in what were once all-male sports. Girls now participate on boys' high school football, baseball, and even wrestling teams.

The National Federation of State High School Associations (NFHS) is the body that oversees and governs the majority of high school athletics in the United States. More than 17,000 high schools are associated with the NFHS, which keeps statistics for participation in interscholastic sports. During the 1971–1972 school year, 294,015 girls participated in a variety of sports, with basketball the most popular sport. In comparison, 3,666,917 boys participated in all sports during the same time period. In the 2008–2009 school year, there were 3,114,091 girls and 4,422,662 boys participating in a variety of sports at the interscholastic level.[1]

Participation for women has increased at the collegiate level as well, and many more women now receive athletic scholarships to colleges and universities. Table 9-1 shows the participation of women in all collegiate divisions from 1991 to 2006. In what sports has participation increased? Decreased? Why? What conclusions can you derive from this data? Does the popularity of a sport coincide with society's interest in that sport? Does participation increase for girls and women if there is a successful role model in the sport, such as Danica Patrick that they can emulate?

Professional sports have also seen an increase in opportunities for women. The Women's National Basketball Association (WNBA) was established in 1996 and has been very successful. It has given elite women college basketball players an opportunity to display their abilities on the professional level, an opportunity that did not exist previously.

Women athletes have made a substantial contribution to sports. Katherine Switzer was one of the pioneers in the realm of women's sports. She played field hockey at Lynchburg College in Virginia and was a dedicated long-distance runner. She was forced to enter the Boston Marathon in 1967 registered as K. V. Switzer instead of Katherine. Officials attempted to oust her out of the race after she had completed two miles.[2] She completed the marathon in 4:20:00. Because of her 1967 run, women were eventually allowed to openly enter and compete in the Boston Marathon.

Olympian Wilma Rudolph beat the odds by winning three Olympic gold medals. Rudolph wore a brace on her left leg because of bouts she had fought with scarlet fever and pneumonia as a young girl. At the age of 16, she won a bronze medal in the Olympics; she followed that by dominating the 1960 Olympic Games. Danica Patrick has been extremely successful in the racing world, notwithstanding comments like Richard Petty's, who said "I just don't think it's a sport for women. . . . And so far, it's proved out. It's really not. It's good for them to come in. It gives us a lot of publicity, it gives them publicity."[3]

Women's individual sports, such as golf, bowling, track and field, and skating, have a longer history than women's team sports. In 1950, the Ladies Professional Golf Association (LPGA) was established. The leading money winner on the LPGA Tour for 2008 was Lorena Ochoa, earning $2,763,193. Annika Sörenstam was the tour's leading money winner from 2001–2005 and was also the leader in 1995, 1997, and 1998. The leading money winner in 1990, Beth Daniel, earned a paltry $863,578.

U.S. women's teams made headlines in the 1996 Olympics, winning gold medals in several sports, including basketball, softball, synchronized swimming, and soccer. The U.S. women's Olympic ice hockey team debuted in 1998 and won the gold medal over the Canadians. In the 2000 Olympics held in Sydney, Australia, women competed in the same number of team sports as men.

Young girls are now being recognized publicly for their achievements in sports. The National Baseball Hall of Fame and Museum asked Katie Brownwell to donate her Little League jersey after she pitched a perfect game for her team, the Dodgers. By the way, she also struck out all 18 batters, never reaching a three-ball count for any batter. Maria Pepe, who opened the doors for girls to play in Little League via her Supreme Court case, was present at the ceremony.[4]

---

[1] National Federation of State High School Associations, http://www.nfhs.org.
[2] Katherine Switzer, *First Women's Strides in Boston Still Echoing,* The New York Times, April 15, 2007.
[3] *Petty hasn't Changed Views on Women Racers,* ESPN.com, June 1, 2006.
[4] Richard, Sandomir, *TV SPORTS; For Unsung Female Athletes, A Top-Notch, Revealing 'Passion to Play,'* The New York Times, October 7, 1994.

TABLE 9-1

PARTICIPATION OPPORTUNITIES FOR FEMALE ATHLETES: ALL DIVISIONS (1991 TO 2006)

Percentage Of Schools That Offer Each Sport

	2006	2004	03	02	01	00	99	98	97	96	95	94	93	92	91
Archery	0.2	0.2	0.2	0.5	0.5	0.3	0.2	0.2	0.2	0.5	0.6	0.5	0.5	0.5	0.3
Badminton	0.4	0.3	0.3	0.1	0.1	0.5	0.5	0.2	0.2	0.3	0.3	0.7	0.5	0.9	0.9
Basketball	98.4	98.3	97.9	98.8	98.6	99.6	98.0	98.2	98.3	98.3	97.5	97.8	97.8	97.2	97.1
Bowling	3.2	3.3	3.2	2.6	2.2	1.4	1.2	0.9	0.8	0.5	0.3	0.3	0.8	0.5	0.3
Crew/Rowing	15.2	14.0	13.9	16.2	15.7	15.6	14.6	12.4	11.2	11.7	10.4	10.4	10.4	5.6	8.6
Cross Country	89.2	88.8	87.9	86.5	85.0	87.8	86.2	86.0	83.1	85.2	83.0	82.6	79.9	80.1	69.0
Fencing	5.9	4.6	4.6	5.8	5.8	5.1	5.1	5.5	5.2	4.6	4.3	4.6	4.8	7.0	7.2
Field Hockey	28.0	28.2	27.8	27.0	26.7	27.4	26.7	26.6	26.0	27.1	26.9	28.2	28.0	28.1	28.9
Golf	52.2	48.7	46.4	48.6	46.8	43.4	40.6	35.1	31.9	30.4	26.7	26.1	22.9	24.0	22.9
Gymnastics	9.5	11.0	11.0	12.0	12.0	11.7	11.9	10.3	10.1	11.2	11.1	10.8	10.9	11.5	11.3
Ice Hockey	9.7	8.8	8.7	8.5	7.9	6.8	5.8	4.6	3.6	2.8	2.6	2.4	2.2	2.4	2.7
Lacrosse	30.6	28.5	27.6	26.7	26.2	26.0	24.1	21.7	20.5	20.9	18.7	17.1	16.6	16.0	16.1
Riding/Equest	3.6	3.6	3.3	3.6	3.6	3.9	3.7	3.2	3.0	2.8	2.6	3.4	3.2	2.4	2.2
Riflery	3.4	2.8	3.0	3.8	3.9	3.6	3.6	3.2	3.2	4.2	4.0	2.6	2.2	2.2	2.4
Sailing	3.8	3.2	3.3	3.1	2.7	2.9	2.9	2.4	2.6	3.5	3.5	3.9	3.9	3.8	3.6
Skiing	5.7	5.8	6.0	5.0	4.8	4.6	4.6	4.2	4.1	4.6	4.9	4.9	5.2	5.7	5.6
Soccer	89.4	88.6	87.5	87.9	86.0	84.0	81.6	78.5	75.8	68.9	61.8	55.5	49.7	45.8	44.4
Softball	87.1	86.4	85.5	86.2	85.0	82.5	79.8	81.2	79.0	77.0	74.5	75.9	74.2	72.4	70.6
Squash	3.4	3.8	3.8	3.1	3.1	3.2	3.1	3.6	3.6	3.4	3.4	3.6	3.6	3.9	3.6
Swim/Dive	50.9	48.7	47.9	52.0	51.5	52.9	51.2	45.7	44.7	48.1	47.4	48.6	47.8	51.1	51.1
Synch Swim	1.3	0.5	0.5	1.0	1.2	1.4	1.4	0.9	0.9	0.8	0.8	0.7	0.5	1.2	1.4
Tennis	85.1	85.2	84.2	87.7	86.7	87.8	84.7	88.0	86.6	87.8	86.4	85.3	82.9	85.8	85.0
Track & Field	67.4	67.4	67.2	67.5	67.7	68.1	67.2	64.9	64.0	65.8	63.7	65.0	63.3	66.4	64.3
Volleyball	95.2	94.6	93.8	85.4	94.7	95.2	94.2	93.5	92.1	92.4	90.9	91.5	90.6	91.1	89.1
Water Polo	5.9	6.5	6.0	6.0	5.3	—	—	—	—	—	—	—	—	—	—

Source: Courtesy of The Women's Sports Foundation.

The gap in opportunities between boys and girls has begun to shrink because of laws such as Title IX as well as attitude changes in our society about the role of girls and women and their ability to participate and compete in the sports world. Case 9-1, *State v. Hunter*, 300 P.2d 455 (Or. 1956), illustrates the mind-set of that period when dealing with women's participation in sports. Consider the crime with which the defendant was charged. What reasons were given as to why women should be banned from wrestling?

📖 CASE 9-1   *State v. Hunter*

300 P.2d 455 (Or. 1956)

TOOZE, Justice.

Defendant Jerry Hunter, a person of the feminine sex, was charged . . . with the crime of 'participating in wrestling competition and exhi-bition,' in violation of the provisions of ORS 463.130.

The complaint, omitting formal parts, charged as follows:

'Jerry Hunter is accused by W. L. Bradshaw, District Attorney, by this Complaint of the Crime of Person of Female Sex Participating in Wrestling Competition and Exhibition committed as follows: The said Jerry Hunter on the 25th day of October, A.D., 1955, in the County of Clackamas and State of Oregon, then and there being a person not of the male sex, to-wit: of the female sex, did then and there unlawfully and willfully participate in a wrestling competition and wrestling exhibition, said act of defen-dant being contrary to the statute in such cases made and provided, and against the peace and dignity of the State of Oregon.'

. . . [D]efendant asserts on this appeal that the statute involved in this prosecution is unconstitutional and void . . .

'1. It denies to defendant the equal protection of the laws in viola-tion of Section 1 of the Fourteenth Amendment to the U. S. Constitu-tion, and it grants other citizens and classes of citizens privileges or immunities which upon the same terms do not equally belong to defendant and all other citizens, in violation of Section 20, Article 1 of the Constitution of the State of Oregon.' . . .

ORS 463.010 to 463.990, inclusive, provides for the creation of boxing and wrestling commissions, for registration of boxers and wrestlers, authorizes certain prize fights and wrestling exhibitions, with cer-tain regulations pertaining to the same, invests the commissions cre-ated with certain powers, including the rule-making power, provides for licensing, for penalties, and, in general, assumes to cover the entire field involved in boxing and wrestling exhibitions. ORS 463.130 provides as follows:

'Wrestling competitions; females barred; licensing; fees. (1) . . . *No person other than a person of the male sex shall participate in or be*

*licensed to participate in any wrestling competition or wrestling
exhibition.'* . . .

The principal question for decision is whether the foregoing ban
against women wrestlers constitutes an unreasonable exercise of the
police power of the state and violates Art. XIV, § 1, of the U.S.
Constitution and Art. 1, § 20, of the Oregon Constitution. Is the
classification contained in the statute arbitrary and unconstitutional, or is it based upon a reasonable distinction having a fair and
substantial relation to the object of the legislation and, therefore,
is constitutional?

Class legislation is permissible if it designates a class that is reasonable and natural and treats all within the class upon the basis of
equality. We take judicial notice of the physical differences between
men and women. These differences have been recognized in many legislative acts, particularly in the field of labor and industry, and most
of such acts have been upheld as a proper exercise of the police power
in the interests of the public health, safety, morals, and welfare.
As we said in State v. Baker, 50 Or. 381, 385, 92 P. 1076, 1078, 13
L.R.A.,N.S., 1040:

'By nature citizens are divided into the two great classes of men and
women, and the recognition of this classification by laws having for
their object the promoting of the general welfare and good morals does
not constitute an unjust discrimination.'

The Baker case involved a statute which prohibited women from entering
and remaining in a saloon. The statute was upheld.

Moreover, there is no inherent right to engage in public exhibitions
of boxing and wrestling. Both sports have long been licensed and regulated by penal statute and, in some cases, absolutely prohibited. It
is axiomatic that the Fourteenth Amendment to the U.S. Constitution
does not protect those liberties which civilized states regard as
properly subject to regulation by penal law. . . .

In addition to the protection of the public health, morals, safety,
and welfare, what other considerations might have entered the legislative mind in enacting the statute in question? We believe that we are
justified in taking judicial notice of the fact that the membership of
the legislative assembly which enacted this statute was predominately
masculine. That fact is important in determining what the legislature
might have had in mind with respect to this particular statute, in
addition to its concern for the public weal. It seems to us that its
purpose, although somewhat selfish in nature, stands out in the
statute like a sore thumb. Obviously it intended that there should be
at least one island on the sea of life reserved for man that would be
impregnable to the assault of woman. It had watched her emerge from

long tresses and demure ways to bobbed hair and almost complete
sophistication; from a creature needing and depending upon the protection and chivalry of man to one asserting complete independence. She
had already invaded practically every activity formerly considered
suitable and appropriate for men only. In the field of sports she had
taken up, among other games, baseball, basketball, golf, bowling,
hockey, long distance swimming, and racing, in all of which she had
become more or less proficient, and in some had excelled. In the business and industrial fields as an employee or as an executive, in the
professions, in politics, as well as in almost every other line of
human endeavor, she had matched her wits and prowess with those of
mere man, and, we are frank to concede, in many instances had outdone
him. In these circumstances, is it any wonder that the legislative
assembly took advantage of the police power of the state in its decision to halt this ever-increasing feminine encroachment upon what for
ages had been considered strictly as manly arts and privileges? Was
the Act an unjust and unconstitutional discrimination against woman?
Have her civil or political rights been unconstitutionally denied her?
Under the circumstances, we think not.

The judgment is affirmed.

Source: Courtesy of Westlaw; reprinted with permission.

Should girls be allowed to participate with boys in Little League baseball? That was the question presented in Case 9-2, *Fortin v. Darlington Little League, Inc.*, 514 F.2d 344 (1st Cir. 1975).
What reasons can you give for and against such participation?

📖 CASE 9-2 *Fortin v. Darlington Little League, Inc.*

514 F.2d 344 (1st Cir. 1975)

CAMPBELL, Circuit Judge.

This case concerns the right of a girl to play Little League baseball.
In the spring of 1974, ten year old Allison "Pookie" Fortin and her
father went to Slater Field, a City of Pawtucket park, where Pookie
sought to participate in the baseball program of the Darlington Little
League, Inc., American Division ("Darlington"). Pookie was a Pawtucket
resident and otherwise eligible; she was turned down because of her
sex. Defendant McCluskie, president of Darlington, told the Fortins
that a boys-only policy was dictated by the national Little League
organization. If Pookie were accepted, McCluskie feared that Darlington's Little League charter would be revoked, and the inexpensive
insurance provided by the national organization lost.

After she was rejected, Pookie and her father brought suit under
42 U.S.C. § 1983 and related statutes against Darlington and McCluskie
and also against Dragon, Pawtucket's Director of Parks and Recreation,
who maintains Slater Field and controls permission to use its baseball
diamonds. They asserted that denying Pookie the same places of public
accommodation and recreational activities as the male children of
Pawtucket taxpayers enjoy violated the equal protection clause of the
fourteenth amendment. Plaintiffs requested a declaration and injunction
allowing Pookie to play on the same terms as boys.

. . . .

. . . Reviewing the facts in this context, we are of the view that the
court's conclusion is not supported, and for reasons hereafter stated
we reverse. First, however, we briefly summarize the evidence presented
at the trial:

1. Pookie's father, a physician, testified that she was "physically fit and
   able to play baseball."
2. The Little League program she would have entered, had Darlington accepted her, was shown to sponsor three tiers of teams, accommodating
   players of different levels of maturity and ability. Younger boys, 8-9,
   play on the so-called minor league teams, of which there are eight.
   There are also several instructional league teams for boys of lesser
   ability. Boys of 10-12 are "drafted" into the seven Little League teams,
   although some older boys may never reach that level if they lack
   the ability. Darlington has a policy of accepting physically handicapped
   boys, placing them in teams and positions suited to their skills.
3. Darlington presented the deposition of Dr. Crane, an orthopedist who
   treated Brown University teams and who also had coached Little League
   baseball. Ninety percent of his experience with athletes had been with
   males. Dr. Crane felt the average girl could not safely compete with
   boys, although there might be some exceptions. His opinion seems to have
   rested mostly on the observation that girls, being more sedentary, were
   likely to be in poorer condition than boys. However, he also felt that
   girls, by reason of the design of their pelvis, walked with more unstable gait; that girls lacked the capacity to throw overhand; and that
   girls might be more likely to sustain bone-end fractures since they
   would be growing faster than boys during the 8-12 period.
4. Plaintiffs' main expert, Dr. Mathieu, was a board certified pediatrician who was medical director of the City of Providence School Department.
   She felt girls of Little League age could safely play baseball with
   boys. She testified that girls 8-12 are generally larger and as strong
   or stronger than boys of a similar age. They are no more subject to
   fractures or other injuries, no more unstable on their feet, are neu-
   rologically similar, and have the same amount of fat. The only notable

physical difference at these ages is that girls have a lesser respiratory capacity, although Dr. Mathieu did not believe the difference would affect their ability to play baseball.

5. A radiologist called by plaintiffs testified that girls' bones are no different from boys,' and that skeletally girls are no more subject to injury or unstable.

6. The president and coaches of Darlington testified to a belief that girls would detract from the game; might cause boys to play less aggressively and more protectively; had a lower "boiling point"; would be more prone to injury and, if in need of first aid, would embarrass the male coaches; and would prefer to play with other girls.

7. Darlington's only witness with experience with mixed teams said that boys on his teams had been encouraged to hold back because girls were less able to protect themselves. He thought that girls were injured more often than boys.

We find this evidence meager support for the court's finding of "material physical differences . . . regarding musculature, bone strength, strength of ligaments and tendons, pelvic structure, gait and reaction time . . . that . . . could undoubtedly result in serious injuries to girls. . . ." Dr. Crane, it is true, deposed that boys generally were stronger, being, he thought, more active. His basis for comparison, however, was entirely impressionistic. He admitted never having observed girls playing baseball and to a medical practice with emphasis upon male patients. He further agreed, with only a few qualifications, that the bones and bodies of girls were essentially as resistant to blows as those of boys, and that girls from 10-12 would experience a growth spurt ahead of boys. No statistical data whatever was presented tending to show greater female than male susceptibility to injury in the 8-12 group, and it is difficult to tell how much of Dr. Crane's deposition rested on personal views, to which he admitted, that it was the normal activity of a young lady to keep off baseball fields and play with dolls, and how much on science.

The court, moreover, gave no reason for totally rejecting the contrary testimony of Dr. Mathieu, a pediatrician with excellent credentials who would seem to have had more chance to examine children of both sexes in the relevant age groups than Dr. Crane. . . .

Darlington, moreover, accepts boys of all degrees of physical condition, including handicapped boys. Even Dr. Crane believed that a few girls could compete at the level of boys, and it is reasonable to suppose that handicapped and unathletic boys would be less proficient than many girls. Girls found to lack conditioning or ability to play safely could, like similarly situated boys, be retained on instructional or junior league teams rather than advanced to little league teams.

In addition, it seems most unlikely that a girl's parents would encourage or permit her to participate—or that the girl would wish to participate—in a program found to be too fast or rough for her. Should girls find Little League baseball too demanding, the problem would seem self-regulating in that the girls would withdraw.

Finally, we take notice not only that girls have for some time played Little League baseball in many communities but that Congress has amended the national Little League charter for the express purpose of encouraging and permitting girls to play on equal terms with boys. To uphold the district court would require us to accept the likelihood that both the policy in other communities and the judgment of Congress have resulted or will result in disproportionate physical injury to girls. We cannot conceive of Congress consciously adopting, and the Little League accepting, a policy likely to result in widespread injury; indeed Congress' action implies a finding by that body that girls are capable of playing Little League baseball without undue risk. The amendment of course removes Darlington's worry as to the availability of insurance for girl players.

We conclude that the court's stated reason for finding Darlington's exclusion of girls "rational"—namely, that injury will undoubtedly occur due to the physical differences between boys and girls—is unsupported. Our decision relates, of course, solely to the age group in question. It seems likely that as girls and boys mature, greater physical differences affecting athletic ability exist. But the evidence is essentially uncontroverted that the years 8–12 are those during which girls come close to matching boys in size and physical potential.

The other reasons cited by Darlington, the alleged preferences of coaches and players, the sense of what is or is not fit for girls to do, and the like, seem to us inadequate reasons to deny Pookie an opportunity to play on equal terms. These fall more under the heading of those "archaic and overbroad generalizations" rejected by the Supreme Court. Other arguments, such as that girls do not deserve an opportunity since later they will move in other athletic channels, do not impress us as justifying their exclusion during the years that they possess essentially equal capacity to enjoy this healthy and beneficial form of recreation. Darlington, we recognize, is staffed by volunteers who, it is asserted, do not wish to coach girls. But while Darlington could adopt any policy it wishes if it did not rely on the large-scale use of city facilities, the latter factor impresses it with the City's duty to deal equally.

Central to our decision, of course, are such factors as the ages of the children concerned, the uniqueness of the opportunity, and recent congressional assessment of the situation. Nothing we say is meant to

preclude recognition of bona fide distinguishing factors between the
sexes in some sports at some ages and in some circumstances.

The judgment of the district court is reversed and the case is
remanded for entry of a suitable declaratory judgment and, if
required, an injunction . . . to admit the female plaintiff to
[Darlington's] programs upon the same terms and conditions
available . . . to all others.

Source: Courtesy of Westlaw; reprinted with permission.

Do you agree with the court's finding in *Fortin* that between the ages of 8 and 12 girls closely
match boys in size and physical potential? Should there be age limits for girls who want to play
baseball in an all-boys league? For an opposite holding, see *Magill v. Avonworth Baseball Conference*,
364 F. Supp. 1212 (W.D. Pa. 1973). In that case the court found that a refusal to allow a ten-year-old
girl to play Little League baseball was not discriminatory. The court stated:

The directors, male and female, were unanimous in their opinions that baseball is a contact sport at
times and at times the contact is violent. We can take judicial notice of that fact and find that baseball
is a contact sport. There is no question that a runner who tries to beat a throw to the plate is frequently
blocked by a catcher. The contact is severe if not violent. The directors spoke of their concern with
wild pitchers and, of course, we know the consequences of trying to steal second or third. The directors have had a great deal of experience with boys' baseball and have formed the opinion after mature
consideration that girls would not fare well in physical contact with the boys. They admit that there are
excellent girl athletes but contend that they should not be placed in physical contact with boys. This is
a class action intended to force integration of the sexes generally in the baseball program and the
directors believe this unwise.[5]

Problem 9-1

You are the president of the local chapter of Pony League Baseball for boys aged 13 and 14.
A 14-year-old girl has requested she be able to play in the boys' Pony League games. There is
no current local policy relating to girls' participation in Pony League Baseball. Some of the parents of the boys have said they would withdraw their sons from the league if girls were allowed
to play. How would you handle this situation? Draft a policy that will cover this scenario.

CONSTITUTIONAL ISSUES IN GENDER EQUITY

Women have sued under multiple legal theories when asserting claims of sex discrimination in
sports, including the Equal Protection Clause of the Fourteenth Amendment to the U.S. Constitution.
State action must be present to prevail under this theory. Women have also pursued discrimination

---

[5] *Magill*, 364 F. Supp. at 1216.

claims under the Equal Rights Amendment (ERA) of some states' constitutions. State ERAs have been extremely helpful in assisting women who have been denied the opportunity to participate in sports.[6]

There have been many cases dealing with the issue of whether girls can play on boys' teams. Courts have recognized that separate teams are justified if the sport is a contact sport. The general rule states that when only one team is available and the sport is deemed a non-contact sport, both sexes must be allowed to try out for the team. If women are given the opportunity to compete on their own, then it is less likely they will be allowed to compete with men. Title IX regulations (discussed later in this chapter) allow an athletic department to field separate teams for each sex if team selection is based on a competitive skill or the sport is deemed a contact sport. If a particular sport is not sponsored for one sex and the sex that has been excluded has a history of limited opportunity in the sport, then the sex being excluded must be allowed to try out for the team.[7] Under Title IX such sports as boxing, wrestling, rugby, ice hockey, basketball, and football have been deemed contact sports.

What happens if a girl wants to try out for the boys' high school football team? Should she be allowed to try out? Should she be allowed to play? That was the issue in Case 9-3, *Lantz by Lantz v. Ambach,* 620 F. Supp. 663 (D.C. N.Y.1985), involving a 16-year-old girl who wanted to try out for her high school football team.

📖 CASE 9-3 *Lantz by Lantz v. Ambach*

620 F. Supp. 663 (D.C. N.Y.1985)

STANTON, District Judge.

Plaintiff Jacqueline Lantz, a 16-year-old healthy female student in her junior year at Lincoln High School, Yonkers, New York wants to play football. Lincoln High School has no girls' football team, so she attempted to try out for the junior varsity football squad. Her attempts were blocked by a regulation. . . . The regulation, 8 N.Y.C.R.R. § 135.4(c)(7)(ii)(c)(2) states:

"There shall be no mixed competition in the following sports: basketball, boxing, football, ice hockey, rugby and wrestling."

Suing under the Civil Rights Act, 42 U.S.C. § 1983, plaintiff claims the regulation violates . . . her right to equal protection of the laws as guaranteed by the Fourteenth Amendment to the United States Constitution. She seeks a declaratory judgment that the regulation as written violates that statute and that clause of the Fourteenth Amendment, and an injunction requiring the defendants to delete the regulation and permit her to try out for the junior varsity squad. . . .

---

[6] *See* A. Faraone, *The Florida Equal Rights Amendment: Raising the Standard Applied to Gender Under the Equal Protection Clause of the Florida Constitution,* 1 FLA. COASTAL L.J. 421 (2000).

[7] 45 C.F.R. § 86.41.

The Supreme Court has stated that discrimination among applicants on the basis of their gender is subject to scrutiny under the Equal Protection clause of the Fourteenth Amendment, and will be upheld only where there is "exceedingly persuasive justification" showing at least that the classification serves "important governmental objectives and that the discriminatory means employed are substantially related to the achievement of those objectives." Here the governmental objective is to protect the health and safety of female students, and there is no quarrel with the importance of that objective. To demonstrate that the regulation is substantially related to that objective, the Commissioner and the Board of Regents have offered data establishing that "as a general rule, senior high school students (age 15 through 18) are more physically developed, stronger, more agile, faster and have greater muscular endurance than their female counterparts," medical opposition to girls' participation on boys' teams in such contact sports as football (which Dr. Falls described as a "collision" sport) because of the risk of injury in such participation, and the testimony of Dr. Willie to the effect, among other points, that the present regulation enhances safety by permitting simple and uniform administration across the state.

But these data, however refined, inevitably reflect averages and generalities. The Commissioner and the Regents say, "It makes no difference that there might be a few girls who wish to play football who are more physically fit than some of the boys on the team." Yet it does make a difference, because the regulation excludes all girls. No girl— and simply because she is a girl—has the chance to show that she is as fit, or more, to be on the squad as the weakest of its male members. Where such cases exist, the regulation has no reasonable relation to the achievement of the governmental objective. In such a case, the effect of the regulation is to exclude qualified members of one gender because they are presumed to suffer from an inherent handicap or to be innately inferior. Thus the regulation's operation is too broad, and must give way to the facts in particular cases.

. . . Jacqueline Lantz obviously has no legal entitlement to a starting position on the Lincoln High School Junior Varsity football squad, since the extent to which she plays must be governed solely by her abilities, as judged by those who coach her. But she seeks no such entitlement here.

Instead she seeks simply a chance, like her counterparts, to display those abilities. She asks, in short, only the right to try.

To the extent that the challenged regulation deprives her of the opportunity to try out for the junior varsity football squad, it operates to abridge her right under Section 1 of the Fourteenth Amendment to the Constitution of the United States, and the defendants will be enjoined from complying with it or enforcing it.

. . . ORDERED that the defendant Board of Education, its agents and
employees arrange for a prompt determination whether plaintiff Jacqueline Lantz is eligible for junior varsity football pursuant to the
same standards that are applied to male candidates and, if she is
found eligible, direct that she be permitted to try out for the
squad. . . .

Source: Courtesy of Westlaw; reprinted with permission.

Is girls' half-court basketball equivalent to boys' full-court basketball? In Case 9-4, *Dodson v. Arkansas Activities Ass'n et al.*, 468 F. Supp. 394 (E.D. Ark. 1979), a federal court in Arkansas was faced with that issue in 1979.

📖 CASE 9-4 *Dodson v. Arkansas Activities Ass'n et al.*

468 F. Supp. 394 (E.D. Ark. 1979)

OPINION

ARNOLD, District Judge.

Diana Lee Dodson brought this suit on January 25, 1977. At the time
she was 14 years old and in the ninth grade in the public schools of
Arkadelphia, Arkansas. She was a good basketball player and had played
on her junior high girls' team in the eighth grade. There are three
defendants: the school district in which Diana Lee's school is
located, the superintendent of schools of that district, and the
Arkansas Activities Association. The Association is a voluntary group
of schools, mostly public, to which the Arkadelphia schools belong,
together with most, if not all, other public junior and senior high
schools in Arkansas.

This suit challenges the constitutionality of the rules for girls'
junior and senior high basketball laid down by the defendant Association. There is no question of state action. . . . It is, at least for
present purposes, subject to the Equal Protection Clause of the Fourteenth Amendment.

The question presented is whether the differences in girls' and boys'
junior and senior high basketball rules, as laid down by the Association for play in Arkansas, are so lacking in justification, and so
injurious to the girls, as to deprive them of the equal protection of
the laws. This Court holds that the rules place girl athletes in
Arkansas at a substantial disadvantage as compared to boy athletes,
that no sufficient justification is offered to justify this disparity,
and that the resulting discrimination is unconstitutional. A decree
will be entered requiring defendants to erase the differences between
the two sets of rules.

Girls' basketball, as played in Arkansas, is markedly different from boys.' It is variously referred to as "half-court," "six on six," or "three on three," while the boys' game is known as "full-court" or "five on five." Girls' teams have six players, while boys' have five. Three girls are forwards, almost always on offense, and three are guards, almost always on defense. No players may cross the center line in the middle of the court. The three guards must always stay in the half of the court where the other team scores. The forwards must stay in the half of the court where their own team scores. Only a forward can shoot or score points. If a guard is fouled, she does not get a free throw. The ball goes to the other end of the court, and one of the forwards does the shooting. In "full court" or "boys' rules," by contrast, all five players may range the full length of the court. They all play defense when the other team has the ball, and they all play offense when their own team has the ball. Any player may shoot and score points, both field goals and free throws.

There are some other differences between the two games, but the difference just described is a major one. Arkansas girls simply do not get the full benefit and experience of the game of basketball available to Arkansas boys. Although substitution is possible, and a girl may play both guard and forward at various times, such changes appear to be the exception rather than the rule. Most girls are typed as either a guard or a forward and remain so. A five-person, full-court game requires a more comprehensive and more complex strategy. It also provides more intensive physical training and conditioning, because, if for no other reason, players on a five-person team have to run up and down the full length of the court, not just half of it. Players of the full-court game also learn to shoot from farther out, because there are five opponents, not just three, trying to keep them away from the basket. Various expert witnesses at the trial summarized the effect of these rules on girls in Arkansas. They are a disservice to the youngsters coming up. Girls are learning half of the game.

All this might not matter so much were it not for the effects on the girls after graduation. Those whose ambition it is to play basketball in college, perhaps even on scholarship, are at a marked disadvantage. College basketball is full-court, for women as well as men. For that matter, almost no one plays half-court any more. Most Arkansas private schools play full-court for boys and girls. International competition is full-court. Every state except Arkansas, Iowa, Oklahoma, and Tennessee is full-court in secondary school. (Texas was apparently in the process of changing when this case was tried. It seems now to play full-court.) If an Arkansas girl wishes to compete for a position on a college team, she must overcome substantial obstacles. Most of her opposition will have played full-court in high school. The lack of training and conditioning, the psychological barrier of the center line, which she has been schooled not to cross, and, in the case of guards, the lack of shooting experience all . . . make the Arkansas girl less able to compete. The disadvantage is tremendous. It takes about a year for a half-court girl with talent to adjust to the difference in games. Even the University of Arkansas does most of its recruiting out of state, for just this reason. The primary basketball player will be from outside of the state of Arkansas, which will be a disadvantage to those young girls who are in this state going to high school.

In view of these disparities a movement understandably arose among some schools to change the rules to permit girls to play full-court. This kind of decision is made by vote of the membership of the Arkansas Activities Association. The vote is by mail ballot. . . . The Association had about 508 memberships at the time this case was tried, but only those with girls' basketball teams were entitled to vote on this issue. The record does not disclose how many eligible votes there were on the question. A vote taken in August 1976 was 117 to 114 to change to full-court. This decision was reversed, however, in January 1977 by a vote of 147 to 116. . . .

The fact that girls in Arkansas secondary schools are treated differently, or less advantageously, than boys, of course, is not at all conclusive of the claim asserted. The Equal Protection Clause does not forbid differences as such. It remains to ask, what justification is offered for the difference? We lay at once to one side any suggestion that girls are not strong enough, or large enough, to play the orthodox full-court game. No such suggestion is made by any party, and in any event the record is overwhelmingly to the contrary. Both the experience in most other states, and the testimony at the trial of this cause, show beyond doubt that no physiological or anatomical reason makes girls unable, or any less able, to play five on five. Indeed, defendants' counsel expressly stated on the record that no physiological differences between males and females . . . prohibit females from playing five on five basketball. Some defense witnesses offered various reasons for preferring half-court: more girls can play, games tend to be higher-scoring (or at any rate more shots are attempted), the center-line barrier requires more agility and skill of movement, and the like. These considerations may have merit in their own way. Half-court may in fact be a better game. But if it's better for the girls, it's better for the boys as well. None of the reasons proffered is at all relevant to a gender-based classification. And significantly, no official of the Association relied at trial on any of these reasons.

The real reason for the difference, and in fact the only operative
reason, is simply that girls' rules have always been this way in
Arkansas. Lee Cassady, director of the Association, candidly testified
as follows:

> Q. Do you know why the girls have been classified to play under
> these certain rules (rules which are different from boys' rules)?
>
> A. In our state it has been kind of a traditional development.
> It was not done originally for any particular reason, other than
> that these were the girls' rules that were being played by girls'
> teams and sponsored by women for girls.

Other evidence supports Mr. Cassady's conclusion. According to
Dr. Downing, when basketball was invented by one Naismith in 1892,
girls and women at once became interested in the game, but they played
on a court divided into Three (not just two) equal parts. There were
nine players on a team, three in each of the three divisions. Why?
Because girls and women wore bustles, long trains, and high starched
collars. They just couldn't get up and down the court fast enough.
Over the years, the game evolved. Girls and women changed first to
half-court, and then, in most states, to full-court.

What constitutional standard is to be applied? The Supreme Court has
recently reaffirmed the standard. In Orr v. Orr, 440 U.S. 268, 99
S.Ct. 1102, 59 L.Ed.2d 306 (1979), the Court said: "To withstand
scrutiny under the equal protection clause, 'classifications by gender
must serve important governmental objectives and must be substantially
related to achievement of those objectives.'"

It is at once apparent that the justification offered here does not
even come close to meeting that test. Simply doing things the way
they've always been done is not an "important government objective,"
if indeed it is a legitimate objective at all. Change for its own
sake is no doubt to be avoided, and tradition is a healthy thing.
But tradition alone, without supporting gender-related substantive
reasons, cannot justify placing girls at a disadvantage for no
reason other than their being girls. The Association's decision to
go back to half-court may have been reached by a democratic process,
at least among school administrators. That circumstance cannot save
it from constitutional condemnation. The Equal Protection Clause is
a limitation on governmental action, no matter how fair the process
that led to it.

It is proper to add a word about what this case is not about. It is
not about whether girls could or should play against boys. The question is whether girls are entitled to play full-court against each

other. Nor is the case concerned with discrimination between Arkansas girls and, say, Mississippi girls. (Mississippi plays full-court.) That kind of discrimination is not cognizable under the Equal Protection Clause, because it results from the action of two separate sovereigns. The point here is that Arkansas boys are in a position to compete on an equal footing with boys elsewhere, while Arkansas girls, merely because they are girls, are not. Nor does this Court hold that there is a constitutional right to play basketball, or to score points. Arkansas schools have chosen to offer basketball. Having taken that step, they may not limit the game's full benefits to one sex without substantial justification.

. . . It is by the Court this 4th day of April, 1979, CONSIDERED, ORDERED, ADJUDGED, and DECREED,

That the defendants, and each of them, their agents, servants, and employees, and all persons acting in concert with them, be, and they are hereby, permanently enjoined and restrained from enforcing as to girls playing junior and senior high school basketball in Arkansas, any rules different from those enforced as to boys.

Source: Courtesy of Westlaw; reprinted with permission.

In Case 9-5, *Israel v. West Virginia Secondary Schools Activities Comm'n*, 388 S.E.2d 480 (W. Va. 1989), a high school girl who was an outstanding baseball player wanted to play on the boys' baseball team.

📖 CASE 9-5 *Israel v. West Virginia Secondary Schools Activities Comm'n*

388 S.E.2d 480 (W. Va. 1989)

MILLER, Justice:

Erin Israel, by her next friend, Patricia Israel, appeals from a final order of the Circuit Court of Pleasants County, entered February 11, 1988, denying her request for a declaratory judgment, injunctive relief, and damages on the basis of alleged gender discrimination. On appeal, Ms. Israel asserts that she was discriminated against in violation of the Equal Protection Clause of the Fourteenth Amendment of the United States Constitution and its state counterpart, Article III, Section 17 of the West Virginia Constitution, as well as the Human Rights Act, W.Va. Code, 5-11-1, *et seq.* (1987).

Ms. Israel has a great deal of experience playing baseball. She began playing baseball at the age of six in the local park and recreation league where she learned the basic fundamentals of the game. At the age of nine, Ms. Israel progressed into the Little League system.

Her Little League coach testified that Ms. Israel's skills were always above average. He stated that "[s]he was very aggressive, understood the game, its concepts, and its technique." While playing Little League, Ms. Israel was nominated for every all-star team. At the age of thirteen, she became the first female to ever play on a Pony League team in Pleasants County. When Ms. Israel was a freshman at St. Mary's High School, and expressed a desire to play on the all-male baseball team, the high school baseball coach told her he had no objections to her playing for him and promised to give her a fair tryout. In February, 1984, Ms. Israel tried out for the all-male high school baseball team. She was prohibited from playing on the team because of a regulation promulgated by the Secondary Schools Activities Commission (SSAC).

The Board of Education of the County of Pleasants (Board) is a member of the SSAC. The SSAC is a nonprofit organization created by W.Va. Code, 18-2-25 (1967), which authorizes county boards of education to delegate their supervisory authority over interscholastic athletic events and band activities to the SSAC. . . . In the exercise of its delegated authority, the SSAC adopted Rule No. 3.9, which provides:

"If a school maintains separate teams in the same or related sports (example: baseball or softball) for girls and boys during the school year, regardless of the sports season, girls may not participate on boys' teams and boys may not participate on girls' teams. However, should a school not maintain separate teams in the same or related sports for boys and girls, then boys and girls may participate on the same team except in contact sports such as football and wrestling."

Shortly after Ms. Israel tried out to play on the baseball team, she was informed by St. Mary's' assistant principal that she was ineligible to play on the baseball team because St. Mary's had a girls' softball team. The assistant principal explained that if the school allowed Ms. Israel to play baseball, it would be in violation of Rule 3.9 and would be barred from playing in state tournaments. After numerous futile efforts to have the rule changed through the internal mechanisms provided by the SSAC, Ms. Israel filed a complaint with the Human Rights Commission. . . .

The Commission issued Ms. Israel a right-to-sue letter, and she filed this action against the SSAC and the Board on April 18, 1986, in the Circuit Court of Pleasants County. The circuit court exonerated the Board, finding that it had made a good-faith effort to have the SSAC change the rule and that if the Board had ignored Rule 3.9, it would have been subject to severe sanctions by the SSAC. Ms. Israel does not appeal this ruling. She does appeal the circuit court's decision that the SSAC rule was valid.

. . . .

II. Equal Protection

Equal protection of the law is implicated when a classification treats similarly situated persons in a disadvantageous manner. The claimed discrimination must be a product of state action as distinguished from a purely private activity.

A. Fourteenth Amendment Equal Protection

In analyzing gender-based discrimination, the United States Supreme Court has been willing to take into account actual differences between the sexes, including physical ones.

Under the United States Constitution, a gender-based discrimination is subject to a level of scrutiny somewhere between the traditional equal protection analysis and the highest level of scrutiny utilized for suspect classes. The intermediate level of scrutiny as applied to gender-based discrimination was stated in *Craig v. Boren*, 429 U.S. 190, 197, . . . (1976): "[C]lassifications by gender must serve important governmental objectives and must be substantially related to achievement of those objectives" in order to withstand an equal protection challenge.

Under the middle-tier analysis for gender-based discrimination claims, courts have recognized that it is constitutionally permissible under certain circumstances for public schools to maintain separate sports teams for males and females so long as they are substantially equivalent. This result has been justified by one or more of the following reasons: (1) there are physical and psychological differences between males and females; (2) the maintenance of separate teams promotes athletic opportunities for women; and, as a corollary to (2), (3) if there were not separate teams, men might dominate in certain sports. . . .

While courts have recognized the concept of substantial equivalency in the area of interscholastic sports, this does not mean that mere superficial equivalency will be found constitutional under equal protection principles. We are not cited nor have we found a case precisely on point. Several courts have held that Little League baseball teams must, under equal protection principles, permit female players to try out. . . .

From the record in this case, we find that the games of baseball and softball are not substantially equivalent. There is, of course, a superficial similarity between the games because both utilize a similar format. However, when the rules are analyzed, there is a substantial disparity in the equipment used and in the skill level required. The difference begins with the size of the ball and its delivery, and differences continue throughout. The softball is larger and must be thrown underhand, which forecloses the different types of pitching that can be accomplished in the overhand throw of a baseball.

There are ten players on the softball team and nine on a baseball team. The distance between the bases in softball is sixty feet, while in baseball it is ninety feet. The pitcher's mound is elevated in baseball and is not in softball. The distance from the pitcher's mound to home plate is sixty feet in baseball and only forty feet in softball. In baseball, a bat of forty-two inches is permitted, while in softball the maximum length is thirty-four inches.

Moreover, the skill level is much more demanding in baseball because the game is played at a more vigorous pace. There are more intangible rewards available if one can make the baseball team. For a skilled player, such as the record demonstrates Ms. Israel to be, it would be deeply frustrating to be told she could not try out for the baseball team, not because she did not possess the necessary skills, but only because she was female. The entire thrust of the equal protection doctrine is to avoid this type of artificial distinction based solely on gender.

We agree with the SSAC that by providing a softball team for females, it was promoting more athletic opportunities for females. However, this purpose does not satisfy the equal protection mandate requiring substantial equivalency. We do not believe that by permitting females to try out for the boys' baseball team, a mass exodus from the girls' softball team will result. There are obvious practical considerations that will forestall such a result. Gender does not provide an automatic admission to play on a boys' baseball team. The team is selected from those who apply and possess the requisite skill to make the team. What we deal with in this case is an opportunity to have a chance to try out for the team. Aside from the baseball-softball dichotomy, other athletic events ordinarily operate on the same rules such that the substantial equivalency issue would be unlikely to arise. . . .

Reversed and remanded.

Source: Courtesy of Westlaw; reprinted with permission.

Problem 9-2

You have just secured a new job as athletic director of the Johnson County Independent School District. One of the first issues you must face is whether girls should be able to try out for and play boys' football for grades 9 to 12. There is a girls' flag football sport at several high schools in the district. However, two girls have requested they be allowed to try out for and play junior varsity and varsity football, respectively. You must draft a policy for such activities that will be approved by the school district. You must consider whether you will have a different policy for junior varsity and varsity participants. Furthermore, your proposed policy must withstand any constitutional challenges. What legal considerations are present?

TITLE IX

History and Overview

Prior to 1970 there had been very few legal challenges addressing sex discrimination in athletics. In the early 1970s, women began using the Fourteenth Amendment for sex discrimination claims. Title IX, federal legislation that was passed in 1972, gave women the statutory remedy needed to address problems dealing with sex discrimination; its purpose is to eliminate discrimination in federally funded activities. The passage and implementation of Title IX has done more to advance women's rights in sports than any other piece of legislation. The statute states in part, "No person in the United States shall, on the basis of sex, be excluded from participation in, be denied the benefits of, or be subjected to discrimination under any education program or activity receiving Federal financial assistance."[8] Title IX has been hugely successful in opening doors for female athletes. Participation in women's sports has increased greatly since the passage of Title IX at both interscholastic and collegiate levels.

The Department of Health, Education, and Welfare (HEW) was given the task of implementing Title IX. Approximately three years after Title IX was passed, regulations were passed and became effective.[9] The Office of Civil Rights (OCR) under the Department of Education is responsible for enforcing Title IX. The OCR's job is to ensure that universities that receive federal funds are in compliance with the requirements of Title IX. The OCR also has a compliance review program for selected recipients. During the review process the OCR is able to identify and resolve sex discrimination issues that may not have been addressed through the compliance process. Many universities and colleges have established guidelines for the development of a Title IX action plan, and many will provide their gender equity plan if requested. Universities and colleges have committees that work directly with athletes in addressing issues of gender equity. Some even will invite OCR representatives or Title IX consultants to visit the campus and assist them in the evaluation and development of policies intended to ensure gender equity.

---

[8] 20 U.S.C. § 1681(a).
[9] 45 C.F.R. Part 86.

In 1979 the Department of Civil Rights established a three-prong test for compliance with Title IX. The test was later clarified in 1996 and again in 2005. It states:

(1)   whether intercollegiate level participation opportunities for male and female students are provided in numbers substantially proportionate to their respective enrollment (the "substantial proportionality prong");

(2)   where the members of one sex have been and are underrepresented among intercollegiate athletics, where the institution can show a history and continuing practice of program expansion which is demonstrably responsive to the developing interest and abilities of the members of that sex (the "history of continuing expansion prong"); or

(3)   where the members of one sex are underrepresented among intercollegiate athletes, and the institution cannot show a continuing practice of program expansion such as cited above, where it can be demonstrated that the interests and abilities of the members of the sex have been fully and effectively accommodated by the present program.

A school can comply with Title IX by meeting the requirements of one of the tests.[10]

Title IX has had a major effect on colleges and universities since its inception. Many have made substantial changes within their athletic programs to ensure compliance with Title IX. In 2006, for example, James Madison University (JMU) voted to dismantle ten athletic teams to comply with federal law.[11] Seven men's varsity teams (outdoor and indoor track, cross country, archery, gymnastics, swimming, and wrestling) and three women's varsity teams (archery, fencing, and gymnastics) were discontinued to comply with Title IX. JMU had been out of compliance with federal law because women made up 61% of enrolled students, whereas female athletic participation was only 50%. With the new plan in place, female athletic participation is predicted to increase to 61%.[12]

In *Kelly v. Board of Trustees of the University of Illinois*, 35 F.3d 265 (7th Cir. 1994), the court ruled that the university did not violate Title IX when it eliminated the men's swimming team and not the women's. The university cited budget constraints along with the need for compliance with Title IX and the gender equity policy of the Big Ten Conference. The court found that Illinois could do away with men's programs without violating Title IX because men's interests are permanently met when

---

[10] *See* Roberts v. Colorado State Board of Agriculture, 998 F.2d 824 (10th Cir. 1993); Choike v. Slippery Rock Univ. of Pa. of the State Sys. of Higher Educ., 2006 WL 2060576 (W.D. Pa. July 21, 2006); Pederson v. La. State Univ., 213 F.3d 858 (5th Cir. 2000); Horner v. Ky. High Sch. Athletic Ass'n, 43 F.3d 265 (6th Cir. 1994).

[11] Associated Press, *James Madison to Drop Teams for Title IX Compliance*, ESPN.com, September 29, 2006.

[12] James Madison University, *JMU Enacts Proportionality Plan to Comply with Title IX*, Sept. 29, 2006, http://www.jmu.edu/jmuweb/general/news/general7490.shtml.

[13] *See* Miami University Wrestling Club v. Miami University, 302 F.3d 608 (6th Cir. 2002) (granting summary judgment for the university on the plaintiff's claims under Title IX and Equal Protection arguments after the university eliminated the men's soccer, tennis, and wrestling teams); Chalenor v. University of North Dakota, 291 F.3d 1042 (8th Cir. 2002) (granting summary judgment for the university on the plaintiff's claims for violation of Title IX after men's wrestling was canceled).

[14] D. Klinker, *Why Conforming with Title IX Hurts Men's Collegiate Sports*, 13 Seton Hall J. Sport L. 73 (2003).

substantial proportionalities exist. Men's participation in athletics at the University of Illinois was at 76.6%, which was more than substantially proportional to their enrollment (56%).

Some athletic programs have been cut in an attempt to comply with Title IX requirements.[13] The fairness of having to cut certain sports programs to comply with Title IX has been subject to debate.[14] In a memo of July 11, 2003, Assistant Secretary of Civil Rights Gerald Reynolds wrote regarding the compliance of intercollegiate athletics with Title IX, "OCR hereby clarifies that nothing in Title IX requires the cutting or reduction of teams in order to demonstrate compliance with Title IX, and that the elimination of teams is a disfavored practice."

Grove City College v. Bell, 46 U.S. 555 (1984), was a landmark case in the history of Title IX. In that case, the court ruled that only programs that received direct financial assistance were subject to Title IX. The holding of *Grove City* was not the intent of Congress when it passed Title IX, so the Civil Rights Restoration Act of 1987 was eventually passed, which further clarified the applicability of Title IX to athletes. Almost all colleges, universities, elementary, and secondary school districts are covered under Title IX. The Civil Rights Restoration Act further supported congressional intent to protect against sex discrimination in institutions receiving federal funds by indicating that a "program" or "activity" includes the entire range of programs in a federally funded institution, not just specifically funded programs as set forth in *Grove City College*.

The Equity Athletics Disclosure Act (EADA) was passed in 1994 and requires public disclosure of financial records relating to athletic expenditures by universities and colleges. The Department of Education is required to report to Congress on gender equity in college athletics; it relies on information received through the EADA in making that report. The university or college must list all participants in athletics, the operating expenses for both men's and women's programs, the number of scholarships awarded, the revenue received, coaches' salaries, and recruiting expenses. This statute allows the NCAA and the public to closely monitor gender equity issues and graduation rates for student-athletes. Many universities and school districts now have a specific job position that has the responsibility of ensuring Title IX compliance. What qualifications are necessary for a Title IX compliance officer? What should be the main responsibility of such officers? To whom should they report? What would their daily duties be?

Case 9-6, *Cohen v. Brown University*, 101 F.3d 155 (1st Cir. 1996), may be the most significant case ever decided under Title IX. After the Ivy League university announced that it was going to eliminate four women's sports but stated that the teams could still qualify as unfunded club sports, the university was sued. The Brown student body was 52% male and 47% female, with 63% of its student-athletes male. The Court of Appeals for the First Circuit ruled against Brown, stating that the university was not in compliance with Title IX and that a university must fully and effectively accommodate the interests of women students to ensure Title IX compliance.

📖 CASE 9-6 *Cohen v. Brown University*

101 F.3d 155 (1st Cir. 1996)

BOWNES, Senior Circuit Judge.

This is a class action lawsuit charging Brown University, its president, and its athletics director (collectively "Brown") with discrimination against women in the operation of its intercollegiate athletics program, in violation of Title IX of the Education Amendments of 1972. The plaintiff class comprises all present, future, and potential Brown University women students who participate, seek to participate, and/or are deterred from participating in intercollegiate athletics funded by Brown.

This suit was initiated in response to the demotion in May 1991 of Brown's women's gymnastics and volleyball teams from university-funded varsity status to donor-funded varsity status. Contemporaneously, Brown demoted two men's teams, water polo and golf, from university-funded to donor-funded varsity status. As a consequence of these demotions, all four teams lost, not only their university funding, but most of the support and privileges that accompany university-funded varsity status at Brown.

Subsequently, after hearing fourteen days of testimony, the district court granted plaintiffs' motion for a preliminary injunction, ordering, *inter alia*, that the women's gymnastics and volleyball teams be reinstated to university-funded varsity status, and prohibiting Brown from eliminating or reducing the status or funding of any existing women's intercollegiate varsity team until the case was resolved on the merits. A panel of this court affirmed the district court's decision granting a preliminary injunction to the plaintiffs. In so doing, we upheld the district court's analysis and ruled that an institution violates Title IX if it ineffectively accommodates its students' interests and abilities in athletics . . . regardless of its performance with respect to other Title IX areas.

On remand, the district court determined after a lengthy bench trial that Brown's intercollegiate athletics program violates Title IX and its supporting regulations. The district court ordered Brown to submit within 120 days a comprehensive plan for complying with Title IX, but stayed that portion of the order pending appeal. The district court subsequently issued a modified order, requiring Brown to submit a compliance plan within 60 days. This action was taken to ensure that the Order was "final" for purposes of this court's jurisdiction, and to expedite the appeal process. Finding that Brown's proposed compliance plan was not comprehensive and that it failed to comply with the . . . order, the district court rejected the plan and ordered in its place specific relief consistent with Brown's stated objectives in formulating the plan. The court's remedial order required Brown to elevate and maintain at university-funded varsity status the women's gymnastics, fencing, skiing, and water polo teams. The district court's decision to fashion specific relief was made, in part, to avoid protracted litigation over the compliance plan and to expedite the appeal on the issue of liability. The district court entered final judgment. . . . This appeal followed. . . .

We find no error in the district court's factual findings or in its interpretation and application of the law in determining that Brown violated Title IX in the operation of its intercollegiate athletics program. We therefore affirm in all respects the district court's analysis and rulings on the issue of liability. We do, however, find error in the district court's award of specific relief and therefore remand the case to the district court for reconsideration of the remedy in light of this opinion.

. . . Brown therefore should be afforded the opportunity to submit another plan for compliance with Title IX. The context of the case has changed in two significant respects since Brown presented its original plan. First, the substantive issues have been decided adversely to Brown. Brown is no longer an appellant seeking a favorable result in the Court of Appeals. Second, the district court is not under time constraints to consider a new plan and fashion a remedy so as to expedite appeal. Accordingly, we remand the case to the district court so that Brown can submit a further plan for its consideration.

VIII.

There can be no doubt that Title IX has changed the face of women's sports as well as our society's interest in and attitude toward women athletes and women's sports. In addition, there is ample evidence that increased athletics participation opportunities for women and young girls, available as a result of Title IX enforcement, have had salutary effects in other areas of societal concern.

One need look no further than the impressive performances of our country's women athletes in the 1996 Olympic Summer Games to see that Title IX has had a dramatic and positive impact on the capabilities of our women athletes, particularly in team sports. These Olympians represent the first full generation of women to grow up under the aegis of Title IX. The unprecedented success of these athletes is due, in no small measure, to Title IX's beneficent effects on women's sports, as the athletes themselves have acknowledged time and again. What stimulated this remarkable change in the quality of women's athletic competition was not a sudden, anomalous upsurge in women's interest in sports, but the enforcement of Title IX's mandate of gender equity in sports.

Affirmed in part, reversed in part, and remanded for further proceedings. . . .

Source: Courtesy of Westlaw; reprinted with permission.

Equality of Facilities

To what extent do the facilities for men's and women's sports have to be "equal" under Title IX? In Case 9-7, *Mason v. Minnesota State High School League,* 2004 WL 1630968 (D. Minn. 2004), the dispute was whether the venue for the girls' hockey team was equal to that of the boys' team.

📖 CASE 9-7 *Mason v. Minnesota State High School League*

2004 WL 1630968 (D. Minn. 2004)

TUNHEIM, J.

Plaintiffs, high school students who participate in girls' hockey, brought this lawsuit against the Minnesota State High School League ("the League") alleging that its administration of the girls' state hockey tournament is not substantially equal to its administration of the boys' state hockey tournament, and that such inequity violates Title IX, 20 U.S.C. § 1681(a) . . .

Plaintiffs request an injunction requiring the League to move the girls' tournament to the Xcel Energy Center ("Xcel"), where the boys' tournament is held. Defendant moves for summary judgment, arguing that there is no legally sufficient basis for granting plaintiffs' requested injunction. For the reasons discussed below, the Court denies defendant's motion for summary judgment.

Factual Background

The League began sponsoring girls' hockey in 1994 and held its first state tournament in February of 1995 at Aldrich Arena in Maplewood, Minnesota. Aldrich is used for high school hockey league and play-off games and is also open to the public for recreational skating. Because attendance at that tournament exceeded Aldrich's capacity of 3,400, the League sought a new venue for the 1996 tournament. From 1996 to 2002, the State Fair Coliseum hosted the girls' tournament. The Coliseum, which offered a 5,200 seating capacity, was built in 1951 to host horse shows and livestock judging. Because it was not originally designed as a hockey arena, the spectator seating is approximately 10 feet from the ice. Conversely, in a standard hockey arena fans sit quite close to the ice, where they are able to generate excitement by pounding on the boards and cheering.

In 2000, the Office for Civil Rights ("OCR") received a discrimination complaint regarding the location of the girls' tournament and opened an investigation. In response to the investigation, the League explored alternative sites, including Mariucci Arena at the University of Minnesota. At this time, the University was building Ridder Arena specifically for its women's hockey team. The League requested permission from OCR to continue holding the girls' tournament at the Coliseum until construction was completed on Ridder. Both the 2001 and 2002 tournaments were held at the Coliseum, after the State Fair made some improvements to the facility. In 2002, twelve teams participated and a total of 15,551 people attended the tournament.

During these same years, the boys' hockey tournament, which drew between 106,307 and 120,133 total fans, was held in the St. Paul Civic Center (1995-98), Target Center (1999-2000), and Xcel (2001-present). Xcel is home to Minnesota's National Hockey League team, the Minnesota Wild, and has been called one of the nation's finest hockey arenas.

In 2001, the League sent a request for proposal ("RFP") to potential hosts of several high school tournaments, including girls' hockey. Bids were solicited for eight different tournaments to be held between Fall 2003 and Winter 2008. The RFP sought a venue with a seating capacity of 4,000 for the girls' tournament. The University of Minnesota submitted a bid for the girls' tournament to use Ridder Arena. Xcel did not submit a bid for girls' hockey, but did bid for the girls' dance team tournament, which Xcel had hosted in the past. The League scheduled the dance team competition for the same dates as the girls' hockey tournament.

The League ultimately accepted the bid for Ridder Arena despite its 2,700-3,200 seating capacity, which is below both the requested 4,000 and below Aldrich's capacity of 3,400. The League argues that Ridder's proposal is consistent with the RFP, which actually specified 4,000 per *session*. The League reasons that since there are two games per session, Ridder's capacity is actually in the requested range. In contrast to Ridder's relatively small capacity, Xcel has a seating capacity of 17,759, which may be reduced to 9,295 by closing off the upper level. Some of the League's tournaments use the lower bowl option, including Class A boys' hockey.

Plaintiffs point to several additional differences between the facilities. Xcel is home to Minnesota's professional hockey team, has padded stadium seating, and employs advanced technologies such as a large, full-color scoreboard and closed-circuit televisions in concession areas and suites. Ridder is home to the University of Minnesota's women's hockey team, has unpadded stadium seating and bench seating, and does not have a scoreboard capable of video-replay. The locker rooms are also distinguishable. Xcel's locker rooms average nearly double the size of Ridder's, are carpeted, and include full shower/restroom facilities. At Ridder, some locker rooms are shared, restrooms are shared, and some teams must use locker rooms at nearby

Mariucci Arena. There are also differences in publicity, parking availability, and proximity to local attractions, hotels, and restaurants.

In December 2002, OCR notified the League that it had closed its monitoring of the case. OCR had toured both Ridder and Xcel and summarized its findings, concluding that Ridder was an adequate venue for the girls' hockey tournament and satisfied the League's commitment to resolve the discrimination complaint. Plaintiffs contend that those findings are based on errors of fact and an incomplete investigation. For example, OCR's comparison was based on availability of 12,000 parking spaces near Ridder, but fewer than 5,000 spaces are actually available within five blocks of that arena. Plaintiffs also allege that OCR misapplied its Title IX policy interpretation. . . .

Analysis

. . . .

II. Legal Standard

A. Title IX, 20 U.S.C. § 1681(a)

Title IX of the Education Act prohibits sex discrimination in any educational program or activity receiving federal funds. The regulations implementing Title IX provide:

> No person shall, on the basis of sex, be excluded from participation in, be denied the benefits of, be treated differently from another person or otherwise be discriminated against in any interscholastic, intercollegiate, club or intramural athletics offered by a recipient [of federal funds], and no recipient shall provide any such athletics separately on such basis.
>
> 34 C.F.R. § 106.41(a)

The regulations specify certain areas for consideration when determining whether athletics programs meet Title IX's requirements. Responsibility for interpretation and implementation of the Education Act is delegated to the Department of Education's Office for Civil Rights ("OCR"). . . .

The policy interpretation does not require identical treatment or opportunities if the overall effect of any differences is negligible. The program components must be equal or equal in effect. . . .

III. Application

Plaintiffs have satisfied their burden to survive summary judgment. The facts, as alleged by plaintiffs, raise questions as to whether the League treats the girls' ice hockey team in a manner "substantially equal" to that of the boys' team. Construing the facts in a light most favorable to plaintiffs, which the Court must do for purposes of this motion, defendant has not shown that the gender classification is "exceedingly persuasive," that the arenas are "equal or equal in effect," and that the "overall effect" of this difference is negligible.

The Court agrees with plaintiffs' contention that factual questions exist over whether the League is providing equal competitive facilities to the girls and boys hockey players. Differences in treatment, according to OCR's policy interpretation, are permissible under Title IX only if the differences [do] not limit the potential for women's athletics events to rise in spectator appeal . . .

. . . Here, there is no dispute that the seating capacity of Ridder is less than that of Aldrich Arena, which was abandoned as a site for the girls' tournament in part because of insufficient seating capacity. Plaintiffs suggest that Xcel's lower bowl option may provide sufficient capacity for current attendance and room for growth while simultaneously addressing the League's concern of maintaining an exciting, loud state tournament atmosphere. Notwithstanding this concern, the League holds other events at Xcel—such as girls' volleyball and dance team—that draw smaller or comparable crowds. Additionally, the League accommodates the smaller Class A boys' hockey tournament at Xcel by using the lower bowl option.

Although the OCR policy interpretation recognizes that crowd size may influence the allocation of resources to a particular team or event, it permits such differences only when it does not limit the potential for women's athletic events to rise in spectator appeal. The evidence presented on this record could lead a fact-finder to conclude that the capacity of Ridder impermissibly restricts the growth of girls' ice hockey. There is also a question whether the League's decision to hold the girls' tournament at Ridder is "substantially related" to its goal of maintaining a "state tournament atmosphere."

Plaintiffs have established a material fact dispute as to whether differences in seating, locker rooms, scoreboards, and variety of available concessions make Ridder impermissibly inferior to Xcel as a state hockey tournament venue. The parties do not dispute that Xcel, with its full-color scoreboard, private locker room facilities, and closed-circuit televisions, is more lavish than Ridder. Defendant, however, points out that Ridder offers benefits to the girls' team that are not available to the boys at Xcel, such as use of weight room and training room facilities and equipment. Ultimately, the question whether these differences constitute illegal gender discrimination is one for a factfinder.

```
ORDER

. . . IT IS HEREBY ORDERED that defendant's motion for summary judgment
is DENIED.
```

Source: Courtesy of Westlaw; reprinted with permission.

Problem 9-3

   You have recently been named Title IX coordinator for a Division I athletic program. The athletic director has asked you to draft a two-page summary outlining a Title IX compliance plan. Draft a short memorandum highlighting the significant portions of a Title IX plan that will withstand scrutiny. What information do you need to draft such a plan? What will be your major concerns and the focus and goals of the plan?

   In Case 9-8, *Daniels v. School Bd. of Brevard County, Fla.*, 995 F. Supp. 1394 (M.D. Fla. 1997), disparity existed between the high school programs for girls' softball and boys' baseball. The school board submitted a plan addressing those disparities. The following court decision addressed whether the plan was compliant with Title IX, along with some other matters as well.

CASE 9-8   *Daniels v. School Bd. of Brevard County, Fla.*

995 F. Supp. 1394 (M.D. Fla. 1997)

I. Introduction

```
On November 25, 1997, the Court entered an Order determining that the
Defendant, School Board of Brevard County, was violating Title IX . . .
based on disparities between the girls' softball and boys' baseball
programs at Merritt Island High School ("MIHS"). In the Order, the
Court identified specific inequalities with respect to the following
matters: electronic scoreboard, batting cage, bleachers, signs, bath-
room facilities, concession stand/press box/announcer's booth, and
field lighting . . . . [T]he Court directed the School Board to submit
a plan concerning how it proposed to remedy the deficiencies identi-
fied in the Order. The School Board has filed its plan. . . .
```

II. The School Board's Plan

```
Preliminarily, the School Board notes that it has sent a directive
to all secondary school principals, advising them that effective
```

immediately all principals, athletic directors, coaches and booster clubs are to be advised that district policy henceforth requires that each principal shall be responsible for insuring that regardless of the source of funding, whether it be school district, school, or booster club, the expenditures that support male and female athletic teams shall be on an equitable basis. Henceforth a principal may not accept or approve, either directly or indirectly, funding which fosters a disparate, inequitable status between male and female athletic teams.

. . . However, the School Board proposes not to spend any funds to remedy the inequities identified in the prior Order. In that regard, the School Board states:

> [T]he plan here being submitted by the School Board does not involve the expenditure of funds by the School Board of Brevard County or Merritt Island High School. The Defendant assumes that the Court understands and can fully appreciate the financial limitations and tight budgetary constraints under which the School Board is forced to operate. Any monies spent on athletics must obviously be taken from another area of operations which is already lacking in funds.

The School Board believes that the immediate expenditure of funds to eliminate the inequities the Court has determined exist between the boys' baseball program and the girls' softball program at Merritt Island High School would create more problems than it would solve. In reaching the decision not to expend funds to eliminate the inequities the Defendant is not unmindful of the fact that before the Court has even issued an injunction in this case the Daniels family has already filed a separate class action asking that the School Board be required to install new softball fields at three other Brevard County high schools which presently use off-campus fields for practice and games. That new suit also suggests that there are inequalities between the boys' facilities and girls' facilities used by students from Brevard County high schools other than Merritt Island High School and that they need to be remedied.

The School Board proposes the following remedial measures regarding the specific inequities identified in the prior Order:

Electronic Scoreboard

The School Board says it is not feasible to move the electronic scoreboard on the boys' baseball field back and forth between the baseball field and the girls' softball field. Accordingly, the Board proposes to disallow use of the scoreboard on the boys' field until such time as the girls' field has a comparable scoreboard.

Batting Cage

The School Board contends that the design and structure of the batting cage on the boys' field precludes moving it back and forth between the two fields. The Board proposes to co-locate the girls' and boys' separate pitching machines so that both teams can use the batting cage on alternate weeks.

Bleachers

The School Board maintains it is not feasible to relocate bleachers from the boys' field to the girls' field. Accordingly, "[u]ntil such time as funds may be raised for the purchase of additional bleachers or bleachers are donated so that the girls' field has bleachers essentially equal in number and quality to the boys' bleachers," the School Board proposes to rope off the boys' bleachers so that the only area used during games shall be equivalent in size and seating number to those bleachers which presently exist on the girls' softball field.

Signs

The School Board proposes altering the "Merritt Island Baseball" sign facing the student parking lot, to read "Merritt Island Baseball and Softball." Alternatively, the Board proposes to either eliminate all lettering or change the sign to "Merritt Island Athletics." The School Board also proposes to remove the donated "Home of the Mustangs" sign which faces the boys' baseball diamond, and to leave in place a second, gender neutral sign located outside the boys' field.

Bathroom Facilities

The School Board proposes to remove a portion of the fence separating the boys' and girls' fields, so as to permit equal access to the restrooms.

Concession Stand/Press Box/Announcer's Booth

The Board proposes to close down this building until such time as a comparable facility is constructed on the girls' field.

Lighting

The School Board has already approved the installation of lights on the MIHS girls' softball field. The Board anticipates the installation process will be complete by the beginning of the girls' season. If it is not, the Board proposes to disallow use of the lights on the boys' field until the lights on the girls' field are in place.

III. Plaintiffs' Response to the Plan

Plaintiffs' basic position is that the School Board should be required to remedy the inequities by spending the funds necessary to improve the MIHS girls' softball program, rather than denying the boys' baseball team facilities it already enjoys. Plaintiffs commend the Board's new policy regarding booster club funding; however, they maintain that this policy will essentially freeze present inequities. Plaintiffs also assert that the School Board's "take it away from the boys" approach is actually designed to generate "backlash" against the girls' softball team. Further, Plaintiffs contend that the Board's plan is inadequate to remedy the perception of inequality because even if the boys are not allowed to use certain facilities—such as the electronic scoreboard, bleachers, lighting and concession stand/press box/announcer's booth—those facilities will remain in place as symbols of inequality. Accordingly, Plaintiffs urge the Court to require the School Board to either completely remove those facilities from the boys' field or provide the girls with equal facilities on their field. Finally, Plaintiffs decry the School Board's claim of "tight budgetary constraints;" they maintain that the Board is slated to receive at least $43 million from the Florida Department of Education for capital improvements.

IV. Analysis

In giving the School Board the opportunity to submit a plan, the Court had hoped for constructive input, such as a long-range fiscal plan to remedy the inequities identified in the Court's prior Order. Unfortunately, the Board's plan leaves much to be desired; it creates the impression that the Board is not as sensitive as it should be regarding the necessity of compliance with Title IX. The Court is inclined to agree with Plaintiffs that many of the Board's proposals seem more retaliatory than constructive. The Board's approach essentially imposes "separate disadvantage," punishing both the girls and the boys, rather than improving the girls' team to the level the boys' team has enjoyed for years. The Court is sensitive to the financial constraints imposed upon public educational institutions in this day and age; that is yet another reason the Court gave the Board an opportunity to submit a remedial plan, rather than simply entering an injunction decreeing the expenditure of funds by a date certain. However, the fact remains that Plaintiffs have presented substantial evidence that the School Board has violated, and continues to violate, Act of Congress mandating gender equality in public education.

However, the inquiry does not end here. Before the School Board's response to the Court's November 25 Order was due, Plaintiffs altered the playing field dramatically by filing a separate suit seeking class action status and challenging the Board's treatment of girls' softball on a county-wide basis. In this second suit, Plaintiffs complain, *inter alia*, of the fact that three of the ten high schools in Brevard County have boys' baseball fields, but no girls' softball fields. On the heels of this filing, a different group of parents and children commenced yet another action claiming gender equity violations with respect to girls' softball programs throughout the county.

As a result of these latest two cases, the Title IX focus has expanded from the softball facilities at one high school to girls' softball programs throughout Brevard County. In the instant suit, two high school girls and a parent sought to force expenditures to improve one softball field. The two subsequent cases presumably seek to force, *inter alia*, the construction of softball fields at three other high schools. These developments dramatically alter the potential financial impact on the School Board.

At this juncture, the Court cannot make a reasoned determination concerning the amount of additional funds the School Board should be required to expend to remedy the inequities present at Plaintiffs' particular high school. The extent to which the Board must further appropriate funds to correct the situation at MIHS must be considered in the context of the two related cases which seek class action treatment and the expenditure of funds on a county-wide basis. Accordingly, with the exception of lighting on the MIHS girls' softball field, which the School Board has already committed to install, for the moment, the Court will impose injunctive measures which do not require additional funding.

V. Preliminary Injunction

Based on the foregoing, it is ORDERED as follows:

1. Before January 26, 1998, the School Board shall make the following changes at Merritt Island High School:
   a. Remove a portion of the fence separating the boys' baseball field and girls' softball field, so that the restroom facilities are readily accessible to players and spectators at both fields.

b. Co-locate the girls' and boys' pitching machines so that both teams can use the batting cage, and establish a schedule allowing both teams equal use of the cage.

c. Change the "Merritt Island Baseball" sign facing the student parking lot, so that it reads "Merritt Island Baseball and Softball," and remove the donated "Home of the Mustangs" sign which faces the boys' baseball diamond.

d. Install lighting on the girls' softball field.

2. During the pendency of this action and the two related cases, the School Board is not required to deny the boys' baseball team and its spectators use of the electronic scoreboard, existing bleachers and the concession stand/press box/announcer's booth. FN 1.

FN 1. Of course, this ruling assumes that the players and spectators of the girls' team are free to patronize the concession stand.

The Board is also not required to deny the boys' baseball team use of the lights on the baseball field, since the Board is required to install lighting on the girls' softball field by January 26, 1998. Finally, the Board is not required to remove the gender-neutral sign located outside the boys' baseball field.

Source: Courtesy of Westlaw; reprinted with permission.

Contact Versus Non-contact Sports

Courts have usually made a distinction between contact and non-contact sports when considering the participation of women in sports. Women will usually be allowed to participate on men's teams if the sport is deemed a non-contact sport and no women's team is available. If there is no team for one sex in a particular sport, and the excluded sex has had a history of limited opportunity, then the excluded sex must be allowed to try out for the existing team. If women have the opportunity to compete, then courts are usually less willing to allow them to participate on men's teams. The HEW regulations under Title IX allow athletic departments that receive federal funding to establish separate teams if the sport is deemed a contact sport or is based on competitive skill.[15]

In Case 9-9, *Mercer v. Duke University,* 190 F.3d 643 (4th Cir. 1999), the university argued that because football is a contact sport, the school need not allow the plaintiff to try out for the team. However, the court found that once the plaintiff was allowed to try out, she should have been given an equal opportunity to make the squad. The trial court awarded her $1 in compensatory damages and $2 million in punitive damages, finding that Duke had engaged in intentional discrimination. The punitive damages award was vacated by the Fourth Circuit Court of Appeals. Mercer was awarded $1 in compensatory damages.[16] In July 2004, the plaintiff was awarded $349,243 in attorneys' fees.[17]

---

[15] 45 C.F.R. § 86.41(b).

[16] *See,* Nicole Mitchell, *Encyclopedia of the Title IX and Sports,* Greenwood Publishing, 2007, pp.76–78.

[17] Mercer v. Duke University, 301 F. Supp. 2d 454 (M.D. N.C. 2004).

📖 CASE 9-9 *Mercer v. Duke University*

190 F.3d 643 (4th Cir. 1999)

LUTTIG, Circuit Judge:

Appellant Heather Sue Mercer challenges the federal district court's holding that Title IX provides a blanket exemption for contact sports and the court's consequent dismissal of her claim that Duke University discriminated against her during her participation in Duke's intercollegiate football program. For the reasons that follow, we hold that where a university has allowed a member of the opposite sex to try out for a single-sex team in a contact sport, the university is, contrary to the holding of the district court, subject to Title IX and therefore prohibited from discriminating against that individual on the basis of his or her sex.

I.

Appellee Duke University operates a Division I college football team. During the period relevant to this appeal (1994–98), appellee Fred Goldsmith was head coach of the Duke football team and appellant Heather Sue Mercer was a student at the school.

Before attending Duke, Mercer was an all-state kicker at Yorktown Heights High School in Yorktown Heights, New York. Upon enrolling at Duke in the fall of 1994, Mercer tried out for the Duke football team as a walk-on kicker. Mercer was the first—and to date, only—woman to try out for the team. Mercer did not initially make the team, and instead served as a manager during the 1994 season; however, she regularly attended practices in the fall of 1994 and participated in conditioning drills the following spring.

In April 1995, the seniors on the team selected Mercer to participate in the Blue-White Game, an intrasquad scrimmage played each spring. In that game, Mercer kicked the winning 28-yard field goal, giving the Blue team a 24-22 victory. The kick was subsequently shown on ESPN, the cable television sports network. Soon after the game, Goldsmith told the news media that Mercer was on the Duke football team, and Fred Chatham, the Duke kicking coach, told Mercer herself that she had made the team. Also, Mike Cragg, the Duke sports information director, asked Mercer to participate in a number of interviews with newspaper, radio, and television reporters, including one with representatives from "The Tonight Show."

Although Mercer did not play in any games during the 1995 season, she again regularly attended practices in the fall and participated in conditioning drills the following spring. Mercer was also officially listed by Duke as a member of the Duke football team on the team roster filed with the NCAA and was pictured in the Duke football yearbook.

During this latter period, Mercer alleges that she was the subject of discriminatory treatment by Duke. Specifically, she claims that Goldsmith did not permit her to attend summer camp, refused to allow her to dress for games or sit on the sidelines during games, and gave her fewer opportunities to participate in practices than other walk-on kickers. In addition, Mercer claims that Goldsmith made a number of offensive comments to her, including asking her why she was interested in football, wondering why she did not prefer to participate in beauty pageants rather than football, and suggesting that she sit in the stands with her boyfriend rather than on the sidelines.

At the beginning of the 1996 season, Goldsmith informed Mercer that he was dropping her from the team. Mercer alleges that Goldsmith's decision to exclude her from the team was on the basis of her sex because Goldsmith allowed other, less qualified walk-on kickers to remain on the team. Mercer attempted to participate in conditioning drills the following spring, but Goldsmith asked her to leave because the drills were only for members of the team. Goldsmith told Mercer, however, that she could try out for the team again in the fall.

On September 16, 1997, rather than try out for the team again, Mercer filed suit against Duke and Goldsmith, alleging sex discrimination in violation of Title IX of the Education Amendments of 1972, 20 U.S.C. §§ 1681–1688, and negligent misrepresentation and breach of contract in violation of North Carolina law. . . .

From the district court's order dismissing her Title IX claim for failure to state a claim upon which relief can be granted and its order denying the motion to alter judgment, Mercer appeals.

II.

Title IX prohibits discrimination on the basis of sex by educational institutions receiving federal funding. . . .

The district court held, and appellees contend on appeal, that, under this regulation, "contact sports, such as football, are specifically excluded from Title IX coverage." We disagree. . . .

We therefore construe the second sentence of subsection (b) as providing that in non-contact sports, but not in contact sports, covered institutions must allow members of an excluded sex to try out for single-sex teams. Once an institution has allowed a member of one sex to try out for a team operated by the institution for the other sex in a contact sport, subsection (b) is simply no longer applicable, and the institution is subject to the general anti-discrimination provision of subsection (a). . . .

Accordingly, because appellant has alleged that Duke allowed her to try out for its football team (and actually made her a member of the team), then discriminated against her and ultimately excluded her from participation in the sport on the basis of her sex, we conclude that she has stated a claim under the applicable regulation, and therefore under Title IX. We take to heart appellees' cautionary observation that, in so holding, we thereby become "the first Court in United States history to recognize such a cause of action." Where, as here, however, the university invites women into what appellees characterize as the "traditionally all-male bastion of collegiate football," we are convinced that this reading of the regulation is the only one permissible under law.

The district court's order granting appellees' motion to dismiss for failure to state a claim is hereby reversed, and the case remanded for further proceedings.

REVERSED AND REMANDED

Source: Courtesy of Westlaw; reprinted with permission.

Problem 9-4

Mary Williams was an outstanding placekicker for her high school football team. She wants to try out for her college football team but is not allowed to do so. The university cites federal law that states that educational institutions are allowed to maintain separate teams in contact sports. Mary argues that because she is a placekicker only, a non-contact position, she should therefore be allowed to try out. Is she correct? Does the school have to let her try out for the team? Should rules be different for placekickers as opposed to other players?

Retaliation Under Title IX

The Supreme Court case in Case 9-10, *Jackson v. Birmingham Bd. Of Educ.*, 125 S.Ct. 1497 (2005), dealt with the issue of whether an individual who was not the direct victim of sex discrimination under Title IX could sustain a cause of action for retaliatory conduct.

CASE 9-10   *Jackson v. Birmingham Bd. of Educ.*

125 S.Ct. 1497 (2005)

O'CONNOR, J., delivered the opinion of the Court, in which STEVENS, SOUTER, GINSBURG and BREYER JJ., joined. THOMAS, J., filed a dissenting opinion, in which REHNQUIST, C.J., and SCALIA and KENNEDY, JJ., joined.

Roderick Jackson, a teacher in the Birmingham, Alabama, public schools, brought suit against the Birmingham Board of Education (Board) alleging that the Board retaliated against him because he had complained about sex discrimination in the high school's athletic program. Jackson claimed that the Board's retaliation violated Title IX of the Education Amendments of 1972. . . . We consider here whether the private right of action implied by Title IX encompasses claims of retaliation. We hold that it does where the funding recipient retaliates against an individual because he has complained about sex discrimination.

I.

. . . .

According to the complaint, Jackson has been an employee of the Birmingham school district for over 10 years. In 1993, the Board hired Jackson to serve as a physical education teacher and girls' basketball coach. Jackson was transferred to Ensley High School in August 1999. At Ensley, he discovered that the girls' team was not receiving equal funding and equal access to athletic equipment and facilities. The lack of adequate funding, equipment, and facilities made it difficult for Jackson to do his job as the team's coach.

In December 2000, Jackson began complaining to his supervisors about the unequal treatment of the girls' basketball team, but to no avail. Jackson's complaints went unanswered, and the school failed to remedy the situation. Instead, Jackson began to receive negative work evaluations and ultimately was removed as the girls' coach in May 2001. Jackson is still employed by the Board as a teacher, but he no longer receives supplemental pay for coaching.

After the Board terminated Jackson's coaching duties, he filed suit in the United States District Court for the Northern District of Alabama. He alleged, among other things, that the Board violated Title IX by retaliating against him for protesting the discrimination against the girls' basketball team. The Board moved to dismiss on the ground that

Title IX's private cause of action does not include claims of retaliation. The District Court granted the motion to dismiss.

The Court of Appeals for the Eleventh Circuit affirmed.

. . . .

II.

A.

Title IX prohibits sex discrimination by recipients of federal education funding. The statute provides that "[n]o person in the United States shall, on the basis of sex, be excluded from participation in, be denied the benefits of, or be subjected to discrimination under any education program or activity receiving Federal financial assistance." 20 U.S.C. § 1681(a). More than 25 years ago, in *Cannon v. University of Chicago*, 441 U.S. 677, 690–693, 99 S.Ct. 1946, 60 L.Ed.2d 560 (1979), we held that Title IX implies a private right of action to enforce its prohibition on intentional sex discrimination. In subsequent cases, we have defined the contours of that right of action. We have also held that the private right of action encompasses intentional sex discrimination in the form of a recipient's deliberate indifference to a teacher's sexual harassment of a student. . . .

In all of these cases, we relied on the text of Title IX, which, subject to a list of narrow exceptions not at issue here, broadly prohibits a funding recipient from subjecting any person to "discrimination" "on the basis of sex." 20 U.S.C. § 1681. Retaliation against a person because that person has complained of sex discrimination is another form of intentional sex discrimination encompassed by Title IX's private cause of action. Retaliation is, by definition, an intentional act. It is a form of " discrimination" because the complainant is being subjected to differential treatment. Moreover, retaliation is discrimination "on the basis of sex" because it is an intentional response to the nature of the complaint: an allegation of sex discrimination. We conclude that when a funding recipient retaliates against a person because he complains of sex discrimination, this constitutes intentional "discrimination" "on the basis of sex," in violation of Title IX.

The Court of Appeals' conclusion that Title IX does not prohibit retaliation because the "statute makes no mention of retaliation," 309 F.3d, at 1344, ignores the import of our repeated holdings construing "discrimination" under Title IX broadly. Though the statute does not mention sexual harassment, we have held that sexual harassment is intentional discrimination encompassed by Title IX's private right of action. . . .

Congress certainly could have mentioned retaliation in Title IX expressly, as it did in § 704 of Title VII of the Civil Rights Act of 1964. . . . Title VII, however, is a vastly different statute from Title IX . . . and the comparison the Board urges us to draw is therefore of limited use. Title IX's cause of action is implied, while Title VII's is express. Title IX is a broadly written general prohibition on discrimination, followed by specific, narrow exceptions to that broad prohibition. See 20 U.S.C. § 1681. By contrast, Title VII spells out in greater detail the conduct that constitutes discrimination in violation of that statute. Because Congress did not list *any* specific discriminatory practices when it wrote Title IX, its failure to mention one such practice does not tell us anything about whether it intended that practice to be covered.

. . . .

The Board cites a Department of Education regulation prohibiting retaliation "against any individual for the purpose of interfering with any right or privilege secured by [Title IX]," 34 CFR § 100.7(e) (2004) . . . and contends that Jackson . . . seeks an "impermissible extension of the statute" when he argues that Title IX's private right of action encompasses retaliation. This argument, however, entirely misses the point. We do not rely on regulations extending Title IX's protection beyond its statutory limits; indeed, we do not rely on the Department of Education's regulation at all, because the statute *itself* contains the necessary prohibition. . . . [T]he text of Title IX prohibits a funding recipient from retaliating against a person who speaks out against sex discrimination, because such retaliation is intentional "discrimination" "on the basis of sex." We reach this result based on the statute's text. . . . [W]e hold that Title IX's private right of action encompasses suits for retaliation, because retaliation falls within the statute's prohibition of intentional discrimination on the basis of sex.

C.

Nor are we convinced by the Board's argument that, even if Title IX's private right of action encompasses discrimination, Jackson is not entitled to invoke it because he is an "indirect victi[m]" of sex discrimination. The statute is broadly worded; it does not require that the victim of the retaliation must also be the victim of the discrimination that is the subject of the original complaint. If the statute provided instead that "no person shall be subjected to discrimination on the basis of *such individual's* sex," then we would agree with the Board. However, Title IX contains no such limitation. Where the retaliation occurs because the complainant speaks out about sex discrimination, the "on the basis of sex" requirement is satisfied. The complainant is himself a victim of discriminatory retaliation, regardless of whether he was the subject of the original complaint. . . .

Congress enacted Title IX not only to prevent the use of federal dollars to support discriminatory practices, but also to provide individual citizens effective protection against those practices. We agree with the United States that this objective "would be difficult, if not impossible, to achieve if persons who complain about sex discrimination did not have effective protection against retaliation." If recipients were permitted to retaliate freely, individuals who witness discrimination would be loathe to report it, and all manner of Title IX violations might go unremedied as a result.

Reporting incidents of discrimination is integral to Title IX enforcement and would be discouraged if retaliation against those who report went unpunished. Indeed, if retaliation were not prohibited, Title IX's enforcement scheme would unravel. Recall that Congress intended Title IX's private right of action to encompass claims of a recipient's deliberate indifference to sexual harassment. Accordingly, if a principal sexually harasses a student, and a teacher complains to the school board but the school board is indifferent, the board would likely be liable for a Title IX violation. But if Title IX's private right of action does not encompass retaliation claims, the teacher would have no recourse if he were subsequently fired for speaking out. Without protection from retaliation, individuals who witness discrimination would likely not report it, indifference claims would be short-circuited, and the underlying discrimination would go unremedied.

Title IX's enforcement scheme also depends on individual reporting because individuals and agencies may not bring suit under the statute unless the recipient has received "actual notice" of the discrimination. If recipients were able to avoid such notice by retaliating against all those who dare complain, the statute's enforcement scheme would be subverted. We should not assume that Congress left such a gap in its scheme.

Moreover, teachers and coaches such as Jackson are often in the best position to vindicate the rights of their students because they are better able to identify discrimination and bring it to the attention of administrators. Indeed, sometimes adult employees are "the only effective adversar[ies]" of discrimination in schools.

D.

The Board is correct in pointing out that, because Title IX was enacted as an exercise of Congress' powers under the Spending Clause, "private damages actions are available only where recipients of federal funding had adequate notice that they could be liable for the conduct at issue." When Congress enacts legislation under its spending power, that legislation is "in the nature of a contract: in return for federal funds, the States agree to comply with federally imposed conditions." As we have recognized, "[t]here can . . . be no knowing acceptance [of the terms of the contract] if a State is unaware of the conditions [imposed by the legislation on its receipt of funds]."

The Board insists that we should not interpret Title IX to prohibit retaliation because it was not on notice that it could be held liable for retaliating against those who complain of Title IX violations. We disagree. Funding recipients have been on notice that they could be subjected to private suits for intentional sex discrimination under Title IX since 1979. . . .

. . . .

Thus, the Board should have been put on notice by the fact that our cases . . . have consistently interpreted Title IX's private cause of action broadly to encompass diverse forms of intentional sex discrimination. Indeed, retaliation presents an even easier case than deliberate indifference. It is easily attributable to the funding recipient, and it is always—by definition—intentional. We therefore conclude that retaliation against individuals because they complain of sex discrimination is intentional conduct that violates the clear terms of the statute . . . and that Title IX itself therefore supplied sufficient notice to the Board that it could not retaliate against Jackson after he complained of discrimination against the girls' basketball team.

The regulations implementing Title IX clearly prohibit retaliation and have been on the books for nearly 30 years. A reasonable school board would realize that institutions covered by Title IX cannot cover up violations of that law by means of discriminatory retaliation. . . .

To prevail on the merits, Jackson will have to prove that the Board retaliated against him *because* he complained of sex discrimination. The amended complaint alleges that the Board retaliated against Jackson for complaining to his supervisor, Ms. Evelyn Baugh, about sex discrimination at Ensley High School. At this stage of the proceedings, "[t]he issue is not whether a plaintiff will ultimately prevail but whether the claimant is entitled to offer evidence to support the claims." Accordingly, the judgment of the Court of Appeals for the

Eleventh Circuit is reversed, and the case is remanded for further proceedings consistent with this opinion.

Source: Courtesy of Westlaw; reprinted with permission.

Problem 9-5

You are the general counsel for Academics University, an NCAA Division I football powerhouse. You have been asked to perform some research and prepare a subsequent memorandum of law concerning the liability of the university and its board of regents. The university wants to know under what circumstances the board of regents, the university, and its coaches could be held liable for the criminal acts of student-athletes. You are to specifically examine Title IX and cases relating to its interpretation. What steps should be taken to limit liability?

NOTES AND DISCUSSION QUESTIONS

Overview

1. ESPN has ranked the top ten greatest moments in women's sports as follows:
   (i)   President Nixon signs Title IX into law (July 23, 1972).
   (ii)   Billie Jean King wins the Battle of the Sexes (Sept. 20, 1973).
   (iii)   The United States defeats China to win the 1999 World Cup.
   (iv)   Wilma Rudolph blazes to three golds in the 1960 Olympics.
   (iv)   Maria Pepe plays Little League baseball (1972).
   (vi)   Shirley Muldowney, Janet Guthrie, and Julie Krone ride into history (1976–93).
   (vii)   Amelia Earhart flies solo nonstop across the Atlantic (May 20–21, 1932).
   (viii) Katherine Switzer runs in disguise in the Boston Marathon (April 19, 1967).
   (ix)   Babe Didrikson sets four world records at AAU championships (July 16, 1932).
   (x)   Huskies hoopsters go undefeated, capture 2002 NCAA title (March 31, 2002).

Constitutional Issues in Gender Equity

2. Under what circumstances should women be allowed to participate in a sport dominated by men? Should there be restrictions? Historically, how have women been discriminated against? When are separate sports teams required or allowed? What are the advantages and disadvantages of having same-sex teams?

3. What could Formula One boss Bernie Ecclestone have meant when he said the following in an interview: "You know, I've got one of the wonderful ideas that women should be dressed in white like all the other domestic appliances"?[18] Is there actually a debate about Danica Patrick's ability to drive a race car? Why are remarks such as Richard Petty's and Ecclestone's made? How does it harm the progress of women in sports?

---

[18] Associated Press, *F1's Ecclestone 'Trying to Make Amends' to Patrick,* USA Today, June 25, 2005.

4. Did you agree with the decision in the *Israel* case, Case 9-5? Are softball and baseball different enough to allow the plaintiff to play on the boys' baseball team?

5. Do you agree with the court's rationale in *Dodson v. Arkansas Activities Ass'n*? Is flag football the "equivalent" of padded football?

6. In *National Organization for Women v. Little League Baseball*, 318 A.2d. 33 (N.J. Super. Ct. App. Div. 1975), the question of whether girls should play Little League baseball was at issue. Little League attempted to defend the position that girls should not be allowed to play because of the physical difference between girls and boys.[19] The court, in allowing girls to play, stated:

> We conclude there was substantial credible evidence in the record to permit the Division to find as a fact that girls of ages 8–12 are not as a class subject to a materially greater hazard of injury while playing baseball than boys of that age group. We will therefore not disturb that finding of the administrative agency. Thus the factor of safety does not militate for a determination that the nature of Little League baseball reasonably restricts participation in it at the 8–12 age level to boys. We regard the psychological testimony on both sides as too speculative to rest any fact-finding on it. In any case, we are clear that there is no substantial psychological basis in the record to warrant a conclusion that the game is reasonably restricted to boys in this age bracket, as against the evident statutory policy against sex discrimination in places of public accommodation.[20]

Based on this reasoning, should girls be allowed to participate on boys' high school and college baseball teams as well if they possess the requisite skill?

On December 26, 1974, the Federal Little League Baseball Charter was amended by Public Law No. 93-551 (December 26, 1974, 88 Stat. 1744, 93 Congress). The amended charter deleted the word "boys" from each place it appeared in the original charter and replaced it with "young people." The phrase "citizenship, sportsmanship and manhood" was replaced with "citizenship and sportsmanship." The stated purpose of the amendment indicated that Little League "shall be open to girls as well as boys." Approximately five million girls have participated in Little League baseball and softball since 1970.[21]

7. Women in coaching have historically been subject to discrimination. They have not been given the same opportunities to coach as men and have received less pay and benefits, and even less acknowledgment, than men for performing the same job. Title IX and Title XII have both been instrumental in allowing women coaches to achieve equality with their male counterparts. Pat Summitt, coach of the University of Tennessee women's basketball team, obtained a contract in excess of $1.4 million per year in salary.[22] Because of the rise in the

---

[19] *National Organization for Women v. Little League Baseball*, 318 A.2d. at 35.

[20] *Id.* at 36–37.

[21] Little League Online, *Little League to Mark 30th Anniversary of Decision Allowing Girls to Play*, Nov. 4, 2003, http://www.littleleague.org/media/newsarchive/06_2003/03_30thgirls.htm. *Also see*, Mark Hyman, *Challenges for Girls Playing High School Baseball*, The New York Times, March 1, 2009.

[22] Bryan Mullen, *Pat Summitt's Road to 1,000 Wins,* The Tennessean, February 2, 2009.

popularity of women's sports, girls and women have slowly been given opportunities to coach at the high school and college levels.[23]

8. In *Buick v. Illinois High School Ass'n*, 351 F. Supp. 69 (D.C. Ill. 1972), two female students were denied an opportunity to try out for the boys' swim team. The court held that the rule did not violate the Equal Protection Clause of the Fourteenth Amendment, citing physical differences between boys and girls as the basis of its opinion. In *Clinton v. Nagy*, 411 F. Supp. 1396 (D.C. Ohio 1974), the court granted the plaintiffs' motion for a temporary restraining order when a 12-year-old girl wanted to play football on a team licensed by the city.

9. Much has been written about discrimination against women in golf. See, Nancy Kamp, *Gender Discrimination at Private Golf Clubs*, 5 SPORTS LAWYERS JOURNAL 89 (1998); Charles Charpentier, *An Unimproved Lie: Gender Discrimination Continues at Augusta National Golf Club*, 11 VILLANOVA SPORTS AND ENTERTAINMENT LAW JOURNAL 111 (2004); and Barbara Osborne, *Gender, Employment, and Sexual Harassment Issues in the Golf Industry*, 16 JOURNAL OF LEGAL ASPECTS OF SPORT 25 (2006).

Title IX

10. In *Pederson v. Louisiana State Univ.*, 201 F.3d 388 (5th Cir. 2000), the Court of Appeals found that LSU officials engaged in intentional discrimination against female athletes under Title IX. The court stated:

> In addition to the district court's evaluation of LSU's attitudes as "archaic," our independent evaluation of the record and the evidence adduced at trial supports the conclusion that Appellees persisted in a systematic, intentional, differential treatment of women. For instance, in meetings to discuss the possibility of a varsity women's soccer team, Dean referred to Lisa Ollar repeatedly as "honey," "sweetie," and "cutie" and negotiated with her by stating that "I'd love to help a cute little girl like you." Dean also opined that soccer, a "more feminine sport," deserved consideration for varsity status because female soccer players "would look cute running around in their soccer shorts." Dean, charismatically defending LSU's chivalry, later told the coach of the women's club soccer team that he would not voluntarily add more women's sports at LSU but would "if forced to." Among many other examples, Karla Pineda testified that, when she met with representatives of the Sports and Leisure Department to request the implementation of an intramural fast-pitch softball team, she was told that LSU would not sponsor fast-pitch softball because "the women might get hurt."

> LSU perpetuated antiquated stereotypes and fashioned a grossly discriminatory athletics system in many other ways. For example, LSU appointed a low-level male athletics department staff member to the position of "Senior Women's Athletic Administrator,"

---

[23] *See* Fuhr v. School Dist. of City of Hazel Park, 131 F. Supp. 2d 947 (E.D. Mich. 2001) (the court denied defendant's motion for summary judgment on plaintiff's claims of sexual discrimination after she was passed over for the position of boys' varsity basketball coach in favor of a male teacher). *Also see* Wynn v. Columbus Municipal Separate School District, 692 F. Supp. 672 (N.D. Miss. 1998) (plaintiff who alleged Title VII violation was awarded back pay and was placed into the athletic director's position); *also see* Lowrey v. Texas A&M University System, 11 F. Supp. 2d 895 (S.D. Tex. 1998) (A coach sued for retaliation in violation of Title IX).

which the NCAA defines as the most senior woman in an athletic department. LSU consistently approved larger budgets for travel, personnel, and training facilities for men's teams versus women's teams. The university consistently compensated coaches of women's teams at a rate far below that of its male team coaches.[24]

What must a plaintiff show to prove intentional discrimination in accordance with Title IX? How can attitudes about women in sports be changed?

11. For further discussion of the *Mercer* case *see* A. Crouse, *Equal Athletic Opportunity: An Analysis of* Mercer v. Duke University *and a Proposal to Amend the Contact Sport Exception to Title IX*, 84 MINNESOTA LAW REVIEW 1655 (2000).

12. Is it ethical that a women's basketball coach at a major university is paid less than the men's basketball coach? Consider noted women's basketball programs such as those of the University of Tennessee, Baylor University, or Old Dominion. Should the women's coach in such places make more than the men's coach because the women's program is more popular on campus?

13. In *Harper v. Board of Regents, Illinois State University*, 35 F. Supp. 2d 1118 (C. D. Ill. 1999), Illinois State University (ISU) eliminated the men's wrestling and soccer teams after an NCAA peer review committee determined that the university had failed to achieve gender equity in its athletic programs. The plaintiffs sued ISU, alleging that the reduction of men's programs was a Title IX violation. The court was "not unsympathetic to the hardship incurred by the members of the wrestling and soccer teams or their disappointment in not being able to pursue their sport of their choice at their chosen institution"; however, it still granted summary judgment for ISU on the plaintiffs' Title IX claims.

14. What do you think about the proposal submitted by the school board in Case 9-8, *Daniels v. School Bd. of Brevard County, Fla.*? Was the remedy ordered by the court fair to all parties? What steps would you have taken to ensure compliance with Title IX? The plaintiffs argued that the school board's plan was a "take it away from the boys" plan that was actually designed to create a backlash against the girls' softball team. Do you agree with that statement? All things being equal, how would you decide whether the words "baseball" or "softball" should appear first on the "Meritt Island Baseball" sign facing the student parking lot? Should there be two signs, one for boys' games and one for girls' games? Was the court order consistent with the application of Title IX? If the boys and girls should have "equal" scoreboards, why shouldn't the boys be denied use of the electronic scoreboard until the girls' team can get one as well?

15. What factors are considered in determining whether a university is in compliance with Title IX regulations?

16. In Case 9-10, *Jackson v. Birmingham Bd. of Educ.*, the court expanded the scope of Title IX to include protection to whistle blowers in addition to direct victims of discrimination under the act. Do you believe this was part of the intent of the act when it was passed? Are there any drawbacks to extending protection to those who were not directly discriminated against? What damages would such plaintiffs be entitled to if they could prove their case?

17. In *NCAA v. Smith*, 525 U.S. 459 (1999), the court was faced with the issue of whether the NCAA as an organization is subject to Title IX. A student-athlete sued the NCAA, stating

---

[24] *Pederson*, 201 F.3d at 412.

that the NCAA was in violation of Title IX by refusing to allow her to enroll in a graduate program at a university where she did not receive her undergraduate degree. The Supreme Court held that the NCAA is not subject to Title IX on the basis that it receives dues from its members, which in turn receive federal financial assistance.

18. Shana Eriksson was a member of the equestrian team at California State University. She died in 2004 after she was thrown from a horse. At the time of her death she was riding unsupervised because her coach had resigned six weeks earlier and no new coach had yet been named. Her parents sued on her behalf, claiming that the university was liable for her death under Title IX. They alleged that the university failed to provide adequate facilities, funding, and coaching staff for the team, saying that the university was attempting to comply with Title IX and was not doing very well.[25] Summary judgment was granted for the defendant, and the plaintiff appealed. Can a university be held liable in tort under Title IX?

19. In *Miller v. University of Cincinnati*, 2006 WL 3591958 (S.D. Ohio 2006), the court granted plaintiffs' motion to certify as a class action. The plaintiffs requested that the court certify a class consisting of "[a]ll present, prospective and future participants in the women's athletics program at the University of Cincinnati."[26] The plaintiffs alleged they were denied the equal opportunity to compete for and receive athletic scholarships and were denied equal access to athletic benefits in training equipment, supplies, coaching, locker rooms, and recruitment of athletes, along with other benefits, in violation of Title IX. The court, in partially granting plaintiffs' motion, stated:

> Limiting the class under consideration to current and future members of the University of Cincinnati women's rowing team provides a specific group that was allegedly harmed during a particular ongoing time frame in a particular location in a particular way, facilitating the Court's ability to ascertain its membership in an objective manner. . . .[27]

> . . . .

> The Court will thus certify a class of "all current and future members of the University of Cincinnati women's rowing team" conditioned upon the filing and granting of this motion.[28]

Who are the appropriate parties in a lawsuit alleging Title IX violations?

20. In *Butler v. National Collegiate Athletic Association*, 2006 WL 2398683 (D. Kan. 2006), the plaintiff alleged a Title IX violation when he missed an opportunity to participate in football at Northwestern Missouri State University (NMSU). His girlfriend had become pregnant and he decided to work and take care of his daughter instead of attending NMSU and playing football there. NCAA rules limit a student-athlete to four seasons of intercollegiate competition within five consecutive years. The plaintiff eventually transferred to the University of Kansas and played football there in the fall of 2005. NCAA rules do

---

[25] IBL Class Action Reporter, March 18, 2004, Vol. 6, No. 55; Eriksson v. CSU, Super. Ct. No. 04CECG02226 MBS.
[26] *Miller*, 2006 WL 3591958 at 1.
[27] *Id.* at 6
[28] *Id.* at 7.

provide for a one-year extension in the eligibility rules for female students who are pregnant. Butler argued that if he had been female, he could have taken advantage of the extra year. The court disagreed, stating:

> As defendants point out, the pregnancy exception allows a waiver "for reasons of pregnancy," which appear to be different from reasons of maternity or paternity. . . . The Court finds no substantial likelihood of success on the merits of plaintiff's Title IX claim.[29]

Does the plaintiff have an Equal Protection argument under the Constitution? Should male student-athletes be given an extension of their eligibility for caring for a child?

SUGGESTED READINGS AND RESOURCES

Carpenter, Linda Jean, & Acosta, R. Vivian. *Title IX*. Champaign, IL: Human Kinetics, 2005.

Cayleff, Susan E. *Babe: The Life and Legend of Babe Didrikson Zaharias*. Urbana: University of Illinois Press, 1996.

Cohen, Greta L. *Women in Sport: Issues and Controversies*, 2nd rev. ed. Reston, VA: National Association for Girls and Women in Sport, 2001.

Deboer, Kathleen J. *Gender and Competition: How Men and Women Approach Work and Play Differently*. Monterey, CA: Coaches Choice Books, 2004.

Fields, Sarah K. *Female Gladiators: Gender, Law, and Contact Sport in America*. Urbana: University of Illinois Press, 2004.

Gavora, Jessica. *Tilting the Playing Field: Schools, Sports, Sex, and Title IX*. San Francisco: Encounter Books, 2001.

A Hero for Daisy (50 Eggs Productions/Redtree Productions 1999).

Messner, Michael A. *Taking the Field: Women, Men and Sports*. Minneapolis: University of Minnesota Press, 2002.

Oglesby, Carole A. (ed.). *Encyclopedia of Women and Sport in America*. Phoenix, AZ: Oryx Press, 1998.

Porto, Brian L. *A New Season: Using Title IX to Reform College Sports*. Westport, CT: Praeger, 2003.

Salter, David F. *Crashing the Old Boys' Network: The Tragedies and Triumphs of Girls and Women in Sports*. Westport, CT: Praeger, 1996.

Scranton, Sheila, & Flintoff, Anne (eds.). *Gender and Sport: A Reader*. New York: Routledge, 2001.

Simon, Rita. *Sporting Equality: Title IX Thirty Years Later*. New Brunswick, NJ: Transaction, 2005.

Smith, Lissa (ed.). *Nike Is a Goddess: The History of Women in Sports*. New York: Atlantic Monthly Press, 1999.

Streissquth, Thomas. *Wilma Rudolph*. Minneapolis, MN: Twenty-First Century Books, 2006.

Tokarz, Karen. *Women, Sports, and the Law: A Comprehensive Research Guide to Sex Discrimination in Sports*. Buffalo, NY: W.S. Hein, 1986.

Wushanley, Ying. *Playing Nice and Losing: The Struggle for Control of Women's Intercollegiate Athletics, 1960–2000*. Syracuse, NY: Syracuse University Press, 2004.

---

[29] 2006 WL 2398683, p. 3

REFERENCE MATERIALS

American Association of University Women, St. Lawrence Branch. *History of Women in Sports Timeline*, http://www.northnet.org/stlawrenceaauw/timeline.htm.

Anderson, Deborah J., Cheslock, John J., & Ehrenberg, Ronald G. *Gender Equity in Intercollegiate Athletics: Determinants of Title IX Compliance.* Cornell University, Feb. 9, 2004.

Avery, Jane C. *Validity, Under Federal Law, of Sex Discrimination in Athletics.* 23 AMERICAN LAW REPORTS FEDERAL 664 (2006).

Burk, Martha, & Plumly, Natasha. *Who Owns Sports? The Politics of Title IX.* 14 MARQUETTE SPORTS LAW REVIEW 49 (2003).

Champion, Walter T. *Sports Law: Cases, Documents, and Materials.* New York: Aspen, 2005.

Charpentier, Charles. *An Unimproved Lie: Gender Discrimination Continues at Augusta National Golf Club.* 11 VILLANOVA SPORTS AND ENTERTAINMENT LAW JOURNAL 111 (2004).

Civil Rights § 339, 15 AMERICAN JURISPRUDENCE 2d.

Coakley, Jay. *Sports in Society: Issues and Controversies,* 8th ed. Boston: McGraw-Hill, 2004.

Conway, L. *NCAA Sports Participation Numbers Show Largest Increase in Fourteen Years.* NCAA News Release, June 7, 2000.

Cozzillio, Michael J., & Hayman, Robert L., Jr. *Sports and Inequality.* Durham, NC: Carolina Academic Press, 2005.

Cozzillio, Michael J., & Levinstein, Mark S. *Sports Law: Cases and Materials.* Durham, NC: Carolina Academic Press, 1997.

Epstein, Adam. *Sports Law.* Clifton Park, NY: Thomson/Delmar Learning, 2003.

Faraone, Andrea. *The Florida Equal Rights Amendment: Raising the Standard Applied to Gender Under the Equal Protection Clause of the Florida Constitution.* 1 FLORIDA COASTAL LAW JOURNAL 421 (2000).

French, Peter A. *Ethics and College Sports: Ethics, Sports and the University.* Lanham, MD: Rowman & Littlefield, 2004.

George, B. Glenn. *Title IX and the Scholarship Dilemma.* 9 MARQUETTE SPORTS LAW REVIEW 273 (1999).

Goplerud, C. Peter, III. *Title IX: Part Three Could Be the Key.* 14 MARQUETTE SPORTS LAW REVIEW 123 (2003).

Hatlevig, Elisa. *Title IX Compliance: Looking Past the Proportionality Prong.* 12 SPORTS LAWYERS JOURNAL 87 (2005).

Heckman, Diane. *Scoreboard: A Concise Chronological Twenty-Five Year History of Title IX Involving Interscholastic and Intercollegiate Athletics.* 7 SETON HALL JOURNAL OF SPORT LAW 391 (1997).

Institutional and Financial Assistance Information for Students, 20 U.S.C.A. § 1092.

Kamp, Nancy. *Gender Discrimination at Private Golf Clubs.* 5 SPORTS LAW JOURNAL 89 (1998).

Klinker, David. *Why Conforming with Title IX Hurts Men's Collegiate Sports.* 13 SETON HALL JOURNAL OF SPORT LAW 73 (2003).

Marburger, Daniel R., & Hogshead-Makar, Nancy. *Is Title IX Really to Blame for the Decline in Intercollegiate Men's Nonrevenue Sports?* 14 MARQUETTE SPORTS LAW REVIEW 65 (2003).

Masteralexis, Lisa Pike, Barr, Carol A., & Hums, Mary A. *Principles and Practice of Sport Management,* 2d ed. Sudbury, MA: Jones and Bartlett, 2005.

Mitten, Matthew J., Davis, Timothy, Smith, Rodney, & Berry, Robert. *Sports Law and Regulations: Cases, Materials and Problems*. New York: Aspen, 2005.

Mowrey, R. *More Than a Game: One Woman's Fight for Gender Equity in Sport*. 14 MARQUETTE SPORTS LAW REVIEW 259 (2003).

National Coalition for Women and Girls in Education. *Title IX Athletics Policies: Issues and Data for Education Decision Makers*. Aug. 27, 2002, http://www.ncwge.org/PDF/Title_IX_Coalition_Report_Final.pdf.

Nondiscrimination on the Basis of Sex in Education Programs and Activities Receiving or Benefiting from Federal Financial Assistance, 45 C.F.R. 86.

Osborne, Barbara. *Gender, Employment, and Sexual Harassment Issues in the Golf Industry*. 16 JOURNAL OF LEGAL ASPECTS OF SPORT 25 (2006).

Pemberton, Cynthia. *Wrestling with Title IX*. 14 MARQUETTE SPORTS LAW JOURNAL 163 (2003).

Pinarski, Annemarie. *When Coaches "Cross the Line": Hostile Athletic Environment Sexual Harassment*. 52 RUTGERS LAW REVIEW 911 (2000).

Porto, Brian L. *Suits by Female College Athletes Against Colleges and Universities Claiming That Decisions to Discontinue Particular Sports or to Deny Varsity Status to Particular Sports Deprive Plaintiffs of Equal Educational Opportunities Required by Title IX (20 U.S.C.A. §§1681–1688)*. 129 AMERICAN LAW REPORTS FEDERAL 571 (2005).

Reich, J. Brad. *All the Athletes Are Equal, but Some Are More Equal Than Others: An Objective Evaluation of Title IX's Past, Present, and Recommendation for Its Future*. 108 PENN STATE LAW REVIEW 525 (2003).

Sharp, Linda A., Moorman, Anita, M., & Clauseen, Cathryn L. *Sport Law: A Managerial Approach*. Scottsdale, AZ: Holcomb Hathaway, 2007.

Simon, Rita J. (ed.). *Sporting Equality: Title IX Thirty Years Later*. New Brunswick, NJ: Transaction, 2005.

Stevens, Lisa Yonka. *The Sport of Numbers: Manipulating Title IX to Rationalize Discrimination Against Women*. 2004 BRIGHAM YOUNG UNIVERSITY EDUCATION AND LAW JOURNAL 155 (2004).

Suggs, Welch. *A Place on the Team: The Triumph and Tragedy of Title IX*. Princeton, NJ: Princeton University Press, 2005.

Tatum, Lynne. *Girls in Sports: Love of the Game Must Begin at an Early Age to Achieve Equality*. 12 SETON HALL JOURNAL OF SPORT LAW 281 (2002).

Wilde, T. Jesse. *Gender Equity in Athletics: Coming of Age in the 90's*. 4 MARQUETTE SPORTS LAW JOURNAL 217 (1994).

Yuracko, Kimberly. *One for You and One for Me: Is Title IX's Sex-Based Proportionality Requirement for College Varsity Athletic Positions Defensible?* 97 NORTHWESTERN UNIVERSITY LAW REVIEW 731 (2003).

THE NATIONAL COLLEGIATE ATHLETIC ASSOCIATION (NCAA)

College sports in America are both popular and lucrative. Collegiate student-athletes compete in a variety of sports, including baseball, football, basketball, ice hockey, golf, rodeo, fencing, water polo, gymnastics, riflery, bowling, volleyball, track and field, wrestling, and lacrosse. Millions of fans attend college sporting events and watch them on television every year. Participation in and the viewing of college athletics is a national pastime and can also be extremely lucrative for some of those involved.

Several associations govern intercollegiate athletics in the United States; however, this chapter focuses solely on the National Collegiate Athletic Association (NCAA) because it is the most powerful of the associations and is the primary rule-making body for collegiate athletics in the United States. The chapter examines the organization and structure of the NCAA and the various challenges that have been brought against the NCAA's rule-making processes, enforcement procedures, eligibility rules, and alleged antitrust violations. It also explores the unique relationship that exists among student-athletes, universities and colleges, and the NCAA.

STRUCTURE AND ORGANIZATION

The NCAA is the primary organization governing collegiate athletics in the United States. It is a private organization that administers the athletic programs of many universities and colleges. The NCAA was founded in 1906 during the presidency of Theodore Roosevelt. The Intercollegiate Football Rules Committee, founded in 1894 by the then college football powerhouses of Harvard, Yale, the University of Pennsylvania, and Princeton, had been the regulating body for college football in 1905. That year, 62 colleges sent representatives to a meeting called by New York University Chancellor MacCraken because of his concern about injuries and deaths in college football. (During the 1907 season there were 11 student-athlete deaths and 98 serious injuries of student-athletes.)[1] The meeting culminated with the formation of the Intercollegiate Athletic Association of the United States,

---

[1] *Football's Death Record of 1907*, The New York Times, November 24, 1907.

which would, several years later, become known as the NCAA. The NCAA now sponsors athletic championships in a wide variety of sports.

Headquartered in Indianapolis, Indiana, the NCAA has a very large staff consisting of departments for championships, business, compliance, enforcement, publishing, and legislative services, to mention a few. Its membership comprises more than 1,250 institutions, which are organized into separate divisions based on competitiveness: Divisions I, II, and III. Division I is divided further into I-A and I-AA. Division I offers full athletic scholarships and is the most competitive. Division II offers athletic scholarships as well, and the student-athletes compete at an intermediate level. Division III has no scholarships and is the least competitive of the divisions but may be the most collegial. Schools compete in different divisions based on student population and athletic participation. Both small private schools and large public universities play in NCAA Division I-A football. For example, Ohio State University in Division I-A has an undergraduate student population in excess of 50,000 while Rice University, has an undergraduate population of approximately 3,000 students. The owls compete in Division I-A football in Conference USA. NCAA Division I-A college football has 120 teams.

The NCAA has expressed its fundamental policy in Article 1.3 of its constitution:

1.3.1 Basic Purpose. The competitive athletics programs of member institutions are designed to be a vital part of the educational system. A basic purpose of this Association is to maintain intercollegiate athletics as an integral part of the educational program and the athlete as an integral part of the student body and, by so doing, retain a clear line of demarcation between intercollegiate athletics and professional sports.[2]

The stated purposes of the NCAA are as follows:

(a) To initiate, stimulate and improve intercollegiate athletics programs for student-athletes and to promote and develop educational leadership, physical fitness, athletics excellence and athletics participation as a recreational pursuit;

(b) To uphold the principle of institutional control of, and responsibility for, all intercollegiate sports in conformity with the constitution and bylaws of this Association;

(c) To encourage its members to adopt eligibility rules to comply with satisfactory standards of scholarship, sportsmanship and amateurism;

(d) To formulate, copyright and publish rules of play governing intercollegiate athletics;

(e) To preserve intercollegiate athletics records;

(f) To supervise the conduct of, and to establish eligibility standards for, regional and national athletics events under the auspices of this Association;

(g) To cooperate with other amateur athletics organizations in promoting and conducting national and international athletics events;

(h) To legislate, through bylaws or by resolutions of a Convention, upon any subject of general concern to the members related to the administration of intercollegiate athletics; and

(i) To study in general all phases of competitive intercollegiate athletics and establish standards whereby the colleges and universities of the United States can maintain their athletics programs on a high level.[3]

---

[2] NATIONAL COLLEGIATE ATHLETIC ASSOCIATION, 2009–2010 NCAA DIVISION I MANUAL 1 (2009).

[3] *Id.* at 1. © National Collegiate Athletic Association. 2006–2008. All rights reserved.

The NCAA is governed by a detailed set of manuals containing its bylaws for each division and is directed by an 18-member council, an executive committee, and paid staff members. Division I-A powerhouse conferences and universities constitute the majority of the membership appointments for the management council and the board of directors.

The NCAA Division I board of directors is composed of 18 CEOs from member institutions. Eleven are from the 11 Division I-A conferences, and 7 are selected from the 20 Division I-AA and I-AAA conferences. The duties and responsibilities of the board of directors at the Division I level are set forth in the NCAA constitution as follows:

> The Board of Directors shall:
>
> (a) Establish and direct general policy;
> (b) Establish a strategic plan;
> (c) Adopt administrative bylaws and regulations;
> (d) Adopt operating bylaws and rules and/or delegate limited legislative powers to the Management Council . . .;
> (e) Delegate to the Management Council responsibilities for specific matters it deems appropriate;
> (f) Ratify, amend or rescind the actions of the Management Council (see Constitution 4.5);
> (g) Assure that there is gender and ethnic diversity among its membership, the membership of the Management Council . . . and the membership of each of the other bodies in the administrative structure;
> (h) Require bodies in the administrative structure to alter (but not expand) their membership to achieve diversity;
> (i) Approve an annual budget;
> (j) Approve regulations providing for the expenditure of funds and the distribution of income consistent with the provisions of Constitution 4.01.2.2;
> (k) Approve regulations providing for the administration of championships;
> (l) Advise the Executive Committee concerning the employment of the Association's president and concerning the oversight of his or her employment; and
> (m) Be responsible for the administration, compilation and disclosure of information concerning the Academic Progress Rate (APR) and Academic Performance Census (APC).[4]

The NCAA is concerned about the graduation rates of its participants.[5] The student-athlete is arguably a student first, who is attending the university on a scholarship to receive a degree from the institution, and secondly an athlete. The NCAA has several programs and policies in place to increase the graduation rates of student-athletes and ensure their academic progress. Bylaw 23.01 attempts to ensure academic excellence for member institutions and student-athletes:

23.01 General Principles

23.01.1 Purpose of the Academic Performance Program. The central purpose of the academic performance program is to ensure that the Division I

---

[4] *Id.* at 23. © National Collegiate Athletic Association. 2006–2008. All rights reserved.
[5] 2006 graduation rates for NCAA Division I schools can be found at http://www.ncaa.org/grad_rates/.

membership is dedicated to providing student-athletes with an exemplary educational and intercollegiate-athletics experience in an environment that recognizes and supports the primacy of the academic mission of its member institutions, while enhancing the ability of male and female student-athletes to earn a four-year degree.

23.01.2 Nature of Reward and Penalty Structure. The Division I membership is committed to providing higher education for a diverse body of male and female student-athletes within the context of an institution's academic and admissions standards for all students through a system that rewards those institutions and teams that demonstrate commitment toward the academic progress, retention and graduation of student-athletes and penalizes those that do not.

23.01.3 Disclosure Requirements.

23.01.3.1 Academic Progress Rate—Disclosure. An institution shall not be eligible to enter a team or individual competitor in an NCAA championship unless it has submitted, by the applicable deadline, its academic progress rate (APR) in a form approved and administered by the Committee on Academic Performance.

. . . .

23.2 Penalties and Rewards

23.2.1 Penalties. The Committee on Academic Performance shall notify an institution or team when it fails to satisfy the appropriate academic standards as outlined in the academic performance program. The institution shall then apply the applicable penalty pursuant to the policies of the academic performance program.

Source: National Collegiate Athletic Association, *2009–2010 NCAA Division I Manual* (2009). © National Collegiate Athletic Association. 2008–2010. All rights reserved.

The NCAA uses a measure known as the Academic Progress Rate (APR) for each Division I member institution. This measure takes into account the eligibility of student-athletes and their graduation and retention rates. Schools that fail to meet the minimum cut-off score set by the NCAA are subject to sanctions.[6]

The NCAA sets forth the rules and regulations with which all member institutions, coaches, and student-athletes must abide. The bylaws published by the NCAA give guidance regarding a myriad of issues relating to collegiate sports, including eligibility, drug testing, use of agents, recruiting, the amateur status of student-athletes, and financial aid. As members of the association, all institutions

---

[6] Steve Wieberg, *NCAA Hands Down Postseason Bans Over Poor APR Scores*, USA Today, May 7, 2009.

are required to comply with all NCAA regulations. If an institution fails to follow NCAA bylaws, then the NCAA is empowered to take appropriate measures against the institution in an attempt to ensure its compliance and can penalize the member institution for any major or minor violation. All individuals employed by member institutions have a duty to cooperate with an NCAA investigation. The institution may begin its own investigation into any alleged violations as well and may do so in an attempt to fend off the NCAA's investigation and mitigate any penalty that may be assessed. Many institutions will immediately begin their own investigation once they have received notice from the NCAA that the athletic program is being investigated.[7] The NCAA's enforcement powers are extensive and have been used in the past to penalize those universities that violate NCAA rules. Some have argued that the NCAA has been too harsh in enforcing its bylaws and needs to be reformed.[8]

Athletic conferences are also members of the NCAA. Universities and colleges are divided into various conferences for athletic purposes.[9] In recent years there has been an extensive reorganization of collegiate athletic conferences. Member institutions have attempted to switch conferences to align themselves with powerhouse athletic programs. The primary motivating force behind the moves is college football. The Big Ten Conference now has 11 teams. In 1996 the former Southwest Conference (SWC) merged with all the members of the Big Eight Conference to establish a new conference, the Big Twelve. The SWC at one time comprised eight Texas universities and the University of Arkansas. Its makeup was unique: it had major public universities such as the University of Texas at Austin and also four private universities, Southern Methodist University, Baylor, Rice, and Texas Christian University. The conference broke up for several reasons, not the least being multiple rule violations by some of its members.[10] The Big East Conference and the Atlantic Coast Conference have also had members leave and establish a new makeup for the conferences in the past few years.

In collegiate sports, competition in a powerful, elite conference can mean substantial revenues for the university as well as increased exposure, resulting in better recruiting for the university sports teams and ultimately more students. Elite conferences receive more bowl game invitations as well as entry into the Bowl Championship Series (BCS) sweepstakes. Lawsuits have resulted as a result of universities changing conferences. In *Boston College v. Big East Conference*, 18 Mass. L. Rptr. 177 (Mass. Super. 2004), the court noted how significant college sports has become to the university campus and the resultant struggle to keep the proper focus on academics:

> The situation that underlies this case is a poster child for the dilemma faced by America's colleges and universities in maintaining the proper balance between their primary mission of academic excellence and the operation of big-time intercollegiate athletic programs. Boston College has chosen to leave the Big East Conference, in which it is one of the Football Schools, and join the Atlantic Coast Conference. At issue is the validity of efforts by the Big East to quintuple the economic penalty and more than

---

[7] Jessica Nunez, *University of Michigan Hires a Firm to Assist its Football Program Investigation*, MLive.com, September 2, 2009.

[8] *See* DON YEAGER, THE NCAA'S INJUSTICE FOR ALL (1991); *Also see* Sherry Young, *The NCAA Enforcement Program and Due Process: The Case for Internal Reform*, 43 SYRACUSE L. REV. 747 (1992).

[9] For further study of the makeup of athletic conferences and NCAA football in general, see Greg Katz, *Conflicting Fiduciary Duties Within Collegiate Athletic Conferences: A Prescription for Leniency*, 47 B.C. L. REV. 345 (2006).

[10] N. Brooks Clark, *4 Southern Methodist*, SI Vault, September 1, 1982.

double the pre-withdrawal notice period, all designed to discourage Conference members from leaving the Conference and punishing them if they do so. In the litigation process spawned, respected college and university presidents charge each other with bad faith, with breaches of fiduciary duties, with misrepresentations and with worse. And any penalty, particularly one of $5 million, must be paid from funds that otherwise would be available for the academic program or scholarship aid.[11]

The NCAA sponsors championships in a wide variety of sports, which are viewed by millions on television and at live sporting events. The Final Four in NCAA basketball has become a staple in the spring, with "March Madness" taking over prime time television and offices for three weeks with even the U.S. President completing his "bracket."[12] College hockey has its own playoffs known as the "Frozen Four." The NCAA sponsors the annual College Baseball World Series in Omaha, Nebraska, where star college players vie for the College World Series Championships. The University of West Virginia won the NCAA National Title in the 2009 Rifle Championships.[13] The Bowl Championship Series in NCAA Division I-A football has become one of the most watched sporting events of the year in the United States. College football is an extremely popular sport in America. NCAA Division I college football drew 43,456,151 fans in the 2008 season. For all divisions of NCAA football in the 2008 season, a total of 48,839,003 viewed games.[14] To gain some perspective, 22,256,502 fans attended NFL games during 2007.[15] Table 10-1 lists the schools with the leading attendance at games during the 2008 college football season.

Big-time college sports is a lucrative business. The NCAA's total operating revenue for 2008–2009 was $661,000,000.[16] Elite NCAA athletic programs can generate in excess of more than $100 million in revenue. The athletic department of the University of Texas generated approximately $120 million in revenue for the 2007–2008 seasons.[17] The Big Ten Conference has a 24-hour Big Ten channel, a joint venture with Fox Sports. This allows the 11 teams in the Big Ten Conference to increase exposure for their universities and sports programs as well as increasing revenues.

NCAA Division I-A football is by far the biggest revenue-producing sport in intercollegiate athletics. Premier college teams compete for the National Championship of college football, which results in massive payouts to the member institutions in the BCS. The projected payouts for the teams involved in the 2009 BCS bowls were $17.5 million for each team. The format of the BCS has been questioned extensively and debated by some as an antitrust violation.[18] Not only do the teams in the

---

[11] *Boston College*, 18 Mass. L. Rptr. at 177.

[12] Andy Katz, *Presidential Pick'Em at the White House*, ESPN.com, March 18, 2009. It is estimated that U.S. offices lost $1.7 billion in loss productivity during the 2008 NCAA basketball tournament. David Sweet, *$1.7B in Lost Work? That's March Madness*, MSNBC.com, March 19, 2008.

[13] NCAA, *NCAA Rifle History*, http://www.ncaa.com/history/rifle.

[14] NCAA, *2008 National College Football Attendance*, http://web1ncaa.org/web_files/stats/football_records/Attendance/2006.pdf.

[15] NFL *Sets Attendance Record in 2007*, NFL.com, 2008.

[16] NCAA, *Revised Budget for Fiscal Year Ended August 31, 2009*, http://www1.ncaa.org/2008-09+BUDGET+(Budget+moves+in+08-09)_FINAL.pdf.

[17] John Maher, *Longhorns Earn No. 1 Ranking . . . in Revenue*, The Austin American-Statesman, June 16, 2009.

[18] *See* David Moreland, *The Antitrust Implications of the Bowl Championship Series: Analysis Through Analogous Reasoning*, 21 Ga. St. U. L. Rev. 721 (2005); Katherine McClelland, *Should College Football's Currency Read "In BCS We Trust" or Is It Just Monopoly Money? Antitrust Implications of the Bowl Championship Series*, 37 Tex. Tech L. Rev. 167 (2004).

TABLE 10-1

2008 NCAA Division I FBS Football Attendance Team Leaders				
Rank	*School*	*Games*	*Attendance*	*Average*
1	Michigan	7	759,997	108,571
2	Penn St.	7	757,775	108,254
3	Ohio St.	7	734,830	104,976
4	Tennessee	7	710,136	101,448
5	Texas	7	686,324	98,046
6	Georgia	6	556,476	92,746
7	LSU	8	739,065	92,383
8	Alabama	7	644,966	92,138
9	Florida	7	633,807	90,544
10	Auburn	7	608,402	86,915
11	Southern Galifornia	6	520,756	86,793
12	Oklahoma	6	510,448	85,075
13	Nebraska	8	680,564	85,071
14	Texas A&M	7	575,351	82,193
15	Wisconsin	7	567,616	81,088
16	Notre Dame	6	484,770	80,795
17	South Carolina	7	563,703	80,529
18	Clemson	7	546,004	78,001
19	Florida St.	7	545,773	77,968
20	Michigan St.	7	524,005	74,858

Source: NCAA.org

National Championship game receive a large payout, but they are also able to generate large revenue streams from other sources as a result of their success. The 2005 National Champion, Texas Longhorns, set a record for licensing royalties with $8.2 million in 2005–2006.[19] The school has approximately 450 licenses. The former record was held by the University of Michigan in 1993–1994 with $6.2 million, set during the "Fab Five" basketball era.

Unfortunately, problems have arisen in college sports as a result of several factors, including the increase in revenues and the opportunity for student-athletes to play professionally. Recruiting scandals have hurt some universities, whereas others have been damaged by the actions of unscrupulous agents or boosters of athletic programs. The NCAA has been aggressive in penalizing universities that have violated NCAA bylaws. It has passed bylaws to regulate agents, student-athletes, and boosters in an attempt to ensure the integrity of college athletes and college sports. The NCAA certainly

---

[19] Associated Press, *Longhorns Knock Off Tar Heels to Lead Nation in Merchandising Revenue*, USA Today, August 26, 2006.

has had its critics as well. Andrew Zimbalist, the Robert A. Woods Professor of Economics at Smith College, has published several books, including *Baseball and Billions*. He noted the following with regard to the NCAA and its member schools:

> With big bucks dangling before their eyes, many NCAA schools find the temptations of success too alluring to worry about the rules. Schools cheat. They cheat by arranging to help their prospective athletes pass standardized tests. They cheat by providing illegal payments to their recruits. They cheat by setting up special rinky-dink curricular so their athletes can stay qualified. And when one school cheats, others feel compelled to do the same. Then the NCAA passes new rules to curtail the cheating. Sometimes these rules are enforced, sometimes not, but rarely is the penalty harsh enough to be a serious deterrent. The solution, it turns out, is more rules. The NCAA Manual has grown in size from 161 pages in 1970–71 to 579 pages in 1996–97 (and the pages increased in size from $6 \times 8\,^1/_2$ inches prior to 1989 to $8\,^1/_2 \times 11$ inches after). In 1989–99, the Manual became so long that the NCAA broke it into three volumes, with 1,268 pages (some are repeats).
>
> So what is "the clear line of demarcation between intercollegiate athletics and professional sports"? It certainly is not the presence or absence of commercialism and corporate interests. Rather, two differences stand out. First, unlike their handsomely remunerated coaches and athletic directors (ADs), college athletes don't get paid. Second, the NCAA and its member schools, construed to be amateur organizations promoting an educational mission, do not pay taxes on their millions from TV deals, sponsorships, licensing or Final Four tickets.
>
> The tension between professional and amateur in college sports creates a myriad of contradictions. And, as the NCAA can well attest, contradictions in 1990s America mean litigation.[20]

Much is at stake in college sports for student-athletes, coaches, administrators, and universities. The NCAA will continue to try to find the right combination of administration and enforcement to strike create the ideal balance between academics and athletic success.

ACTIONS AGAINST THE NCAA

The NCAA has been sued many times by numerous individuals and entities who have asserted a variety of legal theories against the NCAA. For instance, former UCLA basketball star Ed O'Bannon filed a class-action lawsuit against the NCAA in 2009 asserting that former student-athletes should be compensated for the NCAA's use of their images and likeness in advertisements, video games, and NCAA related apparel.[21] In Case 10-1, *National Collegiate Athletic Ass'n v. Hornung*, 754 S.W.2d 855 (Ky. 1988), the NCAA was pitted against former Heisman Trophy winner Paul Hornung. Hornung was a standout running back at Notre Dame. Hornung sued the NCAA, alleging that it interfered with a contract he had entered into with the television station WTBS to announce college football games.

---

[20] Andrew A. Zimbalist, Unpaid Professionals, Commercialism and Conflict in Big Time College Sports 13, 1999, pp.4–5.

[21] Pete Thamel, *NCAA. Sued Over Licensing Practices*, The New York Times, July 21, 2009. *For further study see,* Don Yaeger, *Undue Process: The NCAA's Injustice for All*, Sagamore Publishing, Inc. 1991.

📖   CASE 10-1   *National Collegiate Athletic Ass'n v. Hornung*

754 S.W.2d 855 (Ky. 1988)

LAMBERT, Justice.

Paul Hornung, upon his claim against movant, the National Collegiate Athletic Association (NCAA), for intentional interference with a prospective contractual relation. . . . This Court . . ., upon examination of the evidence, concludes that the trial court erred in failing to sustain the NCAA's motion for directed verdict.

Upon his retirement from professional football, Hornung began a career as a sports broadcaster. From the mid-1960's until 1980, he held a number of positions in which he worked as a play-by-play announcer and color analyst of college and professional football games. During this period, Hornung participated, without objection from the NCAA, in broadcasting college football games.

In 1980 and 1981, Hornung hosted a series of weekly television broadcasts called "Football Saturday Live," a talk show about college football, for WTBS in Atlanta. During that time, in 1981, WTBS learned that the NCAA was soliciting bids for a "supplementary series" of college football games to be broadcast on a cable network. During negotiations with WTBS which followed, the NCAA insisted on having a right to approve the announcers for the series. An agreement was reached and WTBS obtained the right to telecast nineteen games in each of the 1982 and 1983 seasons for a sum of money in excess of $17 million. As a part of the agreement, the NCAA was granted the right to approve or disapprove any announcer or color analyst used on the broadcasts.

. . . While negotiations were underway between the NCAA and WTBS, Hornung was informed by Robert Wussler, president of WTBS, that an agreement appeared to have been reached for the supplementary series and that Hornung's name would be submitted for approval. Hornung offered no objection to the submission of his name. He was also informed that the supplementary series of live games would replace "Football Saturday Live" and that on the new series, he would be the color analyst.

On March 29, 1982, the NCAA Television Committee met in New Orleans to make plans for the upcoming season including broadcast plans for the supplementary series. The Committee was comprised of nineteen men and women who were associated with member universities and conferences. All members were present at the meeting. Also present were WTBS president Robert Wussler and Terry Hanson, executive producer of sports at WTBS. During the meeting, WTBS submitted the names of four persons whom it proposed as announcers for the supplementary series. Hornung was one of the persons named. The Committee briefly discussed the proposed announcers and then voted unanimously to disapprove Hornung, and one other person who had been proposed, as announcers for the supplementary series.

About three weeks after the meeting, Wiles Hallock, Chairman of the NCAA Television Committee, was contacted by a reporter from an Atlanta newspaper. In response to a question from the reporter, Hallock stated that "[T]he Committee objected to Hornung because 'ever since Paul graduated from Notre Dame he had been associated with professional football and perhaps does not represent college football.'" This statement was widely published.

After Hornung's rejection by the Committee, Mr. Hanson of WTBS requested a letter from the NCAA to confirm its disapproval of Hornung. His stated reason for wanting such a letter was "we have a relationship with Paul Hornung . . . that I want to protect and we have to have that in writing before I'll deem it official." In response to this request, on April 22, 1982, the NCAA wrote WTBS as follows:

> Paul Hornung: Paul Hornung was not approved for 1982. The Committee believes he is closely identified with professional football, that he had at least one undesirable public situation while a professional player, that the image which he projects or is projected for him does not personify college football.

WTBS furnished a copy of this letter to Hornung who contacted Billy Reed of the *Courier-Journal* and read portions of the letter to him. Based in part on the letter, Reed wrote a newsstory about Hornung's rejection and the story was published in the *Courier-Journal* on May 11, 1982.

At trial, Committee Chairman Hallock testified that the reasons for Hornung's disapproval were:

"My own experience with the Committee, and you find this in the Constitution and Bylaws of the NCAA, was first of all to protect the objective of keeping a strong demarcation between amateur college football and professional football. There are strong resolutions and actions within the NCAA Bylaws, statements against gambling. I felt very definitely that the combination of the identification, the primary identification since—pretty much since Paul Hornung graduated in 1956 was with professional football. I felt personally that the unfortunate suspension of Mr. Hornung for gambling activity was not something that the NCAA wanted to simply overlook in the selection of people to represent college football on television. I had a personal feeling that the national image as continually being represented by

Miller Beer of Paul Hornung's life-style was not in keeping with any positive—certainly any positive quality that the NCAA was interested in condoning in any way. Those were my personal feelings."

It is undisputed that during his professional football career Hornung was suspended for gambling activity and that in the Miller Lite Beer commercial, Hornung was portrayed as a playboy. These were certainly legitimate matters for consideration by the NCAA. In view of Hornung's long and outstanding career in the National Football League, it is not unreasonable to hold the opinion that he is more closely associated with professional football than college football. Contrary to Hornung's argument, its acceptance of advertising revenue from the Miller Brewing Company does not render the NCAA's objection to the commercial incredible. The objection was not Hornung's promotional activity on behalf of the brewing company; it was the image portrayed in the commercial. Likewise, Hornung's previous broadcast of college football games is irrelevant as the NCAA did not have "announcer approval rights" as it had here. Finally, Hallock's vote in 1985, three years after the Committee vote, in favor of Hornung's election to membership in the College Football Hall of Fame and the fact that the Committee took only ten minutes to disapprove Hornung do not conflict with the testimony given by Hallock. From the foregoing, we conclude that Hornung failed to prove that the NCAA "improperly" interfered with his prospective contractual relation with WTBS.

The NCAA was entitled to assert its right even to the detriment of Hornung's prospective contractual relation. If the NCAA believed that employment of Hornung was contrary to its interest, even if such belief was mistaken, it was justified in disapproving Hornung pursuant to the terms of the agreement with WTBS. . . .

Source: Courtesy of Westlaw; reprinted with permission.

State Action

It is a basic tenet that any governmental action must comply with the constitutional rights of individuals. Private actors do not have such concerns.[22] In the statutory remedy for constitutional violations, 42 U.S.C. § 1983, Congress made it clear that the conduct at issue must have occurred "under the color of state law." When a governmental rule, such as a statute, is challenged, basic constitutional principles such as equal protection and due process apply. Alternatively, when the rules of a private entity are challenged, the law of private associations is applied.[23] An individual who is alleging a denial of his or her constitutional rights must first establish that the action being taken is one by a governmental entity. If the plaintiff cannot establish "state action" on the part of the entity, then the constitutional claim will fail.

---

[22] Burton v. Wilmington Parking Authority, 365 U.S. 715, 722 (1961) (holding the protections of the Fourteenth Amendment do not extend to "private conduct abridging individual rights").

[23] Rewolinski v. Fisher, 444 So.2d 54, 58 (Fla. 3d DCA), *review denied*, 453 So.2d 43 (Fla.1984).

In some cases state action is easy to establish. If a plaintiff is challenging a statute passed by Congress, the state action requirement is clearly met. Other cases are not quite as clear. Amateur athletic associations such as the United States Olympic Committee and the NCAA are private actors but, under certain circumstances, may perform similar functions as a governmental entity. Can an organization that performs "state-like" functions be deemed a "state actor," thereby invoking constitutional considerations? It is well established that high school athletic associations are considered state actors.[24] What about the NCAA? Is it a state actor? That was the issue in Case 10-2, *National Collegiate Athletic Ass'n v. Tarkanian*, 488 U.S. 179 (1988), involving Jerry Tarkanian, "the Shark," a successful NCAA basketball coach formerly at the University of Nevada, Las Vegas (UNLV).

CASE 10-2 *National Collegiate Athletic Ass'n v. Tarkanian*

488 U.S. 179 (1988)

Justice STEVENS delivered the opinion of the Court.

. . . [I]n September 1977 UNLV informed Tarkanian that it was going to suspend him. No dissatisfaction with Tarkanian, once described as "the 'winningest' active basketball coach," motivated his suspension. Rather, the impetus was a report by the NCAA detailing 38 violations of NCAA rules by UNLV personnel, including 10 involving Tarkanian. The NCAA had placed the university's basketball team on probation for two years and ordered UNLV to show cause why the NCAA should not impose further penalties unless UNLV severed all ties during the probation between its intercollegiate athletic program and Tarkanian.

Facing demotion and a drastic cut in pay, Tarkanian brought suit in Nevada state court, alleging that he had been deprived of his Fourteenth Amendment due process rights in violation of 42 U.S.C. § 1983. Ultimately Tarkanian obtained injunctive relief and an award of attorney's fees against both UNLV and the NCAA. NCAA's liability may be upheld only if its participation in the events that led to Tarkanian's suspension constituted "state action" prohibited by the Fourteenth Amendment and was performed "under color of" state law within the meaning of § 1983. We granted certiorari to review the Nevada Supreme Court's holding that the NCAA engaged in state action when it conducted its investigation and recommended that Tarkanian be disciplined. We now reverse.

---

[24] Louisiana High School Athletic Ass'n v. St. Augusta High School, 396 F.2d. 234 (5th Cir. 1968); Brentwood Academy v. Tennessee Secondary School Athletic Ass'n, 531 U.S. 288, 295, 121 S. Ct. 924, 148 L. Ed. 2d 807 (2001); Graham v. Tennessee Secondary Athletic Ass'n, 1995 U.S. Dist. Lexis 3211 (E.D. Tenn. 1995). For a contrary opinion, see Burrows v. Ohio High School Athletic Ass'n, 891 F.2d 122 (6th Cir. 1989), (holding the association did not engage in state action).

In this case Tarkanian argues that the NCAA was a state actor because it misused power that it possessed by virtue of state law. He claims specifically that UNLV delegated its own functions to the NCAA, clothing the Association with authority both to adopt rules governing UNLV's athletic programs and to enforce those rules on behalf of UNLV. Similarly, the Nevada Supreme Court held that UNLV had delegated its authority over personnel decisions to the NCAA. Therefore, the court reasoned, the two entities acted jointly to deprive Tarkanian of liberty and property interests, making the NCAA as well as UNLV a state actor.

These contentions fundamentally misconstrue the facts of this case. In the typical case raising a state-action issue, a private party has taken the decisive step that caused the harm to the plaintiff, and the question is whether the State was sufficiently involved to treat that decisive conduct as state action. This may occur if the State creates the legal framework governing the conduct, if it delegates its authority to the private actor, or sometimes if it knowingly accepts the benefits derived from unconstitutional behavior. Thus, in the usual case we ask whether the State provided a mantle of authority that enhanced the power of the harm-causing individual actor.

This case uniquely mirrors the traditional state-action case. Here the final act challenged by Tarkanian—his suspension—was committed by UNLV. A state university without question is a state actor. When it decides to impose a serious disciplinary sanction upon one of its tenured employees, it must comply with the terms of the Due Process Clause of the Fourteenth Amendment to the Federal Constitution. *Thus when UNLV notified Tarkanian that he was being separated from all relations with the university's basketball program, it acted under color of state law within the meaning of 42 U.S.C. § 1983.*

The mirror image presented in this case requires us to step through an analytical looking glass to resolve the case. Clearly UNLV's conduct was influenced by the rules and recommendations of the NCAA, the private party. But it was UNLV, the state entity, that actually suspended Tarkanian. Thus the question is not whether UNLV participated to a critical extent in the NCAA's activities, but whether UNLV's actions in compliance with the NCAA rules and recommendations turned the NCAA's conduct into state action. . . .

Finally, Tarkanian argues that the power of the NCAA is so great that the UNLV had no practical alternative to compliance with its demands. We are not at all sure this is true, but even if we assume that a private monopolist can impose its will on a state agency by a threatened refusal to deal with it, it does not follow that such a private party is therefore acting under color of state law. . . .

In final analysis the question is whether "the conduct allegedly causing the deprivation of a federal right [can] be fairly attributable to
the State." *Lugar*, 457 U.S., at 937, 102 S. Ct., at 2753. It would be
ironic indeed to conclude that the NCAA's imposition of sanctions
against UNLV—sanctions that UNLV and its counsel, including the Attorney General of Nevada, steadfastly opposed during protracted adversary
proceedings—is fairly attributable to the State of Nevada. It would be
more appropriate to conclude that UNLV has conducted its athletic program under color of the policies adopted by the NCAA, rather than that
those policies were developed and enforced under color of Nevada law.

The judgment of the Nevada Supreme Court is reversed, and the case is
remanded to that court for further proceedings not inconsistent with
this opinion.

It is so ordered.

Source: Courtesy of Westlaw; reprinted with permission.

THE STUDENT-ATHLETE RELATIONSHIP

Student-athletes have challenged a variety of NCAA bylaws on several grounds. Courts, however, have generally given judicial deference to the NCAA's authority and have been hesitant to
place limitations on its regulation of intercollegiate athletics.[25] It is a general rule that courts will not
interfere in the affairs of a private association unless it can be shown that the organization violated
its own rules, fraud is present, or the rules are deemed arbitrary or unconscionable.[26] A Florida case
dealing with recruiting violations stated the general rule regarding private association law, citing
National Collegiate Athletic Association v. Brinkworth, 680 So.2d 1081, 1084 (Fla. 3d DCA 1996):

> We continue to adhere to the rule that courts should exercise limited interference with the internal
> affairs and rules of a voluntary membership association:
>
> Under Florida law a court may intervene in the internal affairs of a private association only in
> exceptional circumstances. "It is a well established proposition in Florida law that ordinarily courts will
> not intervene in the internal affairs of labor unions or other voluntary associations[.]" *Rewolinski v.
> Fisher*, 444 So.2d 54, 58 (Fla. 3d DCA), *review denied*, 453 So.2d 43 (Fla.1984) (citations omitted).
>
> Thus, "the results of internal association processes are subject to judicial reversal only if (1) the
> association's action adversely affects 'substantial property, contract or other economic rights' and the
> association's own internal procedures were inadequate or unfair, or if (2) the association acted mali-
> ciously or in bad faith." *Id.* (summarizing *McCune v. Wilson*, 237 So.2d 169 (Fla.1970)); *see also
> Sult v. Gilbert*, 148 Fla. 31, 3 So.2d 729 (1941).

---

[25] NCAA v. Tarkanian, 488 U.S. 179 (1988).
[26] Mozingo v. Oklahoma Secondary School Activities Ass'n, 575 P.2d 1379 (Okla. App. 1978).

Plaintiffs are usually only successful in challenging the NCAA if they can show that the NCAA was in violation of its own bylaws, regulations, or policies. Barring those factors, courts have been hesitant to intervene and substitute their judgment for that of the NCAA's. In summary, "it is up to the NCAA to interpret its own rules, not the judiciary."[27] As long as the rules and regulations are reasonable and are applied in a fair and consistent manner, courts will not interfere.

Defining and exploring the relationship of the student-athlete to the university and to the NCAA is basic to the understanding of how the law views the NCAA and student-athletes. The student-athlete is faced with challenges on and off the field as he or she is participating in collegiate sports and also attempting to earn a college degree. Student-athletes enter into a contract with the university when they sign a letter of intent and when they accept a scholarship offer from that university.

In the cases presented in this section, the defendants were universities and, in one case, a high school district. These cases explore a variety of issues dealing with the national letter of intent, scholarships, academic advising, and other hurdles encountered by student-athletes in their attempts to obtain a degree and maintain eligibility to participate in collegiate athletes. Litigation has arisen over the extent of the obligations of the student-athlete, the university, and its employees. Student-athletes have attempted to enlarge the responsibility of the university, whereas universities have defended their position, stating that they have met their contractual obligations as prescribed by law.

The role of the university student-athlete has been summarized as follows:

> Legal scholars and others have acknowledged that intercollegiate sports comprise a multimillion dollar entertainment industry. Television contracts, ticket sales, merchandising, and public speaking engagements are just a few of the many sources of revenue acquired under such programs. Educators such as Murray Sperber have characterized the current state of college athletics as a "huge commercial entertainment conglomerate."
>
> At least one researcher has noted that, although a university's main purpose is purportedly to educate its students, and that even those schools with "big-time" athletic programs would continue to exist in the absence of their athletic teams, the university as a whole may derive benefits from its athletic program in the form of increased applications for admissions, publicity, visibility, and alumni donations stemming from winning teams. As a result, the NCAA's Knight Commission discovered that athletic programs are given special, often unique, status within the university, with the best coaches often receiving an income many times that of most full professors. The Knight Commission also found that, although successful athletic programs appear to promise a quick route to revenue, recognition, and renown for a university, the intrinsic educational value of such programs often becomes "engulfed by the revenue stream they generate and overwhelmed by the accompanying publicity."
>
> Lee Goldman notes that "[w]ith millions of dollars in tournament or bowl revenues and alumni contributions at stake, schools often place intense pressure on coaches to succeed. Job retention and salary bonuses are increasingly tied to winning, not graduation rates." Such an environment, according to Goldman, creates a "win-at-all-costs" mentality that can threaten the educational pursuits of student-athletes. This win-at-all-costs mind-set has led at least one commentator to observe that, for many universities, the student-athlete no longer exists, because the academic mission of universities has been supplanted by the athletic mission. All this commercialism and potential for abuse, according to

---

[27] NCAA v. Brinkworth, 680 So.2d 1081, 1084 (citing Regents of the University of Minnesota v. National Collegiate Athletic Ass'n, 560 F.2d 52, 372 (8th Cir.), *cert. denied*, 434 U.S. 978, 98 S. Ct. 600, 54 L. Ed. 2d 472 (1977)).

researchers, has given rise to a multitude of public policy issues concerning the direction and purpose of intercollegiate athletics and the best interests of student-athletes.

Thus, although athletic scholarships may provide an important means for many of today's youth to obtain a valuable college education and enhance their athletic ability, numerous studies have discovered that, in the context of many sports programs, the importance of academic achievement is often overlooked by coaches and athletic departments. Entangled in the web of revenue spun by successful intercollegiate athletic programs, many coaches and athletic departments fail to ensure that their student-athletes are provided with sufficient opportunity to achieve their educational goals.[28]

Given the increasing focus on sports as a business at the collegiate level, legal issues have arisen between student-athletes and universities. The following cases explore some of the issues involved.

Educational Malpractice

Some student-athletes participate in athletics at a university but never receive a degree from the institution. There are a myriad of horror stories of student-athletes who were heavily recruited to a well-known university and then never performed either on the playing field or in the classroom.[29] Can a student-athlete who was recruited to the university to play athletics who never graduated sue the university or coach based on the theory of educational malpractice? Many cases have discussed the issue of educational malpractice.[30] In *Tolman v. Cencor Career Colleges, Inc.*, 851 P.2d 203 (Colo. Ct. App. 1993), the court discussed the issue of educational malpractice for the first time in the state of Colorado. In denying plaintiff's claim, the court stated:

> Since education is a collaborative and subjective process whose success is largely reliant on the student, and since the existence of such outside factors as a student's attitude and abilities render it impossible to establish any quality or curriculum deficiencies as a proximate cause to any injuries, we rule that there is no workable standard of care here and defendant would face an undue burden if forced to litigate its selection of curriculum and teaching methods. *Ross v. Creighton University, supra; Peter W. v. San Francisco Unified School District, supra.* Accordingly, as a matter of law, we decline to impose such a duty here and uphold the summary judgment refusing to recognize plaintiffs' tort claims premised on educational malpractice entered by the trial court.[31]

---

[28] M. L. Emerick, *The University/Student-Athlete Relationship: Duties Giving Rise to a Potential Educational Hindrance Claim*, 44 UCLA L. Rev. 874–77 (1997).

[29] For a further discussion of educational malpractice, see J. Smith, *Tort Liability of Public Schools and Institutions of Higher Learning for Educational Malpractice*, 1 Am. L. Rep. 4th 1139 (1980).

[30] *See* Miller v. Loyola University of New Orleans, 829 So.2d 1057 (La. App. Ct. 2002) (law student's claim for educational malpractice failed after he alleged that the university failed to provide complete and satisfactory instruction in a course on ethics); Hutchins v. Vanderbilt University, 55 Fed. Appx. 308, 310 (6th Cir. 2003) ("courts are not inclined to review educational malpractice claims or breach of contract claims based on educational service") at 310. For a case holding a defendant liable on an educational malpractice claim, see Andre v. Pace University, 618 N.Y.S.2d 975 (N.Y. City Ct. 1994) (awarding the plaintiffs punitive damages on their claims for educational malpractice and finding defendants "liable in negligence for failing to competently and properly teach the promised Pascal course and . . . responsible for all appropriate damages flowing therefrom").

[31] *Tolman, 851 P.2d at 205.*

In *Page v. Klein Tools Inc.*, 461 Mich. 703, 610 N.W. 2d 900 (2000), the court granted summary judgment to a trade school after an apprentice linesman (not an offensive lineman) alleged that the school had failed to instruct him properly during a three-week course on climbing utility poles. In another Michigan case, *Napela v. Plymouth-Canton Community School District*, 207 Mich. App. 580, 525 N.W.2d 897 (1994), the court found in favor of all defendants (a film distribution company, a school district, a teacher, a principal, and other school faculty) on claims for educational malpractice brought by the parents of a second grader who tragically hanged himself after watching a film at school. The film was about an amputee who had attempted suicide before learning to deal with his disability.

Can an individual maintain a claim for educational malpractice against a university? If so, what would the plaintiff have to prove to prevail? Kevin Ross was an "academic casualty" while at Creighton University. He sued the university for educational malpractice, among other theories, in Case 10-3, *Ross v. Creighton University*, 957 F.2d 410 (7th Cir. 1992).

📖 CASE 10-3　*Ross v. Creighton University*

957 F.2d 410 (7th Cir. 1992)

RIPPLE, Circuit Judge.

Kevin Ross filed suit against Creighton University (Creighton or the University) for negligence and breach of contract arising from Creighton's alleged failure to educate him. The district court dismissed Mr. Ross' complaint for failure to state a claim. For the following reasons we affirm in part and reverse in part the judgment of the district court.

I. Background

A. Facts

. . . Mr. Ross' complaint reveals the following story.

In the spring of 1978, Mr. Ross was a promising senior basketball player at Wyandotte High School in Kansas City, Kansas. Sometime during his senior year in high school, he accepted an athletic scholarship to attend Creighton and to play on its varsity basketball team.

Creighton is an academically superior university. Mr. Ross comes from an academically disadvantaged background. At the time of his enrollment at Creighton, Mr. Ross was at an academic level far below that of the average Creighton student. For example, he scored in the bottom fifth percentile of college-bound seniors taking the American College Test, while the average freshman admitted to Creighton with him scored in the upper twenty-seven percent. According to the complaint, Creighton realized Mr. Ross' academic limitations when it admitted him, and, to induce him to attend and play basketball, Creighton assured Mr. Ross that he would receive sufficient tutoring so that he "would receive a meaningful education while at CREIGHTON."

Mr. Ross attended Creighton from 1978 until 1982. During that time he maintained a D average and acquired 96 of the 128 credits needed to graduate. However, many of these credits were in courses such as Marksmanship and Theory of Basketball, and did not count towards a university degree. Mr. Ross alleges that he took these courses on the advice of Creighton's Athletic Department, and that the department also employed a secretary to read his assignments and prepare and type his papers. Mr. Ross also asserts that Creighton failed to provide him with sufficient and competent tutoring that it had promised.

When he left Creighton, Mr. Ross had the overall language skills of a fourth grader and the reading skills of a seventh grader. Consequently, Mr. Ross enrolled, at Creighton's expense, for a year of remedial education at the Westside Preparatory School in Chicago. At Westside, Mr. Ross attended classes with grade school children. He later entered Roosevelt University in Chicago, but was forced to withdraw because of a lack of funds. In July 1987, Mr. Ross suffered what he terms a "major depressive episode," during which he barricaded himself in a Chicago motel room and threw furniture out the window. To Mr. Ross, this furniture "symbolized" Creighton employees who had wronged him.

B. District Court Proceedings

Mr. Ross filed suit against Creighton in Cook County (Illinois) Circuit Court for negligence and breach of contract. . . .

Mr. Ross' complaint advances three separate theories of how Creighton was negligent towards him. First, he contends that Creighton committed "educational malpractice" by not providing him with a meaningful education and preparing him for employment after college. Second, Mr. Ross claims that Creighton negligently inflicted emotional distress upon him by enrolling him in a stressful university environment for which he was not prepared, and then by failing to provide remedial programs that would have helped him survive there. Third, Mr. Ross urges the court to adopt a new cause of action for the tort of "negligent admission," which would allow recovery when an institution admits, and then does not adequately assist, a woefully unprepared student. The complaint also sets forth a contract claim, alleging that Creighton contracted to provide Mr. Ross "an opportunity . . . to obtain a meaningful college education and degree, and to do what was reasonably necessary . . . to enable [Mr. Ross] to obtain a meaningful college education and degree." It goes on to assert that Creighton breached this contract by failing to provide Mr. Ross adequate tutoring; by not requiring Mr. Ross to attend tutoring sessions; by not allowing him to "red-shirt," that is, to forego a year of basketball, in order to work on academics; and by failing to afford Mr. Ross a reasonable opportunity to take advantage of tutoring services. Mr. Ross also alleges that Creighton breached a promise it had made to him to pay for a college education.

II. Analysis

. . . .

B. The Negligence Claims

Mr. Ross advances three separate theories of how Creighton was negligent towards him: educational malpractice for not educating him, a new tort of "negligent admission" to an educational institution, and negligent infliction of emotional distress. We believe that, on the facts of this case, Illinois law would deny Mr. Ross recovery on all three theories.

1. Educational Malpractice

Illinois courts have never ruled on whether a tort cause of action exists against an institution for educational malpractice. However, the overwhelming majority of states that have considered this type of claim have rejected it.

Courts have identified several policy concerns that counsel against allowing claims for educational malpractice. First, there is the lack of a satisfactory standard of care by which to evaluate an educator. Theories of education are not uniform, and different but acceptable scientific methods of academic training [make] it unfeasible to formulate a standard by which to judge the conduct of those delivering the services. Second, inherent uncertainties exist in this type of case about the cause and nature of damages. Factors such as the student's attitude, motivation, temperament, past experience and home environment may all play an essential and immeasurable role in learning. Consequently, it may be a practical impossibility [to] prov[e] that the alleged malpractice of the teacher proximately caused the learning deficiency of the plaintiff student. A third reason for denying this cause of action is the potential it presents for a flood of litigation against schools. As the district court noted, education is a service rendered on an immensely greater scale than other professional services. The sheer number of claims that could arise if this cause of action were allowed might overburden schools. This consideration also suggests that a common-law tort remedy may not be the best way to deal with the problem of inadequate education. A final reason courts have cited for denying this cause of action is that it threatens to embroil the courts into overseeing the day-to-day operations of schools. This oversight might be particularly troubling in the university setting where it necessarily implicates considerations of academic freedom and autonomy.

. . . [T]he Illinois Supreme Court would refuse to recognize the tort of educational malpractice. We therefore affirm the district court's dismissal of Mr. Ross' claim based on that theory.

2. "Negligent Admission"

In his complaint, Mr. Ross alleges that Creighton owed him a duty "to recruit and enroll only those students reasonably qualified and able to academically perform at CREIGHTON." He then contends that Creighton breached this duty by admitting him, not informing him of how unprepared he was for studies there, and then not providing tutoring services or otherwise enabling him to receive a meaningful education. As a result, Mr. Ross underwent undue stress, which brought about, among other things, the incident at the motel.

We believe that Illinois would reject this claim for "negligent admission" for many of the same policy reasons that counsel against recognizing a claim for educational malpractice.

Source: Courtesy of Westlaw; reprinted with permission.

When Kevin Ross left Creighton University after four years he was reading at a second grade level. He could not read a menu or write a check after he left Creighton. At Creighton, Ross averaged 4.2 points a game for his career and had a 0.54 grade point average in his last semester at Creighton. Ross blamed the 1987 incident in which he threw furniture, a television set, and an air conditioner from the eighth floor of the Quality Inn in downtown Chicago, on the recurring nightmares he had of his experiences while at Creighton.[32] While admitting no liability, Creighton University settled the lawsuit with Ross for $30,000.[33]

Academic Advising

Most students at universities seek academic advising throughout their college careers to assist them in matriculating at an acceptable rate. Student-athletes rely on the advice of many individuals in the academic world, ranging from tutors and professors to advisors and coaches, to assist them in navigating the extensive rules and regulations dealing with eligibility and academics. To what extent should a student-athlete rely on this advice? What if the advice is incorrect, misleading, or

---

[32] Jack Curry, *Suing for Second Chance to Start Over*, The New York Times, January 30, 1990.

[33] *Kevin Ross Settles Suit with Creighton*, Jet Magazine, May 18, 1992, p. 48.

in some cases was even fraudulent? What is the responsibility of those charged with the duty of advising student-athletes to properly advise these students? What is the responsibility of the student-athlete? In Case 10-4, *Brown v. Compton Unified School District*, 80 Cal. Rptr. 2d 171 (Cal. Ct. App. 1998), a school counselor improperly advised a high school student-athlete about NCAA rules, which caused the student-athlete, James Brown Jr., to lose his college scholarship. He sued the school district, among other defendants, alleging that they were liable.

CASE 10-4 *Brown v. Compton Unified School District*

80 Cal. Rptr. 2d 171 (Cal. Ct. App. 1998)

EPSTEIN, J.

James Brown Jr. received a full basketball scholarship from the University of Southern California. That scholarship was revoked because Brown did not fulfill all of the eligibility requirements of the National Collegiate Athletic Association (NCAA). In response, Brown sued his high school counselor and the school district (collectively, respondents). The trial court granted respondents' motion for judgment on the pleadings. We affirm because both parties are immune from liability for negligent misrepresentations.

Factual and Procedural Summary

In a complaint, Brown alleged causes of action for negligence and breach of an oral contract against Compton Unified School District and Ms. Rae Bonner. According to the complaint, Brown enrolled in Manuel Dominguez High School as a senior with the "expressed purpose" of taking the required classes to satisfy the NCAA eligibility requirements and of participating in the Manuel Dominguez High School basketball program. The school is a part of the defendant school district. Ms. Bonner, Brown's counselor, advised him to enroll in a particular science course. The course did not meet the NCAA requirements. Failure to complete the required science class resulted in revocation of a basketball scholarship to the University of Southern California after Brown was enrolled at the University.

Brown further alleged that Compton Unified School District expressly and impliedly provided in pertinent part that his transfer to Manuel Dominguez High School and the playing of interscholastic men's basketball for said school would not jeopardize, compromise or threaten his ability to fulfill those high school educational prerequisites mandated by the NCAA for athletes to subsequently participate in its intercollegiate athletic program. According to the complaint, Brown transferred in reliance on those statements.

The complaint incorporates by reference a letter from the high school principal to the NCAA Academic Requirements Committee. The letter states that Brown's failure to take the required science class is "completely the result of misadvisement on the part of one of our school's academic counselors." . . . "Dominguez High School must assume responsibility for misadvising James Brown. It is true that our counselors are overworked and not experts in interpreting NCAA rules; however, this is a mistake that should not have been made. James simply followed the advise [sic] given to him by a school authority."

Finding no duty, the trial court granted respondents' motion for judgment on the pleadings. . . .

Discussion

. . . On appeal, Brown combines his actions for negligence and breach of contract. The critical allegation is that he lost an athletic scholarship to the University of Southern California because of the admitted mistake by Ms. Bonner and the high school. Brown argues that a special relationship existed between himself and the school district because the district induced him to transfer and assured him that the Manuel Dominguez High School would allow him to satisfy the NCAA requirements for athletic eligibility. Brown further contends that he relied on the promise he would be placed in courses that satisfy NCAA requirements. According to Brown, the relative ease of calculating damages militates in favor of imposing a duty. Finally, Brown argues that neither Ms. Bonner nor the school district is immune.

The issue of duty is close. Policy considerations preclude "an actionable 'duty of care' in persons and agencies who administer the academic phases of the public educational process. . . . To hold them to an actionable 'duty of care,' in the discharge of their academic functions, would expose them to the tort claims—real or imagined—of disaffected students and parents in countless numbers. They are already beset by social and financial problems which have gone to major litigation, but for which no permanent solution has yet appeared. The ultimate consequences, in terms of public time and money, would burden them—and society—beyond calculation." This strong policy consideration may outweigh the allegation that Brown undertook a change in circumstances in reliance on the school district. That question in turn raises an issue whether the school district was authorized to incur the obligation.

But even if a duty to Brown were assumed, both Ms. Bonner and the school district are immune from liability for misrepresentations. . . . Brown pled, in essence, that Ms. Bonner negligently misrepresented that the science class in which she counseled him to enroll would meet NCAA eligibility guidelines. As Brown put it in his argument opposing the motion for judgment on the pleadings: "The plaintiff timely filed a governmental tort claim against defendants which alleged they failed to properly counsel him as promised and negligently advised that the science class in issue would satisfy NCAA requirements." Under sections 822.2 and 818.8 both Ms. Bonner and Compton Unified School District are immune from that negligent misrepresentation. . . .

The judgment is affirmed.

Source: Courtesy of Westlaw; reprinted with permission.

Problem 10-1

Jake Lamont was recruited heavily by many large universities to play basketball. He chose University of Oklahoma because of its excellent basketball program and also because of its outstanding journalism school. Jake wants to be a sports writer after college. The coaches who recruited him promised to help him get an internship with a national newspaper if he came to OU to play basketball. After his freshman year, OU hired a new basketball coach, and Jake's playing time was reduced to less than five minutes per game. The new coach never attempted to get him any internships, and after Jake graduated from OU he could not find a job in his field for over a year. Does Jake have any basis for a lawsuit against the coach? Against the university?

Recruiting and the National Letter of Intent

The recruiting of student-athletes for college athletics is a big business. Top universities vie for star high school players in football, basketball, baseball, and ice hockey, as well as many other sports. Universities have a major financial stake in signing top prospects. A highly sought after prospect can bring prestige and generate revenue for the university and its athletic programs. Many publications tout the incoming freshman class for major universities in a variety of sports. High school student-athletes now even hold press conferences to announce where they will attend college.

The NCAA has extensive bylaws that regulate the recruiting of student-athletes, and publishes guidelines for coaches to assist them in the recruiting process.[34] There are numerous examples (too many to cite here) of alumni, boosters, and coaches who have placed pressure on student-athletes to join the athletic programs of their institutions. Numerous universities have been sanctioned by the NCAA for engaging in illegal recruiting. Star student-athletes from the high school ranks want to know where their competition is going to play their college sport to assist them in making a decision about where to sign.

---

[34] *See,* NCAA Division I Football Coaches Off-Campus Recruiting Guide, Effective August 1, 2009. Available at NCAA.org

The National Letter of Intent (NLI) is a binding agreement between a student-athlete and an institution in which the institution agrees to provide a student-athlete (who gains admission to the university and is eligible for financial aid) aid for one academic year in exchange for the student-athlete's agreement to attend the university for one academic year. The NLI is a voluntary program for both student-athletes and institutions. No student-athlete or parent is required to sign the National Letter of Intent. The NCAA eligibility center manages the daily operations of the NLI program while the Collegiate Commissioners Association provides governance oversight of the program. The program has over 600 participating institutions. All universities that participate in the NLI program agree not to recruit a student-athlete once he or she has signed an NLI with another college or university. The NLI must be accompanied by an institutional financial aid agreement. If the student-athlete fails to enroll at the institution for a full academic year, he or she may be subject to penalties, which could include a loss of eligibility. The NLI meets the basic criteria for an enforceable contract: offer, acceptance, and consideration.[35]

In Case 10-5, *Fortay v. University of Miami*, 1994 WL 62319 (D.N.J. 1994), a recruit sued multiple defendants, alleging a variety of causes of actions, when he became disenchanted with the University of Miami's football program and its recruiting process. The plaintiff alleged that the University of Miami and its employees made promises to him during the recruiting process and that it failed to keep its promise.[36] The case was eventually settled prior to a trial.

📖 CASE 10-5   *Fortay v. University of Miami*

1994 WL 62319 (D.N.J. 1994)

WOLIN, District Judge.

A. The Parties

1. Plaintiff

. . . In February, 1989, Fortay, the starting quarterback at East Brunswick High School, and consensus high school All-American, chose to accept a scholarship from the University of Miami to study and to play football. Fortay was enrolled as student-athlete at the university from the fall of 1989 until August 1991, when he transferred to Rutgers University in New Jersey ("Rutgers"). . . .

2. Defendants

Defendant University of Miami ("UM"), is a private university with a faculty of approximately 1700 and with an enrollment in excess of 13,700 students. . . .

---

[35] *See*, Michael J. Cozzillio, *The Athletic Scholarship and the College National Letter of Intent: A Contract by Any Other Name*, Wayne law review, 1989.

[36] Rick Reilly, *See You in Court, SI Vault, August 30, 1993.*

B. Statement of Facts

. . . .

1. Recruitment and Signing by UM

In the spring of 1988, Fortay's junior year of high school, most of the major college football teams began to initiate recruiting contacts with Fortay.

Over the course of 1988, Fortay would receive numerous letters from UM personnel touting UM's (1) elite football program and its penchant for developing NFL-quality quarterbacks, (2) academic requirements for scholarship athletes, (3) health and training facilities, and (4) academic and vocational resources.

During the first weekend of December, 1988, Fortay visited UM to meet the staff and view the school. On or about December 20, 1988, Fortay made a verbal commitment to attend UM, which the UM football staff acknowledged by mailgram and letter.

Prior to making the verbal commitment, Fortay received visits at home in New Jersey (1) on two occasions by Dave Campo ("Campo"), defensive backfield coach for UM's football team, and (2) on one occasion, collectively, by Campo, Jimmy Johnson ("Coach Johnson"), UM's head football coach, Gary Stevens ("Stevens"), and Art Kehoe ("Kehoe"). During the group visit to the Fortay home, certain promises were made to Fortay, the extent and subject of which are in dispute. FN1.

> FN1: According to the Fortays, during this meeting with Coach Johnson and the others, Fortay was told that if he made a verbal commitment to Miami, recruitment of other quarterbacks in his class would cease. According to Stevens, Campo and Kehoe, none of the UM personnel guaranteed Fortay the starting quarterback position and a career in the NFL, but merely promised a scholarship, the opportunity to compete for the starting job early in his career and the chance to travel with the team.

On February 8, 1989, Fortay and his father, Peter Fortay, met with Stevens at East Brunswick High School in New Jersey and signed a Letter of Intent formalizing Fortay's decision to enroll at UM in exchange for an athletic scholarship. Fortay made the formal commitment to UM based on the belief that he would be the starting quarterback at UM and the team would be built around him.

2. The Coaching Change

In February 1989, just after Fortay had signed the Letter of Intent, Coach Johnson announced that he was leaving UM for the head coaching

job with the NFL's Dallas Cowboys. Following Coach Johnson's announcement, Fortay received, at home, letters from Coach Johnson and defendant Jankovich and nearly daily phone calls from defendant Scott,
designed mostly to reassure Fortay about his decision to enroll at UM
and to apprise him of the status of the coaching staff.

Prior to March 8, 1988, UM announced the hiring of Coach Erickson to
replace Coach Johnson at the helm of the UM football program. Following UM's announcement, Coach Erickson contacted Fortay by phone and by
letter to assure him that the commitments, goals and play system of
Coach Johnson's regime would not be changed.

Unhappy with this change in circumstances, Fortay and his father trav-
elled to Miami to procure a release from the Letter of Intent. UM
refused to release Fortay from the Letter of Intent.

In April 1989, Fortay decided to honor the Letter of Intent rather
than to enroll elsewhere and lose two years of eligibility.

3. Fortay at UM: A Football Dream Gone Bust

During his first collegiate season, Fortay was "red-shirted," meaning
that he was not on the active roster, but would be able to practice
and learn the offense without losing a year of eligibility. However,
Fortay lost his red-shirt status, and a year of eligibility, after
UM's starting quarterback suffered an injury and Fortay played in two
regular season games. Contrary to Erickson's assurances, he received
no more playing time that season beyond his appearances in the two
games.

During spring practices in 1990, Fortay was competing with Gino Torretta for the back-up position. Apparently, the competition for the
spot was intense. Fortay became dissatisfied after sensing that Coach
Erickson favored Torretta. Fueled by his son's concerns, Peter Fortay
flew to Miami to discuss the situation with Coach Erickson, who again
made assurances as to Fortay's future. Subsequently, to save Fortay's
eligibility, Coach Erickson red-shirted Fortay for the 1990 season.

Ultimately, Torretta was named UM's starting quarterback for the 1991
season, despite the fact that Fortay outperformed Torretta in spring
and fall practices. Five days later, Fortay packed his bags and transferred to Rutgers, losing a year of eligibility in the process under
NCAA regulations.

C. The Complaint

Based on the foregoing allegations and averments, Fortay filed a
twenty-five count complaint in search of actual, compensatory and
punitive damages for the broken promises of stardom at UM and in the

NFL and the injury, embarrassment and humiliation suffered as a result of the Pell Grant scandal.

In Count One, Fortay asserts UM and the individual defendants negligently misrepresented that he would become UM's starting quarterback, luring him to sign with and enroll at UM.

Count Four contains a request for punitive damages and alleges that defendants, having negligently "lured and courted" Fortay into believing that UM football would lead him to stardom in the NFL, "wantonly and willfully" disregarded Fortay's quarterbacking skills in selecting Torretta for the starting quarterback position in 1991.

Counts Six through Eight allege that prior to December 21, 1988, UM and Fortay entered into a contract under which Fortay would attend UM. Fortay asserts that UM, its athletic department and staff, and the individual defendants breached their contractual duties to plaintiff by violating federal and NCAA regulations and failing to provide Fortay the promised education and athletic training.

Based upon the alleged contract, Count Nine asserts that defendants breached the implied covenant of good faith and fair dealing by failing to supervise Fortay's athletic career and education. . . .

Count Fourteen alleges that defendants intentionally, recklessly and negligently inflicted upon Fortay severe emotional distress through their allegedly outrageous conduct.

. . . Counts Twenty and Twenty-One allege that defendants negligently breached the duties owed to Fortay under the Letter of Intent.

Count Twenty-Two alleges that UM violated NCAA regulations governing a member institution's responsibility for the conduct of its coaching staff.

Source: Courtesy of Westlaw; reprinted with permission.

What evidence does Fortay need to prevail in his lawsuit? Do you agree with Fortay's position or are those "just the breaks"?

Problem 10-2

Lawrence Jacobs, a quarterback, is an All-State football player. To induce him to select the University of Nebraska, the head coach at Nebraska tells him the team and the offense will be centered around him and that the offense will pass the ball 60% of the offensive plays. The coach tells him he is going to be one of the greatest quarterbacks in school history. Jacobs signs a national letter of intent to play at Nebraska. Ten days after he signs the letter of intent, the coach leaves to take the head coaching job at another university. Can Jacobs be released from his letter of intent? Does he have a cause of action against the university or the coach for breach of contract? What is his legal recourse against the university? Against the coach?

Scholarships

Athletic scholarships are available to men and women at the collegiate level in a variety of sports, including football, baseball, golf, bowling, tennis, soccer, swimming and diving, fencing, rowing, basketball, volleyball, track and field, rodeo, lacrosse, water polo, and wrestling. The NCAA delineates the financial limits of scholarships and sets forth criteria that must be met for a scholarship athlete to be eligible to participate. By accepting a scholarship, the student-athlete enters into a relationship with the university whereby the student agrees to play a particular sport for the university, which in turn guarantees the scholarship award to the athlete. A scholarship might include tuition, room and board, and books. The question of whether a student-athlete is considered an employee of the school has been the subject of much debate,[37] as has the issue of whether student-athletes should be paid.[38]

A scholarship is a contract that requires the student-athlete meet certain obligations which include: attending games and practice, following the rules of the NCAA as well as conference and university rules, and maintaining certain academic standards. If the student-athlete fails to fulfill the requirements of the scholarship, then the university may revoke it. It has been argued that the athletic scholarship is an unconscionable contract and unfair to the student athlete.[39]

Courts have generally ruled that student-athletes and universities enter into a contractual relationship when they enter into a scholarship agreement:

> It should be noted that the relationship between a college athlete who accepts an athletic scholarship and the college which awards such an athletic scholarship is contractual in nature. The college athlete agrees to participate in a sport at the college, and the college in return agrees to give assistance to the athlete. The athlete also agrees to be bound by the rules and regulations adopted by the college concerning the financial assistance. Most of these rules and regulations are promulgated by athletic associations whose membership is composed of the individual colleges. The individual athlete has no voice or participation in the formulation or interpretation of these rules and regulations governing his scholarship, even though these materially control his conduct on and off the field. Thus in some circumstances the college athlete may be placed in an unequal bargaining position.[40]

To state a valid claim against a university for breach of contract based on a scholarship, the student-athlete "must point to a specific contract provision that [the university] failed to honor."[41] Prior to the signing of the letter of intent, the NCAA requires the university offering the scholarship to provide the student-athlete with a statement listing the terms and conditions of the scholarship, its amount, and the duration of the scholarship.

---

[37] *See* Robert N. Davis, *The Courts and Athletic Scholarships*, 67 N.D. L. Rev. 163 (1991); C. Peter Goplerud III, *Pay for Play for College Athletes: Now, More Than Ever*, 38 S. Tex. L. Rev. 1081 (1997).

[38] *See* Eric Sobocinski, *College Athletes: What Is Fair Compensation?*, 7 Marq. Sports L. J. 257 (1996).

[39] *See* Sean M. Hanlon, *Athletic Scholarships as Unconscionable Contracts of Adhesion. Has the NCAA Fouled Out?*, 13 Sports Law J. 41 (2006); Daniel Nestel, *Athletics: An Imbalance of Power Between the University and the Student Athlete*, 53 Ohio St. L. J. 1401 (1992).

[40] Gulf South Conference v. Boyd, 369 So.2d 553, 558 (Ala. 1979).

[41] Ross v. Creighton University, 957 F.2d 410, 416 (7th Cir. 1992).

Roan Sterling was a student at the University of Maine and also a member of its football team. He was charged with assault and disorderly conduct under Maine state law after he had assaulted a teammate during an on-campus altercation. After a hearing, he was found to have violated the University of Maine's Student Conduct Code. The football coach withdrew a portion of his scholarship based on his violation of the student conduct code. The coach sent a letter to Sterling stating in part: "It has been my policy to cancel room-and-board privileges for our student athletes when they are unable to conduct themselves properly on campus. We will not supply scholarship money to a student athlete who cannot live under the disciplinary code of the University of Maine and its football program."[42]

The State of Maine filed criminal charges against Sterling. He in turn filed a motion to dismiss the criminal complaint on the basis that the withdrawal of his scholarship had placed him in "jeopardy" and furthermore that "the prosecution of the present complaint would place him twice in jeopardy for the same offense in violation of the State and Federal Constitution."[43] The trial court granted his motion, finding that the partial revocation of the scholarship "could only be characterized as penal," and dismissed the case.[44] The state subsequently appealed the case, arguing that the withdrawal of the scholarship did not constitute punishment because it "effectuated the purposes of the student disciplinary code and protected the integrity of the public educational system."[45] In reversing the lower court's opinion, the court stated:

> In the instant case, it cannot be disputed that Sterling, a student at a state-supported university, has no absolute right to obtain or retain an athletic scholarship. Rather, the scholarship is a privilege to which certain rights and responsibilities attach and which may be granted or withheld for valid reasons involving safeguarding the integrity of the institution. It is essential to the integrity of a university that students at that university observe its code of conduct. We find no merit in Sterling's contention that because he "remained a student and a participant in the football program" the withdrawal of a portion of his athletic scholarship cannot be ascribed a remedial purpose to protect the integrity of the University. The State need not use precise formulas as it pursues remedial sanctions. The withdrawal of a portion of Sterling's athletic scholarship was remedial for the purpose of protecting the integrity of the University and its athletic programs. Accordingly, we determine the trial court erred in concluding that the partial revocation of Sterling's athletic scholarship was "punishment" for the purposes of the double jeopardy analysis.[46]

In Case 10-6, *Taylor v. Wake Forest University*, 191 S.E.2d 379 (N.C. Ct. App. 1972), a student-athlete had his scholarship terminated. What obligations did the student-athlete fail to fulfill under the scholarship?

---

[42] State v. Sterling, 685 A.2d 432, 433 (Me. 1996).

[43] *Id*. at 433.

[44] *Id*.

[45] *Id*. at 433.

[46] *Id*. at 434 (citation omitted).

📖 CASE 10-6 *Taylor v. Wake Forest University*

191 S.E.2d 379 (N.C. Ct. App. 1972)

This action was instituted for the recovery of educational expenses incurred by George J. Taylor, father, and Gregg F. Taylor, son, after alleged wrongful termination of an athletic scholarship issued to Gregg F. Taylor by Wake Forest University.

As early as December 1965, football coaches at Wake Forest were in communication with Gregg Taylor soliciting his enrollment at Wake Forest. This interest was engendered by the football playing ability of Gregg Taylor. Not only was Wake Forest interested in him, but other colleges and universities were likewise showing an interest. As a result of this interest and negotiations, Gregg Taylor and his father, George Taylor, on 27 February 1967, submitted an application entitled, 'Atlantic Coast Conference Application For A Football Grant-In-Aid Or A Scholarship.'

This application was accepted by Wake Forest on 24 May 1967. It provided in part:

> This Grant, if awarded, will be for 4 years provided I conduct myself in accordance with the rules of the Conference, the NCAA, and the Institution. I agree to maintain eligibility for intercollegiate athletics under both Conference and Institutional rules. Training rules for intercollegiate athletics are considered rules of the Institution, and I agree to abide by them.
>
> If injured while participating in athletics supervised by a member of the coaching staff, the Grant or Scholarship will be honored; and the medical expenses will be paid by the Athletic Department.
>
> This grant, when approved, is awarded for academic and athletic achievement and is not to be interpreted as employment in any manner whatsoever.

At the time of the execution of the agreement between the Taylors and Wake Forest, some of the rules of the NCAA prohibited:

(a) Gradation or cancellation of institutional aid during the period of its award on the basis of a student-athlete's prowess or his contribution to a team's success.

(b) Gradation or cancellation of institutional aid during the period of its award because of an injury which prevents the recipient from participating in athletics.

    (c) Gradation or cancellation of institutional aid during the period of its award for any other athletic reason, except that such aid may be gradated or cancelled if the recipient (1) voluntarily renders himself ineligible for intercollegiate competition, or (2) fraudulently misrepresents any information on his application, letter-of-intent or tender, or (3) engages in serious misconduct warranting substantial disciplinary penalty.

    Any such gradation or cancellation of aid is permissible only if (1) such action is taken by the regular disciplinary and/or scholarship awards authorities of the institution, (2) the student has had an opportunity for a hearing, and (3) the action is based on institutional policy applicable to the general student body.

At the time the contract was entered into, Wake Forest did not have a written Grant-In-Aid policy. This policy was not put in writing until January 1969. One of the written policy provisions was to the effect that financial aid could be terminated for '(r)efusal to attend practice sessions or scheduled work-out that are a part of the athletic program or to act in such a manner as to disrupt these sessions.' The Wake Forest Athletic Director set out in an affidavit: "(T)he policy of requiring student athletes to regularly attend practice sessions was in effect at the defendant University when the first scholarship was granted more than 30 years ago."

In compliance with the contract entered into, Gregg Taylor enrolled and became a student at Wake Forest at the beginning of the Fall Session 1967. He participated in the football program during the Fall of 1967.

At the end of that semester, his grade average was 1.0 out of a possible 4.0. Wake Forest required a 1.35 grade average after freshman year, a 1.65 grade average after sophomore year, and a 1.85 grade average after junior year. The 1.0 grade average received by Gregg Taylor for the first semester of his freshman year in the Fall of 1967 was thus below the grade average required by Wake Forest. Gregg Taylor notified the football coach on 6 February 1968 that he would not participate in regular practice sessions of the football team during the Spring of 1968 until his grades had improved. For the second semester of his freshman year, which was the Spring of 1968, Gregg Taylor obtained a 1.9 grade average. This brought his grade average above what Wake Forest required even after junior year. Despite this improvement in his grade average, Gregg Taylor decided that he would not further participate in the football program, and in the fall of his sophomore year, which was the Fall of 1968, Gregg Taylor attained a 2.4 grade average. Gregg Taylor continued in his refusal to participate in the football program.

Wake Forest notified Gregg Taylor on or about 1 May 1969 that a hearing would be held on 14 May 1969 before the Faculty Athletic Committee as to whether his scholarship should be terminated. At this hearing Gregg Taylor was notified that the Faculty Athletic Committee would recommend to the Scholarship Committee that his scholarship be terminated because of his failure to participate in the football program at Wake Forest. Thereafter, the Scholarship Committee of Wake Forest accepted the recommendation of the Faculty Athletic Committee, and on 10 July 1969, the Scholarship Committee notified Gregg Taylor that his scholarship had been terminated as of the end of the 1968–1969 academic year, which was the end of Gregg Taylor's sophomore year.

Gregg Taylor continued to attend Wake Forest during the 1969–1970 academic year, which was his junior year, and likewise, the academic year of 1970–1971, which was his senior year; and he received an undergraduate degree from Wake Forest in June 1971.

As a result of the termination of the scholarship, expenses in the amount of $5500 were incurred during those two academic years. It is for this sum of $5500 that this action was instituted.

The defendant Wake Forest moved for summary judgment pursuant to Rule 56 of the Rules of Civil Procedure on the ground that there was no genuine issue as to any material fact and that the defendant was entitled to judgment as a matter of law. This motion was allowed, and the plaintiffs appealed. . . .

CAMPBELL, Judge.

Plaintiffs contend that there was a genuine issue as to a material fact and that a jury should determine whether Gregg Taylor acted reasonably and in good faith in refusing to participate in the football program at Wake Forest when such participation interfered with reasonable academic progress.

The plaintiffs' position depends upon a construction of the contractual agreement between plaintiffs and Wake Forest. As stated in the affidavit of George J. Taylor, the position of the plaintiffs is that it was orally agreed between plaintiffs and the representative of Wake Forest that: "(I)n the event of any conflict between educational achievement and athletic involvement, participation in athletic activities could be limited or eliminated to the extent necessary to assure reasonable academic progress." And plaintiffs were to be the judge as to what 'reasonable academic progress' constituted.

We do not agree with the position taken by plaintiffs. The scholarship application filed by Gregg Taylor provided:". . . I agree to maintain eligibility for intercollegiate athletics under both Conference and Institutional rules. Training rules for intercollegiate athletics are considered rules of the Institution, and I agree to abide by them."

Both Gregg Taylor and his father knew that the application was for 'Football Grant-In-Aid Or A Scholarship,' and that the scholarship was 'awarded for academic and athletic achievement.' It would be a strained construction of the contract that would enable the plaintiffs to determine the 'reasonable academic progress' of Gregg Taylor. Gregg Taylor, in consideration of the scholarship award, agreed to maintain his athletic eligibility and this meant both physically and scholastically. As long as his grade average equaled or exceeded the requirements of Wake Forest, he was maintaining his scholastic eligibility for athletics. Participation in and attendance at practice were required to maintain his physical eligibility. When he refused to do so in the absence of any injury or excuse other than to devote more time to studies, he was not complying with his contractual obligations.

The record disclosed that Wake Forest fully complied with its agreement and that Gregg Taylor failed to do so. There was no 'genuine issue as to any material fact' and summary judgment was proper.

Source: Courtesy of Westlaw; reprinted with permission.

Problem 10-3

Steven Sims is a student-athlete at the University of Nevada. He is an excellent student and has a 3.94 grade point average (GPA) while attending the university as a pre-med student. He is also an All-Conference performer as a punter. He is very serious about being a physician and following in his mother's footsteps. He has no ambition to play professional football. During the season of his senior year, he is studying for the entrance exam to medical school, which is taking a majority of his time. He continues his studies in the fall as well as playing football.

The team has a new coach for Steven's senior year. Steven informs the coach that he needs to arrive 45 minutes late for all practices because he is taking a course that helps him prepare for the medical school entrance exam. The coach does not like the idea but grants him permission. After the first two games of the season, Steven is punting poorly, so the coach tells him he can no longer be 45 minutes late to practice. Steven offers to stay 45 minutes after practice, but the coach says no, citing the need for all players to practice together. Steven fails to appear on time for the next practice; when he shows up 45 minutes late, the coach tells him to leave. The next day Steven receives an email from the coach that says: "It is required that you appear at all practices on time. The university has provided you with a scholarship and you must do your part to hold up your end of the bargain. Your punting has suffered as a result of your lack of practice and you are hurting the team's chance to win games. I hope you will take to heart this advice and do the right thing. To retain your scholarship status you must practice as requested. I understand your desire to be a doctor but your obligations right now lie with your school and teammates."

What are the player's legal obligations? Can the school revoke his scholarship? What legal advice would you give this student-athlete?

ELIGIBILITY AND NCAA RULES

Numerous NCAA bylaws govern the complicated relationship involving the NCAA, the student-athlete, and the university. It is basic that student-athletes must be eligible to participate before they can play a sport at a member institution. The cases in this section deal with the interpretation of specific NCAA bylaws dealing with eligibility issues. In each case a student-athlete challenged a particular NCAA bylaw and its application to his or her specific situation. There is voluminous material discussing the NCAA bylaws and their application to the student-athlete, but the cases presented in this section provide an overview of the type of bylaws dealing with eligibility that have been challenged by student-athletes and the results of those challenges.

Participation: Right or Privilege?

Does a collegiate student-athlete have a protected liberty interest in his or her athletic reputation? A few courts have held that a collegiate athlete does have a constitutionally protected property right to participate in college athletics.[47] However, other cases have held that participation in college athletics is not a constitutionally protected interest.[48] Most courts have held that no property right exists to participate at the interscholastic level.[49]

In *National Collegiate Athletic Ass'n v. Yeo*, 114 S.W.3d 584 (Tex. App. 2003), the court determined that the plaintiff had a constitutionally protected property interest in her athletic career as a swimmer. The plaintiff was a former Olympian from Singapore who transferred from the University of California–Berkeley to the University of Texas. The court found that the University of Texas, as a state actor, had a duty to protect her liberty interest and failed to do so.

What student-athletes are entitled to claim a protected property interest? Would they have to be a drafted player in a major sport or an Olympic medal winner? For a similar case holding, see *Hall v. University of Minnesota*, 530 F. Supp. 104 (D. Minn. 1982), where the court found a limited property right for a student-athlete who was an outstanding basketball player. The court indicated the plaintiff's interest as "the plaintiff's ability to obtain a 'no cut' contract with the National Basketball Association."[50]

Amateur Rules

The NCAA has many policies relating to the amateur status of a student-athlete. NCAA bylaws deal with issues relating to the use of agents, outside employment for student-athletes, promotional activities, and involvement with professional teams. The NCAA is an amateur sports association and clearly has a vested interest in preserving amateurism. If a student-athlete is being compensated for his or her services, that individual can no longer be deemed an amateur under NCAA rules. NCAA bylaws allow student-athletes to be an amateur in one sport but a professional in another, however.

---

[47] *See* Hall v. University of Minnesota, 530 F. Supp. 104 (D.Minn. 1982); Behagen v. Intercollegiate Conference of Faculty Representatives, 346 *F. Supp. 602* (D.C.Minn. 1972).

[48] *Colorado Seminary (University of Denver) v. NCAA*, 570 F.2d 320, 321 (10th Cir. 1978); Parisch v. NCAA, 506 F.2d 1208, 1034 (5th Cir. 1975).

[49] Indiana High School Athletic Ass'n v. Carlberg, 694 N.E.2d 222 (Ind. 1998); Spring Branch I.S.D. v. Stamos, 695 S.W.2d 556, 560, 27 Ed. Law Rep. 605 (Tex. 1985).

[50] *Hall*, 530 F. Supp. at 108.

The following NCAA bylaws govern eligibility for student-athletes dealing with professional teams.

12.1.3 Amateur Status if Professional in Another Sport. A professional athlete in one sport may represent a member institution in a different sport. However, the student-athlete cannot receive institutional financial assistance in the second sport.

12.2 Involvement with Professional Teams

12.2.1 Tryouts.

12.2.1.1 Tryout Before Enrollment. A student-athlete remains eligible in a sport even though, prior to enrollment in a collegiate institution, the student-athlete may have tried out with a professional athletics team in a sport or received not more than one expense-paid visit from each professional team (or a combine including that team), provided such a visit did not exceed 48 hours and any payment or compensation in connection with the visit was not in excess of actual and necessary expenses. The 48-hour tryout period begins at the time the individual arrives at the tryout location. At the completion of the 48-hour period, the individual must depart the location of the tryout immediately in order to receive return transportation expenses. A tryout may extend beyond 48 hours if the individual self-finances additional expenses, including return transportation. A self-financed tryout may be for any length of time.

. . . .

12.2.1.2 Tryout After Enrollment. After initial full-time collegiate enrollment, an individual who has eligibility remaining may try out with a professional athletics team (or participate in a combine including that team) at any time, provided the individual does not miss class. The individual may receive actual and necessary expenses in conjunction with one 48-hour tryout per professional team (or a combine including that team). The 48-hour tryout period shall begin at the time the individual arrives at the tryout location. At the completion of the 48-hour period, the individual must depart the location of the tryout immediately in order to receive return transportation expenses. A tryout may extend beyond 48 hours if the individual self-finances additional expenses, including return transportation. A self-financed tryout may be for any length of time, provided the individual does not miss class.

Source: National Collegiate Athletic Association, *2009–2010 NCAA Division I Manual* (2009). © National Collegiate Athletic Association. 2008–2010. All rights reserved.

Academic Eligibility

NCAA student-athletes are honored not only for their athletic achievements but also for their work in the classroom. The College Sports Information Directors of America selects academic All-American teams in twelve sports.[51] There is also an Academic All-American Hall of Fame. Some notable members are as follows:[52]

- Byron White, Colorado 1938, U.S. Supreme Court Justice
- Bill Bradley, Princeton 1965, U.S. senator
- Tom McMillen, Maryland 1974, U.S. senator
- John Wooden, Purdue 1932, coach and author

The NCAA desires to sustain academic integrity as well as maintain excellent sports programs. The association has specific academic rules dealing with the initial eligibility requirements for playing sports, and much litigation has ensued over these requirements. In *Cureton v. National Collegiate Athletic Ass'n*, 198 F.3d 107 (3rd Cir. 1999), the plaintiffs sued the NCAA under Title VI of the Civil Rights Act of 1964, alleging that NCAA Proposition 16 unfairly discriminated against them on the basis of race. Proposition 16 was initiated by the NCAA in an attempt to improve the graduation rates of athletes. A high school student's GPA and SAT or ACT scores were combined on a sliding scale, which allowed students with a lower test score but who had a higher GPA to qualify. Proposition 16 replaced Proposal 48, which required a minimum GPA of 2.0 and an SAT score of 700. Furthermore, Proposition 16 placed a greater emphasis on the standard test score than Proposal 48 had. After considering several proposals, the NCAA had settled on Proposition 16, believing it was the best tool to raise the graduation rates of athletes. In *Cureton*, the plaintiffs claimed that the NCAA had engaged in intentional discrimination based on a disparate impact theory. The district court found that Proposition 16 had a disparate impact on African American athletes and permanently enjoined the NCAA from enforcing the rule. The NCAA appealed, and the lower court's decision was reversed by the Third Circuit.[53]

The following NCAA bylaws govern the initial academic eligibility requirements for student-athletes entering the NCAA.

14.3 Freshman Academic Requirements

14.3.1 Eligibility for Financial Aid, Practice and Competition. A student-athlete who enrolls in a member institution as an entering freshman with no previous full-time college attendance shall meet the following academic requirements, as certified by an initial-eligibility clearinghouse approved by the Executive Committee, and any applicable institutional and conference regulations, to be considered a qualifier

---

[51] College Sports Information Directors of America, www.cosida.com.

[52] *Id.*

[53] For a further review, see Eli Oates, Cureton v. NCAA: *The Recognition of Proposition 16's Misplaced Use of Standardized Tests in the Context of Collegiate Athletics as a Barrier to Educational Opportunity for Minorities*, 35 WAKE FOREST L. REV. 445 (2000). *Also see* Pryor v. National Collegiate Athletic Ass'n, 288 F.3d 548 (3rd Cir. 2002).

and thus be eligible for financial aid, practice and competition during the first academic year in residence. . . .

14.3.1.1 Qualifier. A qualifier is defined as one who is a high-school graduate and who presented the following academic qualifications:

(a) A minimum cumulative grade-point average as specified in Bylaw 14.3.1.1.1 (based on a maximum 4.000) in a successfully completed core curriculum of at least 14 academic courses per Bylaw 14.3.1.2, including the following:

English	4 years
Mathematics (two years of mathematics courses at the level of Algebra I or higher)	2 years
Natural or physical science (including at least one laboratory course if offered by the high school) (Computer science courses containing significant programming elements that meet graduation requirements in the area of natural or physical science also may be accepted.)	2 years
Additional courses in English, mathematics, or natural or physical science	1 year
Social science	2 years
Additional academic courses [in any of the above areas or foreign language, computer science, philosophy or nondoctrinal religion (e.g., comparative religion) courses]	3 years

. . . .

(b) A minimum combined score on the SAT verbal and math sections or a minimum sum score on the ACT as specified in Bylaw 14.3.1.1.1.

14.3.1.1.1 Initial-Eligibility Index. Freshmen may establish eligibility using the following eligibility index:

Core GPA	SAT	Sum ACT
3.550 & above	400	37
3.525	410	38
3.500	420	39
3.475	430	40
3.450	440	41

3.425	450	41
3.400	460	42
3.375	470	42
3.350	480	43
3.325	490	44
3.300	500	44
3.275	510	45
3.250	520	46
3.225	530	46
3.200	540	47
3.175	550	47
3.150	560	48
3.125	570	49
3.100	580	49
3.075	590	50
3.050	600	50
3.025	610	51
3.000	620	52
2.975	630	52
2.950	640	53
2.925	650	53
2.900	660	54
2.87	670	55
2.850	680	56
2.825	690	56
2.800	700	57
2.775	710	58
2.750	720	59
2.725	730	59
2.700	730	60
2.675	740-750	61

2.650	760	62
2.625	770	63
2.600	780	64
2.575	790	65
2.550	800	66
2.525	810	67
2.500	820	68
2.475	830	69
2.450	840–850	70
2.425	860	70
2.400	860	71
2.375	870	72
2.350	880	73
2.325	890	74
2.300	900	75
2.275	910	76
2.250	920	77
2.225	930	78
2.200	940	79
2.175	950	80
2.150	960	80
2.125	960	81
2.100	970	82
2.075	980	83
2.050	990	84
2.025	1000	85
2.000	1010	86

. . . .

14.3.1.2 Core-Curriculum Requirements. For purposes of meeting the core-curriculum requirement to establish eligibility at a member institution, a "core course" must meet all the following criteria:

(a) A course must be a recognized academic course and qualify for high-school graduation credit in one or a combination of the following areas: English, mathematics, natural/physical science, social science, foreign language or nondoctrinal religion/philosophy;

(b) A course must be considered college preparatory by the high school . . .;

(c) A mathematics course must be at the level of Algebra I or a higher level mathematics course;

(d) A course must be taught by a qualified instructor as defined by the appropriate academic authority . . .; and

(e) A course must be taught at or above the high school's regular academic level (i.e., remedial, special education or compensatory courses shall not be considered core courses). . . .

Source: National Collegiate Athletic Association, *2008–2010 NCAA Division I Manual* 146–50 (2008). © National Collegiate Athletic Association. 2008–2010. All rights reserved.

The student-athlete must complete certain core courses to be a "qualifier" under NCAA guidelines. Student-athletes and advisors must be careful to ensure that a student-athlete is taking the proper courses for credit. In Case 10-7, *Hall v. National Collegiate Athletic Ass'n*, 985 F. Supp. 782 (N.D. Ill. 1997), a student and his mother sued a university and the NCAA after the student, Reggie Hall, was declared ineligible and lost his scholarship for his freshman year. The lawsuit concerned four courses he took while enrolled at a private university: The four courses were: Microsoft Office, Microsoft Works, Scripture, and Ethics and Morality. The case explores the details of each course and whether or not those courses were acceptable to the NCAA to make Hall a "qualifier" under NCAA rules.

📖 CASE 10-7 *Hall v. National Collegiate Athletic Ass'n*

985 F. Supp. 782 (N.D. Ill. 1997)

KEYS, United States Magistrate Judge.

Reginale Hall ("Reggie") is a 6'7" tall, eighteen year old African-American who excels at basketball, and aspires to play professionally some day. Reggie graduated from Providence St. Mel High School ("St. Mel" on June 1, 1997. St. Mel is a private, Catholic high school with a student body comprised entirely of African-Americans. Reggie was highly recruited nationally by a number of colleges and universities, including Bradley University ("Bradley") in Peoria. He is currently a freshman at Bradley.

. . . .

II. The Dispute

The matter at bar involves, for the most part, a dispute over four courses that Reggie took while enrolled at St. Mel. The inclusion or exclusion of the four courses—Microsoft Office, Microsoft Works, Scripture, and Ethics/Morality—is critical to the Court's analysis of the propriety of the NCAA's ultimate determination that Reggie is ineligible to play Division I basketball this year.

III. NCAA Eligibility Requirements

Pursuant to the bylaws, the NCAA has established minimum academic eligibility requirements that a new college student must fulfill in order to attain the status of "qualifier." As a "qualifier" a student is eligible to practice with intercollegiate teams, compete in intercollegiate events, and receive financial aid or scholarships. NCAA members are prohibited from permitting "nonqualified" students—those who fail to attain either aforementioned status—to practice with the intercollegiate teams, to compete in intercollegiate events, or to receive financial aid (other than purely need based).

To be a "qualifier," NCAA eligibility requirements for Division I competition mandate that the student have taken at least thirteen high school "core courses" and that the student have achieved a specified minimum grade point average ("GPA") in those "core courses," as well as a specified minimum score on either the Scholastic Aptitude Test ("SAT") or American College Testing Program ("ACT"). Those specified GPA and standardized test minimums are determined on a sliding scale basis; the higher the test score, the lower the required core GPA. If a student has more than thirteen "core courses," the core GPA is computed from the thirteen highest grades.

IV. "Core Courses"

The NCAA must approve of any class claimed by a high school to be a "core course." The NCAA generally defines "core courses" as recognized academic courses (as opposed to vocational or personal-service courses) offering fundamental instructional components in specified areas of study. At least 75% of the instructional content of such a course must be in one or more of the required areas of study, set forth in the NCAA bylaws, like English, mathematics, natural science, and social science. In addition to these areas of study, a student must also take "additional core courses" in at least one of the following subjects: foreign language, computer science, philosophy, or comparative religion.

In order to qualify as core courses, religion classes must be non-doctrinal. St. Mel's Ethics/Morality class syllabus, however, was entitled "Growing in Christian Morality." Course work included prayer, chapel visits, journal/reflection, and study of the Christian vision of morality.

Reggie's guidance counselor at St. Mel, Art Murnan, had serious doubts about whether the Scripture class "would get through or not." The textbook for that course was The New American Bible, with the New Catholic translation. The textbook's table of contents included an introduction to the Catholic Study Edition, a history of how the Bible came about, the purpose of the Bible, how to study the Bible, a list of the Catholic Popes, suggested readings for the liturgical year, and Sunday readings of holy scripture.

As to the two Microsoft computer courses at issue, it was Mr. Murnan's understanding that, as long as a computer class went beyond keyboarding and word processing, it qualified as a core course. However, the NCAA Initial-Eligibility Clearinghouse ("Clearinghouse"), which is an independent contractor with the NCAA, and not a party to this lawsuit, stated that, for a computer science course to count as an "additional core course," "at least 75 percent of the instruction in the course must go beyond keyboarding and word processing *and* must be in areas such as the development and implementation of electronic spreadsheets, electronics networking, database management and computer programming."

According to the Microsoft Office course syllabus, one of the goals of the class was "to develop enough keyboarding skill to be able to do useful work in a timely manner." The other goal was "to demonstrate the knowledge and understanding of the basic functions of Microsoft Office; these are included but are not limited to: Word Processing. . . ." St. Mel's principal, in a December 1996 letter he sent to the Clearinghouse, said that "[t]here is no keyboarding practice in this class." Contrastingly, the course syllabus stated that "[k]eyboarding practice will be included in the course work." Additionally, the Microsoft Office course syllabus, for the first quarter, included: keyboarding skills, correct posture for typing, intermediate keyboarding, introduction to the software, word processing, and advanced word processing. Nothing in the entire first quarter qualified as computer science under the Clearinghouse's definition. In fact, according to the syllabus, 50% of the class was spent on instruction/skills explicitly excluded from the NCAA's definition. Therefore, even if the remaining 50% of the semester was spent entirely on fulfilling "core" computer science components (and it is not at all clear that the remaining instruction would have), that remainder would cover only 50% of the course—thereby falling short of the 75% necessary to count as a core class.

Similarly, the Microsoft Works course syllabus for the first quarter included keyboarding, posture, intermediate keyboarding, and formatting diskettes. St. Mel's principal, in that same letter to the Clearinghouse, dated December 1996, said that "[t]here is no keyboarding practice in this class." Again, the course syllabus stated that "[k]eyboarding practice will be included in the course work."

Given the foregoing, the Court finds that the Clearinghouse, and ultimately the NCAA, was correct in determining that these four courses did not fulfill the requirements of core courses, and that such determination was not made arbitrarily or in bad faith. Furthermore, the Halls have not proven that either the Clearinghouse, or NCAA, applied the core course criteria differently to applicants of different races.

Source: Courtesy of Westlaw; reprinted with permission.

ENFORCEMENT

The NCAA has an extensive web of bylaws that member institutions, their employees, and student-athletes must abide by and comply with. These same bylaws give the NCAA enforcement power to ensure compliance. The enforcement bylaws empower the NCAA Committee on Infractions (COI), set forth the policies and procedures of enforcement proceedings, delineate available penalties, and grant a right to appeal to member institutions. The stated mission of the NCAA's enforcement program is set forth in Bylaw 19.01.1:

> It shall be the mission of the NCAA enforcement program to eliminate violations of NCAA rules and impose appropriate penalties should violations occur. The program is committed to fairness of procedures and the timely and equitable resolution of infractions cases. The achievement of these objectives is essential to the conduct of a viable and effective enforcement program. Further, an important consideration in imposing penalties is to provide fairness to uninvolved student-athletes, coaches, administrators, competitors, and other institutions.[54]

Each NCAA member is responsible for conducting its athletic program in a manner consistent with NCAA rules and regulations. NCAA bylaws give the organization the necessary authority to investigate alleged violations of its rules. The NCAA's COI investigates and renders decisions regarding infractions by member institutions. The committee is able to conduct investigations into any conduct that it believes is in violation of NCAA rules and regulations. A member institution is able to conduct its own internal investigation as well, and the NCAA looks favorably upon any action taken by member institutions in good faith to remedy improper conduct. Any discipline rendered as a result of an investigation must be performed in a fair and legal manner.

The first step in the investigation process is evaluating the gathered information to determine whether it is credible. If it is not deemed credible, the case will be closed. If it is determined that the information is credible, then the member institution will be notified that an investigation will be

---

[54] NCAA, *supra* note 1, at 337.

TABLE 10-2

Processing of a Typical NCAA Infractions Appeals Case
1. Institution (or involved party) indicates it will appeal certain findings or penalties to NCAA Infractions Appeals Committee by submitting written notice of appeal to NCAA president not later than 15 calendar days from the date of the public release of the Committee on Infractions' report.
2. Infractions Appeals Committee acknowledges receipt of timely appeal. Institution (or involved party) is provided a 30-day period to submit response in support of appeal.
3. After receiving institution's (and/or involved party's) response, the Committee on Infractions' coordinator of appeals is provided a 30-day period to respond to the institution's (or involved party's) written appeal.
4. Institution (and/or involved party) is provided 14 days to provide a rebuttal to Committee on Infractions' response.
5. Infractions Appeals Committee reviews the institution's (and/or involved party's) appeal and the Committee on Infractions' response. This review is completed either through a hearing or on the written record. Hearings include the institution's (and/or involved party's) representatives as well as the Committee on Infractions' coordinator of appeals, the chair of the Committee on Infractions (observer) and enforcement staff representatives (observers).
6. Infractions Appeals Committee decision is announced.

Source: © National Collegiate Athletic Association, 2008. All rights reserved. Reprinted with permission.

initiated. The notice will generally provide the school with details concerning the investigation, including names of witnesses, when the violation or violations occurred, and the individuals involved.

After the investigation is complete, the COI conducts a hearing. The committee then prepares a public report that details the infractions, actions taken by the member institution in its attempts to remedy the infraction or infractions, and the discipline rendered by the committee. The member institution has the right to appeal the decision of the committee. Table 10-2 outlines how the appeal of an NCAA infractions case is advanced.

A wide range of penalties is available to the NCAA if violations are found, including loss of scholarships, forfeiture of tournament money, ineligibility for postseason play, limitations on television appearances and recruiting, public censure, financial penalties, and the expungement of team or individual records.[55] The NCAA also has the power to give the "death penalty" to a sports program, a term that became more widely known after Southern Methodist University's football program was cancelled for a period of time because of NCAA violations.

Member institutions usually rely on the advice of in-house counsel and outside law firms that specialize in handling NCAA compliance cases if an investigation is initiated. Outside attorneys typically can handle the workload of an NCAA investigation easier than the in-house lawyer for the institution because they have more available resources.[56] Some NCAA members take it upon themselves to penalize their program in the hope that the NCAA will render less harsh disciplinary measures.[57]

---

[55] NCAA Bylaw 19.5.2.2; *See*, Associated Press, *NVAA: Florida State to lose Scholarships, Might Forfeit Games*, CBSSports.com March 6, 2009.

[56] For further discussion, see Gene Marsh, *Weighing the Interests of the Institution, the Membership and Institutional Representative in an NCAA Investigation*, Fla. L. Rev. (2003).

[57] *See* Rodney K. Smith, *The National Collegiate Athletic Association's Death Penalty: How Educators Punish Themselves and Others*, 62 Ind. L. J. 985 (1986).

How often do violations occur? In NCAA Division I-A football from 1980 to 2004, there were approximately 91 major infractions involving 57 different schools.[58] Some of the universities involved are among the elite academic schools in the United States.

Case 10-8, *Bassett v. National Collegiate Athletic Association*, 2006 WL 1312471 (E.D.Ky. 2006), explores the disciplinary powers of the NCAA levied against a coach who allegedly violated NCAA rules while employed at the University of Kentucky.

📖 CASE 10-8 *Bassett v. National Collegiate Athletic Association*

2006 WL 1312471 (E.D.Ky. 2006)

JOSEPH M. HOOD, District Judge.

Background

On November 19, 2000, Plaintiff resigned from his position as assistant coach of the University of Kentucky's ("UK") football team. Earlier that day, UK's Athletic Director, Larry Ivy, confronted Plaintiff with allegations of impropriety. At the end of their meeting, Ivy presented Plaintiff with a choice of two options: (1) resign and, in exchange, no further action would be taken on the allegations made against him, or (2) face an investigation, potential criminal prosecution, and sure dismissal. Plaintiff chose to resign and now claims that if he had known UK would initiate an inquiry into his conduct, he never would have made that choice.

On January 4 and 5, 2001, UK Compliance Officer Sandy Bell, UK General Counsel Dick Plymale, Southeastern Conference ("SEC") Commissioner Roy Kramer, and SEC investigator Bill Seviers interviewed Plaintiff as part of UK's internal investigation of NCAA rules violations. UK submitted the results of this investigation to the NCAA enforcement staff on February 28, 2001. NCAA enforcement staff issued letters of official inquiry to Plaintiff, UK, and former head football coach Hal Mumme. In response to the allegations contained in the official inquiry, Plaintiff's counsel sent a letter to the NCAA on October 12, 2001. Plaintiff explained that he would be unable to attend the hearing on the infractions and that the letter would be "his only response to the allegations." In the letter, Plaintiff stated that he declined to be interviewed by the NCAA because the NCAA would not agree to limit the scope of the interview to pending allegations and would not agree to a telephone interview. The NCAA released its Infractions

---

[58] K. Alexa Otto, *Major Violations and NCAA 'Powerhouse' Football Programs: What Are the Odds of Being Charged?*, 15 J. Legal Aspects Sport 39 (2005).

Report on January 31, 2002. The NCAA found that due to Plaintiff's involvement in certain violations of NCAA rules, if he seeks employment at any NCAA member school between January 31, 2002 and January 30, 2010, both he and the member institution shall be requested to appear before the NCAA's infractions committee to consider whether the institution should be subject to the NCAA's show cause procedures. According to Plaintiff, this show cause order "render[ed him] unemployable as a college coach even beyond the ban."

. . . Plaintiff contends that the NCAA has intentionally and improperly interfered with his prospective contractual relations by issuing an eight-year show cause order which effectively forbids its members to hire him. According to Plaintiff, UK's investigation and subsequent self-report to the NCAA was based upon evidence gathered through deceit. Because Plaintiff was not afforded due process during UK's investigation, the NCAA's reliance upon UK's self-report led to an unjust punishment.

Kentucky has adopted the tort of tortious interference with prospective contractual relations from Restatement (Second) of Torts § 766B, which provides:

> One who intentionally and improperly interferes with another's prospective contractual relation (except a contract to marry) is subject to liability to the other for the pecuniary harm resulting from loss of the benefits of the relation, whether the interference consists of
>
> (a) inducing or otherwise causing a third person not to enter into or continue the prospective relation or
>
> (b) preventing the other from acquiring or continuing the prospective relation.

Several courts have recognized the NCAA's role in college athletics. The NCAA argues that its issuance of a show cause order was entirely proper because, in order to uphold the purposes of its association, it must be allowed to enforce its rules by penalizing violators. Both UK and Plaintiff had agreed to abide by the NCAA's regulations and to report any possible violations to the NCAA. Defending its decision, the NCAA explains that Plaintiff's admissions that he violated numerous NCAA rules, not any impropriety on the part of its association, led to the issuance of the show cause order. The NCAA notes that Plaintiff refused to attend the hearing on his infractions and refused to submit to an interview unless the NCAA agreed to his conditions. Plaintiff responded to the NCAA's official inquiry in an October 12, 2001, letter in which he admitted many of the violations levied against him. In his November 15, 2001, letter supplementing that response, Plaintiff claimed that UK's investigation of Plaintiff was carried out without due process and he requested that the NCAA take into account the manner in which the evidence of his misconduct was obtained when making its determination. Fully aware of Plaintiff's objections to UK's investigation, the NCAA issued its show cause order. The NCAA defends this order and contends that its determinations as to Plaintiff's misconduct are entitled to "a presumption of correctness—particularly when they stem from conceded violations of NCAA regulations." Stating that Plaintiff has not presented any evidence that the NCAA's actions were improper or unjustified, the NCAA asks that summary judgment be granted in its favor.

. . . The NCAA is a voluntary association of over 1200 public and private colleges and universities that enacts legislation to govern college athletics. As noted, the NCAA enforces its rules to advance its legitimate interest in regulating athletics at its member institutions. The show cause order serves to penalize Plaintiff for his rules infractions by making it more difficult, if not impossible according to Plaintiff, to obtain employment at a member institution. Such an order also advances the NCAA's interests by serving as a deterrent to other individuals who may consider violating NCAA regulations. . . .

One of the NCAA's stated purposes evidences society's interest in allowing it to enforce its rules: "A basic purpose of this Association is to maintain intercollegiate athletics as an integral part of the educational program and the athlete as an integral part of the student body and, by so doing, retain a clear line of demarcation between intercollegiate athletics and professional sports." (NCAA Constitution, Art. 1.3.) The NCAA's bylaws on recruiting inducements, academic fraud, and ethical conduct, for example, clearly reflect society's general interests in promoting fairness, honesty, and morality. The Court cannot envision how society would be served by allowing an individual who admittedly violated numerous NCAA rules to re-enter the college coaching field.

Taking all of these factors into account, the Court finds that Plaintiff has not shown that the NCAA acted improperly when it issued its show cause order. After Plaintiff conceded that he violated the NCAA's rules on recruiting inducements, impermissible tryouts, falsification of recruiting records, and unethical conduct, the NCAA was justified in enforcing those rules through a show cause order. Plaintiff had agreed to comply with those rules, and the NCAA exercised its right to enforce its rules by sanctioning him. Throughout this litigation, Plaintiff has blamed others for his misfortune and never acknowledged how evidence of his own impropriety, including his admissions that he violated NCAA regulations, influenced the NCAA's decision. To prevail, Plaintiff must show that the NCAA's actions were improper; Plaintiff has failed to do so and the NCAA has offered substantial evidence that it was justified in issuing the show cause order.

Source: Courtesy of Westlaw; reprinted with permission.

Was the plaintiff in Case 10-8, *Bassett v. National Collegiate Athletic Association*, "railroaded" by the NCAA as he claims? Does the "self-help" policy of the NCAA encourage member institutions to find a scapegoat? What is the NCAA's show cause power discussed in this case?[59] Relevant NCAA bylaws dealing with enforcement read as follows:

32.2 Preliminary Review of Information

32.2.1 Enforcement Staff to Receive Complaints and Conduct Investigations. It is a responsibility of the NCAA enforcement staff to conduct investigations relative to a member institution's failure to comply with NCAA legislation or to meet the conditions and obligations of membership. Information that an institution failed to meet these obligations shall be provided to the enforcement staff and, if received by the committee or Association's president, will be channeled to the enforcement staff.

32.2.1.1 Staff Initiation of Investigation. The enforcement staff may initiate an investigation on its own motion when it receives information that an institution is or has been in violation of NCAA legislation.

32.2.1.2 Self-Disclosure by an Institution. Self-disclosure shall be considered in establishing penalties, and, if an institution uncovers a violation prior to its being reported to the NCAA and/or its conference, such disclosure shall be considered as a mitigating factor in determining the penalty.

Source: National Collegiate Athletic Association, *2006-2007 NCAA Division I Manual* 441-42 (2006). © National Collegiate Athletic Association. 2006-2008. All rights reserved.

Most universities have compliance departments that ensure that all individuals connected to the program understand and follow the rules. Compliance departments are in the business of educating staff, coaches, boosters, alumni, and student-athletes about compliance issues. Member institutions desire a good working relationship with the NCAA so they can be informed quickly of any potential violations. Most athletic programs issue guidelines so that individuals connected with the program know what steps to take if they become aware of a violation.

---

[59] *See* NCAA Bylaw 19.02.1.

Problem 10-4

You are an employee in the athletic department at a major university. You become aware of what you believe is a major violation of NCAA rules involving improper payment of money to recruits. You have been told by an athletic trainer for the football team that an energetic booster has paid student-athletes for work they did not do and also provided them with transportation. What is your obligation to report such a violation? What ethical duties are present when faced with such a violation? Draft a memo to your athletic director concerning the violation covering all the essential elements.

ANTITRUST ISSUES

Prior to 1970 there were virtually no challenges to the NCAA on antitrust grounds. Since then antitrust lawsuits have been brought against the NCAA by student-athletes, competing athletic bodies, coaches, boosters, alumni, and cheerleaders. For many years the NCAA had been immune from scrutiny under the Sherman Antitrust Act because courts were concerned with amateurism and education rather than commercialism. However, courts have now recognized that the NCAA does involve itself in commercial endeavors. The NCAA has faced multiple antitrust challenges in which plaintiffs have alleged anticompetitive behavior.[60]

Most courts have held that the NCAA is not in violation of antitrust laws because the association does not enter into the marketplace and therefore does not regulate an industry. The NCAA has taken the position that its bylaws are noncommercial rules "since there is no trade or commerce in student-athletes."[61] Courts have held that NCAA regulation of intercollegiate athletics is on a national scope and displays an interstate character for the purpose of antitrust law.[62] However, courts have generally had difficulty determining that the NCAA's rule-making, regulating, and enforcement activities constitute trade or commerce for the purposes of the Sherman Act. Many courts have upheld NCAA bylaws on the basis that they protect amateurs in college athletes.[63] However, the NCAA is not exempt from antitrust scrutiny.[64]

Although the NCAA has been more successful than not in antitrust litigation, in *NCAA v. Board of Regents of the University of Oklahoma*, 468 U.S. 85 (1983), the plaintiff prevailed. The case involved NCAA television broadcasts of collegiate football games. The United States Supreme Court found anticompetitive behavior on the part of the NCAA when the University of Oklahoma and the University of Georgia asserted that the NCAA had unreasonably restricted trade in the televising of college football games. The Court found that the restraints placed on NCAA member institutions were anticompetitive because there was no reasonable procompetitive basis for restricting the viewing

---

[60] *See* Law v. NCAA, 134 F.3d 1010 (10th Cir. 1998) (college basketball coaches with "restricted earnings status" brought a class action lawsuit challenging NCAA's rules limiting a coach's annual compensation); Banks v. NCAA, 977 F.2d 1081 (7th Cir. 1992) (exploring whether hiring an agent is an antitrust violation).

[61] In re NCAA I-A Walk-on Football Players Litigation, 391 F. Supp. 2d 1144, 1148 (2005).

[62] Hennessey v. NCAA, 848 F.2d 1338 (5th Cir. 1977).

[63] Smith v. NCAA, 139 F.3d 180 (3rd Cir. 1998).

[64] *Bd. of Regents of Univ. of Oklahoma*, 468 U.S. at 98–100; 104 S. Ct. 2948.

of college football games on television. At that time, the NCAA had restricted the televising of NCAA football to two television stations that were to carry 14 games each.

In *Banks v. NCAA*, 977 F.2d 1081 (7th Cir. 1997), the court was faced with the issue of an athlete who desired to return to college football after declaring himself available for the NFL draft. He had not been selected in the NFL draft and subsequently brought a lawsuit seeking to have his eligibility reinstated. He alleged that the NCAA rules that prevented him from reentry into the college ranks were in violation of the Sherman Act as an unreasonable restraint of trade. The Seventh Circuit Court of Appeals found that the former college player had failed to set forth any anticompetitive effect on a relevant market.

In Case 10-9, *McCormack v. National Collegiate Athletic Ass'n*, 845 F.2d 1338 (5th Cir. 1988), the plaintiffs alleged that the NCAA was guilty of antitrust violations when it administrated the "death penalty" to Southern Methodist University (SMU) football for violations committed by its athletic program. Alumni and cheerleaders brought a lawsuit against the NCAA alleging damages under the Sherman Act. In the following opinion, the court ruled that the loss of an opportunity to cheer for the Mustangs failed to constitute an injury to business or property; therefore, the cheerleaders lacked standing to sue under the antitrust laws.

📖 CASE 10-9 *McCormack v. National Collegiate Athletic Ass'n*

845 F.2d 1338 (5th Cir. 1988)

ALVIN B. RUBIN, Circuit Judge:

Finding that the football program of Southern Methodist University had exceeded restrictions on compensation for student athletes, the National Collegiate Athletic Association suspended the program for the 1987 season and imposed other penalties. A group of SMU alumni, football players, and cheerleaders challenges that action, contending that the NCAA violated the antitrust and civil rights laws by promulgating and enforcing rules restricting the benefits that may be awarded student athletes. While we give the loyal students and alumni credit for making a college try, we affirm the judgment dismissing their complaint. . . .

I.

The NCAA found that Southern Methodist University had violated its rules limiting compensation for football players to scholarships with limited financial benefits. It accordingly suspended the SMU football program for the entire 1987 season and imposed restrictions on it for the 1988 season. David R. McCormack, an attorney and SMU alumnus, then filed this class action suit on behalf of SMU "as an institution," its graduates and current students, several members of its football team, and several cheerleaders.

The complaint, as amended, charges antitrust violations in that (1) the restrictions on compensation to football players constitute illegal price-fixing in violation of the Sherman Act and (2) the suspension of SMU constitutes a group boycott by other NCAA members. The suspension, the complaint alleges, has destroyed the football players' careers and caused the cheerleaders "considerable emotional anguish and distress" by depriving them of the opportunity to conduct their cheerleading activities at games.

In addition, all of the plaintiffs assert that the NCAA has repeatedly imposed penalties on the college football program of SMU in unequal fashion and without due process of law, thereby damaging "the image of the University as an academic institution," endangering "[its] existence . . . as an academic institution," and causing it to lose revenues from donors. The NCAA's actions, it is alleged, have deprived McCormack and others of "their right to associate together in support of the University by attendance at the football games of the University," while the football players have been "forced to discontinue their athlete-academic duties" at SMU and the cheerleaders have lost the opportunity to lead cheers at football games.

Not every person who complains of injury as a result of violation of the antitrust laws has standing to assert claims under the statutes. Only a person injured "in his business or property" may seek damages for violation of the antitrust laws, and only a person who can show a significant threat of such injury from impending violations can obtain injunctive relief. Even a plaintiff injured in his business or property must, in order to sue for damages, show "antitrust injury," that is, "injury of the type the antitrust laws were designed to prevent and that flows from that which makes defendants' acts unlawful." Finally, even if the plaintiff meets these requirements, the court must consider whether he is a "proper plaintiff" to sue for damages, examining such factors as (1) whether the plaintiff's injuries or their causal link to the defendant are speculative, (2) whether other parties have been more directly harmed, and (3) whether allowing this plaintiff to sue would risk multiple lawsuits, duplicative recoveries, or complex damage apportionment.

Neither McCormack nor any of the cheerleaders satisfies these requirements. The cheerleaders assert only the loss of the opportunity to lead cheers, which clearly does not qualify as an injury to business or property. The only injuries McCormack alleges are the devaluation of his degree, the loss of the opportunity to see football games, and the damage to his contact and association with current and prospective student athletes derived from his membership in the Mustang Club, "an athletic fund-raising organization." Of these three, only the first is even arguably an injury to business or property. Although the Supreme Court has emphasized that "property" in this context "has a naturally broad and inclusive meaning," We cannot conclude that the devaluation of McCormack's degree is an injury for which the antitrust laws were designed to afford a remedy. The alleged connection, moreover, between the NCAA's actions and the devaluation of his degree presents the sort of "speculative" and "abstract" causal chain that the Supreme Court has held insufficient to support antitrust standing.

The claims of the football-player plaintiffs rest on a different basis. They contend that they have suffered an injury to their business, playing football: that they in effect sell their labor to SMU and that the NCAA rules restrict the amount that SMU or any other competing university can pay them, thus eliminating their opportunity to offer those services to the highest bidder . . . the selling of one's labor is a commercial interest.

The NCAA argues that, despite the holding in Board of Regents, its eligibility rules are not subject to the antitrust laws because, unlike the television restrictions in Board of Regents, the eligibility rules have purely or primarily noncommercial objectives. The NCAA's argument finds some support in the caselaw, but we need not address it here. Assuming, without deciding, that the antitrust laws apply to the eligibility rules, it does not follow that the rules violate those laws. The Sherman Act does not forbid every combination or conspiracy in restraint of trade, only those that are unreasonable. We hold that the NCAA's eligibility rules are reasonable and that the plaintiffs have failed to allege any facts to the contrary.

Source: Courtesy of Westlaw; reprinted with permission.

A student-athlete playing collegiate sports who was not originally offered a sports scholarship is referred to as a "walk-on" player. Many walk-on players have been successful in playing college football at its most competitive level. The most famous walk-on player in the history of football has to be Daniel E. "Rudy" Ruettiger, who played football at Notre Dame and whose story was told by Hollywood in the film *Rudy* (TriStar Pictures 1993). There are over 22,000 football scholarships available in NCAA football,[65] but the NCAA restricts the number of scholarships at Division I-A football to 85 for each university. To retain Division I status, a school must have 76.5 football scholarship players. In Case 10-10, *In re NCAA I-A Walk-on Football Players Litigation*, 398 F. Supp. 2d 1144 (W.D. Wash. 2005), several walk-on players challenged the NCAA on antitrust grounds over the number of scholarships offered.

CASE 10-10 *In re NCAA I-A Walk-on Football Players Litigation*

398 F. Supp. 2d 1144 (W.D. Wash. 2005)

COUGHENOUR, District Judge.

. . . Plaintiffs' Amended Complaint sets forth their argument as follows: the NCAA and Division I-A schools, in the name of "cost-containment," have entered into an "agreement" or "rule," codified in Bylaw 15.5.5, which "artificially restrains the number of scholarships that a school may award to football team roster members." This practice, they allege, is an unlawful horizontal restraint of trade that violates Section 1 of the Sherman Act, 15 U.S.C. § 1, and is a monopolization of the "big-time college football market" in violation of Section 2 of the Sherman Act, 15 U.S.C. § 2.

The NCAA now moves the Court for judgment on . . . the basis of the following arguments: (1) NCAA rules preserving amateurism and protecting fair competition have been uniformly upheld under the Sherman Act. . . .

IV. Section 1 of the Sherman Act

A. Trade or Commerce

The NCAA first argues that its bylaws are non-commercial rules since there is no trade or commerce in student athletes. In making this argument, the NCAA attempts to characterize this case as challenging the NCAA's protection of amateurism in so-called "big-time college football." . . . [T]he NCAA concludes the scholarship limits at issue in this case fall clearly within the types of NCAA rulemaking which courts have repeatedly found are not subject to the Sherman Act.

The law is clear that athletes may not be "paid to play." Accordingly, courts have regularly upheld NCAA bylaws protecting amateurism in college athletics. . . .

Source: Courtesy of Westlaw; reprinted with permission.

---

[65] AthleticScholarships, http://www.athleticscholarships.net.

NOTES AND DISCUSSION QUESTIONS

Actions Against the NCAA

1. In Case 10-1, *NCAA v. Hornung*, the NCAA did not want Paul Hornung to announce college football games because of a past gambling issue. The NCAA has a specific rule (Bylaw 10.3) that relates to gambling:

> Staff members of a member conference, staff members of the athletics department of a member institution and student-athletes shall not knowingly:
>
> **a.** Provide information to individuals involved in organized gambling activities concerning intercollegiate athletics competition;
>
> **b.** Solicit a bet on any intercollegiate team;
>
> **c.** Accept a bet on any team representing the institution;
>
> **d.** Solicit or accept a bet on any intercollegiate competition for any item (e.g., cash, shirt, dinner) that has tangible value; or
>
> **e.** Participate in any gambling activity that involves intercollegiate athletics or professional athletics, through a bookmaker, a parlay card or any other method employed by organized gambling.[66]

Hornung, once deemed football's "Golden Boy," had been suspended from the National Football League for one year for gambling. He had had a great career at Notre Dame, was the number-one draft pick of the Green Bay Packers, and led the NFL in scoring from 1959 to 1961.[67]

2. In *Howard University v. NCAA*, 510 F.2d 213 (D.C. Cir. 1975), a case prior to *Tarkanian*, the NCAA was held to be a state actor. *Howard* dealt with a soccer player who had been declared ineligible by the NCAA. The association sanctioned Howard University as a result of the violation. The court, in finding state action on the part of the NCAA, stated:

> Approximately half of the NCAA's 655 institutional members are state- or federally supported. Since financial contribution to the NCAA is based upon institutional size, and since public universities generally have the largest student bodies, the public institutions provide the vast majority of the NCAA's capital (the NCAA's annual administrative budget at the time of the suit being $1.3 million). Principal power in the Association lies with the Convention, which is made up of representatives of the member institutions. The Convention elects the governing Council and the NCAA's principal officers, adopts and amends the constitution and Bylaws, and reviews all Council and committee actions. As can be seen from this description, the state instrumentalities are a dominant force in determining NCAA policy and in dictating NCAA actions. That conclusion is buttressed by reference to the record before us which documents that both the President and Secretary-Treasurer were representatives of public instrumentalities and that state instrumentalities traditionally provided the majority of the members of

---

[66] NCAA, *supra* note 1, at 52.

[67] See Paul Hornung, Golden Boy: Girls, Games, and Gambling at Green Bay (And Notre Dame Too) (2004).

the governing Council and the various committees. Thus, governmental involvement, while not exclusive, is 'significant,' and all NCAA actions appear 'impregnated with a governmental character.'

The NCAA's regulation and supervision over intercollegiate athletics is extensive and represents an immeasurably valuable service for its member institutions. The NCAA conducts championship events in most sports for the benefit of its member institutions. The Association regulates the amateur status of student-athletes, sets financial aid policies, prescribes playing and practice seasons, fixes minimum academic standards, establishes standards for approved extra events and determines eligibility for intercollegiate competition and NCAA championships. The NCAA also negotiates television contracts, the proceeds of which, $13,000,000 annually, flow directly to the participating schools, primarily the public universities. The foregoing analysis indicates that the NCAA and its member public instrumentalities are joined in a mutually beneficial relationship, and in fact may be fairly said to form the type of symbiotic relationship between public and private entities which triggers constitutional scrutiny.[68]

Do you agree with the court's analysis in *Howard*? What was different about the NCAA's makeup at the time the *Howard* case was decided as opposed to today? One of the arguments made by the court in *Howard* in support of state action by the NCAA was the $13 million it received in television contracts annually. The association clearly receives in excess of that today. Does that affect your decision concerning the NCAA and state action?

3. When the NCAA approved a 12th football game for the I-A schools, fees for games against certain Division I-A teams ballooned. The University of Florida paid $450,000 to host a football game against Charleston Southern University in 2009. Florida will pay Florida Atlantic $500,000 and Furman $450,000 for 2011 games. Those games seem like bargains when you consider University of Georgia is paying $975,000 to host North Texas in 2013. Edward Aschoff, *Scheduling Games as Part of Business*, The Gainesville Sun, GatorSports.com, September 10, 2009.

4. What is the basis for courts determining that the NCAA is not a state actor? Under what circumstances could the NCAA become a state actor?

The Student-Athlete Relationship

5. Review the allegations of the plaintiff's complaint set forth in Case 10-5, *Fortay v. University of Miami*. Do you believe that the plaintiff could have prevailed on these allegations before a jury or a judge? What would he have to prove to win? What guidelines should be in place for coaches and universities regarding the recruiting of student-athletes? Given the rapid movement of coaches, should the NLI allow a student-recruit to revoke his or her signature without the penalty of losing eligibility?

The University of Miami does have a solid history of being "Quarterback U." George Mira, Bernie Kosar, Jim Kelly, Vinny Testaverde, and Rex Grossman were stand-out quarterbacks at Miami and played NFL football. Jim Kelly is in the Pro Football Hall of Fame. Fortay's competition, Gino Torretta, won the Heisman Trophy at the University of Miami in

---

[68] *Howard University*, 510 F.2d at 219–20 (citations omitted).

1992, passed for more than 3,000 yards in his senior season, and also played in the NFL. Todd Marinovich was also part of the freshman quarterback class, along with Fortay and Torretta. Torretta played in the NFL from 1993 to 1997, and Marinovich was in the NFL from 1991 to 1992.

6. If a university heavily recruits a student-athlete, does it have ethical obligations to that student-athlete to ensure his or her success in the classroom? What steps should the school take to ensure academic progress for its student-athletes?

7. In Case 10-4, *Brown v. Compton*, the court debated whether an academic advisor owed a legal duty to a student-athlete. The court eventually held that the advisor and school district were immune for their actions. Should there be a legal duty in these situations? What damages could Brown claim? How would he be required to mitigate his damages? What is the basis of granting immunity under these circumstances? Should school districts have an individual who is trained and familiar with the NCAA process to assist student-athletes with the transition to college? Assuming the immunity hurdle could be overcome, would the University of Southern California have standing to sue the school district and counselor for damages for loss of a star player?

8. What is the purpose behind the national letter of intent? How does it help schools recruit student-athletes? What changes, if any, would you propose to the NLI? Could it be considered an "unconscionable contract"? For further information, see Stacie Meyer, *Unequal Bargaining Power: Making the National Letter of Intent More Equitable*, 15 MARQUETTE SPORTS LAW REVIEW 227 (2004).

9. Chad Elsey sued Baylor University and Coach David Bliss after he was recruited by Coach Bliss to transfer from SMU to play basketball. He enrolled in Baylor in 1999 and played for the Bears for two years after sitting out one year. In his lawsuit, Elsey claimed Bliss told him that if he came to Baylor he, Bliss, would pay for law school and any other degree Elsey was interested in pursuing as long as Elsey worked diligently toward the degree. Elsey also claims Bliss told him he had "connections" at the law school and could ensure his admittance. Bliss and Baylor denied all allegations. Bliss eventually resigned from Baylor.[69]

10. In *Matthews v. National Collegiate Athletic Ass'n*, 79 F. Supp. 2d 1199 (E.D. Wash. 1999), a student sued the NCAA, Washington State University, and the PAC 10 Conference over violations of the Americans with Disabilities Act and due process. The court stated the following in finding for the defendants:

> *Due Process Claim*. Plaintiff also brings a 42 U.S.C. § 1983 claim for violation of his due process rights due to the NCAA's denial of his application for a waiver of the 75/25 Rule without communicating directly with Plaintiff or holding a pre- or post-decision hearing.
>
> The Supreme Court has held that the NCAA is not a state actor. *National Collegiate Athletic Association v. Tarkanian*, 488 U.S. 179, 109 S. Ct. 454, 102 L.Ed.2d 469 (1988). The facts are somewhat dissimilar. Basketball coach Jerry Tarkanian claimed a violation of his due process rights when the University of Nevada, Las Vegas, suspended him from coaching.

---

[69] *See* 5(4) LEGAL ISSUES IN COLLEGIATE ATHLETICS, Feb. 2004. *See,* Viv Bernstein, *COLLEGE BASKETBALL; Baylor Coach Bliss Resigns; Violations Discovered*, The New York Times, August 9, 2003.

Tarkanian was suspended because the NCAA placed UNLV on probation and threatened further penalties unless UNLV severed its ties with Tarkanian because Tarkanian had violated 10 NCAA rules. The Court held that the NCAA neither exercised nor held governmental power when it threatened to expel a state university from membership if the university did not take specified action. *Tarkanian*, 488 U.S. at 197, 109 S. Ct. 454. Instead, the university chose to conduct its athletic program in compliance with the NCAA's policies in order to maintain NCAA membership. *Id.* at 199, 109 S. Ct. 454.

In the instant case, Plaintiff's concern is the lack of communication between himself and the NCAA, and the lack of a hearing to discuss the NCAA's determination. This concern does not change the fact the NCAA is a private, unincorporated association rather than a state actor. Furthermore, the NCAA "does not take action against student-athletes, but only against member institutions." Decl. of Kevin C. Lemmon at 1. This stance agrees with the determination of the *Tarkanian* court—the individual member institutions choose to comply with the NCAA's rules. An NCAA determination is communicated to the affected member institution rather than to a non-complying individual so that the member institution can make a decision regarding its compliance with NCAA regulations. Plaintiff had no procedural guarantee of a direct communication with the waiver committee; indeed, such communication was never contemplated. In any case, the NCAA is not a state actor. While WSU's decision not to use Plaintiff in intercollegiate football games undoubtedly was a direct result of the NCAA's determination, the NCAA did not make the ultimate decision to sideline Plaintiff.[70]

Eligibility and NCAA Rules

11. Describe the circumstances under which a claim for educational malpractice might exist. Suppose a student-athlete is promised a personal tutor during the recruiting process but is never provided one. Is that enough to sustain a cause of action? For further study, see T. DeMitchell, *Statutes and Standards: Has the Door to Educational Malpractice Been Opened?*, 2003 BRIGHAM YOUNG UNIVERSITY EDUCATION AND LAW JOURNAL 485 (2003).

12. In *Bloom v. National Collegiate Athletic Ass'n*, 93 P.3d 621 (Colo. App. 2004), the court upheld NCAA rules preventing student-athletes from being paid for advertisements and product endorsements. Do you agree with the rule? Should student-athletes be able to endorse a product while still a student at the university?

    Jeremy Bloom presented evidence that the source of his acting opportunities was directly related to his good looks and camera presence, not his athletic ability. What evidence would he have to present at trial to sustain such a proposition? For another case dealing with a student-athlete turned actor, see *Autry v. National Collegiate Athletic Ass'n*, 96-CH-3275 (Cir. Ct. Cook Cty. Ill. 1996). Autry was a drama major at Northwestern University

---

[70] *Matthews*, 79 F. Supp. 2d. at 1207–08.

and received an offer to appear in a movie. The NCAA stated that his appearance in the movie would violate NCAA bylaws and jeopardize his eligibility. His appeal was eventually granted and he appeared in the movie.[71]

What is the purpose of the NCAA bylaw at issue in the *Bloom* case? Bloom argued that the NCAA allows member institutions to commercially endorse athletic equipment by having student-athletes wear equipment with companies' identifying logos during NCAA competition. Is this a valid argument? Why does the NCAA allow a student-athlete to participate professionally in one sport while retaining eligibility in another?

13. University of Iowa quarterback Drew Tate made a hole-in-one at a charity golf tournament event in 2006. The feat entitled him to $25,000 toward the purchase of a new car. Tate indicated he was going to use the prize money for a new Harley Davidson motorcycle. He was later forced to forgo the money due to NCAA regulations. He was informed by Iowa Athletic Director Bob Bowsley that he would be unable to accept the prize because he had one year of eligibility left. To Tate's credit, he acknowledged the role Iowa football had played in his entrance to the tournament. Should Tate be allowed to keep the prize? What interests is the NCAA protecting in not allowing Tate to collect his prize? What if Tate had won $25,000 on a "scratch-off" ticket at his local convenience store? Would the result be the same? *See*, Iowa QB Sinks Hole-In-One, But has to Forgo Prize, ESPN.com, June 5, 2006.

14. Should college players be paid participants? What advantages are there to paying college football players? What disadvantages are there? *See*, Rick Telander, *The Hundred Yard Lie: The Corruption of College Football and What We Can Do to Stop it*, Simon & Schuster Inc., 1989, Chapter 2, Playing for Free is Noble.

15. Do you agree with the NCAA rules regarding agents? Do you believe agents should be able to make contracts with student-athletes prior to the expiration of their eligibility? Is the regulation of agents a job more suited for the university where the student-athlete is matriculating? The NCAA's general rule relating to agents states that an individual will be deemed ineligible if he or she has agreed orally or in writing to be represented by an agent. How will the NCAA monitor oral promises between agents and student-athletes? *See*, T. Matthew Lockhart, *Oliver v. NCAA: Throwing a Contractual Curveball at the NCAA's 'Veil of Amateurism,'* University of Dayton Law Review, Vol. 35 Number 1, 2010.

16. An excellent film displaying college recruiting practices is *Hoop Dreams* (Fine Line Features 1994). The film follows the lives of two basketball recruits from the Chicago area. Contrast this film with the movie *Blue Chips* (Paramount Pictures 1994), starring Shaquille O'Neal.

Enforcement

17. Do you believe the NCAA has been too aggressive in disciplining member institutions for violations? What are the association's major tools for investigations? *See generally*, Michael L. Buckner, *Athletic Investigation Handbook: A Guide for Institutions and Involved Parties During the NCAA Enforcement Process*, iUniverse, Inc., 2004.

---

[71] *See* http://imdb.com.title/tt0119055/fullcredits.

18. NCAA Bylaws allow the NCAA to seek restitution from a member institution that permits ineligible student-athletes to compete in its programs. The NCAA is entitled to a laundry list of options under the rule. The NCAA restitution bylaw was at issue in *National Collegiate Athletic Ass'n v. Lasege*, 53 S.W.3d 77 (Ky. 2001).

19. The NCAA publishes the *Athletics Certification Self-Study Instrument*, which provides guidance to member institutions in preparing for an on-campus evaluation by the NCAA.

Antitrust Issues

20. How is antitrust law applied differently at the amateur level as compared with professional sports?

21. In 1989 the NCAA created a Cost Reduction Committee, which proposed a bylaw restricting Division I basketball coaching staffs to four members: one head coach, two assistant coaches, and one entry-level or "restricted earnings" coach. Another proposed bylaw limited the salary of a restricted-earnings coach in Division I sports other than football to $12,000 for the school year and $4,000 for the summer. These NCAA rules became effective in 1992. The plaintiffs in *Law v. National Collegiate Athletic Ass'n*, 134 F.3d 1010 (10th Cir. 1992), *cert. denied*, 119 S. Ct. 65 (Oct. 5 1998), challenged the restrictions in a class action lawsuit. In 1996 a federal district court enjoined the NCAA from enforcing the compensation limitations. The court stated:

> The NCAA asserts that the REC Rule will help to maintain competitive equity by preventing wealthier schools from placing a more experienced, higher-priced coach in the position of restricted-earnings coach. . . .
>
> While the REC Rule will equalize the salaries paid to entry-level coaches in Division I schools, it is not clear that the REC Rule will equalize the experience level of such coaches. Nowhere does the NCAA prove that the salary restrictions enhance competition, level an uneven playing field, or reduce coaching inequities. Rather, the NCAA only presented evidence that the cost reductions would be achieved in such a way so as to maintain without "significantly altering," "adversely affecting," or "disturbing" the existing competitive balance. The undisputed record reveals that the REC Rule is nothing more than a cost-cutting measure and shows that the only consideration the NCAA gave to competitive balance was simply to structure the rule so as not to exacerbate competitive imbalance. Thus, on its face, the REC Rule is not directed towards competitive balance nor is the nexus between the rule and a compelling need to maintain competitive balance sufficiently clear on this record to withstand a motion for summary judgment.[72]

The NCAA eventually settled the case by paying the plaintiffs $54.5 million in April 1999. The NCAA devised a plan whereby each Division I member school would share settlement proceeds. *Court Approves Revised Plan for Allocation of Settlement Funds to Restricted Earnings Coaches*, "You Make the Call . . .", Marquette University Law School, National Sports Law Institute, Volume 3, Issue 2, Fall 2000.

---

[72] *Law, 134 F.3d* at 1014.

22. The manufacturing of baseball bats is a big business. Baseball is still considered the national pastime, and million of kids play baseball year round in the United States. Players use both aluminum bats and wooden bats at the amateur level for both softball and baseball. However, there have been safety concerns about using aluminum bats at certain levels of competition.[73]

Andrew Sanchez was a college baseball pitcher at California State Northridge who suffered severe brain damage when he was struck by an opposing player's line drive. He filed a lawsuit against the bat manufacturer, the NCAA, and other defendants, asserting a variety of causes of action, including that the NCAA knew aluminum bats created an increased risk of harm to players. Several other players have been killed or injured from the use of aluminum bats.[74] NCAA rules allow the use of both aluminum and wood bats in NCAA baseball.

In *Baum Research and Development Co., Inc. v. Hillerich & Bradsby Co., Inc.*, 31 F. Supp. 2d 1016 (E.D. Mich. 1999), the maker of composite bats alleged that the defendants conspired to arrange for the standards for baseball bats used in the NCAA to exclude the plaintiff from the market. Baum stated that the lack of regulation by the NCAA was squeezing the company out of the market. The court found that the absence of rules by the NCAA relating to the types of bats used actually fostered competition. For further study, see C. M. McCallister, *Aluminum Bat Manufacturers Anticompetitive Trade Practices in Collegiate Baseball: A Case Review*, 2 DePaul Journal of Sports Law and Contemporary Problems (2004). For an indepth discussion of the dynamics of the aluminum bat, see D. Russell, *The Sweet Spot of a Hollow Baseball or Softball Bat*, 116 Journal of the Acoustical Society of America 2602 (2004).

23. What happens when a student graduates and begins graduate school at another university but still has eligibility remaining? That issue is addressed by NCAA Bylaws and is discussed in *Smith v. NCAA*, 139 F.3d 180 (3rd Cir. 1998). In that case a student-athlete challenged NCAA bylaw on antitrust grounds. She alleged that the NCAA's passage and enforcement of a bylaw was an unreasonable restraint of trade and had an adverse anticompetitive effect on her ability to play college athletics. The court found in favor of the NCAA, stating that NCAA rules were not subject to the Sherman Act.

SUGGESTED READINGS AND RESOURCES

Dunnavant, Keith. *The Fifty-Year Seduction: How Television Manipulated College Football, from the Birth of the Modern NCAA to the Creation of the BCS*. New York: Thomas Dunne Books, 2004.

Einhorn, Eddie, with Rapoport, Ron. *How March Became Madness: How the NCAA Tournament Became the Greatest Sporting Event in America*. Chicago: Triumph Books, 2005.

Hegle, John. *The SMS Lady Bears and the House of Stiles: The Season Jackie Stiles Became the Greatest Scorer in NCAA Women's Basketball History and the SMS Lady Bears Earned Their Second Trip to the NCAA Women's Final Four*. Springfield, MO: Lady Bears Book, 2002.

---

[73] Eric Adelson, *Bat Controversy Lingers over NCAA*, ESPN.com, March 29, 2000.

[74] *See* Ira Bericon, *Metal Bats Are an Issue of Life and Death*, New York Times, July 16, 2006. For further study see Matthew R. Wilmot, *Baseball Bats in the High Tech Era: A Products Liability Look at New Technology, Aluminum Bats and Manufacturer Liability*, 16 Marq. Sports L. Rev. 353 (2006).

Knapp, Ron. *Top 10 Stars of the NCAA Men's Basketball Tournament*. Berkeley Heights, NJ: Enslow, 2001.

Mayes, Thomas. *Tonya Harding's Case: Contractual Due Process, the Amateur Athlete, and the American Ideal of Fair Play*. 3 UCLA ENTERTAINMENT LAW REVIEW 109 (1995).

National Collegiate Athletic Association. *2005 Men's and Women's Rifle Rules*. Indianapolis, IN: NCAA, 2004.

Sack, Allen, & Staurowsky, Ellen. *College Athletes for Hire: The Evolution and Legacy of the NCAA's Amateur Myth*. Westport, CT: Praeger, 1998.

Thomas, Bubbha. *NCAA National Collegiate Affirmative Action*. Houston, TX: Lightmen Publishing, 2006.

Vitale, Dick. *Dick Vitale's 25 Years of Basketball Memories*. Champaign, IL: Sports Publishing, 2003.

Walker, Yuri N. *Playing the Game of Academic Integrity vs. Athletic Success: The Americans with Disabilities Act (ADA) and Interscholastic Student-Athletes with Learning Disabilities*. 15 MARQUETTE SPORTS LAW REVIEW 601 (2005).

Wallenfeldt, E. C. *The Six-Minute Fraternity: The Rise and Fall of NCAA Tournament Boxing, 1932–60*. Westport, CT: Praeger, 1994.

Wood, Brian D. *Compensating College Athletes: NCAA Division I-A Athletic Directors' and University Presidents' Perceptions*. Proquest/UMI, 2006.

Yaeger, Don, with Tarkanian, Jerry. *Shark Attack: Jerry Tarkanian and His Battle with the NCAA and UNLV*. New York: HarperCollins, 1992.

REFERENCE MATERIALS

Avery, Jane C. *Validity, Under Federal Law, of Sex Discrimination in Athletics*. 23 AMERICAN LAW REPORTS FEDERAL 664 (2006).

Bartlett, Larry D. *The Court's View of Good Conduct Rules for High School Student Athletes*. 2 WEST'S EDUCATION LAW REPORTER 588 (1993).

Berkon, Ira. *Metal Bats Are an Issue of Life and Death*. NEW YORK TIMES, July 16, 2006.

Braig, Kevin. *A Game Plan to Conserve the Interscholastic Athletic Environment After LeBron James*. 14 MARQUETTE SPORTS LAW REVIEW 343 (2004).

Carter, W. Burlette. *The Age of Innocence: The First 25 Years of the National Collegiate Athletic Association, 1906 to 1931*. 8 VANDERBILT JOURNAL OF ENTERTAINMENT AND TECHNOLOGY LAW 211 (2006).

Champion, Walter T. *Fundamentals of Sports Law*. St. Paul, MN: Thomson/West, 2004.

Champion, Walter T. *Sports Law: Cases, Documents, and Materials*. New York: Aspen, 2005.

Champion, Walter T. *Sports Law in a Nutshell*, 2d ed. St. Paul, MN: West Group, 2000.

Clark, Leroy D. *New Directions for the Civil Rights Movement: College Athletics as a Civil Rights Issue*. 36 HOWARD LAW JOURNAL 259 (1993).

14A. CORPUS JURIS SECUNDUM, COLLEGES AND UNIVERSITIES §49, 50 (2009).

Davis, Timothy. *College Athletics: Testing the Boundaries of Contract and Tort*. 29 U.C. DAVIS LAW REVIEW 971 (1996).

Dennie, Christian. *Amateurism Stifles a Student-Athlete's Dream*. 12 SPORTS LAWYERS JOURNAL 221 (2005).

Edelman, Marc. *Reevaluating Amateurism Standards in Men's College Basketball*. 35 UNIVERSITY OF MICHIGAN JOURNAL OF LAW REFORM 861 (2002).

Estevao, Lesley C. *Student-Athletes Must Find New Ways to Pierce the NCAA's Legal Armor*. 12 SETON HALL SPORTS LAW JOURNAL 243 (2002).

Gardner, Kathryn, & McFarland, Allison J. *Legal Precedents and Strategies Shaping Home Schooled Students' Participation in Public School Sports*. 11 JOURNAL OF LEGAL ASPECTS OF SPORTS 25 (2001).

Greenberg, Martin J., & Gray, James T. 1 *Sports Law Practice*, 2d ed. Charlottesville, VA: Lexis Law Publishing, 1998.

Guruli, Erin. *Commerciality of Collegiate Sports: Should the IRS Intercept?* 12 SPORTS LAWYERS JOURNAL 43 (2005).

Habenicht, Andrew M. *Has the Shot Clock Expired?* Pryor v. NCAA *and the Premature Disposal of a "Deliberate Indifference" Discrimination Claim under Title VI of the Civil Rights Act of 1964*. 11 GEORGE MASON LAW REVIEW 551 (2004).

Hanlon, Sean M. *Athletic Scholarships as Unconscionable Contracts of Adhesion: Has the NCAA Fouled Out?* 13 SPORTS LAWYERS JOURNAL 41 (2006).

Hastings, S., Manoloff, R., Sheeran, T., & Stype, G. *Baldwin's Ohio School Law*, rev. ed. Cleveland, OH: Thomson/West, 2003.

Hilliard, Richard R., Shelton, Angel F., & Pearson, Kevin E. *An Update on Recent Decisions Rendered by the NCAA Infractions Appeals Committee: Further Guidance for NCAA Member Institutions*. 28 JOURNAL OF COLLEGE AND UNIVERSITY LAW 605 (2002).

Hunter, Richard J., & Mayo, Ann M. *Issues in Antitrust, the NCAA, and Sports Management*. 10 MARQUETTE SPORTS LAW JOURNAL 69 (1999).

Kansas State University Public Infractions Report. NCAA news release, 1997.

Kitchin, J. *Spring Symposium: Issues Facing College Athletics*. KANSAS JOURNAL OF LAW AND PUBLIC POLICY (1996).

Lapter, Alain. Bloom v. NCAA: *A Procedural Due Process Analysis and the Need for Reform*. 12 SPORTS LAWYERS JOURNAL 255 (2005).

LiCalsi, Michael B. *"The Whole Situation Is a Shame, Baby!" NCAA Self-Regulations Categorized as Horizontal Combinations Under the Sherman Act's Rule of Reason Standard: Unreasonable Restrains of Trade or an Unfair Judicial Test?* 12 GEORGE MASON LAW REVIEW 831 (2004).

Marsh, Gene, & Robbins, Marie. *Weighing the Interests of the Institution, the Membership and Institutional Representatives in an NCAA Investigation*. 55 FLORIDA LAW REVIEW 667 (2003).

Martin, Kenneth. *The NCAA Infractions Appeals Committee: Procedure, Precedent and Penalties*. 9 SETON HALL JOURNAL OF SPORT LAW 123 (1999).

Mawdsley, Ralph D., & Russo, Charles J. *Antitrust Law and Limiting Coaches' Salaries: The Saga of* Law v. NCAA. 131 WEST'S EDUCATIONAL LAW REPORTER 895 (1999).

Mayes, Thomas A. *Tonya Harding's Case: Contractual Due Process, the Amateur Athlete, and the American Ideal of Fair Play*. 3 UCLA ENTERTAINMENT LAW REVIEW 109 (1995).

McCallister, Cary M. *Aluminum Bat Manufacturers Anticompetitive Trade Practices in Collegiate Baseball: A Case Review*. 2 DEPAUL JOURNAL OF SPORTS LAW & CONTEMPORARY PROBLEMS (2004).

Merten, Jenna. *Raising a Red Card: Why Freddy Adu Should Not Be Allowed to Play Professional Soccer*. 15 MARQUETTE SPORTS LAW REVIEW 205 (2004).

Meyer, Stacey. *Unequal Bargaining Power: Making the National Letter of Intent More Equitable.* 15 MARQUETTE SPORTS LAW REVIEW 227 (2004).

Mitten, Matthew J., Davis, Timothy, Smith, Rodney, & Berry, Robert. *Sports Law and Regulations: Cases, Materials and Problems.* New York: Aspen, 2005.

Nagy, Tibor. *The "Blind Look" Rule of Reason: Federal Courts' Peculiar Treatment of NCAA Amateurism Rules.* 15 MARQUETTE LAW REVIEW 331 (2005).

National Collegiate Athletic Association. *NCAA Division II Amateurism Deregulation Guide for Coaches.* Indianapolis, IN: NCAA, 2009.

National Collegiate Athletic Association. *2005–06 Guide for the College-Bound Student-Athlete.* Iowa City, IA: NCAA Initial-Eligibility Clearinghouse, 2005.

National Collegiate Athletic Association Provisional Standards for Testing Baseball Bat Performance. NCAA news release, 1999.

Otto, K. Alexa. *Major Violations and NCAA 'Powerhouse' Football Programs: What Are the Odds of Being Charged?* 15 JOURNAL OF LEGAL ASPECTS OF SPORT 39 (2005).

Raley, John, & McClelland, Mary. *Should College Football's Currency Read "In BCS We Trust" or Is It Just Monopoly Money? Antitrust Implications of the Bowl Championship Series.* 37 TEXAS TECH LAW REVIEW 167 (2004).

Rebuttal Appeals Brief of the University of Alabama to NCAA Infractions Appeal Committees of Portions of Infractions Report #193 of the NCAA Committee on Infractions (2005).

Savage, Jennifer Brooke. Bloom v. National Collegiate Athletic Association: *No Endorsements for a Two Sport Athlete.* HOLLAND & KNIGHT LLP EDUCATION NEWSLETTER, July 29, 2004.

Vaccaro, Don F. *Validity of Regulation of Athletic Eligibility of Students Voluntarily Transferring from One School to Another.* 15 AMERICAN LAW REPORTS 4TH 885 (1982).

Warmbrod, Jodi M. *Antitrust in Amateur Athletics: Fourth and Long: Why Non-BCS Universities Should Punt Rather Than Go for an Antitrust Challenge to the Bowl Championship Series.* 57 OKLAHOMA LAW REVIEW 333 (2004).

Weiler, Paul C., & Roberts, Gary R. *Sports and the Law: Text, Cases, Problems,* 3d ed. St. Paul, MN: Thomson/West, 2004.

Wilmot, Matthew R. *Baseball Bats in the High Tech Era: A Products Liability Look at New Technology, Aluminum Bats, and Manufacturer Liability.* 16 MARQUETTE SPORTS LAW REVIEW 353 (2006).

Yasser, Ray, & Fees, Clay. *Attacking the NCAA's Anti-Transfer Rules as Covenants Not to Compete.* 15 SETON HALL JOURNAL OF SPORTS AND ENTERTAINMENT LAW 221 (2005).

Yasser, Raymond L., McCurdy, James R., Goplerud, C. Peter, & Weston, M. *Sports Law: Cases and Materials,* 4th ed. Cincinnati, OH: Anderson, 2000.

CHAPTER 11

AMATEUR ATHLETICS AND ELIGIBILITY IN INTERSCHOLASTIC SPORTS

Athletic eligibility is the key to participation in amateur sports. Athletes must be deemed eligible by their sports' governing bodies, which differ as to the definition of an amateur athlete. Athletic associations providing eligibility rules dictate who can participate as well as how student-athletes can participate. High school and collegiate competition is considered "restricted" competition.[1] An inter-scholastic athlete may be regulated by a local school district, the state high school athletic association, or both. At the intercollegiate level, athletic conferences and the national governing entity govern the eligibility and rules of participation of the student-athlete. Conversely, Olympic competition is open to all athletes and is controlled by the United States Olympic Committee.[2] This type of competition has been referred to as "unrestricted competition" because it allows all categories of people and groups and is not restricted by age or other criteria.[3]

Eligibility issues are not as prevalent in professional sports as they are at the amateur level. Inter-collegiate and interscholastic athletes are heavily regulated, bringing into play eligibility issues for the amateur athlete that can involve numerous constitutional issues. Several major governing bodies exist for student-athletes. The collegiate athlete could be governed by the National Collegiate Athletic Association (NCAA), the National Association of Interscholastic Athletics (NAIA), or another governing body. All of these entities have rules and regulations concerning eligibility. This chapter focuses on interscholastic athletics and student-athletes participating at the high school level.

Amateur athletics is widely popular in the United States. High school athletic events can some-times draw bigger crowds than a college or pro event. On December 12, 2002, LeBron James and his high school teammates appeared in a game on ESPN2. The game was the most-watched game in ESPN2 history at the time. ESPN now regularly televises high school football and basketball games. National rankings now exist for high school teams in many sports including football, baseball, bas-ketball, and lacrosse.

---

[1] JOHN C. WEISTART, THE LAW OF SPORTS (SUPPLEMENT 1985) (1985).

[2] Walter Champion, *Sports Law: Cases, Documents, and Materials*, Aspen Publishers, 2005, Chapter 8.

[3] *Id.*

Participation in interscholastic athletics is at an all-time high. Thousands of student-athletes participate in a variety of sports at the high school level every year. As a result of this increased participation, extensive regulation has occurred. The premier governing body for high school sports in the United States is the National Federation of State High School Associations (NFHS), founded in 1923. The NFHS comprises the high school athletic or activities associations of 50 states and currently governs more than seven million student-athletes. Its stated purpose is as follows:

> The National Federation of State High School Associations serves its members, related professional organizations, and students by providing leadership for the administration of education-based interscholastic activities, which support academic achievement, good citizenship, and equitable opportunities.

A major issue in amateur sports in the United States is determining the status of the athletes involved. How is an amateur athlete defined? What if a student-athlete plays on or tries out for a professional team? What if a student-athlete gets paid for playing a sport? Is the athlete now considered a professional athlete? Are Olympic athletes considered amateurs or professionals? The term "amateur" has always been subject to debate and is always evolving.[4]

Defining the fine line between an amateur and professional is essential for the participating athletes. Recently the line has become blurred, making it increasingly difficult to define amateur athletics. The Olympics had always been considered a showplace for the amateur athlete, and for many years the United States sent its premier amateur athletes to participate in the Olympic Games. In recent years, however, the United States has sent its best athletes regardless of their professional or amateur status. The "Dream Team" starring NBA superstars Michael Jordan, Magic Johnson, and Larry Bird dominated the 1992 Olympic Games while they were still playing professionally in the NBA. Swimmer Michael Phelps holds the Olympic record for the most gold medals at a single Olympics; he won eight gold medals at the 2008 Beijing games. Before he even began competing as an Olympic swimmer he had already obtained a multimillion-dollar, multiyear endorsement deal with Speedo to market its products.[5] These situations make it difficult to define "amateur athlete" and are in sharp contrast to past practices. For example, Jim Thorpe won gold medals in both the pentathlon and decathlon in the 1912 Olympics. The Olympic Committee took Thorpe's medals from him and removed his name from the record books after it was discovered he had played two semi-professional seasons of baseball.[6] Thorpe's medals were restored to him posthumously in 1982 and his name replaced in the record books.

The definition of an amateur may change from one governing organization to another, allowing an individual to be considered an amateur under one set of rules but a professional under another. An amateur has been defined by one high school athletic association as follows:

```
A.  A student-athlete who represents a member school in an inter-
    scholastic sport shall be an amateur in that sport. An amateur
    athlete is one who engages in athletic competition solely for the
```

---

[4] *What Does 'Amateur Athlete' Mean?*, The Washington Post, July 9, 1996.

[5] Frank Litsky, *Sports Briefing: Swimming; Phelps Signs Lucrative Endorsement Deal*, The New York Times, November 7, 2003.

[6] *See Generally*, Joseph Bruchac, *Jim Thorpe, Original All-American*, Speak, 2008.

physical, mental, social, and pleasure benefits derived therefrom. This rule may be waived for students participating as members of official United States Olympic Teams.

B. A student-athlete forfeits amateur status and eligibility in a sport sanctioned by the Association by:

1. Competing for pay or monetary compensation (allowable travel, meals and lodging expenses may be accepted);

2. Receiving any award, merchandise or prize whose aggregate value exceeds $250 which has not been approved by the school's principal (this section does not apply to awards given by the Association);

3. Capitalizing on athletic fame by receiving money or gifts of monetary value (scholarships paid directly to institutions of higher learning are specifically exempted);

4. Signing a professional playing contract in that sport.

C. Accepting a nominal, standard fee or salary for instructing, supervising or officiating in an organized youth sports program or recreation, playground or camp activities shall not jeopardize amateur status. An organized youth sports program includes both school and non-school programs.[7]

The fine line between amateur and professional was crossed in *Karmanos III v. Baker*, 816 F.2d 258 (1987). A student, his father, and the father's hockey club sued the University of Michigan and the NCAA after the student was declared ineligible under NCAA rules. While a senior in high school in Canada, the plaintiff played ice hockey with the Canadian Major Junior Hockey League. The university representative for intercollegiate athletics at the University of Michigan initiated a hearing before the NCAA's eligibility committee. The representative argued that Karmanos was not a professional hockey player because he had not been compensated. The NCAA declared him ineligible notwithstanding the lack of pay.

The student's father was also a named plaintiff in the lawsuit and argued that NCAA eligibility rules "penalized him for exercising his constitutional right to raise his son."[8] The Sixth Circuit agreed with the court of appeals, which had stated:

> [T]he right to direct the upbringing and education of one's child does not extend so far as to give a father a right to direct his child to play hockey on a professional team without losing his amateur status.[9]

The court ruled in favor of all defendants, finding that the NCAA was not a state actor. Furthermore, the plaintiff agreed on appeal that he did not have a constitutionally protected right to participate in intercollegiate athletics.

---

[7] Wenatchee Public Schools, Student Athlete Handbook, 2009.
[8] *Karmanos III*, 816 F. 2d at 260.
[9] *Karmanos III*, 617 F. Supp. 809, 813 (E.D. Mich. 1985).

CONSTITUTIONAL CONSIDERATIONS

Amateur athletic associations must take into consideration the interests of student-athletes, coaches, players, fans, teams, and referees and their interactions with one another when drafting and enforcing eligibility rules. These rules and regulations can cover a myriad of issues, including student-athlete conduct (on and off the field), grooming standards for athletes, age and semester limitations, grade requirements, and sportsmanship. Interscholastic athletes and their parents have challenged various rules and regulations largely on the constitutional grounds of due process and equal protection.

One of the primary questions to resolve is, Does a student-athlete have a sufficiently important interest in his or her participation in interscholastic athletics to warrant receiving the protections provided by constitutional due process? If the interest is deemed a right rather than a privilege, then constitutional issues come into play. For due process protections to exist, the right must either be a liberty or property interest.

The Fourteenth Amendment has had a significant effect on interscholastic athletics. It states in part: "No State shall make or enforce any law which shall abridge the privileges or immunities of citizens of the United States; nor shall any State deprive any person of life, liberty, or property, without due process of law; nor deny to any person within its jurisdiction the equal protection of the laws."[10]

Right Versus Privilege

Generally, there is no constitutional right to participate in interscholastic athletics.[11] However, a student cannot be arbitrarily denied the opportunity to participate.[12] Some courts have indicated that "a student merely has an expectation, rather than an entitlement to participate in athletics."[13] Cases that have addressed this question at the interscholastic level have not been favorable for the plaintiffs. In *Indiana High School Athletic Ass'n v. Carlberg by Carlberg*, 694 N.E. 2d 222 (Ind. 1998), the court found that the plaintiff did not have a protected interest in athletic participation at the high school level. Courts have cited a variety of reasons supporting their decisions, including the difference between high school and collegiate athletes. One court has stated:

> There is a vast difference between high school football and college football. A high school athlete receives no present economic benefit from playing high school football, his only economic benefit being the possibility of his receiving an offer of a college scholarship. The *Scott* case held that such a possibility was too speculative to recognize as a property right. In contrast, the college athlete receives a scholarship of substantial pecuniary value to engage in college sports. Such scholarships often cover the complete cost of attending a college or university; therefore, the right to be eligible to participate in

---

[10] U.S. Const. amend. XIV, § 1.

[11] IHSAA v. Lawrence Circuit Court, 240 Ind. 114, 162 (1959); Haas v. South Bend Community School Corporation, 289 N.E.2d 495 (1972); Mitchell v. Louisiana High School Athletic Association, 430 F.2d 1155 (5th Cir. 1970); Blue v. Univ. Interscholastic League, 503 F. Supp. 1030 (N.D. Tex 1980); Rutledge v. Ariz. BD of Regents, 660 F.2d 1345 (9th Cir. 1981), *aff'd on other grounds*, 460 U.S. 719 (1983).

[12] Anderson v. Indiana High School Athletic Association, 699 F. Supp. 719 (S.D. Ind. 1988).

[13] Mississippi High School Activities Association, Inc. v. Coleman, 631 So.2d 768, 774 (citing Niles v. University Interscholastic League, 715 F.2d 1027, 1031 (1983), *cert. denied*, 465 U.S. 1028, 104 S.Ct. 1289, 79 L.E.2d 691 (1984)); Walsh v. Louisiana High School Activities Assoc., 616 F.2d 152, 159–60 (5th Cir. 1980).

college athletics cannot be viewed as a mere speculative interest, but is a property right of present economic value. *Cf. Byars v. Baptist Medical Center, Inc., 361 So.2d 350 (Ala.1978), and Carter v. Knapp Motor Co., 243 Ala. 600, 11 So.2d 383 (1943). See also Note, Judicial Review of Disputes Between Athletes and the National Collegiate Athletic Association, 24 Stan.L.Rev. 903 (1972) (hereinafter referred to as Review of NCAA Disputes); and Martin, The NCAA and the Fourteenth Amendment, 11 New Eng.L.Rev. 383 (1976).*[14]

However, the court in *Colorado Springs v. National Collegiate Athletic Ass'n*, 570 F.2d 320 (10th Cir. 1972), expressed a different view:

> We conclude that this appeal is controlled by our decisions in *Albach v. Odle,* 531 F.2d 983 (10th Cir.), and *Oklahoma High School Athletic Ass'n v. Bray,* 321 F.2d 269 (10th Cir.). These two cases, of course, concerned high school athletics, but the same considerations are applicable here. The arguments as to the difference between high school athletic programs and those in the universities have been examined. We have also considered the point that college athletic scholarship arrangements may create a distinction. But all considered, we find no more than a difference in degree. The fundamental positions are the same, the goals are the same, the stakes are pretty much the same. The same relationship also exists between the primary academic functions of the schools in each category and the athletic programs. The differences in degree or magnitude do not lead to a different result. In each, the athletic program is very important, as are the many other diverse functions, programs, and activities not within the academic core. As we held in *Albach v. Odle,* 531 F.2d 983:
>
> > ". . . The educational process is a broad and comprehensive concept with a variable and indefinite meaning. It is not limited to classroom attendance but includes innumerable separate components, such as participation in athletic activity and membership in school clubs and social groups, which combine to provide an atmosphere of intellectual and moral advancement. We do not read *Goss* to establish a property interest subject to constitutional protection in each of these separate components."[15]

Although the opportunity to participate in interscholastic athletics may not be considered a property right, some student-athletes have been successful by showing they were deprived of "the opportunity to qualify" after being suspended from high school athletics.[16]

In *Tiffany v. Arizona Interscholastic Association,* 726 P.2d 231 (Ariz. Ct. App. 1986), the court failed to find a constitutional violation when a 19-year-old student-athlete failed to obtain a hardship waiver to be able to participate. However, the court found that the association had failed to follow its own bylaws and stated:

> . . . [I]n the realm of constitutional law, there are very few absolutes. We are persuaded that under certain circumstances a high school student can properly establish an entitlement to due process protection in connection with a suspension or exclusion from high school athletics. We believe that an appropriate extension of the holding in *Goss v. Lopez* was expressed by the court in *Pegram v. Nelson,* 469 F.Supp. 1134 (M.D.N.C.1979). In that case, a high school student was suspended for ten days and

---

[14] Gulf South Conference v. Boyd, 369 So.2d 553 (Ala. 1979).
[15] *Colorado Springs*, 570 F.2d at 321.
[16] *Anderson v. Indiana High School Athletic Ass'n*, 699 F. Supp. 719 (1988).

was also excluded from after-school activities for a period of four months. The court acknowledged that the "opportunity to participate in extracurricular activities is not, by and in itself, a property interest." *Id.* at 1139. The court recognized, however, that:

> *"Total exclusion* from participation in that part of the educational process designated as extracurricular activities for a *lengthy period of time* could, depending upon the particular circumstances, be a sufficient deprivation to implicate due process."[17]

The U.S. Supreme Court has defined the parameters of the Due Process Clause of the Fourteenth Amendment. The clause provides two basic protections: due process and equal protection. The Fourteenth Amendment covers both procedural due process and substantive due process. Procedural due process addresses the manner used in arriving at a particular decision. Substantive due process deals with the essential fairness of the government action. The federal statute commonly referred to as Section 1983 is also available to plaintiffs asserting constitutional violations.[18]

To establish a Fourteenth Amendment due process violation, a plaintiff must prove that (1) the plaintiff is an individual; (2) that the defendant is a "state actor"; (3) that the plaintiff has a life, liberty, or property interest at stake; and (4) that the state entity failed to provide the plaintiff with the due process required.[19] Intercollegiate athletics are usually viewed differently than interscholastic athletics on constitutional grounds.[20]

In *Florida High School Athletic Ass'n v. Melbourne Central Catholic High School*, 867 So.2d 1281 (Fla. App. 2004), a high school student sued because he was declared ineligible due to a recruiting violation. In reviewing the trial court's ruling, the court stated:

> . . . [T]he trial court identified a possible protectable interest in Morris's potential for an athletic scholarship. However the possibility of a scholarship is not a protectable property interest. *See also Schaill v. Tippecanoe County Sch. Corp.*, 679 F.Supp. 833, 855 (N.D.Ind. 1998) ("[S]tudent's aspirations for a college scholarship from high school sports . . . do not establish any legally protected interests."), *aff'd*, 864 F.2d 1309 (7th Cir. 1988). Assuming that MCC and Morris were entitled to due process, there is no evidence that they were denied the procedure that was due.
>
> . . . [T]here has been no constitutional violation demonstrated in this case. The harshness resulting from the application of a high school athletic association's eligibility rules is not grounds for judicial interference. More importantly, the complaint fails to allege, and the evidence fails to demonstrate, the deprivation by FHSAA of a constitutionally protected right. While FHSAA action is state action for constitutional purposes, *Florida High School Activities Association, Inc. v. Bradshaw*, 369 So.2d 398, 401 (Fla. 2d DCA 1979), we find no constitutional violation here. The federal due process clause does not protect against every alleged injury at the hands of the state. The opportunity to participate in interscholastic athletic activities, standing alone, is not a constitutionally protected right. "If an individual student [Morris] has no constitutionally protected right or privilege to participate in interscholastic sport activities, then it follows that, without more, a school's football team [MCC] as a group has no such constitutionally protected right or privilege." *Bradshaw*, 369 So.2d at 403.

---

[17] *Tiffany*, 726 P.2d at 235.
[18] 42 U.S.C. § 1983 (2005).
[19] Hawkins v. NCAA, 652 F. Supp. 602, 610 (C.D. Ill. 1987).
[20] *See* National Collegiate Athletic Ass'n v. Yeo, 114 S.W.3d 584 (Tex. App. 2003).

Unless athletic association regulations deny an athlete a protected fundamental right or classify him or her on a suspect basis, *e.g.*, religion or race, athletic programs are not subject to federal scrutiny. We agree with the federal courts that a student's interest in participating in interscholastic sports is a mere expectation, and not a constitutionally protected property right.[21]

If a constitutionally protected right is not at stake, no procedural due process is required.[22] If a fundamental right is at stake, then a different analysis would apply.

Does a student have a property right in a cheerleading spot on the high school cheerleading squad? That issue was explored in Case 11-1, *K. Haverkamp v. Unified School District #380, et al.*, 689 F. Supp. 1055 (1986).

📖 CASE 11-1   *K. Haverkamp v. Unified School District #380, et al.*

689 F. Supp. 1055 (1986)

SAFFELS, District Judge.

Plaintiff claims she was deprived of property and liberty without due process of law, that defendants' actions deprived her of her first amendment rights . . .

Plaintiff is a recent January, 1986 graduate of Centralia High School in Centralia, Kansas. Prior to October 21, 1985, plaintiff was the Head Cheerleader for the high school varsity cheerleading squad.

In October, 1985, plaintiff was given the opportunity to journey to Nashville, Tennessee to record an album. She received permission for the journey from defendants Kraushaar and Zumbahlen. However, defendants Dibble and Sleeper, who were pep club sponsors, removed plaintiff from the varsity cheerleading squad. Plaintiff alleges this was because of animosity and ill-feelings by defendants toward her. Defendants Kraushaar and Zumbahlen were informed of plaintiff's removal but refused to take any action on plaintiff's behalf. Plaintiff alleges her removal from the cheerleading squad was done without notice or hearing of any kind, thus violating her right to procedural due process . . .

Plaintiff claims a property interest in her position as Head Cheerleader for the Centralia High School varsity cheerleading squad and also that her journey to Nashville to record an album was protected activity under the First Amendment of the United States Constitution and defendants' retaliatory actions against her violated her first amendment rights . . .

The court will first consider the nature of plaintiff's interest in her position as Head Cheerleader for the high school varsity

---

[21] *Melbourne*, 867 So.2d at 1288–89.
[22] Paul v. Davis, 424 U.S. at 711, 96 S.Ct. at 1165 (1976).

cheerleading squad. Property interests are not created by the United States Constitution, but are created and their dimensions defined by existing rules or understandings that stem from an independent source such as state law. An interest in property arises only when there is a legitimate claim of entitlement to it; merely having an abstract need or desire for the particular benefit or unilateral expectation of it is insufficient.

Defendants argue that no protected property interest exists in the right to participate in extracurricular scholastic activities. The majority of cases discussing interscholastic athletics and other extracurricular activities have rejected the existence of a federally-protected property right. . . . The court notes, however, that there are a group of cases holding that students have constitutionally-protected interests in extracurricular activities. One line of cases holds that participation in athletics gives rise to a property interest because interscholastic athletics can be a springboard to a higher education or a professional career in sports. Another line of cases finding a constitutionally-protected property interest takes the view that interscholastic athletics are an integral part of the total education process. A third group of cases holds that denial of the right to participate in extracurricular activities may amount to a constitutional violation where such denial violates the equal protection clause of the United States Constitution. . . .

In the instant case, the court finds that plaintiff's position as Head Cheerleader or as a member of the varsity cheerleading squad does not rise to the level of a constitutionally-protected property interest. The court declines to follow those few cases holding that a property interest exists because of the potential for future education or professional career opportunities. Any potential opportunities for the future derived from participation in interscholastic athletics amounts only to mere expectations and are insufficient for the creation of a constitutionally-protected property interest. . . . The court elects to follow the majority view holding that federally-protected property interests do not exist in participation in interscholastic extracurricular activities. Therefore, plaintiff's claim on this basis must be dismissed.

Plaintiff asserts that the facts as pled show a denial of equal protection because defendants' actions in removing her from her position as Head Cheerleader deprived her of her rights under the fourteenth amendment. This argument is tied into plaintiff's assertion that defendants deprived her of her right to free speech by retaliating against her by removing her from the cheerleading squad after she journeyed to Nashville to make a record. The court will consider equal protection and first amendment claims together.

Local school boards have broad discretion in the management of school affairs. Federal courts should not ordinarily intervene in the resolution of conflicts which arise in the daily operation of school systems. Local school boards have a legitimate and substantial community interest in promoting respect for authority and traditional values.

However, the discretion of local school boards in matters of education must be exercised in a manner consistent with "the transcendent imperatives of the first amendment." Although first amendment rights are to be applied in light of the special characteristics of the school environment, it cannot be said "that either students or teachers shed their constitutional rights to freedom of speech or expression at the school house gate. . . . [T]he court has repeatedly emphasized the need for affirming the comprehensive authority of the states and of school officials, consistent with fundamental constitutional safeguards, to prescribe and control conduct in the school."

Plaintiff correctly argues that she need not establish an underlying constitutionally-protected property or liberty interest in her position as Head Cheerleader in order to pursue her first amendment retaliation claim. However, the court cannot agree with plaintiff's assertion that defendants' actions deprived her of her first amendment rights. The facts thus alleged do not rise to the level of a constitutional violation. There is no indication that the nature of plaintiff's speech or associations led to her removal from the cheerleading squad nor is there any indication of retaliation by school officials because plaintiff journeyed to Nashville to record an album. The actions of the defendants fall within the discretionary authority available to school officials and did not cause any restrictions on plaintiff's first amendment rights. A student's first amendment rights are to be considered in light of the special characteristics of the school environment. The court cannot find that defendants' actions violate the protections afforded plaintiff through the first amendment. It follows that plaintiff's claim under equal protection and first amendment violations must be dismissed . . .

Source: Courtesy of Westlaw; reprinted with permission.

State Action

Under constitutional law analysis, the plaintiff must first demonstrate that the deprivation of the alleged liberty or property interest was the result of state action. The Fourteenth Amendment excludes private conduct from constitutional scrutiny.[23] High school athletic associations are generally considered

---

[23] Am. Nfs. Ins. Co. v. Sullivan, 526 U.S. 40, 50 (1999).

state actors when they pass regulations regarding a student-athlete's participation in sports.[24] It is thus relatively simple to determine whether state action is involved if the defendant is a public middle school or high school. The question becomes more difficult when the defendant is a private entity engaging in conduct which has the characteristics of a "state actor" or is actually a de facto state actor.

Courts have applied certain tests to determine whether the defendant is a state actor. If there is a close nexus between the state and the challenged action, the defendants may be treated as a state actor. The test was discussed in *Cranley v. National Life Insurance Co. of Vermont*, 318 F.3d 105 (2nd Cir. 2003), in which the court stated:

> "[S]tate action requires *both* an alleged constitutional deprivation 'caused by the exercise of some right or privilege created by the State or by a rule of conduct imposed by the State or by a person for whom the State is responsible,' *and* that 'the party charged with the deprivation must be a person who may fairly be said to be a state actor.'" *American Manufacturers Mutual Insurance Co. v. Sullivan*, 526 U.S. 40, 50, 119 S.Ct. 977, 143 L.Ed.2d 130 (1999) (quoting *Lugar v. Edmondson Oil Co.*, 457 U.S. 922, 937, 102 S.Ct. 2744, 73 L.Ed.2d 482 (1982)) (emphases in original). Under the latter requirement, a plaintiff must show that the allegedly unconstitutional conduct is "fairly attributable" to the state. *American Manufacturers Mutual Insurance Co. v. Sullivan*, 526 U.S. at 50, 119 S.Ct. 977.
>
> For the conduct of a private entity to be "fairly attributable" to the state, there must be "such a 'close nexus between the State and the challenged action' that seemingly private behavior 'may be fairly treated as that of the State itself.'" *Brentwood Academy v. Tennessee Secondary School Athletic Ass'n*, 531 U.S. 288, 295, 121 S.Ct. 924, 148 L.Ed.2d 807 (2001) (quoting *Jackson v. Metropolitan Edison Co.*, 419 U.S. at 351, 95 S.Ct. 449). "The purpose of [the close-nexus] requirement is to assure that constitutional standards are invoked only when it can be said that the State is *responsible* for the specific conduct of which the plaintiff complains." *Blum v. Yaretsky*, 457 U.S. 991, 1004, 102 S.Ct. 2777, 73 L.Ed.2d 534 (1982) (emphasis in original).
>
> The determination of whether the specific conduct of which the plaintiff complains constitutes state action is a "necessarily fact-bound inquiry." *Brentwood Academy v. Tennessee Secondary School Athletic Ass'n*, 531 U.S. at 298, 121 S.Ct. 924 (internal quotation marks omitted). A challenged activity by a private entity may be deemed state action when the state exercises "coercive power," is "entwined in [the] management or control" of the private actor, or provides the private actor with "significant encouragement, either overt or covert," or when the private actor "operates as a willful participant in joint activity with the State or its agents," is "controlled by an agency of the State," has been delegated a "public function" by the state, or is "entwined with governmental policies." *See id.* at 296, 121 S.Ct. 924 (internal quotation marks omitted).
>
> In contrast, conduct by a private entity is not fairly attributable to the state merely because the private entity is a business subject to extensive state regulation or "affected with the public interest." *Jackson v. Metropolitan Edison Co.*, 419 U.S. at 350, 353, 95 S.Ct. 449. . . .[25]

---

[24] Griffin v. Ill. High Sch. Ass'n, 822 F.2d 671, 674 (7th Cir. 1987); Clark v. Ariz. Interscholastic Ass'n, 695 F.2d 1126, 1128 (9th Cir. 1982), *cert. denied*, 464 U.S. 818 (1983); United States v. Mo. State High Sch. Activities Ass'n, 682 F.2d 147, 151 (8th Cir. 1982); Yellow Springs Exempted Village Sch. Dist. Bd. of Educ. v. Ohio High Sch. Athletic Ass'n, 647 F.2d 651 (6th Cir. 1981); Moreland v. W. Pa. Interscholastic Athletic League, 572 F.2d 121, 125 (3rd Cir. 1978).

[25] *Cranley*, 318 F.3d at 111–12.

In *Johnson v. Rodrigues*, 293 F. 3d 1196 (10th Cir. 2002), the court discussed the concept of state action in the context of an adoption case. The court noted that there were four tests used by courts in determining whether state action exists:[26]

- The pursue function test
- The nexus test
- The symbiotic relationship test
- The joint action test

The court in *Johnson* cited to *Brentwood Academy* in discussing the concept of state action entwinement:

> Having stated the foregoing, the Court then introduced a new locution into the legal lexicon for use in determining whether a private party's actions constituted state action—entwinement.
>
> The entwinement down from the State Board is therefore unmistakable, just as the entwinement up from the member public schools is overwhelming. Entwinement will support a conclusion that an ostensibly private organization ought to be charged with a public character and judged by constitutional standards; entwinement to the degree shown here requires it. *Id.* at 302, 121 S.Ct. 924.
>
> Speaking through Justice Souter, the Court found "entwinement in light of the fact that 84 percent of the members of the interscholastic athletic association were public schools." Thus, although the nomenclature is new, its meaning appears to be comparable to what the Court has previously described as a "symbiotic relationship."
>
> This apparently is the most noteworthy difference that prompted the Court to distinguish the facts in *Brentwood* from those in *National Collegiate Athletic Assoc. v. Tarkanian*, 488 U.S. 179, 109 S.Ct. 454, 102 L.Ed.2d 469 (1988). State action was found in *Brentwood*, which involved a private corporation that organized interscholastic athletics and sponsored tournaments among private and public high schools. *Tarkanian* involved an unincorporated association consisting of approximately 960 private and public universities and colleges. The association promulgated rules governing member institutions' recruiting, admissions, academic eligibility and financial aid standards for student athletes. In *Tarkanian* the Court found there was no state action.
>
> Symbiosis is defined as "the living together in more or less intimate association or even close union of two dissimilar organisms" or "the intimate living together of two dissimilar organisms in any of various mutually beneficial relationships; mutual cooperation between persons and groups in a society especially when ecological interdependence is involved." WEBSTER'S THIRD NEW INT'L DICTIONARY OF THE ENGLISH LANGUAGE, UNABRIDGED (1968). Entwinement is defined as "the action of entwining," while the definition of entwine is "to twine together, to interweave, attach or involve inextricably in sentiment or thought." *Id.*[27]

In Case 11-2, *Communities for Equity v. Michigan High School Athletic Association, Inc.*, 377 F.3d 504 (6th Cir. 2004), the court found the Michigan High School Athletic Association to be a state actor. Under what circumstances could you argue that state action does not exist for a high school athletic association?

---

[26] *Johnson*, 293 F.3d at 1203 (citing Gallagher v. "Neil Young Freedom" Concert, 47 F. 3d 1442 (10th Cir. 1995)).

[27] *Johnson*, 293 F. 3d at 1204–05.

CASE 11-2   *Communities for Equity v. Michigan High School Athletic Association, Inc.*

377 F.3d 504 (6th Cir. 2004)

GILMAN, Circuit Judge.

I. Background

A. *Factual Background*

At issue in this case is whether MHSAA's scheduling of athletic seasons and tournaments for six girls' sports—basketball, volleyball, soccer, Lower Peninsula golf, Lower Peninsula swimming and diving, and tennis—violates the law. With the exception of golf, all of these sports are scheduled during the nontraditional season (meaning a season of the year that differs from when the sport is typically played). Although Lower Peninsula girls' golf is played in the spring—the traditional season for golf—the fall season, when the boys play, is more advantageous. No boys' sports are scheduled in nonadvantageous seasons.

Girls have historically played in the less advantageous seasons because of the way that high school athletics developed in Michigan. MHSAA's executive director, John Roberts, explained in a 1990 article titled *Sports and Their Seasons,* published in MHSAA's Bulletin, that "[b]oys' sports were in [MHSAA member] schools first and girls' sports, which came later, were fitted around the pre-existing boys program." . . .

B. *Equal Protection*

1. State Action

The Fourteenth Amendment to the United States Constitution provides that "[n]o State shall make or enforce any law which shall abridge the privileges or immunities of citizens of the United States; nor shall any State deprive any person of life, liberty, or property, without due process of law; nor deny to any person within its jurisdiction the equal protection of the laws." Pursuant to 42 U.S.C. § 1983,

> [E]very person who, under color of any statute, ordinance, regula-
> tion, custom, or usage, of any State or Territory or the District
> of Columbia, subjects, or causes to be subjected, any citizen of
> the United States or other person within the jurisdiction thereof

to the deprivation of any rights, privileges, or immunities secured by the Constitution and laws, shall be liable to the party injured in an action at law, suit in equity, or other proper proceeding for redress. . . .

An entity or individual charged under § 1983 with a Fourteenth Amendment violation must be a "state actor." *LRL Props. v. Portage Metro Hous. Auth.*, 55 F.3d 1097, 1111 (6th Cir.1995) ("To state a claim under the Equal Protection Clause, a § 1983 plaintiff must allege that a state actor intentionally discriminated against the plaintiff because of membership in a protected class.") (quotation marks and citation omitted). As a threshold issue, therefore, we must determine whether MHSAA is a state actor.

In determining that MHSAA is a state actor, the district court relied upon the United States Supreme Court's decision in *Brentwood Academy v. Tennessee Secondary School Athletic Association*, 531 U.S. 288, 121 S.Ct. 924, 148 L.Ed.2d 807 (2001). *Cmtys. for Equity*, 178 F.Supp.2d at 846–848. The *Brentwood Academy* case addressed the issue of whether the Tennessee Secondary School Athletic Association (TSSAA), which was "incorporated to regulate interscholastic athletic competition among public and private secondary schools," engaged in state action when it enforced one of its rules against a member school. *Id.* at 290, 121 S.Ct. 924. Because of "the pervasive entwinement of state school officials in the structure of the association," the Court held that TSSAA's regulatory activity constituted state action. *Id.* at 291, 121 S.Ct. 924. The Court acknowledged that the analysis of whether state action existed was a "necessarily fact-bound inquiry," *id.* at 298, 121 S.Ct. 924 (quotation marks omitted), and noted that state action may be found only where there is "such a close nexus between the State and the challenged action that seemingly private behavior may be fairly treated as that of the State itself." *Id.* at 295, 121 S.Ct. 924.

Public schools constituted 84% of TSSAA's membership, the Court noted, and school faculty and administrators provided TSSAA's leadership. The Court was also influenced by the fact that TSSAA's primary revenue source was gate receipts from tournaments between TSSAA-member schools. In conclusion, the Court stated that, "to the extent of 84% of its membership, the Association is an organization of public schools represented by their officials acting in their official capacity to provide an integral element of secondary public schooling. There would be no recognizable Association, legal or tangible, without the public school officials, who do not merely control but overwhelmingly perform all but the purely ministerial acts by which the Association exists and functions in practical terms." *Id.* at 299–300, 121

S.Ct. 924. The Court also found significant that TSSAA ministerial
employees were treated like state employees by virtue of their eligibility for membership in the state retirement system.

MHSAA's stated purpose, "[t]o create, establish and provide for,
supervise and conduct interscholastic athletic programs throughout the
state," is virtually identical to that of its Tennessee counterpart.
See id. at 290, 121 S.Ct. 924. Like TSSAA, MHSAA's membership is composed primarily of public schools. And, similar to TSSAA, public
school teachers, administrators, and officials dominate MHSAA's leadership. Another common feature is that the bulk of MHSAA's revenue
comes from ticket sales for state championship tournaments. Finally,
MHSAA employees who had state teaching certificates were, until
January of 1988, considered state employees and were therefore eligible to participate in the state's retirement system. Employees who
started working for MHSAA before January of 1988 continue to be
members of the state employees' retirement system. *Cmtys. for Equity*,
178 F.Supp.2d at 813.

We therefore conclude that MHSAA is so entwined with the public
schools and the state of Michigan, and that there is "such a close
nexus between the State and the challenged action," *Brentwood Academy*,
531 U.S. at 295, 121 S.Ct. 924 (quotation marks omitted), that MHSAA
should be considered a state actor. Tellingly, MHSAA argued earlier in
this litigation, before the Supreme Court reversed this court's opinion
in *Brentwood Academy*, 180 F.3d 758 (6th Cir.1999), that "the nature
and function of the MHSAA is virtually identical to that of the
TSSAA." *Cmtys. for Equity*, 178 F.Supp.2d at 847. MHSAA, in sum, has
failed to present any compelling argument to distinguish itself from
TSSAA. We therefore affirm the determination of the district court
that MHSAA is a state actor.

Source: Courtesy of Westlaw; reprinted with permission.

ELIGIBILITY RULES

A wide variety of rules and regulations can affect the interscholastic athlete. Amateur athletes
must guide themselves through a maze of regulations to become and remain eligible to participate in
interscholastic sports. These rules provide stability and organization for amateur sports associations
but can also be a pitfall to student-athletes if they fail to navigate the rules properly. Rules and regulations concerning the eligibility of student-athletes run the gamut from those relating to hair length
to rules for married and pregnant students. This chapter does not address every rule and regulation
that has been challenged but rather examines selected court opinions that display how such rules
function and are interpreted by courts.

Transfer Rules

High school athletic associations have promulgated specific rules and regulations concerning the transfer of students participating in interscholastic athletics. A transfer rule typically provides that a student will have to "sit out," or remain ineligible for a specified time, if he or she transfers from one school or district to another without justification. One of the primary purposes of the transfer rule is to prevent high school athletes from transferring to other schools to create "superteams," as well as to prevent the recruiting of student-athletes.

Administrators support such rules, citing their goal of protecting high school players from the continual harassment of recruiting from coaches, alumni, and wayward boosters. Even at the high school level, competition for top recruits is fierce, and high school coaches can be placed under great pressure to win by a variety of sources. If a coach can land a star player who may assist the team in making it to the state championship, then some coaches will do whatever it takes, even if that means breaking the rules or engaging in unethical conduct to have that star player enrolled in their school to participate in athletics.

Because student-athletes can go directly to some professional sports immediately after high school, the selection of a high school can be crucial for a star student-athlete. The student-athlete and usually his or her parents want the best forum to display his or her talent for professional scouts. Both student-athletes and professional teams have a lot at stake during a high school athletic "career." In today's sporting market, a senior high school baseball player can garner a large signing bonus immediately after high school.

Several cases have addressed specific eligibility rules relating to the transferring of students between school districts. In *Crane v. Indiana High School Athletic Association*, 975 F.2d 1315 (7th Cir. 1992), a high school student challenged a transfer rule promulgated by the Indiana High School Athletic Association (IHSAA), alleging that the association's decision to declare him ineligible violated the Equal Protection Clause of the Fourteenth Amendment and Indiana state law. After the plaintiff's parents divorced, he moved to his father's new home. As a transfer student, he was ruled ineligible by the school district to participate in athletics at his new school for one year.

The court summarized the transfer rule at issue as follows:

> At center stage in this dispute is IHSAA Rule 19, governing transfer eligibility, which is designed to prevent high school students from changing schools for athletic reasons. Under Rule 19, all students who change schools are ineligible to participate in interschool athletics for one year unless the IHSAA declares them eligible pursuant to one of the subsections of the rule. The IHSAA will not grant eligibility to students who transfer to a new school "for primarily athletic reasons" or as a result of "undue influence." A transfer "for primarily athletic reasons" includes transferring to take advantage of a superior athletic team, facility or coach and transferring to avoid punitive action taken by the previous school. "Undue influence" includes any efforts by a school to recruit a student.[28]

The Court of Appeals for the Seventh Circuit held that the association acted "arbitrarily and capriciously" in ruling that the student was ineligible and upheld the lower court's granting of a permanent injunction in favor of the student.

---

[28] *Crane*, 975 F.2d at 1320–21.

Most "no transfer" rules are viewed to be rationally related to a legitimate state interest, namely, preventing the recruitment of student-athletes at the high school level. This type of ineligibility will not usually violate equal protection.[29] State athletic associations are generally granted much deference by courts when implementing transfer rules for student athletes. In *Robbins v. Indiana High School Athletic Ass'n*, 941 F. Supp. 786 (S.D. Ind. 1996), the court held that the transfer rule did not violate the constitutional right of the plaintiff, who wanted to transfer from a public school to a parochial school after her conversion to Catholicism.

In Case 11-3, *Fusato v. Washington Interscholastic Activities Association*, 970 P.2d 774 (Wash. Ct. App. 1999), a foreign student challenged an association's transfer rule on equal protection grounds. The court found in favor of the transfer student. If most athletic associations' transfer rules are upheld, why was this one struck down?

CASE 11-3   *Fusato v. Washington Interscholastic Activities Association*

970 P.2d 774 (Wash. Ct. App. 1999)

BROWN, J.

Tomoe Fusato challenges the Washington Interscholastic Activities Association's (WIAA) residence and transfer rules, which, with few exceptions, forbid students from playing varsity athletics if they did not relocate to a school district with their parents. The superior court reversed the administrative decision against Ms. Fusato and found the WIAA's rules violated the Fourteenth Amendment's Equal Protection Clause. . . . We conclude that although no fundamental right is threatened, the rule of strict scrutiny applies. This is so because the challenged rule discriminatorily impact[s] Ms. Fusato as a member of a suspect class based upon national origin and there is no showing of a compelling state interest being served by these rules. Additionally, the WIAA did not demonstrate that the least restrictive means were used to accomplish the regulatory purposes of their rules. Accordingly, we affirm.

Facts

Ms. Fusato, a Japanese National, moved from Okinawa to live with her aunt and uncle in Kettle Falls [Washington]. The purpose of the move was to experience American culture and help ease the biases prevalent against Americans arising from recent criminal conduct on the part of American servicemen. She was told she was ineligible for varsity sports at Kettle Falls High School under WIAA rules.

---

[29] Steffes v. California Interscholastic Federation, 176 Cal. App. 3d 739 (Cal. App. 1986); Manico v. South Colonie Central School District, 584 N.Y.S.2d 519 (N.Y. Sup. Ct. 1992).

The WIAA, a non-profit organization, regulates interscholastic athletics at 385 secondary schools and does not allow transferring students to be immediately eligible for varsity competition unless they transfer with their "entire family unit." Since Ms. Fusato moved without her parents a "hardship" was required for eligibility. Because neither the District . . . nor the Executive Board of the WIAA found her case to be a hardship . . . her eligibility was denied.

The Stevens County Superior Court, Judge Stewart, on appeal from the WIAA regulatory process, initially entered a temporary restraining order, permitting Ms. Fusato to play varsity sports pending final hearing. Judge Schroeder reviewed and maintained the temporary order at a continuation hearing. Finally, Judge Baker at the hearing on the merits, held the rules excluded a class of students based on national origin. The court further found the rules have a disparate impact based on this suspect class., The court took judicial notice that "almost every foreign exchange students and/or I-20 VISA students—it's almost unheard of in a high school setting—that such foreign students are here with their parents." The court also took judicial notice that "a typical foreign exchange or I-20 VISA student is unable to ever establish a hardship under the transfer rules."

The trial court concluded there was no compelling state interest in the WIAA residence and transfer rules and, accordingly, found them to be in violation of the Equal Protection Clause in the Fourteenth Amendment of the United States Constitution.

At argument, the parties informed the court that Ms. Fusato had returned to Japan and is no longer a student at Kettle Falls High School and no longer subject to WIAA rules.

Analysis

B. Equal Protection

1. Issue. The issue is whether the trial court erred by using strict scrutiny and deciding the WIAA residence and transfer rules violated the Equal Protection Clause of the Fourteenth Amendment.

. . . .

3. Discussion. The challenger of a rule, regulation or statute claiming an equal protection violation may have to meet one of three different legal standards for judging whether a violation exists. *City of Richland v. Michel,* 89 Wash. App. 764, 768-70, 950 P.2d 10 (1998). The choice is based upon the factual context, giving rise to different degrees of scrutiny in ascending order of difficulty of proof: strict, intermediate, or minimum.

One of three standards of review has been employed when analyzing equal protection claims. *Strict scrutiny* applies when a classification affects a suspect class or threatens a fundamental right. *Intermediate or heightened scrutiny*, used by this court in limited circumstances, applies when important rights or semisuspect classifications are affected. The most relaxed (minimum) level of scrutiny, commonly referred to as the *rational basis or rational relationship test*, applies when a statutory classification does not involve a suspect or semisuspect class and does not threaten a fundamental right.

State v. Manussier, 129 Wash.2d 652, 672-73, 921 P.2d 473 (1996), cert. denied, 520 U.S. 1201, 117 S.Ct. 1563, 137 L.Ed.2d 709 (1997) (citations omitted). It normally follows that the party seeking to uphold the rule, regulation, or statute generally prefers the minimum scrutiny standard, using the rational relationship test.

Deciding the degree or standard of scrutiny is our first task. Here, Ms. Fusato argues for strict scrutiny and defends the trial court's decision while the WIAA argues for the lesser minimum scrutiny standard and use of the rational relationship test. When strict scrutiny is involved, the classification will be upheld if it is shown to be necessary to accomplish a compelling state interest. If the complaining party demonstrates strict scrutiny is the proper test under the facts, then the burden shifts to the party seeking to uphold the rule, regulation, or statute "to show the restrictions serve a compelling state interest and are the least restrictive means for achieving the government objective. If no compelling state interest exists, the restrictions are unconstitutional." *First United Methodist Church v. Hearing Examiner,* 129 Wash.2d 238, 246, 916 P.2d 374 (1996).

If neither a suspect class is involved nor a fundamental right is threatened, the appropriate standard of review is the rational basis test. We answer three questions when deciding if the rational relationship test applies.
1. Does the classification apply alike to all members within the designated class?
2. Do reasonable grounds exist to support a distinction between those within and without each class? and
3. Does the class have a "rational relationship" to the purpose of the legislation?

Harris, 120 Wash.2d at 477, 843 P.2d 1056. Because the trial court agreed with Ms. Fusato that the strict scrutiny test applies here, we examine it first.

Washington courts have recognized there is no fundamental right to engage in interscholastic sports. It follows that for Ms. Fusato to prevail, the WIAA residence and transfer rules must discriminate against a suspect class to warrant strict scrutiny review. Suspect classifications include those based on race, national origin, or alienage. U.S. Const. amend. XIV. Ms. Fusato alleges discrimination and disparate impact based on her national origin.

Under the WIAA residence and transfer rules, foreign exchange and I-20 VISA students, persons of identifiable foreign national origins, cannot compete at the varsity level because their parents usually do not accompany them to the United States. Thus, disparate impact based on alienage is present. Therefore, for persons of foreign national origin the sole recourse is to apply for hardship exception under the WIAA rules. WIAA rule 18.22.1 provides:

A. A hardship exists only when some unique circumstances concerning the student's educational[,] physical or emotional status exist and only when such circumstances are beyond the student's or, where applicable, their family unit's or legal guardian's control.

B. The circumstances must be totally different from those which exist for the majority or even a small minority of students (e.g., usual maturation problems or family situations which do not cause severe and abnormal emotional problems, and academic or athletic deficiencies in a school's curriculum or extracurricular activities do not constitute a hardship).

C. There must be no reason to believe that the decision and/or the execution of the decision concerning the student's academic status was for athletic purposes.

D. The burden of providing evidence that a hardship exists shall be borne by the student.

E. There shall be a direct, causal relationship between the alleged hardship and the student's inability to meet the specific eligibility rule(s).

The trial court found[,] and we agree, a typical foreign exchange or I-20 VISA student cannot meet the hardship criteria. While the alleged purpose of the rules is to prevent school "jumping" for athletic purposes and to ensure equal treatment, the practical effect is that some students are severely limited in eligibility based solely on their national origin. . . . [T]he application of the rules to Ms. Fusato does not further their stated purposes.

However, the United States Supreme Court has repeatedly held that disparate impact, alone, does not violate the Fourteenth Amendment. See *Harris v. McRae*, 448 U.S. 297, 324 n. 26, 100 S.Ct. 2671, 65 L.Ed.2d 784 (1980). Specifically, disparate impact of a suspect class does not trigger strict scrutiny unless the party challenging the government action demonstrates an element of purposeful discrimination or intent.

The burden is on the party alleging discrimination to prove the existence of purposeful discrimination. The court must undertake "a sensitive inquiry into such circumstantial and direct evidence of intent as may be available." Circumstantial evidence may suffice to establish purposeful discrimination.

During Ms. Fusato's first administrative hearing, one of the committee members stated in response to an allegation that schools were abusing foreign exchange students:

> I don't really think that was the reason. The abusing of the foreign exchange program was not the problem. The problem was that people were bitching and complaining about the fact that we[']re giving them [foreign students] special privileges and these other people are getting turned down[,] [our] own people within the country, and that's why they changed the rule. I'm sure that's the reason.

For the WIAA to modify its rules to specifically discriminate against foreign exchange or I-20 VISA students in an attempt to make participation fairer for "our students" establishes discriminatory purpose or intent. Thus, strict scrutiny is warranted because we have both discriminatory impact based upon national origin or alienage and discriminatory purpose.

The WIAA now has the heavy burden of proving that it is necessary to discriminate based on national origin to further a compelling interest. It does not seek to meet this burden but argues solely that the rational relationship applies. In view of our rejection of that proposition, our analysis is complete. We decide the strict scrutiny test applies to these facts[,] shifting the burden to the WIAA to show a compelling state interest. We conclude the WIAA has not met its burden to show a compelling state interest was served by the challenged rules. Further, the WIAA has made no effort to demonstrate that the least restrictive regulatory means have been employed to accomplish the stated purposes. Therefore, we hold the challenged residence and transfer rules are invalid under the equal protection clause of the federal constitution and affirm the trial court. . . .

We hold the trial court did not err applying the strict scrutiny test when deciding the WIAA residence and transfer rules violated Ms. Fusato's equal protection rights under the Fourteenth Amendment. Although Ms. Fusato cannot prove a fundamental right is threatened, she established she was a member of a suspect class based upon national origin or alienage. Upon her showing of disparate impact, together with discriminatory purpose or intent, the WIAA was required to meet the burden of showing a compelling state interest was served by the challenged rules. The WIAA failed to meet its burden and made

no effort to demonstrate that the least restrictive regulatory means
were used to accomplish the stated purposes of their rules.

We affirm.

Source: Courtesy of Westlaw; reprinted with permission.

Recruiting Restrictions

High school athletic associations and even some high schools place restrictions on the recruiting of high school athletes. High school athletics is a serious business in some circles, and coaches are under a lot of pressure to win and to sustain a winning program. Although every athletic association's bylaws strictly prohibit the recruiting of interscholastic athletes, illegal recruiting still goes on.[30]

Grade Requirements

Almost all interscholastic athletic programs set forth some form of basic grade requirements to be eligible to participate. School administrators and officers strive to make it a priority that all students in the district achieve academic success. Most associations have passed bylaws that dictate that any student participating in extracurricular activities must achieve a certain grade point average (GPA) to participate.[31] These rules have been commonly referred to as "No Pass, No Play" rules and were initially proposed by state legislatures and athletic associations in an attempt to strike a balance between academics and athletics. The first "No Pass, No Play" law was passed in Texas and withstood a constitutional challenge.[32]

In *Thompson v. Fayette County Public Schools*, 786 S.W.2d 879 (Ky. Ct. App. 1990), the court upheld a rule requiring a minimum 2.0 GPA for those participating in interscholastic sports. The plaintiff failed to prove he had a property right or liberty interest in participation on the high school wrestling team.

In *Fuentes v. Irvine Unified Sch. Dist.*, 30 Cal. Rptr. 2d 521 (Cal. App. 4th Dist. 1994), a cheerleader sued the school after she was disqualified from participating in cheerleading because of a failing grade. The rules required a student to maintain a cumulative 2.5 GPA on a 4.0 scale. Furthermore, if a student earned an "F" in a course, he or she would still be rendered ineligible regardless of whether the student had a 2.5 GPA. The plaintiff flunked chemistry and therefore became ineligible. However, had she been a member of the football team, she would have remained eligible because the academic standards were lower for members of the football team. She argued she had been denied equal protection, equal privileges and immunities, and due process under the California constitution. The defendants attempted to argue that cheerleading was not a "sport" because it was not classified as such by the California Interscholastic Federation. The court, in ruling in favor of the plaintiff, stated:

> Interscholastic sports and cheerleading are both *non* academic extracurricular activities. There is nothing about cheerleading that makes it qualitatively any more or less scholarly than football, baseball or some

---

[30] Joey Knight and Izzy Gould, *Fighting Illegal Athletic Transfers No Easy Feat for Florida School Districts,* St. Petersburg Times, July 24, 2009.

[31] Dirk Johnson, *'No Pass, No Play' Rule Raises Furor*, The New York Times, May 3, 1988.

[32] Spring Branch I.S.D. v. Stamos, 695 S.W.2d 556 (Tex. 1995). For further discussion, see David J. Shannon, *No Pass, No Play: Equal Protection Analysis Under the Federal and State Constitutions*, 63 IND. L.J. 161 (1987).

other sport. Cheerleading, football, and basketball are intertwined in common presentation and popular imagination. Cheerleaders are not mere passive supporters of football and basketball teams, but, like athletes in spectator sports, entertainers in their own right. Once one draws a line between academic and nonacademic extracurricular activities, it is beyond cavil that football, basketball, and cheerleading all fall on the same side of that line.

. . . While we sympathize with the attempt to impose high academic standards on cheerleaders, the distinction between cheerleading and athletics cannot pass. That does not mean the school board must necessarily lower the academic standards for the pep squad. They could raise them for the athletes. That choice is left to the district.[33]

In Case 11-4, *Rousselle v. Plaquemines Parish School Bd.*, 527 So.2d 376 (4th Cir. 1988), a girl who wanted to try out to be a high school cheerleader challenged the GPA requirement on equal protection grounds.

📖 CASE 11-4   *Rousselle v. Plaquemines Parish School Bd.*

527 So.2d 376 (4th Cir. 1988)

PLOTKIN, Judge.

The trial court's issuance of a permanent mandatory injunction ordering and commanding the defendants to allow the plaintiff, Dani Leigh
Rousselle, to participate in cheerleader try-outs at Belle Chasse
High, despite the fact that she does not meet the minimum 1.6 grade
point average requirement, was improper. The record indicates that the
establishment of the minimum grade point average requirement is a
proper exercise of the school's right to supervise the extra-curricular
activities it sponsors.

The plaintiffs' argument that the 1.6 minimum grade point average
requirement violates the Equal Protection clause of the Fourteenth
Amendment of the United States Constitution and Art. I, Section 3 of
the Louisiana Constitution of 1974 because the minimum requirement for
participation in team sports is only 1.5 is without merit. The Equal
Protection Clause guarantees equal treatment only to those who are
similarly situated. When no fundamental rights are involved, classifications which are not suspect, such as the classification between
cheerleaders and team sport players here, are allowed so long as they
are "rationally related" to any legitimate state purpose and are uniformly applied.

Defendants claim that the minimum grade point average requirement is
designed to promote academic excellence. Certainly, this is a legitimate

---

[33] *Fuentes*, 30 Cal. Rptr. 2d at 524–25.

purpose. Additionally, the classification imposed here, which prohibits
students who do not achieve at least a 1.6 average on a 4.0 scale from
participation in cheerleading is rationally related to that legitimate
purpose. Obviously, students who value the opportunity to participate
in cheerleading will exert extra effort to meet the requirements.

Also without merit is the plaintiffs' argument that the requirement
results in improper, non-uniform application of rules in violation
of the Equal Protection guarantee because team sports members are
subject to different requirements. The school has adopted the minimum
1.5 grade point average guarantee established by the Louisiana
High School Athletic Association for those sports subject to the
requirements of the association. Cheerleading is not subject to
those requirements, leaving establishment of minimum requirements
for participation in cheerleading to the individual schools in the
same manner other extra-curricular activities are subject to supervision by individual schools. Since all students wishing to participate
in cheerleading, the only activity at issue here, are subject to the
requirement, it is uniformly applied as required by equal protection
guarantees.

Accordingly, the judgment of the trial court is reversed and the
injunction is dissolved.

Source: Courtesy of Westlaw; reprinted with permission.

The following is an example of a typical bylaw setting forth basic grade requirements for students to be eligible to participate in extracurricular activities, including interscholastic sports.

Standards and Policies for Participation in Extra-Curricular Activities

Extra-curricular activities are an integral part of school life and
are used as a means of developing wholesome attitudes and good human
relations as well as knowledge and skills. Participation in extracurricular activities is a privilege. Care must be taken to ensure
that these activities do not take precedence over the subject matter
area, but remain supplemental to the basic courses. It is desirable
that students participate in such activities to the extent that they
further their educational development. It is of paramount importance
that such participation shall not jeopardize pupil's academic achievement nor exploit their time and talents.

1. **Definition**
   The standards of a given Grade Point Average (GPA) apply to all
   other extra-curricular activities that are unrelated to courses in
   which a grade is given.

2. **Standards for Participation**

   To be eligible for participation in extra-curricular activities, students must meet minimum grade indexes as follows:

   Grade 9 — 2.00 minimum standard to take effect at the end of the first marking period. All new students must have earned final passing grades in at least three of the four core subject areas: Language Arts, Math, Science, Social Studies. One of the final passing grades must be in the area of Language Arts. A repeating . . . District 9th grade student's eligibility will be based on the fourth quarter index of the previous school year. If the student's grade point average is less than 2.00, but equal to or greater than 1.75, for subsequent marking periods the student would retain eligibility for an additional marking period by enrolling in and attending a mandatory study program in the after school program. In athletics the student must also comply with DIAA eligibility regulations.

   Grade 10-12 — The GPA must be 2.00. The minimum standard for the first quarter of the tenth, eleventh and twelfth grades is based on the grade point index of the fourth quarter of the previous year or the final grade for the year; whichever is higher. Summer school may be used to improve the final grades and impact eligibility.

   If a student's GPA is less than 2.00 but higher than or equal to 1.75, then the student may retain eligibility for one marking period by enrolling in and attending a mandatory student program in the after school program. This can be used only once each year that the student is enrolled.

   Students new to the . . . School District will be eligible for the quarter in which they enter. Eligibility under the . . . School District Policy will begin at the end of the quarter they enter . . .

3. **Probation**

   There will be no periods of probation. Students not meeting the minimum standard will be ineligible for participation.

4. **Tutoring**

   After-school tutoring will be provided for all students requesting such help. Students with a GPA *equal to or greater* than 1.75 less than 2.00 are required to enroll in and attend the after school tutoring for one marking period to increase their GPA to 2.00 . . .

In Case 11-5, *Burtt v. Nassau County Athletic Association*, 421 N.Y.S.2d 172 (N.Y. Sup. Ct. 1979), several students sued, arguing that they were victims of a teacher's strike that had caused them to be ruled ineligible. The court found otherwise.

📖 CASE 11-5 *Burtt v. Nassau County Athletic Association*

421 N.Y.S.2d 172 (N.Y. Sup. Ct. 1979)

JAMES F. NIEHOFF, Justice.

In this proceeding under CPLR Article 78, petitioners seek judgment requiring respondents to permit them to participate in varsity interscholastic football competition during the 1979 season as members of the Levittown Memorial High School team.

The petitioners are former members of the class which graduated from the high school in June, 1979 and have been required to repeat certain courses by reason of their having received failing grades therein. They now expect to graduate in January, 1980.

During the school year 1978-1979, while they were members of the senior class, the petitioners were unable to participate in interscholastic football because of the teachers' strike in the Levittown schools which caused the closing of their school in September and October, 1978.

At issue is the interpretation of the regulation of the Commissioner of Education which defines a pupil's eligibility for interschool athletic competition in senior high school grades 9, 10, 11 and 12. The regulation (8 NYCRR s 135, 4(c)(7)(ii)(b)(1)) reads as follows:

> A pupil shall be eligible for senior high school athletic competition only during eight consecutive semesters after his entry in the ninth grade and prior to graduation, unless sufficient evidence is presented by the chief school officer to the league or section to show that the pupil's failure to enter competition during one or more semesters was caused by illness, accident, or other such circumstances deemed acceptable to the league, section or association. A pupil shall be eligible for interschool competition only between his 14th and 19th birthdays. A pupil who attains the age of 19 years on or after September 1 may continue to participate during that school year in all sports.

In *Murtagh v. Nyquist*, 78 Misc.2d 876, 358 N.Y.S.2d 595, the "duration of competition" regulation (then found in 8 NYCRR s 135.4(e)(3)(i)(a)) was found to have an obvious and reasonable basis which was to prevent "red shirting" or the holding back of a pupil for one grade for academic reasons so that he or she could then compete in the fifth year of high school when the pupil is more mature, more physically developed and presumably more proficient. In *Murtagh*, *supra*, the Court held that red shirting is undesirable "because it encourages students interested in athletics to delay completion of their high school education because it provides a vehicle whereby the older 'red shirted' student is competing with younger, less developed students, a situation which could lead to injuries." In *Murtagh*, the petitioner did not claim that he fell within one of the exceptions set forth above and the petition was dismissed.

In the instant proceeding the petitioners do claim that they fall within one of the exceptions set forth in the regulation. They contend that the above-mentioned teacher's strike constitutes "other such circumstances" which should be deemed acceptable as the reason for their failure to enter interscholastic football during their senior year at high school. In sum, the petitioners contend that the regulation in question obviously envisages a situation wherein a senior high school athlete will be attending school for more than eight consecutive semesters after his or her entry into the ninth grade and that the regulation is not concerned with the reason the pupil is still in school beyond eight semesters but only with why the pupil did not compete in athletics during an earlier year's attendance.

While there is a degree of logic to that argument, the respondents have the primary responsibility of interpreting the above quoted regulation in a particular situation and unless the Court is able to characterize their determination as "arbitrary" or "capricious" it may not overturn their determination. After due consideration, the Court is of the opinion that the respondents' interpretation of the regulation in the situation here presented cannot be classified as either an arbitrary or capricious one.

In refusing to grant the petitioners the right to participate any further in varsity interscholastic football competition they pointed out that:

> If these students were approved for participation beyond their original graduation date and beyond the eight consecutive semesters of participation, there would be no rationale for denying a similar request to the perhaps hundreds of other boy and girl athletes in the Levittown School District who were in grades 9 through 12 during the fall of 1978 and who might not have met graduation requirements at the prescribed time. We believe that this might also create an untenable and unfair situation for the schools which would compete against Levittown teams.

The respondents have a responsibility to all member schools and to each student athlete in this County. In endeavoring to discharge that responsibility they have offered the above quoted reason for their action in petitioners' case. Certainly, the respondents are justified in their concern that there would be an adverse impact on athletics in general in this County if an exception to the regulation were to be made for the benefit of the petitioners herein and a precedent thereby established.

Moreover, the awarding of an extension of eligibility to petitioners might well be deemed a reward for academic failure. Undoubtedly, there were other football players who were similarly unable to participate in interscholastic competition during the 1978 season but who, nevertheless, graduated with their class in June, 1979. Why, then, should petitioners, by reason of their scholastic deficiencies, be granted that which their former classmates and teammates did not enjoy? And, why, because of their academic deficiencies should they be able to compete with younger, less developed students?

Indeed, it has been pointed out by respondents that the request for petitioners' extended eligibility was made by the Principal of Levittown Memorial High School on March 27, 1979, "long before students knew if they were going to fail or pass their necessary courses for graduation."

As respondents state: "Even if they did not purposefully fail, it is obvious that the boys and others must have considered this situation carefully. Otherwise why was a request made before the fact?" In their papers on this application, the petitioners have elected not to answer that pertinent question.

The Court fully agrees with the respondents that it is unfortunate that fine young men are placed in this situation where they were denied one year's participation in football because of a strike and that it is most lamentable that the strike occurred and disrupted the students' education.

However, even though the Court deeply regrets that petitioners were thereby deprived of participation in interscholastic football competition during the 1978 season it cannot hold that respondents' action on petitioners' application for extended eligibility is, in effect, lacking in rationality. On the contrary, the Court agrees with respondents that their "responsibility to all member schools and to each student athlete in . . . (this) county has been . . . discharged with integrity by . . . (them)."

The petition is dismissed.

Source: Courtesy of Westlaw; reprinted with permission.

Outside Competition

Many school districts have regulations stating that any students who play on a team outside the school are prohibited from participating in school-sponsored athletics. What is the purpose of such a regulation? Most courts will uphold "outside competition" rules as legitimate, giving high school athletic associations broad authority to restrict student-athletes from competition in leagues outside the school if they also compete for the school. In Case 11-6, *Letendre v. Missouri State High School Activities Association*, 86 S.W.3d 63 (Mo. Ct. App. 2002), the plaintiff was a dedicated swimmer who wanted to swim all the time, including for teams other than the school-sponsored swim team.

CASE 11-6   *Letendre v. Missouri State High School Activities Association*

86 S.W.3d 63 (Mo. Ct. App. 2002)

JAMES R. DOWD, Presiding Judge.

Claire Letendre seeks to enjoin the Missouri State High School Activities Association (MSHSAA) from enforcing by-law 235, which prohibits students from competing on both a school and a non-school team in the same sport during the school team's season. . . . She appeals, claiming that the association's rule violates the Equal Protection clause of the Fourteenth Amendment and her rights of free association under the First Amendment. We affirm.

The MSHSAA is a voluntary association of 750 secondary public, private and parochial schools in Missouri. It is charged with developing uniform and equitable standards of eligibility for students and schools to participate in interscholastic activities. The rules ostensibly work to avoid interference with the educational program of the school by outside activities; to prevent exploitation of high school youth and the programs of member schools by special interest groups; and to provide a means of evaluating and controlling local, state, and national contests affecting secondary schools. . . .

At the time of trial, Claire was a 15 year-old sophomore earning good grades. She did not participate in any school-sponsored sports, clubs, student government, or organized activities, other than a prayer group, because she "loves to swim." Claire has been a member of the private Parkway Swim Club since the age of three, swimming in competitive meets since the age of five. She practices and competes with the private swim club team all year long, participating in regional and national meets that require out-of-state travel. Her swim club's practice schedule is Monday through Friday from 4:30 to 7:30 p.m. and on Saturdays from 6:15 to 9:30 a.m., swimming from 5,000 to 9,000 yards daily. Claire testified that her coach at the Parkway Swim Club enters her in every single event offered during her swim club seasons. Claire claimed her short-term goal is to qualify for the Senior Nationals and, ultimately, the Olympics.

On January 31, 2001, Claire attended a meeting for students interested in joining the school swim team. They discussed health forms, practice times, the season schedule and MSHSAA eligibility rules. On February 12, 2001, Claire attended another school swim team meeting held immediately prior to the first practice. Claire testified that after this meeting she knew she would become ineligible for school swimming if she chose to swim with the club team.

By-law 235(1)(a) provides that "during the sport season a student . . . shall neither practice nor compete as a member of a non-school team nor as an individual participant in organized non-school competition in that same sport."

The by-laws state that a school sports season begins with the "first practice." Unlike other St. Joseph Academy students who also swam for Parkway Swim Club, Claire chose to practice with her swim club team rather than her school team.

Claire filed suit for injunctive relief to bar the MSHSAA from enforcing by-law 235, claiming it violated her rights under the First and Fourteenth Amendments. After a trial on the merits, the court entered judgment, denying Claire injunctive relief and dismissing her suit with prejudice. Claire now appeals.

Since its inception 75 years ago, the MSHSAA has received a mandate to value the best interests of all student athletes. In 1975, the Association identified outside competition during the school year as one of the "principal areas of problems facing high schools and state associations." A reasonable person could conclude that it is not in the best interest of the majority of high school students to compete in the same sport at the same time on two different teams, with different coaches, different rules, different practice schedules, and different competition schedules. The Executive Director of MSHSAA explained that one purpose of the Association is to have standards that will be in the best interest of the larger number of high school students. Here there is substantial evidence to conclude that by-law 235 is rationally related to the legitimate goal of protecting that interest. Claire's Equal Protection argument must fail.

. . . While we might personally believe that a better rule could be drafted, one that would allow a student athlete who is getting good grades, such as Claire, to compete simultaneously on both her school and non-school swim teams, the law does not permit us to interject our

personal beliefs in the name of the Constitution. Claire's constitutional challenges must fail because by-law 235 is rationally related
to the MSHSAA's purpose of drafting rules that protect the welfare of
the greatest number of high school athletes possible. The judgment
of the trial court is, therefore, affirmed.

Source: Courtesy of Westlaw; reprinted with permission.

Personal Conduct Issues

Amateur athletic associations usually promulgate specific conduct rules that a student-athlete
must abide by to remain eligible. Many schools and school districts require students to sign a code
of conduct stating that they agree to certain terms and conditions dealing with sportsmanship and personal conduct so they may participate in a sports program.[34] A typical policy sets forth the various
prohibited activities and the penalties that will be assessed if a student-athlete violates a portion of
the code of conduct or violates sportsmanship rules. The document is usually signed by the student
and, if the student is a minor, his or her parents as well. The code of conduct typically addresses
issues such as the possession or use of weapons, drugs (including steroids), tobacco, as well as
unsportsmanlike conduct.

What happens if a student violates a code of conduct? What punishment will he or she receive
and how will that punishment be carried out? What happens if the student violates the code of conduct
in the off-season? Those are issues that are central to cases dealing with these codes. In Case 11-7,
Smith v. Chippewa Falls Area Unified School Dist., 302 F. Supp. 2d 953 (W.D. Wisc. 2002), a student
was suspended because of his involvement with alcohol, which was considered a violation of the
school athletic code. He argued that he had been denied procedural due process when he was disciplined by the school for this involvement.

CASE 11-7   *Smith v. Chippewa Falls Area Unified School Dist.*

302 F. Supp. 2d 953 (W.D. Wisc. 2002)

CRABB, District Judge.

. . . [P]laintiff Lucas Smith contends that defendants Chippewa Falls
Area Unified School District and Board of Education violated his
rights to due process by removing him from an athletic team without
proper procedures.

Because I find that plaintiff does not have a protected property
interest in participating in interscholastic sports and that defendants afforded him all the process he was due, defendants' motion for
summary judgment will be granted.

---

[34] Larry D. Bartlett, *The Courts' View of Good Conduct Rules for High School Student Athletes*, 82 ED. LAW. REP.
1087 (1993).

Undisputed Facts

A. Incident and Investigation

From 1998 to January 2002, plaintiff attended Chippewa Falls high school. During that time, he participated in various interscholastic sports for the school, including cross country, track and wrestling. At all times relevant to this case, the Chippewa Falls high school adopted an activity handbook that includes a Code of Conduct for student athletes.

Rebecca R. Davis is an assistant principal at the Chippewa Falls high school. On September 24, 2001, during the course of her administrative duties, Davis learned that one of the high school's student athletes had been injured in an automobile accident the previous day. The accident was believed to be alcohol-related. Davis learned that the student had attended a party before the accident at the residence of Walter Henning.

After receiving information suggesting that high school students had been drinking beer at the party, Davis and Michael Blair, the high school's activities director, began an investigation. Davis and Blair interviewed a number of football players who were believed to have attended the party. These students reported that one student drank two beers in the Henning's "pole shed."

Davis contacted Jean Henning, Walter Henning's wife, to let her know that students were being questioned about the party that had taken place at their home. On September 25, Davis and Blair continued to interview football players about the party. After being told that a beer party had taken place in the Henning's pole shed, Davis obtained permission to get two sets of photographs taken at the Henning's party. On September 26, Davis reviewed one of the sets of photographs in which it appeared that students were consuming beer. Plaintiff appeared in one of the photos with another person who held a can of beer toward the camera.

On the afternoon of September 26, plaintiff visited Davis in her office. He appeared upset and nervous because he had heard about the investigation and wanted to know what was going to happen. Davis told plaintiff that he would be contacted the next day as part of the administration's investigation. Plaintiff denied any wrongdoing.

During the evening of September 26, plaintiff's mother, Lorraine Smith, called Davis. Davis told Smith that it appeared that a beer party had taken place at the Henning's residence and the evidence gathered in the course of the investigation indicated that plaintiff had violated the school district's athletic code by attending a party where alcohol was consumed by underage students. Davis told Smith that no final decision would be made regarding her son's involvement until after he was interviewed and that she would contact Smith to inform her of the administration's determination.

On September 27, 2001, Davis received a second set of photos taken at the party. In this set, another photo showed plaintiff inside the pole shed with a group of students. During the school day, Davis's and Blair's investigation focused on plaintiff's attendance at the party. On the basis of the information they collected, Davis and Blair believed that plaintiff had been inside the pole shed for approximately half an hour.

The same day, Davis and Blair questioned plaintiff. Plaintiff admitted being at the pole shed on the night of the party but stated that he was there for only two to five minutes while he was looking for another student. Davis and Blair told plaintiff that his story was not consistent with the version that other students had told them about his attendance, in which plaintiff was present for more than five minutes and had even passed an alcoholic beverage between two other students. Plaintiff acknowledged passing the beverage. Davis and Blair told plaintiff that he would be getting a code violation on the basis of the accounts from others about the party, the two photos showing him inside the pole shed and the responses he made during the interview. Plaintiff became very emotional and tried to persuade Davis and Blair not to issue an athletic code violation. Davis handed plaintiff the two photos and asked him if in the picture he looked like someone who just stopped by to look for someone else. Plaintiff answered, "No." Davis then asked plaintiff what he expected the school administration to do. Plaintiff replied that the consequence of his code violation should not be so great as to disqualify him from competition for the entire wrestling season. Davis and Blair explained that they were not authorized to modify the consequences of a code violation. Plaintiff was told that he would be suspended from competing in athletics under the athletic code.

Davis telephoned plaintiff's father, Scott Smith, and told him of his son's athletic code violation. Scott Smith came to school and spoke with Davis about the possibility of appealing the administration's determination.

C. Determination and Appeals

In a letter dated September 27, 2001, Blair advised plaintiff's parents formally that their son had been suspended from athletic competition for a second violation of the Chippewa Falls athletic code. Under the code, the interview with plaintiff and the letter of suspension constituted the first step in what is referred to as a "Procedure of Due Process Related to Rules of the Athletic Code" for Chippewa Falls' student athletes.

In a letter dated September 28, 2001, plaintiff asked for a building level appeal of the code violation and his suspension. This letter initiated the second step in the athletic code's review procedure.

On October 8, 2001, the building level appeal took place. Plaintiff was present with his parents. . . . At the hearing, Blair distributed information regarding the procedure the appeals committee would follow. He explained that the purpose of the hearing was to determine whether a code violation had occurred. Blair then presented a summary of the information gathered during the investigation and passed around the photographs taken at the party. Plaintiff was given an opportunity to respond to the administration's case; he chose to do so. The appeals committee voted 5-0 to uphold the finding that a code violation had occurred.

In a letter dated October 9 addressed to plaintiff's parents, Blair confirmed that the building level appeal committee had decided to uphold the finding of a code violation. He added that plaintiff could have the decision reviewed at the Board of Education level by submitting a written request for a hearing. Under the athletic code, an appeal at the board level is the third and final step of the code violation review procedure.

In a letter dated October 15, 2001 to plaintiff's parents, Blair acknowledged receipt of plaintiff's request to appeal to the Board of Education level. On October 24, 2001, the board appeal took place at a conference room in the school district's administration building. A quorum of the board was present. Plaintiff attended the appeal with his parents and was represented by a lawyer. Blair presented the administration's case that a violation had occurred and Davis provided a statement to the board. Plaintiff's lawyer presented his case in response. After hearing from both sides and after deliberation, the board announced that it had voted to uphold the administration's determination that plaintiff had committed an athletic code violation. Under the school's athletic code, the board's decision was final. The board's determination also affirmed plaintiff's suspension from competing in interscholastic athletics under the code.

Opinion

Plaintiff contends that defendants denied him procedural due process by making the determination that he violated the school's athletic code and suspending him from interscholastic competition as a consequence. A procedural due process claim against government officials requires proof of inadequate procedures and interference with a liberty or property interest. Plaintiff's claim fails on both fronts. First, it is doubtful that plaintiff has a protected property interest in participating in interscholastic sports. . . . The preponderance of federal district courts considering the issue have held that the opportunity to participate in extracurricular activities is not a protected property interest. . . .

Plaintiff does not develop his argument that he has a protected interest in participating in sports in any meaningful way, other than to assert that he "had a reasonable expectation that he could not be suspended from participation unless there was sufficient evidence submitted that he had violated the Code of Conduct." Accordingly, plaintiff has failed to demonstrate that he has a property interest entitling him to procedural due process protections.

Even if I were to assume that plaintiff has a protected property interest entitling him to due process protections, he has failed to establish that defendants did not afford him appropriate procedures in deciding to suspend him from athletic competition. In connection with the suspension of a student from public school for disciplinary reasons, due process requires "that the student be given oral or written notice of the charges against him and, if he denies them, an explanation of the evidence the authorities have and an opportunity to present his side of the story." Under this standard, a formal hearing is not required.

Regardless what the minimal procedures are that defendants had to follow in suspending plaintiff from the interscholastic sports program, their conduct comported with procedural due process. The undisputed facts establish that plaintiff was afforded procedural due process. He was allowed to engage in "give-and-take" with the school administrators investigating his case at the initial investigation stage and at all levels of appeal provided for in the athletic code. Defendants presented the evidence upon which they reached their determination and plaintiff was permitted to respond to that evidence and to give his own version of the facts. Although plaintiff may believe that defendants' athletic code is draconian, nothing in the undisputed facts supports an inference that defendants' decision to suspend plaintiff from athletic competition was arbitrary and capricious, as plaintiff argues. Instead, taking the facts in the light most favorable to plaintiff, I find that no reasonable jury could find that defendants denied plaintiff procedural due process.

Source: Courtesy of Westlaw; reprinted with permission.

Problem 11-1

Johnny Jones was a star halfback at Millerstone High School. It was the week of the state playoffs and he was celebrating with some friends at a local pizzeria. He left the pizzeria with some friends to go to a local coffee shop. The car he was riding in was stopped by the police for a broken taillight. During the stop it was discovered that alcohol was present in the car. Johnny said he was not aware of the alcohol in the car, and it is uncontroverted that he was not drinking any alcohol. He was sober at the time of the stop. He was arrested for "Minor in Possession" and released on bond.

The next day the school principal discovered what had happened and, pursuant to the policy set forth below, suspended Johnny for the rest of the season. Johnny's parents are livid and have asked you to represent them and Johnny so he can play in the state finals. Many college scouts will be at the game to watch him play. What legal advice would you give to them? What legal maneuvers would you make to try to get Johnny back on the playing field for the state championship? In light of the policy set forth below, what are your best arguments? What legal hurdles are there to overcome?

Regulation-Athletic Code of Conduct

```
Alcohol Policy-Student-athletes are prohibited from hosting/
attending a party that involves alcohol, drugs, marijuana or other
controlled substances. Student-athletes are prohibited from pos-
sessing or purchasing alcohol for themselves or anyone else.
Student-athletes are also prohibited from being present when
alcohol is possessed or consumed by minors.
```

Problem 11-2

You are the athletic director for your local high school athletic association. You have become concerned about episodes of unsportsmanlike conduct that have occurred during basketball and football games in the district between teams. Several parents have talked to you about what they believe to be unsportsmanlike conduct that has occurred both on and off the field before and after games.

Some of these episodes have been vulgar end zone dances after scoring a touchdown, taunting opposing players with the ball, and making obscene gestures at the opposing bench after scoring a touchdown. In several basketball games, players have begun to make a "throat cutting" motion to the opposing bench after completing a dunk. Recently one member of a high school football team took a picture of the opposing quarterback at a party and linked it to a pornographic website and sent it to an e-mail list he obtained of students from the opposing school.

You are now in the position where you have to address these issues. You are required to draft a sportsmanship policy that will pass constitutional muster and addresses conduct that occurs on and off the field. Should your policy cover band members and cheerleaders as well? What about school mascots?

Problem 11-3

Given the following bylaw, which of the incidents listed here would be subject to discipline?

48. Sportsmanship: Taunting

```
48.1 Taunting includes any actions or comments by coaches,
players, or spectators which are intended to bait, anger, embar-
rass, ridicule, or demean others, whether or not the deeds or
words are vulgar or racist. Included is conduct that berates,
needles, intimidates, or threatens based on race, gender, ethnic
origin or background, and conduct that attacks religious beliefs,
size, economic status, speech, family, special needs, or personal
characteristics.
```

```
Examples of taunting include but are not limited to: "trash talk,"
defined as verbal communication of a personal nature directed by a
competitor to an opponent by ridiculing his/her skills, efforts,
sexual orientation, or lack of success, which is likely to provoke
an altercation or physical response; and physical intimidation
outside the spirit of the game, including "in the face" confronta-
tion by one player to another, standing over/straddling a tackled
or fallen player, etc.[35]
```

1. A basketball player tells an opposing player during a timeout that he is a "punk midget" and could "never get a rebound over me."
2. The mascot for the local high school team leads a cheer at the boys' basketball game that ends "and your team is not 'man enough' to beat us."
3. The student section of a local private high school that is playing St. Francis Academy displays a sign that says, "Catholics won the battle but we won the war."
4. After a batter grounds into a double-play, a player on the opposing bench yells at the player, "Try some Slim-Fast next time."
5. With the score tied at 13, the Lee High School kicker lines up to try a 40-yard field goal to win the game. On the opposite sideline, several players from the opposing team gather in a circle and begin to pray.

Age and Season Limitations

School districts will usually limit the number of semesters a student may participate and may also place age limits on participation. Most high school athletic associations have rules that prohibit student-athletes from participating once they reach the age of 19. The reasons for such a rule include

---

[35] Massachusetts Interscholastic Athletic Association, Rules and Regulations Governing Athletics: A Handbook for Principals and Athletic Directors 42, http://www.miaa.net/MIAA-Handbook05-07.pdf.

protecting younger athletes, ensuring that student-athletes complete their education in a timely manner, preventing "red-shirting" (holding students back in order to play sports), and providing equal competition among all athletic squads.[36] Age rules recently have seen multiple challenges by learning and physically impaired student-athletes who challenge the rules based on the Americans with Disabilities Act along with state and federal laws.[37]

In Case 11-8, *Hamilton v. West Virginia Secondary School Activities Com'n*, 182 W.Va. 158 (W. Va. 1989), the practice of red-shirting was at issue.

CASE 11-8 *Hamilton v. West Virginia Secondary Schools Activities Com'n*

182 W.Va. 158 (W. Va. 1989)

NEELY, Justice:

Chris Hamilton appeals to this Court the decision of the Circuit Court of Kanawha County that he is ineligible to participate in inter-scholastic football as a student at Herbert Hoover High School in Clendenin.

Chris Hamilton began playing football in the eighth grade, 1984–85, at Elkview Junior High School in Kanawha County. In the fall of 1985, Mr. Hamilton, then fourteen, began the ninth grade at Elkview. He played football that year, but failed all his major academic courses that year—English, mathematics, science, health, and American studies. The next school year, 1986–87, Mr. Hamilton repeated the ninth grade at Elkview. He did not play football. Since then, he has maintained at least a C average in his courses. Having successfully completed the ninth grade, Mr. Hamilton entered the tenth grade at Herbert Hoover for the 1987–88 school year. He played football for Herbert Hoover that year and the next, 1988–89, when he was in the eleventh grade. The dispute in this case concerns Mr. Hamilton's status for the twelfth grade, the 1989–90 school year. He was eighteen years old at the beginning of his senior year.

On 13 May 1988, when Mr. Hamilton was a high-school sophomore, Herbert Hoover officials wrote to the state Secondary Schools Activities Commission to determine whether Mr. Hamilton would be eligible to play football his senior year. On 19 May 1988, the Commission responded that Mr. Hamilton would not be eligible as a senior, in accordance with the Commission's rules, because he had repeated the ninth grade.

---

[36] Brooke E. Friedrickson, *The Age Nineteen Rule and Students with Disabilities: Discrimination Against Disabled Students with Athletic Ability*, 25 T. Jefferson L. Rev. 635 (2003).

[37] Cruz v. Pennsylvania Interscholastic Athletic Association, Inc., 157 F. Supp. 2d. 485 (E.D. PA 2001).

Mr. Hamilton appealed the ruling to the Commission's Board of Appeals, which on 14 November 1988 sustained the denial of eligibility. On 8 March 1989, Mr. Hamilton brought his appeal before the Commission's highest tribunal, the Board of Review, which upheld the earlier finding.

On 13 June 1989, Mr. Hamilton sought a judicial declaration in the Circuit Court of Kanawha County that he was eligible to play football and an injunction against the Commission's forbidding him to play. On 18 August 1989, the Circuit Court denied the injunction and held that the Commission's rules, as interpreted, served a legitimate purpose and were validly applied to Mr. Hamilton.

Since this past August, the Circuit Court's order has been stayed for purposes of this appeal, and the Commission has been enjoined from prohibiting Mr. Hamilton from playing football. Herbert Hoover coaches decided to allow Mr. Hamilton to play, and he has. Mr. Hamilton is thought by some to be one [of] the top one hundred high-school football players in the United States. At the time this case was argued before this Court, the 1989 football regular season had just ended. With Mr. Hamilton's help, Herbert Hoover achieved a fine record on the field and expected to lock horns with opponents in the state Triple A football playoffs. The case, therefore, is not moot. We now reverse the judgment of the circuit court and enter final judgment in Mr. Hamilton's favor.

The Commission's athletic eligibility rules set out a scheme for determining how many seasons junior-high and high-school students may participate in inter-scholastic athletics. The basic academic qualification for sports—a 2.0 grade average—is set by the state Board of Education. The Commission has also set out rules to insure that athletes make acceptable academic progress. The Commission's rules are aimed at problems peculiar to sports, especially practices that put sports at war with the fundamental academic *raison d'etre* of the schools. The practice at issue here is known as "red-shirting." It is the cynical and pernicious manipulation of a student's academic standing for the derivative athletic glory of adults—over-zealous coaches and parents. The scheme is to take young athletes of star quality, hold them back in school for a year, keep them off the field, and have them use that year to gain bulk, strength, and maturity. When the student is led back to the field after a year, he makes a more impressive show for coaches, parents, fans, and college recruiters. Red-shirting subverts the student's normal academic progress to unworthy and improper ends. It is a corrupt and mean-spirited practice. However, in their zeal to ban it, the Commission has cast its net too wide, taking in those, like Chris Hamilton, who have just had a run of hard luck in the classroom.

To ban red-shirting, the Commission determines eligibility not by the number of years a student *participates* in a sport, but by the number of years he *attends* the school. Thus, if coaches hold a student back and bench him for a year, that year nonetheless counts as a year of eligibility, as if he had played that year. The same is true if a student takes up a sport late in his school years: He can't stay on at the school just to play the sport. There is also an absolute age limit. To play sports in a school year, a student must not have reached age nineteen on September 1st at the beginning of the school year.

What makes the scheme unreasonable is the Commission's refusal to consider the circumstances surrounding a student's being held back. There is no inquiry into actual *intent* to red-shirt. Thus, in Mr. Hamilton's case, he is simply being punished for having failed the ninth grade. Academic failure is punished, modestly, in any case, because a student who does not maintain a C average must sit on the bench until he brings his grades up. The rationale behind that rule is that the student must put academics first. His participation in sports is limited in the semester immediately following his academic failure, so that he must focus on academics that semester. In this case, however, Mr. Hamilton did sit out the year following his academic failure and now would be made to sit out another year. Because Herbert Hoover is a three-year high school, Mr. Hamilton couldn't have played high-school ball in the ninth grade at any rate. In the ninth grade, he could have played only junior-high ball. Thus, the supposed sins of his junior-high career are being held against him in his senior year of high school. He is told he can play only two years of high-school football because, for academic reasons, he repeated a year of junior high. Under the circumstances, the scheme, as applied to Mr. Hamilton, is unfairly and unreasonably punitive. . . .

The legitimate purposes of the Commission's rules—to prevent red-shirting—may be accomplished in a more reasonable and less restrictive way. There must be some inquiry into the intent to red-shirt. The onus may well be on the player to demonstrate that he was held back solely for academic reasons, but Mr. Hamilton has clearly demonstrated that in this case. And in oral argument before this Court, the Commission admitted that they had no reason to believe that Mr. Hamilton did not repeat the ninth grade for legitimate academic reasons. If the Commission limits its enforcement to cases of intentional athletic red-shirting, that is sufficient to protect the best interests of the student. Such a policy, although requiring more inquiry than a *per se* rule, insures that academic progress is not subverted to the ignoble ends of athletic boosters. That, certainly[,] is reasonable. Any possible unfairness to other teams—here, that Mr. Hamilton is a year older than he otherwise would have been as a high-school senior—is prevented by the Commission's unequivocal age limit for participation in inter-scholastic sports.

The Commission's scheme, as applied to Mr. Hamilton, is not within the Commission's legitimate authority to promulgate "reasonable" regulations for school sports. Therefore, we reverse the judgment of the Circuit Court of Kanawha County and enter final judgment in favor of the appellant.

Source: Courtesy of Westlaw; reprinted with permission.

Problem 11-4

During a basketball game between Huntington High School and Capitol High School on January 26, 2007, O.J. Mayo, a student at Huntington High School, was ejected from the game for committing the second of two technical fouls called against him. Under SSAC rules, a student athlete ejected from a basketball game is automatically suspended for two additional games. Following the ejection, O.J. Mayo approached and had physical contact with a referee. That act required an additional sanction for violating the SSAC rule which prohibits players from "lay[ing] hands" on a referee. O.J. Mayo instituted a civil action in the circuit court on January 30, 2007, through which he sought injunctive relief to prohibit the SSAC from enforcing the automatic two-game suspension prompted by his ejection from the January 26, 2007, basketball game.

223 W.Va. 88, 672 S.E.2d 224, O.J. MAYO v. The WEST VIRGINIA SECONDARY SCHOOLS ACTIVITIES COMMISSION, Nov. 13, 2008.

In Case 11-9, *Nichols v. Farmington Public Schools*, 150 Mich. App. 705 (Mich. App. 1986), the court dealt with an age rule that had been passed by the Michigan High School Athletic Association (MHSAA), considering it in conjunction with the Michigan Handicappers Civil Rights Act.

📖 CASE 11-9 *Nichols v. Farmington Public Schools*

150 Mich. App. 705 (Mich. App. 1986)

PER CURIAM.

Plaintiffs, Tim Nichols and his father, Donald Nichols, appeal as of right from an order of the circuit court granting defendants' motion for summary judgment.

Plaintiff Tim Nichols (hereinafter plaintiff), had been a student in defendant Farmington Public Schools during all of his formal education. As a result of a severe hearing impairment, plaintiff is considered to be handicapped as that term applies to the Michigan Handicappers Civil Rights Act. Plaintiff was placed in special education classes until 1976, when he was "mainstreamed" into regular education classes as required by the civil rights act. When the mainstreaming took place, plaintiff was placed in a grade one level below that which his age would normally suggest. Plaintiff claims that this placement was never discussed with his parents and that the ramifications of this decision were not made clear.

Problems with the placement did not arise until plaintiff's senior year, when he was declared ineligible to compete in the varsity basketball program due to a rule of the Michigan High School Athletic Association (MHSAA), which excludes from participation in interscholastic athletics those students who have reached their 19th birthday before September 1 of the academic year in question. Plaintiff turned nineteen on August 16, 1984, thus rendering him ineligible for varsity basketball during his senior year.

On July 25, 1984, plaintiffs filed a complaint alleging that the enforcement of the age rule in this case would violate plaintiff's constitutional rights. They further sought to enjoin defendant Farmington Public Schools from enforcing the MHSAA's age rule. Defendants filed a motion for summary judgment under GCR 1963, 117.2(1), contending that plaintiffs had failed to plead a constitutionally protected right and failed to plead facts which would support a claim that the age rule deprived plaintiff of equal protection or due process. In an opinion and order filed October 30, 1984, the trial court granted defendants' motion.

Plaintiffs also claim a denial of due process as a result of the failure of defendant MHSAA to provide an exception to the age rule in the instant case. Again, we find that plaintiffs' claim is without merit since they failed to follow the procedures available to them. According to defendant MHSAA, it will consider applications for exceptions to its rules when a school system formally requests a waiver to its representation council. Plaintiffs do not contend that they ever requested that the school system file for such a waiver. Furthermore, plaintiffs have presented no argument which would support their contention that the age rule has a "discriminatory effect." As noted in an affidavit submitted with defendants' brief in support of the motion for summary judgment, the age rule serves the following purposes:

"The 'age rule' is one of the basic rules of eligibility of interscholastic athletics throughout the nation. It has many purposes, and
among them are the following:

"1. It treats all students equally regardless of race, creed, origin, sex,
    gifted, or handicapped.
"2. It encourages athletes to complete four years of high school between
    the ages of 15 and 18.
"3. It reduces the opportunity to hold students back (red shirt) for ath-
    letic purposes.
"4. The rule is consistent with the philosophy of interscholastic athlet-
    ics in that a student's primary purpose in attending high school is to
    obtain an education, with participation in athletics secondary.
"5. It tends to create equal competition with established age limitations.
"6. It tends to decrease the opportunity for one team to have several
    'older' students competing against opponents with younger athletes.
"7. There tends to be great maturity differences between students age 15
    or 16 and those going on age 20.
"8. It tends to reduce the opportunity for mismatches in competition. For
    example, a 15-year-old ninth or tenth grader could be competing against
    a student going on age 20, 21, etc.
"9. It reduces the chances for litigation due to mismatches in competition.
"10. It reduces the opportunity for a student who would normally be out of
    high school to take the position of a younger student who is progress-
    ing through high school at a normal rate.
"11. A September 1 deadline, as indicated by the MHSAA HANDBOOK, could be
    considered arbitrary. However, if the date was changed to August 1, it
    would also be arbitrary and there would be students turning 19 years
    of age July 30, who would want the age limit changed to July 1."

We note that even plaintiffs agree that the age rule has a rational
basis. Since plaintiffs have failed to present a basis for reversing
the trial court's order granting the motion for summary judgment, we
must affirm that order.

Affirmed.

Source: Courtesy of Westlaw; reprinted with permission.

Home Schooling

Can those students who live in the school district but do not attend the local high school participate in that school's sports programs? In *Kaptein v. Conrad School District*, 931 P.2d 1311 (Mont.
1997), a student attending a private Christian school sued the school district because she wanted to
participate in the public school program and play on the public school team for reasons of friendship
and "team camaraderie." She had participated in the public school girls' sport program during the

1994–1995 school year but without permission from the school district. When it discovered her participation, the Board of Trustees for the school district stopped her from participating based on the school policy that participation was limited to those students who were enrolled as full-time students. The court framed the issue as follows:

> . . . Thus, in the present context, the right to participate must be balanced against the School District's interests in restricting participation to students enrolled in the public school system. Consistent with the middle-tier analysis conducted in *Bartmess*, we must first determine whether the classification based upon enrolled students is reasonable. We then examine whether the governmental interest in making this classification based upon enrollment is more important than Tami Kaptein's interest in participating in existing extracurricular activities.[38]

Finding in favor of the school district, the court upheld its policy. Litigation has increased as a result of the increase in the number of students being home schooled. Home-schooled students have sued in an attempt to participate in the athletic programs at local high schools. Should they be allowed to participate? There are now many home school athletic associations. For example, California now has the California Athletics for Home Schools (CAHS), an athletic association just for those students being home schooled.

Problem 11-5

Daniel and Christy Jones (hereinafter "the Joneses") are residents of Marion County, West Virginia. The Joneses have elected to home school their children, including their son Aaron. In 2002, when Aaron was approximately eleven years old, he indicated to his parents his desire to participate on the Mannington Middle School wrestling team. Had Aaron been a student in the public school system, he would have been a sixth grade student at Mannington Middle School. The Joneses investigated the possibility of Aaron joining the Mannington Middle School wrestling team and were advised that they needed approval from the West Virginia Secondary School Activities Commission (hereinafter "the WVSSAC"). Upon contacting the WVSSAC, the Joneses were advised that, pursuant to W. Va.C.S.R. § 127-2-3.1, participation in interscholastic athletic activities was limited to students who were enrolled full-time in a WVSSAC participating school. Consequently, since Aaron was not enrolled as a full-time student at Mannington Middle School, he would not be permitted to participate on the wrestling team. The Joneses received similar responses from Dave Stewart, State Superintendent of Schools, and from the Marion County Board of Education.

Jones v. West Virginia State Board of Education
622 S.E.2d 289 (W. Va. 2005)

---

[38] *Kaptein*, 931 P.2d at 1316.

Personal Grooming

School districts and high schools have an interest in maintaining the appearance of their sports teams and the athletes who participate on those teams. To what extent can a school district regulate the appearance of students? Many districts have implemented grooming policies in an attempt to ensure a "neat" appearance for student-athletes.

School dress codes and dress codes for athletic teams have been challenged on constitutional grounds by plaintiffs.[39] In *Davenport v. Randolph County Bd. of Educ.*, 730 F.2d 1395 (11th Cir. 1984), high school students challenged the clean-shaven policy of the football and basketball teams. Plaintiffs were suspended from participating in football for refusing to shave. The policy "prohibited team members from having beards, wearing mustaches extending beyond the corners of their mouths, or growing sideburns below the ear lobes."[40] The court upheld the board's power to regulate grooming, stating that the plaintiffs failed to set forth any circumstances showing the policy was "arbitrary or unreasonable." Mandatory grooming standards generally have been held to not violate the due process rights of students.[41]

Tattoos can fall under the umbrella of personal grooming. Can a high school or athletic association pass a rule that requires student-athletes to cover tattoos during participation? Could a rule regulating tattoos be deemed a sportsmanship rule or a rule dealing with team unity? Suppose the tattoo was of a religious figure or image, and the student-athlete said that the tattoo was a statement of faith on his or her part and gave him or her "strength and motivation" when they played. What constitutional issues would be present under these circumstances? If you were the athletic director for the high school athletic association, how would you draft a policy dealing with tattoos, body piercing, and the wearing of jewelry for participating student-athletes?[42]

How would you have ruled in Case 11-10, *Stotts v. Community Unit School District No. 1*, 230 F.3d 989 (7th Cir. 2000)? What interests are at stake?

📖 CASE 11-10 *Stotts v. Community Unit School District No. 1*

230 F.3d 989 (7th Cir. 2000)

```
BAUER, Circuit Judge.

Jeffrey Stotts was suspended from his high school's basketball team
because he got a tattoo in violation of a rule governing the personal
appearance of boys basketball players. He challenged the constitution-
ality of the rule, and petitioned the district court for a preliminary
injunction. Stotts now appeals the district court's decision to deny
him injunctive relief. We dismiss the case on the ground that it is
moot.
```

---

[39] Jackson v. Dorrier, 424 F. 2d. 213 (6th Cir. 1978).
[40] *Davenport*, 730 F.2d at 1395.
[41] Atruhaus v. Tomy, 310 F. Supp. 192 (N.D. Cal. 1970).
[42] Track Meet, *When the Rules Run Up Against Faith*, The Washington Post, January 16, 2008.

I. Background

After a local disk jockey called the boys varsity basketball team a bunch of "peanut heads," the Board of Education for the Community Unit School District ("Board") issued "appearance guidelines," which only applied to members of the boys basketball team. These guidelines prohibited boys basketball players from having tattoos, body graffiti, and unnatural hair coloring, and addressed their uniforms and other appearance issues. The Board intended the regulation to "restore pride and team spirit and project a positive image of the team to the community." Before the basketball season began, the coaches discussed the new appearance policy with students who came to open gym.

Jeffrey Stotts, a senior who had been a member of the varsity basketball team since his freshman year, subsequently got a tattoo of a dragon on his back. His basketball uniform covered the tattoo unless another player pulled on his shirt. Pursuant to the appearance guidelines, the coach suspended Stotts from the basketball team for the first half of the season. The coach informed Stotts and his parents that Stotts would have to remove the tattoo before he could play with the team again. Stotts appealed his suspension to the Board, which upheld the coach's decision. The Board further notified Stotts that if he failed to have the tattoo removed by the second half of the season, he would be permanently suspended from the basketball team.

Stotts filed suit in the district court challenging the constitutionality of the appearance regulations. He alleged that the regulation and its enforcement violated his First Amendment right to free speech, his Fourteenth Amendment right to equal protection, and his Fourteenth Amendment substantive due process rights. Stotts petitioned the district court for preliminary injunctive relief so that he could play basketball during his senior year of high school. The district court denied Stotts' petition, holding that he failed to demonstrate a likelihood of success on the merits.

While the appeal was pending before this Court, Stotts graduated from high school. Stotts asks this Court to reverse the district court decision.

Source: Courtesy of Westlaw; reprinted with permission.

Can an athletic team require players to conform to a "hair policy"? How long can a student-athlete wear his or her hair and still be eligible to participate? What if student-athletes kept their hair in a ponytail? Can there be different grooming standards for hair for girls and boys? Case 11-11, *Dostert v. Berthold Public School Dist. No. 54*, 391 F. Supp. 876 (N.D. 1975), examines some of these issues.

📖 CASE 11-11 *Dostert v. Berthold Public School Dist. No. 54*

391 F. Supp. 876 (N.D. 1975)

VAN SICKLE, District Judge.

. . . The gravamen of the complaint is that the Plaintiff Mark Dostert is prohibited from engaging fully in certain extracurricular activities at his school because of his refusal to comply with the hair policy adopted by the Superintendent and the Board of Education, the Defendants. . . .

In January, 1974, members of the Board of Education adopted a written 'Hair and Dress Policy' for Berthhold Public School.

As it applies in this case, the policy prohibits male students whose hair does not conform to certain guidelines from taking part in the public performances of extracurricular organizations; i.e., unless a boy's hairline falls 'above the ears, above the eyebrows and off the shirt collar,' he cannot participate in any athletic competition against another school, nor represent the school's FFA (Future Farmers of America) Chapter, nor publicly perform with the band or choir.

Plaintiff Mark Dostert let his hair grow during the summer of 1973. On numerous occasions during the fall and winter of 1973, he was told by Defendant Grindy to cut his hair, since it was in violation of the unwritten policy then in effect. On each occasion Mark trimmed his hair, but he did not trim it completely from over his ears in accordance with the school policy.

Mark received some kidding from his classmates as a result of his hair style. On November 29, 1973, an incident occurred in which a number of senior boys wrestled Mark to the floor of the vocational agriculture shop and started cutting his hair with a scissors. The incident was reported to the sheriff's office by Mark and his parents, and the students were reprimanded by Superintendent Grindy.

On or about January 26, 1974, shortly after the school assembly at which the written policy was announced to the students, Mark was playing at a basketball game with the school band and was told by Defendant Grindy that he could not play with the band after that performance; he was also told to report to the Superintendent's office the following Monday. It was at the basketball game or in the Superintendent's office that Mark was told that he could no longer participate in the public performances of any extracurricular organizations.

Prior to this time, Mark had been a participant in athletic programs at the school and had been a member of the FFA and the band. On or shortly after January 26, 1974, however, Mark's participation in these activities was substantially curtailed. Mark was allowed to practice with the athletic teams and the band, and allowed to be a member of the FFA; but he could not represent or perform with any of these groups in public. It is conceded that the sole reason for Mark's partial suspension from participation in extracurricular activities was his failure to comply with the school hair policy.

It should be noted that there was uncontradicted testimony that the length of Mark's hair at the time of the trial was the longest it has been since he began violating the school's hair policy. His hair was clean, well-groomed and neat. The only violation of the hair policy was the way his hair fell over his ears so that only the very bottom of his ear lobes would show.

Defendants, cognizant of their burden of showing justification for their hair policy, presented several reasons. Essentially, four justifications were presented:

1. Since students have no constitutional right to participate in extracurricular activities, as opposed to academic programs, a school can impose a hair policy as a condition of participation;
2. The band director and the FFA adviser asserted that judges in band and FFA contests might take long hair into consideration in marking down the school in general appearance;
3. The basketball coach asserted that long hair can interfere with one's play on the basketball court;
4. The football coach (and the basketball coach to some degree) asserted that a hair policy was necessary in building successful athletic teams, in that it contributed to the discipline, dedication and unity of team members. . . .

Our starting point must be the Eighth Circuit opinion in *Bishop v. Colaw, 450 F.2d 1069 (8th Cir. 1971)*. It was in that case that this Circuit recognized that a student possesses 'a constitutionally protected right to govern his appearance while attending public high school.' Bishop at 1075. Once a student has established that a school rule infringes upon his right to govern his personal appearance, however, the inquiry concerning the constitutionality of the challenged rule does not end. 'Personal freedoms are not absolute; they must yield when they intrude upon the freedoms of others. Our task, therefore, is to weigh the competing interests asserted here. In doing so, we proceed from the premise that the school administration carries the burden of establishing the necessity of infringing upon (a student's) freedom in order to carry out the educational mission of the (school).' Bishop, 1075-76.

Defendants first attempt to justify the hair policy by asserting that, since it is enforced merely by prohibiting violators from fully participating in extracurricular activities-and not by expelling or suspending them from any classes-the constitutional rights of the students are not violated. Participation in extracurricular activities is labelled by the Defendants as a privilege. Thus, since students have no right to participate in extracurricular activities in the first place, it is argued that they can be prohibited from participating in them because they fail to comply with the hair policy. This 'right-privilege' argument misses the point. The Plaintiffs' constitutional challenge of the hair policy cannot be answered by an argument that participation in extracurriculars is a privilege and not a right. Regardless of whether participation in extracurriculars is a 'privilege' or a 'right,' it is still a fact that, in excluding Mark from fully participating in extracurriculars because of his long hair, the Defendants are infringing upon his constitutional right to govern his own appearance. The right of a student to govern his own appearance applies to all school-controlled activities, and not just to school academic programs. *Long v. Zopp, 476 F.2d 180 (4th Cir. 1973)* and *Dunham v. Pulsifer, 312 F.Supp. 411 (D.Vt.1970)*.

Insofar as Mark's participation in the school band and the FFA is concerned, the Defendants contend the hair policy is justified by the fact that Mark's hair might cause the school to be marked down for general appearance in band competitions and FFA contests.

With regard to the school band, the Defendants submitted into evidence an official publication of the North Dakota High School Activities Association showing that 'Stage Presence and Appearance' is a factor in the judging of band competitions. The band director could not recite any specific instance where a band had actually been marked down because any of its members had long hair; he did recite a hearsay opinion, however, that this was something very subjective with the judges and that they might take long hair into consideration in judging a band's overall appearance. We believe that this asserted justification has not been established sufficiently to meet the burden imposed upon the Defendants by Bishop.

Alternatively, the school administration has failed to show why this problem could not be solved by imposing a less restrictive rule than requiring students to cut their hair. There was no showing that requiring students to comb their hair under their band caps or requiring them to wear short-hair wigs would not solve the problem of the band's 'general presence and appearance.'

With regard to the FFA, the Defendants submitted into evidence a copy of the FFA State Code of Ethics, which reads, in pertinent part:

'Hair should be neat, clean, well groomed and of reasonable or moderate length.'

Although the school's FFA adviser could point to no specific instance where a participant in an FFA contest had been marked down for his hair length, he voiced the opinion that this might occur and affect the team's score. However, when confronted with Plaintiffs' exhibit of the Oct.-Nov. '74 issue of the National FFA magazine, with the national organization's president on the cover (whose hair style is very comparable to Mark's), the adviser admitted that the FFA Code of Ethics was probably less restrictive than the school's hair policy. He also admitted that Mark's hair was evenly trimmed, so that there is some question as to whether Mark's hair fails to meet the FFA standards of being 'neat, clean, well groomed and of reasonable or moderate length.' At any rate, the FFA adviser stated that an acceptable short-hair wig would meet his demands. Consequently, the Defendants' contention that the hair policy is justified because the school FFA chapter would otherwise be marked down in contests with other chapters is without merit in the light of Bishop's requirement of 'less restrictive rules.'

Insofar as Mark's participation on the basketball team is concerned, the Defendants contend that the hair policy is justified, among other reasons, because long hair can interfere with one's play. The basketball coach testified that, although he had no objection to hair covering the ear, the line had to be drawn somewhere; at some point long hair would interfere with play. However, the coach admitted that hair bands would solve this problem; and, since this would be a less restrictive rule accomplishing the same purpose, Bishop dictates that this asserted justification for the hair policy must also fail.

The most substantial justification for the hair policy advanced by the Defendants is that, insofar as athletics is concerned, it is necessary in building successful teams. A hair policy is said to contribute to the discipline, dedication and unity of an athletic team.

The football coach testified to the effect that, if everyone sacrifices the right to determine his own appearance, the team will be that much more dedicated and unified. Teamwork will be enhanced. Everyone on the team will feel equal and become more integrated into the team. The team will have a high morale and be more spirited. On the other hand, if someone can get away with breaking a rule, the other team members will lose respect for the coach and question why they themselves should sacrifice for the team. Thus the rule itself becomes more important than its actual content.

Bishop has nothing directly to say about this asserted justification. So we must resort to the weighing process set out in Bishop; that is, we must weigh Mark's interest in governing his own hair length with the school's interest in the extra degree of success its athletic programs might enjoy if all team members were more disciplined and dedicated as a result of having uniform hair lengths.

To weigh these competing interests, we must state the scale to be used. The school administration carries the burden of establishing the necessity of infringing upon Mark's freedom in order to carry out its educational mission. *Bishop, 450 F.2d 1075-76.* The Defendants have more than the mere burden of showing that requiring uniformity of hair length is rationally related to obtaining an extra degree of success for their athletic programs. They must show that requiring uniformity of hair length is necessary to obtain an extra degree of success, and that their interest in obtaining this extra degree of success is such a compelling part of the public educational mission as to outweigh Mark's constitutionally protected interest in determining his own hair length. We do not think the Defendants have met their burden.

There are conjectures by the football coach (and the basketball coach to a lesser extent) that an extra measure of athletic success will result from requiring all the members of a school team to have uniform hair lengths. The speculative quality of these opinions, however, brings little weight to the justification.

Even if an athletic team's success could be increased by requiring all its members to have uniform hair lengths, we do not think that winning is such an important interest that it outweighs all others. Winning should not be the 'be-all and the end-all.' And it certainly should not be of more importance in the educational process than the teaching of toleration of individual differences. 'Toleration of individual differences is basic to our democracy, whether those differences be in religion, politics, or life-style.' *Bishop, 450 F.2d at 1077.*

'It would be a bit frightening if a naked emphasis on conformity were to prevail in our public schools. Today's high school student will find that the world beyond his graduation is filled with pressures directed toward conformity. He will certainly not be deprived of the experience. While conformity to reasonable rules of conduct is essential, conformity for its own sake is dangerous. . . . .' *Dunham v. Pulsifer, supra, 312 F.Supp. at 420.*

We recognize that discipline is a trait well worth cultivating in students. We also recognize that, over and above any effect it might have on winning, the inculcation of discipline is a legitimate educational goal and an important element in any athletic program.

'Anyone who has ever played a competitive team sport knows the importance of team discipline. The coach must be able to control within reasonable limits those aspects of a player's behavior which relate to his performance as a contributing member of the team. Training and health rules must be obeyed by all., conduct at practice sessions must be in precise conformity with schedules and objectives. During the actual competition, the coach's instructions must be accepted without question. The coach's right to regulate the lives of his team members does have limits, however. A coach may not demand obedience to a rule which does not in some way further other proper objectives of participation and performance. It is bootstrap reasoning indeed to say that disobedience of any rule weakens the coach's authority or shows a lack of desire on the part of the competitor thus justifying obedience to any rule however arbitrary.

'If the rule is otherwise reasonable or, if in this case, it advances a compelling governmental interest vested in the school board, then it should be obeyed. But an otherwise arbitrary or unjustified regulatory classification cannot pull itself up by the bootstrap of its own existence. *Breen v. Kahl, 419 F.2d 1034, 1038 (7th Cir. 1969).' Dunham v. Pulsifer, supra, 312 F.Supp. at 420.*

Thus, we hold that the school has failed in its attempt to justify its hair policy on the ground that it is necessary to the success of its athletic programs.

In summary, the justifications presented by the school administrators fail to demonstrate the necessity of the hair policy. Accordingly, we hold that the hair policy is invalid and enjoin the Defendants from enforcing it against Plaintiff Mark Dostert.

Source: Courtesy of Westlaw; reprinted with permission.

It is reasonable to believe that schools can regulate the appearance of student-athletes during the season, but what about the off-season? How far can a school or school district go in enforcing personal appearance standards for student-athletes in the off-season? That issue was addressed in Case 11-12, *Long v. Zopp*, 476 F.2d 180 (4th Cir. 1973).

📖 CASE 11-12 *Long v. Zopp*

476 F.2d 180 (4th Cir. 1973)

Before RUSSELL and FIELD, Circuit Judges, and BRYAN, District Judge.

PER CURIAM:

Massie v. Henry (4th Cir. 1972), 455 F.2d 779, found it constitutionally impermissible for public schools to impose "hair codes" on their students. The football coach at Greenbrier East High School, however, decreed that all members of the football squad at that school should observe a "hair code" prescribed by him, not merely during football season, but throughout the school year, under penalty of being denied their "letter" for participation as a member of the team. The plaintiff was a student at Greenbrier East High School and a member of the football squad who, by his participation, earned a right to a "letter" in football. He had observed the "hair code" ordered by the football coach during the football season but allowed his hair to grow beyond the prescribed length thereafter. Because of his noncompliance with the "hair code" in the off-season school year, he was denied at the end of the school year his football "letter" and an invitation to the Athletics Banquet by the coach. This action of the coach, on appeal, was sustained by the school authorities. The plaintiff seeks by this action to void as an unconstitutional deprivation this denial of his right to a football "letter" by the school authorities. The District Court dismissed his action. We reverse.

The doctrine of *Massie* is equally applicable to all school-controlled activities. It extends to school athletic programs, as well as to school academic programs. Awards, properly earned in either field, cannot be used as instruments to enforce compliance with a "hair code," for the enforcement of which there is no compelling necessity. Assuming *arguendo* that there might be some hygienic or other reason to support a "hair code," as promulgated by the football coach during football season, such reason would plainly not justify the enforcement of the code after the football season had ended. The action of the football coach was accordingly in violation of the principles enunciated in *Massie*. *See* Dunham v. Pulsifer (D.C. Vt.1970) 312 F.Supp. 411. The plaintiff is entitled to injunctive relief. Under the circumstances, we do not feel a monetary award is warranted.

Reversed with instructions.

Source: Courtesy of Westlaw; reprinted with permission.

Problem 11-6

Please evaluate the following personal grooming policy. Would it withstand a constitutional challenge?

Personal Appearance and Grooming

Participation in competitive athletics is completely voluntary on the part of all students. To participate in athletics in FISD, there are certain standards, which must be maintained. One such standard is acceptable grooming and personal appearance.

1. Uniformity: Athletes do much traveling to other schools, towns, communities, restaurants, etc., as representatives of the FISD; therefore, they should be groomed in a manner of which our community, school, and sponsors will be proud. We expect our athletes to set the example for our school in the area of grooming and personal appearance.

2. Self-Discipline: One of the rewards of being an athlete is learning to discipline himself/herself. There is no better way to acquire self-discipline than to make sacrifices. Giving up untidy fads of dress and appearance is a very small sacrifice.

3. Hair: In accordance with school policy, hair shall be clean, well groomed, and out of the eyes and shall be styled in a way that is not distracting and/or designed to be conspicuous. The athlete's hair should be neatly trimmed to meet his/her coach's satisfaction. Bleaching and dying of hair a different color is unacceptable!!! Facial hair such as mustaches, beards, goatees, and extremely long sideburns are not allowed.

4. Dress: The athlete should be neatly dressed which includes shoes and socks and complies with all other school rules relating to dress not covered in these policies.

5. Body Art/Piercing: The athletic department realizes that sometimes athletes will have tattoos and body piercing. However, tattoos should not be visible when representing FISD as an athlete. The same holds true for earrings, belly button rings, and the like. Examples deemed inappropriate include: practice, games, banquets, and at tournaments. Tattoos should simply have tape or a band-aid over them, while the body jewelry can simply be taken off.

Source: Frisco ISD Athletic Policies.

Problem 11-7

What are your thoughts regarding the following typical provision which is included in most high school athletic handbooks for student-athletes?

Disrespect to Teacher or Coach

Any act of disrespect by an athlete to his/her teacher, coach, or member of school administration will be handled on an individual basis. Punishment may call for expulsion from athletic activities for one calendar year from date of incident. His/Her return would be determined by his/her conduct during the period of the expulsion.

Source: Frisco ISD Athletic Policies.

Family and Privacy

Athletic associations have propounded rules and regulations regarding a plethora of eligibility issues. The majority of those rules have passed constitutional muster. However, if an eligibility rule infringes on a fundamental right under the U.S. Constitution, the rule will be struck down as unconstitutional.[43] In *Starkey v. Board of Education of Davis County School District*, 381 P.2d 718 (1963), the Board of Education instituted a rule prohibiting married students from participating in extracurricular activities. The court found that one of the board's justifications of the rule, the problem of the large number of dropouts, was not without merit. The Supreme Court of Utah upheld the rule, finding that it bore a reasonable relationship to the problem of dropouts and therefore was not an abuse of discretion by the board. Any rule that prohibits a student from participating that infringes on a fundamental right must show a compelling state interest to survive constitutional scrutiny.

Case 11-13, *Kissick v. Garland Independent School District*, 330 S.W.2d 708 (Tex. Civ. App. 1959), dealt with a rule denying participation to married students and previously married students and restricting them wholly to classroom work.

📖 CASE 11-13   *Kissick v. Garland Independent School District*

330 S.W.2d 708 (Tex. Civ. App. 1959)

YOUNG, Justice.

In proceedings for injunction, Jerry Kissick, individually and on behalf of his minor son, Jerry Kissick, Jr., sought to restrain enforcement of a resolution of defendant District providing that 'married students or previously married students be restricted wholly to classroom work; that they be barred from participating in athletics or other exhibitions, and that they not be permitted to hold class offices or other positions of honor. Academic honors such as Valedictorian and Salutatorian are excepted.' Temporary relief was denied upon hearing with this appeal.

Young Kissick is a resident of defendant District and student of Garland Public School—a letter man on its 1958 football team. He testified to having married in March 1959 at 16 years of age to a girl, age 15, continuing to hold that status at the present school and football season, but then barred from further participation in athletic activities perforce of said regulation; that he had planned to continue on the team during succeeding years of High School, looking to an athletic scholarship and college.

The resolution was attacked as discriminatory, unreasonable and unconstitutional in that, among other things, same is given retroactive effect, applying to those students who were married prior to August 24, 1959. It is admitted that physical education is a required course of the school; the playing of football being sufficient to obtain credit

---

[43] Bell v. Lone Oak Independent School District, 507 S.W.2d 636 (Tex. Ct. Civ. App. 1979).

for that compulsory course; also that the resolution was passed, in the main, to discourage juvenile marriages among students; the school system not having separate facilities for accommodation of married students.

Appellee District adduced evidence in support of the resolution, summarized as follows: that the School has a Parent-Teachers' Association composed of 12 units; its President, Mrs. Mosser, testifying that the group had made an extensive study of 'teen-age' marriages in the School, the resolution being in accord with their recommendations; that their study had included the ill effect of married students participating in extra-curricular activities with unmarried students; noting that there had been an alarming increase in juvenile marriages in the Garland School. Mrs. Mullins and Mrs. Mitchell of P.T.A. testified to the same effect. Mr. Raymond Fletcher, Board member, professional psychologist, and of past teaching experience, stated that a survey among parents of junior and senior high school students indicated a definite need for the resolution; a poll by way of post cards sent to them favoring the resolution by a percentage of nine to one. He said that problems existing in connection with married students participating in school activities such as overnight athletic trips, band trips, etc., was detrimental to efficiency of the system; that in the District last year (1958) there was a total of 62 married students; of these, 24 students had dropped out of school, and of the remainder, at least one-half experienced a drop of at least 10 points in grades; the study further demonstrating a conflict in the general diffusion of knowledge 'as witnessed by the drop in grades and lack of opportunity to teach some of them because of their actual dropping out of school.'

Points of appeal involve questions of law; in substance that the resolution in question was void (1) as arbitrary, capricious, discriminatory and unreasonable; (2) violative of public policy in that it penalizes marriage; (3) violative of the 14th Amendment, U.S. Constitution and Art. 1, Sec. 3, State Constitution, Vernon's Ann.St., because it denies equal protection of the law; (4) denies due process of law under the same Federal Amendment, also Art. 1, Sec. 19, Texas Constitution; (5) is violative of Art. 1, Sec. 16 State Constitution, because retroactive in its effect on appellant; and (6) the Court's error in failing to hold the resolution prospective in nature, and not applicable to Jerry Kissick, Jr., since he was married prior to its passage.

Generally relevant to the regulation under attack are the following constitutional and statutory references: that in Texas scholastic age is over six and under eighteen at beginning of the school year. Art. 2902, Vernon's Ann.Civ.St.; 37-B Tex.Jur. p. 404. Children over eighteen years of age and under twenty-one (also under six years) are not free school students as a matter of right, but may be admitted to benefits of public school on such terms as the trustees may deem proper and just, but not otherwise. Art. 2904, V.A.C.S.; 37 Tex.Jur. p. 404. Art. 7, Sec. 1, State Constitution provides: 'a general diffusion of knowledge being essential to the preservation of the liberties and rights of the people it shall be the duty of the Legislature of the State to establish and make suitable provision for the support and maintenance of an efficient system of public free schools.'

2780 V.A.C.S., states in part: 'said trustees shall adopt such rules, regulations and by-laws as they may deem proper; and the public free schools of such independent district shall be under their control; and they shall have the exclusive power to manage and govern said schools. . . .'

With regard to authority of school trustees, it is uniformly held that 'the courts will not interfere in such matters unless a clear abuse of power and discretion is made to appear.' 3-B Tex.Jur. pp. 414-415. . . .

Appellant asserts that such resolution is violative of public policy in that it penalizes persons because of marriage. Consistent with limitations and requirements of State Statutes, both civil and criminal, the point is overruled. Art. 4603, V.A.C.S., provides that 'males under sixteen and females under fourteen years of age shall not marry.' Art. 404, Vernon's Ann.Penal Code, makes it a criminal offense for the County Clerk to issue a marriage license to males under twenty-one or females under eighteen without consent of parents or guardian, or in lieu thereof the County Judge, under penalty of a $1,000 fine. Art. 4605, V.A.C.S., places similar restrictions on issuance of a marriage license to males under twenty-one and females under eighteen. And in the summer of 1959 our Legislature evidenced its concern over the problem of 'teen-age' marriages by amending Art. 4605. Issuance of license to marry was prohibited to such underage applicants except 'upon the consent and authority *expressly given* by the parent or guardian of such underage applicant *in the presence of the authority issuing such license,*' . . . (emphasis ours); also requiring that application therefor be on file in the County Clerk's office for not less than three days prior thereto.

As appellant states, it is indeed the policy of the law to look with favor upon marriage and to seek in all lawful ways to uphold this most important of social institutions; every intendment being in favor of matrimony. Gress v. Gress, Tex.Civ.App., 209 S.W.2d 1003. The principle however is referable to those of lawful age (male twenty-one, female eighteen). On the other hand, the legislative policy is otherwise insofar as an underage marriage is concerned; it being clearly manifest that by the cited Statutes a public policy is announced unfavorable to and in outright discouragement of 'underage applicants' for matrimony.

. . . [A]ppellant cites constitutional provisions, both State and Federal, with which, he says, the regulation is in conflict. Sufficient grounds for overruling same may be found in the principles underlying the disposition of *Board of Trustees of University of Mississippi v. Waugh*, 105 Miss. 623, 62 So. 827, L.R.A.1915D, 588; *Waugh v. Board of Trustees of University of Mississippi*, 237 U.S. 589, 35 S.Ct. 720, 59 L.Ed. 1131, and *Wilson v. Abilene Independent School District*, Tex.Civ.App., 190 S.W.2d 406, involving, generally, the exclusion of fraternity and sorority houses. We will simply refer to the extensive discussions in these cases for conclusions adverse to the propositions here contended for. Incidentally, in Wilson's appeal, supra, the resolution adopted by Abilene School District applied to students who had belonged to fraternities prior to its adoption.

But appellant points out that the object prohibited in above cited cases related solely to extra-curricular activities; whereas the instant situation involves a compulsory school course (physical education)—the playing of football satisfying that requirement. Obviously, in the case of Jerry Kissick, Jr., his eligibility for the team was contingent upon physical condition and scholastic grades as determined by the governing athletic authority. And with especial reference to point 5 (retroactive law) the question here posed is of whether the playing of football, coupled with an athletic scholarship potential, is such a scholastic right as entitles one to protection of Art. 1, Sec. 16, State Constitution. 'A statute cannot be said to be retroactive law prohibited by the Constitution unless it can be shown that the application of the law would take away or impair vested rights acquired under existing law.' *McCain v. Yost,* 155 Tex. 174, 284 S.W.2d 898, 900. Manifestly, the thing here contended for amounts to no such right. It must be classed as contingent or expectant in contrast to a vested right which is an *immediate fixed right* of present or future enjoyment. 9 Tex.Jur. p. 528. Apart from these considerations Jerry Kissick, Jr., had a constitutional right to attend the Garland School and take part in its functions subject to such reasonable rules and regulations as might be adopted by the School Board from time to time.

We now recur to the first and controlling issue of law raised by appellant; of whether the resolution was 'arbitrary, capricious, discriminatory, unreasonable and void.' Undoubtedly it had a direct relationship to objectives sought to be accomplished by school authorities—that of discouraging the marriage of 'teen-age' students. A similar problem was faced by the School in *State ex rel. Thompson v. Marion County Board of Education, Tenn.*, 302 S.W.2d 57, 58. There the Board had passed a resolution to the effect that any student who married during the school term should be automatically expelled 'for the remainder of the current term.' If the marriage took place during vacation, such student should not be allowed to attend school 'during the term next succeeding.' Under said order, the married student could resume attendance at any later full term. In upholding this regulation as not amounting to an abuse of discretion the Tennessee Supreme Court made the following observation, with which we agree: 'Boards of Education, rather than Courts, are charged with the important and difficult duty of operating the public schools. So, it is not a question of whether this or that individual judge or court considers a given regulation adopted by the Board as expedient. The Court's duty, regardless of its personal views, is to uphold the Board's regulation unless it is generally viewed as being arbitrary and unreasonable. Any other policy would result in confusion detrimental to the progress and efficiency of our public school system.'

All points of appeal upon consideration are overruled and judgment of the trial court affirmed.

Source: Courtesy of Westlaw; reprinted with permission.

In *Perry v. Grenada Municipal Separate School District*, 300 F. Supp. 748 (N.D. Miss. 1969), two unwed mothers sued because the high school had a policy of not admitting unwed mothers. The issue before the court was "whether the policy of the school board of denying admission to unwed mothers violates the Equal Protection Clause of the Fourteen Amendment of the Constitution."[44] The court ruled that the plaintiffs should not be excluded from the school.

> In the present age of enlightenment no one can deny the importance of education to our youth. As was stated in the Dixon case: 'It requires no argument to demonstrate that education is vital and, indeed, basic to civilized society. Without sufficient education the plaintiffs would not be able to earn an adequate livelihood, to enjoy life to the fullest, or to fulfill as completely as possible the duties and responsibilities of good citizens.' *Dixon v. Alabama State Board of Education, 294 F.2d at 157.*
>
> The plaintiffs have introduced evidence which tends to show that unwed mothers, who are allowed to continue their education, are less likely to have a second illegitimate child. In effect the opportunity to pursue their education gives them a hope for the future so that they are less likely to fall into the snare of repeat illegitimate births. On the other hand the Court is aware of the defendants' fear that the presence of unwed mothers in the schools will be a bad influence on the other students vis-à-vis their presence indicating society's approval or acquiescence in the illegitimate births or vis-à-vis the association of the unwed mother with the other students.
>
> The Court can understand and appreciate the effect which the presence of an unwed pregnant girl may have on other students in a school. Yet after the girl has the baby and has the opportunity to realize her wrong and rehabilitate herself, it seems patently unreasonable that she should not have the opportunity to go before some administrative body of the school and seek readmission on the basis of her changed moral and physical condition. Certainly this would be the cause if a girl had been raped and forced to bear the child of another.[45]

Does the *Perry* case reflect societal values of 1969? Could the school district make the same argument today in attempting to exclude unwed mothers from participating in interscholastic sports?

---

[44] *Perry* 300 F. Supp. at 750.
[45] *Perry*, 300 F. Supp. at 752.

In *Nieshe v. Concrete School District*, 127 P.3d 713 (Wash. Ct. App. 2005), the plaintiff became pregnant during her senior year of high school. To graduate, she needed to pass a course entitled Current World Problems. She finished the course with a 58.8 average; a grade of 60 was needed to pass the course. She was informed by the principal a few hours before her graduation ceremony was to take place that she would not graduate. She graduated a month later. Three years after she was prevented from graduating, she filed a lawsuit against the school district. A jury awarded her $5,000 on a claim that her due process rights had been violated and also awarded her $30,864 for attorney fees. The school district appealed. On appeal, the court found that the plaintiff did not state a constitutional claim because "attending a high school ceremony is not a federally protected right."[46]

FREE SPEECH RIGHTS OF STUDENT-ATHLETES

The cases in this section deal specifically with the free speech rights of student-athletes in the interscholastic setting. One of the most famous moments in the history of sport involving "speech conduct" occurred when amateur athletes Tommy Smith and Juan Carlos accepted their medals in the 1968 Summer Olympics and raised their right fists in the symbol of "black power" while on the medal stand.[47] The athletes were suspended by the United States Olympic Committee for their actions. Suppose the speech or speech conduct on the part of the student that is at issue involves an expression of the student's religious beliefs. How should such speech be treated?

Free speech for athletes (and students in general) is more limited at the interscholastic level than at the professional level. Interscholastic students' freedom of speech rights can be summarized as follows:

> It is well-settled that students do not "shed their constitutional rights to freedom of speech of expression at the schoolhouse gate." *Tinker v. Des Moines Sch. Dist.*, 393 U.S. 503, 506, 89 S.Ct. 733, 21 L.Ed.2d 731 (1969). However, it is equally clear that school authorities have a strong and valid interest in maintaining school discipline and in carrying out their educational mission. The First Amendment rights of public school students "are not automatically coextensive with the rights of adults in other settings." *Bethel Sch. Dist. v. Fraser*, 478 U.S. 675, 682, 106 S.Ct. 3159, 92 L.Ed.2d 549 (1986). Accordingly, in the pursuit of pedagogical goals, school authorities are entitled to regulate speech in a way that would be impermissible outside the school context.
>
> The Supreme Court and the Ninth Circuit have recognized that courts are not necessarily in the best position to determine whether speech restrictions at school are appropriate.
>
> There are three distinct areas of student speech that the Supreme Court has identified: (1) obscene, vulgar, and plainly offensive speech; (2) speech that bears the imprimatur of the school; and (3) speech that falls into neither of these two categories. In *Fraser*, the Supreme Court held that a school's interest in prohibiting vulgar and lewd speech outweighs whatever First Amendment interests a student might have. *Fraser*, 478 U.S. at 683-85, 106 S.Ct. 3159. The Supreme Court has also held that when a school sponsors an activity in such a way that students and others may reasonably perceive the activity as bearing the school's imprimatur, the school has the right to restrict student. *Hazelwood Sch. Dist. v. Kuhlmeier*, 484 U.S. 260, 273, 108 S.Ct. 562, 98 L.Ed.2d 592 (1988). Speech that falls into neither of these two categories is governed by the standards set forth in *Tinker*. *Chandler v. McMinnville Sch. Dist.*, 978 F.2d 524, 529 (9th Cir.1992).

---

[46] *Nieshe*, 127 P.3d at 771.
[47] Joseph M. Sheerman, *Olympic Ouster*, The New York Times, October 16, 1968.

For speech that is neither vulgar, plainly offensive, nor bears the imprimatur of the school, school officials must justify their decision by showing "facts which might reasonably have led school authorities to forecast substantial disruption of or material interference with school activities." *Id.* (quoting *Tinker*, 393 U.S. at 514, 89 S.Ct. 733).[48]

Sportsmanship rules require a student-athlete to represent the team and the school in an honorable manner. The rationale behind sportsmanship rules is based on the fact that the student-athlete represents the school, is seen as a reflection of the school and student-athletes are sometimes considered role models for the rest of the student body. Sportsmanship rules can deal with a student's conduct both on and off the field and can involve student-athlete personal conduct dealing with alcohol use, criminal activity, and even poor attitude towards coaches, teammates, and opponents. High School coaches can be tough on student-athletes and sometimes the students or parents will take issue with how a coach is running a team. Is a student athlete allowed to give his or her opinion about how a practice is conducted or who plays in a game? Under what circumstances can a student-athlete criticize the coach and not suffer repercussions? That was the issue in Case 11-14, *Wildman v. Marshalltown School District*, 249 F.3d 768 (8th Cir. 2001).

📖 CASE 11-14 *Wildman v. Marshalltown School District*

249 F.3d 768 (8th Cir. 2001)

BRIGHT, Circuit Judge.

I. Background

. . . In January 1998, Wildman was a sophomore student at Marshalltown High School in Marshalltown, Iowa, and a member of the school's basketball team. Wildman hoped to play on the varsity team and she testified that Coach Rowles, the high school girls' varsity basketball coach, promised in conversations with her before the season that he would promote her to the varsity team. When the promotion never materialized, Wildman testified that she "became frustrated and decided to write a letter to [her] teammates" and that her "purpose was to find out what they thought of the situation and Coach Rowles." She composed a letter on her home computer and distributed it to her teammates in the school's locker room on Saturday, January 24, 1998. The letter stated:

"To all of my teammates:

"Everyone has done a great job this year and now is the time that we need to make ourselves stronger and pull together. It was a tough loss last night but we will get it back. We have had some bumps in the road

---

[48] Pinard v. Clatskanie School Dist. GJ, 319 F. Supp. 2d 1214, 1217 (D. Or. 2004).

to success but every team does and the time is here for us to smoothen it out. Everyone on this team is important whether they think so or not. After watching last nights [sic] Varsity game and seeing their sophomores play up I think and I think [sic] that some of you are think [sic] the same thing. I think that we have to fight for our position. Am I the only one who thinks that some of us should be playing Varsity or even JV? We as a team have to do something about this. I want to say something to Coach Rowles. I will not say anything to him without the whole teams [sic] support. He needs us next year and the year after and what if we aren't there for him? It is time to give him back some of the bullshit that he has given us. We are a really great team and by the time we are seniors and we ALL have worked hard we are going to have an AWESOME season. We deserve better then [sic] what we have gotten. We now need to stand up for what we believe in!!!" She included below her statement a poem about geese in flight titled "We Makes Me Stronger."

The following week, Wildman's sophomore team coach received a telephone call from Charlotte Baltes, a parent of one of Wildman's teammates, who expressed concern about the letter her daughter brought home from the locker room. Coach Rowles received a copy of the letter from another player's parent, Diana Swanson, who worked as the attendance secretary at the high school. Both coaches, who stated in their depositions that they were alarmed by the letter's tone and language, met with athletic director Funk and principal Stephens to discuss how to handle the matter. On January 29, 1998, the coaches met with Wildman alone to discuss the letter with her. They told her the letter was disrespectful and demanded that she apologize to her teammates. Wildman claims that they did not ask her to explain what she hoped to accomplish with her letter. She contends that she did not advocate a strike or boycott but that the school did not give her a chance to explain herself before setting the condition for her continued participation in the basketball program. The coaches gave her twenty-four hours to apologize, and, if she did not, she would not be allowed to return to the team. Wildman refused to apologize and did not practice with the team or play in the season's remaining six games. She also complains that she was not invited to attend the post-season awards banquet and that Coach Rowles declined to give her a participation award because "she did not finish the season." Following the school year, Wildman and her family moved to another school district where she enrolled in high school.

On September 2, 1999, Wildman brought this suit for damages. On November 2, 1999, the defendants filed a motion for summary judgment. On April 6, 2000, the district court granted defendants' motion for summary judgment, holding that Wildman's letter materially interfered or substantially disrupted a school activity. . . .

II. Discussion

. . . Wildman argues that the First Amendment prevents the school from disciplining her for distributing a letter which was a personal communication to other students containing her personal expression. Both parties agree that, as the Supreme Court acknowledged in *Tinker v. Des Moines Indep. Cmty. Sch. Dist.*, 393 U.S. 503, 506, 89 S.Ct. 733, 21 L.Ed.2d 731 (1969), students do not "shed their constitutional rights to freedom of speech or expression at the schoolhouse gate." . . .

However, this right to express opinions on school premises is not absolute. It is well within the parameters of school officials' authority to prohibit the public expression of vulgar and offensive comments and to teach civility and sensitivity in the expression of opinions. . . .

Marshalltown had in place a handbook for student conduct in 1997-1998, as well as a Marshalltown Bobcat Basketball Handbook, drafted by Coach Rowles and distributed to Wildman and her teammates at the start of the season. Both handbooks indicated that disrespect and insubordination will result in disciplinary action at the coach's discretion. Appellees argue that they acted properly and lawfully in their reaction to Wildman's letter. They point to their interest in affording Wildman's teammates an educational environment conducive to learning team unity and sportsmanship and free from disruptions and distractions that could hurt or stray the cohesiveness of the team.

Wildman admits that her speech contained one profane word but contends that because there was no specific evidence of a material disruption of a school activity, her speech is protected. We disagree with the claim of protection.

The parties perhaps could have achieved with minimal creativity and flexibility a solution more amicable or less humiliating to the student. However, the school sanction only required an apology. The school did not interfere with Wildman's regular education. A difference exists between being in the classroom, which was not affected here, and playing on an athletic team when the requirement is that the player only apologize to her teammates and her coach for circulating an insubordinate letter. FN1. We agree with the district court's conclusions that the letter did suggest, at the least, that the team unite in defiance of the coach (where Wildman wrote that the coach "needs us next year and the year after and what if we aren't there for him?" and "[i]t is time to give him back some of the bullshit that he has given us" and "[w]e now need to stand up for what we believe in" and "I think that we have to fight for our position") and that the actions taken by the coaches in response were reasonable. Moreover, coaches deserve a modicum of respect from athletes, particularly in an academic setting.

> FN1. This unfortunate stalemate over the letter and her apology brings to mind the biblical Proverb: "Pride goeth before destruction, and an haughty spirit before a fall." *Proverbs* 16:18.

This suit does not present a case like *Seamons v. Snow,* 206 F.3d 1021 (10th Cir.2000), cited by Wildman for the proposition that dismissal of a high school player from an athletic team for refusing to apologize for the exercise of free speech rights amounts to an unconstitutional action. In that case, the Tenth Circuit Court of Appeals reversed the district court's summary judgment dismissal and remanded because of disputed issues of fact. The student athlete in *Seamons* asserted that the football coach asked the player to apologize to the football team for reporting to the police and to school authorities a hazing incident in which the player was assaulted in the high school locker room by a group of his teammates, forcibly restrained, and bound to a towel rack with adhesive athletic tape. The coach presented a different version, claiming that the player's ultimate failure to be involved with the football team was unrelated to his speech or refusal to speak. The court determined that "[t]here [were] ample facts in the record to indicate that Brian's suspension and dismissal from the football team were directly related to his failure to apologize for reporting the assault." *Seamons,* 206 F.3d at 1028. Implicitly the court acknowledged that Brian's report of the assault was protected free expression.

In contrast, Wildman's letter, containing the word "bullshit" in relation to other language in it and motivated by her disappointment at not playing on the varsity team, constitutes insubordinate speech toward her coaches. Here, in an athletic context void of the egregious conduct which spurred the football player's speech about the hazing incident in *Seamons* and where Wildman's speech called for an apology, no basis exists for a claim of a violation of free speech.

III. Conclusion

Accordingly, we affirm the summary judgment of dismissal of Wildman's claim of alleged violation of her rights under the Free Speech Clause of the First Amendment.

Source: Courtesy of Westlaw; reprinted with permission.

NOTES AND DISCUSSION QUESTIONS

Constitutional Considerations

1. How should an amateur athlete be defined? Should there be a uniform definition to simplify matters? Section 103 of the United States Amateur Sports Act of 1978 defines an amateur as follows: "As used in this Act, the term . . . 'amateur athlete' means any athlete who meets the eligibility standards established by the national governing body for the sport in which the athlete competes. . . ."

2. Amateur sports are extremely popular in the United States. Millions of people participate in a variety of sports, including tennis, volleyball, Little League baseball, Pony League and high school baseball, softball, football, track and field, bowling, and lacrosse. This list is certainly not comprehensive. Very few high school or collegiate athletes play or will play professional sports. It is only the elite few who have a professional career in athletics.

3. What is the distinction between a "right to participate" and an "opportunity to participate"? Under what circumstances could a high school athlete have a right to participate instead of a privilege? What interscholastic athletes can you name who might have acquired that right in high school? What would the student-athlete have to prove to acquire such a right?

4. President Dwight Eisenhower played football against Jim Thorpe while at the U.S. Military Academy. He said of Thorpe in a speech in 1961, "Here and there, there are some people who are supremely endowed. He never practiced in his life, and he could do anything better than any other football player I ever saw." *See*, Greg Botelho, *Roller-Coaster Life of Indian Icon, Sports' First Star*, CNN, July 13, 2004.

5. How does one determine whether state action is present? What tests have been used by courts to determine state action? *See*, Dionne L. Koller, *Frozen in Time: The State Action Doctrine's Application to Amateur Sports*, St. John's Law Review, Vol. 82, 2008.

6. In *Brentwood Academy v. Tennessee Secondary School Athletic Ass'n*, 531 U.S. 288 (2001), the court determined that the Tennessee Secondary School Athletic Association was a state actor based on the "entwinement" test.

7. Why are most high school athletic associations considered state actors, whereas the NCAA is not?

8. In *Griffin High School v. Illinois High School Ass'n*, 822 F.2d 671 (7th Cir. 1987), a voluntary state athletic association that was composed of over 80% of public high schools was deemed to be a state actor. However, in *Burrows v. Ohio High School Athletic Association*, 891 F.2d 122, 125 (6th Cir. 1989), the court found a high school athletic association similar to the NCAA and therefore not a state actor.

Eligibility Rules

9. Did you agree with the court in *Fusato v. Washington Interscholastic Activities Association*? On what legal basis can a transfer rule be challenged? When should a hardship waiver be granted to a student? If you were drafting a hardship waiver, what would you include? If a student can show that he or she is transferring schools for a reason other than being recruited, should the student be allowed to transfer?

10. What is the purpose of a rule limiting the opportunity to participate to a certain number of semesters? In Kanongata'a v. Wash. Interscholastic Activities Ass'n, 2006 U.S. Dist. LEXIS

41152, the plaintiff was 20 years old and playing high school football. Should there be a cap on age regardless of a rule limiting semesters? What exceptions should be made for those students with learning disabilities? Was the defendant's four-year "season limitation" rule upheld? Why or why not? What factors should be taken into consideration when drafting such a rule?

11. Not everyone can be a high school honor student. Should there be academic qualifications to be able to participate in extracurricular activities? Maybe you agree with Judge Harshbarger in his dissenting opinion in *Bailey v. Truby*, 321 S.E.2d 302 (W. Va. 1984), involving a rule requiring students to maintain a C grade point average to participate in extracurricular activities:

> . . . The majority concluded that the State Board has constitutional authority to erect an academic hurdle to participation in interscholastic *athletic* activities and other undefined nonacademic extracurricular activities, but then suggests that the State Board's policy is unlawful to the extent that it places an educational barrier limiting participation in *academic* extracurricular activities.

> The Court indicates that children can participate in student government, music and drama productions and the like without keeping a C average as is required of their counterparts who participate in interscholastic athletic activities, and possibly cheerleading. My brothers would let a flautist flunk without forfeiting his or her flute. But pity the poor punter who did not pass.

> The Court embraces elitism in the name of academic excellence and is focusing too narrowly upon academic or intellectual functions and ignoring, even condemning, other important extracurricular activities. In *Pauley v. Kelly*, W.Va., 255 S.E.2d 859 (1979), we recognized that a thorough and efficient system of schools encompassed an education that develops the minds and bodies of students to prepare them for useful and happy occupations, recreation, and citizenship. Given these broad objectives, why are "mind" building extracurricular activities of higher intrinsic value than "body" developers?

> If I were to fashion any rule, it would be that if a student satisfies the State Board's academic and attendance requirements for graduation with his or her class, all school programs would be open. There should be only one class of student. All efforts to emphasize quality and excellence should be promoted and there should be no chains upon children who want to try to make a mark in the world with whatever talents they possess.

> Even more troubling is the majority's failure to mention the rank unfairness resulting from the dual policy actions of the State Board and the Kanawha County Board of Education. A student in Kanawha County could not participate in interscholastic activities if he failed to comply with the local board's academic requirements, a C average and no F's, while similarly situated students in every other county in the state could participate who had just the C average. If the State Board of Education had enacted a regulation requiring a C average to participate in extracurricular activities and had added an additional no-F policy applicable only to Kanawha County students, I suggest few lawyers, and probably no lay people, could find any conceivable set of facts to make the regulation rational.

> This outright unequal treatment of students by the government is manifestly arbitrary and discriminatory. The state and county policies in tandem are so fundamentally unfair as to violate substantive due process.

But, basically, my dissent is predicated upon what I propose to be the utter nonsense of the C rule and the F rule: although they sound worthy, their result is to place a higher academic achievement duty upon children who choose to participate in school-related extracurricular activities, than is required of those young people who spend their after-school hours loitering and practicing idleness!

Of course, this is barely a legal argument: school officials are entitled to be just as silly as we are, on occasion. And there has been, since the majority decision, but hardly because of it, moderation of the rules by both the Kanawha County and State boards—one suspects prompted by irate coaches and parents.[49]

12. In *Thompson v. Fayette County Public Schools*, 786 S.W.2d 827 (Ky. App. 1990), parents of a student-athlete sued a school district when their son was excluded from the wrestling team. The school board's policy stated that a student was required to maintain a 2.0 grade point average to participate in extracurricular activities.[50] The court upheld the policy, which it said "is designed to minimize outside activities which distract from academic endeavors while providing incentive to make acceptable grades so the eligibility may again be restored."[51] The court further stated that it was not trying to embarrass the student but was concerned that "the educational property right is not squandered or misused."[52]

13. Could a school or school district pass a rule limiting the number of sports a student can participate in? Would such a rule be upheld? What would be the rationale for passing such a rule?

14. In *Mitchell v. Louisiana High School Athletic Association*, 430 F.2d 1155 (5th Cir. 1970), some parents of student-athletes sued over regulations limiting the number of semesters student-athletes could participate after their children lost their eligibility to participate in athletics. The students involved in the case had successfully completed the course requirements for eighth grade, but chose to repeat the eighth grade voluntarily. The lawsuit alleged that the eight-semester rule was unconstitutional and violated the equal protection clause. The district court found the rule to be unconstitutional, but on appeal the association prevailed.

   The appeals court found that the rules of the LHSAA were constitutional and provided for fair competition for all its members. The court further noted that the eight-semester rule was put into place to prevent high schools "from failing talented senior athletes in order to retain a veteran team."[53] The rule was adopted "when it appeared that some high school coaches were obtaining the same result by having promising athletes repeat pre-high school grades."[54] The court ruled in favor of the association, finding that the regulations were reasonably related to a legitimate state interest.

15. In Case 11-6, *Letendre v. Missouri State High School Activities Association*, the court found that the association's rule regarding participation for a student-athlete outside the high school was reasonable. What is the purpose of such a rule? The court indicated that the director

---

[49] Bailey v. Truby, 174 W.Va. 8; 321 S.E.2d 302; 20 Ed. Law Rep. 980.
[50] *Thompson*, 786 S.W.2d at 881.
[51] *Id*. at 882.
[52] *Id*. at 881.
[53] *Mitchell*, 430 F.2d at 1158
[54] *Id*.

of the athletic association testified that athletes participating in extracurricular sports outside the school program created a greater potential for harm than students involved in "music, speech, debating and academics. . . ." To what could he have been alluding? Why are exceptions made for Olympic competition? The plaintiff in *Letendre* just wanted to swim. She was not involved in any school activities other than swimming. What harm is she posing to the association if she swims in a club other than the high school team?

The majority of cases dealing with outside competition rules have found the rules to be reasonable.[55]

16. In *Marshall v. Alabama High School Athletic Association, et al.*, 717 So. 2d 404 (1998), the parent of a student was sanctioned by the defendant association because he assaulted the referee after the game. The parent was prevented from going to future games. On appeal, the association's rule was upheld as reasonable.

17. In *Manico v. South Colonie Central School District*, 584 N.Y.S.2d 519 (N.Y. Sup. Ct. 1992), the plaintiff, a member of the varsity wrestling team, stole eight packages of muffins from the school cafeteria and gave them to a junior varsity wrestling team member. He was caught and apologized. He was suspended from the wrestling team for two days, during which he would miss a crucial match. The court, finding in favor of the student-wrestler, stated, "[T]he case is not about muffins; it is about due process and jurisdiction." The court found the suspension to be arbitrary and capricious and said it must be annulled.

18. In *Kite v. Marshall*, 661 F.2d 1027 (5th Cir. 1981), a rule dealing with attendance at summer camps was at issue. The rule prohibited students who attended athletic training camps from participating in interscholastic sports. The rule stated:

> Training Camps Forbidden—Any student who attends a special athletic training camp in football or basketball shall be ineligible for a period of one year from the date he enrolls in the camp for any athletic contest in the League. This does not apply to bona fide summer camps giving an over-all activity program to the campers or students.

This section had been amended to limit the ineligibility to the sport involved in the special training.[56]

The University Interscholastic League (UIL) argued that the rule was in place to ensure competition among its member schools.[57] The court summarized the UIL's argument, stating, "Several reasons are advanced in support of section 21, including the need to control overzealous coaches, parents and communities, the achieving of a competitive balance between those who can afford to attend summer camp and those who cannot, the avoidance of various excessive pressures on students, and the abrogation of the use of camps as recruiting mechanisms."[58]

In reversing the lower court's ruling, the Court of Appeals for the Fifth Circuit did not find that the rule violated the Due Process or Equal Protection Clauses.

---

[55] *See* Caso v. New York Public High School Athletes Ass'n, 78 A.D.2d 41, 434 S.W.2d 60 (N.Y. App. Div, 1980); *Also see* Zuments v. Colo. High School Athletics Ass'n, 737 P.2d 1113 (Colo. Ct. App. 1987).

[56] *Kite*, 661 F.2d at 1027, 1030.

[57] *Id.* at 1029.

[58] *Id. at 1030.*

19. The Texas Supreme Court upheld the Texas "No Pass, No Play" statute as constitutional. Students were required to maintain a 70 average in all classes to be able to participate in extracurricular activities.[59] It is clear that athletic associations can establish rules regarding grades and academic progress. What grade point average should a student achieve to remain eligible to participate?

20. In *Reid v. Kenowa Hills Public Schools*, 261 Mich. App. 17, 680 N.W.2d 62 (2004), the plaintiffs were home schooling their children "in order to fulfill their God-given responsibility to raise children that know, love and serve God and their fellow-man" and also to "ensure that the education provided to their children integrates their religious beliefs on a curriculum-wide basis and to minimize the influence of other world views (e.g. secular humanism/scientific naturalism) and other persons (e.g. peers and other authority figures) which threaten to undermine those sincerely held religious beliefs."[60] The plaintiff asserted, among many theories, that the defendant's policy that students must attend the school to participate in athletics violates "their right to freely practice their religion."[61] The court found in favor of the defendants because the plaintiffs were free to be home schooled and there was no connection between the plaintiffs' right of freedom of religion and the enrollment requirement. *See*, Darryl C. Wilson, *Home Field Disadvantage: The Negative Impact of Allowing Home-Schoolers to Participate in Mainstream Sports*, Virginia Journal of Sports and the Law, Vol. 3, No. 1, 2001; *Also see, Should Homeschoolers be Allowed on Team?*, ABC News, January 22, 2009.

21. Should home schoolers be allowed to participate in local school athletics? What are the primary arguments for and against their participation? The formation of athletic associations just for home schoolers is becoming more popular. Do you agree with the argument that student-athletes need to attend the school for which they are playing so they can be a good example for other students? If the student's parents are taxpayers in the district, isn't a portion of that tax money going toward athletics? *See*, Joshua Roberts, *Dispelling the Rational Basis for Homeschooler Exclusion from High School Interscholastic Athletes*, Journal of Law and Education, January 2009.

22. In Case 11-13, *Kissick v. Garland Independent School District*, the court found that the married student rule infringed upon the student's constitutional rights. What compelling state interest was at issue in *Kissick*? What regulations, if any, may athletic associations pass with regard to pregnant students?

Free Speech Rights of Student-Athletes

23. Under what circumstances should a student-athlete be allowed to criticize a coach or administrator? Should there be different rules for high school student-athletes and college athletes?

24. In *Rottman v. Pennsylvania Interscholastic Athletic Ass'n*, 349 F. Supp. 2d 922 (W.D. Pa. 2004), the plaintiff was the head varsity basketball coach at North Catholic High School. She was suspended for one year for violating anti-recruiting rules. She sued, alleging that the

---

[59] Spring Branch Independent School District v. Stamos, 695 S.W.2d 556 (Tex. 1985).

[60] *Reid*, 261 Mich. App. 17 at 20.

[61] *Id.* at 26.

rules infringed on her free speech rights. The plaintiff argued that the anti-recruiting rule should be subject to a "strict scrutiny" test because it operated as a "complete ban on coach/prospective student speech."[62] The court ruled in favor of the district, stating in part:

> The Anti-Recruiting Rule passes constitutional muster under the intermediate scrutiny test. We find from the credible evidence that it serves the substantial government interests of prioritizing academics over athletics, protecting young student-athletes from exploitation, and ensuring an even playing field among competing schools. The Rule is narrowly drawn to serve those interests: it proscribes only recruiting of students, in whole or in part, for athletic purposes.
>
> Finally, the Rule allows alternative avenues of communication regarding the North Catholic athletic programs. The Rule does not prevent plaintiff from talking about her basketball program, rather it proscribes the manner and circumstances in which she may do so. The court found Mr. Cashman, the Executive Director of the PIAA, to be a credible witness and finds that the Rule does not prohibit plaintiff from speaking about her basketball program at open houses at the school and answering questions regarding the basketball program there; the Rule does not preclude North Catholic from putting information about the basketball program on the school's website along with information about all of its activities and programs; the Rule does not prohibit placing information about the basketball program in written literature about the school or discussing it at a general assembly of eighth graders; the Rule does not prohibit coaches from holding skills clinics and speaking at school dinners. Indeed, the record reflects that North Catholic and plaintiff have engaged in all of these exact informational activities without sanction from the PIAA.
>
> What the Rule forbids, among other things, is plaintiff's repeated approaching of Ms. Austin, as a representative of North Catholic High School's basketball team, after her stellar on-court performances at St. Bartholomew's grade school, to talk with her about basketball and North Catholic. Plainly, the Rule is not a content ban on speech regarding a school's basketball program.
>
> Instead, the Rule seeks to curb the secondary effects of speech directed at students, and their parents, regarding athletic programs by proscribing the time, place, and manner of such speech and does so in a constitutionally permissible way.[63]

25. In *Pinard v. Clatskanie School District, GJ*, 319 F. Supp. 2d 1214 (D. Or. 2004), a high school student brought an action under Section 1983 after he had been suspended from the basketball team. He started a petition that stated:

> As of February 12, 2001, the Clatskanie Tigers Boys Varsity Basketball Team would like to formally request the immediate resignation of coach Jeff Baughman. As a team, we no longer feel comfortable playing for him as a Coach. He has made derogative remarks, made players uncomfortable playing for him, and is not leading the team in the right direction. We feel that as a team and as individuals we would be better off if we were to finish the season with a replacement coach.

---

[62] *Rottman*, 349 F. Supp. 2d at 931.
[63] *Id*. at 931–32.

We, the undersigned, believe this is in the best interest of the team, school, town, and for the players and fans. We would appreciate the full cooperation of all the parties involved.

The court found in favor of the school district because the plaintiff's speech was not a political invitation or a matter of public concern.[64]

26. For another case involving a married student rule, see *Beeson v. Kiona County School Dist. Re-1*, 567 P.2d 801 (Colo. App. 1977). The lower court found in favor of the defendant school district, and the plaintiff appealed. The plaintiff stated that the rule against allowing married students to participate had cost her the opportunity for a college scholarship in basketball. The judgment of the district court was reversed, and the board's policy was deemed invalid as a denial of equal protection under the Fourteenth Amendment.

SUGGESTED READINGS AND RESOURCES

Bissinger, H. G. *Friday Night Lights: A Town, a Team, and a Dream*. Reading, MA: Addison-Wesley, 1990.

Crawford, Bill. *All American: The Rise and Fall of Jim Thorpe*. Hoboken, NJ: John Wiley & Sons, 2004.

Lincoln, Chris. *Playing the Game: Inside Athletic Recruiting in the Ivy League*. White River Junction, VT: Nomad Press, 2004.

Lullo, Robert J. *Prospect Gold: A Guide to Athletic Recruiting and Scholarships*. Express Publishing, Berkshire, United Kingdom, 2003.

Sack, Allen L., & Staurowsky, Ellen J. *College Athletes for Hire: The Evolution and Legacy of the NCAA's Amateur Myth*. Westport, CT: Praeger, 1998.

Stowers, Carlton. *Where Dreams Die Hard: A Small American Town and Its Six-Man Football Team*. Cambridge, MA: Da Capo Press, 2006.

Wallace, Don. *One Great Game: Two Teams, Two Dreams, in the First Ever National Championship High School Football Game*. New York: Simon & Schuster Trade, 2005.

Washburn, Jeff. *Tales from Indiana High School Basketball*. Champaign, IL: Sports Publishing, 2004.

REFERENCE MATERIALS

Alaska School Activities Association. *Bylaws & Constitution*. In *2008–2009 Handbook*. Anchorage, AK: ASAA.

Amendola, Francis, et al. *XXII. Particular Applications of Due Process Guaranty. I. Schools and Education. 3. Students. a. In General*. 16D CORPUS JURIS SECUNDUM *Constitutional Law* § 1984 (2006).

Bartlett, Larry D. *The Court's View of Good Conduct Rules for High School Student Athletes*. 82 WEST'S EDUCATION LAW REPORTER 1087 (1993).

---

[64] *Pinard*, 319 F. Supp. 2d at 1219.

Braig, Kevin P. *A Game Plan to Conserve the Interscholastic Athletic Environment After LeBron James*. 14 MARQUETTE SPORTS LAW REVIEW 343 (2004).

Champion, Walter T. *Fundaments of Sports Law*. St. Paul, MN: Thomson/West, 2004.

Champion, Walter T. *Sports Law: Cases, Documents, and Materials*. New York: Aspen, 2005.

Champion, Walter T. *Sports Law in a Nutshell*, 2d ed. St. Paul, MN: West Group, 2000.

Clark, Leroy D. *New Directions for the Civil Rights Movement: College Athletics as a Civil Rights Issue*. 36 HOWARD LAW JOURNAL 259 (1993).

Dean, Charles J. *Home-Schoolers' Bid to Play Sports Tabled*. BIRMINGHAM NEWS, Feb. 9, 2006.

Gardner, Kathryn, & McFarland, Allison J. *Legal Precedents and Strategies Shaping Home Schooled Students' Participation in Public School Sports*. 11 JOURNAL OF LEGAL ASPECTS OF SPORTS 25 (2001).

Greenberg, Martin J., & Gray, James T. *1–2 Sports Law Practice*, 2d ed. Charlottesville, VA: Lexis Law Publishing, 1998.

Hastings, S., Manoloff, R., Sheeran, T., & Stype, G. *Baldwin's Ohio School Law*, rev. ed. Cleveland, OH: Thomson/West, 2003.

Illinois High School Association. *Pontiac Penalized for Recruiting Rules Violations*. IHSA Announcements, Aug. 28, 2002, http://www.ihsa.org/announce/2002-03/020828.htm.

Lidz, Franz. *The Brands Twins, Who Live to Inflict Pain on the Mat, Are on Track for the Atlanta Olympics*. SI Vault, June 3, 2006, http://www.sportsillustrated.cnn.com/vault/article/magazine/MAG1008196/index.htm.

Lifland, William T., & Katz, Elai. *Football Scholarship Restrictions Could Restrain Trade*. 235 NEW YORK LAW JOURNAL 3 (2006).

Merten, Jenna. *Raising a Red Card: Why Freddy Adu Should Not Be Allowed to Play Professional Soccer*. 15 MARQUETTE SPORTS LAW REVIEW 205 (2004).

Mitten, Matthew J., Davis, Timothy, Smith, Rodney, & Berry, Robert. *Sports Law and Regulations*. New York: Aspen, 2005.

Schools and School Districts. XX. Interscholastic Athletics and Associations. 78A CORPUS JURIS SECUNDUM § 817 (2006).

Vaccaro, Don F. *Validity of Regulations of Athletic Eligibility of Students Voluntarily Transferring from One School to Another*. 15 AMERICAN LAW REPORTS 4TH 885 (1982).

Weiler, Paul C., & Roberts, Gary R. *Sports and the Law: Text, Cases, Problems*, 3d ed. St. Paul, MN: Thomson/West, 2004.

Yasser, Raymond L., McCurdy, James R., Goplerud, C. Peter, & Weston, M. *Sports Law: Cases and Materials*, 4th ed. Cincinnati, OH: Anderson, 2000.

CHAPTER 12

DRUG TESTING
IN SPORTS

The use of drugs in sports, and the drug testing procedures that have been instituted as a result, have been a major focus at the professional and amateur levels in recent years. Many episodes of drug use in sports have brought attention to this issue, involving both performance-enhancing drugs and recreational drugs. The number of athletes who have used performance-enhancing drugs has increased greatly in recent years. There are too many to note but there are a few well-known episodes.[1] On February 17, 2003, 23-year-old Steve Belcher, a pitcher with the Baltimore Orioles, collapsed and died during spring training. Belcher's family filed a lawsuit against Nutraquest, the manufacturer of Xenadrine RFA-1, a dietary supplement containing ephedra, for $600 million. The case was eventually settled for approximately $1 million.[2] Ken Caminiti admitted to the use of steroids during his Most Valuable Player season with the San Diego Padres in 1996. He later pleaded guilty to cocaine possession and died of an overdose-induced heart attack in 2004.[3] The tragic death of Len Bias from a cocaine overdose brought much attention to the sports world (see Case 5-1). Bias had been selected as the second overall pick in the 1986 NBA draft by the Boston Celtics. Canadian sprinter Ben Johnson won a gold medal at the 1988 Olympics in the 100 meter run but forfeited the medal three days later after he tested positive for the banned anabolic steroid Stanozolol.[4] Olympic track star Marion Jones plead guilty to lying to federal investigators after she denied using performance-enhancing drugs. She told a federal judge that she was "a liar and a cheat."[5] Former University of Texas great and Heisman Trophy winner Ricky Williams failed four drug tests in the NFL and was suspended from the league. He was eventually allowed back in the NFL but Williams was forced to repay $8.6 million to the Miami Dolphins that he had received in a signing bonus from the club.[6]

---

[1] *See, Timeline: A Century of Drugs and the Athlete*, USA Today, March 1, 2007.
[2] *See generally*, Deanna Rusch, *Major League Baseball & Drug Testing: A Legal critique of the Current Policy and a Look at the Future of Drug Testing in the MLB*, Williamette Sports Law Journal, Spring 2005.
[3] Associated Press, *'96 MVP Admitted Steroid Use, Fought Drug Problem*, ESPN Classic, November 3, 2004.
[4] *TRACK AND FIELD: Johnson Fails Another Test*, The New York Times, November 16, 1999.
[5] Associated Press, *Jones Pleads Guilty, Admits Lying About Steroids*, NBC Sports, October 5, 2007.
[6] *Miami Dolphins LTD. v. Williams*, 356 F.Supp.2d 1301.

More recently, baseball has encountered a steroid problem and instituted new rules relating to performance-enhancing drugs. Jose Canseco's book *Juiced* (2006) alleged major steroid use in baseball and has led to much debate in baseball circles regarding the use of performance-enhancing drugs.[7] *Game of Shadows* was published in 2006 and alleged that outfielder Barry Bonds used steroids just before he began his assault on baseball's all-time home run record. Two of baseball's most visible stars, Alex Rodriguez and Manny Ramirez have both been involved with steroid use. Rodriguez first denied steroid use but later admitted it.[8] Ramirez was suspended for fifty games in 2009 for the use of performance-enhancing drugs.[9]

Every professional sport has instituted some form of drug testing and monitoring program. Heavily regulated sports such as horse racing and boxing can require mandatory drug testing without much debate. In sports that engage in collective bargaining, such as football, hockey, baseball, and basketball, drug testing programs are the result of the combined inputs of management and labor through the process of collective bargaining. The regulation of drug testing and drug use in professional sports is quite different from amateur sports. Both, however, present unique legal issues.

Drug use has increased at the interscholastic level as well, becoming a concern for high schools and even for middle schools. Schools and school districts have instituted drug policies for student-athletes and those participating in extracurricular activities.[10] Constitutional challenges have been raised to many schools' drug testing schemes, and several of those challenges have reached the U.S. Supreme Court. Drug testing policies at the high school level have led to a myriad of constitutional challenges relating to equal protection rights and the Fourteenth and Fourth Amendments. The Supreme Court has attempted to fashion the law by balancing the constitutional rights of individuals against concerns regarding drug use by students.

The National Collegiate Athletic Association (NCAA) has a vested interest in ensuring that competition is drug free and has instituted its own drug testing policies. The NCAA requires all student-athletes to sign a consent form to retain their eligibility to participate in sports. The NCAA has been forceful in administering its drug policy for both street drugs and performance-enhancing substances. The association also has dealt with constitutional challenges to its policies.

Drug testing has affected the international stage as well. The U.S. Olympic Committee regulates the use of street drugs such as marijuana and cocaine as well as performance-enhancing drugs. The World Anti-Doping Agency (WADA) has also been aggressive in ensuring that drug use is outlawed in sports. WADA and the International Olympic Committee (IOC) have created a long list of banned substances for which athletes are tested.[11] The IOC has always taken a proactive approach regarding the use of performance-enhancing drugs. It established the very first testing of athletes in the 1968 Winter Games. In 1975, anabolic steroids were added to the IOC's list of banned substances.

Many studies have shown that athletes are using performance-enhancing drugs at an alarming rate.[12] Some experts believe that a doping problem exists at all levels of sports competition. Professional

---

[7] *See generally*, Howard Bryant, *Juicing the Game: Drugs, Power, and the Fight for the Soul of Major League Baseball*, Penguin Group, 2005.

[8] Associated Press, *A-Rod Steroids Report a Baseball Shocker*, CBS News, February 7, 2009.

[9] Ken Gumick, *Manny Suspended 50 Games for PED Use*, MLB.com, May 8, 2009.

[10] Associated Press, *Texas Picks Company to Run Massive Steroids Testing Program*, ESPN, January 22, 2008.

[11] For further study see Framl Osch, *International Sports Law Perspectives, Harmonization of Anti-Doping Code Through Arbitration: The Case Law of the Court of Arbitration for Sport*, 12 Marquette Sports Law Rev. 675 (2002).

[12] G. A. Green, F. D. Uryazc, T. A. Petr, & C. D. Bray, *NCAA Study of Substance Use and Abuse Habits of College Student-Athletes*, 11 Clinical Journal of Sport Medicine 51 (2001).

and amateur sports associations have taken different approaches in trying to combat the problem of doping in sports. This chapter presents an overview of drug use in sports and what has been done at the professional, amateur, and international levels to control it.

PROFESSIONAL SPORTS

Professional athletes are usually deemed employees of the team or league. When professional athletes organize in labor unions, they receive protection under the National Labor Relations Act. Any drug testing program implemented in professional sports must therefore be agreed to by management and labor through the collective bargaining process.[13] The National Labor Relations Act requires that owners and unions "meet at reasonable times and confer in good faith with respect to wages, hours, and other terms and conditions of employment." The National Labor Relations Board (NLRB) determined in *Johnson-Bateman Co.*, 295 N.L.R.B. 180, 182 (1989), that drug testing is a subject of mandatory bargaining between management and labor. For example, Major League Baseball owners could not impose a drug testing policy on players without first entering into good-faith negotiations with the MLB Players Association (MLBPA). Because drug programs are mandatory subjects of collective bargaining, teams or leagues cannot unilaterally institute a drug testing program. Even though Major League Baseball undertook just such an effort in the 1980s.[14]

Professional athletes have a great deal at stake in a short professional career. A career can be cut short by a positive drug test, which may subsequently result in discipline by the team or commissioner or in suspension from the league. If an athlete is endorsing a particular product and tests positive for drug use, there is a very good chance the athlete will lose the endorsement contract. In fact, many contracts allow a team or sponsor to deny a bonus payment upon the finding of a positive drug test. The league or team is also concerned about the overall image of the league and wants to assure its fans and the public that the players do not use drugs. That is a conflict that is not easily resolved but has to be hammered out through collective bargaining. Players unions are concerned about the image of players as well as the effect that suspensions might have on a player's career. Unions have argued for a "stair-step" approach to player discipline, in which discipline ranges from rehabilitation to suspension from the league.

A drug testing scheme at the professional level generally sets forth, among other policies, what players can be tested, the procedure by which the testing is done, what substances are banned by the league, and the discipline imposed for a violation of the drug testing policy. In any drug testing policy for professional leagues, several matters need to be considered by both parties:

- What drugs are prohibited under the policy? Who makes the decision about which drugs are prohibited? How can a drug become prohibited by the league?
- Will random testing of all players occur? If not, how does one determine who is to be tested? Will probable cause be used as a standard for testing?

---

[13] Mark M. Rabuano, *An Examination of Drug-Testing as a Mandatory Subject of Collective Bargaining in Major League Baseball*, University of Pennsylvania Journal of Labor and Employment Law, Vol. 4.2, 200.

[14] *For further study see*, Matt Mitten, *Legal Issues Arising of Blood Testing for Human Growth Hormone*, Marquette Law School Legal Studies Paper No. 09-30, 2009.

- What disciplinary measures are to be taken if an athlete is found to be in violation of the league policy? What are the penalties for repeat offenders of the league's drug policy? What are the appropriate fines and suspensions for violations of the policy?
- How are the tests conducted and by whom? What are the procedures for maintaining the integrity of the samples?
- What are the procedures for challenging the test results?

The four major sports in America have instituted policies regarding performance-enhancing drugs. Major League Baseball was under enormous pressure to control the use of performance-enhancing drugs after the release of the Mitchell Report. As a result, Major League Baseball and the MLBPA were able to come to an agreement to strengthen the league's policy. The following are highlights of the current MLB drug policy.

MAJOR LEAGUE BASEBALL'S

JOINT DRUG PREVENTION AND TREATMENT PROGRAM

8. DISCIPLINE

A. Player Fails to Comply with Treatment Program

1. If the Treatment Board determines . . . that a Player has failed to comply with his Treatment Program . . . that information shall be disclosed to the Commissioner and the Player shall be subject to the following discipline by the Commissioner:
    - (a) First failure to comply at least a 15-game but not more than a 25-game suspension;
    - (b) Second failure to comply: at least a 25-game but not more than a 50-game suspension;
    - (c) Third failure to comply: at least a 50-game but not more than a 75-game suspension;
    - (d) Fourth failure to comply: at least a one-year suspension; and
    - (e) Any subsequent failure to comply by a Player shall result in the Commissioner imposing further discipline on the Player. The level of the discipline will be determined consistent with the concept of progressive discipline.

B. Player Tests Positive for a Performance Enhancing Substance

1. First positive test result: a 50-game suspension;
2. Second positive test result: a 100-game suspension; and
3. Third positive test result: permanent suspension from Major League and Minor League Baseball; provided, however, that a Player so suspended may apply, no earlier than one year following the imposition of the suspension, to the Commissioner for discretionary reinstatement after a minimum period of two years. . . .

C. Player Tests Positive for a Stimulant

1. First positive test result: follow-up testing . . .
2. Second positive test result: a 25-game suspension;
3. Third positive test result: an 80-game suspension; and
4. Fourth and subsequent positive test result: a suspension for just cause by the Commissioner, up to permanent suspension from Major League and Minor League Baseball, which penalty shall be subject to challenge before the Arbitration Panel.

D. Conviction for the Possession or Use of Prohibited Substance

A Player who is convicted or pleads guilty (including a plea of *nolo contendere* or similar plea but not including an adjournment contemplating dismissal or a similar disposition) to the possession or use of any Prohibited Substance (including a criminal charge of conspiracy or attempt to possess or use) shall be subject to the following discipline:

1. For a first offense: at least a 60-game but not more than an 80-game suspension, if the Prohibited Substance is a Performance Enhancing Substance, or at least a 15-game but not more than a 30-game suspension, if the Prohibited Substance is a Drug of Abuse (including a Stimulant);
2. For a second offense: at least a 120-game but not more than a one-year suspension, if the Prohibited Substance is a Performance Enhancing Substance, or at least a 30-game but not more than a 90-game suspension, if the Prohibited Substance is a Drug of Abuse (including a Stimulant);
3. For a third offense involving a Performance Enhancing Substance: permanent suspension from Major League and Minor League Baseball; provided, however, that a Player so suspended may apply, no earlier than one year following the imposition of the suspension, to the Commissioner for discretionary reinstatement after a minimum period of two years.
4. If the Prohibited Substance is a Drug of Abuse (including a Stimulant), a third offense shall result in a one-year suspension, and any subsequent offense shall result in a suspension for just cause by the Commissioner, up to permanent suspension from Major League and Minor League Baseball, which penalty shall be subject to challenge before the Arbitration Panel.

E. Participation in the Sale or Distribution of a Prohibited Substance

A Player who participates in the sale or distribution of a Prohibited Substance shall be subject to the following discipline:

1. For a first offense: at least an 80-game but not more than a 100-game suspension. . . .
2. For a second offense involving a Performance Enhancing Substance: permanent suspension from Major League and Minor League Baseball; provided,

however, that a Player so suspended may apply, no earlier than one year following the imposition of the suspension, to the Commissioner for discretionary reinstatement after a minimum period of two years. . . .

3. If the Prohibited Substance is a Drug of Abuse (including a Stimulant), a second offense shall result in a two-year suspension, and any subsequent offense shall result in disciplinary action for just cause by the Commissioner, up to permanent suspension from Major League and Minor League Baseball, which penalty shall be subject to challenge before the Arbitration Panel.

F. Marijuana

A Player on the Administrative Track for the use or possession of marijuana shall not be subject to suspension. The Player will be subject to fines, which shall be progressive and which shall not exceed $25,000 for any particular violation.

H. Suspensions

1. For purposes of this Section 8, a "game" shall include all championship season games, the All-Star Game and post-season games in which the Player would have been eligible to play, but shall not include spring training games. . . .[15]

The NFL's drug policy clearly states that there is no place for prohibited substances in football and that steroid use is banned. Drug testing is frequently performed in the NFL. Players are subject to random drug testing by the league throughout the year, from preseason to postseason. The NBA's list of prohibited drugs includes marijuana, steroids, cocaine, and PCP. The NBA's policy is harsher for those violators who use street drugs than for those using performance-enhancing drugs. If there is reasonable cause to believe a player is using drugs, the league or the Players Association can request a conference with the player and an independent expert. The independent expert will determine whether reasonable cause exists for testing and will authorize testing if appropriate. First-year players can be tested once during training camp and three times during the regular season. Veteran players are also subject to testing. A veteran player may be required to undergo random testing during training camp and at other times for reasonable cause. Discipline under the NBA policy varies depending on the type of drug used. Marijuana and steroids are treated differently. A player has the opportunity to apply for reinstatement with approval by the league and the Players Association.

In 2005 the National Hockey League announced the start of a program dealing with the use of performance-enhancing substances. Every NHL player will be subjected to no more than two random tests every year, with at least one of the tests to be conducted for the entire team. If a player tests positive, a 20-game suspension without pay results. The player can also be referred to the league's substance abuse/behavioral health program for evaluation, education, and further possible treatment. A second positive offense results in a 60-game suspension. The player is suspended

---

[15] MLBPA.org

permanently for a third positive test, and the player can apply for reinstatement after two years if suspended for a third time. A summary of the NHL's drug testing program for performance-enhancing drug substances is as follows:

Testing Procedures: Following their orientation session on the program, every NHL player will be subject to up to three "no-notice" tests from the start of training camp through the end of the Regular Season. Testing is conducted as follows: 10 teams will be subject to one no-notice test, 10 teams will be subject to two no-notice tests, and 10 teams will be subject to three no-notice tests.

Sample-Collecting Authority: Comprehensive Drug Testing, Long Beach California

Test Laboratory: INRS-Institute Armand-Frappier, Laval Quebec

Disciplinary Penalties: Positive tests for performance-enhancing substances will result in mandatory discipline as follows:

- For the first positive test, a 20-game suspension without pay and mandatory referral to the NHLPA/NHL Substance Abuse and Behavioral Health Program for evaluation, education, and possible treatment.
- For the second positive test, a 60-game suspension without pay.
- For the third positive test, a permanent suspension. A player receiving a third positive test and a permanent suspension from play in the League will, however, be eligible to apply for reinstatement after two years. The application would be considered by the Committee.[16]

Montreal Canadiens goalie Jose Theodore tested positive for a banned substance in 2006 pre-Olympic screening. The team doctor for the Canadiens stated that Theodore had been using a hair-growth agent, which caused the positive test. Theodore was not subject to discipline by the NHL because the pre-Olympic test was not part of the NHL program. He had been taking Propecia for eight years, a known hair-growth stimulant. Propecia is also known as a masking agent for performance-enhancing drugs. In response, Theodore said, "I always like my hair real long and I like to keep it long as long as possible." Theodore also added that he is 5′11″ and 182 pounds, stating, "If you look at me with no shirt, if I'm taking steroids then I should change the guy that gave them to me because it's not working."[17]

As can be expected, there has been much debate about the seriousness and enforcement of drug testing policies at the professional level. Major League Baseball has not been the only professional sports league criticized for its drug policy. WADA Chairman Dick Pound alleged that perhaps one-third of NHL players were taking performance-enhancing drugs. This was vehemently denied by the league and the NHLPA. NHL Deputy Commissioner Bill Daly said that there was absolutely "no basis in fact" for the allegations. Pound, who is a lawyer, is on a campaign to clean up sports. He is a former vice president of the IOC and was a participant in the 1960 Olympic Games in Germany.

Many youngsters look to athletes as role models and dream of becoming a sports superstar at some point in their life. It thus follows that society should be concerned when drug use becomes a major issue in sports, because drugs such as steroids can have serious effects on young athletes' future health and careers.[18]

---

[16] *Source:* National Hockey League Players Association.
[17] Associated Press, *Theodore Tests Positive, Blames Result on Propecia*, ESPN, February 9, 2006.
[18] *See* E. T. Walker, *Missing the Target: How Performance-Enhancing Drugs Go Unnoticed and Endanger the Lives of Athletes*, 10 VILL. SPORTS & ENT. L.J. 181 (2003).

The concern about drug use in professional sports has led many different groups to initiate some form of drug testing program or procedures. In December 2005, the World Wrestling Federation announced it would begin random drug testing to detect illegal drugs after one of its stars, Eddie Guerrero, died before a show.[19] The Tennis Anti-Doping Program has a set of rules that apply to all levels of tennis. The program is administered for the governing body of tennis by International Drug Testing Management, located in Sweden. The Tennis Anti-Doping Program 2009 information sheet states in part:

> Any player who provides an analytically positive urine sample receives fair and due process. Players are considered innocent until proven guilty. They are allowed to continue playing pending a decision on their case by an independent Tennis Anti-Doping Tribunal. The appeals process extends to include possible hearings before the Court of Arbitration for Sport (CAS). When a player is determined to have committed a doping offense, a public announcement is made and the penalties may be retroactive to the date of the positive sample.[20]

The following is the testimony of former Houston Rockets Vice President of Basketball Operations/Athletic Trainer Keith Jones before Congress regarding drug use in the NBA.

Chairman Davis and Members of the Committee:

I am the Vice President of Basketball Operations/Athletic Trainer for the Houston Rockets of the National Basketball Association, and have served as head athletic trainer for the Rockets since 1996. Prior to that, I spent six seasons as head trainer for the Los Angeles Clippers, one season as assistant trainer for the Orlando Magic, and several seasons working as a trainer with football teams in the NFL, USFL, and NCAA. I also worked as the team trainer for the gold medal-winning United States Senior Men's National Basketball Team during the 2000 Summer Olympics in Sydney, Australia, and in the same capacity for the 1998 World Championship of Basketball in Greece and the 1999 Tournament of the Americas in Puerto Rico.

I appreciate the opportunity to testify before the Committee.

In my role as head athletic trainer for the Rockets, and in conjunction with our team physicians, strength and conditioning coaches, and other staff, I am in charge of our team's efforts to prevent, evaluate, manage, and rehabilitate injured or ill players. I interact with Rockets players on a daily basis, am present in the locker and training rooms throughout the season, travel with the team, and attend all practices and games. It is my job to be intimately familiar with the health status of every member of our team and to help them perform on the playing court at the peak of their physical and mental abilities.

I have worked as a trainer in the NBA for 17 years, and have learned a great deal in that period about the physical abilities of professional basketball players and the physical and mental obstacles they face over the course of their careers. I also worked as a trainer of various professional and college football teams prior to joining the NBA, and am therefore in a position to compare and contrast the physical attributes that allow players to succeed in basketball and, separately, in football.

During my tenure in the NBA, I have never observed an NBA player using an anabolic steroid or an illicit performance-enhancing drug. I have never been asked by a player to supply such a substance, nor, of course, would I do so if asked. Steroids and other banned performance-enhancers have no place

---

[19] Associated Press, *Pro Wrestling to Institute Random Drug Testing*, ESPN, December 4, 2005.
[20] Tennis Anti-Doping Program, Information in Tennis Anti-Doping Program, 2009. *Source:* www.itftennis.com.

in the NBA. They carry enormous health risks to athletes, provide no significant advantage to NBA players, and are banned by the NBA's drug policy. Any benefits that a player might receive from using such a substance are greatly outweighed by their costs.

In my experience, steroids and performance-enhancing drugs are not part of the culture of NBA basketball. I cannot say with certainty why this is so, but I believe it to be true. It may be because, from the moment a player begins to develop as a basketball player in AAU and high school, through and including his career in the NBA, the primary emphasis from coaches—and the primary focus from players—is on basketball skill and ability, rather than physical strength, power, or speed. It may be because basketball rewards quickness, agility, and dexterity, and promotes a lean body type, rather than favoring muscle mass, bulk and the larger body types often seen in football and baseball. It may be because steroids and performance-enhancing substances can have the effect of increasing a player's weight and changing his body structure, making it more difficult for him to feel where he is on the court, in the air, or in relation to other players. It may be because of the increased risk of injury and long-term adverse health effects, and the resulting advice of doctors and trainers in our league to avoid these substances. In more recent years, it may be because the NBA's drug policy serves to deter players from getting involved with these drugs.

No matter the reason, it is my belief that steroids and performance enhancing drugs are not used in any meaningful amount by NBA players.

Even though the NBA does not currently have a problem with steroids and performance-enhancing drugs, I fully support the NBA's inclusion of these substances within its anti-drug policy. If we want to ensure that these drugs stay out of our game, it is important to send the message to players that steroids and performance-enhancing substances are banned and to have an effective testing program.[21]

The issue of drugs in sports calls into question the integrity of sports. Is it unethical or engaging in unfair play if some players are using illegal drugs and others are not?[22] Is it fair to allow certain players to use drugs and perform at a higher level when other players do not use drugs? Players understand that the better they perform, the more money they will make. In today's commercial sports market, players have a huge incentive to hit more home runs, score more touchdowns, or jump higher then the next athlete because their next contract will be directly tied to their performance. An increase in home runs and other statistics may bring more fans to the game, but in the long run, is it good for sports?

Drug Use in Major League Baseball

In the spring of 1984, Commissioner Bowie Kuhn attempted to institute league-wide regulations concerning drug use. In June 1984, team owners approved a program involving both owners and the MLBPA that set forth punishment and treatment for players who used drugs. When Peter Ueberroth assumed the role of commissioner, he terminated the regulations and instituted his own mandatory drug testing program that covered management, umpires, and all minor league players. Major League players were not covered under the plan. He later attempted to unilaterally institute voluntary drug testing, but the MLBPA rejected the plan. In 1986 Ueberroth tried to introduce a clause into the MLB

---

[21] *Steroid Use in Sports Part III: Examining the National Basketball Association's Steroid Testing Program: Hearing Before the Committee on Government Reform, U.S. House of Representatives*, 109th Cong. 55–57 (2005) (prepared statement of Keith Jones, V.P. of Basketball Operations/Athletic Trainer, Houston Rockets).

[22] Edited by Jan Boxill, *Sports Ethics and Anthology*, Blackwell Publishing, 2003.

standard player contract that required mandatory drug testing, but the MLBPA filed a grievance in response. An arbitrator found in favor of the MLBPA. After that arbitration decision, baseball had no drug testing program until the 2002 season.

In the arbitration decision in Case 12-1, *In the Matter of Arbitration Between Major League Baseball Players Association and the Commissioner of Major League Baseball, Suspension of Steve Howe*, the arbitrator was determining whether the discipline imposed by the commissioner for drug use by a professional baseball player, Steve Howe, was appropriate. Howe was a former standout pitcher at the University of Michigan and the Los Angeles Dodgers who was a perpetual violator of the league's drug policy.

CASE 12-1   *In the Matter of Arbitration Between Major League Baseball Players Association and the Commissioner of Major League Baseball, Suspension of Steven Howe*

As in any disciplinary matter, the burden of establishing just cause is on those imposing discipline. While the Commissioner has a "reasonable range of discretion" in such matters, the penalty he imposes in a particular case must be "reasonably commensurate with the offense" and "appropriate, given all the circumstances." Moreover, "offenders must be viewed with a careful eye to the specific nature of the offense, and penalties must be carefully fashioned with an eye toward responsive, consistent and fair discipline." There must, in other words, be "careful scrutiny of the individual circumstances and the particular facts relevant to each case."

The need for scrutiny is at its zenith here simply because of the nature of the penalty at issue. Contrary to the analogy counsel seeks to draw, the Commissioner is not an employer who has decided for himself that he will no longer retain an employee who is then free to go elsewhere in the same industry. The Commissioner's imposition of Baseball's "ultimate sanction, lifetime ineligibility" means that no employer in Baseball may hire Howe no matter what he thinks of his ability, his good faith or his chances of successfully resisting the addiction with which he has been plagued. Thus, the burden on the Commissioner to justify his action transcends that of the ordinary employer inasmuch as he can effectively prevent a player's employment by any one at any level of his chosen profession.

. . . .

Discussion and Analysis

. . . .

I fully understand Baseball's institutional interest and its need, in so far as possible, to keep its workplaces free of drugs and to deter

drug use among players wherever it might occur. I also appreciate the
pressures brought to bear on Baseball by those who only see the
"athlete-as-hero." But those considerations, as important as they are,
must be examined in the light of the just cause standard. Under that
standard, Baseball's conduct, as well as Howe's, is subject to review.

In justifying his decision, the Commissioner told the Panel that Baseball had done all that could have been done and that Howe had simply
"squandered" the many chances Baseball had given him. If Baseball had,
in fact, done all it could, both before Howe's 1990 return to the game
and after, the imposition of a lifetime ban would be more understandable. But it is obvious that reality and what the Commissioner perceived to be the case is quite different.

We now know that Howe has an underlying psychiatric disorder that was
never diagnosed or treated; that this disorder has been a contributing
factor to his use of drugs; and that, absent treatment for the condition, he remains vulnerable to such use.

We also know that in 1990 the Commissioner's medical adviser cautioned
against Howe's return unless he was tested every other day of the year
throughout his professional career and that Baseball did not heed this
clear warning even though the Commissioner suggested in his March 1990
decision that such testing be imposed.

These two factors cast a very different light on the nature of the
chance Howe was given in 1990 and, indeed, on the nature of the
chances he had been given in earlier years.

It was clear from Dr. Riordan's report that in his expert view continuous testing, including testing in the off-season, was essential if
Howe was to succeed in resisting drugs during his career while also
seeking to overcome his addiction through therapeutic means. In his
decision allowing Howe to return, the Commissioner quoted Dr. Riordan's
report at some length. The Commissioner's order that Howe play in the
minors for a year, his directions regarding testing and his declaration that Howe would be immediately banned if he tested positive were
all based on Dr. Riordan's cautionary advice. But the stringent, year-
round testing requirement, as we have seen, was not implemented and
Howe was unfortunately set on a course without the strategic safeguard
Dr. Riordan considered indispensable to his success.

If that safeguard had been firmly in place and if Howe had never been
presented with an opportunity to vary its regularity, an opportunity
Dr. Riordan had clearly meant to foreclose, it is not at all likely,
given the certainty of detection such a regimen would have imposed,
that the events of December 19 would have occurred.

While Howe can certainly be faulted for seeking to delay testing at a time of his admittedly increasing sense of vulnerability, the Office of the Commissioner cannot escape its measure of responsibility for what took place in 1991. Based on medical advice the Commissioner had solicited, the need for continuous testing was obvious. To give Howe "yet another chance" of returning to the game without implementing those conditions was not, in my judgment, a fair shot at success.

As to Howe's undiagnosed psychiatric condition and the inadequacy of his prior treatment, the Commissioner considers it unfair to place on his Office the burden of reviewing a player's medical history before imposing discipline. As I pointed out in *Reyes,* a decision rendered three months before the Commissioner's action here, I fail to see the unfairness of such a requirement. Certainly, as the Association attempted to point out prior to the imposition of discipline in this case, it is not unfair to expect a exceptionally scrupulous review of the record when the matter under consideration is a lifetime ban.

What bears repeating here is that the Commissioner does not stand in the isolated position of an individual employer. He can bar the employment of a player at any level of the game regardless of the opinion or wishes of any one of a great number of potential employers. That is an awesome power. With it comes a heavy responsibility, especially when that power is exercised unilaterally and not as the result of a collectively bargained agreement as to the level of sanctions to be imposed for particular actions.

Here, there was little consideration of the medical records and no discernible pre-decision attempt to probe beneath their surface and ascertain if Howe had been properly diagnosed and treated. Even though Dr. Riordan's 1990 report signaled the possibility of a previously undiagnosed and untreated illness affecting Howe's behavior, by 1992, when discipline was to be imposed as a result of Howe's subsequent actions, the Commissioner considered medical matters of little importance when measured against Baseball's interests. But as made manifest by the opinions of Drs. Wender and Kleber, both impartial medical experts, such matters were highly important in that they served to explain events.

It cannot be known what the Commissioner might have done if he had been fully aware of the facts regarding Howe's condition and previous treatment. What we do know is that those facts were not before him and that virtually no effort was made to ascertain them. When considering the permanent expulsion of a player, this failure to examine all the circumstances, irrespective of the cause, is not, in my view, consistent with his responsibility.

The Commissioner seeks to justify his exclusive reliance on institutional considerations by resting Howe's permanent expulsion on an obligation to deter repeated drug use by others. He argues that there was no alternative, that a less severe sanction would have sent the wrong message to players who will view anything short of a lifetime ban as a license to take up and repeatedly use drugs. This hardly seems the case. All available evidence supports the proposition that drug use in organized Baseball is not what it appeared to be some years ago. As the Association pointed out in Nixon there has not been an "initial offender" in the Major Leagues since 1989 and those who unfortunately repeated an offense are concededly no more than a handful.

To everyone's credit, all this has been accomplished without the imposition of a lifetime ban and, given continued education and awareness at both the minor and Major League levels, this steady progress toward a drug free environment is quite likely to continue. When the industry's goal is the complete elimination of drugs, it can be argued, of course, that a single instance of use is one too many. What cannot legitimately be questioned, however, is the commitment of the industry and the Players Association. No member of the public can seriously contend, given the record, that Baseball's attitude toward drugs is light hearted or that the manner in which the industry and the Association have previously dealt with the problem has imperiled the integrity of the game.

One further observation on the reasoning the Commissioner advanced in this proceeding is appropriate. Deterrence, however laudable an objective, should not be achieved at the expense of fairness. What was considered vital to Howe's sobriety at this point in his life should have been implemented. Moreover, the Office of the Commissioner should have looked closely at all the circumstances in order to ascertain and evaluate his condition and the adequacy of his treatment before deciding what discipline to impose. These failings lead me to conclude that the Commissioner's action in imposing a lifetime ban was without just cause.

What remains, given this conclusion, is the penalty that should be imposed in lieu of a lifetime ban. . . .

. . . As previously stated, Howe now recognizes, despite his efforts of recent years, that he bears a responsibility for the events of autumn and early winter of 1991 and that what occurred then, however the responsibility of others is assessed, was an "unacceptable failure" on his part. Considering that fact and weighing all other aspects of this unique case, including his conviction on the federal charge, it's my judgment that the interests of deterrence and fairness as well as punishment would be realized if the penalty imposed by the former Commissioner is reduced to time served and Howe is thereafter given a fair opportunity to succeed. A suspension of this length, 119 days, entails a substantial monetary loss to Howe; almost $400,000 in base salary and a lost opportunity to earn upwards of $1,500,000.00 in contract bonuses. A penalty of this magnitude should serve as a clear warning that drug use will continue to be treated with severity. At the same time, a chance to compete coupled with appropriate treatment and rigorous safeguards will give Howe what he was not adequately given in the past.

As is evident from these proceedings, no one can predict whether Howe will succeed even with the treatment and safeguards provided for in the Award. It is not at all certain, as the impartial medical evaluations reflect, that he is quite ready to accept full responsibility for his actions or that he fully understands, even at this juncture, the complex reasons for his behavior. While fundamental fairness requires that his permanent expulsion be set aside, only with his understanding and acceptance of responsibility will his future truly be secure.

Grievance upheld.

Source: Courtesy of Westlaw; reprinted with permission.

The following can be placed in the category of immediate results of the steroid testing program instituted in 2002: Matt Lawton, right fielder of the New York Yankees, admitted that he took the veterinary steroid boldenone before he was suspended for ten games for violating Major League Baseball's steroid policy. Lawton told a sports reporter he had been playing poorly and was injured, so he turned to steroids. He injected the steroids on September 20 and the next day he hit a home run in his first at bat. He admits it was "stupid" to take steroids but that he was desperate. He told *Sports Weekly,* "I wasn't playing well enough to be on a Little League roster, let alone be on the roster of the New York Yankees. I just wasn't physically able to do the job. I had never been in the playoff hunt before. So I did something that will always haunt me."[23] Lawton was an All-Star in 2000 and 2004.

The late Ken Caminiti was not shy about admitting to using steroids during his 1996 MVP season with the San Diego Padres. Caminiti was also a recovering alcoholic and had pled guilty to cocaine possession. Tragically, he died in 2004 of a heart attack due to a drug overdose. In Caminiti's MVP season, he hit 40 home runs, with 130 RBIs, and batted .326. He had a lifetime batting average of .272 but never hit more than 29 home runs in a season other than his MVP season.

However one accounts for it, there has been an onslaught of home runs in the Major Leagues over the past few years. From 1900 to 1997, only two players hit 60 or more home runs in a single season: Babe Ruth did it in 1927 when he hit 60 runs, and Roger Maris did it in 1961 when he hit 61. From 1998 to 2001, the 60-home-run mark was eclipsed six times, and the 70-home-run mark twice. From 1962 to 1990, only three players in baseball even reached 50 home runs: Willie Mays with 52 in 1965, George Foster with 52 in 1977, and Cecil Fielder with 51 in 1991. From 1995 through 2007, twenty-three players have hit more than 50 home runs. What can account for this increase? Table 12-1 lists the single-season leaders for home runs in Major League Baseball.

---

[23] *Lawton Failed Test After Taking Veterinary Steroid,* ESPN, December 22, 2005.

TABLE 12-1

MLB Single-Season Home Run Leaders					
Name	*Home Runs*	*Year*	*Team*	*League*	*Rank*
Barry Bonds	73	2001	San Francisco Giants	NL	1
Mark McGwire	70	1998	St. Louis Cardinals	NL	2
Sammy Sosa	66	1998	Chicago Cubs	NL	3
Mark McGwire	65	1999	St. Louis Cardinals	NL	4
Sammy Sosa	64	2001	Chicago Cubs	NL	5
Sammy Sosa	63	1999	Chicago Cubs	NL	6
Roger Maris	61	1961	New York Yankees	AL	7
Babe Ruth	60	1927	New York Yankees	AL	8
Babe Ruth	59	1921	New York Yankees	AL	9
Jimmie Foxx	58	1932	Philadelphia Athletics	AL	10
Hank Greenberg	58	1938	Detroit Tigers	AL	
Ryan Howard	58	2006	Philadelphia Phillies	NL	
Mark McGwire	58	1997	Oakland Athletics	AL	
			St. Louis Cardinals	NL	
Luis Gonzalez	57	2001	Arizona Diamondbacks	NL	14
Alex Rodriguez	57	2002	Texas Rangers	AL	

Note: Chart courtesy of Baseball Almanac (www.baseball-almanac.com). Reprinted with permission.

Report to the Commissioner of Baseball of an Independent Investigation into the Illegal Use of Steroids and Other Performance-Enhancing Substances by Players in Major League Baseball   On March 30, 2006, MLB Commissioner Bud Selig requested former Maine Senator George Mitchell to investigate the allegations that many MLB players had used steroids or other performance-enhancing drugs. Mitchell's charge from the commissioner was "to determine, as a factual matter, whether any Major League players associated with [the Bay Area Laboratory Co-Operative] or otherwise used steroids or other illegal performance-enhancing substances at any point after the substances were banned by the 2002–2006 collective bargaining agreement." Mitchell was authorized to expand his investigation beyond players involved with the Bay Area Laboratory Co-Operative (BALCO) if necessary and "to follow the evidence wherever it may lead."

Mitchell accepted the charge of Commissioner Selig on the condition that he be given "total independence" both during the investigation and in compiling the report. The commissioner agreed to this condition. Selig also agreed that the Mitchell Report would be made public when it was completed.

At the outset of the investigation, Mitchell declared that he would conduct a "deliberate and unbiased examination of the facts that would comport with American values of fairness." He retained the law firm of DLA Piper US, LLP, to assist him in the investigation requested by the commissioner. Mitchell's investigation was thorough. He and his team sifted through over 115,000 pages of documents that had been provided to them by a variety of sources, including the Office of the Commissioner of

Major League Baseball and all the Major League teams. Approximately 20,000 other electronic documents from these sources were also reviewed by Mitchell and his legal team. Over 700 witnesses were interviewed during the investigation, and over 550 of those witnesses were "current or former club officials, managers, coaches, team physicians, athletic trainers or resident security agents." Sixteen individuals from the Commissioner's Office were interviewed, including Commissioner Bud Selig and Chief Operating Officer Robert DuPuy. Senator Mitchell and his staff attempted to contact almost 500 former players for the investigation. Only 68 agreed to be interviewed. Mitchell also attempted to contact the Players Association during his investigation, but stated in his report that "[t]he Players Association was largely uncooperative." Mitchell stated that he asked each player to meet with him through his designated representative or the Players Association so that each would have a chance to respond to the allegations contained in the report. He noted, "Almost without exception they declined to meet or talk with me."

Mitchell's goal in preparing his report was "to provide a thorough, accurate, and fair accounting of what I learned in this investigation about the illegal use of performance-enhancing substances by players in Major League Baseball." His investigation led Mitchell to the conclusion that the use of anabolic steroids and other performance-enhancing substances was "widespread" and threatened the integrity of the game of baseball. Mitchell further found that baseball's response to the crisis had been "slow to develop" and was "initially ineffective," but that baseball's response had "gained momentum" after the institution of the 2002 drug testing program. Senator Mitchell found that all 30 Major League teams had players involved with performance-enhancing substances at some point. The report named 78 players, most notably baseball's all-time home run leader Barry Bonds, star pitcher Roger Clemens, and Clemens's former teammate Andy Pettitte. However, the report recommended that the commissioner take no action against players who were found to have used steroids in the past.

The Mitchell Report contained many recommendations "to prevent the illegal use of performance-enhancing substances in Major League Baseball." Senator Mitchell offered these recommendations as a "set of principles and best practices that presently characterize a state-of-the-art drug testing program." He noted, however, that no drug testing program is perfect. He added that every program should be updated regularly to keep pace with constantly changing challenges and best practices. In summary, the Mitchell Report states that there should be a higher priority on aggressive investigation, enhanced educational programs, and continued drug testing. Senator Mitchell was uncertain how this would actually happen, considering the combative relationship between management and the players union.

The following recommendations were offered by the Mitchell Report to enhance the investigative capabilities of Major League Baseball.[24]

1. The Commissioner should establish a Department of Investigations.
2. The Commissioner's Office should more effectively cooperate with law enforcement agencies.
3. The Commissioner's Office should actively use the clubs' powers, as employer, to investigate violations of the joint program.

---

[24] George J. Mitchell, Report to the Commissioner of Baseball of an Independent Investigation into the Illegal Use of Steroids and Other Performance Enhancing Substances by Players in Major League Baseball 287–94 (Dec. 13, 2007).

4. All clubs should have clear, written, and well-publicized policies for reporting information relating to possible performance-enhancing substance violations.

5. Packages sent to players at Major League ballparks should be logged.

The following recommendations were offered as unilateral actions that the commissioner could take to address the issue of performance-enhancing drugs that did not require collective bargaining.[25]

1. Background investigations of prospective clubhouse personnel.

2. Random drug testing of clubhouse personnel.

3. A hotline for reporting anonymous tips.

4. Testing of top draft prospects prior to the Major League Baseball draft.

Changes to the educational program designed to inform players about the dangers of performance-enhancing substances were also recommended:[26]

1. The design and implementation of the educational program should be centralized with the independent program administrator.

2. Spring training programs should include testimonials and other speakers and presentations.

3. Explain the health risks in context and provide education on alternative methods to achieve the same results.

4. Players need to understand the non-health effects of buying performance-enhancing substances from street dealers and "Internet pharmacies."

The report's recommendations for further improvement of the Joint Drug Prevention and Treatment Program were as follows:

1. The program should be independent.

2. The program should be transparent.

3. There should be adequate year-round, unannounced drug testing.

4. The program should be flexible enough to employ best practices as they develop.

5. The program should continue to respect the legitimate rights of players.

6. The program should have adequate funding.

Congress became especially interested in steroid use in baseball in 2005 and again in 2008, holding hearings in which players and baseball management personnel testified before Congress regarding the use of steroids and illegal drugs in the sport. Bud Selig, the Commissioner of Baseball, expressed his concern about drug use in baseball in his testimony before Congress in 2008:

> On March 30, 2006, I asked Senator Mitchell to conduct a comprehensive investigation of the illegal use of performance enhancing substances in Baseball. Mr. Chairman, I decided to do this investigation so that no one could ever say that Baseball had something to hide because I certainly did not. Baseball accepts the findings of this investigation, and Baseball will act on its recommendations.
>
> Before I turn to the Mitchell Report, it is important to recall the progress we have made. Baseball now has the strongest drug testing program in professional sports. Our penalty structure of 50 games,

---

[25] *Id.* at 295–96.

[26] *Id.* at 298–302.

100 games and life is the toughest. We test for stimulants, including amphetamines. We have year-round, unannounced testing, including testing on game days, both before and after games. We use the Olympic-certified laboratories in Montreal for our testing and the day-to-day administration of the program has been delegated to an Independent Program Administrator. A whole generation of players has grown up under our strict Minor League testing policy, which is entering its eighth season. As a result of all of this, our positive tests have declined significantly from 96 in the 2003 survey test to just two steroid positives in 2006 and three in 2007. This improvement is similar to what we have observed in our Minor League program under which the positive rate declined from nine percent in 2001 to less than one-half of one percent in 2007. Just last week, I met with a group of 12 certified athletic trainers from Major League Clubs who assured me that we have changed the culture in Clubhouses regarding steroid use.

Ever since we last reopened our agreement in 2005, our program has continued to improve. Along with the MLBPA, we have tightened our collection procedures by adding chaperones to monitor players. We also often test players after a game, rather than before a game, to deter stimulant use. And the Commissioner's Office has placed emphasis on discipline for non-analytical positives. We had three disciplines for non-analytical positives in 2007 alone.

Because of these facts, I feel that Baseball is dealing effectively with the present and will continue to evolve to deal with the future. Nonetheless, I felt a need to appoint Senator Mitchell to deal with the past.

As I said in March 2006, "nothing is more important to me than the integrity of the game of baseball." I strongly believed 21 months ago, and I continue to believe today, that Baseball needed to fully, honestly and publicly confront the use of performance enhancing substances by players. I knew that an investigation would be an extraordinarily difficult undertaking. I knew that an investigation would be painful for all of those associated with the sport. No other sport had confronted its past in such a way. But I knew that Baseball must undertake that journey in order to preserve the integrity of our game and maintain credibility with the millions of baseball fans throughout the world. I want to thank this Committee for its role in helping to focus us all on the dangers of performance enhancing substances and for its patience as we at Baseball moved forward with this important investigation.

The investigation had a second purpose, as well. I am committed to keeping Major League Baseball's program the strongest in professional sports. I believed in March 2006 that our current drug program would be effective in curtailing the use of detectable steroids by players. Indeed, Senator Mitchell confirmed that our current program has been effective in that detectable steroid use appears to have declined. I also knew from experience that the development of a state-of-the art drug program is an evolutionary process. I knew that our work on this important issue was not done. By rigorously examining Baseball's experience with performance enhancing substances, my desire was for Senator Mitchell to provide us with recommendations and insights to help make additional progress in the on-going battle against the illegal use of performance enhancing substances in sports, recognizing, of course, our collective bargaining obligations. . . .

Senator Mitchell's thorough and detailed report elicited from me a range of reactions. I am a life-long baseball fan. I have devoted the last 45 years to the game. As a fan of the game of baseball and a student of its history, I am deeply saddened and disappointed by the conduct of the players and many other individuals described by the Senator in his report. On the other hand, as the Commissioner of Baseball, with the responsibility for protecting the integrity of the game for future generations, I am optimistic that Senator Mitchell's report is a milestone step in dealing with Baseball's past and the problems caused by these dangerous and illegal substances in both amateur and professional sports. Senator Mitchell's report helps bring understanding of and hopefully closure to the rumors and speculation that have swirled around this issue. Perhaps more important, Senator Mitchell's report—including his twenty recommendations which I fully embrace—helps point a way forward as we continue the battle against the illegal use of performance enhancing substances.

I want to be clear that I agree with the conclusions reached by Senator Mitchell in his report, including his criticisms of Baseball, the union and our players. I have personally agonized over what could have been done differently and I accept responsibility. In 1994, during a very difficult round of collective bargaining that included a lengthy strike, we proposed to the union a joint drug program that included steroids as prohibited substances. We made this proposal in an effort to be proactive, and I can assure you that we did not appreciate the magnitude of the problem that would develop. Senator Mitchell has suggested that the Clubs did not give this proposal the highest priority, but the Major League Baseball Players Association was fiercely and steadfastly opposed to any form of random drug testing. Even if the Clubs had taken a harder line on drugs, the Union would not have agreed and the strike could have lasted even longer. Unfortunately, the next round of bargaining did not occur until 2002, and, therefore, we did not have an opportunity to address the problem before it became more significant . . .

In closing, Senator Mitchell quoted a veteran Major League Player in the report as saying that "Major League Baseball is trying to investigate the past so that they can fix the future." Even prior to the issuance of the Mitchell Report, we had made great strides in reducing the number of players who use performance enhancing substances. I am confident that by adopting Senator Mitchell's recommendations, by constantly working to improve our drug program regardless of the effort or the cost, by pursuing new strategies to catch drug users, and by enhancing our educational efforts, we can make additional progress in our on-going battle against the use of performance enhancing substances in Baseball. Senator Mitchell's report identified the principal goals of his investigation: "to bring to a close this troubling chapter in baseball's history and to use the lessons learned from the past to prevent future use of performance enhancing substances." The lessons from the past serve only to strengthen my commitment to keep Major League Baseball's program the strongest and most effective in sports.[27]

One of the Major League players who testified before Congress was Rafael Palmeiro, who was considered a star player in baseball and a potential Hall of Famer. He played 20 seasons and had 569 lifetime home runs, ranking him fifth on the all-time home run list in baseball. He unequivocally stated before Congress in the following testimony that he had never used steroids; however, he later tested positive for steroid use.

Good morning, Mr. Chairman and Members of the Committee. My name is Rafael Palmeiro and I am a professional baseball player. I'll be brief in my remarks today. Let me start by telling you this: I have never used steroids. Period. I don't know how to say it any more clearly than that. Never. The reference to me in Mr. Canseco's book is absolutely false.

I am against the use of steroids. I don't think athletes should use steroids and I don't think our kids should use them. That point of view is one, unfortunately, that is not shared by our former colleague, Jose Canseco. Mr. Canseco is an unashamed advocate for increased steroid use by all athletes.

My parents and I came to the United States after fleeing the communist tyranny that still reigns over my homeland of Cuba. We came seeking freedom, knowing that through hard work, discipline,

---

[27] Statement of Commissioner Allan H. Selig Before the House Committee on Oversight and Government Reform, Jan. 15, 2008.

and dedication, my family and I could build a bright future in America. Since arriving to this great country, I have tried to live every day of my life in a manner that I hope has typified the very embodiment of the American Dream. I have gotten to play for three great organizations—the Chicago Cubs, Texas Rangers, and Baltimore Orioles—and I have been blessed to do well in a profession I love. That blessing has allowed me to work on projects and with charities in the communities where I live and play. As much as I have appreciated the accolades that have come with a successful career, I am just as honored to have worked with great organizations like the Make-a-Wish Foundation, Shoes for Orphans Souls, and the Lena Pope Home of Fort Worth.

The League and the Player's Association recently agreed on a steroid policy that I hope will be the first step to eradicating these substances from baseball. Congress should work with the League and the Player's Association to make sure that the new policy now being put in place achieves the goal of stamping steroids out of the sport. To the degree an individual player can be helpful, perhaps as an advocate to young people about the dangers of steroids, I hope you will call on us. I, for one, am ready to heed that call.[28]

Legal Challenges to Drug Testing

Fewer challenges have been made to drug testing at the professional level than at the amateur level, mainly because many drug testing procedures in professional sports have been agreed to during the collective bargaining process.

In Case 12-2, *Long v. National Football League,* 870 F. Supp. 101 (W.D. Pa. 1994), an NFL player challenged the league's anabolic steroid policy on constitutional grounds. He sued several defendants, including the NFL and the NFL Commissioner, in his failed attempt to challenge the policy.

📖 **CASE 12-2** *Long v. National Football League*

870 F. Supp. 101 (W.D. Pa. 1994)

ZIEGLER, Chief Judge.

This civil action arises from an incident which took place while plaintiff, Terry Long, was a member of The Pittsburgh Steelers football team. Long's urine was tested for the presence of anabolic steroids pursuant to a policy adopted by the National Football League. He was then suspended pursuant to the same policy because the test results were positive.

Plaintiff has alleged violations of the Fourth and Fourteenth Amendments of the United States Constitution, Article I, section 8 of the Pennsylvania Constitution, and various state law claims for the injury that he allegedly suffered as a result of defendants' actions. Plaintiff has asserted claims against The National Football League, Paul

---

[28] Testimony of Rafael Palmeiro before the Committee on Government Reform, United States House of Representatives, Mar. 17, 2005.

Tagliabue in his capacity as the Commissioner of the National Football League, the Pittsburgh Steelers organization, the City of Pittsburgh, Sophie Masloff in her capacity as the Mayor of the city of Pittsburgh, and the Stadium Authority of the City of Pittsburgh. . . .

Defendants contend that Long's claims for violation of the Fourth and Fourteenth Amendments should be dismissed because they fail to state a claim upon which relief can be granted. Specifically, they argue that plaintiff has failed to allege sufficient facts to support a constitutional claim against the NFL, the Steelers and Paul Tagliabue, as private actors.

Because the language of the Fourteenth Amendment is directed at the states, a violation occurs only by conduct that may be fairly characterized as "state action." Private conduct, however unfair, is not actionable under the Amendment. *National Collegiate Athletic Assoc. v. Tarkanian,* 488 U.S. 179, 191, 109 S.Ct. 454, 461, 102 L.Ed.2d 469 (1988). We must determine whether the amended complaint sufficiently alleges that the conduct of the National Football League in testing and suspending plaintiff constitutes "state action" or is "fairly attributable to the state."

Stressing that the facts of each case are important, the Supreme Court has developed various tests to determine whether conduct by a private party constitutes state action. Two of the tests are relevant here. The first is the symbiotic relationship test. . . . Under the symbiosis analysis, conduct will be considered state action if the state has "so far insinuated itself into a position of interdependence with [the acting party] that it must be recognized as a joint participant in the challenged activity. . . ."

Here, plaintiff alleges that a symbiotic relationship exists between the City of Pittsburgh and the Steelers. The allegations upon which plaintiff's conclusion is based are as follows: (1) the city directly benefits from collection of an amusement tax on the sale of tickets; (2) the city provides numerous services for the Steelers; (3) the city guaranteed the initial bond issuance for the construction of Three Rivers Stadium and (4) city council appoints the board members to the Stadium Authority of the City of Pittsburgh.

Defendants argue, and we agree, that the alleged facts, even if true, fail to establish a symbiotic relationship between the state and the private actors. First, the allegations of financial support and a regulatory framework are not enough to establish "state action." . . .

We do not suggest that financial gain is a separate and distinct test. It is an important element in the mix of information to be considered in determining whether a mutually dependent relationship exists between two parties so that the behavior of one may be attributed to the other. Long's amended complaint falls short of stating a claim for constitutional violations under the symbiotic relationship test because it does not set forth sufficient facts which would allow us to fairly attribute the conduct of the NFL and the Steelers to the state. The business association alleged between the parties is simply too attenuated to attribute the conduct of which plaintiff complains to the state. Further, we disagree that the Steelers' use of the stadium establishes such a relationship. . . . [T]he stadium hosts a variety of events, including baseball games and musical concerts.

. . . Plaintiff here has also failed to allege facts which would support a cause of action based on the state's influence over the policy or decisions of the NFL or the Steelers. . . .

The Supreme Court has created a second test to determine whether conduct may fairly be attributed to the state. Unlike the symbiotic relationship test which looks at the overall relationship among the parties, the close nexus test attempts to determine whether the state may be deemed responsible for the specific conduct of which the plaintiff complains. Under this test, the complaining party must show a sufficiently close nexus between the state and the challenged action to establish state action. A state normally is not responsible for a private decision unless it has exercised coercive power or has provided such significant encouragement, either overt or covert, that the choice must be deemed that of the state.

Plaintiff alleges that the City of Pittsburgh, Mayor Masloff and the Stadium Authority each "acquiesced and/or consented to, supported and upheld the conduct of the other defendants complained of herein." Defendants correctly assert that acquiescence or indirect involvement is not enough to show the requisite state action. We hold that plaintiff's allegations do not meet the standard of the nexus test. Nothing in the amended complaint suggests that either the City, the Mayor or the Stadium Authority formulated the standards or controlled the decisions of the NFL or the Steelers. A close review of the amended complaint reveals that plaintiff was suspended based on independent medical conclusions and policy objectives of the National Football League, neither of which were influenced by the state. Plaintiff fails to allege that the state in any way influenced or implemented the substance abuse policies adopted by the NFL by which plaintiff was suspended. We will dismiss Counts I and II of plaintiff's amended complaint alleging violations of the Fourth and Fourteenth Amendments because plaintiff has failed to allege sufficient facts which would allow us to fairly attribute the conduct of the private parties to the state.

Source: Courtesy of Westlaw; reprinted with permission.

In *Williams v. National Football League and John Lombardo, M.D.*, 582 F.3d 863, the United States Court of Appeals for the eighth circuit upheld a lower court ruling that prohibited the NFL from suspending two Minnesota Viking players who violated the league's anti-doping policy, stating they could contest the suspension through the courts. The court of appeals held that the league's collective bargaining agreement with the NFLPA did not prevent Kevin Williams and Pat Williams from challenging the league's drug testing program under Minnesota State Law.[29] It ruled that the Minnesota drug testing and consumable products laws were not preempted by section 301 of the Federal Labor Management Relations Act ("LMRA").[30]

In Case 12-3, *U.S. District Court, Southern District of New York*, the NBA was arguing against the release of information relating to former NBA player Stanley Roberts. In 1999 the NBA announced that Roberts had been expelled from the league because he tested positive for illegal drugs.[31] Roberts attempted to sign a contract with a team in Turkey, but the Federation Internationale de Basketball (FIBA) stated that Roberts was banned from FIBA competition for two years based on the positive NBA drug test. Roberts sued FIBA in Germany. In the process of defending that lawsuit, FIBA requested the court to send a subpoena to the NBA to retrieve the documents relating to the suspension of Roberts. The following is the opinion relating to that requested subpoena.

📖 CASE 12-3 *In the Matter of the Application of Federation Internationale de Basketball for a Subpoena Pursuant to 28 U.S.C. § 1782*

U.S. District Court, Southern District of New York

LEWIS A. KAPLAN, District Judge.

The principal question presented by this application is whether a provision of the private collective bargaining agreement between the National Basketball Association ("NBA") and the National Basketball Players Association ("NBPA"), which provides that the details of drug tests administered to NBA players shall remain confidential, should result in the denial of an application by Federation Internationale de Basketball ("FIBA") for discovery of tests results administered to a former NBA player in order to defend itself in the German courts against a lawsuit brought by that player.

The collective bargaining agreements ("CBAs") between the NBA and the NBPA have contained an Anti-Drug Program since 1983. The current version of the program permits testing of players for drug use in limited circumstances and provides, among other things, for the expulsion from the league of those who test positive for so-called Drugs of Abuse. It provides also that the NBA and its affiliates "are prohibited from

---

[29] Michael S. Schmidt, *Ruling May Weaken Doping Plans in Pro Sports,* The New York Times, September 19, 2009.
[30] Associated Press, *Other Sports Leagues Support NFL,* ESPN.com, July 14, 2009.
[31] *Stanley Roberts Signs with Raptors,* ESPN.com, September 30, 2003.

publicly disclosing information about the diagnosis, treatment, prognosis, test results, compliance, or the fact of participation of a player in the Program" except "as reasonably required in connection with the suspension or disqualification of a player."

On November 24, 1999, the NBA announced, as permitted by the CBA, "that Stanley Roberts of the Philadelphia 76ers had been expelled from the league because he tested positive for an amphetamine-based designer drug, a substance prohibited by the Anti-Drug Program agreed to by the NBA and the NBPA."

Following his expulsion from the NBA, Roberts sought employment in Europe as a professional basketball player. As he allegedly was on the verge of signing a $500,000 per year contract to play for a team in Istanbul, FIBA—the rules of which authorize it to ban a player based on a positive drug test administered by the NBA—announced that Roberts was banned from FIBA competition worldwide for two years. Claiming that his prospective Turkish contract fell through as a result of the FIBA ban, Roberts pursued an internal appeals procedure before FIBA. When this proved fruitless, he sued FIBA in the District Court in Munich, Germany, and sought a preliminary injunction barring FIBA from barring him from FIBA competition. He argued, among other things, that he did not in fact violate the NBA's anti-drug rules, that FIBA in any event was not entitled to rely on the press announcement of the NBA test results, and in any case that the FIBA anti-drug policy is not enforceable as a matter of German law because it was not reflected in FIBA's Articles of Association.

In February 2000, the Munich court granted Roberts' application for a preliminary injunction, apparently on the ground that the FIBA anti-drug policy was unenforceable because it was not reflected in its charter. FIBA appealed, and the appeal is scheduled to be heard on October 26, 2000. The parties agreed at oral argument that Roberts seeks to sustain the preliminary injunction in the German appellate court on the ground that the Munich District Court was correct in its view of the German law issue concerning the proper location of the anti-drug policy but, in any case, on the alternative grounds that Roberts did not in fact violate the NBA policy and that FIBA in any case should not be permitted to rely upon the NBA's determination.

On October 20, 2000, FIBA moved by order to show cause for an order, pursuant to 28 U.S.C. § 1782, authorizing issuance of a subpoena commanding that the NBA produce documents relating to (1) Roberts' alleged violation of the NBA drug program (including documents relating to the positive drug test), and (2) any grievance instituted by Roberts under the CBA in connection with the alleged drug violation and the NBA's expulsion of Roberts.

II.

Section 1782(a) provides in relevant part that: "The district court of the district in which a person resides or is found may order him to . . . produce a document or other thing for use in a proceeding in a foreign . . . tribunal. . . . The order may be made . . . upon the application of any interested person and may direct that the document or other thing be produced, before a person appointed by the court."

Here, the NBA resides within the Southern District of New York. The documents in question are sought for use in a proceeding in foreign tribunal, the Court of Appeals in Munich, Germany. The application is made by FIBA, the defendant-appellant in the German action, and therefore by an interested person. Hence, the fundamental prerequisites to relief are satisfied. . . .

Confidentiality

. . . [T]he NBA asserts that the information in question is confidential under the terms of the CBA between it and the players' association and therefore should not be disclosed. Indeed, it argues that the NBPA's willingness to agree to an anti-drug program in the future would be destroyed if this Court were to grant the requested relief. It goes so far as to contend that the NBA would be unable to maintain any anti-drug program at all if the absolute confidentiality of these test results were breached.

The NBA's position is unpersuasive, particularly in the circumstances of this case. Even if the mutual expectations of confidentiality implicit in the CBA were sufficient to defeat disclosure pursuant to compulsory process in a different situation, the NBA ignores the significance of the fact that it is Roberts—who has the only relevant privacy interest—who has put his compliance with the NBA program in issue by commencing litigation against FIBA in which he flatly denies any violation of the NBA program. Just as the attorney-client and other privileges are waived where the party entitled to confidentiality puts the substance of the privileged matter at issue, any privacy interest an NBA player or former player may have in the confidentiality of his own drug test results must yield where he voluntarily injects the accuracy or existence of those results into litigation brought by him.

The NBA's confidentiality argument would fail even apart from Roberts' role in injecting the test results into the German litigation. It is a fundamental proposition of American law "that 'the public . . . has a right to every man's evidence,' except for those persons protected by a constitutional, common-law, or statutory privilege. . . ." And while there are circumstances in which private interests in confidentiality may be sufficient to preclude compelled production, at least in civil litigation, even of some relevant evidence, this is not such a case.

The most basic point is that the CBA does not require that the fact of a positive drug test and expulsion be kept confidential. To the contrary, it explicitly authorizes publication of that information. All that is left, it appears, is the clinical detail about the nature of the test and the level of drugs found in the relevant bodily fluid. There simply is not a very great privacy interest in the details once the basic facts are known, as they are here.

In any case, the private interests of the NBA simply are not sufficient to warrant denial of this application on confidentiality grounds. The NBA's concern is only that the NBPA may resist inclusion of an anti-drug program in the next CBA. But the object of the law here is not to make the NBA's collective bargaining easier. Both sides have enormous stakes in reaching agreement on a future CBA. No doubt they will be able to do so, sooner or later.

. . . In this case, FIBA genuinely needs the requested information in view of Roberts' attempt in Germany to controvert the NBA's finding that he violated its anti-drug policy. The information sought is entirely factual or nearly so; FIBA seeks principally clinical test results and details concerning the test(s) themselves. And the Court simply is not persuaded that disclosure of this information, at least in circumstances in which the bottom line result that the player tested positive for drug use already is public and in which the former player voluntarily placed his compliance with the NBA policy at issue elsewhere, is likely to cause any serious harm either to the interests of the NBA or to the public. The worst that might happen is that the NBPA might decline to continue the anti-drug program with which it has lived for seventeen years, a position that could result in substantial public opprobrium and large economic losses for the players should such a position result in a strike or lockout. Neither the risk of such action nor even its realization is sufficient to justify a conclusion that the federal courts should create an evidentiary privilege for drug test results of NBA players.

III.

FIBA's motion is granted in all respects. The NBA is directed to produce the documents described in the subpoena attached to applicant's moving papers forthwith.

SO ORDERED.

Source: Courtesy of Westlaw; reprinted with permission.

Proposed Federal Legislation

During the first session of the 109th Congress, seven bills were presented addressing issues relating to drug use in sports.[32] The Clean Sports Act of 2005, introduced by Senator John McCain, was written to establish minimum drug testing standards in the major professional sports leagues. All of the proposed bills levied stiffer punishments for those who use illegal drugs than the penalties set forth in the collective bargaining agreements of the major sports leagues. The bill proposed by Senator McCain set the penalties as follows:

```
(7) PENALTIES-

    (A) GENERAL RULE-

        (i) FIRST VIOLATION- Except as provided in subparagraph (B), a pro-
            fessional athlete who tests positive shall be immediately sus-
            pended for a minimum of 2 years for a first violation. All
            suspensions shall include a loss of pay for the period of the
            suspension.
        (ii) SECOND VIOLATION- A second violation shall result in a lifetime
            ban of the professional athlete from all major professional
            leagues.

    (B) EXCEPTIONS-

        (i) KNOWLEDGE OF THE ATHLETE- A major professional league may im-
            pose a lesser penalty than provided in subparagraph (A) or no
            penalty if the professional athlete establishes that he did not
            know or suspect, and could not reasonably have known or sus-
            pected even with the exercise of utmost caution, that he had
            used the prohibited substance.[33]
```

The findings and purpose of the bill, set forth in Section 2, read as follows:

```
(a) Findings- Congress finds the following:
    (1) The use of anabolic steroids and other performance-enhancing sub-
        stances by minors is a public health problem of national significance.
    (2) Experts estimate that over 500,000 teenagers have used performance-
        enhancing substances, which medical experts warn can cause a litany
        of health problems for individuals who take them, in particular
        children and teenagers.
    (3) The adverse health effects caused by steroids and other performance-
        enhancing substances include stunted growth, scarring acne, hair
        loss, dramatic mood swings, hormonal and metabolic imbalances,
        liver damage, a higher risk of heart disease and stroke later in
        life, as well as an increased propensity to demonstrate aggressive
        behavior, commit suicide, and commit crimes.
```

---

[32] Lynn Zinser, *McCain Offers Measure for Testing in Pro Sports*, The New York Times, May 25, 2005.

[33] Clean Sports Act of 2005, §§ 4(b)(7)(A) & (B).

(4) Professional athletes are role models for young athletes and influence the behavior of children and teenagers.

(5) Congressional testimony by parents of minors who used performance enhancing drugs, as well as medical and health experts, indicates that the actual or alleged use of performance-enhancing substances by professional athletes results in the increased use of these substances by children and teenagers.

(6) Surveys and studies suggest a connection between the actual or alleged use of performance-enhancing substances by college and professional athletes and the increased use of these substances by children and teenagers.

(7) The real or perceived tolerance of the use of performance-enhancing substances by professional athletes has resulted in both increased pressure on children and teenagers to use performance-enhancing drugs in order to advance their athletic careers and to professional sports['] loss of integrity.

(8) The adoption by professional sports leagues of strong policies to eliminate the use of performance-enhancing substances would result in the reduced use of these substances by children and teenagers.

(9) Minimum drug testing standards for professional sports established by Federal law would ensure the adoption of strong policies to eliminate the use of performance-enhancing substances in professional sports.

(10) Minimum drug testing standards for professional sports established by Federal law would help return integrity to professional sports. . . .

(b) Purpose- The purpose of this Act is to protect the integrity of professional sports and the health and safety of athletes generally by establishing minimum standards for the testing of steroids and other performance-enhancing substances by professional sports leagues.[34]

Billy Hunter, executive director of the National Basketball Players Association (NBPA), testified as follows before a congressional subcommittee on May 18, 2005, regarding the Drug Free Sports Act of 2005 (H.R. 1862):

I appreciate the Subcommittee's interest in and concern about the use of steroids by professional athletes and others, particularly young adults and children, as evidenced by the legislation, H.R. 1862, introduced by several members of this Subcommittee. I would like to begin by clearly stating the position of the NBPA. As a former state prosecutor and United States Attorney, I have participated in the prosecution of numerous drug cases and have a keen understanding of and insight into drug use and abuse. While we strongly believe that the use of steroids and other performance enhancing drugs are virtually non-existent in the NBA, we are committed to ensuring that the use of such drugs does not ever become an issue of concern.

---

[34] Clean Sports Act of 2005, §§ 2(a) & (b).

To that end, in the 1999 Collective Bargaining Agreement between the NBPA and NBA we introduced in our Anti-Drug Program a steroid testing protocol that provides for random testing of all incoming players four (4) times during their rookie seasons and tests veteran players once during the training camp period. Since testing for steroids and other performance enhancing drugs was instituted in 1999 there have been approximately 4200 tests conducted, with only 23 initial laboratory positive tests (less than one (1) percent).

Of the 23 tests that were initially laboratory positives, only 3 satisfied the additional steps that are required for a sample to be confirmed as positive under our Anti Drug Program, either because the player was terminated from employment prior to confirmation of his test result or because the Medical Director found a reasonable medical explanation for the test result. The three (3) players who had confirmed positive tests were immediately suspended.

Additionally, all players are subject to reasonable cause testing. If either the NBA or the NBPA has information that gives it reasonable cause to believe that a player is using, in possession of, or distributing steroids, then they may present such information to an Independent Expert, who is empowered to immediately decide whether reasonable cause exists to test the player. If reasonable cause is found, the player is subject to being tested up to four (4) times during a six week period following the order to test. The testing during this period may be administered at any time, without any prior notice to the player.

It is vitally important in the efforts to control the usage of steroids and other performance enhancing drugs that the list of banned substances for which players are tested remains current. Accordingly, in our Program that list is updated regularly by our Prohibited Substances Committee, comprised of three independent drug testing experts and a representative from both the NBPA and NBA. The Committee will ban a substance that is either declared illegal by the Federal Government or found to be harmful to players and improperly performance enhancing. Under our Anti-Drug Program at least seventeen (17) substances have been added to the list of prohibited substances since 1999.

While our Anti-Drug Program has always had a strong emphasis on education and treatment rather than punishment, with a standard of progressive discipline for violators, the Anti Drug Program does provide for substantial penalties for those who are caught using steroids and other performance enhancing drugs. A first time offender is automatically suspended for five (5) games and is required to enter an education, treatment and counseling program established by the Program's Medical Director. For a second offense the player is suspended for ten (10) games and required to reenter the education, treatment and counseling program. For a third offense, the player is suspended for twenty five (25) games (nearly a third of the 82 game NBA season) and is again required to enter the education, treatment and counseling program. Further, any player who fails to comply with the treatment program, as prescribed by the Medical Director, by engaging in behavior that demonstrates either a mindful disregard of his treatment responsibilities or by testing positive for steroids, suffers additional penalties, up to and including an indefinite suspension.

Another key component of our Anti-Drug Policy is our emphasis on education, treatment and counseling. During each season, every NBA player is required to attend and participate in a meeting where the dangers of steroid and performance enhancing drug use are discussed by drug counselors. Also, all rookie players are required to attend a week long Rookie Transition Program, before the start of their first NBA season, during which numerous topics are addressed in detail, including the dangers of using steroids and performance enhancing drugs. Finally, the program's Medical Director supervises a national network of medical professionals, located in every NBA city, available to provide counseling and treatment to players.

With the additional scrutiny that the use of steroids and other performance enhancing drugs has received in society, and particularly in professional sports, such as baseball, football and track and field, since our ground breaking agreement was reached in 1999, there has been discussion that our agreement requires modification. While I am reluctant to discuss the specifics of these discussions in great detail due to the sensitive, evolving, and complicated nature of collective bargaining negotiations, I represent to you that I have had numerous discussions with Commissioner Stern and the NBA about making significant changes in our next CBA to deal with the growing societal problem of the use of steroids and other performance enhancing drugs. We want to send a strong and unequivocal message to society in general and our young fans in particular that we do not condone, support or accept the use of performance enhancing drugs in our sport. To that end, we have indicated a willingness to significantly increase both the frequency of testing that our players undergo, and increase the penalties imposed upon the violators. We continue to believe that collective bargaining is the most appropriate forum for the resolution of these issues and are confident that the changes that are currently under consideration will address in a meaningful way the concerns of the Subcommittee, as embodied in the pending legislation, H.R. 1862. Congress has long given deference to parties operating under collective bargaining agreements to develop their own solutions to problems, properly recognizing that the parties bound by a collective bargaining agreement have a longstanding relationship with unique problems and problem solving methods that are often difficult to comprehend by those outside the relationship. While we fully believe in and support the Subcommittees' and Congress' goal of eliminating the use of steroids and performance enhancing drugs in sports, we believe this goal is best accomplished by the leagues and players working together to accomplish this universal objective. We think that the players, supported by the leagues, are best able to demonstrate to everyone, especially our young fans that the only way to become a professional athlete is by cultivating and nurturing their talent, determination, and desire and by working harder than everyone else.

I want to thank the Subcommittee for the opportunity to appear before you today.[35]

AMATEUR SPORTS

Unlike professional sports, there are constitutional considerations at issue in the drug testing of athletes involved in amateur sports. In today's society, drugs are present among high school students and, in some cases, even younger students. Some amateur athletes seeking to emulate their role models have turned to performance-enhancing drugs. Recreational and street drugs also pose a problem in amateur athletics.

Interscholastic Drug Testing

The interscholastic education level is generally understood to include students from grades 6 through 12. This covers middle school and high school students. The National Federation of State High School Associations does not require a high school to have a drug testing program. Nonetheless, many school districts have implemented a drug testing policy for athletes and other students who

---

[35] *The Drug Free Sports Act of 2005: Hearings on H.R. 1862 Before the Subcommittee on Commerce, Trade and Consumer Protection of the H. Committee on Energy and Commerce,* 109th Cong. 76–78 (2005) (prepared statement of G. William Hunter, Executive Director, National Basketball Players Association).

participate in extracurricular activities.[36] These policies vary from testing for marijuana to testing specifically for performance-enhancing drugs.

Some drug testing programs have been instituted at the state level. For example, in New Jersey high school athletes whose teams qualify for championship games have been required to undergo random drug testing for steroids. This plan was announced by acting Governor Richard J. Codey, who stated: "This is a growing threat, one we can't leave up to individual parents, coaches or schools to handle." In instituting the plan, the governor referred to data compiled by the National Institute on Drug Abuse, which found that 3.4% of all high school students nationwide admitted to using steroids at least once a year. The use among eighth graders was approximately 2%.[37]

The rights of students were discussed in the landmark case *Tinker v. Des Moines*, 393 U.S. 503 (1969). The court stated in part: "First Amendment rights, applied in light of the special characteristics of the school environment, are available to teachers and students. It can hardly be argued that either students or teachers shed their constitutional rights to freedom of speech or expression at the schoolhouse gate. This has been the unmistakable holding of this Court for almost 50 years."[38]

Prior to 1995, lower federal courts were split on the issue of drug testing in high schools and whether or not such a policy was a violation of the constitutional rights of students.[39] The question presented is, Under what circumstances will an interscholastic drug testing policy violate a student-athlete's right to be free from unreasonable search and seizures under the Fourth Amendment to the U.S. Constitution? The Fourth Amendment guarantees "[t]he right of the people to be secure in their persons, house, papers, and effects, against unreasonable searches and seizures." The constitutional prohibition applies only to an "unreasonable" search. However, the Supreme Court has set forth various exceptions to the warrant requirement of the Fourth Amendment. The "special needs" doctrine is such an exception.

In *Vernonia School District v. Acton*, 515 U.S. 646, 653 (1995), the Supreme Court stated the following regarding the special needs doctrine in relation to interscholastic students: "We have found 'special needs' to exist in the public school context. There, the warrant requirement 'would unduly interfere with the maintenance of the swift and informal disciplinary procedures [that are] needed,' and 'strict adherence to the requirement that searches be based upon probable cause' would undercut 'the substantial need of teachers and administrators for freedom to maintain order in the schools.'"[40] Furthermore it has been stated, "A school official may properly conduct a search of a student's person if the official has a reasonable suspicion that a crime has been or is in the process of being committed or reasonable cause to believe that the search is necessary to maintain school discipline or enforce school policies."[41]

Searches performed at a public school will almost always involve state actors, and a constitutional analysis will follow. The U.S. Supreme Court has stated that an unconstitutional search occurs "when an expectation of privacy that society is prepared to consider reasonable is infringed."[42] In general,

---

[36] A.J. Perez, *Texas Testing Program Screens for Less Steroids as Debate Rages*, USA Today, August 20, 2008.

[37] Associated Press, *NJ Faces Random Drug Testing*, Dec. 27, 2005.

[38] *Tinker*, 393 U.S. 503 at 506.

[39] *See* Schaill v. Tippecanoe County Sch. Corp., 864 F.2d 1309 (7th Cir. 1988); Brooks v. East Chambers Consol. Independent Sch. Dist., 730 F. Supp. 759 (S.D. Tex. 1989); Moule by & Through Moule v. Paradise Valley Unified Sch. Dist., 863 F. Supp. 1098 (D. Ariz. 1994).

[40] *Vernonia*, 515 U.S. at 653.

[41] *New Jersey v. T.L.O.*, 469 U.S. 325, 329 (1985).

[42] *United States v. Jacobsen*, 466 U.S. 109, 113 (1984).

courts have determined that drug testing for athletic teams is permissible based on a student-athlete's diminished expectation of privacy. Student-athletes are sometimes required to submit to physical examinations as well as disrobe in front of other student-athletes when participating in athletics in school. Students also use public restrooms and communal locker rooms when they participate in physical education classes. Thus, courts have reasoned that a student who chooses to participate in sports has a diminished expectation of privacy.

One of the major concerns about the implementation of a drug testing policy is requiring a urinalysis test as a prerequisite for participation in a school-sponsored activity. Students often assert that drug testing procedures infringe on their right to participate. Under the law, however, it is clear that participation in sports at the interscholastic level is a privilege and not a right. *Schaill ex rel. Kross v. Tippecanoe County School Corporations*, 864 F.2d 1309, 1310 (7th Cir. 1988), dealt with high school basketball players who had been required to provide urine samples after school officials had received information that players had been involved in drug use. The school board chose to implement a random drug testing program for all interscholastic athletes and cheerleaders based on the results of five positive drug tests. The Seventh Circuit found the drug testing policy to be reasonable on several grounds, including that drug testing was done in college athletics and at the Olympics and that the students had notice of the testing and gave their consent.

In Case 12-4, *Vernonia School District 47J v. Acton*, 515 U.S. 646 (1995), the Supreme Court ruled that the Fourth Amendment permitted a school policy that prevented students from participating in interscholastic sports unless they agreed to random drug testing. A seventh grader wanted to try out for the football team. Like all other students who wanted to participate in sports, he was required to sign a consent form even though no one had suspected him of using drugs. He and his parents refused to sign the form, and he was prevented from playing football. They sued the school district for failing to allow their son to participate.

📖 CASE 12-4 *Vernonia School District 47J v. Acton*

515 U.S. 646 (1995)

Justice SCALIA delivered the opinion of the Court.

The Student Athlete Drug Policy adopted by School District 47J in the town of Vernonia, Oregon, authorizes random urinalysis drug testing of students who participate in the District's school athletics programs. We granted certiorari to decide whether this violates the Fourth and Fourteenth Amendments to the United States Constitution. . . .

The Policy applies to all students participating in interscholastic athletics. Students wishing to play sports must sign a form consenting to the testing and must obtain the written consent of their parents. Athletes are tested at the beginning of the season for their sport. In addition, once each week of the season the names of the athletes are placed in a "pool" from which a student, with the supervision of two adults, blindly draws the names of 10% of the athletes for random testing. Those selected are notified and tested that same day, if possible. . . .

Fourth Amendment rights, no less than First and Fourteenth Amendment rights, are different in public schools than elsewhere; the "reasonableness" inquiry cannot disregard the schools' custodial and tutelary responsibility for children. For their own good and that of their classmates, public school children are routinely required to submit to various physical examinations, and to be vaccinated against various diseases. . . .

Legitimate privacy expectations are even less with regard to student athletes. School sports are not for the bashful. They require "suiting up" before each practice or event, and showering and changing afterwards. Public school locker rooms, the usual sites for these activities, are not notable for the privacy they afford. The locker rooms in Vernonia are typical: No individual dressing rooms are provided; shower heads are lined up along a wall, unseparated by any sort of partition or curtain; not even all the toilet stalls have doors. . . .

Taking into account all the factors we have considered above—the decreased expectation of privacy, the relative unobtrusiveness of the search, and the severity of the need met by the search—we conclude Vernonia's Policy is reasonable and hence constitutional. . . .

The Ninth Circuit held that Vernonia's Policy not only violated the Fourth Amendment, but also, by reason of that violation, contravened Article I, § 9, of the Oregon Constitution. Our conclusion that the former holding was in error means that the latter holding rested on a flawed premise. We therefore vacate the judgment, and remand the case to the Court of Appeals for further proceedings consistent with this opinion.

It is so ordered.

Justice Ginsburg, concur[s]. . . .

Justice O'Connor, with whom Justice Stevens and Justice Souter join, [dissents]. . . .

Source: Courtesy of Westlaw; reprinted with permission.

In *Board of Education of Ind. Sch. Dist. No. 92 of Pottawatomie County v. Earls*, 536 U.S. 822 (2002), the Supreme Court allowed urinalysis drug testing of all students who participated in extracurricular activities. Consequently, *Earls* expanded the decision of *Vernonia* by allowing a school district to test more students with less of a basis than that set forth in *Vernonia*.

The following is a standard consent form used at the high school level to obtain consent for drug testing from a student and his or her parents.

In the interest of the safety of student athletes and student drivers, [High School] has adopted a drug policy specifically for

these students. The policy requires that student athletes and drivers be subject to random drug tests. A copy of this policy is
attached to this form. Please read it carefully and retain it for
your records. A student will not be permitted to participate in any
athletic activity or drive until this consent form is signed and on
file with the school.

I, _____ (name of student) have read the [High School]
Student Athlete and Student Driver Random Drug and Alcohol Testing
Policy and do so consent to submit to a chemical test should I be
required to do so. I further consent to allow [High School] to test
the specimen I provide for illegal drug and/or alcohol content. I
realize that if my test is positive for drug and/or alcohol use I
will be subject to the consequences in accordance with the provisions
of the Student Athlete and Student Driver Random Drug and Alcohol
Testing Policy. I further consent to and agree to other terms and
conditions of the Student Athlete and Student Driver Random Drug and
Alcohol Testing Policy.

_____

Student Signature Student Name (printed)

Date: _____

We/I the undersigned Parent(s)/Guardian(s) of_____ (name
of student) have read the Student Athlete and Student Driver Random
Drug and Alcohol Testing Policy and do consent to all provisions
thereof.

_____   _____

Student's Parent/Guardian Signature Student's Parent/Guardian Name
(printed)

Date: _____

Problem 12-1

You are the new athletic director for the Miller Independent School District. One of your
tasks is to draft a new drug testing policy for the six high schools in your district. What should
be included in such a policy? How do you draft such a policy and ensure there are no constitutional violations?

Problem 12-2

Victoria Dixon is an honor student and member of the ninth-grade chess team at her high school. The school district has recently instituted a drug testing procedure whereby "all students involved in extracurricular activities in school will be subject to random drug testing throughout the year." The first draft of the policy included only athletic teams, but after the parents of some of the football team members complained, the board changed the policy to include all students in extracurricular activities. The board stated, "There is no rampant drug use in high schools in the district at the current time but this policy is instituted to ensure that drug use does not occur." Victoria and her parents refuse to sign a drug testing consent form, and she is removed from the team. She and her parents file a lawsuit in federal court challenging the policy. What legal considerations are present? What defenses does the school district have in implementing such a policy?[43]

The National Collegiate Athletic Association

The NCAA began a drug testing program for all student-athletes in 1986 to ensure that all participants in collegiate athletics are on a level playing field and are healthy and safe. A student-athlete who fails a drug test administered by the NCAA is subject to suspension for one year. The student-athlete has the right to appeal any decision handed down by the NCAA. The NCAA also requires mandatory random drug testing during postseason intercollegiate athletic activities. The NCAA drug testing policy has been challenged on various grounds.

In *Hill v. National Collegiate Athletic Ass'n*, 865 P.2d 633 (Cal. 1994), the California Supreme Court held that the NCAA had not violated the privacy rights of student-athletes with its mandatory drug testing program. A lower court had found in favor of student-athletes from Stanford University who had sued, stating that the NCAA drug testing violated their right of privacy under the California state constitution. The Superior Court of California permanently enjoined the NCAA from enforcing its policy against the plaintiffs and other Stanford athletes. On appeal, the NCAA stated that its program was justified because it was protecting the health and safety of the athletes as well as "safeguarding the integrity of intercollegiate athletic competition."[44] The court agreed with the NCAA on appeal, reversing the lower court's decision and upholding its drug testing program.[45] The court stated in part:

> Finally, the practical realities of NCAA-sponsored athletic competition cannot be ignored. Intercollegiate sports is, at least in part, a business founded upon offering for public entertainment athletic contests conducted under a rule of fair and rigorous competition. Scandals involving drug use, like those involving improper financial incentives or other forms of corruption, impair the NCAA's reputation in the eyes of the sports-viewing public. A well announced and vigorously pursued drug testing program serves to: (1) provide a significant deterrent to would-be violators, thereby reducing the probability of damaging public disclosure of athlete drug use; and (2) assure student athletes, their schools, and the public that fair competition remains the overriding principle in athletic events. Of course, these outcomes also serve the NCAA's overall interest in safeguarding the integrity of intercollegiate athletic competition.[46]

---

[43] Bob Egelko, *Drug Tests for Chess Club? Judge Says No*, San Francisco Chronicle, May 7, 2009.
[44] *Hill*, 865 P.2d at 659.
[45] *Id.* at 661.
[46] *Id.* at 661.

In addressing the NCAA's health and safety argument, the court stated:

> The NCAA also has an interest in protecting the health and safety of student athletes who are involved in NCAA-regulated competition. Contrary to plaintiffs' characterization, this interest is more than a mere "naked assertion of paternalism." The NCAA sponsors and regulates intercollegiate athletic events, which by their nature may involve risks of physical injury to athletes, spectators, and others. In this way, the NCAA effectively creates occasions for potential injury resulting from the use of drugs. As a result, it may concern itself with the task of protecting the safety of those involved in intercollegiate athletic competition. This NCAA interest exists for the benefit of all persons involved in sporting events (including not only drug-ingesting athletes but also innocent athletes or others who might be injured by a drug user), as well as the sport itself.[47]

Under NCAA bylaws, student-athletes must sign a consent form demonstrating their understanding of the drug testing program and their willingness to participate in the program. Each student-athlete must sign the consent form before the school year or he or she cannot participate in intercollegiate competition. The following is the consent form that must be signed by an NCAA Division I athlete to participate in intercollegiate athletics:

Consent Form: 2009-2010

```
Form 09-3d Academic Year 2009-10
Drug-Testing Consent- NCAA Division I


Required by:
NCAA Constitution 3.2.4.7 and NCAA Bylaws 14.1.4 and 30.5.

Purpose:
To assist in certifying eligibility.


Requirement to sign Drug Testing Consent Form.


Name of your institution:

_____


You must sign this form to participate (i.e., practice or compete) in
intercollegiate athletics per NCAA Constitution 3.2.4.7 and NCAA
Bylaws 14.1.4 and 30.5. If you have any questions, you should discuss
them with your director of athletics.
```

---

[47] *Id.*

Consent to Testing.

You agree to allow the NCAA to test you in relation to any participation by you in any NCAA championship or in any postseason football game certified by the NCAA for the banned drugs listed in Bylaw 31.2.3 (attached). Additionally, if you participate in a NCAA Division I sport, you also agree to be tested on a year-round basis.

Consequences for a positive drug test.

By signing this form, you affirm that you are aware of the NCAA drug-testing program, which provides:

1. A student-athlete who tests positive shall be withheld from competition in all sports for a minimum of 365 days from the drug-test collection date and shall lose a year of eligibility;
2. A student-athlete who tests positive has an opportunity to appeal the positive drug test;
3. A student-athlete who tests positive a second time for the use of any drug, other than a "street drug" shall lose all remaining regular-season and postseason eligibility in all sports. A combination of two positive tests involving street drugs (marijuana, THC or heroin) in whatever order, will result in the loss of an additional year of eligibility;
4. The penalty for missing a scheduled drug test is the same as the penalty for testing positive for the use of a banned drug other than a street drug; and
5. If a student-athlete immediately transfers to a non-NCAA institution while ineligible and competes in collegiate competition within the 365 day period at a non-NCAA institution, the student-athlete will be ineligible for all NCAA regular-season and postseason competition until the student-athlete does not compete in collegiate competition for a 365 day period.

Signatures.

By signing below, I consent:

1. To be tested by the NCAA in accordance with NCAA drug-testing policy, which provides among other things that:
   a. I will be notified of selection to be tested;
   b. I must appear for NCAA testing or be sanctioned for a positive drug test; and
   c. My urine sample collection will be observed by a person of my same gender;
2. To accept the consequences of a positive drug test;
3. To allow my drug-test sample to be used by the NCAA drug-testing laboratories for research purposes to improve drug-testing detection; and

4. To allow disclosure of my drug-testing results only for purposes related to eligibility for participation in NCAA competition. I understand that if I sign this statement falsely or erroneously, I violate NCAA legislation on ethical conduct and will jeopardize my eligibility.

Source: © National Collegiate Athletic Association. 2008-2010. All rights reserved.

In any drug testing scheme, one of the ongoing issues is what drugs should be banned. The following document sets forth the NCAA's list of banned drugs for the 2009–2010 school year.

2009-2010 NCAA Banned-Drug Classes

The NCAA bans the following classes of drugs:

a. Stimulants
b. Anabolic Agents
c. Alcohol and Beta Blockers (banned for rifle only)
d. Diuretics and Other Masking Agents
e. Street Drugs
f. Peptide Hormones and Analogues
g. Anti-estrogens
h. Beta-2 Agonists

Note: Any substance chemically related to these classes is also banned. The institution and the student-athlete shall be held accountable for all drugs within the banned drug class regardless of whether they have been specifically identified.

Drugs and Procedures Subject to Restrictions:

a. Blood Doping.
b. Local Anesthetics (under some conditions).
c. Manipulation of Urine Samples.
d. Beta-2 Agonists permitted only by prescription and inhalation.
e. Caffeine if concentrations in urine exceed 15 micrograms/ml.

NCAA Nutritional/Dietary Supplements Warning:

Before consuming any nutritional/dietary supplement product, review the product and its label with your athletics department staff. Dietary supplements are not well regulated and may cause a positive drug test result. Student-athletes have tested positive and lost their eligibility using dietary supplements. Many dietary supplements are contaminated with banned drugs not listed on the label. Any product containing a dietary supplement ingredient is taken at your own risk. **It is your responsibility to check with athletics staff** before **using any substance.**

Some Examples of NCAA Banned Substances in each class

Note: **There is no complete list of banned drug examples!!**

Check with your athletics department staff to review the label of any product, medication or supplement before you consume it.

Stimulants:
amphetamine (Adderall); caffeine (guarana); cocaine; ephedrine; fenfluramine (Fen); methamphetamine; methylphenidate (Ritalin); phentermine (Phen); synephrine (bitter orange); etc.

exceptions: phenylephrine and pseudoephedrine are not banned.

Anabolic Agents:
boldenone; clenbuterol; DHEA; nandrolone; stanozolol; testosterone; methasterone; androstenedione; norandrostenedione; methandienone; etiocholanolone; trenbolone; etc.

Alcohol and Beta Blockers (banned for rifle only):
alcohol; atenolol; metoprolol; nadolol; pindolol; propranolol; timolol; etc.

Diuretics and Other Masking Agents:
bumetanide; chlorothiazide; furosemide; hydrochlorothiazide; probenecid; spironolactone (canrenone); triameterene; trichlormethiazide; etc.

Street Drugs:
heroin; marijuana; tetrahydrocannabinol (THC).

Peptide Hormones and Analogues:
human growth hormone (hGH); human chorionic gonadotropin (hCG); erythropoietin (EPO); etc.

Anti-Estrogens :
anastrozole; clomiphene; tamoxifen; formestane; etc.

Beta-2 Agonists:
bambuterol; formoterol; salbutamol; salmeterol; etc.

Any substance that is chemically related to the class of banned drugs, unless otherwise noted, is also banned.
Source: NCAA.org

Case 12-5, *Brennan v. Bd. Of Trustees for Univ. Of Louisiana Systems*, 691 So.2d 324 (La. Ct. App. 1997), concerns a challenge to the NCAA drug testing policy in which a student sued, stating that his expectation of privacy had been violated as a result of the drug testing procedures.

CASE 12-5 *Brennan v. Bd. of Trustees for Univ. of Louisiana Systems*

691 So.2d 324 (La. Ct. App. 1997)

LOTTINGER, Chief Judge.

Plaintiff, John Patout Brennan (Brennan), a student-athlete at the University of Southwestern Louisiana (USL), tested positive for drug use in the second of three random drug tests administered by the National Collegiate Athletic Association (NCAA). Brennan requested and received two administrative appeals in which he contended that the positive test results were "false" due to a combination of factors, including heavy drinking and sexual activity the night before the test, and his use of nutritional supplements. Following the unsuccessful appeals, USL complied with the NCAA regulations and suspended Brennan from intercollegiate athletic competition for one year. Brennan brought this action against USL's governing body, the Board of Trustees for University of Louisiana Systems (Board of Trustees), seeking to enjoin enforcement by USL of the suspension.

In his petition, Brennan alleged that, by requiring him to submit to the NCAA's drug testing program, USL violated his right of privacy and deprived him of a liberty and property interest without due process in contravention of Article I, Sections 2 and 5 of the Louisiana Constitution. The NCAA moved to intervene on the grounds that the drug testing policies and procedures that Brennan placed at issue were developed, administered, conducted and enforced by the NCAA. The intervention was granted.

Following a two day trial, the trial judge entered oral reasons for judgment. Initially, the trial judge stated that he would "pretermit any consideration of the several constitutional issues . . . since those issues are mooted by the court's decision." The trial judge then concluded that Brennan was entitled to the preliminary injunction because "the subject test results on the plaintiff based on the one blood sample taken from him was flawed, and therefore that sample should not have been the basis of . . . disciplinary action against the plaintiff. . . ."

The Board of Trustees and the NCAA appealed and assigned the following error:

Having declined to address the only causes of action asserted by Brennan, and having failed to find that Brennan was likely to succeed on the merits of any other cognizable cause of action, it was improper for the district court to issue a preliminary injunction in favor of Brennan.

Validity of the Drug Test

Prior to discussing the assignment of error, it is necessary to review the trial judge's finding that the drug test results were flawed.

After reviewing the record in this case in its entirety, we conclude that the trial judge committed manifest error in finding that the drug test results were flawed. . . .

Upon close review, we find that the record does not contain a reasonable factual basis for the trial judge's conclusion that the test results were flawed. . . . Considering the evidence contained in the record, we conclude that the trial judge was clearly wrong in finding that the test results were flawed.

Preliminary Injunction

Having concluded that the trial judge erred in finding that the test results were flawed, we now consider whether it was proper to issue a preliminary injunction in favor of Brennan. . . .

A. Brennan's Constitutional Claims

Brennan claims that his constitutional rights to privacy and due process were violated. The Louisiana Constitution's protection of privacy provisions contained in Article 1, § 5 does not extend so far as to protect private citizens against the actions of private parties. Thus, in order to prevail on the merits of either constitutional claim, Brennan must first show that USL was a state actor when it enforced the NCAA's rules and recommendations.

1. State Action . . .

In the present case, Brennan asserts that USL, not the NCAA, violated his constitutional rights to privacy and due process. Without question, USL is a state actor even when acting in compliance with NCAA rules and recommendations. While we conclude that there is state action in this case, the preliminary injunction could only be issued on the constitutional claims if Brennan made a prima facie showing that he had a privacy interest which was invaded or that he had a property or liberty interest which was entitled to due process protection.

2. Brennan's Privacy Interest

In determining whether USL violated Brennan's right of privacy, we are guided by the California Supreme Court's recent decision in

Hill v. National Collegiate Athletic Association, 7 Cal.4th 1, 26
Cal.Rptr.2d 834, 865 P.2d 633 (Cal.1994). Therein several student-
athletes filed suit against the NCAA challenging its drug testing program
as an invasion of the right of privacy. *Id.* 26 Cal.Rptr.2d at 838-39, 865
P.2d at 637. While the court recognized that the drug testing program
impacts privacy interests, it reasoned that there was no constitutional
violation when the student-athletes' lower expectations of privacy were balanced against the NCAA's countervailing interests. *Id.* . . .

Although Brennan filed suit against USL, the state actor, rather than
the NCAA, we conclude, as did the court in *Hill,* that there was no
violation of a privacy interest. Brennan, like the student-athletes in
Hill, has a diminished expectation of privacy. Additionally, we note
that USL shares the NCAA's interests in ensuring fair competition in
intercollegiate sports as well as in protecting the health and safety
of student-athletes. While a urine test may be an invasion of privacy,
in this case, it is reasonable considering the diminished expectation
of privacy in the context of intercollegiate sports and there being a
significant interest by USL and the NCAA that outweighs the relatively
small compromise of privacy under the circumstances.

Because Brennan could not make a prima facie showing that he had a
privacy interest which was unjustly violated, he could not prevail on
the merits of the right of privacy claim.

3. Brennan's Property or Liberty Interest . . .

In sum, Brennan could not make a prima facie showing that he would
prevail on the merits of either constitutional claim; therefore, these
claims could not be the basis for the issuance of the preliminary
injunction.

B. Brennan's Tort Claim

Although Brennan could not prevail on the constitutional claims, he
contends that the factual allegations in his petition are sufficient
to support a cause of action in tort. . . .

Assuming, for purposes of discussion only, that USL had a duty to warn
Brennan, the record establishes that Brennan received adequate information and warnings to protect his eligibility. . . .

In the present case, Brennan affirmed that he was aware of the NCAA's
drug testing policy. He was told verbally and in writing to inquire
about the program if he had any questions. Brennan was told that if he
was taking anything at all, prescription or non-prescription, to check
with the USL athletic department. Although Brennan had ample opportunity

to inquire about ingesting nutritional supplements, he chose to ingest the supplements without seeking advice from anyone. . . .

Conclusion

For the foregoing reasons, the judgment of the trial court issuing the preliminary injunction is reversed. Costs of this appeal are assessed against the appellee.

REVERSED.

Source: Courtesy of Westlaw; reprinted with permission.

INTERNATIONAL SPORTS

Drug use and testing have also become concerns at the international level. Athletes participating in international games, including the Olympics, are subjected to testing. Richard Pound, Chairman of the World Anti-Doping Agency, has stated that "doping is the single most important problem facing sport today. If we didn't win the fight, Olympic-standard sport will not survive . . . because the public will have no respect for it. Cheats make what should be a triumph of human achievement into a hollow pretence."[48] In the 2002 Summer games in Athens, Adrian Annus, a Hungarian athlete, was stripped of his gold medal in the hammer throw for failing to take a follow-up test. He was ordered to take another test upon his return to Hungary but failed to appear for that test. When he returned to Hungary, he announced his retirement and eventually was forced to return the gold medal he had won. After the Summer Olympic Games in 2004, U.S. sprinter Michelle Collins was given an eight-year suspension and had to forfeit all her winnings since 2002. A Court of Arbitration for Sport panel found that her involvement in the BALCO scandal amounted to a coverup. Because she had used drugs over an extended period of time, the panel doubled the penalty for her over the other athletes involved in the BALCO affair.

What responsibility does a professional athlete have for substances that enter his or her body? To what extent should an athlete trust and rely upon medical professionals for advice about the use of certain substances?

📖 CASE 12-6 *Arbitration CAS 2008/A/1488 P.v. International Tennis Federation (ITF), award of 22*

Tennis
Doping (hydrocholorthiazide; amiloride)
Duty of care of the athlete
Significant fault or negligence
Application of the transitional provisions of the 2009 WADA Code

---

[48] John Cross & Jane Simon, *Have Olympics Been Ruined by Drug Cheats?*, Aug. 13, 2004, http://www.mirror.co.uk.

1. In consideration of the fact that athletes are under a constant duty to personally manage and make certain that any medication being administered is permitted under the anti-doping rules, the prescription of a particular medicinal product by the athlete's doctor does not excuse the athlete from investigating to their fullest extent that the medication does not contain prohibited substances. If the doctor is not a specialist in sports medicine and not aware of anti-doping regulations, it is of even greater importance that the athlete be significantly more diligent in his/her efforts to ensure that the medication being administered does not conflict with the Code.

2. While it is understandable for an athlete to trust his/her medical professional, reliance on others and on one's own ignorance as to the nature of the medication being prescribed does not satisfy the duty of care as set out in the definitions that must be exhibited to benefit from finding No Significant Fault or Negligence. It is of little relevance to the determination of fault that the product was prescribed with "professional diligence" and "with a clear therapeutic intention." To allow athletes to shirk their responsibilities under the anti-doping rules by not questioning or investigating substances entering their body would result in the erosion of the established strict regulatory standard and increased circumvention of anti-doping rules.

3. A player's ignorance or naivety cannot be the basis upon which he or she is allowed to circumvent the very stringent and onerous doping provisions. There must be some clear and definitive standard of compliance to which all athletes are held accountable.

P. ("the player") is a 23 year old Spanish professional tennis player. The International Tennis Federation (ITF) is the international governing body for the sport of tennis worldwide.

On 19 June 2007 P. was requested to provide a urine sample at the Wimbledon Lawn Tennis Championships Qualifying Tournament in Roehampton, Great Britain. On 12 September 2007, the player was notified by the ITF's Anti-Doping Programme Administrator, Staffan Sahlström, that the results of her A Sample testing had returned an Adverse Analytical Finding ("AAF") for Hydrocholorthiazide and Amiloride. These substances are Prohibited Substances under the Tennis Anti-Doping Programme ("TADP") as category "S5. Diuretics and other masking agents."

By letter dated 26 September 2007, the player accepted that the A sample had returned an AAF and waived her right to have her B sample tested.

In the same letter, the player advanced the explanation that she ingested a medication called Ameride for therapeutic purposes. The medication was prescribed in June 2007 by her physician, Dr. Neus Tomas Benedicto, a specialist in Nutrition and Food Science, who had been treating P. for the past year for "liquid retention and overweight." On the doping control form completed at the time of the collection, however, P. did not declare that she was taking the medication Ameride.

On 1 October 2007 the ITF filed a formal charge against the player for the commission of a doping violation under article C.1 of the TADP.

On 11 October 2007, in light of the formal charge, the player voluntarily withdrew from competition and confessed to having committed a doping offence, and explained that *"pre menstrual symptoms, HTA and oedemas"* were the medical reasons which required her to ingest the medicine Ameride.

On 25 January 2008 the ITF's Independent Anti-Doping Tribunal ("the Tribunal") confirmed the doping offence, declared that P. would be subject to a two-year period of ineligibility commencing 11 October 2007, ordered that P.'s individual results be disqualified in respect of the Wimbledon Qualifiers and subsequent competitions up until the date the player voluntarily withdrew from competition on 11 October 2007, and held that all prize money and ranking points obtained by P. by reason of her participation in these competitions be forfeited.

By e-mail dated 29 January 2008, counsel for the player informed the Tribunal of a factual error included in the player's written submissions which incorrectly attributed medical qualifications to the player which, in fact, are those of her doctor and not those of the athlete.

On 31 January 2008 the Tribunal declined to alter their decision and held that even with the factual error being rectified, the player could not demonstrate that she bore No significant Fault or Negligence and stated that although the error was *"regrettable . . . it is not critical to the decision."*

On 15 February 2008 the player filed her Statement of Appeal with the CAS against the decision reached by the Tribunal on 25 January 2008. The Appellant requested that the CAS Panel decide that:

"the mandatory period of 2 years' ineligibility is reduced according to what is stated in clauses M.5.1, and alternatively as a subsidiary, in accordance with clauses M.5.2 of the Tennis Anti-Doping Programme."

On 28 February 2008 the Appellant filed her Appeal Brief and requested from the CAS that the period of ineligibility be reduced. . . .

On 20 June 2008 a hearing was held at the CAS headquarters in Lausanne, Switzerland. . . .

LAW

Discussion

7. The question the Panel must determine in this appeal is whether P., in the circumstances of this case, demonstrated that she bore No Significant Fault or Negligence, for her admitted doping offence. Therefore establishing the possibility that this Panel might exercise its discretion to reduce the period of ineligibility.

8. The TADP and the WADC provide that to benefit from finding of No Significant Fault, the athlete must first meet the condition precedent of establishing how the prohibited substance entered into his or her system. The Panel notes that the ITF accepted P.'s explanation and confirms the first instance tribunal's conclusion. The Appellant has therefore met this first threshold requirement.

9. In order to determine whether a period of ineligibility can be reduced under . . ., the Panel must assess whether the athlete's fault or negligence was not significant when viewed in the totality of the circumstances of the case.

10. This Panel finds that neither in P.'s written submissions, nor at the hearing before the Panel, did she provide any evidence that she had advised Dr. Neus Tomas of her very strict responsibilities as an athlete and the onerous provisions under the TADP and the Code to which she was subject. Her own testimony during the hearing revealed that she merely asked the doctor if any of the ingredients in the medication would cause her performance to improve. The player did not bring the List of Prohibited Substances with her to the doctor, and she did not indicate that she was subject to random drug testing for a variety of different substances.

11. Her inquiry into whether the drug would result in her improved performance reveals that P. was sufficiently cognizant of her obligations under the TADP and the Code. Given this awareness, P. should have been able to understand that questioning whether the substance will improve one's performance is not synonymous to enquiring whether the drug contains any substances that are prohibited under the Code. Article B.4 of TADP provides that it is the sole responsibility of each player to ensure that anything that he or she ingests or uses as medical treatment does not infringe on the provisions of the Code.

12. In consideration of the fact that athletes are under a constant duty to personally manage and make certain that any medication being administered is permitted under the anti-doping rules, the prescription of a particular medicinal product by the athlete's doctor does not excuse the athlete from investigating to their fullest extent that the medication does not contain prohibited substances.

13. The Respondent cited a number of cases in support of its position that P. did not demonstrate that she bore no significant fault or negligence

in this case. The ITF specifically referred to cases where the athlete was able to establish how the substance entered into his or her system, yet was unable to show that he or she bore no significant fault or negligence in its ingestion in support of such a determination. In CAS OG 04/003, the CAS confirmed that it was not reasonable to accept and ingest a product without having properly examined and investigated the product for prohibited substances; and in *ITF v. Neilsen,* the Anti-Doping Tribunal dismissed the player's plea of No Significant Fault or Negligence, stating that the player *"did not take any steps at all to check whether his medication infringed the anti-doping rules."* Similarly in this circumstance the Panel finds that P. has not demonstrated that she took any responsibility in verifying that her prescribed medication did not violate the anti-doping regulations of the TADP or the Code.

14. The facts accepted by the Tribunal demonstrate that P. had been a patient of Dr. Neus Tomas for one year, a specialist in nutrition and food science. However, there is no evidence to suggest that the doctor was familiar with the provisions of the TADP or had knowledge of the WADC List of Prohibited Substances. The player testified during the hearing that she asked her doctor who prescribed Ameride, if there were any ingredients in the drug that would improve her performance. She testified that the doctor answered no, that if anything it would have the opposite effect. She further stated that she always sent her mother to pick up her prescriptions at the pharmacy and she always instructed her mother to ask if there were any ingredients in the medication that would cause her to test positive.

15. In light of the fact that Dr. Neus Tomas was not a specialist in sports medicine and not aware of anti-doping regulations, it was of even greater importance that P. be significantly more diligent in her efforts to ensure that the medication being administered did not conflict with the Code. For any professional athlete, the most rudimentary of actions would have been to query the doctor prescribing the medication as to its composition and whether the substances complied with the Code.

16. P. relies on the argument that her doping violation was unintentional. The player's Appeal Brief directs the Panel to consider the violation's unintentional nature and P.'s lack of awareness as to the constituents of the administered medication, which she argues, reflects her intention to treat her physical ailments, and not to enhance her performance. The Panel is unable to accept these assertions in these circumstances as the basis that P. bore No Significant Fault or Negligence. First, while it is understandable for an athlete to trust his or her medical professional, reliance on others and on one's own ignorance as to the nature of the medication being prescribed does not satisfy the duty of care as set out in the definitions that must be exhibited to benefit from finding No Significant Fault or Negligence according to TADP Article M.5.2.

17. Secondly, it is of little relevance to the determination of fault that the product was prescribed with "professional diligence" and "with a clear therapeutic intention" as submitted by the Appellant. P.'s fault cannot be considered insignificant given that she did not conduct a thorough investigation into the composition of the drug and did not take even the most elementary of steps and advise her medical professional that she cannot ingest any Prohibited Substances. To allow athletes to shirk their responsibilities under the anti-doping rules by not questioning or investigating substances entering their body would result in the erosion of the established strict regulatory standard and increased circumvention of anti-doping rules.

18. As such a result is undesirable, the Panel must concur with the Tribunal's finding that *"the player clearly failed to comply with the duty of utmost caution, or to exercise any reasonable level of care to comply with the anti-doping programme."* . . .

19. In the view of the Panel, based on the Tribunal's above reasons and the Panel's own findings, the particular circumstances of this case do not amount to exceptional circumstances within which P.'s fault can be described as insignificant. The Player had at her disposal several different methods to ensure that the prescribed medication did not infringe on the anti-doping rules, yet she failed to any steps whatsoever. Furthermore, in addition to failing to take any precautions, the Panel further relies on the player's failure to declare that she was taking this medication on her doping control form as support for the finding that P. fault cannot be described as insignificant. The lack of investigation and the non disclosure of the medication on the doping control form were acts that the player could have avoided and are not actions that can illustrate No Significant Fault or Negligence. Taking into account the circumstances of the case and, in particular the Appellant's testimony, the Panel takes the view that the application of the sanctions provided for in the TADP is not disproportionate.

20. Indeed as was evidenced during the hearing, the player appeared truly ignorant of all the readily available resources at her disposal. While this is truly regrettable, the Panel finds that a player's ignorance or naivety cannot be the basis upon which he or she is allowed to circumvent these very stringent and onerous doping provisions. There must be some clear and definitive standard of compliance to which all athletes are held accountable.

21. It is therefore the conclusion of this Panel that the decision of the ITF's Independent Anti-Doping Tribunal's was in the circumstances, the correct one, and is upheld by this Panel. The Panel accepts the Tribunals determination that there existed no circumstances in this case that would warrant the elimination or the reduction of the presumptive two year period of ineligibility and upholds the Tribunal's decision and reasons in awarding the sanction.

Source: Courtesy of Westlaw; reprinted with permission.

NOTES AND DISCUSSION QUESTIONS

1. Should there be different rules and penalties for the use of illegal street drugs as opposed to performance-enhancing drugs? If so, what should be the standard? Should it differ with regard to amateur and professional sports?

2. Do you believe that the use of performance-enhancing drugs should be legalized? If such drugs were legal, would that not place all athletes on the same competitive level?

Professional Sports

3. Do you agree with Major League Baseball's drug policy? If not, what should be changed? If you were drafting a drug policy for professional sports, what would you include? Do you think that the new drug testing program in baseball is harsh enough for its violators? If not, what is the appropriate discipline for violations of the policy? *See*, Robert D. Manfred, Jr., *Symposium: Doping in Sports: Legal and Ethical Issues: Federal Labor Law Obstacles to Achieving a Completely Independent Drug Program in Major League Baseball*, Marquette Sports Law Review, Fall, 2008; Kirk Radomski, *Bases Loaded*, Hudson Street Press, 2009.

4. Rafael Palmeiro tested positive for steroids after testifying before Congress that he had never used steroids. On his 2004 Topps trading card, it states "Bound for Glory." Is he indeed bound for glory? Should he be inducted into Baseball's Hall of Fame notwithstanding steroid use? Shoeless Joe Jackson and Pete Rose have not made it into the Baseball Hall of Fame because of involvement in gambling. Should Palmeiro's conduct be treated the same? Is it in the "best interests of baseball" to exclude him?

5. Running back Onterrio Smith had a history of violating the NFL's drug policy. In May 2005 while traveling through Minneapolis–St. Paul International Airport, he was briefly detained by authorities after a search of his belongings revealed a device called "The Original Whizzinator." The "Whizzinator," named for obvious reasons, is a device used to beat drug tests. Should Smith have suffered any consequences from the NFL as a result of this incident? *See*, Chris Littman, *Onterrio Smith's Whizzinator on the Auction Block*, The Sporting News, August 28, 2009.

6. ESPN has noted the individuals and entities in sports who have received the most "second chances." Steve Howe was number one on the list. Dwight Gooden and Darryl Strawberry were listed two and four, respectively, both given second chances after drug problems.[49]

7. Leonard Little of the St. Louis Rams was found guilty of involuntary manslaughter when he became intoxicated on his birthday and killed another driver. He was suspended from the league for eight games. What discipline should the commissioner have taken as a result of his actions? Should every league have a policy dealing with alcohol use by players? If so, what should it be? *See*, Josie Karp, *Rams Linebacker Little Coping with Fatal Past*, CNN Sports Illustrated, January 28, 2000.

8. Do you believe Congress should be involved in setting regulations for drug testing in professional sports? What role does collective bargaining play with regard to any bill that would

---

[49] Jeff Merron, *If at First You Don't Succeed. . . .*, ESPN.com, 2007, http://espn.go.com/page2/s/list/secondchances.html.

be passed by Congress? Should Congress be involved in setting standards for drug testing at the collegiate and interscholastic levels?

9. The sanction for violation of antidoping rules in the Australian Football League is the loss of two years of eligibility and a lifetime ban for a second violation.[50] Do you agree with this penalty? Should American sports institute the same provisions for violations?

10. Former Pittsburgh Steeler Terry Long passed away in 2005. A revised death certificate listed his death as suicide from drinking antifreeze.[51] In March of 2005 Long had been indicted on federal grand jury charges for arson to his own chicken processing business. He played right guard for the Pittsburgh Steelers from 1984 to 1991. He was small for an offensive lineman in the NFL but was one of the league's most powerful linemen. He was a fourth-round selection by the Steelers from East Carolina University, where he had been an All-American.

11. Do you believe that players who take performance-enhancing drugs are "cheating"? Do you agree with the rationale given by former MVP Ken Caminiti? Who is actually hurt by a player taking performance-enhancing drugs? What ethical issues do drugs in sports present?

12. Mark McGwire admitted using the substance androstenedione ("andro") during his home run rampage in the 1990s. On October 22, 2004, the Anabolic Steroid Control Act of 2004 classified andro as a controlled substance, thereby making its use as a performance-enhancing drug illegal. At the time McGwire was using andro, it was only banned by the NFL. McGwire testified in front of Congress during the hearings regarding steroid use in baseball. When asked if he had ever used steroids, he responded that he would not talk about the past. Baseball has now banned the use of andro as well. How do you think this will affect the possible introduction of McGwire into the Baseball Hall of Fame? How should professional sports address a situation in which a player was using a drug that is later banned? *See,* Associated Press, *Andro Story on McGwire in 1998 Caught Baseball's Attention,* USA TODAY, December 13, 2007.

13. Unfortunately, baseball players have not always taken drugs seriously. Bill "the Spaceman" Lee pitched for the Red Sox and talked extensively about drug use in his book *The Wrong Stuff* (1984). Pittsburgh Pirates pitcher Doc Ellis talked about a no-hitter he threw on LSD in his book *Dock Ellis, In the Country of Baseball* (1989). *See,* Jerry Crasnick, *Ex-Pitcher Ellis Dies of Liver Disease,* ESPN, December 20, 2008.

14. Drug testing is highly regulated in sports such as boxing and horse racing. In *Stephenson v. Louisiana State Racing Commission,* 907 So.2d 925 (4th Cir. 2005), the state racing commission suspended a veterinarian's license and racing privilege for two years and fined him $10,000. The court of appeals found that the evidence supported the commission's finding that the veterinarian had injected the horse with a substance from home prior to the race:

> A thorough reading of the hearing transcript reveals that there was substantial circumstantial evidence to support a finding that Dr. Stephenson injected the horse, Delightster, with some substance within the prohibitive four-hour time period. The two investigators on the scene both testified that they saw Dr. Stephenson holding an empty

---

[50] *See* Australian Football League, Anti-Doping Code, as amended, Section 12.1, *Imposition of Ineligibility for Prohibited Substances and Prohibited Methods.*

[51] *NFL Roundup: Document Says Former Steeler Drank Antifreeze in Suicide,* New York Times, Jan. 27, 2006.

syringe against the horse's neck. Dr. Stephenson first attempted to conceal the syringe, and then hesitated to surrender it to the investigators. Dr. Stephenson freely admitted that the syringe had contained AMP mixed with a vitamin, thus the fact that the drug analysis proved negative for illegal substances is of no moment. Whether this substance was an illegal narcotic or a vitamin cocktail, injecting any horse with any substance within four hours of post time is a violation of the rules.

Additionally, it taxes the imagination to believe it was mere coincidence that Dr. Stephenson had on his person two syringes, one containing AMP with vitamin B12 in Exhibit A, and the other thiamine mixed with calcium or magnesium in Exhibit B, the two substances Carl Giesse testified he suggested Dr. Stephenson give his horse. Clearly this "coincidence" was not lost on the Commission either as Commissioner Neck pointed out at the hearing.

Dr. Stephenson attempted to explain away the fact that he had an empty syringe in his hand when the investigators found him by stating that he was using it as a "pointing device." According to Dr. Stephenson, he was attempting to explain the symptoms of colic to an illegal alien groom who did not speak English. When this explanation is coupled with Dr. Stephenson's other testimony that the syringe had merely fallen out of his pocket as he attempted to sound the horse's belly with his naked ear, it is easy to see why the Commission gave little credence to either explanation for the presence of the syringe.[52]

15. The Clean Sports Act of 2005 never became law, although it is possible that it will be reintroduced in later sessions of Congress. For further study see, Lindsay J. Taylor, *Congressional Attempts to "Strike Out" Steroids: Constitutional Concerns About the Clean Sports Act*, University of Arizona Law Review, Vol. 49, 2007, p. 961.

Amateur Sports

16. The Supreme Court has succinctly held: "Urination is 'an excretory function' traditionally shielded by great privacy."[53] With this precept in mind, what factors must be taken into consideration when drafting a drug testing policy for a public high school?

17. At what age or grade should drug testing start?

18. The decision in the *Earls* case expands the decision of *Vernonia* by allowing school districts to test more students with no direct evidence of drug use by students present. Under what circumstances should schools be allowed to test student-athletes? What about those who participate in "competitive" extracurricular activities? How would you define extracurricular activity? How would you treat members of the school's debate team?

19. The Supreme Court's decision in *Earls* mentions that a study shows that students who engage in extracurricular activities at schools are less likely to have substance abuse problems.[54]

---

[52] *Stephenson*, 907 So.2d 925 at 931.
[53] Skinner v. Railway Labor Executives' Ass'n, 489 U.S. 602, 626 (1989).
[54] *See* N. ZILL, C. NORD, & L. LOOMIS, ADOLESCENT TIME USE, RISKY BEHAVIOR, AND OUTCOMES: AN ANALYSIS OF NATIONAL DATA 52 (1995).

Do you agree with this proposition? If you do agree, wouldn't the proper course of action be to test all students who are not involved in extracurricular activities? What would be the effect of that? What legal ramifications would result?

20. The school board policy found in *Earls* applied to athletes, cheerleaders, and even members of the Future Homemakers of America. Under what circumstances could the Future Home-makers of America be considered a "competitive" extracurricular activity? Where would you draw the line with regard to drug testing high school students?

21. Four Supreme Court justices disagreed with the *Earls* decision. Justices Ginsburg, Stevens, O'Connor, and Souter dissented, with Ginsburg drafting the dissenting opinion. O'Connor also wrote a short dissenting opinion, in which Souter joined. In her dissenting opinion, Ginsburg discussed the policy of random drug testing. She seemed to attack the arguments made by the majority in somewhat of a tongue-in-cheek fashion:

> At the margins, of course, no policy of random drug testing is perfectly tailored to the harms it seeks to address. The School District cites the dangers faced by members of the band, who must "perform extremely precise routines with heavy equipment and instruments in close proximity to other students," and by Future Farmers of America who "are required to individually control and restrain animals as large as 1500 pounds." For its part, the United States acknowledges that "the linebacker faces a greater risk of serious injury if he takes the field under the influence of drugs than the drummer in the halftime band," but parries that "the risk of injury to a student who is under the influence of drugs while playing golf, cross country, or volleyball (sports covered by the policy in Vernonia) is scarcely any greater that the risk of injury to a student . . . handling a 1500-pound steer (as [Future Farmers of America] members do)." One can demur to the Government's view of the risks drug use poses to golfers, ("golf is a low intensity activity"), for golfers were surely as marginal among the linebackers, sprinters, and basketball players targeted for testing in Vernonia as steer-handlers are among the choristers, musicians, and academic-team members subject to urinalysis in Tecumseh. Notwithstanding nightmarish images of out-of-control flatware, livestock run amok, and colliding tubas disturbing the peace and quiet of Tecumseh, the great majority of students the School District seeks to test in truth are engaged in activities that are not safety sensitive to an unusual degree. There is a difference between imperfect tailoring and no tailoring at all.[55]

Do you agree with the observations and arguments of the dissent in *Earls*?

22. Some courts have found that drug testing of student-athletes without any suspicion of the use of drugs is unconstitutional. In *Trinidad School District No. 1 v. Lopez*, 963 P. 2d 1095 (Colo. 1998), a band member challenged the school board's policy of suspicionless urinalysis drug tests for sixth- through twelfth-grade students participating in extracurricular activities. In finding that the policy was unconstitutional, the court stated: "'Although band members wear uniforms, they do not undergo the type of public undressing and communal showers required of students athletes.' The court here finds this fact significant. Furthermore, the court holds that 'the type of voluntariness to which the *Vernonia* Court referred does not apply to

---

[55] *Earls*, 536 U.S. 822 at 851–52.

students who want to enroll in a for-credit class that is part of the school's curriculum.'" Also see *Gardner ex rel. Gardner v. Tulia Independent School District*, 183 F. Supp. 2d 854 (N. D. Tex. 2000), in which a policy mandating suspicionless drug testing for all students in grades 7 through 12 who were engaged in extracurricular activity was considered in violation of the Fourth Amendment.

23. The National Center for Drug Free Sport uses handheld computers to track the approximately 25,000 drug tests it evaluates yearly for college athletics. The Dolphin 7900 is used to record an athlete's digital signature and to scan the bar codes that are attached to sample containers. There are plans for the Dolphin to be able to take the athlete's picture to further substantiate the integrity of all samples that are taken. The National Center for Drug Free Sports has found that using paper for compiling test data had created possibilities of human error, but that the use of handheld computers virtually eliminated all error.[56]

24. For other cases dealing with drug testing at the collegiate level, see *University of Colorado v. Derdeyn*, 863 P.2d 929 (Colo. 1993) (holding a university's random drug testing of students to be unconstitutional), and *O'Halloran v. University of Washington*, 679 F. Supp. 997 (W.D. Wash. 1998) (holding that the NCAA's use of a monitored urine test did not unreasonably infringe upon a student's right of privacy).

25. What about those students who are not involved in athletics but are involved in extracurricular activities in public school such as the debate team, chess club, choir, Fellowship of Christian Athletes, or the Future Farmers of America? In *Board of Education of Indep. Sch. Dist. No. 92 of Pottawatomie County v. Earls*, 536 U.S. 822 (2002), the U.S. Supreme Court examined the constitutionality of a school policy that required drug testing for all students who participated in "competitive" extracurricular activities. The Court stated:

> Given the nationwide epidemic of drug use, and the evidence of increased drug use in Tecumseh schools, it was entirely reasonable for the School District to enact this particular drug testing policy. We reject the Court of Appeals' novel test that "any district seeking to impose a random suspicionless drug testing policy as a condition to participation in a school activity must demonstrate that there is some identifiable drug abuse problem among a sufficient number of those subject to the testing, such that testing that group of students will actually redress its drug problem." Among other problems, it would be difficult to administer such a test. As we cannot articulate a threshold level of drug use that would suffice to justify a drug testing program for schoolchildren, we refuse to fashion what would in effect be a constitutional quantum of drug use necessary to show a "drug problem."
>
> Finally, we find that testing students who participate in extracurricular activities is a reasonably effective means of addressing the School District's legitimate concerns in preventing, deterring, and detecting drug use. While in *Vernonia* there might have been a closer fit between the testing of athletes and the trial court's finding that the drug problem was "fueled by the 'role model' effect of athletes' drug use," such a finding was not essential to the holding. *Vernonia* did not require the school to test the group of students most likely to use drugs, but rather considered the constitutionality

---

[56] *Computerworld*, Feb. 13, 2006.

of the program in the context of the public school's custodial responsibilities. Evaluating the Policy in this context, we conclude that the drug testing of Tecumseh students who participate in extracurricular activities effectively serves the School District's interest in protecting the safety and health of its students.[57]

International Sports

26. Should U.S. athletes be subject to international drug testing standards? The International Baseball Federation (IBAF) tested for banned substances in the World Baseball Classic (WBC) in 2006. There were some concerns about which substances were to be tested for. The IBAF was sanctioning the WBC and therefore was required to adhere to the World Anti-Doping Code.

SUGGESTED READINGS AND RESOURCES

Canseco, Jose. *Juiced: Wild Times, Rampant 'Roids, Smash Hits, and How Baseball Got Big.* New York: Regan Books, 2005.

Carroll, Will. *The Juice: The Real Story of Baseball's Drug Problems.* Chicago: Ivan R. Dee, 2005.

Diacin, Michael J., Parks, Janet B., & Allison, Pamela C. *Voices of Male Athletes on Drug Use, Drug Testing, and the Existing Order in Intercollegiate Athletics.* 26 JOURNAL OF SPORT BEHAVIOR 1 (2003).

Finley, Laura, & Finley, Peter. *Piss Off! How Drug Testing and Other Privacy Violations Are Alienating America's Youth.* Monroe, ME: Common Courage Press, 2005.

Galas, Judith C. *Drugs and Sports.* San Diego, Lucent Books, 1997.

Hallam, Michael A. *A Casualty of the "War on Drugs": Mandatory, Suspicionless Drug Testing of Student Athletes in* Vernonia School District 47J v. Acton. 74 NORTH CAROLINA LAW REVIEW 833 (1996).

Houlihan, Barrie. *Sport, Policy and Politics: A Comparative Analysis.* New York: Routledge, 1997.

Miller Eric N. *Suspicionless Drug Testing of High School and College Athletes After* Acton: *Similarities and Differences.* 45 UNIVERSITY OF KANSAS LAW REVIEW 301 (1996).

Newton, David E. *Drug Testing: An Issue for School, Sports, and Work.* Springfield, NJ: Enslow, 1999.

Taylor, William N. *Anabolic Steroids and the Athlete,* 2d ed. Jefferson, NC: McFarland, 2002.

Waddington, Ivan. *Sport, Health and Drugs: A Critical Sociological Perspective.* New York: Routledge, 2000.

Wagman, Nancy D. *Are We Becoming a Society of Suspects?* Vernonia School District 47J v. Acton: *Examining Random Suspicionless Drug Testing of Public School Athletes.* 3 VILLANOVA SPORTS AND ENTERTAINMENT LAW JOURNAL 325 (1996).

Wilson, Wayne, & Derse, Edward (eds.). *Doping in Elite Sport: The Politics of Drugs in the Olympic Movement.* Champaign, IL: Human Kinetics, 2001.

---

[57] *Earls*, 536 U.S. 822 at 836–838.

REFERENCE MATERIALS

Anderson, Paul M. *The Supreme Court Sets the Standard: Drug Testing at the Interscholastic Level*. 4 Texas Review of Entertainment and Sports Law 1 (2003).

Arena Football League. *Collective Bargaining Agreement Between Arena Football League, LLC, and Arena Football League Players Association*. Jan. 9, 2004.

Australian Football League. *Anti-Doping Code*. Amended Jan. 1, 2008, http://www.afl.com.au/portals/0/afl_docs/afl_hq/policies/anti-doping%20code%20january%202008.pdf.

Champion, Walter T. *Fundamentals of Sports Law*. St. Paul, MN: Thomson/West, 2005.

Danaher, Scott. *Drug Abuse in Major League Baseball: A Look at Drug Testing in the Past, in the Present, and Steps for the Future*. 14 Seton Hall Journal of Sports and Entertainment Law 305 (2004).

Franz, Joseph C. *Legal Issues: Options Should Be Explored Before Starting Student Drug-Testing Program*. 24 IAA Magazine (1997).

Gorman, Christopher A. *Public School Students' Fourth Amendment Rights After* Vernonia *and* Earls: *Why Limits Must Be Set on Suspicionless Drug Screening in the Public Schools*. 29 Vermont Law Review 147 (2004).

GovTrack.us, http://www.govtrack.us.

Green, Gary A., Uryazc, Frank D., Petr, Todd A., & Bray, Corey D. *NCAA Study of Substance Use and Abuse Habits of College Student-Athletes*. 11 Clinical Journal of Sport Medicine 51 (2001).

Higbee, Kari L. *Students' Privacy Rights: Drug Testing and Fourth Amendment Protections*. 41 Idaho Law Review 361 (2005).

International Judo Federation. *Regulations and Procedure Concerning Drug Tests*. http://www.intjudo.eu/.

Johnson, Eric C. *Arguments Concerning the Efforts to Detect Chemical Enhancements in Top-Level Chess Competitions*. ChessNews.org, Oct. 26, 2001, http://www.chessnews.org/arguments.htm.

Major League Baseball's Joint Drug Prevention and Treatment Program. 2005. http://www.mlb.com/pa/pdf/jda.pdf.

Meldrum, Russell. *Drug Use by College Athletes: Is Random Testing an Effective Deterrent?* 5 Sport Journal 1 (2002).

Nafziger, James. *Circumstantial Evidence of Doping: BALCO and Beyond*. 16 Marquette Sports Law Review 45 (2005).

National Basketball Players Association. *Collective Bargaining Agreement*. July 30, 2005, http://www.nbpa.com/cba_articles.php.

National Collegiate Athletic Association. *Drug-Testing Program, 2006–07*. Indianapolis, IN: NCAA.

National Football League Players Association. *NFL Collective Bargaining Agreement, 2006–2012*. March 8, 2006, http://nflplayers.com/images/fck/NFL%20COLLECTIVE%20BARGAINING%20AGREEMENT%202006%20-%202012.pdf.

National Hockey League. *Collective Bargaining Agreement Between National Hockey League and National Hockey League Players' Association, July 22, 2005–September 15, 2011*. July 22, 2005, http://www.nhl.com/cba/2005-CBA.pdf.

Osei, David K. *Doping, Juicing, and Executive Bypass Oversight: A Case Study of Major League Baseball's Steroid Scandal.* 4 VIRGINIA SPORTS AND ENTERTAINMENT LAW JOURNAL 155 (2004).

Pelkey, Charles. *CAS Rejects Hamilton Appeal.* VeloNews.com, Feb. 11, 2006.

Rabuano, Mark. *An Examination of Drug-Testing as a Mandatory Subject of Collective Bargaining in Major League Baseball.* 4 UNIVERSITY OF PENNSYLVANIA JOURNAL OF LABOR AND EMPLOYMENT LAW 439 (1999).

Sports Drug Testing Act 2003. Queensland, Australia, 2003, http://www.legislation.qld.gov.au/LEGISLTN/ACTS/2003/03AC021.pdf.

Stewart, Laura S. *Has the United States Anti-Doping Agency Gone Too Far? Analyzing the Shift From 'Beyond a Reasonable Doubt' to 'Comfortable Satisfaction.'* 13 VILLANOVA SPORTS AND ENTERTAINMENT LAW JOURNAL 207 (2006).

Tennis Anti-Doping Program. 2009.

Tygart, Travis T. *Winners Never Dope and Finally, Dopers Never Win: USADA Takes Over Drug Testing of United States Olympic Athletes.* 1 DEPAUL JOURNAL OF SPORTS LAW AND CONTEMPORARY PROBLEMS 124 (2003).

Walker, E. Tim. *Missing the Target: How Performance-Enhancing Drugs Go Unnoticed and Endanger the Lives of Athletes.* 10 VILLANOVA SPORTS AND ENTERTAINMENT LAW JOURNAL 181 (2003).

Wendt, John T. *The Year of the Steroid: Are New Testing Regimes Enough?* 22 ENTERTAINMENT AND SPORTS LAWYER 8 (2005).

Wilson, Stephen. *Rogge: IOC 'Very Satisfied' with Games.* SEATTLE POST-INTELLIGENCER, Feb. 26, 2006.

World Anti-Doping Agency. *The World Anti-Doping Code.* Montreal: World Anti-Doping Agency, 2003. http://www.wada-ama.org/rtecontent/document/code_v3.pdf.

Zehrbach, Gareth D., & Mead, Julie F. *Urine as "Tuition": Are We There Yet?* 194 EDUCATION LAW REPORTS 775 (2005).

INTERNATIONAL SPORTS

OVERVIEW

Sports have exploded on the international level. Athletes across the globe compete in a myriad of international events, including the FIFA World Cup, the World Cup of Cricket, the Olympics, the British Open, the Ryder Cup, the World Baseball Classic, Wimbledon, and the Tour de France, just to mention a few. The Olympics have always been the mainstay of international sports, but now major sports such as baseball, football, basketball, and hockey have become more international and well known to millions around the world.[1] Professional sports in the United States have become increasingly more international in nature. The NBA is a very international sport with NBA teams drafting international players on a regular basis. The NHL has always been an international sport and the NFL and MLB are following suit after realizing the numerous international opportunities to promote their respective sports.

A few sports, such as football (soccer), basketball, and track and field, have achieved popularity on a worldwide basis. Other sports are unique to the culture of particular countries. Hockey is popular in Scandinavia, Canada, and the United States, for example. Baseball is very popular in Central America and the Caribbean, Japan, and the United States. The Aussies have their own exciting game of Australian Rules Football. Cricket is a great sport that is played extensively in the United Kingdom, New Zealand, Pakistan, and India. Soccer is a worldwide phenomenon, albeit the United States has been slow to adopt it as a national sport. However, the popularity of the 1994 World Cup gave soccer a boost in the United States. Youth participation in soccer is at an all-time high. Table tennis, running, tennis, golf, skiing, rugby, and cycling are sports enjoyed by millions of individuals globally.

This book has mainly focused on U.S. sports law, but many of the same issues exist on the international level as well. Noted international sports law expert James A. R. Nafziger has stated succinctly the role and future of international sports law:

> The globalization of sports competition is a sign of our times. Inspired by the modern Olympic Games, nurtured by communications technology, and fueled by high-profile professional athletes and commercial

---

[1] For further studies *see,* James A.R. Nafziger, *The Future of International Sports Law,* August 31, 2006. The article is based on Dr. Nafziger's presentation at the Symposium on The Future of Sports Law, at the Willamette University College of Law, March 17, 2006.

interests, the process of globalization continues apace. In this process international sports law is gradually assuming a prominent role.[2]

Professional sports leagues have begun to realize the many corporate opportunities that exist on a worldwide level and have capitalized on marketing their sport to a worldwide audience. For example, the 2009 Super Bowl between the Cardinals and the Steelers was broadcast to 232 countries in 34 languages. In 2005, the Arizona Cardinals and the San Francisco 49ers played the first regular-season game outside the United States, in Mexico City. The game drew 103,467 fans to Azteca Stadium, the largest crowd ever to watch an NFL game. The NFL has now begun to play regular season games in countries other than the United States to increase the popularity of the NFL brand. NFL Commissioner Roger Goodell has stated the NFL will continue playing games in international forums with an eye toward expansion that could lead to placing an NFL franchise in London.[3] The NBA also has plans to place an expansion team in Europe in the near future.[4] The NFL selected Beijing for a game between the Seahawks and the Patriots on August 8, 2007. The game served as a kick-off to the one-year countdown to the XXIX Olympic Games in China. The NFL has signed two new national broadcasting contracts, which gives it a presence in three major European markets: France, Germany, and the United Kingdom.

The NHL has always had an international flavor. The NHL's Montreal Canadiens and Detroit Red Wings played a series of postseason exhibition games in Europe in 1938. On January 27, 1965, Sweden's Ulf Sterner became the first European to play in the NHL. In 1969, the NHL drafted its first European player. In the 1989–1990 NHL season, 12% of the players were European; in 1995, that figure rose to 20.8% and in 2000, it was 31.8%. In that same year, 123 European players were selected in the NHL entry draft, a total of 42% of all players chosen. Although the majority of NHL franchises are located in the United States, NHL players are overwhelmingly from other countries other than the United States. In 2008 nineteen countries were represented in the NHL.[5] To show deference to international play, in 2002 the NHL suspended play during the regular season for 12 games during the Winter Games in Salt Lake City, in which 125 NHL players participated. The 2004 NHL lockout created a myriad of legal and economic issues for all parties involved. After the lockout was announced, many players left to play in Europe. A total of 388 NHL players played on European teams during the strike. Legal issues facing NHL players included insurance matters, tax and immigration issues, contract matters, and restrictions against foreign players.[6]

In 2006 the United States hosted the World Baseball Classic in San Diego, with 16 countries participating. Japan defeated Cuba in the finals. The United States had originally attempted to block Cuban participation in the games, arguing that it conflicted with its trade embargo in place against that country. On the amateur level, foreign teams win the Little League World Series on a regular basis. Although strides have been made to internationalize baseball, there have been setbacks as well. Major League Baseball moved the Montreal Expos to Washington D.C. in 2005, and baseball and softball are no longer recognized as Olympic sports.[7]

---

[2] James A. R. Nafziger, *The Future of International Sports Law*, 42 WILLAMETTE L. REV. 861 (2006).

[3] Associated Press, *Goodell Expects Multiple Games to be Played Overseas,* Fort Wayne Journal Gazette, October 24, 2009.

[4] Associated Press, *Stern Lays Out Vision for NBA Expansion in Europe,* ESPN, March 27, 2008.

[5] *NHL Landscape Changes,* International Ice Hockey Federation, October 5, 2008.

[6] For further examination, see Anders Etgen Reitz, *The NHL Lockout: The Trickle-Down Effect on European Hockey*, 13 SPORTS LAW. J. 179 (2006).

[7] Vicki Michaelis, *Baseball, Softball Bumped from Olympics,* USA Today, July 8, 2005.

JURISDICTION

Many legal issues present themselves for athletes who participate on an international level. Determining the rights of athletes who are participating at the international level involves a web of institutions, organizations, governing bodies, and decision makers. How can athletes challenge a decision by an international body dealing with his or her eligibility or drug testing? What laws apply under such circumstances? Can a decision of an international tribunal be binding on a non-resident athlete? Could an athlete appeal such a ruling? If so, where is the appeal heard, and what law should be applied? How do U.S. courts view a decision from an international body? These and many more issues and questions are present at the international level for athletes and can be both complicated and confusing.

In Case 13-1, *Reynolds v. International Amateur Athletic Federation*, an athlete appealed his suspension by the International Amateur Athletic Federation (IAAF). Track and field star Harry "Butch" Reynolds tested positive for a drug that had been banned by the IAAF. Several legal issues were presented in the case. Does a U.S. court have jurisdiction over an international federation based on the activities of its U.S. member national governing body (NGB)? If the NGB functions as the agent of the international federation in the United States, does personal jurisdiction exist?

 CASE 13-1 *Reynolds v. International Amateur Athletic Federation*

23 F.3d 1110 (6th Cir. 1994)

LIVELY, Senior Circuit Judge.

The International Amateur Athletic Federation (IAAF) appeals the district court's denial of its motion to quash garnishment proceedings and vacate a default judgment and permanent injunction previously entered by the district court. As it did before the district court, the IAAF argues on appeal that the district court had neither subject matter jurisdiction nor personal jurisdiction over the IAAF in the proceedings resulting in the default judgment and permanent injunction.

I.

A.

Harry "Butch" Reynolds is a world-class sprinter who regularly participates in international track and field meets. Reynolds currently holds the individual world record in the 400 meters, is a member of the world record holding 4×400 relay team, and is a gold and silver medalist from the 1988 Olympics.

On August 12, 1990, Reynolds ran in the "Hercules '90" meet in Monte Carlo, Monaco. Immediately after the competition, Reynolds was tested for illegal performance-enhancing drugs as part of a random drug test conducted after all international track meets. Two different samples of Reynolds' urine were sent to Paris for analysis. Each sample contained trace amounts of the steroid Nandrolone, a drug banned by international track regulations created by the IAAF.

The IAAF is an unincorporated association based in London, England, and is made up of track and field organizations representing 205 nations and territories. Its purpose is to coordinate and control track and field athletes and competitions throughout the world. The IAAF has no offices in the United States, and holds no track meets in Ohio, where Reynolds brought this action. One member of the IAAF is The Athletics Congress of the United States, Inc. (TAC), the United States national governing body for track and field. After Reynolds' positive drug test, the IAAF banned him from all international track events for two years, thereby eliminating his hopes for competing in the 1992 Olympics in Barcelona. . . .

B.

Reynolds immediately brought suit in the Southern District of Ohio, arguing that the drug test was given negligently, and provided an erroneous result. The court dismissed one claim and stayed the remainder of the case after finding that Reynolds failed to exhaust administrative remedies provided by the Amateur Sports Act, *36 U.S.C. §§ 371-396 (1988)* and TAC. Reynolds appealed the district court's decision. This court agreed with the exhaustion requirement but vacated the judgment and directed that the entire case be dismissed for lack of subject matter jurisdiction. *Reynolds v. TAC, 935 F.2d 270 (6th Cir.1991)* (Table).

In an attempt to exhaust his administrative remedies, Reynolds participated in an independent arbitration before an AAA panel in June of 1991. Reynolds took this action under the Amateur Sports Act and the United States Olympic Committee Constitution. The AAA arbitrator rendered a decision fully exonerating Reynolds; the arbitrator found strong evidence that the urine samples provided to the Paris laboratory were not Reynolds'. However, the IAAF refused to acknowledge the arbitrator's decision because the arbitration was not conducted under IAAF rules. Accordingly, the IAAF refused to lift Reynolds' two year suspension.

Reynolds then appealed his suspension to TAC, as required by IAAF rules. TAC held a hearing on September 13, 1991. After thoroughly examining the evidence and deliberating for two weeks, the TAC Doping Control Review Board completely exonerated Reynolds . . .

Still not satisfied, the IAAF reopened Reynolds' case pursuant to IAAF Rule 20(3)(ii), which allows the IAAF to conduct an independent arbitration where it appears that one of its member foundations such as

TAC has "misdirected itself." The IAAF arbitration was held on May 10 and 11, 1992, in London, England (the London Arbitration). The parties to the arbitration proceeding were the IAAF and TAC. Reynolds attended and testified at the hearing, and Reynolds' attorneys participated in the proceedings before the IAAF arbitration board, including examining and cross-examining witnesses. At the conclusion of the hearing, the IAAF arbitral panel found that the drug tests were valid, and that there was "no doubt" as to Reynolds' guilt. As a result, the panel upheld Reynolds' two year suspension.

II.

A.

Soon after the IAAF made its final decision, Reynolds filed the present action in the Southern District of Ohio alleging four different state law causes of action: breach of contract, breach of contractual due process, defamation, and tortious interference with business relations. Reynolds sought monetary damages, and a temporary restraining order that would allow him to compete in races leading to the U.S. Olympic trials on June 20, 1992. The IAAF refused to appear in the case, stating in a letter to Reynolds' attorney that the district court had no jurisdiction over the IAAF. The district court issued a temporary restraining order that prevented the IAAF from interfering with Reynolds' attempt to make the Olympic tryouts. Despite IAAF threats to both Reynolds and TAC, Reynolds ran in a few races and qualified to compete in the U.S. Olympic trials in New Orleans.

On June 17, 1992, the district court held a preliminary injunction hearing to decide if Reynolds should compete in the June 20 Olympic trials. The IAAF refused to appear, but TAC intervened to oppose Reynolds. On June 19, the district court issued a preliminary injunction after finding that it had personal jurisdiction over the IAAF and that Reynolds was likely to succeed on the merits of his claims. That afternoon, TAC filed a motion with the Sixth Circuit Court of Appeals, asking for an emergency stay of the district court's decision. At 7:00 that evening, Judge Siler granted the stay. *Reynolds v. IAAF, 968 F.2d 1216 (6th Cir.1992)*(Table). The next morning, Reynolds filed an emergency motion with Supreme Court Justice John Paul Stevens, asking for an order vacating Judge Siler's emergency stay. Justice Stevens granted Reynolds' request, finding that the District Court's opinion was "persuasive." *Reynolds v. IAAF, 505 U.S. 1301, 112 S.Ct. 2512, 120 L.Ed.2d 861 (1992)*.

Despite these rulings, the IAAF announced that every athlete who competed with Reynolds at the U.S. Olympic trials would be ineligible to compete in the Barcelona Olympics. Reynolds' events were temporarily postponed while TAC filed an application to the full Supreme Court to vacate Justice Stevens' stay. The Court denied TAC's request, and Reynolds was eventually allowed to compete in the Olympic trials, after an agreement was reached between the U.S. Olympic Committee and the IAAF. Reynolds made the Olympic team as an alternate for the 400 meter relay. However, the IAAF refused to let Reynolds compete at the 1992 Olympics, and TAC removed him from the U.S. Olympic team roster. Moreover, the IAAF increased Reynolds' two year suspension by four months as punishment for participating in the U.S. Olympic trials.

B.

On September 28, 1992, Reynolds filed a supplemental complaint with the district court, outlining the above events. The IAAF did not respond to Reynolds' complaint and TAC did not appear in the default proceedings. After the IAAF was given full notice, the court entered a default judgment in Reynolds' favor. Soon afterward, the district court held a hearing to determine damages. Again, the IAAF was provided notice but refused to appear. On December 3, 1992, the district court issued an opinion awarding Reynolds $27,356,008, including treble punitive damages. The district court found that the IAAF "acted with ill will and a spirit of revenge towards Mr. Reynolds." . . .

The district court found that it had diversity jurisdiction in this case because Reynolds is a citizen of Ohio and the IAAF is a foreign association. The IAAF is an unincorporated association, and the district court reasoned that the IAAF is deemed to be a citizen of all states where its members are domiciled. The court held that diversity jurisdiction was proper because no IAAF members are citizens of Ohio.

The district court also found that it had personal jurisdiction over the IAAF. The court held that the Ohio long-arm statute was satisfied because the IAAF transacted business with Reynolds in Ohio, and the IAAF's public announcement of Reynolds' positive drug test adversely affected Reynolds in Ohio. The court held that the IAAF had the required minimum contacts with Ohio after finding that TAC acted as the IAAF's agent in the United States.

C.

On February 17, 1993, Reynolds began garnishment proceedings against four corporations with connections to the IAAF. The IAAF finally appeared at a garnishment hearing before the district court, and later filed a "Motion to Quash Garnishment Proceedings and To Vacate the

Default Judgment" pursuant to *FED.R.CIV.P. 60(b)(4)*. In its motion, the IAAF contended that the court lacked personal and subject matter jurisdiction. Before the motion was decided, the IAAF filed a recusal motion, arguing that previous opinions by the court put the district judge's impartiality into question.

The district court denied all motions on July 13, 1993. . . .

The IAAF appeals from denial of its motions. Because it contends that the district court lacked jurisdiction in the earlier proceedings, the IAAF seeks to reverse the money judgment and injunction as well.

III.

Because we have concluded that the district court lacked personal jurisdiction over the IAAF, the sole defendant in this case, it is not necessary to consider the other issues presented and argued by the parties.

A.

The district court found that it had personal jurisdiction over the IAAF under Ohio's long-arm statute. . . .

The IAAF contends that holding it amenable to suit in an Ohio court would offend principles of international comity and put international cooperation at risk. Under this theory, the IAAF should not be required to bear the expense of litigating cases around the world when its only contact with a forum is an athlete's residence. Instead, the IAAF argues that only the courts of England, where it is located, have jurisdiction to review its arbitral proceedings. Reynolds counters that his interest in a convenient forum substantially outweighs the inconvenience to the IAAF. Over half of the IAAF's four year $174.5 million budget is received from United States corporations, one of the IAAF's officers resides in the U.S., and its other officers regularly visit the U.S.

2. Tortious Injury

Reynolds claimed that the false IAAF drug report was both defamatory and interfered with his contractual relationships. . . .

Nevertheless, unless TAC had minimum contacts with Ohio in relation to the "contract" between the IAAF and Reynolds, the court erred in premising jurisdiction of TAC's agency. . . .

In short, the IAAF is based in England, owns no property and transacts no business in Ohio, and does not supervise U.S. athletes in Ohio or elsewhere. Its contacts with Reynolds in Ohio are superficial, and are insufficient to create the requisite minimum contacts for personal jurisdiction . . .

The leading case on this issue is *Calder v. Jones, 465 U.S. 783, 104 S.Ct. 1482, 79 L.Ed.2d 804 (1984)*. In *Calder,* a professional entertainer sued the writers and editors of a Florida magazine for libel in a California court. . . . Because the defendants' intentional actions were aimed at California and the brunt of the harm was felt there, the Court concluded that the defendants could reasonably anticipate being haled into court in California.

We find *Calder* distinguishable for several reasons. First, the press release concerned Reynolds' activities in Monaco, not Ohio. Second, the source of the controversial report was the drug sample taken in Monaco and the laboratory testing in France. Third, Reynolds is an international athlete whose professional reputation is not centered in Ohio. Fourth, the defendant itself did not publish or circulate the report in Ohio; Ohio periodicals disseminated the report. Fifth, Ohio was not the "focal point" of the press release. The fact that the IAAF could foresee that the report would be circulated and have an effect in Ohio is not, in itself, enough to create personal jurisdiction. Finally, although Reynolds lost Ohio corporate endorsement contracts and appearance fees in Ohio, there is no evidence that the IAAF knew of the contracts or of their Ohio origin. *Calder* is a much more compelling case for finding personal jurisdiction.

Reynolds argues, however, that his claims arose out of the IAAF's connection with Ohio because the IAAF intentionally defamed him and interfered with his Ohio business relationships. Under this theory, the IAAF knew that the worldwide media would carry the report and that the brunt of the injury would occur in Ohio.

Even accepting that the IAAF could foresee that its report would be disseminated in Ohio, however, the IAAF would not be subject to personal jurisdiction in Ohio. The press release that the IAAF issued in London did not directly accuse Reynolds of using forbidden substances. It recited the fact that the Paris laboratory had reported a positive drug test and that Reynolds had been suspended and offered a hearing. We cannot hold that this act of the IAAF satisfied the requirements of the Ohio statute, or that permitting the IAAF to be sued in Ohio for the press release would comport with due process. . . .

VI.

TAC was carrying out its statutory duty under the Amateur Sports Act and was not acting as the IAAF's agent when it intervened. There is no indication that the IAAF authorized or even requested TAC to appear. Indeed, the IAAF had consistently refused to appear and had taken the position that the district court lacked jurisdiction over the entire proceeding. We conclude that TAC appeared solely in its role as the national governing body under the Amateur Sports Act.

Conclusion

In conclusion, we do not believe that holding the IAAF amenable to suit in an Ohio court under the facts of this case comports with "traditional notions of fair play and substantial justice." The IAAF stated in its brief and at oral argument that it will not challenge the jurisdiction of English courts to determine the validity of the London Arbitration award if Reynolds seeks to have it set aside in the courts of that country.

Our decision renders the IAAF's recusal motion moot.

The district court abused its discretion by denying the IAAF's *Rule 60(b)(4)* motion for relief. The judgment of the district court is **REVERSED**. Upon **REMAND** the district court will dismiss this action for lack of personal jurisdiction over the IAAF.

Source: Courtesy of Westlaw; reprinted with permission.

THE OLYMPIC GAMES

When international sports events are mentioned, the Olympics are the first to come to mind. The Olympics have been a showcase for athletic competition as far back as the time of the Ancient Greeks. The Olympics started in 776 BC in the valley of Olympus to honor the mythical Greek god Zeus. The Olympics were discontinued in 393 AD and reestablished in their modern form in 1892. The Winter Games began in 1924 and were held in the same year as the Summer Games until 1992. Unfortunately, the games were cancelled due to world wars in 1916, 1940, and 1944.

The Summer Olympics have 38 sports with approximately 300 events, and the Winter Games consist of 7 sports and about 84 events. More than 2,600 athletes competed in 84 events in the 2006 Winter Games in Turin, Italy, and more than 80 countries were represented. Four sports have requested entrance in the 2014 Winter Olympics Games: ski archery, mountaineering, orienteering, and bandy. Bandy has been described as field hockey on ice skates.[8] For the 2012 Summer Games, many sports are attempting to be recognized, including tug-of-war and korfball.[9] Tug-of-war was previously on the Olympic program.[10] Baseball and softball were the first sports eliminated from Olympic competition since polo in 1936. The Olympics have become widely popular in recent years. Television networks engage in heated competition to acquire the rights to broadcast the games.

---

[8] American Bandy Association, http://www.usabandy.com.

[9] *See* http://www.korfball.com and http://www.englandkorfball.co.uk.

[10] International Olympic Committee, *Sports of the Past: Tug-of-War*, http://www.olympic.org/uk/sports/past/index_uk.asp.

Structure of the Olympic Movement

The Olympic movement consists of multiple governing bodies in a complicated structure that is both international and domestic. The International Olympic Committee (IOC) has the responsibility of overseeing and monitoring Olympic activities throughout the world. The IOC recognizes international sports federations (IFs) and national Olympic committees (NOCs). IFs define eligibility for international competition and administer Olympic programs for a particular sport. An NOC is the sole authority for representing a particular country at the Olympic Games. NOCs in turn recognize national governing bodies (NGBs), which administer each Olympic sport and selection of athletes for that sport. The U.S. Olympic Committee (USOC) is the U.S. representative to the IOC. Olympic athletes are under the authority of the IOC, IF, NOC, and NGB and are therefore subject to their rules and regulations, and their discipline, if necessary.

REPRESENTATIVE CASES

The 1980 Summer Games were held in Moscow, the first Olympic Games to be held in a communist country. Approximately 65 countries, led by the United States, boycotted the 1980 Games, citing the 1979 Soviet invasion of Afghanistan as the reason for the boycott. Approximately 80 nations did participate in the Games.[11] President Jimmy Carter had attempted to persuade the IOC to move or even cancel the Summer Games because of the invasion by the Soviets. Some countries, such as France and Britain, participated in the Games but still supported the boycott. Case 13-2, *DeFrantz v. U.S. Olympic Committee,* 492 F. Supp. 1181 (D.C. D.C. 1980), deals with athletes who sued the USOC, stating that they should have been allowed to participate in the 1980 Olympic Games. The plaintiffs attempted to enjoin the USOC from boycotting the 1980 Games. The court held that the plaintiffs had failed to state a viable claim under the Amateur Sports Act of 1978 or for alleged constitutional violations.

📖 CASE 13-2 *DeFrantz v. U.S. Olympic Committee*

492 F. Supp. 1181 (D.C. D.C. 1980)

JOHN H. PRATT, District Judge.

Plaintiffs, 25 athletes and one member of the Executive Board of defendant United States Olympic Committee (USOC), have moved for an injunction barring defendant USOC from carrying out a resolution, adopted by the USOC House of Delegates on April 12, 1980, not to send an American team to participate in the Games of the XXIInd Olympiad to be held in Moscow in the summer of 1980. Plaintiffs allege that in preventing American athletes from competing in the Summer Olympics, defendant has exceeded its statutory powers and has abridged plaintiffs' constitutional rights.

---

[11] Ronald Smothers, *OLYMPICS; Bitterness Lingering Over Carter's Boycott*, The New York Times, July 19, 1996.

. . . According to its Rules and By-laws, the International Olympic Committee (IOC) governs the Olympic movement and owns the rights of the Olympic games. IOC Rules provide that National Olympic Committees (NOC) may be established "as the sole authorities responsible for the representation of the respective countries at the Olympic Games," so long as the NOC's rules and regulations are approved by the IOC. The USOC is one such National Olympic Committee.

The USOC is a corporation created and granted a federal charter by Congress in 1950. This charter was revised by the Amateur Sports Act of 1978. Under this statute, defendant USOC has "exclusive jurisdiction" and authority over participation and representation of the United States in the Olympic Games. . . .

On December 27, 1979, the Soviet Union launched an invasion of its neighbor, Afghanistan. That country's ruler was deposed and killed and a new government was installed. . . .

President Carter termed the invasion a threat to the security of the Persian Gulf area as well as a threat to world peace and stability and he moved to take direct sanctions against the Soviet Union. These sanctions included a curtailment of agricultural and high technology exports to the Soviet Union, and restrictions on commerce with the Soviets. The Administration also turned its attention to a boycott of the summer Olympic Games as a further sanction against the Soviet Union.

. . . [On April 12, 1980], [a]fter what USOC President Kane describes in his affidavit as "full, open, complete and orderly debate by advocates of each motion," the House of Delegates, on a secret ballot, passed by a vote of 1,604 to 798, a resolution which provided in pertinent part:

> RESOLVED that since the President of the United States has advised the United States Olympic Committee that in light of international events the national security of the country is threatened, the USOC has decided not to send a team to the 1980 Summer Games in Moscow . . .

> FURTHER RESOLVED, that if the President of the United States advises the United States Olympic Committee, on or before May 20, 1980, that international events have become compatible with the national interest and the national security is no longer threatened, the USOC will enter its athletes in the 1980 Summer Games.

1. The Amateur Sports Act of 1978

Plaintiffs allege in their complaint that by its decision not to send an American team to compete in the summer Olympic Games in Moscow,

defendant USOC has violated the Amateur Sports Act of 1978. . . .
Reduced to their essentials, these allegations are that the Act does
not give, and that Congress intended to deny, the USOC the authority
to decide not to enter an American team in the Olympics, except perhaps for sports-related reasons, and that the Act guarantees to certain athletes a right to compete in the Olympic Games . . .

The principal substantive powers of the USOC are found in s 375(a) of
the Act. In determining whether the USOC's authority under the Act
encompasses the right to decide not to participate in an Olympic contest, we must read these provisions in the context in which they were
written. In writing this legislation, Congress did not create a new
relationship between the USOC and the IOC. Rather, it recognized an
already long-existing relationship between the two and statutorily
legitimized that relationship with a federal charter and federal
incorporation. The legislative history demonstrates Congressional
awareness that the USOC and its predecessors, as the National Olympic
Committee for the United States, have had a continuing relationship
with the IOC since 1896. Congress was necessarily aware that a
National Olympic Committee is a creation and a creature of the International Olympic Committee, to whose rules and regulations it must
conform. The NOC gets its power and its authority from the IOC, the
sole proprietor and owner of the Olympic Games.

In view of Congress' obvious awareness of these facts, we would expect
that if Congress intended to limit or deny to the USOC powers it
already enjoyed as a National Olympic Committee, such limitation or
denial would be clear and explicit. No such language appears in the
statute. Indeed, far from precluding this authority, the language of the
statute appears to embrace it. For example, the "objects and purposes"
section of the Act speaks in broad terms, stating that the USOC shall
exercise "exclusive jurisdiction" over ". . . all matters pertaining
to the participation of the United States in the Olympic Games. . . ."
We read this broadly stated purpose in conjunction with the specific
power conferred on the USOC by the Act to "represent the United
States as its national Olympic committee in relations with the International Olympic Committee," and in conjunction with the IOC Rules
and By-laws, which provide that "representation" includes the decision to participate. In doing so, we find a compatibility and not a
conflict between the Act and the IOC Rules on the issue of the
authority of the USOC to decide whether or not to accept an invitation to field an American team at the Olympics. The language of the
statute is broad enough to confer this authority, and we find that
Congress must have intended that the USOC exercise that authority in
this area, which it already enjoyed because of its long-standing

relationship with the IOC. We accordingly conclude that the USOC has the authority to decide not to send an American team to the Olympics.

Plaintiffs next argue that if the USOC does have the authority to decide not to accept an invitation to send an American team to the Moscow Olympics, that decision must be based on "sports-related considerations." In support of their argument, plaintiffs point to ss 392(a)(5) and (b) of the Act, which plaintiffs acknowledge "are not in terms applicable to the USOC," but rather concern situations in which national governing bodies of various sports, which are subordinate to the USOC, are asked to sanction the holding of international competitions below the level of the Olympic or Pan American Games in the United States or the participation of the United States athletes in such competition abroad. These sections provide that a national governing body may withhold its sanctions only upon clear and convincing evidence that holding or participating in the competition "would be detrimental to the best interests of the sport." Plaintiffs argue by analogy that a similar "sports-related" limitation must attach to any authority the USOC might have to decide not to participate in an Olympic competition. We cannot agree.

The provision on which plaintiffs place reliance by analogy is specifically concerned with eliminating the feuding between various amateur athletic organizations and national governing bodies which for so long characterized amateur athletics. As all parties recognize, this friction, such as the well-publicized power struggles between the NCAA and the AAU, was a major reason for passage of the Act, and the provisions plaintiffs cite, among others, are aimed at eliminating this senseless strife, which the Senate and House Committee reports indicate had dramatically harmed the ability of the United States to compete effectively in international competition. In order to eliminate this internecine squabbling, the Act elevated the USOC to a supervisory role over the various amateur athletic organizations, and provided that the USOC establish procedures for the swift and equitable settlement of these disputes. As indicated above, it also directed that the national governing bodies of the various sports could only withhold their approvals of international competition for sports-related reasons. Previously, many of these bodies had withheld their sanction of certain athletic competitions in order to further their own interests at the expense of other groups and to the detriment of athletes wishing to participate.

In brief, this sports-related limitation is intimately tied to the specific purpose of curbing the arbitrary and unrestrained power of various athletic organizations subordinate to the USOC not to allow athletes to compete in international competition below the level of the Olympic Games and the Pan American Games. This purpose has nothing to do with a decision by the USOC to exercise authority granted by the IOC to decide not to participate in an Olympic competition.

. . . We therefore conclude that the USOC not only had the authority to decide not to send an American team to the summer Olympics, but also that it could do so for reasons not directly related to sports considerations.

. . . .

b. Athletes Statutory Right to Compete in the Olympics

. . . Plaintiffs argue that the Report of the President's Commission on Olympic Sports, which was the starting point for the legislation proposed, and the legislative history support their argument that the statute confers an enforceable right on plaintiffs to compete in Olympic competition. Again, we are compelled to disagree with plaintiffs.

The legislative history and the statute are clear that the "right to compete," which plaintiffs refer to, is in the context of the numerous jurisdictional disputes between various athletic bodies, such as the NCAA and the AAU, which we have just discussed, and which was a major impetus for the Amateur Sports Act of 1978. Plaintiffs recognize that a major purpose of the Act was to eliminate such disputes. However, they go on to argue that the Presidential report, which highlighted the need for strengthening the USOC in order to eliminate this feuding, made a finding that there is little difference between an athlete denied the right to compete because of a boycott and an athlete denied the right to compete because of jurisdictional bickering.

The short answer is that although the Congress may have borrowed heavily from the Report on the President's Commission, it did not enact the Report. Instead, it enacted a statute and that statute relates a "right to compete" to the elimination of jurisdictional disputes between amateur athletic groups, which for petty and groundless reasons have often deprived athletes of the opportunity to enter a particular competition. . . .

The Senate Report makes clear that the language relied on by plaintiffs is not designed to provide any substantive guarantees, let alone a Bill of Rights. Further, to the extent that any guarantees of a right to compete are included in the USOC Constitution as a result of this provision, they do not include a right that amateur athletes may compete in the Olympic Games despite a decision by the USOC House of Delegates not to accept an invitation to enter an American team in the competition. This provision simply was not designed to extend so far. Rather, it was designed to remedy the jurisdictional disputes among amateur athletic bodies, not disputes between athletes and the USOC itself over the exercise of the USOC's discretion not to participate in the Olympics. . . .

. . . Because we conclude that the rights plaintiffs seek to enforce do not exist in the Act, and because the legislative history of the Act nowhere allows the implication of a private right of action, we find that plaintiffs have no implied private right of action under the Amateur Sports Act of 1978 to maintain this suit.

Case dismissed.

Source: Courtesy of Westlaw; reprinted with permission.

Most courts agree with the *DeFrantz* ruling finding that no private cause of action exists under the Amateur Sports Act, now referred to as the Stevens Act.[12] However, in Case 13-3, *Sternberg v. U.S.A. National Karate-Do Federation*, 123 F. Supp. 2d 659 (E.D. N.Y. 2000), the court found that even if the plaintiff failed to specifically state a private cause of action, one could be implied from the act. In this case, an athlete sued the U.S.A. National Karate-Do Federation, the national governing body for the sport of karate, alleging violations of Title IX, the Amateur Sports Act, and the Fifth Amendment to the U.S. Constitution.

📖 CASE 13-3 *Sternberg v. U.S.A. National Karate-Do Federation*

123 F. Supp. 2d 659 (E.D. N.Y. 2000)

WEINSTEIN, Senior District Judge.

I. Introduction

This case raises a question of apparent first impression with respect to the rights of female athletes to compete in the Olympics. Plaintiff seeks redress for alleged violations of Title IX of the Education Amendments of 1972 ("Title IX"), the Amateur Sports Act ("Sports Act"), and the Fifth Amendment to the United States Constitution. Defendant moves to dismiss the complaint. . . . The motion is denied for the reasons stated below.

---

[12] *See* Slaney v. Int'l Amateur Athletic Federation, 244 F.3d 580 (7th Cir. 2001); *also see* Walton-Floyd v. USOC, 965 S.W.2d 35 (Tex. Ct. App. 1998); Cantrell v. United States Soccer Federation, 924 P.2d 789 (Okla. App. 1996).

II. Facts

The United States Olympic Committee ("Olympic Committee") is a not-for-profit corporation that was chartered pursuant to the Amateur Sports Act of 1978. Defendant concedes that the Olympic Committee receives substantial sums of money from the federal government.

The Olympic Committee recognizes the United States of America National Karate Do Federation ("Karate Federation") as the national governing body for the sport of karate. While the Karate Federation does not receive any direct federal funding, the Olympic Committee did provide over forty million dollars to all national governing sports bodies, including the Karate Federation, in 1999. Without specifying an exact amount, Plaintiff alleges that the Karate Federation received direct and indirect funding from the Olympic Committee, and thus from the United States government.

Plaintiff is a member of the Karate Federation. She was selected as a member of the 1998 Women's Kumite (Karate sparring) Team after training in one of the Federation's camps. In 1998, she traveled to Brazil, expecting to compete for a position on the United States Women's Kumite Team in the World Championships. Prior to the competition, the Karate Federation withdrew the Women's Kumite Team. The Men's Kumite Team participated in the World Championship. Plaintiff filed a grievance with the Karate Federation.

According to the plaintiff, Terrance Hill, the Women's Kumite Team coach, told her that the team was withdrawn because two members refused to participate and the Federation could not field a team without the requisite number of members. Plaintiff, however, alleges the two teammates referred to by coach Hill denied that they had refused to participate, indicated that they did not participate only because coach Hill and the Federation discouraged them, and that coach Hill did not want the team to participate for fear of the risk of injury to women.

It is plaintiff's view that the Federation did not conduct an impartial and unbiased investigation of her complaint. She contends that Dr. Julius Thiry, the president of the Karate Federation, assigned Thomas Burke, his personal Karate student and personal attorney, to investigate her claim; Dr. Thiry in turn arranged for a grievance board comprised almost entirely of his personal Karate students. Dr. Thiry allegedly attempted to prejudice Plaintiff's witnesses, pressured her husband to influence her to drop her grievance, and threatened her husband with the loss of his position as chairman of the Karate Federation Referee Council. After this lawsuit was brought, the Karate Federation removed Plaintiff's husband from his position as chairman of the Karate Federation Referee Council; he is not a party to the suit.

III. Law and Application

. . . .

D. *Ted Stevens Olympic and Amateur 1978 Amateur Sports Act of 1978 (36 U.S.C. §§ 220501 et. seq.) ("Sports Act")*

One of the primary purposes of the 1978 Amateur Sports Act is to "encourage and provide assistance to women in amateur athletic activity." 36 U.S.C.A. § 220503 (1994). As a national governing body, the Karate Federation has a duty, without regard to gender, to provide amateur athletes with an equal opportunity to participate in amateur athletic competition; discrimination on the basis of sex is forbidden. The duties of the Federation as "a national governing body" include providing "equitable support and encouragement for participation by women where separate programs for male and female athletes are conducted on a national basis." The Federation must designate individuals to represent the United States in international amateur athletic competitions and allow such individuals to compete in such competitions, provided that the organization conducting the competition meets the requirements of the Sports Act. It is not contested that the Karate Federation is a national sports governing body subject to the Sports Act and to its anti-discrimination provisions.

1. Private Right of Action Under the Sports Act

Even if a statute does not specifically provide for a private cause of action, one may be implied. In deciding whether Congress designed the Sports Act to permit a private remedy for violations the following four *Cort* factors must be considered:

(1) whether the *plaintiff is "one of the class for whose especial benefit the statute was enacted . . .*—that is, does the statute create a federal right in favor of the plaintiff"; (2) whether there is "any indication of legislative *intent,* explicit or implicit, to create such a remedy or deny one" ; (3) whether it is "*consistent with the underlying purposes of the legislative scheme* to imply such a remedy for the plaintiff"; and (4) whether the cause of action is "one traditionally relegated to state law, in *an area basically the concern of the States,* so that it would be inappropriate to infer a cause of action based solely on federal law." Alaji Salahuddin v. Alaji, 232 F.3d 305 (2d Cir.2000) (citing *Cort v. Ash,* 422 U.S. at 78, 95 S.Ct. 2080) (emphasis added).

In analyzing these factors, cases subsequent to *Cort* have refined the inquiry looking to the "dispositive question" of Congressional design to create a private right of action. . . . Plaintiff's case meets the first, third and fourth prongs of the *Cort* inquiry. *Cort*, 422 U.S. at 78, 95 S.Ct. 2080.

The plaintiff is a female, "one of the class for whose especial benefit the statute was created." The purpose of the Sports Act includes encouraging and providing "assistance to amateur athletic activities for women." 36 U.S.C.A. § 220503(12). The language of this statute—which expressly identifies the class Congress intended to benefit—is consistent with that found in statutes enacted to protect specific classes of people. The statute dictates that national sports governing bodies provide an equal opportunity to amateur athletes to participate in amateur athletic competition without discrimination on the basis of sex. Plaintiff is a female amateur athlete seeking redress for violation of that duty of non-discrimination.

A private remedy is consistent with the "underlying purposes of the legislative scheme". One of the primary goals of the Sports Act is to "encourage and provide assistance to women in amateur athletic activity." The duties of the Federation include providing "equitable support and encouragement for participation by women where separate programs for male and female athletes are conducted on a national basis." Like Title VI and Title IX, the Sports Act seeks to accomplish two related objectives—to "avoid the use of federal resources to support discriminatory practices" and "protect individual citizens against those practices." Private federal enforcement furthers these purposes. It is the athlete who suffers the discrimination who has a strong incentive to sue on her own behalf, thus giving practical and effective content to the statute. Congress's words were not purely precatory.

The subject matter does not involve an area traditionally relegated to the States. As pointed out in *Cannon*, "the Federal Government and the federal courts have been the 'primary and powerful reliances' in protecting citizens against [discrimination on the basis of sex]."

Critical is the second *Cort* factor—the design of Congress to provide a private remedy. An "explicit legislative purpose" to deny a private cause of action is controlling. Here there is no congressional expression. Nonetheless, a private right of action may still be implied from a statute prohibiting conduct deleterious to individuals.

The legislative history of the Sports Act does not indicate that Congress wished to foreclose a private right of action. Prior to passage of the Sports Act, Congress removed the athlete's "bill of rights," which would have explicitly granted a private right of action to anyone who was discriminatorily denied the right to participate in specific events. This history has led some courts to conclude that plaintiffs have no private right of action under the Sports Act.

Yet, the "bill of rights" might have been eliminated because it was too detailed and Congress was reluctant to interject itself too deeply into sports concepts that were still developing. The court of appeals for the Second Circuit has not yet addressed the matter.

Arguably, Congress struck the "bill of rights" to prevent countless lawsuits from disgruntled would-be athletes. Fear of such lawsuits could hinder teams from making decisions based purely on athletic ability. Thus, Congress might simply have sought to eliminate a *broad* private right of action. There is no indication, however, that the athlete's "bill of rights" was removed from the legislation to prevent women from exercising a private right of action under the Sports Act in cases involving gross gender discrimination of the type plaintiff alleges. Such suits would be limited in scope since, for example, they would not involve competition between males on men's teams or between females on women's teams.

Congress has enunciated a strong policy against discrimination on the basis of gender. Where the conduct involves discrimination between men and women, there is a strong presumption that this national policy is reflected in the creation of a private right of action.

The legislative history does not demonstrate that the athlete's "bill of rights" was removed to prevent women from exercising a private right of action under the Sports Act in cases involving discrimination. The other three *Cort* factors point toward an implied private right of action. A narrow right of action regarding sex discrimination by national governing sports bodies may be implied. . . .

Source: Courtesy of Westlaw; reprinted with permission.

One of the more infamous moments in sports history was the assault by Tonya Harding and her associates on fellow ice skater Nancy Kerrigan. Harding hired a "hitman" (Jeff Gillooly, her ex-husband) to "take out" her skating rival, Nancy Kerrigan. Kerrigan was clubbed in the knee just outside a Detroit, Michigan, ice rink on January 6, 1994. She suffered injuries that forced her withdrawal from the 1994 U.S. Nationals. Without Kerrigan competing, Harding won the U.S. Figure Skating Nationals. By virtue of her victory she earned a spot on the U.S. Olympic team. On January 14, 1994, three people were charged with the assault of Kerrigan, including Tonya Harding's bodyguard.[13] On January 28, 1994, Harding admitted she had learned about the plot against her rival a week after it happened.

On February 1, 1994, Harding's ex-husband pleaded guilty to racketeering in connection with the assault on Kerrigan. He also named Harding as a conspirator. He was sentenced to two years and a $100,000 fine. In March of 1994, Harding pleaded guilty to hindering the investigation of the attack on Kerrigan. In exchange for no jail time, she agreed to pay a $100,000 fine, set up a $50,000 fund

---

[13] Jere Longman, *FIGURE SKATING; Three Men Indicted in Kerrigan Assault*, The New York Times, March 22, 1994.

to benefit the Special Olympics, reimburse the prosecutor's office for $10,000 in costs, perform 500 hours of community service, undergo a psychiatric evaluation, and resign from the USFSA.

The U.S. Figure Skating Association (USFSA) began disciplinary proceedings against Harding for unethical conduct for her part in the incident. In July of 1994, the USFSA stripped Harding of her 1994 National Championship and banned her for life. Harding sued the USFSA for breach of contract, Case 13-4, *Harding v. U.S. Figure Skating Ass'n*, 851 F. Supp. 1476 (D. Ore. 1994). The USOC Code of Conduct requires that all members of the U.S. Olympic team conduct themselves "in conformity with traditions of the Olympic Games." Harding's lawsuit attempted to enjoin the USFSA from holding a disciplinary hearing that could result in her dismissal from the Olympics. Harding agreed to drop her lawsuit for damages if she was allowed to compete in the Olympic Games. NGBs and the USOC are given much discretion when attempting to resolve participation disputes relating to athletes. They must, however, follow their own internal rules and regulations in the process.

On February 25, 1995, Kerrigan won the silver medal at the Winter Olympics; Harding finished in eighth place.

📖 CASE 13-4 *Harding v. U.S. Figure Skating Ass'n*

851 F. Supp. 1476 (D. Ore. 1994)

PANNER, District Judge.

Plaintiff Tonya Harding brought this diversity action for breach of contract against defendant United States Figure Skating Association, Inc. I enjoined defendant from holding a planned disciplinary hearing in Colorado on March 10, 1994. When the parties were unable to agree upon a new date for the disciplinary hearing, I extended that injunction to preclude defendant from holding the hearing prior to June 27, 1994. Defendant has now moved for reconsideration of my earlier ruling along with a motion to dismiss this action. I grant both motions, though not for the reasons urged by defendant.

Discussion

. . . At the time this action was filed, plaintiff was a member of the defendant United States Figure Skating Association. Plaintiff paid her dues, and agreed to comply with the rules of that association. The parties mutually agreed to certain rules that would govern any disciplinary proceeding against a member of the association.

Defendant's bylaws provide that when disciplinary charges are filed against a member, that member has thirty days to file a reply. The bylaws further provide that "upon receipt of the reply, the Hearing Panel shall set a place and date for a hearing that is reasonably convenient for all parties." Article XXVII, § 3(c)(iv). Defendant violated this rule by unilaterally setting a time and date for the hearing that was just three days after the reply was due. Defendant acted contrary to its bylaws by setting the date before it received the reply. Furthermore, in view of the complexity of the charges, March 10 was not a date "reasonably convenient for all parties."

I reviewed *in camera* the evidence defendant intended to present at the disciplinary hearing. The evidence was complex, involving the actions of several dozen individuals over a period of weeks. The evidence included statements by alleged co-conspirators, each of whom may have had a motive to misrepresent plaintiff's role in this matter. Moreover, because the Rules of Evidence do not apply at this disciplinary hearing, the documents defendant proposed to use were replete with hearsay, newspaper clippings, conclusions, an anonymous letter, forensic opinions, affidavits, media interviews, and similar items that would not be admissible in a court of law. In addition, it was intimated that plaintiff's defense might include a form of the "battered wife" defense, which would require extensive investigation by experts and interviews with persons who have known plaintiff and her former husband over a period of many years. Finally, the Hearing Panel that would decide the charges against plaintiff was the same panel that acted as a *de facto* grand jury in the decision to file charges against plaintiff in the first place. Based on my fourteen years of experience as a trial judge, and thirty years of experience as a trial lawyer before taking the bench, it was immediately apparent that plaintiff could not possibly prepare a defense to those charges in the time allotted. The hearing date established by defendant was not "reasonably convenient for all parties," as required by defendant's bylaws.

When one party to a contract is given discretion in the performance of some aspect of the contract, that discretion must be exercised in good faith. The date set by defendant was arbitrary and manifestly unreasonable, and would severely prejudice plaintiff's chances of obtaining a fair hearing. Plaintiff immediately advised defendant that this date was not convenient and requested an extension of time. Defendant denied the request because it wanted to conduct the hearing prior to the World Championships so it could remove plaintiff from the United States delegation for that event. Plaintiff then exhausted her internal appeals within the association before filing this action for injunctive relief.

The courts should rightly hesitate before intervening in disciplinary hearings held by private associations, including the defendant United States Figure Skating Association. Intervention is appropriate only in the most extraordinary circumstances, where the association has clearly breached its own rules, that breach will imminently result in *serious* and irreparable harm to the plaintiff, and the plaintiff has exhausted all internal remedies. Even then, injunctive relief is limited to correcting the breach of the rules. The court should not intervene in the merits of the underlying dispute.

This is one of those rare cases where judicial intervention was appropriate. It appeared at the time that had defendant not been enjoined from holding the hearing on March 10, plaintiff would have suffered serious irreparable harm. Defendant argued that the matter was not ripe because the outcome of the hearing was unknown. If the only issue was whether plaintiff should have been allowed to skate in the World Championships in Japan later that month, defendant's point might have been well taken, since injunctive relief could still be sought at the conclusion of the disciplinary hearing. In this particular case, however, merely holding the hearing on March 10 would have caused plaintiff to suffer irreparable harm. In order to maintain her right to contest the decision of the Hearing Panel, plaintiff would have been obliged to appear before the panel and prematurely present her defense without having adequate time to prepare for that hearing. If the Hearing Panel found her guilty as charged, the resultant publicity could have severely prejudiced her chances for a fair trial in any future criminal case. Plaintiff would also have been obliged to decide upon and publicly disclose a defense strategy for both the civil and criminal matters before she had time to conduct full discovery and interview witnesses. Finally, the entire testimony, including information that has heretofore not been made public, would inevitably have been leaked to the media, despite defendant's best intentions to maintain the confidentiality of the proceedings, thereby further poisoning plaintiff's chance of obtaining a fair trial in the criminal proceeding. Under the circumstances, plaintiff's attorneys might well have advised their client not to attend the hearing. In that case, plaintiff would likely have forfeited any right to contest the results of the hearing. Her failure to contest the charges would have also resulted in her being found guilty in the court of public opinion.

I rejected plaintiff's suggestion that the disciplinary hearing be postponed until after resolution of the criminal charges against her. Defendant is a private association, not a governmental body. Plaintiff's constitutional right against self-incrimination is not implicated unless she is compelled to testify either before or by a governmental body.

I nonetheless concluded that plaintiff was entitled to additional time to prepare for the hearing. The harm to plaintiff greatly outweighed the harm to defendant from postponing the hearing. Defendant has an interest in enforcing its rules and promptly disciplining violators, and ensuring that only qualified skaters represent the United States at the World Championships. However, the United States Olympic Committee

("USOC") charter requires that resolution of disputes be both swift *and* equitable. 36 U.S.C. § 382b. In this case, equity was sacrificed for speed. Plaintiff exhausted all her internal remedies before filing suit. Defendant's bylaws provide for accelerated binding arbitration, but only to review the decision of the Hearing Panel *after* it finds plaintiff guilty and orders she be expelled from the Figure Skating Association. In most cases that would have been sufficient to protect the member's interests. This case was the exception. Defendant's bylaws do not provide for emergency arbitration of a dispute as to the timing of the disciplinary hearing. Under the unique circumstances of this case, which included the circus atmosphere generated by an international media frenzy, the complexity of the accusations against plaintiff, and the close connection between the disciplinary proceeding and possible criminal charges against plaintiff, defendant's internal remedies were inadequate to prevent the imminent injury to plaintiff.

. . . Next, defendant argues that 36 U.S.C. § 374(3) vests the USOC and its officially recognized national governing bodies, such as defendant, with exclusive jurisdiction over amateur athletics. In fact, that section refers only to participation of the United States in the Olympic Games and Pan-American Games, neither of which are implicated here. Moreover, I did not order defendant to include plaintiff as a member of the United States delegation to the World Championships, or take any position upon the merits of the disciplinary proceeding. I merely ordered defendant to comply with the requirement in its own bylaws that the hearing be set at a time reasonably convenient for all parties, thus ensuring plaintiff could obtain a fair hearing.

Defendant also argues that the Figure Skating Association's bylaws provide an exclusive administrative procedure for resolution of disputes. However, that procedure works only so long as defendant follows it. Defendant's argument boils down to an assertion that plaintiff has no remedy even if defendant refuses to follow its own procedures. I disagree. The procedures governing disciplinary hearings are binding upon both the Figure Skating Association and its members. . . .

Although I conclude this court has jurisdiction and the injunction was properly issued, I now grant defendant's motion for reconsideration because the circumstances requiring the injunction no longer exist. Plaintiff has resigned from the Figure Skating Association and pled guilty to the criminal charges. A disciplinary hearing has been set for June 29, a date that is reasonably convenient for all parties in accordance with defendant's bylaws. There is no reason to exercise continued jurisdiction over this matter, or to enjoin defendant any longer than absolutely necessary. Any intervention by the courts in the internal affairs of the Figure Skating Association should be restricted to that necessary to vindicate the rights at issue. Accordingly, the injunction dated March 31, 1994 is vacated, and the action dismissed as moot.

Source: Courtesy of Westlaw; reprinted with permission.

In Case 13-5, *American Horse Show Ass'n v. Ward*, 186 Misc.2d 571 (N.Y. 2000), the American Horse Show Association (now the U.S. Equestrian Association), the NGB for equestrian sports in the United States, sought to prevent a former member who had been indicted for insurance fraud related to the killing of four horses from attending any association events.

CASE 13-5 *American Horse Show Ass'n, Inc. v. Ward*

186 Misc.2d 571 (N.Y. 2000)

Richard F. Braun, J.

. . . Plaintiff is the national governing body for equestrian sports in this country, and promulgates rules governing horse shows and competitions which are recognized by plaintiff. Defendant was a member of plaintiff and agreed to be bound by the rules. Defendant is an accomplished equestrian who was a World Cup finalist several times.

In July 1994, defendant and others were indicted by a Grand Jury of the United States District Court for the Northern District of Illinois for crimes involving the killing of four horses in order to collect insurance proceeds for the horses. On March 19, 1996, defendant pleaded guilty to one count of criminal conspiracy to commit wire fraud. Defendant admitted that he conspired with three others to kill a horse in order to enable one of them to file a false insurance claim as to that horse. Defendant further admitted that he told the horse killer to keep quiet about the people who hired the killer to slaughter the horses, and, if he kept quiet about defendant's friends and business associates, defendant would pay him money. Defendant also admitted that he later spoke with the horse killer and that defendant said that he would kill the horse killer if he did anything to hurt defendant. Defendant was sentenced to serve 33 months in prison, to be followed by three years of probation, and to make restitution of $200,000 to one of the defrauded insurance companies.

Defendant was charged by plaintiff with violating plaintiff's rule III, article 302.6 and rule VII, article 702 (a), (d) and (f). Rule III, article 302.6 provides:

"Following a hearing, the AHSA's Hearing Committee may deny or suspend the privilege to participate in or go upon the grounds of Recognized competitions, and/or deny, expel or suspend the privileges of membership in the AHSA to any person, whether or not a member of the AHSA, whom an indictment, information or charge (criminal, administrative, or civil) has asserted, or whom any civil, criminal or administrative court or tribunal has found, to have committed or participated in any plan or conspiracy to commit, any act of cruelty or abuse to a horse, whether or not any such alleged or actual act, plan, or conspiracy occurred on the grounds of a Recognized competition, or was in conjunction with, or was an element of some other offense, actual or alleged. For purposes of this subsection, cruelty and abuse shall include, but shall not be limited to, any of the acts enumerated in Art. 302.4, and, in addition, killing, crippling, abandoning, mistreating, neglecting, or any other form of abuse of a horse. (See Art. 614)."

Rule VII, article 702 provides in pertinent part:

"A violation is any act prejudicial to the best interests of the AHSA, including but not limited to the following:

" (a) Violation of the rules of the AHSA . . .
" (d) Acting or inciting or permitting any other to act in a manner contrary to the rules of the AHSA, or in a manner deemed improper, unethical, dishonest, unsportsmanlike or intemperate, or prejudicial to the best interests of the sport and the AHSA . . .
" (f) Physical assault upon a person and/or cruelty to a horse defined in Art. 302."

A hearing was scheduled on the charges and held on July 10, 1996. Defendant did not appear at the hearing. Before the hearing, defendant's attorney sent a letter to plaintiff stating that, in light of defendant's having pleaded guilty to one charge of the indictment and his admissions regarding his role in the death of one horse, defendant was resigning his membership with plaintiff, effective immediately. The letter further stated that defendant did not intend to appear at the hearing or offer any evidence on his behalf. The charges were sustained by plaintiff. Defendant was immediately expelled from his membership in plaintiff, barred from competing in international competitions, and excluded from all competition grounds either as an exhibitor, participant, or spectator. Defendant was given the right to apply to plaintiff for reinstatement no earlier than August 29, 2009.

By order of Justice DeGrasse of this court, dated June 16, 1999, plaintiff was granted a preliminary injunction enjoining defendant from participating, attending, or spectating at all equestrian competitions recognized by plaintiff. Defendant violated the order by appearing at horse shows in the United States, and by order of Justice

DeGrasse, dated March 21, 2000, was held in contempt of court for violating the June 16, 1999 order.

Defendant then moved to modify the June 16, 1999 preliminary injunction order to allow him to attend events recognized by plaintiff in which defendant's son, also an outstanding American equestrian, participates. By order, dated June 7, 2000, Justice DeGrasse denied the motion.

. . . The second defense is that plaintiff lacks jurisdiction over defendant. Defendant explains in his opposition papers that he means that the lack of jurisdiction is due to defendant's having resigned from plaintiff before the hearing. However, as stated by plaintiff's Secretary General in her May 6, 1999 affidavit, defendant agreed to be bound by plaintiff's rules, including those as to violations and penalties. Defendant's resignation from plaintiff did not deprive plaintiff of the power to penalize defendant for his violation of the rules committed while he was a member. Furthermore, rule III, article 302.6 applies to "any person, whether or not a member of the [plaintiff]." Rule VII, article 701 makes article 702 (a), (d) and (f) applicable to "any person who acts in a manner in violation of the rules of the [plaintiff] or deemed prejudicial to the best interests of the sport and the [plaintiff]." Thus, the defense should be dismissed.

. . . The equities balance in favor of plaintiff who wants to keep defendant, with his past, away from horse shows and competitions. Although defendant would like to see his son at equestrian competitions, unfortunately for defendant's son defendant is not permitted to do so. Defendant should have considered the consequences of his actions before he put himself in the position in which he is now.

. . . As requested by plaintiff, defendant should be permanently enjoined from violating plaintiff's determination against him and from attending as a participant, competitor, or spectator any of plaintiff's recognized competitions. . . .

Source: Courtesy of Westlaw; reprinted with permission.

The U.S. Olympic Committee has been involved in a variety of lawsuits dealing with eligibility issues, intellectual property, and premises liability.[14] In Case 13-6, *United States Olympic Committee v. Toy Truck Lines, Inc.*, 237 F.3d 1331 (Fed Cir. 2001), the defendant attempted to

---

[14] *See* Michels v. USOC, 741 F.2d 155 (7th Cir. 1984) (holding a weightlifter had no cause of action under the Amateur Sports Act after he was suspended by the International Weightlifting Federation for impermissible testosterone levels); Ziegelmeyer v. U.S. Olympic Committee, 2006 WL 3359149 (N.Y. 2006) (finding an Olympic speedskater assumed the risk when she fell during practice and was injured when she hit the boards surrounding the rink).

register the mark PAN AMERICAN for miniature and toy model trucks with the U.S. Trademark Office. The trademark examiner found the mark to be registerable. The USOC subsequently filed an opposition to the registration stating that the USOC owned the names PAN AMERICAN GAMES, USA PAN AM TEAM, and PAN AM GAMES and seeking to have the defendant's trademark cancelled. The court found in favor of the USOC based on the Amateur Sports Act.

📖 CASE 13-6 *U.S. Olympic Committee v. Toy Truck Lines, Inc.*

237 F.3d 1331 (Fed Cir. 2001)

PAULINE NEWMAN, Circuit Judge.

Appellant United States Olympic Committee ("USOC") appeals the decision of the Trademark Trial and Appeal Board of the United States Patent and Trademark Office, dismissing USOC's opposition to Toy Truck Lines' application for registration of the mark PAN AMERICAN for "miniature toy trucks and scale model trucks" in International Class 28. The Board erred in declining to consider the intervening enactment of the Olympic and Amateur Sports Act ("OASA"), 36 U.S.C. § 220501 *et seq.*, and applicable precedent.

Discussion

On May 30, 1995 Toy Truck Lines filed an application for registration, based on intent-to-use, of the mark PAN AMERICAN on "miniature toy trucks and scale model trucks." The trademark examiner ruled that the mark was registrable, and passed the application to publication. On May 2, 1997 the USOC timely filed an opposition to the registration, based on its ownership and use of the marks PAN AMERICAN GAMES, USA PAN AM TEAM, and PAN AM GAMES, registered in 1996 and 1997 for use with a variety of goods, typically jewelry, clothing, flags, and promotional novelties, although not on toy and scale model trucks. The USOC argued that the proposed registration would violate sections 2(a) and 2(d) of the Trademark Act. 15 U.S.C. § 1052(a) (prohibiting the registration of marks which falsely suggest a connection with persons, institutions, beliefs, or national symbols); 15 U.S.C. § 1052(d) (prohibiting the registration of marks which would be likely to cause confusion with a previously registered mark).

In its opposition as initially filed the USOC relied on portions of the Amateur Sports Act of 1978, 36 U.S.C. § 371 *et seq.*, which charged the USOC with promotion of the Olympic movement in the United States, including responsibility for financing and controlling the representation of the United States in the Pan American Games. As then in effect, section 110 of the Amateur Sports Act of 1978, 36 U.S.C. § 380, invested the USOC with certain exclusive rights to the use of the word OLYMPIC and related terms in trade:

36 U.S.C. § 380(a). Without the consent of the Corporation [USOC], any person who uses for the purpose of trade, to induce the sale of any goods or services . . .

(3) any trademark, trade name, sign, symbol, or insignia falsely representing association with, or authorization by, the International Olympic Committee or the Corporation; or

(4) the words "Olympic", "Olympiad", "Citius Altius Fortius", or any combination or simulation thereof tending to cause confusion, to cause mistake, to deceive, or to falsely suggest a connection with the Corporation or any Olympic activity;

shall be subject to suit in a civil action by the Corporation for the remedies provided in the Act of July 5, 1946 (60 Stat. 427; popularly known as the Trademark Act of 1946).

See generally O-M Bread, Inc. v. United States Olympic Comm., 65 F.3d 933, 36 USPQ2d 1041 (Fed.Cir.1995) (discussing the Amateur Sports Act of 1978 and its predecessor statute).

In 1998, during the pendency of the opposition, Congress enacted the Olympic and Amateur Sports Act ("OASA"), 36 U.S.C. § 220501 *et seq.*, amending the 1978 Amateur Sports Act. The 1998 Act enlarged the exclusive rights of the USOC as follows:

36 U.S.C. § 220506. Exclusive right to name, seals, emblems, and badges.

(a) Exclusive right of [the USOC].—Except as provided in subsection (d) of this section, the [USOC] has the exclusive right to use—

. . . .

(4) the words "Olympic," "Olympiad," "Citius Altius Fortius," "Paralympic," "Paralympiad," "Pan-American," "America Espirito Sport Fraternite," or any combination of those words.

. . . .

(c) Civil action for unauthorized use. . . . [T]he corporation may file a civil action against a person . . . if the person, without the consent of the corporation, uses for the purpose of trade, [or] to induce the sale of any goods or services

. . . .

> (3) the words described in subsection (a)(4) of this section, or any combination or simulation of those words tending to cause confusion or mistake, to deceive, or to falsely suggest a connection with the corporation or any Olympic, Paralympic, or Pan American Games activity; or
>
> (4) any trademark, trade name, sign, symbol, or insignia falsely representing association with, or authorization by, the International Olympic Committee, the International Paralympic Committee, the Pan American Sports Organization, or the corporation.

Although the USOC cited the 1998 statute in its brief, the Board declined to consider it and the USOC's arguments based thereon, stating: "While opposer refers to the recent amendments to 36 U.S.C. § 380 in its brief, this statute is not a pleaded ground in the opposition and it has not been so considered." The Board then held that the opposition's asserted grounds of violation of sections 2(a) and 2(d) of the Lanham Act had not been established, *i.e.*, that the USOC did not prove that the mark PAN AMERICAN on toy trucks would falsely suggest a connection to the USOC or the Pan American games, and that the USOC did not prove that Toy Truck's intended use of this mark would be likely to cause confusion as to the source or sponsorship of the toy and model trucks. On these grounds the Board dismissed the USOC's opposition.

It was improper for the Board to refuse to consider the 1998 enactment. The general rule is that a tribunal must apply the law as it exists at the time of the decision. Although this rule is subject to exceptions when justice requires, such as when vested rights are materially affected by the change in law, no such reason has been proffered by Toy Truck Lines. Since this application was based solely on "intent to use," with no representation of actual use, there is no suggestion of the existence of any vested property right or investment in trademark use. In this case there is no suggestion that application of the 1998 Act would impair any rights possessed before the enactment, increase Toy Truck's liability, or impose new duties for any past conduct. The Board was promptly advised of the new statute and its direct relationship to trademark use of "Pan American." The USOC's opposition to Toy Truck's application for registration could not be denied without consideration of the effect of the 1998 Act.

The unambiguous statutory language of § 220506(a)(4) reserves to the USOC the commercial use (other than "grandfathered" uses) of the disputed words PAN AMERICAN, without requiring any showing of likelihood of confusion or false connection. As the Court stated in *San Francisco Arts & Athletics, Inc. v. United States Olympic Comm.*, 483 U.S. 522, 531, 107 S.Ct. 2971, 97 L.Ed.2d 427 (1987). . . . :

The protection granted to the USOC's use of the Olympic words and symbols differs from the normal trademark protection in two respects: the USOC need not prove that a contested use is likely to cause confusion, and an unauthorized user of the word does not have available the normal statutory defenses.

Id. at 531, 107 S.Ct. 2971. Accordingly, the Board's findings that there is no likelihood of confusion or false suggestion of connection are irrelevant to the issue. It was incorrect for the Board to dismiss the USOC's opposition to Toy Truck's registration, for as a matter of law the USOC must prevail. We reverse the Board's dismissal of the USOC's opposition, and remand for further proceedings consistent with this decision. . . .

REVERSED AND REMANDED.

Source: Courtesy of Westlaw; reprinted with permission.

THE TED STEVENS OLYMPIC AND AMATEUR SPORTS ACT

The Ted Stevens Olympic and Amateur Sports Act, 36 U.S.C.A. §§ 220501–220529 (formerly known as the Amateur Sports Act of 1978), gives the USOC the authority to serve as the U.S. coordinating body for international amateur athletic competitions. It was created as a response to the President's Commission on Olympic Sports. The purpose of the act is to coordinate amateur athletic activity, give amateur athletes certain rights, and provide a mechanism for national governing bodies. The act amends statutory provisions that relate to the USOC and states that the USOC can recognize any amateur sport group or NGB that files an application and is eligible. Only one NGB can be recognized for each sport. An NGB must be incorporated as a domestic, nonprofit corporation with the purpose of advancing "amateur" athletic competitions. The act also gives detailed information about an NGB's duties and provides guidance on Olympic competitions.

The following are significant portions of the act.

§ 220501. Short Title and Definitions

(a) **Short title.**—This chapter may be cited as the "Ted Stevens Olympic and Amateur Sports Act."

(b) **Definitions.**—For purposes of this chapter—

   (1) "amateur athlete" means an athlete who meets the eligibility standards established by the national governing body or paralympic sports organization for the sport in which the athlete competes.

   (2) "amateur athletic competition" means a contest, game, meet, match, tournament, regatta, or other event in which amateur athletes compete.

   (3) "amateur sports organization" means a not-for-profit corporation, association, or other group organized in the United States that sponsors or arranges an amateur athletic competition.

    (4) "corporation" means the United States Olympic Committee.

    (5) "international amateur athletic competition" means an amateur athletic competition between one or more athletes representing the United States, individually or as a team, and one or more athletes representing a foreign country.

    (6) "national governing body" means an amateur sports organization that is recognized by the corporation. . . .

    (7) "paralympic sports organization" means an amateur sports organization which is recognized by the corporation. . . .

§ 220503. Purposes

The purposes of the corporation are—

    (1) to establish national goals for amateur athletic activities and encourage the attainment of those goals;

    (2) to coordinate and develop amateur athletic activity in the United States directly related to international amateur athletic competition, to foster productive working relationships among sports-related organizations;

    (3) to exercise exclusive jurisdiction, directly or through constituent members of committees, over—

        (A) all matters pertaining to United States participation in the Olympic Games, the Paralympic Games, and the Pan-American Games, including representation of the United States in the games; and

        (B) the organization of the Olympic Games, the Paralympic Games, and the Pan-American Games when held in the United States; . . .

      . . . .

    (8) to provide swift resolution of conflicts and disputes involving amateur athletes, national governing bodies, and amateur sports organizations, and protect the opportunity of any amateur athlete, coach, trainer, manager, administrator, or official to participate in amateur athletic competition; . . .

§ 220505. Powers

(a) Constitution and bylaws.—The corporation shall adopt a constitution and bylaws. . . .

(b) General corporate powers.—The corporation may—

    (1) adopt and alter a corporate seal;

    (2) establish and maintain offices to conduct the affairs of the corporation;

(3) make contracts;

(4) accept gifts, legacies, and devises in furtherance of its corporate purposes;

(5) acquire, own, lease, encumber, and transfer property as necessary to carry out the purposes of the corporation;

(6) borrow money, issue instruments of indebtedness, and secure its obligations by granting security interests in its property;

(7) publish a magazine, newspaper, and other publications consistent with its corporate purposes;

(8) approve and revoke membership in the corporation;

(9) sue and be sued, except that any civil action brought in a State court against the corporation and solely relating to the corporation's responsibilities under this chapter shall be removed, at the request of the corporation, to the district court of the United States in the district in which the action was brought, and such district court shall have original jurisdiction over the action without regard to the amount in controversy or citizenship of the parties involved, and except that neither this paragraph nor any other provision of this chapter shall create a private right of action under this chapter; and

(10) do any other act necessary and proper to carry out the purposes of the corporation.

(c) Powers related to amateur athletics and the Olympic Games.—The corporation may—

(1) serve as the coordinating body for amateur athletic activity in the United States directly related to international amateur athletic competition;

(2) represent the United States as its national Olympic committee in relations with the International Olympic Committee and the Pan-American Sports Organization and as its national Paralympic committee in relations with the International Paralympic Committee;

(3) organize, finance, and control the representation of the United States in the competitions and events of the Olympic Games, the Paralympic Games, and the Pan-American Games, and obtain, directly or by delegation to the appropriate national governing body, amateur representation for those games;

(4) recognize eligible amateur sports organizations as national governing bodies for any sport that is included on the program of the Olympic Games or the Pan-American Games, or as paralympic sports organizations for any sport that is included on the program of the Paralympic Games;

(5) facilitate, through orderly and effective administrative procedures, the resolution of conflicts or disputes that involve any of its members and any amateur athlete, coach, trainer, manager, administrator, official, national governing body, or amateur sports organization and that arise in connection with their eligibility for and participation in the Olympic Games, the Paralympic Games, the Pan-American Games, world championship competition, the Pan-American world championship competition, or other protected competition as defined in the constitution and bylaws of the corporation; . . .

§ 220509. Resolution of Disputes

(a) General.—The corporation shall establish and maintain provisions in its constitution and bylaws for the swift and equitable resolution of disputes involving any of its members and relating to the opportunity of an amateur athlete, coach, trainer, manager, administrator, or official to participate in the Olympic Games, the Paralympic Games, the Pan-American Games, world championship competition, or other protected competition as defined in the constitution and bylaws of the corporation. . . .

§ 220512. Complete Teams

In obtaining representation for the United States in each competition and event of the Olympic Games, Paralympic Games, and Pan-American Games, the corporation, either directly or by delegation to the appropriate national governing body or paralympic sports organization, may select, but is not obligated to select (even if not selecting will result in an incomplete team for an event), athletes who have not met the eligibility standard of the national governing body and the corporation, when the number of athletes who have met the eligibility standards of such entities is insufficient to fill the roster for an event.

. . . .

Subchapter II. National Governing Bodies

§ 220521. Recognition of Amateur Sports Organizations as National Governing Bodies

(a) General authority.—For any sport which is included on the program of the Olympic Games, the Paralympic Games, or the Pan-American Games, the corporation is authorized to recognize as a national governing body (in the case of a sport on the program of the Olympic Games or Pan-American Games) or as a paralympic sports organization (in the case of a sport on the program of the Paralympic Games for which a national governing body has not been designated under section 220522(b)) an amateur sports organization which files an application and is eligible for such recognition in accordance with the provisions of subsection (a) or (b) of section 220522. The corporation may recognize only one national governing body for each sport for which an application is made and approved. . . .

(b) Public hearing.—Before recognizing an organization as a national governing body, the corporation shall hold at least 2 public hearings on the application. . . .

§ 220523. Authority of National Governing Bodies

(a) Authority.—For the sport that it governs, a national governing body may—

(1) represent the United States in the appropriate international sports federation;

. . . .

(3) serve as the coordinating body for amateur athletic activity in the United States;

. . . .

(5) conduct amateur athletic competition, including national championships, and international amateur athletic competition in the United States, and establish procedures for determining eligibility standards for participation in competition. . . ;

(6) recommend to the corporation individuals and teams to represent the United States in the Olympic Games, the Paralympic Games, and the Pan-American Games; and

(7) designate individuals and teams to represent the United States in international amateur athletic competition (other than the Olympic Games, the Paralympic Games, and the Pan-American Games) and certify, in accordance with applicable international rules, the amateur eligibility of those individuals and teams. . . .

§ 220524. General Duties of National Governing Bodies

. . . .

§ 220527. Complaints Against National Governing Bodies

. . . .

§ 220529. Arbitration of Corporation Determinations

(a) **Right to review.**—A party aggrieved by a determination of the corporation . . . may obtain review by any regional office of the American Arbitration Association.

COURT OF ARBITRATION FOR SPORT

With the sporting world becoming more international, a body was necessary to handle disputes arising from international sports events on a worldwide basis. National courts are not the most convenient places to resolve the kinds of disputes that might occur on an international level in the sporting world. In *Michels v. USOC*, 741 F.2d 155, 159 (7th Cir. 1984) (J. Posner, concurring), the court stated, "[T]here can be few less suitable bodies than the federal courts for determining the eligibility, or the procedures for determining the eligibility, of athletes to compete in the Olympic Games." Numerous problems can arise concerning jurisdiction and choice of law. Therefore, the IOC established the Court of Arbitration for Sport (CAS) in 1984.[15] The purpose of the CAS is to provide a central specialized authority to decide sports-related disputes.

The CAS is based in Switzerland and subject to Swiss law. It handles both professional and amateur sports and possesses broad jurisdiction over various types of sports-related disputes. The CAS hears cases dealing with athlete discipline, eligibility, and commercial disputes. The CAS does not resolve disputes related to the rules of the game, scheduling of competition, or prescribed dimensions of the playing field. The CAS addresses issues dealing with eligibility, suspension of athletes, athlete drug testing, television rights, licensing, sponsorship, and the nationality of athletes for purposes of competition. Even though it is referred to as a court, the CAS is actually an international alternative dispute resolution body that uses arbitration as a method to resolve disputes. The CAS is governed by the Code of Sports-Related Arbitration. Participants can also choose mediation as a method to attempt to resolve the dispute.

The World Anti-Doping Agency (WADA) has designated the CAS as the exclusive body concerning all doping issues that occur during international events. It is also the exclusive body for resolving disputes relating to the Olympics. The IOC as well as all Olympic IFs have agreed to use the CAS to resolve disputes. The international federations and NGBs require all athletes who have a dispute with an IF to submit to the jurisdiction of the CAS to resolve their disputes. The Olympic Athlete Entry Form requires all Olympians to agree to the jurisdiction of the CAS to resolve all disputes that occur during the Olympic Games. Article 74 of the Olympic Charter reads as follows:

> Any dispute arising on the occasion of, or in connection with, the Olympic Games shall be submitted exclusively to the Court of Arbitration for Sport, in accordance with the Code of Sports-Related Arbitration.

---

[15] TAS/CAS, http://www.tas-cas.org.

The CAS consists of at least 150 arbitrators from over 35 countries who specialize in sports law and arbitration. Each arbitrator is appointed for a four-year term. Although arbitrators are not bound to comply with the principle of stare decisis, they usually do.

The CAS has a mediation system in place as well. The CAS mediation rules define mediation as follows:

> CAS Mediation is a non-binding and informal procedure, based on a mediation agreement in which each party undertakes to attempt in good faith to negotiate with the other party, and with the assistance of a CAS mediator, with a view to settling a sports-related dispute.[16]

In 1996 the Ad hoc Division of the CAS was created, which has the task of settling disputes on short notice during the Olympics.[17] Decisions must be submitted within 24 hours unless the time limit is extended by the president of the Ad hoc Division.

The CAS can also issue advisory opinions that are known as "Consultation Proceedings." Rule 60 states:

> The IOC, the IFs, the NOCs, WADA, the associations recognized by the IOC and the OCOGs, may request an advisory opinion from the CAS about any legal issue with respect to the practice or development of sport or any activity related to sports. The request for an opinion shall be addressed to the CAS and accompanied by any document likely to assist the Panel entrusted with giving the opinion.[18]

Although the CAS is based in Switzerland, it also has locations in Sydney, Australia, and New York. Swiss law governs all CAS proceedings. Parties are allowed to be represented by counsel during all CAS proceedings. Parties may also select an arbitrator who will hear the dispute, except when the case is in the Ad hoc Division.

The advantages of the CAS procedures are much like other dispute resolution processes. They provide confidentiality, flexibility, and can result in reduced costs for all parties. CAS decisions are final and binding on the parties. They can be enforced internationally by the New York Convention on the Recognition and Enforcement of foreign Arbitral Awards.

The CAS can award damages as well as costs against parties.[19] A CAS decision can only be appealed to the Swiss Federal Supreme Court .[20] A substantial body of law has been developed by the CAS, which hears a variety of cases.[21]

Athlete Oscar Pistorius has confronted obstacles his entire life. He was born without fibulas (the long thin outer bone between the knee and the ankle) and his legs were amputated below the knee when he was eleven months old. That did not prevent him from becoming a world-class athlete. In 2004 he suffered an injury while playing rugby and began running competitively to rehabilitate himself. In the 2004 Paralympics Games in Athens he won the 200 meters. In Case 13-7, *Arbitration*

---

[16] Article 1, para 1 of the CAS Mediation Rules.

[17] For further study *see,* Richard H. McLaren, *International Sports Law Perspective: Introducing the Court of Arbitration for Sport: The Ad Hoc Division at the Olympic Games,* Marquette Sports Law Review, Fall, 2001.

[18] Rule 60, D. Special Provisions Applicable to the Consultation Proceedings, Tribunal Arbitral Du Sport.

[19] For further studies *see,* James A.R. Nafziger, *International Sports Law as a Process for Resolving Disputes,* International and Comparative Law Quarterly, 1996, pp. 130=149.

[20] *Switzerland's Federal Code on Private International Law,* Art. 191, 2. Court of Appeal, (December 18, 1987).

[21] CAS decisions can be viewed at www.tas-cas.org/. For further examination of the CAS, see R. McLaren, *The CAS Ad Hoc Division at the Athens Olympic Games,* 15 Marq. Sports L. Rev. 175 (2004); also see Ian Blacksaw, Robert Siekmann, & Janwillem Soek, The Court of Arbitration for Sport, 1984–2004 (2006).

CAS 2008/A/1480 Pistorius v. IAAF, Pistorius appealed to the CAS to overturn a ruling by the IAAF that prevented him from competing because the IAAF said his carbon fiber blades gave him a mechanical advantage over other runners.[22]

📖 CASE 13-7 *Arbitration CAS 2008/A/1480 Pistorius v. IAAF, Award of 16 May 2008*

Athletics

Eligibility for an athlete with disabilities to compete in IAAF-sanctioned events alongside able-bodied athlete

No proven biochemical or metabolic advantage over other athletes due to the prosthesis

1. IAAF Rule 144.2(e) states that "For the purposes of this Rule, the following shall be considered assistance, and are therefore not allowed: [. . .] (e) Use of any technical device that incorporates springs, wheels, or any other element that provides the user with an advantage over another athlete not using such a device." Where there is no sufficient evidence of any metabolic advantage in favour of a disabled athlete-a double-amputee using a prosthesis-due to the fact that the disabled athlete uses the same oxygen amounts as able-bodied runners at a sub-maximal running speed and no evidence that the biomechanical effects of using this particular prosthetic device gives the athlete an advantage over other athletes not using the device, the disabled athlete cannot be banned to compete in international IAAF-sanctioned events alongside able-bodied athlete.

The Appellant, Oscar Pistorius ("Mr. Pistorius") is a citizen of, and resident in, the Republic of South Africa. He is a professional athlete competing in 100, 200 and 400 meter sprints.

The Respondent, the International Association of Athletics Federations (IAAF; the "Federation"), governs the sport of athletics throughout the world and recognized as such by the International Olympic Committee . . .

In this arbitration, Mr. Pistorius appeals Decision No. 2008/01 of the IAAF Council on 14 January 2008 (the "IAAF Decision") that the "Cheetah" prosthetic legs worn by Mr. Pistorius, who has been a double amputee since he was eleven months old, constituted a technical device and provided him with an advantage over an able-bodied athlete in violation of IAAF Competition Rule 144.2(e).

---

[22] Joshua Robinson, *Ruling Halts Amputee Sprinter's Olympic Bid,* The New York Times, January 15, 2008.

As a result of the IAAF Decision, Mr. Pistorius is banned from competing against able-bodied athletes in IAAF-sanctioned events . . .

For participation in sporting activities Mr. Pistorius uses a prosthesis known as the *Cheetah Flex-Foot*, supplied by a company headquartered in Iceland, Össur HF ("Össur"). The *Cheetah Flex-Foot* is designed for single and double transtibial (below-the-knee) and transfemoral (above-the-knee) amputees who intend to run at recreational and/or competitive levels. It has been used by many single and double amputees, almost unchanged, since 1997 . . .

The IAAF official who had been given responsibility by the President of the IAAF to evaluate whether Mr. Pistorius' prostheses contravened the new Rule 144.2(e) was Dr. Elio Locatelli . . .

In order to take the evaluation further Dr. Locatelli asked Professor Peter Brüggemann at the Institute of Biomechanics and Orthopaedics at the German Sport University in Cologne if he could conduct a biomechanical study to demonstrate whether or not Mr. Pistorius' prosthetic limbs gave him an advantage over other athletes . . .

Prof. Brüggemann and his colleagues Messrs Arampatzis and Emrich issued the Cologne Report on 15 December 2007. The abstract of the Report contained the following conclusory passage:

> The hypothesis that the transtibial amputee's metabolic capacity is higher than that of the healthy counterparts was rejected. The metabolic tests indicated a lower aerobic capacity of the amputee than of the controls. In the 400 m race the handicapped athlete's VO2 uptake was 25% lower than the oxygen consumption of the sound controls, which achieved about the same final time. The joint kinetics of the ankle joints of the sound legs and the "artificial ankle joint" of the prosthesis were found to be significantly different. Energy return was clearly higher in the prostheses than in the human ankle joints. The kinetics of knee and hip joints were also affected by the prostheses during stance. The swing phase did not demonstrate any advantages for the natural legs in relation with artificial limbs. In total the double transtibial amputee received significant biomechanical advantages by the prosthesis in comparison to sprinting with natural human legs. The hypothesis that the prostheses lead to biomechanical disadvantages was rejected. Finally it was shown that fast running with the dedicated Cheetah prosthesis is a different kind of locomotion than sprinting with natural human legs. The "bouncing" locomotion is related to lower metabolic cost.

On 14 January 2008, the IAAF Council issued a Decision which included the following findings:

running with these prostheses requires a less-important vertical
movement associated with a lesser mechanical effort to raise the
body, and the energy loss resulting from the use of these prostheses is significantly lower than that resulting from a human
ankle joint at a maximal sprint speed.

Based on these findings the IAAF ruled that the *Cheetah Flex-Foot* pros-
thetics used by Mr. Pistorius were to be considered as a . . . *technical
device that incorporates springs, wheels or any other element that provides the user with an advantage over valid athletes,* and therefore
contravened Rule 144.2(e).

Mr. Pistorius was thus declared ineligible to compete in IAAF-sanctioned
events with immediate effect.

In his Statement of Appeal, Mr. Pistorius requested the CAS to vacate
the IAAF Decision, and to determine that he may participate in competitions held under the IAAF Rules using his *Cheetah* prosthetic limbs.

Law

The Issues to be Determined

5. The issues raised by Mr. Pistorius in his appeal may be
   categorised under [as] . . . (iv) Was the IAAF Decision wrong
   in determining that Mr. Pistorius' use of the *Cheetah Flex-Foot*
   device contravenes Rule 144.2(e)?

The Panel's Analysis

*Issue (iv) Was the IAAF Council's Decision wrong in determining that
Mr. Pistorius' use of the Cheetah Flex-Foot device contravenes Rule
144.2(e)?*

31. The Panel's point of departure for this part of the analysis is
    Rule 144.2(e), adopted by the IAAF's Council at its meeting in
    Mombasa, Kenya on 26 March 2007. As stated above, it reads as fol-
    lows:

    > For the purposes of this Rule, the following shall be consid-
    > ered assistance, and are therefore not allowed: [. . .] (e)
    > Use of any technical device that incorporates springs, wheels,
    > or any other element that provides the user with an advantage
    > over another athlete not using such a device.

32. Without implying any criticism of the draftsman, who faced an extra-
    ordinarily difficult task, the Panel considers that this provision

is a masterpiece of ambiguity. What constitutes a *technical device*? For the purposes of the present enquiry, the Panel is prepared to assume that a passive prosthetic such as the *Cheetah Flex-Foot* is to be considered as a "technical device," even though this proposition may not be wholly free from doubt.

33. What constitutes a device that *incorporates springs*? Technically, almost every non-brittle material object is a "spring" in the sense that it has elasticity. Certainly the *Cheetah Flex-Foot* is a "spring," but does it *incorporate* a "spring"? A natural human leg is itself a "spring."

34. Then there is the critical question of the meaning of an *advantage . . . over another athlete*. It was urged on the Panel by the IAAF's counsel that the ordinary and natural meaning of the word *advantage* is absolute, in the sense that if a *technical device* is used, and is determined (presumably by an appropriate and fair process) to provide an athlete with any *advantage*, however small, in any part of a competition, that device must render that athlete ineligible to compete regardless of any compensating disadvantages.

35. The Panel does not accept this proposition. Of course, athletes should not be forced to compete against persons who use powered aids such as motors, wheels, springs (as in "pogo sticks," for example), or other active propulsive devices. This is not in doubt, and interpreted in this way the new Rule 144.2(e) is a sensible and appropriate rule. But to propose that a passive device such as the *Cheetah Flex-Foot* as used by Mr. Pistorius should be classified as contravening that Rule without convincing scientific proof that it provides him with *an overall net advantage* over other athletes flies in the face of both legal principle and common-sense. The rule specifically prohibits a technical device that . . . *provides the user with an advantage over an athlete not using that device*. If the use of the device provides more disadvantages than advantages, then it cannot reasonably be said to provide an advantage over other athletes, because the user is actually at a competitive disadvantage. That is the only sensible reading of the terms of Rule 144.2(e).

36. The Panel notes that this interpretation of Rule 144.2(e) was effectively adopted by Dr. Locatelli of the IAAF in his testimony at the hearing, when he said that the rule would not prohibit Mr. Pistorius from running in 100-metre or 200-metre races. Dr. Locatelli said that such distances did not allow Mr. Pistorius to catch up from his slower start. Thus, Dr. Locatelli focused on the overall effect of the prosthesis and not on whether Mr. Pistorius had an advantage at only one point in the race.

37. Unfortunately, as Prof. Brüggemann made clear during the hearing, the IAAF did not ask him to determine whether or not Mr. Pistorius' use of the *Cheetah Flex-Foot* prosthesis provided him with an overall net advantage or disadvantage. The Cologne Report therefore does not address the central question that the Panel is required to answer in this appeal.

The Panel's Assessment of the Evidence

42. As shown in the quotation above from the abstract to the Cologne Report, and as stated in the IAAF Decision, the finding of an advantage in using the *Cheetah Flex-Foot* prosthesis comes principally from two elements of the Cologne Report: First, Mr. Pistorius, in using the device, does not have as much vertical force with each step; in other words, he runs in a flatter manner than able-bodied runners. All the experts agreed that these measurements were valid. Second, Mr. Pistorius uses less metabolic energy in running, perhaps as a result of that flatter running. These test results were challenged.

43. The experts presented by Mr. Pistorius conducted their own tests on him and on able-bodied athletes as controls at a laboratory in Houston in February 2008 (the "Houston Report"). Among other things, tests set out in the Houston Report found that Mr. Pistorius used the same oxygen amounts as able-bodied runners at a submaximal running speed, and thus did not have a metabolic advantage. Other tests also showed that Mr. Pistorius fatigued normally. Again, the experts agreed that these test results were valid. The Houston Report also tested the amount of energy loss from the *Cheetah Flex-Foot* prosthesis against the intact human leg, which includes tendons and other elements that generate positive energy (and which, for obvious reasons, an amputated athlete would not have). It is common ground that the Cologne Report did not measure any of these elements.

44. In summary, the Panel determines that the IAAF has not met its "on the balance of probability" burden of proof that Rule 144.2(e) is contravened by Mr. Pistorius' use of the *Cheetah Flex Foot* prosthesis for several reasons. First, as noted above, a violation would only occur if the user of the prosthesis gained an *overall net advantage* over other runners, and the IAAF did not ask Prof. Brüggemann and his colleagues to make that determination. The terms of reference put to Prof. Brüggemann and his team by the IAAF did not propose the appropriate question.

45. The testing protocol that he prepared for the purposes of writing the Cologne Report, on the basis of his instructions from the

IAAF, was not designed to provide a scientific opinion as to whether Mr. Pistorius' *Cheetah Flex-Foot* prosthesis provided him with an overall net advantage over other athletes not using such devices. The point was stated clearly by Dr. Locatelli in one of his press interviews, when he said . . . *we are looking for advantages, not for disadvantages*. The experts also agreed at the hearing that *neither the Cologne nor Houston studies have quantified all of the possible advantages or disadvantages of Mr. Pistorius in a 400m race*.

46. Secondly, the Panel is not persuaded that there is sufficient evidence of any metabolic advantage in favour of a double amputee using the *Cheetah Flex-Foot*. Certainly, the evidence presented in the Cologne Report is not capable of satisfying the burden of proof that is acknowledged by the IAAF. The IAAF seemed to recognize this fact at the hearing as it focused on the biomechanical aspects of the Cologne Report, and it acknowledged that most of the metabolic findings, including its blood lactate measurements, were not conclusive.

47. Similarly, the IAAF has not proven the other basis of the IAAF Decision: namely that the biomechanical effects of using the particular prosthetic device give Mr. Pistorius an advantage over other athletes not using the device. Thus, the Cologne Report's finding, on which the IAAF Decision relied, that Mr. Pistorius uses less vertical force and runs in a flatter manner may be a *disadvantage* rather than *an advantage*.

48. In addition, while the Cologne Report found less energy loss in the *Cheetah Flex-Foot* prosthesis than in the human ankle, the scientific experts all agreed that the energy "lost" in the ankle could be transferred elsewhere in the body, through tendons, ligaments and muscles etc, because the human body does not like to lose energy. They agreed that that such a transfer cannot be properly measured or currently understood. Thus, based on current scientific knowledge, it appears to be impracticable to assess definitively whether the *Cheetah Flex-Foot* prosthesis acts as more than, or less than, the human ankle and lower leg, in terms of "spring-like" quality.

49. Moreover, the scientific experts agreed that *a mechanical advantage provided by a prosthetic leg would be expected to lead to a metabolic advantage for a runner*. As noted above, neither the Cologne Report nor the Houston Report showed such a metabolic advantage.

50. In the light of the Panel's analysis of the facts, the scientific expert opinions and the legal principles involved, the Panel has no doubt in finding that the IAAF has failed to satisfy the burden of proof that it accepts. It follows that Mr. Pistorius' appeal must be upheld.

The Court of Arbitration for Sport Rules

1. The IAAF having failed to satisfy the applicable burden of proof that it expressly acknowledged, the appeal filed by Oscar Pistorius on 13 February 2008 must be upheld.

2. Accordingly, the IAAF Council's Decision no. 2008/1 of 14 January 2008 is revoked with immediate effect, and the athlete is currently eligible to compete in IAAF-sanctioned events while wearing the Össur *Cheetah Flex-Foot* prosthesis model as used in the Cologne tests and presented as an exhibit at the Hearing of this appeal.

In the following Case 13-8, the question of eligibility was at issue in the Ad hoc Division at the 2008 Beijing Olympics.

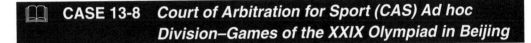

CASE 13-8 *Court of Arbitration for Sport (CAS) Ad hoc Division–Games of the XXIX Olympiad in Beijing*

CAS Arbitration No. OG 08/006

1. Introduction

1.1 This is an application by the National Olympic Committee of Moldova ("MNOC") to set aside the decision of the International Olympic Committee ("IOC"), dated 7 August 2008, in terms of which it held that one Mr. Octavian Gutu was not eligible to represent the Republic of Moldova in the Beijing 2008 Olympic Games.

2. The Facts

2.1 The basis of the written application submitted to ad hoc Division of the Court of Arbitration for Sport ("CAS") and placed before this Panel for adjudication is that Mr. Gutu is a citizen of Moldova, where he was born and educated and of which the government has financially supported him. He has represented Moldova as a swimmer and was a national swimming champion there in 2008. At the 2007 Swimming World Championships held in Melbourne, Australia, however, he represented Romania. This representation, the MNOC stated, was "without any approval by Moldova" and was hence "illegal." As such he should be divested of all awards arising from his performances at the championships and he should be allowed to represent Moldova once again.

2.2 The difficulty arising from this succinct presentation of the facts is that it omits to append any supporting documentation, in the form of an identity certificate, passport or the like, to identify Mr. Gutu and to indicate his nationality. It likewise omits to indicate under what circumstances he was able to represent Romania in the Swimming World Championships of 2007 without the necessary approval of the relevant authorities of Moldova or Romania and without the sanction of FINA.

2.3 At the hearing of the application a document signed by one Mr. G Popovici, the Secretary General of the MNOC and Chef de Mission of the Moldova Olympic Team to Beijing, was submitted. It was dated 6 August 2008 and was directed to one Mr. P Miró, the Director of the NOC Relations Department of the IOC. From this it appears that Mr. Gutu represented Moldova in the Athens 2004 Olympic Games. His participation in the Swimming World Championships of 2007 on behalf of Romania was without the permission of the Moldova Swimming Association and he has not, since that time, represented Romania. It is then baldly stated, without reference to any dates, times or specific events, that he complied with the Beijing Olympic standard and won the championship of Moldova in 2008. Furthermore the RNOC and the Romanian Swimming Association do not object to his representing Moldova at the Olympic Games.

2.4 In this regard Mr. Popovici referred to a letter dated 11 June 2008 from the Romanian Swimming and Modern Pentathlon Federation to the President of the MNOC stating that Mr. Gutu is not a member of the Romanian Olympic team and as such it had no objection to his participation on behalf of Moldova in the Beijing Olympics. The RNOC likewise, in a letter to the MNOC dated 9 July 2008, voiced no opposition to his participating in the Beijing Olympics as a member of the Moldova team. Significantly, no mention was made of the fact that he represented Romania in the 2007 World Swimming Championships and whether or not, as the MNOC has suggested, such representation was not approved and was hence illegal.

2.5 Mr. Cai submitted, without tendering any evidence or supporting documentation, that Mr. Gutu in fact has dual nationality, namely that of Moldova and Romania. He realised, however, that he was not entitled to represent Romania in the 2007 World Swimming Championships without the necessary permission and for that reason was prepared to have his participation at such championships invalidated. As a citizen and national of Moldova he was entitled to represent it in the Olympics.

2.6 In his argument on behalf of the IOC Mr. Stupp relied on Rule 42 of the Olympic Charter, the bye-law to which requires a period of

three years to lapse since the competitor in question last represented his former country. This period may be reduced or waived
only with the approval of the relevant National Olympic Committees and the relevant International Federation. In the present
case the said time period has not expired and there has been no
approval by FINA placed before the Panel. In this regard it may
be pointed out that the CAS office attempted to communicate with
FINA with a view to inviting it to participate in the hearing.
Unfortunately no contact was made and the hearing proceeded without
any input from FINA.

3. Jurisdiction

. . . .

3.2 The jurisdiction of the CAS ad hoc Division arises out of Rule 59
of the Olympic Charter.

4. Applicable Law

4.1 Sections 1 and 2 of the Bye-Law to Rule 42 of the Olympic Charter
read thus: *1. A competitor who is a national of two or more countries at the same time may represent either one of them, as he may
elect. However, after having represented one country in the
Olympic Games, in continental or regional games or in world or
regional championships recognised by the relevant IF, he may not
represent another country unless he meets the conditions set forth
in paragraph 2 below that apply to persons who have changed their
nationality or acquired a new nationality.*

*2. A competitor who has represented one country in the Olympic
Games, in continental or regional games or in world or regional
championships recognised by the relevant IF, and who has changed
his nationality or acquired a new nationality, may participate in
the Olympic Games to represent his new country provided that at
least three years have passed since the competitor last represented his former country. This period may be reduced or even cancelled, with the agreement of the NOCs and IF concerned, by the
IOC Executive Board, which takes into account the circumstances of
each case.*

5. Consideration of the Facts and the Applicable Law

5.1 When these Charter provisions are considered against the background of the facts set forth above, it is quite clear that the

MNOC has come nowhere near establishing that Mr. Gutu is entitled to participate in the Beijing Olympic Games as a member of the Olympic Team of Moldova. It may well be that the RNOC and MNOC have not opposed his participation, but there is clearly no indication whatever that the relevant international federation, FINA, has considered and approved it. In any event the glaring omissions in the application render the proper consideration thereof difficult, if not impossible.

5.2 The fact that Mr. Gutu is allegedly prepared to have his participation for Romania in the 2007 Swimming World Championships invalidated, is quite irrelevant for purposes of the present application. The provisions of the cited Bye-Law to Rule 42 of the Olympic Charter is couched in peremptory terms and this Panel has no authority to waive any part thereof. For the rest the legality or otherwise of Mr. Gutu's participation for Romania at such Championships is a matter for the consideration of FINA and not this Panel.

5.3 In this regard the Panel understands that the drafters of the Charter had the following objective: the holder of dual or multiple nationalities should not be entitled to switch allegiance from the one to the other at his or her convenience. This would make it possible for an athlete to move, opportunistically, from one team to another should the former not select him or her and the latter be willing to include him or her in its national team. Such conduct would not be compatible with the spirit of Rule 42 of the Olympic Charter.

6. Decision

In view of these considerations it must be held that the MNOC has failed to persuade this Panel that it is entitled to the relief sought.

MISCELLANEOUS INTERNATIONAL ISSUES

Many players on U.S. sports teams are born outside the United States. In Case 13-9, *Grimson v. I.N.S.* Stu Grimson, "the Grim Reaper," one of hockey's tough guys and long considered one of the league's elite fighters,[23] sued the Immigration and Naturalization Service (INS) over the denial of his visa petition. Grimson played in the NHL from 1998 to 2002, appearing in 729 regular games.

---

[23] Elliott Teaford, *Tough Love*, Los Angeles Times, December 14, 1998.

He racked up a very impressive 2,113 penalty minutes during his career, ranking him 41st on the all-time penalty minutes leaders in NHL history.

Grimson had sought classification as a priority worker of extraordinary skill with the INS and was denied. He appealed, claiming that his skill as a hockey player allowed him to achieve national fame and should qualify him as an alien with extraordinary ability under U.S. law. Grimson graduated from the University of Memphis Law School in 2005 and completed his undergraduate degree in economics at the University of Minnesota while playing in the NHL. (Perhaps this case, which took several years to resolve, encouraged Grimson to study the law.)

CASE 13-9 *Grimson v. INS*

934 F. Supp. 965 (N.D. Ill. 1996)

GETTLEMAN, District Judge.

This case, much like the National Hockey League playoffs and the Energizer Bunny, just keeps going and going and going. Plaintiff Allan Stuart Grimson, a citizen of Canada, has filed a complaint for declaratory and injunctive relief pursuant to 28 U.S.C. §§ 2201, 1361, seeking to overturn defendant Immigration and Naturalization Service's ("INS") denial of his visa petition. For the reasons set forth below . . . the decision of the INS is reversed.

Procedural History

. . . Plaintiff is a professional hockey player. He has played in the "professional leagues" since the 1982–83 season when he began playing for the Regina, Saskatchewan team in the now defunct World Hockey League. He has been playing in the NHL since the 1989 season. He is currently a member of the Detroit Red Wings, one of the better teams in the league.

Plaintiff initially filed a visa petition with defendant INS on January 20, 1993, seeking classification as a priority worker of extraordinary ability pursuant to 8 U.S.C. § 1153(b)(1)(A). The petition was denied by the Director of the INS Northern Service Center on the ground that plaintiff had failed to demonstrate that he was a player of extraordinary ability as defined by the INS. Plaintiff appealed to the Administrative Appeals Unit ("AAU"), contending that he had achieved sustained national and international acclaim as a professional hockey player, and that the Northern Service Center had recently classified four other hockey players of comparable ability as aliens of extraordinary ability.

The AAU affirmed the denial of plaintiff's petition, holding that, "while the record indicates that the petitioner had played several seasons with an NHL team, it has not been established that the petitioner has achieved the sustained national or international acclaim required for classification as an alien with extraordinary ability, that he is one of the small percentage who have risen to the very top of his field of endeavor, or that his entry into the United States would substantially benefit prospectively the United States."

On March 23, 1995, this court issued a memorandum opinion and order again remanding the case to the INS for further evidentiary proceedings. This court specifically directed plaintiff to submit and defendant to consider evidence regarding the necessity of a player with plaintiff's style of play and abilities, and evidence comparing his skill, salary level and other abilities to those of comparable players in the NHL, players who fulfill the same role for their respective teams. In addition, the court directed defendant to consider plaintiff's argument that a sustained career in the NHL demonstrates extraordinary ability.

Consistent with this court's instruction, on remand plaintiff submitted evidence of his current salary and contract with the Detroit Red Wings, a table from the *Hockey News* showing the 1996 players' salaries, newspaper and magazine articles about plaintiff, and an affidavit from Darren Pang, former renown[ed] NHL goal tender and current television broadcaster and NHL analyst for ESPN. Pang is a recognized expert on NHL hockey. Pang's affidavit lists all the "enforcers" in the league and their current salaries. It also sets forth the necessity for an enforcer, and indicates that most teams carry two such players on their rosters. Finally, Pang's affidavit indicates that plaintiff is currently the third rated and third highest paid enforcer in the NHL (the other two being paid more because of their goal scoring ability), and that plaintiff was rated the fifth best enforcer in 1993 when he filed his original petition.

Standard of Review

This court's review in this case is limited to the determination of whether the INS's denial of plaintiff's visa petition constituted an abuse of discretion. The test for abuse of discretion in an immigration case is as follows:

> The decision must be upheld unless it was made without a rational explanation, inexplicably departs from established policies, or rests on an impermissible basis such as invidious discrimination against a particular race or group.

Discussion

As in plaintiff's previous case, this case turns on the interpretation of "extraordinary ability" as used in the priority worker category under 8 U.S.C. § 1153(b)(1)(A)(i), which provides:

(b) Preference allocation for employment-based immigrants

Aliens subject to the worldwide level specified in section 1151(d) of this title for employment-based immigrants in a fiscal year shall be allotted visas as follows:

(1) Priority workers

Visas shall first be made available in a number not to exceed 28.6 percent of such worldwide level, plus any visas not required for the classes specified in paragraphs (4) and (5), to qualified immigrants who are aliens described in any of the following subparagraphs (A) through (c):

(A) Aliens with extraordinary ability

An alien is described in this subparagraph if—

(i) the alien has extraordinary ability in the sciences, arts, education, business, or athletics which has been demonstrated by sustained national or international acclaim and whose achievements have been recognized in the field through extensive documentation.

The statute itself does not define extraordinary ability; however, the regulations promulgated by the INS define the term as "a level of expertise indicating that the individual is one of that small percentage who has risen to the very top of the field of endeavor." A petition for relief under this section must be accompanied by evidence that the alien has "sustained national or international acclaim and that his or her achievements have been recognized in the field of expertise." The regulations set forth various types of evidence that may be submitted to meet this evidentiary burden, including the documentation of memberships and associations which require outstanding achievements, major media publications relating to the alien's work in the field at issue, and evidence that the alien has commanded a large salary in relation to others in the field.

On remand from this court, the Director again completely rejected all plaintiff's evidence and denied his petition. . . .

Next, the Director rejected plaintiff's argument that a sustained career in professional hockey and four years in the NHL should be considered as evidence of extraordinary ability. The Director determined that plaintiff had failed to present evidence that four years in the

NHL as an enforcer qualified as a sustained career. The Director then rejected those portions of Pang's affidavit in which he attested that plaintiff's $300,000 salary in 1993 ranked him among the highest paid enforcers, and that plaintiff was considered among the top five enforcers in the league at that time. The basis for rejecting this evidence was that the affidavit contained no backup information for what the Director determined to be conclusory statements. The affidavit, however, indicates Mr. Pang's background and extensive knowledge of the NHL. He clearly states that he is familiar with plaintiff and the other enforcers in the league, and gives a basis for his opinions. He further states that if called to testify, he would testify that in his opinion in 1993 plaintiff was one of the top five enforcers in the league, and was so considered among his peers.

It is apparent to this court that at the heart of defendant's refusal to grant plaintiff a visa (as it has to other comparable NHL players) is its distaste for the role he plays on a hockey team. As stated in the Director's decision, "the service has never argued that the role of enforcer is not prevalent in the NHL. The *necessity* of such a role appears to be debatable. The service does argue that the sport itself has never condoned the kind of activity that petitioner is known for, as evidenced by the number of penalty minutes he is charged." The decision further states, "[A]t the time the petition was filed, the petitioner's main claim to fame was that he held the record for the most penalty minutes in a game. The amount of penalties the petitioner amasses is indicative of the amount of fighting he does but quantity does not equate to extraordinary ability." Despite this language, however, the only evidence presented to the Director was that plaintiff was the fifth best enforcer in the league at the time he filed his petition. The decision to simply ignore this evidence was an abuse of discretion.

Moreover, it is apparent from the above quoted language that the Director simply rejects the notion that an enforcer can have extraordinary ability limited to the role that he plays on a hockey team. Indeed, as set forth in defendant's memorandum in support of his cross-motion for summary judgment, defendant's position remains that because plaintiff engages in conduct which is "disfavored," his abilities cannot properly be considered as a factor supportive of his claim to be an athlete of extraordinary ability. This court disagrees. The only evidence that was presented to the Director indicates that the role of an enforcer is necessary to the success of an NHL hockey team. The fact that a player is penalized for fighting does not mean that it is not both a necessary and accepted element of the game. Indeed, if it was not a necessary and accepted element of the game, the league would simply ban fighting altogether. Moreover, plaintiff presented evidence that his role as an enforcer entails much more than fighting. Pang's affidavit indicates that the role of an enforcer is to fight when necessary, but also to protect the team stars from being roughed up by the opposing team. An enforcer also serves as a deterrent to fighting, depending upon the reputation of the team's enforcer.

The fact remains that plaintiff has presented evidence sufficient to demonstrate that he is currently among the top three players in the world at what he does, and in 1993, when he filed his petition, he was among the top five players in the world. It goes without saying that there are countless players attempting to replace him every day. Yet, in 1993 he was, and remains today, among the best in the world. He has reached the very top of his field of endeavor. There is virtually no evidence in the record (let alone substantial evidence) to support defendant's finding that plaintiff is not among the best in the world, or that he is not an athlete of extraordinary ability.

The court concludes that the decision to reject plaintiff's role and unquestioned ability as an enforcer was without rational explanation, and that there was not substantial evidence for the factual finding that plaintiff is not at the top of his field of endeavor. Accordingly, plaintiff's motion for summary judgment is granted, defendant's cross-motion is denied, and defendant is ordered to issue plaintiff the visa he seeks.

Conclusion

For the reasons set forth above, defendant is ordered to issue a visa to plaintiff.

Source: Courtesy of Westlaw; reprinted with permission.

In the following Case 13-10, *Lee v. Ziglar*, 237 F. Supp. 2d 914 (N.D. ILL 2002), international baseball star Man Soo Lee sought a visa as a baseball coach but his application was denied.

📖 CASE 13-10 *Lee v. Ziglar*

237 F. Supp. 2d 914 (N.D. ILL 2002)

CASTILLO, J.

Plaintiff Man Soo Lee ("Lee") brings this action against James W. Ziglar, Commissioner of the Immigration and Naturalization Service (INS), challenging the INS' denial of Lee's application for an immigrant visa. Lee is an acclaimed baseball player from Korea and is currently part of the coaching staff of the Major League Baseball team, the Chicago White Sox. Lee petitioned the INS for an immigrant visa, claiming that he was a worker with extraordinary ability, who therefore deserved priority treatment under § 203(b)(1)(A) of the Immigration and Naturalization Act ("INA"). Lee's petition was denied. Both parties now move for summary judgment. After careful consideration, we deny Lee's motion for summary judgment, and grant the INS' motion for summary judgment.

Relevant Facts

Lee, a citizen of Korea, currently resides in Illinois. Lee is arguably one of the most famous baseball players in Korean history. He played for sixteen seasons as a catcher for the Samsung Lions from 1982-1997. During that time Lee hit a total of 252 home runs with a career batting average of .297. Until 1999, he held the Korean record for the most career home runs. Lee's other achievements as a Korean baseball player includes All Star Game appearances, the Triple Crown Title, season MVP and five Golden Glove awards. Lee secured a coaching position with the Chicago White Sox for the 2000 season and a tempo-rary visa in the P-1 category.

On April 17, 2000, Lee filed a petition with the INS Nebraska Ser-vice Center, seeking an immigrant visa as a professional baseball coach. . . . In July 2000, the INS sent Lee a request for additional evidence to establish that Lee is "an alien of extraordinary abil-ity" and "is one of that small percentage who have risen to the very top of the field of endeavor." Lee responded by providing evidence of his great success as a baseball player. The INS sent Lee a letter in September 2000 requesting additional evidence that he sustained national or international acclaim as a *coach*. Lee responded by argu-ing that under the statute he was not required to submit evidence that he is an acclaimed *coach*. Lee contended that he need only establish his extraordinary ability as a baseball player and his intention to continue to work in the "area of his extraordinary ability." Lee also submitted letters from White Sox Manager Jerry Manuel and White Sox Pitcher Bob Howry to support his argument that his experience as a baseball player is relevant to the experience and skills needed to coach major league baseball.

The Director of the INS Northern Service Center denied Lee's peti-tion, noting that although Lee appeared to have been an accomplished baseball player, he had not achieved national or international acclaim as a coach. The Director observed that Lee, as an ex-player, might be well-suited for a coaching position, but that the visa classification demands a much higher showing than simply being well-equipped for a given occupation. On appeal, the INS Administrative Appeals Office (AAO) sustained the denial of Lee's petition. The AAO observed that Lee never offered evidence that he received national or international acclaim as a coach, or that he was within the small percentage at the very top of the field of coaching. The AAO further noted that even though Lee will be working in the field of baseball, he will not be doing so as a player, which is the only area in which Lee has demonstrated extraordinary ability. (*Id.* at 070.) Lee's appeal is now before this Court.

Legal Standards

The Court is bound by an abuse of discretion standard in reviewing the INS' decision to deny Lee's visa petition. Therefore, we must defer to the INS' decision unless it: (1) is made without a rational explanation, (2) inexplicab[l]y departs from established policies, or (3) rests on an impermissible basis.

Analysis

Lee attempts to gain permanent residence in the United States as an "alien of extraordinary ability" under § 203(b)(1)(A). To obtain an immigrant visa under this classification, the applicant must show that:

> (i) the alien has extraordinary ability in the sciences, arts, education, business, or athletics which has been demonstrated by sustained national or international acclaim and whose achievements have been recognized in the field through extensive documentation,

> (ii) the alien seeks to enter the United States to continue to work in the area of extraordinary ability, and

> (iii) the alien's entry to the United States will substantially benefit prospectively the United States.

The INS regulations interpreting § 203(b)(1)(A) define extraordinary ability as "a level of expertise indicating that the individual is one of that small percentage who have risen to the very top of the field of endeavor." The regulations further specify the type of evidence which may be presented to support a finding of "extraordinary ability," including documentation of nationally or internationally recognized awards, documentation of membership in associations in the field for which classification is sought and publications about the alien's work in the field.

In support of his petition for a visa as a coach of extraordinary ability, Lee offered evidence that he was an outstanding foreign professional baseball player. Lee presented letters from top officials in the Korean Baseball Organization ("KBO") supporting his claim, a certificate from the KBO confirming Lee's career statistics and receipt of national awards and newspaper articles relating to Lee's baseball career. The INS does not dispute that Lee might qualify as an alien of extraordinary ability as a baseball *player*. The INS argues, however, that Lee failed to establish extraordinary ability as a baseball *coach*.

The INS' determination that Lee was not an alien of extraordinary ability as a baseball coach was reasonable. Our review of the record reveals that Lee has not distinguished himself as a coach to such an extent that he has achieved national or international acclaim or risen to the very top of the baseball coaching profession. In fact, the record only shows Lee's achievements as a player, not a coach, which are markedly different roles. Lee even admits that he does not claim to be a coach who has risen to the top of the field. The INS' distinction between extraordinary ability as a coach and a player is a reasonable one, entitled to deference. As such, the INS did not abuse its discretion in determining that Lee was not an alien of extraordinary ability. . . .

The INS also found that Lee failed to establish that he was "seeking to enter the United States to continue to work in the area of extraordinary ability." The INS contends that because Lee is coaching, rather than playing, he is not continuing to work in the "area of extraordinary ability." Lee argues that because he is coaching a major league *baseball team*, he is thus continuing to work in his "area" of extraordinary ability-baseball.

Once again, the INS' interpretation of "area of extraordinary ability" is a reasonable one and thus binding on this Court. It is reasonable to interpret continuing to work in one's "area of extraordinary ability" as working in the same profession in which one has extraordinary ability, not necessarily in any profession in that field. For example, Lee's extraordinary ability as a baseball player does not imply that he also has extraordinary ability in all positions or professions in the baseball industry such as a manager, umpire or coach. The regulations regarding this preference classification are extremely restrictive, and not expanding "area" to include everything within a particular field cannot be considered unreasonable.

Moreover, the INS' decision was not an abuse of discretion. The decision was a rational one based on the INS' reasonable interpretation of § 203(b)(1)(A) of the INA and did not rest on an impermissible basis. The decision denying Lee's petition is also consistent with the INS' established policy. In reviewing other INS denials similar to Lee's, we found that the INS consistently denies petitions of players seeking a visa as a coach . . .

The INS has explicitly stated that the "area" of athletics should not be considered as a whole to include every occupation involving athletics. Furthermore, in a case similar to the instant one, where a soccer player petitioned for an immigrant visa as a soccer coach, the AAO commented that the general assertion that former players often enjoy success as coaches "cannot establish that [a] particular alien has already earned national or international acclaim as a[ ] coach." Therefore, the INS' decision that Lee's past achievements as a baseball player do not imply that he likewise possesses an extraordinary ability as a coach is in accord with established INS policy. In short, the INS' construction of § 203(b)(1)(A) was reasonable and the agency's application of the statute to Lee's petition was not an abuse of discretion.

Conclusion

For the reasons set forth above, the INS' decision denying Lee an immigrant visa is affirmed. Lee is no doubt an acclaimed baseball player who during his lengthy career contributed much to Korean baseball. The visa classification for extraordinary ability is an extremely restrictive one, however, and absent an abuse of discretion, the Court must defer to the INS' reasonable interpretation of the statute. Therefore, Lee's motion for summary judgment is denied, and the INS' motion for summary judgment is granted.

Source: Courtesy of Westlaw; reprinted with permission.

NOTES AND DISCUSSION QUESTIONS

1. What sport do you think has the most international appeal? What are the major sports leagues doing on an international level to increase their appeal? Would an NBA division in Europe be feasible? What other major sports could function on a full-scale international level? What legal issues would a professional league have to concern itself with if it were to expand its regular-season schedule to Europe or other overseas venues?

2. Foreign-born baseball players dominate MLB. In 2006, the Boston Red Sox signed Japanese pitcher Daisuke Matsuzaka for $52 million over six years, paying a record-breaking $51.1 million to the Seibu Lions just for the exclusive right to speak with him about signing a contract, which would be refunded if they were unable to sign him. See, Associated Press, *Red Sox's Winning Bid for Matsuzaka: $51.1 Million*, ESPN, November 14, 2006.

3. Track and field star Butch Reynolds was required to exhaust all of his administrative remedies before the district court could accept the case.[24] The *Reynolds* case displays the procedural quagmire that some athletes are placed in by a decision of an international or national sporting body. How would you propose to resolve such a case?

4. In *Slaney v. IAAF*, 244 F.3d 580 (7th Cir. 2001), *cert. denied*, 534 U.S. 828 (2001), a female track participant was disciplined for a positive drug test that indicated the possibility of blood doping violations. When she sued the IAAF and the USOC on state and civil RICO (Racketeer Influenced and Corrupt Organizations Act) claims, the courts granted the defendants' motion to dismiss.

The Olympic Games

5. After reviewing Case 13-3, *Sternberg v. U.S.A. National Karate-Do Federation*, under what circumstances can a court find an implied cause of action under the Ted Stevens Olympic and Amateur Sports Act? Why do courts frown upon giving individuals a private cause of action under the act? Should athletes who participate on an international level have an athletes' Bill of Rights?

6. Unfortunately, the Olympics have been a place of tragedy as well. On September 5, 1972, eight Palestinians from the Black September faction broke into the Israeli quarters at the Olympic village dressed as athletes. Some athletes were able to escape, but two were killed and nine were taken hostage. Chaos ensued while the entire world watched on television, hoping for the best. After a shootout with the German police, nine Israeli athletes, five Palestinians, and a Munich policeman were killed. Despite this tragic set of events, the Olympic Games continued.

7. In *Oldfield v. Athletic Congress*, 779 F.2d 505 (9th Cir. 1985), a former Olympic athlete who signed a professional performance contract sued the Athletic Congress and the U.S. Olympic Committee, among others, challenging his disqualification from further participation in amateur athletics. The lower court granted summary judgment for all defendants, and the plaintiff—a shot-putter—appealed. The plaintiff acknowledged that there was no private cause of action under the Amateur Sports Act of 1978 but argued that one should be implied. The court noted:

> Oldfield narrows his attack and contends that, because the section containing the private right of action was deleted in response to pressure from high school and college organizations, we should infer that Congress intended to eliminate only the private right of action of student athletes. Such a distinction finds no support in the statute: all the provisions in the Act concerning resolution of disputes and conflicts refer to amateur athletes in general.[25]

---

[24] *See also* Barnes v. IAAF, 862 F. Supp. 1537 (S.D. W. Va. 1993). For a further discussion of *Reynolds*, see Eric Fastiff, *The Proposed Hague Convention on the Recognition and Enforcement of Civil and Commercial Judgments: A Solution to Butch Reynolds' Jurisdiction and Enforcement Problems*, 28 Cornell Intl. L.J. 469 (1995).

[25] *Oldfield*, 779 F.2d at 507.

8. The USOC does permit the use of the word "Olympics" for the Special Olympics for athletes with disabilities, as well as the Junior Olympics for youth.[26]

9. The USOC is considered a private entity and not a state actor. In *San Francisco Arts and Athletics, Inc. v. U.S. Olympic Committee*, 483 U.S. 522 (1987), the USOC and IOC sued under the Amateur Sports Act to prevent the defendants from using the word "Olympics." San Francisco Arts and Athletics was promoting the "Gay Olympic Games" and was using those words on its letterhead, mailings, and other materials. The U.S. Supreme Court ruled in favor of the USOC. The USOC has had a trademark in the word "Olympic" since 1986, and the Amateur Sports Act gave statutory protection to the USOC for use of the word. Furthermore, the court found that "the USOC is a 'private' corporatio[n] established under Federal law.' 36 U.S.C. §1101(46).'"[27] The court found that the USOC was not a governmental actor. National governing bodies are also not state actors.[28]

10. *Martinez v. U.S. Olympic Committee*, 802 F.2d 1275 (10th Cir. 1986), involved a 21-year-old boxer, Benjamin Davis, who died from severe brain stem injuries. He had participated in a Golden Gloves tournament and collapsed during his second fight. The court noted that the lawsuit was the first brought under the Amateur Sports Act for injuries in an event sponsored by the USOC. The court, in finding in favor of the defendant (the USOC), stated:

> The Act states that purposes of the USOC include promotion and support for amateur athletic activities, promotion of public participation in amateur athletic activities, and assistance to organizations in the development of amateur athletic programs. 36 U.S.C. § 374(5), (6) and (7). We find no indication in the Act that Congress intended the USOC to be liable to athletes injured while competing in events that were not fully controlled by the USOC. Therefore, we uphold the district court's dismissal of Martinez's suit because she failed to state a federal cause of action on which the court could grant relief.[29]

11. The first games for disabled athletes were held in 1948 in England. In the 1960 Olympics in Rome, an Olympic-style competition was held for disabled athletes. Since that time, games have been held every four years. The Paralympian movement has grown extensively since its inception. In *Shepherd v. U.S. Olympic Committee*, 2006 WL 3333677 (D. Colo. 2006), the plaintiff alleged discrimination against the USOC based on Title III of the Americans with Disabilities Act (ADA) and Section 504 of the Rehabilitation Act. The court discussed *PGA Tour, Inc. v. Martin* (see Case 7-5) in arriving at its decision. What rights are owed to disabled athletes by the USOC?

In *Shepherd*, the plaintiff alleged that the USOC operated "places of public accommodation," thereby making it a covered entity under Title III of the ADA. The plaintiff stated that Section (L), "a gymnasium, health spa, bowling alley, golf course, or other place of exercise or recreation," was applicable. Casey Martin made the same argument in *PGA Tour, Inc. v. Martin*. Martin prevailed on his argument, but the court in *Shepherd* said *Martin* would be inapplicable. What was the basis for the *Shepherd* court's decision? What is different about *Martin* as opposed to *Shepherd* with regard to claims under Title III of the ADA? Suppose

---

[26] Special Olympics, www.specialolympics.org/.

[27] *San Francisco Arts*, 483 U.S. at 542.

[28] *Behagen v. Amateur Basketball Ass'n of the United States*, 884 F.2d 524 (10th Cir. 1989).

[29] *Martinez*, 802 F.2d at 1281.

the Paralympics facility were open to the public. Would that change your opinion with regard to whether Title III of the ADA is applicable?

12. In *Stop the Olympic Prison v. U.S. Olympic Committee*, 489 F. Supp. 1112 (S.D.N.Y. 1980), the plaintiffs printed a "Stop the Olympic Prison" poster in protest against the use of the Lake Placid Olympic Village as a prison after the Olympics were over. The court held that the use of the village was not in violation of trademark law because the posters were not sold commercially and there was no likelihood of confusion.

The Court of Arbitration for Sport

13. What are your impressions of the Court of Arbitration for Sport? What disadvantages are there to this type of dispute resolution system? How would you limit its jurisdiction? What types of disputes should it handle? Should all Olympic athletes be required to use the CAS as the exclusive method for resolving Olympic disputes?

Miscellaneous International Issues

14. In *Russell v. INS*, 2001 WL 11055 (N.D. Ill. 2001), the plaintiff was a professional hockey player who filed a petition with the INS for permanent residency as an alien with extraordinary athletic ability. The INS denied his application, and he subsequently filed a lawsuit against the INS. The court noted that the plaintiff must "demonstrate at least three of ten factors established by INS regulation, including, for example, the receipt of nationally recognized awards for excellence in the field, a high salary in relation to others in the field, and the establishment of a distinguished reputation within the field. *See* 8 C.F.R. § 204.5(h)(3)."[30] The court relied upon the *Grimson* decision in granting the INS's motion for summary judgment. The court stated that in *Grimson* the petitioner had submitted several affidavits from former and present NHL players discussing the plaintiff's skill as a hockey player. Darren Pang, former NHL goalie and a current ESPN announcer, deemed Grimson "one of the top three enforcers in the world."[31] Russell was described by Pang as being steady, consistent and reliable, and a "strong defensive defenseman."[32] Those adjectives do not amount to extraordinary.

15. In *In re X*, 1998 WL 2027159, the court denied the petition of a skier who made his application as a ski coach. The petition submitted numerous articles about his success as a skier. On appeal, counsel for petitioner argued that under the statute extraordinary skill may be established "in the sciences, arts, education, business, or athletics." He argued that athletics should be viewed as a broad category. The court disagreed, stating:

> This argument is untenable. By the same argument, a zoologist could seek entry to work as a nuclear physicist because both occupations fall within the heading of "sciences." Taking an example from athletics, by counsel's reasoning, if Michael Jordan were an alien seeking admission, he could cite his legendary basketball career as support for his petition to enter

[30] *Russell v. INS*, 2001 WL 11055 (N.D. Ill. 2001).
[31] *Grimson*, 934 F. Supp. at 967.
[32] *Russell*, 2001 WL at *5.

and work as a baseball player, even though Mr. Jordan's career in minor-league baseball was short-lived and undistinguished except for a degree of novelty value. The purpose of the extraordinary ability visa classification is not to reward an individual for his or her past accomplishments, but to bring the most renowned aliens in various fields into the United States so that the aliens can mutually benefit themselves and the nation by continuing the work which has heretofore brought them renown.[33]

SUGGESTED READINGS AND RESOURCES

Blacksaw, Ian S. *Mediating Sports Disputes: National and International Perspectives*. The Hague: Asser Press, 2002.

Blacksaw, Ian S., Siekmann, Robert, & Soek, Janwillem. *The Court of Arbitration for Sport, 1984–2004*. West Nyack, NY: Cambridge University Press, 2006.

Blanpain, Roger. *The Legal Status of Sportsmen and Sportswomen Under International, European and Belgian National and Regional Law*. The Hague: Kluwer Law International, 2003.

Do You Believe in Miracles? The Story of the 1980 U.S. Hockey Team. Home Box Office, 2001.

Foer, Franklin. *How Soccer Explains the World: An Unlikely Theory of Globalization*. New York: HarperCollins, 2004.

Greenspan, Bud. *100 Greatest Moments in Olympic History*, special children's collector's edition. Los Angeles: General Publishing Group, 1995.

Hilton, Christopher. *Hitler's Olympics: The 1936 Berlin Olympic Games*. Stroud: Sutton Publishing, 2006.

Kaufmann-Kohler, Gabrielle. *Arbitration at the Olympics: Issues of Fast-Track Dispute Resolution and Sports Law*. The Hague: Kluwer Law International, 2001.

Nafziger, James A. *International Sports Law*, 2d ed. Ardsley, NY: Transnational Publishers, 2004.

The Olympic Games: Athens 1896–Athens 2004. New York: DK Publishing, 2004.

Senn, Alfred Erich. *Power, Politics and the Olympic Games*. Champaign, IL: Human Kinetics, 1999.

Siekmann, Robert, & Soek, Janwillem (eds.). *Arbitral and Disciplinary Rules of International Sports Organisations*. The Hague: Springer, 2001.

Siekmann, Robert, & Soek, Janwillem. *Basic Documents of International Sports Organisations*. The Hague: Martinus Nijhoff, 1998.

Siekmann, Robert, & Soek, Janwillem. *The European Union and Sport: Legal and Policy Documents*. The Hague: Asser Press, 2005.

Siekmann, Robert, Soek, Janwillem, & Bellani, Andrea. *Doping Rules of International Sporting Organisations*. The Hague: Asser Press, 1999.

Wise, Aaron, & Meyer, Bruce. *International Sports Law and Business*. The Hague: Kluwer Law International, 1997.

Young, David C. *A Brief History of the Olympic Games*. Malden, MA: Blackwell, 2004.

---

[33] *In re X*, 1998 WL 2027159.

REFERENCE MATERIALS

Abrams, Roger I. *Keep Your Eye on the Pelota: Sports Arbitration at the Jai-Alai Fronton.* 16 MARQUETTE SPORTS LAW REVIEW 1 (2005).

Champion, Walter T. *Fundamentals of Sports Law.* St. Paul, MN: Thomson/West, 2004.

Dougiello, Leslie Ann. Jacobs v. United States Track & Field: *Inequitable Procedures Win Gold in Olympic Arbitration.* 24 QUINNIPIAC LAW REVIEW 887 (2006).

Etter, Lauren. *What Makes a Sport Olympic?* WALL STREET JOURNAL, Feb. 18–19, 2006, A7.

Frankel, Matthew J. *Major League Problems: Baseball's Broken System of Cuban Defection.* 25 BOSTON COLLEGE THIRD WORLD LAW JOURNAL 383 (2005).

Gilson, Eric T. *Exploring the Court of Arbitration for Sport.* 98 LAW LIBRARY JOURNAL 503 (2006).

Jodouin Anik L. *The Sport Dispute Resolution Centre of Canada: An Innovative Development in Canadian Amateur Sport.* 15 JOURNAL OF LEGAL ASPECTS OF SPORT 295 (2005).

Kane, Darren. *Twenty Years On: An Evaluation of the Court of Arbitration for Sport.* 4 MELBOURNE JOURNAL OF INTERNATIONAL LAW 10 (2003).

Keller-Smith, Sara Lee, & Affrunti, Sherri A. *Going for the Gold: The Representation of Olympic Athletes.* 3 VILLANOVA SPORTS & ENTERTAINMENT LAW JOURNAL 443 (1996).

Kroll, Jason. *Second Class Athletes: The USOC's Treatment of its Paralympians.* 23 CARDOZO ARTS & ENTERTAINMENT LAW JOURNAL 307 (2005).

Mayes, Thomas A. *Tonya Harding's Case: Contractual Due Process, the Amateur Athlete, and the American Ideal of Fair Play.* 3 UCLA ENTERTAINMENT LAW REVIEW 109 (1995).

McLaren, Richard. *The CAS Ad Hoc Division at the Athens Olympic Games.* 15 MARQUETTE SPORTS LAW REVIEW 175 (2004).

Menke, Frank G. *The Encyclopedia of Sports.* New York: A. S. Barnes, 1953.

Miller, Trey. *Opening the Floodgates: The Effects of Flexible Immigration Laws in International Basketball Players Seeking Employment in the NBA.* 11 SPORTS LAWYERS JOURNAL 195 (2004).

Mitten, Matthew J., Davis, Timothy, Smith, Rodney, & Berry, Robert. *Sports Law and Regulation: Cases, Materials, and Problems.* New York: Aspen, 2005.

Morrow, Heather. E. *The Wide World of Sports Is Getting Wider: A Look at Drafting Foreign Players into U.S. Professional Sports.* 26 HOUSTON JOURNAL OF INTERNATIONAL LAW 649 (2004).

Nafziger, James A. R. *The Future of International Sports Law.* 42 WILLIAMETTE LAW REVIEW 861 (2006).

Nish, Noelle K. *How Far Have We Come? A Look at the Olympic and Amateur Sports Act of 1998, the United States Olympic Committee, and the Winter Olympic Games of 2002.* 13 SETON HALL JOURNAL OF SPORT LAW 53 (2003).

Olatawura, Ola. *The "Theatre of Dreams"?—Manchester United FC, Globalization, and International Sports Law.* 16 MARQUETTE SPORTS LAW REVIEW 287 (2006).

Opie, Hayden. *Australian Medico-Legal Issues in Sport: The View from the Grandstand.* 13 MARQUETTE SPORTS LAW REVIEW 113 (2002).

Opie, Hayden. *The Sport Administrator's Charter:* Agar v. Hyde. 12 SETON HALL JOURNAL OF SPORT LAW 199 (2002).

Panagiotopoulos, Dimitrios. *International Sports Rules' "Implementation-Decisions" Executability: The* Bliamou *Case.* 15 MARQUETTE SPORTS LAW REVIEW 1 (2004).

Platt, Jim, with Buckley, James, Jr. *Sports Immortals: Stories of Inspiration and Achievement.* Chicago: Triumph Books, 2002.

Reitz, Anders Etgen. *The NHL Lockout: The Trickle-Down Effect on European Hockey.* 13 Sports Lawyers Journal 179 (2006).

Ross, Stephen F. *Player Restraints and Competition Law Throughout the World.* 15 Marquette Sports Law Review 49 (2004).

Savarese, Kristin L. *Judging the Judges: Dispute Resolution at the Olympic Games.* 30 Brooklyn Journal of International Law 1107 (2005).

Sherwin, Peter, & Holinstat, Steven. *Federal Court Rejects Russian Team's Attempt to Prevent Hockey Sensation Ovechkin from Playing in the NHL.* 23 WTR Entertainment & Sports Law 3 (2006).

Soek, Janwillem. *The Court of Arbitration for Sport (1984–2004).* The Hague: Asser International Sports Law Centre.

United States Olympic Committee. *Code of Conduct,* 2006. http://assets.teamusa.org/assets/documents/attached_file/filename/13521/usoc_code_of_conduct_2.1.06_IN_EFFECT_updated_6.24.09.pdf.

Yasser, Raymond L., McCurdy, James R., Goplerud, C. Peter, & Weston, M. *Sports Law: Cases and Materials,* 4th ed. Cincinnati, OH: Anderson, 2000.

CASE INDEX

INDEX